MICROSOFT
Office 2000

Advanced Concepts and Techniques

WORD 2000   EXCEL 2000   ACCESS 2000   POWERPOINT 2000

Gary B. Shelly
Thomas J. Cashman
Misty E. Vermaat

Contributing Authors
Mary Z. Last
Philip J. Pratt
James S. Quasney
Susan L. Sebok
Joy L. Starks

MICROSOFT

Office 2000

Advanced Concepts and Techniques

WORD 2000   EXCEL 2000   ACCESS 2000   POWERPOINT 2000

Gary B. Shelly
Thomas J. Cashman
Misty E. Vermaat

Contributing Authors
Mary Z. Last
Philip J. Pratt
James S. Quasney
Susan L. Sebok
Joy L. Starks

COURSE TECHNOLOGY
ONE MAIN STREET
CAMBRIDGE MA 02142

Thomson Learning™

SHELLY
CASHMAN
SERIES®

Australia • Canada • Denmark • Japan • Mexico • New Zealand • Philippines
Puerto Rico • Singapore • South Africa • Spain • United Kingdom • United States

TRADEMARKS

Course Technology and the Open Book logo are registered trademarks and CourseKits is a trademark of Course Technology.

SHELLY CASHMAN SERIES® and **Custom Edition**® are trademarks of Thomson Learning. Some of the product names and company names used in this book have been used for identification purposes only and may be trademarks or registered trademarks of their respective manufacturers and sellers. Thomson Learning and Course Technology disclaim any affiliation, association, or connection with, or sponsorship or endorsement by, such owners.

DISCLAIMER

Course Technology reserves the right to revise this publication and make changes from time to time in its content without notice.

"Microsoft and the Microsoft Office User Specialist Logo are registered trademarks of Microsoft Corporation in the United States and other countries. Course Technology is an independent entity from Microsoft Corporation, and not affiliated with Microsoft Corporation in any manner. This textbook may be used in assisting students to prepare for a Microsoft Office User Specialist Exam. Neither Microsoft Corporation, its designated review company, nor Course Technology warrants that use of this textbook will ensure passing the relevant Exam.

"Use of the Microsoft Office User Specialist Approved Courseware Logo on this product signifies that it has been independently reviewed and approved in complying with the following standards: 'Acceptable coverage of all content related to the Microsoft Office Exam entitled "Microsoft Word 2000 Core Exam, Microsoft Excel 2000 Core Exam, Microsoft Access 2000 Core Exam, and Microsoft PowerPoint 2000 Core Exam;" and sufficient performance-based exercises that relate closely to all required content, based on sampling of text."

PHOTO CREDITS: Microsoft Office Word 2000 *Project 4, pages WD 4.2-3* Graduates, Courtesy of Image Club; Graphs and charts, Courtesy of BP Amoco; Businessman, Courtesy of Photo Disc, Inc.; *Project 5, pages WD 5.2-3* Woman reading magazine, mailbox, basketball, Courtesy of PhotoDisc, Inc.; Man and woman athletes, Courtesy of Digital Stock; Italy photos, Courtesy of Corel Corporation; *Project 6, pages WD 6.2-3* Pirate ship, Courtesy of Hector Arvizu; Horse, telephone lines, satellite dish, hand on mouse, hand on keyboard, Courtesy of PhotoDisc, Inc.; *page WD 6.5* Networked computers, globe, Courtesy of Dynamic Graphics, Inc.; **Microsoft Office Excel 2000** *Project 4, pages E 4.2-3* Couple reviewing notes, mortgage printout, home, hand on keyboard, Courtesy of PhotoDisc, Inc.; *page E 4.5* Pig, money, Courtesy of Corel Corporation; *Project 5, pages E 5.2-3* Senior citizen pool players, man, woman, group of people working, Courtesy of PhotoDisc, Inc.; *page E 5.5* Skates, hockey equipment, Courtesy of MetaTools, *Project 6, pages E 6.2-3* Ambulance, women praying, emergency medics, family, Courtesy of PhotoDisc, Inc.; Country Companies Insurance Group brochure, Courtesy of Country Life Insurance Company; *page E 6.5* Sound systems, conductor, globe, Courtesy of Corel Corporation; **Microsoft Office Access 2000** *Project 4, pages A 4.2-3* Laptop, woman using a cell phone, hiker, pager, background sky, truck and sign, surveyor, Courtesy of PhotoDisc, Inc.; Satellite, Courtesy of Philips Car Systems, Inc.; Vehicle navigational equipment, Courtesy Magellan Corporation; NavTalk Pilot, Courtesy of Garmin International; *page A 4.5* Island paradise, Courtesy of Dynamic Graphics, Inc.; *Project 5, pages A 5.2-3* Thumbprint, Courtesy of Corel Professional Photos CD-ROM Image usage; Magnifying glass, police car, police, investigators, Courtesy of PhotoDisc, Inc.; *Project 6, pages A 6.2-3* Man working on a laptop, group of workers, man at a computer, woman at a computer, group of workers at a computer, woman on the telephone, laptop and telephone, Courtesy of PhotoDisc, Inc.; *page A 6.5* Boats in a marina, Courtesy of Digital Stock; **Microsoft Office PowerPoint 2000** *Project 3, pages PP 3.2-3* Businessman, woman at computer, teacher and students, Courtesy of PhotoDisc, Inc.; *page PP 3.5* Couple kayaking, Courtesy of PhotoDisc, Inc.; *Project 4, pages PP 4.2-3* Hawaiian vacation brochure, fish, Courtesy of MetaTools, BMW, Courtesy of BMW North America, Inc.; *page PP 4.5* Palm trees, Courtesy of MetaTools; Couple on the beach, Courtesy of Corel Corporation.

ISBN 0-7895-4649-3 (Perfect bound)
ISBN 0-7895-5629-4 (Hard cover)

5 6 7 8 9 10   BC   04 03 02 01

MICROSOFT
Office 2000

Advanced Concepts and Techniques

WORD 2000   EXCEL 2000   ACCESS 2000   POWERPOINT 2000

C O N T E N T S

Microsoft Word 2000

● **PROJECT 6**

CREATING A PROFESSIONAL NEWSLETTER

● **INTEGRATION FEATURE**

MERGING FORM LETTERS TO E-MAIL ADDRESSES USING AN ACCESS TABLE

Microsoft Excel 2000

Microsoft Access 2000

● PROJECT 4

REPORTS, FORMS AND COMBO BOXES

● PROJECT 5

ENHANCING FORMS WITH OLE FIELDS, HYPERLINKS, AND SUBFORMS

Microsoft PowerPoint 2000

Integration Case Studies

Appendix A

MICROSOFT OFFICE 2000 HELP SYSTEM — MO A.1

Appendix B

PUBLISHING OFFICE WEB PAGES TO A WEB SERVER — MO B.1

Appendix C

RESETTING THE MENUS AND TOOLBARS — MO C.1

Appendix D

MICROSOFT OFFICE USER SPECIALIST CERTIFICATION PROGRAM — MO D.1

Preface

The Shelly Cashman Series® offers the finest textbooks in computer education. We are proud of the fact that our Microsoft Office 4.3, Microsoft Office 95, and Microsoft Office 97 textbooks have been the most widely used books in computer education. Each edition of our Office textbooks has included innovations, many based on comments made by the instructors and students who use our books. The Microsoft Office 2000 books continue with the innovation, quality, and reliability that you have come to expect from the Shelly Cashman Series.

In our Office 2000 books, you will find an educationally sound and easy-to-follow pedagogy that combines a step-by-step approach with corresponding screens. All projects and exercises in this book are designed to take full advantage of the Office 2000 enhancements. The popular Other Ways and More About features offer in-depth knowledge of Office 2000. The project openers provide a fascinating perspective of the subject covered in the project. The project material is developed carefully to ensure that students will see the importance of learning Office 2000 applications for future course work.

Objectives of This Textbook

Microsoft Office 2000: Advanced Concepts and Techniques is intended for a one-quarter or one-semester advanced computer applications course. This book assumes that the student is familiar with the fundamentals of Microsoft Word, Microsoft Excel, Microsoft Access, and Microsoft PowerPoint. These topics are covered in the companion textbook *Microsoft Office 2000: Introductory Concepts and Techniques*. The objectives of this book are:

- To extend the students' basic knowledge of Microsoft Word 2000, Microsoft Excel 2000, Microsoft Access 2000, and Microsoft PowerPoint 2000.
- To help students demonstrate their proficiency in the Microsoft Office applications by preparing them to pass the Core level Microsoft Office User Specialist Exam for Microsoft Word 2000, Microsoft Excel 2000, Microsoft Access 2000, and Microsoft PowerPoint 2000.
- To acquaint students with the proper procedures to create more advanced documents, workbooks, databases, and presentations suitable for course work, professional purposes, and personal use
- To develop an exercise-oriented approach that allows students to learn by example
- To encourage independent study, and help those who are working alone in a distance education environment

Approved by Microsoft as Courseware for the Microsoft Office User Specialist Program – Core Level

This book, when used in combination with the companion textbook *Microsoft Office 2000: Introductory Concepts and Techniques* in a two-semester sequence, has been approved by Microsoft as courseware for the Microsoft Office User Specialist (MOUS) program. After completing the projects and exercises in this book and its companion book, students will be prepared to take the Core level Microsoft Office User Specialist Exams for Microsoft Word 2000, Microsoft Excel 2000, Microsoft Access 2000, and Microsoft PowerPoint 2000. By passing the certification exam for a Microsoft software application, students demonstrate their proficiency in that application to employers. This exam is offered at participating centers, participating corporations, and participating employment agencies. See Appendix D for additional information on the MOUS program and for a table that includes the Word 2000, Excel 2000, Access 2000, and PowerPoint 2000 MOUS skill sets and corresponding page numbers where a skill is discussed in the book or visit the Web site www.mous.net.

The Shelly Cashman Series Microsoft Office User Specialist Center Web page (Figure 1) has more than fifteen Web pages you can visit to obtain additional information on the MOUS Certification program. The Web page (www.scsite.com/off2000/cert.htm) includes links to general information on certification, choosing an application for certification, preparing for the certification exam, and taking and passing the certification exams.

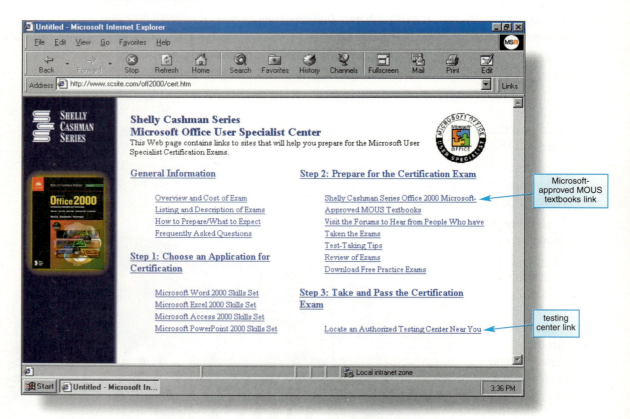

FIGURE 1

The Shelly Cashman Approach

Features of the Shelly Cashman Series Office 2000 books include:

- **Project Orientation:** Each project in the book presents a practical problem and complete solution in an easy-to-understand approach.

- **Step-by-Step, Screen-by-Screen Instructions:** Each of the tasks required to complete a project is shown using a step-by-step, screen-by-screen approach. The steps are accompanied by full-color screens.

- **Thoroughly Tested Projects:** Every screen in the book is correct because it is produced by the author only after performing a step, resulting in unprecedented quality.

- **Other Ways Boxes and Quick Reference Summary:** Office 2000 provides a variety of ways to carry out a given task. The Other Ways boxes displayed at the end of most of the step-by-step sequences specify the other ways to do the task completed in the steps. Thus, the steps and the Other Ways box make a comprehensive reference unit. In addition, a Quick Reference Summary, at the back of this book and also available on the Web, summarizes the ways application-specific tasks can be completed.

- **More About Feature:** These marginal annotations provide background information that complements the topics covered, adding depth and perspective to the learning process.

- **Integration of the World Wide Web:** We have integrated the World Wide Web into the students' Office 2000 learning experience in different ways. For example, we have added (1) More Abouts that send students to Web sites for up-to-date information and alternative approaches to tasks; (2) a MOUS information Web page and a MOUS map Web page so students can better prepare for the Microsoft Office Use Specialist (MOUS) Certification examinations; (3) an Office 2000 Quick Reference Summary Web page that summarizes the ways to complete tasks (mouse, menu, shortcut menu, and keyboard); and (4) project reinforcement Web pages in the form of true/false, multiple choice, and short answer questions, and other types of student activities.

(a) First Page of Newsletter

(b) Second Page of Newsletter

FIGURE 6-1

WD 6.5

More About 2000

Digitizing

Digitizing produces some dazzling objects that add interest to presentations. Many artists have traded their paint brushes and easels for the mouse and monitor. To view some of their creations, visit the PowerPoint 2000 More About Web page (www.scsite.com/pp2000/more.htm) and click Digitizing.

Other Ways

1. On Insert menu point to Picture, click WordArt on Picture submenu
2. Right-click toolbar, click WordArt, click Insert WordArt button

Microsoft **Office 2000**

Organization of This Textbook

Microsoft Office 2000: Advanced Concepts and Techniques consists of three projects each on Microsoft Word 2000, Microsoft Excel 2000, and Microsoft Access 2000, two projects on Microsoft PowerPoint 2000, four short Integration Features following each application, three capstone Integration Case Study exercises, four appendices, and a Quick Reference Summary. A short description of each follows.

Microsoft Word 2000

This textbook begins by providing detailed instruction on how to use the advanced commands and techniques of Microsoft Word 2000. The material is divided into three projects and the integration feature as follows:

Project 4 – Creating a Document with a Table, Chart, and Watermark In Project 4, students work with a multi-page document that has a title page. Students learn how to add an outside border with color and shading; download clip art from the Microsoft Clip Gallery Live Web page; center text vertically on a page; insert a section break; insert an existing Word document into an open document; change the starting page number in a section; create a header different from a previous header; chart a Word table; modify and format the chart; add picture bullets to a list; create a table using the Draw Table feature; change the direction of text in table cells; change the alignment of table cell text; center a table; and insert a picture as a watermark.

Project 5 – Generating Form Letters, Mailing Labels, and Envelopes In Project 5, students learn how to generate form letters, mailing labels, and envelopes from a main document and a data source. Topics include creating and editing the form letter, mailing label, and envelope main documents and their associated data source; using a template to create a letter; inserting merge fields into a main document; printing a document in landscape orientation; creating an outline numbered list; using an IF field; inserting a Fill-in field; displaying and printing field codes; merging and printing the documents; selecting data records to merge and print; sorting data records to merge and print; and inserting a bar code on the mailing labels and envelopes.

Project 6 – Creating a Professional Newsletter In Project 6, students learn how to use Word's desktop publishing features to create a newsletter. Topics include creating and formatting a WordArt drawing object; adding ruling lines; inserting the current date into a document; formatting a document into multiple columns; justifying a paragraph; formatting a character as a drop cap; inserting a column break; linking an object into a Word document; placing a vertical rule between columns; inserting and positioning a text box; changing character spacing; shading a paragraph; balancing columns; inserting a picture into a document; positioning a graphic between columns; using the Format Painter button; and highlighting text.

Integration Feature – Merging Form Letters to E-Mail Addresses Using an Access Table In the Integration Feature, students identify an existing Access database table as the data source for a main document. Then, students send the merged documents to e-mail addresses – attaching the form letter as a Word document to each e-mail message.

Microsoft Excel 2000

Following the three advanced projects and integration feature on Microsoft Word 2000, this textbook presents three advanced projects and an integration feature on Microsoft Excel 2000. The topics presented are as follows:

Project 4 – Financial Functions, Data Tables, Amortization Schedules, and Hyperlinks In Project 4, students learn how to use financial functions and learn more about analyzing data in a worksheet. Topics include applying the PMT function to determine a monthly payment; the PV function to determine the amount due on a loan at the end of a year; adding a hyperlink to a Web page; using names to reference cells; protecting a worksheet; and analyzing data by (1) goal seeking, (2) creating a data table, and (3) creating an amortization schedule.

Project 5 – Creating, Sorting, and Querying a Worksheet Database In Project 5, students learn how to create, sort, and filter a database. Topics include using a data form to create and maintain a database; creating subtotals; finding, extracting, and deleting records that pass a test; outlining a worksheet; and applying database and lookup functions.

Project 6 – Creating Templates and Working with Multiple Worksheets and Workbooks In Project 6, students learn to create a template and consolidate data into one worksheet. Topics include building and copying a template; multiple worksheets; 3-D cell references; customized formats; styles; charting; WordArt; adding notes to a cell; adding a header and footer; creating and modifying lines and objects; changing page setup characteristics; and finding and replacing data.

Integration Feature – Linking an Excel Worksheet to a Word Document In the Integration Feature, students are introduced to linking a worksheet to a Word document. Topics include a discussion of the differences among copying and pasting, copying and embedding, and copying and linking; opening multiple applications; saving and printing a document with a linked worksheet; and editing a linked worksheet in a Word document.

Microsoft Access 2000

Following the three advanced projects and integration feature on Microsoft Excel 2000, this textbook provides detailed instruction on advanced topics in Microsoft Access 2000. The topics are divided into three projects and one integration feature as follows:

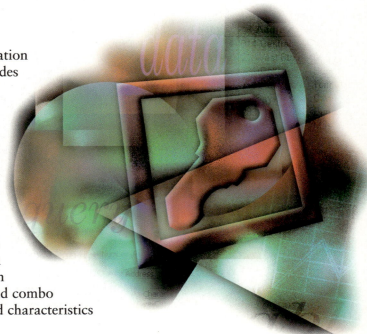

Project 4 – Reports, Forms, and Combo Boxes In Project 4, students learn to create custom reports and forms. Topics include creating queries for reports; using the Report Wizard; modifying a report design; saving a report; printing a report; creating a report with groups and subtotals; removing totals from a report; and changing the characteristics of items on a report. Other topics include creating an initial form using the Form Wizard; modifying a form design; moving fields; and adding calculated fields and combo boxes. Students learn how to change a variety of field characteristics such as font styles, formats, and colors.

Project 5 – Enhancing Forms with OLE Fields, Hyperlinks, and Subforms In Project 5, students learn to use date, memo, OLE, and hyperlink fields. Topics include incorporating these fields in the structure of a database; updating the data in these fields and changing table properties; creating a form that uses a subform to incorporate a one-to-many relationship between tables; manipulating subforms on a main form; incorporating date, memo, OLE, and hyperlink fields in forms; and incorporating various visual effects in forms. Students also learn to use the hyperlink fields to access Web pages and to use date and memo fields in a query.

Project 6 – Creating an Application System Using Macros, Wizards, and the Switchboard Manager In Project 6, students learn how to create a switchboard system, which is a system that allows users to access tables, forms, and reports simply by clicking buttons. Topics include creating and running macros; creating and using Lookup Wizard fields; using the Input Mask Wizard; and creating and using a switchboard system.

Integration Feature – Integrating Excel Worksheet Data into an Access Database In the Integration Feature, students learn how to embed an Excel worksheet in an Access database and how to link a worksheet to a database. Topics include embedding worksheets; linking worksheets; and using the resulting tables.

Microsoft PowerPoint 2000

The final Microsoft Office 2000 software application covered in this textbook is Microsoft PowerPoint 2000. The material is presented in two advanced projects and an integration feature as follows:

Project 3 – Using Embedded Visuals to Enhance a Slide Show In Project 3, students create a presentation from a Microsoft Word outline and then enhance it with embedded visuals. Topics include creating a slide background using a picture; customizing graphical bullets; creating and embedding an organization chart; creating and formatting a PowerPoint table; scaling objects; ungrouping and modifying clip art; and applying slide transition and text preset animation effects.

Project 4 – Creating a Presentation Containing Interactive OLE Documents In Project 4, students customize the presentation created in Project 3 by updating the information on the slides and using object linking and embedding to create a slide containing action buttons and hyperlinks. Topics include creating a WordArt object; adding special text effects; modifying organization chart content and formatting; modifying a PowerPoint table; hiding a slide; using guides to position and size objects; adding a summary slide automatically; and running a slide show to display a hidden slide in an active interactive document.

Integration Feature – Importing Clips from the Microsoft Clip Gallery Live Web Site In the Integration Feature, students are introduced to downloading clips from a source on the Internet and adding them to a presentation. Topics include connecting to the Clip Gallery Live Web site, searching for and downloading motion and sound clips to Microsoft Clip Gallery 5.0; importing clips into a presentation; and positioning the clips on a slide.

Integration Case Studies

Following the four major Office applications are case studies on integration. In the Integration Case Studies, students use the concepts and techniques presented in the projects and integration features in this book to integrate the major Office 2000 applications. The first case study requires students to link an existing Excel worksheet to a Word document and then link corresponding Excel charts to a PowerPoint presentation. The second case study requires students to use an existing Access database table as the data source in a Word form letter; students also are asked to use WordArt to create the letterhead for the form letter. The third case study requires the students to create an Access database table and then convert the table to a Word document and an Excel worksheet. Files are provided to the student for the first and second case studies.

Appendices

Appendix A presents a detailed step-by-step introduction to the Microsoft Office Help system. Students learn how to use the Office Assistant, as well as the Contents, Answer Wizard, and Index sheets in the Help window. Appendix B describes how to publish Office Web pages to a Web server. Appendix C shows students how to reset the menus and toolbars in any Office application. Appendix D introduces students to the Microsoft Office User Specialist (MOUS) Certification program and includes a MOUS map that lists a page number in the book for each of the MOUS activities.

Microsoft Office 2000 Quick Reference Summary

This book concludes with a detailed Quick Reference Summary. In the Microsoft Office 2000 applications, you can accomplish a task in a number of ways, such as using the mouse, menu, shortcut menu, and keyboard. The Quick Reference Summary provides a quick reference to each task presented in this textbook.

End-of-Project Exercises

A notable strength of the Shelly Cashman Series Office 2000 books is the extensive student activities at the end of each project. Well-structured student activities can make the difference between students merely participating in a class and students retaining the information they learn. The activities in the Shelly Cashman Series Office 2000 books include the following.

- **What You Should Know** A listing of the tasks completed within a project together with the pages where the step-by-step, screen-by-screen explanations appear. This section provides a perfect study review for students.

- **Project Reinforcement on the Web** Every project has a Web page accessible from www.scsite.com/off2000/reinforce.htm. The Web page includes true/false, multiple choice, and short answer questions, and additional project-related reinforcement activities that will help students gain confidence in their Office 2000 abilities.

- **Apply Your Knowledge** This exercise requires students to open and manipulate a file on the Data Disk for the Office 2000 books. To obtain a copy of the Data Disk, follow the instructions on the inside back cover of this textbook.

- **In the Lab** Three in-depth assignments per project require students to apply the knowledge gained in the project to solve problems on a computer.

- **Cases and Places** Up to seven unique case studies that require students to apply their knowledge to real-world situations.

Shelly Cashman Series Teaching Tools

A comprehensive set of Teaching Tools accompanies this textbook in the form of a CD-ROM. The CD-ROM includes an Instructor's Manual and teaching and testing aids. The CD-ROM (ISBN 0-7895-4636-1) is available through your Course Technology representative or by calling one of the following telephone numbers: Colleges and Universities, 1-800-648-7450; High Schools, 1-800-824-5179; and Career Colleges, 1-800-477-3692. The contents of the CD-ROM are listed below.

- **Instructor's Manual** The Instructor's Manual is made up of Microsoft Word files. The files include lecture notes, solutions to laboratory assignments, and a large test bank. The files allow you to modify the lecture notes or generate quizzes and exams from the test bank using your own word processing software. Where appropriate, solutions to laboratory assignments are embedded as icons in the files. When an icon appears, double-click it and the application will start and the solution will display on the screen. The Instructor's Manual includes the following for each project: project objectives; project overview; detailed lesson plans with page number references; teacher notes and activities; answers to the end-of-project exercises; test bank of 110 questions for every project (25 multiple-choice, 50 true/false, and 35 fill-in-the-blank) with page number references; and transparency references. The transparencies are available through the Figures in the Book. The test bank questions are numbered the same as in Course Test Manager. Thus, you can print a copy of the project test bank and use the printout to select your questions in Course Test Manager.

- **Figures in the Book** Illustrations of the figures and tables in the textbook are available in Figures in the Book. Use this ancillary to create a slide show from the illustrations for lecture or to print transparencies for use in lecture with an overhead projector.

- **Course Test Manager** Course Test Manager is a powerful testing and assessment package that enables instructors to create and print tests from the large test bank. Instructors with access to a networked computer lab (LAN) can administer, grade, and track tests online. Students also can take online practice tests, which generate customized study guides that indicate where in the textbook students can find more information for each question.

- **Course Syllabus** Any instructor who has been assigned a course at the last minute knows how difficult it is to come up with a course syllabus. For this reason, sample syllabi are included for each of the Office 2000 products that can be customized easily to a course.

- **Lecture Success System** Lecture Success System files are for use with the application software, a personal computer, and projection device to explain and illustrate the step-by-step, screen-by-screen development of a project in the textbook without entering large amounts of data.

- **Instructor's Lab Solutions** Solutions and required files for all the In the Lab assignments at the end of each project are available.

- **Lab Tests/Test Outs** Tests that parallel the In the Lab assignments are supplied for the purpose of testing students in the laboratory on the material covered in the project or testing students out of the course.

- **Project Reinforcement** True/false, multiple choice, and short answer questions, and additional project-related reinforcement activities for each project help students gain confidence in their Office 2000 abilities.

- **Student Files** All the files that are required by students to complete the Apply Your Knowledge exercises are included.
- **Interactive Labs** Eighteen hands-on interactive labs that take students from ten to fifteen minutes each to step through help solidify and reinforce mouse and keyboard usage and computer concepts. Student assessment is available in each interactive lab by means of a Print button. The assessment requires students to answer questions.

Microsoft Office 2000 Supplements

Three supplements can be used in combination with the Shelly Cashman Series Microsoft Office 2000 books. These supplements reinforce the concepts and techniques presented in the books.

Microsoft Office 2000 Workbook

This highly popular supplement (ISBN 0-7895-4690-6) includes a variety of activities that help students recall, review, and master Office 2000 concepts and techniques. The workbook complements the end-of-project material in the textbook *Microsoft Office 2000: Introductory Concepts and Techniques* with a guided project outline, a self-test consisting of true/false, multiple choice, short answer, fill-in, and matching questions, an entertaining puzzle, and other challenging exercises.

Course Assessment Live

Course Assessment Live (ISBN 0-619-00147-X) is a performance-based testing program that measures students' proficiency in Microsoft Office 2000. Previously known as SAM, Course Assessment Live is available for Office 2000 in both live and simulated environments. You can use Course Assessment Live to place students into or out of courses, monitor their performance throughout a course, and help prepare them for the MOUS certification exams.

Course CBT

Enhance your students' Office 2000 classroom learning experience with self-paced computer-based training on CD-ROM (ISBN 0-619-00151-8). Course CBT engages students with interactive multimedia and hands-on simulations that reinforce and complement the concepts and skills covered in the textbook. All the content is aligned with the Microsoft Office User Specialist (MOUS) certification program, making it a great preparation tool for the certification exams. Course CBT also includes extensive pre- and post-assessments that test students' mastery of skills. These pre- and post-assessments automatically generate a custom learning path through the course that highlights only the topics with which students need help.

Microsoft **Office 2000**

Acknowledgments

The Shelly Cashman Series would not be the leading computer education series without the contributions of outstanding publishing professionals. First, and foremost, among them is Becky Herrington, director of production and designer. She is the heart and soul of the Shelly Cashman Series, and it is only through her leadership, dedication, and tireless efforts that superior products are made possible. Becky created and produced the award-winning Windows series of books.

Under Becky's direction, the following individuals made significant contributions to these books: Doug Cowley, production manager; Ginny Harvey, series specialist and developmental editor; Ken Russo, senior Web designer; Mike Bodnar, associate production manager; Mark Norton, Web designer; Stephanie Nance, graphic artist and cover designer; Meena Mohtadi, production editor; Ellana Russo, Marlo Mitchem, Chris Schneider, Hector Arvizu, and Kenny Tran, graphic artists; Jeanne Black and Betty Hopkins, Quark experts; Nancy Lamm and Lyn Markowicz, copy editors; Marilyn Martin, Mary Steinman, and Kim Kosmatka, proofreaders; Cristina Haley, indexer; Sarah Evertson of Image Quest, photo researcher; Susan Sebok and Ginny Harvey, contributing writers; and Bill Daley, manuscript reviewer.

Special thanks go to Richard Keaveny, managing editor; Jim Quasney, series consultant; Lora Wade, product manager; Meagan Walsh, associate product manager; Francis Schurgot, Web product manager; Scott Wiseman, online developer; Rajika Gupta, marketing manager; and Erin Bennett, editorial assistant.

Gary B. Shelly
Thomas J. Cashman
Misty E. Vermaat

Shelly Cashman Series – Traditionally Bound Textbooks

The Shelly Cashman Series presents the following computer subjects in a variety of traditionally bound textbooks. For more information, see your Course Technology representative or call 1-800-648-7450. For Shelly Cashman Series information, visit Shelly Cashman Online at **www.scseries.com**

COMPUTERS	
Computers	Discovering Computers 2000: Concepts for a Connected World, Web and CNN Enhanced
	Discovering Computers 2000: Concepts for a Connected World, Web and CNN Enhanced Brief Edition
	Teachers Discovering Computers: A Link to the Future, Web and CNN Enhanced
	Discovering Computers 98: A Link to the Future, World Wide Web Enhanced
	Discovering Computers 98: A Link to the Future, World Wide Web Enhanced Brief Edition
	Exploring Computers: A Record of Discovery 2e with CD-ROM
	Study Guide for Discovering Computers 2000: Concepts for a Connected World, Web and CNN Enhanced
	Essential Introduction to Computers 3e (32-page)

WINDOWS APPLICATIONS	
Microsoft Office	Microsoft Office 2000: Essential Concepts and Techniques (5 projects)
	Microsoft Office 2000: Brief Concepts and Techniques (9 projects)
	Microsoft Office 2000: Introductory Concepts and Techniques (15 projects)
	Microsoft Office 2000: Advanced Concepts and Techniques (11 projects)
	Microsoft Office 2000: Post Advanced Concepts and Techniques (11 projects)
	Microsoft Office 97: Introductory Concepts and Techniques, Brief Edition (6 projects)
	Microsoft Office 97: Introductory Concepts and Techniques, Essentials Edition (10 projects)
	Microsoft Office 97: Introductory Concepts and Techniques, Enhanced Edition (15 projects)
	Microsoft Office 97: Advanced Concepts and Techniques
Microsoft Works	Microsoft Works 4.5[1] • Microsoft Works 3.0[1]
Windows	Microsoft Windows 98: Essential Concepts and Techniques (2 projects)
	Microsoft Windows 98: Introductory Concepts and Techniques (3 projects)
	Microsoft Windows 98: Introductory Concepts and Techniques Web Style Edition (3 projects)
	Microsoft Windows 98: Complete Concepts and Techniques (6 projects)
	Microsoft Windows 98: Comprehensive Concepts and Techniques (9 projects)
	Introduction to Microsoft Windows NT Workstation 4
	Microsoft Windows 95: Introductory Concepts and Techniques (2 projects)
	Introduction to Microsoft Windows 95 (3 projects)
	Microsoft Windows 95: Complete Concepts and Techniques
Word Processing	Microsoft Word 2000[2] • Microsoft Word 97[1] • Microsoft Word 7[1] Corel WordPerfect 8 • Corel WordPerfect 7 • WordPerfect 6.1[1]
Spreadsheets	Microsoft Excel 2000[2] • Microsoft Excel 97[1] • Microsoft Excel 7[1] • Microsoft Excel 5[1] • Lotus 1-2-3 97[1]
Database	Microsoft Access 2000[2] • Microsoft Access 97[1] • Microsoft Access 7[1]
Presentation Graphics	Microsoft PowerPoint 2000[2] • Microsoft PowerPoint 97[1] • Microsoft PowerPoint 7[1]
Desktop Publishing	Microsoft Publisher 2000[1]

PROGRAMMING	
Programming	Microsoft Visual Basic 6: Complete Concepts and Techniques[1]
	Microsoft Visual Basic 5: Complete Concepts and Techniques[1]
	QBasic • QBasic: An Introduction to Programming • Microsoft BASIC
	Structured COBOL Programming

INTERNET	
Browser	Microsoft Internet Explorer 5: An Introduction • Microsoft Internet Explorer 4: An Introduction Netscape Navigator 4: An Introduction
Web Page Creation	HTML: Complete Concepts and Techniques[1] • Microsoft FrontPage 98: Complete Concepts and Techniques[1] • Netscape Composer • JavaScript: Complete Concepts and Techniques[1]

SYSTEMS ANALYSIS	
Systems Analysis	Systems Analysis and Design, Third Edition

DATA COMMUNICATIONS	
Data Communications	Business Data Communications: Introductory Concepts and Techniques, Second Edition

[1]Also available as an Introductory Edition, which is a shortened version of the complete book

[2]Also available as an Introductory Edition, which is a shortened version of the complete book and also as a Comprehensive Edition, which is an extended version of the complete book

Shelly Cashman Series – Custom Edition® Program

If you do not find a Shelly Cashman Series traditionally bound textbook to fit your needs, the Shelly Cashman Series unique **Custom Edition** program allows you to choose from a number of options and create a textbook perfectly suited to your course. Features of the **Custom Edition** program are:

- Textbooks that match the content of your course
- Windows- and DOS-based materials for the latest versions of personal computer applications software
- Shelly Cashman Series quality, with the same full-color materials and Shelly Cashman Series pedagogy found in the traditionally bound books
- Affordable pricing so your students receive the **Custom Edition** at a cost similar to that of traditionally bound books

The table on the right summarizes the available materials.

For more information, see your Course Technology representative or call one of the following telephone numbers: Colleges and Universities, 1-800-648-7450; High Schools, 1-800-824-5179; and Career Colleges, 1-800-477-3692.

For Shelly Cashman Series information, visit Shelly Cashman Online at **www.scseries.com**

COMPUTERS	
Computers	Discovering Computers 2000: Concepts for a Connected World, Web and CNN Enhanced
	Discovering Computers 2000: Concepts for a Connected World, Web and CNN Enhanced Brief Edition
	Discovering Computers 98: A Link to the Future, World Wide Web Enhanced
	Discovering Computers 98: A Link to the Future, World Wide Web Enhanced Brief Edition
	A Record of Discovery for Exploring Computers 2e (available with CD-ROM)
	Study Guide for Discovering Computers 2000: Concepts for a Connected World, Web and CNN Enhanced
	Essential Introduction to Computers 3e (32-page)
OPERATING SYSTEMS	
Windows	Microsoft Windows 98: Essential Concepts and Techniques (2 projects)
	Microsoft Windows 98: Introductory Concepts and Techniques (3 projects)
	Microsoft Windows 98: Introductory Concepts and Techniques Web Style Edition (3-project)
	Microsoft Windows 98: Complete Concepts and Techniques (6 projects)
	Microsoft Windows 98: Comprehensive Concepts and Techniques (9 projects)
	Microsoft Windows 95: Introductory Concepts and Techniques (2 projects)
	Introduction to Microsoft Windows NT Workstation 4
	Introduction to Microsoft Windows 95 (3 projects)
	Microsoft Windows 95: Complete Concepts and Techniques
DOS	Introduction to DOS 6 (using DOS prompt)
WINDOWS APPLICATIONS	
Microsoft Office	Microsoft Office 2000: Brief Concepts and Techniques (5 projects)
	Microsoft Office 97: Introductory Concepts and Techniques, Brief Edition (396-pages)
	Microsoft Office 97: Introductory Concepts and Techniques, Essentials Edition (672-pages)
	Object Linking and Embedding (OLE) (32-page)
	Microsoft Outlook 97 • Microsoft Schedule+ 7
	Using Microsoft Office 97 (16-page)
	Using Microsoft Office 95 (16-page)
	Introduction to Integrating Office 97 Applications (48-page)
	Introduction to Integrating Office 95 Applications (80-page)
Word Processing	Microsoft Word 2000* • Microsoft Word 97* • Microsoft Word 7* Corel WordPerfect 8 • Corel WordPerfect 7 •
Spreadsheets	Microsoft Excel 2000* • Microsoft Excel 97* • Microsoft Excel 7* Lotus 1-2-3 97* • Quattro Pro 6
Database	Microsoft Access 2000* • Microsoft Access 97* • Microsoft Access 7*
Presentation Graphics	Microsoft PowerPoint 2000* • Microsoft PowerPoint 97* Microsoft PowerPoint 7*
INTERNET	
Internet	The Internet: Introductory Concepts and Techniques (UNIX)
Browser	Netscape Navigator 4 • Netscape Navigator 3
	Microsoft Internet Explorer 5 • Microsoft Internet Explorer 4
	Microsoft Internet Explorer 3
Web Page Creation	Netscape Composer

*Also available as a mini-module

Microsoft **Word 2000**

Microsoft Word 2000

P R O J E C T

Creating a Document with a Table, Chart, and Watermark

You will have mastered the material in this project when you can:

O B J E C T I V E S

- Add an outside border with color and shading to a paragraph
- Download clip art from the Microsoft Clip Gallery Live Web page
- Add a shadow to characters
- Center text vertically on a page
- Return formatting to the Normal style
- Insert a section break
- Insert an existing Word document into an open document
- Save an active document with a new file name
- Create a header different from a previous header
- Change the starting page number in a section
- Create a chart from a Word table
- Modify a chart in Microsoft Graph
- Format a chart in Word
- Add picture bullets to a list
- Use the Draw Table feature to create a table
- Change the direction of text in table cells
- Change alignment of text in table cells
- Insert a picture as a watermark
- Format a watermark

The Successful Job Search

A Look at Prospective Companies

As you near completion of your formal education, your activities begin to focus on the pursuit of employment and securing your future. Part of a successful job search involves researching a prospective company. Its financial situation, hiring plans, and growth strategies are important factors to consider in deciding whether to apply. In an interview, recruiters determine an applicant's familiarity with the corporation by asking such questions as, What do you know about the corporation?

An easy way to locate such relevant information is through the corporation's annual report. This document contains narratives explaining the corporation's mission, vision for expansion, and significant developments. These features are enhanced and supplemented by the plethora of charts and graphs reflecting the company's activities during the year compared to previous years.

An annual report is similar to the sales proposal you will create in Project 4. Both documents are tailored to specific audiences. Each publication contains an attractive title page, tables, charts, and a variety of design elements. The sales proposal in this project contains a graphic watermark that

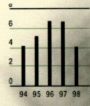

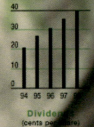

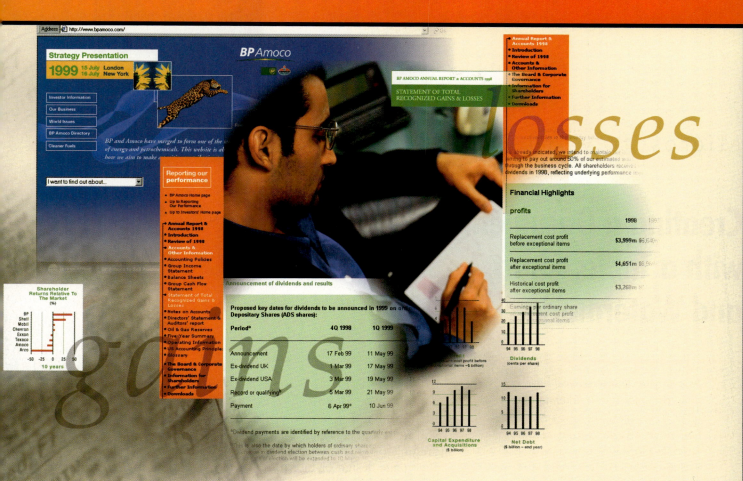

displays behind the first and second pages of the proposal. Companies sometimes use their logos or other graphics as watermarks on documents to add visual appeal.

Say you are an engineering major looking for a career with an international corporation known for research and development. At your college's placement office, you locate the annual report for BP Amoco, a large integrated petroleum and chemical company.

Turning to the inside cover, you glance at the table containing BP Amoco's financial and operating highlights. From your perusal of the report, you find that BP and Amoco have merged to form BP Amoco, one of the world's leading providers of energy and petrochemicals. You find information about the proposal to merge the two companies, its combined markets, financial highlights, brands, and the board of directors. You determine reported revenues and shareholders' cash dividends. Graphs and charts distributed throughout the report depict the tracked data.

In addition to the charts and graphs comprising the annual report, the document

contains features on environmental and social issues and highlights the company's worldwide exploration. You conclude that this is a successful company.

Although the report is distributed to shareholders once a year, production takes nearly six months and requires a team approach involving personnel throughout the corporation. For example, while managers are writing their reports about activities in their departments, photographers are capturing images of oil fields and personnel throughout the world, accountants are gathering financial data, and design team members are planning the document's organization. As press time nears, personnel review manuscripts for accuracy and legality, produce charts and graphs, scan photos, and design pages. Computers allow last-minute changes to be made so the document is as accurate as possible.

Certainly a document such as this company's annual report, complete with charts, tables, and graphs, provides the opportunity for job seekers to analyze their prospects with any prospective employer.

Microsoft Word 2000

Creating a Document with a Table, Chart, and Watermark

PROJECT 4

CASE PERSPECTIVE

As a marketing major, you have a part-time job preparing marketing pieces for local businesses. The owners of Super Sounds, a disc jockey service, have hired you to design a sales proposal that they can mail to homes in the surrounding communities.

In your first meeting with Juan and Nora Garcia, you learn as much as possible about Super Sounds. The Garcias explain they have been in business since 1990 and have performed for a variety of special events. They take pride in providing outstanding service in all areas including experienced disc jockeys, exceptional sound quality, thorough event planning, an extensive music library, and eye-catching special effects. Juan and Nora explain they have received excellent reviews from all of their clients. Together, you decide that a table and chart summarizing the performance ratings would be fitting in the proposal.

Juan and Nora also show you their business Web site, from which they say you can use any information you deem appropriate. At the conclusion of your meeting, you inform the Garcias that you will complete the proposal for their review within a week.

Introduction

In all probability, sometime during your professional life, you will find yourself placed in a sales role. You might be selling a tangible product, such as vehicles or books, or a service, such as Web page design or interior decorating. Within an organization, you might be selling an idea, such as a benefits package to company employees or a budget plan to upper management. To sell an item, whether tangible or intangible, you often will find yourself writing a proposal. Proposals vary in length, style, and formality, but all are designed to elicit acceptance from the reader.

A proposal may be one of three types: planning, research, or sales. A **planning proposal** offers solutions to a problem or improvement to a situation. A **research proposal** usually requests funding for a research project. A **sales proposal** offers a product or service to existing or potential customers.

Project Four — Sales Proposal

Project 4 uses Word to produce the sales proposal shown in Figures 4-1a, 4-1b, and 4-1c. The sales proposal is designed to persuade the reader to hire Super Sounds, a disc jockey service, for his or her next special event. The proposal has a colorful title page to attract the reader's attention. To add impact, the body of the sales proposal has a watermark behind the text and uses tables and a chart to summarize data.

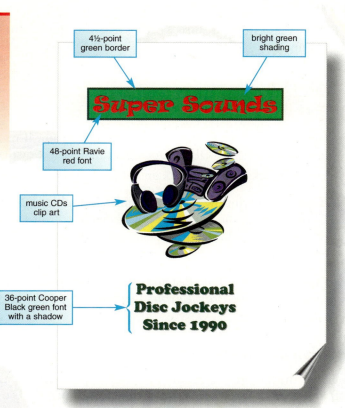

4½-point green border

bright green shading

48-point Ravie red font

music CDs clip art

36-point Cooper Black green font with a shadow

(a) Title Page

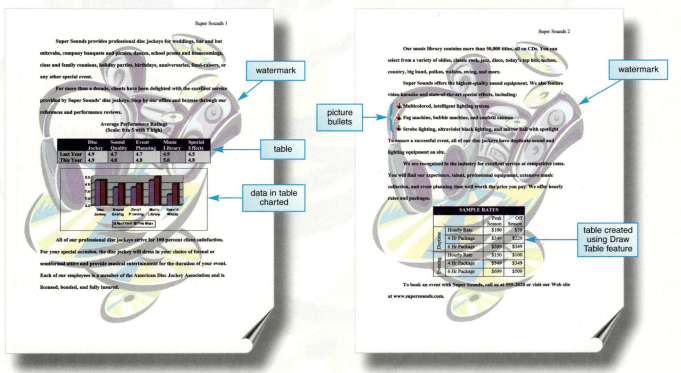

watermark

table

data in table charted

(b) First Page of Body of Sales Proposal

watermark

picture bullets

table created using Draw Table feature

(c) Second Page of Body of Sales Proposal

FIGURE 4-1

More About

Sales Proposals

A sales proposal may be solicited or unsolicited. If someone else requests that you develop the proposal, it is solicited, whereas if you write the proposal because you recognize a need, the proposal is unsolicited. A sales proposal is successful if it addresses how its product or service meets the reader's needs better than the competition does.

Starting Word

Follow these steps to start Word or ask your instructor how to start Word for your system.

TO START WORD

1 Click the Start button on the taskbar.

2 Click New Office Document on the Start menu. If necessary, click the General tab when the New Office Document dialog box displays.

3 Double-click the Blank Document icon in the General sheet.

4 If the Word window is not maximized, double-click its title bar to maximize it. Click View on the menu bar and then click Print Layout. If the Office Assistant displays, right-click it and then click Hide on the shortcut menu.

Office starts Word. After a few moments, an empty document titled Document1 displays in the Word window. Because this project contains tables, you will use print layout view; thus, the Print Layout View button on the horizontal scroll bar is recessed.

Resetting Menus and Toolbars

To set the menus and toolbars so they appear exactly as shown in this book, reset your menus and toolbars as outlined in Appendix C or follow these steps.

TO RESET MENUS AND TOOLBARS

1 Click View on the menu bar and then point to Toolbars. Click Customize on the Toolbars submenu.

2 When the Customize dialog box displays, click the Options tab, make sure the top three check boxes have check marks and then click the Reset my usage data button. When the Microsoft Word dialog box displays, click the Yes button.

3 Click the Toolbars tab. Click Standard in the Toolbars list and then click the Reset button. When the Reset Toolbar dialog box displays, click the OK button.

4 Click Formatting in the Toolbars list and then click the Reset button. When the Reset Toolbar dialog box displays, click the OK button. Click the Close button.

Zooming Text Width

As you have learned, when you **zoom text width**, Word displays text on the screen as large as possible in print layout view without extending the right margin beyond the right edge of the document window. Perform these steps to zoom text width.

TO ZOOM TEXT WIDTH

1 Double-click the move handle on the Standard toolbar so the entire toolbar displays. Click the Zoom box arrow on the Standard toolbar.

Click Text Width in the Zoom list.

Word computes the zoom percentage based on a variety of settings (see Figure 4-2 on the next page). Your percentage may be different depending on your system configuration.

Displaying Formatting Marks

You have learned that it is helpful to display formatting marks that indicate where in the document you pressed the ENTER key, SPACEBAR, and other keys. Follow this step to display formatting marks.

TO DISPLAY FORMATTING MARKS

 If the Show/Hide ¶ button on the Standard toolbar is not already recessed, click it.

Word displays formatting marks on the screen (Figure 4-2).

Creating a Title Page

A **title page** should be designed to attract the reader's attention. The title page of the sales proposal in Project 4 (Figure 4-1a on page WD 4.5) contains color, shading, an outside border, shadowed text, clip art, and a variety of fonts and font sizes. The steps on the following pages discuss how to create this title page.

Formatting and Entering Characters

The first step in creating the title page is to enter the company name, centered using 48-point Ravie red font as described below.

TO FORMAT CHARACTERS

1. Double-click the move handle on the Formatting toolbar to display the entire toolbar. Click the Center button on the Formatting toolbar.
2. Click the Font box arrow on the Formatting toolbar. Scroll to and then click Ravie (or a similar font) in the list of available fonts.
3. Click the Font Size box arrow on the Formatting toolbar. Scroll to and then click 48.
4. Click the Font Color button arrow on the Formatting toolbar. Click Red on the color palette.
5. Type Super Sounds and then press the ENTER key.

Word enters the company name, Super Sounds, in 48-point Ravie red font (Figure 4-2).

Adding an Outside Border in Color with Shading

The next step is to surround the company name with a border. You want a 4½-point green outside border with shading in light green. One method of specifying the point size, color, shading, and placement of a border is to use the **Tables and Borders toolbar**. To display the Tables and Borders toolbar, you click the **Tables and Borders button** on the Standard toolbar. When you click the Tables and Borders button, the

More About

Title Pages

Formal proposals often require a specific format for the title page. Beginning about 3-4" from the top margin, the following components are each centered and on separate lines: title; the word, for; reader's name, position, organization, and address; the word, by; your name, position, and organization; and the date the proposal was written.

More About

Borders

You can add a border to any edge of a paragraph. That is, borders may be added above or below a paragraph, to the left or right of a paragraph, or any combination of these sides. To add the most recently defined border, click the Border button on the Formatting toolbar. To change border specifications, use the Tables and Borders toolbar.

Tables and Borders toolbar displays in the Word window and the Tables and Borders button on the Standard toolbar is recessed. Also, if your screen is not already in print layout view, Word switches to print layout view.

Perform the following steps to add a 4½-point green outside border around the company name.

Steps To Border a Paragraph

1 Click somewhere in line 1 to position the insertion point in the company name. Double-click the move handle on the Standard toolbar to display the entire toolbar. Point to the Tables and Borders button on the Standard toolbar (Figure 4-2).

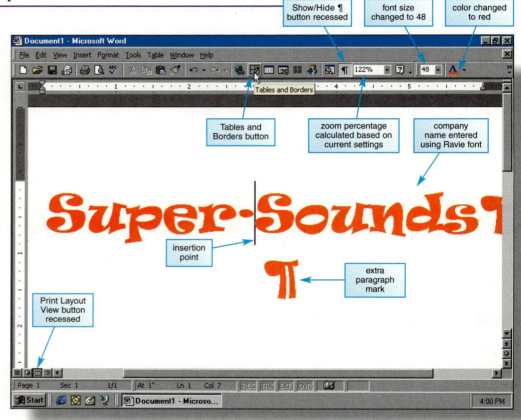

FIGURE 4-2

2 Click the Tables and Borders button. If the Tables and Borders toolbar is floating in the Word window, point to its title bar.

The Tables and Borders toolbar displays (Figure 4-3). Depending on the last position of this toolbar, it may be floating or it may be docked.

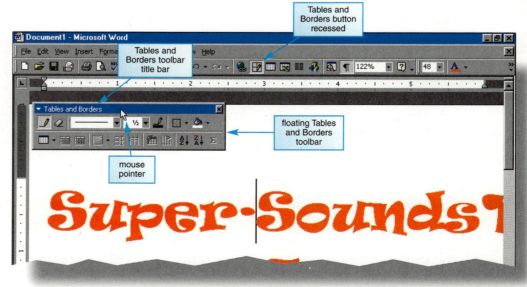

FIGURE 4-3

**3** If the Tables and Borders toolbar is floating in the Word window, double-click the title bar of the Tables and Borders toolbar.

Word docks the Tables and Borders toolbar below the Standard and Formatting toolbars.

4 Click the Line Weight box arrow on the Tables and Borders toolbar and then point to 4 ½ pt.

Word displays a list of available line weights (Figure 4-4).

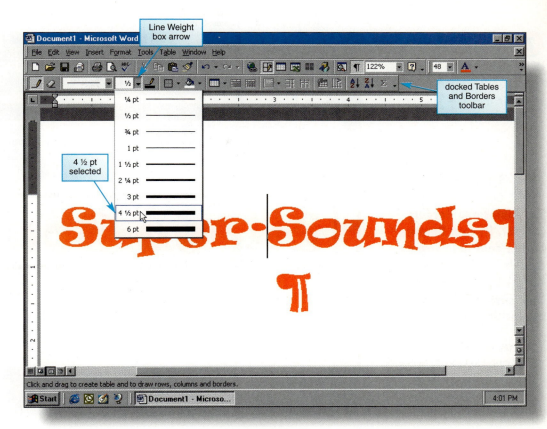

FIGURE 4-4

5 Click 4 ½ pt.

Word changes the line weight to 4 ½ point.

6 Click the Border Color button on the Tables and Borders toolbar. Point to Green on the color palette.

Word displays a color palette for border colors (Figure 4-5).

FIGURE 4-5

7 **Click Green.**

Word changes the color of the border to green, as shown in the Line Style box and on the Border Color button.

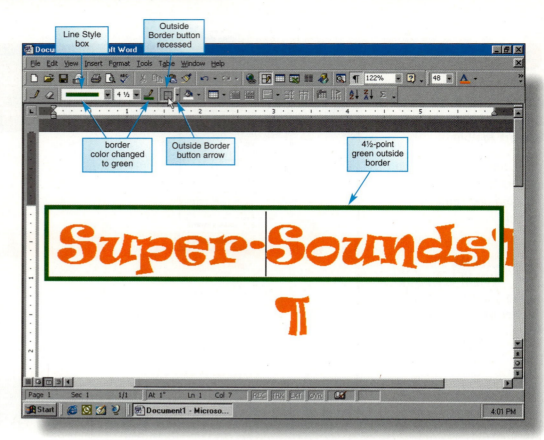

FIGURE 4-6

8 **Click the Outside Border button on the Tables and Borders toolbar. (If your Border button does not show an outside border, click the Border button arrow and then click the Outside Border button.)**

Word places a 4½-point green outside border around the company name (Figure 4-6). The Outside Border button on the Tables and Borders toolbar is recessed.

9 **Click the Shading Color button arrow on the Tables and Borders toolbar. Point to Bright Green on the color palette.**

Word displays a color palette for shading (Figure 4-7).

10 **Click Bright Green.**

Word shades the current paragraph bright green. To ensure that the next border you draw is not 4½-point green with shading, you should reset the line weight, color, and shading settings to their defaults.

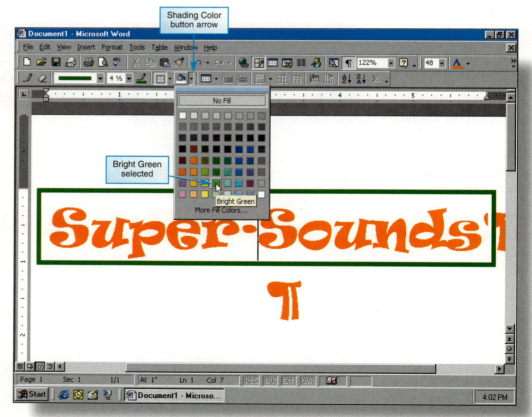

FIGURE 4-7

Position the insertion point on the paragraph mark on line 2. Click the Line Weight box arrow on the Tables and Borders toolbar and then click ½ pt. Click the Border Color button on the Tables and Borders toolbar and then click Automatic. Click the Shading Color button arrow and then click No Fill. Point to the Tables and Borders button on the Standard toolbar (Figure 4-8).

Click the Tables and Borders button.

The Tables and Borders toolbar no longer displays on the Word screen, and the Tables and Borders button no longer is recessed.

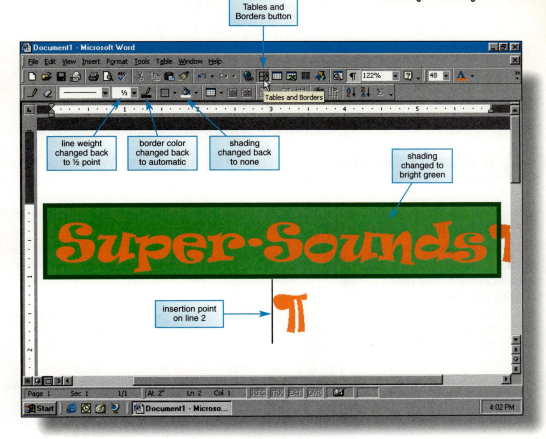

FIGURE 4-8

In an earlier project, you learned the Formatting toolbar also contains a Border button. Word provides two Border buttons. If you want to place a border using the same settings as the most recently defined border, then you simply click the Border button on the Formatting toolbar. If you want to change the size, color, shading, or other settings of the border, then you must use the Tables and Borders toolbar or the Borders and Shading dialog box.

Inserting Clip Art from the Web into a Word Document

You may recall that Word 2000 includes a series of predefined graphics called **clip art** that you can insert into a Word document. This clip art is located in the Clip Gallery, which contains a collection of **clips**, including clip art, photographs, sounds, and video clips.

If you cannot locate an appropriate clip art image in Word's Clip Gallery and have access to the Web, Microsoft provides a special Web page with additional clips, called the **Clip Gallery Live**. Navigating the Clip Gallery Live Web page is similar to using Word's Clip Gallery; that is, you can search for clips based on keywords you enter or you can display categories of clips. If you locate a clip you like, you can download it from the Clip Gallery Live Web page into Word's Clip Gallery.

The next series of steps illustrate how to download a music CDs clip art image from Microsoft's Clip Gallery Live Web page and then insert the clip art image into the Word document.

Note: The following steps assume you are using Microsoft Internet Explorer as your browser and that you have access to the Web. If you are not using Internet Explorer, you may need to perform a different set of steps. Your browser's handling of pictures on the Web will be discovered in Step 6 on page WD 4.14. If necessary, you may be directed to follow the steps on page WD 4.15 to import the clip art image from the Data Disk. If you do not have access to the Web, go directly to the steps on page WD 4.15.

 To Download Clip Art from Microsoft's Clip Gallery Live Web Page

1 **With the insertion point on line 2, press the ENTER key. Click Insert on the menu bar, point to Picture, and then point to Clip Art.**

The insertion point is on line 3 in the document (Figure 4-9).

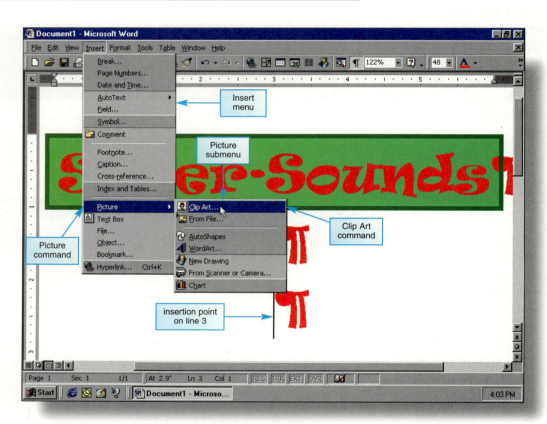

FIGURE 4-9

2 **Click Clip Art. If necessary, click the Pictures tab when the Insert ClipArt window opens. Point to the Clips Online button.**

Word opens the Insert ClipArt window (Figure 4-10).

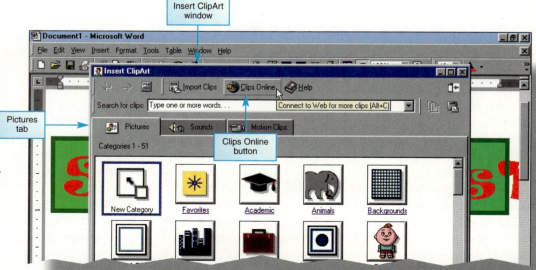

FIGURE 4-10

3 Click the Clips Online button. If a Connect to Web for More Clip Art, Photos, Sounds dialog box displays, click its OK button. If necessary, maximize your browser window. If Microsoft displays an End-User License Agreement (EULA) in the Clip Gallery Live window, read the EULA and then click the Accept button.

If you currently are not connected to the Web, Word connects you using your default browser. Microsoft Clip Gallery Live displays in a new window.

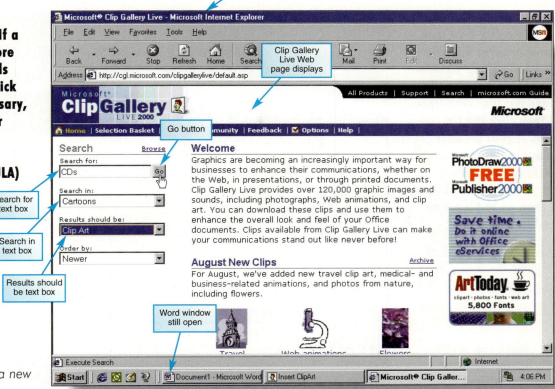

FIGURE 4-11

4 Click the Search for text box. Type CDs and then click the Search in box arrow. Click Cartoons. Click the Results should be box arrow and then click Clip Art. Point to the Go button (Figure 4-11).

5 Click the Go button. Point to the Click To Download icon below the clip you want to download.

*Clip Gallery Live displays the clip art associated with key-words you entered (Figure 4-12). The size of each clip art file displays below its image. To download a file into the Clip Gallery, you click the **Click To Download icon** that displays below the clip.*

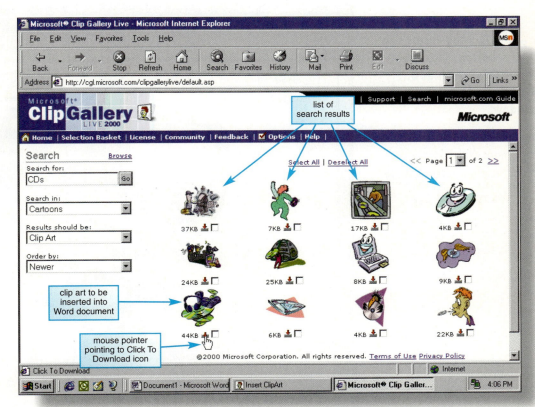

FIGURE 4-12

6 Click the Download This Clip Now icon. (If your browser displays a dialog box asking whether you want to open the file or save the file, click Open and then click the OK button. If your browser displays a dialog box and Open is not an option, close your browser window, and then go to Step 3 on page WD 4.15)

Your browser downloads the file into the Downloaded Clips category of Word's Clip Gallery.

7 When the Insert ClipArt window redisplays, click the downloaded music CDs image and then point to the Insert clip button on the Pop-up menu (Figure 4-13).

8 Click the Insert clip button. Close the Insert ClipArt window. Close your browser window.

Word inserts the clip into your document at the location of the insertion point (Figure 4-14).

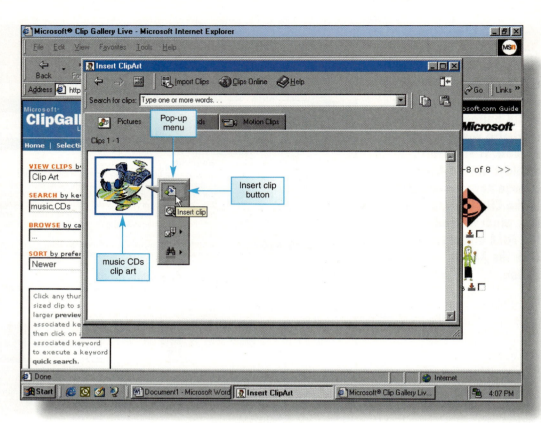

FIGURE 4-13

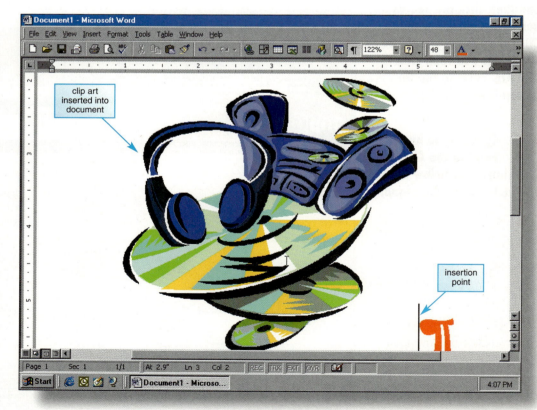

FIGURE 4-14

If you do not have access to the Web, you can import the clip art file into Word's Clip Gallery from the Data Disk as described in the following steps. If you did not download the Data Disk, see the inside back cover for instructions for downloading the Data Disk or see your instructor.

TO IMPORT CLIP ART FROM THE DATA DISK

1 With the insertion point on line 2, press the ENTER key.

2 Click Insert on the menu bar, point to Picture, and then click Clip Art. If necessary, click the Picture tab when the Insert ClipArt window opens.

3 Insert the Data Disk into drive A. Click the Import Clips button in the Insert ClipArt window.

4 When the Add clip to Clip Gallery dialog box displays, click the Look in box arrow and then click 3½ Floppy (A:). Click the file name EN00424_ and then click the Import button. When the Clip Properties dialog box displays, type music CDs, and then click the OK button.

5 When the Insert ClipArt window redisplays, click the music CDs image and then click the Insert clip button on the Pop-up menu. Close the Insert ClipArt window.

Word inserts the clip into your document at the location of the insertion point (see Figure 4-14).

Entering and Formatting the Company Slogan

The next step is to enter the company slogan below the graphic on the title page. The slogan is 36-point Cooper Black green font. The characters also are formatted with a shadow. A **shadow** is a light gray duplicate image that displays on the lower-right edge of a character or object.

Because you display the Font dialog box to add a shadow to characters, you can change the font, font size, and font color all at once using the Font dialog box, instead of using the Formatting toolbar. Perform the following steps to format the slogan using the Font dialog box.

 **To Format and Enter the Company Slogan**

1 **With the insertion point positioned as shown in Figure 4-14, press the ENTER key twice. Right-click the paragraph mark at the end of the document and then point to Font on the shortcut menu.**

Word displays a shortcut menu (Figure 4-15). The insertion point is immediately in front of the last paragraph mark in the document (line 5).

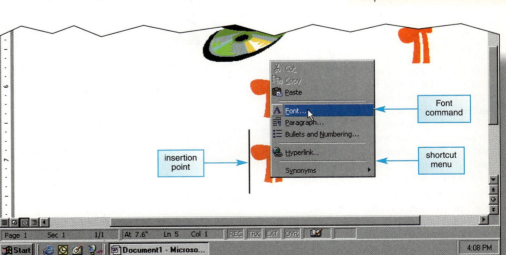

FIGURE 4-15

2 **Click Font. If necessary, click the Font tab when the Font dialog box displays. Scroll through the Font list and then click Cooper Black (or a similar font). Scroll through the Size list and then click 36. Click the Font color box arrow and then click Green. Click Shadow in the Effects area. Point to the OK button.**

The Preview area reflects the current selections (Figure 4-16).

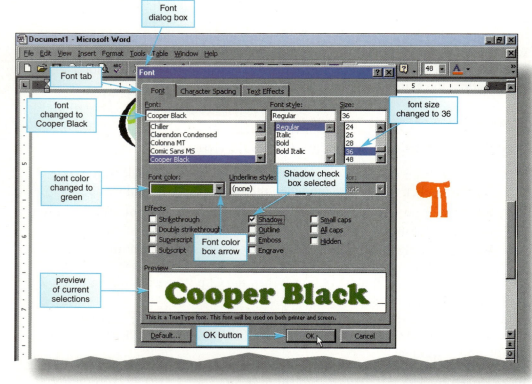

FIGURE 4-16

3 **Click the OK button. Type** Professional **and then press the ENTER key. Type** Disc Jockeys **and then press the ENTER key. Type** Since 1990 **to complete the slogan.**

Word displays the company slogan formatted to 36-point Cooper Black green font with a shadow (Figure 4-17).

Other Ways

1. Click Font box arrow then select desired font, click Font Size box arrow then select desired font size, click Font Color button arrow then click Green, right-click selected text, click Font on shortcut menu, click Font tab, click Shadow, click OK button

2. On Format menu click Font, click Font tab, select desired font in Font list, select desired font size in Size list, click Color box arrow then select desired color, click Shadow, click OK button

FIGURE 4-17

In addition to a shadow, the Font dialog box (Figure 4-16) contains many other effects you can add to characters in a document. Table 4-1 illustrates the result of each of these effects.

Centering the Title Page Text Vertically on the Page

For visual appeal, you would like to center the text on the title page vertically; that is, between the top and bottom margins. You have learned that the default top margin in Word is one inch, which includes a one-half inch header. Notice in Figure 4-17 that the insertion point, which is at the end of the title page text, is 8.7" from the top of the page. Thus, the space at the bottom of the page currently is approximately two and one-third inches.

Perform the following steps to center text vertically on a page.

Table 4-1 Character Effects Available in Font Dialog Box		
TYPE OF EFFECT	PLAIN TEXT	FORMATTED TEXT
Strikethrough	Super Sounds	~~Super Sounds~~
Double strikethrough	Professional	~~Professional~~
Superscript	102	10^2
Subscript	H20	H_2O
Shadow	Disc Jockey	Disc Jockey
Outline	Disc Jockey	Disc Jockey
Emboss	Disc Jockey	Disc Jockey
Engrave	Disc Jockey	Disc Jockey
Small caps	Disc Jockey	DISC JOCKEY
All caps	Disc Jockey	DISC JOCKEY
Hidden	Disc Jockey	

 To Center Text Vertically

1 **Click File on the menu bar and then point to Page Setup (Figure 4-18).**

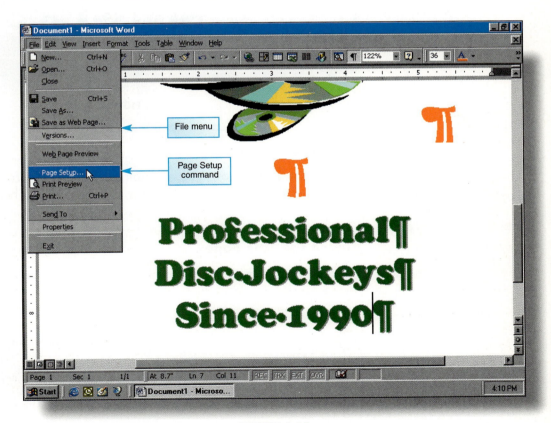

FIGURE 4-18

2 Click Page Setup. If necessary, click the Layout tab when the Page Setup dialog box displays. Click the Vertical alignment box arrow and then click Center. Point to the OK button.

Word displays the Page Setup dialog box (Figure 4-19). The vertical alignment is changed to Center.

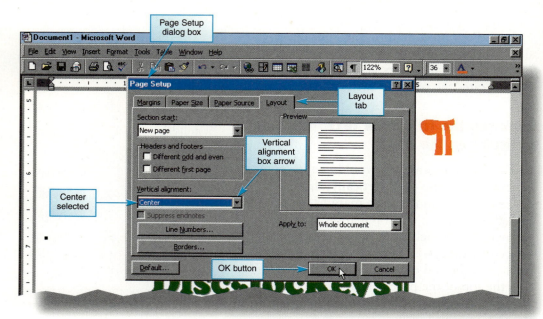

FIGURE 4-19

3 Click the OK button.

Word centers the text on the title page vertically (Figure 4-20).

FIGURE 4-20

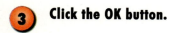

The status bar shows the insertion point now is 9" from the top of the document (Figure 4-20), which means the empty space above and below the text totals approximately two inches.

Saving the Title Page

Save the title page by performing the following steps.

TO SAVE A DOCUMENT

1 Insert a floppy disk into drive A. Click the Save button on the Standard toolbar.

2 Type Super Sounds Title Page in the File name text box.

3 Click the Save in box arrow and then click 3½ Floppy (A:).

4 Click the Save button in the Save As dialog box.

Word saves the document on a floppy disk in drive A with the file name Super Sounds Title Page (Figure 4-21).

The title page for the sales proposal is complete. The next step is to insert a draft of the proposal after the title page.

Inserting an Existing Document into an Open Document

Assume you already have prepared a draft of the body of the proposal and saved it with the file name Super Sounds Draft. You would like the draft to display on a separate page below the title page. Once the two documents display on the screen together as one document, you would like to save this active document with a new name so each of the original documents remains intact.

You want the inserted pages of the sales proposal to use the Times New Roman font and be left-aligned. That is, you want to return to the Normal style. Because the text to be entered at the insertion point currently is formatted for paragraphs to be centered using 36-point Cooper Black green font with a shadow, you should apply the Normal style as shown in the steps below.

More About 2000

Drafting a Proposal

All proposals should have an introduction, body, and conclusion. The introduction could contain the subject, purpose, statement of problem, need, background, or scope. The body may include available or required facilities, cost, feasibility, methods, timetable, materials, or equipment. The conclusion summarizes key points or requests some action.

 Steps ## To Apply the Normal Style

1 **Be sure the insertion point is on the paragraph mark on line 7 and then press the ENTER key. Double-click the move handle on the Formatting toolbar to display the entire toolbar. Click the Style box arrow on the Formatting toolbar and then point to Normal.**

Word displays the list of available styles (Figure 4-21). Notice the paragraph mark on line 8 is formatted the same as the slogan because when you press the ENTER key, formatting is carried forward to the next paragraph.

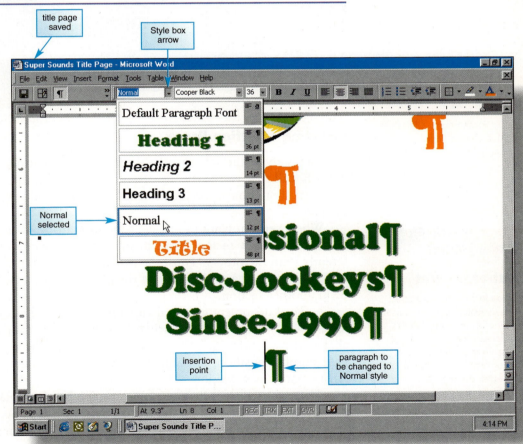

FIGURE 4-21

2 **Click Normal.**

Word returns the paragraph mark at the location of the insertion point to the Normal style (Figure 4-22). That is, the paragraph mark is left-aligned and the text to be entered is 12-point Times New Roman. Depending on your installation of Word, the Normal style might be a different font or font size.

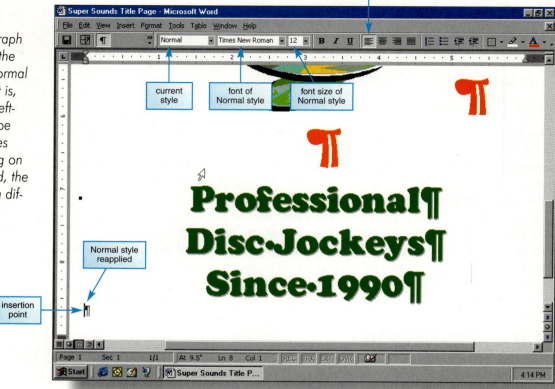

FIGURE 4-22

Section Breaks

To see formatting associated with a section, double-click the section break. This displays the Layout sheet in the Page Setup dialog box. In this dialog box, you can click the Borders button to add a border to a section.

Inserting a Section Break

The body of the sales proposal requires different page formatting than the title page. Recall that you vertically centered the text on the title page. The body of the proposal should have top alignment; that is, it should begin one inch from the top of the page.

Whenever you want to change page formatting for a portion of a document, you must create a new **section** in the document. Each section then may be formatted differently than the others. Thus, the title page formatted with vertical alignment must be in one section, and the body of the proposal formatted with top alignment must be in another section.

A Word document can be divided into any number of sections. All documents have at least one section. If during the course of creating a document, you need to change the top margin, bottom margin, page alignment, paper size, page orientation, page number position, or contents or position of headers, footers, or footnotes, you must create a new section.

When you create a new section, a **section break** displays on the screen as a double dotted line separated by the words, Section Break. Section breaks do not print. When you create a section break, you specify whether or not the new section should begin on a new page.

The body of the sales proposal is to be on a separate page after the title page. Perform the following steps to insert a section break that begins the new section on the next page of the document.

To Insert a Next Page Section Break

1 Be sure the insertion point is positioned on the paragraph mark on line 8 (see Figure 4-22). Click Insert on the menu bar and then point to Break (Figure 4-23).

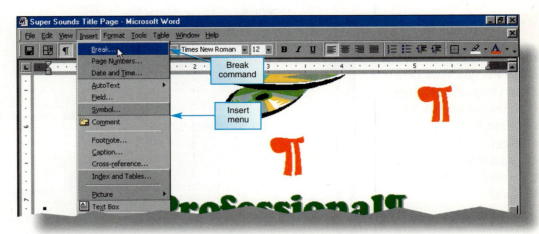

FIGURE 4-23

2 Click Break. When the Break dialog box displays, click Next page in the Section break types area. Point to the OK button.

Word displays the Break dialog box (Figure 4-24). The Next page option instructs Word to place the new section on the next page.

3 Click the OK button.

Word inserts a next page section break in the document (see Figure 4-26 on the next page).

FIGURE 4-24

The insertion point and paragraph mark are placed in the new section, which Word places on a new page. Notice in Figure 4-25 on the next page that the status bar indicates the insertion point is on page 2 in section 2. Also, the insertion point is set at 5.4" because earlier you changed the page formatting to vertical alignment. You want the body of the proposal to have top alignment. Thus, follow the steps on the next page to change the alignment of section 2 from center to top.

To Align Text with Top of Page

1 **Be sure the insertion point is in section 2. Click File on the menu bar and then click Page Setup. If necessary, click the Layout tab when the Page Setup dialog box displays. Click the Vertical alignment box arrow and then click Top. Point to the OK button.**

Word displays the Page Setup dialog box (Figure 4-25).

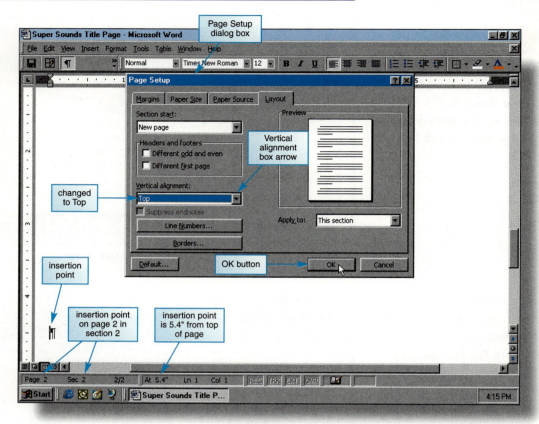

FIGURE 4-25

2 **Click the OK button. Scroll up so the bottom of page 1 and the top of page 2 display in the document window.**

Word changes the vertical alignment to top (Figure 4-26). Notice the status bar indicates the insertion point now is positioned 1" from the top of the page, which is the top margin setting.

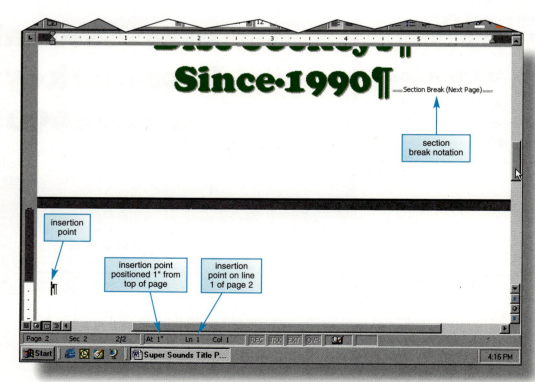

FIGURE 4-26

Word stores all section formatting in the section break. Notice in Figure 4-26 that the section break notation displays on the screen as the words, Section Break (Next Page). You can delete a section break and all associated section formatting by selecting the section break notation, right-clicking the selection, and then clicking Cut on the shortcut menu. To select a section break, point to its left until the mouse pointer changes direction and then click. If you accidentally delete a section break, you can bring it back by clicking the Undo button on the Standard toolbar.

Inserting a Word Document into an Open Document

The next step is to insert the draft of the sales proposal after the section break. The draft is located on the Data Disk. If you did not download the Data Disk, see the inside back cover for instructions for downloading the Data Disk or see your instructor.

If you created a Word file at an earlier time, you may have forgotten its name. For this reason, Word provides a means to display the contents of, or **preview**, any file before you insert it. Perform the following steps to preview and then insert the draft of the proposal into the open document.

Files

In the Insert and Open File dialog boxes, click the Views button arrow to change how the files display in the dialog box. Click the Tools button arrow and then click Delete to delete the selected file. Click the Tools button arrow and then click Properties to display a variety of information about the selected file.

 To Insert a Word Document into an Open Document

1 If necessary, insert the Data Disk into drive A. Be sure the insertion point is positioned on the paragraph mark immediately below the section break. Click Insert on the menu bar and then point to File (Figure 4-27).

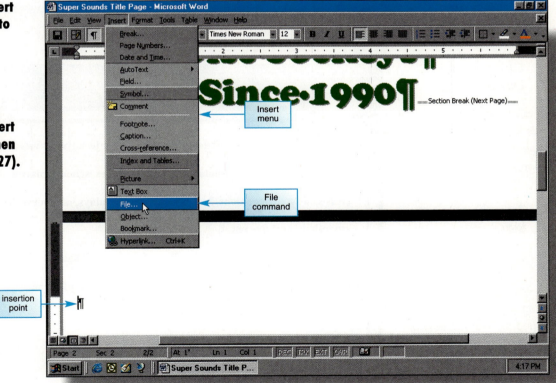

FIGURE 4-27

2 **Click File. When the Insert File dialog box displays, click the Look in box arrow and then click 3½ Floppy (A:). Click the Views button arrow and then click Preview. Click Super Sounds Draft and then point to the Insert button.**

Word displays the Insert File dialog box (Figure 4-28). A list of Word documents on the Data Disk displays. The contents of the selected file (Super Sounds Draft) display on the right side of the dialog box.

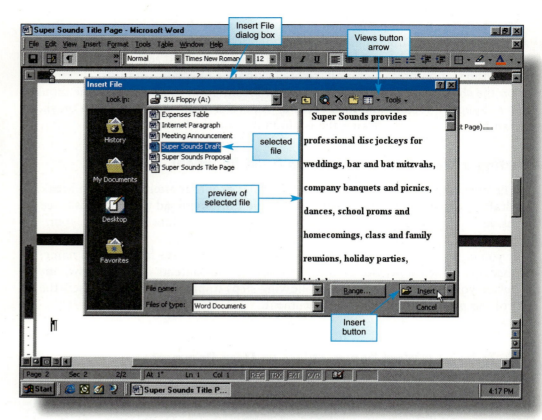

FIGURE 4-28

3 **Click the Insert button.**

Word inserts the file, Super Sounds Draft, into the open document at the location of insertion point.

4 **Press the SHIFT+F5 keys.**

Word positions the insertion point on line 1 of page 2, which was its location prior to inserting the new Word document (Figure 4-29). Pressing the SHIFT+F5 keys instructs Word to return the insertion point to your last editing location.

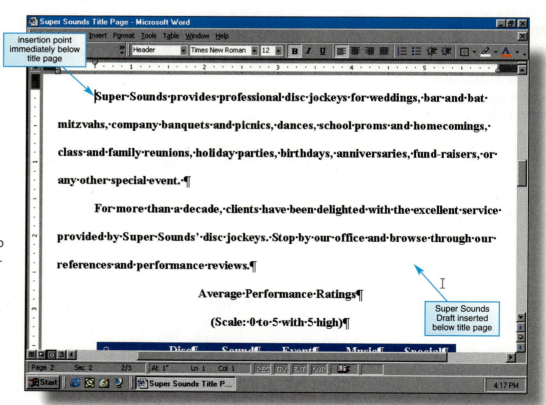

FIGURE 4-29

Word inserts the entire document at the location of the insertion point. If the insertion point, therefore, is positioned in the middle of the open document when you insert another Word document, the open document continues after the last character of the inserted document.

As illustrated in Figure 4-28, previewing files before opening them is very useful if you have forgotten the name of a particular file. For this reason, you can preview files by clicking the Views button arrow in both the Open and Insert File dialog boxes.

Saving the Active Document with a New File Name

The current file name on the title bar is Super Sounds Title Page, yet the active document contains both the title page and the draft of the sales proposal. Because you might want to keep the title page as a separate document called Super Sounds Title Page, you should save the active document with a new file name. If you save the active document by clicking the Save button on the Standard toolbar, Word will assign it the current file name. You want the active document to have a new file name. Thus, use the following steps to save the active document with a new file name.

TO SAVE AN ACTIVE DOCUMENT WITH A NEW FILE NAME

① If necessary, insert the floppy disk containing your title page into drive A.

② Click File on the menu bar and then click Save As.

③ Type Super Sounds Proposal in the File name text box. Do not press the ENTER key.

④ If necessary, click the Save in box arrow and then click 3½ Floppy (A:).

⑤ Click the Save button in the Save As dialog box.

Word saves the document on a floppy disk in drive A with the file name Super Sounds Proposal (see Figure 4-31 on page WD 4.28).

Printing Certain Pages in a Document

The title page is the first page of the proposal. The body of the proposal is the second and third pages. To see a hard copy of the body of the proposal, perform the following steps.

TO PRINT A DOCUMENT

① Ready the printer.

② Click File on the menu bar and then click Print.

③ When the Print dialog box displays, click Pages in the Page range area. Type 2-3 and then click the OK button.

Word prints the draft of the sales proposal (Figure 4-30a on the next page).

SHIFT+F5

Word remembers your last three editing or typing locations. Thus, you can press the SHIFT+F5 keys up to three times to move the insertion point to previous editing locations in your document. This feature works even after you save and then re-open a document.

File Save As

You can press F12 to display the Save As dialog box when you want to assign a new file name to an existing file.

Printing Colors

If you have a black-and-white printer and print a document with colors, the colors other than black or white will print in shades of gray.

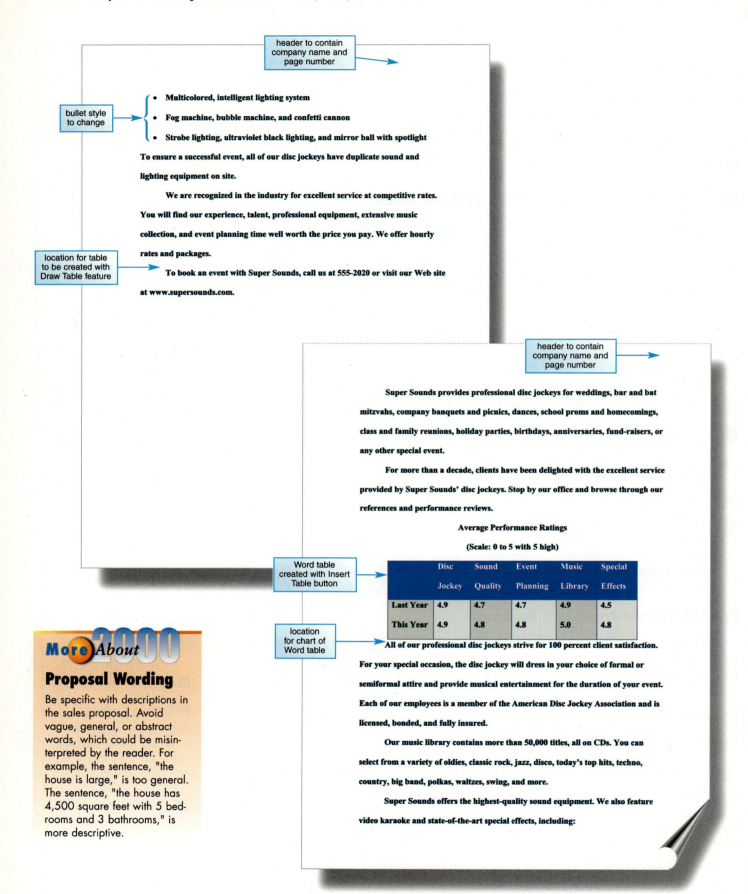

header to contain company name and page number

bullet style to change

- **Multicolored, intelligent lighting system**
- **Fog machine, bubble machine, and confetti cannon**
- **Strobe lighting, ultraviolet black lighting, and mirror ball with spotlight**

To ensure a successful event, all of our disc jockeys have duplicate sound and lighting equipment on site.

We are recognized in the industry for excellent service at competitive rates. You will find our experience, talent, professional equipment, extensive music collection, and event planning time well worth the price you pay. We offer hourly rates and packages.

location for table to be created with Draw Table feature

To book an event with Super Sounds, call us at 555-2020 or visit our Web site at www.supersounds.com.

header to contain company name and page number

Super Sounds provides professional disc jockeys for weddings, bar and bat mitzvahs, company banquets and picnics, dances, school proms and homecomings, class and family reunions, holiday parties, birthdays, anniversaries, fund-raisers, or any other special event.

For more than a decade, clients have been delighted with the excellent service provided by Super Sounds' disc jockeys. Stop by our office and browse through our references and performance reviews.

Average Performance Ratings

(Scale: 0 to 5 with 5 high)

Word table created with Insert Table button

	Disc Jockey	Sound Quality	Event Planning	Music Library	Special Effects
Last Year	4.9	4.7	4.7	4.9	4.5
This Year	4.9	4.8	4.8	5.0	4.8

location for chart of Word table

All of our professional disc jockeys strive for 100 percent client satisfaction. For your special occasion, the disc jockey will dress in your choice of formal or semiformal attire and provide musical entertainment for the duration of your event. Each of our employees is a member of the American Disc Jockey Association and is licensed, bonded, and fully insured.

Our music library contains more than 50,000 titles, all on CDs. You can select from a variety of oldies, classic rock, jazz, disco, today's top hits, techno, country, big band, polkas, waltzes, swing, and more.

Super Sounds offers the highest-quality sound equipment. We also feature video karaoke and state-of-the-art special effects, including:

More About 2000

Proposal Wording

Be specific with descriptions in the sales proposal. Avoid vague, general, or abstract words, which could be misinterpreted by the reader. For example, the sentence, "the house is large," is too general. The sentence, "the house has 4,500 square feet with 5 bedrooms and 3 bathrooms," is more descriptive.

FIGURE 4-30a Super Sounds Draft

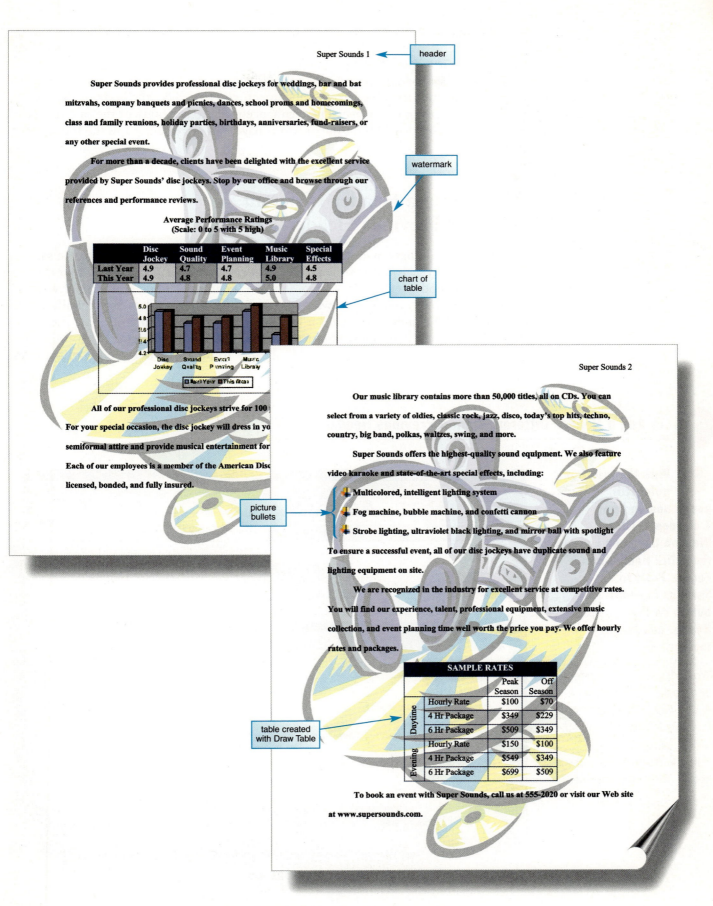

FIGURE 4-30b Body of Sales Proposal with Enhancements

When you remove the document from the printer, review it carefully. Depending on the printer driver you are using, wordwrap may occur in different locations from those shown in Figure 4-30a on the previous page.

By adding a header, charting the table, changing the bullets to picture bullets, and inserting another table into the document, you can make the body of the proposal more pleasing to the eye. These enhancements to the body of the sales proposal are shown in Figure 4-30b on the previous page and are discussed in the following pages.

Creating a Header Different from the Previous Header

You want the company name and page number to display on the body of the sales proposal; however, you do not want this header on the title page. Recall that the title page and the body of the sales proposal are in separate sections. You do not want a header in section 1, but you do want a header in section 2. When you initially create a header, Word assumes you want it in all sections. Thus, when you create the header in section 2, you must instruct Word to not place it in section 1.

Perform the following steps to add a header to the pages in the body of the sales proposal.

 Steps To Add a Header Different from a Previous Header

1 With the insertion point still positioned on line 1 of page 2, click View on the menu bar and then click Header and Footer. Point to the Same as Previous button on the Header and Footer toolbar.

Word displays the Header and Footer toolbar (Figure 4-31). Notice the Same as Previous button is recessed, which, when recessed, instructs Word to place the header in the previous section also.

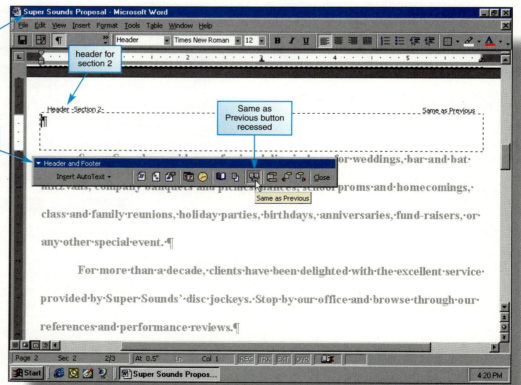

FIGURE 4-31

2 **Click the Same as Previous button. Point to the right edge of the header area and then double-click when a right-align icon displays next to the I-beam. Type** Super Sounds **and then press the SPACEBAR. Click the Insert Page Number button on the Header and Footer toolbar.**

Word displays the header for section 2 (Figure 4-32). The Same as Previous button no longer is recessed.

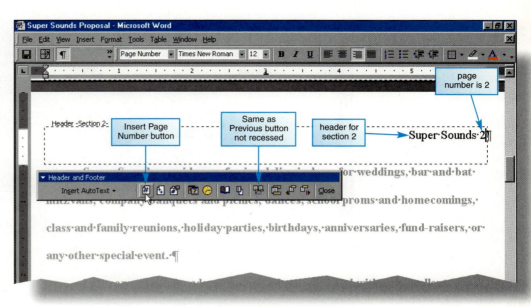

FIGURE 4-32

The next step is to change the starting page number in a section. Leave the header displaying on the screen for the next series of steps.

Changing the Starting Page Number in a Section

In Figure 4-32, the page number is a 2 because Word begins numbering pages from the beginning of the document. You want to begin numbering the body of the sales proposal with a number 1. Thus, you need to instruct Word to begin numbering the pages in section 2 with the number 1.

Perform the following steps to page number differently in a section.

 ## To Page Number Differently in a Section

1 **With the header displayed on the screen, click Insert on the menu bar and then point to Page Numbers (Figure 4-33).**

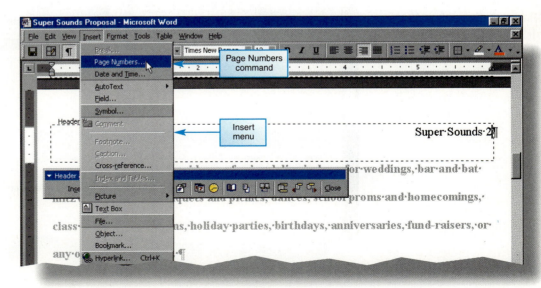

FIGURE 4-33

2 Click Page Numbers. When the Page Numbers dialog box displays, point to the Format button.

Word displays the Page Numbers dialog box (Figure 4-34).

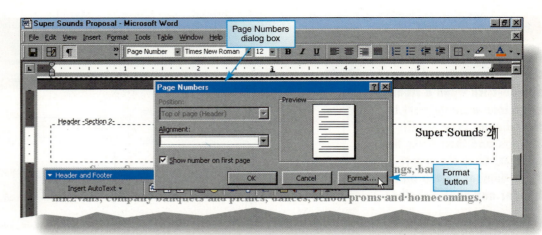

FIGURE 4-34

3 Click the Format button. When the Page Number Format dialog box displays, click Start at in the Page numbering area and then point to the OK button.

Word displays the Page Number Format dialog box (Figure 4-35). By default, the number 1 displays in the Start at box.

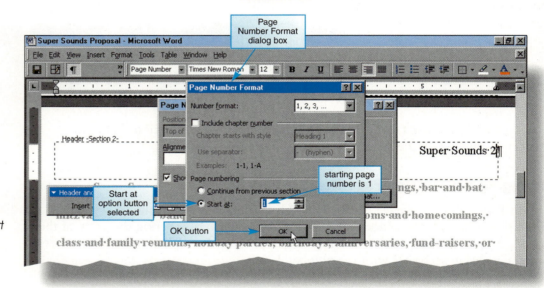

FIGURE 4-35

4 Click the OK button. When the Page Numbers dialog box is visible again, click its Close button.

Word changes the starting page number for section 2 to the number 1 (Figure 4-36).

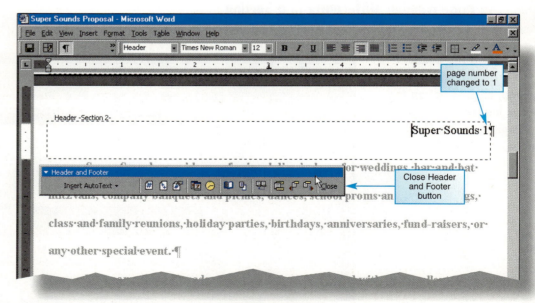

FIGURE 4-36

The next step is to close the header area as described in the following step.

TO CLOSE THE HEADER AREA

1 Click the Close Header and Footer button on the Header and Footer toolbar.

Word removes the Header and Footer toolbar from the screen.

Charting a Table

The sales proposal draft contains a Word table (see Figure 4-30a on page WD 4.26) that was created using the Insert Table button on the Standard toolbar. This table contains three rows and six columns. The first row identifies the performance category; the second and third rows show the average performance ratings for last year and this year, respectively. The first column identifies the year, and the remaining columns show the average performance rating for each performance category.

You would like to create a chart of this table (see Figure 4-30b on page WD 4.27) to show graphically the average performance ratings for Super Sounds. The following pages explain how to modify the table, chart its contents, modify the chart, and then format the chart.

Changing Line Spacing

You would like to modify the paragraph containing the table title so that it is single-spaced, instead of double-spaced. Perform the following steps to single-space this paragraph.

TO SINGLE-SPACE A PARAGRAPH

1 Scroll down to display the table title. Click in the table title, Average Performance Ratings.

2 Press CTRL+1 (the numeral one).

Word removes the blank line between the first and second lines of the table title (Figure 4-37).

More *About*

Word 2000 Features

For more information on features and capabilities of Word 2000, visit the Word 2000 More About Web page (www.scsite.com/wd2000/more.htm) and then click Features and Capabilities of Word 2000.

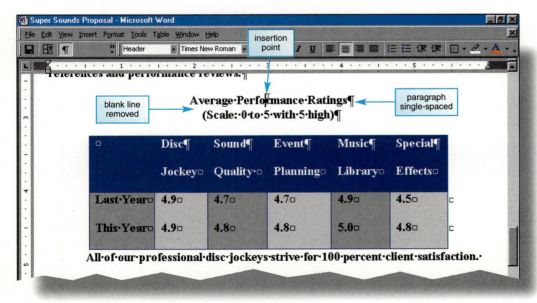

FIGURE 4-37

You also would like the contents of the table to be single-spaced, instead of double-spaced. To accomplish this, you first select the entire table and then change the line spacing to single, as shown in the following steps.

Steps **To Change Line Spacing in a Table**

1 **Position the insertion point somewhere in the table. Click Table on the menu bar, point to Select, and then point to Table (Figure 4-38).**

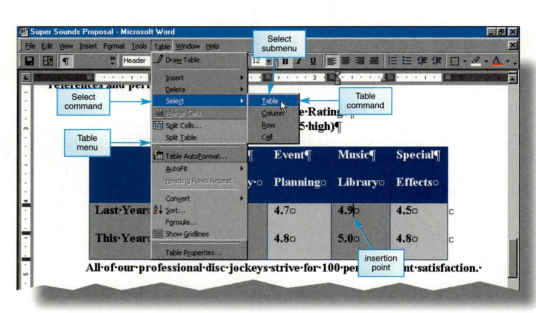

FIGURE 4-38

2 **Click Table to select the entire table. Press CTRL+1 (the numeral one).**

Word single-spaces the contents of the table (Figure 4-39).

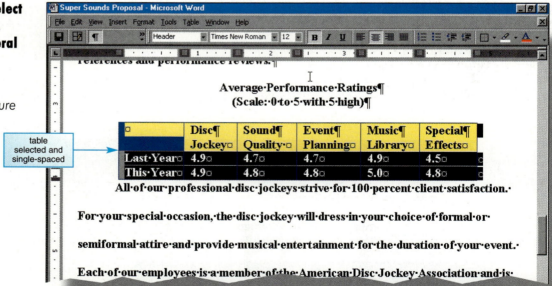

FIGURE 4-39

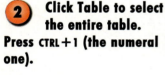

Other Ways

1. On Format menu click Paragraph, click Indents and Spacing tab, click Line spacing box arrow, click Single, click OK button

Leave the table selected for the next series of steps.

Creating a Chart from a Word Table

When you create a Word table, you easily can chart the data using an embedded charting application called **Microsoft Graph 2000**. Because Graph is an embedded application, it has its own menus and commands. With these commands, you can modify the appearance of the chart.

To create a chart from a Word table, the top row and left column of the table must contain text labels, and the other cells in the table must contain numbers. The table in the Super Sounds Draft meets these criteria.

To chart a Word table, you first select it and then chart it. The table in this document still is selected from the previous steps. Thus, perform the following steps to chart a selected table.

 To Chart a Table

1 With the table selected as shown in Figure 4-39, click Insert on the menu bar, point to Picture, and then point to Chart (Figure 4-40).

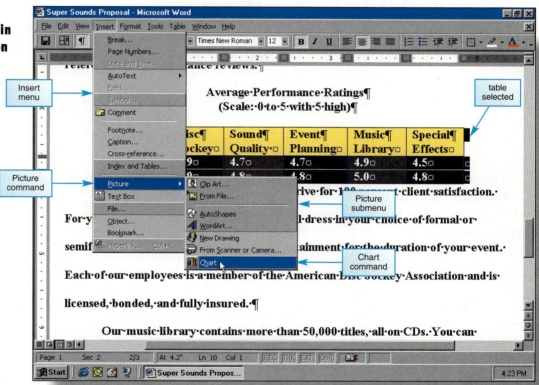

FIGURE 4-40

2 **Click Chart.**

Word starts the Microsoft Graph 2000 application (Figure 4-41). Graph creates a chart of the selected table.

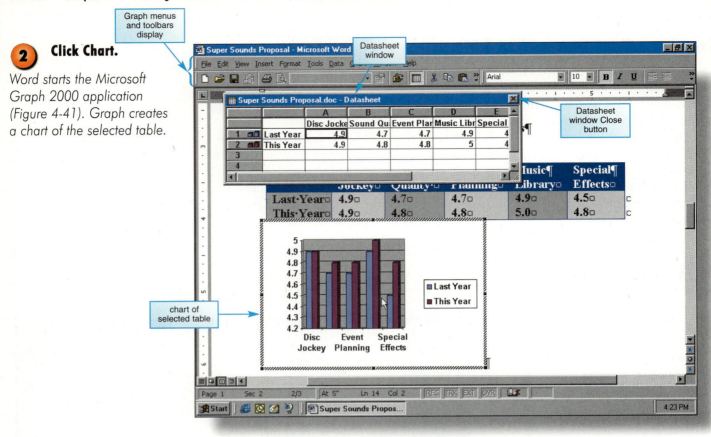

FIGURE 4-41

3 **If Graph displays a Datasheet window, click the Close button in the upper-right corner of the Datasheet window.**

Word closes the Datasheet window (Figure 4-42).

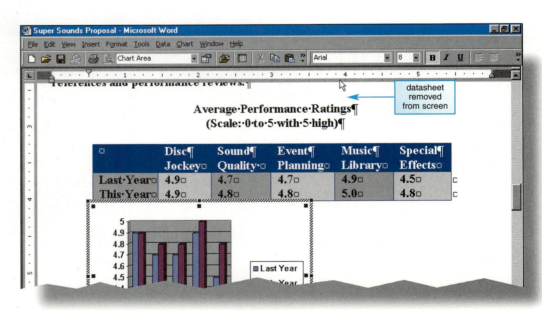

FIGURE 4-42

The menus on the menu bar and buttons on the toolbars change to Graph menus and toolbars. The Graph program is running inside your Word program.

Graph places the contents of the table into a **Datasheet window**, also called a **datasheet** (see Figure 4-41). Graph then charts the contents of the datasheet. Although you can modify the contents of the datasheet, it is not necessary in this project; thus, you close the Datasheet window.

Changing the Chart in Graph

You would like to change the format of the numbers on the value axis, move the legend so it displays below the chart, and resize the chart.

The **value axis** is a vertical axis along the left edge of the chart. Most numbers along the value axis display with one position after the decimal point; however, the top number displays as a whole number with no positions after the decimal point.

Perform the following steps so that all the numbers on the value axis display with one position after the decimal point.

 To Format Numbers on the Value Axis of a Chart

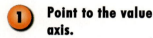 **Point to the value axis.**

Graph displays the ScreenTip, Value Axis (Figure 4-43).

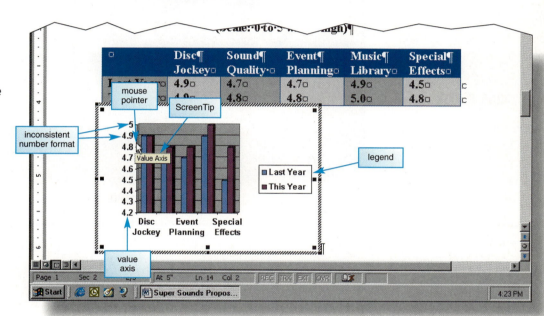

FIGURE 4-43

2 **Right-click the value axis. Point to Format Axis on the shortcut menu.**

Graph displays a shortcut menu (Figure 4-44).

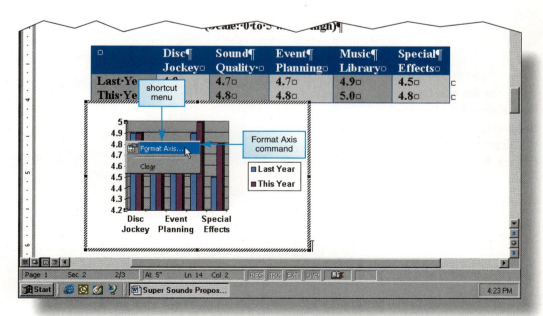

FIGURE 4-44

3 Click Format Axis. If necessary, click the Number tab when the Format Axis dialog box displays. Click Number in the Category list and then click the Decimal places down arrow once. Point to the OK button.

Graph displays the Format Axis dialog box (Figure 4-45). The Sample area displays a sample number formatted using the current selections.

4 Click the OK button.

Graph formats the value axis labels to one position after the decimal point (see Figure 4-46 below).

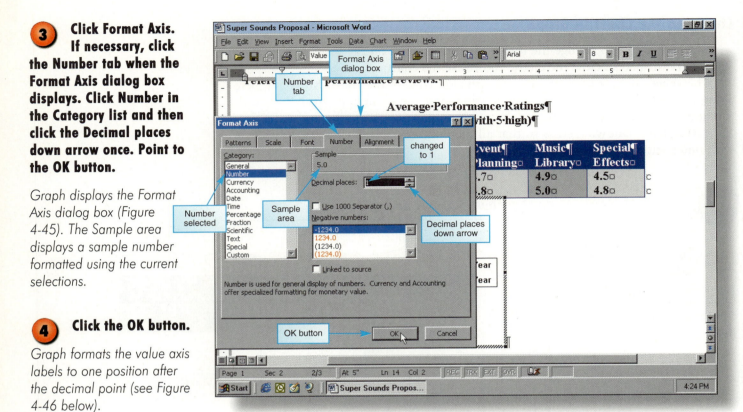

FIGURE 4-45

The next step in changing the chart is to move the legend so it displays below the chart instead of to the right of the chart. The **legend** is a box on the right side of the chart that identifies the colors assigned to categories in the chart. Perform the following steps to move the legend in the chart.

To Move Legend Placement in a Chart

1 Point to the legend in the chart and then right-click. Point to Format Legend on the shortcut menu (Figure 4-46).

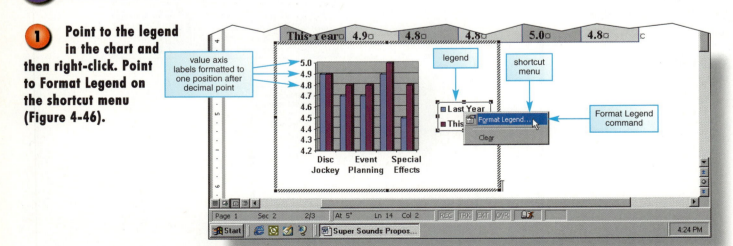

FIGURE 4-46

2 **Click Format Legend. If necessary, click the Placement tab when the Format Legend dialog box displays. Click Bottom in the Placement area and then point to the OK button.**

Graph displays the Format Legend dialog box (Figure 4-47).

3 **Click the OK button.**

Graph places the legend below the chart (see Figure 4-48 below).

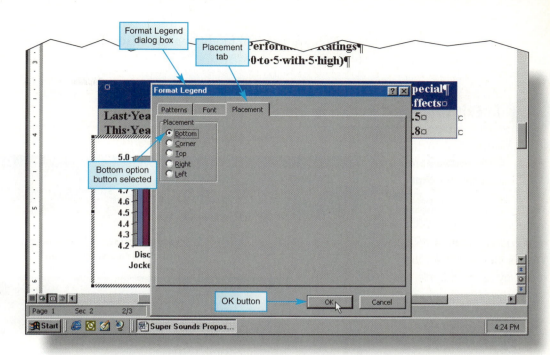

FIGURE 4-47

Notice that the Sound Quality and Music Library labels currently do not show on the category axis (the horizontal axis) because the chart is too narrow. Thus, the next step is to resize the chart so it is wider.

You resize a chart the same way you do any other graphical object. That is, you drag the chart's sizing handles as shown in the following steps.

Steps To Resize a Chart

1 **Point to the right-middle sizing handle and drag to the right as shown in Figure 4-48.**

2 **Release the mouse button.**

Graph resizes the chart (see Figure 4-49 on the next page).

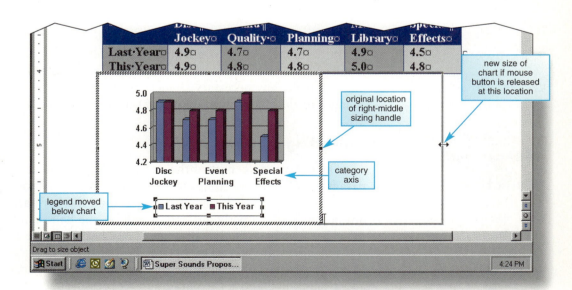

FIGURE 4-48

You are finished modifying the chart. The next step is to exit Graph and return to Word.

 ## To Exit Graph and Return to Word

 1 **Click somewhere outside the chart.**

Word closes the Graph application (Figure 4-49). Word's menus and toolbars redisplay below the title bar.

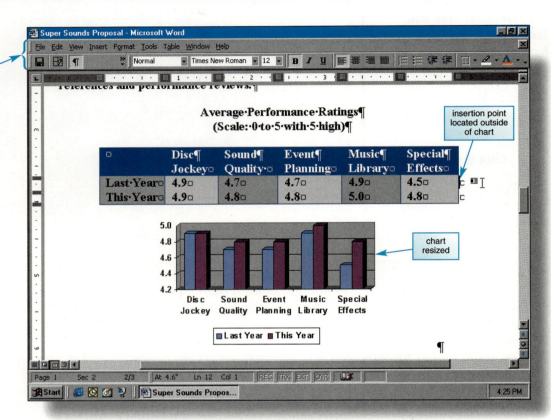

FIGURE 4-49

If, for some reason, you wanted to modify an existing chart in a document, you would double-click the chart to reopen the Microsoft Graph 2000 application. Then, you can make any necessary changes to the chart. When you are finished making changes to the chart, click anywhere outside the chart to return to Word.

Formatting the Chart in Word

The chart now is part of the paragraph below the table. Thus, you can apply any paragraph alignment settings to the chart. The chart should be centered. If you select the chart and then click the Center button on the Formatting toolbar, the chart will not be centered properly. Instead, it will be one-half inch to the right of the center point because first-line indent is set at one-half inch (see Figure 4-50).

You also want to add an outside border to the chart and add a blank line between the chart and the table. Because the chart is part of the paragraph, you will add a blank line above the paragraph by pressing the **CTRL+0** keys.

Perform the following steps to center, outline, and add a blank line above the chart.

Blank Lines

You can use menus instead of using shortcut keys to add a blank line above a paragraph. Click Format on the menu bar, click Paragraph, click the Indents and Spacing tab, change the Spacing Before box to 12 pt, and then click the OK button. To add a blank line after a paragraph, change the Spacing After box to 12 pt.

Steps To Format a Chart

1 Click anywhere in the chart.

Word selects the chart (Figure 4-50). A selected chart displays surrounded by a selection rectangle that has sizing handles at each corner and middle location.

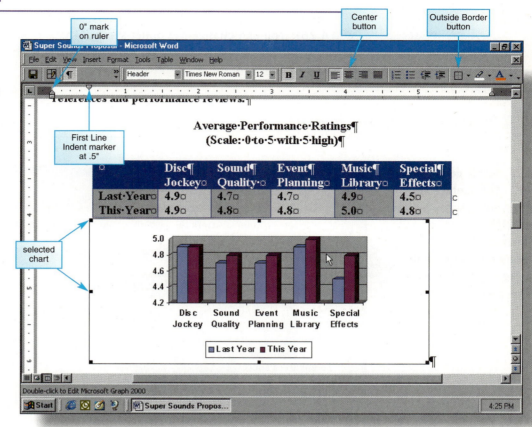

FIGURE 4-50

2 Drag the First Line Indent marker to the 0" mark on the ruler. Click the Center button on the Formatting toolbar. Click the Outside Border button on the Formatting toolbar. Press CTRL+0 (the numeral zero) to insert a blank line above the paragraph containing the chart. Click outside the chart to deselect it.

Word centers the chart between the left and right margins, places an outside border around the chart, and inserts a blank line above the chart (Figure 4-51).

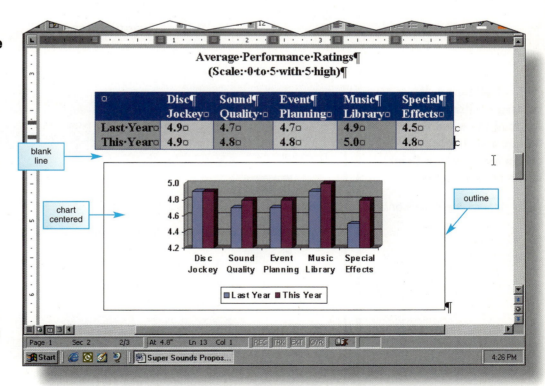

FIGURE 4-51

Customizing Bullets in a List

The draft of the sales proposal contains a bulleted list (see Figure 4-30a on page WD 4.26). You can change the bullet symbol from a small, solid circle to a graphical object as shown in Figure 4-30b on page WD 4.27. Perform the following steps to change the bullets in the list to picture bullets.

Steps To Add Picture Bullets to a List

1 Scroll down and then select the paragraphs in the bulleted list. Right-click the selection. Point to Bullets and Numbering on the shortcut menu (Figure 4-52).

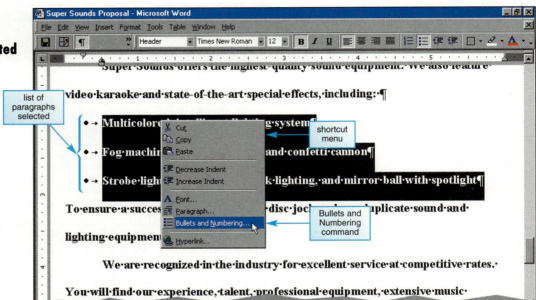

FIGURE 4-52

2 Click Bullets and Numbering. If necessary, click the Bulleted tab when the Bullets and Numbering dialog box displays. Point to the Picture button.

Word displays the Bullets and Numbering dialog box (Figure 4-53).

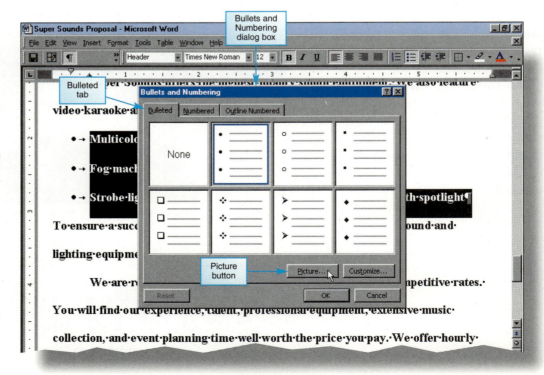

FIGURE 4-53

3 **Click the Picture button. If necessary, click the Pictures tab when the Picture Bullet dialog box displays. Click the desired picture bullet and then point to the Insert clip button on the Pop-up menu.**

Word displays the Picture Bullet dialog box (Figure 4-54). The selected picture bullet has a box around it, indicating it is selected.

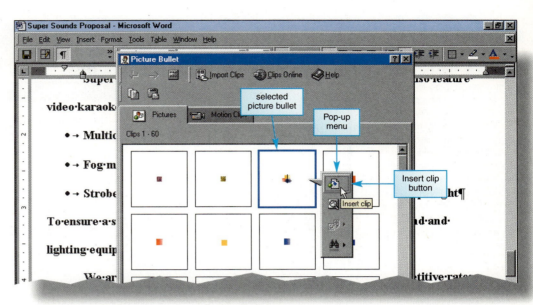

FIGURE 4-54

4 **Click the Insert clip button. When the Word window is visible again, click outside the selection to remove the highlight.**

Word changes the default bullets to picture bullets on the paragraphs (Figure 4-55).

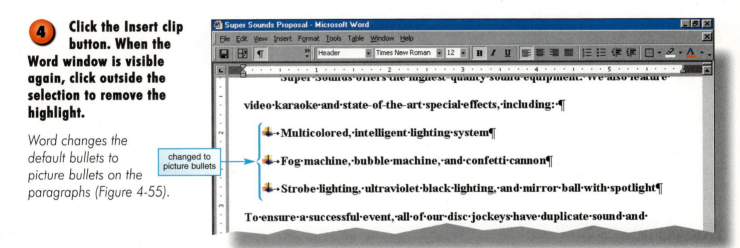

FIGURE 4-55

In addition to picture bullets, the Bullets and Numbering dialog box (Figure 4-53) provides a number of other bullet styles. To use one of these styles, simply click the desired style in the dialog box and then click the OK button.

Creating a Table Using the Draw Table Feature

Before the last paragraph of the sales proposal draft, you are to insert a table (Figure 4-30b on page WD 4.27). You have learned that a Word table is a collection of rows and columns and that the intersection of a row and a column is called a cell. Cells are filled with data.

When you want to create a simple table, one with the same number of rows and columns, use the Insert Table button on the Standard toolbar to create the table. This table, however, is more complex (Figure 4-56 on the next page). It contains a varying number of columns per row. To create a complex table, use Word's **Draw Table feature.**

Other Ways

1. Select the list, on Format menu click Bullets and Numbering, click Bullets tab, click Picture button, click desired bullet style, click OK button

More About

Bullet Symbols

For more bullet symbols, click Bullets and Numbering on the Format menu, click the Bulleted tab, click the Customize button, click the Bullets button, select desired bullet symbol, and click the OK button.

More About

Aligning Text

You may be tempted to vertically-align text by pressing the SPACEBAR. The problem is that word processing software uses variable character fonts; that is, the letter w takes up more space than the letter l. Thus, when you use the SPACEBAR to vertically-align text, the column has a wavy look because each character does not begin at the same location.

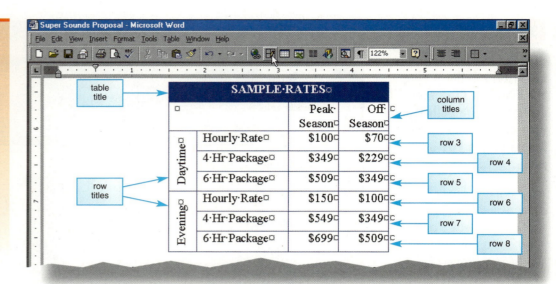

FIGURE 4-56

The following pages discuss how to create a complex table using Word's Draw Table feature.

More About

Draw Table

If you make a mistake while drawing a table, remember you always can click the Undo button to undo your most recent action.

Drawing a Table

The first step is to draw an empty table in the document. To do this, you use the **Draw Table button** on the Tables and Borders toolbar. The Tables and Borders toolbar contains a **Draw Table button** that, when recessed, changes the mouse pointer shape to a pencil. To draw the boundary, rows, and columns of the table, you drag the pencil pointer on the screen.

Perform the following steps to draw the table shown in Figure 4-56. If you make a mistake while drawing the table, remember that you can click the Undo button on the Standard toolbar to undo your most recent action.

 **To Draw a Table**

1 **Position the insertion point at the beginning of the last paragraph (before the word, To). Double-click the move handle on the Standard toolbar to display the entire toolbar. If it is not already recessed, click the Tables and Borders button on the Standard toolbar to display the Tables and Borders toolbar. If it is not already recessed, click the Draw Table button on the Tables and Borders toolbar. Move the mouse pointer, which is the shape of a pencil, into the document window to the location shown in Figure 4-57.**

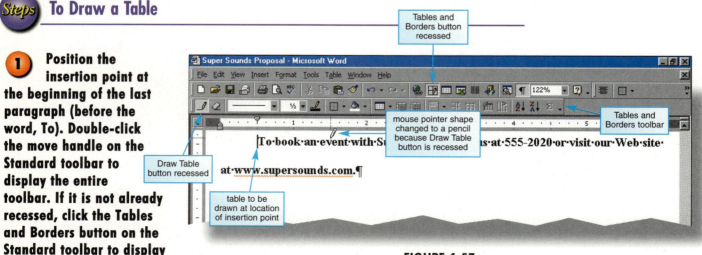

FIGURE 4-57

2 Drag the pencil pointer downward and to the right until the dotted rectangle is positioned similarly to the one shown in Figure 4-58.

Word displays a dotted rectangle that indicates the table's size (Figure 4-58).

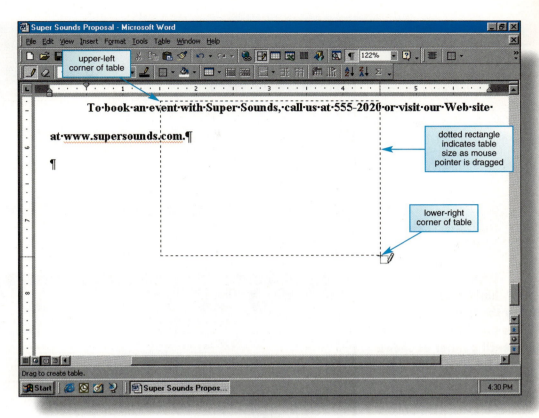

FIGURE 4-58

3 Release the mouse button. If necessary, scroll to display the entire table in the document window. If Word wraps the text around the table, click Edit on the menu bar, click Undo, and then begin these steps again - moving the pencil pointer closer to the word, event.

Word draws the table border. The Outside Border button on the Tables and Borders toolbar is recessed.

4 Position the pencil pointer as shown in Figure 4-59.

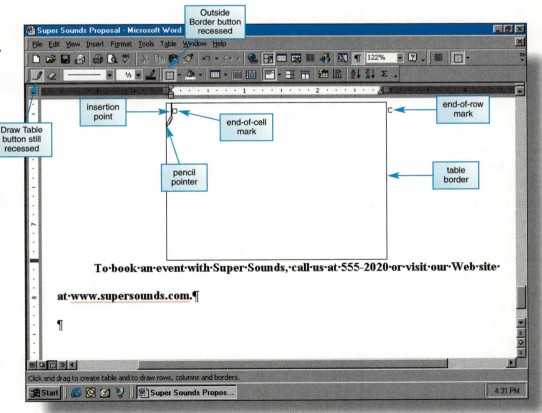

FIGURE 4-59

5 **Drag the pencil pointer to the right to draw a horizontal line.**

Word draws a horizontal line, which forms the bottom border of the first row in the table (Figure 4-60).

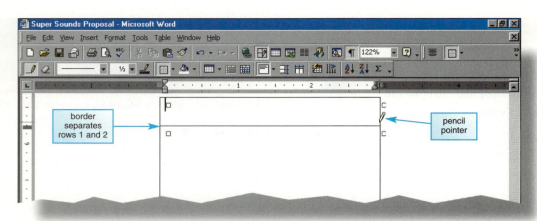

FIGURE 4-60

6 **Draw another horizontal line below the first as shown in Figure 4-61. Then, position the pencil pointer as shown in Figure 4-61.**

Word draws a second horizontal line to form the bottom border of the second row in the table (Figure 4-61). The pencil pointer is positioned to draw the first column.

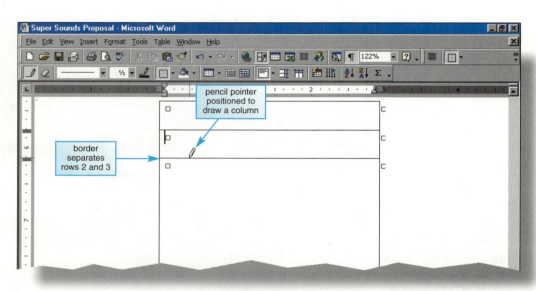

FIGURE 4-61

7 **Draw three vertical lines to form the column borders similar to those shown in Figure 4-62.**

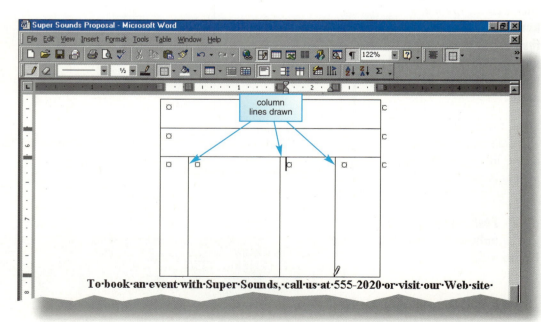

FIGURE 4-62

8 Draw five horizontal lines to form the row borders similar to those shown in Figure 4-63.

The empty table displays as shown in Figure 4-63.

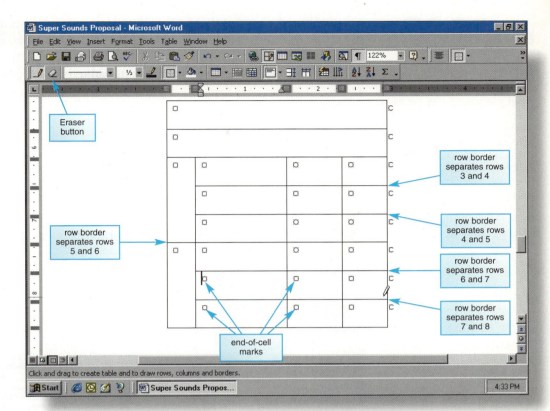

FIGURE 4-63

If, after drawing rows and columns in the table, you want to remove and redraw a line, click the **Eraser button** on the Tables and Borders toolbar (Figure 4-63) and then drag the mouse pointer (an eraser shape) through the line to erase. Click the Eraser button again to turn the eraser pointer off.

All Word tables that you draw have a .5-point border. To change this border, you can use the Tables and Borders toolbar as described earlier in this project.

You have learned that each row has an **end-of-row mark** (see Figure 4-59 on page WD 4.43), which is used to add columns to the right of a table, and each cell has an **end-of-cell mark**, which is used to select a cell. Notice the end-of-cell marks currently are left-aligned in each cell (Figure 4-63), which indicates the data will be left-aligned in the cells.

To format a table or data in a table, first you must select the cell(s) and then apply the appropriate formats. Because selecting table text is such a crucial function of Word tables, techniques to select these items are described in Table 4-2.

1. On Table menu click Draw Table, use pencil pointer to draw table

Table 4-2 Techniques for Selecting Items in a Table

ITEM TO SELECT	ACTION
Cell	Click the left edge of the cell.
Row	Click to the left of the row.
Column	Click the column's top gridline or border.
Cells, rows, or columns	Drag through the cells, rows, or columns.
Text in next cell	Press the TAB key.
Text in previous cell	Press the SHIFT+TAB keys.
Entire table	Click the table, click Table on the menu bar, point to Select, and then click Table.

Table Wrapping

When you draw a table, Word may wrap the text of the document around the table. To remove the text wrapping, right-click the table, click Table Properties, click the Table tab, click None in Text wrapping area, and then click the OK button. To have Word automatically wrap text around the table, hold down the CTRL key while you draw the table.

Because the text of the draft of the sales proposal is double-spaced and bold, the table also is formatted to double-spaced and bold. You want the table to be single-spaced and not bold. Thus, perform the following steps to change the line spacing of the table from double to single and remove the bold format from the cells in the table.

TO CHANGE TABLE FORMATS

1 Be sure the insertion point is somewhere in the table.

2 Click Table on the menu bar, point to Select, and then click Table.

3 Press CTRL+1 (the numeral one) to single-space the rows in the table.

4 Press CTRL+B to remove the bold format from the cells in the table.

Word changes the table line spacing to single and removes the bold format (Figure 4-64).

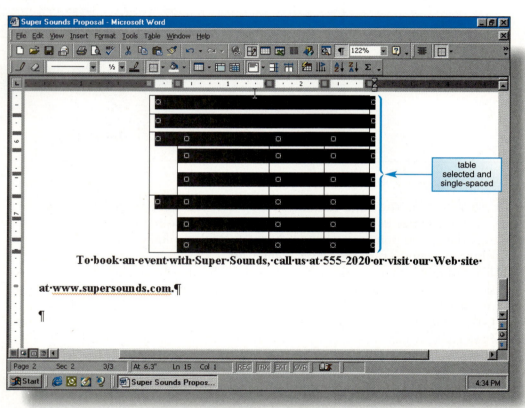

FIGURE 4-64

Because you drew the table borders with the mouse, some of the rows may be varying heights. Perform the following step to make the row spacing in the table even.

Table Line Spacing

If you have distributed rows evenly and then want to change line spacing, you first must do the following: select the table, right-click the selection, click Table Properties on the shortcut menu, click the Row tab, remove the check mark from the Specify height check box, and then click the OK button.

Steps **To Distribute Rows Evenly**

1 **With the table still selected, click the Distribute Rows Evenly button on the Tables and Borders toolbar.**

Word makes the height of the selected rows uniform (Figure 4-65).

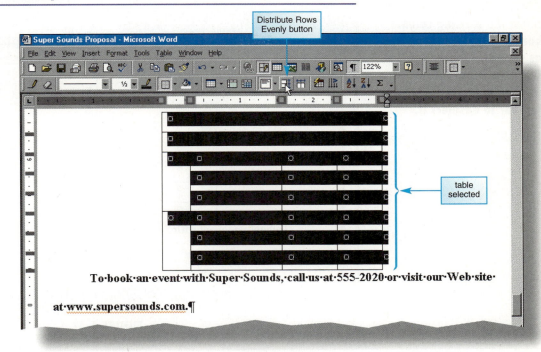

FIGURE 4-65

Two additional lines for column headings are required in the table. Perform the following steps to continue drawing the table.

Steps **To Draw More Table Lines**

1 **Click inside the table to remove the highlight. Click the Draw Table button on the Tables and Borders toolbar. Position the pencil pointer as shown in Figure 4-66.**

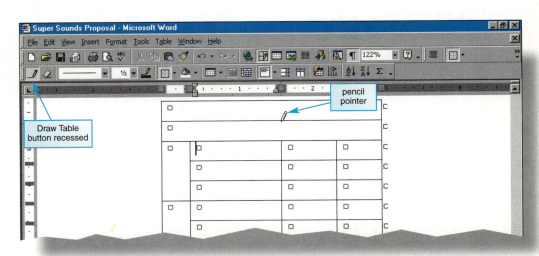

FIGURE 4-66

Other Ways

1. Select cells, on Table menu point to AutoFit, on AutoFit menu click Distribute Rows Evenly
2. Drag row boundaries (borders) on table
3. Drag Adjust Table Row markers on vertical ruler
4. On Table menu click Table Properties, click Row tab, enter desired height, click OK button

2 Draw a line downward until you reach the existing column border. Draw a second line as shown in Figure 4-67. Click the Draw Table button on the Tables and Borders toolbar to deselect it.

The table is drawn completely (Figure 4-67).

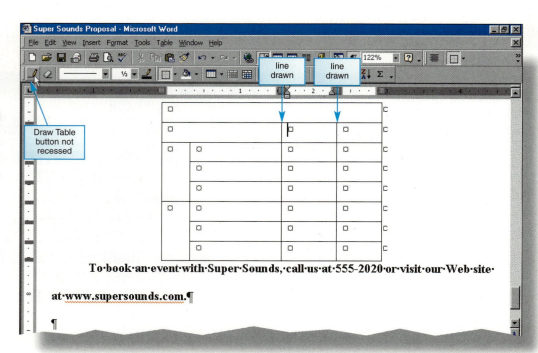

FIGURE 4-67

The last two columns in the table must be the same width. Because you drew the borders of these columns, they may be varying widths. Perform the following steps to evenly size these columns.

 To Distribute Columns Evenly

1 Point to the left of the cell shown in Figure 4-68 until the mouse pointer changes to a right-pointing solid arrow.

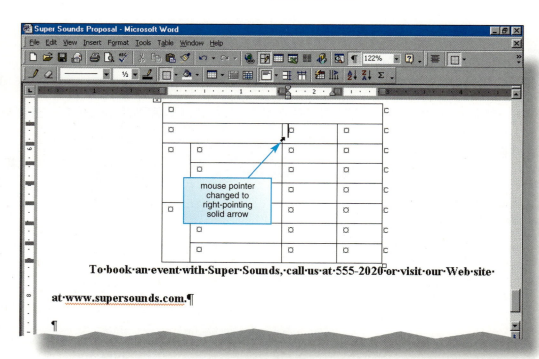

FIGURE 4-68

2 Drag through the 14 cells shown in Figure 4-69 and then click the Distribute Columns Evenly button on the Tables and Borders toolbar.

Word applies uniform widths to the selected columns (Figure 4-69).

3 Click outside the selection to remove the highlight.

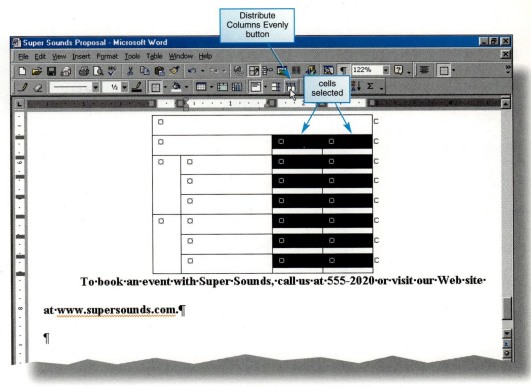

FIGURE 4-69

Entering Data into the Table

The next step is to enter the data into the table. To advance from one column to the next, press the TAB key. To advance from one row to the next, also press the TAB key; do not press the ENTER key. The ENTER key is used to begin new paragraphs within a cell. Perform the following steps to enter the data into the table.

TO ENTER DATA INTO A TABLE

1 Click in the first cell of the table. Double-click the move handle on the Formatting toolbar to display the entire toolbar. Click the Center button on the Formatting toolbar. Type SAMPLE RATES and then press the TAB key twice.

2 Type Peak Season and then press the TAB key. Type Off Season and then press the TAB key.

3 Type Daytime and then press the TAB key. Type Hourly Rate and then press the TAB key. Type $100 and then press the TAB key. Type $70 and then press the TAB key twice. Type 4 Hr Package and then press the TAB key. Type $349 and then press the TAB key. Type $229 and then press the TAB key twice. Type 6 Hr Package and then press the TAB key. Type $509 and then press the TAB key. Type $349 and then press the TAB key.

4 Type Evening and then press the TAB key. Type Hourly Rate and then press the TAB key. Type $150 and then press the TAB key. Type $100 and then press the TAB key twice. Type 4 Hr Package and then press the TAB key. Type $549 and then press the TAB key. Type $349 and then press the TAB key twice. Type 6 Hr Package and then press the TAB key. Type $699 and then press the TAB key. Type $509 as the last entry.

The table data is entered (Figure 4-70 on the next page).

The table data is entered (Figure 4-70 on the next page).

Other Ways

1. Select cells, on Table menu point to AutoFit, on AutoFit menu click Distribute Columns Evenly
2. Drag column boundaries (borders) on table
3. Drag Move Table Column markers on horizontal ruler
4. On Table menu click Table Properties, click Column tab, enter desired width, click OK button

More About

Table Columns

When the insertion point is in a table, the ruler displays column markers that indicate the beginning and ending of columns. A column boundary is the vertical gridline immediately to the right of a column in the table itself. To resize a column width, drag the column boundary in the table or the column marker on the ruler. Holding down the ALT key while dragging markers displays column width measurements.

Microsoft **Word 2000**

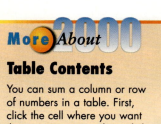

More About 2000

Table Contents

You can sum a column or row of numbers in a table. First, click the cell where you want the sum to appear. Then, click Formula on the Table menu. If you agree with the formula Word proposes in the Formula dialog box, click the OK button; otherwise, delete the formula and then build your own formula using the Paste Function list box.

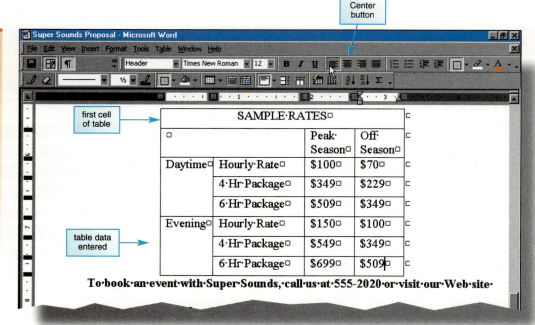

FIGURE 4-70

The next step is to rotate the row heading text, Daytime and Evening, so it displays vertically instead of horizontally.

Formatting the Table

The data you enter in cells displays horizontally. You can change the text so it displays vertically. Changing the direction of text adds variety to your tables. Perform the following steps to display the row heading text vertically.

 To Vertically Display Text in a Cell

1 **Select the row heading text cells containing the words, Daytime and Evening. Point to the Change Text Direction button on the Tables and Borders toolbar.**

The cells to be formatted are selected (Figure 4-71).

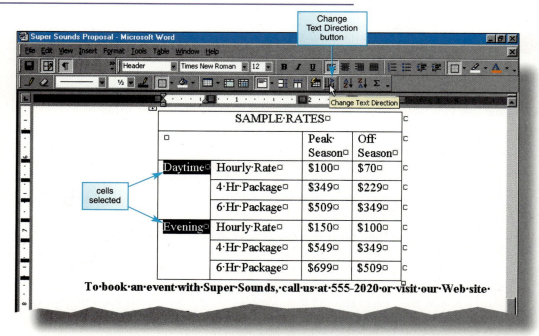

FIGURE 4-71

2 **Click the Change Text Direction button twice.**

Word displays the text vertically so you read it from bottom to top (Figure 4-72).

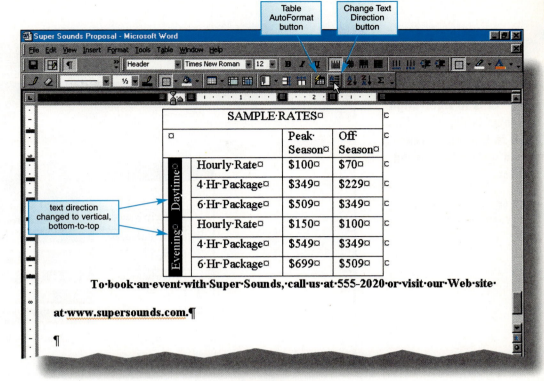

FIGURE 4-72

The first time you click the Change Text Direction button, Word displays the text vertically so you read it from top to bottom. The second time you click the Change Text Direction button, Word displays the text vertically so you read it from bottom to top (Figure 4-72). If you click the button a third time, the text would display horizontally again.

Perform the following steps to format the table using the Table AutoFormat command.

TO AUTOFORMAT A TABLE

1 Click somewhere in the table. Click the Table AutoFormat button on the Tables and Borders toolbar (see Figure 4-72).

2 When the Table AutoFormat dialog box displays, scroll through the Formats list and then click Grid 8. Be sure these check boxes contain check marks: Borders, Shading, Font, Color, Heading rows, and First column. All other check boxes should be cleared.

3 Click the OK button.

Word formats the table using the Grid 8 format (Figure 4-73 on the next page).

Just as with paragraphs, you can left-align, center, or right-align the end-of-cell marks in a table. The data you enter into the cells is left-aligned, by default. You can change the alignment just as you would for a paragraph. Before changing the alignment, you must select the cell(s). Perform the steps on the next page to right-align the end-of-cell marks for cells containing dollar amounts.

Shading

You can shade paragraphs or the cells in a table. To do this, click the cell(s) or paragraph(s) to shade, click the Shading Color button arrow on the Tables and Borders toolbar, and then click the desired shade color on the shade palette. To remove shading, click No Fill on the shade palette.

Steps To Right-Align Cell Contents

1 Drag through the cells to right-align as shown in Figure 4-73. Point to the Align Right button on the Formatting toolbar.

Word selects the cells to format (Figure 4-73).

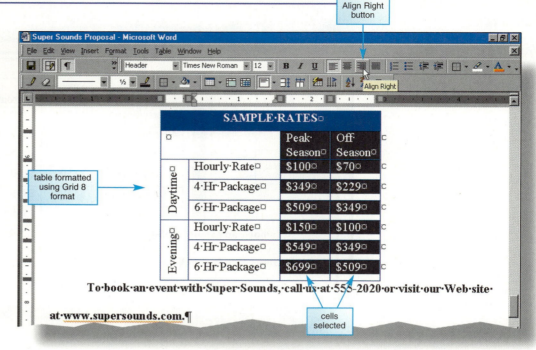

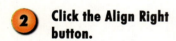

FIGURE 4-73

2 Click the Align Right button.

Word right-aligns the data and end-of-cell marks in the selected area (Figure 4-74).

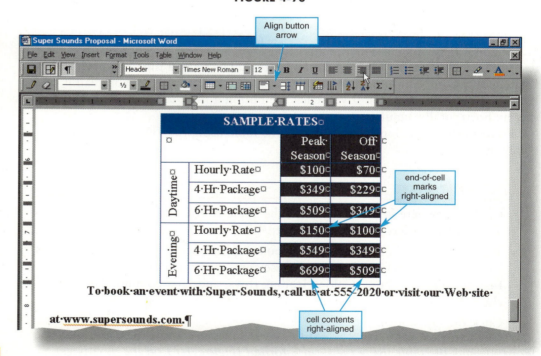

FIGURE 4-74

In addition to aligning text horizontally in a cell (left, centered, or right), you can center it vertically using the Align button arrow on the Tables and Borders toolbar. If you wanted to center text vertically, or both vertically and horizontally, you could click the Align button arrow and then click the appropriate button. Table 4-3 illustrates the various alignment options.

Table 4-3 Cell Alignment Options

Align Top Left	Hourly Rate		
Align Top Center		Hourly Rate	
Align Top Right			Hourly Rate
Align Center Left	Hourly Rate		
Align Center		Hourly Rate	
Align Center Right			Hourly Rate
Align Bottom Left	Hourly Rate		
Align Bottom Center		Hourly Rate	
Align Bottom Right			Hourly Rate

More About

Cell Alignment

Cell alignment options also are available on the Table menu. Right-click the cell(s) to align, point to Cell Alignment on the shortcut menu, and then click the desired cell alignment icon.

Working with Tables

At times you might want to insert additional rows or columns in a table. To add a row to the end of a table, position the insertion point in the bottom-right corner cell and then press the TAB key.

Depending on the task you want to perform in a table, the function of the Table button on the Standard toolbar changes, and the commands on the Table menu and associated shortcut menu change. To **add rows** in the middle of a table, select the row below where the new row is to be inserted, then click the Insert Rows button (the same button you clicked to insert a table); or click Insert Rows on the shortcut menu; or click Table on the menu bar, point to Insert, and then click Rows Above. To **add a column** in the middle of a table, select the column to the right of where the new columns is to be inserted and then click the Insert Columns button (the same button you clicked to insert a table); click Insert Columns on the shortcut menu; or click Table on the menu bar, point to Insert, and then click Columns to the Left. To add a column to the right of a table, select the end-of-row marks at the right edge of the table, then click the Insert Columns button; click Insert Columns on the shortcut menu; or click Table on the menu bar, point to Insert, and then click Columns to the Right.

If you want to **delete row(s)** or **delete column(s)** from a table, select the row(s) or column(s) to delete and then click **Delete Rows** or **Delete Columns** on shortcut menu, or click Table on the menu bar, click Delete, and then click the appropriate item to delete.

The final step in formatting the table is to add a blank line between the table and the paragraph below it, as described in the following step.

More About

Moving Tables

To move a table to a new location, point to the upper-left corner of the table until the table move handle displays (a small box containing a four-headed arrow). Point to the table move handle and then drag the table to its new location.

More About

Resizing Tables

If you wanted to resize a table, you would click the Draw Table button on the Tables and Borders toolbar to turn off the Draw Table feature and then drag the table or column boundaries to their new locations.

TO ADD A BLANK LINE ABOVE A PARAGRAPH

 1 Position the insertion point in the last paragraph of the proposal and then press CTRL+0 (the numeral zero). Double-click the move handle on the Standard toolbar to display the entire toolbar. Click the Tables and Borders button on the Standard toolbar.

Word adds a blank line above the paragraph (Figure 4-75 on the next page). Word removes the Tables and Borders toolbar from the window.

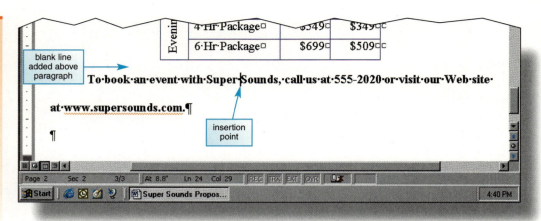

FIGURE 4-75

Creating a Watermark

A **watermark** is text or a graphic that displays on top of or behind the text in a document. For example, a catalog may print the words, Not Available, on top of sold-out items. A product manager may want the word, Draft, to print behind his or her first draft of a five-year plan. Some companies use their logos or other graphics as watermarks on documents to add visual appeal to the document.

To create a watermark in a document, you add the text or graphic to the header in the section you want the watermark. Then, you resize and position the watermark where you want it to display. You can move the watermark anywhere on the page; its location is not restricted to the area at the top or bottom of the page.

In this project, the owners of Super Sounds would like the music CDs graphic to display on the pages of the body of the proposal. Perform the following steps to create this watermark.

To Create a Watermark of a Graphic

1 **Click View on the menu bar and then click Header and Footer. When the header area displays on the screen, press the END key, press the ENTER key twice, and then press CTRL+E to center the insertion point and paragraph mark. Click Insert on the menu bar, point to Picture, and then point to Clip Art.**

Word centers the insertion point on line 3 of the header (Figure 4-76).

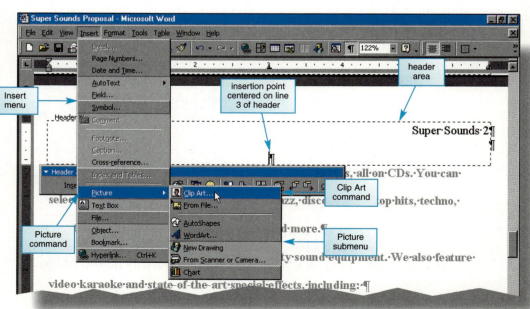

FIGURE 4-76

2 **Click Clip Art. In the Insert ClipArt window, click the Downloaded Clips category, click the music CDs graphic, click the Insert clip button on the Pop-up menu, and then close the Insert ClipArt window. When the graphic displays in the header of the document, click it to select it. (If the Picture toolbar does not display, click View on the menu bar, point to Toolbars, and then click Picture.) Point to the Format Picture button on the Picture toolbar (Figure 4-77).**

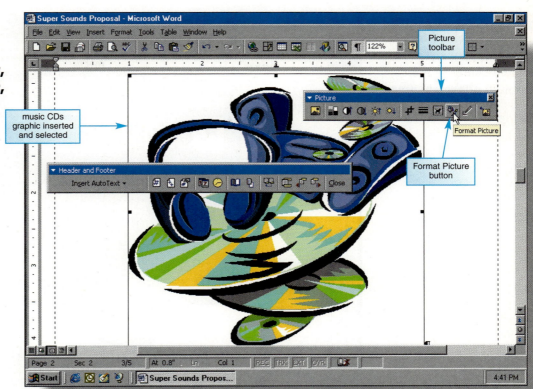

FIGURE 4-77

3 **Click the Format Picture button. When the Format Picture dialog box displays, if necessary, click the Picture tab. Click the Color box arrow and then click Watermark.**

Word displays the Format Picture dialog box (Figure 4-78). The Watermark setting adjusts the brightness and contrast so the graphic displays faded.

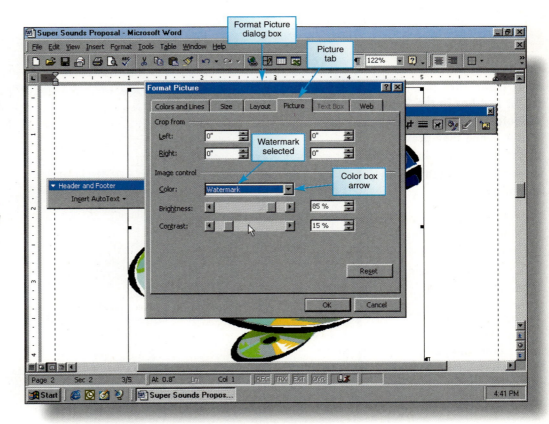

FIGURE 4-78

4 **Click the Layout tab. Click Behind text in the Wrapping style area and Center in the Horizontal alignment area.**

These settings instruct Word to place the text in front of the image, which is to be centered horizontally on the page (Figure 4-79).

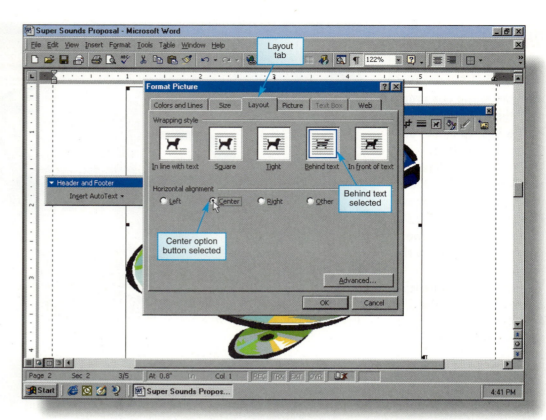

FIGURE 4-79

5 **Click the Size tab. Click Lock aspect ratio to remove the check mark. Triple-click the Height text box in the Size and rotate area to select it. Type** 9.5 **and then press the TAB key. Type** 7 **in the Width text box. Point to the OK button.**

By deselecting Lock aspect ratio, you can vary the height and width measurements from their original proportions (Figure 4-80).

6 **Click the OK button. Click the Close Header and Footer button on the Header and Footer toolbar.**

The watermark displays faded behind the body proposal.

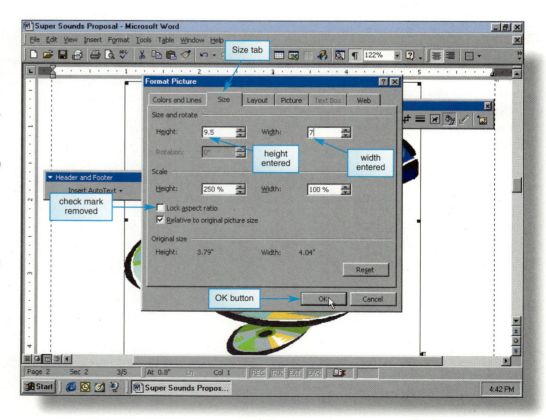

FIGURE 4-80

If you want to remove a watermark, you would delete it from the header or footer.

To see how the watermark looks in the entire document, view the document in print preview as described in the following steps.

TO PRINT PREVIEW A DOCUMENT

1 Click the Print Preview button on the Standard toolbar. If necessary, click the Multiple Pages button on the Print Preview toolbar and then click the third icon in the first row of the grid (1 × 3 Pages) to display all three pages of the proposal as shown in Figure 4-81.

2 When finished viewing the document, click the Close Preview button on the Print Preview toolbar.

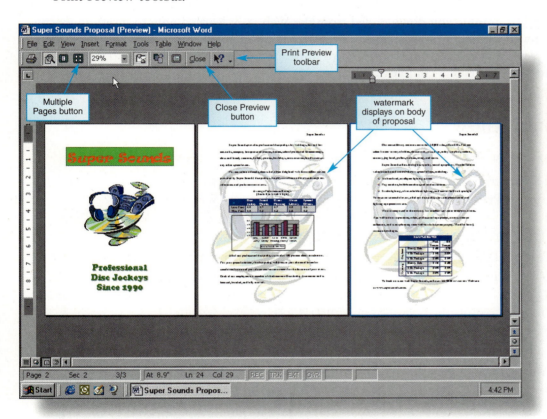

FIGURE 4-81

Checking Spelling, Saving Again, and Printing the Sales Proposal

Check the spelling of the document by clicking the Spelling and Grammar button on the Standard toolbar. Save the document one final time by clicking the Save button on the Standard toolbar, then print the sales proposal by clicking the Print button. The printed document displays as shown in Figure 4-1 on page 4.5.

Project 4 now is complete. Follow this step to quit Word.

TO QUIT WORD

1 Click the Close button in the Word window.

The Word window closes.

More About

Quick Reference

For a table that lists how to complete the tasks covered in this book using the mouse, menu, shortcut menu, and keyboard, visit the Shelly Cashman Series Office Web page (www.scsite.com/off2000/qr.htm) and then click Microsoft Word 2000.

More About

Printing

If you want to save ink, print faster, or decrease printer overrun errors, lower the printer resolution. Click File on the menu bar, click Print, click the Properties button in the Print dialog box, click the Graphics tab, click the Resolution box arrow, click a lower resolution than that displayed currently, click the Apply button, click the OK button, and then click the Close button.

More About

Microsoft Certification

The Microsoft Office User Specialist (MOUS) Certification program provides an opportunity for you to obtain a valuable industry credential - proof that you have the Word 2000 skills required by employers. For more information, see Appendix D or visit the Shelly Cashman Series MOUS Web page at www.scsite.com/off2000/cert.htm.

CASE PERSPECTIVE SUMMARY

As promised, you finish the sales proposal for Super Sounds within a week and set up an appointment to meet with Juan and Nora Garcia. Juan and Nora are quite impressed with the proposal. They mention that your creativity with colors and graphics makes this proposal much more appealing than any other they have seen. In fact, they would like to incorporate your work into their Web site. You point out that you have experience developing Web pages and would be willing to update theirs, if they would like. Without hesitation, they offer you the job.

Project Summary

Project 4 introduced you to creating a proposal with a title page, table, chart, and a watermark. First, you created a title page that contained a graphic you downloaded from the Web. You learned how to insert an existing Word document into the active document. You inserted a header for the body of the proposal that was different from the title page header. Next, you charted an existing Word table. You added picture bullets to a list. Then, you used the Draw Table feature to create a complex table.

What You Should Know

Having completed this project, you now should be able to perform the following tasks:

▶ Add a Blank Line Above a Paragraph *(WD 4.53)*
▶ Add a Header Different from a Previous Header *(WD 4.28)*
▶ Add Picture Bullets to a List *(WD 4.40)*
▶ Align Text with Top of Page *(WD 4.22)*
▶ Apply the Normal Style *(WD 4.19)*
▶ AutoFormat a Table *(WD 4.51)*
▶ Border a Paragraph *(WD 4.8)*
▶ Center Text Vertically *(WD 4.17)*
▶ Change Line Spacing in a Table *(WD 4.32)*
▶ Change Table Formats *(WD 4.46)*
▶ Chart a Table *(WD 4.33)*
▶ Close the Header Area *(WD 4.31)*
▶ Create a Watermark of a Graphic *(WD 4.54)*
▶ Display Formatting Marks *(WD 4.7)*
▶ Distribute Columns Evenly *(WD 4.48)*
▶ Distribute Rows Evenly *(WD 4.47)*
▶ Download Clip Art from Microsoft's Clip Gallery Live Web Page *(WD 4.12)*
▶ Draw a Table *(WD 4.42)*
▶ Draw More Table Lines *(WD 4.47)*
▶ Enter Data into a Table *(WD 4.49)*
▶ Exit Graph and Return to Word *(WD 4.38)*
▶ Format a Chart *(WD 4.39)*
▶ Format and Enter the Company Slogan *(WD 4.15)*
▶ Format Characters *(WD 4.7)*
▶ Format Numbers on the Value Axis of a Chart *(WD 4.35)*
▶ Import Clip Art from the Data Disk *(WD 4.15)*
▶ Insert a Next Page Section Break *(WD 4.21)*
▶ Insert a Word Document into an Open Document *(WD 4.23)*
▶ Move Legend Placement in a Chart *(WD 4.36)*
▶ Page Number Differently in a Section *(WD 4.29)*
▶ Print a Document *(WD 4.25)*
▶ Print Preview a Document *(WD 4.57)*
▶ Quit Word *(WD 4.57)*
▶ Reset Menus and Toolbars *(WD 4.6)*
▶ Resize a Chart *(WD 4.37)*
▶ Right-align Cell Contents *(WD 4.52)*
▶ Save a Document *(WD 4.18)*
▶ Save an Active Document with a New File Name *(WD 4.25)*
▶ Single-space a Paragraph *(WD 4.31)*
▶ Start Word *(WD 4.6)*
▶ Vertically Display Text in a Cell *(WD 4.50)*
▶ Zoom Text Width *(WD 4.6)*

Apply Your Knowledge

➕ Project Reinforcement at www.scsite.com/off2000/reinforce.htm

1 **Working with Tables**

Instructions: Start Word. Open the document, Weekly Sales Report, on the Data Disk. If you did not download the Data Disk, see the inside back cover for instructions for downloading the Data Disk or see your instructor.

The document contains a table created with the Draw Table feature. You are to modify the table so it looks like Figure 4-82.

Perform the following tasks.

1. Select the cell containing the title, Shoe World. Center it, bold it, and change its font size to 28. If necessary, click the Tables and Borders button on the Standard toolbar to display the Tables and Borders toolbar. Click the Shading Color button arrow on the Tables and Borders toolbar and then click Plum. Click the Font Color button arrow on the Formatting toolbar and then click White.

Shoe World

		Monday	Tuesday	Wednesday	Thursday	Friday	Total
		Weekly Sales Report					
Zone 1	Chicago	45,443	34,221	41,202	40,112	38,556	199,534
	Dallas	67,203	52,202	39,668	45,203	43,223	247,499
	San Francisco	68,778	60,980	49,127	57,009	31,101	266,995
Zone 2	Boston	79,985	68,993	45,024	54,897	71,992	320,891
	Detroit	45,494	41,220	22,101	29,445	34,003	172,263
	Miami	57,925	56,898	49,056	51,119	54,395	269,393
Total Weekly Sales		364,828	314,514	246,178	277,785	273,270	1,476,575

FIGURE 4-82

2. Select the row containing the subtitle, Weekly Sales Report. Center and bold the subtitle. Click the Font Color button arrow on the Formatting toolbar and then click Teal.

3. Select the cells containing the row headings, Zone 1 and Zone 2. Click the Change Text Direction button on the Tables and Borders toolbar twice.

4. Select the cells containing the column headings, Monday, Tuesday, Wednesday, Thursday, and Friday. Click Table on the menu bar, point to AutoFit, and then click AutoFit to Contents. These columns now are as wide as the column headings.

5. Select the cell containing the label, Total Weekly Sales, and the cell immediately to its right. Click the Merge Cells button on the Table and Borders toolbar.

6. Click the cell in the last row to contain the total weekly cells for Monday and then click the AutoSum button on the Tables and Borders toolbar. Repeat this process for each cell in the bottom row of the table. If the totals do not fit in the existing column widths, drag the column borders to the right to increase the width of the affected columns.

7. Click the cell to contain the Total Sales for Miami. Click the AutoSum button on the Tables and Borders toolbar. Repeat this process for each cell in the rightmost column of the table – working your way up the table. If your totals are incorrect, click Table on the menu bar, click Formula, be sure the formula is =SUM(LEFT), and then click the OK button.

8. Center the cells containing the column headings, e.g, Monday, Tuesday, etc.

9. Right-align the cells containing numbers.

10. Select the rows below the subtitle, Weekly Sales Report, and then click the Distribute Rows Evenly button on the Tables and Borders toolbar.

11. Bold the cells in the last row and also in the rightmost column.

12. Click File on the menu bar and then click Save As. Use the file name Revised Weekly Sales Report.

13. Print the revised document.

In the Lab

1 Creating a Proposal Using the Draw Table Feature

Problem: The owner of The Computer Doctor has hired you to prepare a sales proposal describing his services (Figures 4-83a and 4-83b), which will be mailed to all community residents.

Instructions:

1. Create the title page as shown in Figure 4-83a. The computer is located in the Cartoons category of the Clip Gallery or search for the keywords, sick computer, to locate the image of the computer. Resize the graphic to 175% of the original size (approximately 3.5" wide and 3" high). *Hint:* Click the Format Picture button on the Picture toolbar and then click the Size tab.

FIGURE 4-83a

In the Lab

2. Center the title page vertically. Insert a section break. Return to the Normal style. Change the vertical alignment for the second section to top. Adjust line spacing to double. If necessary, change the font size to 12 for the body of the proposal.
3. Enter the body of the proposal as shown in Figure 4-83b. The body of the proposal has a list with red picture bullets and a table created with the Draw Table feature. Single-space the table. Change the alignment of the row titles, Software and Hardware, to Align Center Left. *Hint:* Use the Align button arrow on the Tables and Borders toolbar. Select the table and shade it Light Turquoise using the Shading Color button arrow on the Tables and Borders toolbar.
4. Check the spelling. Save the document with Computer Doctor Proposal as the file name. View and print the document in print preview.

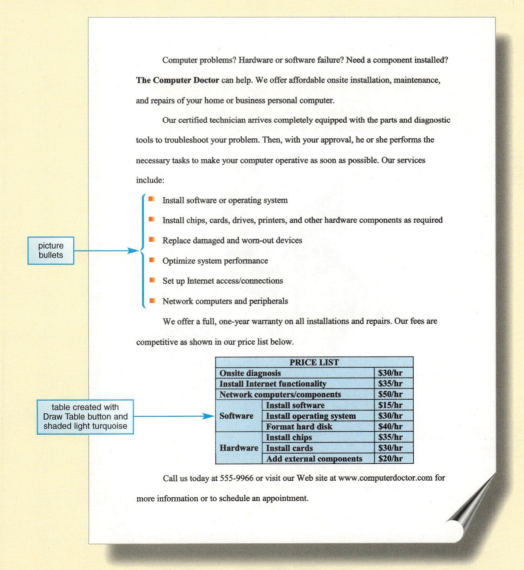

FIGURE 4-83b

In the Lab

2 Creating a Proposal Using Downloaded Clip Art and a Chart

Problem: Your neighbor owns Entertainment Enterprises and has hired you to create a sales proposal for Sunshine the Clown. You develop the proposal shown in Figures 4-84a and 4-84b.

Instructions:

1. Create the title page as shown in Figure 4-84a. Download the clip art from Microsoft's Clip Gallery Live Web page. To reach this file, type clown in the SEARCH by keyword text box. If you do not have access to the Web, you can import the file (file name PE03690_) from the Data Disk. If you did not download the Data Disk, see the inside back cover for instructions for downloading the Data Disk or see your instructor.

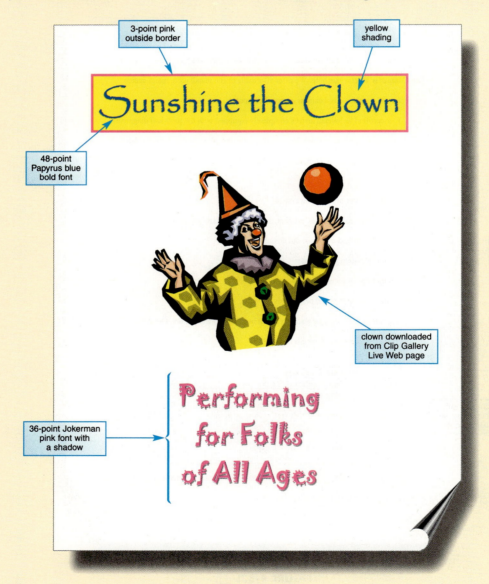

FIGURE 4-84a

In the Lab

2. Center the title page vertically. Insert a section break. Return to the Normal style. Change the Vertical alignment for the second section to top. Adjust line spacing to double. If necessary, change the font size to 12 for the body of the proposal.

3. Create the body of the proposal as shown in Figure 4-84b. The body of the proposal has picture bullets and a table created with the Insert Table button. The table contains five columns and two rows and is formatted using the Grid 3 AutoFormat option. Center the table between the page margins. Chart the table. Change the chart type to Pie with a 3-D visual effect. *Hint*: Right-click when the ScreenTip is Chart Area and then click Chart Type on the shortcut menu.

4. In the second section of the document, create a watermark of the clown graphic.

5. Check the spelling. Save the document with Sunshine Proposal as the file name. View and print the document in print preview.

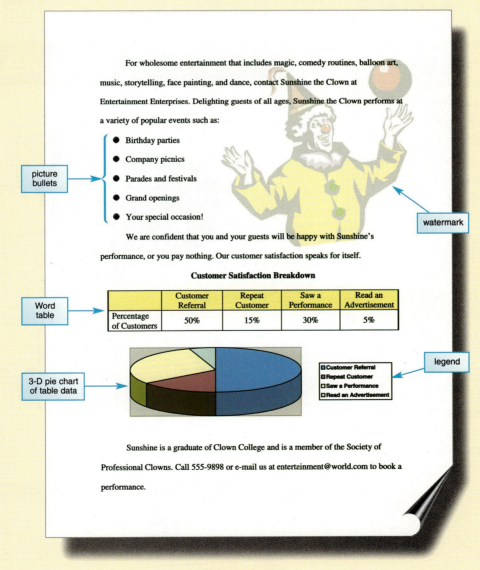

FIGURE 4-84b

In the Lab

3 Enhancing a Draft of a Proposal

Problem: You work for the marketing director at Antique Autos. You create a title page (Figure 4-85a) for an informal sales proposal that your boss has drafted (Figures 4-85b and 4-85c) to be sent to prospective customers around the country. You decide to add picture bullets, another table, a chart, and a watermark to the body of the proposal.

This lab uses the Data Disk. If you did not download the Data Disk, see the inside back cover for instructions for downloading the Data Disk or see your instructor.

Instructions:

1. Create the title page as shown in Figure 4-85a. *Hint:* Use the Format dialog box to apply the wave double underline and the outline format to the text. The antique car clip art is located at Microsoft's Clip Gallery Live Web page. To reach this file, type `antique car` in the SEARCH by keyword text box. If you do not have access to the Web, you can import the file (file name TN00288_) from the Data Disk.

2. Center the title page vertically. Insert a section break. Return to the Normal style. Insert the draft of the body of the proposal below the title page using the File command on the Insert menu. The draft is called Antique Autos Draft on the Data Disk. The draft of the body of the proposal is shown in Figures 4-85b and 4-85c. Be sure change the alignment to Top for section 2.

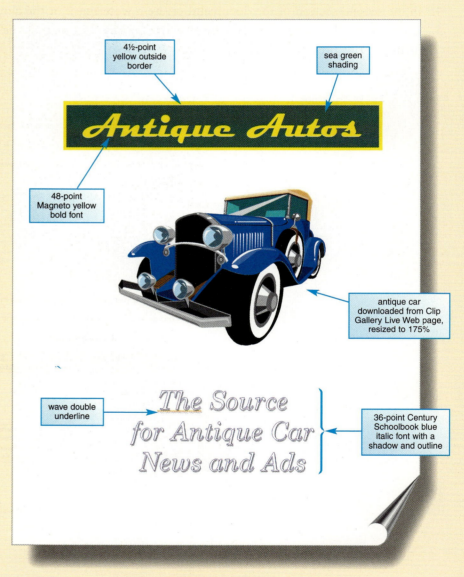

FIGURE 4-85a

In the Lab

Antique Autos is a weekly publication containing old car news and advertisements for antique cars and parts. Each issue lists dates of upcoming auctions, shows, swap meets, and other events; offers restoration tips, tricks, and suggestions; relates fellow antique car owner stories; and includes pages of ads for cars, parts, and books for sale or trade.

A one-year subscription to *Antique Autos* entitles you to the following benefits:

- 52 issues of *Antique Autos*
- Members-only Visa credit card offer
- Discounts from antique auto parts vendors
- *Antique Autos* members-only Web site
- *Antique Autos* chat room access
- Group insurance

The group *Antique Autos* insurance offers the lowest premiums you will find anywhere.

To qualify for these great deals, your vehicle must be used primarily for shows, parades, exhibitions, or other public-interest activities. You also must have the automobile appraised and submit a recent color photograph of the vehicle with your application.

Whether you own an antique car, are in the market for one, or simply are an old car enthusiast, you will find every issue of *Antique Autos* filled with interesting and informative articles and loaded with outstanding deals.

printout of Antique Autos Draft file

bullet style to be changed to picture bullets

location for table using Draw Table feature

FIGURE 4-85b

Subscribers who advertise in *Antique Autos* Classifieds find tremendous success selling their vehicles.

Recent *Antique Autos* Classified Sales

	Asking Price	Selling Price
1918 Model T Ford Speedster	$4,350	$4,350
1919 Studebaker	$19,000	$18,500
1936 Chevrolet Pickup	$2,500	$2,225
1953 Buick Roadmaster Wagon	$35,000	$35,000
1958 Imperial Convertible	$22,500	$22,500
1965 Thunderbird	$5,200	$5,000

location for chart of Classified Sales table

A one-year subscription to *Antique Autos* is $35. Mention this article and receive a 10-percent discount on your first year's price. Do not miss another issue! Call 708-555-2020 today or e-mail us at antiqueautos@net.com to subscribe.

FIGURE 4-85c

(continued)

In the Lab

Enhancing a Draft of a Proposal *(continued)*

3. On the first page of the body of the proposal, change the style of the bullet characters in the list to picture bullets.

4. On the first page of the body of the proposal, use the Draw Table button to create a table that is similar to Figure 4-86 below the third paragraph in the proposal. Single-space the table, adjusting table borders to fit all text as necessary. *Hint*: Use Help to learn about resizing tables. Format the table using the Grid 8 AutoFormat option.

Sample Antique Auto Insurance Premiums		1st Car	2nd Car	3rd Car
Liability ($300,000 single limit)		$15.00	$10.00	$5.00
Medical Payments ($1,000 limit)		$3.00	$2.00	$1.00
Physical Damage	Comprehensive	$0.35 per $100 of appraisal value		
	Collision	$0.40 per $100 of appraisal value		
Uninsured/Underinsured Motorist		determined by state		

FIGURE 4-86

5. On the second page of the body of the proposal, create a chart of the Recent Antique Autos Classified Sales table. Change the chart type to Cylinder. Enlarge the chart so all the labels are visible.

6. Add a header to section 2 of the proposal.

7. Create a watermark in section 2 of the proposal using the antique auto graphic.

8. Save the active document with the file name Antique Autos Proposal using the Save As command on the File menu.

9. View the document in print preview. Print the document from within print preview.

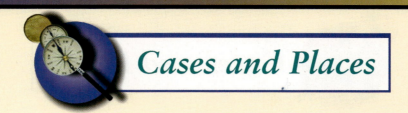

Cases and Places

1 ▶   As assistant to the promotions director, you have been assigned the task of preparing a sales proposal that recruits new members to the Camper Club. The title page is to contain the name, Camper Club, followed by an appropriate camping graphic, and then the slogan, Experiencing Outdoor Adventures with Friends. The body of the proposal should contain the following: first paragraph – Looking for adventures in the great outdoors? Want to meet new friends? Do you like to camp? The Camper Club is looking for new members. As a member you are entitled to a variety of benefits.; list with picture bullets – Monthly Issue of Camper Club, Reduced rates at campgrounds across the country, Discounts on Camp America orders, Low-rate recreational vehicle insurance protection, Listings of Camper Club Chapter members in your area, Participation in Camper Club Chapter outings; next paragraph – The Camper Club currently has more than 50,000 members nationwide. Upon membership, you will be sent a current catalog of all members across the nation; the data for the table is shown in Figure 4-87; last paragraph - A membership costs just $25 per year. Mention this article when you join and receive a 20 percent discount on your first year's membership. Call 708-555-1818, e-mail us at camperclub@hill.com, or visit our Web site at www.camperclub.com to join today!

Sample Chapter Breakdowns			Male	Female
Southern Indiana		Adult	75	79
		Teen	23	27
		Child	35	32
Northern Texas		Adult	101	98
		Teen	33	40
		Child	56	43

FIGURE 4-87

2 ▶▶   Assume you are running for an office in your school's Student Government Association. You plan to design a sales proposal to post around campus that sells *you*; that is, it explains why you are the best candidate for the job. Create a proposal that outlines your interests, summarizes your activities, and highlights your accomplishments. It also may present your background, education, and other pertinent experiences. Use whatever personal information you believe is relevant to the office being sought. Place your name, an appropriate graphic, and a slogan on the title page. Be sure the body of the proposal includes the following items: a list with picture bullets, a table, a chart, and a watermark.

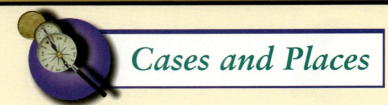

Cases and Places

3 ▶▶ During the course of a semester, you utilize several facilities on campus. These may include registration, advising, cafeteria, day care, computer facilities, career development, fitness center, library, bookstore, student government, and/or the tutoring center. Select an item from this list, or one of your own, that you feel needs improvement at your school. Visit the library or surf the Internet for guidelines on preparing a planning proposal. Develop a planning proposal you could submit to the Dean of Students that recommends some action the school could take to improve the situation. Design an appropriate title page. Be sure the body of the proposal includes the following items: a list with picture bullets, a table, a chart, and a watermark.

4 ▶▶ Assume your school is creating or modifying a core curriculum, which is a list of courses that every enrolled student must complete prior to graduation – regardless of major. Much discussion/controversy centers on the list of *essential* courses. As an active member of the Student Government Association, you have been asked for your recommendations on which classes you feel should be in the core curriculum and why. Visit the library or surf the Internet for guidelines on preparing a planning proposal. Develop a planning proposal that recommends a core curriculum to your school's Curriculum Committee. Design an appropriate title page. Be sure the body of the proposal includes the following items: a list with picture bullets, a table, a chart, and a watermark.

5 ▶▶▶ You have been assigned the task of writing a proposal to request funds to landscape or enhance the landscape on the grounds at your school. The proposal should describe the current condition of the grounds, as well as the proposed landscaping designs (e.g, trees, grass, sod, flowers, shrubs, etc.). Provide a minimum of two alternative cost quotations, with sources of the quotations cited. Visit the library or surf the Internet for guidelines on preparing a research proposal. Draft a research proposal that presents your findings, suggests two alternatives, and then recommends your suggested design to your school's decision-making body. Design an appropriate title page. Be sure the body of the proposal includes the following items: a list with picture bullets, a table, a chart, a header with a page number, and a watermark.

6 ▶▶▶ Your school has a budget for student trips. You have been assigned the task of writing a proposal to request funds for your entire class to attend an out-of-town conference. Locate a conference that appeals to you. The proposal should describe the conference, its relevance, and all associated costs (e.g., travel, conference, meals, lodging, supplies, etc.). For travel and lodging, provide a minimum of two alternative cost quotations, with sources of the quotations cited. Visit the library or surf the Internet for guidelines on preparing a research proposal. Draft a research proposal that presents your findings, suggests the cost alternatives, and then recommends the best package to your school's decision-making body. Design an appropriate title page. Be sure the body of the proposal includes the following items: a list with picture bullets, a table, a chart, a header with a page number, and a watermark.

Microsoft **Word 2000**

Microsoft Word 2000

Generating Form Letters, Mailing Labels, and Envelopes

You will have mastered the material in this project
when you can:

- Explain the merge process
- Explain the terms, data field and data record
- Use a template to create a letter
- Create a data source
- Print a document in landscape orientation
- Switch from a data source to the main document
- Insert merge fields into the main document
- Create an outline numbered list
- Use an IF field in the main document
- Insert a Fill-in field in the main document
- Merge and print form letters
- Selectively merge and print form letters
- Sort a data source
- Address mailing labels
- Address envelopes

True to Form

Personalization Yields a Definite Response

Sorting your mail is a lingering task in this age of personalized junk mail. At times, it is hard to determine which letters have merit. You dare not discard them all for fear of tossing an important notice or missing an official date. In the stack of correspondence are credit card applications, clothing catalogs, free vacations to interesting places, announcements of sales and grand openings, free subscriptions, sweepstakes forms, and other envelopes, all with your name on them.

The U.S. Postal Service calls these unsolicited offers "bulk business mail," and they are big business. As much as we complain about this mail, Americans are responding to these pitches in record numbers.

Part of the reason for this success is the sellers' ability to send form letters and offers tailored to individuals' specific interests and buying habits. The personalized Eagle Run Golf Club form letters and corresponding mailing labels and envelopes you will

create in Project 5 are an example of this capability. Individuals and business executives are more likely to open and read a personalized letter than a standard bulk mail letter.

Where do these marketers get your name? How do they know you just bought a house, had a baby, or like to golf? Whether you like it or not, specific details of all phases of your life are fields in highly specialized databases used to churn out four million tons of personalized letters every year.

Much of the data in these databases comes from public records in local governmental offices: birth certificates, business licenses, and marriage certificates. Real estate records contain the owner, price, and date sold of every parcel of land. State and federal tax lien information, civil lawsuits, and bankruptcy filings are easily obtainable. Records are generated each time you use or apply for a credit card. Consumers volunteer information when they describe their family size, income, and hobbies on product warranty cards. Telephone books and U.S. Postal Service address change forms also are major sources of profitable data.

Companies research, compile, and rent this data to marketers at the rate of $50 to $150 per 1,000 names. List makers boast they have more than 10,000 customized lists for rent, including those containing the names and addresses of 35 million college students, 750,000 professors, 7 million credit card holders, and 5 million pet owners.

Companies can rent several lists and search for the same names appearing on each one. For example, a financial institution marketing credit cards to affluent homeowners with good credit histories can merge lists with Census Bureau records of people living in specific areas, the buying habits of people in these neighborhoods, and credit reports showing good credit risks. Some companies may use up to 100 lists to fine-tune the names in an attempt to find appropriate mail prospects.

These targeted mailings are an efficient way for direct marketers to find nearly 100 times as many consumers as they would by running a television ad. With this success, be prepared to receive even more personalized solicitations.

Microsoft Word 2000

Generating Form Letters, Mailing Labels, and Envelopes

C A S E   P E R S P E C T I V E

Rosa Rodriguez, marketing director of Eagle Run Golf Club, recently contracted your services as a Word specialist to work with her assistant, Ahmed, to promote the new golf course and its services. Ahmed is to send a letter to a mailing list of local residents notifying them of the Grand Opening Celebration. Instead of typing a separate letter to each person on the mailing list, you suggest to Ahmed that he use Word to create a form letter because much of the information in the letters is identical. He can create a separate file containing the names and addresses of each person in the mailing list; this file is called a data source. Then, Word allows merging the data source with the form letter so that an individual letter prints for each person in the mailing list. Ahmed also intends to address mailing labels and envelopes for each person in the data source.

For those people who become a member during the Grand Opening Celebration, Rosa wants two separate discount rates, with the lower rate being offered to students. That is, students receive a 75 percent discount and all other people receive a 25 percent discount.

Introduction

An individual or business executive is more likely to open and read a personalized letter than a standard Dear Sir or Dear Madam letter. Because typing individual letters to many people is a time-consuming task, you can generate personalized letters in Word by creating a form letter. Form letters are used regularly in both business and personal correspondence. The basic content of a group of **form letters** is similar; however, items such as name, address, city, state, and postal code change from one letter to the next. Thus, form letters are personalized to the addressee.

Form letters usually are sent to a group of people. **Business form letters** include announcements of sales to customers or notices of benefits to employees. **Personal form letters** include letters of application for a job or invitations to participate in a sweepstakes giveaway. With Word, you easily can address envelopes or mailing labels for the form letters.

Project Five — Form Letters, Mailing Labels, and Envelopes

Project 5 illustrates how to create a business form letter and address corresponding mailing labels and envelopes. The form letter is sent to local residents, informing them of Eagle Run Golf Club's upcoming Grand Opening Celebration. For those people who become a member during the Grand Opening Celebration, a varying discount rate applies, depending on whether or not the new member is a student.

The process of generating form letters involves creating a main document for the form letter and a data source, and then merging, or *blending*, the two together into a series of individual letters as shown in Figure 5-1.

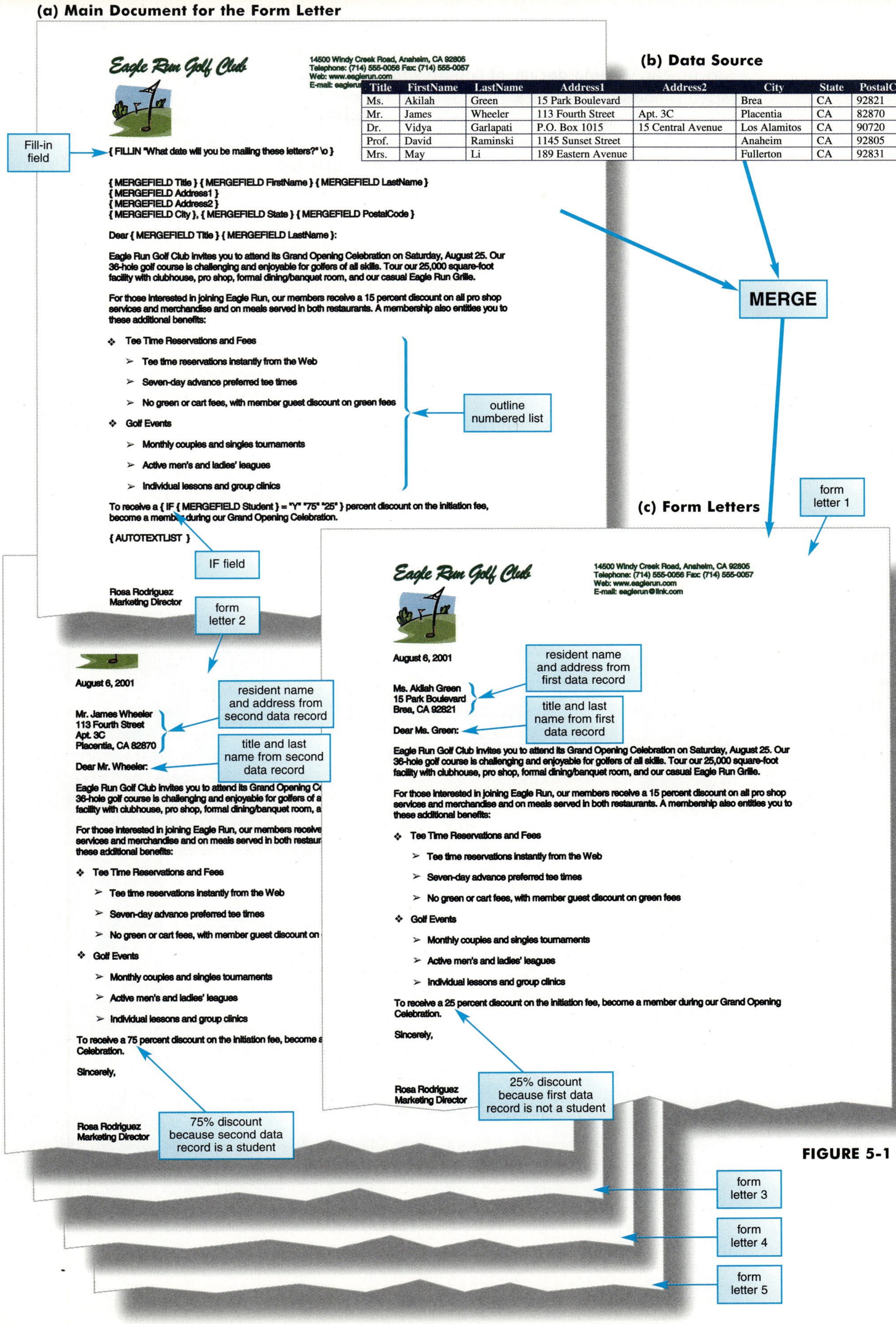

(a) Main Document for the Form Letter

Eagle Run Golf Club

14500 Windy Creek Road, Anaheim, CA 92805
Telephone: (714) 555-0056 Fax: (714) 555-0057
Web: www.eaglerun.com
E-mail: eaglerun@link.com

(b) Data Source

Title	FirstName	LastName	Address1	Address2	City	State	PostalCode	Student
Ms.	Akilah	Green	15 Park Boulevard		Brea	CA	92821	N
Mr.	James	Wheeler	113 Fourth Street	Apt. 3C	Placentia	CA	82870	Y
Dr.	Vidya	Garlapati	P.O. Box 1015	15 Central Avenue	Los Alamitos	CA	90720	N
Prof.	David	Raminski	1145 Sunset Street		Anaheim	CA	92805	N
Mrs.	May	Li	189 Eastern Avenue		Fullerton	CA	92831	Y

Fill-in field → { FILLIN "What date will you be mailing these letters?" \o }

{ MERGEFIELD Title } { MERGEFIELD FirstName } { MERGEFIELD LastName }
{ MERGEFIELD Address1 }
{ MERGEFIELD Address2 }
{ MERGEFIELD City }, { MERGEFIELD State } { MERGEFIELD PostalCode }

Dear { MERGEFIELD Title } { MERGEFIELD LastName }:

Eagle Run Golf Club invites you to attend its Grand Opening Celebration on Saturday, August 25. Our 36-hole golf course is challenging and enjoyable for golfers of all skills. Tour our 25,000 square-foot facility with clubhouse, pro shop, formal dining/banquet room, and our casual Eagle Run Grille.

For those interested in joining Eagle Run, our members receive a 15 percent discount on all pro shop services and merchandise and on meals served in both restaurants. A membership also entitles you to these additional benefits:

❖ Tee Time Reservations and Fees

➢ Tee time reservations instantly from the Web

➢ Seven-day advance preferred tee times

➢ No green or cart fees, with member guest discount on green fees

❖ Golf Events

➢ Monthly couples and singles tournaments

➢ Active men's and ladies' leagues

➢ Individual lessons and group clinics

outline numbered list

To receive a { IF { MERGEFIELD Student } = "Y" "75" "25" } percent discount on the initiation fee, become a member during our Grand Opening Celebration.

{ AUTOTEXTLIST }

IF field

Rosa Rodriguez
Marketing Director

MERGE

(c) Form Letters

form letter 1

form letter 2

August 6, 2001

resident name and address from second data record

Mr. James Wheeler
113 Fourth Street
Apt. 3C
Placentia, CA 82870

title and last name from second data record

Dear Mr. Wheeler:

Eagle Run Golf Club invites you to attend its Grand Opening Ce 36-hole golf course is challenging and enjoyable for golfers of a facility with clubhouse, pro shop, formal dining/banquet room, a

For those interested in joining Eagle Run, our members receive services and merchandise and on meals served in both restaura these additional benefits:

❖ Tee Time Reservations and Fees

➢ Tee time reservations instantly from the Web

➢ Seven-day advance preferred tee times

➢ No green or cart fees, with member guest discount on

❖ Golf Events

➢ Monthly couples and singles tournaments

➢ Active men's and ladies' leagues

➢ Individual lessons and group clinics

To receive a 75 percent discount on the initiation fee, become a Celebration.

Sincerely,

Rosa Rodriguez
Marketing Director

75% discount because second data record is a student

Eagle Run Golf Club

14500 Windy Creek Road, Anaheim, CA 92805
Telephone: (714) 555-0056 Fax: (714) 555-0057
Web: www.eaglerun.com
E-mail: eaglerun@link.com

August 6, 2001

resident name and address from first data record

Ms. Akilah Green
15 Park Boulevard
Brea, CA 92821

title and last name from first data record

Dear Ms. Green:

Eagle Run Golf Club invites you to attend its Grand Opening Celebration on Saturday, August 25. Our 36-hole golf course is challenging and enjoyable for golfers of all skills. Tour our 25,000 square-foot facility with clubhouse, pro shop, formal dining/banquet room, and our casual Eagle Run Grille.

For those interested in joining Eagle Run, our members receive a 15 percent discount on all pro shop services and merchandise and on meals served in both restaurants. A membership also entitles you to these additional benefits:

❖ Tee Time Reservations and Fees

➢ Tee time reservations instantly from the Web

➢ Seven-day advance preferred tee times

➢ No green or cart fees, with member guest discount on green fees

❖ Golf Events

➢ Monthly couples and singles tournaments

➢ Active men's and ladies' leagues

➢ Individual lessons and group clinics

To receive a 25 percent discount on the initiation fee, become a member during our Grand Opening Celebration.

Sincerely,

Rosa Rodriguez
Marketing Director

25% discount because first data record is not a student

FIGURE 5-1

form letter 3

form letter 4

form letter 5

Microsoft Word 2000

Merging is the process of combining the contents of a data source with a main document. A **main document** contains the constant, or unchanging, text, punctuation, spaces, and graphics. In Figure 5-1a on the previous page, the main document represents the portion of the form letter that repeats from one merged letter to the next. Conversely, the **data source** contains the variable, or changing, values for each letter. In Figure 5-1b, the data source contains five different people. Thus, one form letter is generated for each person listed in the data source.

Using a Template to Create a Letter

You can type a letter from scratch into a blank document window, as you did with the cover letter in Project 2; or you can use the letter wizard and let Word format the letter based on your responses to the wizard; or you can use a letter template. You have learned that a **template** is similar to a form with prewritten text. In the case of the letter template, Word prepares a letter with text and/or formatting common to all letters. Then, you can customize the resulting letter by selecting and replacing prewritten text.

Word provides three styles of wizards and templates: Professional, Contemporary, and Elegant. Perform the following steps to use the Professional Letter template to create a letter.

Writing Letters

For more information on writing letters, visit the Word 2000 More About Web page (www.scsite.com/wd2000/more.htm) and then click Writing Letters.

 To Create a Letter Using a Word Template

1 **Click the Start button on the taskbar and then click New Office Document. If necessary, click the Letters & Faxes tab when the New Office Document dialog box displays. Click the Professional Letter icon.**

Office displays several wizard and template icons in the Letters & Faxes sheet in the New Office Document dialog box (Figure 5-2). You have learned that icons without the word, Wizard, below them are templates. A sample of the Professional Letter template displays in the Preview area.

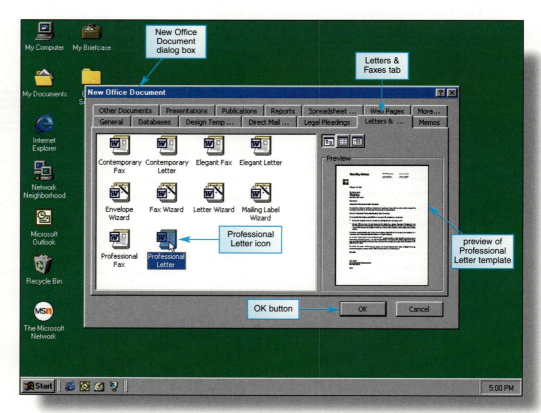

FIGURE 5-2

2 Click the OK button.

Office starts Word, which in turn creates a professional style letter by using the Professional Letter template and displays the letter in a document window in print layout view (Figure 5-3). Because the letter template instructs Word to display the current date in the letter, your date line more than likely will display a different date.

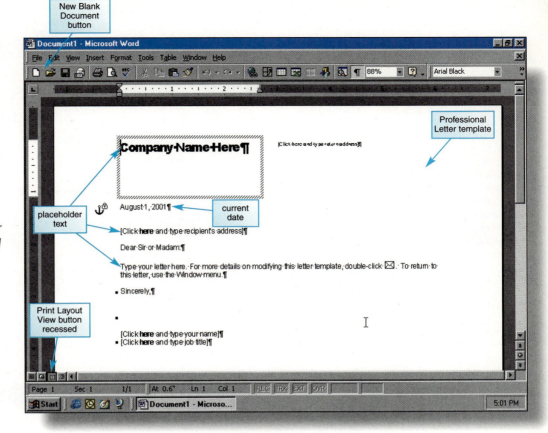

FIGURE 5-3

You have learned that a template displays prewritten text, called **placeholder text**, that you select and replace to personalize the document. Figure 5-3 identifies some of the placeholder text created by the Professional Letter template.

You learned in Project 3 that with Word on the screen, you can create a new document using the New Blank Document button (Figure 5-3) on the Standard toolbar. When you click this button, Word uses the Blank Document template located in the General sheet in the New dialog box. If you want to use a different template or a wizard, you cannot use the New Blank Document button; instead, you must display the New dialog box by clicking File on the menu bar and then clicking New.

The Professional Letter template is based on a **block style** letter; that is, all components below the company name in the letter begin flush with the left margin. In Project 3, you learned that all business letters have common elements such as a date line, inside address, message, and signature block.

In creating the template, Word uses different styles to represent various elements of the letter. You have learned that a style is a customized format that Word applies to characters or paragraphs. Figure 5-4 on the next page identifies the styles used in the Professional Letter template. The Style box on the Formatting toolbar displays the name of the style associated with the location of the insertion point (see Figure 5-6 on page WD 5.10). When you modify the cover letter, the style associated with the location of the insertion point will be applied to the text you type.

Other Ways

1. In Microsoft Word, on File menu click New, click Letters & Faxes tab, double-click Professional Letter template

More About 2000

New Documents

When you click File on the menu bar and then click New, Word displays the New dialog box. When you click the Start button and then click New Office Document, Office displays the New Office Document dialog box. The New Office Document dialog box contains all the tabbed sheets in Word's New dialog box, in addition to those sheets associated with other Office applications.

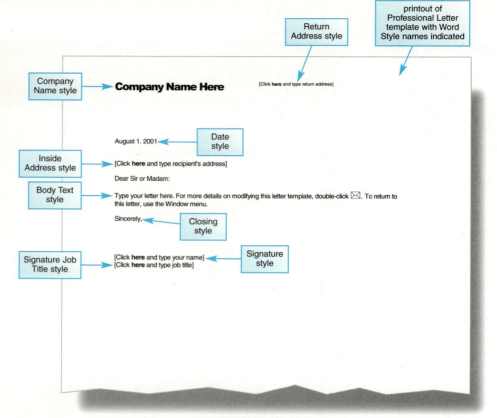

FIGURE 5-4

Business Letters

All business letters must contain the following items from top to bottom: date line, inside address, body or message, and signature block. Many business letters contain additional items such as a special mailing notations, attention line, salutation, subject line, complimentary close, reference initials, and enclosure notation.

Resetting Menus and Toolbars

To set the menus and toolbars so they appear exactly as shown in this book, you should reset your menus and toolbars as outlined in Appendix C or follow these steps.

TO RESET MENUS AND TOOLBARS

1. Click View on the menu bar and then point to Toolbars. Click Customize on the Toolbars submenu.

2. When the Customize dialog box displays, click the Options tab, make sure the top three check boxes have check marks and then click the Reset my usage data button. When the Microsoft Word dialog box displays, click the Yes button.

3. Click the Toolbars tab. Click Standard in the Toolbars list and then click the Reset button. When the Reset Toolbar dialog box displays, click the OK button.

4. Click Formatting in the Toolbars list and then click the Reset button. When the Reset Toolbar dialog box displays, click the OK button. Click the Close button.

Word resets the menus and toolbars.

Zooming Text Width

As you have learned, when you **zoom text width**, Word displays text on the screen as large as possible in print layout view without extending the right margin beyond the right edge of the document window. Perform the following steps to zoom text width.

TO ZOOM TEXT WIDTH

1 Double-click the move handle on the Standard toolbar to display the entire toolbar. Click the Zoom box arrow on the Standard toolbar.

2 Click Text Width in the Zoom list.

Word computes the zoom percentage based on a variety of settings (see Figure 5-5). Your percentage may be different depending on your system configuration.

Displaying Formatting Marks

You have learned that it is helpful to display formatting marks that indicate where in the document you pressed the ENTER key, SPACEBAR, and other keys. Follow this step to display formatting marks.

TO DISPLAY FORMATTING MARKS

1 If the Show/Hide ¶ button on the Standard toolbar is not already recessed, click it.

Word displays formatting marks in the document window, and the Show/Hide ¶ button on the Standard toolbar is recessed (see Figure 5-5).

Selecting and Replacing Template Placeholder Text

The first step in personalizing the letter is to create the company letterhead. As this is the golf club's grand opening, they do not yet have any preprinted letterhead. Thus, you create a letterhead by filling in the placeholder text as indicated in the letter template. Select, format, and then replace the text as shown in the following steps.

To Select and Replace Placeholder Text

1 **Drag through the placeholder text, Company Name Here.**

The placeholder text displays surrounded by a frame (Figure 5-5). Word frames the company name to provide flexibility in its location. Frames are discussed in more depth in the next project.

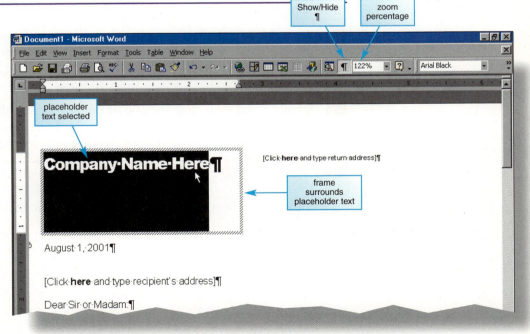

FIGURE 5-5

2 **Double-click the move handle on the Formatting toolbar to display the entire toolbar. Click the Font box arrow. Scroll to and then click Script MT Bold, or a similar font, in the Font list. Click the Font Size box arrow and then click 24. Click the Font Color button arrow and then click Green. Type** Eagle Run Golf Club **and then press the ENTER key.**

Word displays the company name in 24-point Script MT Bold green font (Figure 5-6).

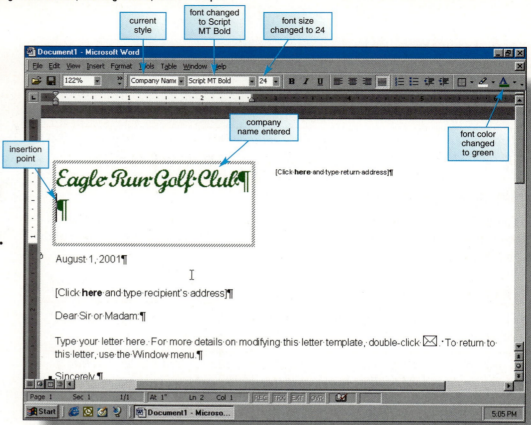

FIGURE 5-6

The next step is to insert a graphic of a golf course from the Clip Gallery below the company name, and then reduce the size of the graphic to 25 percent of its original size. Perform the following steps to insert the golf course graphic.

TO INSERT CLIP ART

1 With the insertion point on line 2 as shown in Figure 5-6, click Insert on the menu bar, point to Picture, and then click Clip Art.

2 When the Insert ClipArt window opens, click the Search for clips text box. Type golf course and then press the ENTER key.

3 Scroll to and then click the clip of the golf course that matches the one shown in Figure 5-7. Click the Insert clip button on the Pop-up menu. Click the Close button on the Insert ClipArt window's title bar.

Word inserts the golf course image into the document.

Perform the following steps to resize the graphic to 25 percent of its original size.

To Resize a Graphic

1 **Click the graphic to select it. If the Picture toolbar does not display on the screen, right-click the graphic and then click Show Picture Toolbar on the shortcut menu. Point to the Format Picture button on the Picture toolbar (Figure 5-7).**

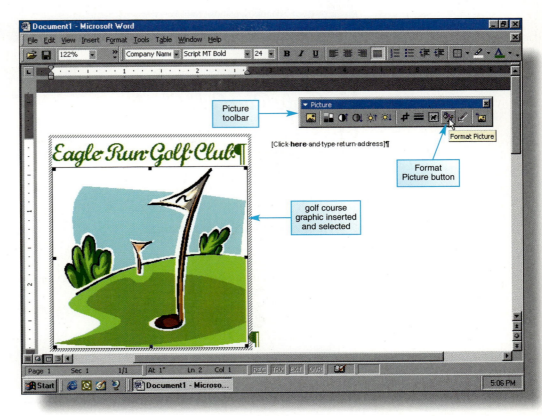

FIGURE 5-7

2 **Click the Format Picture button. When the Format Picture dialog box displays, click the Size tab. In the Scale area, drag through the text in the Height box. Type** 25 **and then press the TAB key. If necessary, type** 25 **in the Width box. Point to the OK button.**

Word displays the Format Picture dialog box (Figure 5-8).

FIGURE 5-8

3 **Click the OK button.**

Word resizes the graphic to 25 percent of its original size (Figure 5-9).

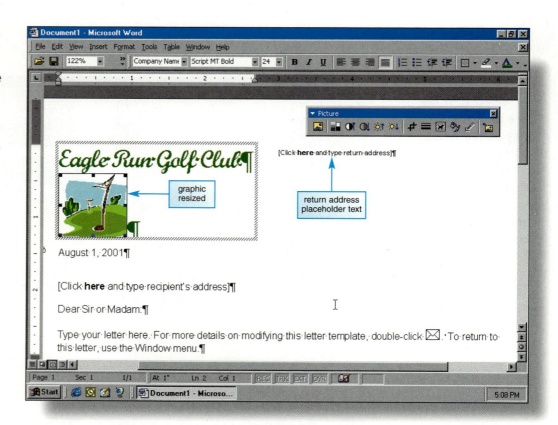

FIGURE 5-9

If, for some reason, you wanted to delete a graphic, you would select it and then press the DELETE key or click the Cut button on the Standard toolbar.

The next step is to enter the return address in 9-point Arial green font as described in the steps below.

TO SELECT AND REPLACE MORE PLACEHOLDER TEXT

1 Click the placeholder text, Click **here** and type return address (see Figure 5-9).

2 Click the Font Size box arrow on the Formatting toolbar and then click 9.

3 Click the Font Color button on the Formatting toolbar to change the color of the return address paragraph to green.

4 Type 14500 Windy Creek Road, Anaheim, CA 92805 and then press the ENTER key.

5 Type Telephone: (714) 555-0056 Fax: (714) 555-0057 and then press the ENTER key.

6 Type Web: www.eaglerun.com and then press the ENTER key. Press the CTRL+Z keys to undo the hyperlink AutoFormat of the Web address.

7 Type E-mail: eaglerun@link.com to finish the return address.

Word displays the return address in 9-point Arial green font (Figure 5-10).

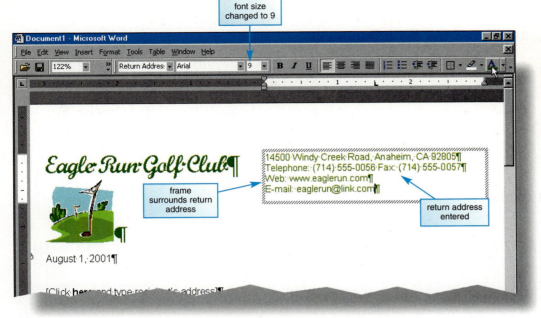

FIGURE 5-10

Because you have performed several tasks, you should save the document as described in the following steps.

TO SAVE THE LETTER

1. Insert your floppy disk into drive A.

2. Double-click the move handle on the Standard toolbar to display the entire toolbar. Click the Save button on the Standard toolbar.

3. Type `Eagle Run Grand Opening` in the File name text box. Do not press the ENTER key after typing the file name.

4. If necessary, click the Save in box arrow and then click 3½ Floppy (A:).

5. Click the Save button in the Save As dialog box.

Word saves the document on a floppy disk on drive A with the file name, Eagle Run Grand Opening (see Figure 5-11 on the next page).

You are ready to begin typing the body of the form letter. To do this, you work with two documents: the form letter, which contains constant text, and the data source, which contains varying data. The next series of steps illustrate how to link these two documents together so that you can work between them.

Identifying the Main Document and Creating the Data Source

Creating form letters requires merging a main document with a data source. To create form letters using Word's mail merge, you perform these tasks: (1) identify the main document, (2) create or specify the data source, (3) enter the main document for the form letter, and (4) merge the data source with the main document to generate and print the form letters. The following pages illustrate these tasks.

Identifying the Main Document

The first step in the mail merge process is to identify the document you will use as the main document. If it is a new document, you can click the New Blank Document button on the Standard toolbar to open a new document window. Because the main document in this project is the Eagle Run Grand Opening file, you should leave the current document open. With the main document file open, you must identify it as such to Word's mail merge, as shown in these steps.

Steps ## To Identify the Main Document

1 **Click Tools on the menu bar and then point to Mail Merge (Figure 5-11).**

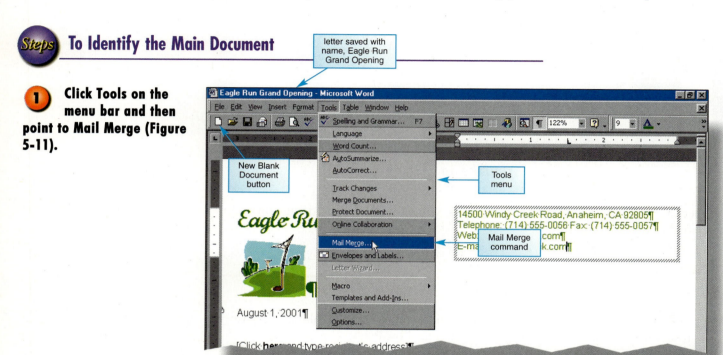

FIGURE 5-11

2 **Click Mail Merge. When the Mail Merge Helper dialog box displays, point to the Create button.**

Word displays the Mail Merge Helper dialog box (Figure 5-12). Using this dialog box, you identify the main document and can create the data source. Notice the instructions at the top of this dialog box.

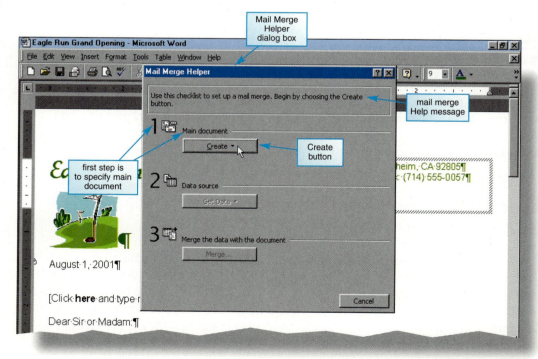

FIGURE 5-12

3 **Click the Create button. Point to Form Letters.**

Word displays a list of main document types (Figure 5-13).

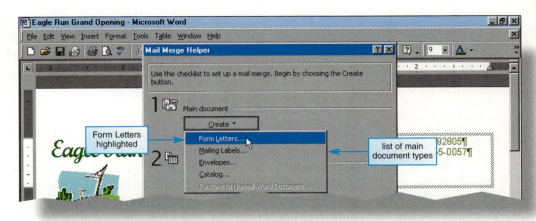

FIGURE 5-13

4 **Click Form Letters.**

Word displays a Microsoft Word dialog box asking if you want to use the active document window for the form letters (Figure 5-14). The Active Window button will use the current open document, Eagle Run Grand Opening, for the main document, whereas the New Main Document button opens a new document window for the main document – a procedure similar to clicking the New Blank Document button on the Standard toolbar.

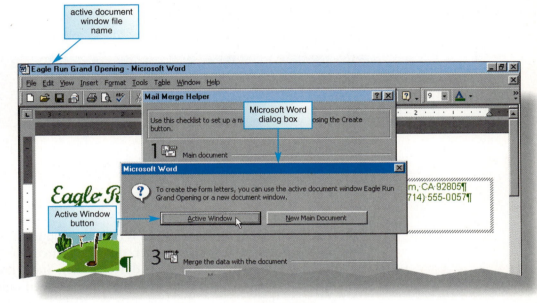

FIGURE 5-14

5 **Click the Active Window button.**

Word returns to the Mail Merge Helper dialog box (Figure 5-15). The merge type is identified as Form Letters and the main document is A:\Eagle Run Grand Opening.doc. An Edit button now displays in the Mail Merge Helper dialog box so you can modify the contents of the main document.

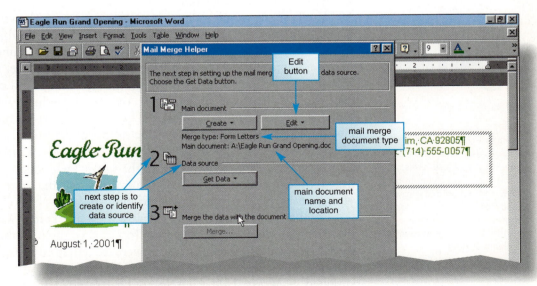

FIGURE 5-15

At this point, you will not enter the main document text; you simply identify it. As indicated in the Mail Merge Helper dialog box, the next step is to create or identify the data source. After you create the data source, you will enter the main document text.

Creating a Data Source

A data source can be a Word table (Figure 5-16). You have learned that a **Word table** is a series of rows and columns. The first row of a data source is called the **header row.** Each row below the header row is called a **data record.** Data records contain the text that varies from one merged document to the next. The data source for this project contains five data records. In this project, each data record identifies a different person. Thus, five form letters will be generated from this data source.

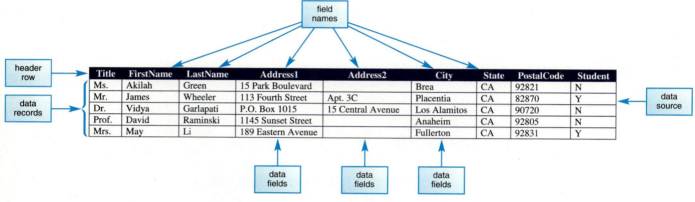

Title	FirstName	LastName	Address1	Address2	City	State	PostalCode	Student
Ms.	Akilah	Green	15 Park Boulevard		Brea	CA	92821	N
Mr.	James	Wheeler	113 Fourth Street	Apt. 3C	Placentia	CA	82870	Y
Dr.	Vidya	Garlapati	P.O. Box 1015	15 Central Avenue	Los Alamitos	CA	90720	N
Prof.	David	Raminski	1145 Sunset Street		Anaheim	CA	92805	N
Mrs.	May	Li	189 Eastern Avenue		Fullerton	CA	92831	Y

FIGURE 5-16

Each column in the data source is called a **data field.** A data field represents a group of similar data. In this project, the data source contains nine data fields: Title, FirstName, LastName, Address1, Address2, City, State, PostalCode, and Student.

In a data source, each data field must be identified uniquely with a name, called a **field name.** For example, FirstName is the name of the field (column) containing the first names. Field names are placed in the header row of the data source to identify the name of each column.

The first step in creating a data source is to decide which fields it will contain. That is, you must identify the information that will vary from one merged document to the next. In this project, each record contains up to nine different fields for each person: a courtesy title (e.g., Mrs.), first name, last name, first line of street address, second line of street address (optional), city, state, postal code, and student. The student field contains the value, Y (for Yes), or the value, N (for No), depending on whether the recipient is a student. The discount percent on the membership initiation fee is determined based on the value of the student field.

For each field, you must decide on a field name. Field names must be unique; that is, no two field names may be the same. Field names may be up to 40 characters in length, can contain only letters, numbers, and the underscore (_), and must begin with a letter. Field names cannot contain spaces.

Because data sources often contain the same fields, Word provides you with a list of 13 commonly used field names. To improve the readability of field names, Word uses a mixture of uppercase and lowercase letters to separate words within the field name (remember spaces are not allowed). You will use eight of the 13 field names supplied by Word: Title, FirstName, LastName, Address1, Address2, City, State, and PostalCode. You will delete the other five field names from the list supplied by Word. That is, you will delete JobTitle, Company, Country, HomePhone, and

WorkPhone. In this project, the only field that Word does not supply is the Student field. Thus, you will add a field name called Student.

Fields and related field names may be listed in any order in the data source. The order of fields has no effect on the order in which they will print in the main document.

Perform the following steps to create a new data source.

More About 2000

Mail Merge Helper

If the Mail Merge Helper is not on the screen, click Tools on the menu bar and then click Mail Merge.

To Create a Data Source in Word

1 **In the Mail Merge Helper dialog box, click the Get Data button and then point to Create Data Source.**

Word displays a list of data source options (Figure 5-17). You can create your own data source in Word; use a data source already created in Word; or use a file from another program such as Access, Excel, or Outlook as a data source.

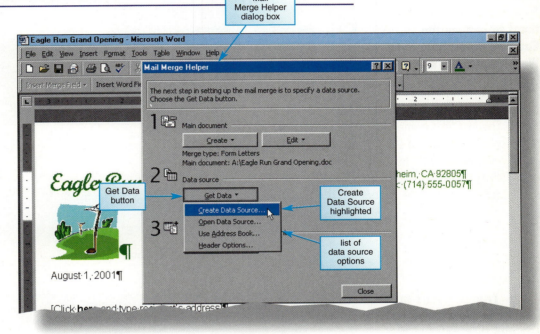

FIGURE 5-17

2 **Click Create Data Source. When the Create Data Source dialog box displays, click JobTitle in the Field names in header row list. Point to the Remove Field Name button.**

Word displays the Create Data Source dialog box (Figure 5-18). In the Field names in header row list, Word displays a list of commonly used field names. You can remove a field name from this list if you do not want it in the header row of your data source. JobTitle is highlighted for removal.

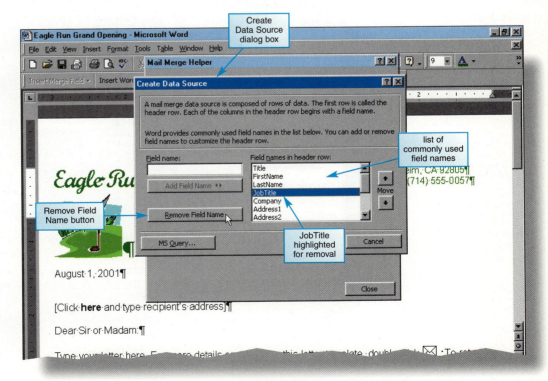

FIGURE 5-18

③ **Click the Remove Field Name button to remove the JobTitle field. Click the Remove Field Name button again to remove the Company field. Scroll to the bottom of the list and then click Country. Click the Remove Field Name button three times to remove the Country, HomePhone, and WorkPhone field names.**

Word removes five field names from the list (Figure 5-19). The last field name removed, WorkPhone, displays in the Field name text box. The next step is to add the Student field name to the list.

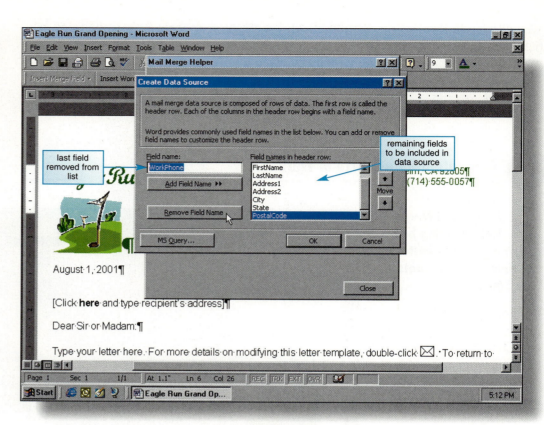

FIGURE 5-19

④ **Type** Student **in the Field name text box and then point to the Add Field Name button (Figure 5-20).**

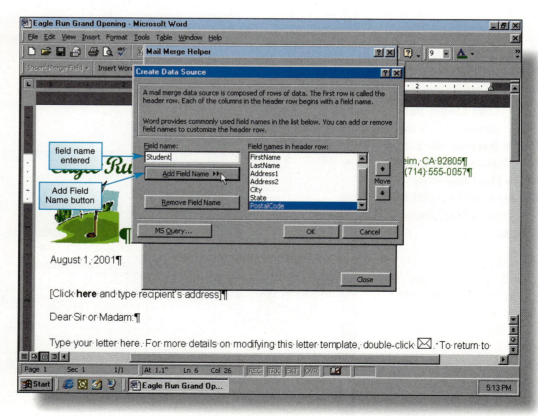

FIGURE 5-20

5 **Click the Add Field Name button. Point to the OK button.**

Word adds the Student field name to the bottom of the Field names in header row list (Figure 5-21).

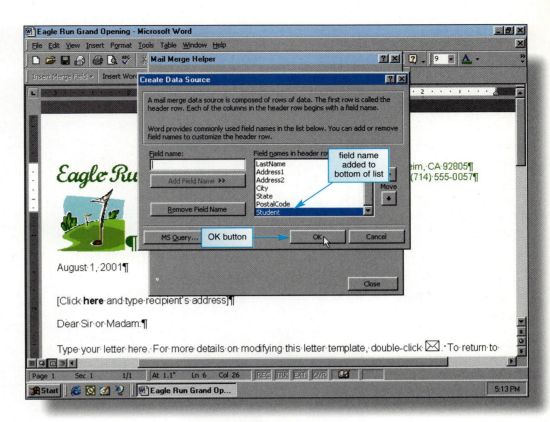

FIGURE 5-21

6 **Click the OK button.**

Word displays the Save As dialog box. You assign a file name to the data source in this dialog box.

7 **Type** Mailing List **and, if necessary, change the drive to 3½ Floppy (A:). Point to the Save button in the Save As dialog box.**

The data source for this project will be saved with the file name, Mailing List (Figure 5-22).

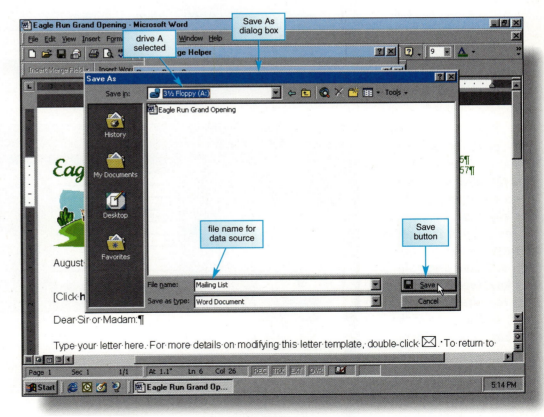

FIGURE 5-22

8 **Click the Save button in the Save As dialog box.**

A Microsoft Word dialog box displays asking if you would like to edit the data source or edit the main document at this point (Figure 5-23). Because you want to add data records to the data source, you will edit the data source now.

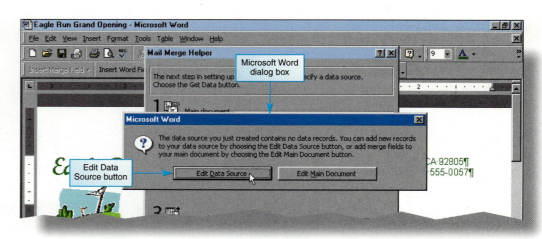

FIGURE 5-23

9 **Click the Edit Data Source button.**

Word displays a Data Form dialog box (Figure 5-24). You can use this dialog box to enter the data records into the data source. Notice the field names from the header row display along the left edge of the dialog box with an empty text box to the right of each field name. The insertion point is in the first text box.

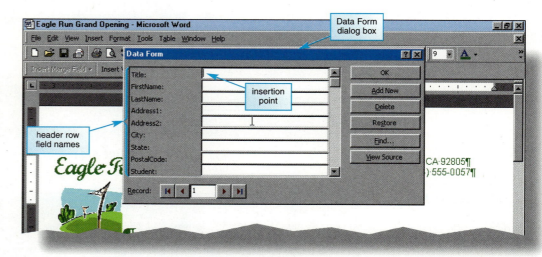

FIGURE 5-24

10 **Type** Ms. **and then press the ENTER key. Type** Akilah **and then press the ENTER key. Type** Green **and then press the ENTER key. Type** 15 Park Boulevard **and then press the ENTER key twice. Type** Brea **and then press the ENTER key. Type** CA **and then press the ENTER key. Type** 92821 **and then press the ENTER key. Type** N **(Figure 5-25).**

If you notice an error in a text box, click the text box and then correct the error as you would in the document window.

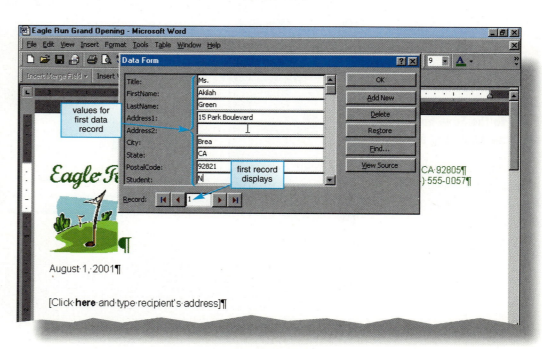

FIGURE 5-25

11 Press the ENTER key to display a blank data form for the second data record. Type Mr. and then press the ENTER key. James and then press the ENTER key. Type Wheeler and then press the ENTER key. Type 113 Fourth Street and then press the ENTER key. Type Apt. 3C and then press the ENTER key. Type Placentia and then press the ENTER key. Type CA and press the ENTER key. Type 82870 and then press the ENTER key. Type Y (Figure 5-26).

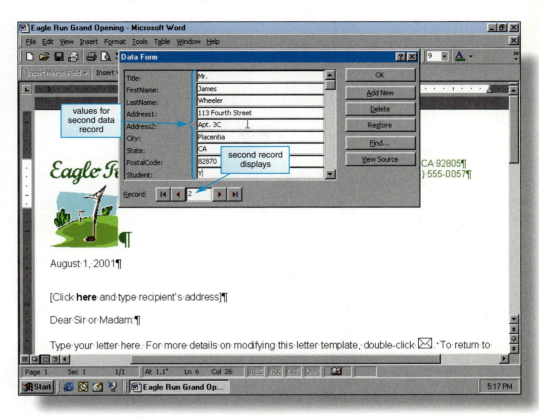

FIGURE 5-26

12 Press the ENTER key to display a blank data form for the third data record. Type Dr. and then press the ENTER key. Type Vidya and then press the ENTER key. Type Garlapati and then press the ENTER key. Type P.O. Box 1015 and then press the ENTER key. Type 15 Central Avenue and then press the ENTER key. Type Los Alamitos and then press the ENTER key. Type CA and press the ENTER key. Type 90720 and then press the ENTER key. Type N (Figure 5-27).

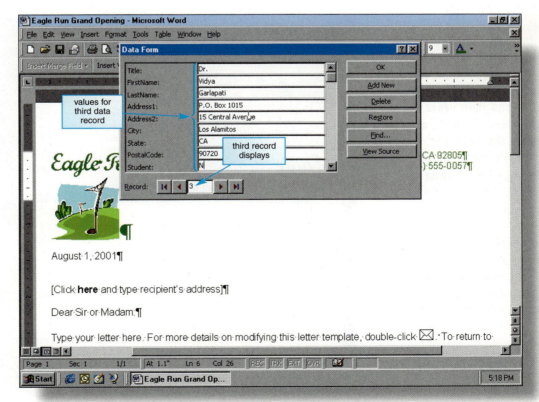

FIGURE 5-27

13 Press the ENTER key to display a blank data form for the fourth data record. Type `Prof.` and then press the ENTER key. Type `David` and then press the ENTER key. Type `Raminski` and then press the ENTER key. Type `1145 Sunset Street` and then press the ENTER key twice. Type `Anaheim` and then press the ENTER key. Type `CA` and then press the ENTER key. Type `92805` and then press the ENTER key. Type `N` (Figure 5-28).

FIGURE 5-28

14 Press the ENTER key to display a blank data form for the fifth data record. Type `Mrs.` and then press the ENTER key. Type `May` and then press the ENTER key. Type `Li` and then press the ENTER key. Type `189 Eastern Avenue` and then press the ENTER key twice. Type `Fullerton` and then press the ENTER key. Type `CA` and then press the ENTER key. Type `92831` and then press the ENTER key. Type `Y` and then point to the View Source button (Figure 5-29).

The functions of other buttons in this dialog box are discussed in the next section.

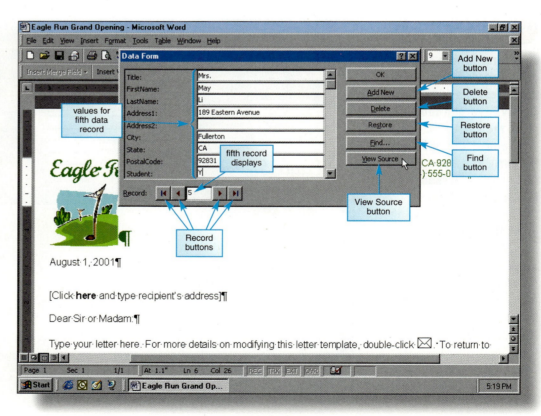

FIGURE 5-29

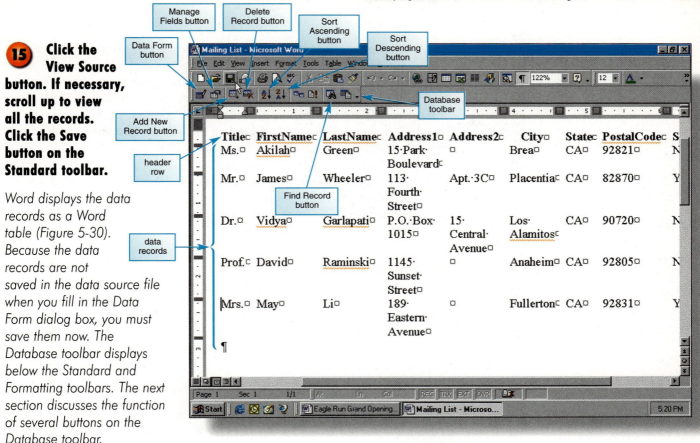

FIGURE 5-30

15 **Click the View Source button. If necessary, scroll up to view all the records. Click the Save button on the Standard toolbar.**

Word displays the data records as a Word table (Figure 5-30). Because the data records are not saved in the data source file when you fill in the Data Form dialog box, you must save them now. The Database toolbar displays below the Standard and Formatting toolbars. The next section discusses the function of several buttons on the Database toolbar.

Your data source table may display **gridlines** that separate the rows and columns. You have learned that gridlines do not print. Some users display gridlines to help identify rows and columns in a table. If you want to hide the gridlines, click somewhere in the table, click table on the menu bar, and then click Hide Gridlines.

All of the data records have been entered into the data source and saved with the file name, Mailing List. If, when you are entering your data records into the Data Form dialog box, you accidentally click the OK button, Word returns you to the main document. To redisplay the Data Form dialog box and continue adding data records, click the Edit Data Source button on the Mail Merge toolbar shown in Figure 5-34 on page WD 5.26.

Editing Records in the Data Source

If the data source displays as a Word table and you would like to redisplay the Data Form dialog box, click the Data Form button (Figure 5-30) on the Database toolbar. In the Data Form dialog box, you can add, change, or delete data records. To **add a new record**, press the ENTER key with the insertion point in the last field on the form as shown in the previous steps or click the Add New button (Figure 5-29). To **change an existing record**, display it in the Data Form dialog box by clicking the appropriate Record button(s) or using the Find button to locate a particular data item. For example, to find David Raminski, you could click the Find button, enter `Prof.` in the Find What box and then click the OK button. Once you have changed an existing record's data, click the OK button in the Data Form dialog box. To **delete a record**, display it in the Data Form dialog box, and then click the Delete button. If you accidentally delete a data record, click the Restore button to bring it back.

Organizing Data

Organize the information in a data source so it is reusable. For example, you may want to print a person's title, first, middle, and last name (e.g., Mr. Roger A. Bannerman) in the inside address but only the title and last name in the salutation (Dear Mr. Bannerman). Thus, you should break the name into separate fields: title, first, middle initial, and last name.

Modifying Fields

You can add a field name to a data source, change an existing field name, or remove a field by using the Manage Fields dialog box. To display the Manage Fields dialog box, click the Manage Fields button (Figure 5-30) on the Database toolbar.

You also can add, change, and delete data records when you are viewing the source as a Word table as shown in Figure 5-30 on the previous page. Click the Add New Record button on the Database toolbar to add a blank row to the bottom of the table and then fill in the field values. To delete a row, click somewhere in the row and then click the Delete Record button on the Database toolbar. Because the data source is a Word table, you can also add and delete records the same way you add and delete rows in a Word table, which was discussed in Projects 3 and 4. You can edit the data as you would in any other Word table.

The data source now is complete. You have learned in earlier projects that you can use the Table AutoFormat command to format a table. The data source is a table. Thus, perform the following steps to format the data source using the Table AutoFormat command.

TO AUTOFORMAT A TABLE

1 With the insertion point somewhere in the table, click Table on the menu bar and then click Table AutoFormat.

2 When the Table AutoFormat dialog box displays, scroll through the Formats list and then click Grid 8. Be sure these check boxes contain check marks: Borders, Shading, Font, Color, AutoFit, and Heading rows. All other check boxes should be cleared.

3 Click the OK button.

Word formats the table using the Grid 8 format (see Figure 5-16 on page WD 5.16).

Printing a Document in Landscape Orientation

The mailing list table is too wide to fit on a piece of paper in **portrait orientation**; that is, with the short edge of the paper at the top. You can instruct Word to print a document in **landscape orientation** so the long edge of the paper is at the top. Perform the following steps to change the orientation of the Mailing List from portrait to landscape.

Page Orientation

You can change the page orientation for part of a document by selecting the pages to be changed prior to displaying the Page Setup dialog box. With the pages selected, click the Apply to box arrow and then click Selected text in the Paper Size sheet of the Page Setup dialog box. Word inserts a section break before and after the selected pages.

 **To Change Page Orientation**

1 Click File on the menu bar and then point to Page Setup (Figure 5-31).

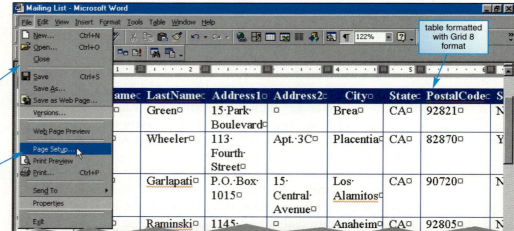

FIGURE 5-31

2 **Click Page Setup. When the Page Setup dialog box displays, click the Paper Size tab. Click Landscape in the Orientation area and then point to the OK button.**

Word displays the Page Setup dialog box (Figure 5-32).

3 **Click the OK button.**

Word changes the print orientation to landscape.

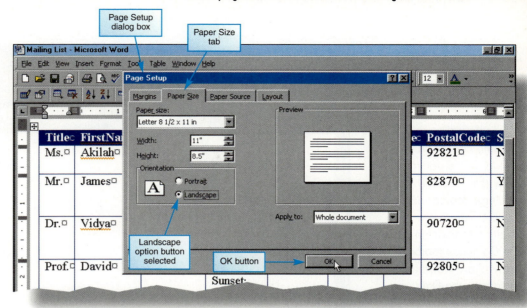

FIGURE 5-32

To print the document, perform the following step.

TO PRINT A DOCUMENT

1 Click the Print button on the Standard toolbar.

Word prints the document in landscape orientation (see Figure 5-16 on page WD 5.16).

Other Ways

1. On File menu click Print, click Properties button, click Paper tab, click Landscape, click OK button

Switching from the Data Source to the Main Document

The next step is to switch from the data source to the main document so that you can enter the contents of the form letter into the main document. Perform the following steps to switch from the data source to the main document for the form letter.

To Switch from the Data Source to the Main Document

1 **Point to the Mail Merge Main Document button on the Database toolbar (Figure 5-33).**

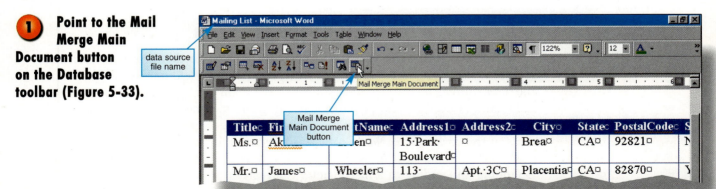

FIGURE 5-33

2 **Click the Mail Merge Main Document button.**

Word displays the main document, Eagle Run Grand Opening, in the document window (Figure 5-34). The Mail Merge toolbar displays below the Standard and Formatting toolbars in place of the Database toolbar. When you are viewing the data source, the Database toolbar displays; when you are viewing the main document, the Mail Merge toolbar displays.

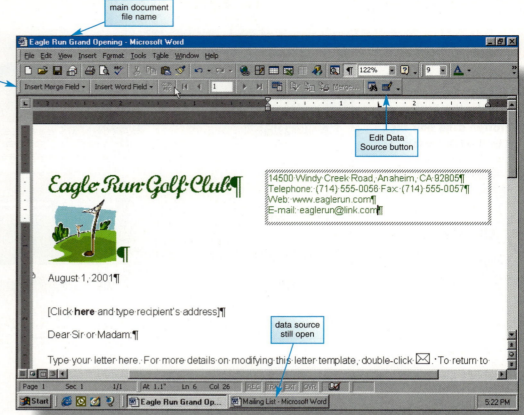

FIGURE 5-34

If, for some reason, you wanted to edit the data source, you would click the Edit Data Source button on the Mail Merge toolbar (Figure 5-34).

Entering the Main Document for the Form Letter

The next step is to create the **main document**, which in this case is the form letter (see Figure 5-1a on page WD 5.5). The steps on the following pages illustrate how to create the main document for the form letter.

The first item to be entered in the main document is the inside address on the letter. The contents of the inside address are located in the data source. Thus, you insert fields from the data source into the main document.

Inserting Merge Fields into the Main Document

In the previous steps, you created the data source for the form letter. The first record in the data source, the header row, contains the field names of each field in the data source. To link the data source to the main document, you must insert these field names into the main document. In the main document, these field names are called **merge fields** because they merge, or combine, the main document with the contents of the data source. When a field is inserted into the main document from the data source, Word surrounds the field name with chevrons. These **chevrons** mark the beginning and ending of a merge field. Chevrons are not on the keyboard; therefore, you cannot type them directly into the document. They display as a result of inserting a merge field with the **Insert Merge Field button** on the Mail Merge toolbar.

Perform the following steps to insert a merge field from the data source.

To Insert a Merge Field into the Main Document

1 If necessary, scroll down and click the placeholder text, Click here and type recipient's address. Click the Insert Merge Field button on the Mail Merge toolbar. In the list of fields, point to Title.

Word displays a list of fields from the data source (Figure 5-35). The field you select will replace the selected placeholder text in the main document.

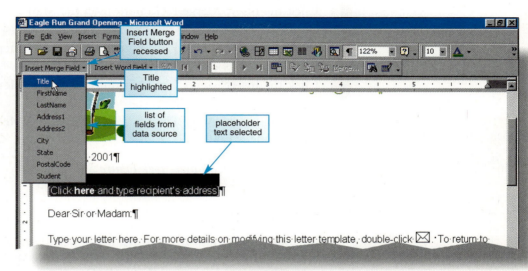

FIGURE 5-35

2 Click Title. When the list of fields disappears from the screen, press the SPACEBAR.

Word displays the field name, Title, surrounded with chevrons in the main document (Figure 5-36). When you merge the data source with the main document, the customer's title (e.g., Mr. or Ms.) will print at the location of the merge field, Title. One space follows the ending chevron after the Title merge field.

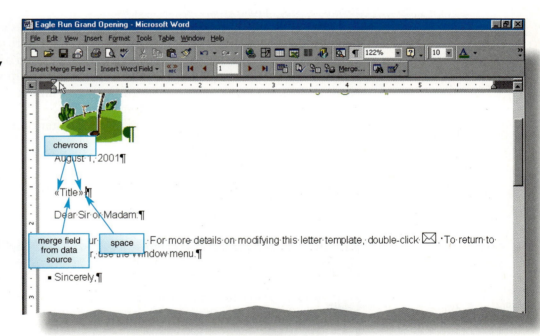

FIGURE 5-36

Perform the following steps to enter the remaining merge fields for the recipient's address.

TO ENTER MORE MERGE FIELDS

1 Click the Insert Merge Field button on the Mail Merge toolbar and then click FirstName. Press the SPACEBAR.

2 Click the Insert Merge Field button on the Mail Merge toolbar and then click LastName. Press the ENTER key.

More *About*

Field Codes

If, when you insert fields into a document, the fields display surrounded by braces instead of chevrons and extra instructions appear between the braces, then field codes have been turned on. To turn off field codes, press the ALT+F9 keys.

3 Click the Insert Merge Field button on the Mail Merge toolbar and then click Address1. Press the ENTER key.

4 Click the Insert Merge Field button on the Mail Merge toolbar and then click Address2. Press the ENTER key.

5 Click the Insert Merge Field button on the Mail Merge toolbar and then click City. Press the COMMA key and then press the SPACEBAR.

6 Click the Insert Merge Field button on the Mail Merge toolbar and then click State. Press the SPACEBAR.

7 Click the Insert Merge Field button on the Mail Merge toolbar and then click PostalCode.

The inside address is complete (see Figure 5-37).

Finding Fields

To find a particular field in a document, click Edit on the menu bar, click Go To, click Field in the Go to what text box, type the field name in the Enter field name text box, and then click the Next button. To move the insertion point to the next field in a document, click the Select Browse Object button on the vertical scroll bar and then click Browse by Field.

Unlinking a Field

The salutation is currently a Word field. When you point to it, a ScreenTip displays and when you right-click it, a list of salutations displays from which you may select one. The salutation currently reads, Dear Sir or Madam (see Figure 5-37). You want the salutation to be personalized to the recipient; that is, the word, Dear, followed by the fields, Title and LastName.

To change the salutation, you must remove the field designation, or **unlink the field**. To do this, you position the insertion point in the field and then press CTRL+SHIFT+F9. When you position the insertion point in a Word field, the entire field is shaded gray. The shading displays on the screen to help you identify fields; the shading does not print on a hard copy. Once you unlink the field, Word removes the gray shading because the text is no longer a field.

Perform the following steps to unlink the salutation field and enter a personalized salutation.

Steps To Unlink a Field

1 **Click in the salutation field.**

The field displays shaded in gray (Figure 5-37).

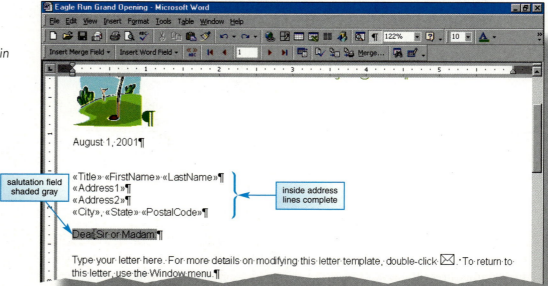

FIGURE 5-37

2 Press CTRL+SHIFT+F9. Click anywhere to remove the highlight.

Word removes the field designation from the salutation.

3 Drag through the text, Sir or Madam, in the salutation. Click the Insert Merge Field button on the Mail Merge toolbar. Point to Title in the list (Figure 5-38).

4 Click Title. Press the SPACEBAR. Click the Insert Merge Field button on the Mail Merge toolbar and then click LastName.

The salutation is complete (see Figure 5-39).

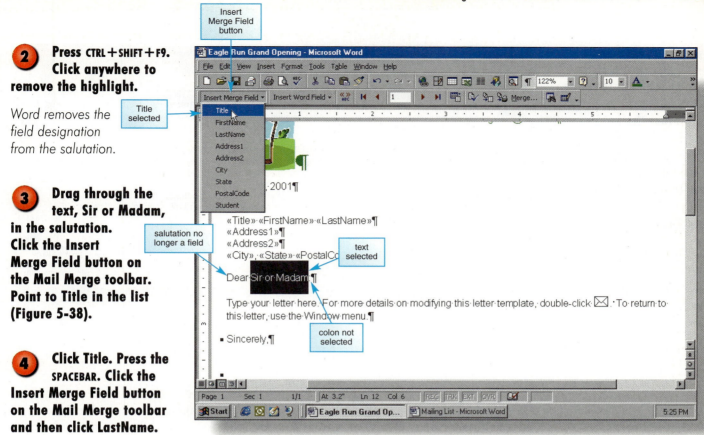

FIGURE 5-38

Entering the Body of a Letter Template

The next step is to enter the first two paragraphs in the body of the form letter. These paragraphs contain constant, or unchanging, text to be printed in each form letter. Perform the following steps to select the placeholder text in the letter template and enter the first two paragraphs of the form letter.

 To Enter the Body of the Letter

1 Scroll down and then triple-click the placeholder text that begins with Type your letter here.

Word selects the entire paragraph in the body of the letter (Figure 5-39).

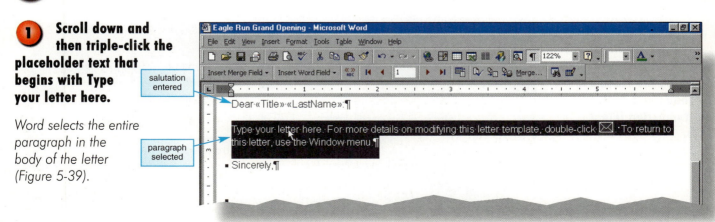

FIGURE 5-39

2 **Type the first paragraph of the body of the form letter as shown in Figure 5-40. Press the ENTER key. Type the second paragraph of the body of the form letter as shown in Figure 5-40. Press the ENTER key.**

Depending on your printer driver, your wordwrap may occur in different locations (Figure 5-40).

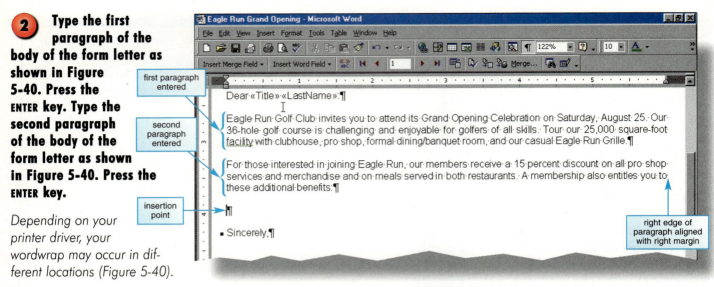

FIGURE 5-40

The paragraphs of the body of the Professional Letter template use the Body Text style. This style specifies single-spacing within paragraphs and double-spacing between paragraphs. Thus, each time you press the ENTER key, Word places a blank line between paragraphs.

The Body Text style also specifies to **justify** paragraphs, which means the left and right edges of the paragraphs are aligned with the left and right margins, respectively, like the edges of newspaper columns.

Creating an Outline Numbered List

The next step is to enter an outline numbered list in the form letter (see Figure 5-1 on page 5.5). An **outline numbered list** is a list that contains several levels of items, with each level displaying a different numeric, alphabetic, or bullet symbol. Perform the following steps to create an outline numbered list that uses bullet symbols.

 To Create an Outline Numbered List

1 **With the insertion point positioned as shown in Figure 5-40, click Format on the menu bar and then point to Bullets and Numbering (Figure 5-41).**

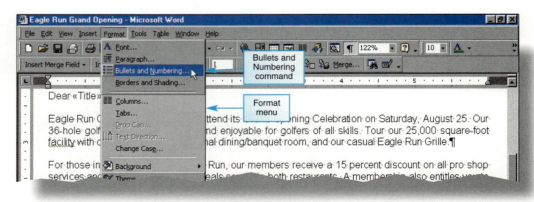

FIGURE 5-41

2 **Click Bullets and Numbering. When the Bullets and Numbering dialog box displays, if necessary, click the Outline Numbered tab. Click the desired number or bullet style in the list and then point to the OK button.**

Word displays the Bullets and Numbering dialog box (Figure 5-42).

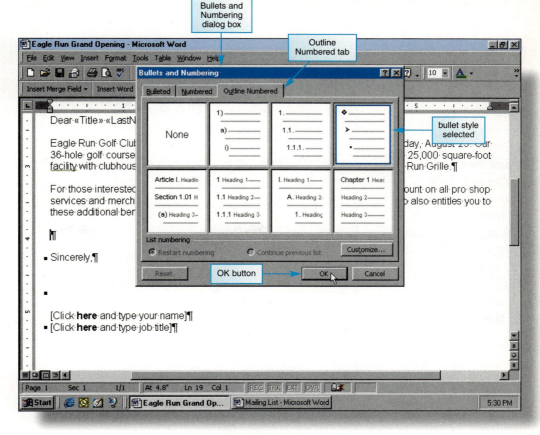

FIGURE 5-42

3 **Click the OK button. Scroll down and then type** Tee Time Reservations and Fees **and then press the ENTER key.**

Word places the first-level bullet symbol on the first list item (Figure 5-43). The first-level bullet symbol also displays on the next line. You want this to be a second-level bullet symbol.

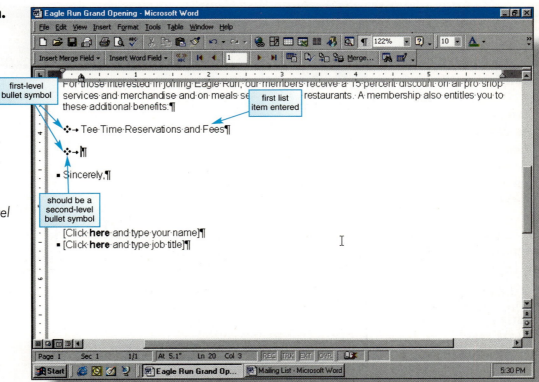

FIGURE 5-43

4 Press the TAB key to demote the current list item so it displays a second-level bullet symbol. Type Tee time reservations instantly from the Web **and then press the ENTER key. Type** Seven-day advance preferred tee times **and then press the ENTER key. Type** No green or cart fees, with member guest discount on green fees **and then press the ENTER key.**

The second level list items are entered (Figure 5-44).

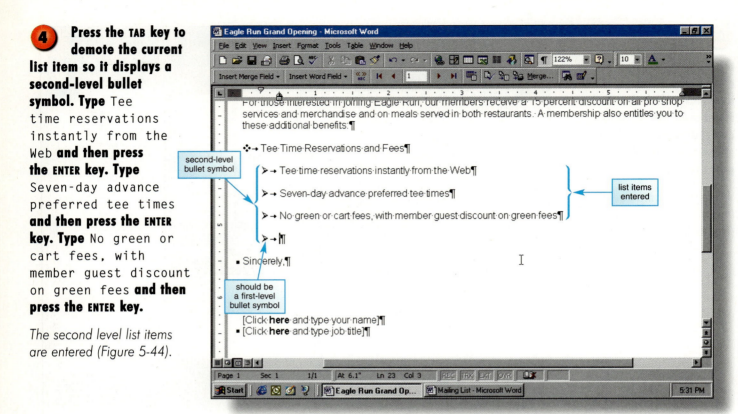

FIGURE 5-44

5 Press the SHIFT+TAB keys to promote the current list item so it displays a first-level bullet symbol. Type Golf Events **and then press the ENTER key. Press the TAB key to demote the current list item. Type** Monthly couples and singles tournaments **and then press the ENTER key. Type** Active men's and ladies' leagues **and then press the ENTER key. Type** Individual lessons and group clinics **and then press the ENTER key. Press the SHIFT+TAB keys.**

The items in the list are entered (Figure 5-45).

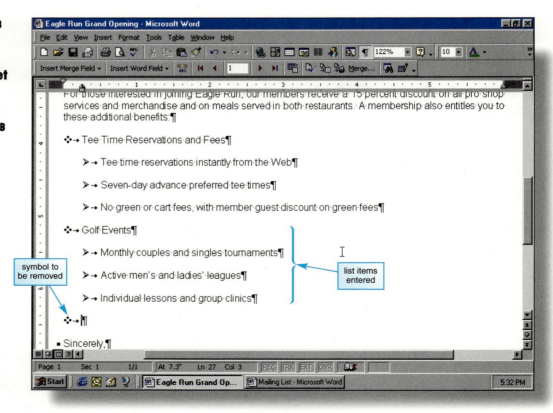

FIGURE 5-45

6 **Double-click the move handle on the Formatting toolbar to display the entire toolbar. Click the Numbering button on the Formatting toolbar.**

Word removes the numbered list bullet symbol from the current paragraph (Figure 5-46).

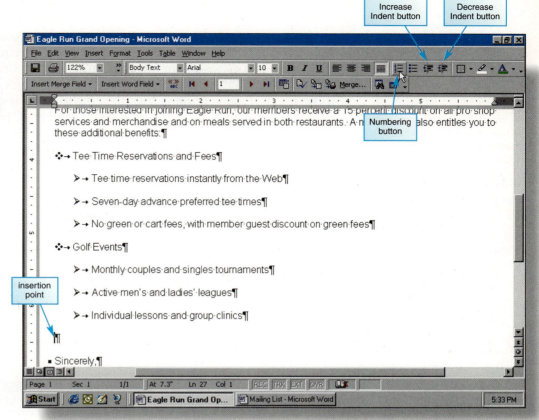

FIGURE 5-46

You also can click the Increase Indent button on the Formatting toolbar to demote a list item in an outline numbered list. Likewise, you can click the Decrease Indent button on the Formatting toolbar to promote a list item.

Using an IF Field to Conditionally Print Text in a Form Letter

In addition to merge fields, you can insert other types of fields in your main document. One type of field is called an **IF field**. One form of the IF field is: If a condition is true, then perform an action. For example, If Mary owns a house, then send her information on homeowner's insurance. This type of IF field is called **If...Then**. Another form of the IF field is: If a condition is true, then perform an action; else perform a different action. For example, If John has an e-mail address, then send him an e-mail message; else send him the note via the postal service. This type of IF field is called **If...Then...Else**.

In this project, the form letter checks whether the person on the mailing list is a student. If he or she is a student, then the discount is 75 percent. If he or she is not a student, then the discount is 25 percent. For Word to determine which discount percent to use, you must enter an If...Then...Else: If Student is equal to Y (for Yes), then print 75 percent as the discount, else print 25 percent as the discount.

The phrase that appears after the word If is called a condition. A **condition** is composed of an expression, followed by a comparison operator, followed by a final expression.

EXPRESSIONS The **expression** in a condition can be a merge field, a number, a series of characters, or a mathematical formula. Word surrounds a series of characters with quotation marks ("). To indicate an empty, or **null**, expression, you place two quotation marks together (" ").

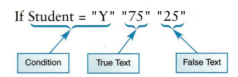

IF Fields

The term, IF field, originates from computer programming. Don't be intimidated by the terminology. An IF field simply specifies a decision. Some programmers refer to it as an IF statement. An IF field can be quite simple or complex. Complex IF fields include nested IF fields, which is a second IF field inside true or false text of the first IF field.

COMPARISON OPERATORS   The **comparison operator** in a condition must be one of six characters: = (equal to or matches the text), <> (not equal to or does not match text), < (less than), <= (less than or equal to), > (greater than), >= (greater than or equal to).

If the result of a condition is true, then the **true text** is evaluated; otherwise, if the result of the condition is false, the **false text** is evaluated. In this project, the first expression in the condition is a merge field (Student); the comparison operator is an equal sign (=); and the second expression is the text "Y". The true text is "75" and the false text is "25". That is, the complete IF field is as follows:

$$\text{If Student} = \text{"Y"} \quad \text{"75"} \quad \text{"25"}$$

Condition   True Text   False Text

Perform the following steps to insert the IF field into the form letter.

Steps: To Insert an IF Field into the Main Document

1   **Scroll down and then type** To receive a **and then press the SPACEBAR. Click the Insert Word Field button on the Mail Merge toolbar. When the list of Word fields displays, point to If...Then...Else.**

A list of Word fields that may be inserted into the main document displays (Figure 5-47).

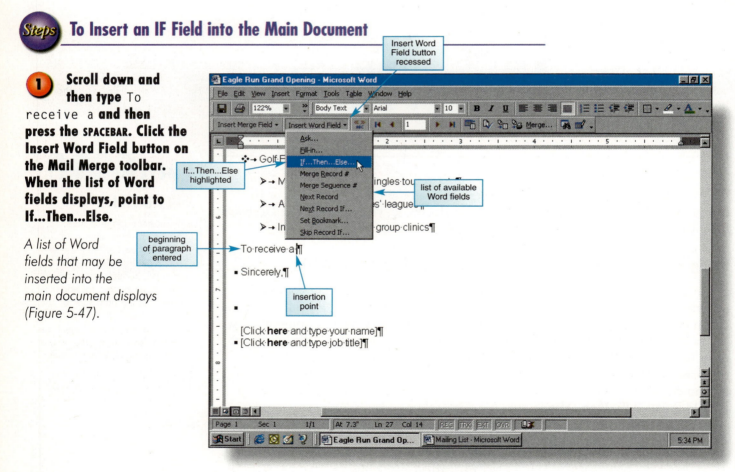

FIGURE 5-47

2 Click If...Then...Else. When the Insert Word Field: IF dialog box displays, point to the Field name box arrow.

Word displays the Insert Word Field: IF dialog box (Figure 5-48). You can specify the condition in the IF area of this dialog box.

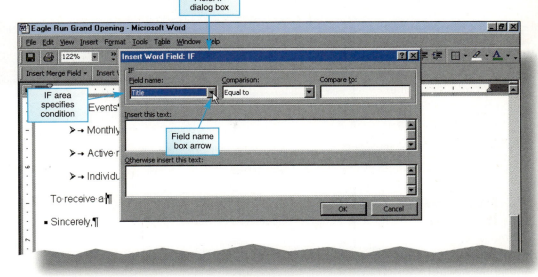

FIGURE 5-48

3 Click the Field name box arrow. Scroll through the list of fields and then point to Student.

Word displays a list of fields from the data source (Figure 5-49).

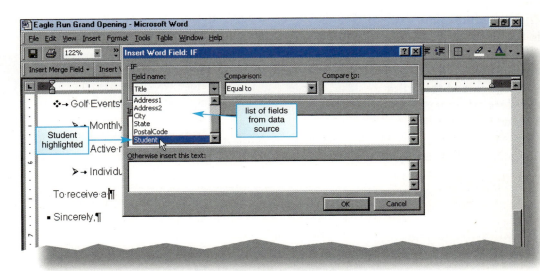

FIGURE 5-49

4 Click Student. Click the Compare to text box. Type Y and then press the TAB key. Type 75 and then press the TAB key. Type 25 and then point to the OK button.

The entries in the Insert Word Field: IF dialog box are complete (Figure 5-50).

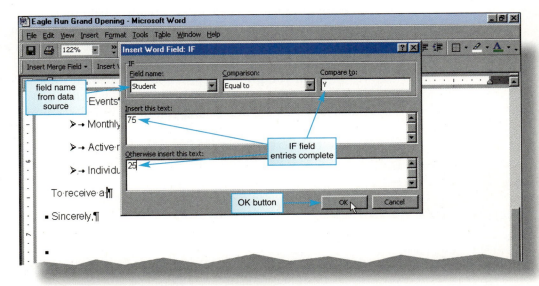

FIGURE 5-50

5 Click the OK button.

Word returns you to the document. The discount percent, 25, displays at the location of the insertion point because the first record in the data source is not a student.

6 Press the SPACEBAR. **Type** percent discount on the initiation fee, become a member during our Grand Opening Celebration. **Click the placeholder text in the signature block, Click here and type your name. Type** Rosa Rodriguez **and then click the placeholder text, Click here and type job title. Type** Marketing Director **(Figure 5-51).**

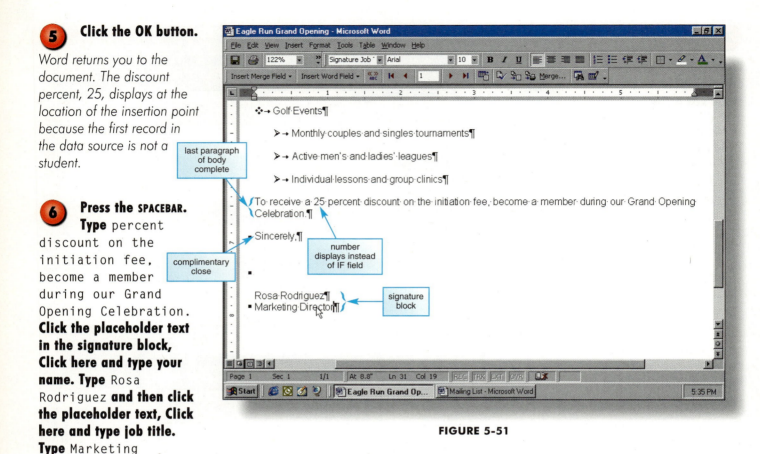

FIGURE 5-51

The next step is to enter a Fill-in field for the mailing date of the letters.

Inserting a Fill-in Field

The Professional Letter template currently displays the date as a field at the top of the form letter. The date is actually a field that Word updates to the current date when it prints the document. You do not, however, want the computer's system date to print on the form letters. Instead, the date that prints at the top of the form letters should be the date the letters are placed in the mail.

When you print the form letters, you want to be able to enter the mailing date at that time. Thus, you insert a **Fill-in field**, which is a Word field that when executed displays a dialog box asking you to fill in information. In this case, when you merge the form letters, the dialog box will ask for the mailing date. Perform the following steps to insert a Fill-in field into the form letter.

To Insert a Fill-in Field

1 Scroll up to display the date in the form letter. Double-click the month or the year to select the entire date field. Click the Insert Word Field button on the Mail Merge toolbar and then point to Fill-in (Figure 5-52).

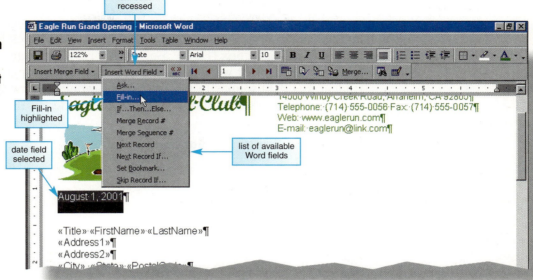

FIGURE 5-52

2 Click Fill-in. When the Insert Word Field: Fill-in dialog box displays, type What date will you be mailing these letters? in the Prompt text box. Click Ask once to select the check box.

Word displays the Insert Word Field: Fill-in dialog box (Figure 5-53). By selecting the Ask once check box, Word will ask the question when you begin the mail merge process – instead of repeatedly for each letter.

3 Click the OK button. When Word displays a sample dialog box showing the prompt question, click the OK button.

Word leaves the date line of the form letter blank (see Figure 5-55 on page WD 5.40).

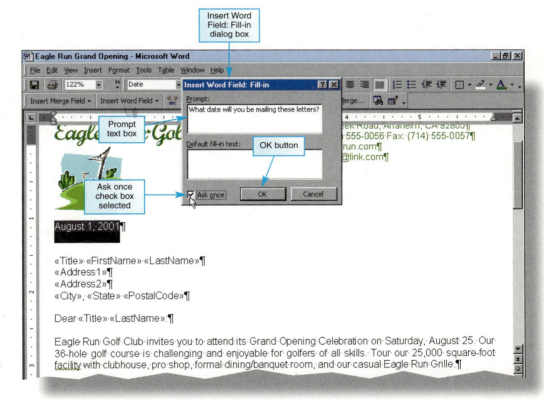

FIGURE 5-53

Other Ways

1. On Insert menu click Field, click Mail Merge in Fields list, click Fill-in in Field names list, enter expression in text box, click OK button

When you merge the form letters, the Fill-in field instructs Word to display the dialog box that requests the mailing date of the form letters so that the correct date prints on the letters.

If you wanted to enter varying responses to a particular question for each record in a data source, you would not check the Ask once check box in the Insert Word Field: Fill-in dialog box (Figure 5-53 on the previous page). For example, a school's advising office might want to enter a specific advising appointment time for each student in a data source. In this case, Word would display the dialog box for each individual form letter, allowing you to enter a different time for each letter.

Saving the Document Again

Because the main document for the form letter now is complete, you should save it again, as described in the following step.

TO SAVE A DOCUMENT AGAIN

 Double-click the move handle on the Standard toolbar to display the entire toolbar. Click the Save button on the Standard toolbar.

Word saves the main document for the form letter with the same name, Eagle Run Grand Opening.

Displaying Field Codes

The Fill-in field and IF field do not display in the document window. At the location of the IF field, the value of the IF field, called the **field results,** displays. That is, the number 25 displays (see Figure 5-51 on page WD 5.36) because the first data record is not a student. At the location of the Fill-in field, nothing displays (see Figure 5-55 on page WD 5.40). Recall that when you merge the letters, Word will display a dialog box requesting you enter a date. At that time, Word will place the date you enter at the location of the Fill-in field – the date line.

The instructions within the Fill-in field and IF field are referred to as **field codes,** and the default for Word is field codes off. Thus, field codes do not print or display unless you turn them on. You use one procedure to display field codes on the screen and a different procedure to print them on a hard copy. To display field codes on the screen, you press the ALT+F9 keys. The procedure for printing field codes is discussed in the next section.

Whether field codes are on or off on your screen has no effect on the print merge process. The following steps illustrate how to turn on field codes so you may see them on the screen. Most Word users only turn on field codes to verify their accuracy. Because field codes tend to clutter the screen, you may want to turn them off after checking their accuracy.

Perform the following steps to turn field codes on for display and then turn them off again.

Locking Fields

If you wanted to lock a field so that its field results cannot be changed, click the field and then press CTRL+F11. To subsequently unlock a field so that it may be updated, click the field and then press CTRL+SHIFT+F11.

Steps To Turn Field Codes On and Off for Display

1 **Press the ALT + F9 keys.**

Word displays the main document with field codes on (Figure 5-54). With field codes on, the term, MERGEFIELD, displays before each field from the data source. The instructions in the Fill-in and IF fields also display. With field codes on, braces surround the fields instead of chevrons.

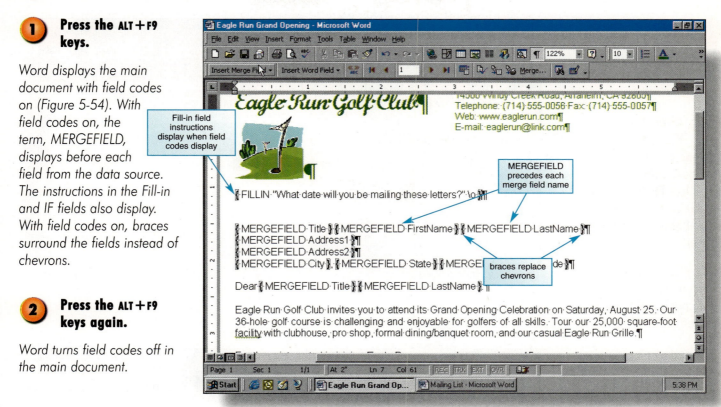

2 **Press the ALT + F9 keys again.**

Word turns field codes off in the main document.

FIGURE 5-54

Printing Field Codes

You also may want to print the field codes version of the form letter so that you have a hard copy of the fields for future reference (see Figure 5-1a on page WD 5.5). When you print field codes, you must remember to turn off the field codes option so that future documents print field results instead of field codes. For example, with field codes on, merged form letters will display field codes instead of data. Perform the steps on the next page to print the field codes in the main document and then turn off the field codes print option for future printing.

To Print Field Codes in the Main Document

1 **Click Tools on the menu bar and then point to Options (Figure 5-55).**

2 **Click Options. When the Options dialog box displays, click the Print tab. Click Field codes in the Include with document area. Point to the OK button.**

Word displays the Options dialog box (Figure 5-56). The Field codes check box is selected.

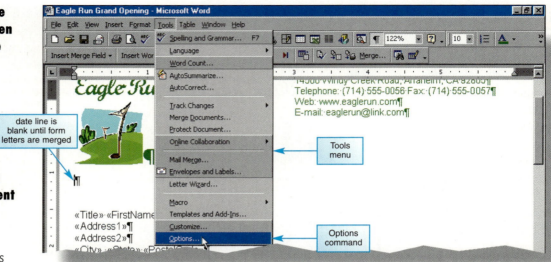

FIGURE 5-55

3 **Click the OK button. Click the Print button on the Standard toolbar.**

Word prints the main document with field codes (see Figure 5-1a on page WD 5.5). Notice the Fill-in and IF field instructions display on the printout.

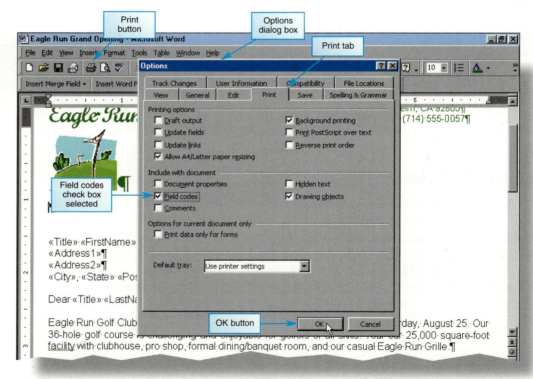

FIGURE 5-56

1. On File menu click Print, click Options button, click Field codes, click OK button, click OK button

2. Press CTRL+P, click Options button, click Field codes, click OK button, click OK button

You should turn off printed field codes so that future documents do not print field codes. Perform the following steps to turn off field codes for printing.

TO TURN FIELD CODES OFF FOR PRINTING

1 Click Tools on menu bar and then click Options.

2 When the Options dialog box displays, if necessary, click the Print tab. Click Field codes in the Include with document area to remove the check mark.

3 Click the OK button.

Word turns off field codes for printed documents.

Merging the Documents and Printing the Letters

The data source and main document for the form letter are complete. The next step is to merge them together to generate the individual form letters as shown in the following steps.

More About

Main Documents

When you open a main document, Word attempts to open the associated data source file, too. If the data source is not in exactly the same location (i.e., drive and folder) as when it was saved originally, Word displays a dialog box indicating that it could not find the data source. When this occurs, click the Find Data Source button to display the Open Data Source dialog box.

 To Merge the Documents and Print the Form Letters

1 **Point to the Merge to Printer button on the Mail Merge toolbar (Figure 5-57).**

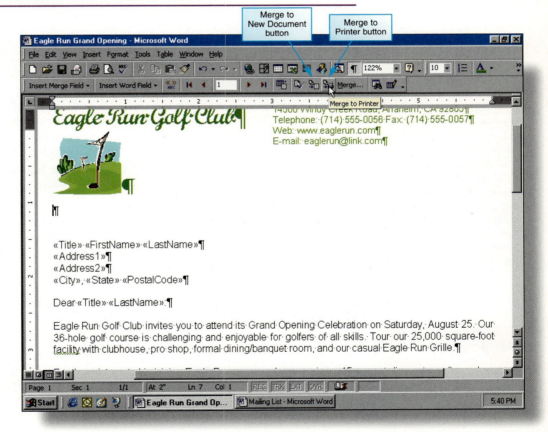

FIGURE 5-57

Click the Merge to Printer button. When the Print dialog box displays, click the OK button. When the Microsoft Word dialog box displays, type August 6, 2001 **and then point to the OK button.**

The Fill-in field instructs Word to display the dialog box requesting the mailing date of the form letters (Figure 5-58).

 Click the OK button.

Word prints five separate letters, one for each person in the data source (see Figure 5-1c on page WD 5.5).

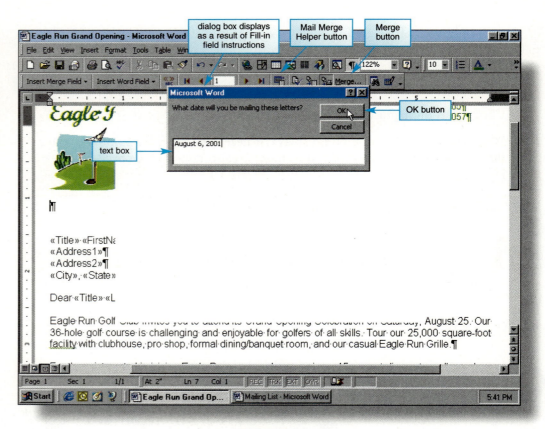

FIGURE 5-58

1. Click Merge button on Mail Merge toolbar, click Merge to box arrow and then click Printer, click Merge button in Merge dialog box

2. Click Mail Merge Helper button on Mail Merge toolbar, click Merge button, click Merge to box arrow and then click Printer, click Merge button in Merge dialog box, click Close button

Conditions

The merge condition is case sensitive, which means the criteria you enter in the Compare to text box (Figure 5-60) must be the same case as the text in the data source. That is, if the data in the data source is in upper case, then the criteria entered in the Filter Records sheet also must be in upper case.

The contents of the data source merge with the merge fields in the main document to generate the form letters. Word prints five form letters because the data source contains five records. The address lines *suppress* blanks. That is, customers without a second address line begin the city on the line immediately below the first address line. Also, the discount percent changes from one letter to the next based on whether or not the person in the mailing list is a student.

If you notice errors in your form letters, you can edit the main document the same way you edit any other document. Then, save your changes and merge again.

Instead of printing the merged form letters, you could send them into a new document window by clicking the Merge to New Document button on the Mail Merge toolbar (see Figure 5-57 on the previous page). With this button, you view the merged form letters in a new document window on the screen to verify their accuracy before printing the letters. When you are finished viewing the merged form letters, you can print them by clicking the Print button on the Standard toolbar. In addition, you also can save these merged form letters in a file. If you do not want to save the merged form letters, close the document window by clicking the Close button at the right edge of the menu bar and then click the No button to not save the document.

Selecting Data Records to Merge and Print

Instead of merging and printing all of the records in the data source, you can choose which records will merge, based on a condition you specify. For example, to merge and print only those people in the mailing list who are students, perform the following steps.

To Selectively Merge and Print Records

1
Click the Merge button on the Mail Merge toolbar. When Word displays the Merge dialog box, point to the Query Options button.

Word displays the Merge dialog box (Figure 5-59).

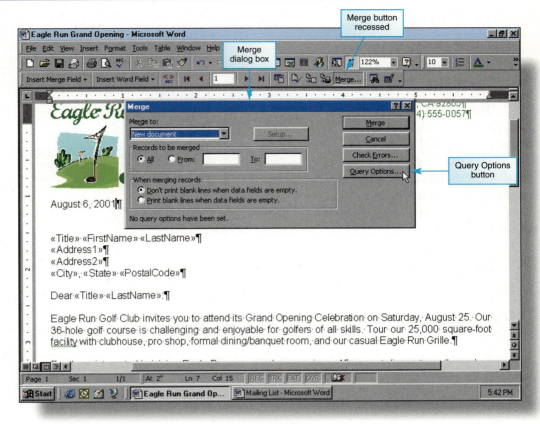

FIGURE 5-59

2
Click the Query Options button. When the Query Options dialog box displays, if necessary, click the Filter Records tab. Click the Field box arrow to display a list of fields from the data source. Scroll to the bottom of the list and then click Student. In the Compare to text box, type Y and then point to the OK button.

Word displays the Query Options dialog box (Figure 5-60). Student displays in the Field box, Equal to displays in the Comparison box, and Y displays in the Compare to box.

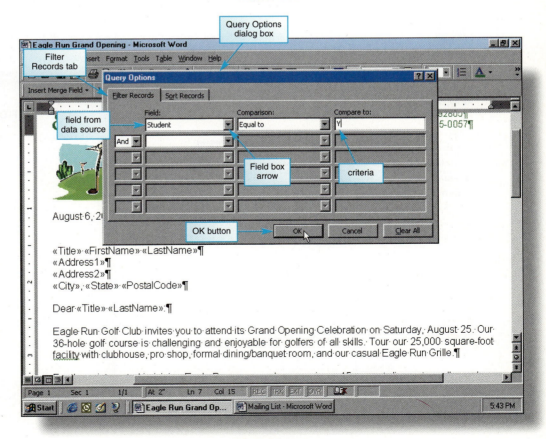

FIGURE 5-60

Microsoft Word 2000

3 **Click the OK button. When the Merge dialog box redisplays, click its Close button.**

Word returns to the Merge dialog box. You close this dialog box.

4 **Click the Merge to Printer button on the Mail Merge toolbar. When Word displays the Print dialog box, click the OK button. When the Microsoft Word dialog box displays, if necessary, type** August 6, 2001 **and then click the OK button.**

Word prints the form letters that match the specified condition: Student is Equal to Y (Figure 5-61). Two form letters print because two people in the mailing list are students.

Eagle Run Golf Club

14500 Windy Creek Road, Anaheim, CA 92805
Telephone: (714) 555-0056 Fax: (714) 555-0057
Web: www.eaglerun.com
E-mail: eaglerun@link.com

August 6, 2001

Mr. James Wheeler
113 Fourth Street
Apt. 3C
Placentia, CA 82870

Dear Mr. Wheeler:

Eagle Run Golf Club invites you to attend its Grand Opening Celebration on Saturday, August 25. Our 36-hole golf course is challenging and enjoyable for golfers of all skills. Tour our 25,000 square-foot facility with clubhouse, pro shop, formal dining/banquet room, and our casual Eagle Run Grille.

For those interested in joining Eagle Run, our members receive a 15 percent discount on all pro shop services and merchandise and on meals served in both restaurants. A membership also entitles you to these additional benefits:

❖ Tee Time Reservations and Fees

➤ Tee time reservations instantly from the Web

➤ Seven-day advance preferred tee times

➤ No green or cart fees, with member guest discount on green fees

❖ Golf Events

➤ Monthly couples and singles tournaments

➤ Active men's and ladies' leagues

➤ Individual lessons and group clinics

To receive a 75 percent discount on the initiation fee, become a member during our Grand Opening Celebration.

Sincerely,

discount percent for student

Rosa Rodriguez
Marketing Director

Eagle Run Golf Club

14500 Windy Creek Road, Anaheim, CA 92805
Telephone: (714) 555-0056 Fax: (714) 555-0057
Web: www.eaglerun.com
E-mail: eaglerun@link.com

August 6, 2001

Mrs. May Li
189 Eastern Avenue
Fullerton, CA 92831

Dear Mrs. Li:

Eagle Run Golf Club invites you to attend its Grand Opening Celebration on Saturday, August 25. Our 36-hole golf course is challenging and enjoyable for golfers of all skills. Tour our 25,000 square-foot facility with clubhouse, pro shop, formal dining/banquet room, and our casual Eagle Run Grille.

For those interested in joining Eagle Run, our members receive a 15 percent discount on all pro shop services and merchandise and on meals served in both restaurants. A membership also entitles you to these additional benefits:

❖ Tee Time Reservations and Fees

➤ Tee time reservations instantly from the Web

➤ Seven-day advance preferred tee times

➤ No green or cart fees, with member guest discount on green fees

❖ Golf Events

➤ Monthly couples and singles tournaments

➤ Active men's and ladies' leagues

➤ Individual lessons and group clinics

To receive a 75 percent discount on the initiation fee, become a member during our Grand Opening Celebration.

Sincerely,

discount percent for student

Rosa Rodriguez
Marketing Director

FIGURE 5-61

Other Ways

1. Click Mail Merge Helper button on Mail Merge toolbar, click Merge button, click Query Options button, enter condition, click OK button, click Merge to box arrow and then click Printer, click Merge button in Merge dialog box, click Close button

You should remove the merge condition so that future merges will not be restricted to Student is Equal to Y.

TO REMOVE A MERGE CONDITION

1 Click the Merge button on the Mail Merge toolbar.

2 Click the Query Options button in the Merge dialog box.

3 Click the Clear All button. Click the OK button.

4 Click the Close button in the Merge dialog box.

Word removes the specified condition.

Sorting Data Records to Merge and Print

If you mail your form letters using the U.S. Postal Service's bulk rate mailing service, the post office requires you to sort and group the form letters by zip code. Thus, follow these steps to sort the data records by zip code.

Steps To Sort the Data Records

1 Click the Merge button on the Mail Merge toolbar. When Word displays the Merge dialog box, click the Query Options button (see Figure 5-59 on page WD 5.43). If necessary, click the Sort Records tab when the Query Options dialog box displays. Point to the Sort by box arrow.

Word displays the Query Options dialog box (Figure 5-62). You can order the data source records by any field.

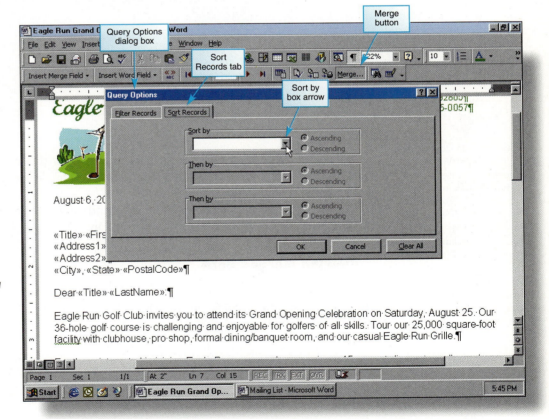

FIGURE 5-62

2   Click the Sort by box arrow to display a list of fields from the data source. Scroll to the bottom of the list and then click PostalCode.

Word displays PostalCode in the Sort by box (Figure 5-63). The Ascending option button is selected. Thus, the smallest postal code (those beginning with zero) will be listed first in the data source and the largest postal code will be last.

3   Click the OK button. When the Merge dialog box redisplays, click its Close button.

The data records are sorted in ascending order by postal code. Future merged documents will print in postal code order.

FIGURE 5-63

Other **Ways**

1. Click the Edit Data Source button on the Mail Merge toolbar, click the View Source button in the Data Form dialog box, click in the PostalCode column of the data source table, click the Sort Ascending button (see Figure 5-30 on page WD 5.23) on the Database toolbar, click the Mail Merge Main Document button on the Database toolbar

If you chose to merge the form letters again at this point, Word would print them in postal code order; that is, James Wheeler's letter would print first and May Li's letter would print last.

Because you want the mailing labels and envelopes to print in order of zip code, leave the sort condition set in the Query Options dialog box.

Viewing Merged Data

You can verify the order of the data records without printing them by using the **View Merged Data button** on the Mail Merge toolbar as shown in the following steps.

Steps ## To View Merged Data in the Main Document

1 ### Click the View Merged Data button on the Mail Merge toolbar.

Word displays the contents of the first data record in the main document, instead of the merge fields (Figure 5-64). The View Merged Data button is recessed.

2 ### Click the View Merged Data button on the Mail Merge toolbar again.

Word displays the merge fields in the main document, instead of the field values.

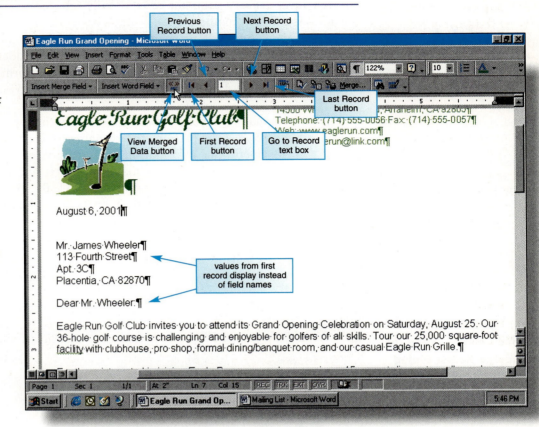

FIGURE 5-64

When you are viewing merged data in the main document (the View Merged Data button is recessed), you can click the **Last Record button** (see Figure 5-64) on the Mail Merge toolbar to display the values from the last record of the data source, the **Next Record button** to display the values from the next consecutive record number, the **Previous Record button** to display the values from the previous record number, or the **First Record button** to display the values from record one. You also can display a particular record by clicking the **Go to Record text box**, typing the record number you would like to display in the main document, and then pressing the ENTER key.

Addressing Mailing Labels

Now that you have merged and printed the form letters, the next step is to print addresses on **mailing labels** to be adhered to envelopes for the form letters. The mailing labels will use the same data source as the form letter, Mailing List. The format and content of the mailing labels will be exactly the same as the inside address in the main document for the form letter. That is, the first line will contain the resident's title, followed by the first name, followed by the last name. The second line will contain his or her street address, and so on.

More *About*

2000

Opening Form Letters

When you open the main document, the associated data source also automatically opens in a separate document window. If, however, you open the data source, only the data source opens. Thus, to generate form letters at a later date, simply open the main document and then click the Merge to Printer button.

Mailing Labels

Instead of addressing mailing labels from a data source, you can print a label(s) for a single address. Click Tools on the menu bar, click Envelopes and Labels, click the Labels tab, type the name and address in the Address text box, click the Options button and select the label type, click the OK button, and then click the Print button in the Envelopes and Labels dialog box.

If your printer can print graphics, you can add a **POSTNET (POSTal Numeric Encoding Technique) delivery-point bar code,** usually referred to simply as a **bar code,** above the address on each mailing label. Using a bar code speeds up delivery by the U.S. Postal Service. A bar code represents the addressee's zip code and first street address.

You follow the same basic steps to create the main document for the mailing labels as you did to create the main document for the form letters. The major difference is that the data source already exists because you created it earlier in this project.

To address mailing labels, you need to specify the type of labels you intend to use. Word will request the manufacturer's name, as well as a product number and name. You can obtain this information from the box of labels. For illustration purposes in addressing these labels, the manufacturer is Avery, and the product name is address labels, which has a product number of 5160. The following pages illustrate how to address these mailing labels from an existing data source.

To Address Mailing Labels from an Existing Data Source

1 **Click Tools on the menu bar and then click Mail Merge. When the Mail Merge Helper dialog box displays, click the Create button. Point to Mailing Labels (Figure 5-65).**

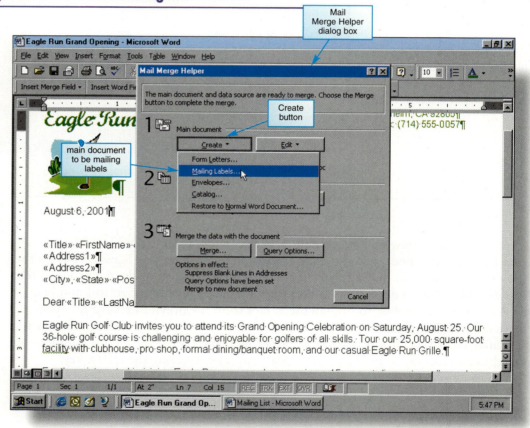

FIGURE 5-65

2 Click Mailing Labels. Point to the New Main Document button in the Microsoft Word dialog box.

A Microsoft Word dialog box displays asking if you want to change the active window main document to mailing labels or if you want to open a new window for the mailing labels (Figure 5-66). You want to open a new document window for the mailing labels.

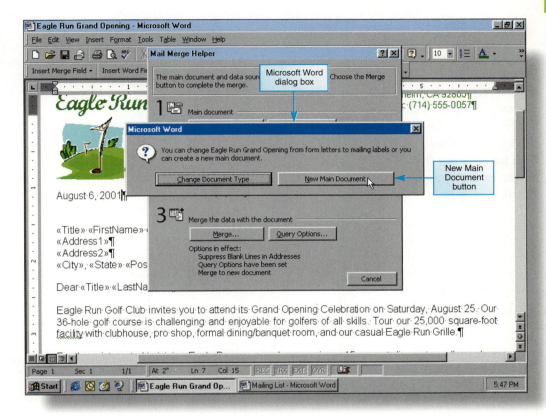

FIGURE 5-66

3 Click the New Main Document button. When the Mail Merge Helper dialog box is visible again, click the Get Data button and then point to Open Data Source.

Word opens a new document window and returns you to the Mail Merge Helper dialog box (Figure 5-67). The merge type is identified as mailing labels for the main document. You will open and use the same data source you created for the form letters.

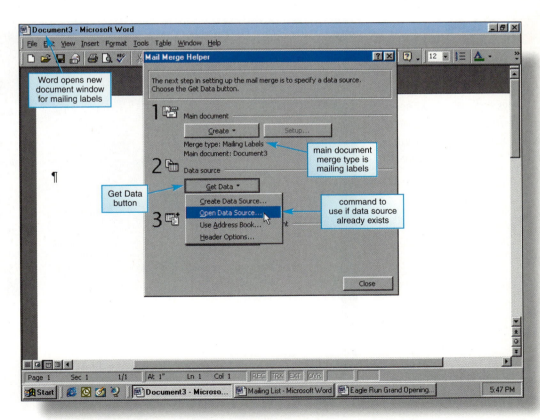

FIGURE 5-67

4 **Click Open Data Source. When Word displays the Open Data Source dialog box, if necessary, click the Look in box arrow and then click 3½ Floppy (A:). Click the file name, Mailing List, and then point to the Open button in the Open Data Source dialog box.**

Word displays the Open Data Source dialog box (Figure 5-68). You use the existing data source, Mailing List, to address the mailing labels.

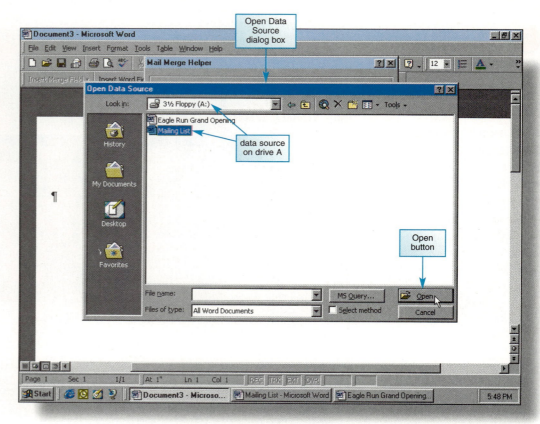

FIGURE 5-68

5 **Click the Open button in the Open Data Source dialog box.**

A Microsoft Word dialog box displays indicating you need to set up the main document, which will be a mailing label layout in this case (Figure 5-69).

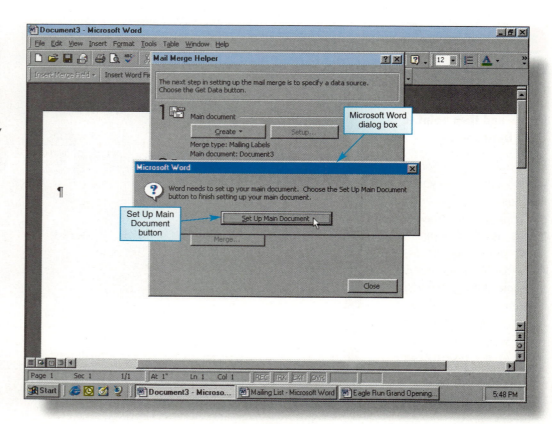

FIGURE 5-69

6 Click the Set Up Main Document button. When the Label Options dialog box displays, click the desired Avery product number in the Product number list. Point to the OK button.

Word displays the Label Options dialog box (Figure 5-70). If you have a dot matrix printer, your printer information will differ from this figure. The Product number list displays the product numbers for all possible Avery mailing label sheets compatible with your printer.

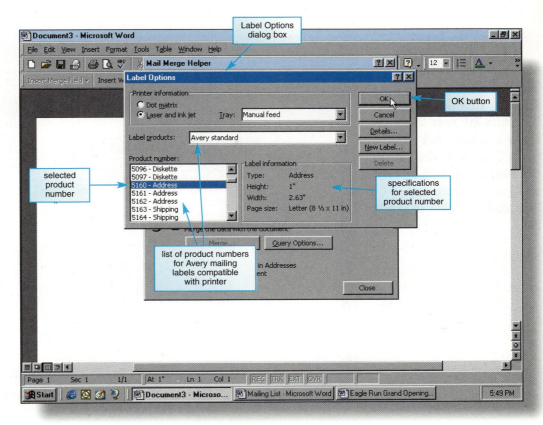

FIGURE 5-70

7 Click the OK button.

Word displays the Create Labels dialog box. You insert merge fields into the Sample label area of this dialog box using a technique similar to how you inserted merge fields into the main document for the form letter.

8 Using the Insert Merge Field button in the Create Labels dialog box, follow Steps 1 and 2 on page WD 5.27 and then Steps 1 through 7 on pages WD 5.27 and WD 5.28 to address the mailing label. Point to the Insert Postal Bar Code button (Figure 5-71).

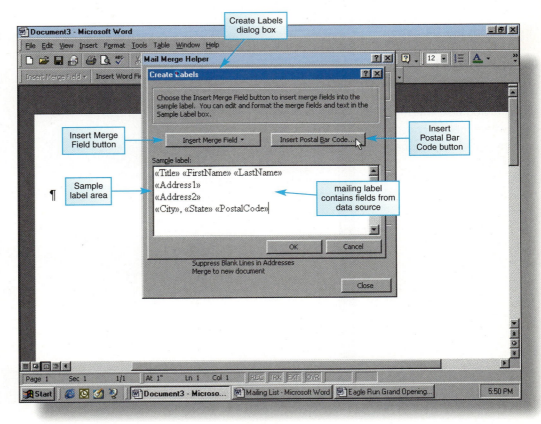

FIGURE 5-71

9 **Click the Insert Postal Bar Code button. When the Insert Postal Bar Code dialog box displays, click the Merge field with ZIP code box arrow and then click PostalCode in the list. Click the Merge field with street address box arrow and then click Address1 in the list.**

Word displays the Insert Postal Bar Code dialog box (Figure 5-72). A bar code contains the zip code and the first address line.

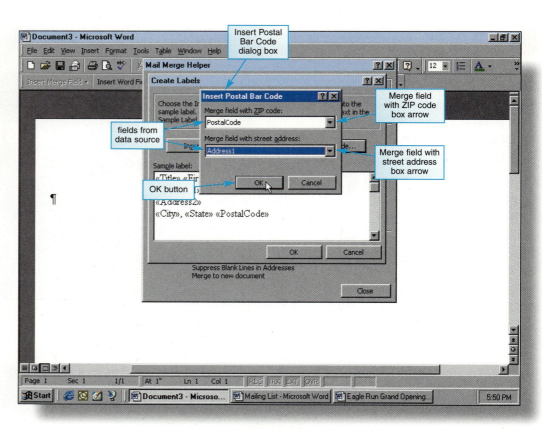

FIGURE 5-72

10 **Click the OK button in the Insert Postal Bar Code dialog box.**

Word returns to the Create Labels dialog box, which indicates where the bar code will print on each mailing label (Figure 5-73).

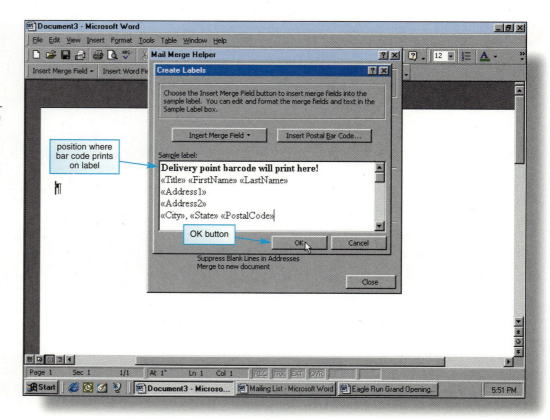

FIGURE 5-73

11 **Click the OK button in the Create Labels dialog box. Click the Close button in the Mail Merge Helper dialog box. When the main document displays in the document window, click the Merge to Printer button on the Mail Merge toolbar. When the Print dialog box displays, click the OK button.**

Word returns to the document window with the mailing label layout as the main document (Figure 5-74). The bar codes will print correctly even if your screen displays an error message or if the merge fields appear misaligned.

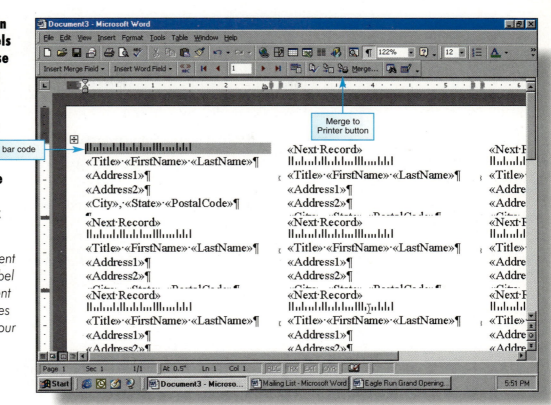

FIGURE 5-74

12 **Retrieve the mailing labels from the printer.**

The mailing labels print as shown in Figure 5-75. The mailing labels print in zip code order because earlier in this project you sorted the data source by zip code.

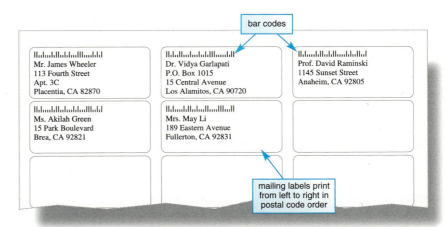

FIGURE 5-75

More About 2000

Bar Codes

If the bar code option is not available, the mailing label size you selected might not be wide enough to accommodate a bar code.

Saving the Mailing Labels

Perform the following steps to save the mailing labels.

TO SAVE THE MAILING LABELS

1 Insert your floppy disk into drive A.

2 Click the Save button on the Standard toolbar.

3 Type the file name `Eagle Run Labels` in the File name text box. Do not press the ENTER key after typing the file name.

4 If necessary, click the Save in box arrow and then click 3½ Floppy (A:).

5 Click the Save button in the Save As dialog box.

Word saves the document on a floppy disk on drive A with the file name, Eagle Run Labels.

More *About*

Mail Merge Helper Button

If the Mail Merge toolbar displays in the Word window, you can click the Mail Merge Helper button on the Mail Merge toolbar to display the Mail Merge Helper dialog box. If the Mail Merge toolbar does not display, click Tools on the menu bar and then click Mail Merge to display the Mail Merge Helper dialog box.

Addressing Envelopes

Instead of addressing mailing labels to affix to envelopes, your printer may have the capability of printing directly onto envelopes. To print the label information directly on envelopes, follow the same basic steps as you did to address the mailing labels. Perform the following steps to address envelopes using an existing data source.

Steps **To Address Envelopes from an Existing Data Source**

1 **Click Tools on the menu bar and then click Mail Merge. When the Mail Merge Helper dialog box displays, click the Create button and then point to Envelopes (Figure 5-76).**

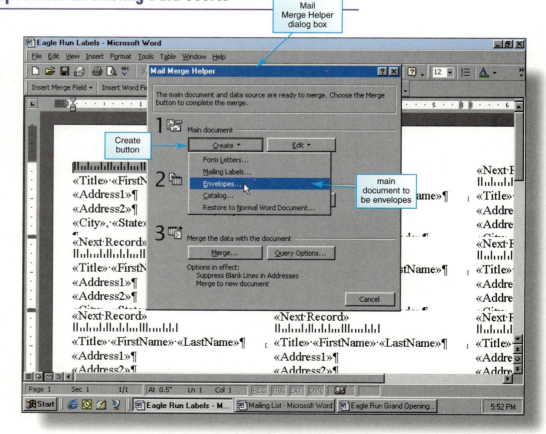

FIGURE 5-76

2 **Click Envelopes. Click the New Main Document button. Click the Get Data button and then click Open Data Source. When the Open Data Source dialog box displays, if necessary, change the Look in location to drive A. Click the file name, Mailing List, and then click the Open button in the Open Data Source dialog box. Click the Set Up Main Document button. If necessary, click the Envelope Options tab when the Envelope Options dialog box displays.**

Word displays the Envelope Options dialog box (Figure 5-77). Depending on your printer, your Envelope Options sheet may differ from this figure.

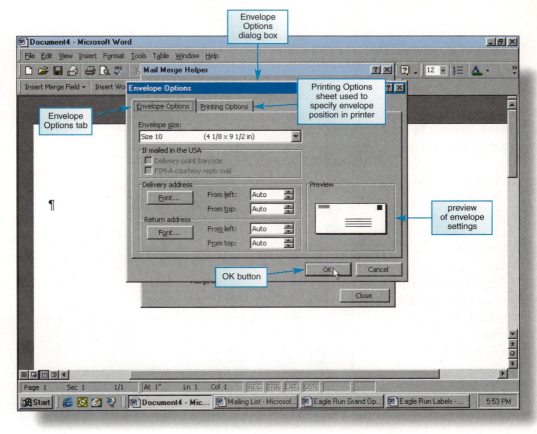

FIGURE 5-77

3 **Click the OK button.**

Word displays the Envelope address dialog box. You insert merge fields into the Sample envelope address area of this dialog box the same way you inserted merge fields into the main document for the mailing labels and the main document for the form letter.

4 **Follow Steps 8 through 11 on pages WD 5.51 through WD 5.53 to address the envelopes with a bar code.**

Word displays the completed envelope layout (Figure 5-78).

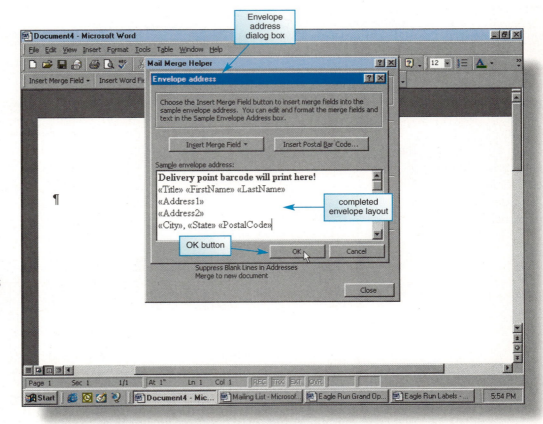

FIGURE 5-78

5 **Click the OK button. When the Mail Merge Helper dialog box displays, click the Close button. When the main document displays in the document window, type** Eagle Run Golf Club **in the return address area. Press the ENTER key. Type** 14500 Windy Creek Road **and then press the ENTER key. Type** Anaheim, CA 92805 **and then click the Merge to Printer button on the Mail Merge toolbar. When the Print dialog box displays, click the OK button.**

Word returns to the document window with the envelope layout as the main document (Figure 5-79). The bar codes will print correctly even if your screen displays an error message.

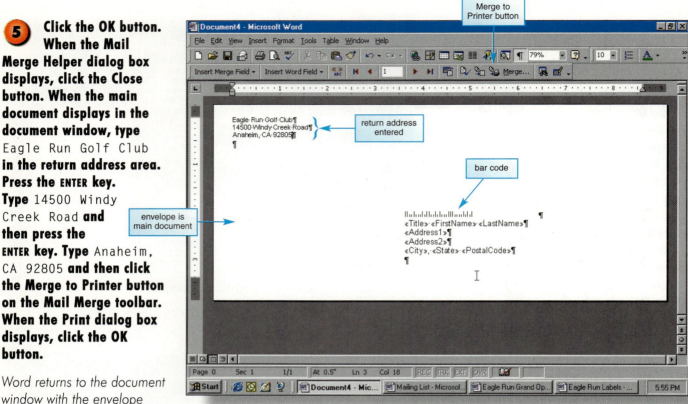

FIGURE 5-79

6 **Retrieve the envelopes from the printer.**

The envelopes print as shown in Figure 5-80. The envelopes print in postal code order because earlier in this project you sorted the data source by postal code.

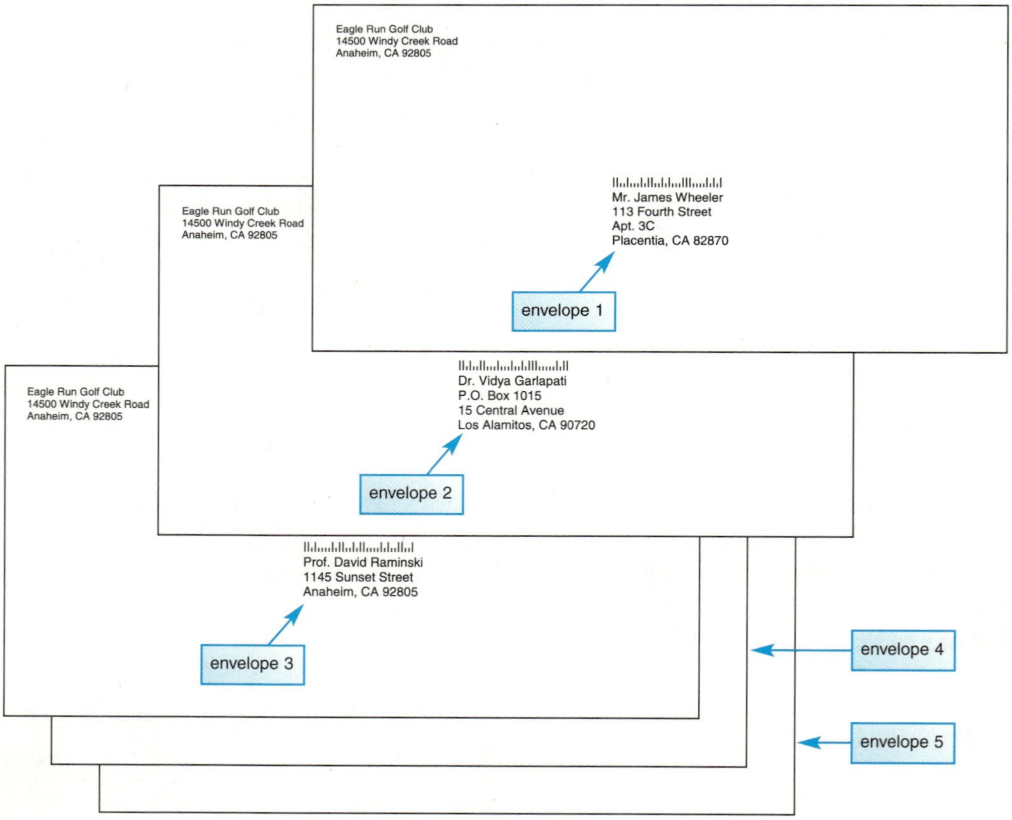

Other Ways

1. Click Mail Merge Helper button on Mail Merge toolbar

FIGURE 5-80

Saving the Envelopes

Perform the following steps to save the envelopes.

TO SAVE THE ENVELOPES

1 Insert your floppy disk into drive A.

2 Click the Save button on the Standard toolbar.

3 Type the file name `Eagle Run Envelopes` in the File name text box. Do not press the ENTER key after typing the file name.

4 If necessary, click the Save in box arrow and then click 3½ Floppy (A:).

5 Click the Save button in the Save As dialog box.

Word saves the document on a floppy disk on drive A with the file name, Eagle Run Envelopes.

Closing All Open Files and Quitting Word

You currently have four files open: Mailing List, Eagle Run Golf Opening, Eagle Run Mailing Labels, and Eagle Run Envelopes. Close all open files at once as described in these steps.

TO CLOSE ALL OPEN DOCUMENTS

1 Press and hold the SHIFT key. While holding the SHIFT key, click File on the menu bar. Release the SHIFT key.

2 Click Close All.

3 If a Microsoft Word dialog box displays, click the Yes button to save any changes made to the individual documents. If you do not want the data records to be saved in sorted order (by postal code), you would click the No button when Word asks if you want to save changes to Mailing List.

Word closes all open documents and displays a blank document window.

Project 5 now is complete. Follow this step to quit Word.

TO QUIT WORD

1 Click the Close button in the Word window.

The Word window closes.

CASE PERSPECTIVE SUMMARY

Ahmed inserts the form letters into the preaddressed envelopes, seals them, and applies necessary postage. He takes the stack of envelopes to the post office to expedite the delivery of the letters. Rosa and her staff prepare diligently for the upcoming celebration.

The Grand Opening Celebration is a smashing success. The weather is quite accommodating – sunny, 85 degrees, and a gentle breeze. More than 1,000 people visit Eagle Run on August 25, touring the club, taking advantage of the pro shop sale, and enjoying fabulous food. Best of all, 257 of the visitors become members during the celebration.

Project Summary

Project 5 introduced you to creating and printing form letters and addressing corresponding mailing labels and envelopes. First, you used a letter template to begin creating the letter, then identified the letter as the main document and created a data source. Next, you entered the main document for the form letter. The form letter included merge fields, an IF field, a Fill-in field, and an outline numbered list. In this project, you learned how to merge and print all the records in the data source, as well as only records that meet a certain criterion. You also learned how to sort the data source records. Finally, you addressed mailing labels and envelopes to accompany the form letters.

What You Should Know

Having completed this project, you should now be able to perform the following tasks:

▶ Address Envelopes from an Existing Data Source *(WD 5.54)*

▶ Address Mailing Labels from an Existing Data Source *(WD 5.48)*

▶ AutoFormat a Table *(WD 5.24)*

▶ Change Page Orientation *(WD 5.24)*

▶ Close All Open Documents *(WD 5.57)*

▶ Create a Data Source in Word *(WD 5.17)*

▶ Create a Letter Using a Word Template *(WD 5.6)*

▶ Create an Outline Numbered List *(WD 5.30)*

▶ Display Formatting Marks *(WD 5.9)*

▶ Enter More Merge Fields *(WD 5.27)*

▶ Enter the Body of the Letter *(WD 5.29)*

▶ Identify the Main Document *(WD 5.14)*

▶ Insert a Fill-in Field *(WD 5.37)*

▶ Insert a Merge Field into the Main Document *(WD 5.27)*

▶ Insert an IF Field into the Main Document *(WD 5.34)*

▶ Insert Clip Art *(WD 5.10)*

▶ Merge the Documents and Print the Form Letters *(WD 5.41)*

▶ Print a Document *(WD 5.25)*

▶ Print Field Codes in the Main Document *(WD 5.40)*

▶ Quit Word *(WD 5.57)*

▶ Remove a Merge Condition *(WD 5.45)*

▶ Reset Menus and Toolbars *(WD 5.8)*

▶ Resize a Graphic *(WD 5.11)*

▶ Save a Document Again *(WD 5.38)*

▶ Save the Envelopes *(WD 5.57)*

▶ Save the Letter *(WD 5.13)*

▶ Save the Mailing Labels *(WD 5.54)*

▶ Select and Replace More Placeholder Text *(WD 5.12)*

▶ Select and Replace Placeholder Text *(WD 5.9)*

▶ Selectively Merge and Print Records *(WD 5.43)*

▶ Sort the Data Records *(WD 5.45)*

▶ Switch from the Data Source to the Main Document *(WD 5.25)*

▶ Turn Field Codes Off for Printing *(WD 5.41)*

▶ Turn Field Codes On or Off for Display *(WD 5.39)*

▶ Unlink a Field *(WD 5.28)*

▶ View Merged Data in the Main Document *(WD 5.47)*

▶ Zoom Text Width *(WD 5.9)*

More About 2000

Microsoft Certification

The Microsoft Office User Specialist (MOUS) Certification program provides an opportunity for you to obtain a valuable industry credential - proof that you have the Word 2000 skills required by employers. For more information, see Appendix D or visit the Shelly Cashman Series MOUS Web page at www.scsite.com/off2000/cert.htm.

Apply Your Knowledge

➕ Project Reinforcement at www.scsite.com/off2000/reinforce.htm

1 Working with a Form Letter

Instructions: Start Word. Open the document, Orland Flowers Holiday Special, on the Data Disk. If you did not download the Data Disk, see the inside back cover for instructions for downloading the Data Disk or see your instructor.

The document is a main document for Orland Flowers and Gifts. You are to print field codes in the main document (Figure 5-81), edit and print a formatted data source in landscape orientation, and then merge the form letters to a file and the printer.

Orland Flowers and Gifts

15220 Oak Avenue, Orland Park, IL 60462
Telephone: (708) 555-0045
Web: www.orlandflowers.com

{ FILLIN "What date will you be mailing these letters?" \o }

{ MERGEFIELD Title } { MERGEFIELD FirstName } { MERGEFIELD LastName }
{ MERGEFIELD Address1 }
{ MERGEFIELD Address2 }
{ MERGEFIELD City }, { MERGEFIELD State } { MERGEFIELD PostalCode }

Dear { MERGEFIELD Title } { MERGEFIELD LastName }:

With the holiday season quickly approaching, now is the time to take advantage of our great prices on flower arrangements and customized gift baskets. We will deliver your order locally or package and send it anywhere in the country.

As a valued customer, we want to thank you for choosing Orland Flowers and Gifts. Simply bring in this letter to receive a { IF { MERGEFIELD PreferredCard } = "Y" "20" "10" } percent discount on any purchase until the end of the year.

{ AUTOTEXTLIST }

Marianne Pulaski
Owner

FIGURE 5-81

Apply Your Knowledge

Project Reinforcement at www.scsite.com/off2000/reinforce.htm

Working with a Form Letter *(continued)*

Perform the following tasks:

1. Click the Print button on the Standard toolbar.
2. Click Tools on the menu bar and then click Options. When the Options dialog box displays, if necessary, click the Print tab. Click Field codes to select the check box and then click the OK button. Click the Print button on the Standard toolbar.
3. Click Tools on the menu bar and then click Options. When the Options dialog box displays, if necessary, click the Print tab. Click Field codes to turn off the check box and then click the OK button.
4. Click the Edit Data Source button on the Mail Merge toolbar and then click the View Source button in the Data Form dialog box to display the data source, Orland Flowers Customer List, as a Word table.
5. Click Table on the menu bar and then click Table AutoFormat. When the Table AutoFormat dialog box displays, scroll through the list of formats, and then click Grid 8. Click the OK button.
6. Click the Add New Record button on the Database toolbar. Add a record containing your personal information; enter Y in the PreferredCard field.
7. Click in the LastName column of the data source. Click the Sort Ascending button on the Database toolbar.
8. Click File on the menu bar and then click Save As. Use the file name Revised Orland Flowers Customer List.
9. Click File on the menu bar and then click Page Setup. When the Page Setup dialog box displays, click the Paper Size tab. Click Landscape in the Orientation area and then click the OK button. Click the Print button on the Standard toolbar.
10. Click the Mail Merge Main Document button on the Database toolbar.
11. Click the Merge to New Document button on the Mail Merge toolbar. Type December 3, 2001 in the text box and then click the OK button. Click the Print button on the Standard toolbar. Click File on the menu bar and then click the Close button. Click the No button in the Microsoft Word dialog box.
12. Click the Merge to Printer button on the Mail Merge toolbar. Click the OK button in the Print dialog box. If necessary, type December 3, 2001 in the text box and then click the OK button.
13. Hold down the SHIFT key while clicking File on the menu bar. Click Close All.

In the Lab

1 **Creating a Data Source, Form Letter, and Mailing Labels**

Problem: Martin Popovich, the director of admissions at Taxton Community College, has asked you to send an orientation announcement letter to all incoming freshman. You decide to use a form letter (Figure 5-82).

Instructions:

1. Use the Professional Letter template to create a letter. Enter the letterhead shown at the top of Figure 5-82 into the appropriate areas of the template.

In the Lab

2. Begin the mail merge process by clicking Tools on the menu bar and then clicking Mail Merge. Specify the current document window as the main document.

Taxton Community College 156 Grand Boulevard, Cambridge, MA 02142
Telephone: (617) 555-8768 Fax: (617) 555-8770
Web: www.taxtoncc.com
E-mail: taxtoncc@mass.com

August 1, 2001

«Title» «FirstName» «LastName»
«Address1»
«Address2»
«City», «State» «PostalCode»

Dear «Title» «LastName»:

Congratulations on your acceptance to Taxton Community College.

We have scheduled an orientation in Alumni Hall from 6:00 p.m. to 9:00 p.m. on Thursday, August 9, for incoming freshmen. Advisors, instructors, and other staff members will be available to familiarize you with the campus and answer your questions. We look forward to meeting with you then.

Sincerely,

Martin Carucci
Director of Admissions

FIGURE 5-82

(continued)

In the Lab

Creating a Data Source, Form Letter, and Mailing Labels *(continued)*

3. Create the data source shown in Figure 5-83.

Title	FirstName	LastName	Address1	Address2	City	State	PostalCode
Mr.	Raul	Ramos	145 Sunset Road	Apt. 4D	Cambridge	MA	02142
Ms.	Crystal	Weaver	13 Western Avenue		Boston	MA	02102
Mr.	Fred	VanWijk	P.O. Box 889	143 Third Street	Boston	MA	02125
Mr.	Ed	Spelbring	103 Oak Avenue		Somerville	MA	01245
Ms.	Dawn	Nitz	P.O. Box 113	15 Center Street	West Medford	MA	02156

FIGURE 5-83

4. Click the View Data Source button in the Data Form dialog box to view the data source in table form. Save the data source with the file name Taxton New Students.

5. Format the data source using the Grid 8 format in the Table AutoFormat dialog box. Print the data source in landscape orientation.

6. Switch to the main document. Save the main document with the file name, Taxton Welcome Letter. Create the main document for the form letter shown in Figure 5-82. Remove the field format from the date at the top of the letter and enter the date, August 1, 2001.

7. Save the main document for the form letter again. Print the main document.

8. Merge and print the form letters.

9. Address mailing labels using the same data source you used for the form letters. Specify a new document window as the main document. Put bar codes on the mailing labels.

10. Save the mailing labels with the name Taxton Mailing Labels. Print the mailing labels.

11. If your printer allows, address envelopes using the same data source you used for the form letters. Specify a new document window as the main document. Put bar codes on the envelopes. Save the envelopes with the name Taxton Envelopes. Print the envelopes.

2 Creating a Form Letter with an IF Field, a Fill-in Field, and an Outline Numbered List

Problem: As the computer specialist at Williams Landscaping, the owner has asked you to send a letter to all former customers, notifying them that the nursery will be moving to a new location. You have decided to use a form letter (Figure 5-84). For business customers, you print the word, business, at the end of the last paragraph of the letter; for home customers, you print the word, home, at the end of the last paragraph of the letter.

Instructions:

1. Use the Professional Letter template to create a letter. Enter the letterhead shown at the top of Figure 5-84 on the previous page into the appropriate areas of the template.

In the Lab

2. Begin the mail merge process by clicking Tools on the menu bar and then clicking Mail Merge. Specify the current document window as the main document.

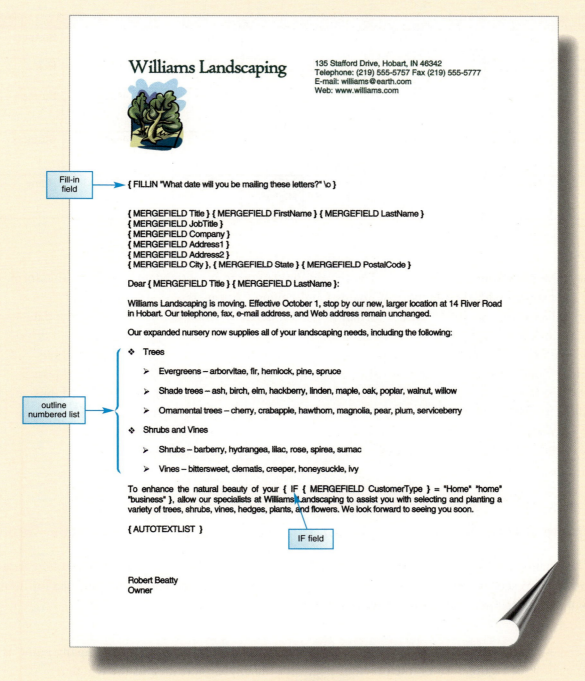

FIGURE 5-84

(continued)

In the Lab

Creating a Form Letter with an IF Field, a Fill-in Field, and an Outline Numbered List *(continued)*

3. Create the data source shown in Figure 5-85.

Title	FirstName	LastName	JobTitle	Company	Address1	Address2	City	State	PostalCode	CustomerType
Mr.	Joel	Puntillo	Grounds Manager	Wilson Plastics	P.O. Box 145		Merrillville	IN	46410	Business
Ms.	Shauna	Gupta			14 Duluth Street		Highland	IN	46322	Home
Dr.	Maria	Lopez			P.O. Box 56	156 Grand Street	Munster	IN	46321	Business
Mrs.	Lisa	Pavlowski	Owner	Hobart Flowers	15 Lincoln Highway		Hobart	IN	46342	Business
Mr.	Arnie	Kristoff			P.O. Box 72	147 Highway Avenue	Griffith	IN	46319	Home

FIGURE 5-85

4. Click the View Data Source button in the Data Form dialog box to view the data source in table form. Save the data source with the file name Williams Landscaping Customers.

5. Format the data source using the Grid 8 format in the Table AutoFormat dialog box. Print the data source in landscape orientation.

6. Switch to the main document. Save the main document with the file name, Williams Landscaping Form Letter. Create the main document for the form letter shown in Figure 5-84. The IF field tests if CustomerType is equal to Home; if it is, then print the word, home; otherwise print the word, business. Use a Fill-in field with the following text for the date: What date will you be mailing these letters?

7. Save the main document for the form letter again.

8. Print the main document with field codes on. Do not forget to turn the field codes off.

9. Merge and print the form letters.

3 Designing a Data Source, Form Letter, and Mailing Labels from Sample Memos

Problem: The benefits coordinator at Geo Consulting, Inc., would like to schedule a benefits enrollment session for all employees. Two separate session times will be scheduled: one for salaried employees and one for hourly employees. Sample drafted memos are shown in Figure 5-86.

Instructions:

1. Use the Professional Memo template to create an interoffice memorandum. Enter the company name as shown at the top of Figure 5-86 on the previous page into the appropriate area of the template.

2. Begin the mail merge process by clicking Tools on the menu bar and then clicking Mail Merge. Specify the current document window as the main document.

3. Decide on field names to use in the data source. Create a data source with five sample employees. Two of the sample employees may be the ones shown in Figure 5-86.

In the Lab

4. Format the data source. Print the data source in landscape orientation.

5. Switch to the main document. Save the main document with the file name, Geo Benefits Memo. Create the main document for the form letter shown in Figure 5-86. The current date should print at the top of the form letter. The IF field tests the EmployeeType: if EmployeeType is Salaried, then the meeting is from 10:00 – 11:00 A.M.; otherwise the meeting is from 2:00 – 3:00 P.M.

Geo Consulting, Inc.

Memo

To: Mr. Jason Carter
Accountant
Office: A-224

From-   Huang Chin
Benefits Coordinator

Date: October 1, 2001

R⊹   2002 Health Benefits Enrollment

Geo Consulting, Inc. health benefits enrollment takes place from October 8 through October 26, 2001. You will receive the benefits enrollment package within the next few days. During open enrollment, you will have the opportunity to review your plan choices and make changes. If you have any questions, please call our office at x272.

Your enrollment session has been scheduled for Monday, October 21, from 10:00 a.m. to 11:00 a.m. If you are unable to attend this general session, please call Gina at x277 to schedule a personal session.

Thank you.

{ PAGE }

FIGURE 5-86a

(continued)

In the Lab

Designing a Data Source, Form Letter, and Mailing Labels from Sample Memos *(continued)*

Geo Consulting, Inc.

Memo

To: Ms. Tashay McCants
Order Entry
Office: B-156

From: Huang Chin
Benefits Coordinator

Date: October 1, 2001

Re: 2002 Health Benefits Enrollment

_____

Geo Consulting, Inc. health benefits enrollment takes place from October 8 through October 26, 2001. You will receive the benefits enrollment package within the next few days. During open enrollment, you will have the opportunity to review your plan choices and make changes. If you have any questions, please call our office at x272.

Your enrollment session has been scheduled for Monday, October 21, from 2:00 p.m. to 3:00 p.m. If you are unable to attend this general session, please call Gina at x277 to schedule a personal session.

Thank you.

{ PAGE }

FIGURE 5-86b

6. Save the main document for the form letter again.
7. Print the main document with field codes. Do not forget to turn off the field codes after printing them.
8. Merge and print the form letters.
9. Address mailing labels using the same data source you used for the form letters. Specify a new document window as the main document.
10. Save the mailing labels with the name Geo Mailing Labels. Print the mailing labels.

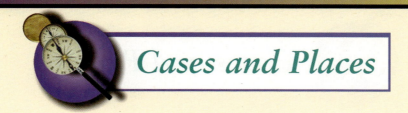

Cases and Places

1 ◗ You are activities chairperson for the Summer Day Camp at your church. Letters must be sent to all parents informing them of the rules for the event. Create a form letter using the following information: Company Name: First United Church; Address: 15 Park Avenue, Oviedo, FL 32765; Telephone: (407) 555-2828; Fax: (407) 555-2929. Create the data source shown in Figure 5-87. Use merge fields to create the inside address and salutation. All recipients live in Oviedo Florida 32765. First paragraph: <u>Summer Day Camp is scheduled from June 25 through June 29 at the church campgrounds. Camp will be from 9:00 A.M. until 3:00 P.M. each day. Your {MERGEFIELD ChildGender} should bring the following items in a backpack to camp.</u> Create an outline numbered list using the bullet character for the following list items: Extra clothes – socks, tennis shoes, sweatshirt, raincoat; Sundries – water bottle, insect repellent, mess kit, sit-upon. Last paragraph – <u>If you have any questions, please contact Geri at 555-2828.</u> Use your name in the signature block. Then, create and address accompanying labels or envelopes for the form letters.

Title	FirstName	LastName	Address1	Address2	ChildGender
Mrs.	Effie	Maniotes	1567 Cedar Boulevard		son
Ms.	Juanita	Espinoza	15 Carroll Street		daughter
Dr.	John	Parker	P.O. Box 1128	1128 Eastern Avenue	daughter
Mrs.	Kimberly	Johnson	998 Sycamore Road		son
Mr.	Mohammed	Ashved	P.O. Box 7786	14 Franklin Road	daughter

FIGURE 5-87

2 ◗◗ You are organizing a block party for Saturday, August 18. The party will begin at 9:00 A.M. and end at 11:00 P.M. Each family is to bring a side dish or dessert that will feed at least 15 people. You need volunteers for setup, games, cooks, and refreshments. Anyone with questions should contact you. Create a form letter announcing the block party and requesting volunteers. Use the text, First Annual Block Party, at the top of the letter with an appropriate clip art image. Obtain the names and addresses of five of your family members and use them as records in the data source. Then, address accompanying labels or envelopes for the form letters.

3 ◗◗ The bookstore at your school will be holding its annual Book Buy Back on May 10 and May 11 from 8:00 A.M. to 5:00 P.M. each day. The books will be bought at 50 percent of their original purchase price. Only books that are being used in the fall semester may be returned. Books must be in a usable condition. Create a form letter announcing the Book Buy Back. Be sure the top of the form letter contains the school name, address, and an appropriate clip art image. Obtain the names and addresses of five of your classmates and use them as records in the data source. Then, address accompanying labels or envelopes for the form letters.

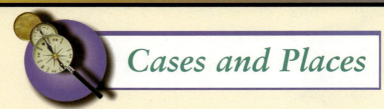

Cases and Places

4 ▶▶ You currently are seeking an employment position in your field of study. You already have prepared a resume and would like to send it to a group of potential employers. You decide to design a cover letter to send along with the resume. Obtain a recent newspaper and cut out three classified advertisements pertaining to your field of study. Locate two job advertisements on the Internet. Create the cover letter for your resume as a form letter. Be sure the top of the cover letter contains your name, address and telephone number, as well as an appropriate clip art image. Use the information in the classified ads from newspapers and the Internet for the data source. The data source should contain potential employers' names, addresses, and position being sought. Then, address accompanying labels or envelopes for the cover letters. Turn in the want ads with your printouts.

5 ▶▶▶ As assistant to the sales manager at your company, you are responsible for providing each salesperson with a company car. This year, you need ten new cars. Obtain the names and addresses of five new car dealerships in your area. Research the types of vehicles that would be best suited as company cars and then create a form letter requesting quotations on these cars. Be sure the letter has an attractive letterhead with an appropriate clip art image. Use dealership names and addresses as records in your data source. Then, address accompanying labels or envelopes for the cover letters.

6 ▶▶▶ If Microsoft Access is installed on your system, you can use it to create a table and then use that table as the data source in a mail merge document. Start Access and then create the table in Project 5 (Figure 5-16 on page WD 5.16) as an Access database table. You may need to use Help in Access to assist you in the procedure for creating and saving a database that contains a table. Exit Access. Start Word. Begin the mail merge process as discussed in Project 5. When specifying the data source, click Open Data Source. In the Open Data Source dialog box, change the file type to MS Access Databases and then click the database name of the file you created in Access. Create the form letter in Project 5 so it uses the fields in the Access database table. Then, address accompanying labels or envelopes for the cover letters.

7 ▶▶▶ If Microsoft Access is installed on your system, you can use it to create a table and then use that table as the data source in a mail merge document. Start Access and then create the table for the In the Lab 2 exercise as an Access table (Figure 5-85 on page WD 5.62). You may need to use Help in Access to assist you in the procedure for creating and saving a database that contains a table. Exit Access. Start Word. Begin the mail merge process as discussed in Project 5. When specifying the data source, click Open Data Source. In the Open Data Source dialog box, change the file type to MS Access Databases and then click the database name of the file you created in Access. Create the form letter in Figure 5-84 on page WD 5.61 so it uses the fields in the Access database table. Then, address accompanying labels or envelopes for the cover letters.

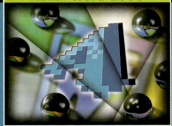

Microsoft Word 2000

Microsoft Word 2000

Creating a Professional Newsletter

You will have mastered the material in this project when you can:

- Define desktop publishing terminology
- Create a WordArt drawing object
- Format a WordArt drawing object
- Add ruling lines above and below paragraphs
- Insert the current date into a document
- Format a document into multiple columns
- Justify a paragraph
- Format a character as a dropped capital letter
- Insert a column break
- Link an object to a Word document
- Place a vertical rule between columns
- Insert a text box
- Change character spacing
- Shade a paragraph
- Position a text box
- Balance columns
- Insert a picture into a document
- Position a graphic between columns
- Use the Format Painter button
- Place a border on a page
- Highlight text

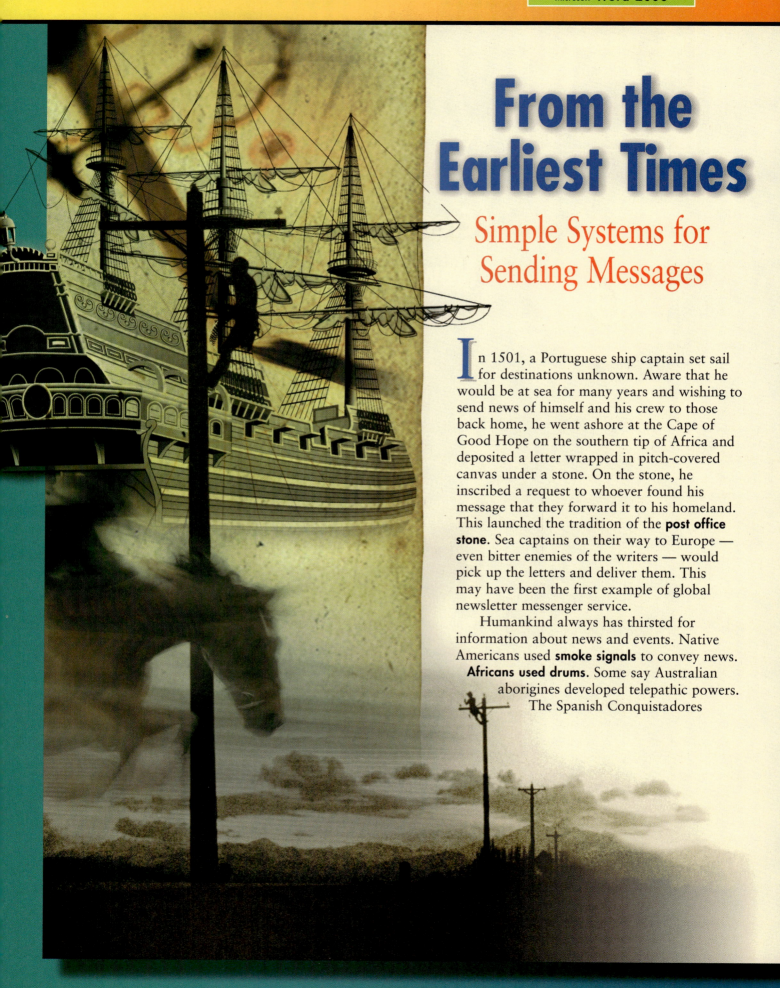

From the Earliest Times

Simple Systems for Sending Messages

In 1501, a Portuguese ship captain set sail for destinations unknown. Aware that he would be at sea for many years and wishing to send news of himself and his crew to those back home, he went ashore at the Cape of Good Hope on the southern tip of Africa and deposited a letter wrapped in pitch-covered canvas under a stone. On the stone, he inscribed a request to whoever found his message that they forward it to his homeland. This launched the tradition of the **post office stone**. Sea captains on their way to Europe — even bitter enemies of the writers — would pick up the letters and deliver them. This may have been the first example of global newsletter messenger service.

Humankind always has thirsted for information about news and events. Native Americans used **smoke signals** to convey news. **Africans used drums**. Some say Australian aborigines developed telepathic powers. The Spanish Conquistadores scratched their news onto **Inscription Rock** in New Mexico. Armies of old relied on mirrors and semaphores. Then, as technology progressed, the means of delivery grew more sophisticated, evolving from **Pony Express** and **telegraph** to modern **fiber-optic cables**, **microwaves**, and **satellite relays**.

Newsletters likewise have evolved into highly specialized vehicles that number in the thousands, addressing everything from astrology to investments to medicine to zoology. No matter what the association, cause, or subject, a newsletter for it is likely to exist. Besides the blizzard of hardcopy newsletters delivered by mail every day, e-mail and Web sites reach millions more.

A good reason for the explosive growth of newsletters is they get results. To unite people, organize an activity, persuade, or simply to pour out one's feelings, an attractive, well-written newsletter can boost sales, promote morale, raise money, or send your personal news to friends during the holiday season.

Snappy content, however, is not good enough. To reach out and seize someone's attention, newsletters must be more than merely attractive. Your newsletter must make a statement, provide appeal, and elicit interest.

In Word 2000, you have the ideal partner for creating eye-catching, dynamic newsletters. Word lets you produce crisp banner headlines; create WordArt drawing objects; manipulate columns, fonts, and blocks of copy at will; insert pictures into documents; link another document to the newsletter, then spice the whole thing with graphics and borders. Once you have the newsletter just right, Word also provides the capability of merging names and addresses from a separate database, such as a student organization, your clients, or your family and friends. You can also e-mail the newsletter to others for approval before making many copies for distribution.

Unlike that sixteenth century ship captain who had to rely on chance that someone would find the mail he deposited under the post office stone, once you finish creating that professional looking newsletter using Word's desktop publishing features, you can whisk it on its way via the Internet or the corner mailbox — without getting pitch on your hands.

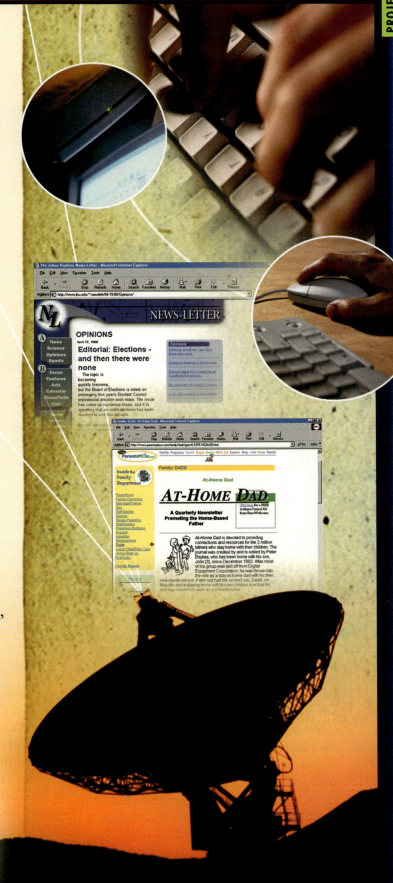

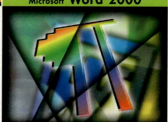

Microsoft **Word 2000**

Microsoft Word 2000

Creating a Professional Newsletter

P R O J E C T

6

C A S E   P E R S P E C T I V E

You are vice president of The Web Club at your school. Because you are majoring in Office Information Systems, you prepare the club's monthly newsletter. Each month, the newsletter contains a feature article and announcements. You decide that this month's feature article will cover communications and modems. You plan to create the article as a Word document, discussing items such as signal conversion; definition of a modem; modem speed; and internal, external, PC Card, fax, and cable modems. The announcements will remind readers about the upcoming field trip, notify them of new club discounts, and inform them of the club's new Web site.

After you create the article, Jamie Navaro, president of The Web Club, will review it. Then, you will insert the Word document into your newsletter in the appropriate column. Your task now is to design the newsletter so the feature article spans the first two columns of page 1 and then continues on page 2. The announcements should be located in the third column of page 1 of The Web Club newsletter.

Introduction

Professional looking documents, such as newsletters and brochures, often are created using desktop publishing software. With **desktop publishing software**, you can divide a document into multiple columns, wrap text around pictures and other objects, change fonts and font sizes, add color and lines, and so on to create an attention-grabbing document. A traditionally held opinion of desktop publishing software, such as Adobe PageMaker or QuarkXpress, is that it enables you to open an existing word processing document and enhance it through formatting not provided in your word processing software. Word, however, provides you with many of the formatting features that you would find in a desktop publishing package. Thus, you can create eye-catching newsletters and brochures directly within Word.

Project Six – Newsletter

Project 6 uses Word to produce the monthly newsletter shown in Figure 6-1. The newsletter is a monthly publication for members of The Web Club. Notice that it incorporates the desktop publishing features of Word. The body of each page of the newsletter is divided into three columns. A variety of fonts, font sizes, and colors add visual appeal to the document. The first page has text wrapped around a pull-quote and the second page has text wrapped around a picture. Horizontal and vertical lines separate distinct areas of the newsletter, including a page border around the perimeter of each page.

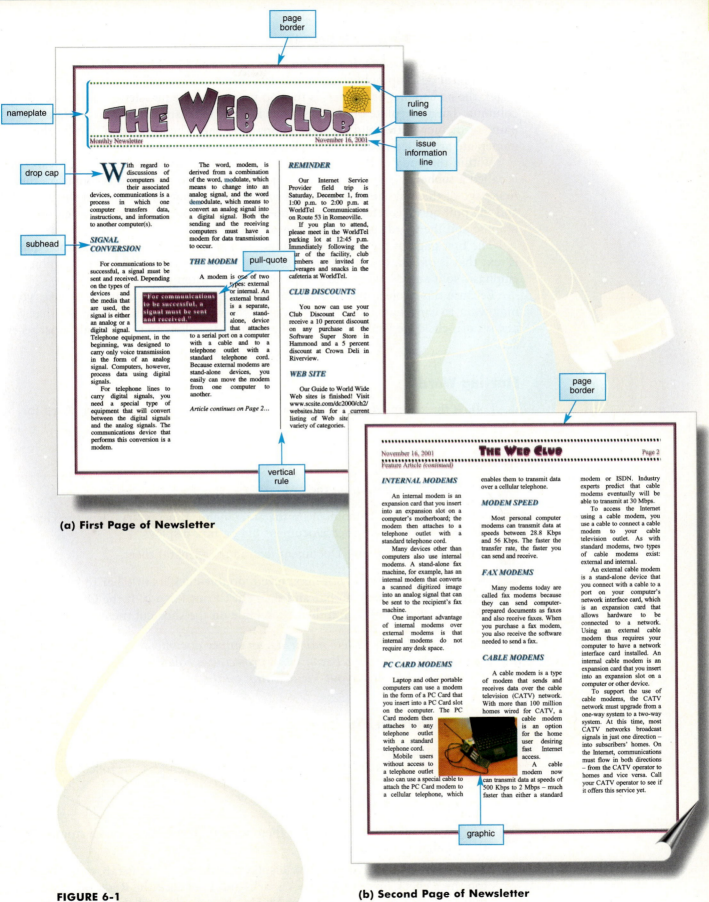

(a) First Page of Newsletter

FIGURE 6-1

(b) Second Page of Newsletter

Desktop Publishing

For more information on desktop publishing, visit the Word 2000 More About Web page (www.scsite.com/wd2000/more.htm) and then click Desktop Publishing.

Desktop Publishing Terminology

As you create professional looking newsletters and brochures, you should understand several desktop publishing terms. In Project 6 (Figure 6-1 on the previous page), the **nameplate**, or **banner**, is the top portion of the newsletter above the three columns. The nameplate on the first page is more extensive because it contains the name of the newsletter and the **issue information line**. The horizontal lines in the nameplate are called **rules**, or **ruling lines**.

Within the body of the newsletter, a heading, such as SIGNAL CONVERSION, is called a **subhead**. The vertical line dividing the second and third columns on the first page of the newsletter is a **vertical rule**. The text that wraps around the picture and the pull-quote is referred to as **wrap-around text**, and the space between the graphic and the words is called the **run-around**.

The first page of the newsletter contains a pull-quote (Figure 6-1a). A **pull-quote** is text that is *pulled*, or copied, from the text of the document and given graphical emphasis so it stands apart and grasps the reader's attention.

Because this project involves several steps requiring you to drag the mouse, you may want to cancel an action if you drag to the wrong location. Remember that you always can click the Undo button on the Standard toolbar to cancel your most recent action.

Starting Word

Follow these steps to start Word or ask your instructor how to start Word for your system.

TO START WORD

1. Click the Start button on the taskbar.

2. Click New Office Document on the Start menu. If necessary, click the General tab when the New Office Document dialog box displays.

3. Double-click the Blank Document icon in the General sheet.

4. If the Word window is not maximized, double-click its title bar to maximize it. Click View on the menu bar and then click Print Layout. If the Office Assistant displays, right-click it and then click Hide on the shortcut menu.

Office starts Word. After a few moments, an empty document titled Document1 displays in the Word window. Because this project uses columns, you will use print layout view; thus, the Print Layout View button on the horizontal scroll bar is recessed.

Resetting Menus and Toolbars

To set the menus and toolbars so they appear exactly as shown in this book, you should reset your menus and toolbars as outlined in Appendix C or follow these steps.

TO RESET MENUS AND TOOLBARS

1. Click View on the menu bar and then point to Toolbars. Click Customize on the Toolbars submenu.

2. When the Customize dialog box displays, click the Options tab, make sure the top three check boxes have check marks and then click the Reset my usage data button. When the Microsoft Word dialog box displays, click the Yes button.

③ Click the Toolbars tab. Click Standard in the Toolbars list and then click the Reset button. When the Reset Toolbar dialog box displays, click the OK button.

④ Click Formatting in the Toolbars list and then click the Reset button. When the Reset Toolbar dialog box displays, click the OK button. Click the Close button.

Word resets the menus and toolbars.

Displaying Formatting Marks

You have learned that it is helpful to display formatting marks that indicate where in the document you pressed the ENTER key, SPACEBAR, and other keys. Follow this step to display formatting marks.

TO DISPLAY FORMATTING MARKS

① If the Show/Hide ¶ button on the Standard toolbar is not already recessed, click it.

Word displays formatting marks in the document window, and the Show/Hide ¶ button on the Standard toolbar is recessed.

Changing All Margin Settings

You have learned that Word is preset to use standard 8.5-by-11-inch paper, with 1.25-inch left and right margins and 1-inch top and bottom margins. For the newsletter in this project, you want all margins (left, right, top, and bottom) to be .75 inch. Perform the following steps to change these margin settings.

TO CHANGE ALL MARGIN SETTINGS

① Click File on the menu bar and then click Page Setup.

② When the Page Setup dialog box displays, if necessary, click the Margins tab. Type .75 in the Top text box and then press the TAB key.

③ Type .75 in the Bottom text box and then press the TAB key.

④ Type .75 in the Left text box and then press the TAB key.

⑤ Type .75 in the Right text box and then point to the OK button (Figure 6-2 on the next page).

⑥ Click the OK button to change the margin settings for this document.

Depending on the printer you are using, you may need to set the margins differently for this project.

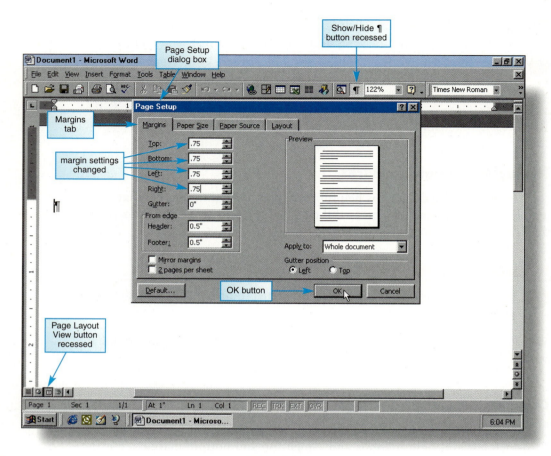

FIGURE 6-2

Zooming Text Width

As you have learned, when you zoom text width, Word displays text on the screen as large as possible in print layout view without extending the right margin beyond the right edge of the document window. Perform the following steps to zoom text width.

TO ZOOM TEXT WIDTH

1 Double-click the move handle on the Standard toolbar so that the entire toolbar displays. Click the Zoom box arrow on the Standard toolbar.

2 Click Text Width in the Zoom list.

Word places the right margin at the right edge of the document window (see Figure 6-3). Word computes the zoom percentage based on a variety of settings. Your percentage may be different depending on your system configuration.

Creating the Nameplate

The nameplate on the first page of this newsletter consists of the information above the multiple columns (see Figure 6-1a on page WD 6.5). The nameplate is composed of the newsletter title, THE WEB CLUB, and the issue information line. The steps on the following pages illustrate how to create the nameplate for the first page of the newsletter in this project.

Nameplates

The nameplate should contain, at a minimum, the title and date of the newsletter. The title should be displayed in as large a font size as possible. You also may include a logo in the nameplate. Many nameplates include a headline outlining the function of the newsletter. Some nameplates also include a short table of contents.

Creating a WordArt Drawing Object

You can insert two types of graphics into a Word document: a picture and a drawing object. A **picture** is a graphic that was created in another program. Examples of pictures are scanned images, photographs, and clip art. In earlier projects, you inserted clip art from the Clip Gallery. Later in this project, you insert a scanned photograph into the newsletter.

A **drawing object** is a graphic you create using Word. You can modify or enhance drawing objects using the Drawing toolbar. You display the Drawing toolbar by clicking the Drawing button on the Standard toolbar (see Figure 6-3).

Examples of drawing objects include shapes, curves, lines, and WordArt objects. With **WordArt**, you can create special effects such as shadowed, rotated, stretched, skewed, and wavy text. This project uses a WordArt drawing object in the nameplate on the first page of the newsletter. Perform the following steps to insert a WordArt drawing object.

More About

WordArt Drawing Objects

Keep in mind that WordArt drawing objects are not treated as Word text. Thus, if you misspell the contents of a WordArt drawing object and then spell check the document, Word will not flag a misspelled word(s) in the WordArt drawing object.

Steps **To Insert a WordArt Drawing Object**

1 If the Drawing toolbar does not display in the Word window, click the Drawing button on the Standard toolbar. Point to the Insert WordArt button on the Drawing toolbar (Figure 6-3).

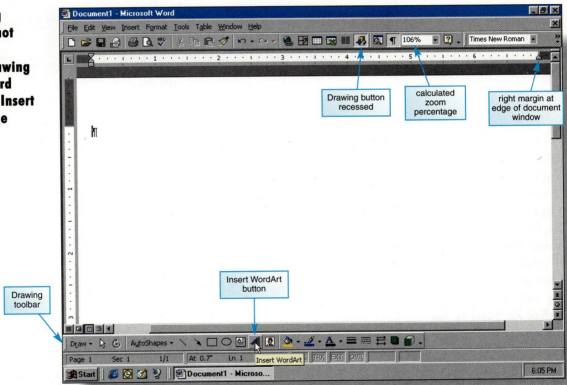

FIGURE 6-3

2 **Click the Insert WordArt button. When the WordArt Gallery dialog box displays, if necessary, click the style in the upper-left corner and then point to the OK button.**

The WordArt Gallery dialog box displays (Figure 6-4). Because you will add your own special text effects, the style in the upper-left corner is selected.

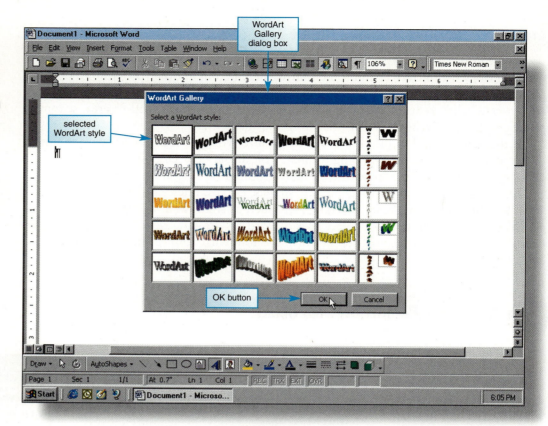

FIGURE 6-4

3 **Click the OK button. When the Edit WordArt Text dialog box displays, type** The Web Club **and then click the Font box arrow in the dialog box. Scroll to and then click Beesknees ITC, or a similar font. Click the Size box arrow in the dialog box, scroll to and then click 72. Point to the OK button.**

The Edit WordArt Text dialog box displays (Figure 6-5). In this dialog box, you enter the WordArt text and change its font, font size, and font style.

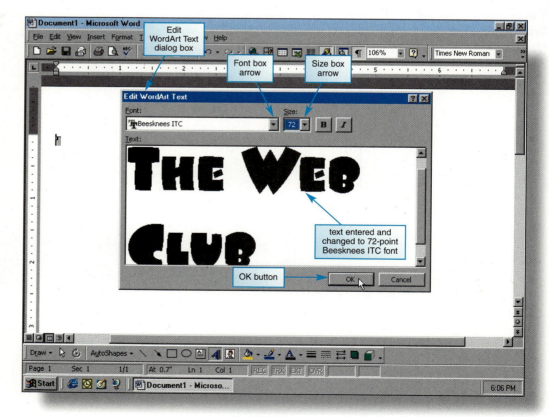

FIGURE 6-5

4 **Click the OK button. If the WordArt toolbar does not display on your screen, right-click the WordArt drawing object and then click Show WordArt Toolbar.**

A WordArt drawing object displays selected in the document window (Figure 6-6). When a WordArt drawing object is selected, the WordArt toolbar displays in the Word window.

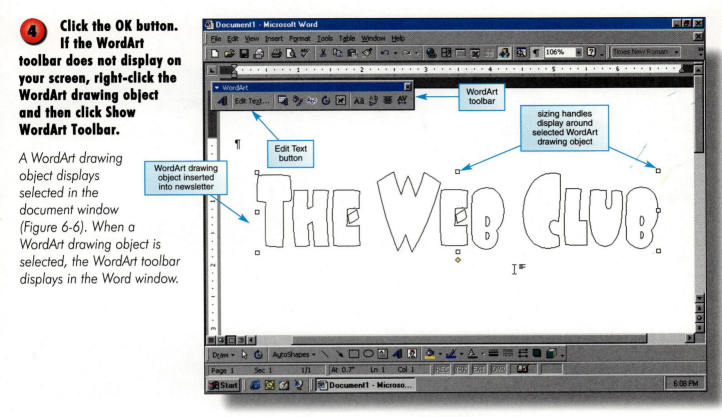

FIGURE 6-6

If a WordArt drawing object is too wide, you can decrease its point size (if it contains text) or you can reduce its width. To change the size (width and height) of a WordArt drawing object, you drag its sizing handles, just as you resize any other graphic. If, for some reason, you wanted to delete the WordArt drawing object, you could right-click it and then click Cut on the shortcut menu, or you could click it and then press the DELETE key.

To change the WordArt text, its font, its font size, or its font style, you would display the Edit WordArt Text dialog box (Figure 6-5) by clicking the Edit Text button on the WordArt toolbar.

Formatting a WordArt Drawing Object

Currently, the WordArt drawing object is a **floating object**, which is one positioned at a specific location in a document or in a layer over or behind text in a document. You can position a floating object anywhere on the page. You do not want the WordArt drawing object to be a floating object; instead, you want it to be an **inline object** that is positioned as part of a paragraph in the Word document at the location of the insertion point.

You change a WordArt drawing object from inline to floating and vice-versa by changing its wrapping style in the Format WordArt dialog box. In this dialog box, you also can change the color of the WordArt drawing object. Perform the steps on the next page to change the wrapping style of the WordArt drawing object and use a gradient (blended) color of violet into lavender.

Steps **To Format a WordArt Drawing Object**

1 **Click the Format WordArt button on the WordArt toolbar. When the Format WordArt dialog box displays, if necessary, click the Layout tab. Click In line with text in the Wrapping style area.**

Word displays the Format WordArt dialog box (Figure 6-7). You change a WordArt drawing object to inline in the Wrapping style area.

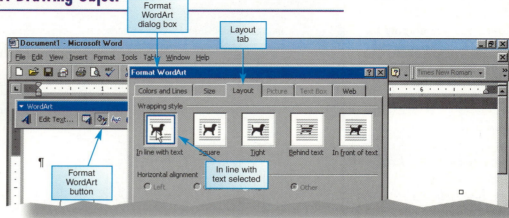

FIGURE 6-7

2 **Click the Colors and Lines tab. Click the Color box arrow in the Fill area and then point to the Fill Effects button.**

The options in the Colors and Lines sheet display (Figure 6-8). You can add a gradient color using the Fill Effects command.

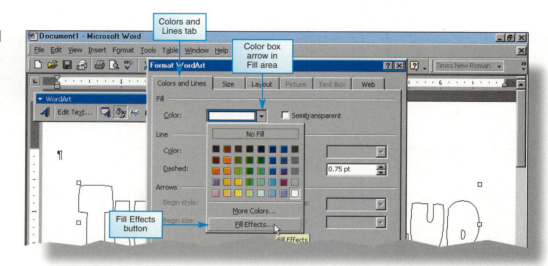

FIGURE 6-8

3 **Click the Fill Effects button. When the Fill Effects dialog box displays, if necessary, click the Gradient tab. Click Two colors in the Colors area and then point to the Color 1 box arrow.**

Word displays the Fill Effects dialog box (Figure 6-9). When you use two colors for a drawing object, color 1 displays at the top of the drawing object and blends down into color 2.

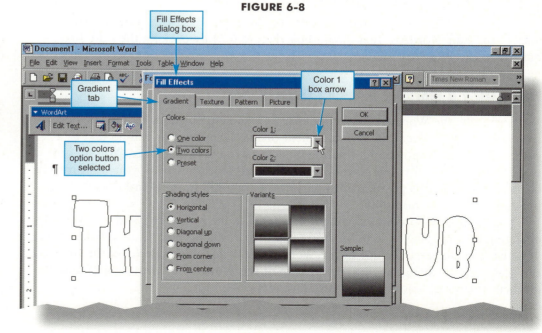

FIGURE 6-9

4 Click the Color 1 box arrow and then click Violet. Click the Color 2 box arrow and then click Lavender. Point to the OK button.

The selected gradient colors for the WordArt object display in the Sample box (Figure 6-10).

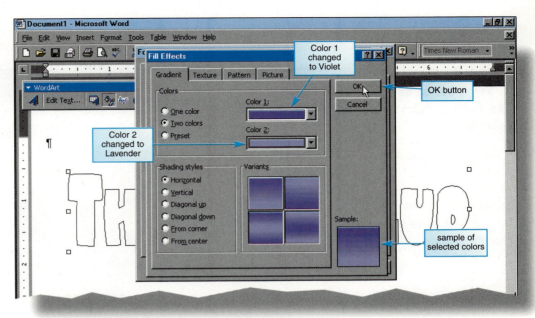

FIGURE 6-10

5 Click the OK button. Click the OK button in the Format WordArt dialog box.

Word formats the WordArt object as inline and changes its colors (Figure 6-11).

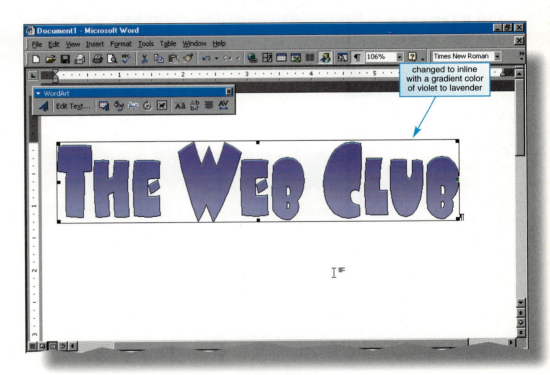

FIGURE 6-11

Changing the WordArt Shape

Word provides a variety of shapes to make your WordArt drawing object more interesting. Perform the steps on the next page to change the WordArt drawing object to a triangular shape.

Other Ways

1. Right-click WordArt object, click Format WordArt on shortcut menu, change desired options, click OK button

2. On Format menu click WordArt, change desired options, click OK button

To Change the Shape of a WordArt Drawing Object

1 **Click the WordArt Shape button on the WordArt toolbar. Point to Triangle Up.**

Word displays a graphical list of available shapes (Figure 6-12). The WordArt drawing object forms itself into the selected shape when you click the shape.

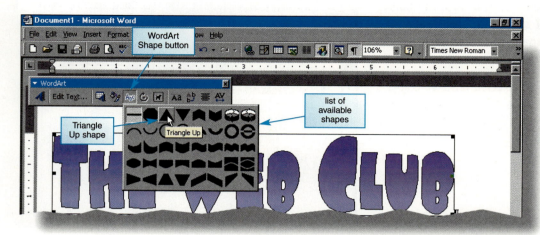

FIGURE 6-12

2 **Click Triangle Up. Click the paragraph mark to the right of the WordArt text.**

The newsletter title displays in a triangular shape (Figure 6-13). The WordArt toolbar no longer displays in the Word window.

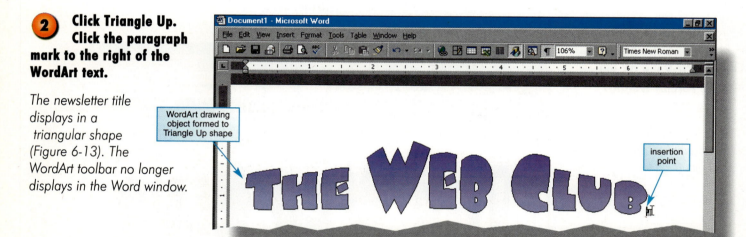

FIGURE 6-13

You will use the Drawing toolbar again later in this project. Thus, leave it displaying in the Word window.

Because you changed the WordArt drawing object from a floating object to an inline object, it is part of the current paragraph. Thus, you can use any of the paragraph alignment buttons on the Formatting toolbar to reposition the object. Perform the following step to center the WordArt drawing object.

TO CENTER AN INLINE OBJECT

1 Double-click the move handle on the Formatting toolbar to display the entire toolbar. Click the Center button on the Formatting toolbar.

Word centers the WordArt drawing object between the left and right margins (see Figure 6-14).

The next step is to add a rule, or ruling line, above the newsletter title.

Adding Ruling Lines

In Word, you use borders to create **ruling lines**. You have learned that borders can be placed on any edge of a paragraph(s), that is, the top, bottom, left, or right edges. Perform the following steps to place a ruling line above the newsletter title.

TO USE BORDERS TO ADD A RULING LINE

1 Double-click the move handle on the Standard toolbar to display the entire toolbar. If necessary, click the Tables and Borders button on the Standard toolbar to display the Tables and Borders toolbar.

2 Click the Line Style box arrow on the Tables and Borders toolbar and then click the first dotted line in the list.

3 Click the Line Weight box arrow on the Tables and Borders toolbar and then click 3 pt.

4 Click the Border Color button on the Tables and Borders toolbar and then click Teal.

5 Click the Border button arrow on the Tables and Borders toolbar and then click Top Border.

The newsletter title and Tables and Borders toolbar display as shown in Figure 6-14.

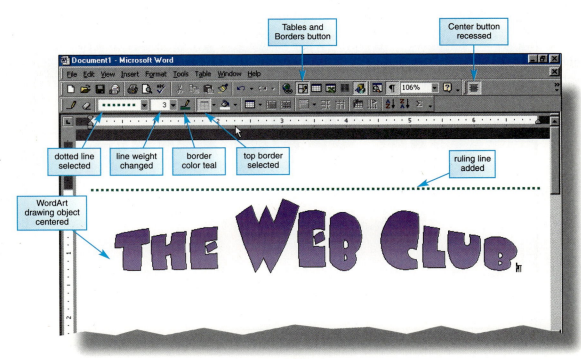

FIGURE 6-14

Because you will use the Tables and Borders toolbar again in the next steps, leave it displaying in the Word window.

The next step is to enter the issue information line. Thus, you will press the ENTER key at the end of the newsletter title so that you can enter the issue information line. You have learned that when you press the ENTER key, Word carries paragraph formatting to the next paragraph. You do not want the issue information line to be formatted the same as the newsletter title line. Instead, you want to apply the Normal style to the paragraph below the newsletter title line. Perform the steps on the next page to apply the Normal style to a paragraph.

To Apply the Normal Style

 1 **If necessary, scroll down. With the insertion point on the paragraph mark in line 1, press the ENTER key. Double-click the move handle on the Formatting toolbar to display the entire toolbar. Click the Style box arrow and then point to Normal (Figure 6-15).**

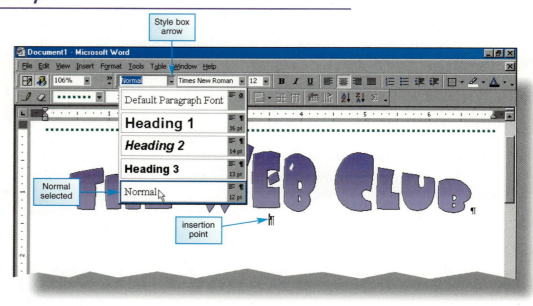

FIGURE 6-15

2 **Click Normal.**

Word applies the Normal style to the current paragraph (Figure 6-16). The paragraph is left-aligned.

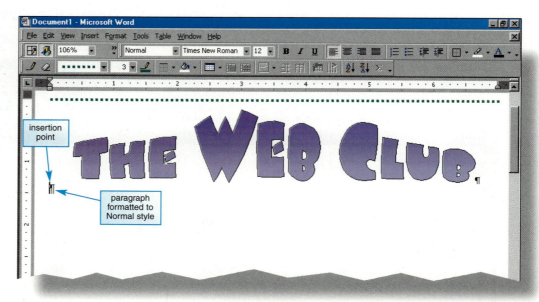

FIGURE 6-16

1. On Format menu click Style, click Normal in Styles list, click Apply button
2. Press CTRL+SHIFT+N

The next step is to enter the issue information line in the nameplate of the newsletter.

Inserting the Current Date into a Document

The issue information line is to contain the text, Monthly Newsletter, at the left margin and the current date at the right margin. You have learned that a paragraph cannot be formatted as both left-aligned and right-aligned. To place text at the right margin of a left-aligned paragraph, you set a tab stop at the right margin.

Perform the following steps to enter text at the left margin and then set a right-aligned tab stop at the right margin.

TO SET A RIGHT-ALIGNED TAB STOP

1 Click the Font Color button arrow on the Formatting toolbar and then click Violet. Type `Monthly Newsletter` on line 2 of the newsletter.

2 Click Format on the menu bar and then click Tabs. When the Tabs dialog box displays, type 7 in the Tab stop position text box, and then click Right in the Alignment area. Click the Set button (Figure 6-17).

3 Click the OK button.

After clicking the OK button, Word places a right-aligned tab stop at the right margin.

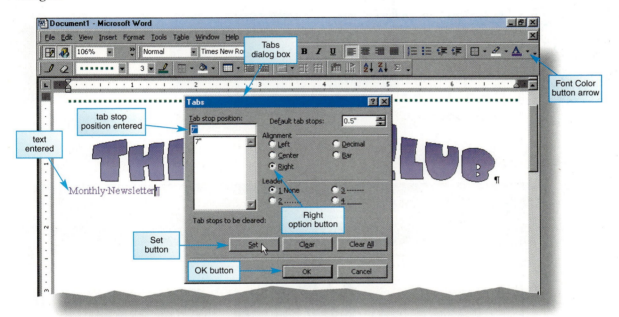

FIGURE 6-17

The next step is to enter the current date at the right margin of the issue information line. Word provides a method of inserting the computer's system date into a document. Perform the following steps to insert the current date into a document.

 To Insert the Current Date into a Document

1 Press the TAB key. Click Insert on the menu bar and then point to Date and Time (Figure 6-18).

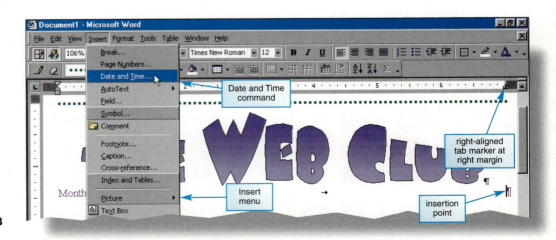

FIGURE 6-18

2 Click Date and Time. When the Date and Time dialog box displays, click the desired format (in this case, November 16, 2001).

Word displays the Date and Time dialog box (Figure 6-19). A list of available formats for dates and times displays. Your screen will not show November 16, 2001; instead, it will display the current system date stored in your computer.

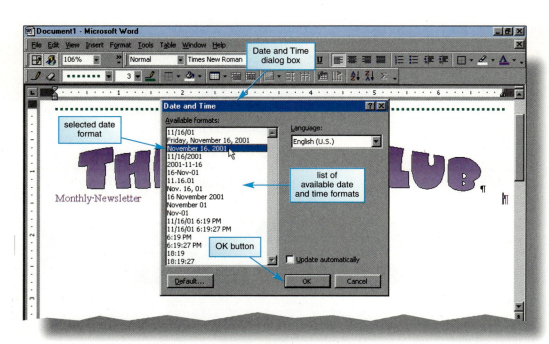

FIGURE 6-19

3 Click the OK button.

Word displays the current date in the newsletter at the right margin (Figure 6-20).

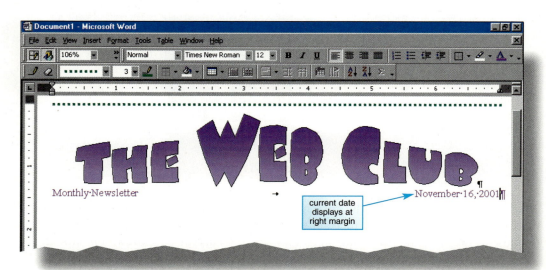

FIGURE 6-20

Dates

If you want Word to display the current date or time when you print a document, make it a field. That is, click the Update automatically check box in the Date and Time dialog box when you insert the current date or time.

The next step is to place top and bottom borders on the issue information line as described in the following steps.

TO ADD MORE RULING LINES

1 Double-click the move handle on the Standard toolbar to display the entire toolbar. If necessary, click the Tables and Borders button on the Standard toolbar to display the Tables and Borders toolbar.

2 Click to the left of the issue information line to select it.

3 Click the Border button arrow on the Tables and Borders toolbar and then click Top Border.

4 Click the Border button arrow on the Tables and Borders toolbar and then click Bottom Border.

5 Click the Tables and Borders button on the Standard toolbar to remove the Tables and Borders toolbar from the Word window.

6 Click in the issue information line to remove the highlight.

Word places a 3-point dotted teal top and bottom border on the issue information line (Figure 6-21).

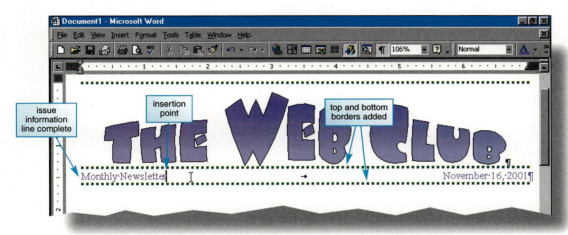

FIGURE 6-21

The next step is to insert a spider web clip art image into the nameplate.

Inserting a Floating Graphic

When you insert a clip art image into a document, Word inserts the picture as part of the current paragraph. You have learned that this is called an inline object. With this format, you change the location of the graphic by setting paragraph options, such as centered, right-aligned, and so on.

In many cases, you want more flexibility in positioning graphics. That is, you want to position a graphic at a specific location in a document; this is called a floating object. In this project, for example, you want the spider web graphic to be positioned in the upper-right corner of the first page of the newsletter. Perform the following steps to insert a clip art image and then change it from an inline to a floating object.

TO INSERT CLIP ART

1 Click Insert on the menu bar, point to Picture, and then click Clip Art.

2 When the Insert ClipArt window opens, click the Search for clips text box. Type spider web and then press the ENTER key.

3 Click the clip that matches the one shown in Figure 6-22 on the next page.

4 Click the Insert clip button on the Pop-up menu.

5 Click the Close button on the Insert ClipArt window's title bar.

Word inserts the spider web graphic at the location of the insertion point as an inline object (Figure 6-22).

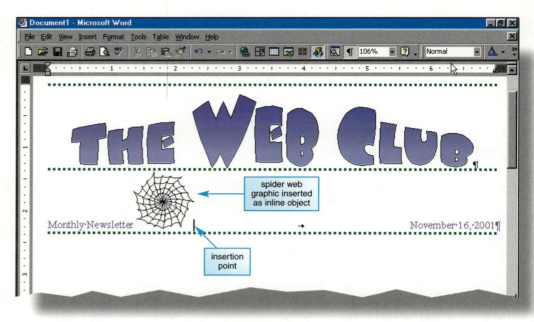

FIGURE 6-22

Depending on the location of your insertion point, your spider web graphic may be in a different position. Perform the following steps to change the spider web graphic from inline to floating.

 To Format a Graphic as Floating

1 **In the document window, click the graphic to select it. If the Picture toolbar does not display, right-click the graphic and then click Show Picture Toolbar. Click the Text Wrapping button on the Picture toolbar and then point to In Front of Text (Figure 6-23).**

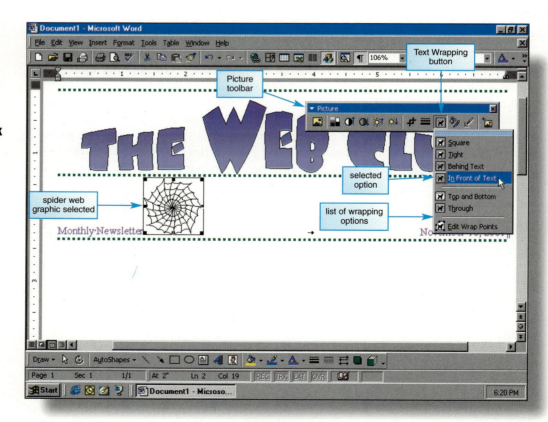

FIGURE 6-23

2 Click In Front of Text.

Word changes the format of the graphic from inline to floating. You can position a floating object anywhere in the document.

3 If necessary, scroll up. Point to the middle of the graphic and drag it to the position shown in Figure 6-24. Resize the graphic by dragging its lower-left sizing handle toward the middle of the graphic.

The graphic is resized and positioned in the upper-right corner of the document (Figure 6-24).

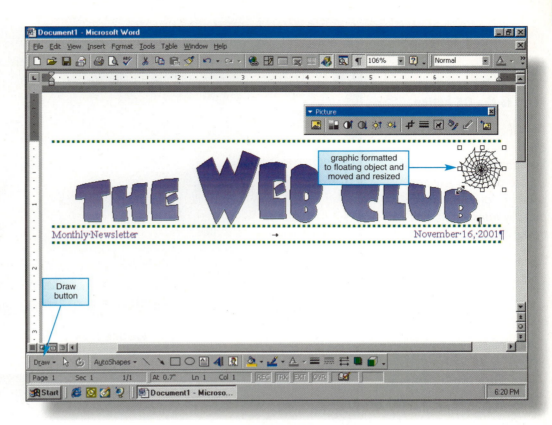

FIGURE 6-24

To place an object behind text, instead of in front of text, you select the Behind Text wrapping style (Figure 6-23). You can change the order of text and graphical objects by clicking the Draw button (Figure 6-24) on the Drawing toolbar, pointing to Order, and then clicking the desired location for the currently selected object.

The next step is to shade the graphic, as shown in the following steps.

 To Shade a Graphic

1 With the graphic still selected, click the Format Picture button on the Picture toolbar. When the Format Picture dialog box displays, if necessary, click the Colors and Lines tab. Point to the Color box arrow in the Fill area.

Word displays the Format Picture dialog box (Figure 6-25).

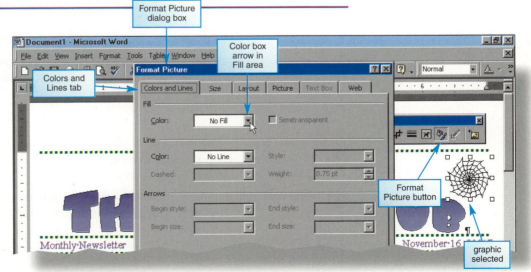

FIGURE 6-25

2   **Click the Color box arrow in the Fill area and then click Gold. Click Semitransparent. Point to the OK button.**

The fill color is gold and a check mark displays in the Semitransparent check box (Figure 6-26). A semitransparent color is one that is partially transparent; that is, not opaque.

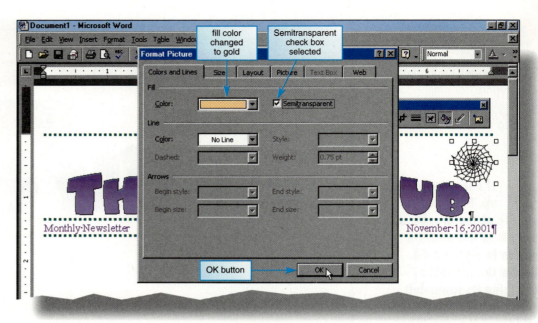

FIGURE 6-26

3   **Click the OK button.**

Word shades the graphic in a partially transparent gold color (Figure 6-27).

FIGURE 6-27

When you press the ENTER key in a bordered paragraph, such as at the end of the issue information line, Word carries the border forward to the next paragraph. Thus, apply the Normal style to the new paragraph to remove the border and other formatting, as described in the following steps.

TO APPLY THE NORMAL STYLE

1   If necessary, scroll down. Position the insertion point at the end of the issue information line. Press the ENTER key.

2   Double-click the move handle on the Formatting toolbar to display the entire toolbar. Click the Style box arrow and then click Normal.

Word applies the Normal style to the current paragraph (Figure 6-28). The paragraph no longer contains any borders and is left-aligned.

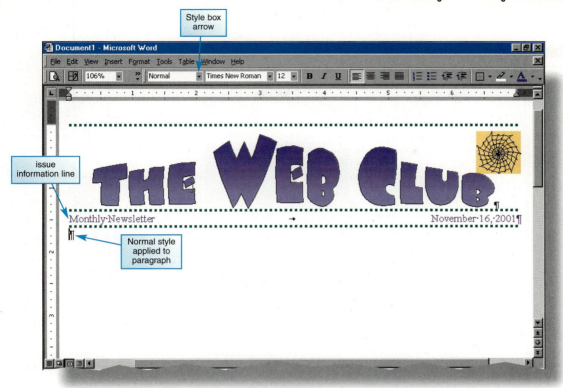

FIGURE 6-28

Formatting the First Page of the Body of the Newsletter

The body of the newsletter in this project is divided into three columns (see Figure 6-1a on page WD 6.5). The characters in the paragraphs are aligned on both the right and left edges – similar to newspaper columns. The first letter in the first paragraph is much larger than the rest of the characters in the paragraph. A vertical rule separates the second and third columns. The steps on the following pages illustrate how to format the first page of the body of the newsletter using these desktop publishing features.

Formatting a Document into Multiple Columns

The text in **snaking columns**, or newspaper-style columns, flows from the bottom of one column to the top of the next. The body of the newsletter in Project 6 uses snaking columns.

When you begin a document in Word, it has one column. You can divide a portion of a document or the entire document into multiple columns. Within each column, you can type, modify, or format text.

To divide a portion of a document into multiple columns, you use section breaks. That is, Word requires that a new section be created each time you alter the number of columns in a document. Thus, if a document has a nameplate (one column) followed by an article of three columns followed by an article of two columns, then the document would be divided into a total of three sections.

In this project, the nameplate is one column and the body of the newsletter is three columns. Thus, you must insert a continuous section break below the nameplate. *Continuous* means you want the new section on the same page as the previous section. Perform the steps on the next page to divide the body of the newsletter into three columns.

Steps: To Insert a Continuous Section Break

1 **With the insertion point on line 3, press the ENTER key twice. Click Insert on the menu bar and then click Break. When the Break dialog box displays, click Continuous in the Section break types area. Point to the OK button.**

Word displays the Break dialog box (Figure 6-29). Continuous means you want the new section on the same page as the previous section.

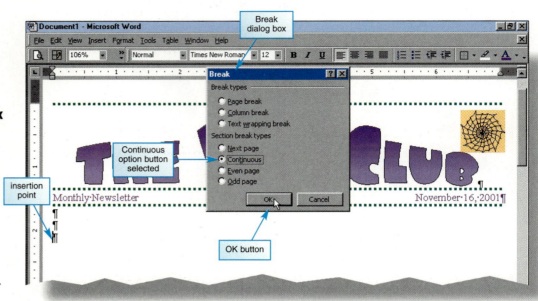

FIGURE 6-29

2 **Click the OK button.**

Word inserts a section break above the insertion point (Figure 6-30). The insertion point now is located in section 2.

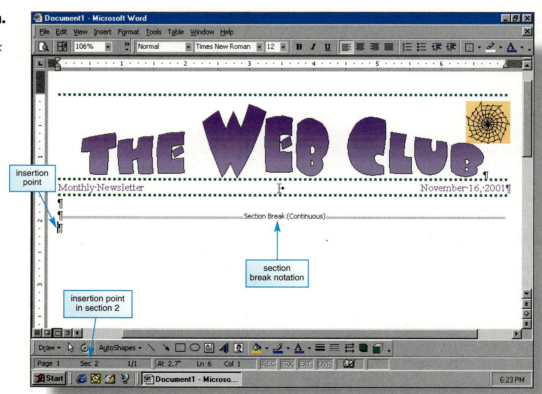

FIGURE 6-30

The next step is to format the second section to three columns, as shown in the following steps.

To Format Columns

1 **If necessary, scroll down. Be sure the insertion point is in section 2. Double-click the move handle on the Standard toolbar to display the entire toolbar. Point to the Columns button on the Standard toolbar (Figure 6-31).**

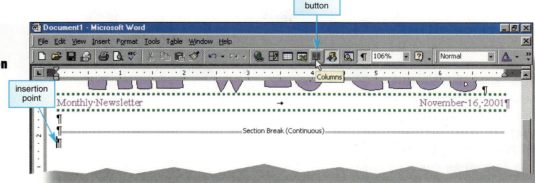

FIGURE 6-31

2 **Click the Columns button. Point to the third column in the columns list graphic.**

Word displays a columns list graphic below the Columns button (Figure 6-32).

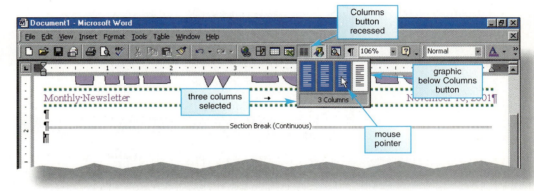

FIGURE 6-32

3 **Click the third column.**

Word divides the section containing the insertion point into three evenly sized and spaced columns (Figure 6-33). Notice that the ruler indicates the width of each column.

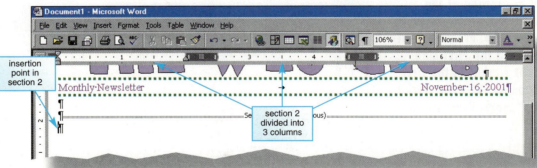

FIGURE 6-33

When you use the Columns button to create columns, Word creates columns of equal width. You can create columns of unequal width by clicking the Columns command on the Format menu.

Justifying a Paragraph

The text in the paragraphs of the body of the newsletter is **justified**, which means that the left and right margins are aligned, like the edges of newspaper columns. The first line of each paragraph is indented .25-inch. Perform the steps on the next page to enter the first paragraph of the feature article using justified alignment.

Microsoft **Word 2000**

To Justify a Paragraph

1 Drag the First Line Indent marker in the first column on the ruler to the .25" mark. Double-click the move handle on the Formatting toolbar to display the entire toolbar. Point to the Justify button on the Formatting toolbar (Figure 6-34).

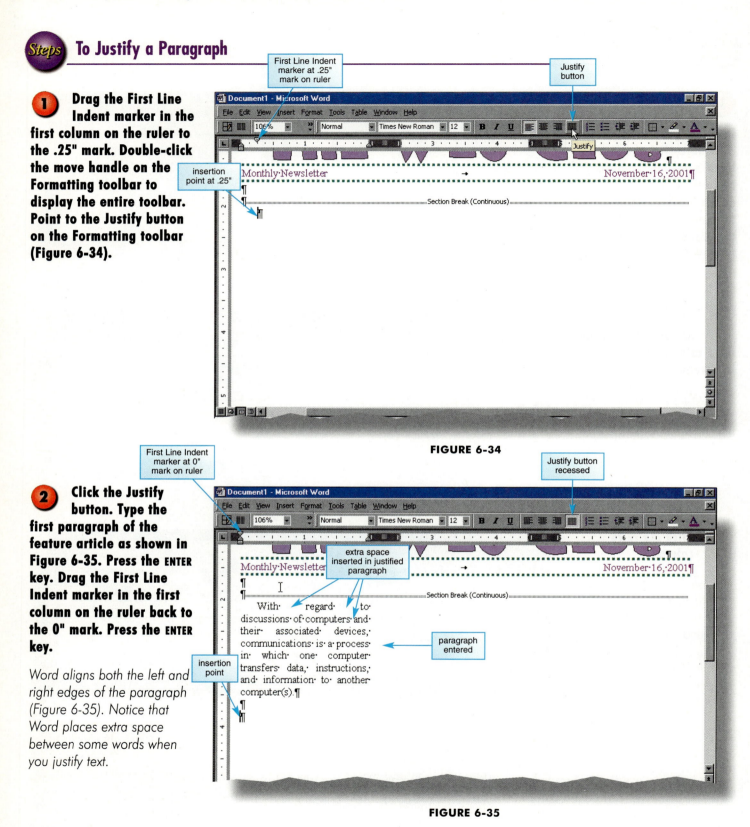

FIGURE 6-34

2 Click the Justify button. Type the first paragraph of the feature article as shown in Figure 6-35. Press the ENTER key. Drag the First Line Indent marker in the first column on the ruler back to the 0" mark. Press the ENTER key.

Word aligns both the left and right edges of the paragraph (Figure 6-35). Notice that Word places extra space between some words when you justify text.

FIGURE 6-35

Saving the Newsletter

Because you have performed several steps, you should save the newsletter as described in the following steps.

TO SAVE THE NEWSLETTER

① Insert a floppy disk into drive A.

② Double-click the move handle on the Standard toolbar to display the entire toolbar. Click the Save button on the Standard toolbar.

③ Type Web Club Newsletter in the File name text box. Do not press the ENTER key.

④ Click the Save in box arrow and then click 3½ Floppy (A:).

⑤ Click the Save button in the Save As dialog box.

Word saves the document on a floppy disk in drive A with the file name Web Club Newsletter.

Inserting the Remainder of the Feature Article

Instead of entering the rest of the feature article into the newsletter for this project, you insert the file named Communications Article into the newsletter. This file contains the remainder of the feature article.

The Communications Article file is located on the Data Disk. If you did not download the Data Disk, see the inside back cover for instructions for downloading the Data Disk or see your instructor. Perform the following steps to insert the Communications Article into the newsletter.

Steps **To Insert a File into the Newsletter**

① **If necessary, insert the Data Disk into drive A. Click Insert on the menu bar and then click File. If necessary, click the Look in box arrow and then click 3½ Floppy (A:). Click Communications Article and then point to the Insert button.**

Word displays the Insert File dialog box (Figure 6-36). The file will be inserted at the location of the insertion point in the document.

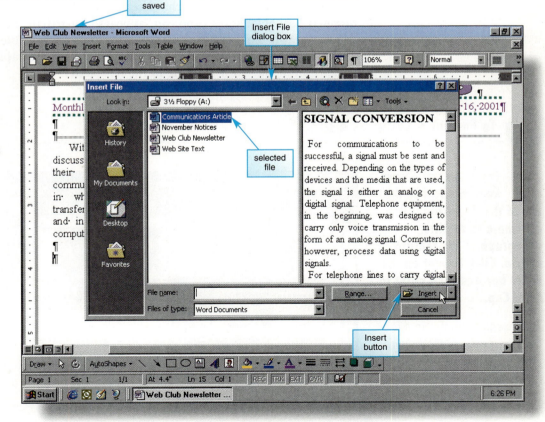

FIGURE 6-36

2 **Click the Insert button.**

Word inserts the file, Communications Article, into the file Web Club Newsletter at the location of the insertion point (Figure 6-37). The text automatically is formatted into columns.

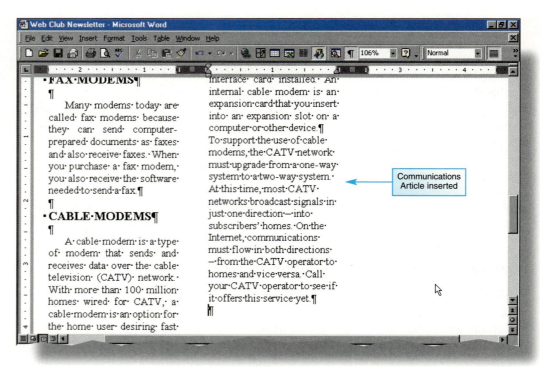

FIGURE 6-37

Formatting a Letter as a Dropped Capital

You can format the first character or word in a paragraph to be dropped. A **dropped capital letter**, or **drop cap**, appears larger than the rest of the characters in the paragraph. The text in the paragraph then wraps around the dropped capital letter. Perform the following steps to create a dropped capital letter in the first paragraph of the feature article in the newsletter.

 To Format a Letter as a Drop Cap

1 **Press the CTRL+HOME keys to scroll to the top of the document. Click anywhere in the first paragraph of the feature article. Click Format on the menu bar and then point to Drop Cap.**

The insertion point is in the first paragraph of the feature article (Figure 6-38).

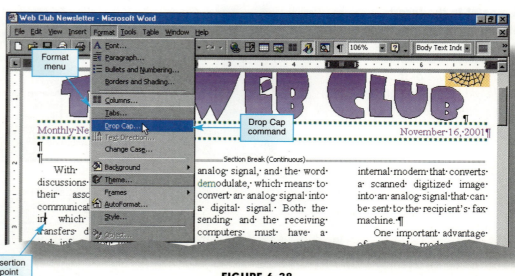

FIGURE 6-38

2 **Click Drop Cap. When the Drop Cap dialog box displays, click Dropped in the Position area. Point to the OK button.**

Word displays the Drop Cap dialog box (Figure 6-39).

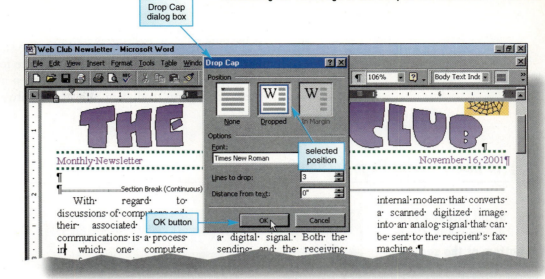

FIGURE 6-39

3 **Click the OK button.**

Word drops the letter W in the word, With, and wraps subsequent text around the dropped capital W (Figure 6-40).

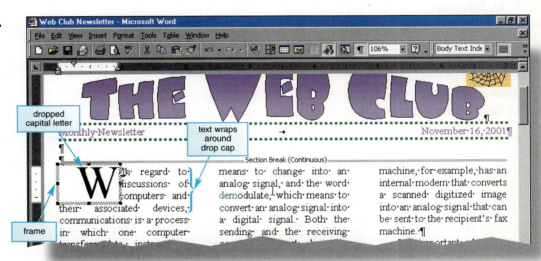

FIGURE 6-40

When you drop cap a letter, Word places a text frame around it. A **text frame** is a container for text that allows you to position the text anywhere on the page. As illustrated in the previous steps, Word can format the frame so that text wraps around it.

To remove the frame from displaying in the document window, you simply click outside the frame to display the insertion point elsewhere in the document.

The next step is to insert a column break before the subhead, INTERNAL MODEMS.

Inserting a Column Break

Notice in Figure 6-1a on page WD 6.5 that the third column is not a continuation of the feature article. The third column contains several club announcements. The feature article continues on the second page of the newsletter (Figure 6-1b). In order for the club announcements to display in the third column, you must force a **column break** at the bottom of the second column. Word inserts column breaks at the location of the insertion point.

More About

Drop Caps

A drop cap often is used to mark the beginning of an article. To format the first word as a drop cap, select the word. An alternative to a drop cap is a stick-up cap, which extends into the left margin, instead of sinking into the first few lines of the text. To insert a stick-up cap, click In Margin in the Drop Cap dialog box.

The first step in continuing the feature article on the second page and placing club announcements into the third column is to force the feature article to continue on the next page with a **next page section break**, and then insert a column break at the bottom of the second column so the announcements always display in the third column.

Steps To Insert a Next Page Section Break

1 Scroll through the document to display the bottom of the second column of the first page in the document window. Click before the I in the INTERNAL MODEMS subhead. Click Insert on the menu bar and then click Break. When the Break dialog box displays, click Next page in the Section break types area.

The insertion point is at the beginning of the INTERNAL MODEMS subhead (Figure 6-41).

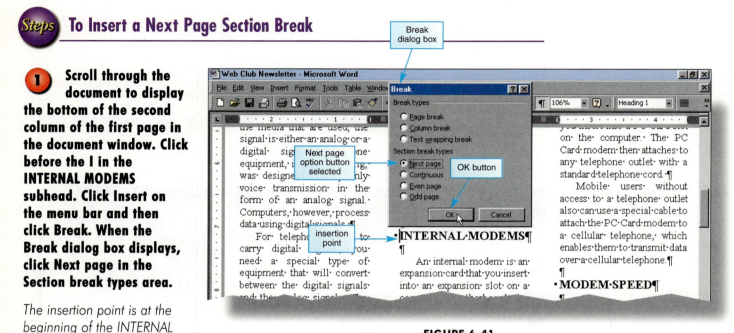

FIGURE 6-41

2 Click the OK button.

Word inserts a section break at the location of the insertion point (Figure 6-42). The rest of the article displays on page 2 of the document because a next page section break includes a page break. On page 1, the bottom of the second column and the entire third column are empty.

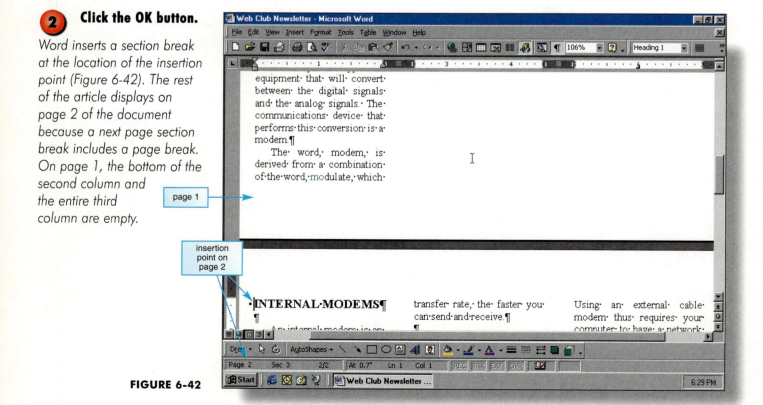

FIGURE 6-42

Because you want the club announcements to begin at the top of the third column, the next step is to insert a column break at the end of the text in the second column as shown in these steps.

To Insert a Column Break

1 **Position the insertion point at the end of the second column on the first page of the newsletter. Press the ENTER key. Drag the First Line Indent marker on the ruler in column 2 to the 0" mark. Press the ENTER key. Press the CTRL+I keys to turn on italics. Type** `Article continues on Page 2…` **and then press the CTRL+I keys again. Press the ENTER key. Click Insert on the menu bar and then click Break. Click Column break in the Break dialog box (Figure 6-43).**

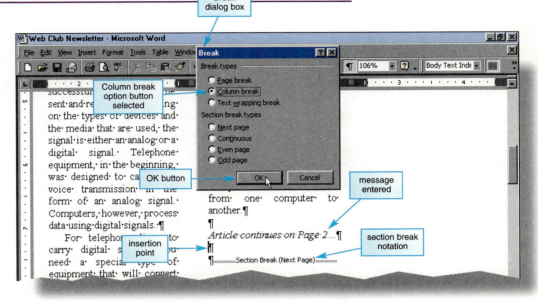

FIGURE 6-43

2 **Click the OK button.**

Word inserts a column break at the bottom of the second column and places the insertion point at the top of the third column (Figure 6-44).

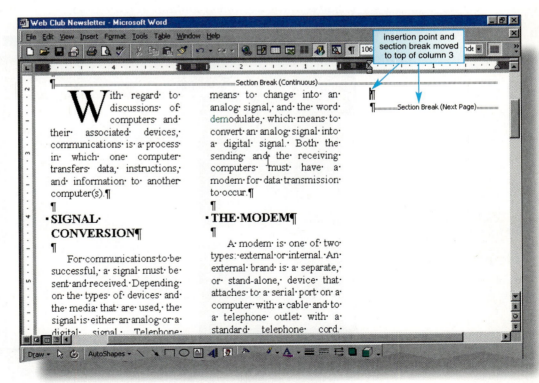

FIGURE 6-44

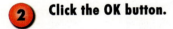

Other Ways
1. Press CTRL+SHIFT+ENTER

To eliminate having to enter the entire column of announcements into the newsletter, you insert the file named November Notices into the third column of the newsletter. This file contains the first two announcements (REMINDER and CLUB DISCOUNTS) for this November issue of the newsletter.

The November Notices file is located on the Data Disk. If you did not download the Data Disk, see the inside back cover for instructions for downloading the Data Disk or see your instructor. Perform the following steps to insert the November Notices file into the newsletter.

TO INSERT A FILE INTO A COLUMN OF THE NEWSLETTER

1 If necessary, insert the Data Disk into drive A. With the insertion point at the top of the third column, click Insert on the menu bar and then click File.

2 When the Insert File dialog box displays, if necessary, click the Look in box arrow and then click 3½ Floppy (A:). Click November Notices.

3 Click the Insert button.

Word inserts the file November Notices into the third column of the newsletter.

Perform the following step to display the entire page in the document window so that you can see the layout of the first page of the newsletter thus far.

TO ZOOM WHOLE PAGE

1 Click the Zoom box arrow and then click Whole Page in the list.

Word displays the first page of the newsletter in reduced form so that the entire page displays in the document window (Figure 6-45).

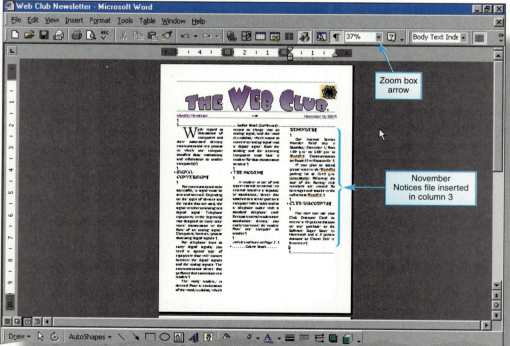

FIGURE 6-45

Perform the following step to return the display to zoom text width.

TO ZOOM TEXT WIDTH

 1 Click the Zoom box arrow and then click Text Width.

Word extends the right margin to the right edge of the document window.

The next step is to enter the subhead for the last announcement in the third column of the first page of the newsletter.

Applying a Style

The subheads, such as REMINDER and CLUB DISCOUNTS, are formatted using the Heading 1 style, which in this case uses 14-point Times New Roman bold font. Instead of changing the font size and font style individually for the new WEB SITE subhead, apply the Heading 1 style as shown in the following steps.

Steps To Apply the Heading 1 Style

1 **With the insertion point at the end of the third column, press the ENTER key. Double-click the move handle on the Formatting toolbar to display the entire toolbar. Click the Style box arrow on the Formatting toolbar and then point to Heading 1.**

Word displays a list of available styles for this document (Figure 6-46).

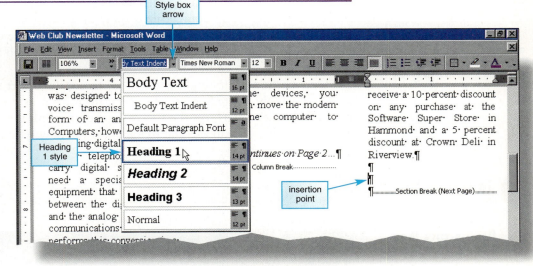

FIGURE 6-46

2 **Click Heading 1. Type WEB SITE and then press the RIGHT ARROW key. Press the ENTER key.**

Word enters the subhead, WEB SITE, and formats it according to the Heading 1 style (Figure 6-47).

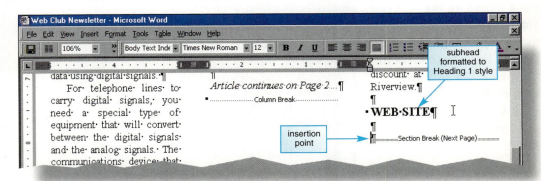

FIGURE 6-47

Many different styles are associated with a document. To view a complete list of available styles for a document, click Format on the menu bar and then click Styles. As you click each style name in the Styles list of the Styles dialog box, a preview of the selected style displays on the right side of the dialog box. To save time while composing a document, use styles to format characters and paragraphs.

The next step is to insert the last announcement in the third column of the first page of the newsletter.

Linking an Object into a Word Document

The last announcement in the third column of the newsletter notifies club members of the new Guide to World Wide Web sites. The text for this announcement is in a file named Web Site Text. Because the contents of this file might change between now and when the newsletter is printed, you want to be sure to use the most updated version of the Web Site Text file. To do this, you will link the Web Site Text file to the Web Club Newsletter.

In this case, the file named Web Site Text is called the **source file**. The file named Web Club Newsletter is called the **destination file**. When you **link** an object, such as a file, the contents of the source file display in the destination file, but the contents of the link actually are stored in the source file. That is, the destination file stores only the location of the source file. When the source file (Web Site Text) is updated, the destination file also can be updated.

One method of linking documents is to copy the text of the source document and then use the Paste Special command to insert it as a linked object into the destination document. Perform the following steps to link the Word document, Web Site Text, that is located on the Data Disk, into the newsletter.

More *About* **2000**

Linking and Embedding

A linked object is one that is updated in the destination file when the source file is updated. By contrast, an embedded object does not change if you change the source file. Thus, an embedded object becomes part of the destination file, whereas a linked object does not. To create an embedded object, click Paste (instead of Paste link) in the Paste Special dialog box.

Steps **To Link an Object**

1 **Double-click the move handle on the Standard toolbar to display the entire toolbar. Click the Open button on the Standard toolbar. If necessary, change the Look in location to drive A. Click Web Site Text and then click the Open button. Click Edit on the menu bar and then point to Select All.**

Word opens the Web Site Text document (Figure 6-48). You want to copy the entire document.

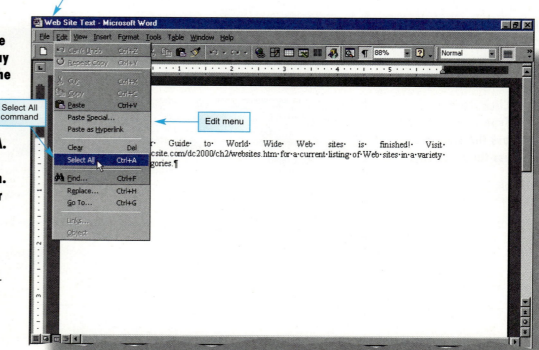

FIGURE 6-48

2 **Click Select All. Click the Copy button on the Standard toolbar. Point to the Web Club Newsletter program button on the taskbar.**

Word highlights the entire document (Figure 6-49). The selection is copied to the Office Clipboard.

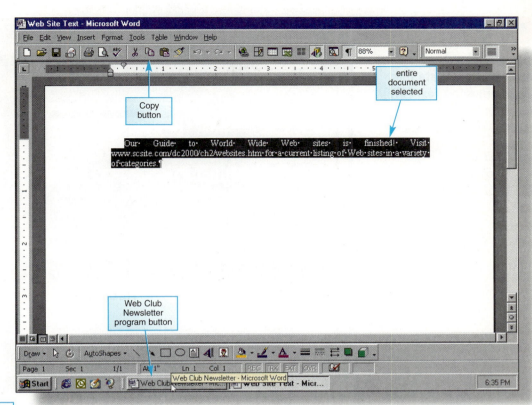

FIGURE 6-49

3 **Click the Web Club Newsletter program button. When the Web Club Newsletter document window displays again, click Edit on the menu bar and the point to Paste Special.**

Word redisplays the Web Club Newsletter (Figure 6-50).

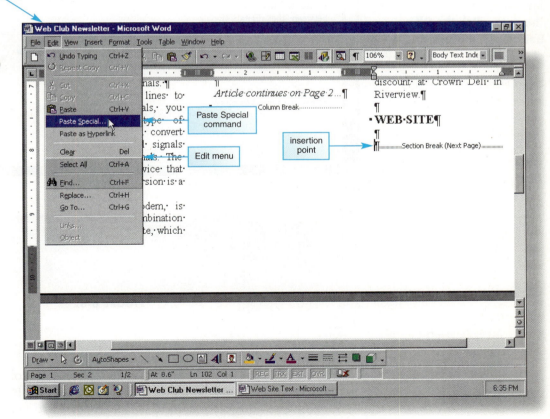

FIGURE 6-50

4 Click Paste Special. When the Paste Special dialog box displays, click Paste link. Click Formatted Text (RTF) in the As list and then point to the OK button.

Word displays the Paste Special dialog box (Figure 6-51).

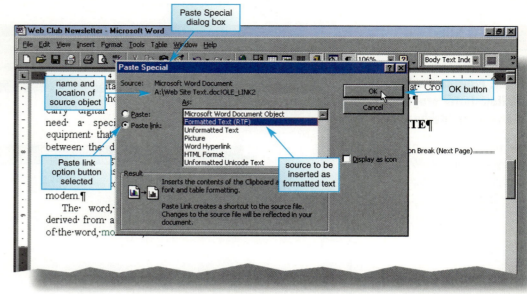

FIGURE 6-51

5 Click the OK button. Drag the First Line Indent marker in the third column of the ruler to the .25" mark. (If Word displays a dialog box indicating it cannot obtain the data, click the OK button and perform these steps again.)

Word links the source into the destination at the location of the insertion point (Figure 6-52).

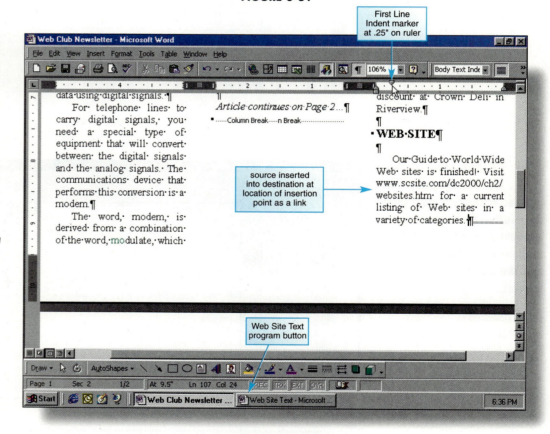

FIGURE 6-52

1. On Insert menu click Object, click Create from File tab, enter file name, click Link to file, click OK button

The contents of the source file display in the third column of the newsletter as a link. Word automatically updates links if the source file changes while the destination file is open. If the destination file is closed, Word updates the links the next time you open or print the destination file. If a link, for some reason, is not updated automatically, click the link and then press F9 to update it manually.

You are finished with the source file. Perform the following steps to close it.

TO CLOSE A FILE

1 Click the Web Site Text program button on the taskbar.

2 When the Web Site Text document window displays, click File on the menu bar and then click Close.

3 If Word displays a dialog box, click the No button.

Word closes the Web Site Text document window and redisplays the Web Club Newsletter document window.

The next step is to place a vertical rule between the second and third columns of the newsletter.

Adding a Vertical Rule Between Columns

In newsletters, you often see a vertical rule separating columns. With Word, you can place a vertical rule between *all* columns by clicking the Columns command on the Format menu and then clicking the Line between check box.

In this project, you want a vertical rule between *only* the second and third columns. To do this, you place a left border spaced several points from the text. You have learned that a point is approximately 1/72 of an inch. Perform the following steps to place a vertical rule between the second and third columns of the newsletter.

Steps To Place a Vertical Rule between Columns

1 **Drag the mouse from the top of the third column down to the bottom of the third column. Click Format on the menu bar and then point to Borders and Shading.**

Word highlights the entire third column of page 1 in the newsletter (Figure 6-53).

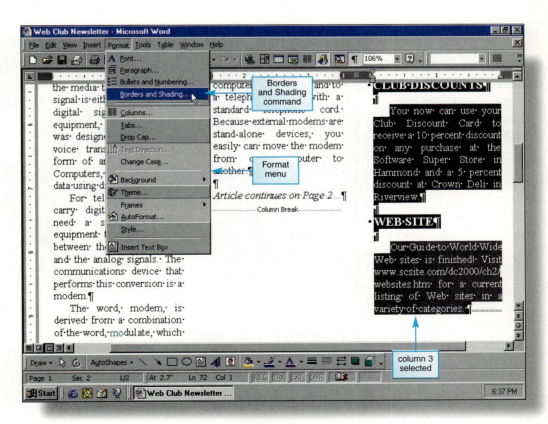

FIGURE 6-53

2 **Click Borders and Shading. When the Borders and Shading dialog box displays, if necessary, click the Borders tab. Click the Left Border button in the Preview area. Point to the Options button.**

Word displays the Borders and Shading dialog box (Figure 6-54). The border diagram graphically shows the selected borders.

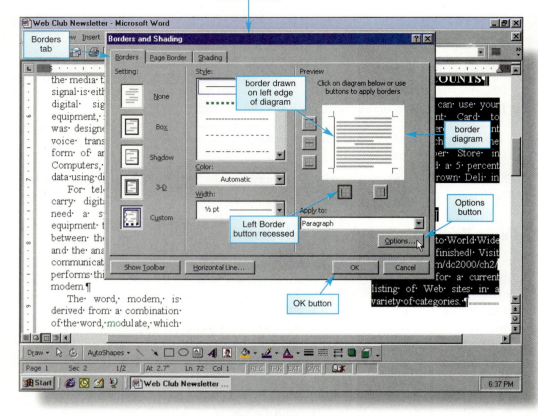

FIGURE 6-54

3 **Click the Options button. When the Border and Shading Options dialog box displays, change the Left text box to 15 pt. Point to the OK button.**

The Preview area shows the border positioned 15 points from the left edge of the paragraph (Figure 6-55).

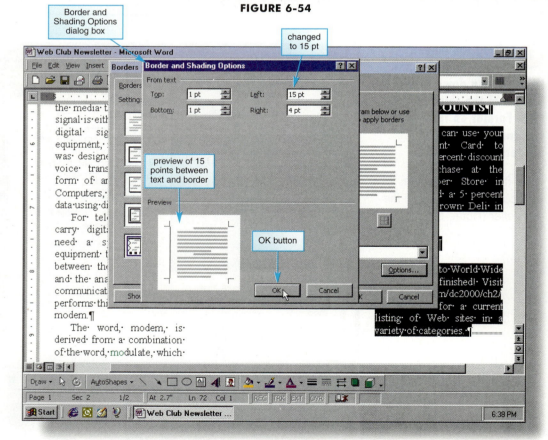

FIGURE 6-55

4 Click the OK button. When the Borders and Shading dialog box is visible again, click its OK button. Click in the second column to remove the selection from the third column.

Word draws a border positioned 15 points from the left edge of the text in the third column (Figure 6-56). The border displays as a vertical rule between the second and third columns of the newsletter.

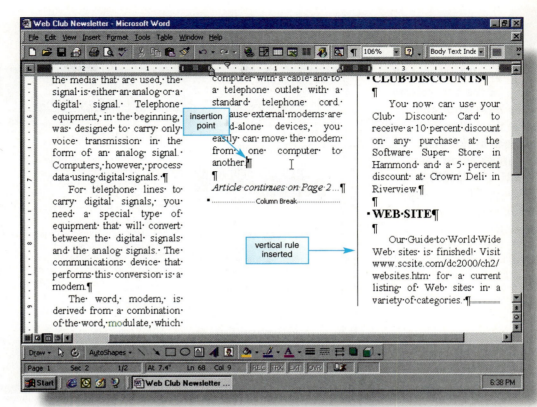

FIGURE 6-56

Creating a Pull-Quote

You have learned that a pull-quote is text *pulled*, or copied, from the text of the document and given graphical emphasis so it stands apart and grasps the reader's attention. The newsletter in this project has a pull-quote on the first page between the first and second columns (see Figure 6-1a on page WD 6.5).

To create a pull-quote, you copy the text in the existing document to the Office Clipboard and then paste it into a column of the newsletter. To position it between columns, you place a text box around it. A **text box**, like a text frame, is a container for text that allows you to position the text anywhere on the page. The difference between a text box and a frame is that a text box has more graphical formatting options than does a frame.

The steps on the following pages discuss how to create the pull-quote shown in Figure 6-1a on page WD 6.5.

Inserting a Text Box

The first step in creating the pull-quote is to copy the sentence to be used in the pull-quote and then insert a text box around it as shown in the steps on the next page.

More About 2000

Pull-Quotes

Because of their bold emphasis, pull-quotes should be used sparingly in a newsletter. Pull-quotes are useful for breaking the monotony of long columns of text. Quotation marks are not required around a pull-quote; however, if you use them, use curly (or smart) quotes instead of straight quotes.

Steps **To Insert a Text Box**

1 Scroll to the middle of the first column of the newsletter and select the entire first sentence of the first paragraph below the SIGNAL CONVERSION subhead. Click the Copy button on the Standard toolbar.

The text for the pull-quote is highlighted (Figure 6-57).

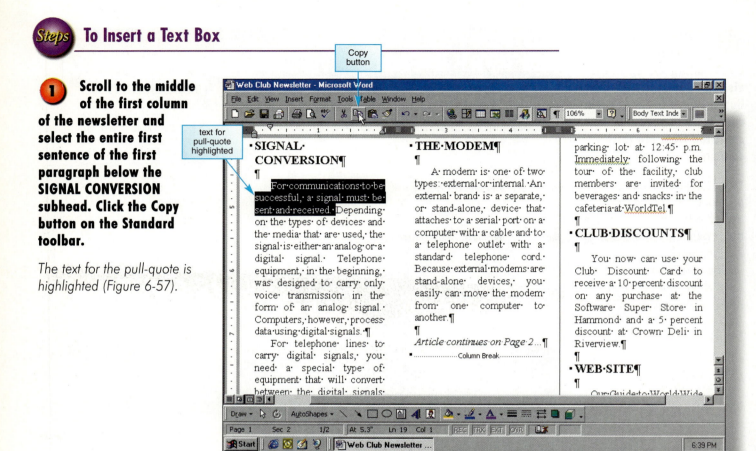

FIGURE 6-57

2 Click the paragraph mark below the SIGNAL CONVERSION subhead. Click the Paste button on the Standard toolbar. Type a quotation mark (") at the end of the pull-quote, and then type a quotation mark (") at the beginning of the pull-quote. Select the entire pull-quote (do not select the paragraph mark). If necessary, click the Drawing button on the Standard toolbar to display the Drawing toolbar. Point to the Text Box button on the Drawing toolbar (Figure 6-58).

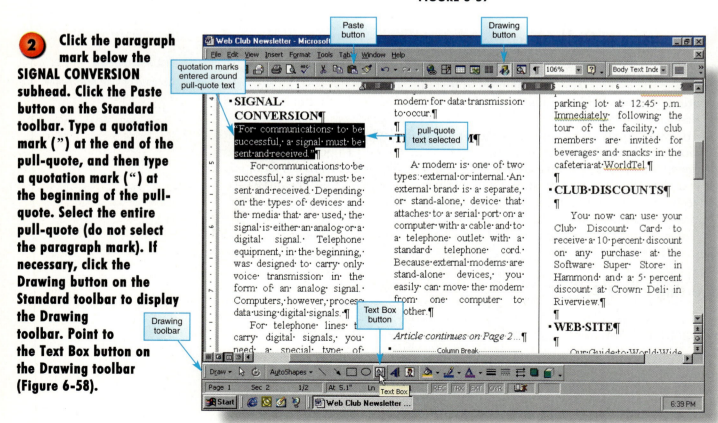

FIGURE 6-58

3 **Click the Text Box button.**

Word places a text box around the pull-quote (Figure 6-59). The pull-quote now may be positioned anywhere on the page.

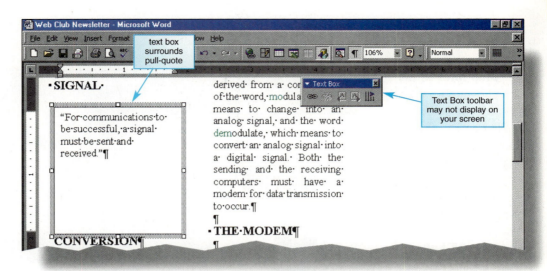

FIGURE 6-59

The next step in formatting the pull-quote is to change the color and increase the weight of the text box as described in the following steps.

To Format a Text Box

1 **Double-click any edge of the text box. When the Format Text Box dialog box displays, if necessary, click the Colors and Lines tab. Click the Color box arrow in the Line area and then click Teal. Change the Weight to 1.5 pt and then point to the OK button.**

Word displays the Format Text Box dialog box (Figure 6-60).

 2 **Click the OK button.**

Word formats the text box to a 1.5-point teal line.

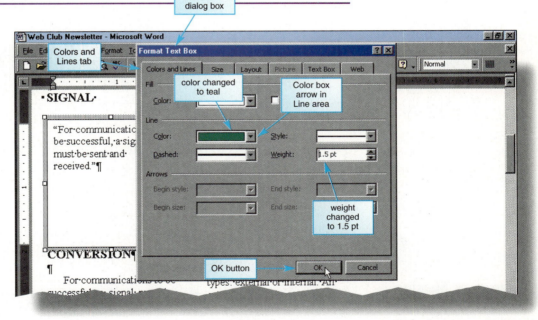

FIGURE 6-60

The next step in formatting the pull-quote is to increase the spacing between the characters, in order to enhance the readability of the text. Perform the steps on the next page to expand the character spacing.

Steps To Increase Character Spacing

1 **Drag through the pull-quote text. Right-click the selection. Click Font on the shortcut menu. When the Font dialog box displays, if necessary, click the Character Spacing tab. Click the Spacing box arrow and then click Expanded. Point to the OK button.**

The Preview area shows the selected text with one point placed between each character (Figure 6-61). Depending on your printer, the characters displayed in the Preview area may differ.

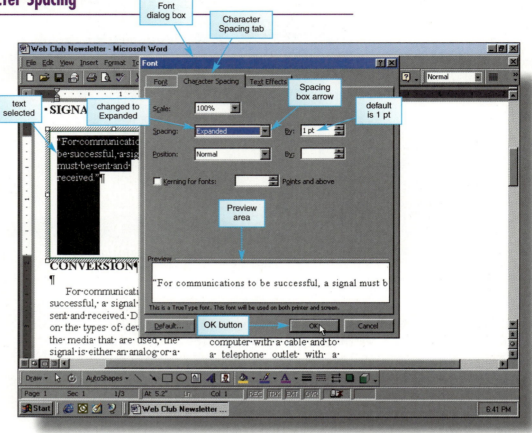

FIGURE 6-61

2 **Click the OK button.**

Word increases the spacing between each character in the pull-quote by one point (see Figure 6-62).

Character Spacing

In addition to increasing the spacing between characters, you also can decrease the spacing between characters in the Character Spacing sheet. To make spacing in a word more proportional, select the word and then click the Kerning for fonts check box in the Character Spacing sheet.

The next step is to bold the characters in the pull-quote as described in the following step.

TO BOLD TEXT

1 Double-click the move handle on the Formatting toolbar to display the entire toolbar. With the pull-quote text still selected, click the Bold button on the Formatting toolbar.

Word bolds the characters in the pull-quote (Figure 6-62). Depending on your printer, the text in your text box may wrap differently than shown in this figure.

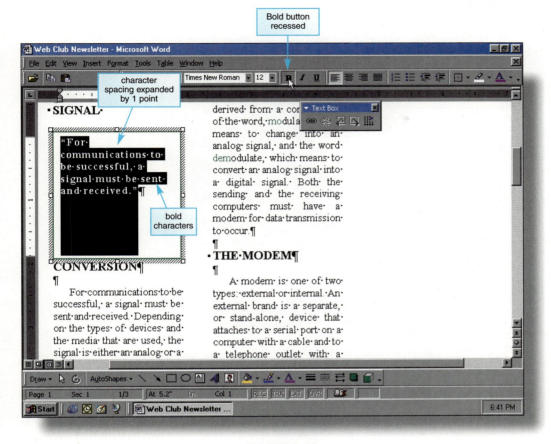

FIGURE 6-62

Notice in Figure 6-62 that the text is positioned closely to the text box on the top and left sides of the text box. You want more space between the pull-quote in the text box and the text box itself. Perform the following steps to increase the left and right indentation and the spacing above and below the paragraph in the text box.

TO CHANGE PARAGRAPH INDENTATION AND SPACING

1 Position the insertion point in the pull-quote text. Click Format on the menu bar and then click Paragraph. If necessary, click the Indents and Spacing tab when the Paragraph dialog box displays.

2 In the Indentation area, change Left to 0.1" and Right to 0.1" to increase the amount of space between the left and right edges of the pull-quote and the text box.

3 In the Spacing area, change Before to 6 pt and After to 12 pt to increase the amount of space above and below the pull-quote (Figure 6-63 on the next page).

4 Click the OK button.

Word changes the paragraph indentation and spacing.

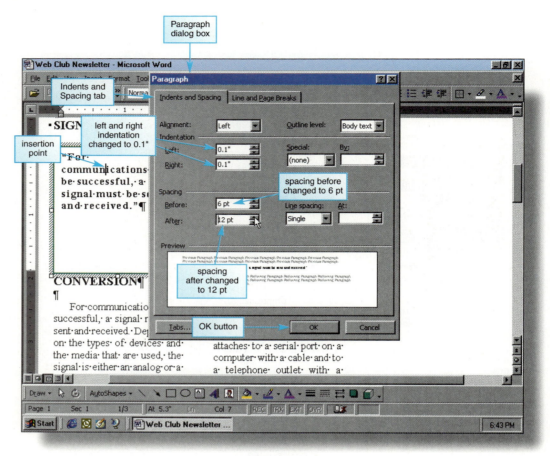

FIGURE 6-63

The next step in formatting the pull-quote is to resize it as described in the following steps.

TO RESIZE A TEXT BOX

1. Drag the right-middle sizing handle to the right to make the pull-quote a bit wider so the pull-quote text looks more balanced.

2. Drag the bottom-middle sizing handle up so the text box looks similar to that shown in Figure 6-65.

Word resizes the text box.

The next step in formatting the pull-quote is to shade the pull-quote paragraph violet as shown in the following steps.

More About

Text Boxes

You learned in Project 4 how to create a graphic watermark. You also can create text watermarks by inserting a text box into the header or footer of the document. To lighten the text so it does not interfere with the document text, change its font color to a lighter shade.

To Shade a Paragraph

1 **Select the pull-quote paragraph in the text box, including the paragraph mark. Click Format on the menu bar and then click Borders and Shading. When the Borders and Shading dialog box displays, if necessary, click the Shading tab. Click Violet. Point to the OK button.**

Word displays the Borders and Shading dialog box (Figure 6-64).

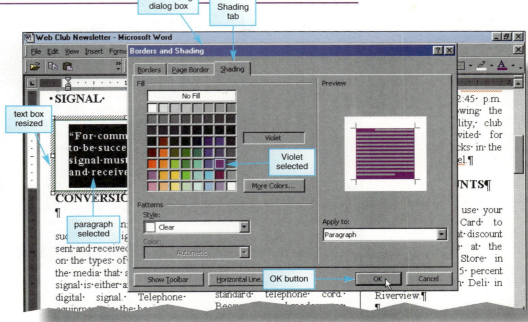

FIGURE 6-64

2 **Click the OK button.**

Word shades the paragraph violet. The characters in the paragraph currently are black, which is difficult to read on a violet background. Thus, change the color of the characters to white.

3 **Click the Font Color button arrow on the Formatting toolbar and then click White. Click outside the selection to remove the highlight.**

Word changes the color of the characters in the pull-quote to white (Figure 6-65).

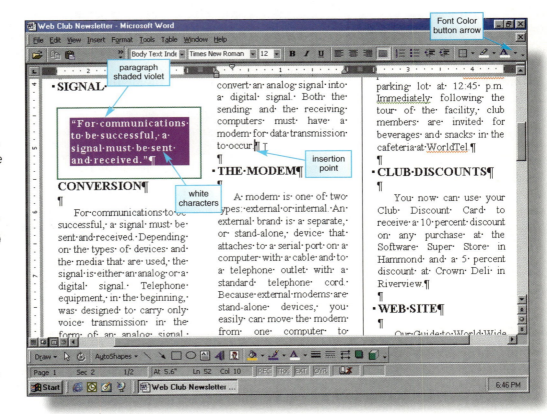

FIGURE 6-65

 Other Ways

1. Click Shadow Color button on Tables and Borders toolbar

The final step is to position the pull-quote between the first and second columns of the newsletter as shown in the steps on the next page.

Steps ▶ **To Position a Text Box**

1 **Click the text box to select it. Point to the text box.**

The mouse pointer has a four-headed arrow attached to it when positioned on a text box (Figure 6-66).

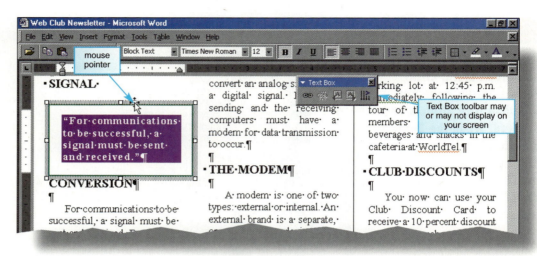

FIGURE 6-66

2 **Drag the text box to its new position (Figure 6-67). You may need to drag it a couple of times to position it similarly to this figure. Depending on your printer, your wordwrap may occur in different locations. Click outside the text box to remove the selection.**

The pull-quote is complete (Figure 6-67).

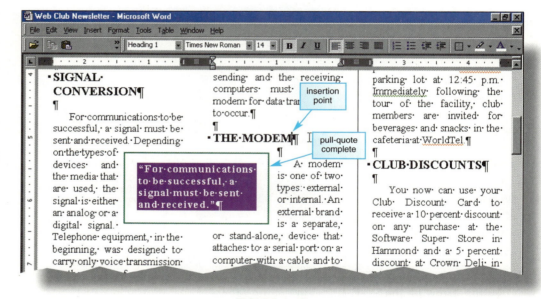

FIGURE 6-67

Perform the following steps to save the document again.

TO SAVE A DOCUMENT

1 Double-click the move handle on the Standard toolbar to display the entire toolbar. With your disk containing the newsletter file in drive A, click the Save button on the Standard toolbar.

Word saves the document again.

The first page of the newsletter is finished, with the exception of the page border, which will be added later in this project. Perform the following steps to print the first page of the newsletter.

TO PRINT A PAGE

1 Click File on the menu bar and then click Print.

2 When the Print dialog box displays, click Current page in the Page range area.

3 Click the OK button.

Word prints the first page of the newsletter (Figure 6-68).

Monthly Newsletter   November 16, 2001

With regard to discussions of computers and their associated devices, communications is a process in which one computer transfers data, instructions, and information to another computer(s).

SIGNAL CONVERSION

For communications to be successful, a signal must be sent and received. Depending on the types of devices and the media that are used, the signal is either an analog or a digital signal. Telephone equipment, in the beginning, was designed to carry only voice transmission in the form of an analog signal. Computers, however, process data using digital signals.

For telephone lines to carry digital signals, you need a special type of equipment that will convert between the digital signals and the analog signals. The communications device that

performs this conversion is a modem.

The word, modem, is derived from a combination of the word, modulate, which means to change into an analog signal, and the word demodulate, which means to convert an analog signal into a digital signal. Both the sending and the receiving computers must have a modem for data transmission to occur.

THE MODEM

"For communications to be successful, a signal must be sent and received."

A modem is one of two types: external or internal. An external brand is a separate, or stand-alone, device that attaches to a serial port on a computer with a cable and to a telephone outlet with a standard telephone cord. Because external modems are stand-alone devices, you easily can move the modem from one computer to another.

Article continues on Page 2...

REMINDER

Our Internet Service Provider field trip is Saturday, December 1, from 1:00 p.m. to 2:00 p.m. at WorldTel Communications on Route 53 in Romeoville.

If you plan to attend, please meet in the WorldTel parking lot at 12:45 p.m. Immediately following the tour of the facility, club members are invited for beverages and snacks in the cafeteria at WorldTel.

CLUB DISCOUNTS

You now can use your Club Discount Card to receive a 10 percent discount on any purchase at the Software Super Store in Hammond and a 5 percent discount at Crown Deli in Riverview.

WEB SITE

Our Guide to World Wide Web sites is finished! Visit www.scsite.com/dc2000/ch2/ websites.htm for a current listing of Web sites in a variety of categories.

FIGURE 6-68

Formatting the Second Page of the Newsletter

The second page of the newsletter (see Figure 6-1b on page WD 6.5) continues the feature article that began in the first two columns of the first page. The nameplate on the second page is much more concise than the one on the first page of the newsletter. In addition to the text in the feature article, page two contains a picture. The following pages illustrate how to format the second page of the newsletter in this project.

Creating the Nameplate on the Second Page

Because the document currently is formatted into three columns and the nameplate is a single column, the next step is to change the number of columns to one at the top of the second page. You have learned that Word requires a new section each time you change the number of columns in a document. Thus, you will insert a section break and then format the section to one column so you can enter the nameplate. Perform the following steps to format and enter the nameplate on the second page of the newsletter.

To Change Column Formatting

1 **Scroll through the document and position the mouse pointer at the upper-left corner of the second page of the newsletter. Click Insert on the menu bar and then click Break. When the Break dialog box displays, click Continuous in the Section break types area.**

Word displays the Break dialog box (Figure 6-69). This section break will place the nameplate on the same physical page as the three columns of the continued feature article.

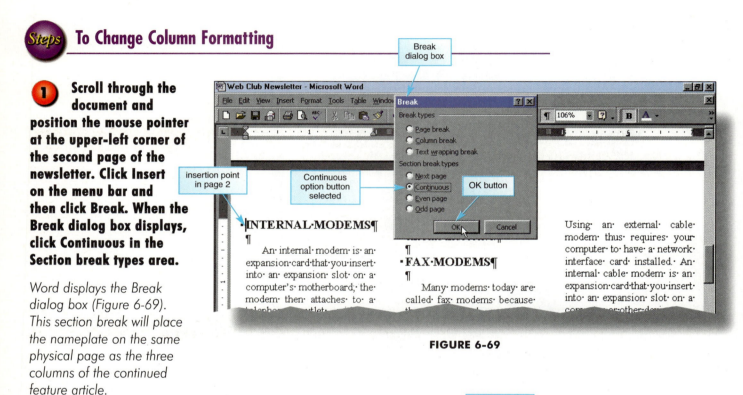

FIGURE 6-69

2 **Click the OK button.**

Word inserts a section break above the insertion point.

3 **Press the UP ARROW key to position the insertion point in section 3 to the left of the section break notation. Click the Columns button on the Standard toolbar. Point to the first column of the columns list graphic.**

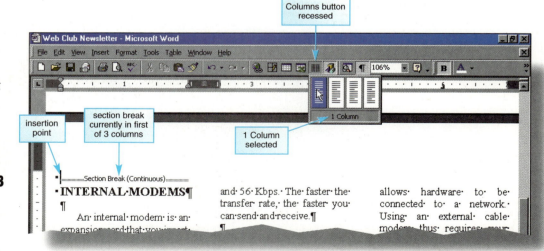

FIGURE 6-70

Word highlights the left column in the columns list graphic and displays 1 Column below the graphic (Figure 6-70). The current section, for the nameplate, will be formatted to one column.

Click the first column in the columns list graphic.

Word formats the current section to one column (Figure 6-71).

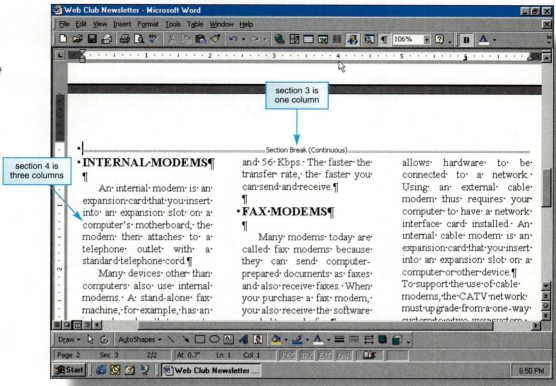

section 3 is one column

section 4 is three columns

FIGURE 6-71

In the nameplate on the second page, the date is to display at the left margin; the newsletter title, The Web Club, is to be centered; and the page number is to display at the right margin. Thus, you set a centered and right-aligned tab stop for the nameplate as described in the following steps.

TO SET TAB STOPS

1 Be sure the insertion point is in section 3. Double-click the move handle on the Formatting toolbar to display the entire toolbar. Click the Style box arrow on the Formatting toolbar and then click Normal.

2 Press the ENTER key twice and then press the UP ARROW key. Click Format on the menu bar and then click Tabs.

3 When the Tabs dialog box displays, type 3.5 and then click Center in the Alignment area. Click the Set button.

4 Type 7 in the Tab stop position text box and then click Right in the Alignment area (Figure 6-72 on the next page). Click the Set button.

5 Click the OK button.

Word places a centered tab marker at the 3.5" mark on the ruler and a right-aligned tab marker at the right margin.

Other Ways

1. On Format menu click Columns, click number of columns in Presets area, click OK button

More About

Columns

If you already have typed text and would like it to be formatted in a different number of columns, select the text, click the Columns button on the Standard toolbar, and then click the number of columns desired in the columns list graphic. Word automatically creates a new section for the newly formatted columns.

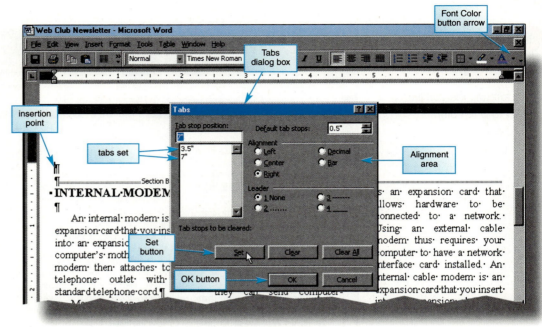

FIGURE 6-72

The next step is to enter the nameplate and a continued message at the top of the first column in the second page of the newsletter.

TO ENTER THE NAMEPLATE AND CONTINUED MESSAGE ON THE SECOND PAGE

1 Click the Font Color button arrow on the Formatting toolbar and then click Violet. Click Insert on the menu bar, click Date and Time, click the date format of month, day, year (November 16, 2001), and then click the OK button.

2 Press the TAB key. Change the font to Beesknees ITC, or a similar font. Change the font size to 24. Type `The Web Club` and then change the font size back to 12. Change the font back to Times New Roman.

3 Press the TAB key. Type `Page 2` and then press the ENTER key.

4 Click somewhere in the line typed in Steps 1 through 3. Double-click the move handle on the Standard toolbar to display the entire toolbar. If necessary, click the Tables and Borders button on the Standard toolbar to display the Tables and Borders toolbar.

5 Click the Line Style box arrow on the Tables and Borders toolbar and then click the first dotted line in the list.

6 Click the Border button arrow on the Tables and Borders toolbar and then click Top Border. Click the Border button arrow on the Tables and Borders toolbar and then click Bottom Border. Click the Tables and Borders button on the Standard toolbar to remove the Tables and Borders toolbar from the Word window.

7 Click the paragraph mark in line 2 (below the dotted line border). Type `Feature Article` and then press the SPACEBAR. Press the CTRL+I keys to turn on italics. Type `(continued)` and then press the CTRL+I keys to turn off italics. Double-click the move handle on the Formatting toolbar to display the entire toolbar. Change the font color back to Automatic.

The nameplate and article continued message for page two are complete (Figure 6-73).

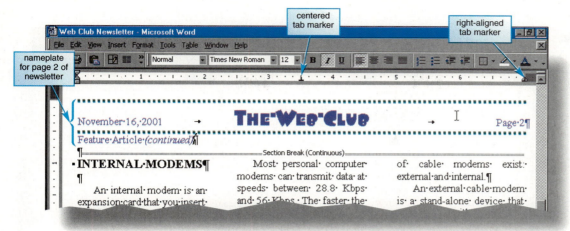

FIGURE 6-73

The next step is to balance the columns on the second page of the newsletter.

Balancing Columns

Currently, the text on the second page of the newsletter fills up the first and second columns completely and spills into a portion of the third column. You would like the text in the three columns to consume the same amount of vertical space; that is, they should be balanced. To balance columns, you insert a continuous section break at the end of the text as shown in the following steps.

Steps To Balance Columns

1 Scroll to the bottom of the text in the third column on the second page of the newsletter and then click the paragraph mark below the text. Click Insert on the menu bar and then click Break. When the Break dialog box displays, click Continuous in the Section break types area. Point to the OK button.

Word displays the Break dialog box (Figure 6-74).

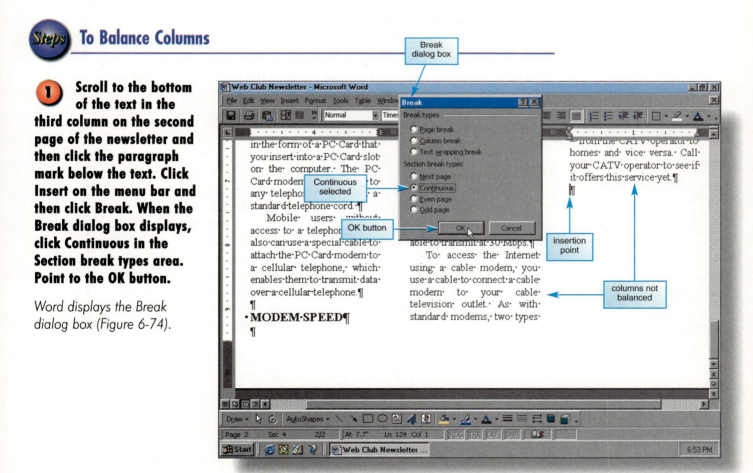

FIGURE 6-74

Click the OK button.

Word inserts a continuous section break, which balances the columns on the second page of the newsletter (Figure 6-75).

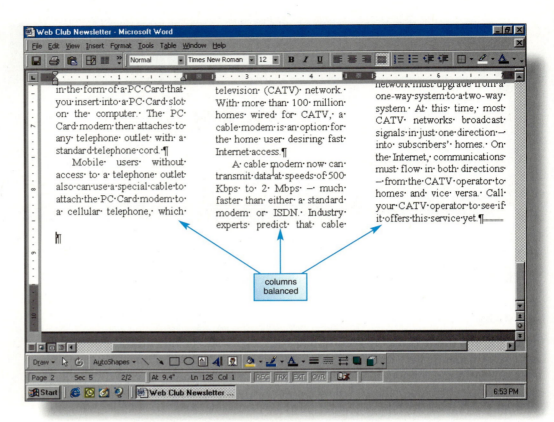

FIGURE 6-75

The next step is to insert a picture between the first and second columns on the second page of the newsletter.

Positioning Graphics on the Page

Graphic files are available from a variety of sources. You have learned that Word 2000 includes a clip gallery and Microsoft has the Clip Gallery Live Web page, both of which provide a host of clip art files. You also can insert a picture or photograph into a Word document. If you have a scanner attached to your computer, Word can insert a scanned picture directly from the scanner; or you can scan the picture into a file and then insert the scanned file into the Word document at a later time.

In this project, you insert a scanned file into the newsletter and position it between the first and second columns on the second page. Like clip art, pictures are inserted as inline. You want the text in the first two columns to wrap around the picture. An inline picture can be moved only from within one column to another; that is, not between columns. Thus, you must change the picture from inline to floating so you can position it between the columns.

The picture is named PC Card and is located on the Data Disk. Perform the following steps to insert the picture and then position it between columns in the newsletter.

Graphics

The use of real photographs in a newsletter adds professionalism to the document. You can insert them yourself if you have a scanner; otherwise, you can work with a print shop. When using photographs, you may need to crop, or trim out, the edges. If you have a scanner, you usually can crop the images using software provided with the scanner.

Steps **To Insert a Picture**

1 Scroll through the document and position the insertion point on the paragraph mark immediately below the PC CARD MODEMS subhead in the first column on the second page of the newsletter. Click Insert on the menu bar, point to Picture, and then point to From File (Figure 6-76).

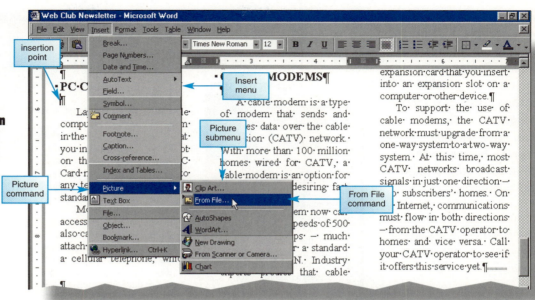

FIGURE 6-76

2 If necessary, insert the Data Disk into drive A. Click From File. When the Insert Picture dialog box displays, if necessary, change the Look in location to drive A. Click PC Card. Point to the Insert button.

Word displays the Insert Picture dialog box (Figure 6-77).

3 Click the Insert button.

Word inserts the picture into your document as an inline object (see Figure 6-78 on the next page).

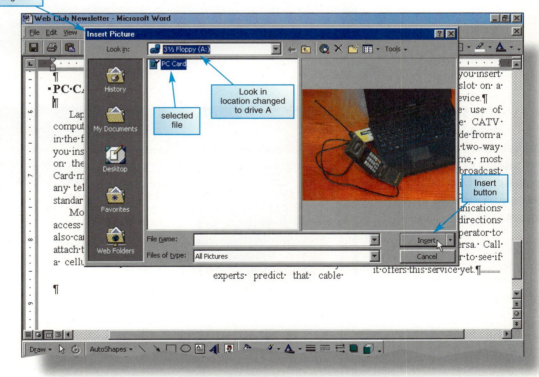

FIGURE 6-77

The next step is to change the graphic from inline to floating and then position it between the first and second columns on the second page of the newsletter.

To Wrap Text Around a Graphic

1 **Click the picture graphic to select it. If the Picture toolbar does not display, right-click the graphic and then click Show Picture Toolbar on the shortcut menu. Click the Text Wrapping button on the Picture toolbar and then point to Square.**

The wrapping styles specify how the text in the document displays with or around the graphic (Figure 6-78).

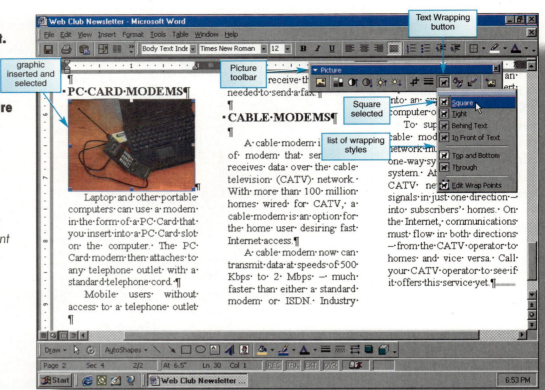

FIGURE 6-78

2 **Click Square. Scroll down to display the graphic. Point to the middle of the graphic so the mouse has a four-headed arrow attached to it.**

Word changes the wrapping style to square so that the text wraps around the graphic (Figure 6-79).

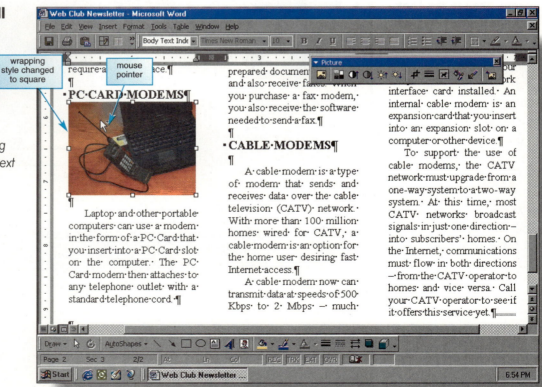

FIGURE 6-79

3 Drag the graphic to the desired location. You may have to drag the graphic a couple of times to position it similarly to Figure 6-80. Click outside the graphic to remove the selection.

As the graphic moves, a dotted border indicates its new location if you release the mouse button at that moment (Figure 6-80). Depending on the printer you are using, your wordwrap may occur in different locations.

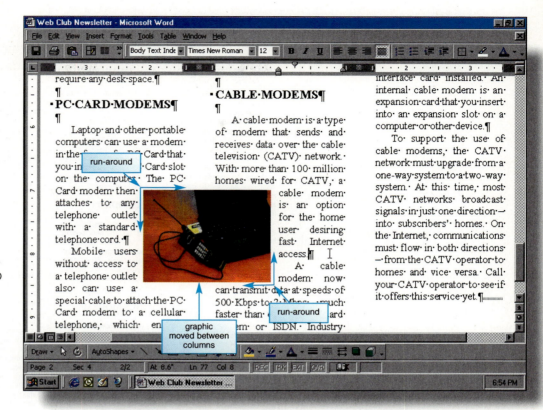

FIGURE 6-80

Notice in Figure 6-80 that the text in columns one and two wraps around the picture. Thus, it is called wrap-around text. The wrap-around forms a square because of the wrapping style set in Step 3. The space between the picture and the wrap-around text is called the run-around.

The second page of the newsletter is complete, with the exception of the page border. Perform the following steps to print the second page of the newsletter.

TO PRINT A PAGE

1 Click File on the menu bar and then click Print.

2 When the Print dialog box displays, click Current page in the Page range area.

3 Click the OK button.

Word prints the second page of the newsletter (Figure 6-81 on the next page).

More About 2000

Run-Around

The run-around should be at least 1/8" and should be the same for all graphics in the newsletter. Adjust the run-around of a selected graphic by clicking the Format Picture button on the Picture toolbar, clicking the Layout tab, clicking the Advanced button, adjusting the Distance from text boxes, and then clicking the OK button.

FIGURE 6-81

THE WEB CLUB newsletter page (shown in Figure 6-81)

November 16, 2001 — THE WEB CLUB — Page 2

Feature Article *(continued)*

INTERNAL MODEMS

An internal modem is an expansion card that you insert into an expansion slot on a computer's motherboard; the modem then attaches to a telephone outlet with a standard telephone cord.

Many devices other than computers also use internal modems. A stand-alone fax machine, for example, has an internal modem that converts a scanned digitized image into an analog signal that can be sent to the recipient's fax machine.

One important advantage of internal modems over external modems is that internal modems do not require any desk space.

PC CARD MODEMS

Laptop and other portable computers can use a modem in the form of a PC Card that you insert into a PC Card slot on the computer. The PC Card modem then attaches to any telephone outlet with a standard telephone cord.

Mobile users without access to a telephone outlet also can use a special cable to attach the PC Card modem to a cellular telephone, which enables them to transmit data over a cellular telephone.

MODEM SPEED

Most personal computer modems can transmit data at speeds between 28.8 Kbps and 56 Kbps. The faster the transfer rate, the faster you can send and receive.

FAX MODEMS

Many modems today are called fax modems because they can send computer-prepared documents as faxes and also receive faxes. When you purchase a fax modem, you also receive the software needed to send a fax.

CABLE MODEMS

A cable modem is a type of modem that sends and receives data over the cable television (CATV) network. With more than 100 million homes wired for CATV, a cable modem is an option for the home user desiring fast Internet access.

A cable modem now can transmit data at speeds of 500 Kbps to 2 Mbps – much faster than either a standard modem or ISDN. Industry experts predict that cable modems eventually will be able to transmit at 30 Mbps.

To access the Internet using a cable modem, you use a cable to connect a cable modem to your cable television outlet. As with standard modems, two types of cable modems exist: external and internal.

An external cable modem is a stand-alone device that you connect with a cable to a port on your computer's network interface card, which is an expansion card that allows hardware to be connected to a network. Using an external cable modem thus requires your computer to have a network interface card installed. An internal cable modem is an expansion card that you insert into an expansion slot on a computer or other device.

To support the use of cable modems, the CATV network must upgrade from a one-way system to a two-way system. At this time, most CATV networks broadcast signals in just one direction – into subscribers' homes. On the Internet, communications must flow in both directions – from the CATV operator to homes and vice versa. Call your CATV operator to see if it offers this service yet.

Enhancing the Newsletter with Color and a Page Border

You already have added color to many of the characters and lines in the newsletter in this project. You also want to color all of the subheads and add a border around each page of the newsletter. The following pages illustrate these tasks.

The first step is to color the dropped capital letter.

TO COLOR THE DROP CAP

1 Scroll to the top of the newsletter and then select the drop cap by clicking to its left.

2 Click the Font Color button arrow on the Formatting toolbar and then click Teal.

Word changes the color of the dropped capital letter to teal (see Figure 6-82).

Using the Format Painter Button

You have learned that subheads are internal headings placed throughout the body of the newsletter, such as SIGNAL CONVERSION and THE MODEM. Thus far, the subheads are bold and have a font size of 14. You also want all of the subheads italicized and colored teal.

Instead of selecting each subhead one at a time and then formatting it to italics and changing its color, you can format the first subhead and then copy its formatting to another location. To copy formatting, use the **Format Painter button** on the Standard toolbar as shown in the following steps.

To Use the Format Painter Button

1 Select the characters in the subhead, SIGNAL CONVERSION. Click the Italic button on the Formatting toolbar. Click the Font Color button on the Formatting toolbar. Click somewhere in the SIGNAL CONVERSION subhead. Double-click the move handle on the Standard toolbar to display the entire toolbar. Click the Format Painter button on the Standard toolbar. Move the mouse pointer into the document window.

Word attaches a paintbrush to the mouse pointer when the Format Painter button is recessed (Figure 6-82). The 14-point Times New Roman teal, bold italic font has been copied by the format painter.

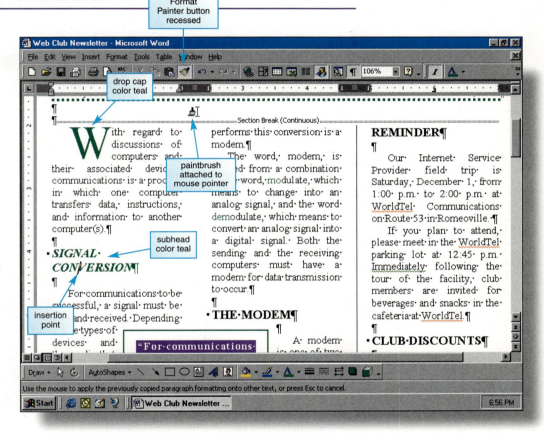

FIGURE 6-82

2 Scroll through the newsletter to the next subhead, THE MODEM. Select the subhead by clicking to its left. Click outside the selection to remove the highlight.

Word copies the 14-point Times New Roman teal, bold italic font to the subhead THE MODEM (Figure 6-83). The Format Painter button on the Standard toolbar no longer is recessed.

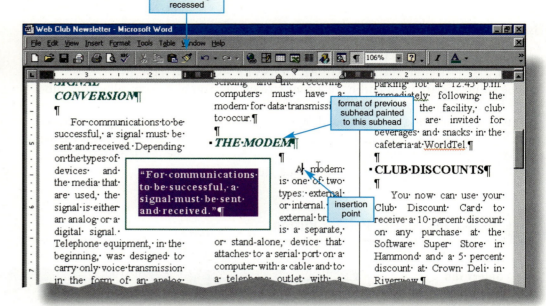

FIGURE 6-83

If you want to copy formatting to multiple locations in a document, double-click the Format Painter button, which will remain recessed until you click it again. Then highlight each location where you want the format copied. When you are finished copying the character formatting, click the Format Painter button again to restore the normal I-beam pointer. Use the Format Painter button to color the remaining subheads in the newsletter as described in the following steps.

TO COLOR THE REMAINING SUBHEADS IN THE NEWSLETTER

1 Position the insertion point in the subhead THE MODEM. Double-click the Format Painter button on the Standard toolbar.

2 Scroll to the second page of the newsletter and then click to the left of the INTERNAL MODEMS, PC CARD MODEMS, MODEM SPEED, FAX MODEMS, and CABLE MODEMS subheads to format them the same as the subhead THE MODEM.

3 Click the Format Painter button on the Standard toolbar to turn off the format painter.

4 Scroll to the top of the third column in the first page of the newsletter. Selec the REMINDER subhead. Double-click the move handle on the Formatting toolbar to display the entire toolbar. Click the Italic button on the Formatting toolbar. Click the Font Color button on the Formatting toolbar.

5 Double-click the move handle on the Standard toolbar to display the entire toolbar. Double-click the Format Painter button on the Standard toolbar.

6 Scroll to and then click to the left of the CLUB DISCOUNTS and WEB SITE subheads.

7 Click the Format Painter button on the Standard toolbar to turn off the format painter.

The subheads in the newsletter are formatted (see Figure 6-1 on page WD 6.5).

The next step in enhancing the newsletter is to add a border around each page.

Adding a Page Border

You have added borders to the edges of a paragraph(s). In Word, you also can add a border around the perimeter of an entire page. Page borders add professionalism to your documents. Perform the following steps to add a violet page border to the pages of the newsletter.

 **To Add a Page Border**

1 **Click Format on the menu bar and then click Borders and Shading. When the Borders and Shading dialog box displays, if necessary, click the Page Border tab. Click Box in the Setting area. Scroll through the Style list and click the style shown in Figure 6-84. Click the Color box arrow and then click Violet. Point to the OK button.**

Word displays the Borders and Shading dialog box (Figure 6-84). The page border is set to a 3-point violet box.

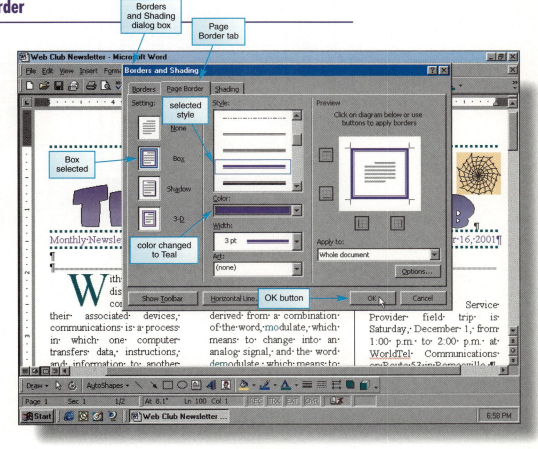

FIGURE 6-84

2 **Click the OK button.**

Word places a page border on each page of the newsletter (see Figure 6-85 on the next page).

To see the borders on the newsletter, display both pages in the document window as described in the following step.

TO ZOOM TWO PAGES

1 Click the Zoom box arrow and then click Two Pages in the list.

Word displays the pages of the newsletter in reduced form so both pages display in the document window (Figure 6-85 on the next page).

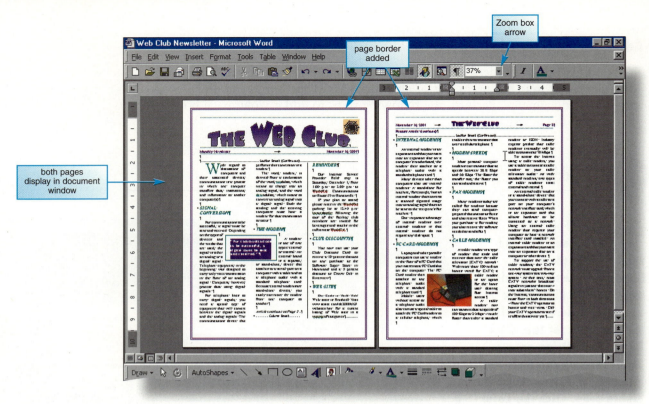

FIGURE 6-85

Perform the following step to return the display to zoom text width.

TO ZOOM TEXT WIDTH

 Click the Zoom box arrow and then click Text Width.

Word extends the right margin to the right edge of the document window.

The newsletter now is complete. You should save the document again and print it as described in the following series of steps.

TO SAVE A DOCUMENT

 With the disk containing the newsletter file in drive A, click the Save button on the Standard toolbar.

Word saves the document again with the name, Web Club Newsletter.

TO PRINT A DOCUMENT

 Click the Print button on the Standard toolbar.

The printed newsletter is shown in Figure 6-1 on page WD 6.5.

Highlighting Text

If you send this document via e-mail so recipients can view it on line, you may wish to highlight text. **Highlighting** alerts the reader to the text's importance, much like a highlight marker does in a textbook. The following steps illustrate how to highlight text yellow.

Steps ## To Highlight Text

1 **Press CTRL + HOME. Double-click the move handle on the Formatting toolbar to display the entire toolbar. Click the Highlight button arrow on the Formatting toolbar and then point to Yellow.**

Word displays a variety of highlight color options (Figure 6-86).

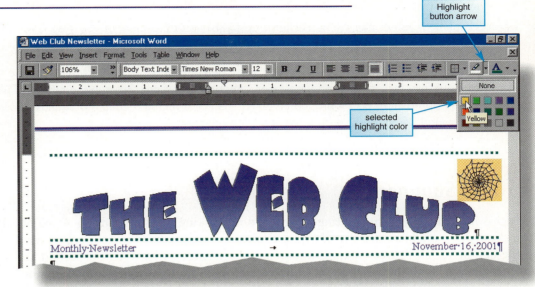

FIGURE 6-86

2 **Click Yellow. Drag through the REMINDER subhead in the document.**

Word highlights the selection yellow (Figure 6-87).

3 **Click the Highlight button to turn highlighting off.**

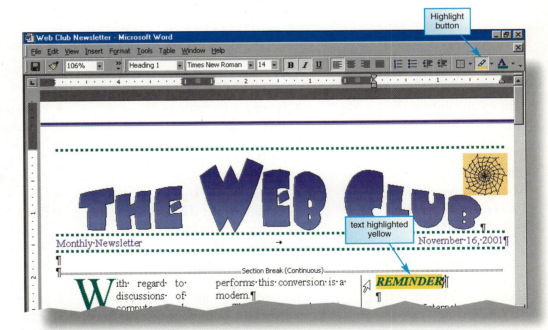

FIGURE 6-87

When the Highlight button is recessed, you can continue selecting text to be highlighted. Notice in Figure 6-86 that Word provides a variety of colors for highlighting text.

TO QUIT WORD

1 Click the Close button in the Word window.

The Word window closes.

Microsoft Certification

The Microsoft Office User Specialist (MOUS) Certification program provides an opportunity for you to obtain a valuable industry credential - proof that you have the Word 2000 skills required by employers. For more information, see Appendix D or visit the Shelly Cashman Series MOUS Web page at www.scsite.com/off2000/cert.htm.

CASE PERSPECTIVE SUMMARY

Upon completion, you e-mail the newsletter to Jamie Navaro, president of The Web Club, for his review. He thinks it looks great and gives you approval to distribute.

You print the newsletter on a color printer and send the color printout to the Duplicating Center to have 1,000 copies made. While the copies are being made, you submit the newsletter to the school's Public Relations department for their approval to post it around campus. Then, you recruit a couple of friends to assist you in posting the newsletter around campus and distributing it to club members.

Project Summary

Project 6 introduced you to creating a professional looking newsletter using Word's desktop publishing features. You created a nameplate using a WordArt drawing object and the current computer date. You formatted the body of the newsletter into three columns and added a vertical rule between the second and third columns. You linked another document to the newsletter. You created a pull-quote, inserted a picture, and learned how to move these graphical objects between columns. Finally, you used the Format Painter button and added a page border to the newsletter.

What You Should Know

Having completed this project, you should now be able to perform the following tasks:

▶ Add a Page Border (WD 6.59)
▶ Add More Ruling Lines (WD 6.18)
▶ Apply the Heading 1 Style (WD 6.33)
▶ Apply the Normal Style (WD 6.16, WD 6.22)
▶ Balance Columns (WD 6.51)
▶ Bold Text (WD 6.42)
▶ Center an Inline Object (WD 6.14)
▶ Change All Margin Settings (WD 6.7)
▶ Change Column Formatting (WD 6.48)
▶ Change Paragraph Indentation and Spacing (WD 6.43)
▶ Change the Shape of a WordArt Drawing Object (WD 6.14)
▶ Close a File (WD 6.37)
▶ Color the Drop Cap (WD 6.56)
▶ Color the Remaining Subheads in the Newsletter (WD 6.58)
▶ Display Formatting Marks (WD 6.7)
▶ Enter the Nameplate and Continued Message on the Second Page (WD 6.50)

▶ Format a Graphic as Floating (WD 6.20)
▶ Format a Letter as a Drop Cap (WD 6.28)
▶ Format a Text Box (WD 6.41)
▶ Format a WordArt Drawing Object (WD 6.12)
▶ Format Columns (WD 6.25)
▶ Highlight Text (WD 6.61)
▶ Increase Character Spacing (WD 6.42)
▶ Insert a Column Break (WD 6.31)
▶ Insert a Continuous Section Break (WD 6.24)
▶ Insert a File into a Column of the Newsletter (WD 6.32)
▶ Insert a File into the Newsletter (WD 6.27)
▶ Insert a Next Page Section Break (WD 6.30)
▶ Insert a Picture (WD 6.53)
▶ Insert a Text Box (WD 6.40)
▶ Insert a WordArt Drawing Object (WD 6.9)
▶ Insert Clip Art (WD 6.19)
▶ Insert the Current Date into a Document (WD 6.17)
▶ Justify a Paragraph (WD 6.26)
▶ Link an Object (WD 6.34)

▶ Place a Vertical Rule Between Columns (WD 6.37)
▶ Position a Text Box (WD 6.46)
▶ Print a Document (WD 6.60)
▶ Print a Page (WD 6.47, WD 6.55)
▶ Quit Word (WD 6.61)
▶ Reset Menus and Toolbars (WD 6.6)
▶ Resize a Text Box (WD 6.44)
▶ Save a Document (WD 6.46, WD 6.60))
▶ Save the Newsletter (WD 6.27)
▶ Set a Right-Aligned Tab Stop (WD 6.17)
▶ Set Tab Stops (WD 6.49)
▶ Shade a Graphic (WD 6.21)
▶ Shade a Paragraph (WD 6.45)
▶ Start Word (WD 6.6)
▶ Use Borders to Add a Ruling Line (WD 6.15)
▶ Use the Format Painter Button (WD 6.57)
▶ Wrap Text around a Graphic (WD 6.54)
▶ Zoom Text Width (WD 6.8, WD 6.33, Word 6.60))
▶ Zoom Two Pages (WD 6.59)
▶ Zoom Whole Page (WD 6.32)

Apply Your Knowledge

⊕ Project Reinforcement at www.scsite.com/off2000/reinforce.htm

1 Linking and Editing an Object

Instruction: Start Word. Open the documents, Play-Dough and Thank You Note, on the Data Disk. If you did not download the Data Disk, see the inside back cover for instructions for downloading the Data Disk or see your instructor.

Performing the steps below, you are to link the Play-Dough document into the Thank You Note document and then modify the source document (Play-Dough). The revised destination document (Thank You Note) is shown in Figure 6-88.

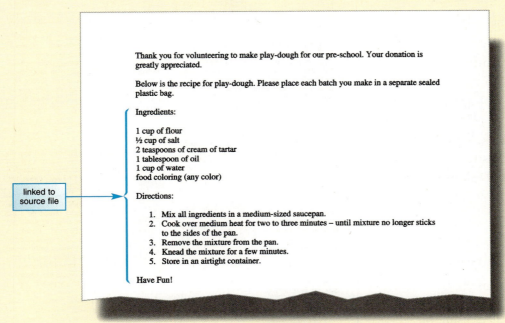

FIGURE 6-88

Perform the following tasks:

1. Click the Play-Dough program button on the taskbar. When the Play-Dough document window displays, click Edit on the menu bar and then click Select All. Click the Copy button on the Standard toolbar.

2. Click the Thank You Note program button on the taskbar. When the Thank You Note document window displays, position the insertion point on line 7. Click Edit on the menu bar and then click Paste Special. When the Paste Special dialog box displays, click Paste link, click Formatted Text (RTF) in the list, and then click the OK button.

3. Click the Play-Dough program button on the taskbar. When the Play-Dough document window displays, click anywhere to remove the selection. Highlight the text between the words, Directions and Have Fun. Click the Numbering button on the Formatting toolbar to number the list of directions.

4. Click the Save button on the Standard toolbar to save the revised Play-Dough file. Close the Play-Dough document window.

5. When the Thank You Note document window redisplays, click somewhere in the directions and then press F9.

6. Save the destination document with the name Revised Thank You Note.

7. Print the revised destination document.

In the Lab

1 Creating a Newsletter with a Picture and an Article on File

Problem: You are an editor of the *Home Photography* newsletter. The December 6th edition is due out next Thursday. The feature article will present options for electronic photographs (Figure 6-89). The newsletter also includes a scanned picture. The feature article and the picture are on the Data Disk. If you did not download the Data Disk, see the inside back cover for instructions for downloading the Data Disk or see your instructor.

Instructions:

1. Change all margins to .75 inch. Depending on your printer, you may need different margin settings.

2. Create the nameplate using the formats identified in Figure 6-89. Create a continuous section break below the nameplate. Format section 2 to two columns.

3. Insert the Electronic Photo Article on the Data Disk into section 2 below the nameplate.

4. Format the newsletter according to Figure 6-89. Use the Format Painter button to automate some of your formatting tasks. Insert the picture named, filmbag, from the Data Disk. Format the picture to square wrapping.

5. Save the document with Home Photography Newsletter as the file name. Print the newsletter.

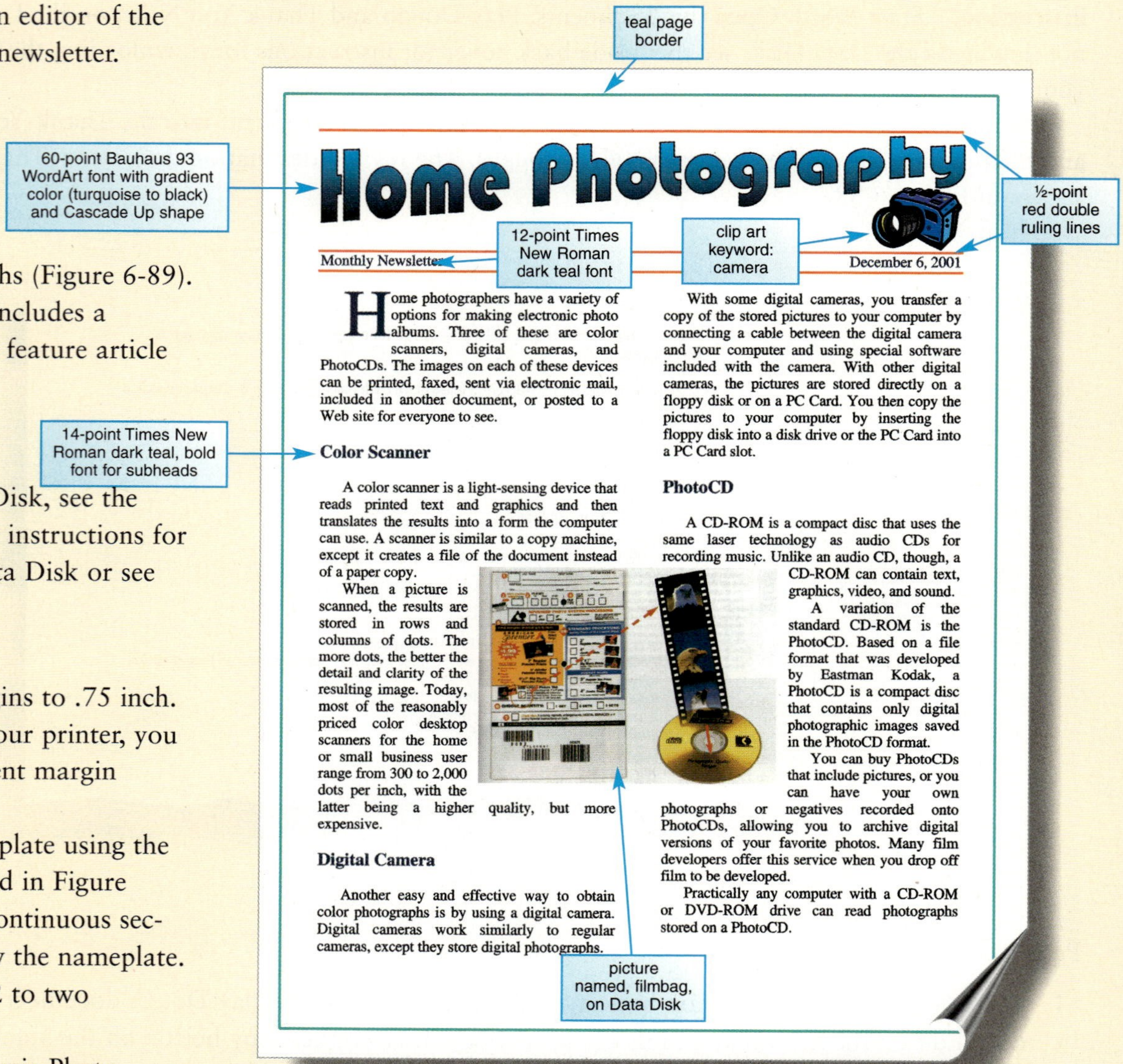

FIGURE 6-89

Figure annotations:
- teal page border
- 60-point Bauhaus 93 WordArt font with gradient color (turquoise to black) and Cascade Up shape
- ½-point red double ruling lines
- 12-point Times New Roman dark teal font
- clip art keyword: camera
- 14-point Times New Roman dark teal, bold font for subheads
- picture named, filmbag, on Data Disk

Home Photography

Monthly Newsletter   December 6, 2001

Home photographers have a variety of options for making electronic photo albums. Three of these are color scanners, digital cameras, and PhotoCDs. The images on each of these devices can be printed, faxed, sent via electronic mail, included in another document, or posted to a Web site for everyone to see.

Color Scanner

A color scanner is a light-sensing device that reads printed text and graphics and then translates the results into a form the computer can use. A scanner is similar to a copy machine, except it creates a file of the document instead of a paper copy.

When a picture is scanned, the results are stored in rows and columns of dots. The more dots, the better the detail and clarity of the resulting image. Today, most of the reasonably priced color desktop scanners for the home or small business user range from 300 to 2,000 dots per inch, with the latter being a higher quality, but more expensive.

Digital Camera

Another easy and effective way to obtain color photographs is by using a digital camera. Digital cameras work similarly to regular cameras, except they store digital photographs.

With some digital cameras, you transfer a copy of the stored pictures to your computer by connecting a cable between the digital camera and your computer and using special software included with the camera. With other digital cameras, the pictures are stored directly on a floppy disk or on a PC Card. You then copy the pictures to your computer by inserting the floppy disk into a disk drive or the PC Card into a PC Card slot.

PhotoCD

A CD-ROM is a compact disc that uses the same laser technology as audio CDs for recording music. Unlike an audio CD, though, a CD-ROM can contain text, graphics, video, and sound.

A variation of the standard CD-ROM is the PhotoCD. Based on a file format that was developed by Eastman Kodak, a PhotoCD is a compact disc that contains only digital photographic images saved in the PhotoCD format.

You can buy PhotoCDs that include pictures, or you can have your own photographs or negatives recorded onto PhotoCDs, allowing you to archive digital versions of your favorite photos. Many film developers offer this service when you drop off film to be developed.

Practically any computer with a CD-ROM or DVD-ROM drive can read photographs stored on a PhotoCD.

In the Lab

2 Creating a Newsletter with a Text Box and an Article on File

Problem: You are responsible for the monthly preparation of *Remodeling*, a newsletter for club members. The next edition is due out in two weeks, which is to discuss the layout, setting, and cutting of tiles for ceramic tile installation (Figure 6-90). This article already has been prepared and is on the Data Disk. If you did not download the Data Disk, see the inside back cover for instructions for downloading the Data Disk or see your instructor. You need to create the text box.

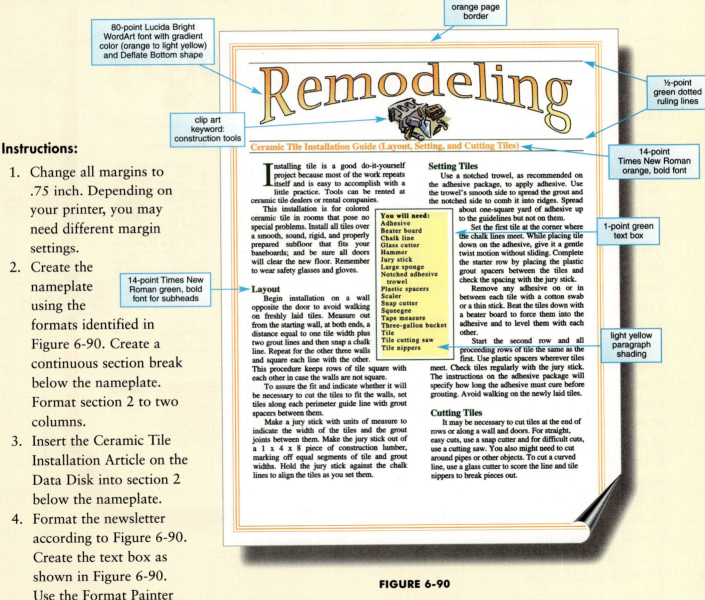

FIGURE 6-90

Instructions:

1. Change all margins to .75 inch. Depending on your printer, you may need different margin settings.
2. Create the nameplate using the formats identified in Figure 6-90. Create a continuous section break below the nameplate. Format section 2 to two columns.
3. Insert the Ceramic Tile Installation Article on the Data Disk into section 2 below the nameplate.
4. Format the newsletter according to Figure 6-90. Create the text box as shown in Figure 6-90. Use the Format Painter button to automate some of your formatting tasks.
5. Save the document with Remodeling Newsletter as the file name. Print the newsletter.

In the Lab

3 Creating a Newsletter from Scratch

Problem: You are a leader of *Young Explorers*, which publishes a newsletter for parents of children in your unit. You prepare a newsletter for distribution at each meeting (Figure 6-91).

Instructions:

1. Change all margins to .75 inch. Depending on your printer, you may need different margin settings.

2. Create the nameplate using the formats identified in Figure 6-91. *Hint*: Use the Shadow button on the Drawing toolbar to apply the shadow effect. Create a continuous section break below the nameplate. Format section 2 to three columns.

3. Enter announcements into section 2 below the nameplate.

4. Insert a continuous section break at the end of the announcements. Format section 3 to one column. Create the table as shown at the bottom of the newsletter.

5. Format the newsletter according to Figure 6-91. Place a vertical rule between all columns in section 2. Use the Line between check box in the Columns dialog box (Format menu) to do this. Use the Format Painter button to automate some of your formatting tasks.

6. Save the document with Young Explorers Newsletter as the file name. Print the newsletter.

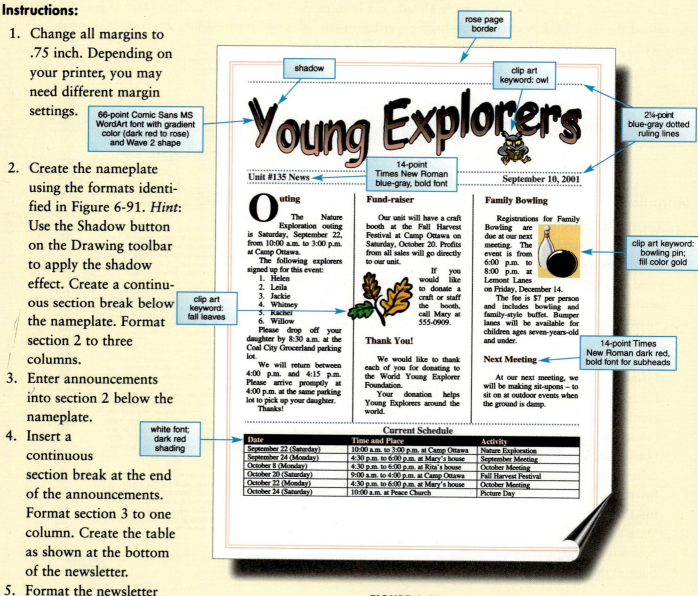

FIGURE 6-91

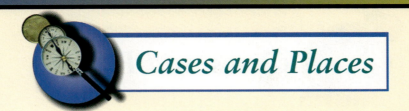

Cases and Places

The difficulty of these case studies varies:
❱ are the least difficult; ❱❱ are more difficult; and ❱❱❱ are the most difficult.

1 ❱   As your final project in CIS 144, you have been assigned the task of creating page WD 4.58 in this textbook. The page contains many desktop publishing elements: shading in the header and CASE PERSPECTIVE SUMMARY sections, extra space between characters in the CASE PERSPECTIVE SUMMARY, drop caps in the Project Summary and What You Should Know subheads, a variety of font sizes and font color, a paragraph border around the CASE PERSPECTIVE SUMMARY, and balanced columns in the What You Should Know section. You may need to resize and move the drop cap frame so it aligns properly with the subheads. To display the half moon bullets, click on the Customize button in the Bullets and Numbering dialog box. Click the Bullet button in the dialog box to locate the half moon bullet, and click the Font button in the dialog box to change the bullet color.

2 ❱❱   You are an editor of *Home Photography*, a one-page newsletter for amateur photographers. Last week's edition is shown in Figure 6-89 on page WD 6.64. The January 3rd edition is due out next Thursday. Your assignment is to decide on a feature article for the next edition of the *Home Photography* newsletter. Use your personal experiences as the basis for your feature article. Your article could address an item such as these: taking pictures, types of cameras, camera features, making photo albums, and so on. The newsletter should contain an appropriate photograph or clip art, a text box, or a pull-quote for the feature article. Enhance the newsletter with WordArt, color, ruling lines, and a page border using colors different from those used in Figure 6-89.

3 ❱❱   You are responsible for the monthly preparation of *Remodeling*, a one-page newsletter for club members. Last month's edition is shown in Figure 6-90 on page WD 6.65. The next edition is due out in two weeks. Your assignment is to decide on a feature article for the next edition of the newsletter. The feature article should address some aspect of remodeling. For example, your feature article could discuss remodeling tools, remodeling projects, remodeling tips, or any other remodeling topic that interests you. Visit a home improvement store for information for your article. The newsletter should contain an appropriate photograph or clip art, a text box, or a pull-quote for the feature article. Enhance the newsletter with WordArt, color, ruling lines, and a page border using colors different from those used in Figure 6-90.

4 ❱❱   You are the editor of *Young Explorers*, a one-page monthly newsletter for the parents of unit members. Last meeting's newsletter is shown in Figure 6-91. The next meeting is on September 24. Your assignment is to develop some announcements for the next meeting of the *Young Explorers*. Your announcements could address items such as these: upcoming events and activities, meeting plans, notices, and so on. The newsletter should contain an appropriate photograph or clip art, a text box, or a pull-quote for the feature article. Enhance the newsletter with WordArt, color, ruling lines, and a page border using colors different from those used in Figure 6-91.

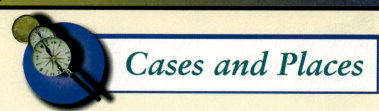

Cases and Places

5 ▶▶▶ You are a member of your child's parent-teacher organization (PTO). The PTO has decided to publish a two-page monthly newsletter to be sent home with all children in the district. You must decide on a title for the newsletter. Your assignment is to design the newsletter and develop the first issue. The newsletter could include a feature article, announcements, information, notices, or other items of interest to parents. Visit a school in your district to obtain information about schools in the district. Use the Internet, school newsletters, PTO meeting minutes, school board meeting minutes, teacher interviews, and parent interviews for information on your article. Enhance the newsletter with WordArt, color, shading, ruling lines, and a page border. Use an appropriate graphic and a pull-quote in the newsletter.

6 ▶▶▶ You are a member of a restaurant and food review club. Because you have a background in desktop publishing, you prepare the monthly two-page newsletter for club members. Your assignment is to design the newsletter and develop the next issue. The newsletter should have a feature article and some announcements for club members. Your feature article could discuss/review a restaurant, a deli, an online or in town grocery store, a recipe, or any other aspect of food or food service. Use the Internet, visit a restaurant, interview restaurant or grocery store patrons, prepare a dish using a new recipe, and so on, to obtain information for the feature article. The feature article should span both pages of the newsletter and club announcements should be on the first page of the newsletter. Enhance the newsletter with WordArt, color, shading, ruling lines, and a page border. Use an appropriate graphic and a pull-quote in the newsletter.

Microsoft **Word 2000**

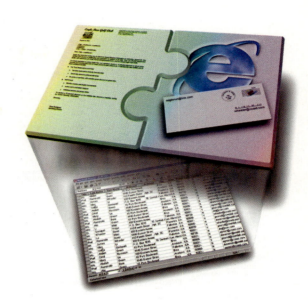

Microsoft Word 2000

Merging Form Letters to E-Mail Addresses Using an Access Table

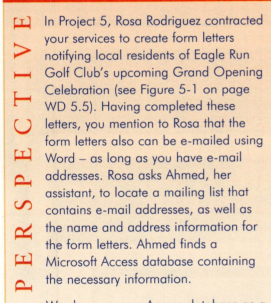

In Project 5, Rosa Rodriguez contracted your services to create form letters notifying local residents of Eagle Run Golf Club's upcoming Grand Opening Celebration (see Figure 5-1 on page WD 5.5). Having completed these letters, you mention to Rosa that the form letters also can be e-mailed using Word – as long as you have e-mail addresses. Rosa asks Ahmed, her assistant, to locate a mailing list that contains e-mail addresses, as well as the name and address information for the form letters. Ahmed finds a Microsoft Access database containing the necessary information.

Word can use an Access database as a data source, providing the fields are set up to match the form letter fields. Because the database is missing the Student field, you explain to Ahmed how to add a new field to a database table and how to enter data into the field. Then, with your assistance, Ahmed sends the form letters to e-mail addresses using the Access database table.

To complete this Integration Feature, you will need the main document for the form letters created in Project 5. (If you did not create the form letters, see your instructor for a copy.)

Introduction

You learned in Project 5 that the basic content of a group of **form letters** is similar; however, items such as name, address, city, state, and postal code change from one letter to the next. Thus, form letters are personalized to the addressee.

The process of generating form letters involves creating a main document for the form letters and a data source, and then merging the two together into a series of individual letters. In Project 5, you set up a Word table as a data source. In addition to Word tables, you can use a Microsoft Outlook contact list, a Microsoft Excel worksheet, a Microsoft Access database table, or a text file as the data source for form letters.

In this Integration Feature, you open the Eagle Run Grand Opening main document file (Figure 1a on the next page). Then, you specify that you will use an Access database table (Figure 1b on the next page) as the data source. The database table, which contains an Email field, is located on the Data Disk. Next, you merge data from the Access database table into the main document, Eagle Run Grand Opening.

In Project 5, you learned that you can send merged documents to the printer or to a new document window. In this Integration Feature, you send the merged documents to e-mail addresses – attaching the form letter as a Word document to each e-mail message. This merge process creates a separate e-mail message for each person in the database table. Figure 1c on the next page shows the five e-mail messages created by this merge. Each message contains an icon that when opened, displays the merged document in a Word window.

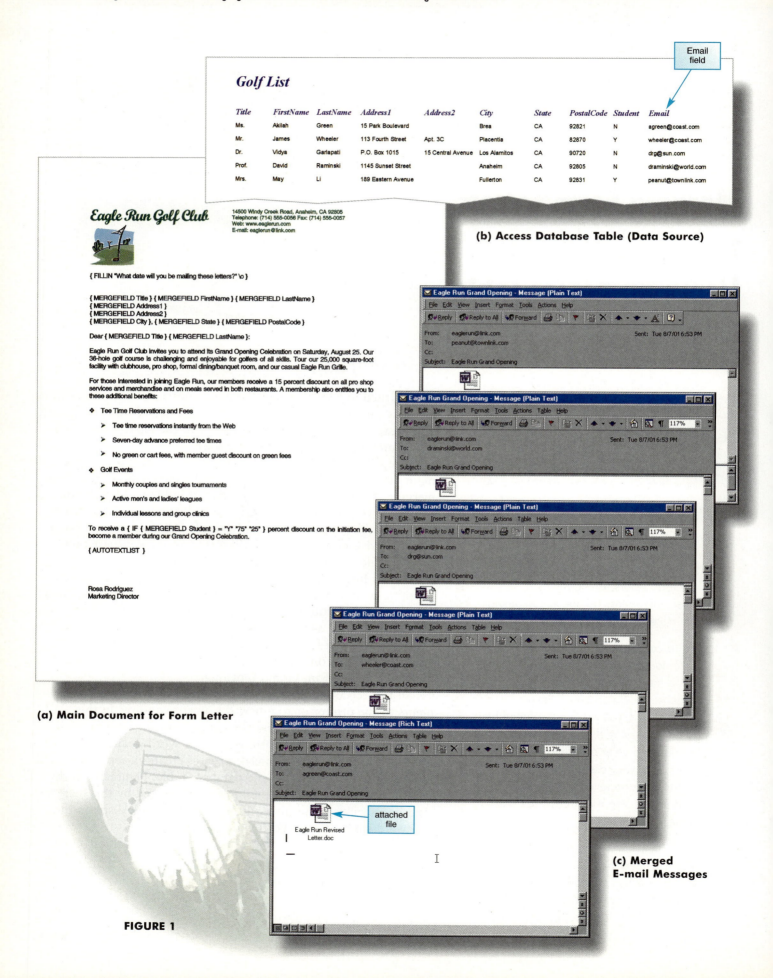

FIGURE 1

Unlinking a Field

The date line in the main document for the form letter currently is a Fill-in field. When you merge the letters, the Fill-in field instructs Word to display a dialog box requesting that you enter the date these letters will be mailed. In Project 5, you indicated that the question should display only once – at the beginning of the merge process. When you merge to e-mail addresses, Word asks the question for each record; thus, you should remove this field designation, or **unlink the field**, so that it displays as regular text.

Perform the following steps to unlink the Fill-in field.

TO UNLINK A FIELD

1 Start Word and then open the Eagle Run Grand Opening file created in Project 5. Reset your toolbars as described in Appendix C.

2 Click in the date field.

3 Press CTRL+SHIFT+F9. Click anywhere in the date field to remove the highlight.

Word removes the field designation from the date (Figure 2).

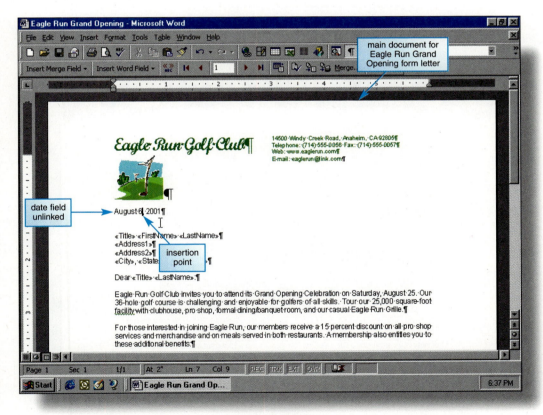

FIGURE 2

Changing the Data Source in a Form Letter

Currently, the data source for the Eagle Run Grand Opening form letter is a Word table that you saved in a file named Mailing List. The data source in this Integration Feature should be an Access database table.

More About

Mailing Lists

For more information on mailing lists available for purchase or download, visit the Word 2000 More About Web page (www.scsite.com/wd2000/more.htm) and then click Mailing Lists.

A **database** is a collection of data organized in a manner that allows access, retrieval, and use of that data. **Database software**, also called a **database management system** (**DBMS**), allows you to create a computerized database; add, change, and delete data; sort and retrieve data from the database; and create forms and reports using the data.

Microsoft Access is database software included with Microsoft Office. In Access, a database consists of a collection of tables, organized in rows and columns. You have learned that a row in a table also is called a **record**; and a column in a table also is called a **field**.

The Access database you will use for this Integration Feature is called Golf Prospects and is located on the Data Disk. The table in the database that you will link to the form letters is called Golf List. If you did not download the Data Disk, see the inside back cover for instructions for downloading the Data Disk or see your instructor.

Perform the following steps to change the data source designation to an Access database table.

Steps To Change a Data Source Designation

1 **Click the Mail Merge Helper button on the Mail Merge toolbar. Click the Get Data button and then point to Open Data Source (Figure 3).**

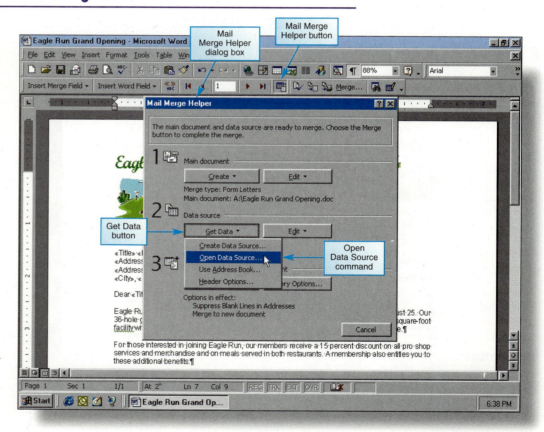

FIGURE 3

2 If necessary, insert the Data Disk into drive A. Click Open Data Source. If necessary, when the Open Data Source dialog box displays, change the Look in location to 3½ Floppy (A:). Click the Files of type box arrow and then click MS Access Databases. Click Golf Prospects in the Look in list and then point to the Open button in the Open Data Source dialog box.

Word displays the Open Data Source dialog box (Figure 4). The Access database you will use is named Golf Prospects.

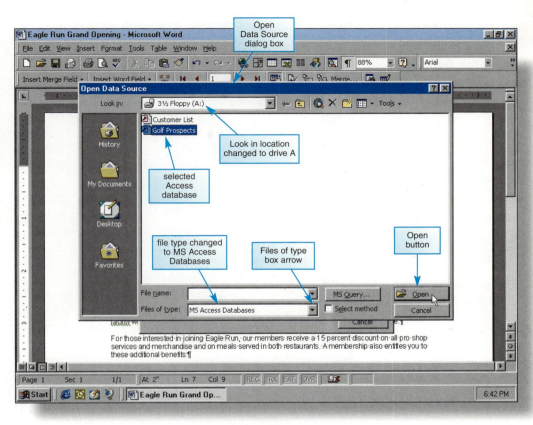

FIGURE 4

3 Click the Open button in the Open Data Source dialog box. If necessary, when the Microsoft Access dialog box displays, click the Tables tab. Click Golf List in the Tables in Golf Prospects list and then point to the OK button.

Word closes the Open Data Source dialog box and starts Microsoft Access; a Microsoft Access dialog box displays, listing the tables in the Golf Prospects database (Figure 5). You select the table to be linked to the form letter.

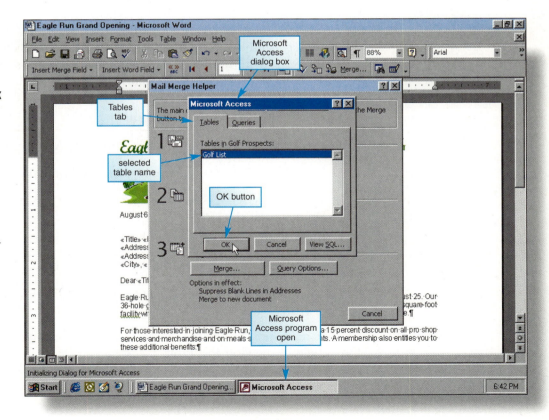

FIGURE 5

4 **Click the OK button. Point to the Close button in the Mail Merge Helper dialog box.**

The Mail Merge Helper dialog box is visible again (Figure 6). Word lists the Access table name as the data source for the form letters.

5 **Click the Close button.**

Word closes the Mail Merge Helper dialog box.

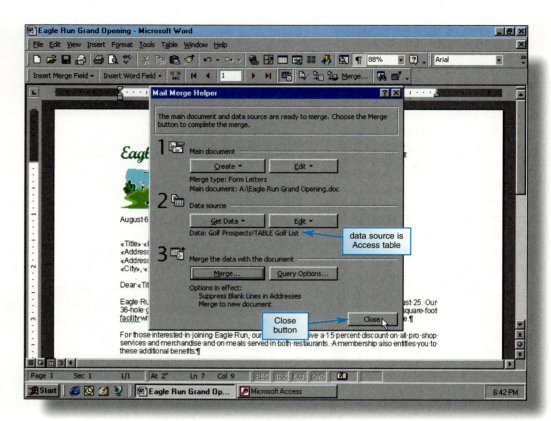

FIGURE 6

The Access table now is the data source for the form letter. To maintain the original form letter with the Word table as the data source, save this form letter with a new file name as described in the following steps.

TO SAVE THE FORM LETTER WITH A NEW FILE NAME

1 If necessary, insert a floppy disk into drive A.

2 Click File on the menu bar and then click Save As.

3 Type the file name `Eagle Run Revised Letter` in the File name text box. Do not press the ENTER key.

4 If necessary, click the Save in box arrow and then click 3½ Floppy (A:).

5 Click the Save button in the Save As dialog box.

Word saves the form letter on a floppy disk in drive A with the file name Eagle Run Revised Letter.

The next step is to merge the documents to the e-mail addresses specified in the Email field of the Golf List table.

Merging to E-Mail Addresses

When you merge to e-mail addresses, you can instruct Word to insert the merged document into the body of the e-mail message or to include the merged document as a separate Word document that is attached to each e-mail message. By sending the merged document as an attachment, you preserve all Word formatting. Thus, perform the following steps to merge the form letters to e-mail addresses, sending each merged document as an attachment to each e-mail message.

More *About*

Merging

To merge only those records that contain an e-mail address, click the Merge button on the Mail Merge toolbar, click the Query Options button, click the Filter Records tab, click the Field box arrow, click the field name that contains the e-mail addresses, click the Comparison box arrow, click is not blank, and then click the OK button.

 To Merge to E-Mail Addresses

1 **Click the Merge button on the Mail Merge toolbar. When the Merge dialog box displays, point to the Merge to box arrow.**

Word displays the Merge dialog box (Figure 7).

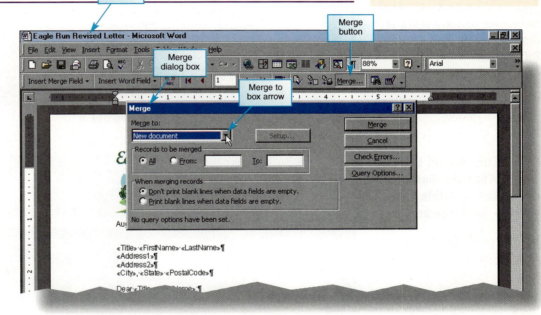

FIGURE 7

2 **Click the Merge to box arrow and then click Electronic mail. Point to the Setup button (Figure 8).**

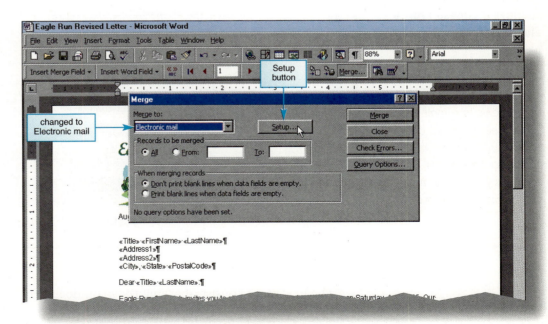

FIGURE 8

3 **Click the Setup button. When Word displays the Merge To Setup dialog box, click the Data field with Mail/Fax address box arrow. Scroll to and then click Email. Press the TAB key and then type** Eagle Run Grand Opening **as the subject line for the e-mail message. Click Send document as an attachment to display a check mark in the check box. Point to the OK button.**

Word displays the Merge To Setup dialog box (Figure 9).

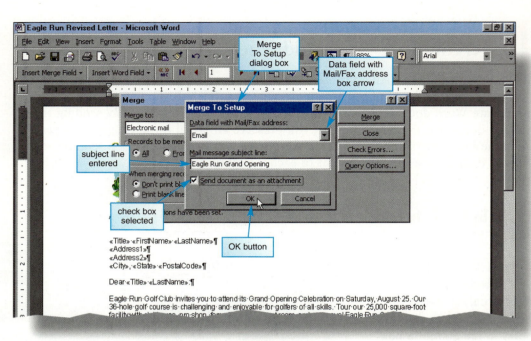

FIGURE 9

4 **Click the OK button. When the Merge dialog box is visible again, point to its Merge button.**

The Merge dialog box is visible again (Figure 10).

5 **Click the Merge button in the Merge dialog box. If Word displays a Choose Profile dialog box, click the OK button.**

Word merges the form letters and distributes them as attachments to e-mail messages (see Figure 1c on page WDI 1.2). If you are not connected to the Internet, Word connects you so the messages can be delivered.

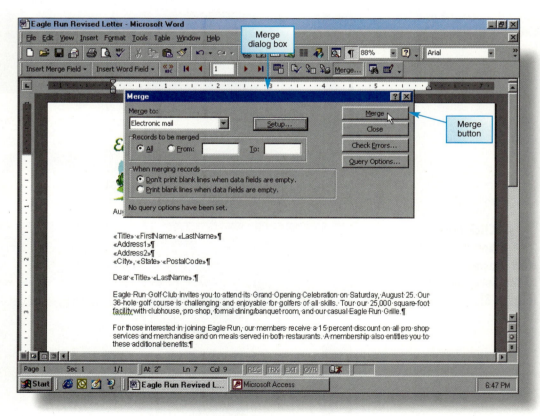

FIGURE 10

The next steps consist of saving the main document again and then quitting Word.

TO SAVE THE MAIN DOCUMENT AGAIN

 Click the Save button on the Standard toolbar.

Word saves the form letters with the name Eagle Run Revised Letter on a disk in drive A.

TO QUIT WORD

 Click the Close button at the right edge of Word's title bar.

The Word window closes.

More *About*

Quick Reference

For a table that lists how to complete the tasks covered in this book using the mouse, menu, shortcut menu, and keyboard, visit the Shelly Cashman Series Office Web page (www.scsite.com/off2000/qr.htm) and then click Microsoft Word 2000.

C A S E   P E R S P E C T I V E   S U M M A R Y

To verify that the merge worked correctly, Ahmed added his own personal information as a record in the Access database table – which means he should have an e-mail message with the subject of Eagle Run Grand Opening in his Inbox. Ahmed starts Outlook and checks his messages. The announcement of the grand opening is there!

Ahmed is amazed at how easy it is to distribute form letters to e-mail addresses. He shows Rosa the e-mail message he sent himself. He informs Rosa that the announcement also has been e-mailed to all the people listed in the Golf List database table. She is impressed.

Integration Feature Summary

This Integration Feature introduced you to specifying an existing Access database as a data source. You also learned how to merge documents and distribute them to e-mail addresses as attachments to the e-mail messages.

More *About*

Microsoft Certification

The Microsoft Office User Specialist (MOUS) Certification program provides an opportunity for you to obtain a valuable industry credential - proof that you have the Word 2000 skills required by employers. For more information, see Appendix D or visit the Shelly Cashman Series MOUS Web page at www.scsite.com/off2000/cert.htm.

In the Lab

1 Using an Access Database Table for a Merge

Problem: Marianne Pulaski, owner of Orland Flowers and Gifts, has an Access database table that she would like you to merge with the form letter shown in Figure 5-81 on page WD 5.59 in Project 5.

Instructions:

1. Open the document, Orland Flowers Holiday Special, on the Data Disk. If you did not download the Data Disk, see the inside back cover for instructions for downloading the Data Disk or see your instructor.
2. Using the Get Data button in the Mail Merge Helper dialog box, specify the data source as the database file called Customer List on the Data Disk. The table name is Customers.
3. Save the main document using Orland Flowers Revised Letter as the file name.
4. Merge the documents to the printer.

2 Distributing Form Letters to E-Mail Addresses

Problem: You created the form letter shown in Figure 5-82 on page WD 5.60 in Project 5. You decide to modify the Word data source to include e-mail addresses and then distribute the letter to the e-mail addresses.

Instructions:

1. Open the Taxton Welcome Letter shown in Figure 5-82. (If you did not create the form letter, see your instructor for a copy.)
2. Switch to the data source so that it displays as a Word table on the screen. Add a field called, Email, to the data source. Enter the following e-mail addresses: ramos@ocean.com, cw@eastern.com, van@worldwide.com, spelbring@somer.com, dawn@ocean.com. Add a row to the table containing your personal information. Save the revised data source with the file name Taxton New Students Revised.
3. Switch to the main document. Merge the form letters to the e-mail addresses, sending the letter as an attachment to the e-mail messages. Print the e-mail message that is delivered to your Inbox.
4. Save the main document using Taxton Revised Letter as the file name.

In the Lab

3 Creating an Access Table for a Merge to E-Mail Addresses

Problem: Robert Beatty, owner of Williams Landscaping, would like you to create an Access database table that he could merge with the form letter shown in Figure 5-84 on page WD 5.61 in Project 5.

Instructions:

1. Start Access. Create a database called Landscaping that contains a table called Landscaping Customers. The data for the table is shown in Figure 5-85 on page WD 5.62 in Project 5. Add an Email field with suitable e-mail adresses. Add a record to the table containing your personal information. You may need to use Help in Access to assist you in the procedure for creating and saving a database that contains a table. Save the table and then quit Access.

2. Start Word. Open the document, Williams Landscaping Form Letter, from your floppy disk. (If you did not create the form letter, see your instructor for a copy.)

3. Using the Get Data button in the Mail Merge Helper dialog box, specify the data source as the database file you created in Step 1.

4. Merge the form letters to the e-mail addresses, sending the letter as an attachment to the e-mail messages. Print the e-mail message that is delivered to your Inbox.

5. Save the main document using Williams Landscaping Revised Letter as the file name.

Microsoft Excel 2000

Microsoft Excel 2000

PROJECT

4

Financial Functions, Data Tables, Amortization Schedules, and Hyperlinks

O B J E C T I V E S

You will have mastered the material in this project when you can:

- Control the colors and thickness of outlines and borders
- Assign a name to a cell and refer to the cell in a formula by using the assigned name
- Determine the monthly payment of a loan using the financial function PMT
- Enter a series of percents using the fill handle
- Create a data table to analyze data in a worksheet
- Add a pointer to a data table using conditional formatting
- Determine a present value of a loan using the PV function
- Create an amortization schedule
- Analyze worksheet data by changing values
- Add a hyperlink to a workbook
- Protect and unprotect cells
- Analyze worksheet data by goal seeking

Making Your Home Where the Living is Best

Worksheets Help Buyers Attain the Goal

After college, many graduates begin their professions; a few travel or defer their careers for other interests, and some marry, buy homes, and start families. Owning a home is part of the American Dream, the ideal of a happy and successful life to which all may aspire. With the current trend continuing, however, in corporate downsizing, fluctuating interest rates, job insecurity, and wage freezes, this dream often remains to some just a desire that seems unattainable.

Creative lending institutions, however, work with customers' purse strings to explore various mortgage options. They often use worksheets such as the WeSavU National Bank Loan Analysis that you will create in this Excel project. The loan analysis in this project evaluates data by applying financial functions and an amortization schedule, and using an additional what-if tool, the data table, to guide consumers and help determine their ability to purchase a home. Another feature of Excel, allows you to add

	B	C	D	E	F	G	H
1		WeSavU National Bank					Amortiza
2	Date	19-Nov-2001	Rate	8.25%	Yr	Beginning Balance	Ending Balan
3	Item	House	Years	15	1	$122,000.00	$117,7
4	Price	$154,000.00	Monthly Pymt	$1,183.57	2	117,702.04	113,0
5	Down Pymt	$32,000.00	Total Interest	$91,042.82	3	113,035.78	107,9
6	Loan Amt	$122,000.00	Total Cost	$245,042.82	4	107,969.66	102,4
7		Varying Interest Rate Table			5	102,469.41	96,4
8	Rate	Monthly Pymt	Total Interest	Total Cost	6	96,497.83	90,0
9		$1,183.57	$91,042.82	$245,042.82	7	90,014.54	82,9
10	7.50%	1,130.96	81,571.91	235,571.91	8	82,975.68	75,3
11	7.75%	1,148.36	84,704.16	238,704.16	9	75,333.64	67
12	8.00%	1,165.90	87,861.20	241,861.20	10	67,036.74	
13	8.25%	1,183.57	91,042.82	245,042.82	11	58,020.88	

hyperlinks to a worksheet, making it possible to click a link in the worksheet to launch your Web browser application and display an associated Web page.

Citibank uses the Client Affordability and CitiShowcase worksheets, online loan forms and question and answer Web pages to help potential borrowers determine a maximum loan amount based on annual income, and establish down payments required to qualify for various mortgage options.

Home shoppers, particularly first-time buyers, often do not know whether they have a sufficient down payment and adequate income to purchase a home. Then they need to know maximum sales prices of homes they can afford. To provide this information, a Citibank loan officer retrieves the Client Affordability Analysis form on a notebook computer and interviews the clients. The officer asks the amount of annual income, monthly debt, and down payment and simultaneously inputs the figures in unprotected worksheet cells. Then the officer inputs current interest rates for particular loans, such as 8.75 percent on a 30-year fixed rate.

At this point, the worksheet program uses financial functions to determine the maximum loan amounts and monthly payments based on the clients' data.

If this client has an approximate sales price in mind, the worksheet will use this figure to determine if the property is affordable. For example, if the home is priced at $150,000, the worksheet computes that this price, coupled with other property expenses, amounts to 35.73 percent of the total gross income.

These figures then are examined using a data table that automates data analysis. Using the $150,000 home, the worksheet computes the annual income required to obtain 30-year fixed, 15-year fixed, and adjustable-rate mortgages with down payments of 25, 20, 10, and 5 percent. For example, the client needs an annual income of $40,365 and a 25 percent down payment of $37,500 to obtain a 30-year fixed mortgage with an interest rate of 8.75 percent and monthly payments of $1,111. Additional analysis indicates that the client needs to earn $57,525 with a 10-percent down payment of $15,000 to obtain a 15-year fixed mortgage at 8.25 percent with monthly payments of $1,583.

Citibank, like most lenders, uses these work-sheets as a starting point to help potential borrowers explore mortgage options. In an attempt to qualify the client for the mortgage, the loan officer considers compensating factors, such as a clean credit history, verifiable job offers, and length of time since graduation, particularly for first-time buyers. A strong financial picture can help make the dream attainable.

Microsoft Excel 2000

Financial Functions, Data Tables, Amortization Schedules, and Hyperlinks

P R O J E C T

4

C A S E   P E R S P E C T I V E

Leslie Alex recently was promoted to manager of financial services for WeSavU National Bank. His immediate challenge is to modernize the archaic procedures the board of directors believes are responsible for the recent slippage in personal loans. His first step is to computerize the procedures in the loan department. Leslie's intent is to have the loan officers generate the monthly payment, total interest, total cost, a table of varying interest rates, and an amortization schedule of a proposed loan when the customer comes in for an interview. The customer then can take home a printed copy of the information to review. He also wants the bank's Statement of Condition available via a hyperlink in case a customer questions the bank's worthiness.

Leslie recently took a one-day course on Microsoft Excel at the local community college. He learned that Excel has many financial functions, what-if tools, and Web capabilities. As Leslie's spreadsheet specialist, he has asked you to create a workbook that will generate the desired loan information, while ensuring that the loan officers will not render the worksheet useless by entering data into the wrong cells.

Introduction

Two of the more powerful aspects of Excel are its wide array of functions and its capability to organize answers to what-if questions. In earlier projects, you were introduced to several functions such as AVERAGE, MAX, SUM, IF, and MIN. In this project, you will learn about financial functions such as the PMT function that allows you to determine a monthly payment for a loan (upper-left side of Figure 4-1a). The upper-left side of Figure 4-1a is called the loan analysis section.

You also learned how to analyze data by using Excel's recalculation feature and goal seeking. This project revisits these two methods of analyzing data and describes an additional what-if tool called data tables. You use a data table to automate your data analyses and organize the answers returned by Excel. The data table section on the lower-left in Figure 4-1a answers 11 different what-if questions. The questions pertain to the effect the 11 different interest rates in column B have on the monthly payment, total interest, and total cost of a loan.

Another important loan analysis tool is the Amortization Schedule section (right side of Figure 4-1a). An amortization schedule shows the beginning and ending balances and the amount of payment that applies to the principal and interest over a period of time.

Another key feature of Excel is its capability to add hyperlinks to a worksheet. Hyperlinks are built-in links (file path names or URLs) to other Office documents or HTML files (Web pages). A hyperlink can be assigned to text in a cell or to an object, such as the stack of dollar bills graphic at the bottom of Figure 4-1a. When you click the stack of dollar bills graphic, Excel starts your browser and displays an HTML file (Figure 4-1b).

Finally, this project introduces you to cell protection. Cell protection ensures that users do not inadvertently change values that are critical to the worksheet.

Excel calculates loan information

all cells, except those in ranges C3:C6 and E2:E3, are protected so user cannot change cells accidentally

Amortization Schedule summarizes monthly payments on an annual basis

loan data in loan analysis section

data table section lists payment data for interest rates between 7.50% and 10.00% in increments of 0.25%

green background highlights row in data table that corresponds to rate in cell E2

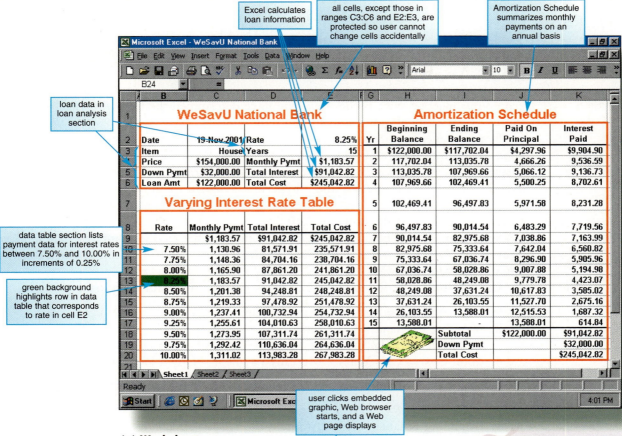

user clicks embedded graphic, Web browser starts, and a Web page displays

(a) Worksheet

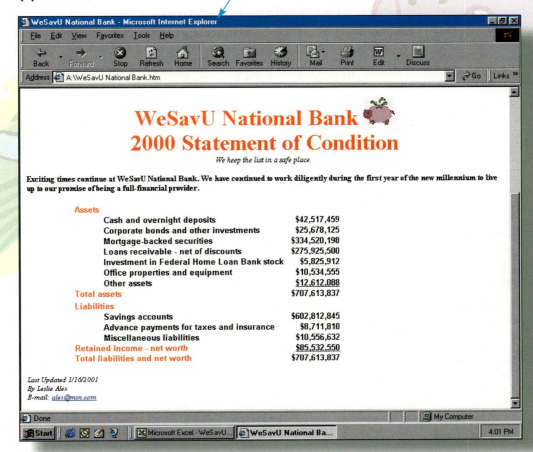

(b) Web Page   **FIGURE 4-1**

More *About*

Good Worksheet Design

Do not create worksheets with the thinking that they are to be used only once. Instead, carefully design worksheets as if they will be on display and evaluated by your fellow workers. Smart worksheet design starts with visualizing the results you need. For additional information on good worksheet design, visit the Excel 2000 More About Web page (www.scsite.com/ex2000/more.htm) and click Smart Spreadsheet Design.

Project Four — WeSavU National Bank Loan Analysis

From your meeting with Leslie Alex, you have determined the following needs, source of data, calculations, and special requirements.

Needs: An easy-to-read worksheet (Figure 4-1a on the previous page) that determines the monthly payment, total interest, and total cost for a loan; a data table that answers what-if questions based on changing interest rates; an amortization schedule that shows annual summaries; and a hyperlink assigned to an object so that when you click the object, the WeSavU National Bank's 2000 Statement of Condition displays (Figure 4-1b on the previous page).

Source of Data: The data (item, price of item, down payment, interest rate, and term of the loan in years) is determined by the loan officer and customer when they initially meet for the loan.

Calculations: The following calculations must be made for each loan:

1. Loan Amount = Price – Down Payment
2. Monthly Payment = PMT function
3. Total Interest = 12 x Years x Monthly Payment – Loan Amount
4. Total Cost = 12 x Years x Monthly Payment + Down Payment

Use the Table command to create the data table. The Amortization Schedule involves the following calculations:

1. Beginning Balance = Loan Amount
2. Ending Balance = PV function (present value) or zero
3. Paid on Principal = Beginning Balance – Ending Balance
4. Interest Paid = 12 x Monthly Payment – Paid on Principal or zero
5. Column Totals = SUM function

Special Requirements: Protect the worksheet in such a way that the loan officers cannot enter data mistakenly into wrong cells. Add a hyperlink to an HTML file containing the bank's Statement of Condition.

Starting Excel and Resetting the Toolbars and Menus

Perform the following steps to start Excel. Steps 4 through 6 resets the toolbars and menus to their installation settings. For additional information on resetting the toolbars and menus, see Appendix B.

More *About*

Starting Excel at Startup

To start Excel when you start Windows, copy the Excel application icon to the Startup folder. Any program in the Startup folder automatically starts when Windows starts.

TO START EXCEL AND RESET THE TOOLBARS AND MENUS

1 Click the Start button on the taskbar.

2 Click New Office Document. If necessary, click the General tab in the New Office Document dialog box.

3 Double-click the Blank Workbook icon.

4 When the blank worksheet displays, click View on the menu bar, click the arrows to display the full menu, point to Toolbars, and then click Customize on the Toolbars submenu.

5 When the Customize dialog box displays, click the Options tab, make sure the top three check boxes have check marks, click the Reset my usage data button, and then click the Yes button.

6   Click the Toolbars tab. Click Standard, click the Reset button, and then click the OK button. Click Formatting, click the Reset button, and then click the OK button. Click the Close button.

The Standard and Formatting toolbars display as shown in Figure 4-1a on page E 4.5.

An alternative to Steps 1 through 3 is to click the Start button, point to Programs, and then click Microsoft Excel on the Programs submenu.

Changing the Font Style of the Entire Worksheet

The first step in this project is to change the font style of the entire worksheet to bold to ensure that the characters in the worksheet stand out.

TO CHANGE THE FONT STYLE OF THE ENTIRE WORKSHEET

1   Double-click the move handle on the Formatting toolbar (see Figure 4-2 on the next page).

2   Click the Select All button immediately above row heading 1 and to the left of column heading A.

3   Click the Bold button on the Formatting toolbar.

As you enter text and numbers onto the worksheet, they will display in bold.

Entering the Section Title, Row Titles, and System Date

The next step is to enter the loan analysis section title, row titles, and system date. To make the worksheet easier to read, the width of column A will be decreased to 0.5 points and used as a separator between the loan analysis section and the row headings on the left. Using a column as a separator between sections on a worksheet is a common technique used by spreadsheet specialists. The width of columns B through E will be increased so the intended values fit. The heights of rows 1 and 2, which contain the titles, will be increased so they stand out. The worksheet title also will be changed from 10-point to 16-point red font.

TO ENTER THE SECTION TITLE, ROW TITLES, AND SYSTEM DATE

1   Click cell B1. Type WeSavU National Bank as the section title and then press the ENTER key. Select the range B1:E1. Click the Merge and Center button on the Formatting toolbar.

2   With cell B1 active, click the Font Size box arrow on the Formatting toolbar and then click 16. Click the Font Color button on the Formatting toolbar to change the color of the font to red.

3   Drag through row headings 1 and 2 and then position the mouse pointer on the bottom boundary of row heading 2. Drag down until the ScreenTip, Height: 27.00 (36.00 pixels), displays.

4   Click cell B2, type Date and then press the ENTER key.

5   Click cell C2. Type =now() and then press the ENTER key.

Global Formatting

To assign formats to all the cells in all the worksheets in a workbook, click the Select All button, then right-click a tab and click Select All Sheets on the shortcut menu. Next, assign the formats. To deselect the sheets, hold down the SHIFT key and then click the Sheet1 tab. You also can select a cell or a range of cells and then select all sheets to assign formats to a cell or a range of cells on all the sheets in a workbook.

Unmerging

The Merge and Center button merges the selected cells and centers the text located in the leftmost cell. To unmerge a cell, you can click the Undo button on the Standard toolbar if the action still is available in the Undo list. If the action is not available in the Undo list, then right-click the merged cell, click Format Cells on the shortcut menu, click the Alignment tab, click the Merge cells check box, click the Horizontal arrow, click General in the list, and click the OK button.

6 Right-click cell C2 and then click Format Cells on the shortcut menu. When the Format Cells dialog box displays, click the Number tab, click Date in the Category list, scroll down in the Type list and click 14-Mar-1998. Click the OK button.

7 Enter the following row titles:

CELL	ENTRY	CELL	ENTRY	CELL	ENTRY
B3	Item	B6	Loan Amt	D4	Monthly Pymt
B4	Price	D2	Rate	D5	Total Interest
B5	Down Pymt	D3	Years	D6	Total Cost

Point with Care

Excel requires that you point to the object (cell, range, or toolbar) on the screen when you right-click to display the corresponding shortcut menu. For example, if you select the range A1:D5, and right-click cell F10, then the shortcut menu pertains to cell F10, and not the selected range A1:D5.

8 Position the mouse pointer on the right boundary of column heading A and then drag to the left until the ScreenTip, Width: .50 (6 pixels) displays.

9 Position the mouse pointer on the right boundary of column heading B and then drag to the right until the ScreenTip, Width: 10.14 (76 pixels) displays.

10 Click the column C heading to select it and then drag through column headings D through E. Position the mouse pointer on the right boundary of column heading C and then drag until the ScreenTip, Width: 12.29 (91 pixels), displays.

11 Click cell C2 to deselect the columns. Click the Save button on the Standard toolbar. Save the workbook on drive A using the file name WeSavU National Bank.

The loan analysis section title, row titles, and system date display as shown in Figure 4-2.

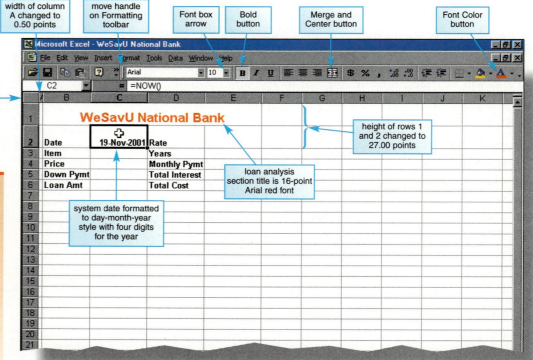

FIGURE 4-2

Left-Handed Mouse Users

Are you a lefty? You can change the functions of the left and right mouse buttons. Double-click the My Computer icon on the desktop, double-click the Control Panel icon, double-click the Mouse icon in Control Panel, depending on your Mouse software, click the Basics tab or Buttons tab, click the appropriate option button, and then click the OK button.

utlining and Adding Borders

In previous projects, you were introduced to outlining using the Borders button on the Formatting toolbar. To control the color and thickness of the outline and borders, use the Border tab in the Format Cells dialog box. The following steps add an outline to the loan analysis section. To further subdivide the row titles and numbers, light borders also are added within the outline as shown in Figure 4-1a on page E 4.5.

Steps **To Add an Outline and Borders to the Loan Analysis Section**

1 **Select the range B2:E6. Right-click the selected range and then point to Format Cells on the shortcut menu (Figure 4-3).**

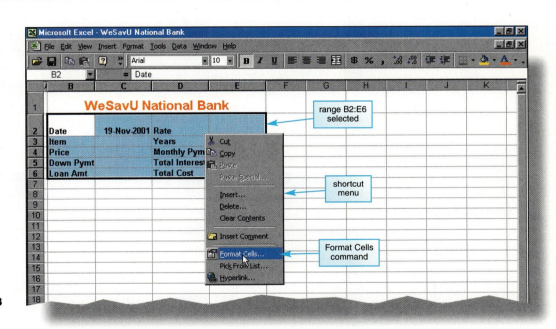

FIGURE 4-3

2 **Click Format Cells. When the Format Cells dialog box displays, click the Border tab. Click the Color box arrow. Click the color red (column 1, row 3) on the palette. Click the heavy border in the Style box (column 2, row 6). Click the Outline button in the Presets area.**

Excel previews the outline in the Border area (Figure 4-4).

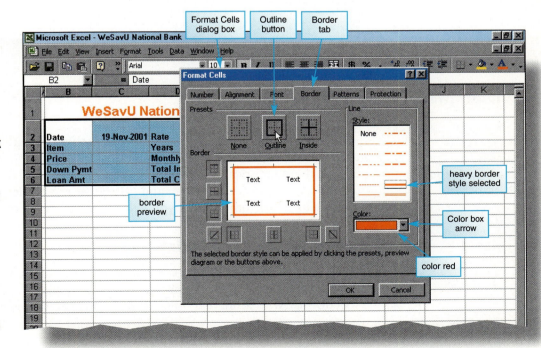

FIGURE 4-4

3 **Click the Color box arrow. Click Automatic (row 1) on the palette. Click the light border in the Style box (column 1, row 7). Click the vertical line button in the Border area.**

Excel previews the vertical border in the Border area (Figure 4-5).

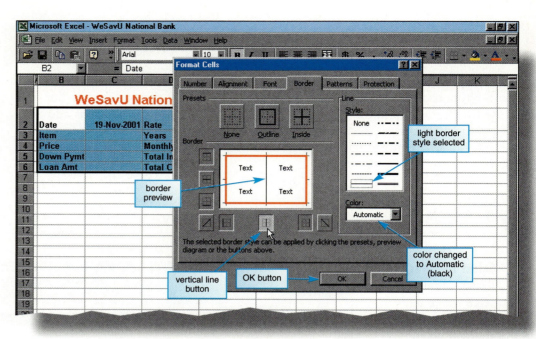

FIGURE 4-5

4 **Click the OK button. Select cell B8 to deselect the range B2:E6.**

Excel adds a red outline with vertical borders to the right side of each column in the range B2:E6 (Figure 4-6).

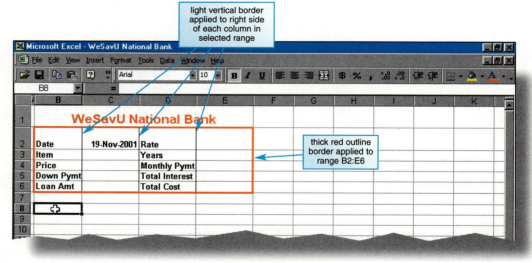

FIGURE 4-6

1. On Format menu click Cells, click Border tab
2. For black borders, click Borders button arrow on Formatting toolbar

As shown in Figure 4-5, you can add a variety of outlines and borders with color to a cell or range of cells to improve its appearance. It is important that you select border characteristics in the order specified in the steps; that is, (1) choose the color; (2) choose the border line style; and (3) choose the border type. If you attempt to do these steps in any other order, you will not end up with the desired borders.

Formatting Cells Before Entering Values

While usually you format cells after you enter the values, Excel also allows you to format cells before you enter the values. The following steps assign the Currency style format with a floating dollar sign to the ranges C4:C6 and E4:E6 before the values are entered.

TO FORMAT CELLS BEFORE ENTERING VALUES

1 Select the range C4:C6. While holding down the CTRL key, select the nonadjacent range E4:E6. Right-click one of the selected ranges.

2 Click Format Cells on the shortcut menu. When the Format Cells dialog box displays, click the Number tab.

3 Click Currency in the Category list box and then click the fourth format, ($1,234.10), in the Negative numbers list box.

4 Click the OK button.

The ranges C4:C6 and E4:E6 are assigned the Currency style format with a floating dollar sign.

As you enter numbers into these cells, the numbers will display using the Currency style format. You also could have selected the range B4:E6 rather than the nonadjacent ranges and assigned the Currency style format to this range, which includes text. The Currency style format has no impact on text.

Entering the Loan Data

As shown in Figure 4-1a on page E 4.5, five items make up the loan data in the worksheet: the item to be purchased, the price of the item, the down payment, the interest rate, and the number of years until the loan is paid back (also called the term of the loan). These items are entered into cells C3 through C5 and cells E2 and E3. The following steps describe how to enter the following loan data: Item - House; Price - $154,000.00; Down Payment - $32,000.00; Interest Rate - 8.25%; and Years - 15.

TO ENTER THE LOAN DATA

1 Click cell C3. Enter House as the item. With cell C3 still active, click the Align Right button on the Formatting toolbar. Click cell C4 and enter 154000 for the price of the house. Click cell C5 and enter 32000 for the down payment.

2 Click cell E2. Enter 8.25% for the interest rate. Click cell E3 and enter 15 for the number of years.

The loan data displays in the worksheet as shown in Figure 4-7.

When to Format

Excel lets you format (1) empty cells before you enter data; (2) when you enter data (through the use of format symbols); (3) incrementally after entering sections of data; and, (4) after you enter all the data. Spreadsheet specialists usually format a worksheet in increments as they build the worksheet, but occasions do exist when it makes sense to format before you enter any data.

Percents

When entering a percent value, remember to append the percent sign (%) or Excel will use a number 100 times greater than the number you thought you entered. An alternative to using the percent sign is to enter the number with the decimal point moved two places to the left.

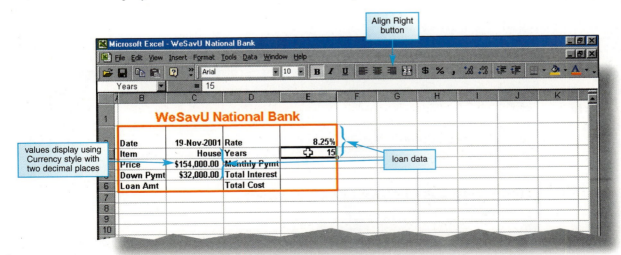

FIGURE 4-7

The values in cells C4 and C5 display using the Currency style with two decimal places, because this format was assigned to the cells prior to entering the values. Excel also automatically formats the interest rate to the Percent style with two decimal places, because the percent sign (%) was appended to 8.25 when it was entered into cell E2.

Calculating the four remaining entries in the loan analysis section of the worksheet - loan amount (cell C6), monthly payment (cell E4), total interest (cell E5), and total cost (cell E6) - require that you enter formulas that reference cells C4, C5, C6, E2, and E3. The formulas will be entered referencing names assigned to cells, such as Price, rather than cell references, such as C4, because names are easier to remember than cell references.

Creating Cell Names Based on Row Titles

Worksheets often have column titles at the top of each column and row titles to the left of each row that describe the data within the worksheet. You can use these titles within formulas when you want to refer to the related data by **name**. Names are created through the use of the **Name command** on the Insert menu. You also can use the same command to define descriptive names that are not column titles or row titles to represent cells, ranges of cells, formulas, or constants.

Naming a cell that you plan to reference in a formula helps make the formula easier to read and remember. For example, the loan amount in cell C6 is equal to the price in cell C4 less the down payment in cell C5. Therefore, according to what you learned in the earlier projects, you can write the loan amount formula in cell C6 as =C4 – C5. By assigning the corresponding row titles in column B as the names of cells C4 and C5, however, you can write the loan amount formula as =Price – Down_Pymt, which is clearer and easier to understand than =C4 – C5.

To name cells, you select the range that encompasses the row titles that include the names and the cells to be named (range B4:C6) and then use the Name command on the Insert menu. This project does not use the names Date and Item to reference cells C2 and C3.

The following steps assign each row title in cells B4 through B6 to their adjacent cell in column C and also assigns each row title in cells D2 through D6 to their adjacent cell in column E.

Steps To Create Names Based on Row Titles

1 **Select the range B4:C6. Click Insert on the menu bar. Point to Name and then point to Create on the Name submenu.**

Excel highlights the range B4:C6. The Insert menu and Name submenu display (Figure 4-8).

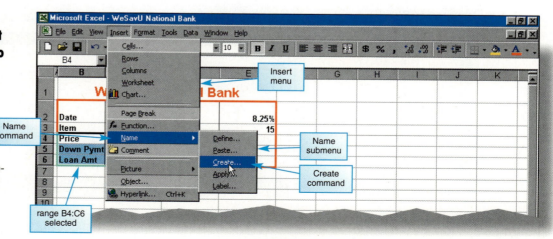

FIGURE 4-8

2 **Click Create. When the Create Names dialog box displays, point to the OK button.**

The Create Names dialog box displays (Figure 4-9). The Left column check box is selected automatically in the Create names in area because the direction of the cells containing text selected in Step 1 is downward.

3 **Click the OK button. Select the range D2:E6. Click Insert on the menu bar, point to Name, and then click Create on the Name submenu. Click the OK button in the Create Names dialog box. Click cell B8 to deselect the range D2:E6**

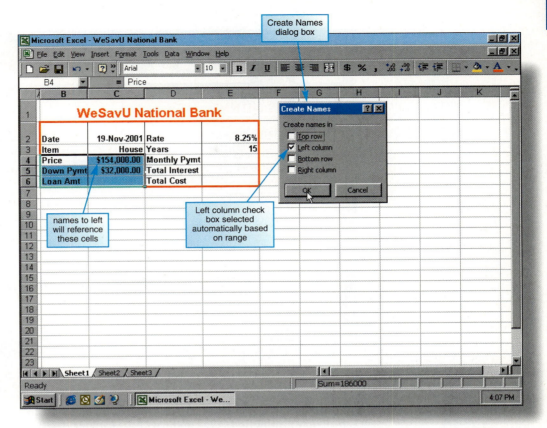

FIGURE 4-9

You now can use the names in the range B4:B6 and D2:D6 in formulas to reference the adjacent cells on the left. Excel is not case-sensitive with respect to names of cells. Hence, you can enter the names of cells in formulas in uppercase or lowercase. Some names, such as Down Pymt in cell B5, include a space because they are made up of two or more words. To use a name in a formula that is made up of two or more words, you replace any space with the **underscore character** (_). For example, Down Pymt is written as down_pymt when you want to reference the adjacent cell C5.

Consider these additional points regarding the assignment of names to cells:

1. A name can be a minimum of one character to a maximum of 255 characters.
2. If you want to assign a name that is not a text item in an adjacent cell, use the **Define command** on the Name submenu (Figure 4-8) or select the cell or range and type the name in the Name box in the formula bar.
3. Names are absolute cell references. This is important to remember if you plan to use the Copy command with formulas that contain names, rather than cell references.
4. The names display in alphabetical order in the Name box when you click the Name box arrow (Figure 4-10 on the next page).
5. Names are **global** to the workbook. That is, a name assigned on one worksheet in a workbook can be used on other sheets in the same workbook to reference the associated cell or range of cells.

Other Ways

1. Select range, press CTRL+SHIFT+F3
2. Select each cell individually, type name in Name box
3. On Insert menu point to Names, click Define, enter name

More About 2000

Names

You can create row and column names at the same time if you have a worksheet with column titles and row titles. Simply select the column titles and row titles along with the cells to name, and then on the Insert menu, click Name and on the Name submenu, click Create. In the Create Name dialog box, click both Top row and Left column, and then click the OK button. As a result, you can use the column title and row title separated by a space to refer to the intersecting cell.

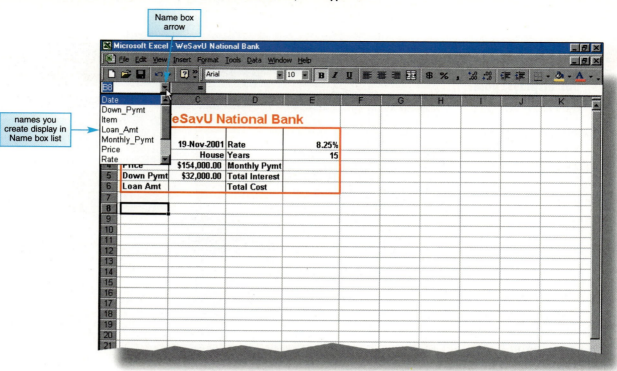

FIGURE 4-10

More *About*

Functions

Functions operate on data, called arguments, which are inserted between parentheses. Functions return to a cell a value, similarly to the way a formula returns a value.

Spreadsheet specialists often assign names to a cell or range of cells so they can select them quickly. If you want to select a cell that has been assigned a name, you can click the Name box arrow (Figure 4-10) and then click the name of the cell you want to select. This method is similar to using the Go To command on the Edit menu or the F5 key to select a cell, but it is much quicker.

Determining the Loan Amount

To determine the loan amount in cell C6, subtract the down payment in cell C5 from the price in cell C4. As indicated earlier, you could do this by entering the formula =C4 – C5 or you can enter the formula = price – down_pymt as shown in the following steps.

 **To Enter the Loan Amount Formula Using Names**

1 **Click cell C6. Type**
=price –
down_pymt.

The formula displays in cell C6 and in the formula bar (Figure 4-11).

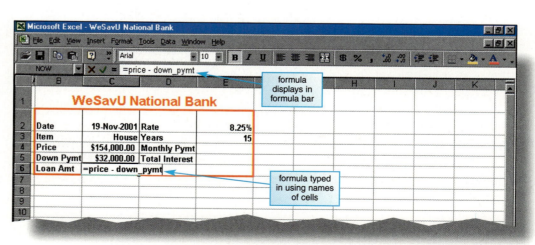

FIGURE 4-11

2 **Press the ENTER key.**

Excel assigns the formula =price – down_pymt to cell C6. The result of the formula ($122,000.00) displays in cell C6 using the Currency style format assigned earlier (Figure 4-12).

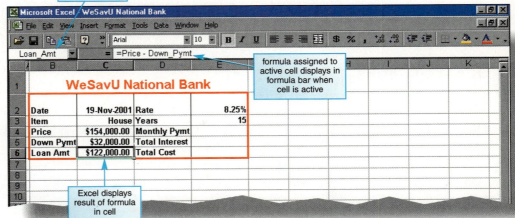

FIGURE 4-12

An alternative to creating names is to use labels. A **label** is a row title or column title, similar to the adjacent names created earlier. Any row title or column title can be used in formulas to reference corresponding cells. It is not necessary to enter commands to assign label names.

The major drawback to using labels in some applications is that they are **relative**, which means the label may very well reference a cell that is nonadjacent to the label. It also is important to note that Excel does not recognize labels in formulas unless you activate label usage. To activate **label usage**, click Tools on the menu bar, click Options, click the Calculation tab, and select Accept labels in formulas. Any row title or column title then can be used in formulas to reference corresponding cells.

Labels are different from names in the following ways: (1) labels are not absolute; (2) they cannot be used on other worksheets in the workbook; (3) they do not show up in the Names box (see Figure 4-10); and (4) you can use them without entering underscores in place of spaces.

Determining the Monthly Payment

The next step is to determine the monthly payment for the loan. You can use Excel's **PMT function** to determine the monthly payment in cell E4. The PMT function has three arguments – rate, payment, and loan amount. Its general form is

=PMT(rate, payment, loan amount)

where rate is the interest rate per payment period, payment is the number of payments, and loan amount is the amount of the loan.

In the worksheet shown in Figure 4-12, cell E2 displays the annual interest rate. Loan institutions, however, calculate interest on a monthly basis. The rate value in the PMT function, thus, is rate / 12 (cell E2 divided by 12), rather than just rate (cell E2). The number of payments (or periods) in the PMT function is 12 * years (12 times cell E3) because there are 12 months, or 12 payments, per year.

Excel considers the value returned by the PMT function to be a debit, and therefore, returns a negative number as the monthly payment. To display the monthly payment as a positive number, you can enter a negative sign before the loan amount. Thus, the loan amount is equal to –loan_amt. The PMT function for cell E4 is

=PMT(rate / 12, 12 * years, – loan_amt)

monthly interest rate   number of payments   loan amount

The PMT Function

An alternative to requiring the user to enter an interest rate in percent form, such as 7.75%, is to allow the user to enter the interest rate as a number without an appended percent sign (7.75) and then divide the interest rate by 1200, rather than 12.

The following steps use the PMT function to determine the monthly payment in cell E4.

 To Enter the PMT Function

 Click cell E4. Type =pmt(rate / 12, 12 * years, -loan_amt) **as the function.**

The PMT function displays in cell E4 and in the formula bar (Figure 4-13).

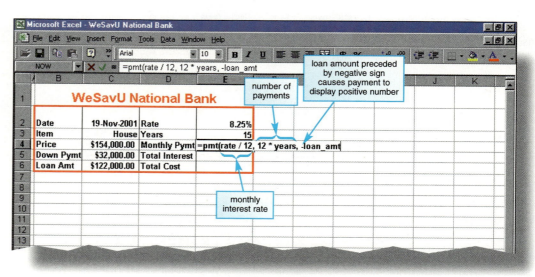

FIGURE 4-13

 Press the ENTER key.

Excel displays the monthly payment $1,183.57 in cell E4, based on a loan amount of $122,000.00 (cell C6) with an annual interest rate of 8.25% (cell E2) for a term of 15 years (cell E3).

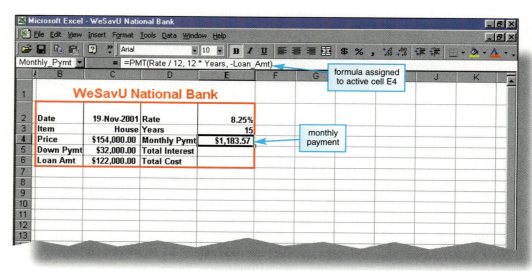

FIGURE 4-14

Other **Ways**

1. Click Paste Function button on Standard toolbar, click Financial in Function category box, click PMT in Function box
2. Click Edit Formula button in formula bar, click Function box arrow in formula bar, click PMT function

You could have entered the PMT function by clicking the Paste Function button on the Standard toolbar. When the Paste Function dialog box displays, click Financial in the Function category list box and then click PMT in the Function name list box. In addition to the PMT function, Excel provides more than 50 additional financial functions to help you solve the most complex finance problems. These functions save you from entering long, complicated formulas to obtain needed results. Table 4-1 summarizes three of the more often used financial functions.

Table 4-1	Financial Functions
FUNCTION	DESCRIPTION
FV(rate, periods, payment)	Returns the future value of an investment based on periodic, constant payments and a constant interest rate.
PMT(rate, periods, loan amount)	Returns the payments for a loan based on periodic, constant payments and a constant interest rate.
PV(rate, periods, payment)	Returns the present value of an investment; that is, the total amount that a series of payments is worth now.

Determining the Total Interest and Total Cost

The next step is to determine the total interest (WeSavU National Bank's gross profit for the loan) and the borrower's total cost of the item being purchased. The total interest (cell E5) is equal to the number of payments times the monthly payment, less the loan amount:

=12 * years * monthly_pymt – loan_amt

The total cost of the item to be purchased (cell E6) is equal to the number of payments times the monthly payment plus the down payment:

=12 * years * monthly_pymt + down_pymt

To enter the total interest and total cost formulas, perform the following steps.

TO DETERMINE THE TOTAL INTEREST AND TOTAL COST

1 Click cell E5. Enter the formula =12 * years * monthly_pymt – loan_amt to determine the total interest.

2 Click cell E6. Enter the formula =12 * years * monthly_pymt + down_pymt to determine the total cost.

3 Click cell B8 to deselect cell E6. Click the Save button on the Standard toolbar to save the workbook using the file name WeSavU National Bank.

Excel displays a total interest (bank's gross profit) of $91,042.82 in cell E5 and a total cost to the borrower of $245,042.82 in cell E6 for the house (Figure 4-15).

More About

Range Finder

Do not forget to check all formulas carefully. You can double-click a cell with a formula and Excel will highlight the cells that provide data to the formula.

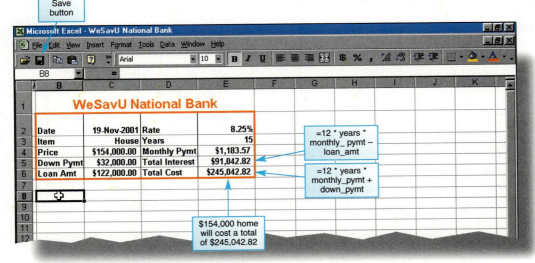

FIGURE 4-15

With the loan analysis section of the worksheet complete, you can use it to determine the monthly payment, total interest, and total cost for any loan data.

Entering New Loan Data

Assume you want to purchase a diamond ring for $7,595.00. You have $2,350.00 for a down payment and you want the loan for a term of 3 years. WeSavU National Bank currently is charging 10% interest for a three-year loan. The following steps show how to enter the new loan data.

More *About*

Testing a Worksheet

It is good practice to test a worksheet over and over again until you are confident it will not fail. Use data that tests the limits of the formulas. For example, you should enter negative numbers, zero, and large positive numbers to test the formulas.

TO ENTER NEW LOAN DATA

1 Click cell C3. Type Diamond Ring and then press the DOWN ARROW key.

2 In cell C4, type 7595 and then press the DOWN ARROW key.

3 In cell C5, type 2350 and then click cell E2.

4 In cell E2, type 10 and then press the DOWN ARROW key.

5 In cell E3, type 3 and then click cell B8.

Excel instantaneously recalculates the loan information in cells C6, E4, E5, and E6 (Figure 4-16).

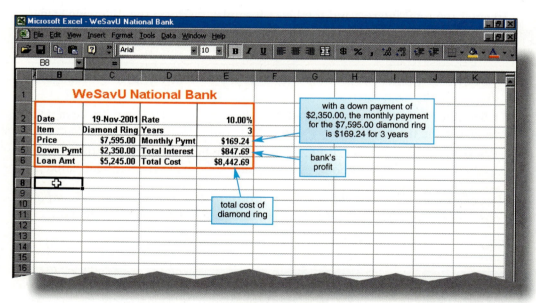

FIGURE 4-16

As you can see from Figure 4-16, the monthly payment for the diamond ring is $169.24. The total interest is $847.69. By paying for the diamond ring over a three-year period, you actually pay a total cost of $8,442.69 for a $7,595.00 diamond ring. As shown in the example, you can use the loan analysis section to calculate the loan information for any loan data.

The next step is to create the data table described earlier and shown in Figure 4-1 on page E 4.5. Before creating the data table, follow these steps to re-enter the original loan data.

TO ENTER THE ORIGINAL LOAN DATA

1 Click cell C3. Type House and then press the DOWN ARROW key.

2 In cell C4, type 154000 and then press the DOWN ARROW key.

3 In cell C5, type 32000 and then click cell E2.

4 In cell E2, type 8.25 and then press the DOWN ARROW key.

5 In cell E3, type 15 and then click cell B8.

Excel instantaneously recalculates all formulas in the worksheet each time you enter a value. The original loan information displays as shown earlier in Figure 4-15 on page E 4.17.

Using a Data Table to Analyze Worksheet Data

You already have seen that if you change a value in a cell, Excel immediately recalculates and displays the new results of any formulas that reference the cell directly or indirectly. But what if you want to compare the results of the formula for several different values? Writing down or trying to remember all the answers to the what-if questions would be unwieldy. If you use a data table, however, Excel will organize the answers in the worksheet for you automatically.

A **data table** is a range of cells that shows the answers generated by formulas in which different values have been substituted. The data table shown below the loan analysis section in Figure 4-17, for example, will display the resulting monthly payment, total interest, and total cost values based on different interest rates in column **B**.

More About 2000

The Purpose of Data Tables

Data tables have one purpose, and that is to organize the answers to what-if questions. You can create two kinds of data tables. The first type involves changing one input value to see the resulting effect on one or more formulas. The second type involves changing two input values to see the resulting effect on one formula.

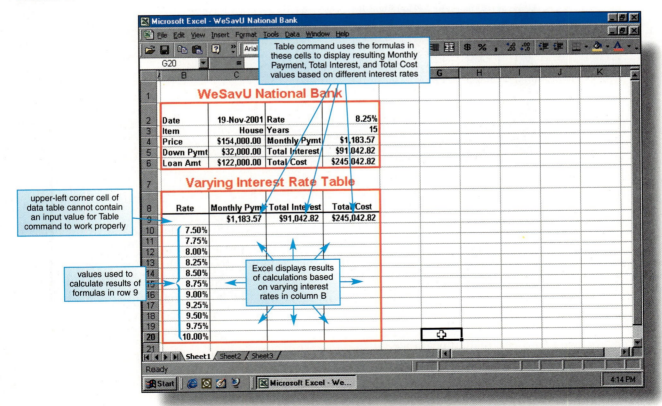

FIGURE 4-17

Data tables are built in an unused area of the worksheet (in this case, the range B7:E20). Within the table, you can vary one or two values and Excel will display the results of the specified formulas in table form. Figure 4-17 on the previous page illustrates the makeup of a one-input data table. With a **one-input data table**, you vary the value in one cell (in this worksheet, cell E2, the interest rate). Excel then calculates the results of one or more formulas and fills the table with the results. A **two-input data table** allows you to vary the values in two cells, but you can apply it to only one formula.

The interest rates that will be used to analyze the loan formulas in this project range from 7.50% to 10.00%, increasing in increments of 0.25%. The one-input data table shown in Figure 4-18 illustrates the impact of varying the interest rate on three formulas: the monthly payment (cell E4), total interest paid (cell E5), and the total cost of the item to be purchased (cell E6). The series of interest rates in column B are called **input values**.

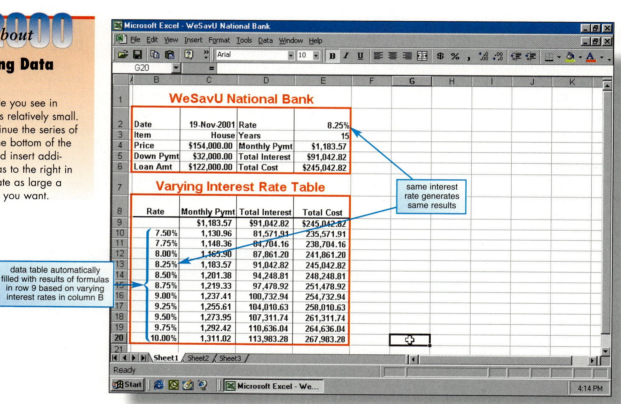

FIGURE 4-18

To construct the data table shown in Figure 4-18, complete the following steps: (1) enter the data table section title and column titles in the range B7:E8; (2) adjust the heights of rows 7 and 8; (3) use the fill handle to enter the series of varying interest rates in column B; (4) enter the formulas in the range C9:E9 for which you want the data table to determine answers; (5) use the **Table command** on the **Data menu** to define the range B9:E20 as a data table and then identify the interest rate in cell B7 as the **input cell**, the one you want to vary; and (6) outline the data table so it has a professional appearance.

TO ENTER THE DATA TABLE TITLE AND COLUMN TITLES

1 Click cell B7. Type `Varying Interest Rate Table` as the data table section title. Press the ENTER key.

2 Click the Font Size box arrow on the Formatting toolbar and then click 16. Click the Font Color button on the Formatting toolbar to change the font color to red. Select the range B7:E7 and click the Merge and Center button on the Formatting toolbar.

3 Enter the column titles from the table on the right in the range B8:E8 as shown in Figure 4-19.

4 Select the range B8:E8 and then click the Center button on the Formatting toolbar to center the column titles.

5 Drag through row headings 7 and 8 and position the mouse pointer on the bottom boundary of row heading 8. Drag down until the ScreenTip, Height: 27.00 (36.00 pixels), displays. Click cell B10 to deselect rows 7 and 8.

CELL	ENTRY
B8	Rate
C8	Monthly Pymt
D8	Total Interest
E8	Total Cost

The data table title and column headings display as shown in Figure 4-19.

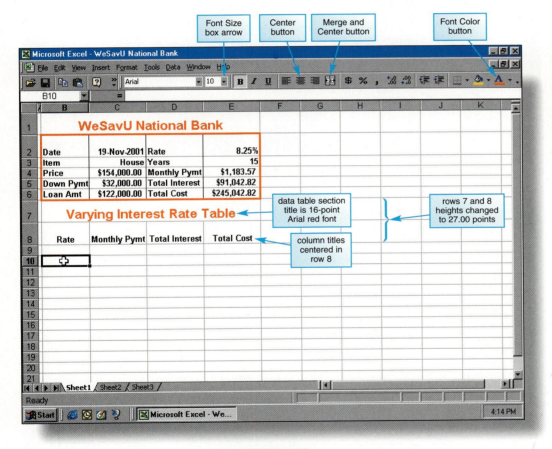

FIGURE 4-19

More About

Data Table Errors

The most common error made by beginning Excel users when creating a one-input data table is to start the input values in the upper-left cell in the data table (see Figure 4-17 on page E 4.19).

Creating a Percent Series Using the Fill Handle

The next step is to create the percent series in column B using the fill handle. These percents will serve as the input data for the data table.

To Create a Percent Series Using the Fill Handle

1 **Click cell B10 and enter** 7.50% **as the first number in the series. Select cell B11 and enter** 7.75% **as the second number in the series.**

2 **Select the range B10:B11 and then point to the fill handle. Drag the fill handle through cell B20 and hold.**

Excel shades the border of the copy and paste area (Figure 4-20). The ScreenTip, 10.00%, displays below the fill handle indicating the last value in the series. This value will display in cell B20.

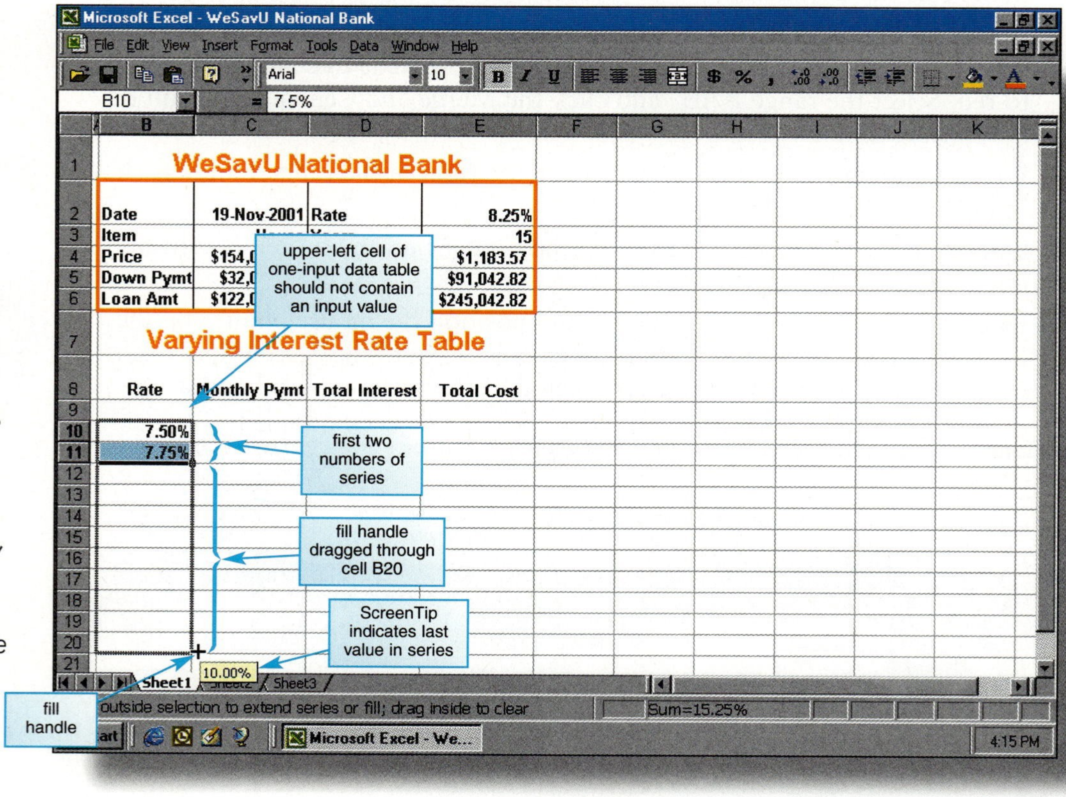

FIGURE 4-20

3 **Release the mouse button. Click cell C9 to deselect the range B10:B20.**

Excel generates the series of numbers from 7.50% to 10.00% in the range B10:B20 (Figure 4-21). The series increases in increments of 0.25%.

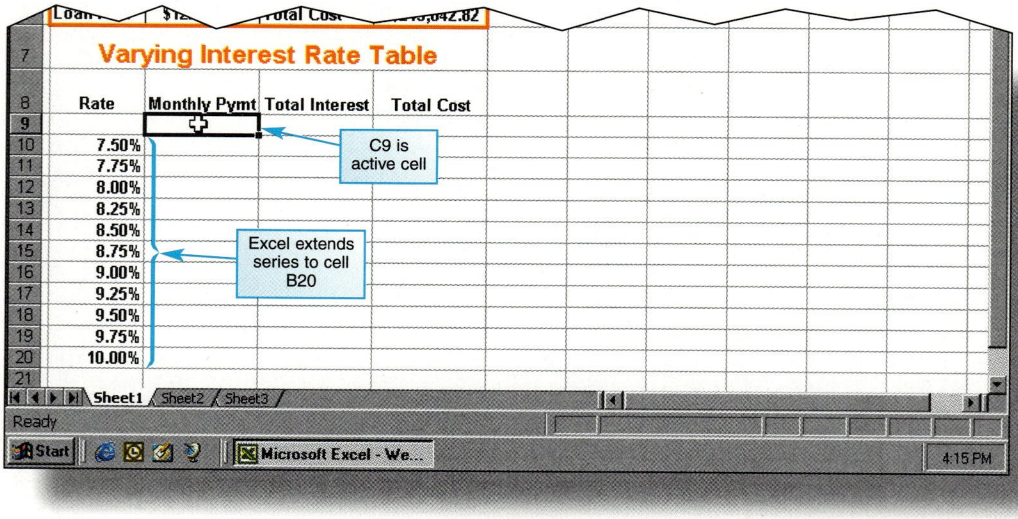

FIGURE 4-21

Excel will use the percents in column B to calculate the formulas to be evaluated and entered at the top of the data table in row 3. This series begins in cell B10, not cell B9, because the cell immediately to the left of the formulas in a one-input data table cannot include an input value.

Entering the Formulas in the Data Table

The next step in creating the data table is to enter the three formulas in cells C9, D9, and E9. The three formulas are the same as the monthly payment formula in cell E4, the total interest formula in cell E5, and the total cost formula in cell E6. The number of formulas you place at the top of a one-input data table depends on the application. Some one-input data tables will have only one formula, while others might have several. In this case, three formulas are affected when the interest rate changes.

Excel provides four ways to enter these formulas in the data table: (1) retype the formulas in cells C9, D9, and E9; (2) copy cells E4, E5, and E6 to cells C9, D9, and E9, respectively; (3) enter the formulas =monthly_pymt in cell C9, =total_interest in cell D9, and =total_cost in cell E9; or (4) enter the formulas =e4 in cell C9, =e5 in cell D9, and =e6 in cell E9.

The best alternative is the fourth one. That is, use the cell references preceded by an equal sign to define the formulas in the data table. This is the best method because: (1) it is easier to enter the cell references; and (2) if you change any of the formulas in the range E4:E6, the formulas at the top of the data table are updated automatically. Using the names of the cells in formulas is nearly as good an alternative. The reason why cell references are preferred over cell names is because if you use cell references, Excel assigns the format of the cell reference (Currency style format) to the cell. If you use cell names, Excel will not assign the format to the cell.

TO ENTER THE FORMULAS IN THE DATA TABLE

1 With cell C9 active, type =e4 and then press the RIGHT ARROW key.

2 Type =e5 in cell D9 and then press the RIGHT ARROW key.

3 Type =e6 in cell E9 and then click the Enter box or press the ENTER key.

The results of the formulas display in the range C9:E9 (Figure 4-22). Excel automatically assigns the Currency style format to cells C9 through E9 based on the formats assigned to cells E4 through E6.

More *About*

Formulas in Data Tables

Any experienced Excel user will tell you that to enter the formulas at the top of the data table, you should enter the cell reference or name of the cell preceded by an equal sign. This ensures that if you change the original formula in the worksheet, Excel automatically will change the corresponding formula in the data table. If you use a cell reference, Excel also copies the format to the cell. If you use a name, Excel does not copy the format to the cell.

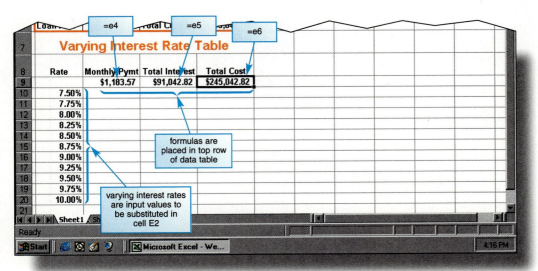

FIGURE 4-22

It is important to understand that the entries in the top row of the data table (row 9) refer to the formulas that the loan department wants to evaluate using the series of percents in column B.

Defining the Data Table

After creating the percent interest rates series in column B and entering the formulas in row 9, the next step is to define the range B9:E20 as a data table.

Steps To Define a Range as a Data Table

1 Select the range B9:E20. Click Data on the menu bar and then point to Table.

The Data menu displays (Figure 4-23). The range to be defined as the data table begins with the formulas in row 9. The section title and column headings in the range B7:E8 are not part of the data table, even though they identify the data table and columns in the table.

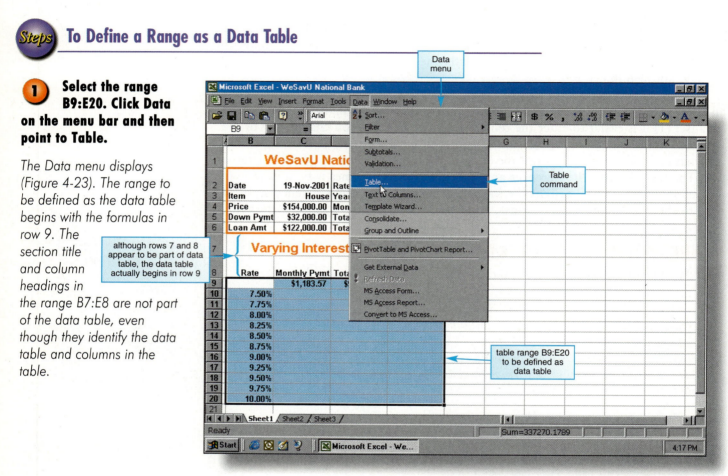

FIGURE 4-23

2 **Click Table. When the Table dialog box displays, click the Column input cell text box. Click cell E2 in the loan analysis section as the input cell and then point to the OK button.**

A marquee surrounds the selected cell E2, indicating it will be the input cell in which values from column B in the data table are substituted in the formula. $E$2 displays in the Column input cell text box in the Table dialog box (Figure 4-24).

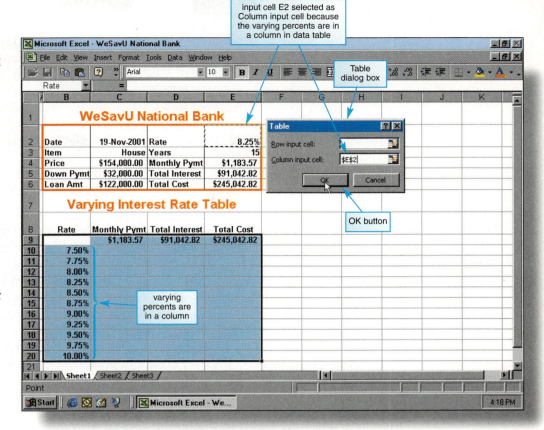

FIGURE 4-24

3 **Click the OK button.**

Excel calculates the results of the three formulas in row 9 for each interest rate in column B and immediately fills columns C, D, and E of the data table (Figure 4-25). The resulting values for each interest rate are displayed in the corresponding rows.

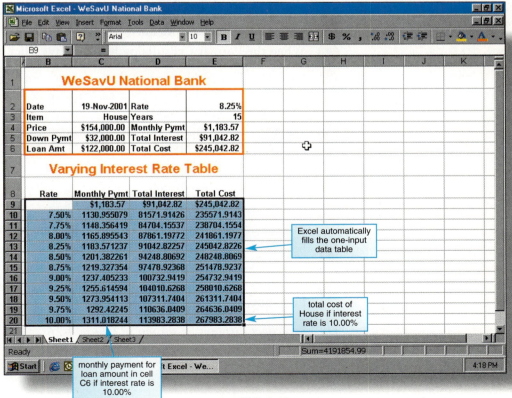

FIGURE 4-25

In Figure 4-25 on the previous page, the data table displays the monthly payment, total interest, and total cost for the interest rates in column B. For example, if the interest rate is 8.25% (cell E2), the monthly payment is $1,183.57 (cell E4). If, however, the interest rate is 9.75% (cell B19), the monthly payment is $1,292.42 rounded to the nearest cent (cell C19). If the interest rate is 7.50% (cell B10), then the total cost of the house is $235,571.91 rounded to the nearest cent (cell E10), rather than $245,042.82 (cell E6). Thus, a 0.75% decrease in the interest rate results in a $9,470.91 decrease in the total cost of the house. The results in the data table in Figure 4-25 will be formatted to the Comma style shortly.

The following list details important points you should know about data tables:

1. The formula(s) you are analyzing must have a cell reference to the input cell.
2. You can have as many active data tables in a worksheet as you want.
3. While only one value can vary in a one-input data table, the data table can analyze as many formulas as you want.
4. To add additional formulas to a one-input data table, enter them in adjacent cells in the same row as the current formulas (row 9 in Figure 4-25) and then define the entire new range as a data table by using the Table command on the Data menu.
5. You delete a data table as you would delete any other item on a worksheet. That is, select the data table and press the DELETE key.

Formatting the Data Table

The next step is to format the data table to improve its readability.

TO OUTLINE AND FORMAT THE DATA TABLE

1 Select the range B8:E20. Right-click the selected range and then click Format Cells on the shortcut menu.

2 When the Format Cells dialog box displays, click the Border tab.

3 Click the Color box arrow. Select red (column 1, row 3) on the palette. Click the heavy border in the Style area (column 2, row 6). Click the Outline button in the Presets area.

4 Click the Color box arrow. Click Automatic (row 1) on the palette. Click the light border in the Style area (column 1, row 7). Click the vertical border button in the Border area.

5 Click the OK button.

6 Select the range B8:E8. Click the Borders button arrow on the Formatting toolbar and then click the Thick Bottom Border button (column 2, row 2).

7 Select the range C10:E20. Click the Comma Style button on the Formatting toolbar. Click cell G20 to deselect the range C10:E20.

8 Click the Save button on the Standard toolbar to save the workbook using the file name, WeSavU National Bank.

The worksheet displays as shown in Figure 4-26.

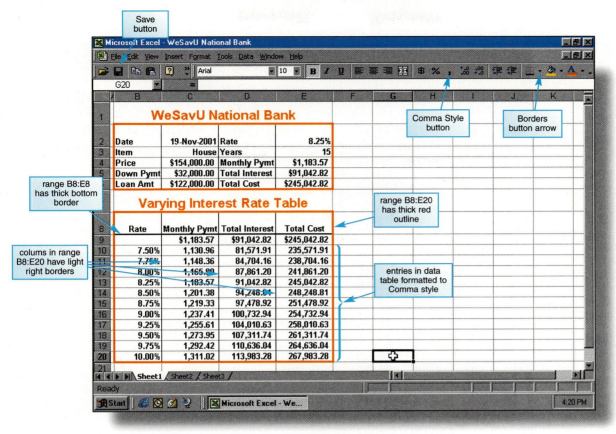

FIGURE 4-26

The data table is complete. Each time you enter new data into the loan analysis section, Excel recalculates all formulas, including the data table.

Adding an Input Value Pointer to the Data Table Using Conditional Formatting

If the interest rate in cell E2 is between 7.50% and 10.00% and its decimal portion is a multiple of 0.25 (such as 8.25%), then one of the rows in the data table agrees exactly with the monthly payment, interest paid, and total cost in the range E4:E6. For example, in Figure 4-26, row 13 (8.25%) in the data table agrees with the results in the range E4:E6, because the interest rate in cell B13 is the same as the interest rate in cell E2. Analysts often look for the row in the data table that agrees with the input cell results. To make this row stand out, you can use **conditional formatting** to color the background of the cell in column B that agrees with the input cell (cell E2) as shown in the steps on the next page.

Conditional Formatting

You can add up to three different conditions to a cell or range of cells. To include additional conditions, click the Add button in the Conditional Formatting dialog box. If more than one condition is true for a cell, then Excel applies the format of the first condition that is true.

To Add an Input Cell Pointer to the Data Table

1 Select the range
B10:B20. Click
Format on the menu bar
and then point to
Conditional Formatting.

*The Format menu displays
(Figure 4-27).*

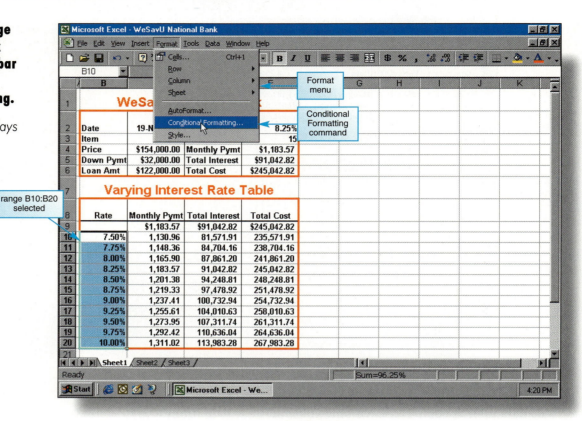

FIGURE 4-27

2 Click Conditional
Formatting. When
the Conditional Formatting
dialog box displays, click
equal to in the middle box
of the Condition 1 area.
Click the box on the right
in the Condition 1 area
(also called value 2 box)
and then click cell E2 in the
loan analysis section. Click
the Format button, click the
Patterns tab, and click the
color green (column 4, row
2) on the color palette.
Click the OK button in the
Format Cells dialog box.

*The Conditional Formatting
dialog box displays as shown
in Figure 4-28.*

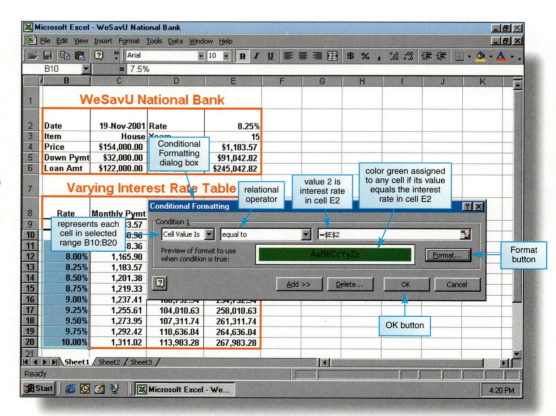

FIGURE 4-28

3 Click the OK button in the Conditional Formatting dialog box. Click cell G20 to deselect the range B10:B20.

Cell B13 in the data table, which contains 8.25%, displays with a green background because 8.25% is the same as the rate in cell E2 (Figure 4-29).

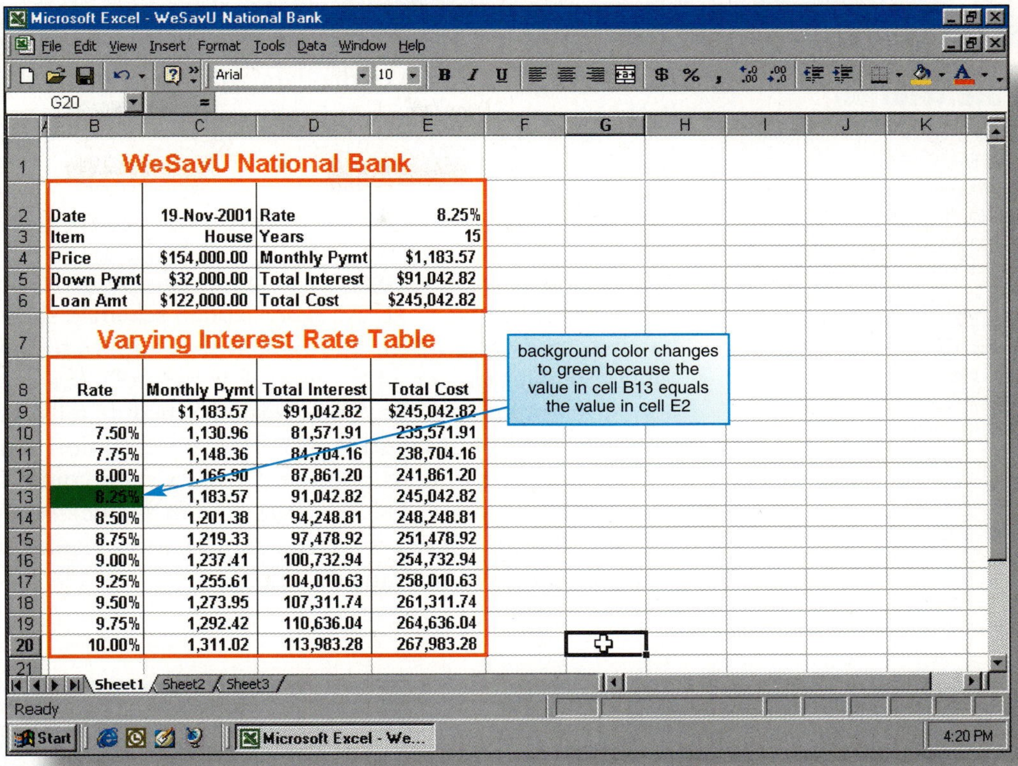

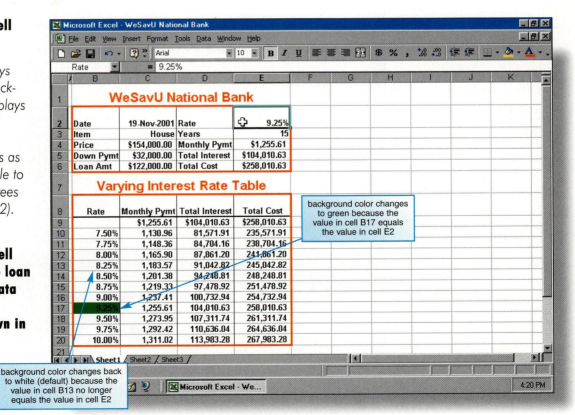

FIGURE 4-29

4 Enter 9.25 in cell E2.

Excel immediately displays cell B17 with a green background and cell B13 displays with a white background (Figure 4-30). Thus, the green background serves as a pointer in the data table to indicate the row that agrees with the input cell (cell E2).

5 Enter 8.25 in cell E2 to return the loan analysis section and data table section to their original states as shown in Figure 4-28.

FIGURE 4-30

More About

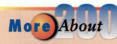

Recalculation

Enter a value in a worksheet and Excel automatically recalculates all formulas and data tables. You can instruct Excel not to recalculate data tables, unless you press function key F9. To change recalculation, click Options on the Tools menu, click the Calculation tab, click Automatic except tables in the Calculation area, and then click the OK button.

When the loan officer using this worksheet enters a different percent in cell E2, the pointer will move or disappear. It will disappear whenever the interest rate in cell E2 is outside the range of the data table or its decimal portion is not a multiple of 0.25.

Creating an Amortization Schedule

The next step in this project is to create the Amortization Schedule shown on the right side of Figure 4-31. An **amortization schedule** shows the beginning and ending balances and the amount of payment that applies to the principal and interest for each year over the life of the loan. For example, if a customer wanted to pay off the loan after two years, the Amortization Schedule tells the loan officer what the payoff would be (cell I4 in Figure 4-31). The Amortization Schedule shown in Figure 4-31 will work only for loans of up to 15 years. You could, however, extend the table to any number of years. The Amortization Schedule also contains summaries in rows 18, 19, and 20. These summaries should agree exactly with the amounts in the loan analysis section in the range B1:E6.

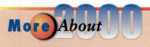

More About

Amortization Schedules

Hundreds of Web sites offer amortization schedules. Use a search engine with your browser to find several sites. Search for amortization schedule. For an example of a Web site that determines an amortization schedule, visit the Excel 2000 More About Web page (www.scsite.com/ex2000/more.htm) and click Amortization Schedule.

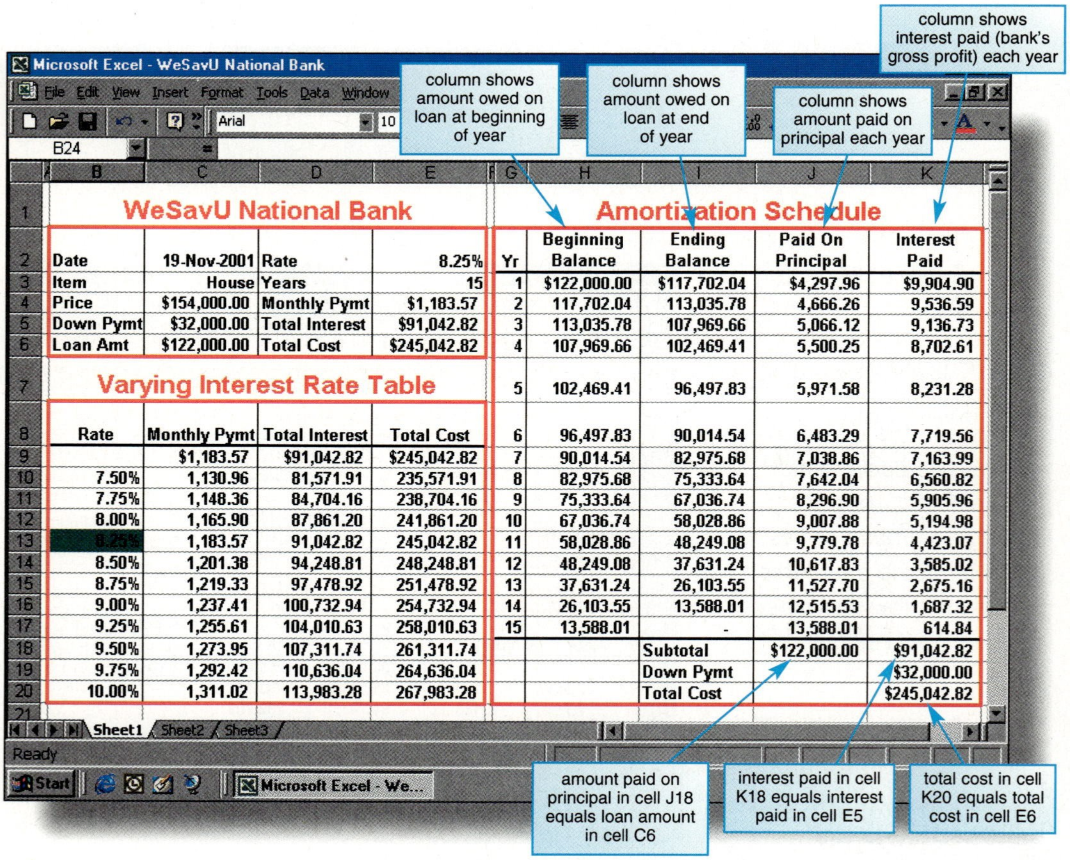

WeSavU National Bank

Date	19-Nov-2001	Rate	8.25%
Item	House	Years	15
Price	$154,000.00	Monthly Pymt	$1,183.57
Down Pymt	$32,000.00	Total Interest	$91,042.82
Loan Amt	$122,000.00	Total Cost	$245,042.82

Varying Interest Rate Table

Rate	Monthly Pymt	Total Interest	Total Cost
	$1,183.57	$91,042.82	$245,042.82
7.50%	1,130.96	81,571.91	235,571.91
7.75%	1,148.36	84,704.16	238,704.16
8.00%	1,165.90	87,861.20	241,861.20
8.25%	1,183.57	91,042.82	245,042.82
8.50%	1,201.38	94,248.81	248,248.81
8.75%	1,219.33	97,478.92	251,478.92
9.00%	1,237.41	100,732.94	254,732.94
9.25%	1,255.61	104,010.63	258,010.63
9.50%	1,273.95	107,311.74	261,311.74
9.75%	1,292.42	110,636.04	264,636.04
10.00%	1,311.02	113,983.28	267,983.28

Amortization Schedule

Yr	Beginning Balance	Ending Balance	Paid On Principal	Interest Paid
1	$122,000.00	$117,702.04	$4,297.96	$9,904.90
2	117,702.04	113,035.78	4,666.26	9,536.59
3	113,035.78	107,969.66	5,066.12	9,136.73
4	107,969.66	102,469.41	5,500.25	8,702.61
5	102,469.41	96,497.83	5,971.58	8,231.28
6	96,497.83	90,014.54	6,483.29	7,719.56
7	90,014.54	82,975.68	7,038.86	7,163.99
8	82,975.68	75,333.64	7,642.04	6,560.82
9	75,333.64	67,036.74	8,296.90	5,905.96
10	67,036.74	58,028.86	9,007.88	5,194.98
11	58,028.86	48,249.08	9,779.78	4,423.07
12	48,249.08	37,631.24	10,617.83	3,585.02
13	37,631.24	26,103.55	11,527.70	2,675.16
14	26,103.55	13,588.01	12,515.53	1,687.32
15	13,588.01	-	13,588.01	614.84
		Subtotal	$122,000.00	$91,042.82
		Down Pymt		$32,000.00
		Total Cost		$245,042.82

FIGURE 4-31

To construct the Amortization Schedule shown in Figure 4-31, complete the following steps: (1) adjust the column widths and enter the titles in the range G1:K2; (2) use the fill handle to create a series of integers in column G that represent the years 1 through 15; (3) enter the formulas in the range H3:K3 and then copy them to the range H4:K17; (4) enter the total formulas; (5) format the numbers; and (6) outline the Amortization Schedule to highlight it.

Changing Column Widths and Entering the Titles

The first step in creating the Amortization Schedule is to adjust the column widths and enter the Amortization Schedule section title and column titles.

TO CHANGE COLUMN WIDTHS AND ENTER TITLES

1 Position the mouse pointer on the right boundary of column heading F and then drag to the left until the ScreenTip, Width: .50 (6 pixels) displays.

2 Position the mouse pointer on the right boundary of column heading G and then drag to the left until the ScreenTip, Width: 3.00 (26 pixels), displays.

3 Drag through column headings H through K to select them. Position the mouse pointer on the right boundary of column heading K and then drag to the right until the ScreenTip, Width: 12.29 (91 pixels) displays.

4 Click cell G1. Type Amortization Schedule as the section title. Press the ENTER key

5 With cell G1 selected, click the Font Size box arrow on the Formatting toolbar and then click 16. Click the Font Color button on the Formatting toolbar to change the font color to red. Select the range G1:K1 and then click the Merge and Center button on the Formatting toolbar.

6 Enter the column titles from the table on the right in the range G2:K2. Where appropriate, press ALT+ENTER to enter the titles on two lines.

7 Select the range G2:K2 and then click the Center button on the Formatting toolbar. Click cell G3.

CELL	ENTRY
G2	Yr
H2	Beginning Balance
I2	Ending Balance
J2	Paid On Principal
K2	Interest Paid

The section title and column headings display as shown in Figure 4-32.

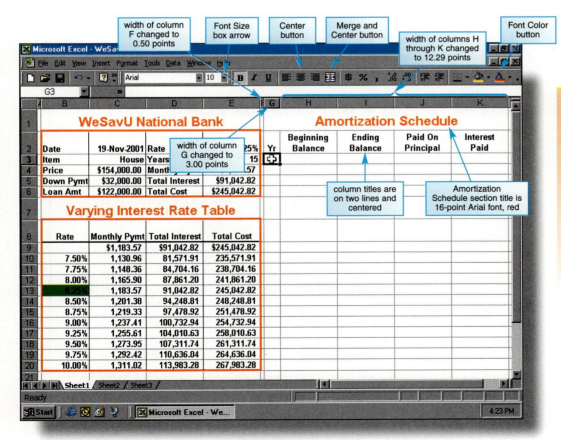

FIGURE 4-32

More About 2000

Column Borders

In this project, columns A and F are used as column borders to divide sections of the worksheet from one another as well as from the row headings. A column border is an unused column with a significantly reduced width. You also can use row borders to separate sections of a worksheet.

Creating a Series of Integers Using the Fill Handle

The next step is to create a series of numbers, using the fill handle, that represent the years during the life of the loan. The series begins with 1 (year 1) and ends with 15 (year 15).

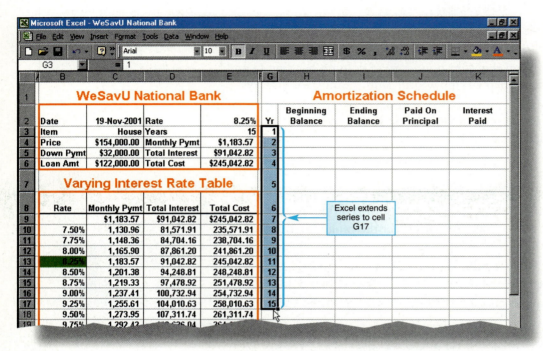

FIGURE 4-33

TO CREATE A SERIES OF INTEGERS USING THE FILL HANDLE

1 With cell G3 active, enter 1 as the initial year. Click cell G4 and enter 2 to represent the next year.

2 Select the range G3:G4 and point to the fill handle. Drag the fill handle through cell G17.

Excel creates the series of integers 1 though 15 in the range G3:G17 (Figure 4-33).

As you will see shortly, the series of integers in the range G3:G17 will play an important role in determining the ending balance and interest paid in the amortization schedule.

Entering the Formulas in the Amortization Schedule

The next step is to enter the four formulas in row 3 that form the basis of the amortization schedule. Later, these formulas will be copied through row 17. The formulas are summarized in Table 4-2.

Table 4-2   Formulas for the Amortization Schedule

CELL	DESCRIPTION	FORMULA	COMMENT
H3	Beginning Balance	=C6	The beginning balance is the initial loan amount in cell C6.
I3	Ending Balance	=PV($E$2 /12, 12 * ($E$3 – G3), -$E$4)	The balance at the end of a year is equal to the present value of the monthly payments paid over the remaining life of the loan.
J3	Paid on Principal	=H3 – I3	The amount paid on the principal is equal to the beginning balance (cell H3) less the ending balance (cell I3).
K3	Interest Paid	=12 * $E$4 – J3	The interest paid during the year is equal to 12 times the monthly payment (cell E4) less the amount paid on the principal (cell J3).

Of the four formulas in Table 4-2, the most difficult to understand is the PV function that will be assigned to cell I3. The **PV function** returns the present value of an annuity. An **annuity** is a series of fixed payments (such as the monthly payment in cell E4) made at the end of a fixed number of terms (months) at a fixed interest rate. You can use the PV function to determine how much the borrower of the loan still owes at the end of each year.

The PV function can determine the ending balance after the first year (cell I3) by using a term equal to the number of months the borrower must still make payments. For example, if the loan is for 15 years (180 months), then the borrower still owes 168 payments after the first year. The number of payments outstanding can be determined from the formula 12 * (E3 – G3) or 12 * (15 – 1), which equals 168. Recall that column G contains integers that represent the years into the loan. After the second year, the number of payments remaining is 156, and so on.

If you assign the PV function to cell I3 as shown in Table 4-2, and you copy it down to the range I4:I17, the ending balances for each year will display properly. If, however, the loan is for less than 15 years, then the ending balances displayed for the years beyond the time the loan is due are invalid. For example, if a loan is taken out for 5 years, then the rows representing years 6 through 15 in the Amortization Schedule should be zero. The PV function, however, will display negative numbers even though the loan has already been paid off.

What is needed here is a way to assign the PV function to the range I3:I17 as long as the corresponding year in column G is less than or equal to the number of years in cell E3. If the corresponding year in column G is greater than the number of years in cell E3, then the ending balance for that year and the remaining years should be zero. As you know from previous projects, the IF function can handle this type of situation. The following IF function displays the value of the PV function or zero in cell I3 depending on whether the corresponding value in column G is less than or equal to the number of years in cell E3. Recall that the dollar signs within the cell references indicate the cell reference is absolute and, therefore, will not change as you copy the function downward.

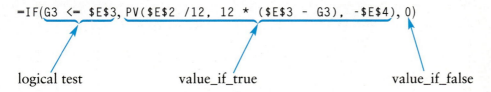

$$\text{=IF(G3 <= \$E\$3, PV(\$E\$2 /12, 12 * (\$E\$3 - G3), -\$E\$4), 0)}$$

logical test   value_if_true   value_if_false

In the above formula, the logical test determines if the year in column G is less than or equal to the term of the loan in cell E3. If the logical test is true, then the IF function assigns the PV function to the cell. If the logical test is false, then the IF function assigns zero (0) to the cell.

The PV function in the IF function includes absolute cell references (cell references with dollar signs) to ensure that these cell references in column E do not change when the If function is later copied down the column. The steps on the next page enter the four formulas shown in Table 4-2 into row 3. Row 3 represents year 1 of the loan.

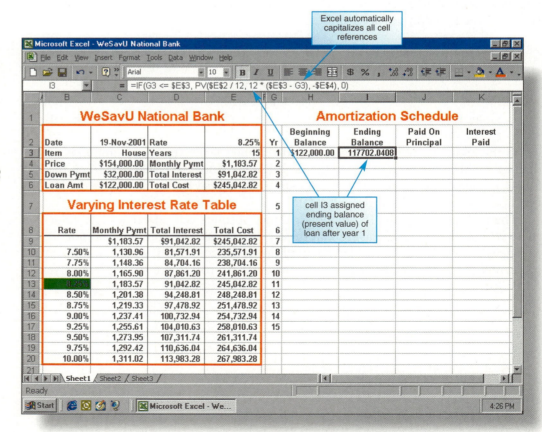

To Enter the Formulas in the Amortization Schedule

1 **Select cell H3. Type** =C6 **and then press the RIGHT ARROW key to enter the beginning balance of the loan. Type** =if(g3 <= e3, pv(e2 / 12, 12 * (e3 – g3), -e4), 0) **as the entry for cell I3.**

The loan amount displays in cell H3 as the first year's beginning balance using the same format as in cell C6. The IF function displays in cell I3 and in the formula bar (Figure 4-34).

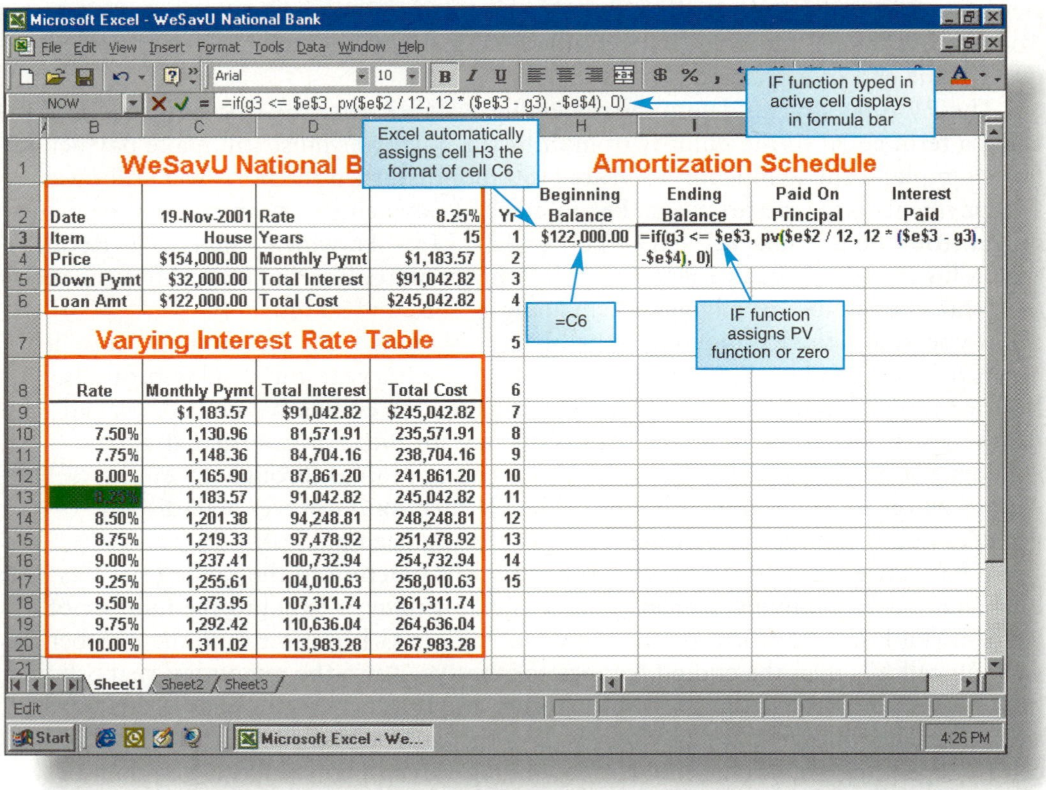

FIGURE 4-34

2 **Press the ENTER key.**

Excel evaluates the IF function in cell I3 and displays the result of the PV function (117702.0408) because the value in cell G3 (1) is less than or equal to the term of the loan in cell E3 (15). With cell I3 active, the formula displays in the formula bar (Figure 4-35). If the borrower wanted to pay off the loan after one year, the cost would be $117,702.04.

FIGURE 4-35

3 **Click cell J3. Type**
=h3 - i3 **and then**
press the RIGHT ARROW **key.**
Type =if(h3 > 0, 12 *
e4 - j3, 0) **in cell**
K3.

The amount paid on the principal after one year displays
in cell J3 using the same format as in cell H3. The IF
function displays in cell K3
and in the formula bar
(Figure 4-36).

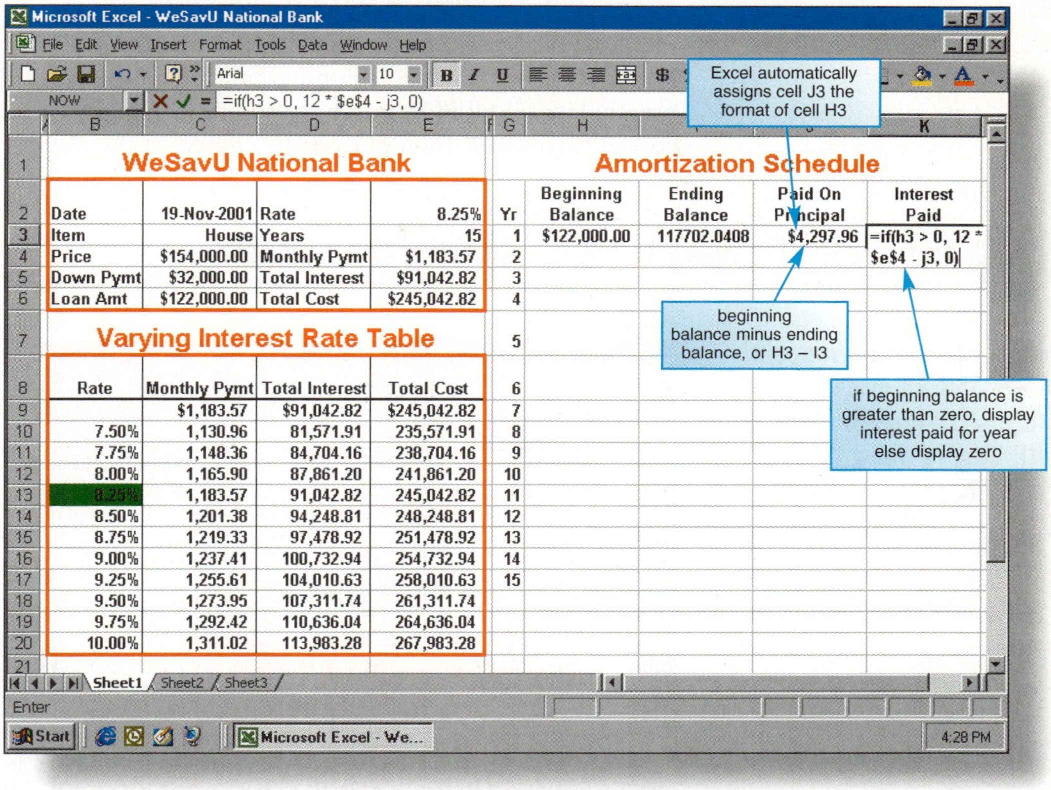

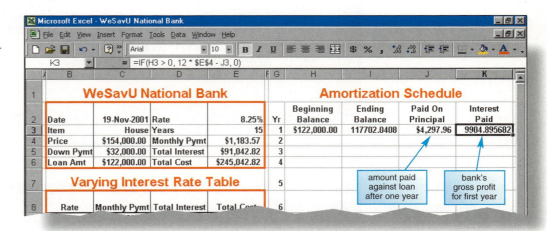

FIGURE 4-36

4 **Press the** ENTER **key.**

The interest paid after
one year displays in cell K3
(Figure 4-37).

FIGURE 4-37

When you enter a formula in a cell, Excel assigns the cell the same format as the
first cell reference in the formula. For example, when you enter =c6 in cell H3, Excel
assigns the format in cell C6 to H3. The same applies to cell J3. Excel assigns the
Currency style format to J3 because cell reference H3 is the first cell reference in the
formula (=H3 – I3) assigned to cell J3 and cell H3 has a Currency style format.
Although this method of formatting also works for most functions, it does not work
for the IF function. Thus, the results of the IF functions in cells I3 and K3 display
using the General format, which is the format of all cells when you open a new
workbook.

With the formulas entered into the first row, the next step is to copy them to the remaining rows in the Amortization Schedule. The required copying is straightforward except for the beginning balance column. To obtain the next year's beginning balance (cell H4), you have to use last year's ending balance (I3). Once cell I3 is copied to cell H4, then H4 can be copied to the range H5:H17.

To Copy the Formulas to Fill the Amortization Schedule

1 **Select the range I3:K3 and then point to the fill handle. Drag the fill handle down through row 17.**

The formulas in cells I3, J3, and K3 are copied to the range I4:K17 (Figure 4-38). Many of the numbers displayed are incorrect because most of the cells in column H do not contain beginning balances.

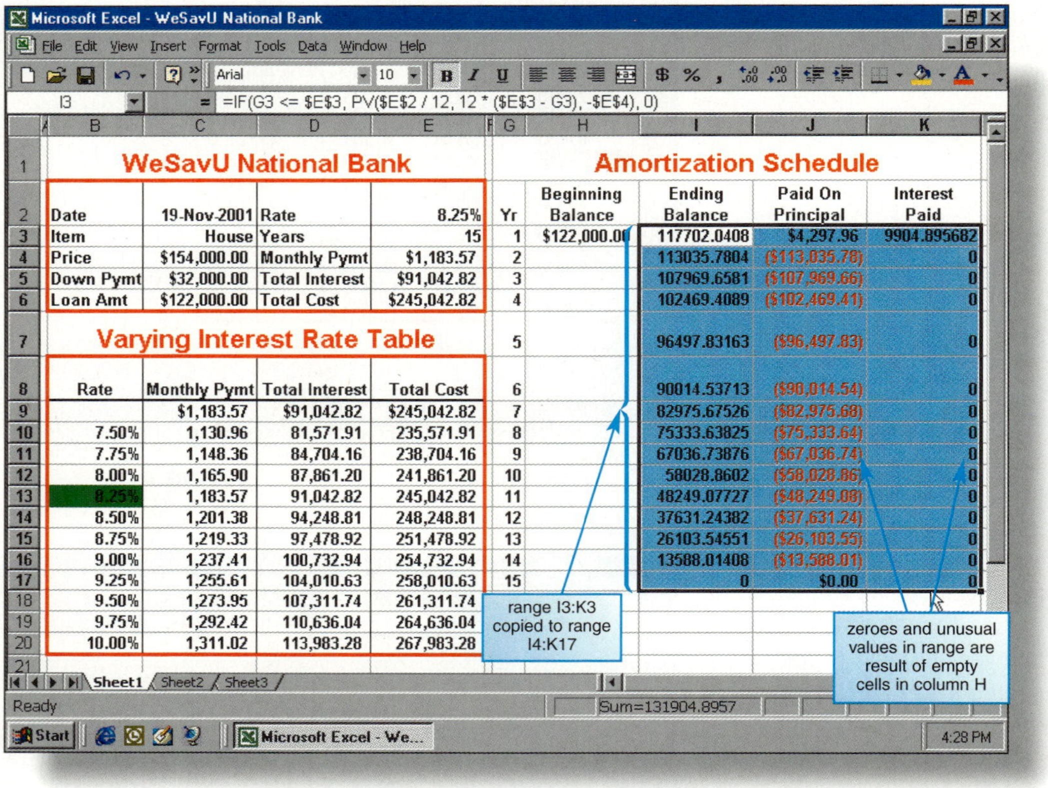

FIGURE 4-38

2 **Select cell H4. Type =I3 and then press the ENTER key.**

The ending balance for year 1 in cell I3 also displays as the beginning balance for year 2 in cell H4 (Figure 4-39).

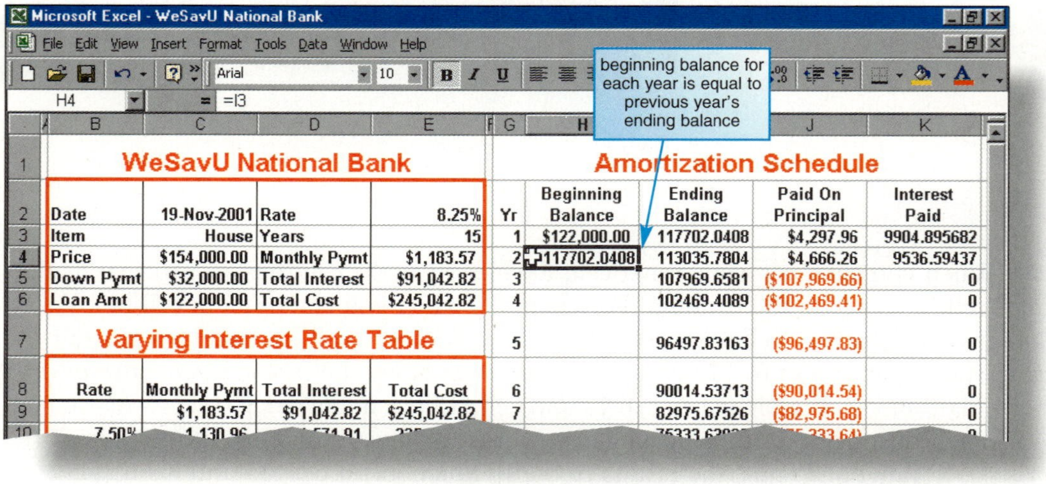

FIGURE 4-39

③ **With cell H4 active, point to the fill handle. Drag the fill handle down through row 17.**

The formula in cell H4 (=I3) is copied to the range H5:H17 (Figure 4-40). Because the cell reference I3 in the formula in cell H4 is relative, Excel adjusts the row portion of the cell reference as it is copied downward. Thus, each new beginning balance in column H is equal to the ending balance of the previous year.

④ **Click the Save button on the Standard toolbar to save the workbook using the file name, WeSavU National Bank.**

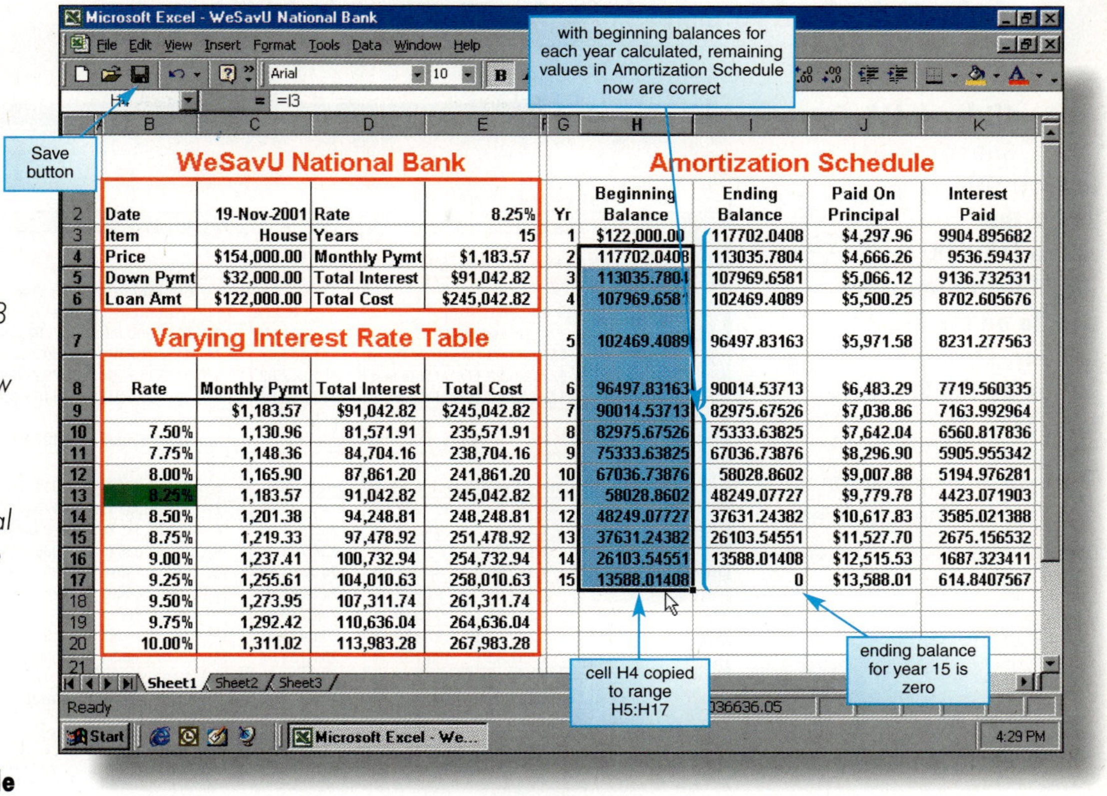

FIGURE 4-40

The numbers that display in the Amortization Schedule in Figure 4-40 are now correct, although they need to be formatted to make them easier to read. Cell I17 shows that at the end of the 15th year, the ending balance is zero, which is what it should be for a 15-year loan.

Entering the Total Formulas in the Amortization Schedule

The next step is to determine the amortization schedule totals in rows 18 through 20. These totals should agree with the totals in the loan analysis section (range B1:E6).

To Enter the Total Formulas in the Amortization Schedule

1 **Click cell I18. Enter** `Subtotal` **as the row title. Select the range J18:K18. Double-click the move handle on the Standard toolbar. Click the AutoSum button on the Standard toolbar.**

The total amount paid on the principal and the total interest paid display in cells J18 and K18, respectively (Figure 4-41)

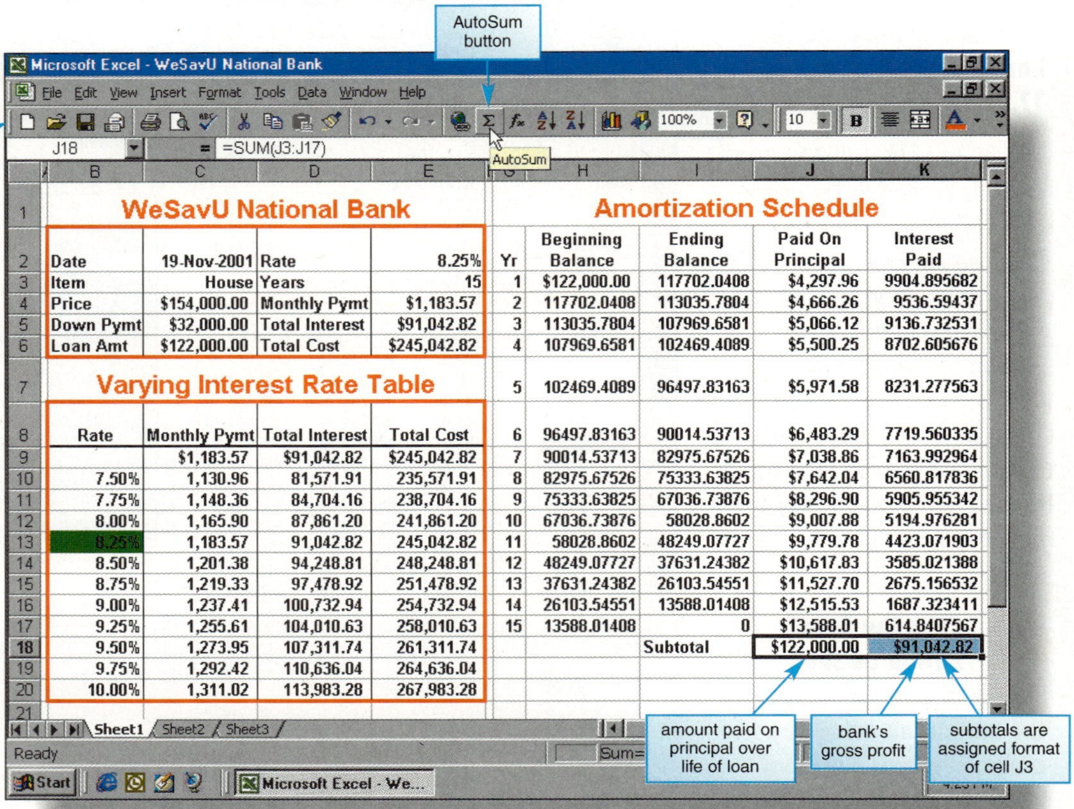

FIGURE 4-41

2 **Click cell I19. Enter** `Down Pymt` **as the row title. Click cell K19 and enter** `=c5` **as the down payment. Click cell I20. Enter** `Total Cost` **as the row title. Click cell K20 and enter** `=j18 + k18 + k19` **as the total cost.**

The amortization schedule totals display as shown in Figure 4-42.

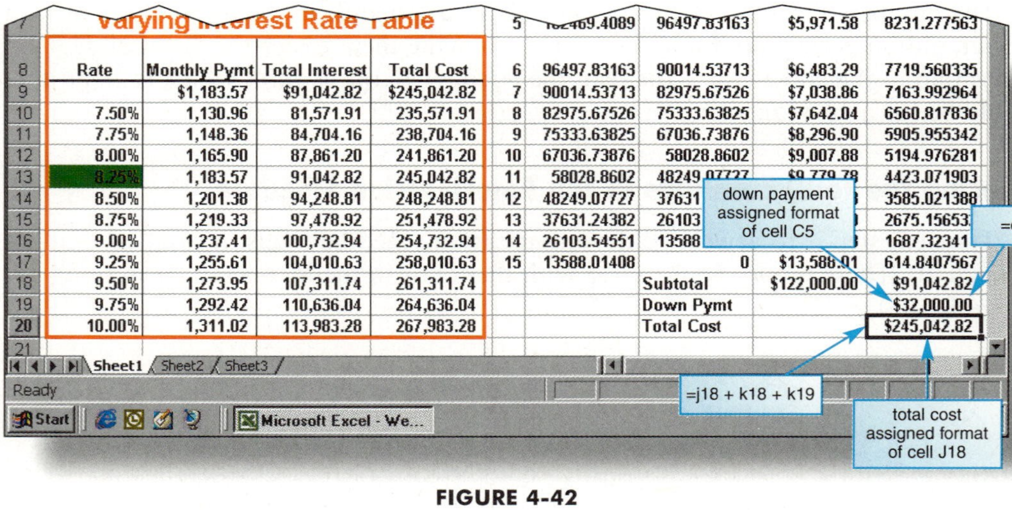

FIGURE 4-42

The formula assigned to cell K20 sums the amounts paid on the principal (cell J18), the total interest paid (cell K18), and the down payment (cell K19).

Here again, Excel assigns the same format to cell J18 as in cell J3, because cell J3 is the first cell reference in =SUM(J3:J17). Furthermore, cell J18 was selected first when the range J18:K18 was selected to determine the sum. Thus, Excel assigned cell K18 the same format as was assigned to cell J18. Finally, cell K19 was assigned the Currency style format, because cell K19 was assigned the formula =C5 and cell C5 has a Currency style format. For the same reason, the value in cell K20 displays in Currency style format.

Formatting New Loan Data

The final step in creating the amortization schedule is to format it so it is easier to read. The formatting is divided into two parts (1) format the numbers; and (2) add an outline and borders.

When the beginning balance formula (=C6) was entered earlier into cell H3, Excel automatically copied the Currency style format along with the value from cell C6 to cell H3. The following steps use the Format Painter button to copy the Currency style format from cell H3 to the range I3:K3. Finally, the Comma Style button on the Formatting toolbar will be used to assign the Comma style format to the range H4:K17.

TO FORMAT THE NUMBERS IN THE AMORTIZATION SCHEDULE

1. Click cell H3. Click the Format Painter button on the Standard toolbar. Drag through the range I3:K3 to assign the Currency style format to the numbers.

2. Double click the move handle on the Formatting toolbar. Select the range H4:K17. Click the Comma Style button on the Formatting toolbar. Select cell H19 to deselect the range H4:K17.

The numbers in the amortization schedule display as shown in Figure 4-43.

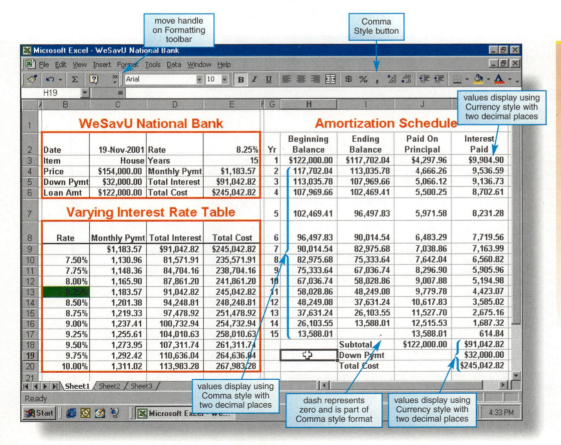

FIGURE 4-43

More About

Round-Off Errors

If you manually add the numbers in column K (range K3:K17) and compare it with the sum in cell K18, you will notice that the total interest paid is $0.01 off. You can use the ROUND function on the formula entered into cell K3 to ensure the total is exactly correct. For information on the ROUND function, click the Paste button on the Standard toolbar, click Math & Trig in the Function category list, scroll down in the Function name list, and then click ROUND.

The Comma Style button on the Formatting toolbar was used purposely to format the body of amortization schedule because it uses the dash to represent zero (see cell I17). If the term of a loan is for less than 15 years, the amortization schedule will include zeros in cells. The dash has a more professional appearance than columns of zeros.

The following steps add the outline and borders to the amortization schedule.

TO ADD AN OUTLINE AND BORDERS TO THE AMORTIZATION SCHEDULE

1 Select the range G2:K20. Right-click the selected range and then click Format Cells on the shortcut menu.

2 When the Format Cells dialog box displays, click the Border tab.

3 Click the Color box arrow. Click red (column 1, row 3) on the palette. Click the heavy border in the Style area (column 2, row 6). Click the Outline button in the Presets area.

4 Click the Color box arrow. Click Automatic (row 1) on the palette. Click the light border in the Style area (column 1, row 7). Click the vertical line button in the Border area.

5 Click the OK button.

6 Select the range G2:K2. Click the Borders button arrow on the Formatting toolbar and then click Thick Bottom Border (column 2, row 2).

7 Select the range G17:K17 and click the Borders button arrow to assign it a thick bottom border.

8 Double-click the move handle on the Standard toolbar. Click the Save button on the Standard toolbar to save the workbook using the file name, WeSavU National Bank.

The worksheet displays as shown in Figure 4-44.

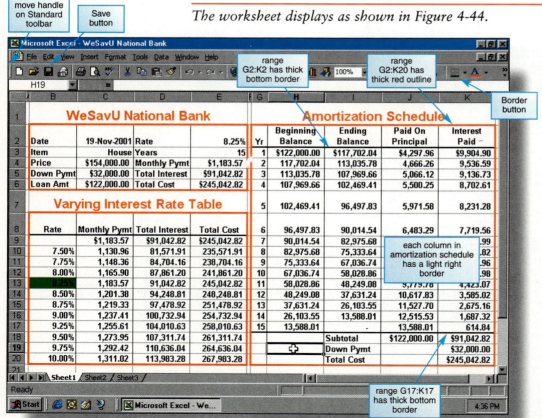

FIGURE 4-44

Entering New Loan Data

With the loan analysis, data table, and Amortization Schedule sections of the worksheet complete, you can use them to generate new loan information. For example, assume you want to purchase a 2002 Camaro for $28,500.00. You have $5,500.00 for a down payment and want the loan for 5 years. WeSavU National Bank currently is charging 9.50% interest for a 5-year automobile loan. The following steps show how to enter the new loan data.

TO ENTER NEW LOAN DATA

1 Click cell C3. Type 2002 Camaro and then press the DOWN ARROW key.

2 In cell C4, type 28500 and then press the DOWN ARROW key.

3 In cell C5, type 5500 and then press the ENTER key.

4 Click cell E2, type 9.50 and then press the DOWN ARROW key.

5 In cell E3, type 5 and then press the DOWN ARROW key. Click cell H19.

Excel automatically recalculates the loan information in cells C6, E4, E5, E6, the data table in the rangeB7:E20, and the Amortization Schedule in the range G3:K20 (Figure 4-45).

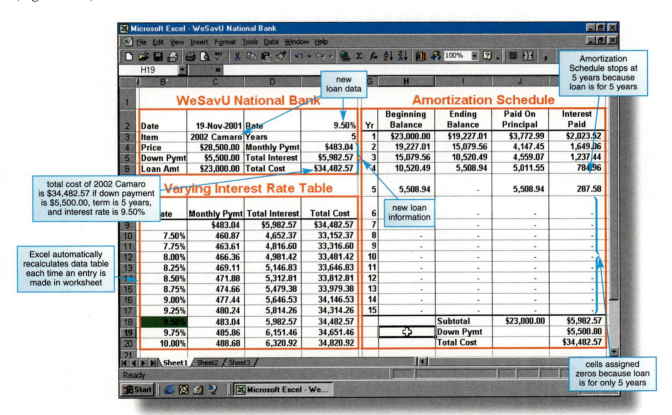

FIGURE 4-45

As you can see from Figure 4-45 on the previous page, the monthly payment for the 2002 Camaro is $483.04 (cell E4). The total interest is $5,982.57 (cell E5). The total cost of the $28,500.00 Camaro is $34,482.57 (cell E6). Because the term of the loan is for five years, rows 6 through 15 in the amortization schedule display a dash (-), which represents zero (0).

The following steps enter the original loan data.

TO ENTER THE ORIGINAL LOAN DATA

1 Click cell C3. Type House and then press the DOWN ARROW key.

2 In cell C4, type 154000 and then press the DOWN ARROW key.

3 In cell C5, type 32000 and then press the ENTER key.

4 Click cell E2, type 8.25 and then press the DOWN ARROW key.

5 In cell E3, type 15 and then click the Enter box or press the ENTER key. Click cell H20.

Excel automatically recalculates the loan information, the data table, and the amortization schedule as shown previously in Figure 4-44 on page E 4.40.

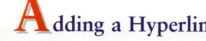dding a Hyperlink to the Worksheet

A **hyperlink** points to the location of a computer on which a destination file is stored. With Excel, you easily can create hyperlinks (Figure 4-46) to other files on your personal computer, your intranet, or the World Wide Web. The destination file (or hyperlinked file) can be any Office document or HTML file (Web page). Two primary worksheet elements exist to which you can assign a hyperlink:

1. **Text** – Enter text in a cell and make the text a hyperlink; text hyperlinks display in the color blue and are underlined.
2. **Embedded graphic** – Draw or insert a graphic, such as clip art, and then make the graphic a hyperlink.

You use the **Hyperlink command** on the shortcut menu to assign the hyperlink to the worksheet element.

Hyperlinks

You can embed hyperlinks into an Excel worksheet that easily connect to important information on your local disk, on your company's intranet, or on the Internet. The information can be a Web page or another Office 2000 document, such as an Excel workbook.

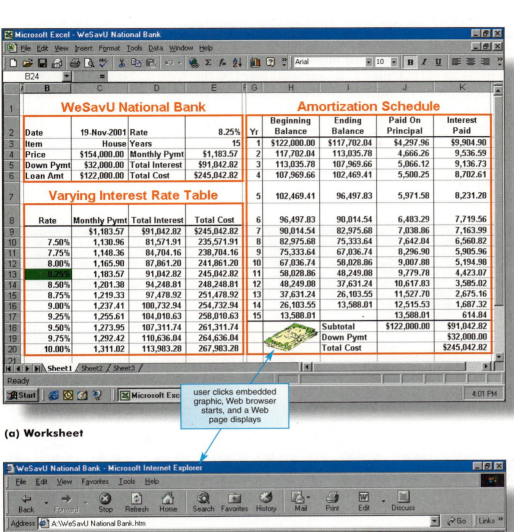

(a) Worksheet

user clicks embedded graphic, Web browser starts, and a Web page displays

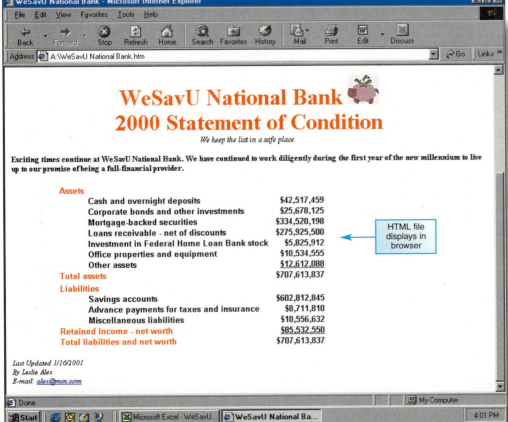

HTML file displays in browser

(b) Web Page   **FIGURE 4-46**

Assigning a Hyperlink to an Embedded Graphic

The following steps show how to assign a hyperlink to a graphic. The destination file is an HTML file (Web page) that contains the WeSavU National Bank's 2000 Statement of Condition. The destination file, WeSavU National Bank.htm, is located on the Data Disk. If you do not have a copy of the Data Disk, see the inside back cover of this book.

 Steps

To Assign a Hyperlink to an Embedded Graphic

1 **Click Insert on the menu bar. Point to Picture and then point to Clip Art on the Picture submenu.**

The Insert menu and Picture submenu display (Figure 4-47).

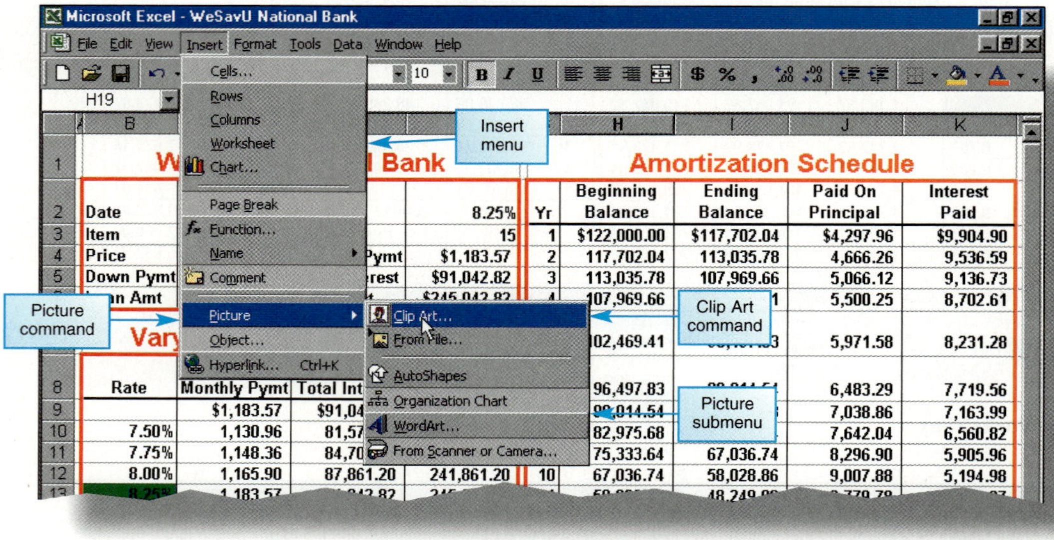

FIGURE 4-47

2 **Click Clip Art. When the Insert ClipArt window displays, point to the Business icon (column 3, row 2) in the Categories list box.**

The Insert ClipArt window displays (Figure 4-48). Each icon in the Categories list box represents a category of clip art.

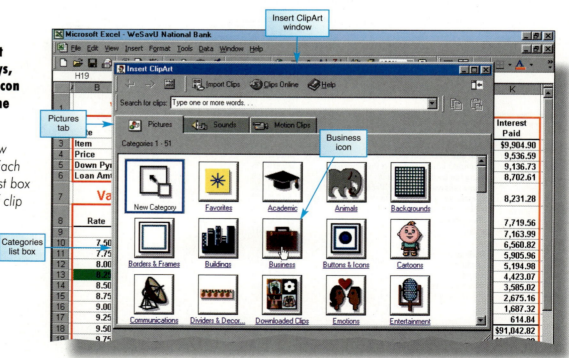

FIGURE 4-48

3 **Click the Business icon. If necessary, scroll down until the stack of dollar bills graphic displays. If the stack of dollar bills graphic is not available, select another one. Right-click the stack of dollar bills graphic and then point to Insert on the shortcut menu.**

The shortcut menu displays (Figure 4-49).

FIGURE 4-49

4 **Click Insert. Click the Close button in the Insert ClipArt window. Scroll down in the worksheet so the stack of dollar bills graphic is in full view.**

Excel embeds the stack of dollar bills graphic below the data in the worksheet (Figure 4-50).

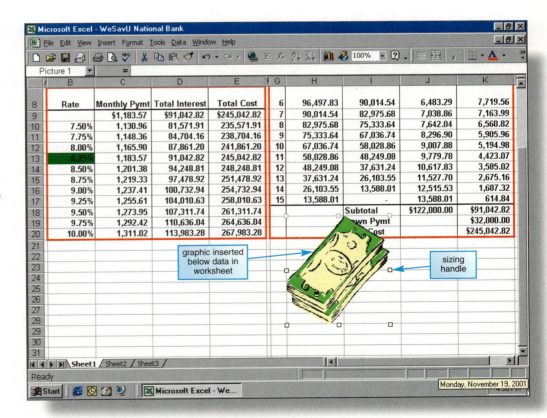

FIGURE 4-50

5 Drag the sizing handles to resize the graphic and then drag it so it displays in the range H18:H20.

The stack of dollar bills graphic displays (Figure 4-51).

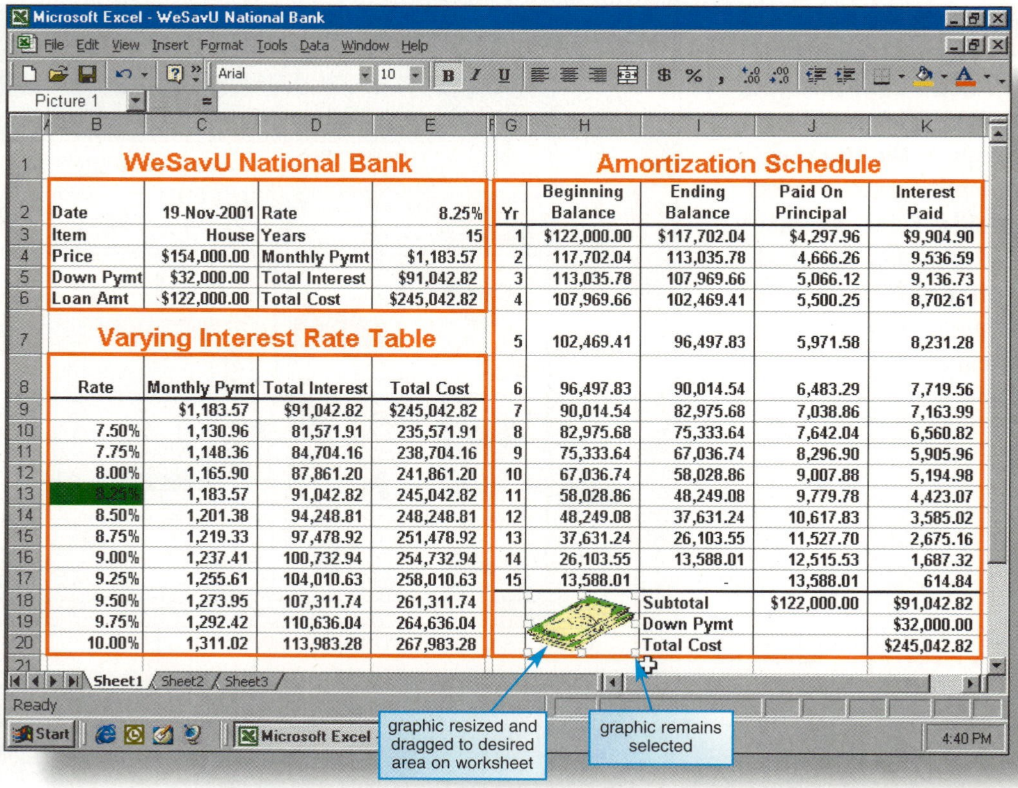

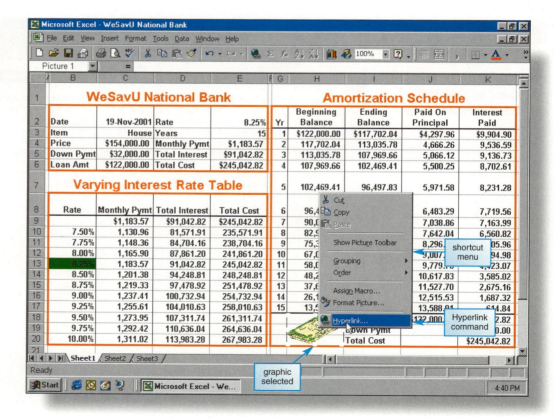

FIGURE 4-51

6 With the stack of dollar bills graphic selected, right-click it and then point to Hyperlink on the shortcut menu (Figure 4-52).

FIGURE 4-52

7 **Click Hyperlink. When the Insert Hyperlink dialog box displays, type** `a:\wesavu national bank.htm` **in the Type the file or Web page name text box. Point to the OK button.**

The Insert Hyperlink dialog box displays (Figure 4-53).

8 **Click the OK button. Click cell J19 to deselect the graphic. Click the Save button on the Standard toolbar to save the workbook using the file name, WeSavU National Bank.**

Excel assigns the hyperlink, a:\WeSavU National Bank.htm, to the stack of dollar bills graphic. Excel saves the workbook using the file name, WeSavU National Bank.

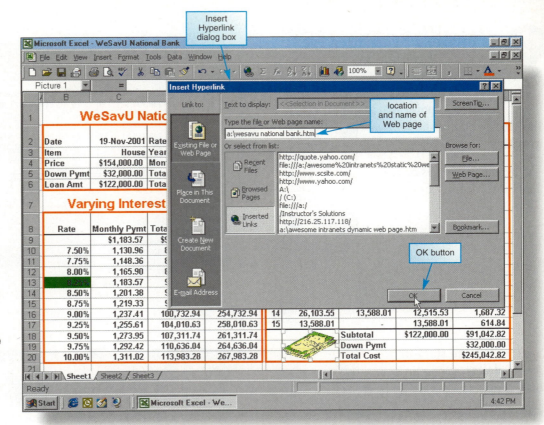

FIGURE 4-53

To edit the hyperlink, right-click the stack of dollar bills graphic to select it, point to Hyperlink on the shortcut menu, and then click Edit Hyperlink or click the Insert Hyperlink button on the Standard toolbar.

Displaying a Hyperlinked File

The next step is to display the hyperlinked file by clicking the stack of dollar bills graphic on the worksheet. Once you assign a hyperlink to an element in your worksheet, you can position the mouse pointer on the element to display the hyperlink as a ScreenTip. Clicking the stack of dollar bills graphic will display the hyperlinked file, as shown in the steps on the next page.

To Display a Hyperlinked File

1 **With the Data Disk in drive A, point to the stack of dollar bills graphic.**

The hyperlink displays as a ScreenTip (Figure 4-54).

FIGURE 4-54

2 **Click the stack of dollar bills graphic.**

Excel starts your browser and displays the HTML file (Web page) as shown in Figure 4-55. The Web page contains the WeSavU National Bank 2000 Statement of Condition. Both the Excel button and browser button display on the taskbar.

3 **When you are finished viewing the Web page, click the Back button to return to Excel.**

The browser closes and the loan analysis worksheet displays in the active window.

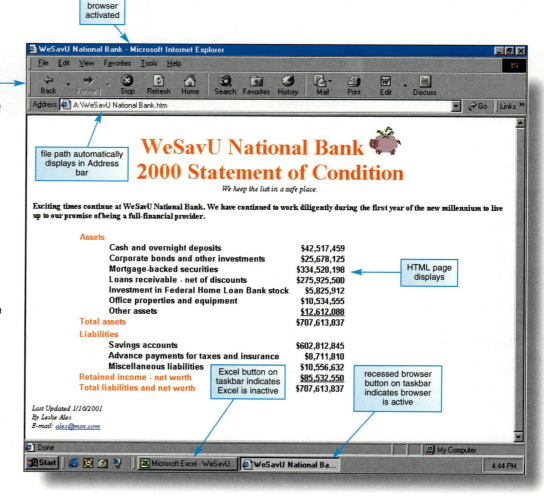

FIGURE 4-55

If the hyperlink does not connect you to the destination file, make sure you typed the correct hyperlink in the Type the file or Web page name text box in the Insert Hyperlink dialog box (Figure 4-53 on the previous page). If you entered the hyperlink correctly and it still does not work, check to be sure the file exists on the Data Disk.

Protecting the Worksheet

When building a worksheet for novice users, you should protect the cells in the worksheet that you do not want changed, such as cells that contain text and formulas.

When you create a new worksheet, all the cells are assigned a locked status, but the lock is not engaged, leaving them unprotected. **Unprotected cells** are cells whose values you can change at any time. **Protected cells** are cells that you cannot change. If a cell is protected and the user attempts to change its value, Excel displays a dialog box with a message indicating the cells are protected.

You should protect cells only after the worksheet has been tested fully and displays the correct results. Protecting a worksheet is a two-step process:

1. Select the cells you want to leave unprotected and change their cell protection settings to an unlocked status.
2. Protect the entire worksheet.

At first glance, these steps may appear to be backwards. Once you protect the entire worksheet, however, you cannot change anything, including the locked status of individual cells.

In the loan analysis worksheet (Figure 4-56), the user should make changes to only five cells: the item in cell C3; the price in cell C4; the down payment in cell C5; the interest rate in cell E2; and the years in cell E3. These cells thus must remain unprotected. The remaining cells and the embedded stack of dollar bills graphic in the worksheet should be protected so they cannot be changed by the user.

The following steps show how to protect the loan analysis worksheet.

More About

Protecting Worksheets

You can move from one unprotected cell to another unprotected cell in a worksheet by using the TAB and SHIFT+TAB keys.

To Protect a Worksheet

1 **Select the range C3:C5. Hold down the CTRL key and then select the nonadjacent range E2:E3. Right-click one of the selected ranges and then point to Format Cells on the shortcut menu.**

The shortcut menu displays (Figure 4-56).

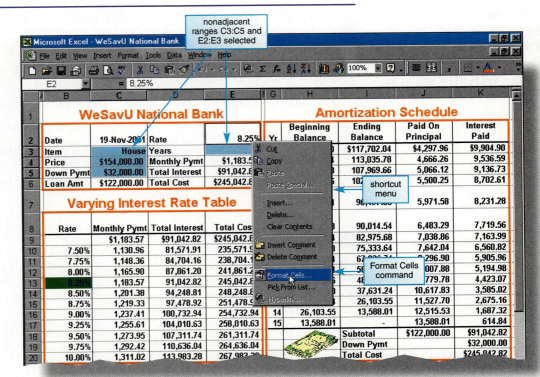

FIGURE 4-56

2 **Click Format Cells. When the Format Cells dialog box displays, click the Protection tab. Click the Locked check box to deselect it.**

The Protection sheet in the Format Cells dialog box displays with the check mark removed from the Locked check box. This means the selected cells will not be protected (Figure 4-57).

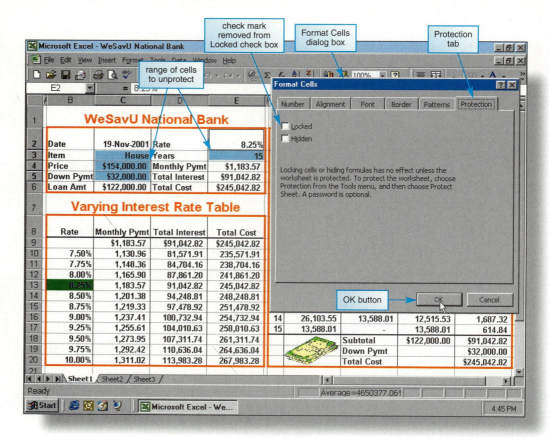

FIGURE 4-57

3 **Click the OK button. Click cell J19 to deselect the ranges C3:C5 and E2:E3. Click Tools on the menu bar. Point to Protection and then point to Protect Sheet on the Protection submenu.**

Excel displays the Tools menu and Protection submenu (Figure 4-58).

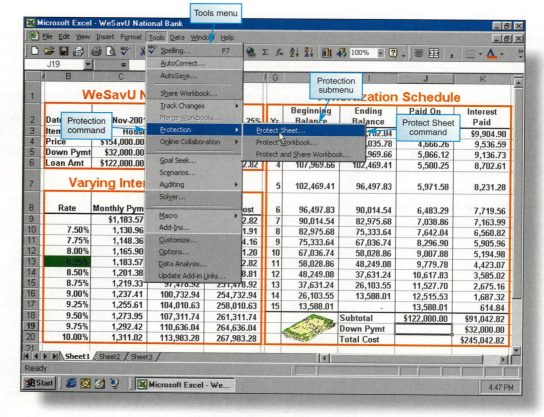

FIGURE 4-58

4 **Click Protect Sheet.**

The Protect Sheet dialog box displays (Figure 4-59). All three check boxes are selected, thus protecting the worksheet from changes to contents (except the cells left unlocked), objects, and scenarios.

5 **Click the OK button. Click the Save button on the Standard toolbar to save the protected workbook.**

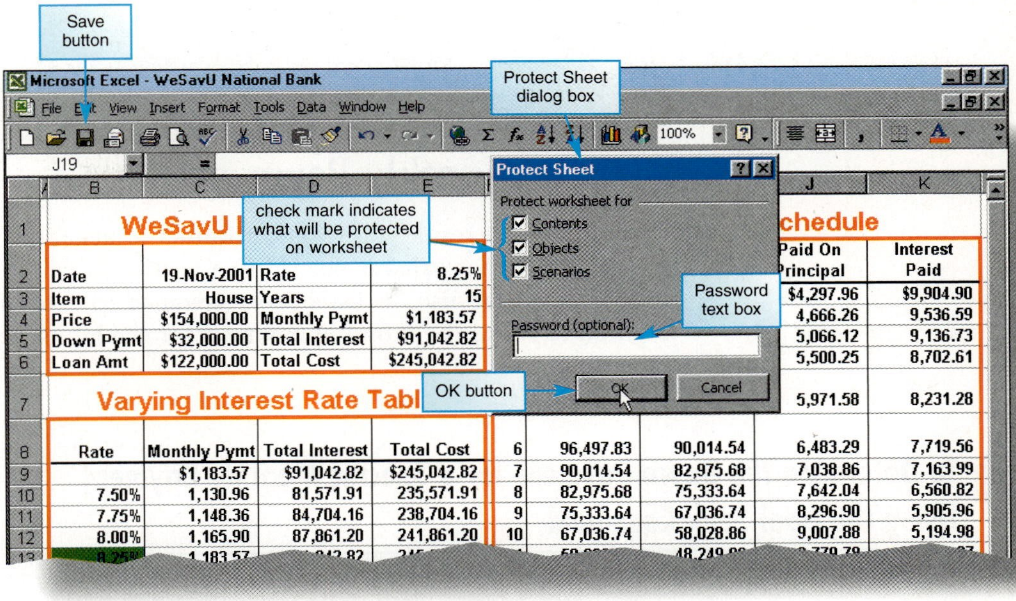

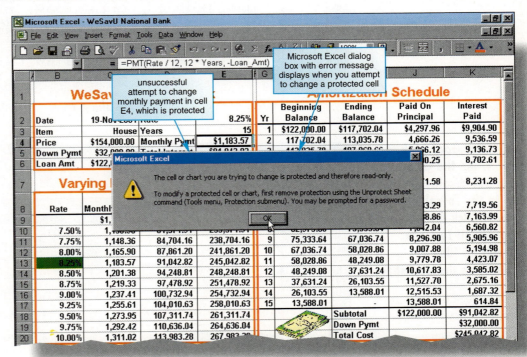

FIGURE 4-59

All the cells in the worksheet are protected, except for the ranges C3:C5 and E2:E3.

The **Protect Sheet dialog box** in Figure 4-58 lets you enter a password. You should create a **password** when you want to keep others from changing the worksheet from protected to unprotected.

If you want to protect more than one sheet, select each one before you begin the protection process or click **Protect Workbook** on the **Protection submenu** that displays (Figure 4-57) when you point to **Protection** on the Tools menu.

Now when this workbook is turned over to the loan officers, they will be able to enter data in only the unprotected cells. If they try to change any protected cell, such as the monthly payment in cell E4, Excel displays a dialog box with a diagnostic message as shown in Figure 4-60.

To change any cells in the worksheet such as titles or formulas, unprotect the document by pointing to Protection on the Tools menu and then clicking **Unprotect Sheet.**

Quick Reference

For a table that lists how to complete the tasks covered in this book using the mouse, menu, shortcut menu, and keyboard, visit the Office 2000 Web page (www.scsite.com/office 2000/qr.htm), and then click Microsoft Excel 2000.

FIGURE 4-60

Goal Seeking to Determine the Down Payment for a Specific Monthly Payment

If you know the result you want a formula to generate, you can use goal seeking to determine what value is needed in a particular cell to produce that result. For example, you can use the **Goal Seek command** to determine what down payment is required to make the monthly payment for the House exactly $1,000.00, rather than the current $1,183.37.

Steps To Determine the Down Payment for a Specific Monthly Payment Using the Goal Seek Command

1 Click cell E4, the cell with the monthly payment amount. Click Tools on the menu bar and then point to Goal Seek.

The Tools menu displays (Figure 4-61).

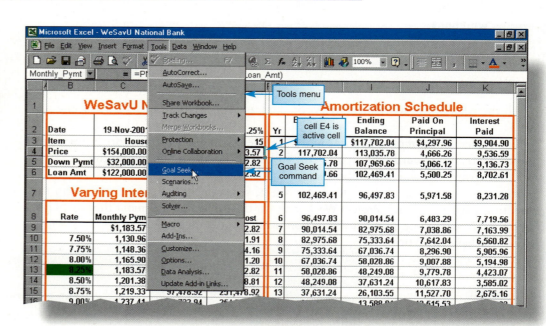

FIGURE 4-61

2 Click Goal Seek. When the Goal Seek dialog box displays, type 1000 in the To value text box. Click the By changing cell text box. Click cell C5 (down payment) on the worksheet.

The Goal Seek dialog box displays as shown in Figure 4-62

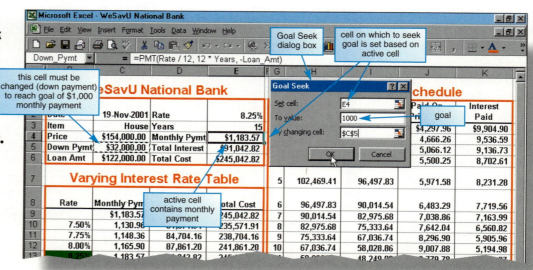

FIGURE 4-62

3 **Click the OK button.**

Excel displays the Goal Seek Status dialog box indicating it has found an answer. Excel also changes the monthly payment in cell E4 to the goal ($1,000.00) and changes the down payment in cell C5 to $50,922.13 (Figure 4-63).

4 **Click the Cancel button in the Goal Seek Status dialog box to undo the changes to the worksheet.**

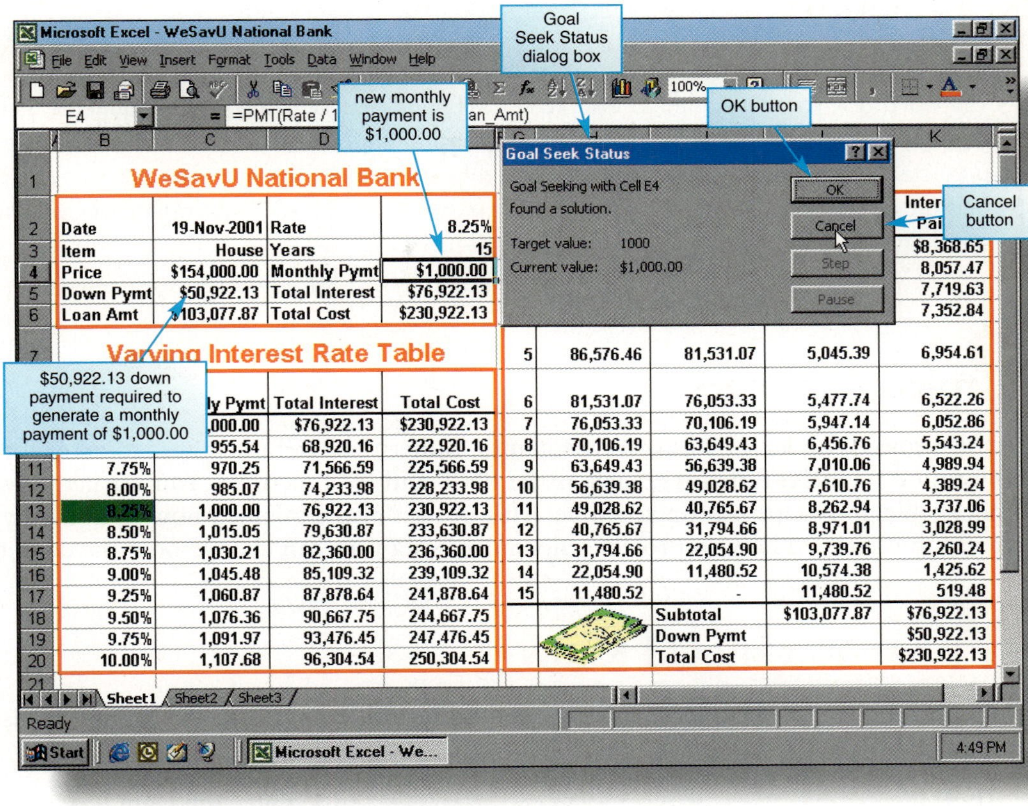

FIGURE 4-63

As shown in Figure 4-63, if you want to pay exactly $1,000.00 a month and the House costs $154,000.00, the interest rate is 8.25%, and the term is 15 years, then you must pay a down payment of $50,922.13, or $18,922.13 more than the original $32,000.00 down payment.

In this goal seeking example, you do not have to reference directly the cell to vary in the formula or function. For example, the monthly payment formula in cell E4 is =PMT(Interest Rate / 12, 12 * Years, – Loan Amount). This formula does not include a direct reference to the down payment in cell C5. Because the loan amount, which is referenced in the PMT function, is based on the down payment, however, Excel is able to goal seek on the monthly payment by varying the down payment.

If you had clicked the OK button instead of the Cancel button in Step 4, then Excel would have made the changes to the worksheet based on the goal seek activity. If you do click the OK button, you can reset the worksheet to the values displayed prior to goal seeking by clicking the Undo button on the Standard toolbar.

Quitting Excel

To quit Excel, follow the steps below.

TO QUIT EXCEL

1 Click the Close button on the right side of the title bar.

2 If the Microsoft Excel dialog box displays, click the No button.

More About 2000

Microsoft Certification

The Microsoft Office User Specialist (MOUS) Certification program provides an opportunity for you to obtain a valuable industry credential - proof that you have the Excel 2000 skills required by employers. For more information, see Appendix D or visit the Shelly Cashman Series MOUS Web page at www.scsite.com/off2000/cert.htm.

More About 2000

Closing Files

If you have multiple workbooks opened, you can close them all at the same time by holding down the SHIFT key when you click the File menu. The Close command changes to Close All. Click Close All and Excel will close all open workbooks.

CASE PERSPECTIVE SUMMARY

The workbook you developed in this project will handle all of Leslie Alex's requirements for the loan department at WeSavU National Bank. The loan information, data table, and Amortization Schedule are easy to read in the protected worksheet, which will help with customer relations. The hyperlink associated with the stack of dollar bills graphic gives the loan officer quick access to the bank's 2000 Statement of Condition to answer customer questions.

Project Summary

In this project you learned how to use names, rather than cell references to enter formulas. You also learned how to use financial functions, such as the PMT and PV functions. You learned how to analyze data by creating a data table and amortization schedule. This project also explained how to add a hyperlink to a worksheet. Finally, you learned how to protect a document so a user can change only the contents of unprotected cells.

What You Should Know

Having completed this project, you now should be able to perform the following tasks:

▶ Add an Input Cell Pointer to the Data Table (E 4.28)

▶ Add an Outline and Borders to the Amortization Schedule (E 4.40)

▶ Add an Outline and Borders to the Loan Analysis Section (E 4.9)

▶ Assign a Hyperlink to an Embedded Graphic (E 4.44)

▶ Change Column Widths and Enter Titles (E 4.31)

▶ Change the Font Style of the Entire Worksheet (E 4.7)

▶ Copy the Formulas to Fill the Amortization Schedule (E 4.36)

▶ Create a Percent Series Using the Fill Handle (E 4.22)

▶ Create a Series of Integers Using the Fill Handle (E 4.32)

▶ Create Names Based on Row Titles (E 4.12)

▶ Define a Range as a Data Table (E 4.24)

▶ Determine the Down Payment for a Specific Monthly Payment Using the Goal Seek Command (E 4.52)

▶ Determine the Total Interest and Total Cost (E 4.17)

▶ Display a Hyperlinked File (E 4.48)

▶ Enter New Loan Data (E 4.18, E 4.41)

▶ Enter the Data Table Title and Column Titles (E 4.21)

▶ Enter the Formulas in the Amortization Schedule (E 4.34)

▶ Enter the Formulas in the Data Table (E 4.23)

▶ Enter the Loan Amount Formula Using Names (E 4.14)

▶ Enter the Loan Data (E 4.11)

▶ Enter the Original Loan Data (E 4.19, E 4.42)

▶ Enter the PMT Function (E 4.16)

▶ Enter the Section Title, Row Titles, and System Date (E 4.7)

▶ Enter the Total Formulas in the Amortization Schedule (E 4.38)

▶ Format Cells before Entering Values (E 4.11)

▶ Format Numbers in the Amortization Schedule (E 4.39)

▶ Outline and Format the Data Table (E 4.26)

▶ Protect a Worksheet (E 4.49)

▶ Quit Excel (E 4.53)

▶ Start Excel and Reset the Toolbars and Menus (E 4.6)

Apply Your Knowledge

Project Reinforcement at www.scsite.com/off2000/reinforce.htm

1 What-If Analysis

Instructions: Start Excel and perform the following tasks.

1. Open the workbook Monthly Loan Payment on the Data Disk. See the inside back cover for instructions for downloading the Data Disk or see your instructor for information on accessing the files required for this book.

2. Use the Name command on the Insert menu to create names for cells in the range B3:B9 using the row titles in the range A3:A9.

3. Determine the loan amount in cell B8 by entering the formula: =Price – Down_Payment.

4. Determine the monthly payment in cell B9 by entering the function =PMT(Interest_Rate/12, 12 * Years, – Loan_Amount).

5. In the data table, assign the formulas in the table on the right to cells E4, F4, and G4.

6. Use the Table command on the Data menu to define the range D4:G11 as a one-input data table. Use cell B6 (interest rate) as the column input cell. The results should display as shown in Figure 4-64.

CELL	FORMULA
E4	=B9
F4	=12 * B7 * B9 + B5
G4	=F4 – B4

7. Add your name, course, computer laboratory assignment number (Apply Your Knowledge 4-1), date, and instructor name in column A beginning in cell A14.

8. Unlock the range B3:B7. Protect the worksheet.

9. Print the worksheet. Press CTRL+LEFT QUOTATION MARK and print the formulas version in landscape using the Fit to print option. Press CTRL+LEFT QUOTATION MARK to display the values version.

10. Save the workbook using the file name, Monthly Loan Payment 2.

11. Determine the monthly payment and print the worksheet for each data set: (a) Item = Summer Home; Price = $124,000.00; Down Payment = $32,000.00; Interest Rate = 8.75%; Years = 15 (b) Item = 25' Sailboat; Price = $32,000.00; Down Payment = $0.00; Interest Rate = 11.50%; Years = 7. You should get the following monthly payment results: (a) $919.49; (b) $556.37.

	A	B	C	D	E	F	G
1	**Determining a Monthly Loan Payment**				**Payments for Varying Interest Rates**		
2							
3	Item	2001 Lexus LX 450			**Monthly Payment**	**Total Cost**	**Total Interest**
4	Price	$78,500.00		Interest	$1,123.60	$92,415.97	$13,915.97
5	Down Payment	$25,000.00		8.50%	1,097.63	90,858.07	12,358.07
6	Interest Rate	9.50%		9.00%	1,110.57	91,634.32	13,134.32
7	Years	5		9.50%	1,123.60	92,415.97	13,915.97
8	Loan Amount	$53,500.00		10.00%	1,136.72	93,203.01	14,703.01
9	Monthly Payment	$1,123.60		10.50%	1,149.92	93,995.42	15,495.42
10				11.00%	1,163.22	94,793.18	16,293.18
11				11.50%	1,176.60	95,596.27	17,096.27

Microsoft Excel - Monthly Loan Payment 2

File Edit View Insert Format Tools Data Window Help

Times New Roman   10   B I U

A11

Sheet1 / Sheet2 / Sheet3

Ready

Start   Microsoft Excel - Mon...   5:01 PM

FIGURE 4-64

In the Lab

1 Linkup.com 401(k) Investment Model

Problem: You are a work study student for Linkup.com, a small start-up e-commerce company that hit it big when the company's investors took the company public. With the number of employees expected to reach 750 by the end of the year and the tight job market, the chief financial officer (CFO) has developed several employee benefit plans to keep current employees and attract new employees. One of the new employee benefits is a 401(k) plan. The CFO has asked you to develop a 401(k) investment model worksheet that will allow each current and prospective employee to see the effect (dollar accumulation) of investing a percent of his or her monthly salary over a period of years (Figure 4-65). The plan calls for the company to match the employee's investment dollar for dollar up to 3%. Thus, if an employee invests 5% of his or her annual salary, then the company matches the first 3%. If an employee invests only 2% of his or her annual salary, then the company matches the entire 2%. The CFO wants a data table to show the future value of the investment for different periods of time.

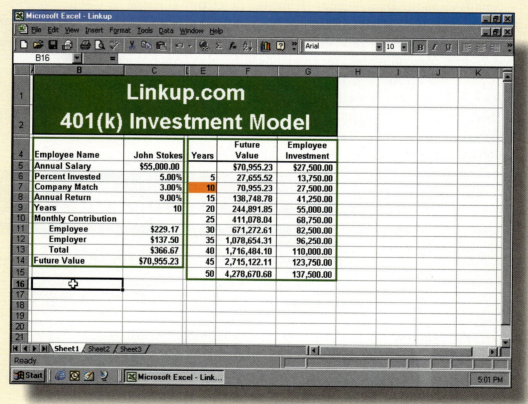

FIGURE 4-65

Instructions: With a blank worksheet on the screen, perform the following tasks.

1. Change the font of the entire worksheet to bold. Change the column widths to the following: A and D = 0.50; B = 20.00; C, F, and G = 13.00. Change the row heights to the following: 1 and 2 = 36.00; 3 = 4.50; and 4 = 27.00.

In the Lab

2. Enter the following worksheet titles: B1 = Linkup.com; B2 = 401(k) Investment Model. Change their font size to 26 point. One at a time, merge and center cells B1 and B2 across columns B through G. Change the background color of cells B1 and B2 to green (column 4, row 2 on the Fill Color palette). Change the font color to white (column 8, row 5 on the Font Color palette). Draw a thick black outline around cells B1 and B2.

3. Enter the row titles in column B, beginning in cell B4 as shown in Figure 4-65. Add the data in Table 4-3 to column C (also see Figure 4-65). Use the dollar and percent symbols to format the numbers in the range C4:C9.

4. Use the Create command on the Name submenu (Insert menu) to assign the row titles in column B (range B4:B14) to the adjacent cells in column C. Use these names to enter the following formulas in the range C11:C14. Step 4e formats the displayed results of the formulas.

   a. Employee Monthly Contribution (cell C11) = Annual_Salary * Percent_Invested / 12

   b. Employer Monthly Contribution (cell C12) = IF(Percent_Invested < Company_Match, Percent_Invested * Annual_Salary / 12, Company_Match * Annual_Salary / 12)

   c. Total Monthly Contribution (cell C13) = SUM(C11:C12)

   d. Future Value (cell C14) = FV(Annual_Return/12, 12 * Years, -Total)

   e. If necessary, use the Format Painter button on the Standard toolbar to assign the Currency style format in cell C5 to the range C11:C14.

   The **Future Value function** in Step 4d returns to the cell the future value of the investment. The **future value** of an investment is its value at some point in the future based on a series of payments of equal amounts made over a number of periods earning a constant rate of return.

5. Add the green outline and black borders to the range B4:C14 as shown in Figure 4-65.

6. Use the concepts and techniques developed in this project to add the data table to the range E4:G15 as follows.

   a. Enter and format the table column titles in row 4.

   b. Use the fill handle to create the series of years beginning with 5 and ending with 50 in increments of 5 in column E, beginning in cell E6.

   c. In cells F5 and G5, use cell references to enter the formulas so Excel will copy the formats. That is, in cell F5, enter the formula =C14. In cell G5, enter the formula: =12 * C11 * C9.

   d. Use the Table command on the Data menu to define the range E5:G15 as a one-input data table. Use cell C9 as the column input cell.

   e. Format the numbers in the range F6:G15 to the Comma style format.

   f. Add the outline and borders as shown in Figure 4-65. Column F in the data table shows the future value of the investment for years 5 through 50 in multiples of 5. Column G shows the amount the employee invests for the specified years.

7. Add an orange pointer to the data table in the Years column that shows the row that equals the results in column C as shown in Figure 4-65.

8. Add your name, course, computer laboratory assignment number (Lab 4-1), date, and instructor name in column B beginning in cell B17.

Table 4-3	Employee Data
TITLE	ITEM
Employee Name	John Stokes
Annual Salary	$55,000.00
Percent Invested	5.00%
Company Match	3.00%
Annual Return	9.00%
Years	10

(continued)

In the Lab

Linkup.com 401(k) Investment Model (*continued*)

9. Spell check the worksheet. Unlock the cells in the range C4:C9. Protect the worksheet.

10. Print the worksheet. Press CTRL+LEFT QUOTATION MARK and print the formulas version in landscape using the Fit to print option. Press CTRL+LEFT QUOTATION MARK to display the values version. Click the Save button on the Standard toolbar to save the workbook using the file name, Linkup.

11. Determine the future value for the data in Table 4-4. Print the worksheet for each data set.

12. You should get the following Future Value results in cell C14: Data Set 1 = $312,917.10; Data Set 2 = $1,105,118.72; and Data Set 3 = $582,511.04.

Table 4-4	Future Value Data		
	DATA SET 1	*DATA SET 2*	*DATA SET 3*
Employee Name	Fred Triples	Al Waiter	Sue Birts
Annual Salary	$75,000.00	$62,500.00	$78,000.00
Percent Invested	6%	8%	2.5%
Company Match	2.5%	3%	2%
Annual Return	8%	9.25%	6%
Years	20	30	40

2 Doug's LA Denim Ltd. Quarterly Income Statement and Break-Even Analysis

Problem: You are a consultant to Doug's LA Denim Ltd. Your area of expertise is cost-volume-profit (CVP) (also called break-even analysis), which investigates the relationship among a product's expenses (cost), its volume (units sold), and the operating income (gross profit). Any money a company earns above the break-even point is called operating income, or gross profit (row 10 in the Break-Even Analysis table in Figure 4-66). You have been asked to prepare a quarterly income statement and a data table that shows revenue, expenses, and income for units sold between 400,000 and 800,000 in increments of 25,000.

Microsoft Excel - Doug's LA Denim Ltd

File Edit View Insert Format Tools Data Window Help

Arial 10 B I U

A25

	A	B	C	E	F	G	H
1	**Doug's LA Denim Ltd.**			**Break-Even**			
2	**Quarterly Income Statement**			**Analysis**			
3	Revenue			Units	Revenue	Expenses	Income
4		Units Sold	639,150		$14,700,450	$13,558,950	$1,141,500
5		Price per Unit	$23	400,000	9,200,000	10,450,000	(1,250,000)
6		Total Revenue	$14,700,450	425,000	9,775,000	10,775,000	(1,000,000)
7	Fixed Expenses			450,000	10,350,000	11,100,000	(750,000)
8		Administrative	$1,250,000	475,000	10,925,000	11,425,000	(500,000)
9		Leasing	1,300,000	500,000	11,500,000	11,750,000	(250,000)
10		Marketing	1,500,000	525,000	12,075,000	12,075,000	0
11		Salary and Benefits	1,200,000	550,000	12,650,000	12,400,000	250,000
12		Total Fixed Expenses	$5,250,000	575,000	13,225,000	12,725,000	500,000
13	Variable Expenses			600,000	13,800,000	13,050,000	750,000
14		Material Cost per Unit	$5	625,000	14,375,000	13,375,000	1,000,000
15		Total Material Cost	$3,195,750	650,000	14,950,000	13,700,000	1,250,000
16		Manufacturing Cost per Unit	$8	675,000	15,525,000	14,025,000	1,500,000
17		Total Manufacturing Cost	$5,113,200	700,000	16,100,000	14,350,000	1,750,000
18		Total Variable Expenses	$8,308,950	725,000	16,675,000	14,675,000	2,000,000
19	Summary			750,000	17,250,000	15,000,000	2,250,000
20		Total Expenses	$13,558,950	775,000	17,825,000	15,325,000	2,500,000
21		Operating Income	$1,141,500	800,000	18,400,000	15,650,000	2,750,000

Sheet1 / Sheet2 / Sheet3

Ready

Start Microsoft Excel - Dou... 5:01 PM

FIGURE 4-66

In the Lab

Instructions: With a blank worksheet on the screen, perform the following tasks.

1. Change the font of the entire worksheet to bold. Change the column widths to the following: A = 21.00; B = 26.00; C = 13.71; D = 0.50; E = 7.14; and F through H = 11.14. Change the heights of rows 1 and 2 to 33.00.

2. Enter the following worksheet titles: A1 = Doug's LA Denim Ltd.; A2 = Quarterly Income Statement. Increase the font size in cell A1 and A2 to 20 points. One at a time, merge and center cells A1 and A2 across columns A through C. Change the background color of cells A1 and A2 to orange (column 2, row 2 on the Fill Color palette). Change the font color to white (column 8, row 5 on the Font Color palette). Add a thick black outline to the range A1:A2.

3. Enter the row titles in columns A and B as shown in Figure 4-66. Change the row titles in column A to 12 point. Add the data shown in Table 4-5 in column C. Use the dollar sign ($) and comma symbol to format the numbers in column C as you enter them.

Table 4-5	Quarterly Income Data	
TITLE	**CELL**	**ITEM**
Units Sold	C4	639,150
Price per Unit	C5	$23
Administrative	C8	$1,250,000
Leasing	C9	$1,300,000
Marketing	C10	$1,500,000
Salary and Benefits	C11	$1,200,000
Material Cost per Unit	C14	$5
Manufacturing Cost per Unit	C16	$8

4. Use the Create command on the Name submenu to assign the row titles in column B to the adjacent cells in column C. Use these names to enter the following formulas in column C:
   a. Total Revenue (cell C6) = Units_Sold * Price_per_Unit or =C4 * C5
   b. Total Fixed Expenses (cell C12) = SUM(C8:C11)
   c. Total Material Cost (cell C15) = Units_Sold * Material_Cost_per_Unit or =C4 * C14
   d. Total Manufacturing Cost (cell C17) = Units_Sold * Manufacturing_Cost_per_Unit or =C4 * C16
   e. Total Variable Expenses (cell C18) = Total_Material_Cost + Total_Manufacturing_Cost or =C15 + C17
   f. Total Expenses (cell C20) = Total_Fixed_Expenses + Total_Variable_Expenses or =C12 + C18
   g. Operating Income (cell C21) = Total_Revenue – Total_Expenses or =C6 – C20

5. If necessary, use the Format Painter button on the Standard toolbar to assign the Currency style format in cell C8 to the unformatted dollar amounts in column C.

6. Add a thick bottom border to the ranges B5:C5, B11:C11, and B17:C17 as shown in Figure 4-66.

7. Use the concepts and techniques developed in this project to add the data table to the range E1:H21 as follows:
   a. Add the data table titles Break-Even in cell E1 and Analysis in cell E2. Merge and center cells E1 and E2 across columns E through H. Increase the font size in cells E1 and E2 to 20 point. Format the background and font colors the same as the titles in cells A1 and A2. Enter the column titles in the range E3:H3 (see Figure 4-66).
   b. Use the fill handle to create the series of units sold in column E from 400,000 to 800,000 in increments of 25,000, beginning in cell E5.
   c. In cells F4, G4, and H4, use cell references to enter the formulas so Excel will copy the formats. That is, in cell F4, enter the formula =C6. In cell G4, enter the formula =C20. In cell H4, enter the formula =C21.

(continued)

In the Lab

Doug's LA Denim Ltd. Quarterly Income Statement and Break-Even Analysis *(continued)*

    d. Use the Table command on the Data menu to define the range E4:H21 as a one-input data table. Use cell C4 (units sold) as the column input cell.

    e. Use the Format Cells command on the shortcut menu to format the range F5:H21 to the Comma style format with no decimal places and negative numbers in red with parentheses. Add the borders shown in Figure 4-66 on page E 4.58.

8. Spell check the worksheet. Add your name, course, computer laboratory assignment number (Lab 4-2), date, and instructor name in column A beginning in cell A24.

9. Unlock the following cells: C4, C5, C14, and C16. Protect the worksheet.

10. Print the worksheet. Press CTRL+LEFT QUOTATION MARK and print the formulas version in landscape using the Fit to print option. Press CTRL+LEFT QUOTATION MARK to display the values version.

11. Save the workbook using the file name, Doug's LA Denim Ltd.

12. Determine the operating income for the data in Table 4-6. Print the worksheet for each data set.

Table 4-6	Operating Income Data			
TITLE	CELL	DATA SET 1	DATA SET 2	DATA SET 3
Units Sold	C4	775,000	425,000	650,000
Price per Unit	C5	$24	$26	$20
Material Cost per Unit	C14	$5	$12	$10
Manufacturing Cost per Unit	C16	$10	$6	$3

13. You should get the following Operating Income results in cell C21: Data Set 1 = $1,725,000; Data Set 2 = ($1,850,000); and Data Set 3 = ($700,000).

3 Confide In Us Loan Analysis and Amortization Schedule

Problem: Each student in your Office 2000 Applications course is assigned a real-world project that involves working with a local company. For your project, you are working with the Confide In Us Loan Company, a subsidiary of WeSavU National Bank. The manager of Confide In Us has asked you to create the loan information worksheet shown in Figure 4-67. She also wants a hyperlink added to the worksheet that displays the WeSavU National Bank 2000 Statement of Condition. Finally, she wants you to demonstrate the goal seeking capabilities of Excel.

In the Lab

	Confide In Us Loan Company				
	A Subsidiary of WeSavU National Bank				
Price	$161,000.00		Rate		8.75%
Down Pymt	$22,500.00		Years		30
Loan Amount	$138,500.00		Monthly Pymt		$1,089.58
Year	Beginning Balance	Ending Balance	Paid On Principal	Interest Paid	
1	$138,500.00	$137,504.49	$995.51	$12,079.45	
2	137,504.49	136,418.30	1,086.19	11,988.77	
3	136,418.30	135,233.16	1,185.14	11,889.82	
4	135,233.16	133,940.06	1,293.10	11,781.86	
5	133,940.06	132,529.16	1,410.90	11,664.06	
6	132,529.16	130,989.74	1,539.42	11,535.54	
7	130,989.74	129,310.08	1,679.66	11,395.30	
8	129,310.08	127,477.41	1,832.67	11,242.29	
9	127,477.41	125,477.79	1,999.62	11,075.34	
10	125,477.79	123,296.01	2,181.78	10,893.19	
11	123,296.01	120,915.49	2,380.53	10,694.43	
12	120,915.49	118,318.10	2,597.38	10,477.58	
13	118,318.10	115,484.11	2,833.99	10,240.97	
14	115,484.11	112,391.95	3,092.16	9,982.80	
15	112,391.95	109,018.11	3,373.84	9,701.12	
16	109,018.11	105,336.93	3,681.18	9,393.78	
17	105,336.93	101,320.41	4,016.52	9,058.44	
18	101,320.41	96,937.99	4,382.41	8,692.55	
19	96,937.99	92,156.36	4,781.63	8,293.33	
20	92,156.36	86,939.15	5,217.22	7,857.74	
21	86,939.15	81,246.66	5,692.48	7,382.48	
22	81,246.66	75,035.61	6,211.05	6,863.91	
23	75,035.61	68,258.77	6,776.85	6,298.11	
24	68,258.77	60,864.58	7,394.19	5,680.77	
25	60,864.58	52,796.81	8,067.77	5,007.19	
26	52,796.81	43,994.10	8,802.71	4,272.25	
27	43,994.10	34,389.50	9,604.60	3,470.36	
28	34,389.50	23,909.97	10,479.54	2,595.42	
29	23,909.97	12,475.79	11,434.18	1,640.78	
30	12,475.79	-	12,475.79	599.18	
		Subtotal	$138,500.00	$253,748.82	
		Down Pymt		$22,500.00	
		Total Cost		$414,748.82	

FIGURE 4-67

Instructions: With a blank worksheet on the screen, perform the following tasks to create the worksheet.

1. Bold the entire worksheet. Enter the worksheet title in cell A1 and change its font to 20-point Franklin Gothic Heavy red (or a similar font style). Enter the worksheet subtitle in cell A2 and change its font to 12-point red Franklin Gothic Medium (or a similar font style). One at a time, merge and center cells A1 and A2 across columns A through E.

(continued)

In the Lab

Confide In Us Loan Analysis and Amortization Schedule *(continued)*

2. Enter the text in the ranges A3:A5 and D3:D5.

3. Enter 161000 (price) in cell B3, 22500 (down payment) in cell B4, 8.75 (interest rate) in cell E3, and 30 (years) in cell E4 (Figure 4-67 on the previous page). Determine the loan amount in cell B5 by using the formula =B3 – B4. Determine the monthly payment in cell E5 by entering the PMT function =PMT(E3 / 12, 12 * E4, – B5)

4. Increase the widths of columns A through E to 15.00. In the range A3:E5, color the background red, the font white, and add a heavy outline to the range.

5. Enter the column titles for the amortization schedule in the range A6:E6. Center the right four column titles. Use the fill handle to generate the series of years in the range A7:A36.

6. Assign the formulas and functions to the cells indicated in Table 4-7.

7. Enter the total titles in the range C37:C39 as shown in Figure 4-67.

8. Copy cell B8 to the range B9:B36. Copy the range C7:E7 to the range C8:E36. Assign the Currency style format to the range B7:E7. Assign the Comma style format to the range B8:E36. Draw the borders shown in Figure 4-67.

9. Add your name, course, laboratory assignment number (Lab 4-3), date, and instructor name in column A beginning in cell A40.

10. Spell check the worksheet. Save the workbook using the file name, Confide In Us Loan Company. Print the worksheet with the loan data and loan information in Figure 4-67. Press CTRL+LEFT QUOTATION MARK and print the formulas version of the worksheet using the Fit to option.

Table 4-7	Cell Assignments
CELL	**FORMULA OR FUNCTION**
B7	=B5
C7	=IF(A7 <= $E$4, PV($E$3 / 12, 12 * ($E$4 – A7), -$E$5),0)
D7	=B7 – C7
E7	=IF(B7 > 0, 12 * $E$5 – D7, 0)
B8	=C7
D37	=SUM(D7:D36)
E37	=SUM(E7:E36)
E38	=B4
E39	=D37 + E37 + E38

11. Insert the clip art graphic shown in the range C3:C5. The clip art file name is famous people.wmf. When the Insert ClipArt window displays, search for the file using its file name. Assign the hyperlink a:\wesavu national bank.htm to the clip art graphic. Display and print the HTML file (Web page). You must have the Data Disk in drive A to display the HTML file.

12. Unlock the ranges B3:B5 and E3:E4. Protect the worksheet. Save the worksheet.

13. Use Excel's goal seeking capabilities to determine the down payment required for the loan data in Figure 4-67 if the monthly payment is set to $800.00. The down payment that results for a monthly payment of $800.00 is $59,309.45. Print the worksheet with the new monthly payment of $800.00. Close the workbook without saving changes.

Cases and Places

The difficulty of these case studies varies:
◗ are the least difficult; ◗◗ are more difficult; and ◗◗◗ are the most difficult.

1 ◗ After visiting several automobile showrooms, Stephanie Rogers has decided she wants to buy a new Honda Prelude. She will pay for the car by making monthly payments over a period of five years. Before she buys the car, Stephanie wants to know her monthly payment and how much she actually will pay for the car with all the interest. Create a worksheet based on the information provided by Stephanie. The cost of the car is $25,500.00; the interest is 10.75% for 5 years. She plans to put $2,500.00 down.

2 ◗ You can calculate the break-even point (number of units you must sell) if you know the fixed expenses, the price per unit, and the expense (cost) per unit. You are employed as a spreadsheet analyst for CD Music Emporium, the leader in CD sales. You have been asked to create a data table that analyzes the break-even point for prices between $5.00 and $10.00 in increments of $0.20. The following formula determines the break-even point:

Break-Even Point = Fixed Expenses / (Price per Unit – Expense per Unit)

Assume Fixed Expenses = $10,000,000; Price per Unit = $5.69; and Expense per Unit = $2.45.

Enter the data and formula into a worksheet and then create the data table. Use the Price per Unit as the input cell and the break-even value as the result. For a unit cost of $8.40, the data table should show a break-even point of 1,680,672.

3 ◗◗ Your aunt Myrna and uncle Frank have decided to save for the down payment on a house, after living for years in a tiny apartment. Frank's buddy, Jeb, who works for the city's Streets and Sanitation department, promises them he can get the pair an annual interest rate of 10% through a special city annuity program. Frank would like you to create a worksheet that determines how much their monthly payment must be so that in four years the value of the account is $25,000. *Hint*: Use the FV function with a monthly savings of $100. Then use the Goal Seek command to determine the monthly payment. Myrna realizes Frank is full of grand schemes that often go awry, so in case Frank's plans change, she has asked you also to compute the monthly payments to accumulate $25,000.00 for years 5 through 10 using the Goal Seek command. Enter the results below the worksheet.

4 ◗◗ Julio Quatorze, owner of Shrub and Trees Landscape Inc., recently purchased a new truck. Julio wants a worksheet that uses a financial function (SLN) to show the truck's straight-line depreciation and a formula to determine the annual rate of depreciation. Straight-line depreciation is based on an asset's initial cost, how long it can be used (called useful life), and the price at which it eventually can be sold (called salvage value). Julio has supplied the following information: Cost = $42,821; Salvage = $12,500; Life = 5 years; and Annual Rate of Depreciation = SLN / Cost.

Julio is not sure how much he will be able to sell the truck for. Create a data table that shows straight-line depreciation and annual rate of depreciation for salvage from $7,000 to $16,000 in $500 increments. Use Help to learn more about the SLN function.

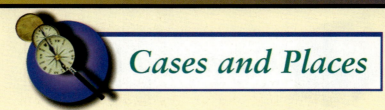

Cases and Places

5 ▶▶ Ukari and Amin's dream for their daughter is that one day she will attend their alma mater, Chelios College. For the next ten years, they plan to make monthly payment deposits to a long-term savings account at a local bank. The account pays 7.25% annual interest, compounded monthly. Create a worksheet for the parents that uses a financial function to show the future value (FV) of their investment and a formula to determine the percentage of the college's tuition saved. Ukari and Amin have supplied the following information: Tuition = $120,000; Rate (per month) = 7.25% / 12; Nper (number of monthly payments) = 10 * 12; Pmt (payment per period) = $300; and percentage of Tuition Saved = FV / Tuition.

Ukari and Amin are not sure how much they will be able to save each month. Create a data table that shows the future value and percentage of tuition saved for monthly payments from $250 to $600, in $50 increments. Insert a clip art file and assign it a hyperlink to the HTML file, WeSavU National Bank.htm, on the Data Disk.

6 ▶▶ Dexter University is offering its faculty a generous retirement package. Professor Michael Holsum has accepted the proposal, but before moving to a warmer climate, he wants to settle his account with the school credit union. Professor Holsum has four years remaining on a five-year car loan, with an interest rate of 9.25% and a monthly payment of $383.00. The credit union is willing to accept the present value (PV) of the loan as a payoff. Develop an amortization schedule that shows how much Professor Holsum must pay at the end of each of the five years. Include the beginning and ending balance, the amount paid on the principal and the interest paid for years two through five. Because he has already paid for the first year, determine only the ending balance (present value) for year one.

7 ▶▶▶ Buying a car not only means finding one you like, but finding one you can afford as well. Many dealerships offer financing plans to prospective buyers. Visit an automobile dealership and pick out your favorite car. Talk to a salesperson about the cost, down payment, amount that must be borrowed, annual loan interest rate, and length of time for which the loan runs. With this information, develop a worksheet to calculate your monthly payment (PMT), total cost, and total interest. Add a data table that shows the effect on the monthly payment for varying interest rates three percentage points on either side of the annual loan interest rate given to you by the salesperson in increments of 0.25%. Also add an amortization schedule similar to the one developed in this project.

Microsoft Excel 2000

P R O J E C T

5

Creating, Sorting, and Querying a Worksheet Database

O B J E C T I V E S

You will have mastered the material in this project when you can:

- Create a worksheet database
- Add computational fields to a database
- Use the VLOOKUP function to look up a value in a table
- Change the range assigned to a Name
- Use a data form to display records, add records, delete records, and change field values in a worksheet database
- Sort a worksheet database on one field or multiple fields
- Display automatic subtotals
- Use a data form to find records that meet comparison criteria
- Filter data to display records that meet comparison criteria
- Use the advanced filtering features to display records that meet comparison criteria
- Apply database functions to generate information about a worksheet database

Security for the Millennium

Be Prepared

From the time you start your first job until the day of your retirement, you will be faced with the age-old concern about your economic security. Corporate America and the world economy continue to change. What was once loyalty to a company, with solid job status and opportunity for advancement, is now the constant threat of downsizing, cutbacks, mergers, and unemployment. The job no longer yields the tenure or relationships it has in the past. Workers fear losing their incomes due to injury or layoffs or company closures. Having sufficient funds for retirement is worrisome, especially when lifetimes may exceed 90 years in the near future. Only 30 percent of Americans, however, are set for retirement at age 55.

The Social Security program was created during the Great Depression to address economic security fears. Today, 95 percent of Americans are protected by the program, and nearly one in five receives Social Security benefits. More than 90 percent of senior citizens receive these funds. In addition, 15 million Americans of all ages receive Social Security disability and survivors benefits as compensation for losing a source of family income when severe injury or death strikes.

Social Security works by using pooled resources, much like an insurance program does. Workers contribute money that is invested in a trust fund. Since the inception of the program, more than $4.5 trillion has been paid into the system, and more than $4.1 trillion has been dispersed. Benefits generally are based on the amount a worker has contributed to the program during his or her career.

The Social Security Administration maintains a database that has a record for every person with a Social Security number. Similar to the SkateJam Sales Representative Database you will create in this Excel project, the SSA database has records that contain fields to store such data as Social Security number, last name, first name, gender, birth date, length of time the worker contributed Social Security funds, wages, date of death, date of disability, and birth date of widow or widower.

The data in these fields can be analyzed in computations, just as you will learn to do in this Excel project. For example, the SSA determines the total number of people who have received or are receiving various benefits and the average amount they receive. Also, the agency uses the data to manage its trust fund by predicting demands for benefits. By sorting records based on birth date, it can determine people who will reach retirement age each year and the amount of benefits they will draw. Using these figures, the SSA realizes that without taking any action, in 2019 the interest and tax revenues generated from the trust funds will be insufficient to meet these retirees' financial demands. If the agency then begins drawing on the trust fund principal, which is expected to grow to $3.3 trillion in 2019, that principal will be exhausted during the next ten years.

Anyone with a Social Security number can call the SSA 800 number to use this database to compute a Personal Earnings and Benefit Estimate Statement that shows Social Security earnings history and estimates how much has been paid in Social Security taxes. It also estimates future benefits and tells how to qualify for them. In addition, the SSA distributes a comparable interactive PC-compatible program, ANYPIA, that allows users to compute these estimates themselves. For details, visit Social Security Online at www.ssa.gov.

Microsoft Excel 2000

Creating, Sorting, and Querying a Worksheet Database

PROJECT 5

CASE PERSPECTIVE

SkateJam, Inc. pioneered the sport of in-line skating in the late 1970s as an off-season training tool for hockey players. The sport quickly caught on with general fitness enthusiasts and the population in general. Today, there are nearly 40 million in-line skaters.

Rosa Blade, who is the national sales manager for SkateJam, oversees one dozen sales representatives spread equally among six states: Arizona, California, Florida, New York, Pennsylvania, and Texas.

Rosa plans to use Excel 2000 to create, maintain, and query a worksheet database containing data about the SkateJam sales representatives. She has learned through the Excel Help system that a database can hold both data and formulas. Furthermore, she learned that Excel 2000 has a lookup function that can be used to grade the performance of sales reps based on the percentage of quota met.

Rosa has assigned you the challenge of creating the database. Besides creating the database, she wants you to demonstrate how to sort and query the database using Excel 2000's database capabilities.

Introduction

A **worksheet database**, also called a **database** or **list**, is an organized collection of data. For example, a list of club members, a list of students attending a college, an instructor's grade book, and a list of company sales representatives are databases. In these cases, the data related to a person is called a **record**, and the data items that make up a record are called **fields**. In a database of sales representatives, each one would have a separate record; some of the fields in the records might be name, hire date, age, and gender. A database record also can include formulas and functions. A field in a database that contains formulas or functions is called a **computational field**. A computational field displays results based on other fields in the database.

A worksheet's row-and-column structure can be used to organize and store a database (Figure 5-1). Each row of a worksheet can be used to store a record and each column to store a field. Additionally, a row of column titles at the top of the worksheet can be used as **field names** that identify each field.

Once you enter a database into a worksheet, you can use Excel to:

▶ Add and delete records
▶ Change the values of fields in records
▶ Sort the records so they display in a different order
▶ Determine subtotals for numeric fields
▶ Display records that meet comparison criteria
▶ Analyze data using database functions

This project illustrates all six of these database capabilities.

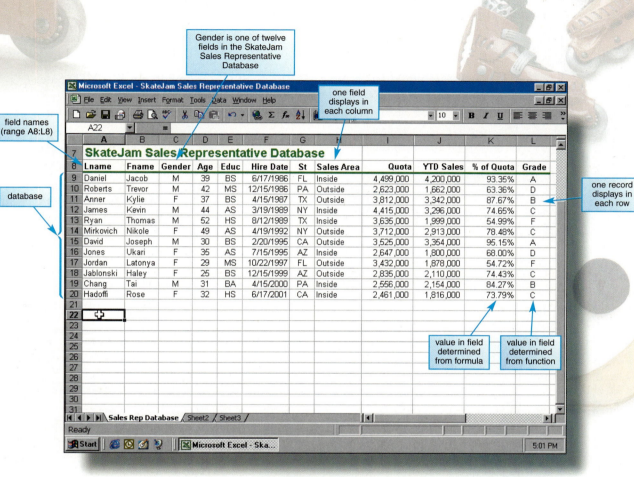

Gender is one of twelve fields in the SkateJam Sales Representative Database

one field displays in each column

field names (range A8:L8)

database

one record displays in each row

value in field determined from formula

value in field determined from function

FIGURE 5-1

Project Five — SkateJam Sales Representative Database

From your meeting with Rosa Blade, you have determined the following needs, source of data, and calculations.

Needs: Create a sales representative database (Figure 5-1). The field names, columns, types of data, and column widths are described in Table 5-1 on the next page. Because Rosa will use the database online as she travels among the offices, it is important that it be readable and that the database is visible on the screen. Therefore, some of the column widths listed in Table 5-1 on the next page are determined from the field names and not the maximum length of the data. The last two fields (located in columns K and L) use a formula and function based on data within each sales representative record.

More About 2000

Worksheet Databases

Although Excel is not a true database management system such as Access, FoxPro, or Oracle, it does give you many of the same capabilities as these dedicated systems. For example, in Excel you can create a database; add, change, and delete data in the database; sort data in the database; query the database; and create forms and reports.

Table 5-1 Database Column Information

COLUMN TITLES (FIELD NAMES)	COLUMN	TYPE OF DATA	COLUMN WIDTH
Lname	A	Text	9.00
Fname	B	Text	7.00
Gender	C	Text	7.00
Age	D	Numeric	5.00
Educ	E	Text	5.00
Hire Date	F	Date	10.00
St	G	Text	5.00
Sales Area	H	Text	10.00
Quota	I	Numeric	11.00
YTD Sales	J	Numeric	11.00
% of Quota	K	YTD Sales / Quota	11.00
Grade	L	VLOOKUP Function	7.00

Once the database is entered into the worksheet, it will be sorted and manipulated to illustrate how quickly information can be generated from a database.

Source of Data: Rosa will supply the sales representative data required for the database.

Calculations: The last two fields in the database in columns K and L are determined as follows:

1. % of Quota in column K = YTD Sales / Quota
2. Grade in column L = VLOOKUP function

The VLOOKUP function will be used to display the grades in column L based on the table in columns N and O in Figure 5-2. The DAVERAGE function will be used to find the average age of males and females in the database (range Q5:T6 in Figure 5-2). Finally, the DCOUNT function will be used to count the number of sales representatives who have a grade of A (range Q7:T7 in Figure 5-2). These two functions require that you set set up a criteria area (range Q1:S3) to tell Excel what items to average and count.

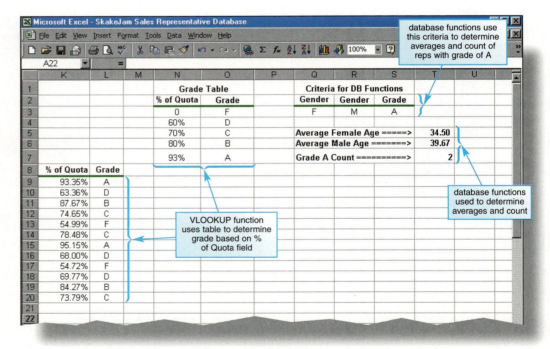

FIGURE 5-2

Starting Excel and Resetting the Toolbars and Menus

Perform the following steps to start Excel. Steps 4 through 6 reset the toolbars and menus to their installation settings. For additional information on resetting the toolbars and menus, see Appendix C.

TO START EXCEL AND RESET THE TOOLBARS AND MENUS

1 Click the Start button on the taskbar.

2 Click New Office Document. If necessary, click the General tab in the New Office Document dialog box.

3 Double-click the Blank Workbook icon.

4 When the blank worksheet displays, click View on the menu bar, point to Toolbars, and then click Customize on the Toolbars submenu.

5 When the Customize dialog box displays, click the Options tab, make sure the top three check boxes have check marks, click the Reset my usage data button, and then click the Yes button.

6 Click the Toolbars tab. Click Standard, click the Reset button, and then click the OK button. Click Formatting, click the Reset button, and then click the OK button. Click the Close button.

The Standard and Formatting toolbars display as shown in Figure 5-1 on page E 5.5.

Creating a Database

The three steps to creating a database in Excel are:

1. Set up the database
2. Assign a name to the range containing the database
3. Enter the data into the database

These steps are similar to what you would do with a traditional database package, such as Access 2000. The following pages illustrate these three steps for creating the SkateJam Sales Representative database.

Setting Up a Database

Setting up the database involves entering field names in a row in the worksheet and changing the column widths so the data will fit in the columns. Follow these steps to change the column widths to those specified in Table 5-1, to change the height of row 7 to 18 points and row 8 to 15 points to emphasize these rows, and to enter and format the database title and column titles (field names).

Although Excel does not require a database title to be entered, it is a good practice to include one on the worksheet to show where the database begins. With Excel, you usually enter the database several rows below the top. These blank rows will be used later to query the database. The following steps also change the name of Sheet1 to Sales Rep Database and save the workbook using the file name SkateJam Sales Representative Database.

TO SET UP A DATABASE

1 Use the mouse to change the column widths as follows: A = 9.00, B = 7.00, C = 7.00, D = 5.00, E = 5.00, F = 10.00, G = 5.00, H = 10.00, I = 11.00, J = 11.00, K = 11.00, and L = 7.00.

2 Click cell A7 and then enter SkateJam Sales Representative Database as the worksheet database title.

More About 2000

Location of the Database

Always leave several rows empty above the database on the worksheet to set up a criteria area for querying the database. Some experienced Excel users also leave several columns to the left empty, beginning with column A, for additional worksheet activities. A range of blank rows or columns on the side of a database is called a moat of cells.

(3) Double-click the move handle on the Formatting toolbar so it displays in its entirety. With cell A7 active, click the Font Size arrow on the Formatting toolbar and then click 14 in the Font list. Click the Bold button on the Formatting toolbar. Click the Font Color arrow on the Formatting toolbar and then click Green (column 4, row 2) on the color palette. Change the height of row 7 to 18.00.

(4) Enter the column titles in row 8 as shown in Figure 5-3. Change the height of row 8 to 15.00.

(5) Select the range A8:J8. Click the Bold button on the Formatting toolbar. Right-click the selected range and then click Format Cells on the shortcut menu. Click the Border tab. Click the Color box arrow in the Line area and then click Green (column 4, row 2) on the color palette. Click the heavy border in the Style box (column 2, row 6). Click the Underline button on the left side of the Border area. Click the OK button.

(6) Click column heading C to select the entire column. Hold down the CTRL key and click column headings D, E, G, and L. Click the Center button on the Formatting toolbar so that all future entries in columns C, D, E, G, and L will be centered.

(7) Right-click column heading F. Click Format Cells on the shortcut menu. When the Format cells dialog box displays, click the Number tab, click Date in the Category list box, scroll down in the Type box box and then click 3/14/1998 to display the future date entries with four-digit years. Click the OK button.

(8) Click column heading I. Drag through column heading J to select both columns. Click the Comma Style button on the Formatting toolbar. Click the Decrease Decimal button on the Formatting toolbar twice so that all future numeric entries in columns I and J will display using the Comma style with zero decimal places. Click cell A10 to deselect columns I and J.

(9) Double-click the Sheet1 tab at the bottom of the screen. Type Sales Rep Database as the sheet name. Press the ENTER key.

(10) Click the Save button on the Standard toolbar. When the Save As dialog box displays, type SkateJam Sales Representative Database in the File name text box. Click 3½ Floppy (A:) in the Save in box and then click the Save button in the Save As dialog box.

The worksheet displays as shown in Figure 5-3.

Toolbars

Are you tired of double-clicking the move handle to display a toolbar in its entirety? If so, you can display the Standard toolbar and Formatting toolbar on separate rows, one below the other. To display both toolbars on separate rows, right-click a toolbar, click Customize on the shortcut menu, click the Options tab in the Customize dialog box, click Standard and Formatting toolbars share one row to deselect it, and click the Close button.

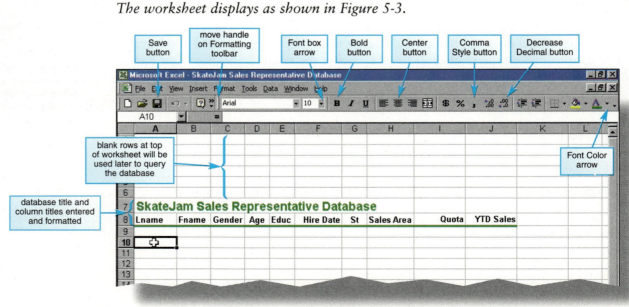

FIGURE 5-3

Compare the column titles in row 8 in Figure 5-1 on page E 5.5 with Figure 5-3. In Figure 5-3, the two computational fields, % of Quota and Grade, are not included in columns K and L. These two fields will be added after the data is entered for the twelve sales representatives. In Excel, computational fields that depend on data in the database usually are entered after the data has been entered.

Naming a Database

Although Excel usually can identify a **database range** when you invoke a database-type command, assigning the name Database to the range eliminates any confusion when commands are entered to manipulate the database. Thus, as you create the SkateJam Sales Representative database shown in Figure 5-1, you first assign the range A8:J9 to the name Database by selecting the range and typing Database in the Name box on the left side of the formula bar. The range assigned to the name Database includes the column titles (row 8) and one blank row (row 9) below the column titles. The blank row is for expansion of the database. As records are added using a data form, Excel automatically expands the named range Database to include the last record. Later, when the database is expanded to include the two computational fields, % of Quota and Grade, the name Database will be redefined to encompass the new fields in columns K and L.

More About

Names

If you delete columns or rows from the range defined as Database, Excel automatically adjusts the range of the name Database.

TO NAME THE DATABASE

1 Select the range A8:J9. Click the Name box in the formula bar and then type Database as the name for the selected range.

2 Press the ENTER key.

The worksheet displays as shown in Figure 5-4.

Using the Name box in the formula bar to name a range is a useful tool for many worksheet tasks. For example, if you name a cell or range of cells that you select often, you then can select the cell or range of cells by clicking the name in the Name box list.

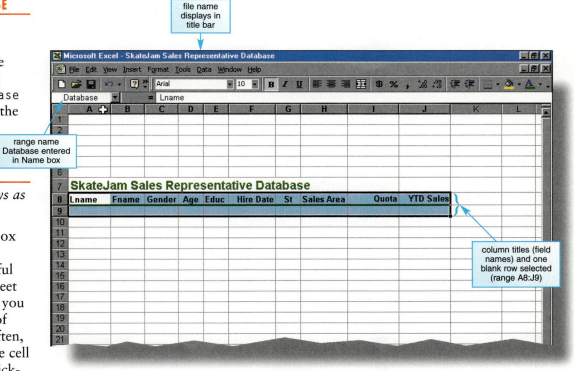

FIGURE 5-4

Entering Records into the Database Using a Data Form

The next step is to use a data form to enter the sales representative records. A **data form** is an Excel dialog box that lists the field names in the database and provides corresponding boxes in which you enter the field values. The steps on the next page add the sales representative records to the database as shown in Figure 5-1. As indicated earlier, the computational fields in columns K and L will be added after the data is in the database.

More About

Naming Ranges

An alternative to using the Name box in the formula bar to name a cell or range of cells is to use the Define command on the Name submenu. The Name command is on the Insert menu.

Steps **To Enter Records into a Database Using a Data Form**

1 **Click cell A9 to deselect the range A8:J9. Click Data on the menu bar and then point to Form.**

The Data menu displays (Figure 5-5).

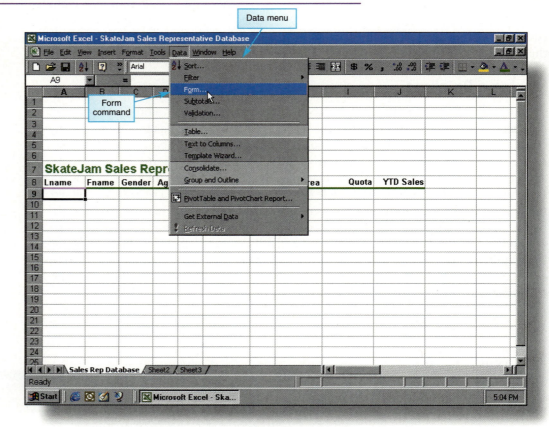

FIGURE 5-5

2 **Click Form.**

Excel displays the data form (Figure 5-6) with the sheet name Sales Rep Database on the title bar. The data form automatically includes the field names and corresponding text boxes for entering the field values. Excel selects the field names in the range A8:J8 because they are at the top of the range named Database.

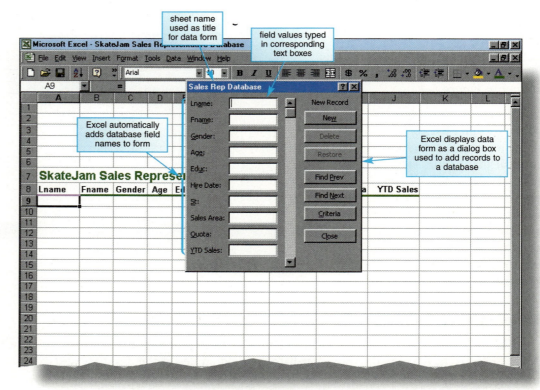

FIGURE 5-6

3 Enter the first sales representative record into the data form as shown in Figure 5-7. Use the mouse or the TAB key to move the insertion point down to the next box. If you make a mistake, use the mouse or the SHIFT+TAB keys to move the insertion point to the previous text box in the data form to edit the entry. Point to the New button.

The first record displays in the data form (Figure 5-7).

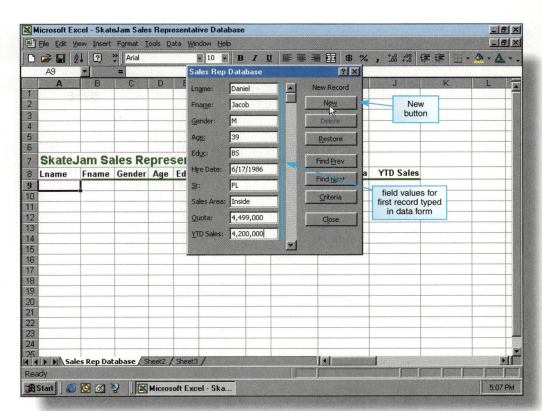

FIGURE 5-7

4 Click the New button. Type the second sales representative record into the data form as shown in Figure 5-8. Point to the New button.

Excel adds the first sales representative record to row 9 in the database range on the worksheet. The second record displays in the data form (Figure 5-8).

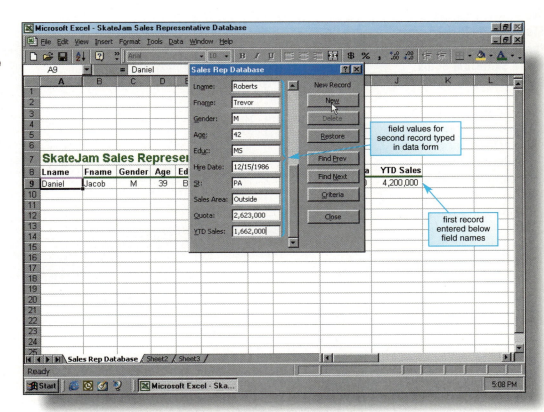

FIGURE 5-8

5 **Click the New button to enter the second sales representative record. Use the data form to enter the next nine sales representative records in rows 11 through 19, as shown in Figure 5-1 on page E 5.5. Type the last sales representative record into the data form as shown in Figure 5-9. Point to the Close button.**

Excel enters the sales representative records into the database range as shown in Figure 5-9. The last record displays in the data form.

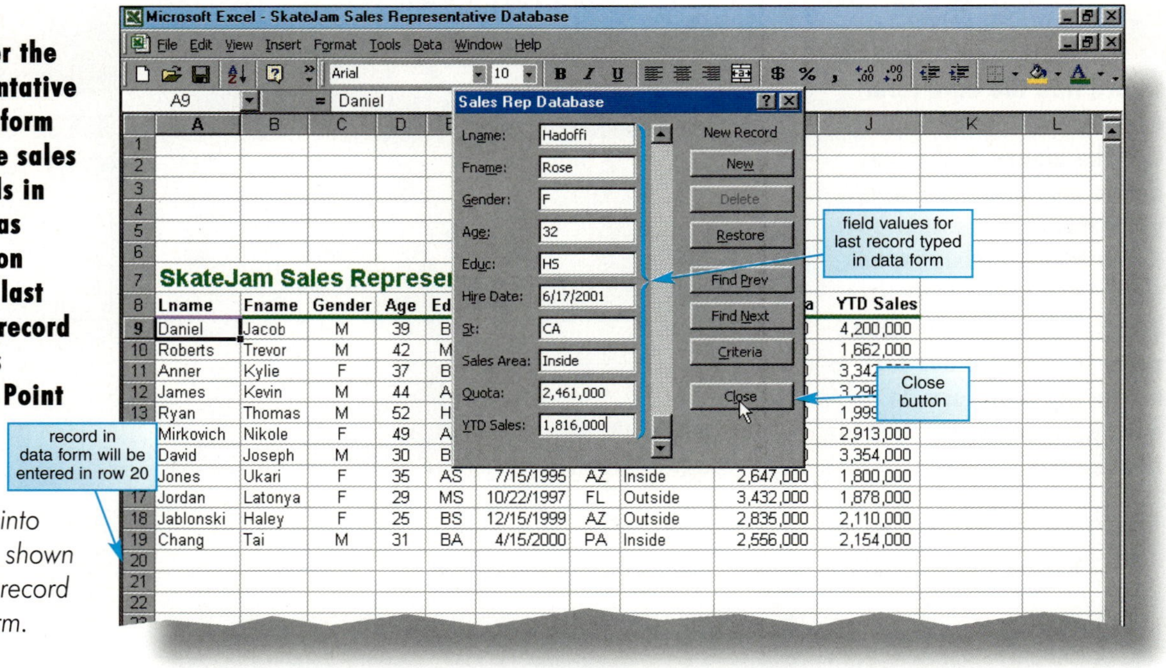

FIGURE 5-9

6 **Click the Close button to complete the record entry. Click the Save button on the Standard toolbar to save the workbook using the file name SkateJam Sales Representative Database.**

The data form closes and Excel enters the last sales representative record in row 20 of the database. The SkateJam Sales Representative Database displays as shown in Figure 5-10.

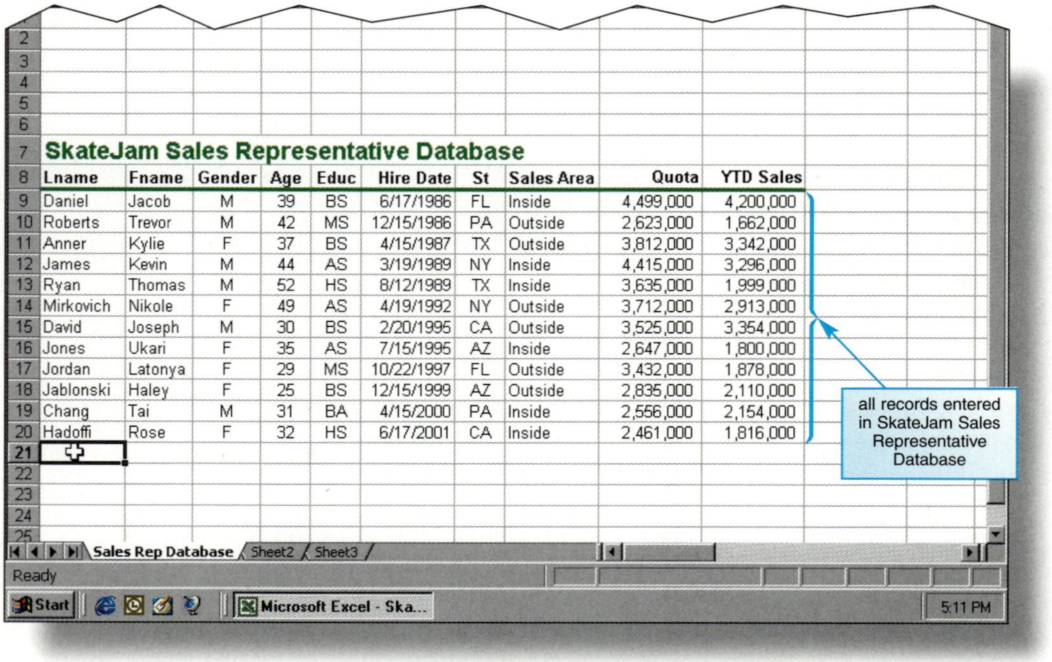

FIGURE 5-10

You also could create the database by entering the records in columns and rows as you would enter data into any worksheet and then assign the name Database to the range (A8:J20). The data form was illustrated here because it is considered to be a more accurate and reliable method of data entry, which automatically extends the range of the name Database to include any new records.

Moving from Field to Field in a Data Form

As described earlier in Step 3 in the previous section on page E 5.11, you can move from field to field in a data form using the TAB key, or you can hold down the ALT key and press the key that corresponds to the underlined letter in the name of the field to which you want to move. An underlined letter in a field name is called an **access key**. Thus, to select the field titled Fname in Figure 5-9, you would hold down the ALT key and press the M key (ALT+M), because M is the access key for the field name Fname.

 dding Computational Fields to the Database

The next step is to add the computational fields % of Quota in column K and Grade in column L. Then the name Database must be changed from the range A8:J20 to A8:L20 so it includes the two new fields.

Adding New Field Names and Determining the % of Quota

The first step in adding the two new fields is to enter and format the two field names in cells K8 and L8, and then enter the first % of Quota formula in cell K9. The formula for the % of Quota in cell K9 is YTD Sales / Quota or =J9 / I9.

Big Brother

Excel is always watching what you are doing. If you enter the data into the database as you entered worksheets in past projects, you will notice Excel entering data automatically for you, based on the data entered into the column. For example, in the St column in Figure 5-11, if you type the letter P in cell G21, Excel will enter PA into the cell. You also can right-click an empty cell under a list of items in a column and click the Pick From List command. Excel will display a list of items in the column from which you can pick to assign to cell G21.

 To Enter New Field Names and the % of Quota Formula

1 Select cell K8. Enter % of Quota as the new field name. Select cell L8. Enter Grade as the new field name. Double-click the move handle on the Standard toolbar to display it in its entirety. Click cell J8. Click the Format Painter button on the Standard toolbar. Drag through cells K8:L8. Select cell K9. Enter =J9 / I9 as the formula.

The new field names display in cells K8 and L8, and the result of the % of Quota formula displays in cell K9 (Figure 5-11).

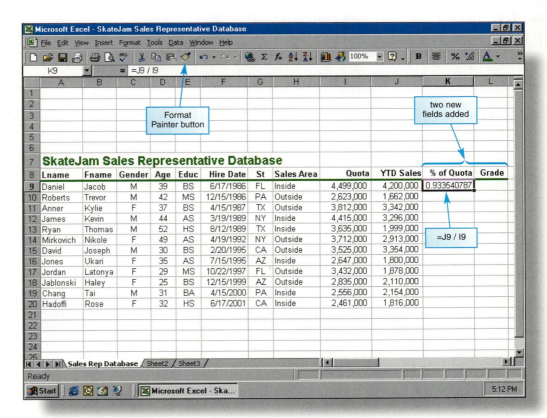

FIGURE 5-11

2 Double-click the move handle on the Formatting toolbar to display it in its entirety. With cell K9 selected, click the Percent Style button on the Formatting toolbar. Click the Increase Decimal button on the Formatting toolbar twice.

The % of Quota in cell K9 displays using the Percent style format with two decimal places (Figure 5-12).

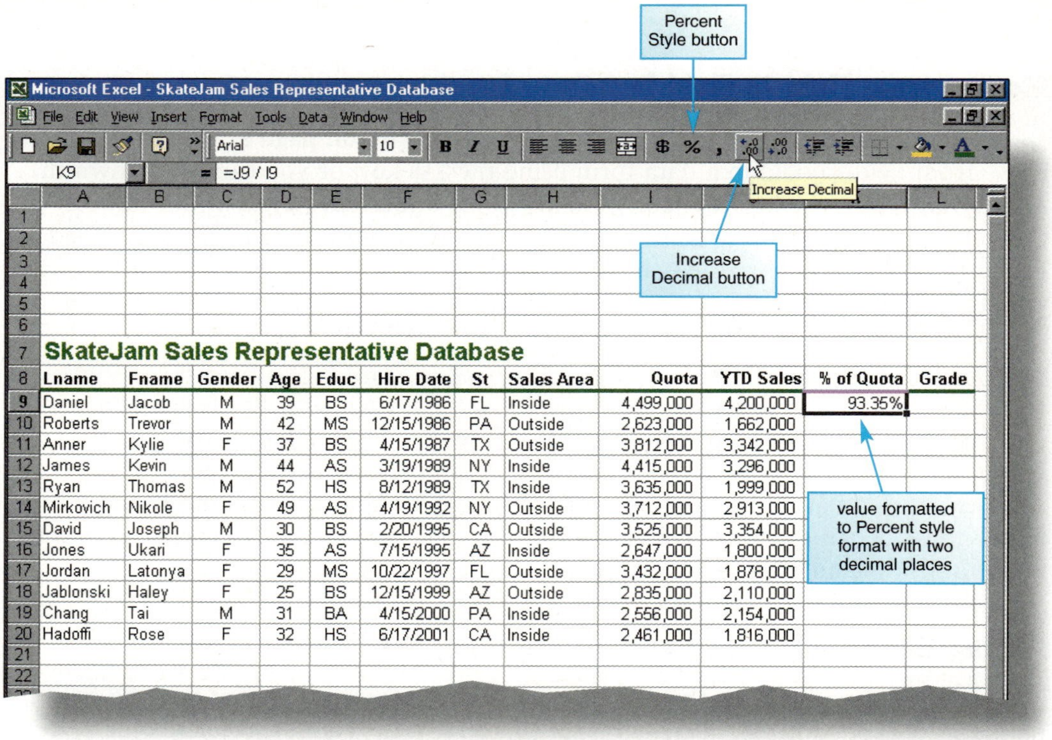

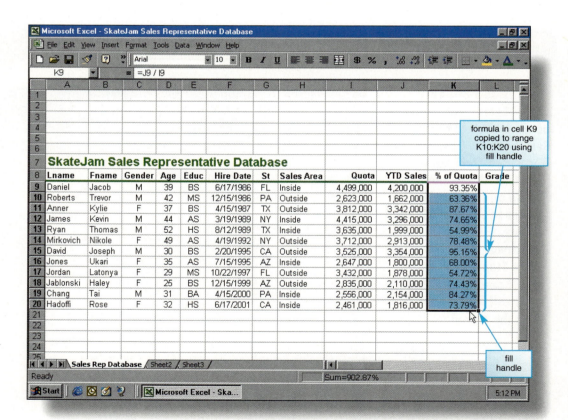

FIGURE 5-12

3 With cell K9 selected, drag the fill handle down through cell K20.

The % of Quota displays for each sales representative (Figure 5-13).

FIGURE 5-13

The entries in the % of Quota column give the user an immediate evaluation of how well each sales representative's YTD Sales are in relation to their annual quota. Many people, however, dislike numbers as an evaluation tool. Most prefer simple letter grades, which when used properly can group the sales representatives in the same way an instructor groups students by letter grades. Excel has functions that allow you to assign letter grades based on a table as explained in the next section.

Using Excel's VLOOKUP Function to Determine Letter Grades

Excel has two lookup functions that are useful for looking up values in tables, such as tax tables, discount tables, parts tables, and grade scale tables. Both functions look up a value in a table and return a corresponding value from the table to the cell assigned the function. The **HLOOKUP function** is used when the table direction is horizontal or across the worksheet. The **VLOOKUP function** is used when a table direction is vertical or down the worksheet. The VLOOKUP function is by far the most often used, because most tables are vertical as is the table in this project.

The grading scale in this project (Table 5-2) is similar to one that your instructor uses to determine your letter grade. In Table 5-2, any score greater than or equal to 93% equates to a letter grade of A. Scores of 80 and less than 93 are assigned a letter grade of B, and so on.

Table 5-2 Typical Grade Table	
% OF QUOTA	**GRADE**
>=93%	A
80% to < 93%	B
70% to < 80%	C
60% to < 70%	D
0 to < 60%	F

The VLOOKUP function requires that the table only indicate the lowest score for a letter grade. Furthermore, the table entries must be in sequence from lowest score to highest scores. Thus, the entries in Table 5-2 must be resequenced for use with the VLOOKUP function so it appears as in Table 5-3.

The general form of the VLOOKUP function is:

=VLOOKUP(search argument, table range, column number)

The VLOOKUP function searches the leftmost column of a table (called the **table arguments**). In Table 5-3, the table arguments are the percents. The VLOOKUP function uses the % of Quota value (called the **search argument**) in the record of a sales representative to search the leftmost column for a particular value and then returns the corresponding value from the specified column (called the **table values**). In this example, the table values are the grades in the second or rightmost column.

Table 5-3 Typical Grade Table Modified for VLOOKUP Function	
% OF QUOTA	**GRADE**
0	F
60%	D
70%	C
80%	B
93%	A

For the VLOOKUP function to work correctly, the table arguments must be in ascending sequence, because the VLOOKUP function will return a table value based on the search argument being less than or equal to the table arguments. Thus, if the % of Quota value is 74.65% (fourth record in database), then the VLOOKUP function returns a grade of C because 74.65% is greater than or equal to 70% and less than 80%.

The steps on the next page show how to enter the table elements in Table 5-3 onto the worksheet and use the VLOOKUP function to determine the letter grade for each sales representative based on his or her % of Quota value.

To Create a Lookup Table and Use the VLOOKUP Function to Determine Letter Grades

1 **Click cell N1 and then enter** Grade Table **as the table title. Click the Bold button on the Formatting toolbar. Drag through cell O1 and then click the Merge and Center button on the Formatting toolbar. Click cell N2. Enter the column titles and table entries in Table 5-3 on page E 5.15 in the range N2:O7. Select columns N and O and increase their width to 10.00. Click cell L8. Click the Format Painter button on the Standard toolbar. Drag through the range N2:O2. Click cell L9 to deselect the range N2:O2.**

The table displays as shown in Figure 5-14.

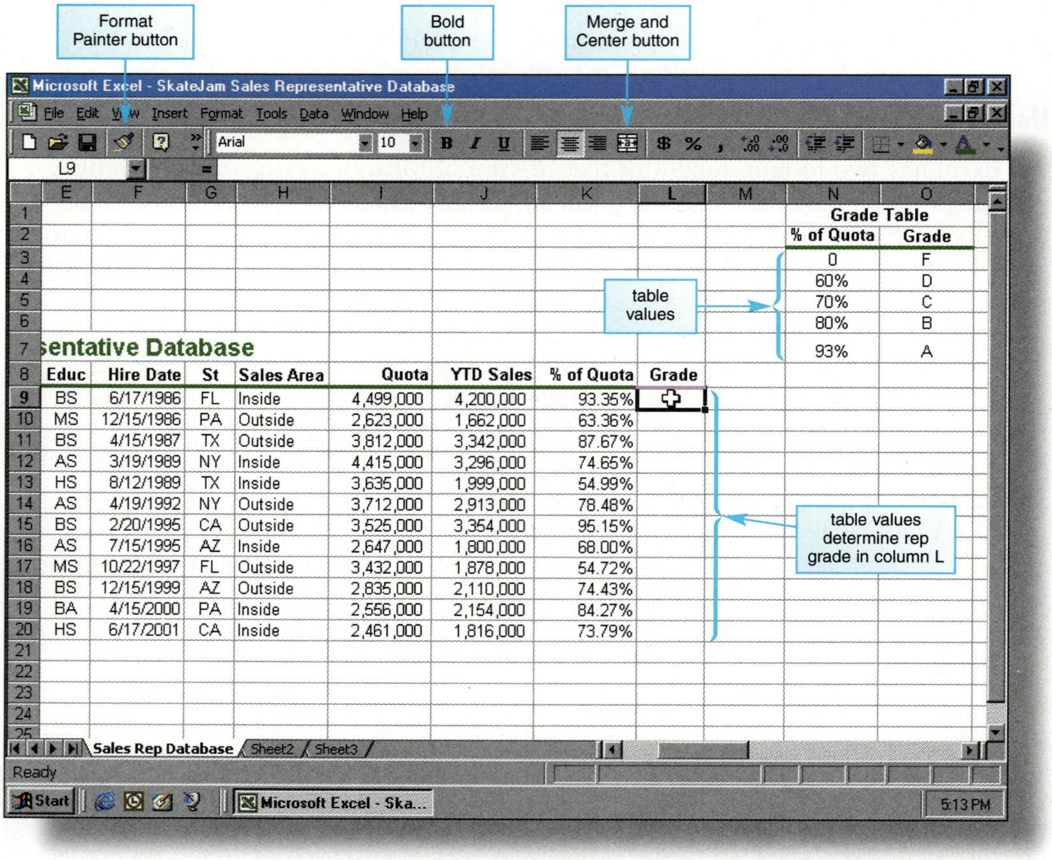

FIGURE 5-14

2 **Type** =vlookup (k9, n3:o7, 2) **in cell L9.**

The VLOOKUP function displays in the cell and in the formula bar (Figure 5-15). In this case, cell K9 is the search argument; n3:o7 is the table range; and 2 is the column number in the table range.

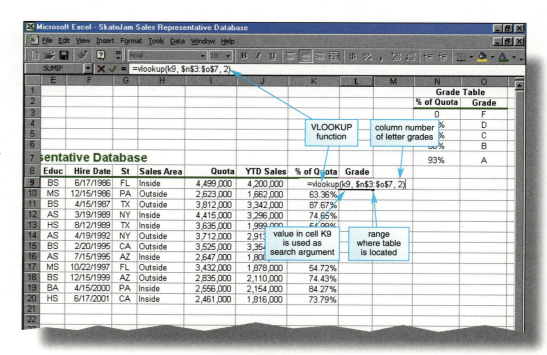

FIGURE 5-15

3 Press the ENTER key.

The VLOOKUP function returns to cell L9 a grade of A for a % of Quota value in cell K9 of 93.35% (Figure 5-16).

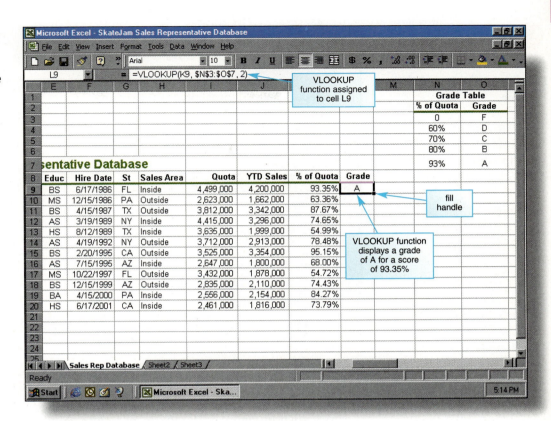

FIGURE 5-16

4 With cell L9 selected, drag the fill handle through cell L20 to copy the function to the range L10:L20.

The VLOOKUP function returns the grades shown in column L from the table of grades in columns N and O for the corresponding % of Quota values in column K (Figure 5-17).

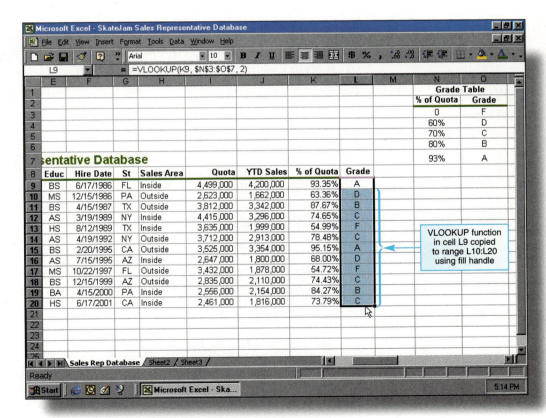

FIGURE 5-17

5 Select cell A22 to deselect the range L9:L20. Scroll down until row 7 is at the top of the window.

The entries for the database are complete (Figure 5-18).

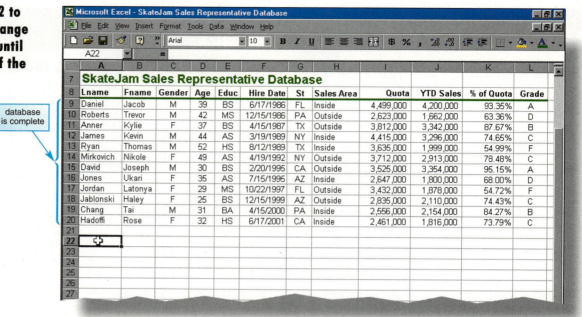

FIGURE 5-18

As shown in Figure 5-18, any % of Quota value below 60 returns a grade of F. Thus, the fifth record (Thomas Ryan) receives a grade of F because his % of Quota value is 54.98%. A percent of 60 is required to move up to the next letter grade. The last record (Rose Hadoffi) receives a grade of C because her % of Quota value is 73.79%, which is equal to or greater than 70% and less than 80%.

From column L in Figure 5-17 on the previous page, you can see that the VLOOKUP function is not searching for a table argument that matches the search argument exactly. The VLOOKUP function begins the search at the top of the table and works downward. As soon as it finds the first table argument greater than the search argument, it returns the previous table value. For example, when it searches the table with the third record (Kylie Anner), it determines the score is less than 93% in the first column in the table and returns the grade of B from the second column in the table, which actually corresponds to 80% in the table. The letter grade of F is returned for any value greater than or equal to 0 (zero) and less than 60. A score less than 0 (zero) would return an error message (#N/A) to the cell assigned the VLOOKUP function.

It is most important that you use absolute cell references for the table range ($N$3:$O$7) in the VLOOKUP function (see the entry in the formula bar shown in Figure 5-16 on the previous page) or Excel will adjust the cell references when you copy the function down through column L in Step 4. This will cause unexpected results in column L.

Redefining the Name Database

The final step in adding the two computational fields to the database is to redefine the name Database. Recall that it was originally defined as the range A8:J9 and it expanded automatically to the range A8:J20 by adding records through the use of the data form. To tie the two new fields to the database, the name Database must be redefined as the range A8:L20. The following steps show how to redefine the range assigned to a name.

More About 2000

The VLOOKUP Function

A score that is outside the range of the table causes the VLOOKUP function to return an error message (#N/A) to the cell. For example, any % of Quota score less than zero in column K of Figure 5-18 would result in the error message being assigned to the corresponding cell.

Steps To Redefine the Name Database

1 **Click Insert on the menu bar. Point to Name and then point to Define on the Name submenu.**

The Insert menu and Name submenu display (Figure 5-19).

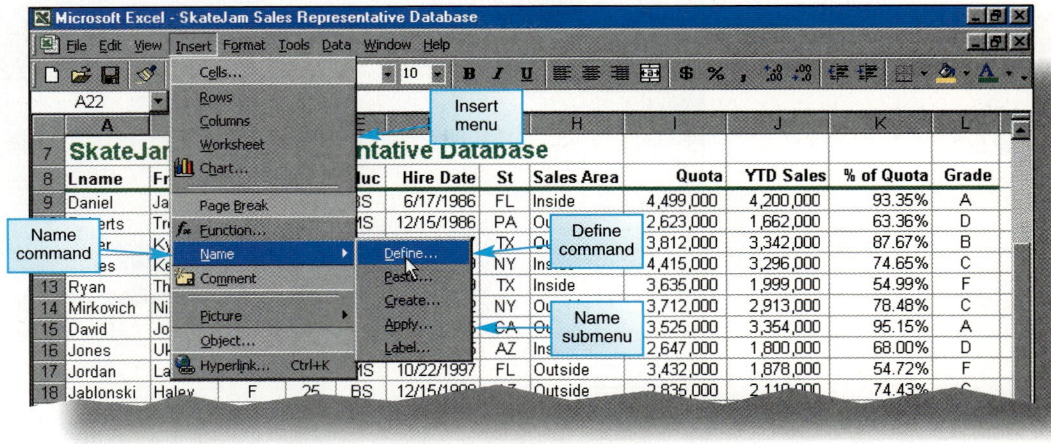

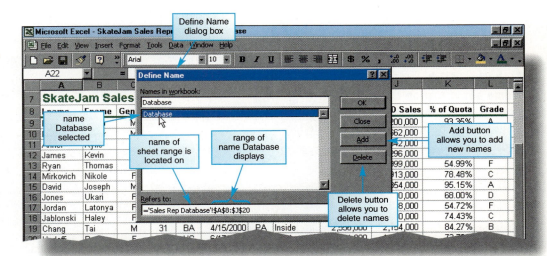

FIGURE 5-19

2 **Click Define. When the Define Name dialog box displays, click Database in the Names in workbook list.**

The Define Name dialog box displays with the name Database selected (Figure 5-20). The Refers to box at the bottom of the dialog box indicates the range assigned to the name Database.

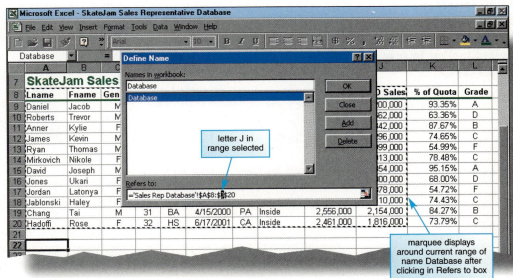

FIGURE 5-20

3 **Drag through the letter J in the range in the Refers to box.**

Excel displays a marquee around the original range assigned to the name Database (Figure 5-21).

FIGURE 5-21

4 Type the letter L to replace the letter J in the Refers to box.

The new range in the Refers to box encompasses the two new fields in column K and L (Figure 5-22).

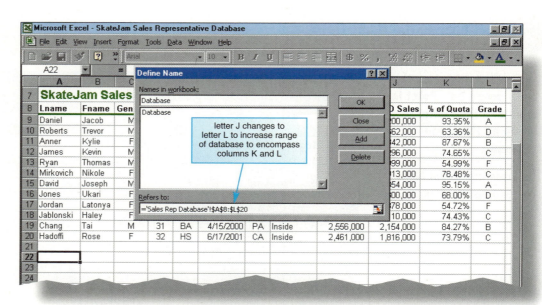

FIGURE 5-22

5 Click the OK button. Click the Name box arrow on the left side of the formula bar and then click the name Database.

Excel highlights the new range (A8:L20) assigned to the name Database (Figure 5-23).

6 Select cell A21 to deselect the range A8:L20. Click the Save button on the Standard toolbar to save the workbook.

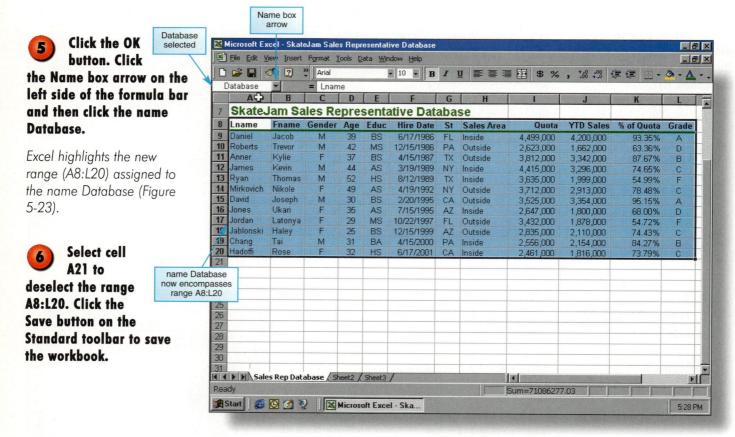

FIGURE 5-23

Not only can you use the Define Name dialog box in Figure 5-22 to redefine names, but you also can use it to define new names through the use of the **Add button**, and you can delete names through the use of the **Delete button**. As shown in Figure 5-23, names are useful in a workbook to select ranges quickly for purposes of copying, printing, and formatting.

Guidelines to Follow When Creating a Database

When you create a database in Excel, you should follow some basic guidelines, as listed in Table 5-4.

Table 5-4 Guidelines for Creating a Database

DATABASE SIZE AND WORKBOOK LOCATION

1. Do not enter more than one database per worksheet.

2. Maintain at least one blank row between a database and other worksheet entries.

3. Do not store other worksheet entries in the same rows as your database.

4. Define the name Database as the database range.

5. A database can have a maximum of 256 fields and 65,536 records on a worksheet.

COLUMN TITLES (FIELD NAMES)

1. Place column titles (field names) in the first row of the database.

2. Do not use blank rows or rows with dashes to separate the column titles (field names) from the data.

3. Apply a different format to the column titles and the data. For example, bold the column titles and display the data below the column titles using a regular style.

4. Column titles (field names) can be up to 32,767 characters in length. The column titles should be meaningful.

CONTENTS OF DATABASE

1. Each column should have similar data. For example, employee hire date should be in the same column for all employees.

2. Format the data to improve readability, but do not vary the format of the data in a column.

Using a Data Form to View Records and Change Data

At any time while the worksheet is active, you can use the **Form command** on the Data menu to display records, add new records, delete records, and change the data in records. When a data form is opened initially, Excel displays the first record in the database. To display the ninth record as shown in Figure 5-24, click the Find Next button until the ninth record displays. Each time you click the **Find Next button**, Excel advances to the next record in the database. If necessary, you can use the **Find Prev button** to go back to a previous record. You also can use the vertical scroll bar in the middle of the data form to move between records.

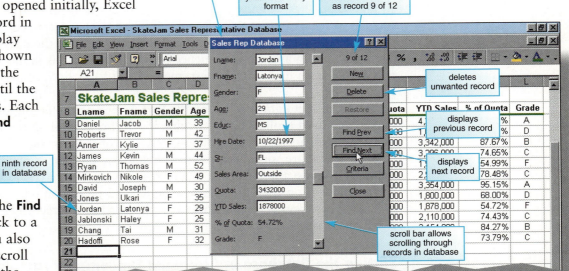

FIGURE 5-24

To change data in a record, you first display it on a data form. Next, you select the fields to change. Finally, you use the DOWN ARROW key or the ENTER key to confirm or enter the field changes. If you change field values on a data form and then select the Find Next button to move to the next record without entering the field changes, these changes will not be made.

To add a new record, click the **New button** on the data form. Excel automatically adds the new record to the bottom of the database and increases the range assigned to the name Database. To delete a record, you first display it on a data form and then click the **Delete button**. Excel automatically moves all records below the deleted record up one row and appropriately redefines the range of the name Database.

Printing a Database

To print the database, follow the same procedures you followed in earlier projects. If the worksheet includes data that is not part of the database you want to print, then follow these steps to print only the database.

TO PRINT A DATABASE

1 Click File on the menu bar and then click Page Setup.

2 Click the Sheet tab in the Page Setup dialog box. Type `Database` in the Print Area text box.

3 Click the OK button.

4 Ready the printer and then click the Print button on the Standard toolbar.

Later, if you want to print the entire worksheet, delete the database range in the Print area text box in the Sheet tab of the Page Setup dialog box.

Sorting a Database

The data in a database is easier to work with and more meaningful if the records are arranged sequentially based on one or more fields. Arranging records in a specific sequence is called **sorting**. Data is in **ascending sequence** if it is in order from lowest to highest, earliest to most recent, or alphabetically from A to Z. For example, the records in the SkateJam Sales Representative Database were entered in order from the earliest hire date to the most recent hire date. Thus, the database shown in Figure 5-25 is sorted in ascending sequence by hire date. Data is in **descending sequence** if it is sorted from highest to lowest, most recent to earliest, or alphabetically from Z to A.

You can sort data by clicking the **Sort Ascending button** or **Sort Descending button** on the Standard toolbar or by clicking the **Sort command** on the Data menu. If you are sorting on a single field (column), use one of the Sort buttons on the Standard toolbar. If you are sorting on multiple fields, use the Sort command on the Data menu. If you use a button to sort, make sure you select a cell in the field on which to sort before you click the button. The field or fields you select to sort the records are called **sort keys**. The first sort example reorders the records by last name in ascending sequence.

Sorting the Database in Ascending Sequence by Last Name

Follow these steps to sort the records in ascending sequence by last name.

To Sort a Database in Ascending Sequence by Last Name

1 **Double-click the move handle on the Standard toolbar to display it in its entirety. Click cell A9 and then point to the Sort Ascending button on the Standard toolbar (Figure 5-25).**

move handle on Standard toolbar

cell selected in column on which to sort

Sort Ascending button

Sort Descending button

Lname	Fname	Gender	Age	Educ	Hire Date	St	Sales Area	Quota	YTD Sales	% of Quota	Grade
Daniel	Jacob	M	39	BS	6/17/1986	FL	Inside	4,499,000	4,200,000	93.35%	A
Roberts	Trevor	M	42	MS	12/15/1986	PA	Outside	2,623,000	1,662,000	63.36%	D
Anner	Kylie	F	37	BS	4/15/1987	TX	Outside	3,812,000	3,342,000	87.67%	B
James	Kevin	M	44	AS	3/19/1989	NY	Inside	4,415,000	3,296,000	74.65%	C
Ryan	Thomas	M	52	HS	8/12/1989	TX	Inside	3,635,000	1,999,000	54.99%	F
Mirkovich	Nikole	F	49	AS	4/19/1992	NY	Outside	3,712,000	2,913,000	78.48%	C
David	Joseph	M	30	BS	2/20/1995	CA	Outside	3,525,000	3,354,000	95.15%	A
Jones	Ukari	F	35	AS	7/15/1995	AZ	Inside	2,647,000	1,800,000	68.00%	D
Jordan	Latonya	F	29	MS	10/22/1997	FL	Outside	3,432,000	1,878,000	54.72%	F
Jablonski	Haley	F	25	BS	12/15/1999	AZ	Outside	2,835,000	2,110,000	74.43%	C
Chang	Tai	M	31	BA	4/15/2000	PA	Inside	2,556,000	2,154,000	84.27%	B
Hadoffi	Rose	F	32	HS	6/17/2001	CA	Inside	2,461,000	1,816,000	73.79%	C

FIGURE 5-25

2 **Click the Sort Ascending button.**

Excel sorts the sales representative database in ascending sequence by last name (Figure 5-26).

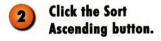
records sorted in ascending sequence by last name

Lname	Fname	Gender	Age	Educ	Hire Date	St	Sales Area	Quota	YTD Sales	% of Quota	Grade
Anner	Kylie	F	37	BS	4/15/1987	TX	Outside	3,812,000	3,342,000	87.67%	B
Chang	Tai	M	31	BA	4/15/2000	PA	Inside	2,556,000	2,154,000	84.27%	B
Daniel	Jacob	M	39	BS	6/17/1986	FL	Inside	4,499,000	4,200,000	93.35%	A
David	Joseph	M	30	BS	2/20/1995	CA	Outside	3,525,000	3,354,000	95.15%	A
Hadoffi	Rose	F	32	HS	6/17/2001	CA	Inside	2,461,000	1,816,000	73.79%	C
Jablonski	Haley	F	25	BS	12/15/1999	AZ	Outside	2,835,000	2,110,000	74.43%	C
James	Kevin	M	44	AS	3/19/1989	NY	Inside	4,415,000	3,296,000	74.65%	C
Jones	Ukari	F	35	AS	7/15/1995	AZ	Inside	2,647,000	1,800,000	68.00%	D
Jordan	Latonya	F	29	MS	10/22/1997	FL	Outside	3,432,000	1,878,000	54.72%	F
Mirkovich	Nikole	F	49	AS	4/19/1992	NY	Outside	3,712,000	2,913,000	78.48%	C
Roberts	Trevor	M	42	MS	12/15/1986	PA	Outside	2,623,000	1,662,000	63.36%	D
Ryan	Thomas	M	52	HS	8/12/1989	TX	Inside	3,635,000	1,999,000	54.99%	F

FIGURE 5-26

Sorting a Database in Descending Sequence by Last Name

Follow the steps on the next page to sort the records in descending sequence by last name.

More About

Manipulating the Database

After naming the database range Database, you still can select a subset of the database, such as the last ten records, before completing an activity such as a sort operation. Excel will manipulate only the data in the selected range.

TO SORT A DATABASE IN DESCENDING SEQUENCE BY LAST NAME

1 If necessary, click cell A9 to make it active.

2 Click the Sort Descending button on the Standard toolbar.

Excel sorts the sales representative database in descending sequence by last name (Figure 5-27).

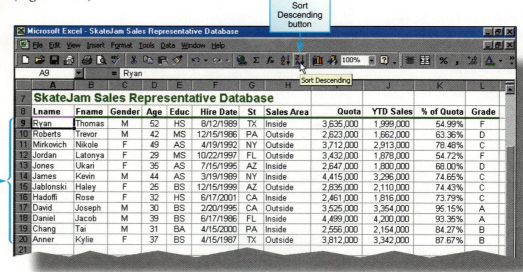

FIGURE 5-27

More About

Sorting

Some Excel users use the fill handle to create a series in an additional field in the database that is used only to reorder the records into their original sequence.

Returning a Database to Its Original Order

When you design a database, it is good practice to include a field that allows you to return the database to its original order. In the case of the SkateJam Sales Representaive database, the records were entered in sequence by hire date. Follow these steps to return the records back to their original order in ascending sequence by hire date.

TO RETURN A DATABASE TO ITS ORIGINAL ORDER

1 Click cell F9.

2 Click the Sort Ascending button on the Standard toolbar.

Excel sorts the sales representative database in ascending sequence by hire date. The database displays in its original order (Figure 5-28).

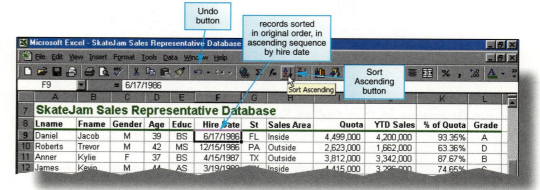

FIGURE 5-28

You also can undo a sort operation by performing one of the following actions:

1. Click the Undo button on the Standard toolbar.
2. Click the Undo Sort command on the Edit menu.

If you have sorted the database more than once, you can click the Undo button multiple times to undo the previous sorts.

Sorting a Database on Multiple Fields

Excel allows you to sort on a maximum of three fields in a single sort operation. For instance, the sort example that follows uses the Sort command on the Data menu to sort the SkateJam Sales Representative database by quota (column I) within education (column E) within gender (column C). The Gender and Educ fields will be sorted in ascending sequence; the Quota field will be sorted in descending sequence.

The phrase, sort by quota within education within gender, means that the records first are arranged in ascending sequence by gender code. Within gender, the records are arranged in ascending sequence by education code. Within education, the records are arranged in descending sequence by the quota.

In this case, gender is the **major sort key** (Sort by field), education is the **intermediate sort key** (first Then by field), and quota is the **minor sort key** (second Then by field).

To Sort a Database on Multiple Fields

1 **With a cell in the database active, click Data on the menu bar and then point to Sort.**

The Data menu displays (Figure 5-29).

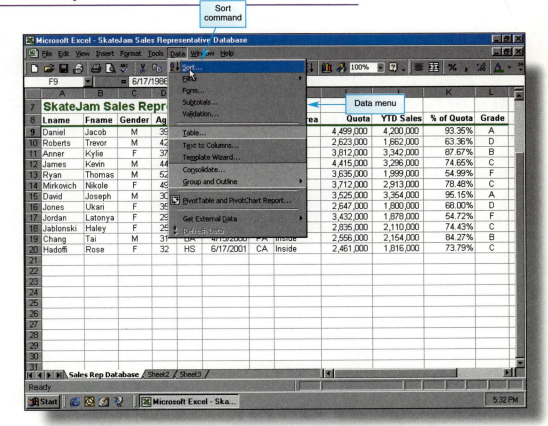

FIGURE 5-29

2 Click Sort. When the Sort dialog box displays, click the Sort by box arrow and then point to Gender in the list.

Excel selects the database and the Sort dialog box displays. The Sort by list includes the field names in the database (Figure 5-30).

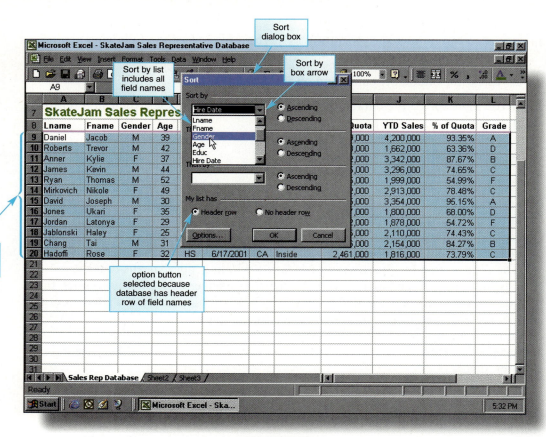

FIGURE 5-30

3 Click Gender. Click the first Then by box arrow and then click Educ. Click the second Then by box arrow and then click Quota. Click Descending in the second Then by area. Point to the OK button.

The Sort dialog box displays (Figure 5-31). The database will be sorted by quota within education within gender.

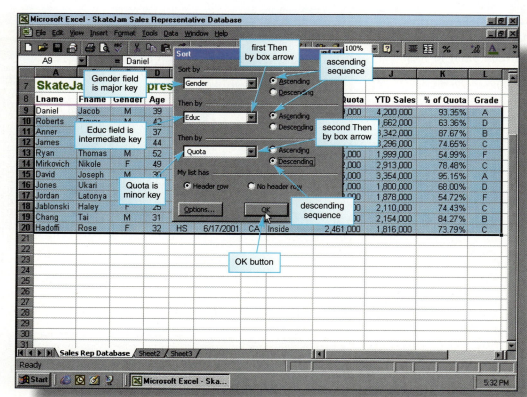

FIGURE 5-31

4 Click the OK button. Excel sorts the SkateJam Sales Representative database by quota within education within gender as shown in Figure 5-32.

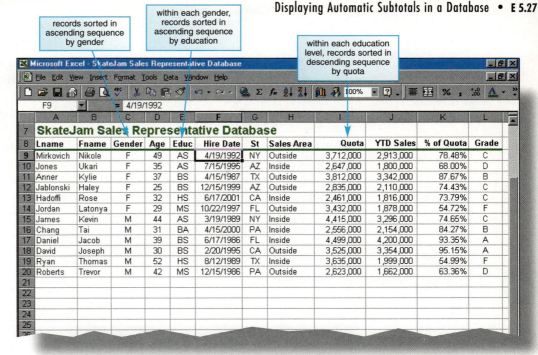

records sorted in ascending sequence by gender

within each gender, records sorted in ascending sequence by education

within each education level, records sorted in descending sequence by quota

FIGURE 5-32

As shown in Figure 5-32, Excel sorts the records in ascending sequence by the gender codes (F or M) in column C. Within each gender code, the records are in ascending sequence by the education codes (AS, BA, BS, HS, and MS) in column E. Finally, within the education codes, the records are sorted in descending sequence by the quotas in column I. Remember, if you make a mistake in a sort operation, you can return the records to their original order by clicking the Undo button on the Standard toolbar.

Because Excel sorts the database using the current order of the records, the previous example could have been completed by sorting on one field at a time using the Sort buttons on the Standard toolbar, beginning with the minor sort key.

Sorting a Database on More than Three Fields

To sort on more than three fields, you must sort the database two or more times. The most recent sort takes precedence. Hence, if you plan to sort on four fields, you sort on the three least important keys first and then sort on the major key. For example, if you want to sort on last name (Lname) within job category (Sales Area) within state (St) within gender (Gender), you first sort on Lname (second Then by column) within Sales Area (first Then by column) within St (Sort by column). After the first sort operation is complete, you sort on the Gender field by clicking one of the cells in the Gender column and then clicking the Sort Ascending button or Sort Descending button on the Standard toolbar.

Displaying Automatic Subtotals in a Database

Displaying **automatic subtotals** is a powerful tool for summarizing data in a database. Excel requires that you sort the database only on the field on which you want subtotals to be based, and then use the **Subtotals command** on the Data menu. When the Subtotal dialog box displays, you select the subtotal function you want to use.

More About

Sort Options

You can sort left to right across rows by clicking the Options button (Figure 5-31 on page E 5.26) and then clicking Sort left to right in the Orientation area. You also can click the Case sensitive check box, which would sort lowercase letters ahead of the same capital letters for an ascending sort.

Sort Algorithms

Numerous sort algorithms are used with computers, such as the Bubble sort, Shaker sort, and Shell sort. For additional information on sorting, visit the Excel 2000 More About Web page (www.scsite.com/ex2000/more.htm) and click Sort Algorithms.

The field on which you sort prior to invoking the Subtotals command is called the **control field**. When the control field changes, Excel displays a subtotal for the numeric fields you select in the Subtotal dialog box. For example, if you sort on the St field and request subtotals for the Quota and YTD Sales fields, then Excel recalculates the subtotal and grand total each time the St field changes to a new state. The most common subtotal used with the Subtotals command is the SUM function, which displays a sum each time the control field changes.

In addition to displaying subtotals, Excel also creates an outline for the database. The following steps shows you how to display subtotals for the Quota field and YTD Sales field by state. Because the insertion of subtotals increases the number of rows, the Zoom box on the Standard toolbar is used to display the entire database.

To Display Subtotals in a Database

1 Select cell G9. Click the Sort Ascending button on the Standard toolbar.

The SkateJam Sales Representative database displays in ascending sequence by state (Figure 5-33).

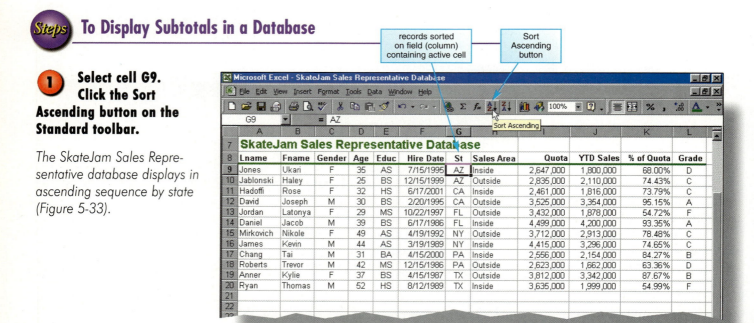

FIGURE 5-33

2 Click Data on the menu bar and then point to Subtotals (Figure 5-34).

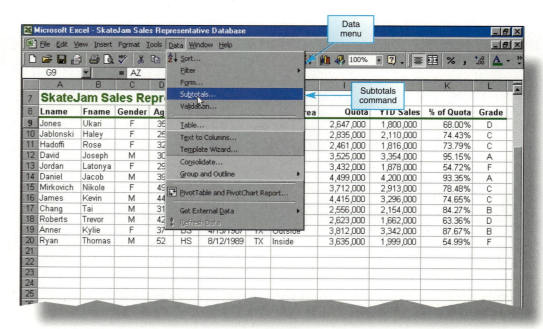

FIGURE 5-34

3 **Click Subtotals. When the Subtotal dialog box displays, click the At each change in box arrow and then click St. If necessary, select Sum in the Use function list. Click the Quota and YTD Sales check boxes in the Add subtotal to list. Point to the OK button.**

The Subtotal dialog box displays (Figure 5-35). The At each change in box contains the St field. The Use function box contains Sum. In the Add subtotal to box, both Quota and YTD Sales are selected.

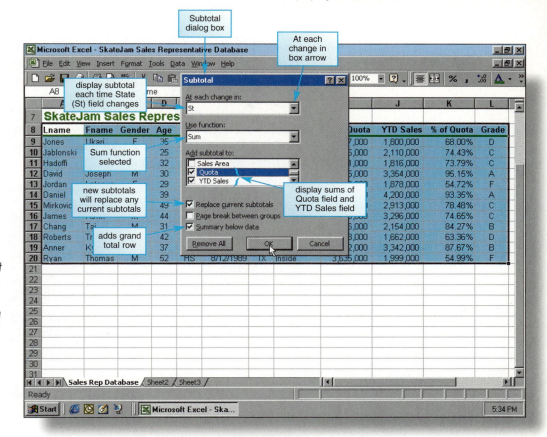

FIGURE 5-35

4 **Click the OK button.**

Excel inserts seven new rows in the SkateJam Sales Representative database. Six of the new rows contain Quota and YTD Sales subtotals for each state (Figure 5-36). The seventh new row displays grand totals for the Quota and YTD Sales fields. Excel also outlines the database, which causes the rightmost column to be outside the window.

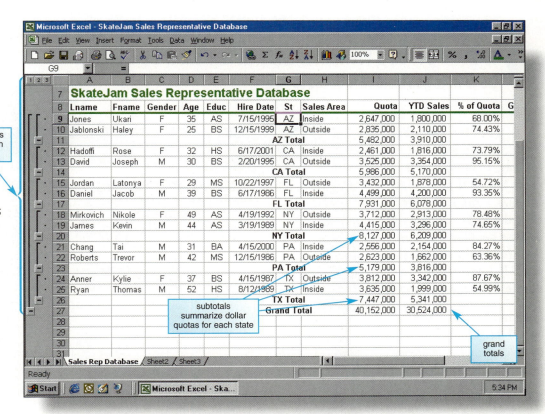

FIGURE 5-36

As shown in Figure 5-36 on the previous page, Excel has added six subtotal rows and one grand total row to the database. The names for each subtotal row are derived from the state names. Thus, in cell G11 of row 11 the text AZ Total names the Quota and YTD Sales totals for Arizona.

In Figure 5-35 on the previous page, the Use function box contains Sum, which instructs Excel to sum the fields selected in the Add subtotal to list. Additional functions are available by clicking the Use function box arrow. The frequently used subtotal functions are listed in Table 5-5.

Table 5-5	Frequently Used Subtotal Functions
SUBTOTAL FUNCTION	**DESCRIPTION**
Sum	Sums a column
Count	Counts the number of entries in a column
Average	Determines the average of numbers in a column
Max	Determines the maximum value in a column
Min	Determines the minimum value in a column

Zooming Out on a Worksheet and Hiding and Showing Detail Data in a Subtotaled Database

The following steps show how to use the Zoom box on the Standard toolbar to reduce the magnification of the worksheet so that all fields display. The steps also illustrate how to use the outline features of Excel to display only the total rows.

To Zoom Out on a Worksheet and Hide and Show Detail Data in a Subtotaled Database

1 **Click the Zoom box on the Standard toolbar. Type** 90 **and then press the ENTER key. Select columns I and J. Double-click the right boundary of column heading J to ensure the grand totals display in row 27. Select cell G9 to deselect the range I and J.**

Excel reduces the magnification of the worksheet so that all columns in the database display (Figure 5-37).

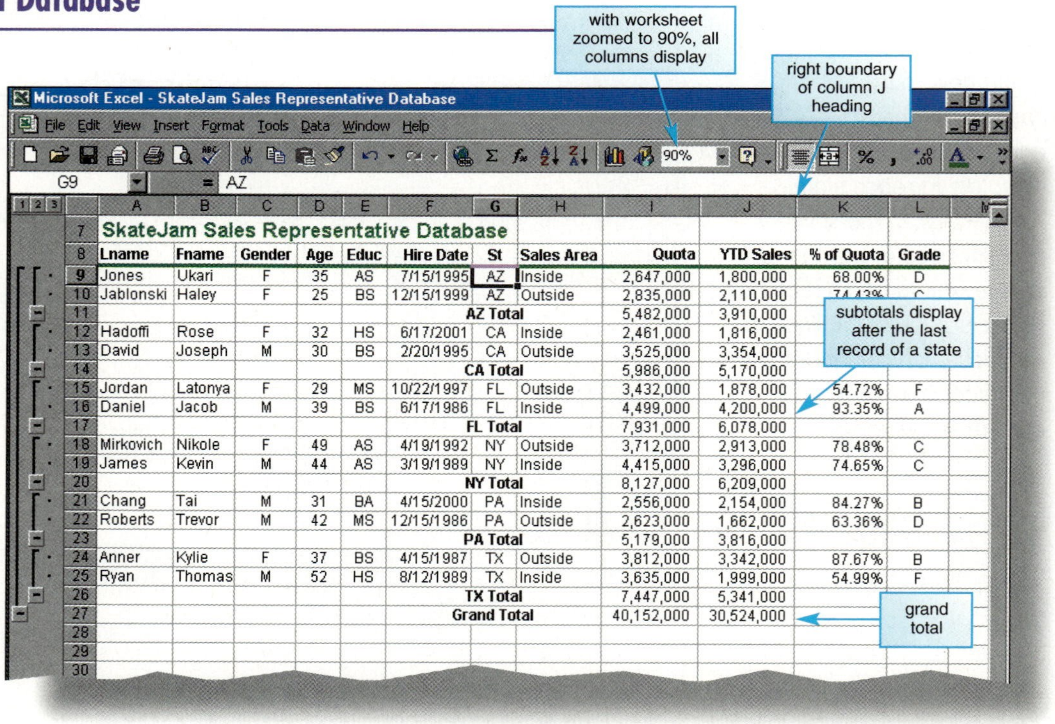

FIGURE 5-37

2 Click the row level 2 symbol on the left side of the screen.

Excel hides all detail rows and displays only the subtotal and grand total rows (Figure 5-38).

3 Click the row level 3 symbol on the left side of the screen to display hidden detail rows. Click the Zoom box arrow on the Standard toolbar and then click 100% in the list.

Excel displays the worksheet in normal size (Figure 5-36 on page E 5.29).

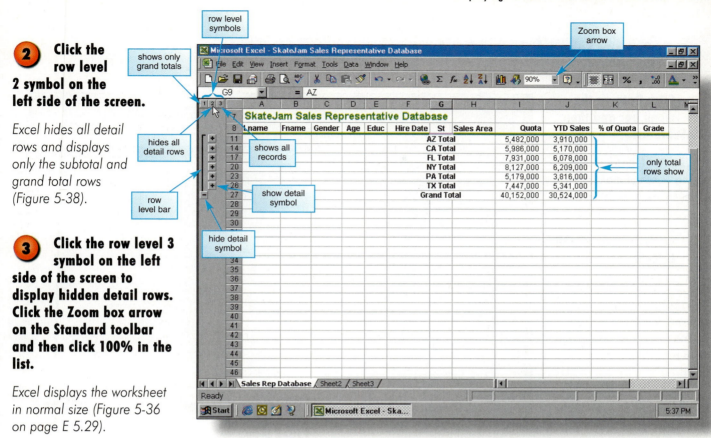

FIGURE 5-38

4 Change the width of columns I and J back to 11.00.

By utilizing the **outlining features** of Excel, you quickly can hide and show detail data. As described in Step 2, you can click the **row level symbols** to expand or collapse the worksheet. Row level symbol 1 hides all rows except the Grand Total row. Row level symbol 2 hides the detail records so the subtotal and grand total rows display as shown in Figure 5-38. Row level symbol 3 displays all rows.

The minus and plus symbols to the left on the row level bar in Figure 5-38 are called the show detail symbol (+) and hide detail symbol (-). If you click the **show detail symbol** (+), Excel displays the hidden detail records. If you click the **hide detail symbol** (-), Excel hides the detail records within the row level bar. The **row level bar** indicates which detail records will be hidden if you click the corresponding hide detail symbol.

You can outline any worksheet by using the **Group and Outline command** on the Data menu.

Removing Subtotals from the Database

You can remove subtotals and the accompanying outline from a database in two ways: you can click the Undo button on the Standard toolbar, or you can click the **Remove All button** in the Subtotal dialog box. The steps on the next page show how to use the Remove All button to remove subtotals from a database.

More *About*

Outlining

When you hide data using the outline features, you can chart the resulting rows and columns as if they were adjacent to one another. Thus, in Figure 5-38, you can chart the quotas by state as an adjacent range even though they are not in adjacent rows when the worksheet displays in normal form.

Steps **To Remove Subtotals from a Database**

1 **Click Data on the menu bar and then click Subtotals.**

Excel selects the database and the Subtotal dialog box displays (Figure 5-39).

2 **Click the Remove All button.**

Excel removes all subtotal and total rows and the outline from the database so it displays as shown previously in Figure 5-33 on page E 5.28.

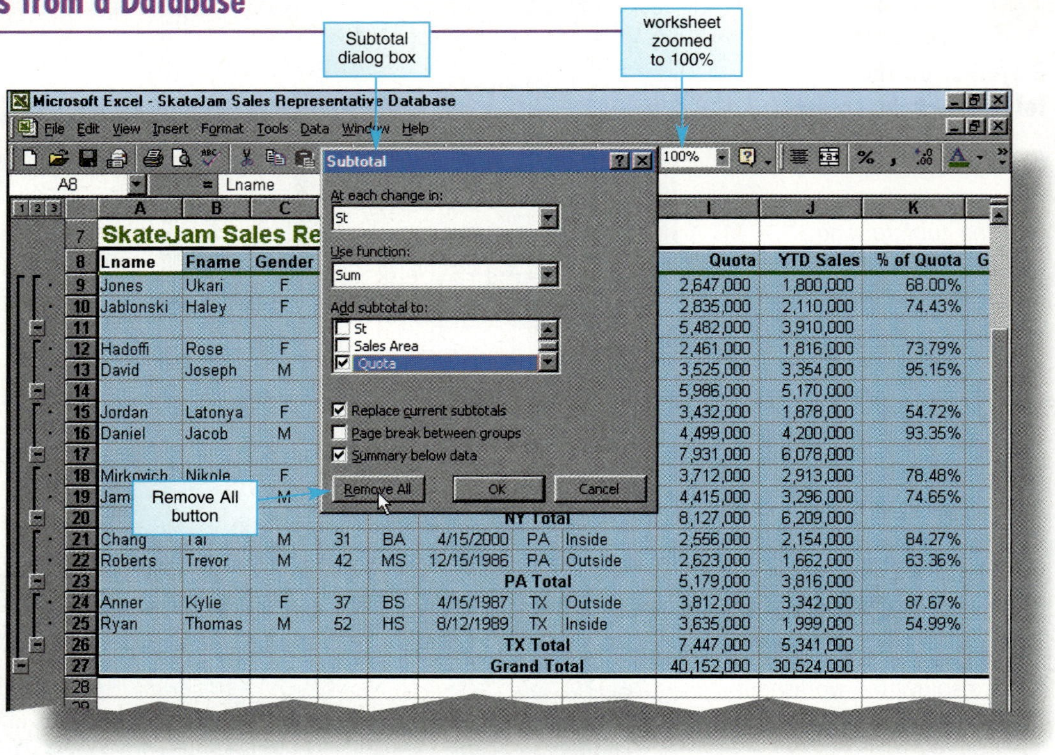

FIGURE 5-39

As shown in the previous sections, Excel makes it easy to add and remove subtotals from a database. Thus, you can generate quickly the type of information that database users need to help them make decisions about products or a company's direction.

Before moving on to the next section, complete the following steps to sort the SkateJam Sales Representative database into its original order in ascending sequence by hire date.

TO SORT THE DATABASE BY HIRE DATE

1 Click cell F9.

2 Click the Sort Ascending button on the Standard toolbar.

The records in the SkateJam Sales Representative database are sorted in ascending sequence by hire date.

Finding Records Using a Data Form

Once you have created the database, you might want to view records that meet only certain conditions, or comparison criteria. **Comparison criteria** are one or more conditions that include the field names and entries in the corresponding boxes in a data form. Displaying records that pass a test is called **querying the database**. For example, you can instruct Excel to find and display only those records that pass the test:

Gender = M **AND** Age >= 42 **AND** Sales Area = Inside **AND** Quota > 2,600,000

More About

Outlining

Use of the Group and Outline command on the Data menu is especially useful with large worksheets where the user can get lost in the sea of numbers. Outlining allows the user to hide the detail records to reduce the complexity of the worksheet.

You use the same relational operators (=, <, >, >=, <=, and <>) to enter comparison criteria on a data form that you used to formulate conditions in IF functions. For a record to display in the data form, it has to pass **all** four parts of the test. Finding records that pass a test is useful for viewing specific records, as well as maintaining the database. When a record that passes the test displays in the data form, you can change the field values or delete it from the database.

To find records in the database that pass a test made up of comparison criteria, you can use the Find Prev and Find Next buttons together with the **Criteria button** in the data form. The following steps illustrate how to use a data form to find records that pass the test described at the bottom of page E 5.32.

More About 2000

Databases

Have you ever wondered how a company got your name in its database? A company's customer or contacts database constitutes a major portion of its assets. Many companies sell their databases to non-competing companies, sometimes for millions of dollars. If one company has your name in its database, then chances are several other companies do too.

Steps: To Find Records Using a Data Form

1 Click Data on the menu bar and then click Form.

The first record in the SkateJam Sales Representative Database displays in the data form (Figure 5-40).

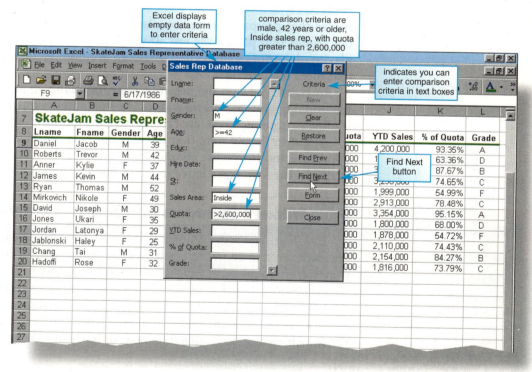

FIGURE 5-40

2 Click the Criteria button in the data form.

Excel clears the field values in the data form and displays a data form with blank text boxes.

3 Enter M in the Gender text box, >=42 in the Age text box, Inside in the Sales Area text box, and >2,600,000 in the Quota text box. Point to the Find Next button.

The data form displays with the comparison criteria entered as shown in Figure 5-41.

FIGURE 5-41

FIGURE 5-43

(continued)

E 5.34 • Project 5 • Creating, Sorting, and Querying a Worksheet Database

Microsoft **Excel 2000**

record 4 of 12
is first record in
database to pass
comparison criteria

In the Lab

Filtering and Sorting the Special Guys Apparel Database *(continued)*

Instructions Part 2: Step through each filter exercise in Table 5-6 and print the results for each in portrait orientation using the Fit to option on the Page Setup dialog box.

To complete a filter exercise, select the appropriate drop-down arrow(s) and option(s) in the lists. Use the (Custom...) option for field names that do not contain appropriate selections. After printing each filtered solution, point to Filter on the Data menu and click Show All on the Filter submenu. After the last filter exercise, remove the drop-down arrows by clicking AutoFilter on the Filter submenu. You should end up with the following number of records for Filters 1 through 12: 1 = 4; 2 = 2; 3 = 2; 4 = 5; 5 = 4; 6 = 7; 7 = 3; 8 = 7; 9 = 4; 10 = 0; 11 = 4; and 12 = 13.

Table 5-6 Special Guys Apparel Filter Criteria

FILTER	REGION	DIVISION	DISTRICT	LNAME	FNAME	HIRE DATE	AGE	GENDER	EDUC	SALES
1	1	B								
2	2	A	1							
3				Begins with S						
4								M		
5							>27 and < 45		BS or MS	
6						After 1/1/2000				
7					Begins with J					
8										>2,500,000
9							>30	M		
10					Ends with E		>50	F	HS	
11							<35	F		
12	All	All	All	All	All	All	All	All	All	All

Instructions Part 3: Sort the database according to the following six sort problems. Print the database for each sort problem in portrait orientation using the Fit to option in the Page Setup dialog box. Begin problems 2 through 6 by sorting on the Hire Date field to put the database back in its original order.

1. Sort the database in ascending sequence by region.
2. Sort the database by district within division within region. All three sort keys are to be in ascending sequence.
3. Sort the database by division within region. Both sort keys are to be in descending sequence.
4. Sort the database by salesperson number within district within division within region. All four sort keys are to be in ascending sequence.

In the Lab

5. Sort the database in descending sequence by sales.

6. Sort the database by district within division within region. All three sort keys are to be in descending sequence.

7. Hide columns J and K by selecting them and pressing CTRL+0 (zero). Print the database. Select columns I and L. Press CTRL+SHIFT+RIGHT PARENTHESIS to display the hidden columns. Close the Special Guys Apparel database without saving changes.

Instructions Part 4: Open the Special Guys Apparel database. Sort the database by district within division within region. Select ascending sequence for all three sort keys. Use the Subtotals command on the Data menu to generate subtotals for sales by region (Figure 5-65). Change column A to best fit. Print the worksheet. Click row level symbol 1 and print the worksheet. Click row level symbol 2 and print the worksheet. Click row level symbol 3. Remove all subtotals. Close the database without saving changes.

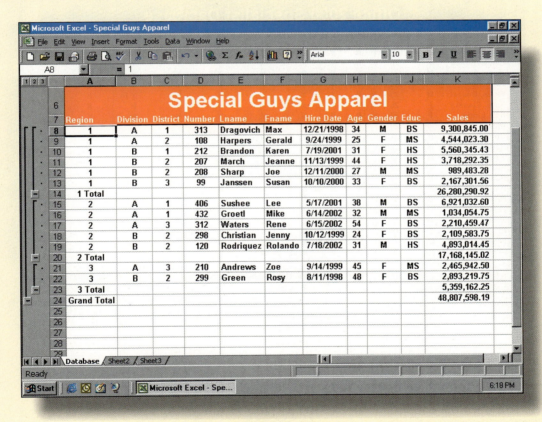

FIGURE 5-65

In the Lab

2 Filtering and Sorting a Database of Office 2000 Specialists

Problem: Office Temps, Inc. specializes in supplying consultants to companies in need of Office 2000 expertise. The president of the company, Juanita Jeffries, developed a database (Figure 5-66) that shows the expertise of each employee the company sends out as a consultant. She has asked you to sort, query, and determine some averages from the database. Carefully label each required printout by using the part number and step. If there are multiple printouts in a step, label them a, b, c, and so on.

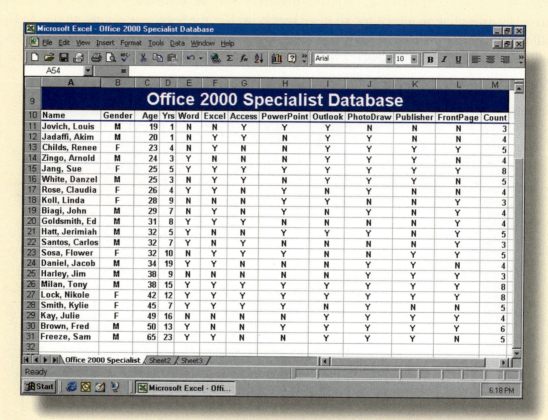

FIGURE 5-66

Instructions Part 1: Perform the following tasks.

1. Start Excel and open the database Office 2000 Specialist Database from the Data Disk. If you do not have a copy of the Data Disk, see the inside back cover of this book for instructions for downloading it.

2. Complete the following tasks.

   a. Sort the records in the database into ascending sequence by name. John Biagi should display first in the database. Arnold Zingo should display last. Print the sorted version in portrait orientation using the Fit to option in the Page Setup dialog box.

   b. Sort the records in the database by age within gender. Select ascending sequence for the gender code and descending sequence for the age. Julie Kay should be the first record. Print the sorted version as indicated in Step 2a.

In the Lab

c. Sort the database by PowerPoint within Access within Excel within Word. Use the Sort Descending button on the Standard toolbar on all fields. Sort first on PowerPoint, then Access, then Excel, and finally Word. Those who are experts in all four applications should rise to the top of the database. Print the sorted version as indicated in Step 2a. Close the workbook without saving it.

Instructions Part 2: If necessary, open the workbook Office 2000 Specialist Database (Figure 5-67). Select a cell within the database range. Use the Form command on the Data menu to display a data form. Use the Criteria button in the data form to enter the comparison criteria for the tasks below Figure 5-67. Use the Find Next and Find Prev buttons in the data form to find the records that pass the comparison criteria. Write down and submit the names of the employees who pass the comparison criteria for items a through d. Close the data form after each query and then reopen it by clicking the Form command on the Data menu. You should end up with the following number of records for items a through d: a = 2; b = 3; c = 5; and d = 2.

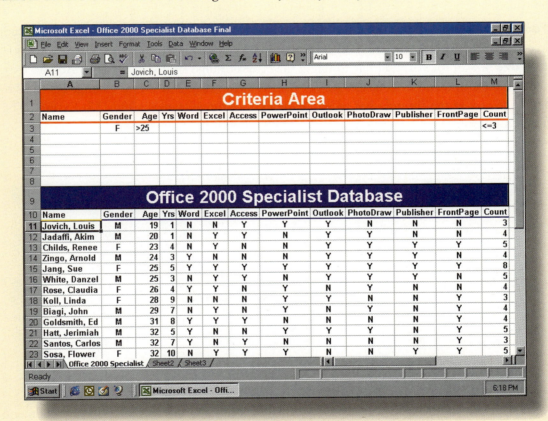

FIGURE 5-67

a. Find all records that represent specialists who are female and are experts in Word and Outlook.

b. Find all records that represent specialists with more than 5 years' experience (Yrs) and who are experts in Word, PhotoDraw, and FrontPage.

c. Find all records that represent male specialists who are at least 26 years old and are experts in Excel.

d. Find all records that represent specialists who have at least 10 years' experience (Yrs) and who are experts in Excel, Access, and PhotoDraw.

(continued)

In the Lab

Filtering and Sorting a Database of Office 2000 Specialists *(continued)*

e. Close and then re-open the data form. All specialists who did not know Publisher were sent to a seminar on the application. Use the Find Next button in the data form to locate the records of these employees and change the Publisher field entry in the data form from the letter N to the letter Y. Make sure you press the ENTER key or press the DOWN ARROW key after changing the letter. Print the worksheet as indicated in Step 2a of Part 1. Close the database without saving the changes.

Instructions Part 3: Open the workbook Office 2000 Specialist Database. Click a cell within the database range. Click Data on the menu bar and then point to Filter. Use the AutoFilter command on the Filter submenu and redo Part 2 a, b, c, and d. Use the Show All command on the Filter submenu before starting items b, c, and d. Print the worksheet as indicated in Step 2a of Part 1 for each problem. Click AutoFilter on the Filter submenu to remove the Auto-Filter arrows. Close the workbook without saving the changes.

Instructions Part 4: Open the workbook Office 2000 Specialist Database. Add a criteria range by copying the database title and field names (range A9:M10) to range A1:M2 (Figure 5-67). Change cell A1 to `Criteria Area`. Use the Name box in the formula bar to name the criteria range (A2:M3) Criteria. Add an extract range by copying the database title and field names (range A9:M10) to range A37:M38. Change cell A37 to `Extract Area`. Use the Name box in the formula bar to name the extract range (range A38:M38) Extract. The top of your worksheet should look similar to the top of the screen shown in Figure 5-68.

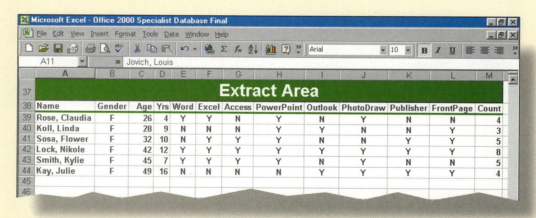

FIGURE 5-68

1. With a cell active in the database range, use the Advanced Filter command on the Filter submenu to extract records that pass the tests in the following items a through e. Print the entire worksheet after each extraction as indicated in Step 2a of Part 1.

   a. Extract the records that represent specialists who are female and older than 25 (Figure 5-68). You should extract six records.

   b. Extract the records that represent male specialists who are experts in Access, but not in PhotoDraw. You should extract three records.

In the Lab

c. Extract the records that represent female specialists who are at least 30 years old and have a count of 8. The field Count in column M uses the **COUNTIF function** to count the number of Ys in a record. A count of 8 means the record represents a specialist with expertise in all areas. You should extract one record.

d. Extract the records that represent specialists whose last name begins with the letter S. You should extract three records.

e. Extract the records that represent specialists who are experts in three applications or less. You should extract four records. Save the workbook using the file name Office 2000 Specialist Database Final. Close the workbook.

Instructions Part 5: Open the workbook Office 2000 Specialist Database Final created in Part 4. If you did not do Part 4, then open the Office 2000 Specialist Database from the Data Disk.

Scroll to the right to display cell O1 in the upper left corner of the window. Enter the criteria in the range O1:Q3 as shown in Figure 5-69. Enter the row titles in cells O5:O7 as shown in Figure 5-69.

Use the database function DAVERAGE and the appropriate criteria in the range O1:Q3 to determine the average age of the males and females in the range. Use the database function DCOUNT and the appropriate criteria in the range O1:Q3 to determine the record count of those who have expertise in Excel. The DCOUNT function requires that you choose a numeric field in the database to count. Print the range O1:R7. Save the workbook using the file name Office 2000 Specialist Database Final.

FIGURE 5-69

In the Lab

3 Creating and Manipulating the Eta Chi Rho Social Club Database

Problem: You are a member of Eta Chi Rho, a social club for adult learners returning to school. The president has asked for a volunteer to create a database made up of the club's members (Figure 5-70). You decide it is a great opportunity to show your Excel skills. Besides including a member's GPA in the database, the president also would like a GPA letter grade assigned to each member.

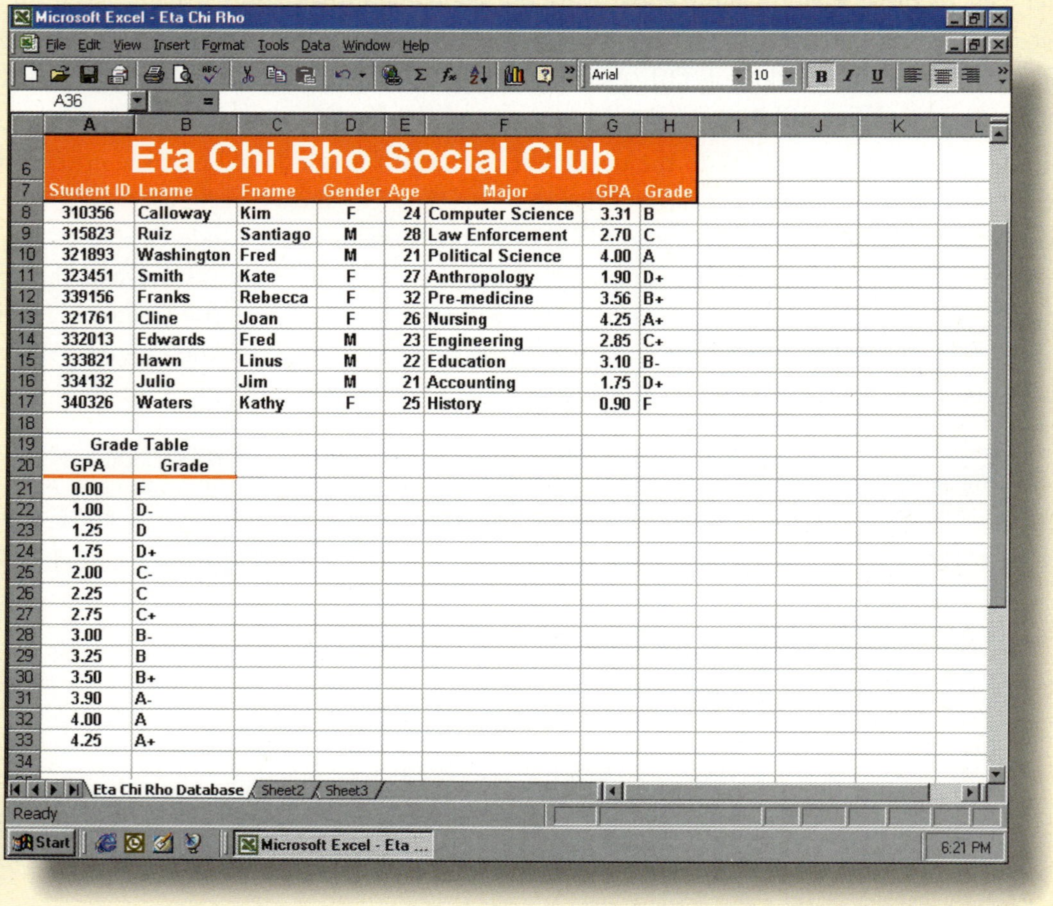

FIGURE 5-70

Instructions Part 1: Use the concepts and techniques developed in this project to create the database shown in the range A6:H17 in Figure 5-70.

1. Enter the database title in cell A6 and the column titles in row 7. Define the range A7:G8 as Database. Format the titles as shown in Figure 5-70.
2. Use the Form command on the Data menu to enter the data shown in the range A8:G17.

In the Lab

3. Enter the Grade table in the range A19:B33. In cell H8, enter the function =vlookup(G8, $A$21:$B$33, 2) to determine the letter grade that corresponds to the GPA in cell G8. Copy the function in cell H8 to the range H9:H17.
4. Redefine the name Database as the range A7:H17.
5. Enter your name, course number, laboratory assignment (Lab 5-3), date, and instructor name in the range F20:F24.
6. Save the workbook using the file name Eta Chi Rho. Print the worksheet. At the bottom of the printout, explain why the dollar signs ($) are necessary in the VLOOKUP function in step 3.

Instructions Part 2: Use a data form to change the following GPAs: 310356 = 2.80; 339156 = 3.4; 340326 = 1.35. Close the data form. The three member's grades should display as C+, B, and D, respectively. Print the worksheet. Close the workbook without saving changes.

Instructions Part 3: Open the workbook Eta Chi Rho. Use the Criteria button and the Find Next and Find Prev buttons in the data form to display records that meet the following criteria:

1. Gender = F; GPA > 3 (Three records pass the test.)
2. Age > 27 (Two records pass the test.)
3. Gender = M; Age < 25 (Four records pass the test.)

Print the worksheet and write down the Student IDs of the records that pass the tests. Close the workbook without saving the changes.

Instructions Part 4: Open the workbook Eta Chi Rho. Sort the database as follows. Print the database after each sort.

1. Sort the database in ascending sequence by last name.
2. Sort the database by Age within Gender. Use descending sequence for both fields.
3. Sort the database by letter grade within Gender. Use ascending sequence for both fields.
   Close the workbook without saving the changes.

Instructions Part 5: Open the workbook Eta Chi Rho. Use the concepts and techniques presented in this project to set up a Criteria area above the database, set up an Extract area below the Grade table, and complete the following extractions. For each extraction, it is important that you select a cell in the database before using the Advanced Filter command. Extract the records that meet the three criteria sets in Part 3 above. Print the worksheet for each criteria set. Extract the records that meet the following criteria: 25 < Age < 30. It is necessary that you add a second field called Age to the immediate right of the Criteria range and redefine the Criteria area to include the new field. Three records pass the final test. Save the workbook with the last criteria set using the file name Eta Chi Rho 2.

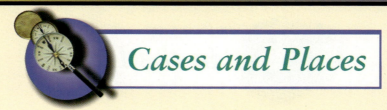

Cases and Places

The difficulty of these case studies varies:
▶ are the least difficult; ▶▶ are more difficult; and ▶▶▶ are the most difficult.

1 ▶ Academic classes, like individuals, may have distinct personalities and characteristics. A database can help reveal a class's idiosyncrasies. Create a Student database from the student data in Table 5-7. Begin the database title (Student Database) in row 7. Use the column headings as the field names in the database. Print the worksheet. Save the workbook. Print the worksheet after each of the following sorts: (1) sort the database in ascending sequence by last name; (2) sort by major within age within gender (all in descending sequence); and (3) sort the database by class in ascending sequence. With the database sorted by class, display subtotals for the number of credit hours. Print the worksheet. Use a data form to find all male students who have earned more than 75 credit hours towards graduation. Write the number who pass the test at the bottom of the Subtotals printout.

Table 5-7	Student Database						
LNAME	*FNAME*	*AGE*	*GENDER*	*STATE*	*CLASS*	*MAJOR*	*CREDIT HRS*
Berlin	Fredrick	21	M	IN	Senior	CIS	110
James	John	18	M	IL	Freshman	ENG	16
Manous	Nick	23	M	MI	Junior	CS	76
Franker	Holly	19	F	IN	Sophomore	CS	33
Steppes	Amos	20	M	IN	Junior	NS	59
Francisco	Julio	19	M	TN	Sophomore	MET	35
Deeks	George	24	M	KY	Senior	EET	112
Kurtz	Len	36	M	KY	Freshman	CS	18
Kelly	Joan	28	F	IL	Junior	EET	72
Winder	Heidi	23	F	MI	Senior	EET	115

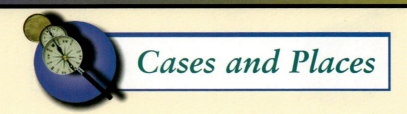

Cases and Places

2 ▸ You work for Abdul's Sports Incorporated. Abdul's Sports sells sporting equipment to high schools and colleges in the Midwest. You have been asked to create an inventory database from the data in Table 5-8. Use the column headings in the table as the field names in the database. Enter the database title Abdul's Sports Inventory Database in cell A8 and enter the database immediately below it. The Amount and Priority fields are computational fields. Amount equals Inventory times Price. The Priority field ranks the items 1 through 5 based on their inventory. The higher the number, the stronger the possibility that the company should put the item on sale or market it better. Create a Priority table in the range J1:K7 from the data shown Table 5-9. Use the VLOOKUP function to determine the rank. Print the worksheet. Save the workbook.

Table 5-8	Abdul's Sports Inventory Database						
ORDER NO	ORDER DATE	PART NO	DESCRIPTION	INVENTORY	PRICE	AMOUNT	PRIORITY
116712	11/2/2001	FD13	Soccer Ball	130	14.75		
128185	11/3/2001	DF13	Racquet	225	24.30		
128185	11/3/2001	SD45	Tennis Ball	375	0.50		
128186	11/4/2001	QW23	Football	22	32.45		
128187	11/4/2001	UT67	Trunks	78	6.50		
128187	11/4/2001	QG56	Hip Pads	25	50.45		
128187	11/4/2001	DE34	Shoulder Pads	115	75.25		
128188	11/4/2001	AD34	Helmet	645	90.50		
128189	11/5/2001	AG19	Jersey	250	15.23		
128189	11/5/2001	WR45	Wristband	195	2.25		
142191	11/5/2001	QH78	Go Cart	140	125.65		

Table 5-9	Priority Categories
INVENTORY	PRIORITY
0	1
50	2
100	3
200	4
300	5

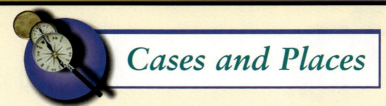

Cases and Places

3 ▶ Open the database created in Cases and Places Exercise 2. Print the database for each of the following: (1) sort the database in ascending sequence by inventory; (2) sort the database by amount (descending) within priority (ascending); and (3) sort the database in ascending sequence by order number. With the database sorted by order number, use the Subtotals command to determine amount subtotals for each order number. Print the worksheet with the subtotals. Use row level symbol 2 to display only subtotals. Print the worksheet.

4 ▶ Open the database created in Cases and Places Exercise 2. Use the concepts and techniques described in this project to filter (query) the database using the AutoFilter and Show All commands on the Filter submenu. Print the worksheet for each of the following independent queries: (1) priority equal to 1; (2) inventory greater than 175; (3) order number equals 128187 and part number equals DE34; and (4) price greater than 50 and amount greater than 15,000. The number of records that display are: (1) 2; (2) 5; (3) 1; and (4) 2.

5 ▶▶ Open the database created in Cases and Places Exercise 1. Use the concepts and techniques presented in this project to create a Criteria area and an Extract area. Use the Advanced AutoFilter command to extract records. Print the Extract area for each of the following: (1) males; (2) females; (3) males older than 21; (4) CS majors with less than 40 credit hours; (5) males less than 21 years old from the state of Indiana (6) female seniors; and (7) students between the ages of 19 and 21, inclusive. The number of records that display are: (1) 7; (2) 3; (3) 3; (4) 2; (5) 1; (6) 1; and (7) 4.

6 ▶▶ Open the database created in Cases and Places Exercise 1. Use the concepts and techniques presented in this project to determine the average age of males; the average age of females; the average number of credit hours accumulated by students from IN. Count the number of students that are seniors.

7 ▶▶▶ You work for the classified ads section of your local newspaper. Your editors have decided to introduce a new service in which readers can call the office and inquire if a particular car is being advertised. The editors have assigned this task to you. Begin by creating a database with fields for car manufacturer, model, year, price, mileage, and engine size. Then enter 20 ads in today's newspaper. If any information is missing, enter NA (not available). Test the project by performing queries to find records of cars from each of the past five years.

Microsoft Excel 2000

PROJECT

6

Creating Templates and Working with Multiple Worksheets and Workbooks

O B J E C T I V E S

You will have mastered the material in this project when you can:

- Create and use a template
- Use the ROUND function
- Utilize custom format codes
- Define, apply, and remove a style
- Copy data among worksheets in a workbook
- Drill an entry through worksheets
- Add a worksheet to a workbook
- Create formulas that use 3-D references to cells in different sheets in a workbook
- Summarize data using consolidation
- Draw a 3-D Cone chart
- Use WordArt to create a title
- Create and modify lines and objects
- Add comments to cells
- Add a header or footer to a workbook
- Change the page margins
- Set print titles and options
- Insert a page break
- Use the Find and Replace commands
- Consolidate data by linking workbooks

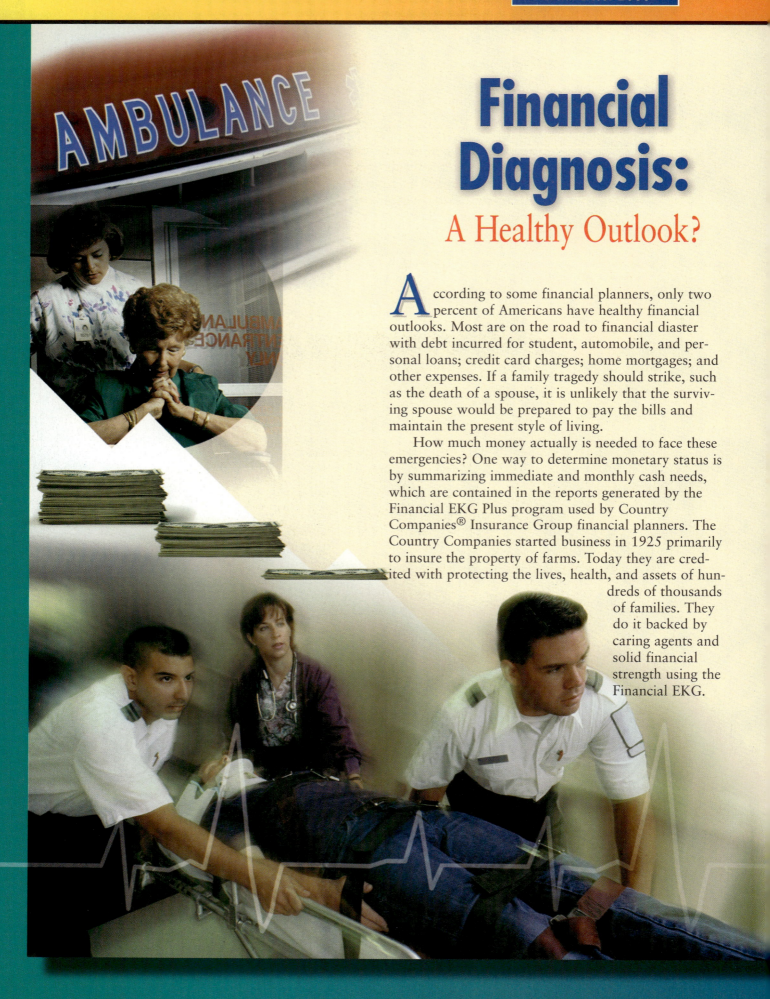

Financial Diagnosis:

A Healthy Outlook?

According to some financial planners, only two percent of Americans have healthy financial outlooks. Most are on the road to financial diaster with debt incurred for student, automobile, and personal loans; credit card charges; home mortgages; and other expenses. If a family tragedy should strike, such as the death of a spouse, it is unlikely that the surviving spouse would be prepared to pay the bills and maintain the present style of living.

How much money actually is needed to face these emergencies? One way to determine monetary status is by summarizing immediate and monthly cash needs, which are contained in the reports generated by the Financial EKG Plus program used by Country Companies® Insurance Group financial planners. The Country Companies started business in 1925 primarily to insure the property of farms. Today they are credited with protecting the lives, health, and assets of hundreds of thousands of families. They do it backed by caring agents and solid financial strength using the Financial EKG.

This worksheet analysis gives a detailed review of the current financial situation, projects the amount needed to meet the family's needs, and then uses these figures in other worksheets to determine how much should be invested each month in various life insurance options to secure the added financial protection.

As in the multiple worksheets in the Home Entertainment Systems profit potential workbook you will create in this Excel project, the Financial EKG uses headers and footers to standardize the worksheet design. On each page, the forms use the company name, Country Companies Financial EKG Plus, and the current date as the header and the text, This proposal was prepared by:, and the insurance agent's name as the footer.

The agent uses the first worksheet to determine the family's immediate cash needs, which is the difference between total cash needed and total cash available. To compute cash needed, the agent enters data for the following fields in the worksheet form: last expenses (medical bills, burial expenses), debt liquidation (loans, credit cards), contingency fund (home-care, child-care), mortgage/rent payment fund (10 years' rent or the mortgage balance), and the educational/vocational fund (four-year undergraduate education). The total cash available is the sum of Social Security death benefits, total liquid assets, and existing life insurance. Normally a cash shortage exists.

The agent then enters data used to compute the surviving spouse's income needs through retirement. He or she estimates how much cash the surviving spouse and child need to maintain their current style of living, the spouse's earnings, and Social Security benefits. The worksheet uses an average four-percent rate of growth on money and computes the total amount of cash the family will need while the child is a minor, during the blackout period between the time the child is 16 and the spouse retires, and during retirement.

When this income need is added to the cash shortage, the total represents the amount that should be invested to cover this family's financial future in time of tragedy.

The Financial EKG then uses another worksheet that references the cell containing this total cash needed. Three life insurance options are reported: term with increasing premiums, whole life with increasing premiums, and whole life with fixed premiums. For each option, the worksheet computes total premiums paid, cash value and dividends, insurance policy value, and monthly income at age 65. For a better understanding of insurance terminology, the Country Companies Web site offers an insurance terms glossary (www.countrycos.com).

These reports help a family prepare for an unexpected loss of income. Thus, by using Financial EKG today, they can be on the road to a healthy financial outlook.

Microsoft **Excel 2000**

Microsoft Excel 2000

Creating Templates and Working with Multiple Worksheets and Workbooks

P R O J E C T
6

C A S E   P E R S P E C T I V E

A creative marketing campaign and unique sales model have helped a recent start-up company, Home Entertainment Systems (HES), grow to become one of the premier small companies in the United States. The company, which sells a variety of home entertainment systems over the World Wide Web, maintains its inventory at its three former stores in Pittsburgh, Indianapolis, and Phoenix. The company's sales model is unique in that customers sign up on the Web to purchase a home entertainment system over a two-week period. The price continues to decrease as more customers buy the system. At the end of two-weeks, a final price is determined.

Even more exciting is that a major competitor recently sent HES's president, Santiago Biagi, a letter of intent to purchase the company. As part of due diligence, the competitor has requested that Santigo supply a report that shows the total gross profit potential based on the month-end inventory.

Santiago has asked you to consolidate the inventory data from the three stores onto one worksheet and to create a chart that compares the gross profit potentials of the systems (Figure 6-1).

Introduction

Many business-type applications, such as the one described in the Case Perspective, require data from several worksheets in a workbook to be summarized on one worksheet. Suppose, for example, your firm maintains data for three different units within the company on three separate worksheets in a workbook. You can click the tabs at the bottom of the Excel window to move from worksheet to worksheet. You can enter formulas on one worksheet that reference cells found on the other worksheets, which allows you to summarize worksheet data. The process of summarizing data found on multiple worksheets on one worksheet is called **consolidation**.

Another important concept is the use of a template. A **template** is a special workbook or worksheet you can create and then use as a pattern to create new, similar workbooks or worksheets. A template usually consists of a general format (worksheet title, column and row titles, and numeric format) and formulas that are common to all the worksheets. For example, in the Home Entertainment Systems workbook, the worksheets for each of the three store locations and the company worksheet are identical (Figure 6-1), except for the data. One way to create the workbook is to first create a template, save it, and then copy it as many times as necessary to a workbook.

Several other techniques are introduced in this project, including rounding, custom format codes, creating a format style, adding comments to a cell, headers and footers, using WordArt to create a title, using the Find and Replace commands, various print options, and linking workbooks.

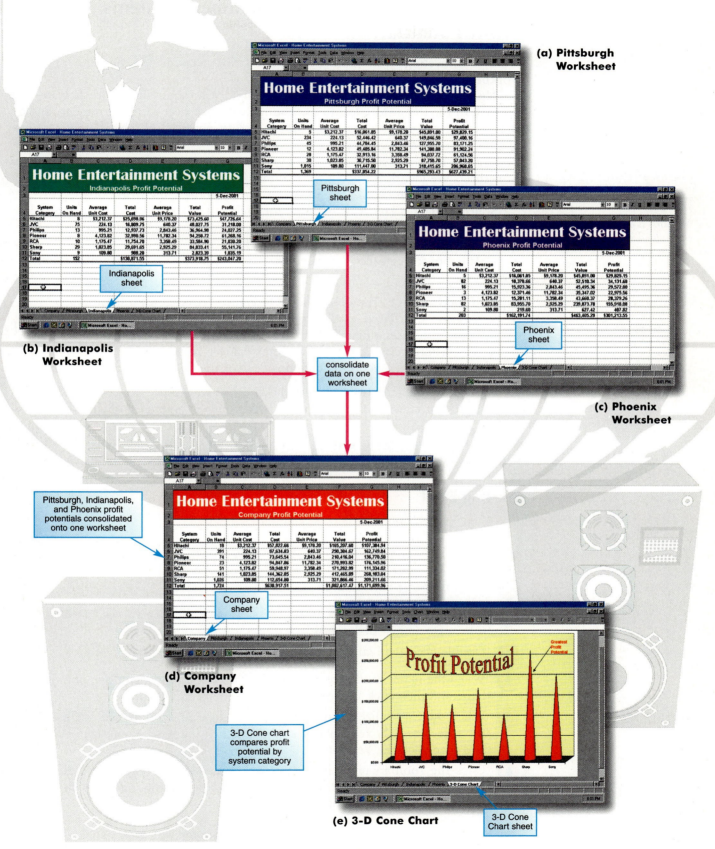

(a) Pittsburgh Worksheet

Pittsburgh sheet

(b) Indianapolis Worksheet

Indianapolis sheet

consolidate data on one worksheet

(c) Phoenix Worksheet

Phoenix sheet

Pittsburgh, Indianapolis, and Phoenix profit potentials consolidated onto one worksheet

Company sheet

(d) Company Worksheet

3-D Cone chart compares profit potential by system category

(e) 3-D Cone Chart

3-D Cone Chart sheet

FIGURE 6-1

Project Six — Home Entertainment Systems Profit Potential

From your meetings with Santiago Biagi, you have accumulated the following workbook specifications:

Needs: The workbook Santiago has in mind will require five worksheets — one for each of the three store locations, a summary worksheet for the company, and a chart on a separate sheet that compares the profit potential of the different systems (Figure 6-1 on the previous page).

Because the three stores have the same seven categories of systems, the inventory worksheets are identical, except for the units on hand. You thus can create a template (Figure 6-2) and then copy it to worksheets in the same workbook.

Source of Data: The units on hand for each system category will be collected from the business managers of the respective stores. The average unit cost of each system category is available from the main office.

Calculations: The following calculations are required for the template (Figure 6-2):

1. Total Cost in column D = Units On Hand * Average Unit Cost
2. Average Unit Price in column E = Average Unit Cost / (1 − .65)
3. Total Value in column F = Units On Hand * Average Unit Price
4. Profit Potential in column G = Total Value − Total Cost
5. Use the SUM function in columns B, D, F, and G to total each column.

After using the template to create the multiple-worksheet workbook, use the SUM function to determine the units on hand totals in column B of the Company sheet (Figure 6-1d).

Graph Requirements: Include a 3-D Cone chart on a separate chart sheet that compares the profit potential for each system category on the Company sheet.

More About 2000

Templates

Templates are most helpful when you need to create several similar or identical workbooks. They help reduce work and ensure consistency. Templates can contain: (1) text and graphics, such as a company name and logo; (2) formats and page layouts, such as styles and custom headers and footers; and (3) formulas or macros.

Starting Excel

To start Excel, follow the steps summarized below.

TO START EXCEL

1 Click the Start button on the taskbar.

2 Click New Office Document. If necessary, click the General tab in the New Office Document dialog box.

3 Double-click the Blank Workbook icon.

4 When the blank worksheet displays, click View on the menu bar, point to Toolbars, and then click Customize on the Toolbars submenu.

5 When the Customize dialog box displays, click the Options tab, make sure the top three check boxes have check marks, click the Reset my usage data button, and then click the Yes button.

6 Click the Toolbars tab. Click Standard, click the Reset button, and then click the OK button. Click Formatting, click the Reset button, and then click the OK button. Click the Close button.

The Standard and Formatting toolbars display as shown in Figure 6-2.

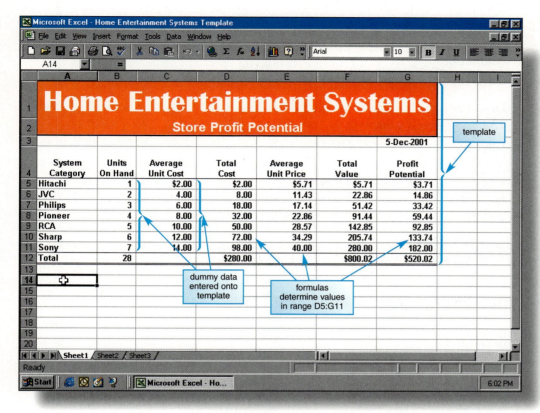

FIGURE 6-2

Creating the Template

Learning how to use templates is important, especially if you plan to use a similar worksheet design or layout for several worksheets or workbooks. In Project 6, for instance, the four worksheets in the inventory workbook (Figure 6-1) are nearly identical. Thus, the first step in building the Home Entertainment Systems workbook is to create and save a template that contains the labels, formulas, and formats used on each of the sheets. Once the template is saved on disk, you can use it every time you begin developing a similar workbook. Because templates help speed and simplify their work, many Excel users create a template for each application on which they work. Templates can be simple — possibly using a special font or worksheet title — or more complex — perhaps utilizing specific formulas and format styles, such as the template for Project 6.

To create a template, you follow the same basic steps used to create a workbook. The only difference between developing a workbook and a template is the way you save the file.

Bolding the Font and Changing the Column Widths of the Template

The first step in this project is to change the font style of the entire template to bold and adjust the column widths as follows: columns A, and C through G = 13.00; and column B = 8.14. Perform the steps on the next page to apply this formatting.

Built-In Templates

A set of templates is available with Excel that provides solutions to common business problems. To view the templates, click New on the File menu, and then click the Spreadsheet Solutions tab. Many more templates that solve a wide range of problems are available at the Microsoft Office Update Site. To download templates, visit the Excel 2000 More About Web page (www.scsite.com/ex2000/more.htm) and click More Excel Add-Ins and Templates.

TO BOLD THE FONT AND CHANGE THE COLUMN WIDTHS IN THE TEMPLATE

1 Click the Select All button immediately above row heading 1 and to the left of column heading A.

2 Click the Bold button on the Formatting toolbar. Click column heading A.

3 Drag the right boundary of column heading A right until the ScreenTip, Width: 13.00 (97 pixels), displays.

4 Click column heading B. Drag the right boundary of column heading B to the left until the ScreenTip, Width: 8.14 (62 pixels), displays.

5 Click column heading C. Drag through to column heading G. Drag the right boundary of column heading G right until the ScreenTip, Width: 13.00 (97 pixels), displays. Click cell A14 to deselect columns C through G.

Excel assigns the Bold font style to all cells in the worksheet. Columns A and C through G have a width of 13.00. Column B has a width of 8.14.

Entering the Template Title and Row Titles

The following steps enter the worksheet titles in cells A1 and A2 and the row titles in column A.

TO ENTER THE TEMPLATE TITLE AND ROW TITLES

1 Click cell A1. Type Home Entertainment Systems and then press the DOWN ARROW key. Type Store Profit Potential and then press the DOWN ARROW key twice to make cell A4 active.

2 Type System and then press ALT+ENTER. Type Category and then press the DOWN ARROW key.

3 With cell A5 active, enter the remaining row titles in column A as shown in Figure 6-3.

The template title and row titles display in column A as shown in Figure 6-3. Because the entry in cell A4 requires two lines, Excel automatically increases the height of row 4.

Entering Column Titles and the System Date

The next step is to enter the column titles in row 4 and the system date in cell G3.

TO ENTER COLUMN TITLES AND THE SYSTEM DATE IN THE TEMPLATE

1 Click cell B4. Type Units and then press ALT+ENTER. Type On Hand and then press the RIGHT ARROW key.

2 Type Average and then press ALT+ENTER. Type Unit Cost and then press the RIGHT ARROW key.

3 With cell D4 active, enter the remaining column titles in row 4 as shown in Figure 6-3.

4 Click cell G3. Type =now() and then press the ENTER key. Select cell A14 to deselect cell G3.

The column titles and system date display as shown in Figure 6-3.

Dummy Numbers

As you develop more sophisticated workbooks, it will become increasingly important that you create good test data to ensure your workbooks are error free. The more you test a workbook, the more confident you will be in the results generated. Select test data that tests the limits of the formulas.

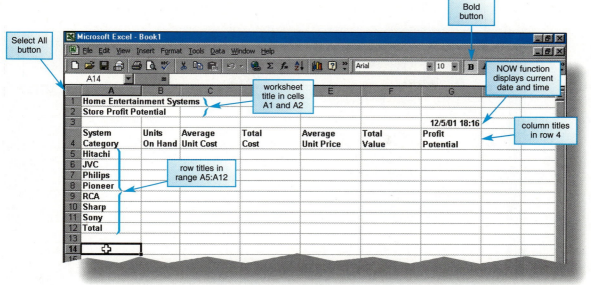

FIGURE 6-3

Entering Dummy Data in the Template

When you create a template, you should use **dummy data** in place of actual data to verify the formulas in the template. Selecting simple numbers such as 1, 2, and 3 allows you to check quickly to see if the formulas are generating the proper results. While creating the Home Entertainment Systems Template in Project 6, dummy data is used for the Units On Hand in the range B5:B11 and the Average Unit Costs in the range C5:C11.

The dummy data is entered by using the fill handle to create a series of numbers in columns B and C. The series in column B begins with 1 and increments by 1; the series in column C begins with 2 and increments by 2. Recall, to create a series you enter the first two numbers so Excel can determine the increment amount. If the cell to the right of the start value is empty and you want to increment by 1, however, you can create a series by entering only one number. Perform the following to create the two series of numbers.

More About

Accuracy

The result of an arithmetic operation, such as multiplication or division, is accurate to the factor or number with the least number of decimal places.

 To Enter Dummy Data in the Template Using the Fill Handle

1 Type 1 in cell B5 and then press the ENTER key. Select the range B5:C5. Drag the fill handle through cells B11 and C11.

Excel surrounds the range B5:C11 with a gray border (Figure 6-4). A ScreenTip displays showing the final value in the series that will be assigned to cell B11.

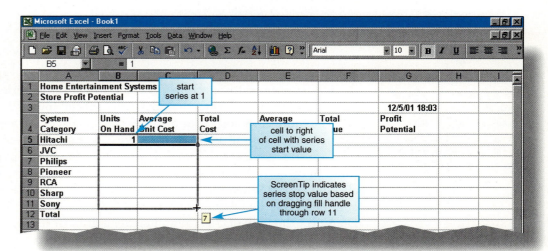

FIGURE 6-4

Microsoft Excel 2000

2 **Release the mouse button.**

Excel creates the series 1 through 7 in increments of 1 in the range B5:B11 (Figure 6-5).

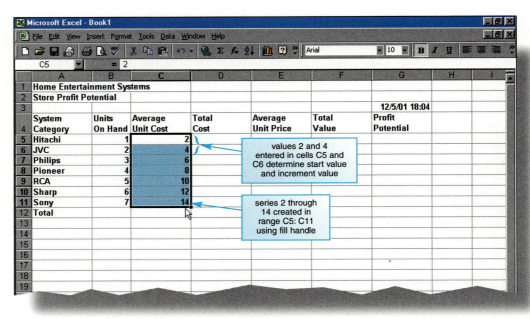

FIGURE 6-5

3 **Click cell C5. Type 2 and then press the DOWN ARROW key. Type 4 and then press the ENTER key. Select the range C5:C6. Drag the fill handle through cell C11 and then release the mouse button.**

Excel creates the series 2 through 14 in increments of 2 in the range C5:C11 (Figure 6-6).

FIGURE 6-6

Other Ways

1. Enter first number, while holding down CTRL key drag through range
2. Enter start value, select range, on Edit menu point to Fill, click Series, enter parameters, click OK button

It is important to remember, if you create a linear series by selecting the cell to the right of the start value, then that selected cell must be empty.

The more common types of series used in Excel are a **date/time series** (Jan, Feb, Mar, etc.), an **AutoFill series** (1, 1, 1, etc.), and a **linear series** (1, 2, 3, etc.). A fourth type of series is a growth series. A **growth series** multiplies values by a constant factor. You can create a growth series by pointing to Fill on the Edit menu and then clicking Series. When the Series dialog box displays, click the Growth option button and then click the OK button. For example, if you enter 2 in cell D5 and 4 in cell D6, select the range D5:D15, and create a growth series, Excel will create the series 2, 4, 8, 16, 32, 64, 128, 256, 512, 1024, 2048 in the range D5:D15.

The ROUND Function and Entering the Formulas in the Template

The next step is to enter the four formulas for the first system category (Hitachi) in the range D5:G5. When you multiply or divide decimal numbers that result in an answer with more decimal places than the format allows, you run the risk of the column totals being a penny or so off. For example, in this project, the Currency and Comma style formats display two decimal places. And yet the formulas result in several additional decimal places that Excel maintains for computation purposes. For this reason, it is recommended that you use the **ROUND function** on formulas that potentially can result in more decimal places than the format displays. The general form of the ROUND function is

=ROUND (number, number of digits)

where the number argument can be a number, a cell reference that contains a number, or a formula that results in a number; and the number of digits argument, which can be any positive or negative number, determines how many places will be rounded. The following is true about the ROUND function:

1. If the number of digits argument is greater than 0 (zero), then the number is rounded to the specified number of digits.
2. If the number of digits argument is equal to 0 (zero), then the number is rounded to the nearest integer.
3. If the number of digits argument is less than 0 (zero), then the number is rounded to the left of the decimal point.

The four formulas to enter are shown in Table 6-1. To illustrate the ROUND function, it is applied to the formula assigned to cell E5.

Table 6-1 Formulas Used to Determine Profit Potential			
CELL	DESCRIPTION	FORMULA	ENTRY
D5	Total Cost	Units On Hand x Average Unit Cost	=B5 * C5
E5	Average Unit Price	ROUND(Average Unit Cost / (1−.65), 2)	=ROUND(C5 / (1−.65), 2)
F5	Total Value	Units on Hand x Average Unit Price	=B5 * E5
G5	Profit Potential	Total Value − Total Cost	=F5 − D5

The most difficult formula to understand in Table 6-1 is the one that determines the average unit price, which also is called the average selling price. To make a net profit, companies must sell their merchandise for more than the unit cost of the merchandise plus the company's operating expenses (taxes, warehouse rent, upkeep, and so forth). To determine what selling price to set for an item, companies often first establish a desired margin.

Most companies look for a margin of 60% to 75%. Home Entertainment Systems, for example, tries to make a margin of 65% on its products. The formula for the average unit price in Table 6-1 helps the company determine the price at which to sell an item so that it ends up with a 65% margin. For example, if an item costs Home Entertainment Systems $1.00, the company must sell it for $2.86 [$1.00 / (1−.65)] to make a 65% margin. Of this $2.86, $1.00 goes to pay the cost of the item; the other $1.86 is the gross profit potential (65% x $2.86 = $1.86).

The steps on the next page use Point mode to enter the four formulas in Table 6-1 in the range D5:G5. After the formulas are entered for the Hitachi system category in row 5, the formulas will be copied for the remaining six system categories.

The Magical Fill Handle

Using the fill handle, you can create different types of series. To select the type of series to create, right-drag the fill handle. When you release the right mouse button, a shortcut menu displays from which you can select the type of series to create.

Fractions

The forward slash (/) has multiple uses. For example, dates often are entered using the slash. In formulas, the slash represents division. What about fractions? To enter a fraction, such as ½, type .5 or 0 1/2 (i.e., type zero, followed by a space, followed by the number 1, followed by a slash, followed by the number 2). If you type 1/2, Excel will store the value in the cell as the date January 2.

Steps To Enter the Formulas Using Point Mode and Determine Totals in the Template

1 **Click cell D5. Type = to start the formula. Click cell B5. Type * (asterisk) and then click cell C5. Click the Enter box in the formula bar.**

The formula =B5*C5 displays in the formula bar and the value 2 (1 x 2) displays as the total cost in cell D5 (Figure 6-7).

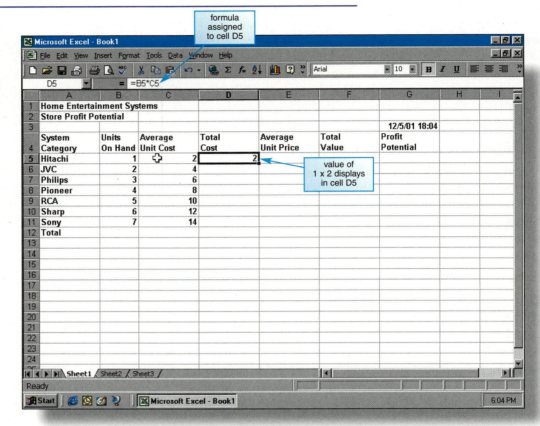

FIGURE 6-7

2 **Click cell E5. Type =round(c5/ (1–.65), 2) and then click the Enter box in the formula bar.**

The value 5.71 (5.7142857 rounded to two decimal places) displays as the average unit price in cell E5 and the formula =ROUND(C5/(1–0.65), 2) displays in the formula bar (Figure 6-8).

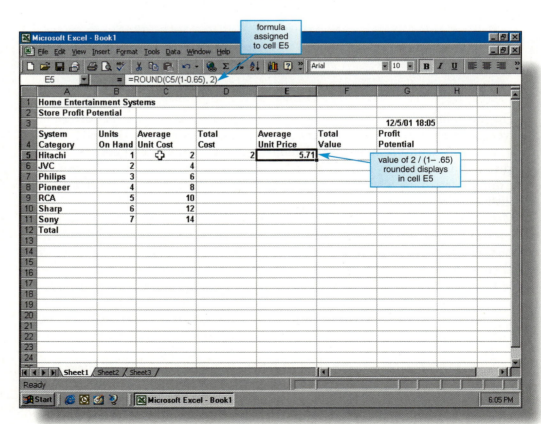

FIGURE 6-8

3 **Click cell F5. Type = to start the formula. Click cell B5. Type * (asterisk) and then click cell E5. Click the Enter box in the formula bar.**

The value 5.71 (1 x 5.71) displays as the total value in cell F5 and the formula =B5*E5 displays in the formula bar (Figure 6-9).

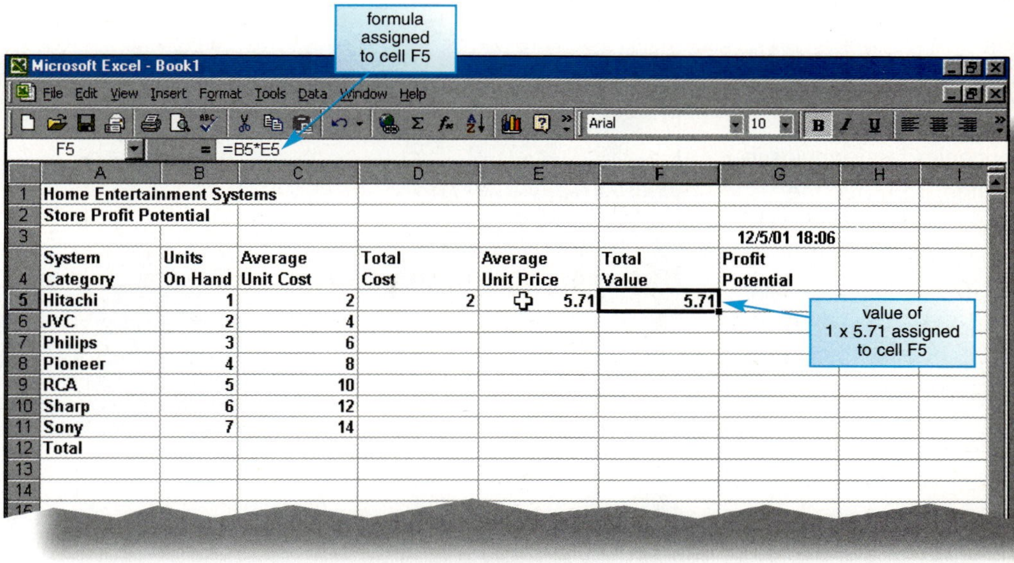

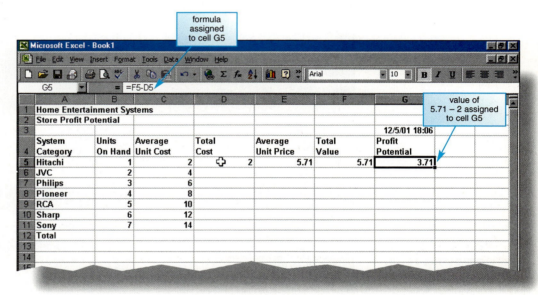

FIGURE 6-9

4 **Click cell G5. Type = to start the formula. Click cell F5. Type – (minus sign) and then click cell D5. Click the Enter box in the formula bar.**

The value 3.71 (5.71 – 2) displays as the profit potential in cell G5 and the formula =F5 – 5 displays in the formula bar (Figure 6-10).

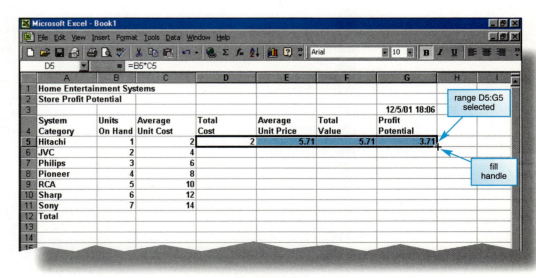

FIGURE 6-10

5 **Select the range D5:G5 and then point to the fill handle.**

The range D5:G5 is selected and the mouse pointer changes to a cross hair when positioned on the fill handle (Figure 6-11).

FIGURE 6-11

6 **Drag down through the range D6:G11.**

Excel copies the formulas in the range D5:G5 to the range D6:G11. Excel automatically adjusts the cell references so each formula references the data in the row to which it is copied (Figure 6-12).

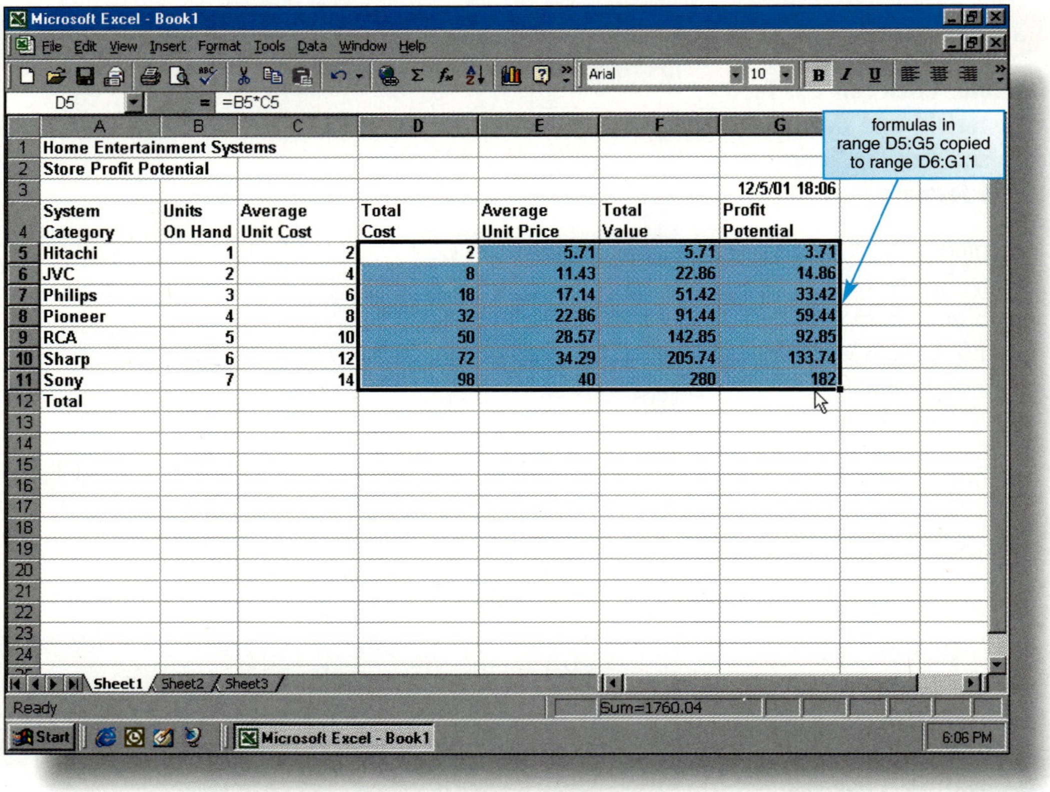

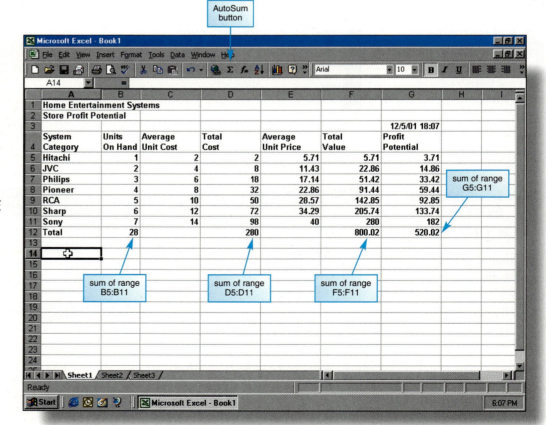

FIGURE 6-12

7 **Click cell B12. Click the AutoSum button on the Standard toolbar twice. Click cell D12. Click the AutoSum button twice. Select the range F12:G12. Click the AutoSum button. Select cell A14 to deselect the range F12:G12.**

The totals for columns B, D, F, and G display in row 12 (Figure 6-13).

FIGURE 6-13

The values Excel generates from the formulas are based on the dummy data entered in columns B and C. After you save and format the template, you will use it to create the Home Entertainment Systems workbook. You then will enter the actual data for the different system categories.

Saving the Template

Saving a template is just like saving a workbook, except that you select Template in the Save as type box in the Save As dialog box. The following steps save the template on drive A using the file name Home Entertainment Systems Template.

 To Save a Template

1 Click the Save button on the Standard toolbar. When the Save As dialog box displays, type Home Entertainment Systems Template in the File name text box. Click the Save as type box arrow and then click Template in the list. Click the Save in box arrow and then click 3½ Floppy (A:). Point to the Save button in the Save As dialog box.

The Save As dialog box displays (Figure 6-14).

2 Click the Save button in the Save As dialog box.

Excel saves the template Home Entertainment Systems on the floppy disk in drive A. The file name Home Entertainment Systems Template displays on the title bar as shown in Figure 6-15 on the next page.

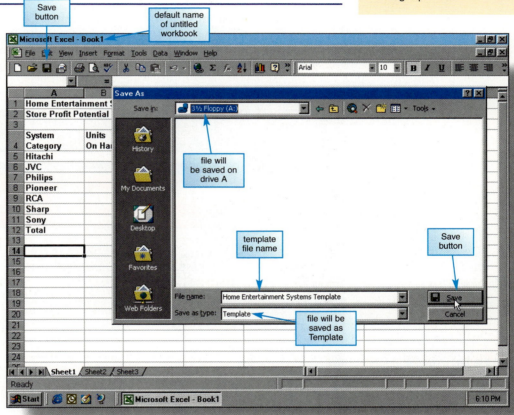

FIGURE 6-14

More About 2000

File Extensions

If the MS-DOS extension .xlt shows in your title bar following the file name, it means that the option not to show the MS-DOS extension is not selected on the View sheet in the Options dialog box in Explorer. You display the Options dialog box in Explorer by clicking View on the menu bar, and then clicking Options.

Other Ways

1. On File menu click Save As, type file name, select Template in Save as type box, select drive or folder, click OK button

2. Press CTRL+S, type file name, select Template in Save as type box, select drive or folder, click OK button

Formatting the Template

The next step is to format the template so it displays as shown in Figure 6-15. As you format the template, keep in mind that each of the sheets for which the template is used contains the same formats. The following list summarizes the steps required to format the template.

1. Change the font of the template title in cells A1 and A2. Center cells A1 and A2 across columns A through G. Change the background color, change the font color, and add a heavy outline border to the range A1:A2.
2. Format the column titles and add borders.
3. Assign the Currency style format with a floating dollar sign to the non-adjacent ranges C5:G5 and D12:G12.
4. Assign a Custom style format to the range C6:G11.
5. Assign a Comma style format to the range B5:B12.
6. Assign borders to rows 4 and 12.
7. Create a format style and assign it to the date in cell G3.

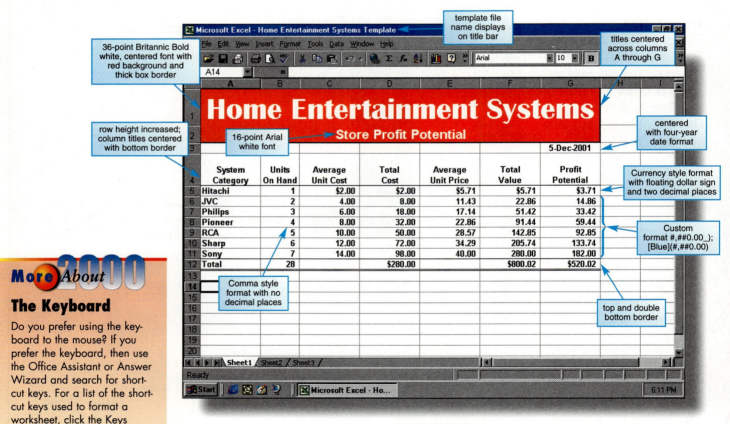

FIGURE 6-15

Formatting the Template Title

The steps used to format the template title include changing cell A1 to 36-point Britannic Bold font (or a similar font); changing cell A2 to 16-point Arial font; centering both titles across columns A through G; changing the title background color to red and the title font to white; and drawing a thick box border around the title area. Perform the following steps to format the template title.

TO FORMAT THE TEMPLATE TITLE

1 Double-click the move handle on the Formatting toolbar.

2 Click cell A1. Click the Font box arrow on the Formatting toolbar and then click Britannic Bold (or a similar font) in the list. Click the Font Size box arrow on the Formatting toolbar and then click 36 in the list. Select the range A1:G1. Click the Merge and Center button on the Formatting toolbar.

3 Click cell A2. Click the Font Size box arrow on the Formatting toolbar and then click 16 in the list. Select the range A2:G2. Click the Merge and Center button on the Formatting toolbar.

4 Select the range A1:A2. Click the Fill Color button arrow on the Formatting toolbar and then click Red (column 1, row 3) on the Fill Color palette.

5 Click the Font Color button arrow on the Formatting toolbar and then click White (column 8, row 5) on the Font Color palette.

6 Click the Borders button arrow on the Formatting toolbar and then click Thick Box Border (column 4, row 3) on the Borders palette.

Merged Cells

When cells are merged, you can activate only the leftmost cell. For example, in Figure 6-16, if you use the Name box or Go To command to activate any of the merged cells A1 through G1, Excel will activate cell A1.

The template title area displays as shown in Figure 6-16.

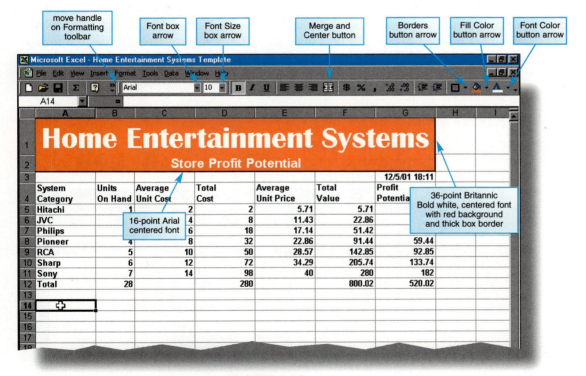

FIGURE 6-16

When you increase the font size, Excel automatically increases the heights of rows 1 and 2 so the tallest letter will display properly in the cells.

Formatting the Column Titles and Total Line

Next, center and underline the column titles and draw a top and double bottom border on the totals in row 12. Perform the steps on the next page to apply this formatting.

TO FORMAT THE COLUMN TITLES AND TOTAL LINE

1 Select the range A4:G4. Click the Center button on the Formatting toolbar. Click the Borders button arrow on the Formatting toolbar and then click Bottom Border (column 2, row 1) on the Borders palette.

2 Point to the boundary below row 4. Drag down until the ScreenTip, Height: 39.00 (52 pixels), displays.

3 Select the range A12:G12. Click the Borders button arrow on the Formatting toolbar and then click Top and Double Bottom Border (column 4, row 2) on the Borders palette.

The column titles in row 4 and the totals in row 12 display as shown in Figure 6-17.

More About

Special Formatting

Excel has formats for ZIP codes, telephone numbers, and Social Security numbers. Click Special in the Category list box in the Format Cells dialog box. The formats will display in the Type list box. These formats automatically will add dashes in the appropriate positions. All you have to do is enter the digits.

Applying Number Formats Using the Format Dialog Box

As shown in Figure 6-15 on page E 6.16, the template for this project follows the standard accounting format for a table of numbers; that is, it displays floating dollar signs in the first row of numbers (row 5) and the totals row (row 12). Recall that while a fixed dollar sign always displays in the same position in a cell (regardless of the number of significant digits), a floating dollar sign always displays immediately to the left of the first significant digit. To assign a fixed dollar sign to rows 5 and 12, you simply select the range and click the Currency button on the Formatting toolbar. Assigning a floating dollar sign, by contrast, requires you to select the desired format in the Format Cells dialog box.

The following steps use the Format Cells dialog box to assign a Currency style with a floating dollar sign and two decimal places to the range C5:G5 and D12:G12.

Steps To Assign a Currency Style Using the Format Dialog Box

1 Select the range C5:G5. While holding down the CTRL key, select the nonadjacent range D12:G12. Right-click one of the selected ranges.

The shortcut menu displays (Figure 6-17).

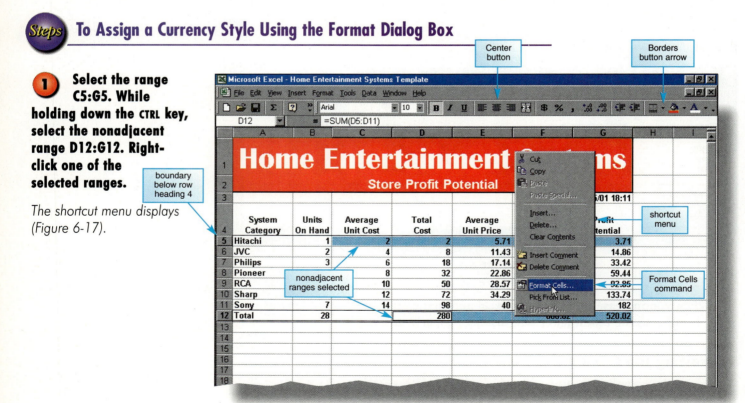

FIGURE 6-17

2 **Click Format Cells on the shortcut menu. When the Format Cells dialog box displays, click the Number tab. Click Currency in the Category list box. Click the fourth item ($1,234.10) in the Negative numbers list box and then point to the OK button.**

The Format Cells dialog box displays as shown in Figure 6-18. The selected format will apply a Currency style with a floating dollar sign and two decimal places to the selected ranges.

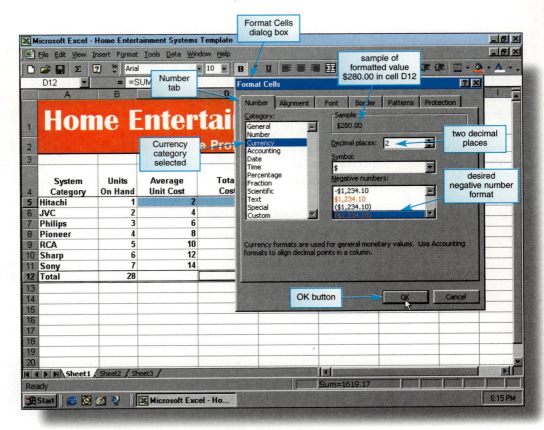

FIGURE 6-18

3 **Click the OK button. Select cell A14 to deselect the nonadjacent ranges.**

Excel assigns the Currency style with a floating dollar sign and two decimal places to the selected ranges (Figure 6-19).

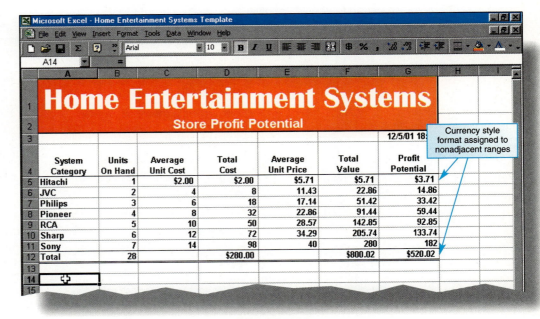

FIGURE 6-19

Other Ways

1. On Format menu click Cells, click Number tab, select format, click OK button

2. Press CTRL+1, click Number tab, select format, click OK button

Creating Customized Formats

Each format symbol within the format code has special meaning. Table 6-2 summarizes the frequently used format symbols and their meanings. For additional information on creating format codes, use the Office Assistant or Answer Wizard and search for, create a custom number format.

Creating a Customized Format Code

Every format style listed in the Category list box in the Number sheet of the Format Cells dialog box shown in Figure 6-18 on the previous page has a format code assigned to it. A **format code** is a series of format symbols (Table 6-2) that define how a format displays. To view the entire list of format codes that come with Excel, select Custom in the Category list box. Before you begin to create your own format codes or modify a customized format code, you should understand their makeup. As shown below, a format code can have up to four sections: positive numbers, negative numbers, zeros, and text. Each section is divided by a semicolon.

$*#,##0.00 ; [Blue]#,##0.00; 0.00; "The answer is "@

for positive numbers   for negative numbers   for zero numbers   for text

A format code need not have all four sections. For most applications, a format code will have only a positive section and possibly a negative section.

Table 6-2	Format Symbols in Format Codes	
FORMAT SYMBOL	**EXAMPLE OF SYMBOL**	**DESCRIPTION**
# (number sign)	###.##	Serves as a digit placeholder. If more digits are to the right of the decimal point than are number signs, Excel rounds the number. Extra digits to the left of the decimal point are displayed.
0 (zero)	0.00	Functions like a number sign (#), except that if the number is less than 1, Excel displays a zero in the ones place.
. (period)	#0.00	Ensures a decimal point will display in the number. The placement of symbols determines how many digits display to the left and right of the decimal point.
% (percent)	0.00%	Displays numbers as percentages of 100. Excel multiplies the value of the cell by 100 and displays a percent sign after the number.
, (comma)	#,##0.00	Displays comma as a thousands separator.
( )	#0.00;(#0.00)	Displays parentheses around negative numbers.
$ or + or −	$#,##0.00;($#,##0.00)	Displays a floating sign ($, +, or −).
* (asterisk)	$*##0.00	Displays a fixed sign ($, +, or −) to the left in the cell followed by spaces until the first significant digit.
[color]	#.##;[Red]#.##	Displays the characters in the cell in the designated color. In the example, positive numbers display in the default color and negative numbers display in red.
" " (quotation marks)	$0.00 "Surplus";-$0.00 "Shortage"	Displays text along with numbers entered in a cell.
_ (underscore)	#,##0.00_)	Skips the width of the character that follows the underline.

The next step is to assign a customized Comma style to the range C6:G11. To assign a customized Comma style, you select the Custom category in the Format Cells dialog box, select a format code close to the desired one, and then modify or customize it. Perform the following steps to assign a customized format code to the range C6:G11. The last step uses buttons on the Formatting toolbar to assign a Comma style with no decimal places to column B.

More *About*

Format Codes

Excel has the same format code capabilities as any programming language, such as COBOL.

 To Create a Custom Format Code

1 Select the range C6:G11 and then right-click it. Click Format Cells on the shortcut menu. When the Format Cells dialog box displays, click Custom in the Category list box. Scroll down and click #,##0.00_);[Red](#,## 0.00) in the Type list box. In the Type text box, change the word Red to Blue. Point to the OK button.

The Format Cells dialog box displays as shown in Figure 6-20. The Custom format has been modified to display negative numbers in blue. Excel displays a sample of the first number in the selected range in the Sample area.

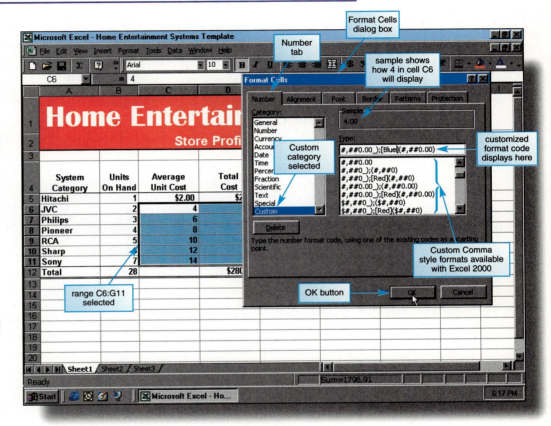

FIGURE 6-20

2 Click the OK button. Select the range B5:B12. Click the Comma Style button on the Formatting toolbar. Click the Decrease Decimal button on the Formatting toolbar twice. Select cell A14.

The numbers in the template display as shown in Figure 6-21. When numbers with more than three whole number digits are entered in the range B5:B12, the Comma style format will show in the range.

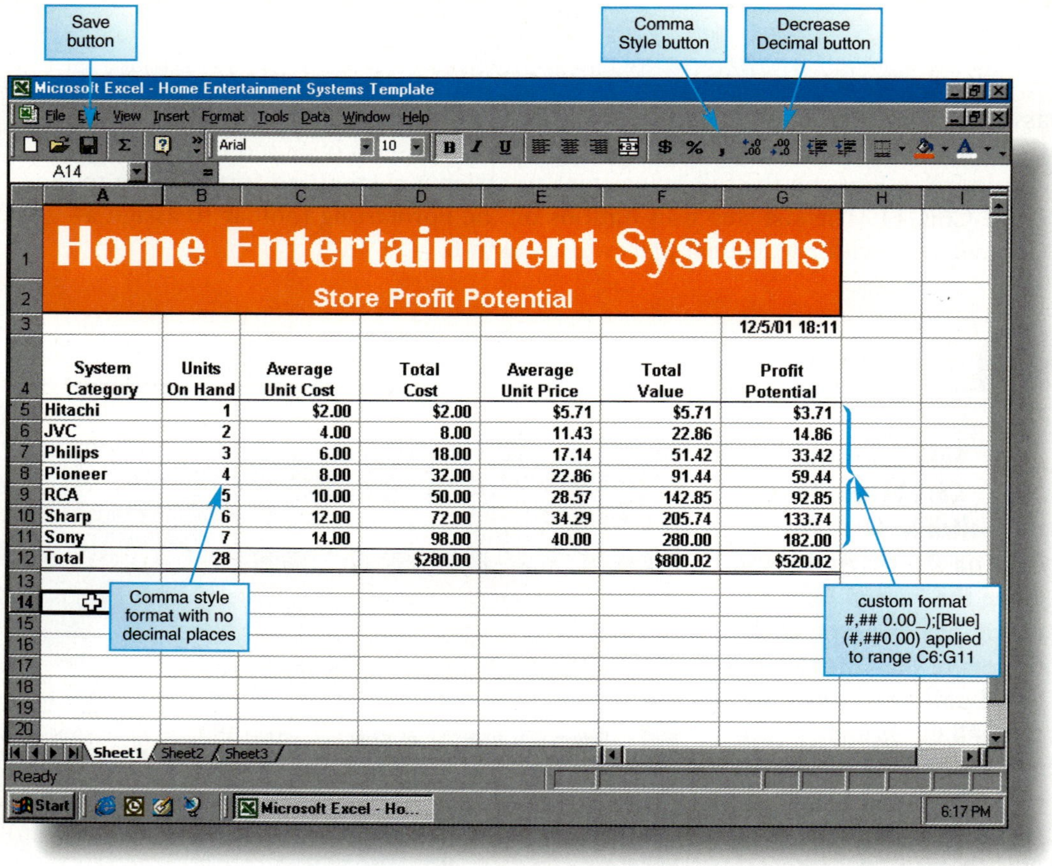

FIGURE 6-21

Other Ways

1. On Format menu click Cells, click Number tab, select format, click OK button
2. Press CTRL+1, click Number tab, select format, click OK button

When you create a new custom format code, Excel adds it to the bottom of the Type list box in the Numbers sheet in the Format Cells dialog box to make it available for future use.

Creating and Applying a Style

A **style** is a group of format specifications that are assigned to a style name. Excel includes several styles as described in Table 6-3. Excel assigns the Normal style to all cells when you open a new workbook.

Using the Style command on the Format menu, you can assign a style to a cell, a range of cells, a worksheet, or a workbook in the same way you assign a format using the buttons on the Formatting toolbar. In fact, the Currency Style button, Comma Style button, and Percent Style button assign the Currency, Comma, and Percent styles in Table 6-3, respectively.

Table 6-3 Styles Available with All Workbooks

STYLE NAME	DESCRIPTION
Normal	Number = General; Alignment = General, Bottom Aligned; Font = Arial 10; Border = No Borders; Patterns = No Shading; Protection = Locked
Comma	Number = (*#,##0.00);_(*(#,##0.00);_(*"-");_(@_)
Comma(0)	Number = (*#,##0_);_(*(#,##0);_(*"-"_);_(@_)
Currency	Number = ($#,##0.00_);_($*(#,##0.00);_($*"-"??_);_(@_)
Currency(0)	Number = ($#,##0_);_($*(#,##0);_($*"-"_);_(@_)
Percent	Number = 0%

With the Style command, you also can add new styles, modify styles, delete styles, and merge styles from other workbooks. You add a new style to a workbook or merge styles when you plan to use a group of format specifications over and over.

The following steps create a new style called Four-Digit Year by modifying the existing Normal style. The new Four-Digit Year style will include the following formats: Number = d-mmm-yyyy; Alignment = Horizontal Center, Bottom Aligned; and Font = Arial 10, Bold.

Normal Style

The Normal style is the format style that Excel initially assigns all cells in a workbook. If you change the Normal style, Excel formats all cells not assigned another style the new format specifications.

 To Create a New Style

1 Click Format on the menu bar and then point to Style.

The Format menu displays as shown in Figure 6-22.

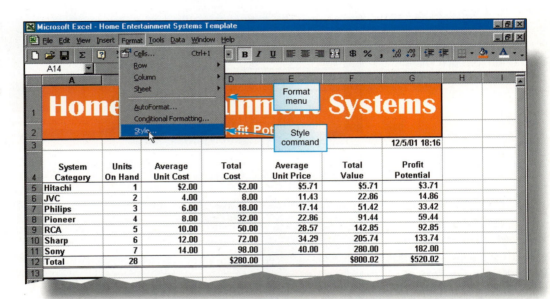

FIGURE 6-22

2 Click Style. When the Style dialog box displays, drag through Normal in the Style name text box and then type Four-Digit Year as the new style name. Point to the Modify button.

The Style dialog box displays with the new style name Four-Digit Year (Figure 6-23).

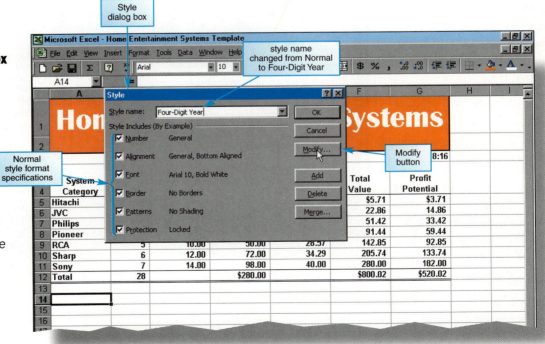

FIGURE 6-23

3 Click the Modify button. When the Format Cells dialog box displays, if necessary, click the Number tab, click Date in the Category list, and then click 14-Mar-1998 in the Type list. Point to the Alignment tab.

The Format Cells dialog box displays (Figure 6-24). The Format Cells dialog box contains a tab for each check box in the Style dialog box.

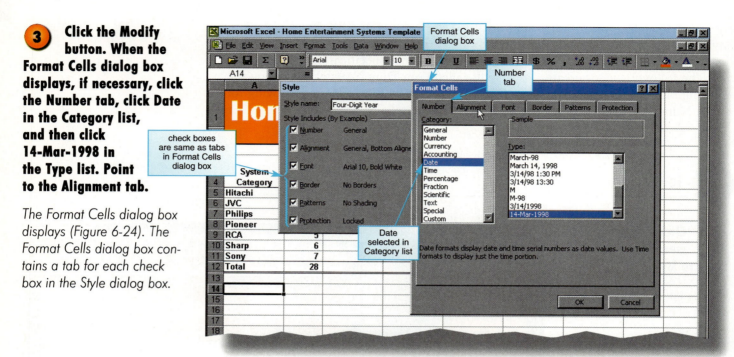

FIGURE 6-24

4 Click the Alignment tab. Click the Horizontal box arrow and then click Center. Click the OK button in the Format Cells dialog box. Click Font, Borders, Patterns, and Protection to deselect the check boxes in the Style Includes area. Point to the Add button.

The Style dialog box displays the formats assigned to the Four-Digit Year (Figure 6-25).

5 Click the Add button to add the new style to the style list available with this template. Click the OK button.

The new style Four-Digit Year becomes part of the list of styles available with the template.

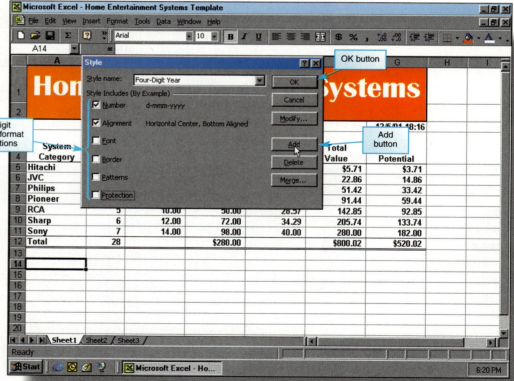

FIGURE 6-25

Other Ways

1. Press ALT+O, press S

Applying a Style

In earlier steps, cell G3 was assigned the NOW function. This project calls for centering the date and displaying it with a four-digit year. To accomplish this task, the following steps assign the Four-Digit Year style to cell G3.

 **To Apply a Style**

1 **Click cell G3. Click Format on the menu bar and then click Style. Click the Style name box arrow and then click Four-Digit Year in the list. Point to the OK button.**

The Style dialog box displays (Figure 6-26).

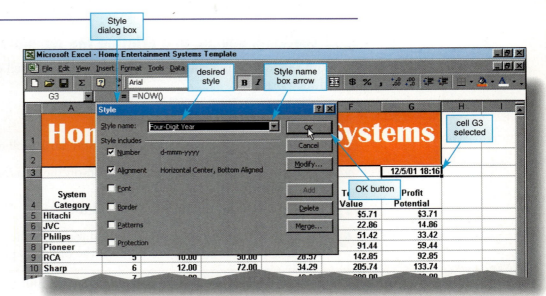

FIGURE 6-26

2 **Click the OK button.**

Excel assigns the Four-Digit Year style to cell G3 (Figure 6-27).

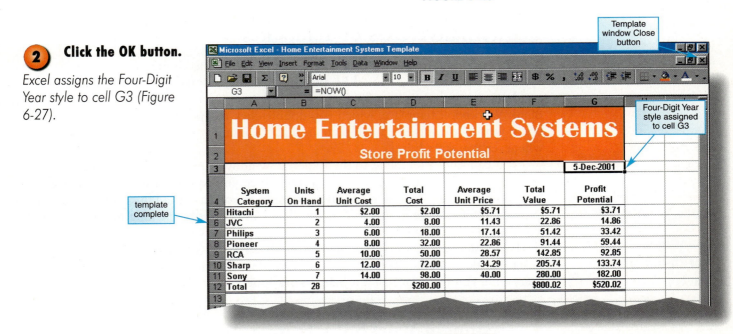

FIGURE 6-27

Keep in mind the following additional points concerning styles:

1. If you assign two styles to a range of cells, Excel adds the second style to the first rather than replacing it.

Other Ways

1. Press ALT+O, press S

2. Do not delete the default styles that come with Excel because some of the buttons on the toolbars are dependent on them.

3. You can merge styles from another workbook into the active workbook through the use of the Merge button in the Style dialog box. You must, however, open the workbook that contains the desired styles before you use the Merge button.

4. The six check boxes in the Style dialog box are identical to the six tabs in the Format Cells dialog box.

Spell Checking, Saving, and Printing the Template

With the formatting complete, the next step is to spell check the template, save it, and then print it.

TO SPELL CHECK, SAVE, AND PRINT THE TEMPLATE

1 Double-click the move handle on the Standard toolbar.

2 Click cell A1. Click the Spelling button on the Standard toolbar. Change any misspelled words.

3 Click the Save button on the Standard toolbar.

4 Click the Print button on the Standard toolbar. Click the Close button on the template title bar (see Figure 6-27 on the previous page).

Excel saves the template using the file name Home Entertainment Systems Template, prints the template, and finally closes the template.

Alternative Uses of Templates

Before continuing on and using the template to create the Home Entertainment Systems workbook, you should be aware of some additional uses of templates. As you have seen when you begin a new Office document, Excel includes a default Blank Workbook template, which you double-click to open a new workbook. This blank workbook acts like a template in that it contains the defaults that you see whenever you start Excel.

You can save a template to the folder: c:\windows\application data\microsoft\templates. Once a template is saved in this folder, you can select it by clicking the New command on the File menu. For example, if you save the Home Entertainment Systems Template file to this folder, you then can open it by clicking the New command on the File menu.

If you save a formatted template in the folder: c:\microsoft office\office\xlstart using the file name Book, Excel uses it as the default Blank Workbook template every time you begin or insert a blank workbook.

Creating a Workbook from a Template

Once you have saved the template on disk, you can begin the second phase of this project: using the template to create the Home Entertainment Systems workbook shown in Figure 6-1 on page E 6.5. As shown by the three tabs at the bottom of Figure 6-28, Excel's default Blank Workbook template includes three worksheets. The Home Entertainment Systems workbook, however, requires four sheets — one for each of the three store locations and one for the company totals. Thus, a worksheet must be added to the workbook. Perform the following steps to add a worksheet to the workbook.

More About

Opening a Workbook at Startup

You can instruct Windows to open a workbook (or template) automatically when you turn on your computer by adding the workbook (or template) to the Startup folder. Use Explorer to copy the file to the Startup folder. The Startup folder is in the Programs folder and the Programs folder is in the Start Menu folder.

Steps **To Open a Template and Add a Worksheet**

1 **Click the Open button on** the Standard toolbar. When the Open dialog box displays, click the Files of type box arrow and click Templates. Click the Look in box arrow and click 3½ Floppy (A:). Double-click Home Entertainment Systems Template.

Excel opens the file, Home Entertainment Systems Template, as shown earlier in Figure 6-27.

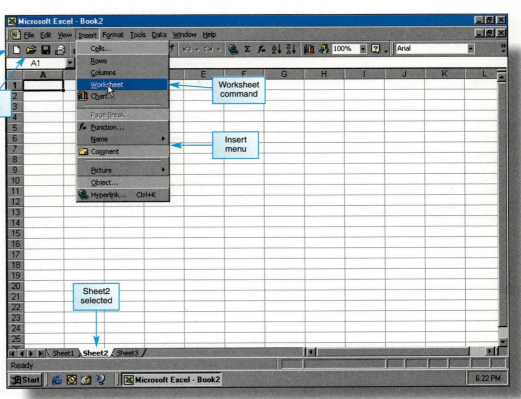

FIGURE 6-28

2 **Click the Sheet2 tab** at the bottom of the screen. Click Insert on the menu bar and then point to Worksheet.

The Insert menu displays (Figure 6-28).

3 **Click Worksheet.**

Excel adds a fourth worksheet between Sheet1 and Sheet2. Recall that Sheet1 contains the template. As shown on the sheet tab, Sheet4 is the name of the new worksheet (Figure 6-29).

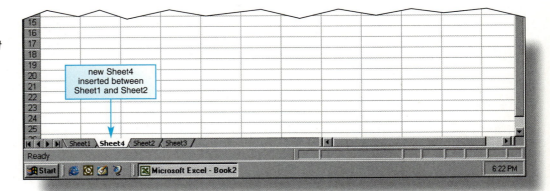

FIGURE 6-29

Other Ways

1. Right-click sheet tab, click Insert, double-click Worksheet icon
2. Right-click sheet tab, click Move or Copy, click Create a copy, click OK button

You can add up to a total of 255 worksheets. An alternative to adding worksheets is to change the default number of worksheets before you open a new workbook. To change the default number of worksheets in a blank workbook, click Options on the Tools menu, click the General tab, and change the number in the Sheets in new workbook box. You also can delete a worksheet by right-clicking the tab of the worksheet you want to delete and then clicking Delete on the shortcut menu.

With four worksheets, you now can copy the template on the Sheet1 worksheet to the three blank worksheets in the workbook.

To Create a Workbook from a Template

1 **Click the Sheet1 tab to display the template. Click the Select All button and then click the Copy button on the Standard toolbar.**

The template is selected as shown in Figure 6-30. The template, including all data and formats, is copied to the Office Clipboard.

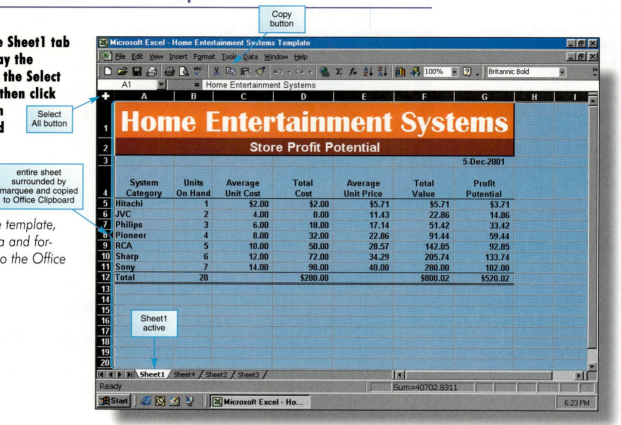

FIGURE 6-30

2 **Click the Sheet4 tab. While holding down the SHIFT key, click the Sheet3 tab so all three blank worksheets are selected. Click the Paste button on the Standard toolbar.**

The template is copied to Sheet4, Sheet2, and Sheet3. Because multiple sheets are selected, the term [Group] follows the template name on the title bar (Figure 6-31).

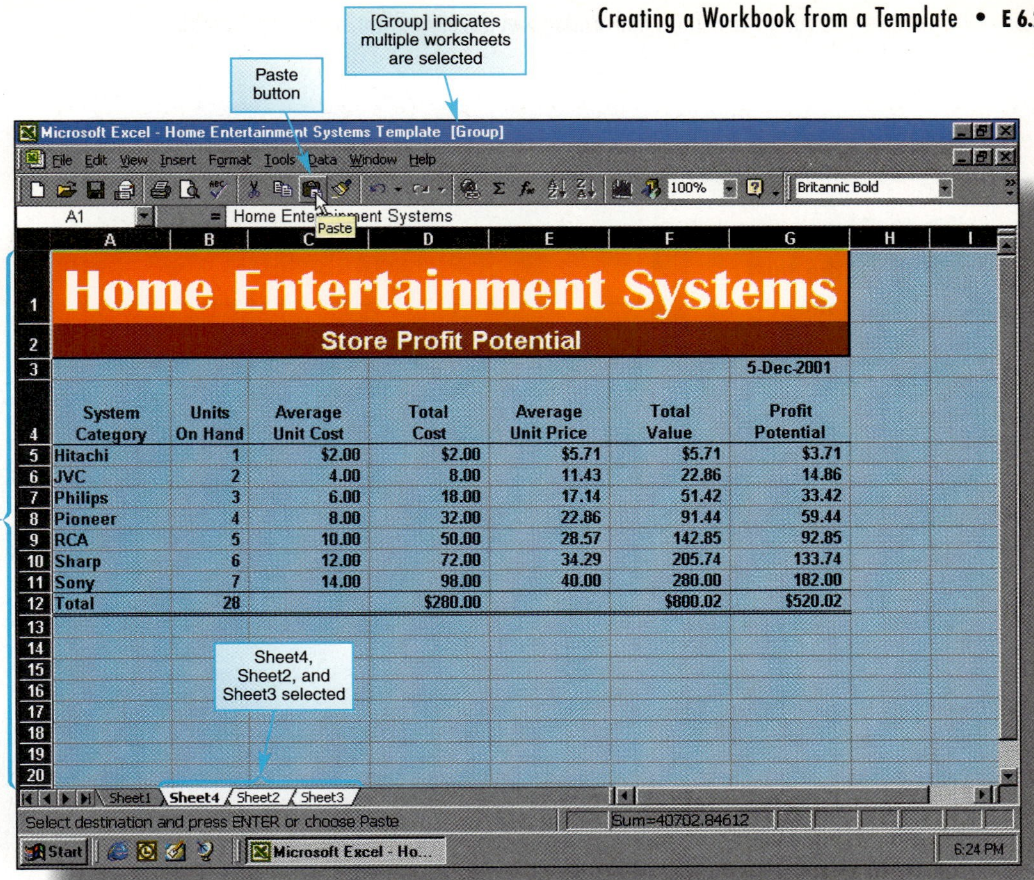

3 **Click the Sheet1 tab. Press the ESC key to remove the marquee surrounding the selection. Hold down the SHIFT key and click the Sheet3 tab. Click cell A14 to deselect the worksheet on each**
sheet. **Hold down the SHIFT key and click the Sheet1 tab. Click Save As on the File menu. Type** Home Entertainment Systems **in the File name text box. Click Microsoft Excel Workbook in the Save as type list. If necessary, click 3½ Floppy (A:) in the Save in list. Click the Save button in the Save As dialog box.**

Excel saves the workbook on drive A using the file name Home Entertainment Systems. Sheet1 is the active worksheet.

FIGURE 6-31

Drilling an Entry Down through Worksheets

The next step is to enter the average unit cost for each system category (Table 6-4) in the range C5:C11. The average unit costs for each category are identical on all four sheets. For example, the average unit cost for the Hitachi category in cell C5 is $3,212.37 on all four sheets. To speed data entry, Excel allows you to enter a number once and drill it through worksheets so it displays in the same cell on all the selected worksheets. This technique is referred to as **drilling an entry**. The steps on the next page drill the seven average unit cost entries in Table 6-4 through all four worksheets.

Table 6-4 Average Unit Cost Entries	
SYSTEM CATEGORY	AVERAGE UNIT COST
Hitachi	3212.37
JVC	224.13
Philips	995.21
Pioneer	4123.82
RCA	1175.47
Sharp	1023.85
Sony	109.80

Steps To Drill an Entry Through Worksheets

1 With Sheet1 active, hold down the SHIFT key and then click the Sheet3 tab. Click cell C5. Type 3212.37 and then press the DOWN ARROW key. Enter the six remaining average unit costs in Table 6-4 on the previous page in the range C6:C11.

All four tabs at the bottom of the screen are selected. The word Sheet1 on the first tab is bold, indicating it is the active sheet. The average unit cost entries display as shown in Figure 6-32.

	System Category	Units On Hand	Average Unit Cost	Total Cost	Average Unit Price	Total Value	Profit Potential
							5-Dec-2001
5	Hitachi	1	$3,212.37	$3,212.37	$9,178.20	$9,178.20	$5,965.83
6	JVC	2	224.13	448.26	640.37	1,280.74	832.48
7	Philips	3	995.21	2,985.63	2,843.46	8,530.38	5,544.75
8	Pioneer	4	4,123.82	16,495.28	11,782.34	47,129.36	30,634.08
9	RCA	5	1,175.47	5,877.35	3,358.49	16,792.45	10,915.10
10	Sharp	6	1,023.85	6,143.10	2,925.29	17,551.74	11,408.64
11	Sony	7	109.80	768.60	313.71	2,195.97	1,427.37
12	Total	28		$35,930.59		$102,658.84	$66,728.25

all four sheets selected

average unit costs entered on Sheet1 also are assigned to the same cells on Sheet4, Sheet2, and Sheet3

Sheet1 / Sheet4 / Sheet2 / Sheet3

FIGURE 6-32

2 Hold down the SHIFT key and then click the Sheet1 tab to deselect Sheet4, Sheet2, and Sheet3. One at a time, click the Sheet4 tab, the Sheet2 tab, and the Sheet3 tab.

The four sheets are identical (Figure 6-33). Each is made up of the data and formats assigned earlier to the template.

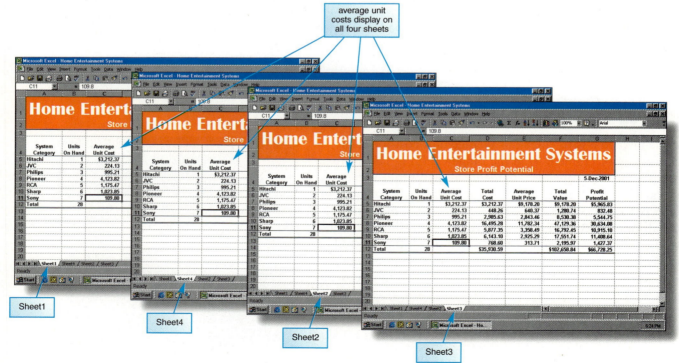

average unit costs display on all four sheets

Sheet1

Sheet4

Sheet2

Sheet3

FIGURE 6-33

In the previous set of steps, seven new numbers were entered on one worksheet. As shown in Figure 6-33, by drilling the entries through the four other worksheets, twenty-eight new numbers now display, seven on each of the four worksheets. This capability of drilling data through worksheets is an efficient way to enter data that is common among worksheets.

Modifying the Pittsburgh Sheet

With the skeleton of the Home Entertainment Systems workbook created, the next step is to modify the individual sheets. The following steps modify the Pittsburgh sheet by changing the sheet name and worksheet subtitle, changing the color of the title area, and entering the units on hand in column B.

TO MODIFY THE PITTSBURGH SHEET

1 Double-click the Sheet4 tab and then type `Pittsburgh` as the sheet name.

2 Double-click cell A2, drag through the word Store, and type `Pittsburgh` to change the worksheet subtitle.

3 Double-click the move handle on the Formatting toolbar to display it in its entirety. Select the range A1:A2. Click the Fill Color button arrow on the Formatting toolbar. Click Blue (column 6, row 2) on the Fill Color palette.

4 Enter the data listed in Table 6-5 in the range B5:B11.

5 Click the Save button on the Standard toolbar.

The Pittsburgh sheet displays as shown in Figure 6-34.

More About

Drilling an Entry

Besides drilling a number down through a workbook, you can drill a format, a function, or a formula down through a workbook.

Table 6-5   Pittsburgh Units on Hand

CELL	UNITS ON HAND
B5	5
B6	234
B7	45
B8	12
B9	28
B10	30
B11	1015

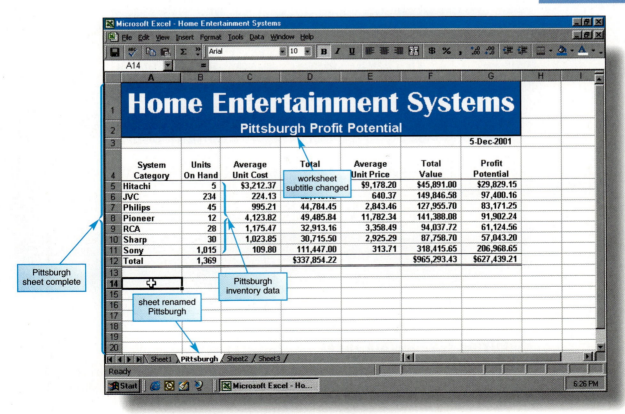

FIGURE 6-34

As you enter the new data, Excel immediately recalculates the formulas on all four worksheets.

Modifying the Indianapolis Sheet

The following steps modify the Indianapolis sheet.

TO MODIFY THE INDIANAPOLIS SHEET

1. Double-click the Sheet2 tab and then type Indianapolis as the sheet name.

2. Double-click cell A2, drag through the word Store, and type Indianapolis as the worksheet subtitle.

3. Select the range A1:A2. Click the Fill Color button arrow on the Formatting toolbar. Click Green (column 4, row 2) on the Fill Color palette.

4. Enter the data in Table 6-6 in the range B5:B11.

5. Click the Save button on the Standard toolbar.

The Indianapolis sheet displays as shown in Figure 6-35.

Table 6-6	Indianapolis Units on Hand
CELL	UNITS ON HAND
B5	8
B6	75
B7	13
B8	8
B9	10
B10	29
B11	9

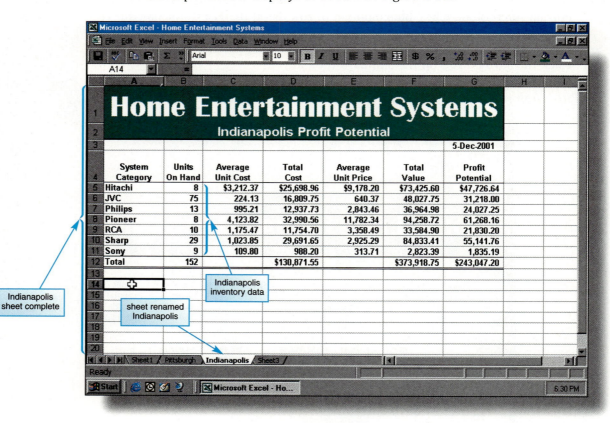

FIGURE 6-35

Modifying the Phoenix Sheet

As with the Pittsburgh and Indianapolis sheets, the sheet name, worksheet subtitle, data, and background colors must be changed on the Phoenix sheet. The following steps modify the Phoenix sheet.

TO MODIFY THE PHOENIX SHEET

1 Double click the Sheet3 tab and then type Phoenix as the sheet name.

2 Double click cell A2, drag through the word store and type Phoenix to change the worksheet subtitle.

3 Select the range A1:A2. Click the Fill Color button arrow on the Formatting toolbar. Click Violet (column 7, row 3) on the Fill Color palette.

4 Enter the data in Table 6-7 in the range B5:B11.

5 Click the Save button on the Standard toolbar.

The Phoenix sheet displays as shown in Figure 6-36.

Table 6-7	Phoenix Units on Hand
CELL	**UNITS ON HAND**
B5	5
B6	82
B7	16
B8	3
B9	13
B10	82
B11	2

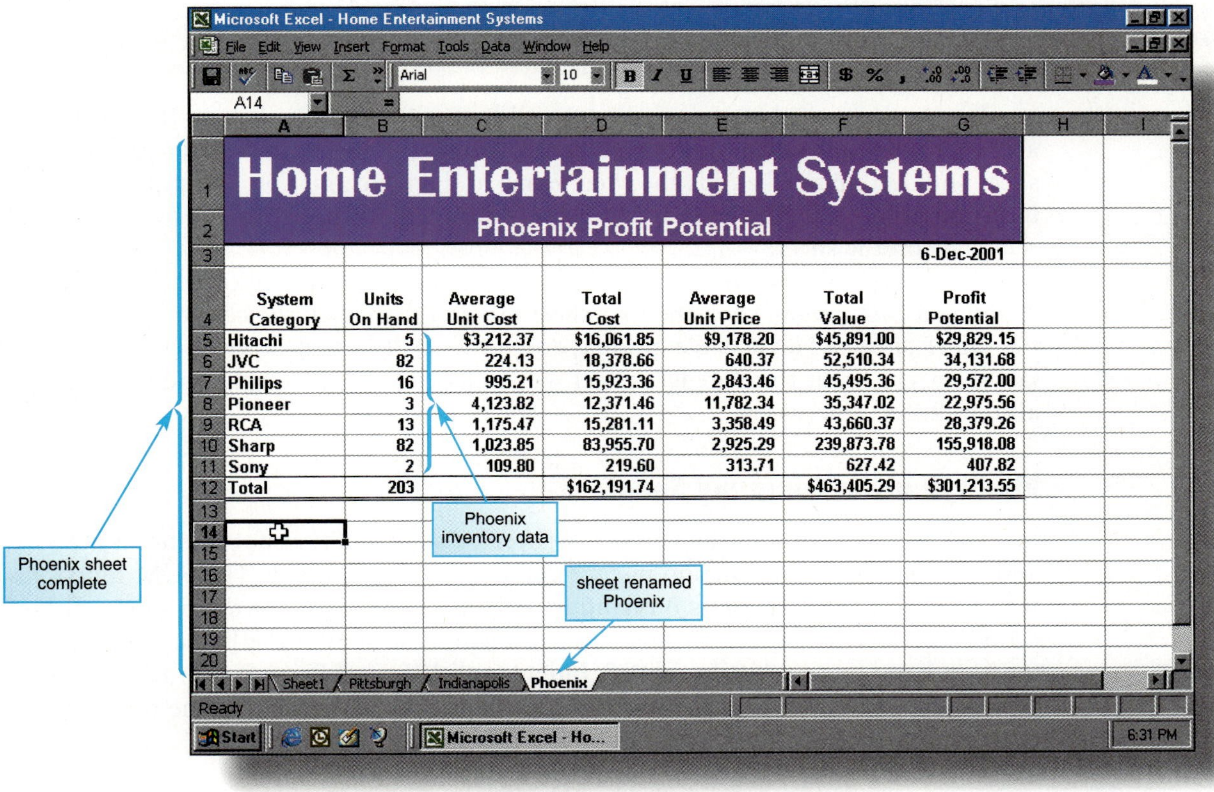

FIGURE 6-36

With the three store sheets complete, the next step is to modify Sheet1, which will serve as the consolidation worksheet containing totals of the data on the Pittsburgh, Indianapolis, and Phoenix sheets. Because this sheet contains totals of the data, you need to understand how to reference cells in other sheets in a workbook before modifying Sheet1.

Referencing Cells in Other Sheets in a Workbook

To reference cells in other sheets in a workbook, you use the sheet name, which serves as the **sheet reference**, and the cell reference. For example, you refer to cell B5 on the Pittsburgh sheet as shown below.

=Pittsburgh!B5

More About

Importing Data

Unit costs often are maintained in another workbook, a file, or a database. If the unit costs are maintained elsewhere, ways exist to link to a workbook or import data from a file or database into a workbook. For information on importing data, see the Get External Data command on the Data menu.

Sheet Tabs

If you right-click a tab, a short-cut menu displays with several commands to modify the workbook. Commands include Insert, Delete, Rename, Move, or Copy. All these commands relate to manipulating sheets in a workbook. For example, you can use this menu to insert a new sheet, delete the active sheet, rename the active sheet, or move or copy the active sheet.

Using this method, you can sum cell B5 on the three store sheets by selecting cell B5 on the Sheet1 sheet and then entering:

= Pittsburgh!B5 + Indianapolis!B5 + Phoenix!B5

A much quicker way to total this is to use the SUM function as follows:

=SUM(Pittsburgh:Phoenix!B5)

The SUM argument (Pittsburgh:Phoenix!B5) instructs Excel to sum cell B5 on each of the three sheets (Pittsburgh, Indianapolis, and Phoenix). The colon (:) between the first sheet and the last sheet means to include these sheets and all sheets in between, just as it does with a range of cells on a sheet. A range that spans two or more sheets in a workbook, such as Pittsburgh:Phoenix!B5, is called a **3-D range**. The reference to this range is a **3-D reference**.

A sheet reference, such as Phoenix!, always is absolute. Thus, the sheet reference remains constant when you copy formulas.

Entering a Sheet Reference

You can enter a sheet reference in a cell by typing it or by clicking the appropriate sheet tab while in Point mode. When you click the sheet tab, Excel activates the sheet and automatically adds the sheet name and an exclamation point after the insertion point in the formula bar. Next, click or drag through the cells you want to reference on the sheet.

If the range of cells to be referenced is located on several worksheets (as when selecting a 3-D range), click the first sheet tab and then click the cell or drag through the range of cells. Next, while holding down the SHIFT key, click the sheet tab of the last sheet you want to reference. Excel will include the cell(s) on the end sheets and all the sheets in between.

Modifying the Company Sheet

This section modifies the Company sheet by changing the sheet name, subtitle, and entering the SUM function in each cell in the range B5:B11. The SUM functions will determine the total units on hand by system category for the three stores. Cell B5 on the Company sheet, for instance, will equal the sum of the Hitachi category units on hand in cells Pittsburgh!B5, Indianapolis!B5, and Phoenix!B5. Before determining the totals, perform the following steps to change the sheet name from Sheet1 to Company and the worksheet subtitle to Company Profit Potential.

3-D References

If you are adding numbers on noncontiguous sheets, hold down the CTRL key rather than the SHIFT key when selecting the sheets.

TO RENAME A SHEET AND MODIFY THE WORKSHEET TITLE

1 Double-click the Sheet1 sheet tab.

2 Type Company and then press the ENTER key.

3 Double-click cell A2, drag through the word Store, and type Company as the worksheet subtitle. Press the ENTER key

Excel changes the name of Sheet1 to Company and the worksheet subtitle to Company Profit Potential.

The following steps enter the 3-D references used to determine the total units on hand for each of the seven system categories.

To Enter and Copy 3-D References

1 **Double-click the move handle on the Standard toolbar to show it in its entirety. Click cell B5 and then click the AutoSum button on the Standard toolbar.**

The SUM function displays without a selected range (Figure 6-37).

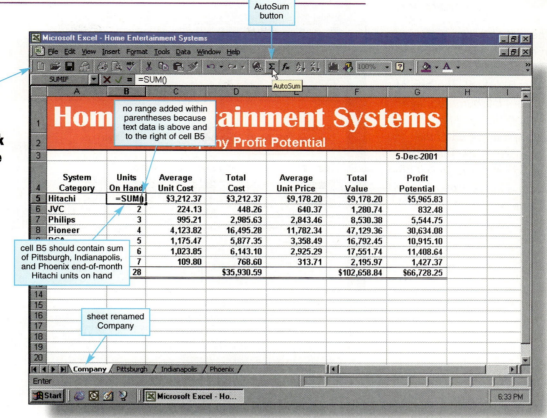

FIGURE 6-37

2 **Click the Pittsburgh tab and then click cell B5. While holding down the SHIFT key, click the Phoenix tab.**

A marquee surrounds cell Pittsburgh!B5 (Figure 6-38). All four sheet tabs are selected; the Pittsburgh tab displays in bold because it is the active sheet. The SUM function displays in the formula bar.

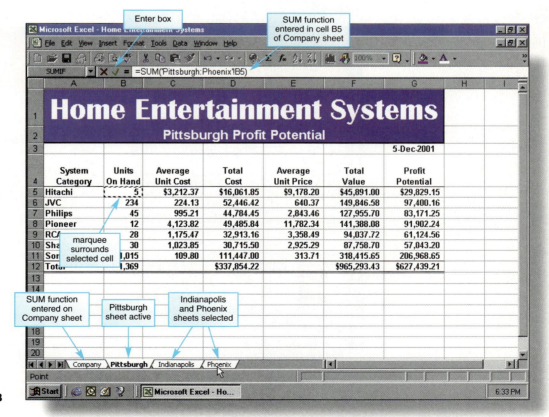

FIGURE 6-38

3 **Click the Enter box in the formula bar.**

The SUM function is entered in cell Company!B5 and the Company sheet becomes the active sheet. The sum of the cells Pittsburgh!B5, Indianapolis!B5, and Phoenix!B5 displays in cell B5 of the Company sheet. The SUM function assigned to cell B5 displays in the formula bar (Figure 6-39).

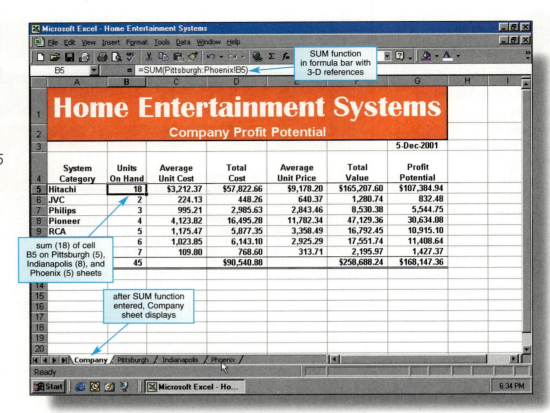

FIGURE 6-39

4 **With cell B5 active, point to the fill handle.**

The mouse pointer changes to a cross hair on the fill handle (Figure 6-40).

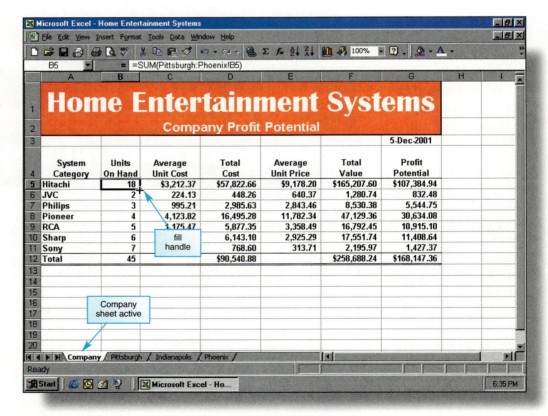

FIGURE 6-40

5 **Drag the fill handle through cell B11.**

Excel copies the SUM function in cell B5 to the range B6:B11 (Figure 6-41). Excel automatically adjusts the cell references in the SUM function to reference the corresponding cells on the other three sheets in the workbook. The total units on hand for each system category displays.

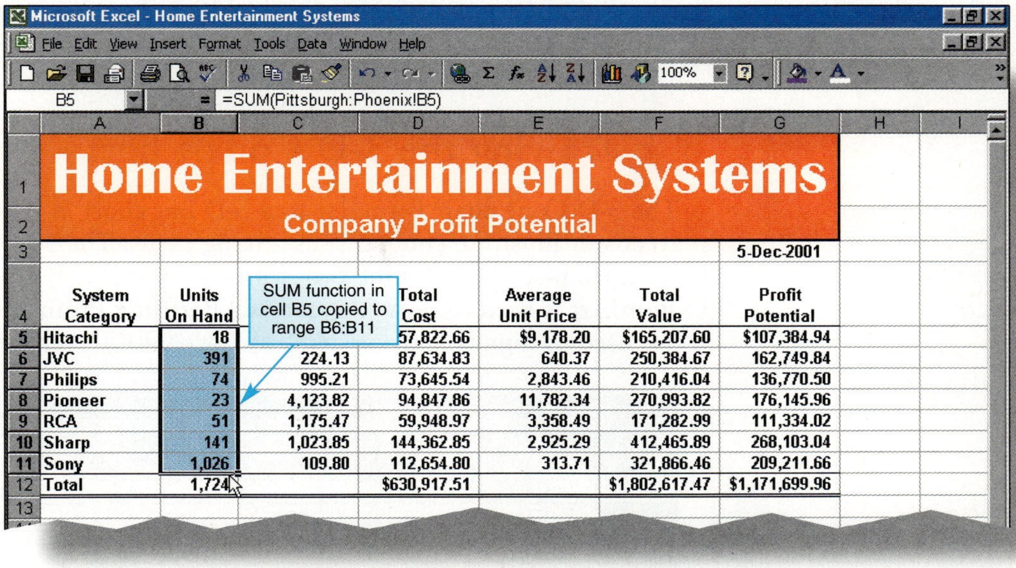

System Category	Units On Hand		Total Cost	Average Unit Price	Total Value	Profit Potential
						5-Dec-2001
Hitachi	18	SUM function in cell B5 copied to range B6:B11	57,822.66	$9,178.20	$165,207.60	$107,384.94
JVC	391	224.13	87,634.83	640.37	250,384.67	162,749.84
Philips	74	995.21	73,645.54	2,843.46	210,416.04	136,770.50
Pioneer	23	4,123.82	94,847.86	11,782.34	270,993.82	176,145.96
RCA	51	1,175.47	59,948.97	3,358.49	171,282.99	111,334.02
Sharp	141	1,023.85	144,362.85	2,925.29	412,465.89	268,103.04
Sony	1,026	109.80	112,654.80	313.71	321,866.46	209,211.66
Total	1,724		$630,917.51		$1,802,617.47	$1,171,699.96

FIGURE 6-41

6 **Click cell A14 to deselect the range B6:B11. Click the Save button on the Standard toolbar to save the Home Entertainment Systems workbook.**

All the formulas on the Company sheet are recalculated based on the total units on hand for each system category. The Company sheet is complete (Figure 6-42).

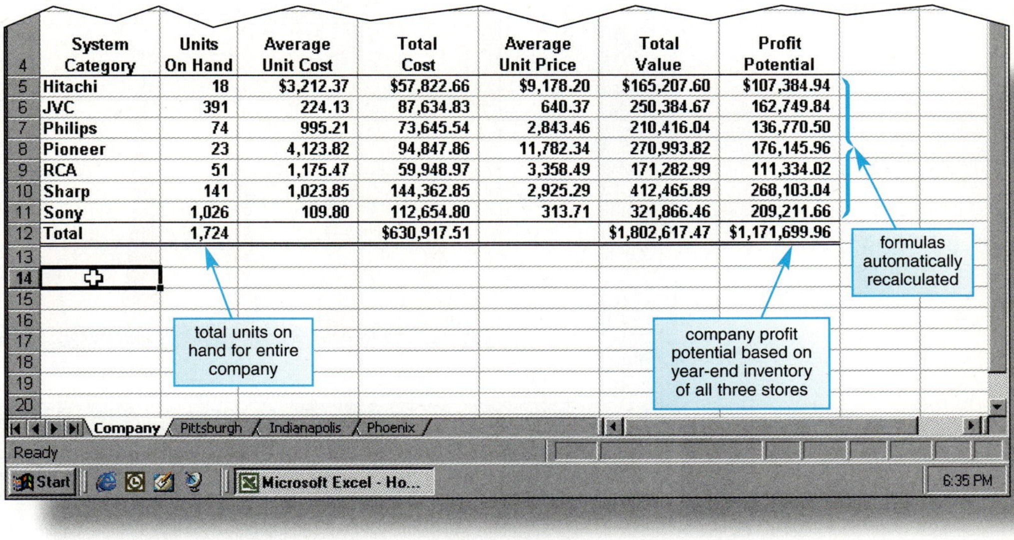

System Category	Units On Hand	Average Unit Cost	Total Cost	Average Unit Price	Total Value	Profit Potential
Hitachi	18	$3,212.37	$57,822.66	$9,178.20	$165,207.60	$107,384.94
JVC	391	224.13	87,634.83	640.37	250,384.67	162,749.84
Philips	74	995.21	73,645.54	2,843.46	210,416.04	136,770.50
Pioneer	23	4,123.82	94,847.86	11,782.34	270,993.82	176,145.96
RCA	51	1,175.47	59,948.97	3,358.49	171,282.99	111,334.02
Sharp	141	1,023.85	144,362.85	2,925.29	412,465.89	268,103.04
Sony	1,026	109.80	112,654.80	313.71	321,866.46	209,211.66
Total	1,724		$630,917.51		$1,802,617.47	$1,171,699.96

total units on hand for entire company

company profit potential based on year-end inventory of all three stores

formulas automatically recalculated

FIGURE 6-42

As shown in cell G12 in Figure 6-42, Home Entertainment Systems has a month-end profit potential of $1,171,699.96, based on the inventory data submitted by the three stores. If a store calls in a correction to the units on hand for any system category, Santiago Biagi, simply has to select the sheet that represents the store and enter the correction. All formulas, including those on the Company sheet, will be recalculated immediately, and Santiago quickly can see the most up-to-date profit potential.

With the four worksheets in the Home Entertainment Systems workbook complete, the next step is to draw a 3-D Cone chart.

Drawing the 3-D Cone Chart

The 3-D Cone chart is similar to a 3-D Bar chart in that it can be used to show trends or illustrate comparisons among items. The 3-D Cone chart in Figure 6-43, for example, compares the profit potential of each of the seven system categories. WordArt is used to draw the curved chart title Profit Potential. A text box and arrow are used to highlight the system category with the greatest profit potential.

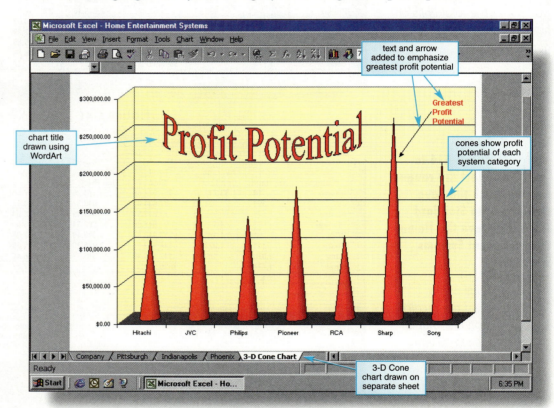

FIGURE 6-43

The following steps create the 3-D Cone chart.

To Draw a 3-D Cone Chart

1 **With the Company sheet active, select the range A5:A11. While holding down the CTRL key, select the range G5:G11. Click the Chart Wizard button on the Standard toolbar. When the Chart Wizard – Step 1 of 4 – Chart Type dialog box displays, click Cone in the Chart type list box. If necessary, click Column with a conical shape (column 1, row 1) in the Chart sub-type area. Point to the Next button.**

The Chart Wizard – Step 1 of 4 – Chart Type dialog box displays as shown in Figure 6-44. The nonadjacent range selection displays behind the dialog box.

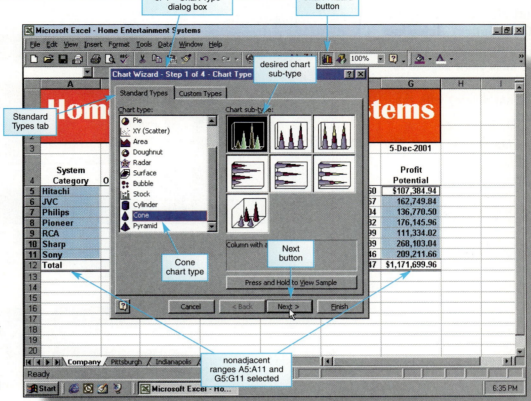

FIGURE 6-44

2 **Click the Next button.**

The Chart Wizard – Step 2 of 4 – Chart Source Data dialog box displays with a sample of the 3-D Cone chart and the nonadjacent data range selection (Figure 6-45). Because nonadjacent ranges are selected down the sheet, Excel automatically determines series are in columns.

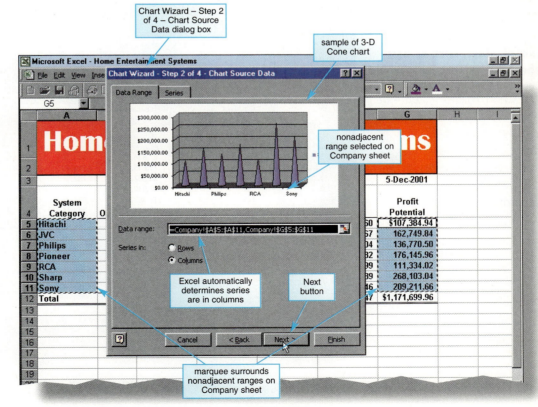

FIGURE 6-45

3 **Click the Next button. When the Chart Wizard – Step 3 of 4 – Chart Options dialog box displays, click the Legend tab. Click Show Legend to deselect it so the legend does not display with the chart.**

The Chart Wizard – Step 3 of 4 – Chart Options dialog box displays (Figure 6-46).

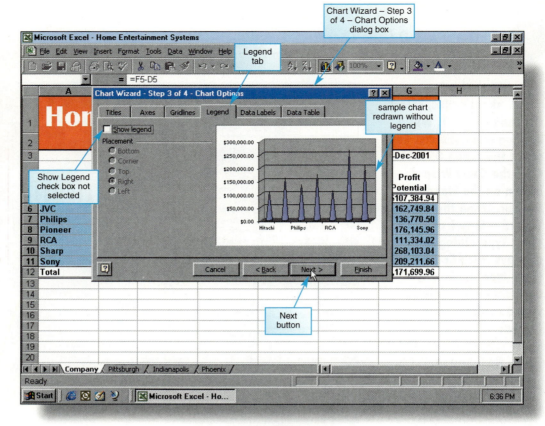

FIGURE 6-46

4 **Click the Next button. When the Chart Wizard – Step 4 of 4 – Chart Location dialog box displays, click As new sheet.**

The Chart Wizard – Step 4 of 4 – Chart Location dialog box displays (Figure 6-47). Because the As new sheet option button is selected, the chart will be drawn on a separate chart sheet.

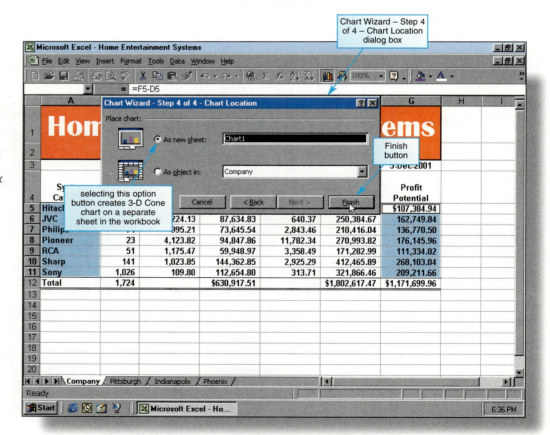

FIGURE 6-47

Click the Finish button.

Excel draws the 3-D Cone chart. The chart sheet, which is named Chart1, is inserted as the first sheet in the workbook (Figure 6-48).

Click the wall behind the cones. Click the Fill Color button arrow on the Formatting toolbar. Click Light Yellow (column 3, row 5). Click one of the cones to select all the cones. Click the Fill Color button arrow on the Formatting toolbar. Click Red (column 1, row 3).

The 3-D Cone chart displays as shown earlier in Figure 6-43 on page E 6.38.

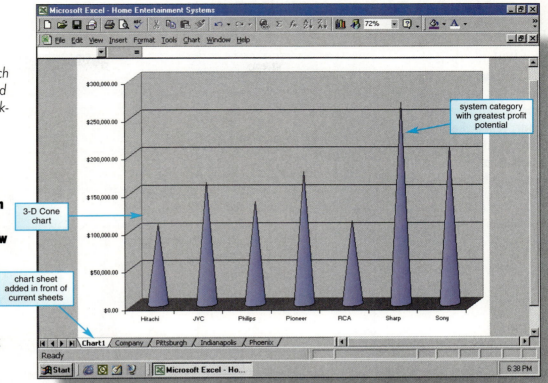

FIGURE 6-48

Double-click the Chart1 tab and then type 3-D Cone Chart **as the sheet name. Press the ENTER key. Drag the 3-D Cone Chart sheet tab to the right of the Phoenix sheet tab.**

Other Ways

1. Select chart range, press F11

The 3-D Cone chart compares the profit potential of the seven system categories. You can see from the chart that the Sharp category has the greatest profit potential and that the Hitachi category has the least profit potential.

Adding a Chart Title Using the WordArt Tool

In earlier projects, you added a chart title by using the Chart Wizard and then formatted it using the Formatting toolbar. This section shows you how to add a chart title and create special text formatting effects using the WordArt tool. The **WordArt tool** allows you to create shadowed, skewed, rotated, and stretched text on a chart sheet or worksheet. The WordArt design is called an **object**. You start the WordArt tool by clicking the WordArt button on the Drawing toolbar. Perform the steps on the next page to add a Chart title using the WordArt tool.

To Add a Chart Title Using the WordArt Tool

1 With the chart sheet displaying on the screen, click the Drawing button on the Standard toolbar. When the Drawing toolbar displays, dock it at the bottom of the screen by dragging it below the tabs.

The Drawing toolbar displays at the bottom of the screen (Figure 6-49).

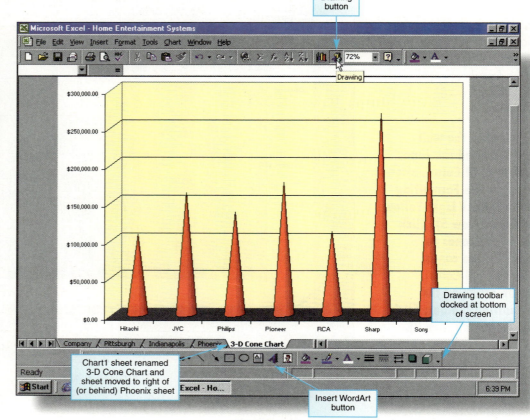

FIGURE 6-49

2 Click the Insert WordArt button on the Drawing toolbar. When the WordArt Gallery dialog box displays, click the design in column 5, row 1 in the Select a WordArt style area. Point to the OK button.

The WordArt Gallery dialog box displays (Figure 6-50).

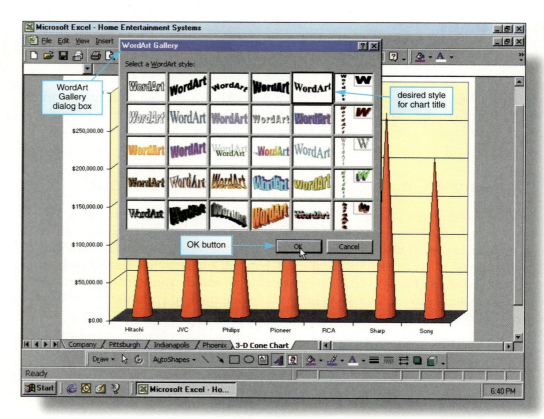

FIGURE 6-50

3 **Click the OK button. When the Edit WordArt Text dialog box displays, type** Profit Potential **as the title of the 3-D Cone chart. Point to the OK button.**

The Edit WordArt Text dialog box displays (Figure 6-51). Profit Potential will be the chart title.

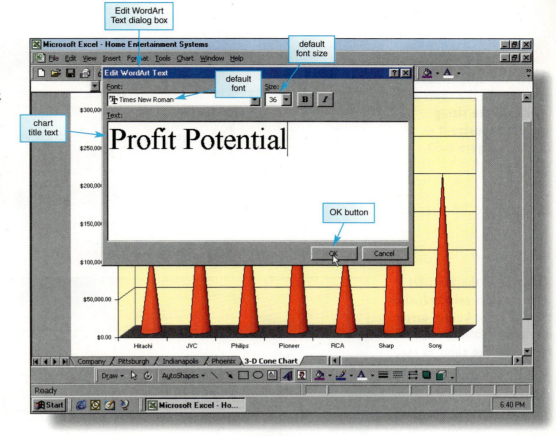

FIGURE 6-51

4 **Click the OK button.**

The WordArt object (Profit Potential) displays in the middle of the chart sheet (Figure 6-52). The WordArt toolbar displays.

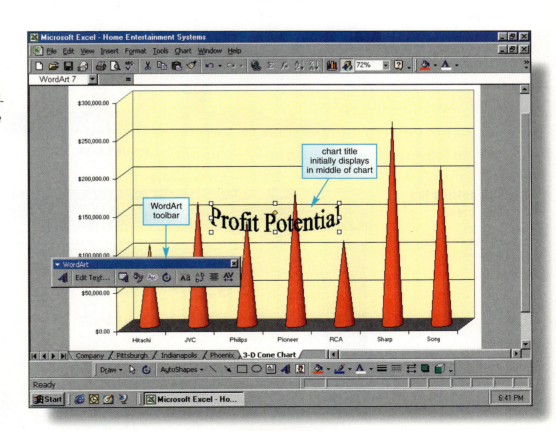

FIGURE 6-52

5 Point to the center of the WordArt object and drag it above the cones in the chart and then drag the sizing handles to resize it as shown in Figure 6-53.

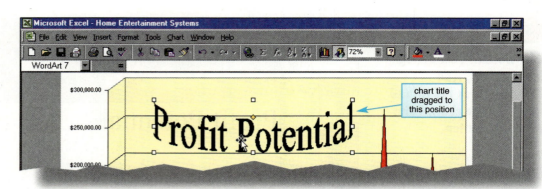

FIGURE 6-53

6 With the WordArt object selected, click the Fill Color button arrow on the Formatting toolbar to change the color to red.

The color of the WordArt object changes to red (Figure 6-54). Even though the title appears to be made up of text, the chart title is an object. Thus, you use the Fill Color button, rather than the Font Color button, to change the color of the object.

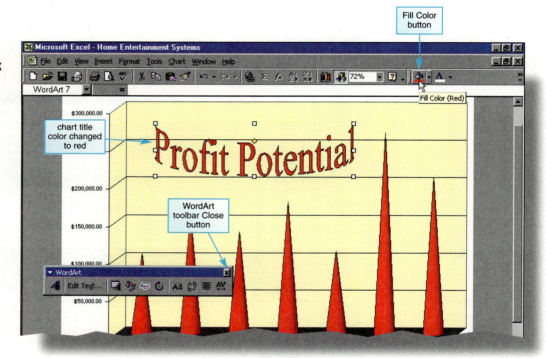

FIGURE 6-54

7 Click outside the chart area.

Excel hides the WordArt toolbar. The chart title is finished (Figure 6-55).

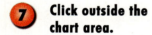

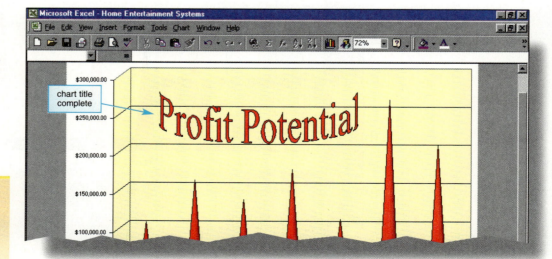

FIGURE 6-55

Other Ways

1. On Insert menu point to Picture, click WordArt on Picture submenu
2. Right-click toolbar, click WordArt, click Insert WordArt button

Once you add a WordArt object to your workbook, you can use the WordArt toolbar to edit it. The buttons on the WordArt toolbar and their functions are described in Table 6-8. Like the other Excel toolbars, you can display or hide the WordArt toolbar by right-clicking any toolbar and then clicking WordArt on the shortcut menu.

Adding a Text Box and Arrow to the Chart

A text box and arrow can be used to **annotate** (callout or highlight) other objects or elements in a worksheet or chart. For example, in a worksheet, you may want to annotate a particular cell or group of cells by adding a text box and arrow. In a chart, you may want to emphasize a column or slice of a Pie chart.

A **text box** is a rectangular area of variable size in which you can add text. You use the sizing handles to resize a text box in the same manner you resize an embedded chart. If the text box has the same color as the background, then the text appears as if it was written freehand because the box itself does not show. An **arrow** allows you to connect an object, such as a text box, to an item that you want to annotate.

To draw a text box, click the **Text Box button** on the Drawing toolbar. Move the cross hair to one corner of the desired location and drag to the diagonally opposite corner. Once the mouse pointer changes to a cross hair, you also can click the upper-left corner of the desired location and Excel will draw a box that you can resize later. To enter text within the box, click the box and begin typing.

To draw an arrow, click the **Arrow button** on the Drawing toolbar. Move the cross hair pointer to one end of the line you want to draw. Drag the mouse pointer to draw the line. The arrowhead appears at the end of the line where you released the mouse button.

The steps on the next page add the text box and arrow shown earlier in Figure 6-43 on page E 6.38.

Table 6-8	Buttons on the WordArt Toolbar	
BUTTON	NAME	FUNCTION
	Insert WordArt	Starts the WordArt tool
Edit Text...	Edit Text	Edits text
	WordArt Gallery	Displays the WordArt Gallery dialog box
	Format Object	Formats an object
Abc	WordArt Shape	Changes the shape of an object
	Free Rotate	Rotates an object
Aa	WordArt Same Letter Heights	Switches between the same and different letter height in an object
Ab b	WordArt Vertical Text	Changes the design from horizontal to vertical
	WordArt Alignment	Changes the alignment of an object
AV	WordArt Character Spacing	Changes the character spacing in an object

More About

Drawing Objects

To draw multiple objects, such as text boxes and arrows, double-click the corresponding button. The button will stay recessed, allowing you to draw more objects, until you click the corresponding button. If you need a series of identical objects, create one object, then use the Copy and Paste buttons.

Steps: To Add a Text Box and Arrow

1 **Click the Text Box button on the Drawing toolbar. Point to the upper-left corner of the planned text box location (Figure 6-56) and then drag the cross hair to the lower-right corner. Type** Greatest Profit Potential **as the text. Drag through the text. Right-click the text and then click Format Text Box. When the Format Text Box dialog box displays, change the font to 12-point red, bold. Click the OK button. If necessary, use the sizing handles to resize the text box.**

The text box displays as shown in Figure 6-56.

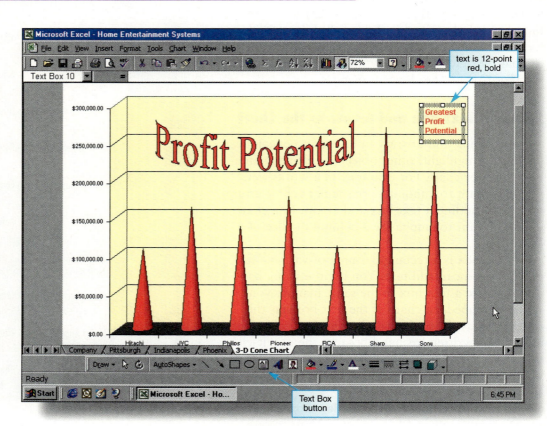

FIGURE 6-56

2 **Click the Arrow button on the Drawing toolbar. Point immediately to the left of the letter P in Profit in the text box. Drag to the cone representing Sharp. Release the mouse button.**

The arrow points to the cone representing Sharp (Figure 6-57).

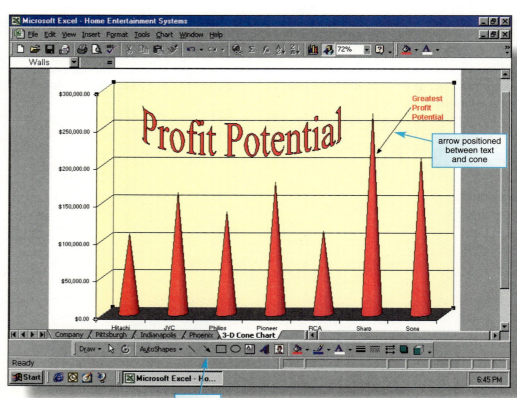

FIGURE 6-57

③ Click the Drawing button on the Standard toolbar to hide the Drawing toolbar.

The 3-D Cone chart is complete (Figure 6-58).

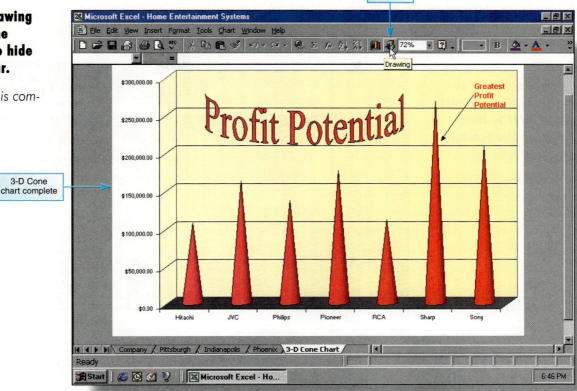

FIGURE 6-58

Besides text boxes, you can use the **AutoShapes button** on the Drawing toolbar to draw more eloquent callouts, such as flowchart symbols, stars and banners, and balloons that are similar to what is used to display words in a comic book.

Adding Comments to a Workbook

Comments, or **notes,** in a workbook are used to describe the function of a cell, a range of cells, a sheet, or the entire workbook. Comments are used to identify entries that might otherwise be difficult to understand.

In Excel, you can assign comments to any cell in the worksheet using the **Comment command** on the Insert menu or the **Insert Comment command** on the short-cut menu. Once a comment is assigned, you can read the comment by pointing to the cell. Excel will display the comment in a **comment box**. In general, overall workbook comments should include the following:

1. Worksheet title
2. Author's name
3. Date created
4. Date last modified (use N/A if it has not been modified)
5. Template(s) used, if any
6. A short description of the purpose of the worksheet

The steps on the next page assign a workbook comment to cell A14 on the Company sheet.

Steps To Assign a Comment to a Cell

1 **Click the Company tab to display the Company sheet. Right-click cell A14. Point to Insert Comment on the shortcut menu.**

The shortcut menu displays (Figure 6-59).

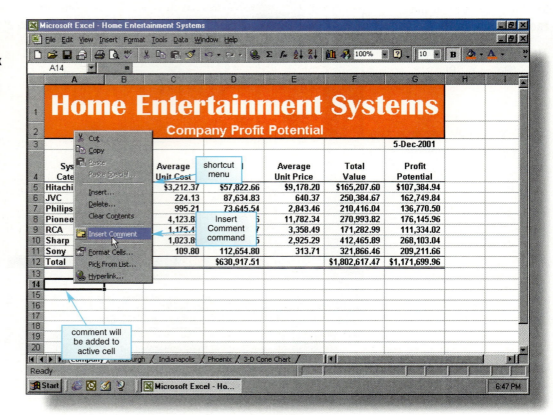

FIGURE 6-59

2 **Click Insert Comment. When the comment box displays, drag the lower-right handle to resize the comment box as shown in Figure 6-60.**

Excel adds a small red triangle, called a comment indicator, to cell A14. A small black arrow attached to the comment box points to the comment indicator (Figure 6-60).

3 **Enter the comment shown in Figure 6-60 in the comment box.**

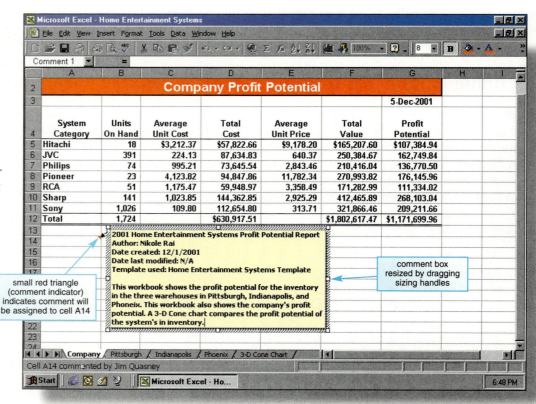

FIGURE 6-60

4 **Click cell A17 and then point to cell A14.**

The comment box displays (Figure 6-61).

5 **Click the Save button on the Standard toolbar to save the workbook.**

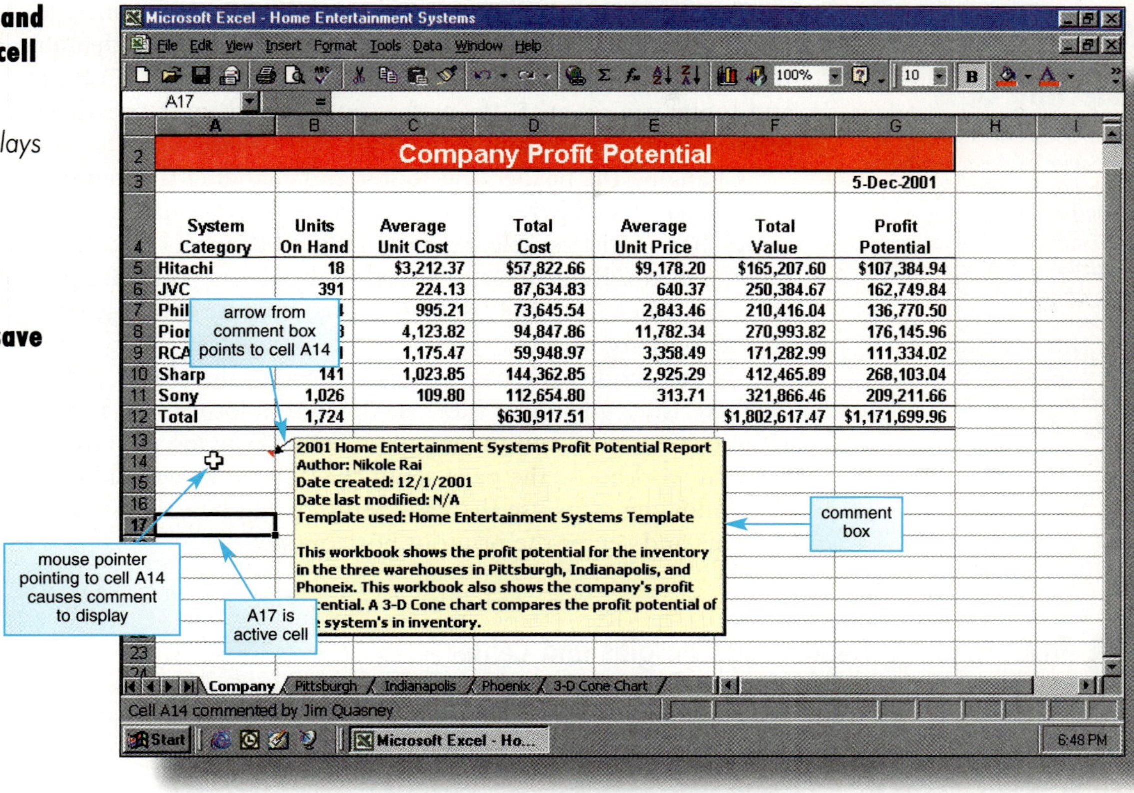

FIGURE 6-61

The **comment indicator** in the upper-right corner of cell A14 indicates the cell has a comment associated with it. To read the comment, point to the cell and the note will display on the worksheet. To edit the comment, right-click the cell and then click **Edit Comment** on the shortcut menu, or click the cell and then press SHIFT+F2. To delete the comment, right-click the cell and then click **Delete Comment** on the shortcut menu.

When working with comments, you have three options regarding their display on the worksheet:

1. **None** – do not display the comment indicator or comment
2. **Comment indicator only** – display the comment indicator, but not the comment unless you point to it
3. **Comment & indicator** – display both the comment indicator and comment at all times

You select one of the three by clicking Options on the Tools menu and making your selection in the Comments area in the View sheet. If you choose None, then the comment will not display when you point to the cell with the comment. Thus, it becomes a hidden comment.

Adding a Header and Changing the Margins

A **header** is printed at the top of every page in a printout. A **footer** is printed at the bottom of every page in a printout. By default, both the header and footer are blank. You can change either so information, such as the workbook author, date, page number, or tab name, prints at the top or bottom of each page.

Other Ways

1. On Insert menu click Comment
2. Press SHIFT+F2

More About 2000

Printing Comments

You can print comments assigned to cells as follows: click File on the menu bar, click Page Setup, in the Page Setup dialog box, click the Sheet tab, click the Comments box arrow, and then click where you want the comments printed in relation to the worksheet printout.

Selecting Cells

If you double-click the top of the heavy border surrounding the active cell, Excel will make the first empty cell below any non-blank cell in the column the active cell. If you double-click the left side of the heavy border surrounding the active cell, Excel will make the first empty cell to the right of any non-blank cell in the row the active cell.

Sometimes you will want to change the margins to increase or decrease the white space surrounding the printed worksheet or chart. The default **margins** in Excel are set to the following: Top = 1"; Bottom = 1"; Left = .75"; Right = .75". The header and footer are set at .5" from the top and bottom, respectively. You also can center a printout horizontally and vertically.

Changing the header and footer and changing the margins are all part of the **page setup**, which defines the appearance and format of a page. To change page setup characteristics, select the desired sheet(s) and click the **Page Setup command** on the File menu. Remember to select all the sheets you want to modify before you change the headers, footers, or margins, because the page setup characteristics will change only for selected sheets.

As you modify the page setup, remember that Excel does not copy page setup characteristics when one sheet is copied to another. Thus, even if you assigned page setup characteristics to the template before copying it to the Home Entertainment Systems workbook, the page setup characteristics would not copy to the new sheet. The following steps use the Page Setup dialog box to change the headers and margins and center the printout horizontally.

 ## To Change the Header and Margins and Center the Printout Horizontally

1 **If necessary, click the Company tab to make it active. While holding down the SHIFT key, click the 3-D Cone Chart tab. Click File on the menu bar and then point to Page Setup.**

Excel displays the File menu (Figure 6-62). The five sheet tabs at the bottom of the window are selected.

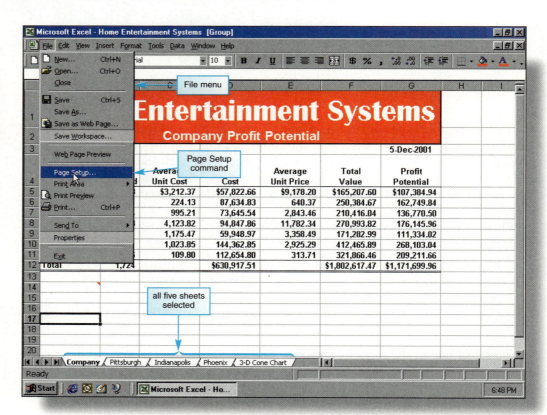

FIGURE 6-62

2 **Click Page Setup. When the Page Setup dialog box displays, click the Header/Footer tab. Point to the Custom Header button.**

Samples of the default header and footer display (Figure 6-63). The entry (none) indicates that the headers and footers are blank.

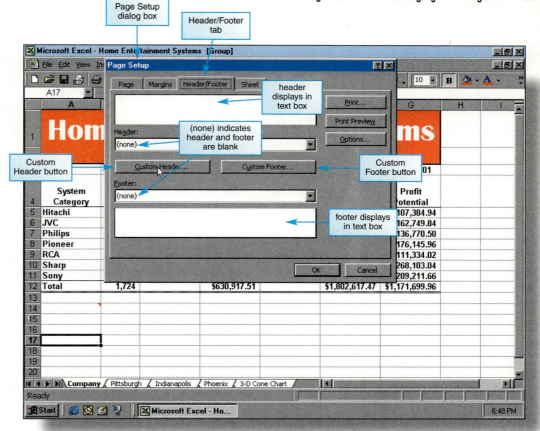

FIGURE 6-63

3 **Click the Custom Header button. When the Header dialog box displays, click the Left section text box. Type** Nikole Rai **and then press the ENTER key. Type** Profit Potential **and then click the Center section text box. Click the Sheet Name button. Click the Right section text box. Type** Page **followed by a space and then click the Page Number button. Type a space and then type** of **followed by a space. Click the Total Pages button. Point to the OK button in the Header dialog box.**

The Header dialog box displays with the new header (Figure 6-64).

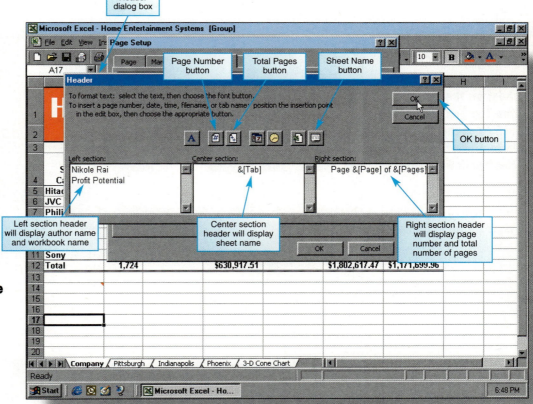

FIGURE 6-64

4 **Click the OK button.**

The Header/Footer sheet in the Page Setup dialog box displays as shown in Figure 6-65.

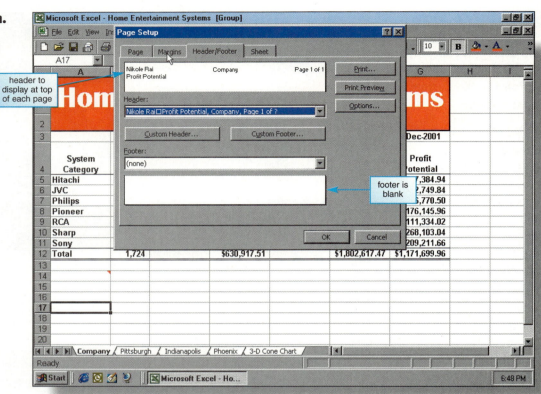

FIGURE 6-65

5 **Click the Margins tab. Click Horizontally in the Center on page area to center the worksheet on the page. Click the Top box and then type** 1.5 **to change the top margin to 1.5". Point to the Print Preview button.**

The Margins sheet in the Page Setup dialog box displays as shown in Figure 6-66.

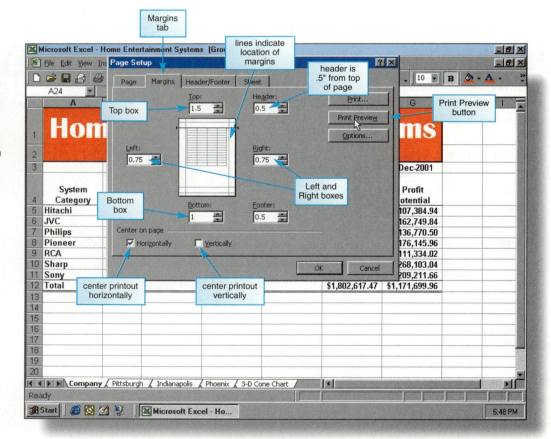

FIGURE 6-66

6 **Click the Print Preview button in the Page Setup dialog box to preview the workbook.**

The Company sheet displays as shown in Figure 6-67. Although difficult to read, the header displays at the top of the page. While the mouse pointer is a magnifying glass, you can click the page to get a better view.

7 **After previewing the printout, click the Close button on the Print Preview toolbar. Click the Save button on the Standard toolbar to save the workbook with the new page setup characteristics.**

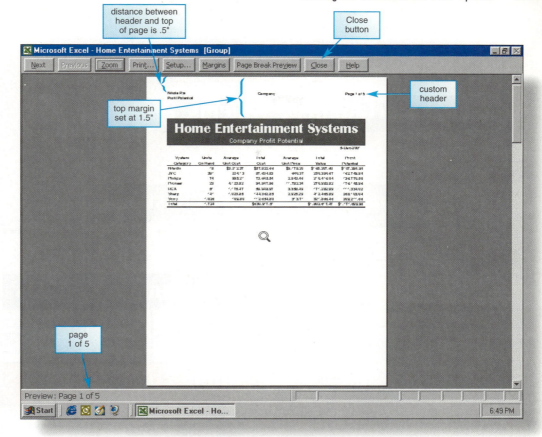

FIGURE 6-67

When you click a button in the Header dialog box (Figure 6-64 on page E 6.51), Excel enters a code (similar to a format code) into the active header section. A code such as &[Page] instructs Excel to insert the page number. Table 6-9 summarizes the buttons, their codes, and their functions in the Header or Footer dialog box.

1. Press ALT+F, press U

Printing the Workbook and Print Options

This section describes how to print the five-page workbook and then describes additional print options available in Excel. The following steps print the workbook.

TO PRINT THE WORKBOOK

1 Ready the printer.

2 If the five sheets in the workbook are not selected, click the Company tab and then, while holding down the SHIFT key, click the 3-D Cone tab.

3 Click the Print button on the Standard toolbar.

4 Hold down the SHIFT key and click the Company tab.

The workbook prints as shown in Figures 6-68a and 6-68b on the next page.

BUTTON	CODE	FUNCTION
A		Displays the Font dialog box
#	&[Page]	Inserts a page number
#	&[Pages]	Inserts a total number of pages
	&[Date]	Inserts the system date
	&[Time]	Inserts the system time
	&[File]	Inserts the file name of the workbook
	&[Tab]	Inserts the tab name

Table 6-9 Buttons in the Header Dialog Box

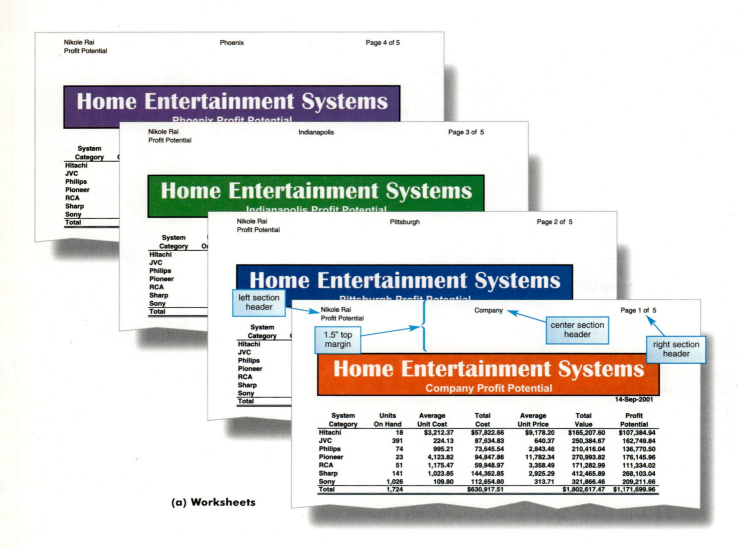

(a) Worksheets

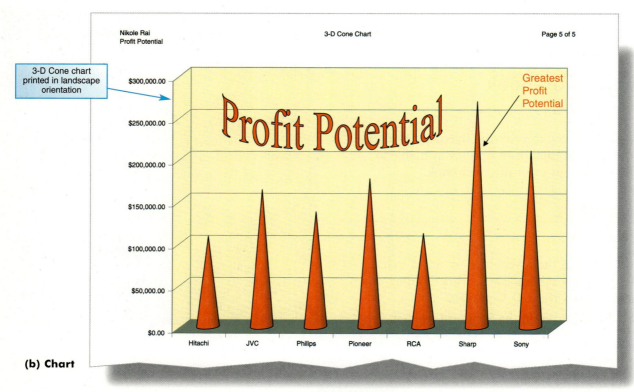

(b) Chart

FIGURE 6-68

Changing Sheet Settings

Up to this point you have been introduced to several different print options, such as changing the orientation, fit to option, changing the margin, adding a header and footer, and centering a worksheet on a page. This section describes additional print options available in the Sheet tab in the Page Setup dialog box (Figure 6-69). These print options pertain to the way the worksheet will appear in the printed copy.

Templates

Applying page setup characteristics to a template will not work because they are not part of the pasted worksheets. Thus, the page setup characteristics assigned to a template apply only to the first sheet in a workbook created by copying the template to multiple worksheets in the workbook.

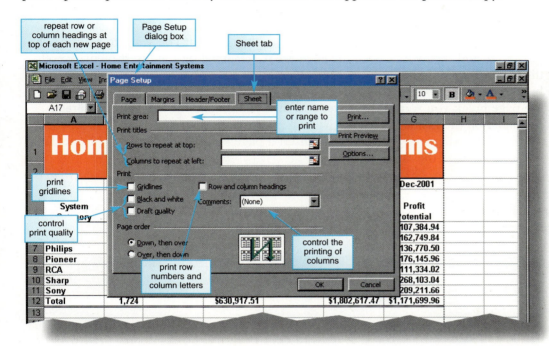

FIGURE 6-69

Table 6-10 summarizes the print options available on the Sheet tab.

Headers and Footers

You can turn off headers and footers for a printout by selecting (none) in the Header box and in the Footer box in the Header/Footer sheet in the Page Setup dialog box. This is true especially when printing charts for slides. If the 3-D Cone Chart (Figure 6-68) prints without the header, then you must select the 3-D Cone Chart sheet individually and add the header.

Table 6-10	Print Options Available Using the Sheet Tab
PRINT OPTION	**DESCRIPTION**
Print area text box	Excel prints from cell A1 to the last occupied cell in a worksheet unless you instruct it to print a selected area. You can select a range to print with the mouse or you can enter a range in the Print area text box. The range can be a name. Noncontiguous ranges will print on a separate page.
Print titles area	This area is used to print row titles and column titles on each page of a worksheet that exceeds a page. You must specify a range, even if you are designating one column (i.e., 1:4 means the first four rows).
Gridlines check box	This check box determines whether gridlines will print.
Black and white check box	A check mark in this check box speeds up printing and saves ink if you have colors in a worksheet and are not printing on a color printer.
Draft quality check box	A check mark in this check box speeds up printing by ignoring formatting and not printing most graphics.
Row and column headings check box	A check mark in this check box instructs Excel to include the column headings (A, B, C, etc.) a and row headings (1, 2, 3, etc.) in the printout.
Page order area	Determines the order in which multipage worksheets will print.

Printing

To speed up printing and save ink of worksheets with background colors, select the Black and White option in the Sheet tab in the Page Setup dialog box.

More About

Page Breaks

If the dotted line representing a page break does not display, click Tools on the menu bar, click Options, click the View tab, and click Page breaks in the Windows option area.

Page Breaks

You can insert page breaks in a worksheet at the top of any row to control how much of a worksheet prints on a page. This is especially useful if you have a worksheet that is several pages long and you want certain parts of the worksheet to print on separate pages. For example, if you had a worksheet comprised of ten departments in sequence and each department had many rows of information, and you wanted each department to begin on a new page, then inserting page breaks would satisfy the requirement.

To insert a page break, you select a cell in the row that you want to print on the next page and then you invoke the **Page Break command** on the Insert menu. Excel displays a dotted line to indicate the beginning of a new page. To remove a page break, you select a cell in the row immediately below the dotted line that indicates the page break you want to remove, and then you invoke the **Remove Page Break command** on the Insert menu.

The following steps show how to insert a page break between rows 11 and 12 and then remove the same page break.

 To Insert and Remove a Page Break

1 **Click cell A12. Click Insert on the menu bar and then point to Page break.**

The Insert menu displays (Figure 6-70).

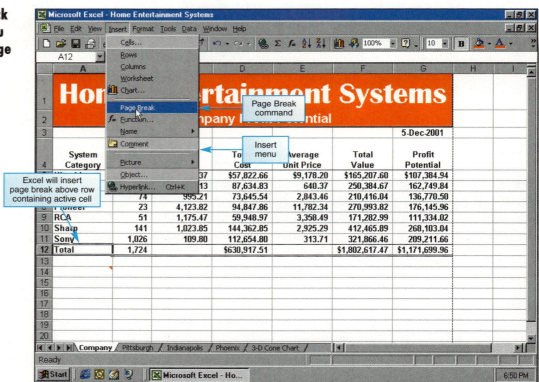

FIGURE 6-70

2 **Click Page Break.**

Excel draws a dotted line above row 12 indicating a page break (Figure 6-71).

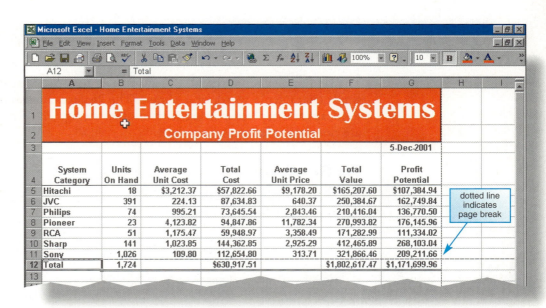

FIGURE 6-71

3 **If necessary, click cell A12. Click Insert on the menu bar and then point to Remove Page break.**

The Insert menu displays (Figure 6-72).

4 **Click Remove Page Break to remove the page break.**

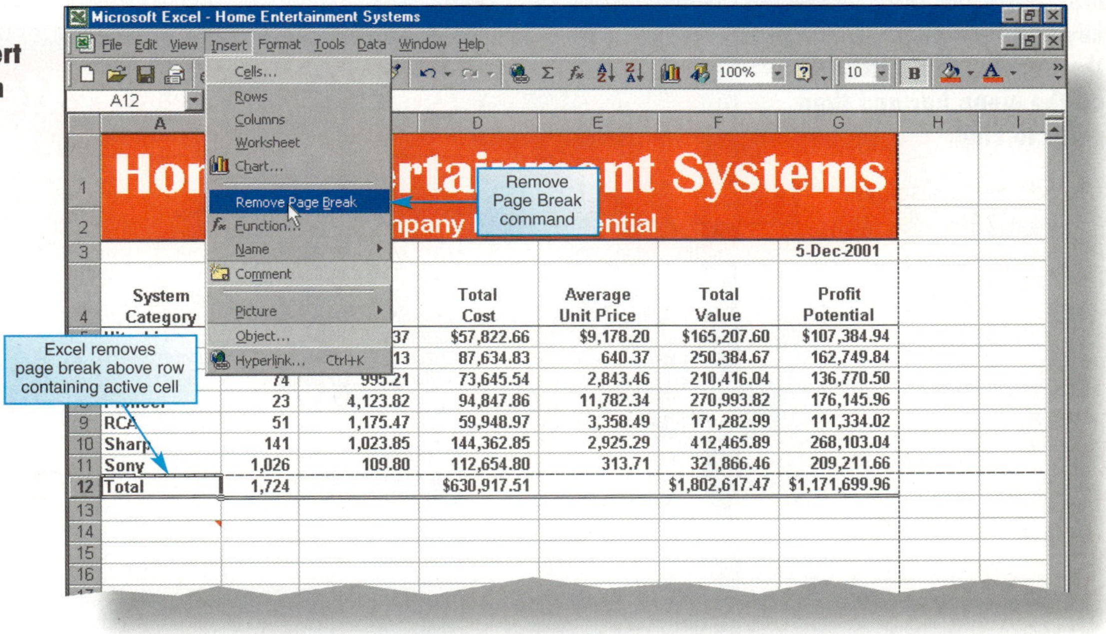

FIGURE 6-72

Other Ways

1. Press ALT+I, press B

You can select any cell in the row immediately below where you want a page break or where you want to remove a page break. You also can select the row heading. The Page Break command on the Insert menu changes to Remove Page Break when you select a cell immediately below a page break symbol.

An alternative to using the Page Break command on the Insert menu to insert page breaks is to click the Print Preview button on the Standard toolbar and then click the **Page Break Preview button**. Once the Page Break preview displays, you can drag the blue boundaries, which represent page breaks, to new locations.

The Find and Replace Commands

The **Find command** on the Edit menu is used to locate a string. A **string** can be a single character, a word, or a phrase. The **Replace command** on the Edit menu is used to locate and replace a string with another string. The Find and Replace commands are not available for a chart sheet.

The Find Command

The following steps show how to locate the string, Sony, in the four worksheets: Company, Pittsburgh, Indianapolis, and Phoenix.

 To Find a String

1 **With the Company sheet active, hold down the SHIFT key and then click the Phoenix tab. Click Edit on the menu bar and then point to Find.**

The Edit menu displays (Figure 6-73).

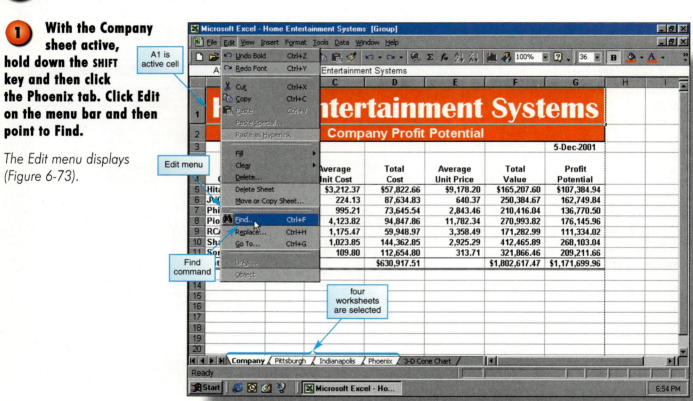

FIGURE 6-73

2 **When the Find dialog box displays, type** Sony **in the Find what text box. Click the Look in box arrow and then select Formulas. Click the Find Next button.**

Excel makes cell A11 the active cell (Figure 6-74). It is the first cell with the string, Sony, that Excel came across searching from the top by rows.

3 **Continue clicking the Find Next button to find the string, Sony, on the four selected sheets. Click the Close button to terminate the Find command. Hold down the** SHIFT **key and then click the Company tab to deselect the other worksheets.**

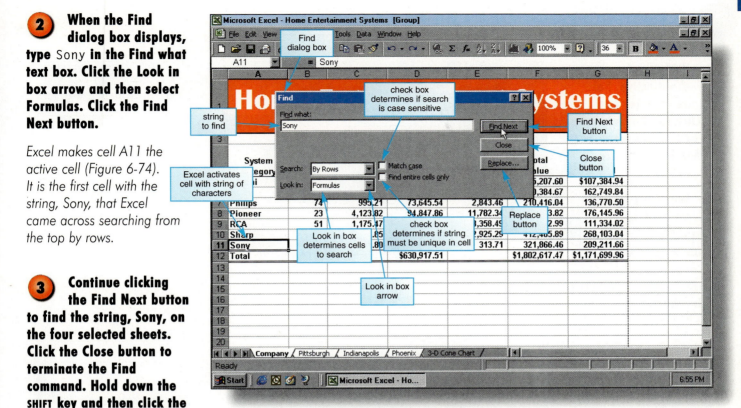

FIGURE 6-74

Other Ways

1. Press CTRL+F

The **Look in box** in the Find dialog box allows you to select Values, Formulas, or Comments. If you select **Values**, Excel will look only in cells that do not have formulas. If you select Formulas, Excel will look in all cells. If you select **Comments**, then it will look only in comments. If you place a check mark in the **Match case check box**, then Excel will stop only on cells that have the string in the same case. For example, sony is not the same as Sony. If you place a check mark in the Find entire cells only check box, then Excel will stop only on cells that have only the string and no other characters.

If the Find command does not find the string you are searching for, then it displays a dialog box indicating it has searched the selected worksheets without success.

The Replace Command

The **Replace command** is similar to the Find command, except that the search string is replaced by a new string. The steps on the next page show how to replace Sony with Sony ET.

More About

The Find Command

You can use the Look in box, Match case check box, and Find entire cells only check box in the Find dialog box to speed up searches, especially in a large worksheet.

To Replace a String with Another String

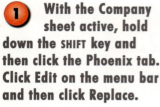 **1** **With the Company sheet active, hold down the SHIFT key and then click the Phoenix tab. Click Edit on the menu bar and then click Replace.**

2 **When the Replace dialog box displays, type** Sony **in the Find what text box and** Sony ET **in the Replace with text box. Click the Find Next button. Point to the Replace button.**

Excel makes cell A11 the active cell (Figure 6-75). It is the first cell with the string, Sony, that Excel came across searching from the top by rows.

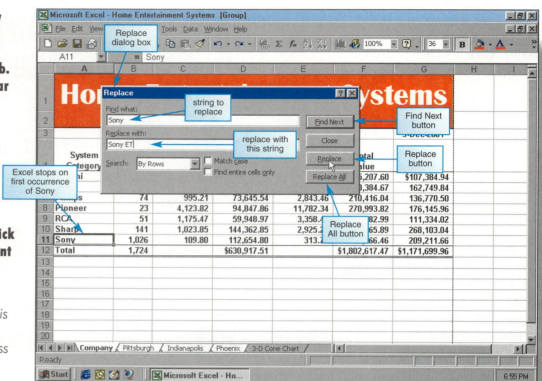

FIGURE 6-75

3 **Click the Replace button.**

Excel replaces the string, Sony, in cell A11 with Sony ET (Figure 6-76).

4 **Continue to click the Find Next button and Replace button to replace the string, Sony, with Sony ET in other cells in the selected worksheets. Click the Close button to terminate the Find command. Hold down the SHIFT key and then click the Company tab to deselect the other worksheets.**

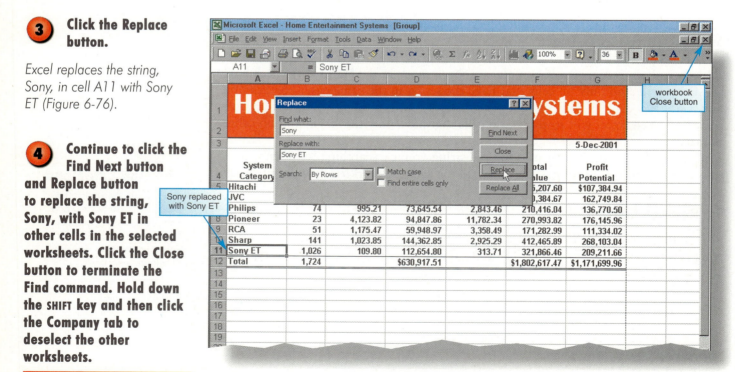

FIGURE 6-76

Other Ways

1. Press CTRL+H

The Replace dialog box also has a Replace All button. If you click the **Replace All button**, Excel immediately replaces all occurrences of Sony with Sony ET throughout the selected worksheets.

Closing the Workbook

The following steps close the Home Entertainment Systems workbook without saving changes.

TO CLOSE THE WORKBOK

1 Click the Close button on the right side of the workbook title bar (Figure 6-76).

2 When the Microsoft Excel dialog box displays, click the No button.

Excel closes the workbook without saving changes. Excel remains active.

Consolidating Data by Linking Workbooks

Earlier in this project, the data from three worksheets were consolidated onto another worksheet in the same workbook using 3-D references. An alternative to this method is to consolidate data from worksheets in other workbooks. Consolidating data from other workbooks also is referred to as **linking**. A **link** is a reference to a cell or range of cells in another workbook. In this case, the 3-D reference also includes a workbook name. For example, the following 3-D reference pertains to cell B5 on the Pittsburgh sheet in the workbook HES Pittsburgh PP located on drive A.

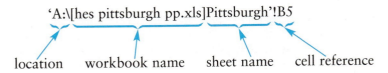

'A:\[hes pittsburgh pp.xls]Pittsburgh'!B5

location   workbook name   sheet name   cell reference

The single quotation marks surrounding the location, workbook name, and sheet name are required if any spaces are in any of the three names. If the workbook you are referring to is in the same folder as the active workbook, then the location (A:\) is not needed. The brackets surrounding the workbook name are required.

To illustrate linking cells between workbooks, the Company, Pittsburgh, Indianapolis, and Phoenix worksheets from the workbook created earlier in this project are on the Data Disk in separate workbooks as described in Table 6-11. In the workbook names in Table 6-11, the HES stands for Home Entertainment Systems and the PP stands for Profit Potential.

The steps on the next page show how to consolidate in the workbook HES Company PP the data in the Units on Hand column (column B) in the three store workbooks.

More *About*

Consolidation

Consolidate data across different workbooks using the Consolidate command on the Data menu. For more information, use the Office Assistant or Answer Wizard or click the Microsoft Excel Help button on the Standard toolbar, click the Index tab, and obtain information on the consolidating data topic.

Table 6-11 Workbook Names	
WORKSHEET IN HOME ENTERTAINMENT SYSTEMS	**SAVED USING THE WORKBOOK NAME**
Company	HES Company PP
Pittsburgh	HES Pittsburgh PP
Indianapolis	HES Indianapolis PP
Phoenix	HES Phoenix PP

Using a Workspace File

If you use a group of Workbooks together, such as in this section, you can save time opening them by creating a workspace file. A workspace file contains the workbook names and folder locations, their positions on the screen, and window sizes. Before you invoke the Save Workspace command on the File menu, open the workbooks you want in the workspace and activate the workbook you want active. Later, when you open the workspace file, it opens all the workbooks in the workspace and displays the one that was active when you created the workspace file.

TO CONSOLIDATE DATA BY LINKING WORKBOOKS

1 Open the workbooks HES Company PP, HES Pittsburgh PP, HES Indianapolis PP, and HES Phoenix PP.

2 Click Window on the menu bar and then click HES Company PP. Click cell B5. Click the AutoSum button on the Standard toolbar.

3 Click Window on the menu bar and then click HES Pittsburgh PP. Click cell B5. Delete the dollar signs ($) in the reference to cell B5 in the formula bar. Click immediately after B5 in the formula bar and then type , (comma).

4 Click Window on the menu bar and then click HES Indianapolis PP. Click cell B5. Delete the dollar signs ($) in the reference to cell B5 in the formula bar. Click immediately after B5 in the formula bar and then type , (comma).

5 Click Window on the menu bar, and then click HES Phoenix PP. Click cell B5. Delete the dollar signs ($) in the reference to cell B5 in the formula bar. Press the ENTER key.

6 With cell B5 active on the Company sheet in the HES Company PP workbook, drag the fill handle down to cell B11.

7 Click the Save button on the Standard toolbar. Click the Print button on the Standard toolbar.

The total units on hand at the three stores for each system category display in the range B5:B11 on the Company sheet in the HES Company PP workbook (Figure 6-77).

Quick Reference

For a table that lists how to complete the tasks covered in this book using the mouse, menu, shortcut menu, and keyboard, visit the Office 2000 Web page (www.scsite.com/office 2000/qr.htm), and then click Microsoft Excel 2000.

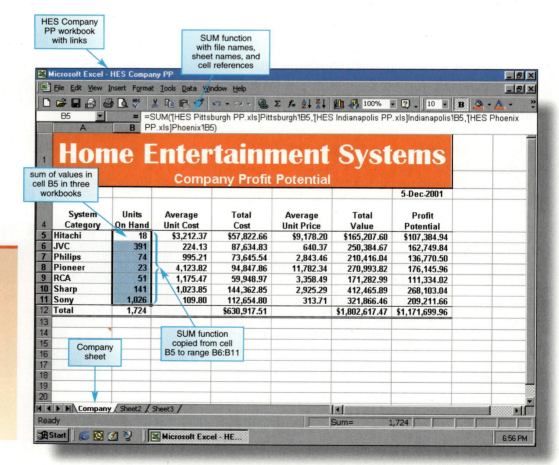

FIGURE 6-77

An alternative to opening all four workbooks and using Point mode, is to open the workbook HES Company PP and use the keyboard to enter the SUM function in cell B5 as shown in the formula bar in Figure 6-77.

It is necessary that you remember these two important points about this SUM function. First, as you build the SUM function for cell B5, the cell reference inserted by Excel each time you click a cell in a workbook is an absolute cell reference ($B$5). You must go into the formula and change these to relative cell references because the SUM function later is copied to the range B6:B11 in Step 6. If the cell references are left as absolute, then the copied function always would refer to cell B5 in the three workbooks no matter where you copy the SUM function. Second, because the three cells being summed in this example are not adjacent to one another, the cell references must be separated by commas in the SUM function.

Updating Links

Later, when you open the HES Company PP workbook, also called the **dependent workbook**, Excel will ask you whether you want to update the links. The linked workbooks are called the **source workbooks**. If the three source workbooks also are open, then Excel will update the links (recalculate) automatically in the HES Company PP workbook when a value is changed in any one of the source workbooks. If the source workbooks are not open, then Excel will display a dialog box that will give you the option to update the links. In the latter case, Excel reads the data in the source workbooks on disk and recalculates formulas in the dependent workbook, but it does not open the source workbooks.

You also can use the Links command on the Edit menu to update the links at any time. For example, with the dependent workbook HES Company PP open, you can invoke the **Links command** on the Edit menu to recalculate, open a source workbook, or change the source workbook. The Links dialog box also displays the names of all the linked workbooks (Figure 6-78).

More About

Microsoft Certification

The Microsoft Office User Specialist (MOUS) Certification program provides an opportunity for you to obtain a valuable industry credential - proof that you have the Excel 2000 skills required by employers. For more information, see Appendix D or visit the Shelly Cashman Series MOUS Web page at www.scsite.com/off2000/cert.htm.

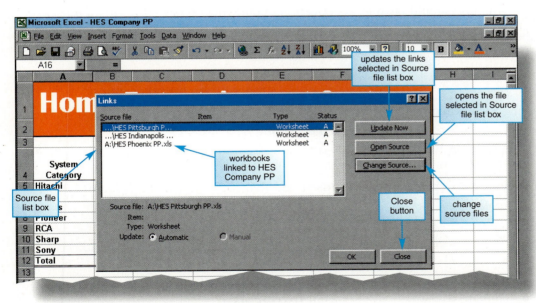

FIGURE 6-78

Quitting Excel

To quit Excel, complete the steps on the next page.

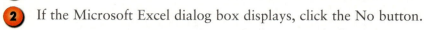
TO QUIT EXCEL

1 Click the Close button on the right side of the title bar.

2 If the Microsoft Excel dialog box displays, click the No button.

CASE PERSPECTIVE SUMMARY

Santiago Biagi, president and CEO of Home Entertainment Systems, is sure to be pleased with many aspects of the workbook developed in this project. The use of multiple sheets, for example, allows for better organization of the data, while the 3-D Cone chart makes it easy to pinpoint the system category with the greatest profit potential. This workbook should answer any due diligence questions put forth by the buyout candidate. Perhaps the best aspect of the way the workbook is used, however, is the use of the template: even if the buyout does not work out, Santiago can use the template in the future to add additional stores to the existing workbook or create new, similar workbooks.

Project Summary

This project introduced you to creating and using a template, customizing formats, creating styles, changing chart types, drawing and enhancing a 3-D Cone chart using WordArt, and annotating using text boxes and arrows. You also learned how to reference cells in other sheets and add comments to a cell. To enhance a print-out, you learned how to add a header and footer and to change margins. Finally, you learned how to customize a printout, add and remove page breaks, use the Find and Replace commands, and link cell entries from external workbooks.

What You Should Know

Having completed this project, you now should be able to perform the following tasks:

▶ Add a Chart Title Using the WordArt Tool (E 6.40)
▶ Add a Text Box and Arrow (E 6.46)
▶ Apply a Style (E 6.25)
▶ Assign a Comment to a Cell (E 6.48)
▶ Assign a Currency Style Using the Format Dialog Box (E 6.18)
▶ Bold the Font and Change the Column Widths in the Template (E 6.8)
▶ Change the Header and Margins and Center the Printout Horizontally (E 6.50)
▶ Close the Workbook (E 6.61)
▶ Consolidate Data by Linking Workbooks (E 6.62)
▶ Create a Custom Format Code (E 6.21)
▶ Create a New Style (E 6.23)
▶ Create a Workbook from a Template (E 6.28)
▶ Draw a 3-D Cone Chart (E 6.39)
▶ Drill an Entry through Worksheets (E 6.30)
▶ Enter and Copy 3-D References (E 6.35)
▶ Enter Column Titles and the System Date in the Template (E 6.8)

▶ Enter Dummy Data in the Template Using the Fill Handle (E 6.9)
▶ Enter the Formulas Using Point Mode and Determine Totals in the Template (E 6.12)
▶ Enter the Template Title and Row Titles (E 6.8)
▶ Find a String (E 6.58)
▶ Format the Column Titles and Total Line (E 6.18)
▶ Format the Template Title (E 6.17)
▶ Insert and Remove a Page Break (E 6.56)
▶ Modify the Indianapolis Sheet (E 6.32)
▶ Modify the Phoenix Sheet (E 6.33)
▶ Modify the Pittsburgh Sheet (E 6.31)
▶ Open a Template and Add a Worksheet (E 6.27)
▶ Print the Workbook (E 6.53)
▶ Quit Excel (E 6.64)
▶ Rename a Sheet and Modify the Worksheet Title (E 6.34)
▶ Replace a String with Another String (E 6.60)
▶ Save a Template (E 6.15)
▶ Spell Check, Save, and Print the Template (E 6.26)
▶ Start Excel (E 6.6)

Apply Your Knowledge

✚ Project Reinforcement at www.scsite.com/off2000/reinforce.htm

1 Consolidating Data in a Workbook

Instructions Part 1: Follow the steps below to consolidate the four quarterly sheets on the Annual Totals sheet in the workbook Annual Payroll. The Annual Totals sheet should display as shown in the lower screen in Figure 6-79.

1. Open the workbook Annual Payroll from the Data Disk. If you do not have a copy of the Data Disk, see the inside back cover of this book.

2. One by one, click the first four tabs and review the quarterly totals. Click the Annual Totals tab.

3. Determine the annual totals by using the SUM function and 3-D references to sum the hours worked and gross pay for each employee. If necessary, use the Format Painter button to copy the format of cell C23 to cell B23 to redisplay the underline in cell B23.

4. Save the workbook using the file name Annual Totals 1.

5. Add a header that includes your name and course number in the Left section, the computer laboratory exercise number (Apply 6-1) in the Center section, and the system date and your instructor's name in the Right section. Add the page number and total number of pages to the footer.

6. Select all five sheets. Use the Page Setup command to center all worksheets on the page and print gridlines. Preview and print the five worksheets. Hold down the SHIFT key and then click the Annual Totals tab to select the sheet. Save the workbook with the new page setup using the same file name as in Step 4.

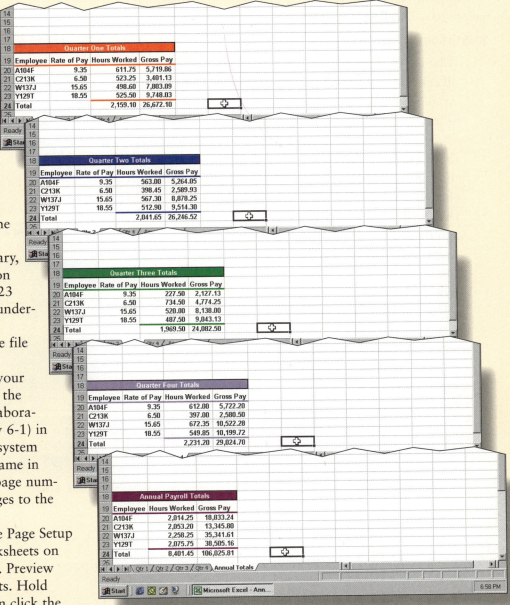

FIGURE 6-79

Instructions Part 2: Open the workbook Annual Payroll from the Data Disk. Save each of the five sheets as separate workbooks using the tab names as the file names. Close all workbooks. Open the Annual Totals workbook. Use 3-D references from the four quarterly workbooks to determine totals on the Annual Totals workbook. Print the Annual Totals workbook.

In the Lab

1 Designing a Template for Swing Productions

Problem: For the first month of your work-study program, you have been answering the telephone at the main office of Swing Productions. Your immediate supervisor knows your real specialty is designing workbooks and wants to utilize your Excel skills. She has asked you to create a template for the management to use when they create new Excel workbooks (Figure 6-80).

Instructions: Start Excel and perform the following steps to create a template.

1. Change the font of all cells to 12-point Arial bold. Increase all row heights to 18.00. (*Hint:* Click the Select All button to make these changes.)

2. Use the Style command on the Format menu to create the format style called Comma (4) as shown in Figure 6-80. Display the Comma style, change the name in the Style name box from Comma to Comma (4), and use the Modify button to change the decimal places to 4 and the font to Arial 12, Bold.

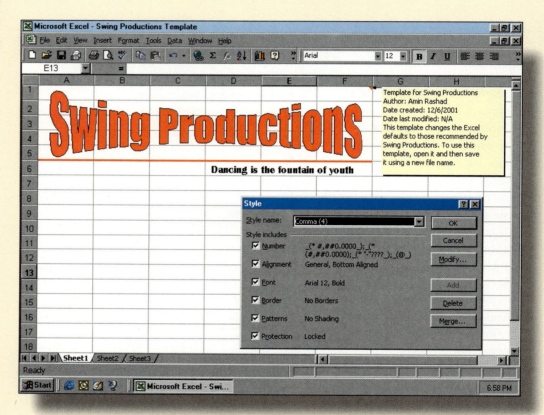

FIGURE 6-80

3. Add a comment to cell F1 to identify the template and its purpose, as shown in Figure 6-80. Include your name as the author.

4. Use WordArt to create the title shown in the range A1:F5. Use the style in column 4, row 1 of the WordArt Gallery dialog box. Change the color of the title to red. Draw a thick red bottom border across the range A5:F5. Add the subtitle in cell D6. Change its font style to Britannic Bold.

5. Enter your name, course, computer laboratory assignment (Lab 6-1), date, time, and instructor's name as the header. Add a page number as the footer.

6. Use the Save As command to save the template, selecting Template in the Save as type list. Save the template using the file name Swing Productions Template.

In the Lab

7. Print the template and comment. To print the comment, click the Sheet tab in the Page Setup dialog box. Click the Comments box arrow and then click At end of sheet. The comment will print on a separate sheet. After the comment prints, deselect printing the comment by clicking the Comment box arrow in the Sheet tab in the Page Setup dialog box and then clicking (None).

8. Close the template and then reopen it. Save the template as a regular workbook using the file name Swing Productions. Close the workbook.

2 Using a Template to Create a Multiple-Sheet Workbook

Problem: Custom Fragrances is a mail-order company that specializes in unique bath oils and perfumes. The company has outlets in three cities — Baltimore, Columbus, and Portland — and a corporate office in Houston. All of the outlets sell their products via the Web, telephone, mail, and walk-in. Every year, the corporate officers in Houston use a template to create a year-end sales analysis workbook. The workbook contains four sheets, one for each of the three outlets and one for the company totals. The Company Totals sheet displays as shown in Figure 6-81.

The template is on the Data Disk. Mr. Malone, the company's chief financial officer (CFO), has asked you to use the template to create the year-end sales analysis workbook.

Instructions Part 1: Perform the following tasks.

1. Open the template, Custom Fragrances Template, from the Data Disk. Add a worksheet to the workbook and then paste the template to the three empty sheets. Save the workbook using the file name Custom Fragrances. Make sure Microsoft Excel Workbook is selected in the Save as type list.

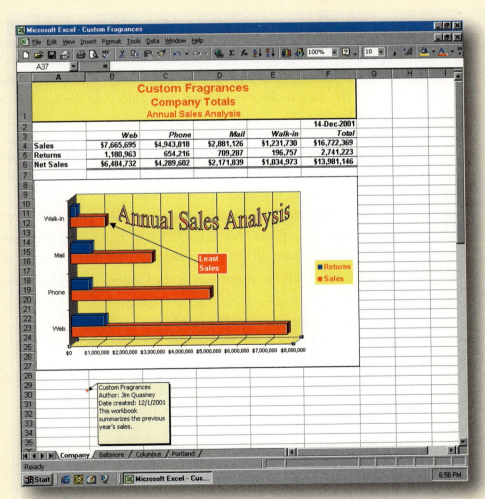

FIGURE 6-81

(continued)

In the Lab

Using a Template to Create a Multiple-Sheet Workbook *(continued)*

2. From left to right, rename the sheet tabs Company, Baltimore, Columbus, and Portland. Enter the data in Table 6-12 onto the three city sheets. On each sheet, change the subtitle in cell A2 to reflect the city. Choose a different background color for each sheet.

3. On the Company sheet, use the SUM function, 3-D references, and the fill handle to total the corresponding cells on the three city sheets. First, compute the sum in cell B4 and then compute the sum in cell B5. Copy the range B4:B5 to the range C4:E5. The Company sheet should resemble the top of Figure 6-81. Save the workbook.

Table 6-12	Custom Fragrances Sales Data			
		BALTIMORE	COLUMBUS	PORTLAND
Web	Sales	2,546,120	3,189,732	1,929,843
	Returns	396,362	572,001	212,600
Phone	Sales	1,732,918	2,381,900	829,000
	Returns	356,821	195,610	101,785
Mail	Sales	987,502	1,328,712	564,912
	Returns	200,675	396,897	111,715
Walk-in	Sales	356,810	578,420	296,500
	Returns	48,349	76,198	72,210

4. Create an embedded Clustered bar chart with a 3-D visual effect in the range A8:F27 on the Company sheet. Chart the range A3:E5 on the Company sheet. Do not include a chart title. If necessary, reduce the font size of the labels on both axes to 8 point. Use the chart colors shown in Figure 6-81. Use the WordArt button on the Drawing toolbar to add the chart title. Add the text box and arrow as shown in Figure 6-81. Save the workbook.

5. Select all four sheets. Change the header to include your name, course, computer laboratory exercise (Lab 6-2), date, and instructor's name. Change the footer to include the page number and total pages. Add the comment shown in cell A30. Preview and then print the entire workbook, including the comment. Save the workbook with the new page setup characteristics.

Instructions Part 2: The following corrections were sent in: (a) Baltimore Walk-in Sales 425,190; (b) Columbus Web Returns 225,115; (c) Portland Mail Sales 725,300. Enter these corrections. The Company Total Net Sales should equal $14,556,800. Print all the worksheets. Do not print the comment.

Instructions Part 3: Select all the worksheets in the Custom Fragrances workbook and do the following:

1. Select cell A1 on the Company sheet. Use the Find command to locate all occurrences of the word Sales. You should find 12 occurrences of the word Sales.

2. Click Find entire cells only in the Find dialog box. Use the Find command to find all occurrences of the word Sales. You should find three occurrences.

3. Use the Replace command to replace the word Web with the acronym WWW on all four sheets. Print all four sheets. Do not save the workbook.

In the Lab

3 Returning Real-Time Stock Quotes to the High-Tech Stock Portfolio Worksheet

Problem: You have been investing in the stock market for the past few years and you maintain a summary of your stock market investments in an Excel workbook (Figure 6-82a). Each day you go through the Business section of the newspaper and manually update the current prices in column G to determine the value of your equities. You recently heard about the Web query capabilities of Excel and have decided to use them to update your stock portfolio automatically.

Instructions: Perform the steps on the next page to have Web queries automatically update the current price in column G and the major indices in the range B12:B15 of Figure 6-82a.

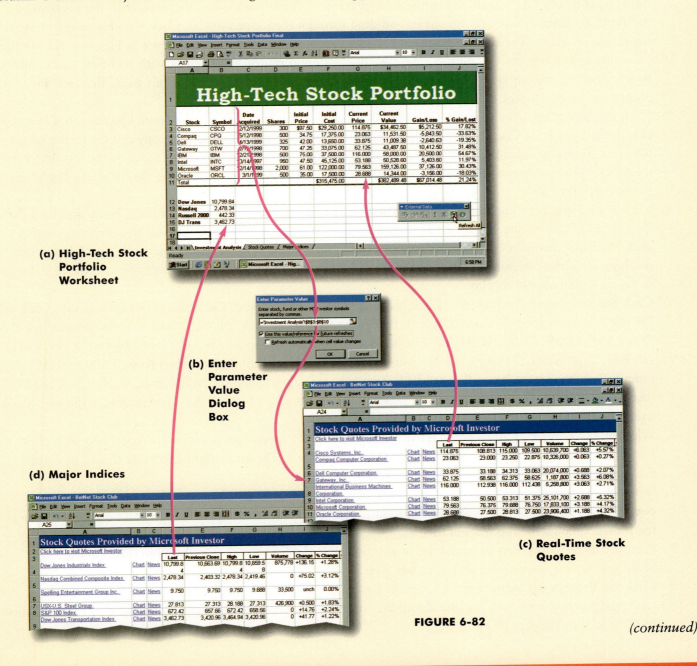

(a) High-Tech Stock Portfolio Worksheet

(b) Enter Parameter Value Dialog Box

(d) Major Indices

(c) Real-Time Stock Quotes

FIGURE 6-82

(continued)

In the Lab

Returning Real-Time Stock Quotes to the High-Tech Stock Portfolio Worksheet *(continued)*

1. Start Excel and open the workbook High-Tech Stock Portfolio on the Data Disk. If you do not have a copy of the Data Disk, see the inside back cover of this book. After reviewing the High-Tech Stock Portfolio worksheet on your screen, you should notice that it lacks current prices in column G and the major indices in the range B12:B15.

2. Click Sheet2 and then click cell A1. Click Data on the menu bar, point to Get External Data, and then click Run Saved Query on the Get External Data submenu. When the Run Query dialog box displays, double-click Microsoft Investor Stock Quotes. When the Returning External Data to Microsoft Excel dialog box displays, click the OK button. When the Enter Parameter Value dialog box displays, click the Investment Analysis tab at the bottom of the screen and drag through the range B3:B10. Click Use this value/reference for future refreshes. The Enter Parameter Value dialog box should display as shown in Figure 6-82b on the previous page. Click the OK button. The Web query should return a worksheet with real-time stock quotes to the Stock Quotes sheet similar to the one shown in Figure 6-82c on the previous page. Rename the Sheet2 tab Stock Quotes.

3. Click the Investment Analysis tab. Click cell G3. Type = (equal sign). Click the Stock Quotes tab. Click cell D4 (the last price for Cisco Systems). Press the ENTER key. Use the fill handle to copy cell G3 to the range G4:G10. You now should have current prices for the stock portfolio that are the same as the last prices on the Stock Quotes sheet in column D. Click cell A17 and save the workbook using the file name High-Tech Stock Portfolio Final.

4. Click Sheet3 and then click cell A1. Click Data on the menu bar, point to Get External Data, and then click Run Saved Query on the Get External Data submenu. When the Run Query dialog box displays, double-click Microsoft Investor Major Indices. When the Returning External Data to Microsoft Excel dialog box displays, click the OK button. Rename the Sheet3 tab Major Indices. A worksheet similar to the one shown in Figure 6-82d should display.

5. Click the Investment Analysis tab. Click cell B12. Type = (equal sign). Click the Major Indices tab. Click cell D4 (the last Dow Jones Industrial Index). Press the ENTER key. Click cell B13. Type = (equal sign). Click the Major Indices tab. Click cell D5 (the last Nasdaq Combined Composite Index). Press the ENTER key. Click cell B14. Type = (equal sign). Click the Major Indices tab. Click cell D10 (the last Russell 2000 Stock Index). Press the ENTER key. Click cell B15. Type = (equal sign). Click the Major Indices tab. Click cell D9 (the last Dow Jones Transportation Index). Press the ENTER key. Click cell A17 and then save the workbook using the file name High-Tech Stock Portfolio Final.

6. With the Investment Analysis sheet active, click View on the menu bar, point to Toolbars, and then click External Data. If necessary, drag the External Data toolbar to the lower-right corner as shown in Figure 6-82a.

7. Select all three worksheets. Use the Page Setup command on the File menu to enter your name, course, computer laboratory assignment (Lab 6-3), date, and instructor name as the header. Add a page number as the footer. Change the top margin to 1.5".

8. Print the three worksheets in landscape orientation. Use the Fit to option in the Page sheet on the Page Setup dialog box to print the sheets on one page.

9. Click the Refresh All button on the External Data toolbar (Figure 6-82a). Print the three worksheets.

10. Click the Stock Quotes tab. Use the Zoom box on the Standard toolbar to shrink the view of the worksheet to 65% so it displays in its entirety.

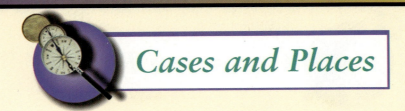

Cases and Places

The difficulty of these case studies varies:
◗ are the least difficult; ◗◗ are more difficult; and ◗◗◗ are the most difficult.

1 ◗ Holly Volley, assistant tennis coach, has jotted down notes on three players (Table 6-13) based on a recent match. Make a template that Coach Volley can use to evaluate her players. Include each statistic, the percentage of winners (winner/total shots), the percentage of errors (errors/total shots), and what Coach Volley calls the "success rate" (percentage of winners − percentage of errors). Use the template to develop a worksheet for each player. Summarize the results on a Team worksheet. Compute the percents on the Team worksheet in a manner similar to the player's worksheets.

Table 6-13 Summary Notes on Players			
ROB RALLY	TOTAL SHOTS	WINNERS	ERRORS
Forehand	192	42	25
Backhand	192	34	26
Volley	15	0	8
Service	98	17	5
Service Return	118	29	17
LORI LOVE	TOTAL SHOTS	WINNERS	ERRORS
Forehand	238	74	62
Backhand	156	65	23
Volley	36	18	3
Service	114	21	0
Service Return	108	60	9
FREDDIE FOREHAND	TOTAL SHOTS	WINNERS	ERRORS
Forehand	198	37	13
Backhand	168	24	39
Volley	102	84	3
Service	72	33	6
Service Return	108	40	46

2 ◗ Stylish Weddings, Inc. has been a successful full-service wedding planning company for 25 years in Chicago, Illinois. After launching its Web site three years ago, the company has attracted so many clients from Europe that the owners opened a shop in Paris. The Chicago and Paris shops' assets last year, respectively, were: cash $317,325 and $132,650; accounts receivable $107,125 and $74,975; marketable securities $196,425 and $76,250; inventory $350,395 and $175,750; and equipment $25,000 and $17,500. The liabilities for each store were: notes payable $28,300 and $26,000; accounts payable $78,450 and $80,125; and income tax payable $62,000 and $20,000. The stockholders' equity was: common stock $731,170 and $268,375 and retained earnings $96,350 and $82,625. Design a template as a balance sheet to reflect the figures above. Include totals for current assets, total assets, current liabilities, total liabilities, total stockholders' equity, and liabilities and stockholders' equity. Use the template to create a balance sheet for each store and consolidated balance sheet for the corporation.

Cases and Places

3 ▶ Progressive Programs sells computer software and supplies. Merchandise is divided into six categories based on profit margin: individual application packages (22%), integrated application packages (9%), entertainment software (16%), system software (25%), learning aids (18%), and supplies (10%). Last year's sales data has been collected for the Harlem Street Store and Zapata Avenue Store as shown in Table 6-14.

Table 6-14 Last Year's Sales for Harlem Street and Zapata Avenue Stores		
	HARLEM STREET STORE	ZAPATA AVENUE STORE
Individual applications	$48,812	$42, 864
Integrated applications	40,135	63, 182
Entertainment software	52, 912	52, 345
System software	12, 769	15, 278
Learning aids	8, 562	11, 397
Supplies	34, 215	24, 921

Develop a template that can be used to determine marketing strategies for next year. Include sales, profit margins, profits (sales x profit margin), total sales, total profits, and functions to determine the most and least sales, profit margins, and profits. Use the template to create a worksheet for each store, a consolidated worksheet for the entire company, and a chart on a separate sheet reflecting the company's profits by category.

4 ▶▶ Gifts for Any Occasion has noticed a sharp increase in business since it started a Web site that allows people to order gifts over the Internet. The Company also started a free gift information service on the Web that has contributed to an additional increase in sales. The owner of Gifts for Any Occasion needs a worksheet representation of the business increases based on the data in Table 6-15. Create a

Table 6-15 Gifts for Any Occasion Sales				
	QTR	CONSUMABLE	NON-CONSUMABLE	OUT OF STATE
2001	1	82,345.25	56,924.65	0
	2	108,540.00	78,213.50	1
	3	113,956.20	82,130.75	0
	4	203,725.80	98,320.60	2
2002	1	412,500.45	303,750.40	27
	2	435,210.75	268,921.50	96
	3	508,383.70	315,245.90	224
	4	723,912.20	375,835.70	309

worksheet for each year and one for the totals, adding a column for quarter totals and a row for item totals. Include the percentage of annual growth (2002 – 2001) / 2001 on the Company Totals worksheet. Add an embedded 3-D Pie chart to the Company Totals worksheet that shows the sales contribution of each quarter to the two-year sales total.

Microsoft Excel 2000

Linking an Excel Worksheet to a Word Document

C A S E   P E R S P E C T I V E

Each month, the director of sales for Home Networks, Inc., LaShondra West, sends out a memorandum to all the regional sales managers in the organization showing the previous month's sales by office. She currently uses Word to produce the memorandum that includes a table of the monthly sales. The wording in the memorandum remains constant month to month. The data in the table changes each month.

LaShondra recently heard of the Object Linking and Embedding (OLE) capabilities of Microsoft Office 2000 and wants to use them to create the basic memorandum (Figure 1a on the next page) using Word and maintain the monthly sales on an Excel worksheet (Figure 1b). Each month, she envisions sending out the Word document with the updated worksheet (Figure 1c). Once the link is established, she can update the worksheet each month, modify the date in the memorandum, and then print and distribute the memorandum to the regional sales managers.

As LaShondra's technical assistant, she has asked you to handle the details of linking the Excel worksheet to the memorandum.

Introduction

With Microsoft 2000, you can incorporate parts of documents or entire documents, called **objects**, from one application into another application. For example, you can copy a worksheet created in Excel into a document created in Word. In this case, the worksheet in Excel is called the **source document** (copied from) and the document in Word is called the **destination document** (copied to). Copying objects between applications can be accomplished in three ways: (1) copy and paste; (2) copy and embed; and (3) copy and link.

All of the Microsoft Office applications allow you to use these three methods to copy objects between applications. The first method uses the Copy and Paste buttons. The latter two use the Paste Special command on the Edit menu and are referred to as **Object Linking and Embedding**, or **OLE**. Table 1 on page EI 1.3 summarizes the differences among the three methods.

You would use copy and link over the other two methods when an object is likely to change and you want to make sure the object reflects the changes in the source document or if the object is large, such as a video clip or sound clip. Thus, if you link a portion or all of a worksheet to a memorandum, and update the worksheet monthly in Excel, any time you open the memorandum in Word, the latest updates of the worksheet will display as part of the memorandum (Figure 1 on the next page).

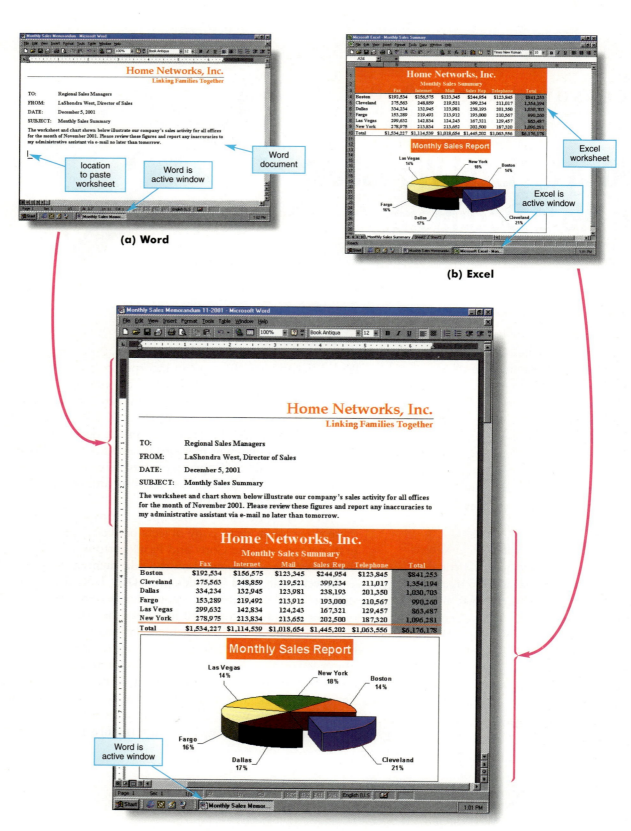

(a) Word

(b) Excel

(c) Word Document and Linked Excel Worksheet

FIGURE 1

Table 1   Three Methods of Copying Objects Between Applications

METHOD	CHARACTERISTICS
Copy and paste	Source document becomes part of the destination document. Object may be edited, but the editing features are limited to those in the destination application. An Excel worksheet becomes a Word table. If changes are made to values in the Word table, any original Excel formulas are not recalculated.
Copy and embed	Source document becomes part of the destination document. Object may be edited in the destination application using source editing features. Excel worksheet remains a worksheet in Word. If changes are made to values in the worksheet with Word active, Excel formulas will be recalculated, but the changes are not updated in the Excel worksheet in the workbook on disk. If you use Excel to change values in the worksheet, the changes will not show in the Word document the next time you open it.
Copy and link	Source document does not become part of the destination document even though it appears to be part of it. Rather, a link is established between the two documents so that when you open the Word document, the worksheet displays as part of it. When you attempt to edit a linked worksheet in Word, the system activates Excel. If you change the worksheet in Excel, the changes will show in the Word document the next time you open it.

Opening a Word Document and an Excel Workbook

Both the Word document (Monthly Sales Memorandum.doc) and the Excel workbook (Monthly Sales Summary.xls) are on the Data Disk. If you do not have a copy of the Data Disk, see the inside back cover of this book. The first step in linking the Excel worksheet to the Word document is to open both the document in Word and the workbook in Excel as shown in the following steps.

Steps **To Open a Word Document and an Excel Workbook**

1 **Insert the Data Disk in drive A. Click the Start button on the taskbar and then click Open Office document on the Start menu. When the Open Office Document dialog displays, click 3½ Floppy (A:) in the Look in box. Select the Excel folder. Double-click the Word file name, Monthly Sales Memorandum.**

Word becomes active and the Monthly Sales Memorandum displays in Normal View (Figure 2).

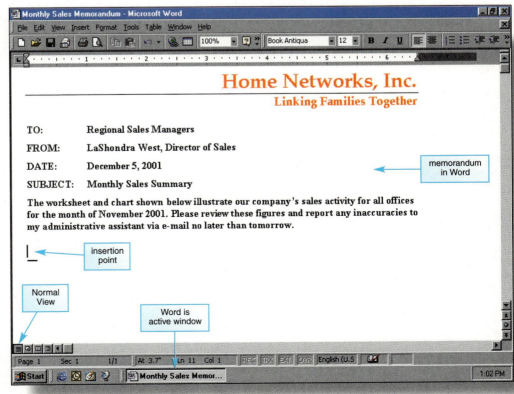

FIGURE 2

2 **Click the Start button on the taskbar and then click Open Office document on the Start menu. When the Open Office Document dialog displays, click 3½ Floppy (A:) in the Look in box. Double-click the Excel file name, Monthly Sales Summary.**

Excel becomes active and the Monthly Sales Summary workbook displays (Figure 3). At this point, Word is inactive. Excel is the active window as shown on the taskbar.

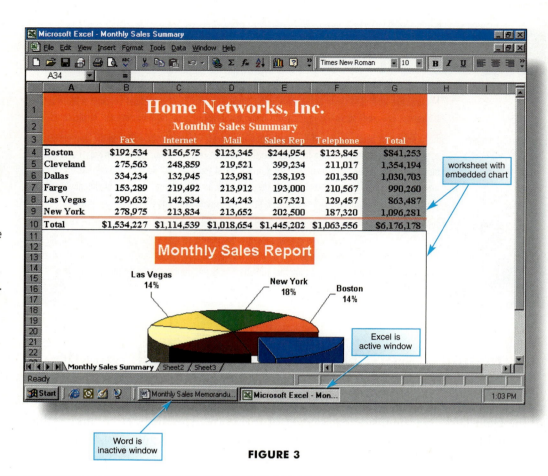

FIGURE 3

Scrap

You can store objects to embed on the desktop, rather than using the Office Clipboard. When you use this technique, the objects are called **scrap**. To accomplish this task, part of the desktop must be visible behind the window of the source application. Next, point to a border of the object and then right-drag it from the source application onto the desktop. Once on the desktop, Windows displays the object as an icon. When the shortcut menu displays, click Create Scrap Here. Next, activate the destination document and then drag the scrap from the desktop onto the destination document and drop it where you want it inserted. To delete a scrap from the desktop, right-click it and then click Delete on the shortcut menu.

With both Word and Excel open, you can switch between the applications by clicking the appropriate button on the taskbar.

Linking an Excel Worksheet to a Word Document

With both applications running, the next step is to link the Excel worksheet to the Word document as shown in the following steps.

To Link an Excel Worksheet to a Word Document

1 **With the Excel window active, select the range A1:G28. Click the Copy button to place the selected range on the Office Clipboard.**

Excel displays a marquee around the range A1:G28 (Figure 4).

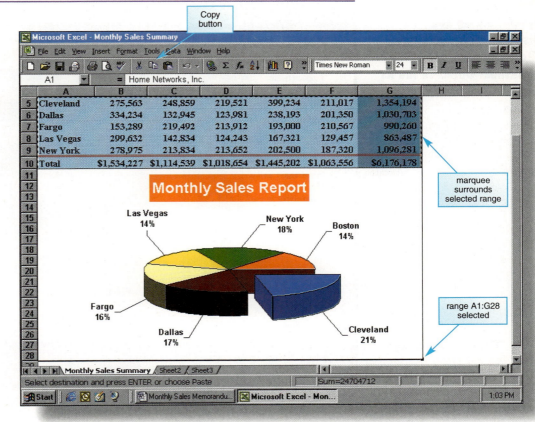

FIGURE 4

2 **Click the Monthly Sales Memorandum button on the taskbar to activate the Word window. Click below the last line of text to position the insertion point where the worksheet will display in the document. Click Edit on the menu bar and then point to Paste Special.**

The Monthly Sales Memorandum document and the Edit menu display on the screen. The insertion point blinks at the bottom of the document (Figure 5).

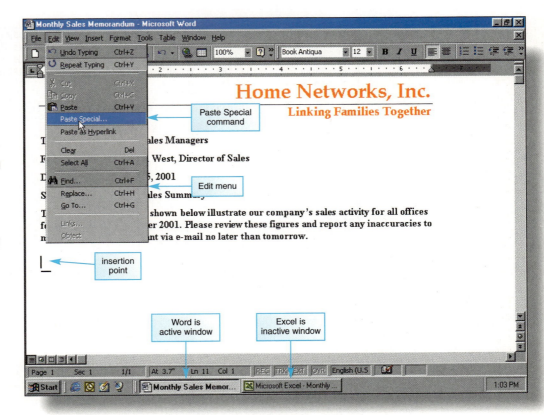

FIGURE 5

3 **Click Paste Special. When the Paste Special dialog box displays, click Paste link, click Microsoft Excel Worksheet Object in the As list box. Point to the OK button.**

The Paste Special dialog box displays (Figure 6).

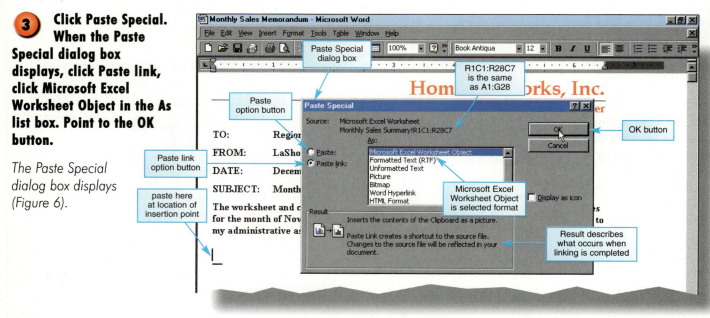

FIGURE 6

4 **Click the OK button.**

Word switches to Print Layout View. The range A1:G28 of the worksheet displays in the Word document beginning at the location of the insertion point (Figure 7).

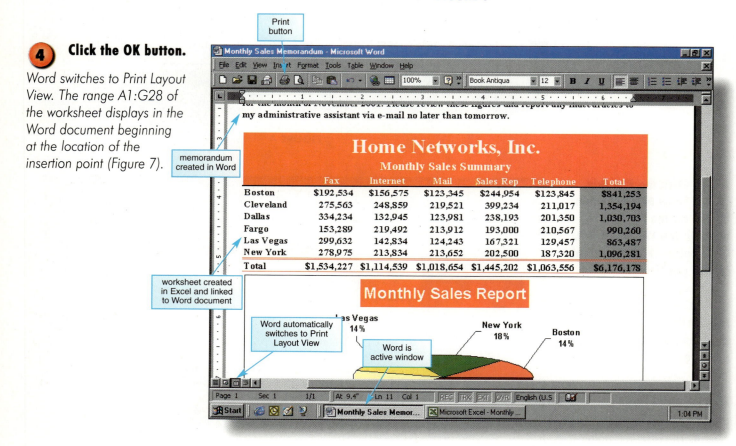

FIGURE 7

The Excel worksheet now is linked to the Word document. If you save the Word document and reopen it, the worksheet will display just as it does in Figure 7. If you want to delete the worksheet, select it and then press the DELETE key. The next section shows how to print and save the memo with the linked worksheet.

Printing and Saving the Word Document with the Linked Worksheet

The following steps print and then save the Word document with the linked worksheet.

To Print and Save the Memo with the Linked Worksheet

1 **With the Word window active, click the Print button on the Standard toolbar.**

The memo and the worksheet print as one document (Figure 8).

2 **Click File on the menu bar and then click Save As. Type** Monthly Sales Memorandum 11-2001 **in the File name text box. Click the OK button.**

Excel saves the Word document on your floppy disk using the file name Monthly Sales Memorandum 11-2001.doc.

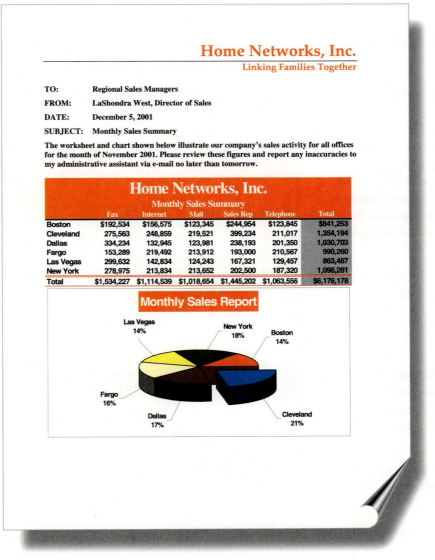

Home Networks, Inc.
Linking Families Together

TO: Regional Sales Managers

FROM: LaShondra West, Director of Sales

DATE: December 5, 2001

SUBJECT: Monthly Sales Summary

The worksheet and chart shown below illustrate our company's sales activity for all offices for the month of November 2001. Please review these figures and report any inaccuracies to my administrative assistant via e-mail no later than tomorrow.

Home Networks, Inc.
Monthly Sales Summary

	Fax	Internet	Mail	Sales Rep	Telephone	Total
Boston	$192,534	$156,575	$123,345	$244,954	$123,845	$841,253
Cleveland	275,563	248,859	219,521	399,234	211,017	1,354,194
Dallas	334,234	132,945	123,981	238,193	201,350	1,030,703
Fargo	153,289	219,492	213,912	193,000	210,567	990,260
Las Vegas	299,632	142,834	124,243	167,321	129,457	863,487
New York	278,975	213,834	213,652	202,500	187,320	1,096,281
Total	$1,534,227	$1,114,539	$1,018,654	$1,445,202	$1,063,556	$6,176,178

Monthly Sales Report

Las Vegas 14%
New York 18%
Boston 14%
Fargo 16%
Dallas 17%
Cleveland 21%

FIGURE 8

If you quit both applications and reopen Monthly Sales Memorandum 11-2001, the worksheet will display in the document even though Excel is not running. Because Word supports object linking and embedding (OLE), it is capable of displaying the linked portion of the Excel workbook without Excel running.

The next section describes what happens when you attempt to edit the linked worksheet while Word is active.

Editing the Linked Worksheet

You can edit any of the cells in the worksheet while it displays as part of the Word document. To edit the worksheet, double-click it. If Excel is running, the system will switch to it and display the linked workbook. If Excel is not running, the system will start it automatically and display the linked workbook. The following steps show how to change the amount sold by the sales rep in Las Vegas (cell E8) from $167,321 to $300,000.

To Edit the Linked Worksheet

1 With the Word window active and the Monthly Sales Memorandum 11-2001 document active, double-click the worksheet. When the Excel window becomes active, double-click the title bar to maximize the window.

Windows switches from Word to Excel and displays the original workbook Monthly Sales Summary.

2 Click cell E8 and then enter 300000 as the new value for the sales rep in Las Vegas.

Excel recalculates all formulas in the workbook and redraws the 3-D Pie chart (Figure 9).

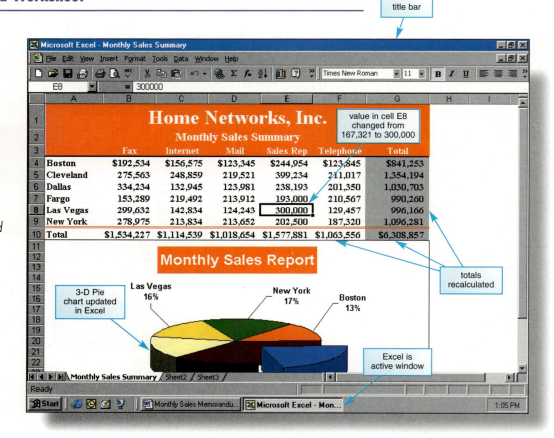

FIGURE 9

3 **Click the Monthly Sales Memorandum button on the taskbar.**

The Word window becomes active. The monthly sales amount for the sales rep in Las Vegas, which was 167,321 now is 300,000. New totals display for the sales reps column, the Las Vegas total, and the company total (Figure 10).

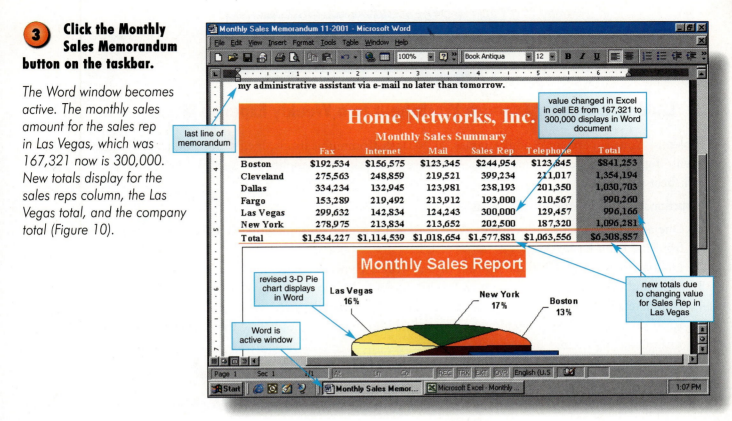

FIGURE 10

As you can see from the previous steps, you double-click a linked object when you want to edit it. Windows will activate the application and display the workbook or document from which the object came. You can then edit the object and return to the destination application. Any changes made to the object will display in the destination document.

If you want the edited changes to the linked workbook to be permanent, you must save the Monthly Sales Summary workbook before quitting Excel.

CASE PERSPECTIVE SUMMARY

As the sales for the previous month are sent in from the various offices to LaShondra, she updates the Excel workbook. She then opens the Word memorandum from the previous month and modifies the date. After saving the Word document, she prints it and distributes the updated version to the regional sales managers.

Integration Feature Summary

This Integration Feature introduced you to Object Linking and Embedding (OLE). OLE allows you to bring together data and information that has been created in different applications. When you link an object to a document and save it, only a link to the object is saved with the document. You edit a linked object by double-clicking it. The system activates the application and opens the file in which the object was created. If you change any part of the object and then return to the destination document, the updated object will display.

In the Lab

1 Linking a Weekly Expense Worksheet to a Weekly Expense Memo

Problem: Your supervisor, Radjika James, at N-Dash Communications, Inc., sends out a weekly memo with expense figures to the district managers. You have been asked to simplify her task by linking the weekly expense worksheet to a memo.

Instructions: Perform the following tasks.

1. One at a time, open the document Weekly Expense Memo and the workbook Weekly Expense Summary from the Data Disk.
2. Link the range A1:E17 to the bottom of the Weekly Expense Memo document.
3. Print and then save the document as Weekly Expense Memo 12-17-01.
4. Double-click the worksheet and use the keyboard to manually increase each of the nine expense amounts by $200. Activate the Word window and print it with the new values. Close the document and workbook without saving them.

2 Linking a Weekly Expense Memo to a Weekly Expense Workbook

Problem: Your supervisor, Radjika James, at N-Dash Communications, Inc., has asked you to link the Word document to the Excel workbook, rather than the Excel workbook to the Word document the way it was done in exercise 1.

Instructions: Complete the following tasks.

1. One at a time, open the document Weekly Expense Memo and the workbook Weekly Expense Summary from the Data Disk.
2. With the Excel window active, insert 18 rows above row 1 and then select cell A1. Activate the Word document and copy the entire document. Embed the Word document at the top of the Weekly Office Expenses worksheet. To embed, click the Paste link option button in the Paste Special dialog box and then select Microsoft Word Document Object in the As list box.
3. Print the Weekly Office Expenses sheet and then save the workbook as Weekly Expense with Memo 12-17-01.
4. With the Excel window active, double-click the embedded document and then delete the first sentence in the paragraph. Activate the Excel window and then print the worksheet with the modified memo. Close the workbook and document without saving them.

Microsoft **Access 2000**

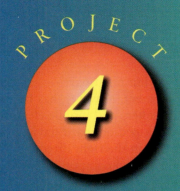

PROJECT

4

Microsoft Access 2000

Reports, Forms and Combo Boxes

You will have mastered the material in this project when you can:

- Create a query for a report
- Use the Report Wizard to create a report
- Use the Report window to modify a report design
- Move between Design view and Print Preview
- Recognize sections in a report
- Save a report
- Close a report
- Print a report
- Create a report with grouping and subtotals
- Change headings in a report
- Move and resize controls on a report
- Use the Form Wizard to create an initial form
- Use the Form window to modify a form design
- Move fields on a form
- Place a calculated field on a form
- Change the format of a field on a form
- Place a combo box on a form
- Place a title on a form
- Change colors on a form
- View data using a form

Navigation Systems

GPS Databases Help You Arrive

The age-old navigation nightmare — getting lost. This traveling torment, however, has become a thing of the past. Automakers and mobile electronics manufacturers have developed onboard navigation systems to help point drivers in the right direction. These pocket-sized navigation system computers use databases that cover the Earth's surface.

These computers collect radio signals emitted from government satellites and calculate the user's position and altitude. Then, they interface with commercial databases and display such useful information as where the closest automated teller machine is located or how long it will take to get to the campground.

The technology is the offspring of once-secret military Cold War technology. The Department of

Defense spent an estimated $10 billion developing the Global Positioning Satellite (GPS) system during the 1970s and launched its first satellite in 1978. Now, 24 GPS satellites orbit high above the Earth.

Expanding on the military's technological successes using the GPS system for bombing missions and navigating during the Gulf War, enterprising engineers developed civilian satellite-navigation systems that use mapped data from databases to guide users in a variety of applications.

Advanced mobile GPS technology allows these systems to map out a route to any known destination on a small color screen positioned near the dashboard and track the precise location of a vehicle as it moves along that route. The systems recalibrate if a motorist makes a wrong turn, and some supply audio directions in addition to the in-dash visual display. The OnStar® system, available with many makes and models, has an emergency function that can be used at the touch of a single button on the OnStar handset. The GPS automatically calculates the vehicle's location and display it on the Advisor' screen so the information can be relayed to an emergency provider with the request for assistance.

In another system, GPS technology in airplanes helps pilots save time and fuel. Databases contain information on airport locations and radio frequencies, and they interact with the satellite signals to compute the aircraft's precise location, direct route to an airport, time enroute, airspeed, and ground speed.

Hikers and boaters benefit from hand held GPS navigating technology. Databases for hikers contain details on popular campgrounds, fishing holes, and hiking trails, and the computer can calculate current position, walking speed, direction to these sites, and estimated time of arrival. GPS systems for boaters display the course traveled, distance to go, miles off course, latitude and longitude, and speed.

Entrepreneurial developers have engineered systems for trucking companies to track the location of their vehicles on the roads, farmers to analyze their crops, police to track drug dealers, and scientists to check movements of the San Andreas fault.

These portable computers and extensive databases are the most important advances in the ancient art of navigation. As they gain acceptance in sporting and traveling activities, they may certainly put an end to the folded maps, detours, stops for directions, and the familiar phrase, "Excuse me, could you tell me how to get to…?"

Microsoft Access 2000

Reports, Forms, and Combo Boxes

P R O J E C T

4

C A S E   P E R S P E C T I V E

Bavant Marine Services has realized several benefits from its database of marinas and technicians. The management and staff of Bavant Marine Services greatly appreciate, for example, the ease with which they can query the database. They hope to realize additional benefits using two custom reports that meet their specific needs. The first report includes the number, name, address, city, state, zip code, and total amount (warranty amount plus non-warranty amount) of each marina. The second report groups the records by technician number. Subtotals of the warranty and non-warranty amounts display after each group, and grand totals display at the end of the report. They also want to improve the data entry process by using a custom form. In addition to a title, the form will contain the fields arranged in two columns and display the total amount, which will be calculated automatically by adding the warranty and non-warranty amounts. To assist users in entering the correct marina type, users should be able to select from a list of possible marina types. To assist users in entering the correct technician number, users should be able to select from a list of existing technicians. Your task is to help Bavant Marine Services with these tasks.

Introduction

This project creates two reports and a form. The first report is shown in Figure 4-1. This report includes the number, name, address, city, state, zip code, and total amount (warranty plus non-warranty) of each marina. It is similar to the one produced by clicking the Print button on the toolbar. It has two significant differences, however.

First, not all fields are included. The Marina table includes a Marina Type field (added in Project 3), a Warranty field, a Non-warranty field, and a Tech Number field, none of which appears on this report. Second, this report contains a Total Amount field, which does not display in the Marina table.

The second report is shown in Figure 4-2 on page A 4.6. It is similar to the report in Figure 4-1 but contains an additional feature, grouping. **Grouping** means creating separate collections of records sharing some common characteristic. In the report shown in Figure 4-2, for example, the records have been grouped by technician number. There are three separate groups: one for technician 23, one for technician 36, and one for technician 49. The appropriate technician number appears before each group, and the total of the warranty and non-warranty amounts for the marinas in the group (called a **subtotal**) displays after the group. At the end of the report is a grand total of the warranty and non-warranty amounts for all groups.

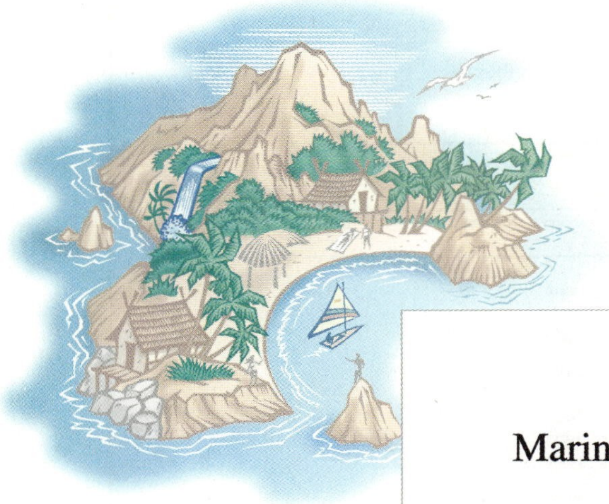

Marina Amount Report

Marina Number	Name	Address	City	State	Zip Code	Total Amount
AD57	Alan's Docks Boat Works	314 Central	Burton	MI	49611	$1,845.75
BL72	Brite's Landing	281 Robin	Burton	MI	49611	$217.00
EL25	Elend Marina	462 River	Torino	MI	48268	$1,092.25
FB96	Fenton's Boats	36 Bayview	Cavela	MI	47926	$1,580.70
FM22	Fedder's Marina	283 Waterfront	Burton	MI	49611	$432.00
NW72	Nelson's Wharf	27 Lake	Masondale	MI	49832	$1,128.50
PM34	Peter's Marina	453 Wilson	Torino	MI	48268	$0.00
TR72	The Reef	92 East Bay	Woodview	MI	47212	$219.00

Tuesday, September 11, 2001 Page 1 of 1

FIGURE 4-1

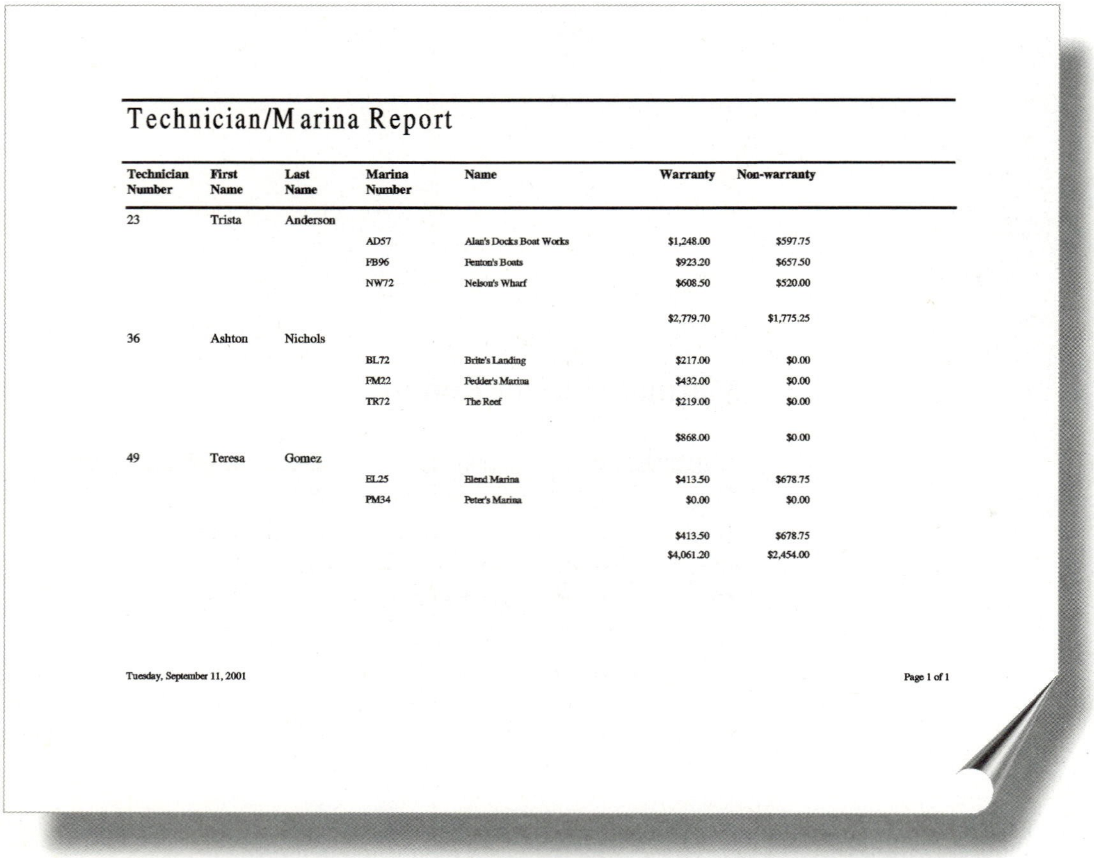

Technician/Marina Report

Technician Number	First Name	Last Name	Marina Number	Name	Warranty	Non-warranty
23	Trista	Anderson				
			AD57	Alan's Docks Boat Works	$1,248.00	$597.75
			FB96	Fenton's Boats	$923.20	$657.50
			NW72	Nelson's Wharf	$608.50	$520.00
					$2,779.70	$1,775.25
36	Ashton	Nichols				
			BL72	Brite's Landing	$217.00	$0.00
			FM22	Fedder's Marina	$432.00	$0.00
			TR72	The Reef	$219.00	$0.00
					$868.00	$0.00
49	Teresa	Gomez				
			EL25	Elend Marina	$413.50	$678.75
			PM34	Peter's Marina	$0.00	$0.00
					$413.50	$678.75
					$4,061.20	$2,454.00

Tuesday, September 11, 2001 — Page 1 of 1

FIGURE 4-2

The **custom form** to be created is shown in Figure 4-3. Although similar to the form created in Project 1, it offers some distinct advantages. Some of the differences are merely aesthetic. The form has a title and the fields have been rearranged in two columns. In addition, two other major differences are present. This form displays the total amount and will calculate it automatically by adding the warranty and non-warranty amounts. Second, to assist users in entering the correct marina type and technician, the form contains **combo boxes**, which are boxes that allow you to select entries from a list. An arrow displays in the Technician Number field, for example. Clicking the arrow causes a list of the technicians in the Technician table to display as shown in the figure. You then can either type the desired technician number or click the desired technician.

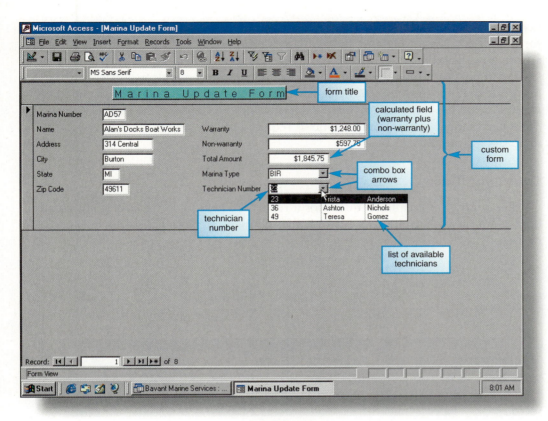

FIGURE 4-3

You are to create the reports requested by the management of Bavant Marine Services. You also must create the form the management deems to be important to the data-entry process.

Opening the Database

Before you create the reports or forms, you must open the database. Perform the following steps to complete this task.

TO OPEN A DATABASE

1 Click the Start button.

2 Click Open Office Document on the Start menu and then click 3½ Floppy (A:) in the Look in box. Make sure the database called Bavant Marine Services is selected.

3 Click the Open button.

The database is open and the Bavant Marine Services : Database window displays.

Report Creation

The simplest way to create a report design is to use the **Report Wizard**. For some reports, the Report Wizard can produce exactly the desired report. For others, however, you must first use the Report Wizard to produce a report that is as close as possible to the desired report. Then use the **Report window** to modify the report and transform it into the correct report. In either case, once the report is created and

More About

Creating a Report

There are two alternatives to using the Report Wizard to create reports. You can use AutoReport to create a very simple report that includes all fields and records in the table or query. Design View also allows you to create a report from scratch.

Using Queries for Reports

Records in a report will appear in the specified order if you have sorted the data in the query. You also can enter criteria in the query to specify that only those records that satisfy the criteria will be included in the report. Reports based on queries open faster than those based on tables.

saved, you can print it at any time. Access will use the current data in the database for the report, formatting and arranging it in exactly the way you specified when the report was created.

If a report uses only the fields in a single table, use the table as a basis for the report. If the report uses extra fields (such as Total Amount), however, the simplest way to create the report is to create a query using the steps you learned in Project 2. The query should contain only the fields required for the report. This query forms the basis for the report.

Creating a Query

The process of creating a query for a report is identical to the process of creating queries for any other purpose. Perform the following steps to create the query for the first report.

 To Create a Query

1 **In the Database window, click Tables on the Objects bar, if necessary, and then click Marina. Click the New Object: AutoForm button arrow on the Database window toolbar. Click Query. Be sure Design View is selected, and then click the OK button. Maximize the Query1 : Select Query window. Resize the upper and lower panes and the Marina field box so that all the fields in the Marina table display.**

2 **Double-click Marina Number. Select Ascending as the sort order for the field. Double-click the names of the fields to include the Name, Address, City, State, and Zip Code**

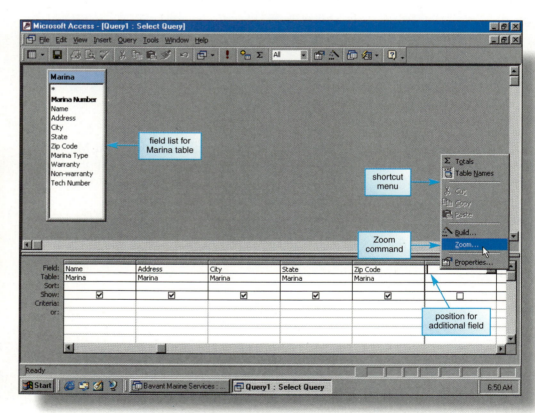

FIGURE 4-4

fields in the design grid. Right-click in the Field row of the column for the additional field (the field after the Zip Code field). Point to Zoom on the shortcut menu.

The shortcut menu for the extra field displays (Figure 4-4).

3 Click Zoom on the shortcut menu. Type
`Total Amount: [Warranty]+[Non-warranty]` **in the Zoom dialog box and point to the OK button (Figure 4-5).**

4 Click the OK button. Click the Close button for the Select Query window and then click the Yes button.

5 Type `Marina Amount Query` **as the name of the query and then click the OK button.**

The query is saved, and the Select Query window closes.

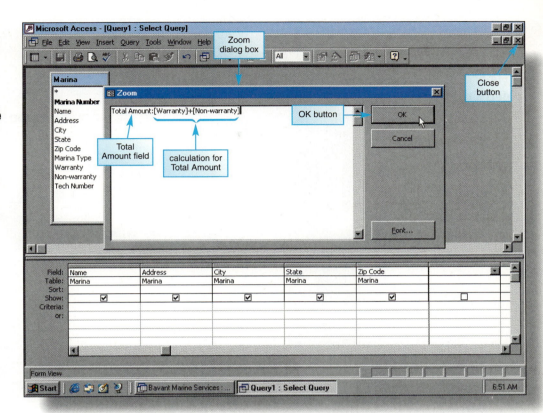

FIGURE 4-5

Creating a Report

Next, you will create a report using the Report Wizard. Access leads you through a series of choices and questions and then creates the report automatically. Perform the following steps to create the report shown in Figure 4-1 on page A 4.5.

Steps To Create a Report

1 In the Database window, click Queries on the Objects bar, if necessary, and then click Marina Amount Query. Click the New Object: AutoForm button arrow on the Database window toolbar and then point to Report (Figure 4-6).

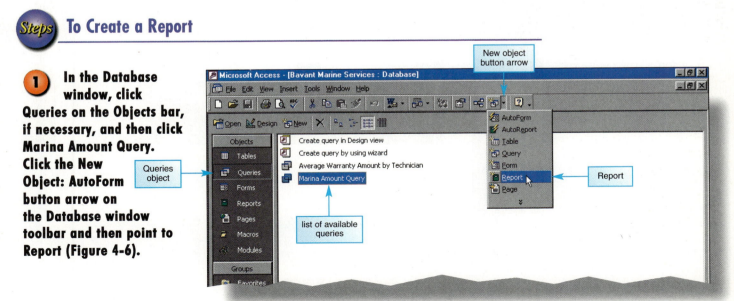

FIGURE 4-6

2 Click Report. Click Report Wizard. If necessary, click the Choose the table or query where the object's data comes from down arrow, and then click Marina Amount Query. Point to the OK button.

The New Report dialog box displays and the Marina Amount Query is selected (Figure 4-7).

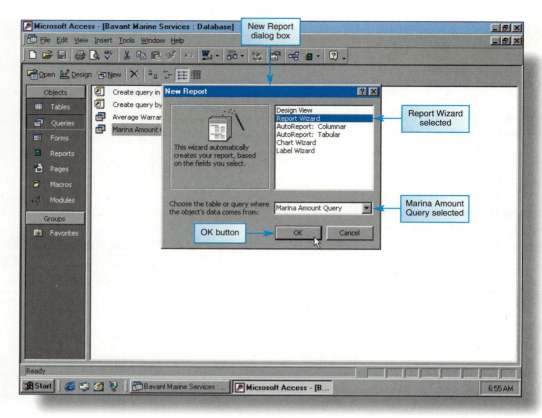

FIGURE 4-7

3 Click the OK button and then point to the Add All Fields button.

The Report Wizard dialog box displays, requesting the fields for the report (Figure 4-8). To add the selected field to the list of fields on the report, use the Add Field button. To add all fields, use the Add All Fields button.

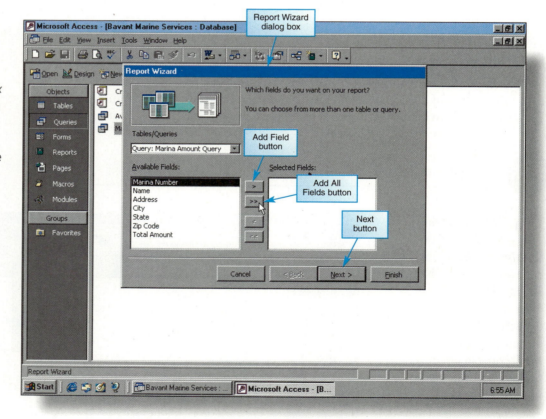

FIGURE 4-8

4 **Click the Add All Fields button to add all the fields, and then click the Next button.**

The next Report Wizard dialog box displays, requesting the field or fields for grouping levels (Figure 4-9). This report will not include grouping levels.

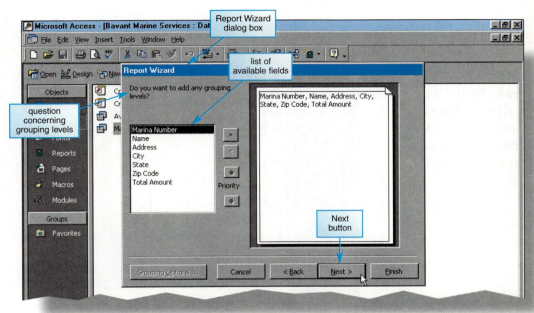

FIGURE 4-9

5 **Click the Next button. The next Report Wizard dialog box displays, requesting the sort order for the report (Figure 4-10). The query already is sorted in the appropriate order, so you will not need to specify a sort order.**

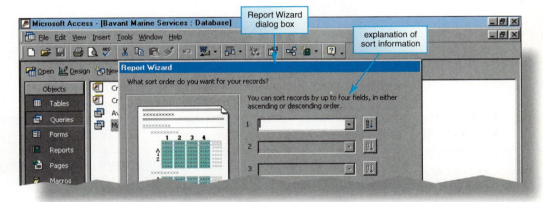

FIGURE 4-10

6 **Click the Next button. The next Report Wizard dialog box displays, requesting your report layout preference (Figure 4-11).**

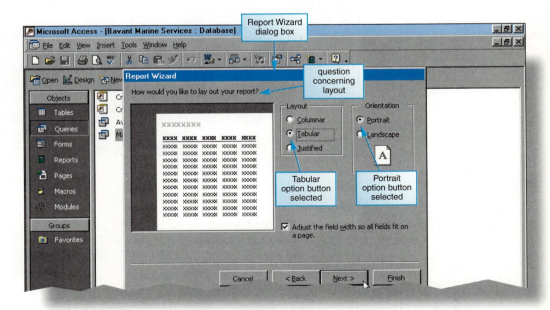

FIGURE 4-11

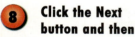 **Be sure the options selected in the Report Wizard dialog box on your screen match those shown in Figure 4-11, and then click the Next button. If Formal is not already selected, click Formal to select it. Point to the Next button.**

The next Report Wizard dialog box displays, requesting a style for the report (Figure 4-12). The Formal style is selected.

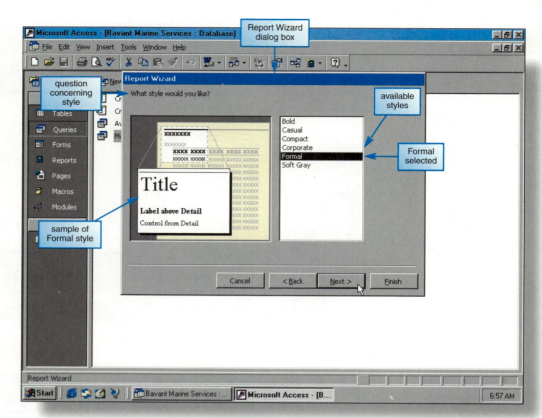

FIGURE 4-12

8 **Click the Next button and then type** Marina Amount Report **as the report title. Point to the Finish button.**

The next Report Wizard dialog box displays, requesting a title for the report (Figure 4-13). Marina Amount Report is entered as the title.

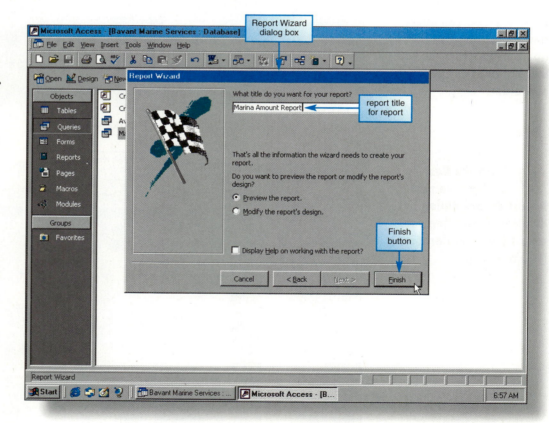

FIGURE 4-13

9 **Click the Finish button.**

The report design is complete and displays in Print Preview (Figure 4-14). (If your computer displays an entire page of the report, click the portion of the report displaying the mouse pointer.)

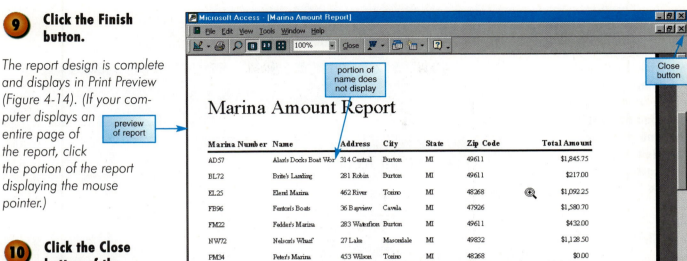

FIGURE 4-14

10 **Click the Close button of the window containing the report to close the report.**

The report no longer displays.

Because of the insufficient amount of space allowed in the report shown in Figure 4-14, some of the data does not display completely. The final portion of the name of Alan's Docks Boat Works does not display, for example. You will need to correct this problem.

Moving to Design View and Docking the Toolbox

Within the Report window, the different possible views are Design view and Print Preview. Use **Design view** to modify the design (layout) of the report. Use **Print Preview** to see the report with sample data. To move from Design view to Print Preview, click the Print Preview button on the Report Design toolbar. To move from Print Preview to Design view, click the button labeled Close on the Print Preview toolbar.

Within Print Preview, you can switch between viewing an entire page and viewing a portion of a page. To do so, click somewhere within the report (the mouse pointer will change shape to a magnifying glass).

In Design view, you can modify the design of the report. A **toolbox** is available in Design view that allows you to create special objects for the report. The toolbox also can obscure a portion of the report. You can use the Toolbox button on the Report Design toolbar to remove it and then return it to the screen when needed. Because you use the toolbox frequently when modifying report and form designs, it is desirable to be able to leave it on the screen, however. You can move the toolbar to different positions on the screen using a process referred to as **docking**. To dock the toolbox in a different position, simply drag the title bar of the toolbox to the desired position. The bottom of the screen usually is a good position for it.

Perform the steps on the next page to move to Design view. You will also remove the **field box** that displays, because you will not need it.

Other Ways

1. On Objects bar click Reports, click New button, and then click Report Wizard to create report
2. On Objects bar click Reports, Create report by using wizard
3. On Insert menu click Report, click Report Wizard to create report

More About 2000

Previewing a Report

You can view two pages at the same time when previewing a report by clicking the Two Pages button on the Print Preview toolbar. You can view multiple pages by clicking View on the menu bar, clicking Pages, and then clicking the number of pages to view.

Steps **To Move to Design View and Dock the Toolbox**

1 **Click the Reports object in the Database window, right-click Marina Amount Report, and then click Design View on the shortcut menu. If a field box displays, click its Close button.**

The report displays in Design view (Figure 4-15).

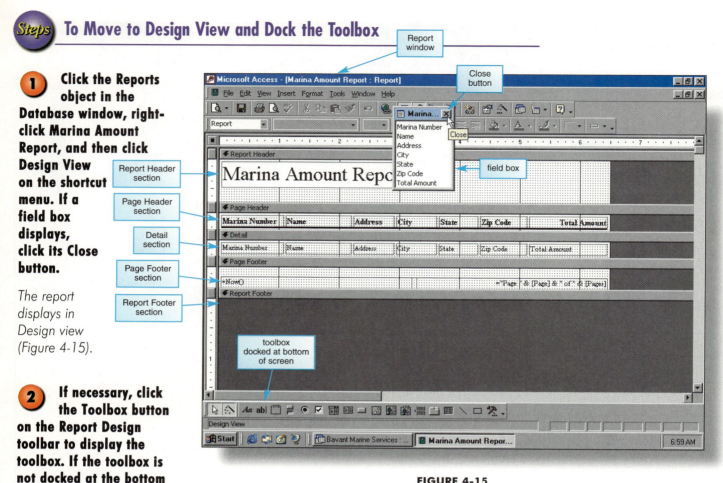

FIGURE 4-15

2 **If necessary, click the Toolbox button on the Report Design toolbar to display the toolbox. If the toolbox is not docked at the bottom of the screen as in Figure 4-15, dock it there by dragging its title bar to the bottom of the screen.**

The field box no longer displays, and the toolbar is docked at the bottom of the screen.

Other Ways

1. With report selected, click Design button

Report Sections

Each portion of the report is described in what is termed a **section**. The sections are labeled on the screen (see Figure 4-15). Notice the following sections: Report Header section, Page Header section, Detail section, Page Footer section, and Report Footer section.

The contents of the **Report Header section** print once at the beginning of the report. The contents of the **Report Footer section** print once at the end of the report. The contents of the **Page Header section** print once at the top of each page, and the contents of the **Page Footer section** print once at the bottom of each page. The contents of the **Detail section** print once for each record in the table.

The various rectangles displaying in Figure 4-15 (Marina Amount Report, Marina Number, Name, and so on) are called **controls**. All the information on a report or form is contained in the controls. The control containing Marina Amount Report displays the report title; that is, it displays the words, Marina Amount Report. The control in the Page Header section containing Name displays the word, Name.

The controls in the Detail section display the contents of the corresponding fields. The control containing Name, for example, will display the marina's name. The controls in the Page Header section serve as **captions** for the data. The Marina

Number control in this section, for example, will display the words, Marina Number, immediately above the column of marina numbers, thus making it clear to anyone reading the report that the items in the column are, in fact, marina numbers.

To move, resize, delete, or modify a control, click it. Small squares called **sizing handles** display around the border of the control. Drag the control to move it, drag one of the sizing handles to resize it, or press the DELETE key to delete it. Clicking a second time produces an insertion point in the control in order to modify its contents.

Changing Properties

Some of the changes you may make will involve using the property sheet for the control to be changed. The **property sheet** for each control is a list of properties that can be modified. By using the property sheet, you can change one or more of the control's properties. To produce the property sheet, right-click the desired control and then click Properties on the shortcut menu.

The problem of the missing data in the report shown in Figure 4-14 on page A 4.13 can be corrected in several ways.

1. Move the controls to allow more space in between them. Then, drag the appropriate handles on the controls that need to be expanded to enlarge them.
2. Use the Font Size property to select a smaller font size. This will allow more data to print in the same space.
3. Use the Can Grow property. By changing the value of this property from No to Yes, the data can be spread over two lines, thus allowing all the data to print. The name of customer AD57, for example, will have Alan's Docks Boat on one line and Works on the next line. Access will split data at natural break points, such as commas, spaces, and hyphens.

The first approach will work, but it can be cumbersome. The second approach also works but makes the report more difficult to read. The third approach, changing the Can Grow property, is the simplest method to use and generally produces a very readable report. Perform the following steps to change the Can Grow property for the Detail section.

More About

Changing Properties

There are a large number of properties that can be changed using the property sheet. The properties determine the structure and appearance of a control. They also determine the characteristics of the data the control contains. For details on a particular property, click the Help button, then click the name of the property.

 To Change the Can Grow Property

1 **Point below the section selector for the Detail section (Figure 4-16).**

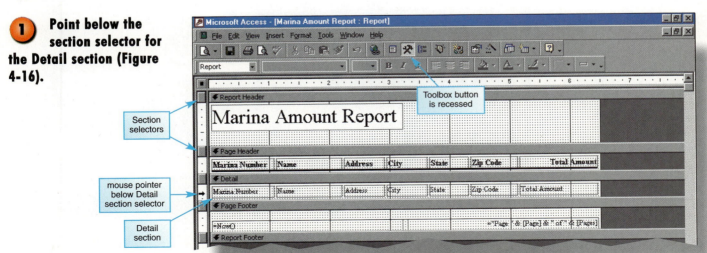

FIGURE 4-16

2 **Right-click and then point to Properties on the shortcut menu.**

The shortcut menu displays (Figure 4-17). All the controls in the Detail section are selected.

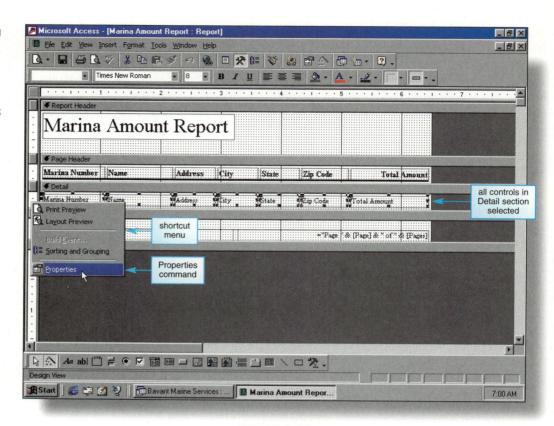

FIGURE 4-17

3 **Click Properties and then click the All tab, if necessary, to ensure that all available properties display. Click the Can Grow property, click the Can Grow box arrow, and then click Yes in the list that displays.**

The Multiple selection property sheet displays (Figure 4-18). All the properties display on the All sheet. The value for the Can Grow property has been changed to Yes.

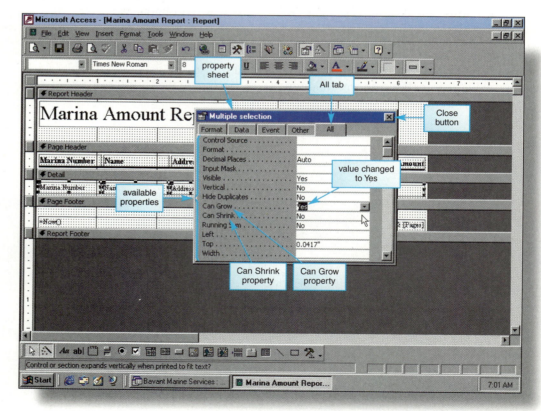

FIGURE 4-18

4 Close the property sheet by clicking its Close button, and then point to the Print Preview button on the Report Design toolbar (Figure 4-19).

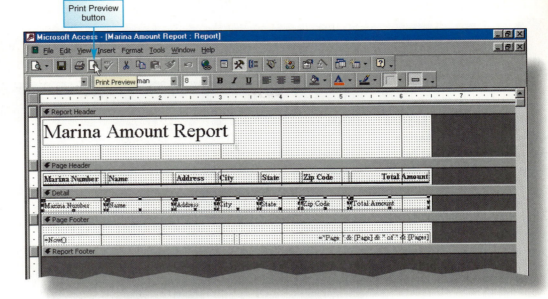

FIGURE 4-19

5 Click the Print Preview button.

A portion of the report displays (Figure 4-20). The names now display completely by extending to a second line. (If your computer displays an entire page, click the portion of the report displaying the mouse pointer in the figure.)

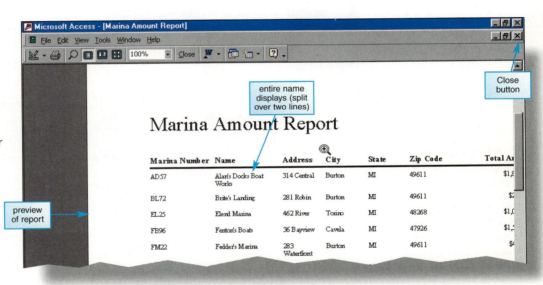

FIGURE 4-20

1. On File menu click Close

Closing and Saving a Report

To close a report, close the window using the window's Close button in the upper-right corner of the window. Then indicate whether or not you want to save your changes. Perform the following step to close the report.

TO CLOSE AND SAVE A REPORT

1 Close the Report window and then click the Yes button to save the report.

Printing a Report

To print a report, right-click the report in the Database window, and then click Print on the shortcut menu. Perform the steps on the next page to print the Marina Amount Report.

Steps To Print a Report

1 **In the Database window, if necessary, click the Reports object. Right-click Marina Amount Report. Point to Print on the shortcut menu.**

The shortcut menu for the Marina Amount Report displays (Figure 4-21).

2 **Click Print.**

The report prints. It should look like the report shown in Figure 4-1 on page A 4.5.

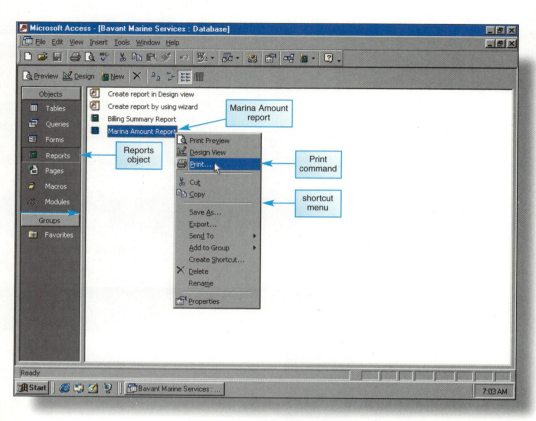

FIGURE 4-21

More About 2000

Grouping in a Report

To force each group to begin on a new page of the report, change the value of the Force-NewPage property for the group header section from None to Before Section. You can change the ForceNew-Page property for any section except the page header and page footer.

Grouping in a Report

Grouping arranges the records in your report. When records are grouped in a report, separate collections of records are created from those that share a common characteristic. In the report shown in Figure 4-2 on page A 4.6, for example, the records are grouped by technician number. Three separate groups were formed, one for each technician.

In grouping, reports typically include two additional types of sections: a group header and a group footer. A **group header** is printed before the records in a particular group are printed, and a **group footer** is printed after the group. In Figure 4-2, the group header indicates the technician number and name. The group footer includes the total of the warranty and non-warranty amounts for the marinas assigned to that technician. Such a total is called a **subtotal**, because it is a subset of the overall total.

Creating a Second Report

As you did when you created the first report, you will use the Report Wizard to create the second report. This time, however, you will select fields from two tables. To do so, you will select the first table (for example, Technician) and then select the fields from this table you would like to include. Next, you will select the second table (for example, Marina) and then select the fields from the second table. Perform the following steps to create the report shown in Figure 4-2 on page A 4.6.

Steps **To Create a Second Report**

1 **In the Database window, click the Reports object and then right-click Create report by using wizard. Click Design View on the shortcut menu. When the Report Wizard dialog box displays, click the Tables/Queries arrow and select Technician. Point to the Add Field button.**

The Report Wizard dialog box displays, requesting the fields for the report (Figure 4-22). Fields from the Technician table display. The Tech Number field is selected.

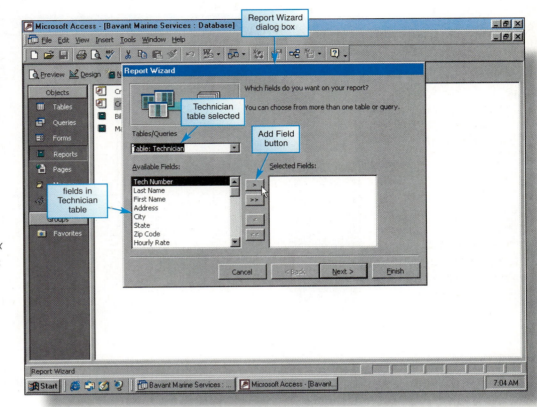

FIGURE 4-22

2 **Click the Add Field button to add the Tech Number field. Add the First Name field by clicking it and then clicking the Add Field button. Add the Last Name field in the same manner. Select the Marina table in the Tables/Queries list box and then point to the Add Field button.**

The Tech Number, First Name, and Last Name fields are selected (Figure 4-23). The fields from the Marina table display in the Available Fields box.

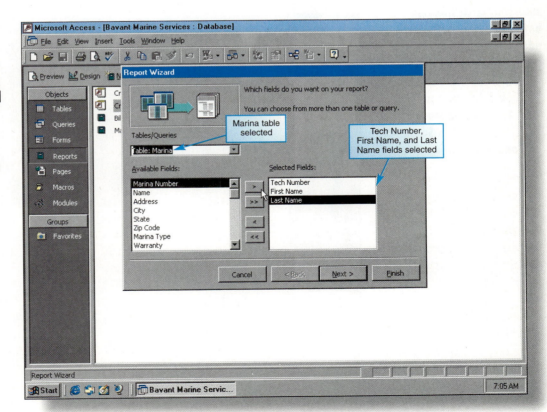

FIGURE 4-23

3 **Add the Marina Number, Name, Warranty, and Non-warranty fields by clicking the field and then clicking the Add Field button. Click the Next button.**

The next Report Wizard dialog box displays (Figure 4-24). Because the Technician and Marina tables are related, the wizard is asking you to indicate how the data is to be viewed; that is, the way the report is to be organized. The report may be organized by Technician or by Marina.

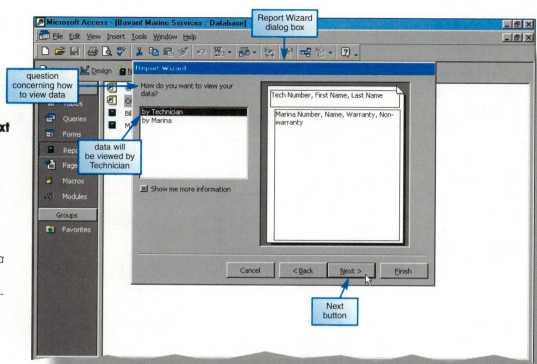

FIGURE 4-24

4 **Because the report is to be viewed by technician and by Technician already is selected, click the Next button. Because no additional grouping levels are required, click the Next button a second time. Click the box 1 arrow and then click the Marina Number field. Point to the Summary Options button.**

The next Report Wizard dialog box displays, requesting the sort order for detail records in the report; that is, the way in which records will be sorted within each of the groups (Figure 4-25). The Marina Number field is selected for the sort order, indicating that within the group of marinas of any technician, the marinas will be sorted by marina number.

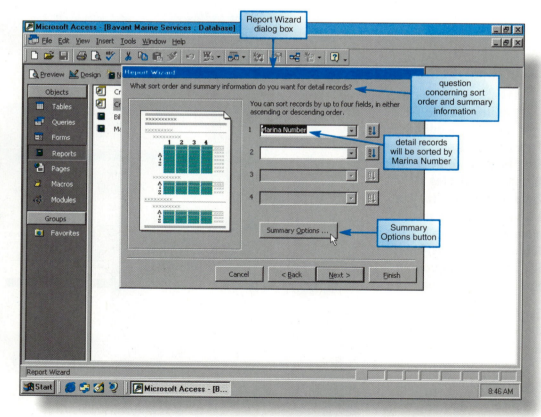

FIGURE 4-25

5 **Click the Summary Options button. Point to the Sum check box in the row labeled Warranty.**

The Summary Options dialog box displays (Figure 4-26). This dialog box allows you to indicate any statistics you want calculated in the report by clicking the appropriate check box.

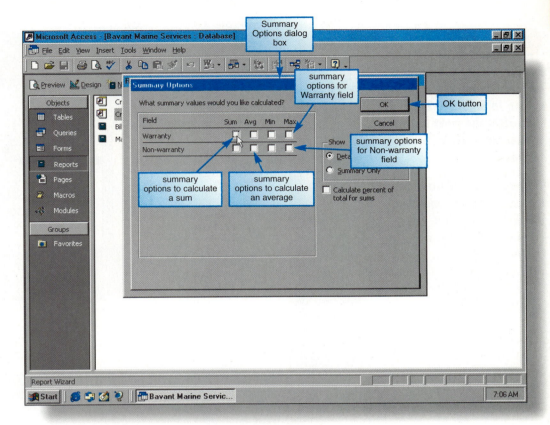

FIGURE 4-26

6 **Click the Sum check box in the Warranty row and the Sum check box in the Non-warranty row. Click the OK button in the Summary Options dialog box, and then click the Next button. Click the Landscape option button.**

The next Report Wizard dialog box displays, requesting your report layout preference (Figure 4-27). The Stepped layout, which is the correct one, already is selected. To see the effect of any of the others, click the appropriate option button. Landscape orientation is selected.

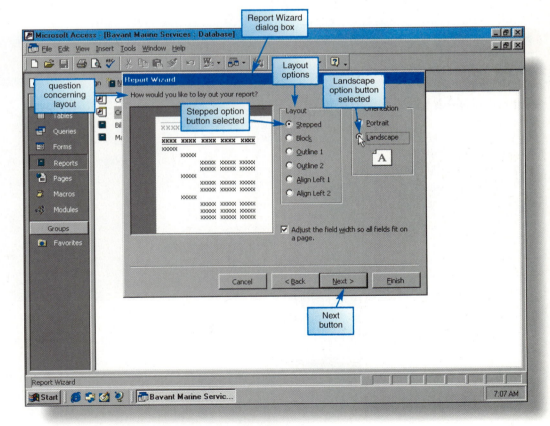

FIGURE 4-27

7 Be sure the options selected in the Report Wizard dialog box on your screen match those shown in Figure 4-27, and then click the Next button. If necessary, click Formal to select it.

The next Report Wizard dialog box displays, requesting a style for the report. The Formal style is selected (Figure 4-28).

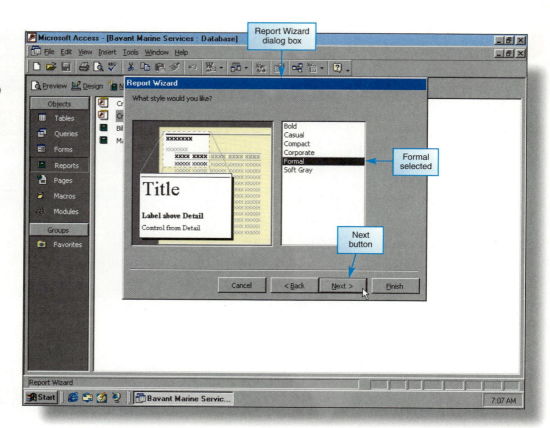

FIGURE 4-28

8 Click the Next button and then type Technician/Marina Report as the report title. Point to the Finish button.

The next Report Wizard dialog box displays, requesting a title for the report (Figure 4-29). Technician/Marina Report is typed as the title.

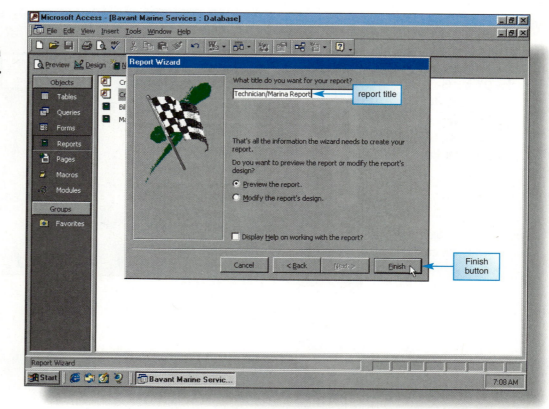

FIGURE 4-29

9 **Click the Finish button.**

The report design is complete and displays in the Print Preview window (Figure 4-30).

10 **Close the report by clicking the Close button for the window containing the report.**

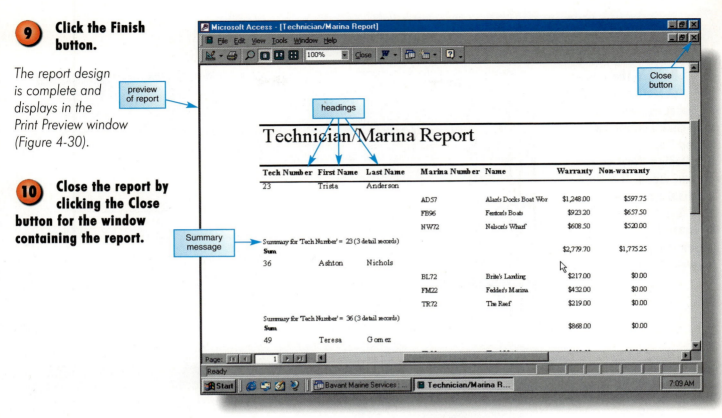

FIGURE 4-30

Reviewing the Report Design

You will find three major differences between the report shown in Figure 4-30 and the one illustrated in Figure 4-2 on page A 4.6. The first is that all the column headings in Figure 4-30 are on a single line, whereas they extend over two lines in the report in Figure 4-2. The first column heading in Figure 4-2 is Technician Number, instead of Tech Number. The second difference is that the report in Figure 4-2 does not contain the message that begins, Summary for Tech Number. There are other messages found on the report in Figure 4-30 that are not on the report in Figure 4-2, but they are included in a portion of the report that does not display. The third difference is that the marina name for Alan's Docks Boat Works does not display completely.

To complete the report design, you must change the column headings and remove these extra messages. In addition, you will move the Warranty and Non-warranty fields to make room for enlarging the Name field. You will then enlarge the Name field so the values display completely.

Removing Unwanted Controls

To remove the extra messages, or any other control, first click the control to select it. Then press the DELETE key to remove the unwanted control. Perform the steps on the next page to remove the unwanted controls from the report.

To Remove Unwanted Controls

1 **Be sure the Reports object is selected in the Database window, right-click Technician/Marina Report, and then click Design View on the shortcut menu. If a field box displays, click its Close button. Point to the control that begins, ="Summary for " (Figure 4-31).**

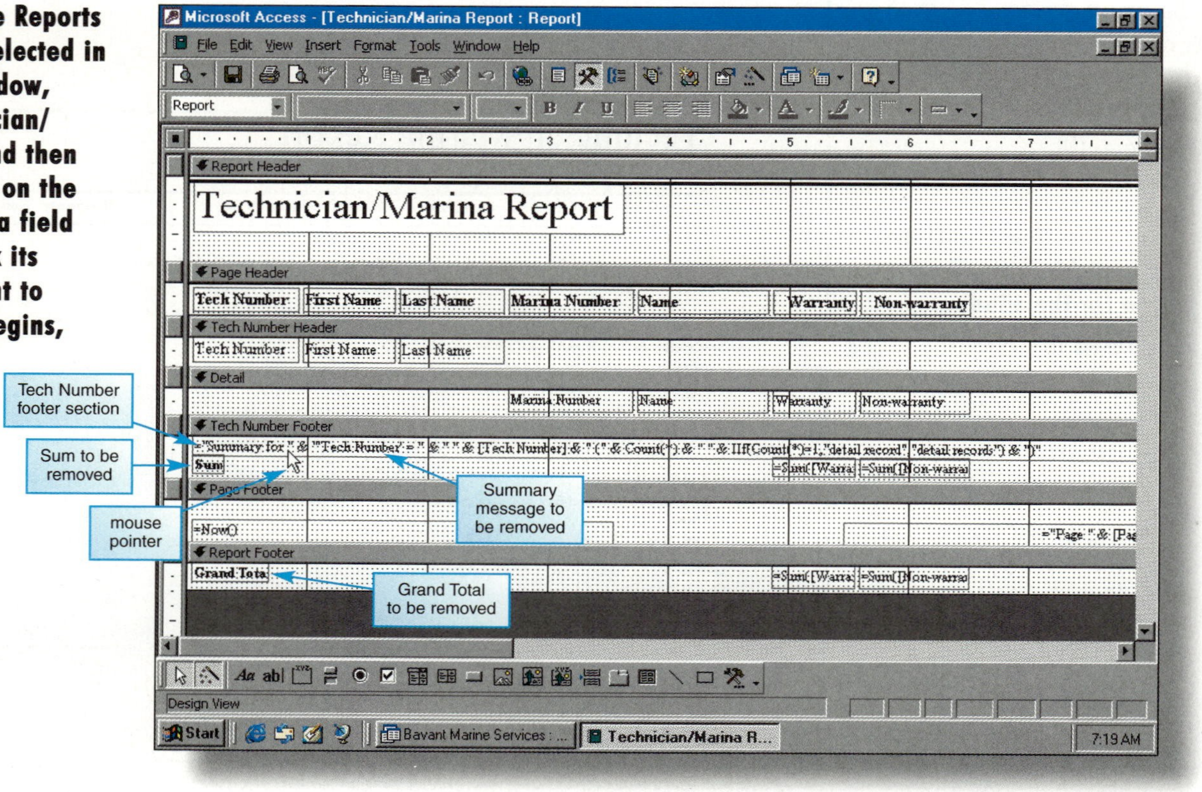

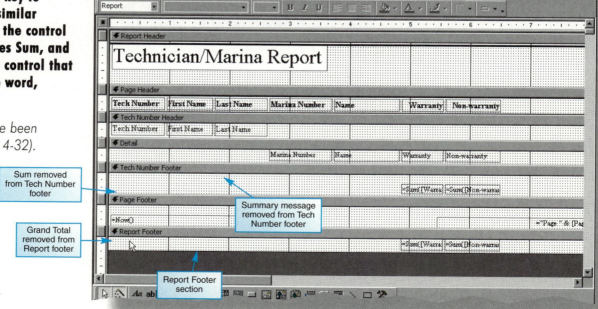

FIGURE 4-31

2 **Click the control to select it, and then press the DELETE key to delete it. In a similar fashion, delete the control below that states Sum, and then delete the control that begins with the word, Grand.**

The controls have been removed (Figure 4-32).

FIGURE 4-32

Enlarging the Page Header Section

The current Page Header section is not large enough to encompass the desired column headings because several of them extend over two lines. Thus, before changing the column headings, you must **enlarge** the Page Header. To do so, drag the bottom border of the Page Header section down. A bold line in the Page Header section immediately below the column headings also must be dragged down.

Perform the following steps to enlarge the Page Header section and move the bold line.

 To Enlarge the Page Header Section

1 **Point to the bottom border of the Page Header section (Figure 4-33). The mouse pointer shape changes to a two-headed vertical arrow with a crossbar.**

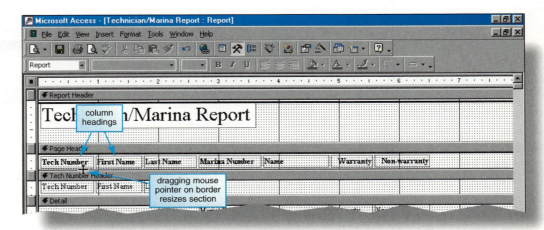

FIGURE 4-33

2 **Drag the mouse pointer down to enlarge the size of the Page Header section to that shown in Figure 4-34 and then drag the bold line in the Page Header section down to the position shown in the figure.**

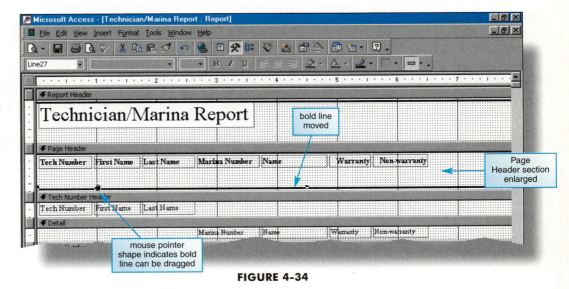

FIGURE 4-34

Changing Column Headings

To change a column heading, point to the position where you would like to display an insertion point. Click once to select the heading. Handles will display around the border of the heading after clicking. Then, click a second time to display the insertion point. Then you can make the desired changes. To delete a character, press the DELETE key to delete the character following the insertion point, or press the BACKSPACE key to delete the character preceding the insertion point. To insert a new character, simply type the character. To move the portion following the insertion point to a second line, press the SHIFT+ENTER keys.

If you click the second time too rapidly, Access will assume that you have double-clicked the heading. Double-clicking a control is another way to produce the control's property sheet. If this happens, simply close the property sheet and begin the process again.

Perform the following steps to change the column headings.

Steps To Change the Column Headings

1 **Point immediately in front of the N in Number in the heading for the first field. Click the column heading for the first field to select it. Click it a second time to produce an insertion point in front of the N, and then press the SHIFT+ENTER keys. Click immediately after the h in Tech and then type** nician **to complete the word, Technician, on the first line.**

The heading is split over two lines, and the heading has been changed to Technician Number (Figure 4-35).

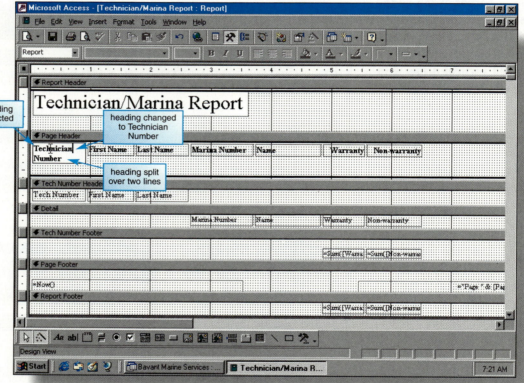

FIGURE 4-35

2 **Use the same technique to split the headings for the First Name, Last Name, and Marina Number fields over two lines.**

The changes to the header now are complete.

Moving and Resizing Controls

To move, resize, delete, or modify a single control, click it. Sizing handles display around the border of the control. To move the control, point to the boundary of the control, but away from any sizing handle. The mouse pointer changes shape to a hand. You then can drag the control to move it. To resize the control, drag one of the sizing handles.

You can move or resize several controls at the same time by selecting all of them before dragging. This is especially useful when controls must line up in a column. For example, the Warranty control in the Page Header should line up above the Warranty control in the Detail section. These controls also should line up with the controls in the Tech Number Footer and Report Footer sections that will display the sum of the warranty amounts.

To select multiple controls, click the first control you wish to select. Then hold down the SHIFT key while you click each of the others. The following steps first will select the controls in the Page Header, Detail, Tech Number Footer, and Report Footer sections that relate to the Warranty amount. You then will move and resize all these controls at once. Next, you will use the same technique to move and resize the controls that relate to the Non-warranty amount. Finally, to ensure enough room for complete names, you will enlarge the Name controls in the Page Header and Detail sections.

 ## To Move and Resize Controls

1 **Click the Non-warranty control in the Page Header section to select it. Hold down the SHIFT key and click the Non-warranty control in the Detail section, the control for the sum of the Non-warranty amounts in the Tech Number Footer section, and the control for the sum of the Non-warranty amounts in the Report Footer section. Release the SHIFT key. Point to the border of the Non-warranty control in the Page Header section but away from any handle. The mouse pointer shape should change to a hand.**

Multiple controls are selected, and the mouse pointer changes to a hand (Figure 4-36).

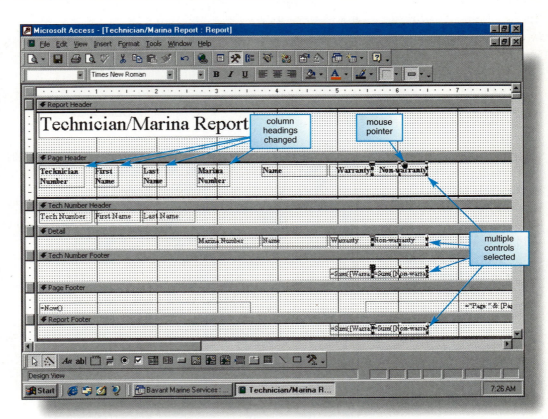

FIGURE 4-36

2 Drag the Non-warranty control in the Page Header section to the position shown in Figure 4-37. Drag the right sizing handle of the Non-warranty control in the Page Header section to change the size of the control to the one shown in the figure. You need not be exact.

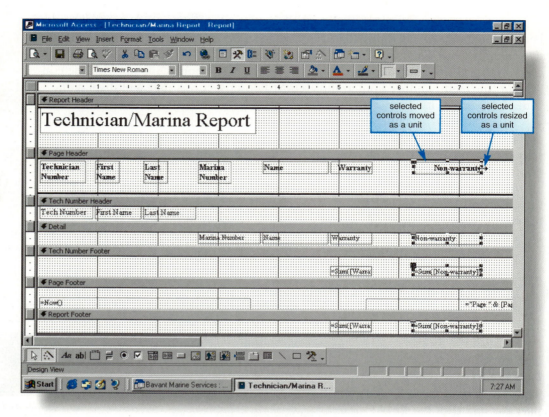

FIGURE 4-37

3 Use the same technique to move the controls for the Warranty field to the position shown in Figure 4-38 and change the size of the controls to those shown in the figure. Use the same technique to change the size of the controls for the Name field to those shown in the figure. Again, you need not be exact.

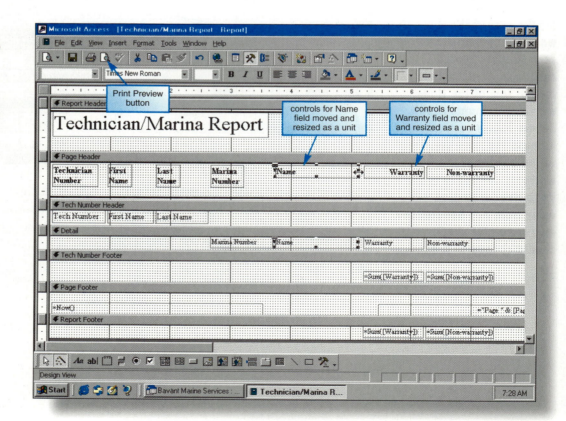

FIGURE 4-38

Previewing a Report

To see what the report looks like with sample data, preview the report by clicking the Print Preview button on the Report Design toolbar as illustrated in the following step.

TO PREVIEW A REPORT

 Click the Print Preview button on the Report Design toolbar. If the entire width of the report does not display, click anywhere within the report.

A preview of the report displays (Figure 4-39). The extra messages have been removed. The column headings have been changed and now extend over two lines.

 Other Ways

1. Click View button on Report Design toolbar
2. Click View button arrow on Report Design toolbar, click Print Preview
3. On View menu click Print Preview

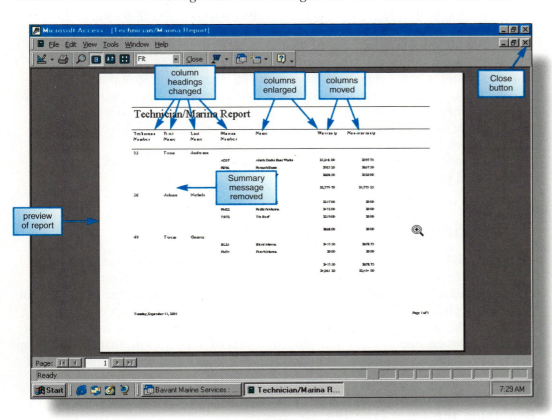

FIGURE 4-39

Closing and Saving a Report

To close a report, close the window using the window's Close button. Then, indicate whether you want to save your changes. Perform the following step to close and save the report.

TO CLOSE AND SAVE A REPORT

 Click the window's Close button to close the window. Click the Yes button to save the design of the report.

Printing a Report

To print the report, right-click the report name in the Database window, and then click Print on the shortcut menu as shown in the step on the next page.

TO PRINT A REPORT

1 Make sure that the Reports object is selected in the Database window. Right-click Technician/Marina Report and then click Print on the shortcut menu.

The report prints. It should look like the report shown in Figure 4-2 on page A 4.6.

Report Design Considerations

When designing and creating reports, keep in mind the following guidelines.

1. The purpose of any report is to provide specific information. Ask yourself if the report conveys this information effectively. Are the meanings of the rows and columns in the report clear? Are the column captions easily understood? Are all abbreviations used in the report clear to those looking at the report?
2. Be sure to allow sufficient white space between groups. If you feel the amount is insufficient, add more space by enlarging the group footer.
3. You can use different fonts and sizes by changing the appropriate properties. It is important not to overuse them, however. Consistently using several different fonts and sizes often gives a cluttered and amateurish look to the report.
4. Be consistent when creating reports. Once you have decided on a general style, stick with it.

Creating and Using Custom Forms

Thus far, you have used a form to add new records to a table and change existing records. When you did, you created a basic form using the New Object: AutoForm button. Although the form did provide some assistance in the task, the form was not particularly pleasing. The standard form stacked fields on top of each other at the left side of the screen. This section covers custom forms that you can use in place of the basic form created by the Form Wizard. To create such a form, first use the Form Wizard to create a basic form. Then modify the design of this form, transforming it into the one you want.

Beginning the Form Creation

To create a form, click the Tables object and select the table. Click the New Object button arrow and then Form. Next, use the Form Wizard to create the form. The Form Wizard will lead you through a series of choices and questions. Access then will create the form automatically.

Perform the steps on the next page to create an initial form. This form later will be modified to produce the form shown in Figure 4-3 on page A 4.7.

Steps **To Begin Creating a Form**

1 **Make sure the Tables object is selected and then click Marina. Click the New Object button arrow, click Form, and then click Form Wizard. Click the OK button and then point to the Add Field button.**

The Form Wizard dialog box displays (Figure 4-40). The Marina Number field is selected.

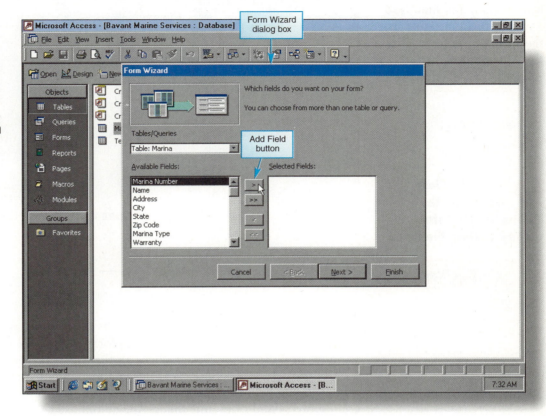

FIGURE 4-40

2 **Use the Add Field button to add all the fields except the Marina Type and Tech Number fields. Then click the Next button. When asked for a layout, be sure Columnar is selected, and then click the Next button again.**

The Form Wizard dialog box displays, requesting a form style (Figure 4-41).

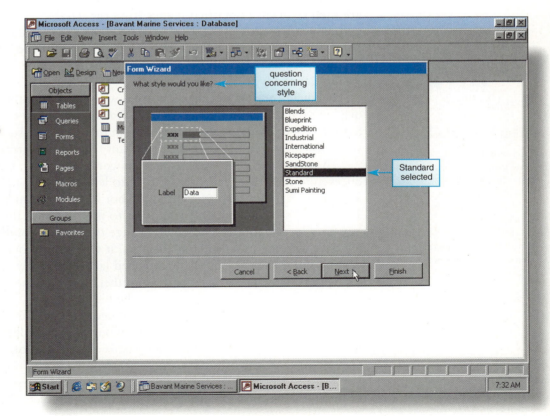

FIGURE 4-41

3 Be sure Standard is selected, click the Next button, and then type Marina Update Form as the title for the form. Click the Finish button to complete and display the form.

The form displays (Figure 4-42).

4 Click the Close button for the Marina Update Form window to close the form.

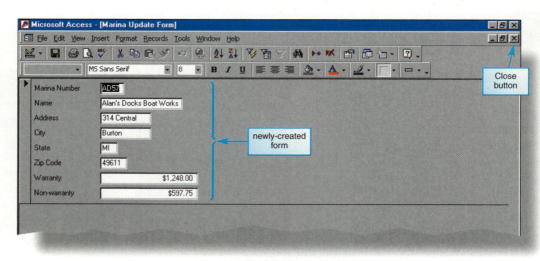

FIGURE 4-42

1. On Objects bar click Forms, click New button, and then click Form Wizard
2. On Objects bar click Forms, click Create form by using wizard
3. On Insert menu click Form, click Form Wizard

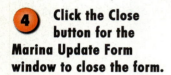

Attached Labels

You can remove an attached label by clicking the label and then pressing the DELETE key. The label will be removed, but the control will remain. To attach a label to a control, create the label, click the Cut button, click the Control, and then click the Paste button.

Modifying the Form Design

To modify the design of an existing form, right-click the form in the Database window, and then click Design View on the shortcut menu. At this time, you can modify the design. The modifications can include moving fields, adding new fields, and changing field characteristics. In addition, you can add special features, such as combo boxes and titles and change the colors used.

Just as with reports, the various items on a form are called **controls**. The three types are bound controls, unbound controls, and calculated controls. **Bound controls** are used to display data that comes from the database, such as the marina number and name. Bound controls have attached labels that typically display the name of the field that furnishes the data for the control. The **attached label** for the Marina Number field, for example, is the portion of the screen immediately to the left of the field. It contains the words, Marina Number.

Unbound controls are not associated with data from the database and are used to display such things as the form's title. Finally, **calculated controls** are used to display data that is calculated from other data in the database, such as the Total Amount, which is calculated by adding the warranty and non-warranty amounts.

To move, resize, delete, or modify a control, click it. Clicking a second time produces an insertion point in the control to let you modify its contents. When a control is selected, handles display around the border of the control and, if appropriate, around the attached label. If you point to the border of the control, but away from any handle, the pointer shape will change to a hand. You then can drag the control to move it. If an attached label displays, it will move along with the control. If you wish to move the control or the attached label separately, drag the large handle in the upper-left corner of the control or label. To resize the control, drag one of the sizing handles; and to delete it, press the DELETE key.

Just as with reports, some of the changes you wish to make to a control will involve using the property sheet for the control. You will use the property sheet of the Total Amount control, for example, to change the format that Access uses to display the contents of the control.

Perform the steps on the next page to modify the design of the Marina Update Form and dock the toolbox at the bottom of the screen, if necessary.

Steps ## To Modify the Form Design

1 In the Bavant Marine Services Database window, click the Forms object. Right-click Marina Update Form and then click Design View on the shortcut menu. Maximize the window, if necessary. If a field box displays, click its Close button. Be sure the toolbox displays and is docked at the bottom of the screen. (If it is not, drag the title bar of the toolbox below the scroll bar at the bottom of the screen and release the left mouse button.)

2 Click the control for the Warranty field, and then move the mouse pointer until the shape changes to a hand. (You will need to point to the border of the control but away from any handle.)

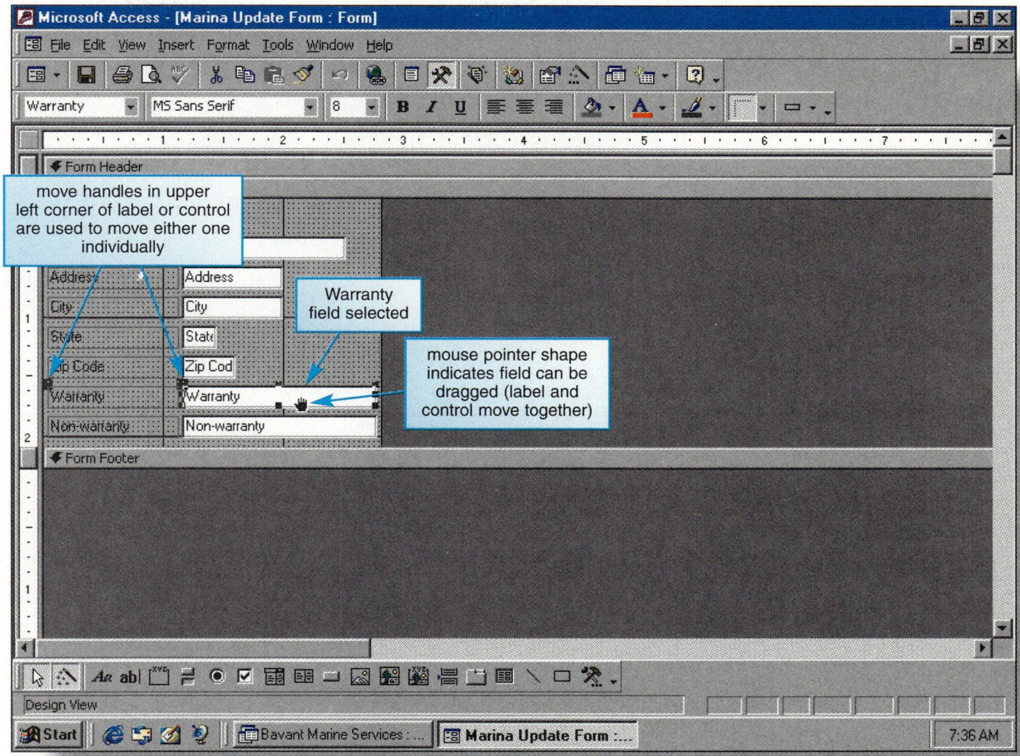

Move handles display, indicating the field is selected (Figure 4-43). The shape of the mouse pointer changes to a hand.

FIGURE 4-43

3 Drag the Warranty field to the approximate position shown in Figure 4-44. The form will expand automatically in size to accommodate the new position for the field.

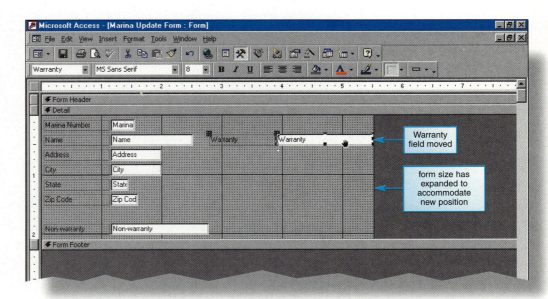

FIGURE 4-44

4 Use the same steps to move the Non-warranty field to the position shown in Figure 4-45.

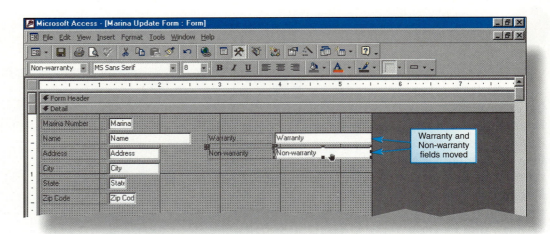

FIGURE 4-45

Adding a New Field

To add a new field, use the Text Box button in the toolbox to add a field. After clicking the Text Box button, click the position for the field on the form, and then indicate the contents of the field. Perform the following steps to add the Total Amount field to the form.

 ## To Add a New Field

1 Point to the Text Box button in the toolbox (Figure 4-46).

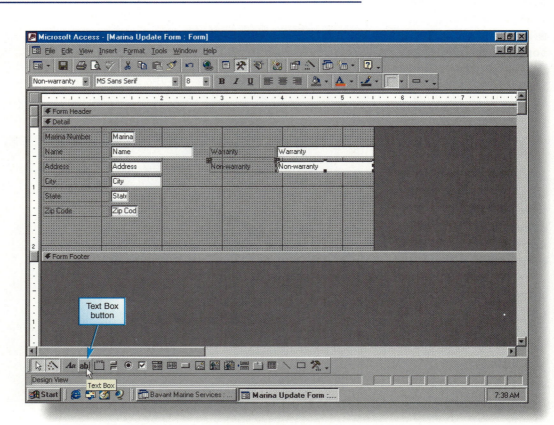

FIGURE 4-46

2 Click the Text Box button in the toolbox, and then move the mouse pointer, which has changed shape to a small plus symbol accompanied by a text box, to the position shown in Figure 4-47.

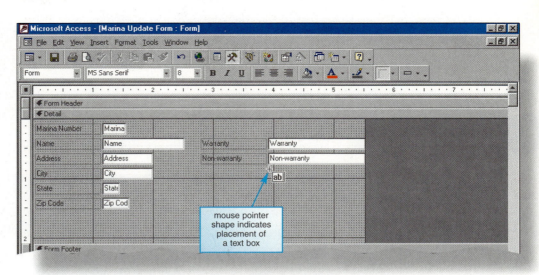

FIGURE 4-47

3 Click the position shown in Figure 4-47 to place a text box. Click inside the text box and type =[Warranty]+[Non-warranty] as the expression in the text box. Click the field label (the box that contains the word Text) twice, once to select it and a second time to display an insertion point. Use the DELETE key or the BACKSPACE key to delete the current entry. Type Total Amount as the new entry.

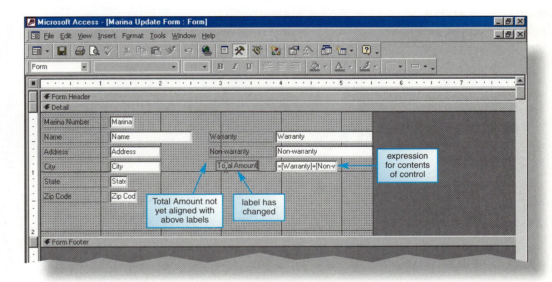

FIGURE 4-48

The expression for the field has been entered and the label has been changed to Total Amount (Figure 4-48).

4 Click outside the Total Amount control to deselect it. Then, click the control to select it once more. Handles will display around the control. Move the label portion so its left edge lines up with the labels for the Warranty and Non-warranty fields by dragging the move handle in its upper-left corner. Click outside the control to deselect it.

Changing the Format of a Field

Access automatically formats fields from the database appropriately because it knows their data types. Usually, you will find the formats assigned by Access to be acceptable. For calculated fields, such as Total Amount, however, Access just assigns a general format. The value will not display automatically with two decimal places and a dollar sign.

More About

Adding a Field

You can receive assistance in entering the expression for a field you are adding by using the Expression Builder. To do so, click the Control Source property on the control's property sheet and then click the Build button. The Expression Builder dialog box will then display.

To change to a special format, such as Currency, which displays the number with a dollar sign and two decimal places, requires using the field's property sheet to change the Format property. Perform the following steps to change the format for the Total Amount field to Currency.

 To Change the Format of a Field

1 Right-click the control for the Total Amount field (the box containing the expression) to produce its shortcut menu and then click Properties on the shortcut menu. Click the All tab, if necessary, so all the properties display, and then click the Format property. Point to the Format box arrow.

The property sheet for the field displays in the Text Box window (Figure 4-49).

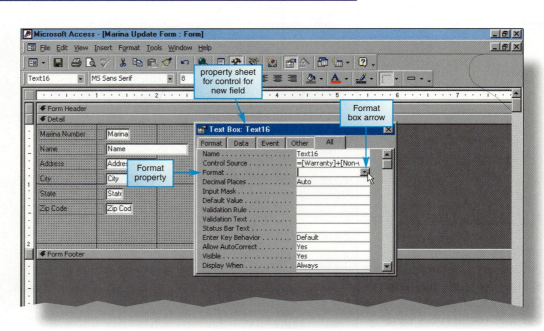

FIGURE 4-49

2 Click the Format box arrow to produce a list of available formats. Scroll down so Currency displays and then click Currency. Close the property sheet by clicking its Close button.

The values in the Total Amount field will display in Currency format, which includes a dollar sign and two decimal places.

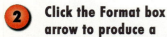 *About* **2000**

Changing a Format

Access assigns formats to database fields, but these formats can be changed by changing the Format property of the fields. The specific formats that are available depend on the data type of the field. The Format list also contains samples of the way the data will display using the various formats.

Combo Boxes

When entering a value for the marina type, there are only three legitimate values: BIR, IWO, and RSO. When entering a technician number, the value must match the number of a technician currently in the technician table. To assist the users in entering this data, the form will contain combo boxes. With a **combo box**, the user can type the data, if that is convenient. Alternatively, the user can click the combo box arrow to display a list of possible values and then select an item from the list.

To place a combo box in the form, use the Combo Box button in the toolbox. If the **Control Wizards button** in the toolbox is recessed, you can use a wizard to guide you through the process of creating the combo box. Perform the steps on the next page to place a combo box for the Marina Type field on the form.

To Place a Combo Box that Selects Values from a List

1 Make sure the Control Wizards button in the toolbox is recessed. Point to the Combo Box button in the toolbox (Figure 4-50).

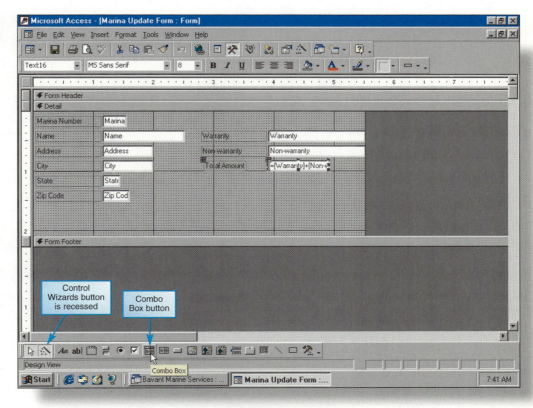

FIGURE 4-50

2 Click the Combo Box button in the toolbox, and then move the mouse pointer, whose shape has changed to a small plus symbol accompanied by a combo box, to the position shown in Figure 4-51.

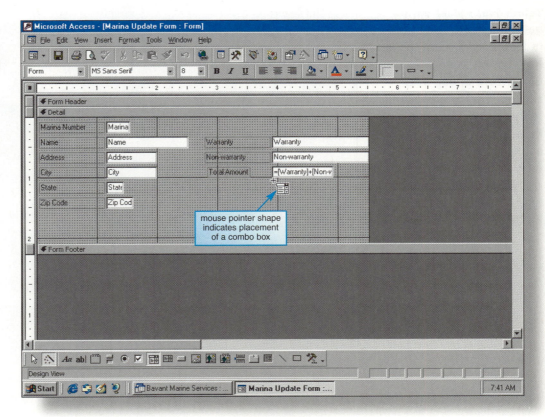

FIGURE 4-51

Microsoft **Access** 2000

3 **Click the position shown in Figure 4-51 to place a combo box.**

The Combo Box Wizard dialog box displays, requesting that you indicate how the combo box is to receive values for the list (Figure 4-52).

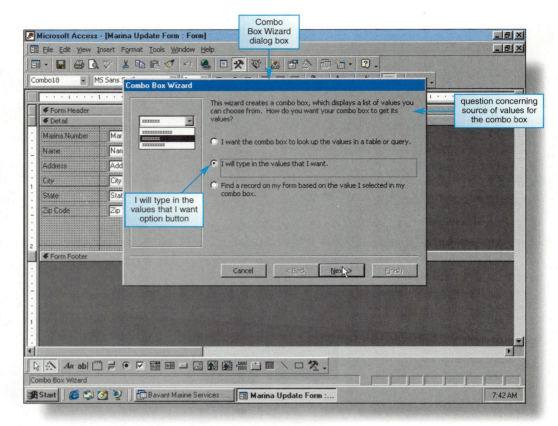

FIGURE 4-52

4 **If necessary, click I will type in the values that I want option button to select it as shown in Figure 4-52. Click the Next button in the Combo Box Wizard dialog box, click the first row of the table (under Col1) and then type** BIR. **Press the DOWN ARROW key and then type** IWO. **Press the DOWN ARROW key again and then type** RSO. **Point to the Next button.**

The list of values for the combo box is entered (Figure 4-53).

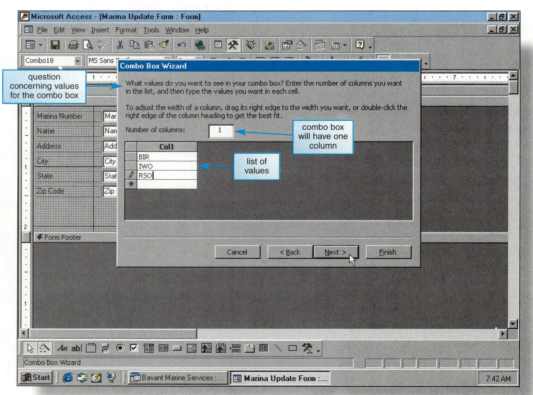

FIGURE 4-53

5 Click the Next button. Click Store that value in this field. Click the Store that value in this field box arrow, and then click Marina Type. Point to the Next button.

The Store that value in this field option button is selected, and the Marina Type field is selected (Figure 4-54).

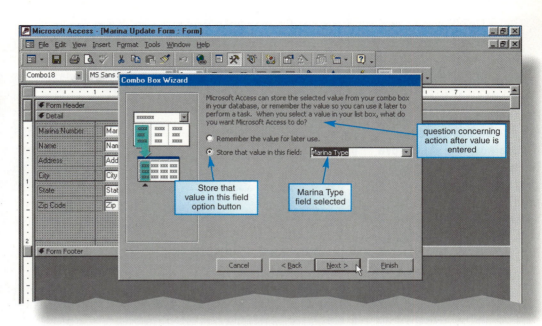

FIGURE 4-54

6 Click the Next button. Type `Marina Type` as the label for the combo box and point to the Finish button.

The label is entered (Figure 4-55).

7 Click the Finish button. Click the label for the combo box, and then move the label so that its left edge aligns with the left edge of the labels for the Warranty, Non-warranty, and Total Amount fields. Select the label and then expand it by double-clicking the handle on its right edge so the entire Marina Type label displays.

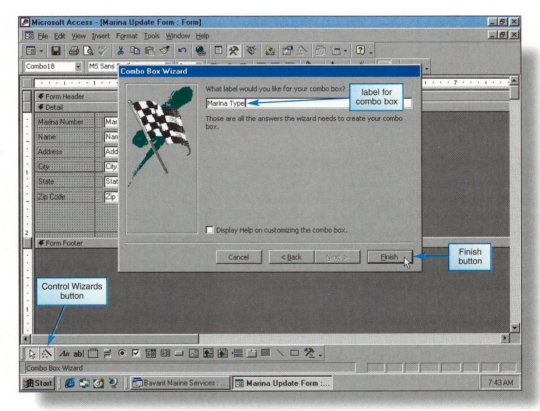

FIGURE 4-55

The steps for placing a combo box to select values from a table are similar to those for placing a combo box to select values from a list. The only difference is the source of the data. Perform the steps on the next page to place a combo box for the Tech Number field on the form.

Microsoft **Access 2000**

To Place a Combo Box that Selects Values from a Related Table

1 With the Control Wizards button in the toolbox recessed, click the Combo Box button in the toolbox, and then move the mouse pointer, whose shape has changed to a small plus symbol accompanied by a combo box, to the position shown in Figure 4-56.

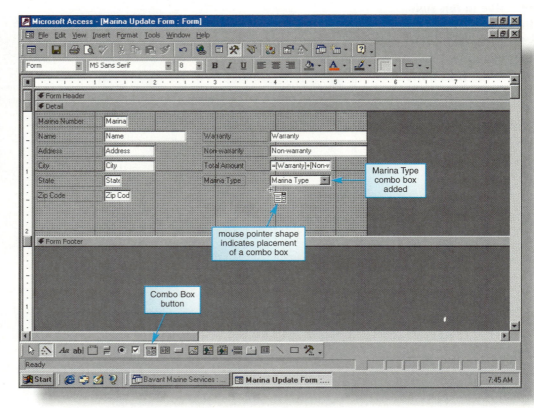

FIGURE 4-56

2 Click the position shown in Figure 4-56 to place a combo box. In the Combo Box wizard, click I want the combo box to look up the values in a table or query if it is not already selected. Click the Next button, click the Technician table, and then point to the Next button.

The Technician table is selected as the table to provide values for the combo box (Figure 4-57).

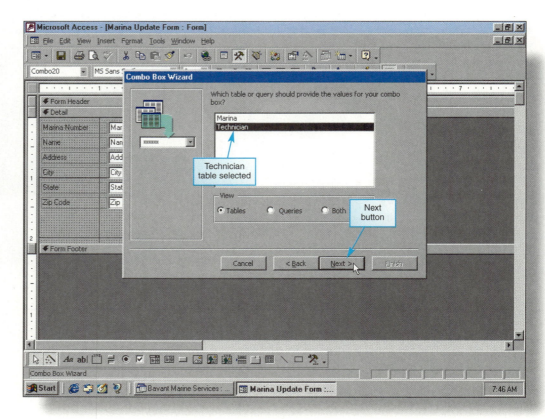

FIGURE 4-57

3 Click the Next button. Click the Add Field button to add the Tech Number as a field in the combo box. Click the First Name field and then click the Add Field button. Click the Last Name field and then click the Add Field button. Point to the Next button.

The Tech Number, First Name, and Last Name fields are selected for the combo box (Figure 4-58).

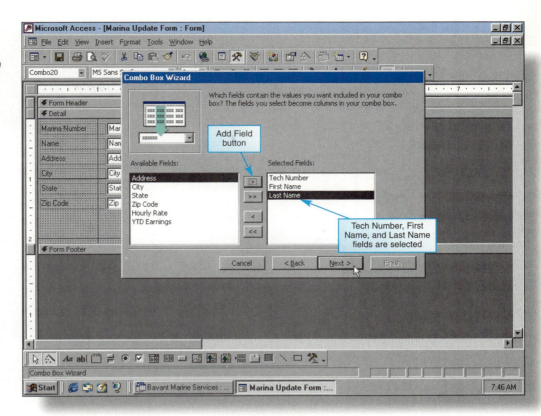

FIGURE 4-58

4 Click the Next button. Point to the Hide key column (recommended) check box.

The next Combo Box Wizard dialog box displays (Figure 4-59). You can use this dialog box to change the sizes of the fields. You also can use it to indicate whether the key field, in this case the Tech Number field, should be hidden.

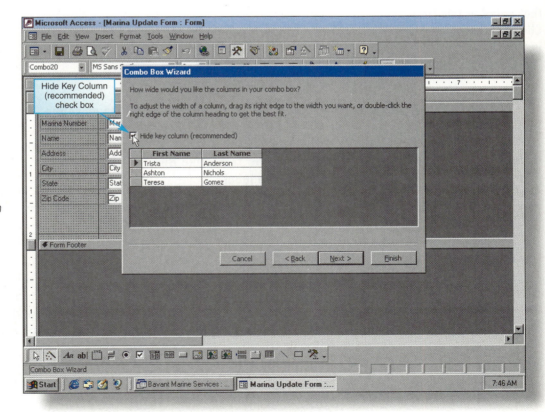

FIGURE 4-59

5 **Click Hide key column (recommended) to remove the check mark to ensure the Tech Number field displays along with the First Name and Last Name fields. Resize each column to best fit the data by double-clicking the right-hand border of the column heading. Click the Next button.**

The Combo Box Wizard dialog box displays, asking you to choose a field that uniquely identifies a row in the combo box (Figure 4-60). The Tech Number field, which is the correct field, is already selected.

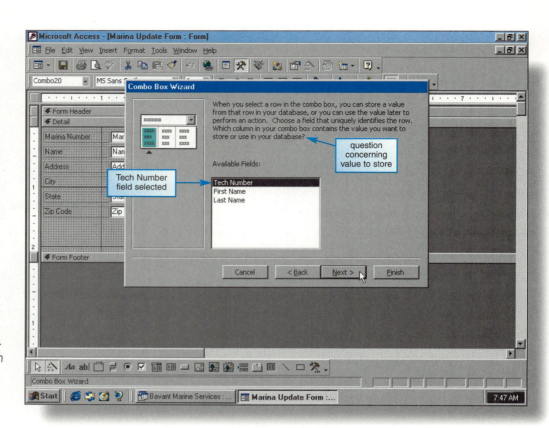

FIGURE 4-60

6 **Click the Next button. Click Store that value in this field. Click the Store that value in this field box arrow, scroll down, and then click Tech Number. Click the Next button. Type** Technician Number **as the label for the combo box.**

7 **Click the Finish button. Click the label for the combo box, and then move the label so its left edge aligns with the left edge of the Marina Type, Warranty, Non-warranty, and Total Amount fields. Select the label and then expand it by double-clicking the handle on its right edge so the entire Technician Number label displays. Click anywhere outside the label to deselect the label.**

Adding a Title

The form in Figure 4-3 on page A 4.7 contains a title, Marina Update Form, that displays in a large, light blue label at the top of the form. To add a title, first expand the Form Header to allow room for the title. Next, use the Label button in the toolbox to place the label in the Form Header. Finally, type the title in the label. Perform the following steps to add a title to the form.

Steps To Add a Title

1 Point to the bottom border of the Form Header. The mouse pointer changes shape to a two-headed vertical arrow with a crossbar as shown in Figure 4-61.

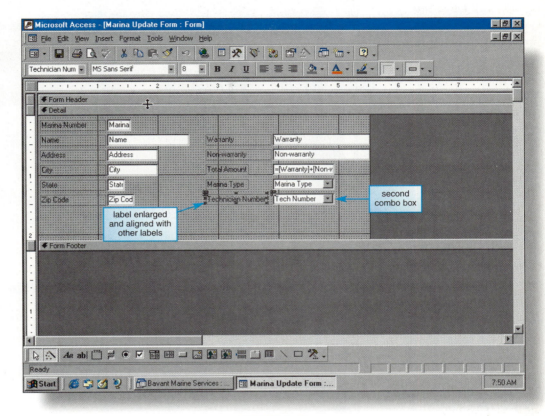

FIGURE 4-61

2 Drag the bottom border of the Form Header to the approximate position shown in Figure 4-62, and then point to the Label button in the toolbox.

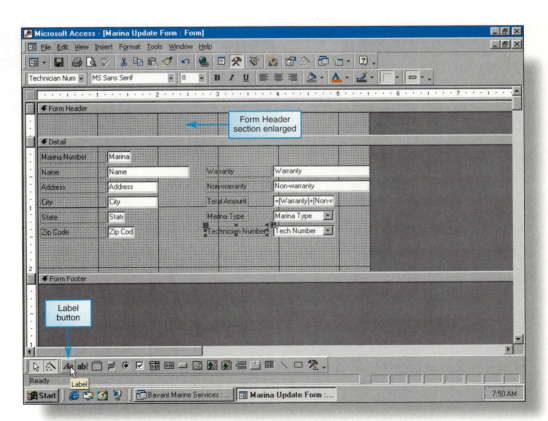

FIGURE 4-62

3 Click the Label button in the toolbox and move the mouse pointer, whose shape has changed to a small plus symbol accompanied by a label, into the position shown in Figure 4-63.

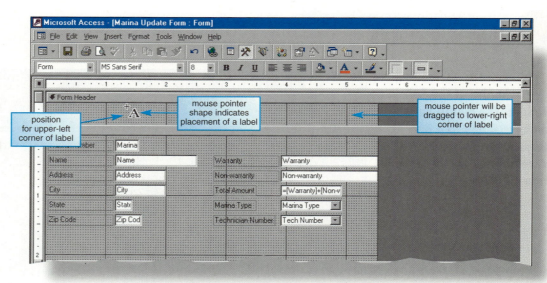

FIGURE 4-63

4 Drag the pointer to the opposite corner of the Form Header to form the label shown in Figure 4-64.

5 Type Marina Update Form as the form title.

The title is entered.

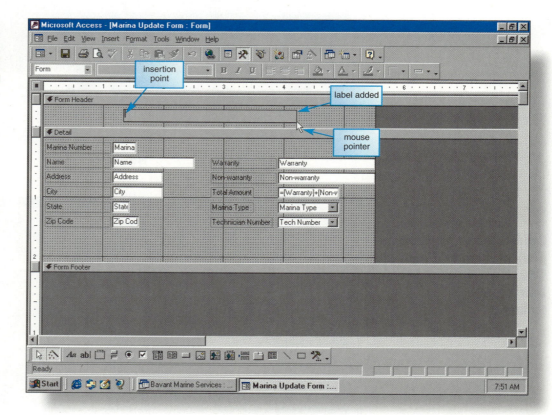

FIGURE 4-64

Enhancing a Title

The form now contains a title. You can enhance the appearance of the title by changing various properties of the label containing the title. The steps on the next page change the color of the label, make the label appear to be raised from the screen, change the font size of the title, and change the alignment of the title within the label.

To Enhance a Title

1 **Click somewhere outside the label containing the title to deselect the label. Deselecting is required or right-clicking the label will have no effect. Next, right-click the label containing the title. Point to Properties on the shortcut menu.**

The shortcut menu for the label displays (Figure 4-65).

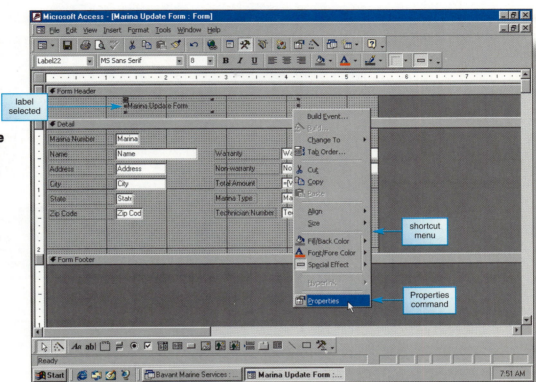

FIGURE 4-65

2 **Click Properties. If necessary, click the All tab on the property sheet. Click Back Color and then point to the Build button (the button with the three dots).**

The property sheet for the label displays. The insertion point displays in the Back Color property (Figure 4-66).

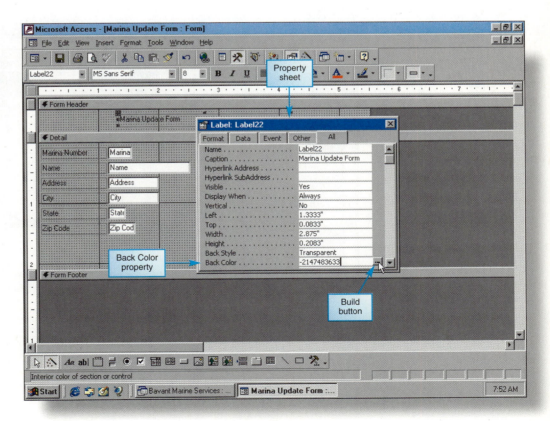

FIGURE 4-66

Microsoft **Access 2000**

3 Click the Build button and then point to the color light blue in the Color dialog box that displays (Figure 4-67).

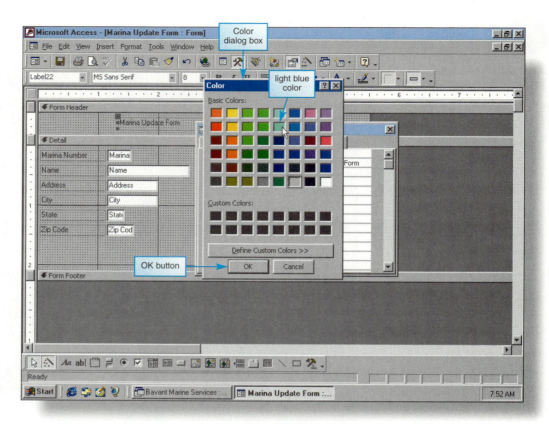

FIGURE 4-67

4 Click the color light blue, and then click the OK button. Scroll down the property sheet, click the Special Effect property, and then click the Special Effect box arrow.

The list of available values for the Special Effect property displays (Figure 4-68).

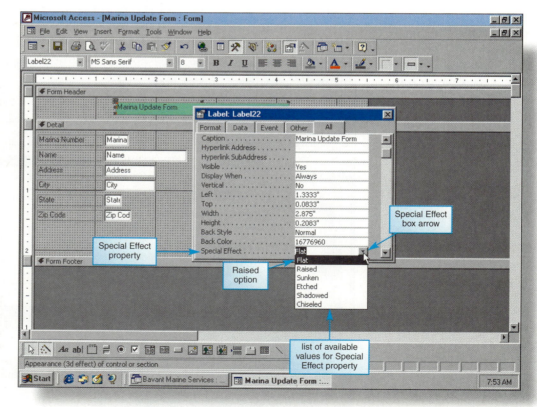

FIGURE 4-68

5 **Click Raised. Scroll down the property sheet and then click the Font Size property. Click the Font Size box arrow. Click 14 in the list of font sizes that displays. Scroll down and then click the Text Align property. Click the Text Align box arrow.**

The list of available values for the Text Align property displays (Figure 4-69).

6 **Click Distribute. Close the property sheet by clicking its Close button. If necessary, use the sizing handles to resize the label so that the entire title displays. Click outside the label to deselect it.**

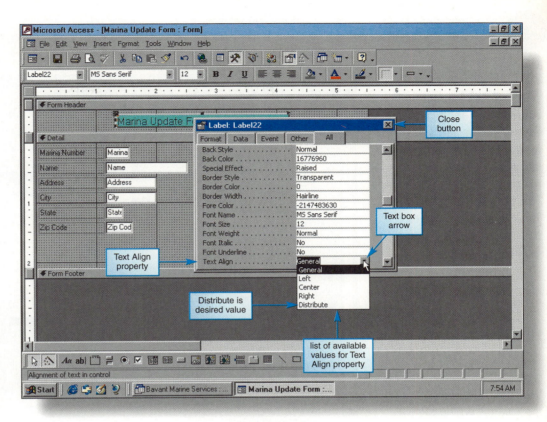

FIGURE 4-69

The enhancements to the title now are complete.

Changing Tab Stops

Users cannot change the value for the total amount. Instead, it will be recalculated automatically whenever the warranty or non-warranty amounts change. Consequently, if users repeatedly press the TAB key to move through the controls on the form, the Total Amount control should be bypassed. In order to force this to happen, change the Tab Stop property for the control from Yes to No as illustrated in the steps on the next page.

Microsoft Certification

The Microsoft Office User Specialist (MOUS) Certification program provides an opportunity for you to obtain a valuable industry credential - proof that you have the Access 2000 skills required by employers. For more information, see Appendix D or visit the Shelly Cashman Series MOUS Web page at www.scsite.com/off2000/cert.htm.

To Change a Tab Stop

1 Right-click the Total Amount control, and then click Properties on the shortcut menu. Click the down scroll arrow until the Tab Stop property displays, click the Tab Stop property, click the Tab Stop box arrow, and then point to No (Figure 4-70).

2 Click No, and then close the property sheet.

The modifications to the control are complete. With this change, tabbing through the controls on the form will bypass the total amount.

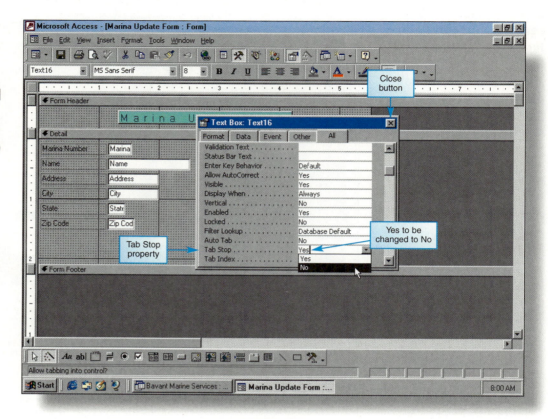

FIGURE 4-70

Other Ways

1. On File menu click Close

Closing and Saving a Form

To close a form, close the window using the window's Close button. Then indicate whether you want to save your changes. Perform the following step to close and save the form.

TO CLOSE AND SAVE A FORM

1 Click the window's Close button to close the window, and then click the Yes button to save the design of the form.

Opening a Form

To open a form, right-click a form in the Database window, and then click Open on the shortcut menu. The form will display and can be used to examine and update data. Perform the following steps to open the Marina Update Form.

Other Ways

1. Select form, click Open button on Database window toolbar
2. Double-click form

TO OPEN A FORM

1 With the Forms object selected, right-click the Marina Update Form to display the shortcut menu. Click Open on the shortcut menu.

The form displays. It should look like the form shown in Figure 4-3 on page A 4.7.

Using a Form

You use this form as you used the form in Project 3, with two differences. Access will not allow changes to the Total Amount, because Access calculates this amount automatically by adding the warranty and non-warranty amounts. The other difference is that this form contains combo boxes.

To use a combo box, click the arrow. Clicking the arrow in the Marina Type combo box produces a list of marina types (Figure 4-71). Clicking the arrow in the Technician Number combo box produces a list of numbers and the names of available technicians display as shown in Figure 4-3. In either case, you can type the appropriate value from the list you see on the screen or you can simply click the value in the list. With either method, the combo box helps you enter the correct value.

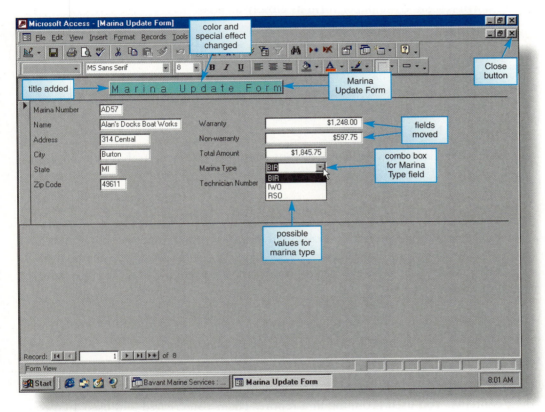

FIGURE 4-71

Closing a Form

To close a form, simply close the window containing the form. Perform the following step to close the form.

TO CLOSE A FORM

 Click the Close button for the Form window.

Form Design Considerations

As you design and create custom forms, keep in mind the following guidelines.

1. Remember that someone using your form may be looking at the form for several hours at a time. Forms that are cluttered or contain too many different effects (colors, fonts, frame styles, and so on) can become very hard on the eyes.
2. Place the fields in logical groupings. Fields that relate to each other should be close to one another on the form.
3. If the data that a user will enter comes from a paper form, make the screen form resemble the paper form as closely as possible.

Closing The Database

The following step closes the database by closing its Database window.

TO CLOSE A DATABASE

 Click the Close button for the Bavant Marine Services : Database window.

C A S E   P E R S P E C T I V E   S U M M A R Y

In Project 4, you assisted the management of Bavant Marine Services by creating two custom reports and a data entry form. You created the first report from a query that used a calculated field. In the second report, you grouped records by technician number and displayed subtotal and grand total amounts. You created a custom form that used a calculated control and combo boxes.

Project Summary

In Project 4, you created two reports and a form. To create the reports, you learned the purpose of the various sections and how to modify their contents. You used grouping in a report. Then, you created and used a custom form. Steps and techniques were presented showing you how to move controls, create new controls, add combo boxes, and add a title. You changed the characteristics of various objects in the form. You also learned general principles to help you design effective reports and forms.

What You Should Know

Having completed this project, you now should be able to perform the following tasks:

▶ Add a New Field *(A 4.34)*

▶ Add a Title *(A 4.42)*

▶ Begin Creating a Form *(A 4.30)*

▶ Change a Tab Stop *(A 4.47)*

▶ Change the Can Grow Property *(A 4.15)*

▶ Change the Column Headings *(A 4.25)*

▶ Change the Format of a Field *(A 4.35)*

▶ Close a Database *(A 4.50)*

▶ Close a Form *(A 4.49)*

▶ Close and Save a Form *(A 4.48)*

▶ Close and Save a Report *(A 4.17, A 4.29)*

▶ Create a Report *(A 4.9)*

▶ Create a Query *(A 4.8)*

▶ Create a Second Report *(A 4.18)*

▶ Enhance a Title *(A 4.44)*

▶ Enlarge the Page Header Section *(A 4.25)*

▶ Modify the Form Design *(A 4.32)*

▶ Move and Resize Controls *(A 4.26)*

▶ Move to Design View and Dock the Toolbox *(A 4.13)*

▶ Open a Database *(A 4.7)*

▶ Open a Form *(A 4.48)*

▶ Place a Combo Box to Select Values from a List *(A 4.37)*

▶ Place a Combo Box to Select Values from a Related Table *(A 4.40)*

▶ Preview a Report *(A 4.29)*

▶ Print a Report *(A 4.17, A 4 29)*

▶ Remove Unwanted Controls *(A 4.23)*

Apply Your Knowledge

Project Reinforcement at www.scsite.com/off2000/reinforce.htm

1 Presenting Data in the Sidewalk Scrapers Database

Instructions: If you are using the Microsoft Access 2000 Complete or the Microsoft Access 2000 Comprehensive text, open the Sidewalk Scrapers database that you used in Project 3. Otherwise, see the inside back cover for instructions for downloading the Access Data Disk or see your instructor for information on accessing the files required for this book. Perform the following tasks.

1. Create the report shown in Figure 4-72. Sort the report by Customer Number.
2. Print the report.
3. Using the Form Wizard, create a form for the Customer table. Include all fields except Worker Id on the form. Use Customer Update Form as the title for the form.

4. Modify the form in the Design window to create the form shown in Figure 4-73. The form includes a combo box for the Worker Id field.
5. Print the form. To print the form, open the form, click File on the menu bar, and then click Print. Click Selected Record(s) as the Print Range. Click the OK button.

Worker/Customer Report

Worker Id	First Name	Last Name	Customer Number	Name	Balance
03	Chris	Carter			
			AL25	Arders, Lars	$45.00
			CI05	Cinco Gallery	$29.00
			MD60	Martinez, Dan	$95.00
					$169.00
07	Louis	Ferrens			
			LK44	Lee, Kim	$0.00
					$0.00
10	John	Lau			
			AT43	Atari Cleaners	$80.00
			JB51	Jordach, Ben	$60.00
			ST21	Styling Salon and Tanning	$40.00
					$180.00
14	Elena	Sanchez			
			CH65	Chan's Bootery	$70.00
			MB02	Meat Shoppe	$0.00
					$70.00
					$419.00

FIGURE 4-72

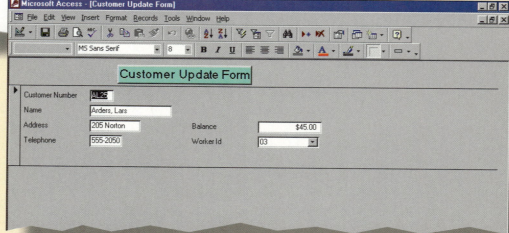

FIGURE 4-73

In the Lab

1 Presenting Data in the School Connection Database

Problem: The Booster's Club already has realized the benefits from the database of items and vendors that you created. The club must now prepare reports for auditors as well as the school board. The club greatly appreciates the validation rules that were added to ensure that data is entered correctly. They now feel they can improve the data entry process even further by creating custom forms.

Instructions: If you are using the Microsoft Access 2000 Complete or the Microsoft Access 2000 Comprehensive text, open the School Connection database that you used in Project 3. Otherwise, see the inside back cover for instructions for downloading the Access Data Disk or see your instructor for information on accessing the files required for this book. Perform the following tasks.

1. Create the On Hand Value Report shown in Figure 4-74 for the Item table. On Hand Value is the result of multiplying On Hand by Cost.
2. Print the report.
3. Create the Vendor/Items report shown in Figure 4-75. Profit is the difference between Selling Price and Cost.
4. Print the report.
5. Create the form shown in Figure 4-76. On Hand Value is a calculated control and is the result of multiplying On Hand by Cost. Include a combo box for Vendor Code.
6. Print the form. To print the form, open the form, click File on the menu bar, and then click Print. Click Selected Record(s) as the Print Range. Click the OK button.

FIGURE 4-74

On Hand Value Report

Item Id	Description	On Hand	Cost	On Hand Value
BA02	Baseball Cap	15	$12.50	$187.50
CM12	Coffee Mug	20	$3.75	$75.00
DM05	Doormat	5	$14.25	$71.25
MN04	Mouse Pad	5	$9.10	$45.50
OR01	Ornament	25	$2.75	$68.75
PL05	Pillow	8	$13.50	$108.00
PN21	Pennant	22	$5.65	$124.30
PP20	Pen and Pencil Set	12	$16.00	$192.00
SC11	Scarf	17	$8.40	$142.80
WA34	Wastebasket	3	$14.00	$42.00

Vendor/Items Report

Vendor Code	Name	Item Id	Description	Selling Price	Cost	Profit
AL	Alum Logo Inc.					
		BA02	Baseball Cap	$15.00	$12.50	$2.50
		MN04	Mouse Pad	$11.00	$9.10	$1.90
		SC11	Scarf	$12.00	$8.40	$3.60
GG	GG Gifts					
		CM12	Coffee Mug	$5.00	$3.75	$1.25
		OR01	Ornament	$4.00	$2.75	$1.25
		PP20	Pen and Pencil Set	$20.00	$16.00	$4.00
		WA34	Wastebasket	$15.00	$14.00	$1.00
TM	Trinkets 'n More					
		DM05	Doormat	$17.00	$14.25	$2.75
		PL05	Pillow	$15.00	$13.50	$1.50
		PN21	Pennant	$7.00	$5.65	$1.35

FIGURE 4-75

FIGURE 4-76

In the Lab

2 Presenting Data in the City Area Bus Company Database

Problem: The advertising sales manager already has realized several benefits from the database you created. The manager now would like to prepare reports from the database. He greatly appreciates the validation rules that were added to ensure that data is entered correctly. He now feels the data entry process can be improved even further by creating custom forms.

Instructions: If you are using the Microsoft Access 2000 Complete or the Microsoft Access 2000 Comprehensive text, open the City Area Bus Company database that you used in Project 3. Otherwise, see the inside back cover for instructions for downloading the Access Data Disk or see your instructor for information on accessing the files required for this book. Perform the following tasks.

1. Create the Advertising Income Report shown in Figure 4-77. Advertising Income is the sum of Balance and Amount Paid. Sort the report by Advertiser Id.
2. Print the report.
3. Create the Sales Rep/Advertiser report shown in Figure 4-78.
4. Print the report.
5. Create the form shown in Figure 4-79. Advertising Income is a calculated control and is the sum of Balance and Amount Paid. Ad Type and Sales Rep Number are combo boxes.

Sales Rep/Advertiser Report

Sales Rep Number	First Name	Last Name	Advertiser Id	Name	Ad Type	Amount Paid	Balance
24	Peter	Chou					
			AC25	Alia Cleaners	SER	$585.00	$85.00
			NO10	New Orient	DIN	$350.00	$150.00
			TM89	Tom's Market	RET	$500.00	$50.00
						$1,435.00	$285.00
29	Elvia	Ortiz					
			BB99	Bob's Bakery	RET	$1,150.00	$435.00
			CS46	Cara's Salon	SER	$660.00	$35.00
			HC11	Hilde's Cards & Gifts	RET	$500.00	$250.00
			MC34	Mom's Cookies	RET	$1,050.00	$95.00
						$3,360.00	$815.00
31	Pat	Reed					
			PJ24	Pajama Store	RET	$775.00	$0.00
			PP24	Pia's Pizza	DIN	$0.00	$50.00
						$775.00	$50.00
						$5,570.00	$1,150.00

FIGURE 4-78

Advertising Income Report

Advertiser Id	Name	City	Balance	Amount Paid	Advertising Income
AC25	Alia Cleaners	Crescentville	$85.00	$585.00	$670.00
BB99	Bob's Bakery	Richmond	$435.00	$1,150.00	$1,585.00
CS46	Cara's Salon	Cheltenham	$35.00	$660.00	$695.00
HC11	Hilde's Cards & Gifts	Crescentville	$250.00	$500.00	$750.00
MC34	Mom's Cookies	Crescentville	$95.00	$1,050.00	$1,145.00
NO10	New Orient	Manyunk	$150.00	$350.00	$500.00
PJ24	Pajama Store	Cheltenham	$0.00	$775.00	$775.00
PP24	Pia's Pizza	Richmond	$50.00	$0.00	$50.00
TM89	Tom's Market	Richmond	$50.00	$500.00	$550.00

FIGURE 4-77

In the Lab

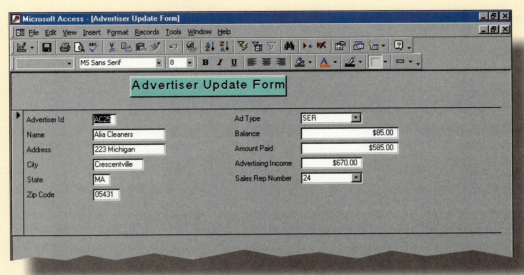

FIGURE 4-79

6. Print the form. To print the form, open the form, click File on the menu bar, and then click Print. Click Selected Record(s) as the Print Range. Click the OK button.

3 Presenting Data in the Resort Rental Database

Instructions: If you are using the Microsoft Access 2000 Complete or the Microsoft Access 2000 Comprehensive text, open the Resort Rentals database that you used in Project 3. Otherwise, see the inside back cover for instructions for downloading the Access Data Disk or see your instructor for information on accessing the files required for this book. Perform the following tasks.

1. Create the City Rental List shown in Figure 4-80. Sort the report in ascending order by city. Within city, the report should be sorted in ascending order by number of bedrooms and number of bathrooms. (*Hint*: Use a query to sort the data and base the report on the query.)
2. Print the report.
3. Create the Owner/Rental Units report shown in Figure 4-81 on the next page. Sort the data by city within each group.

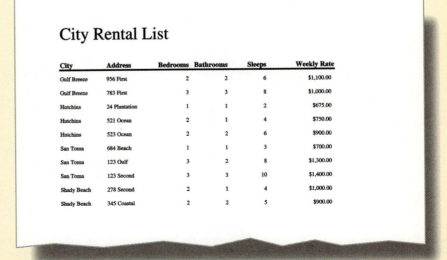

City Rental List

City	Address	Bedrooms	Bathrooms	Sleeps	Weekly Rate
Gulf Breeze	956 First	2	2	6	$1,100.00
Gulf Breeze	783 First	3	3	8	$1,000.00
Hutchins	24 Plantation	1	1	2	$675.00
Hutchins	521 Ocean	2	1	4	$750.00
Hutchins	523 Ocean	2	2	6	$900.00
San Toma	684 Beach	1	1	3	$700.00
San Toma	123 Gulf	3	2	8	$1,300.00
San Toma	123 Second	3	3	10	$1,400.00
Shady Beach	278 Second	2	1	4	$1,000.00
Shady Beach	345 Coastal	2	2	5	$900.00

FIGURE 4-80

(continued)

In the Lab

Presenting Data in the Resort Rental Database *(continued)*

4. Print the report.
5. Create the form shown in Figure 4-82. Owner Id is a combo box.
6. Add the current date to the form. Place the date in the upper right corner of the Form Header section. (*Hint*: Use Help to solve this problem.)
7. Print the form. To print the form, open the form, click File on the menu bar, and then click Print. Click Selected Record(s) as the Print Range. Click the OK button.

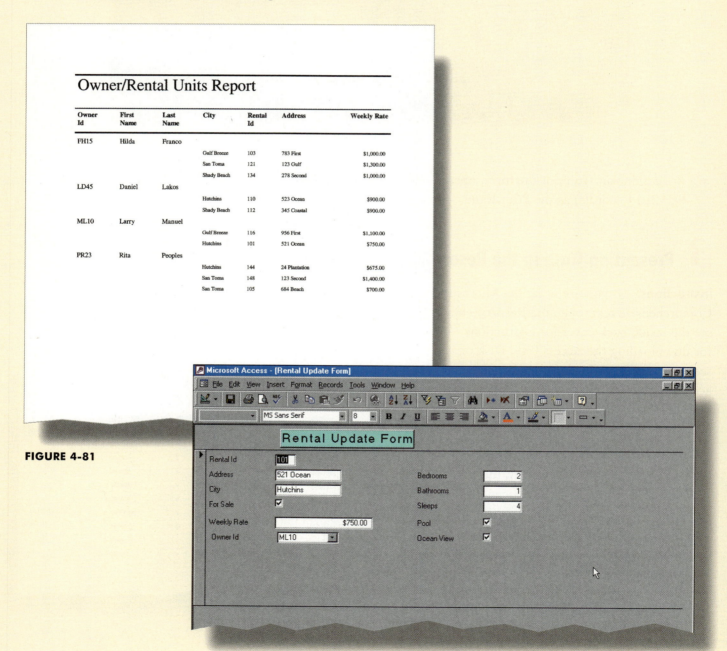

FIGURE 4-81

FIGURE 4-82

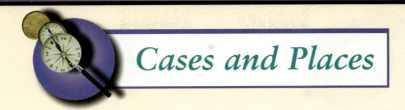

Cases and Places

The difficulty of these case studies varies:
▶ are the least difficult; ▶▶ are more difficult; and ▶▶▶ are the most difficult.

1 ▶ As a fund-raising project, the local college's Computer Science Club sells small computer accessories to students. Disks, disk cases, and mouse pads are some of the items the club sells from a small kiosk in the student computer lab. The club uses a database to keep track of their inventory and suppliers. The Computer Items database is on the Access Data Disk. Use this database and create the report shown in Figure 4-83. (*Hint:* Create a query and base the report on the query.) Print the report.

Supplier/Items Report

Name	Item Id	Description	Cost	Selling Price	Profit
Ergonomics Inc.					
	1663	Antistatic Wipes	$0.15	$0.25	$0.10
	2563	Desktop Holder	$3.85	$4.75	$0.90
Human Interfac					
	1683	CD Wallet	$3.45	$4.00	$0.55
	3923	Disk Cases	$2.20	$2.75	$0.55
	2593	Disks	$0.20	$0.75	$0.55
	6140	Zip Disk Wallet	$11.90	$14.00	$2.10
Mouse Trails					
	3953	Mouse Holder	$0.80	$1.00	$0.20
	5810	Mouse Pad-Logo	$3.45	$5.00	$1.55
	4343	Mouse Pad-Plain	$2.25	$3.00	$0.75

FIGURE 4-83

2 ▶ Using the database from Case Study 1 above, create the data entry form shown in Figure 4-84. Supplier code is a combo box. Inventory Value is a calculated field that is the result of multiplying the number of units on hand by the cost. Print the form.

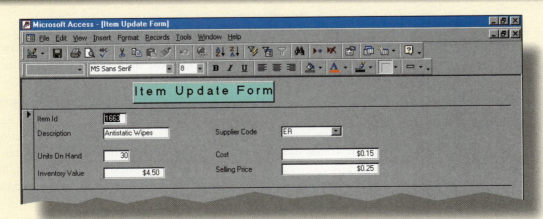

FIGURE 4-84

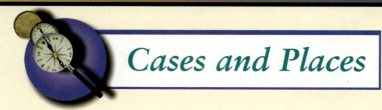

Cases and Places

3 ▶▶ Galaxy Books is a local bookstore that specializes in Science Fiction. The owner uses a database to keep track of the books she has in stock. The Galaxy Books database is on the Access Data Disk. Use this database to create a report similar to the one shown in Figure 4-74 on page A 4.53. Include the book code, book title, author, units on hand, and price fields. Use a calculated control called Stock Value that is the result of multiplying units on hand by price. Sort the report in ascending order by book title. Print the report. Create the report shown in Figure 4-85. The report groups books by publisher and displays the average book price for each publisher. Print the report.

Publisher/Books Report

Publisher Code	Publisher Name	Book Code	Title	Price	
BB	Bertrand Books				
		1019	Stargaze	$5.50	
		3495	Dark Wind	$4.95	
			Average Book Price		$5.23
PB	Pearless Books				
		128X	Comet Dust	$5.95	
		6517	Strange Alien	$8.95	
			Average Book Price		$7.45
SI	Simpson-Ivan				
		0488	Android Wars	$5.95	
		0533	Albert's Way	$4.75	
			Average Book Price		$5.35
VN	VanNester				
		1668	Robots R Us	$6.95	
		3859	No Infinity	$4.75	
		4889	The Galaxy	$6.75	
		7104	Secret Planet	$5.75	
			Average Book Price		$6.05

FIGURE 4-85

4 ▶▶ Using the database from Case Study 3, create a Book Update Form similar to the one shown in Figure 4-76 on page A 4.53. Use a calculated control called Stock Value that is the result of multiplying units on hand by price. Include a combo box for Publisher Code.

5 ▶▶▶ You are the treasurer for the Computer Science Club. Create a database to store information about the club's checking account. Include the check number, check payee, check amount, date written, and a code to indicate the expense category. Use expense categories such as supplies, food, meetings, and entertainment. Create and print a report that lists checks by expense category. In addition, create and print a form to help you update the database easily. Experiment with different styles.

Microsoft **Access 2000**

Microsoft Access 2000

P R O J E C T

5

Enhancing Forms with OLE Fields, Hyperlinks, and Subforms

You will have mastered the material in this project when you can:

- Use date, memo, OLE, and hyperlink fields
- Enter data in date fields
- Enter data in memo fields
- Enter pictures into OLE fields
- Enter Web page names into hyperlink fields
- Change the row and column spacing in tables
- Save table properties
- Create a form with a subform
- Move and resize fields on a form
- Change the styles and colors of labels
- Use special effects on forms
- Add a title to a form
- Use a form that contains a subform
- Use date and memo fields in a query
- Compact a database

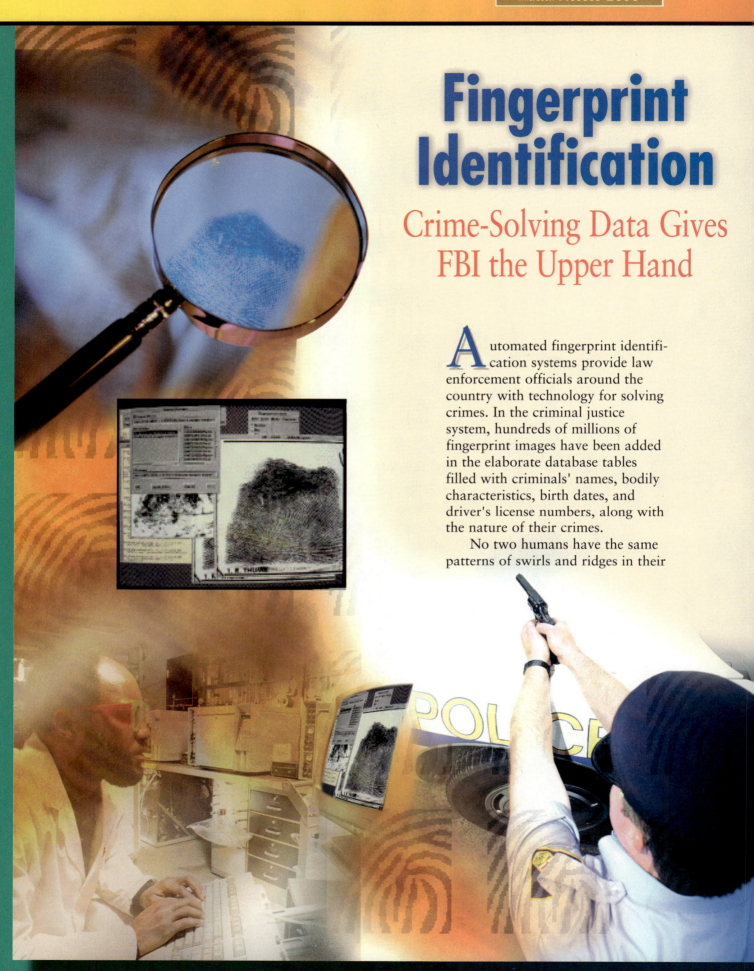

Fingerprint Identification

Crime-Solving Data Gives FBI the Upper Hand

Automated fingerprint identification systems provide law enforcement officials around the country with technology for solving crimes. In the criminal justice system, hundreds of millions of fingerprint images have been added in the elaborate database tables filled with criminals' names, bodily characteristics, birth dates, and driver's license numbers, along with the nature of their crimes.

No two humans have the same patterns of swirls and ridges in their

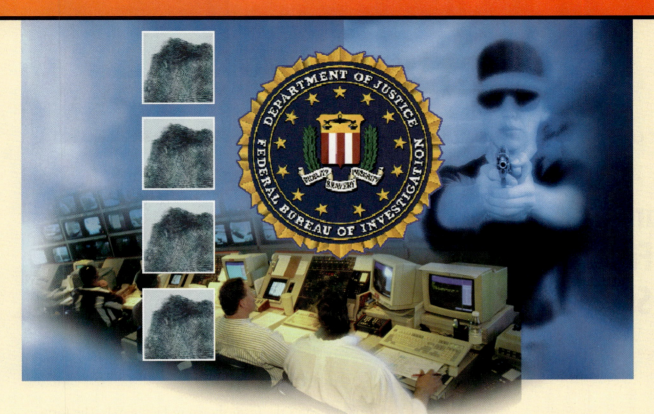

fingerprints, so comparing these unique features has been the most powerful method of identifying people since Babylonians pioneered fingerprinting in 1700 B.C. The fingerprint identification technology is part of the growing field of biometrics, which identifies people based on physical characteristics. Manual comparisons of prints by looking through state and FBI files can take as long as three weeks, but computer database comparisons using search algorithms can make positive identifications in only two hours or less if a suspect is in custody.

The Federal Bureau of Investigation's Integrated Automated Fingerprint Identification System (IAFIS) is one of the largest of its kind, and the biggest single technology investment in FBI history. The system consists of a suite of powerful supercomputers, sophisticated image processing algorithms, and data management tools such as those available with Access 2000. The FBI system is capable of rapidly and accurately searching a national criminal database expected to grow to more than 400 million records by the year 2000. IAFIS is designed to be a rapid-response, paperless system that receives and processes electronic fingerprint images, criminal histories, and related data. Services include remote searches of crime scene fingerprints and remote access to fingerprint images.

Law enforcement officials get the prints when they arrest and book a suspect or when they obtain latent prints at the crime scene. If the subject has been apprehended, the officer rolls the suspect's fingers on a small glass plate connected to a computer. If the suspect has not been identified or apprehended, an evidence technician goes to the crime scene, uses special powders, chemicals, and lasers and lifts and photographs the print. In both cases, the fingerprints are displayed on the computer monitor, traced with a stylus to enhance the lines, scanned, and digitized. These images then are transmitted electronically to the FBI and added to the database.

The FBI receives more than 50,000 requests daily to query the database in an attempt to match prints with images stored in the database. The FBI's system is so elaborate it can handle requests to match partial, smudged, or faint prints.

IAFIS has been a success in helping the FBI nab nearly 3,000 fugitives a month by searching this database. San Francisco investigators cleared nearly 14 times more latent cases during their first year using this system as compared with the previous year.

Working hand in hand, the IAFIS and law enforcement community are apprehending many of the hundreds of thousands of fugitives on America's streets.

Microsoft Access 2000

Enhancing Forms with OLE Fields, Hyperlinks, and Subforms

P R O J E C T

5

C A S E   P E R S P E C T I V E

The management of Bavant Marine Services has found that it needs to maintain additional data on its technicians. Managers need to store the start date of each technician in the database. They also would like for the database to contain a description of the technician's specialties, the technician's picture, and the address of the technician's Web page.

They also would like to have a form created that incorporates some of the new fields along with some existing fields. In addition, the management would like for the form to contain the marina number, name, warranty amount, and non-warranty amount for the marinas of each technician. They would like to be able to display two or three marinas on the screen at the same time, as well as be able to scroll through all the marinas of a technician and be able to access his or her Web Page directly from the form. They will need queries that use the Start Date and Specialties fields as criteria. Finally, they are concerned the database is getting larger than necessary and would like to compact the database to remove any wasted space. You must help Bavant Marine Services make these changes.

Introduction

This project creates the form shown in Figure 5-1. The form incorporates the following features not covered in previous projects:

- New fields display in the form. The Specialties field allows the organization to store a paragraph describing the specialties of the technician. The Specialties entry can be only as long as the organization desires. The Picture field holds a photograph of the technician.
- The Web Page field enables the user to access the Technician's Web Page directly from the database.
- The form not only shows data concerning the technician, but also the technician's marinas. The marinas are displayed as a table on the form.

Project Five — Enhancing the Bavant Marine Services Forms

Before you create the form required by the management of Bavant Marine Services, you must change the structure of the Technician table to incorporate the four new fields: Start Date, Specialties, Picture, and Web Page. Each of these new fields uses a data type you have not encountered before. Then, you must fill in these new fields with the appropriate data. The manner in which this is achieved depends on the field type. After entering data in the fields, you are to create the form including the table of marina data. You will create queries to obtain the answer to two important questions that reference the new fields. Finally, you will compact the database, thus ensuring the database does not occupy more space than is required.

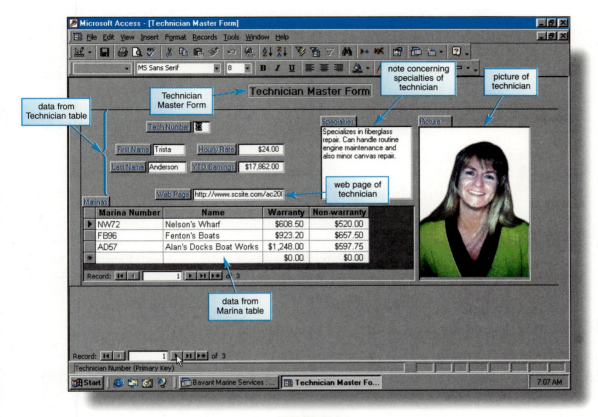

FIGURE 5-1

Opening the Database

Before you can modify the Technician table and create the form, you must open the database. Perform the following steps to complete this task.

TO OPEN A DATABASE

1. Click the Start button.

2. Click Open Office Document, and then click 3½ Floppy (A:) in the Look in box. Make sure the database called Bavant Marine Services is selected.

3. Click the Open button.

The database is open and the Bavant Marine Services : Database window displays.

More *About*

OLE Fields

OLE fields can store data such as Microsoft Word or Excel documents, pictures, sound, and other types of binary data created in other programs. For more information, visit the Access 2000 Project 4 More About page (www.scsite. com/ac2000/more.htm) and click OLE Fields.

Date, Memo, OLE, and Hyperlink Fields

The data to be added incorporates the following data types:

1. **Date (D)** — The field contains only valid dates.
2. **Memo (M)** — The field contains text that is variable in length. The length of the text stored in memo fields is virtually unlimited.
3. **OLE (O)** — The field contains objects created by other applications that support **OLE (Object Linking and Embedding)** as a server. Object Linking and Embedding is a special feature of Microsoft Windows that creates a special relationship between Microsoft Access and the application that created the object. When you edit the object, Microsoft Access returns automatically to the application that created the object.
4. **Hyperlink (H)** — This field contains links to other office documents or to Web Pages. If the link is to a Web Page, the field will contain the **Web page name**.

Adding Fields to a Table

You add the new fields to the Technician table by modifying the design of the table and inserting the fields at the appropriate position in the table structure. Perform the following steps to add the Start Date, Specialties, Picture, and Web Page fields to the Technician table.

 To Add Fields to a Table

1 **If necessary, click Tables on the Objects bar. Right-click Technician, and then point to Design View on the shortcut menu.**

The shortcut menu for the Technician table displays, and the Design View command is highlighted (Figure 5-2).

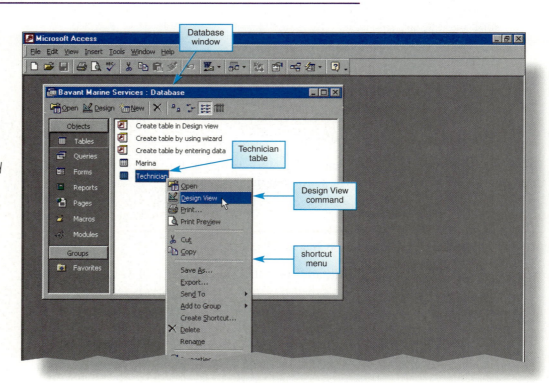

FIGURE 5-2

2 Click Design View on the shortcut menu and then maximize the Microsoft Access – [Technician : Table] window. Point to the position for the new field (the Field Name column in the row following the YTD Earnings field).

The Microsoft Access - Technician : Table] window displays (Figure 5-3).

3 Click the position for the new field. Type Start Date as the field name, press the TAB key, select Date/Time as the data type, press the TAB key, type Start Date as the description, and then press the TAB key to move to the next field.

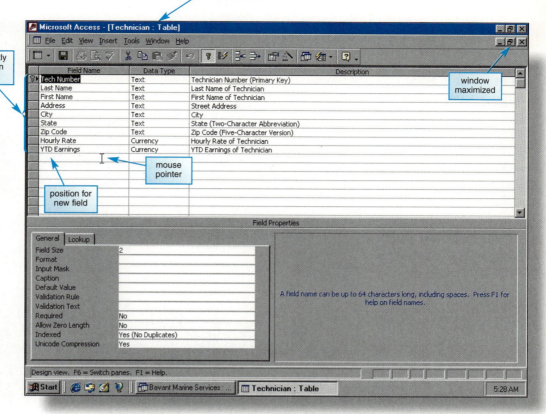

FIGURE 5-3

4 **Type** Specialties **as the field name, press the TAB key, select Memo as the data type, press the TAB key, type** Note Containing Details of Technician's Specialties **as the description, and then press the TAB key to move to the next field. Type** Picture **as the field name, press the TAB key, select OLE Object as the data type, press the TAB key, type** Picture of Technician **as the description, and then press the TAB key to move to the next field. Type** Web Page **as the field name, press the TAB key, select Hyperlink as the data type, press the TAB key, and type** Address of Technician's Web Page **as the description. Point to the Close button.**

The new fields are entered (Figure 5-4).

5 **Close the window by clicking its Close button. Click the Yes button in the Microsoft Access dialog box to save the changes.**

The new fields have been added to the structure.

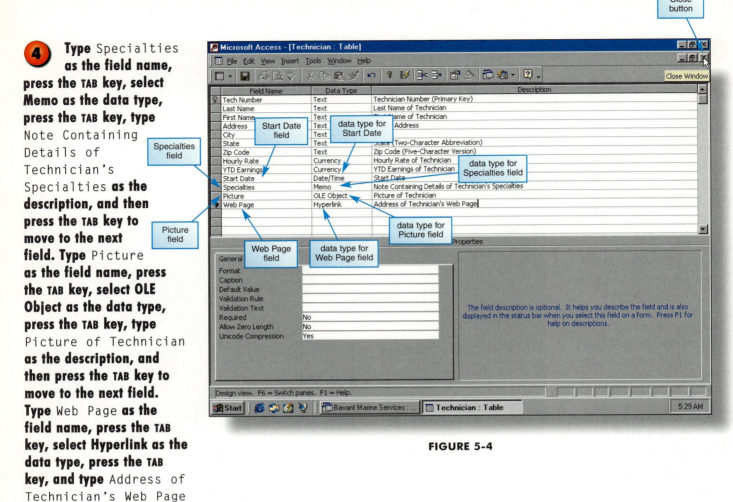

FIGURE 5-4

Updating the New Fields

After adding the new fields to the table, the next task is to enter data into the fields. The manner in which this is accomplished depends on the field type. The following sections cover the methods for updating date fields, memo fields, OLE fields, and Hyperlink fields.

Updating Date Fields

To enter data in **date fields**, simply type the dates and include slashes (/). Perform the following steps to add the Start Dates for all three technicians using Datasheet view.

 To Enter Data in Date Fields

1 **With the Database window on the screen, right-click the Technician table. Point to Open on the shortcut menu.**

The shortcut menu displays, and the Open command is highlighted (Figure 5-5).

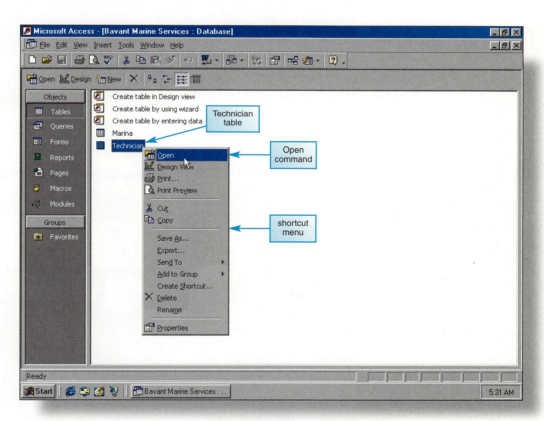

FIGURE 5-5

2 Click Open on the shortcut menu and then, if necessary, maximize the window. Point to the right scroll arrow.

The Technician table displays in Datasheet view in the maximized window (Figure 5-6).

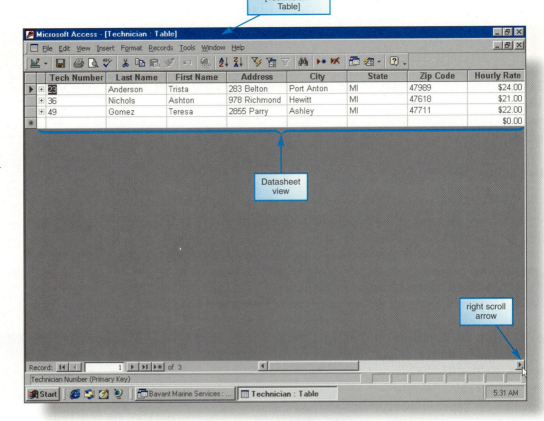

FIGURE 5-6

3 Repeatedly click the right scroll arrow until the new fields display and then click the Start Date field on the first record (Figure 5-7).

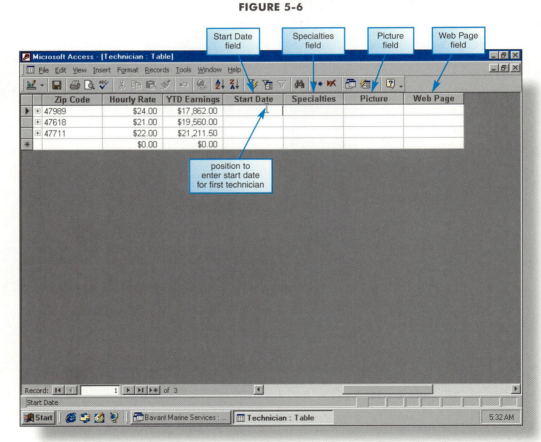

FIGURE 5-7

4 **Type** 9/9/1999 **as the date. Press the DOWN ARROW key. Type** 1/6/2000 **as the Start Date on the second record and then press the DOWN ARROW key. Type** 11/12/2000 **as the date on the third record.**

The dates are entered (Figure 5-8). If the dates do not display with four-digit years, click the Start menu, click Settings and then click Control Panel. Double-click Regional Settings, click the Date tab, and then change the short date style to MM/dd/yyyy. Click the OK button.

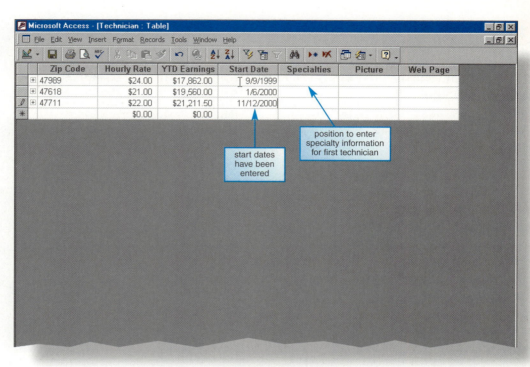

FIGURE 5-8

Updating Memo Fields

To **update a memo field**, simply type the data in the field. With the current spacing on the screen, only a small portion of the memo will display. To correct this problem, you will change the spacing later to allow more room for the memo. Perform the following steps to enter each technician's specialties.

 To Enter Data in Memo Fields

1 **If necessary, click the right scroll arrow so that the Specialties field displays. Click the Specialties field on the first record. Type** Specializes in fiberglass repair. Can handle routine engine maintenance and also minor canvas repair. **as the entry.**

The last portion of the memo displays (Figure 5-9).

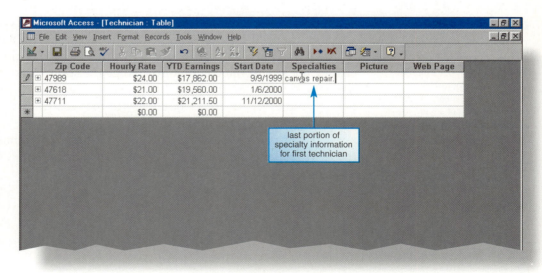

FIGURE 5-9

2 Click the Specialties field on the second record. Type Can handle all types of engine maintenance and repair. Can also do electrical work. **as the entry.**

3 Click the Specialties field on the third record. Type Specializes in electrical problems including electronics repair. Can also handle routine engine maintenance. **as the entry.**

All the Specialties are entered (Figure 5-10). The first portion of the specialty information for the first two technicians displays. Because the insertion point is still in the field for the third technician, only the last portion displays.

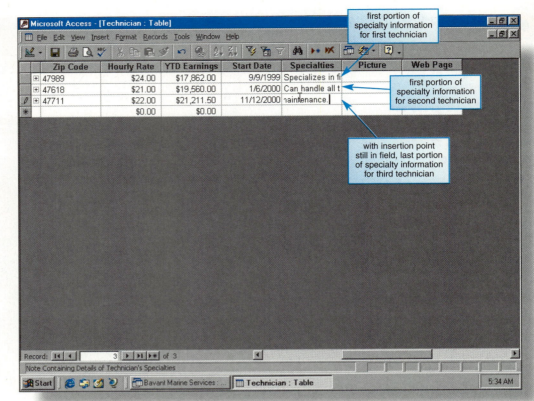

FIGURE 5-10

Changing the Row and Column Size

The Undo command cannot be used to reverse (undo) changes to the row and column size. To undo the changes to the sizes, close the datasheet without saving the changes. Once you have saved changes to row and column size, there is no automatic way to restore the original sizes.

Changing the Row and Column Size

Only a small portion of the information about the specialties displays in the datasheet. To allow more of the information to display, you can expand the size of the rows and the columns. You can change the size of a column by using the field selector. The **field selector** is the bar containing the field name. You position the mouse pointer on the right boundary of the column's field selector and then drag to change the size of the column. To change the size of a row, you use a record's **row selector,** which is the small box at the beginning of each record. You position the mouse pointer on the lower boundary of the record's row selector to select the record and then drag to resize the row.

The steps on the next page resize the column containing the Specialties field and the rows of the table so a larger portion of the Specialties field text will display.

Steps: To Change the Row and Column Size

1 Point to the line between the column headings for the Specialties and Picture columns.

The mouse pointer changes to a two-headed horizontal arrow with a vertical crossbar, indicating you can drag the line to resize the column (Figure 5-11).

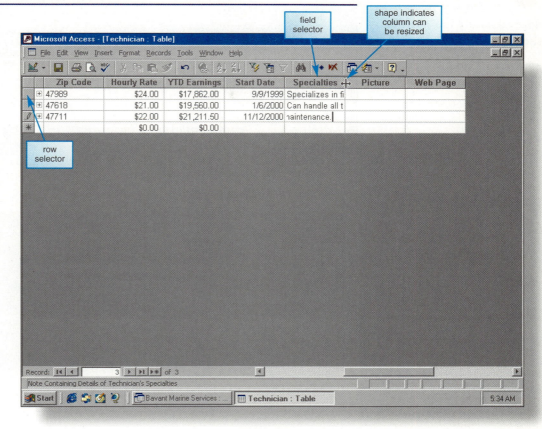

FIGURE 5-11

2 Drag to the right to resize the Specialties column to the approximate size shown in Figure 5-12 and then point to the line between the first and second row selectors as shown in the figure.

The mouse pointer changes to a two-headed arrow with a horizontal bar, indicating you can drag the line to resize the row.

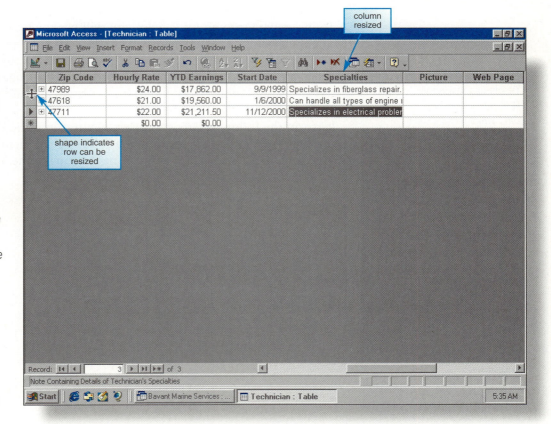

FIGURE 5-12

3 **Drag the edge of the row to approximately the position shown in Figure 5-13.**

All the rows are resized at the same time (Figure 5-13). The specialties now display in their entirety. The last row has a different appearance from the other two because it still is selected.

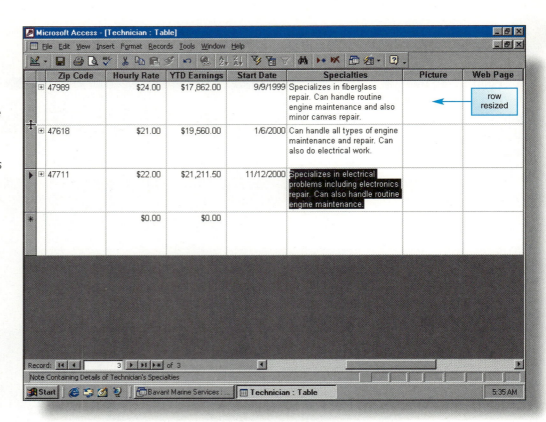

FIGURE 5-13

Other **Ways**

1. Right-click row selector, click Row Height to change row spacing

2. Right-click field selector, click Column Width to change column size

3. On Format menu click Row Height to change row spacing

4. On Format menu click Column Width to change column size.

Updating OLE Fields

To insert data into an OLE field, you will use the **Insert Object command** on the OLE field's shortcut menu. The Insert Object command presents a list of the various types of objects that can be inserted. Access then opens the corresponding application to create the object, for example, Microsoft Drawing. If the object already is created and stored in a file, as is the case with the photographs in this project, you simply insert it directly from the file.

Perform the following steps to insert pictures into the Picture field. The steps assume that the pictures are located in a folder called pictures on drive C:. If your pictures are located elsewhere, you will need to make the appropriate changes.

Note: If your database is on a floppy disk, skip the following steps so that your database will not become too large for your disk.

More About

Updating OLE Fields

OLE fields can occupy a great deal of space. To save space in your database, you can convert a picture from Bitmap Image to Picture (Device Independent Bitmap). To make the conversion, right-click the field, click Bitmap Image Object, click Convert, and then double-click Picture.

To Enter Data in OLE Fields and Convert the Data to Pictures

1 **Ensure the Picture field displays. Right-click the Picture field on the first record. Point to Insert Object on the shortcut menu.**

The shortcut menu for the Picture field displays (Figure 5-14).

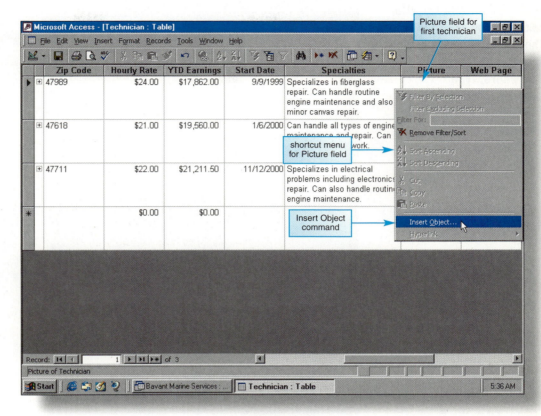

FIGURE 5-14

2 **Click Insert Object. Point to Create from File in the Insert Object dialog box.**

The Insert Object dialog box displays, and the Object Types display in the list box (Figure 5-15).

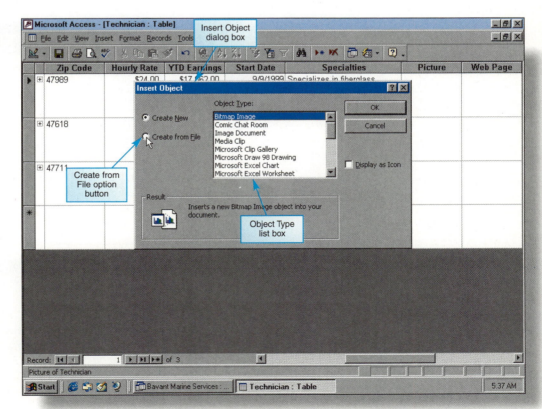

FIGURE 5-15

3 Click Create from File. Type c:\pictures in the File text box and then point to the Browse button. (If your pictures are located elsewhere, type the name and location of the folder where they are located instead of c:\pictures.)

The Create from File option button is selected, and the location of the folder displays in the File text box (Figure 5-16).

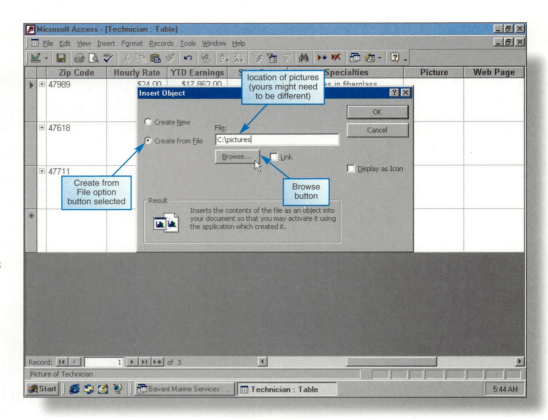

FIGURE 5-16

4 Click the Browse button, and then point to pict1.

The Browse dialog box displays (Figure 5-17). If you do not have the pictures, you will need to locate the folder in which yours are stored.

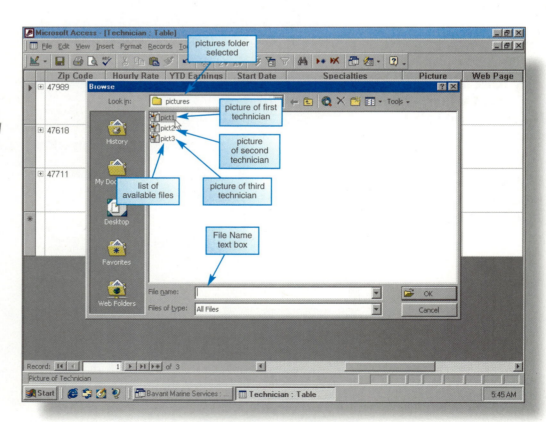

FIGURE 5-17

5 **Double-click pict1 and then point to the OK button.**

The Browse dialog box closes and the Insert Object dialog box displays (Figure 5-18). The name of the selected picture displays in the File text box.

6 **Click the OK button.**

7 **Insert the pictures into the second and third records using the techniques illustrated in Steps 1 through 6. For the second record, select the picture named pict2. For the third record, select the picture named pict3.**

The pictures are inserted.

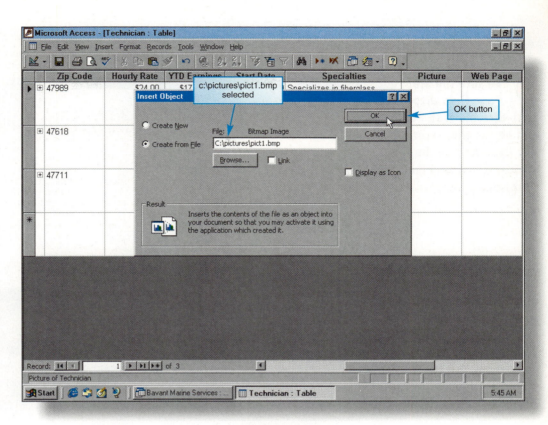

FIGURE 5-18

Updating Hyperlink Fields

To insert data into a Hyperlink field, you will use the **Hyperlink command** on the Hyperlink field's shortcut menu. You then edit the hyperlink. You can enter the Web page name for the appropriate Web Page or specify a file that contains the document to which you wish to link.

Perform the steps on the next page to insert data into the Web Page field.

Other Ways

1. On Insert menu click Object

Steps To Enter Data in Hyperlink Fields

1 **Be sure the Web Page field displays. Right-click the Web Page field on the first record, click Hyperlink on the shortcut menu, and then point to Edit Hyperlink.**

The shortcut menu for the Web Page field displays (Figure 5-19).

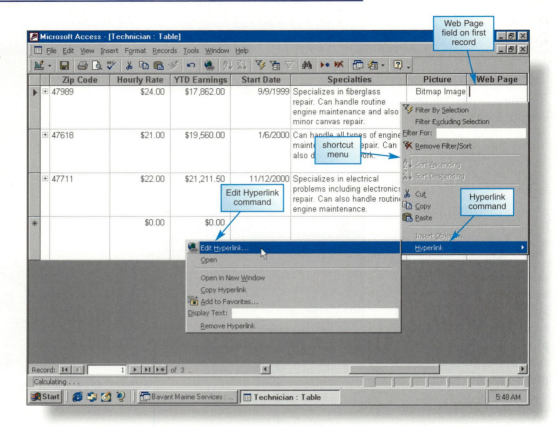

FIGURE 5-19

2 **Click Edit Hyperlink. Type** www.scsite.com/ac2000/tech1.htm **in the Type the file or Web page name text box. Point to the OK button. (If you do not have access to the Internet, type** a:\tech1.htm **in the Type the file or Web page name text box instead of www.scsite.com/ac2000/tech1.htm as the Web page name.)**

The Insert Hyperlink dialog box displays, and a list of Browsed Pages displays in the list box. Your list may be different (Figure 5-20).

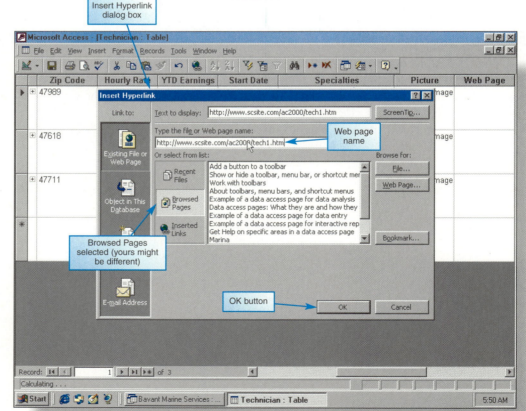

FIGURE 5-20

3 Click the OK button. Use the techniques described in Steps 1 and 2 to enter Web page data for the second and third technicians. For the second technician, type `www.scsite.com/ ac2000/tech2.htm` as the Web page name; and for the third, type `www.scsite.com/ ac2000/tech3.htm` as the Web page name. (If you do not have access to the Internet, type `a:\tech2.htm` for the second technician and `a:\tech3.htm` for the third technician.)

The Web page data is entered (Figure 5-21).

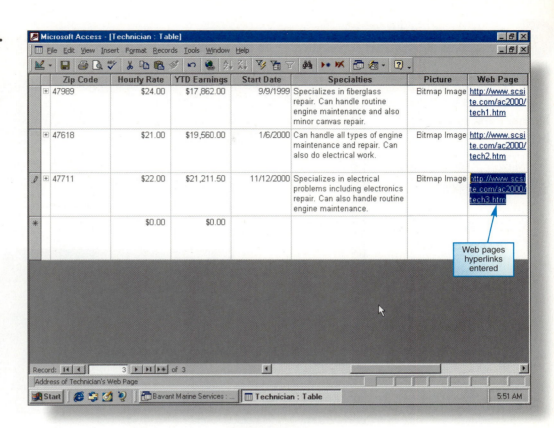

FIGURE 5-21

Other Ways

1. On Insert menu click Hyperlink

Saving the Table Properties

The row and column spacing are **table properties**. When changing any table properties, the changes apply only as long as the table is active *unless they are saved*. If they are saved, they will apply every time the table is opened. To save them, simply close the table. If any properties have changed, a Microsoft Access dialog box will ask if you want to save the changes. By answering Yes, you can save the changes.

Perform the steps on the next page to close the table and save the properties that have been changed.

To Close the Table and Save the Properties

1 **Close the table by clicking its Close button. Point to the Yes button.**

The Microsoft Access dialog box displays (Figure 5-22).

2 **Click the Yes button to save the table properties.**

The properties are saved.

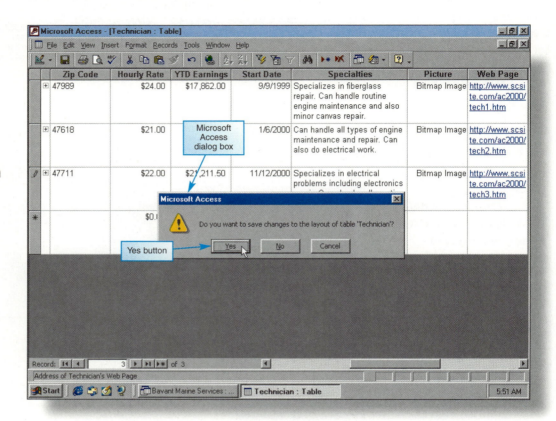

FIGURE 5-22

Although the pictures do not display on the screen, you can view them at any time. To view the picture of a particular technician, point to the Picture field for the technician, and then right-click to produce the shortcut menu. Click Bitmap Image Object on the shortcut menu, and then click Open. The picture will display. Once you have finished viewing the picture, close the window containing the picture by clicking its Close button. You also can view the Web Page for a technician, by clicking the technician's Web Page field.

Subforms

When you create forms with subforms, the tables for the main form and the subform must be related. The relationship must have been previously set in the Relationships window. To see if your tables are related, click the Relationships button. Relationships between tables display as lines connecting the tables.

Advanced Form Techniques

The form in this project includes data from both the Technician and Marina tables. The form will display data concerning one technician. It also will display data concerning the many marinas to which the technician is assigned. Formally, the relationship between technicians and marinas is called a **one-to-many relationship** (*one* technician services *many* marinas).

To include the data for the many marinas of a technician on the form, the marina data must display in a **subform**, which is a form that is contained within another form. The form in which the subform is contained is called the main form. Thus, the **main form** will contain technician data, and the subform will contain marina data.

Creating a Form with a Subform Using the Form Wizard

No special action is required to create a form with a subform if you use the Form Wizard. The Form Wizard will create both the form and subform automatically once you have selected the tables and indicated the general organization of your data. Perform the following steps to create the form and subform.

 To Create a Form with a Subform Using the Form Wizard

1 **With the Database window on the screen and the Forms object selected, right-click Create form by using Wizard and then point to Open on the shortcut menu.**

The shortcut menu displays (Figure 5-23).

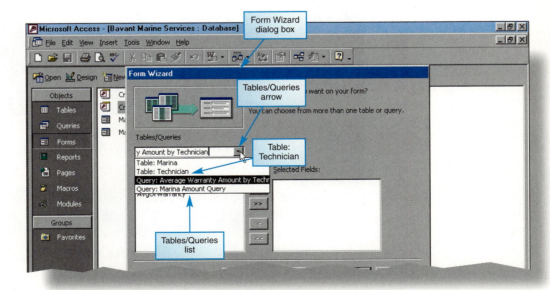

FIGURE 5-23

2 **Click Open on the shortcut menu and then click the Tables/ Queries arrow.**

The list of available tables and queries displays (Figure 5-24).

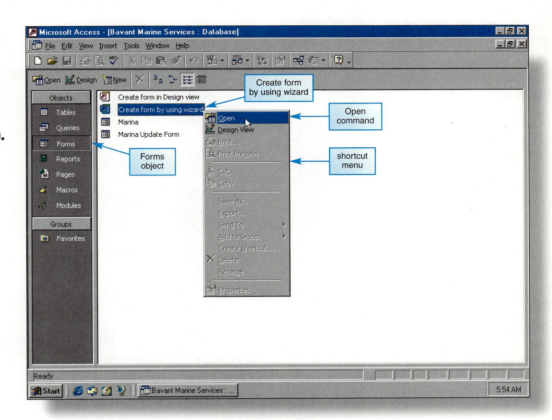

FIGURE 5-24

3 **Click Table: Technician. With the Tech Number field selected in the Available Fields box, click the Add Field button. Select the First Name, Last Name, Hourly Rate, YTD Earnings, Web Page, Specialties, and Picture fields by clicking the field and then clicking the Add Field button. Click the Table/Queries box arrow and then point to Table: Marina.**

The fields from the Technician table are selected for the form (Figure 5-25).

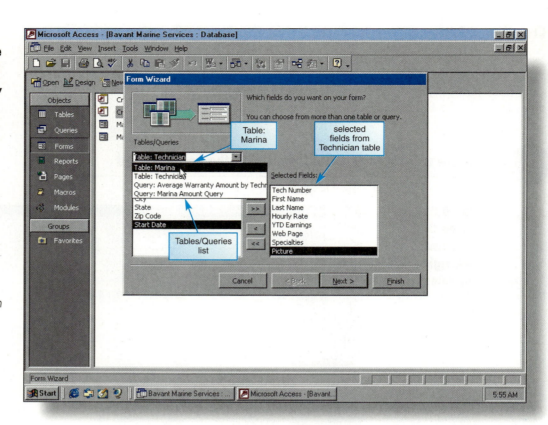

FIGURE 5-25

4 **Click Table: Marina. Select the Marina Number, Name, Warranty, and Non-warranty fields. Point to the Next button.**

All the fields are selected (Figure 5-26).

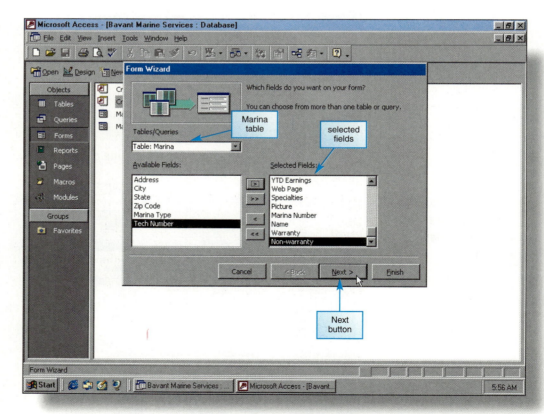

FIGURE 5-26

Click the Next button.

The Form Wizard dialog box displays, requesting how you want to view the data: by Technician or by Marina (Figure 5-27). The highlighted selection, by Technician, is correct. The box on the right indicates visually that the main organization is by Technician, with the Technician fields listed at the top. Contained within the form is a subform that contains marina data.

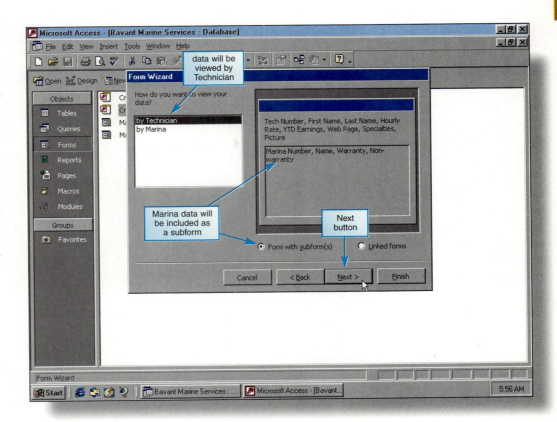

FIGURE 5-27

Click the Next button.

The Form Wizard dialog box displays, requesting the layout for the subform (Figure 5-28). This subform is to display in Datasheet view.

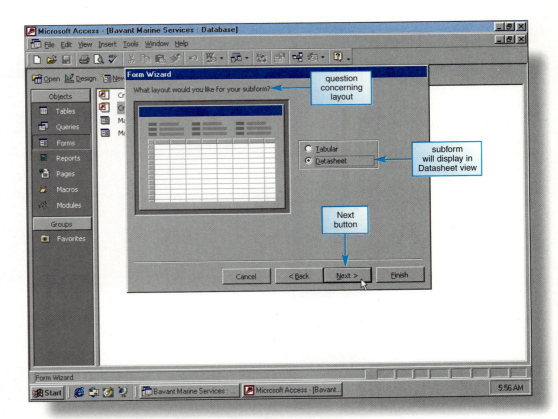

FIGURE 5-28

7 **Be sure Datasheet is selected and then click the Next button. Ensure Standard style is selected.**

The Form Wizard dialog box displays, requesting a style for the report, and Standard is selected (Figure 5-29).

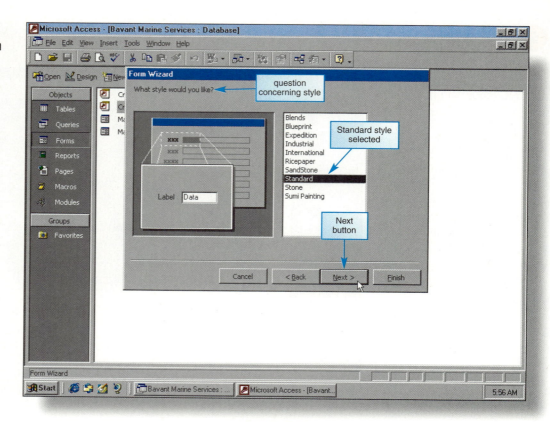

FIGURE 5-29

8 **Click the Next button.**

The Form Wizard dialog box displays (Figure 5-30). You use this dialog box to change the titles of the form and subform.

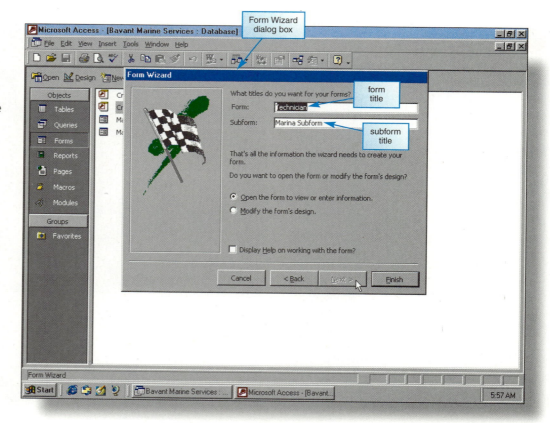

FIGURE 5-30

9 **Type** Technician Master Form **as the title of the form. Click the Subform text box, use the DELETE or BACKSPACE key to erase the current entry, and then type** Marinas **as the name of the subform. Point to the Finish button.**

The titles are changed (Figure 5-31).

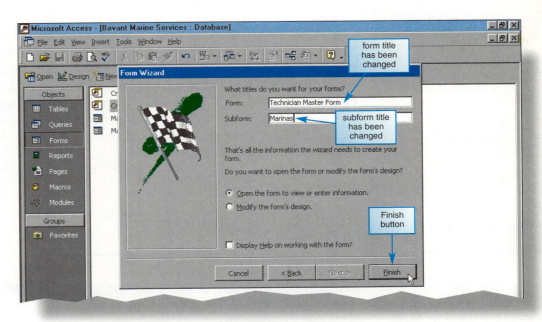

FIGURE 5-31

10 **Click the Finish button.**

The form displays (Figure 5-32).

11 **Close the form by clicking its Close button.**

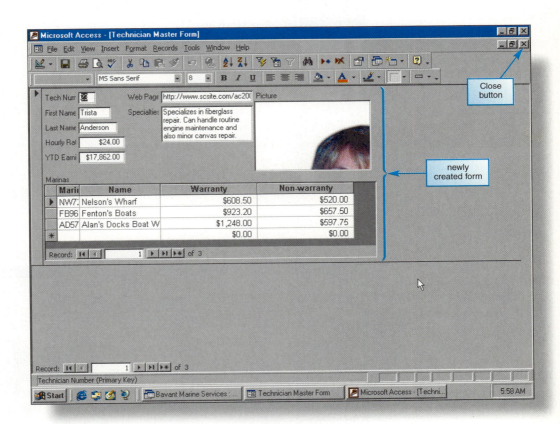

FIGURE 5-32

The form and subform now have been saved as part of the database and are available for future use.

More About

Subform Design

To change the appearance of the subform, make sure the subform control is not selected, double-click inside the subform, right-click the form selector for the subform, click Properties, and then change the DefaultView property.

Modifying the Subform Design

The next task is to modify the spacing of the columns in the subform. The Marina Number column is so narrow that only the letters, Marin, display. Conversely, the Warranty column is much wider than needed. You can correct these problems by right-clicking the subform in the Database window and then clicking Design View. When the design of the subform displays, you then can convert it to Datasheet view. At this point, you resize each column by double-clicking the border to the right of the column name.

Perform the following steps to modify the subform design to improve the column spacing.

Steps To Modify the Subform Design

1 **With the Forms object selected, right-click Marinas. Point to Design View on the shortcut menu.**

The shortcut menu for the subform displays (Figure 5-33).

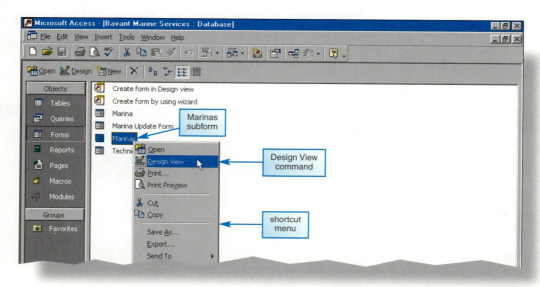

FIGURE 5-33

2 **Click Design View on the shortcut menu. If the field list displays, point to its Close button (Figure 5-34).**

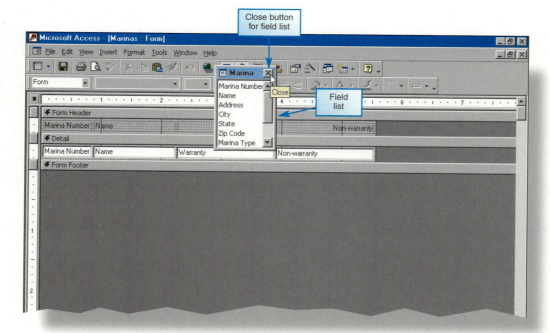

FIGURE 5-34

3 If the field list displays, click its Close button. Point to the View button on the toolbar (Figure 5-35).

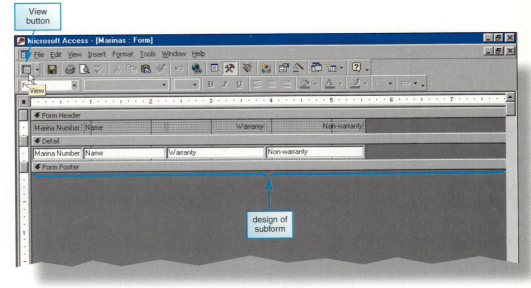

FIGURE 5-35

4 Click the View button to display the subform in Datasheet view. Resize each of the columns by pointing to the right edge of the field selector (to the right of the column name) and double-clicking. Point to the Close button.

The subform displays in Datasheet view (Figure 5-36). The columns have been resized. You also can resize each column by dragging the right edge of the field selector.

5 Close the subform by clicking its Close button.

The changes are made and saved.

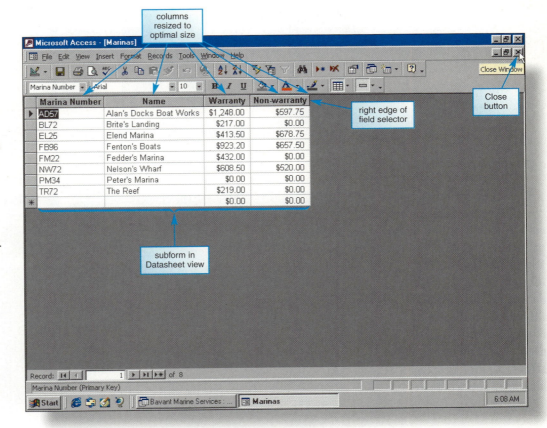

FIGURE 5-36

Modifying the Form Design

The next step is to make several changes to the form. Various objects need to be moved or resized. The properties of the picture need to be adjusted so the entire picture displays. The appearance of the labels needs to be changed, and a title needs to be added to the form.

Right-click the form in the Database window and then click Design View to make these or other changes to the design of the form. If the toolbox is on the screen, make sure it is docked at the bottom of the screen.

Perform the following steps to begin the modification of the form design.

To Modify the Form Design

1 **Right-click Technician Master Form. Point to Design View on the shortcut menu.**

The shortcut menu for the form displays (Figure 5-37).

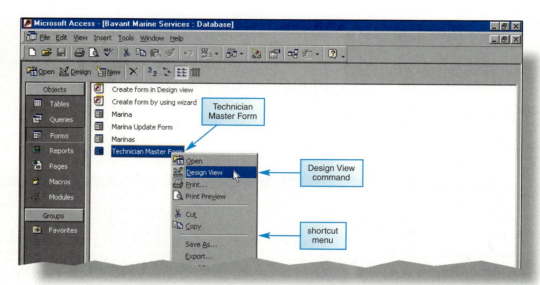

FIGURE 5-37

2 **Click Design View on the shortcut menu. If the toolbox does not display, click the Toolbox button on the toolbar. Make sure it is docked at the bottom of the screen as shown in Figure 5-38). If it is not, drag it to the bottom of the screen to dock it there. Maximize the window.**

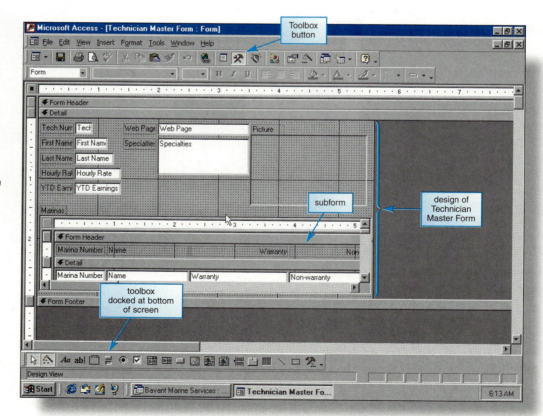

FIGURE 5-38

Moving and Resizing Fields

Fields on this form can be moved or resized just as they were in the form created in the previous project. First, click the field. To move it, move the mouse pointer to the boundary of the field so it becomes a hand, and then drag the field. To resize a field, drag the appropriate sizing handle. The following steps move certain fields on the form. They also resize the fields appropriately.

 To Move and Resize Fields

1 **Click the Picture control, and then move the mouse pointer until the shape changes to a hand.**

The Picture control is selected, and sizing handles display (Figure 5-39).

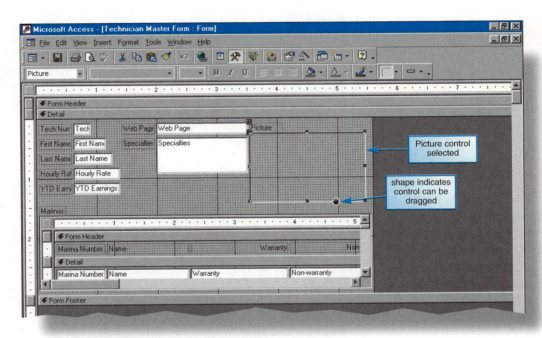

FIGURE 5-39

2 **Drag the Picture control to approximately the position shown in Figure 5-40 and then point to the sizing handle on the lower edge of the control.**

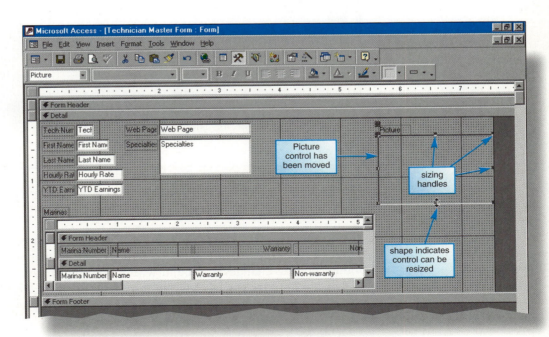

FIGURE 5-40

3 Drag the lower sizing handle to approximately the position shown in Figure 5-41 and then point to the sizing handle on the right edge of the control.

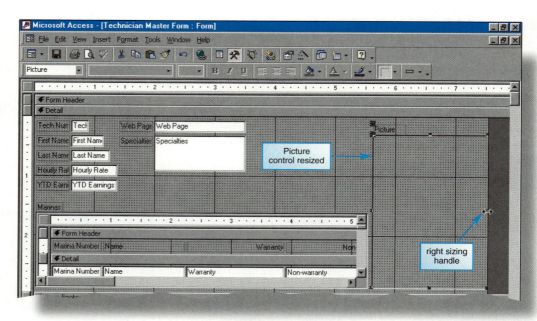

FIGURE 5-41

4 Resize the Picture control to the approximate size shown in Figure 5-42, and then move and resize the Specialties control to the approximate position and size shown in the figure.

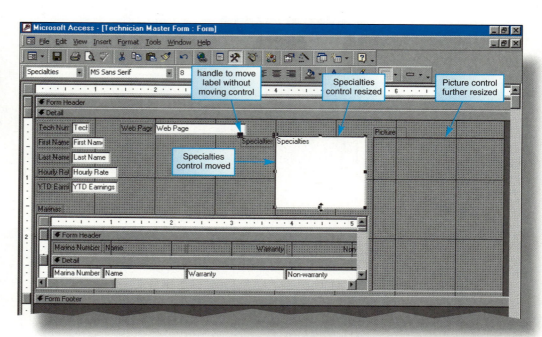

FIGURE 5-42

Moving Labels

To move a label independently from the field with which the label is associated, point to the large, **move handle** in the upper-left corner of the label. The shape of the mouse pointer changes to a hand with a pointing finger. By dragging this move handle, you will move the label without moving the associated field. Perform the step on the next page to move the label of the Specialties field without moving the field itself.

To Move a Label

1 **Click the label for the Specialties field and then drag the handle in the upper-left corner to the position shown in Figure 5-43.**

The shape of the mouse pointer changes to a hand with a pointing finger.

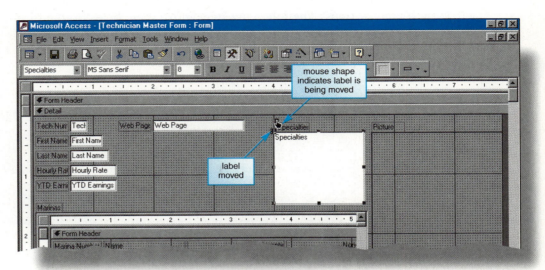

FIGURE 5-43

Resizing a Label

The label for the Specialties field has the last letter cut off. To resize a label, select the label by clicking it, and then drag the appropriate sizing handle. To resize a label to optimum size, select the label and then double-click the appropriate sizing handle. Perform the following steps to resize the label for the Specialties field by double-clicking the sizing handle on the right.

 To Resize a Label

1 **Ensure the label for the Specialties field is selected, and then point to the middle sizing handle on the right edge of the label.**

The shape of the mouse pointer changes to a two-headed arrow (Figure 5-44).

2 **Double-click the sizing handle to expand the label to the appropriate size.**

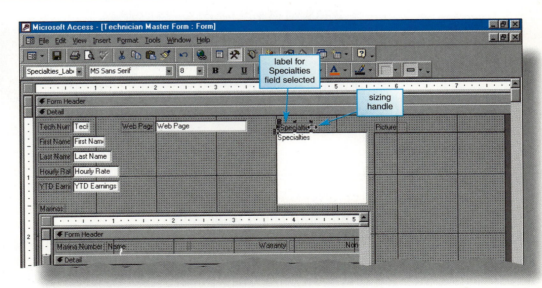

FIGURE 5-44

Moving Remaining Fields

The remaining fields on this form also need to be moved into appropriate positions. The following steps move these fields on the form.

 To Move Fields

1 **Click the Web Page field, move the mouse pointer until the shape changes to a hand, and then drag the field to the position shown in Figure 5-45.**

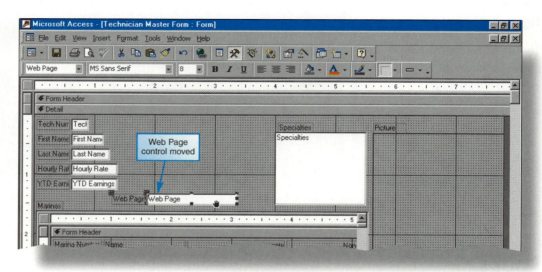

FIGURE 5-45

2 **Drag the YTD Earnings, Hourly Rate, Last Name, First Name, and Tech Number fields to the positions shown in Figure 5-46.**

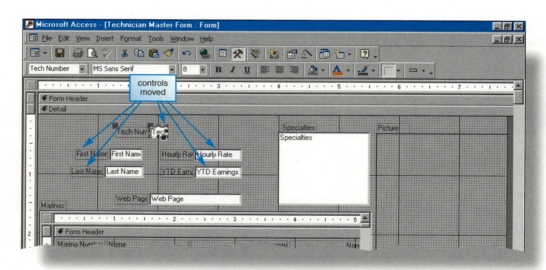

FIGURE 5-46

Changing Label Alignment

The labels for the Tech Number, First Name, Last Name, Hourly Rate, YTD Earnings, and Web Page fields illustrated in Figure 5-1 on page A 5.5 are **right-aligned**, that is, aligned with the right margin. Because the labels are currently left-aligned, the alignment needs to be changed. To change the alignment, right-click the label to display the shortcut menu, click Properties, and then scroll to display the Text Align property. Click Text Align. In the property sheet, you can select the appropriate alignment.

In some cases, you will want to make the same change to several objects, perhaps to several labels at one time. Rather than making the changes individually, you can select all the objects at once, and then make a single change. Perform the following steps to change the alignment of the labels.

 To Change Label Alignment

1 **If the label for the Tech Number field is not already selected, click it. Select the labels for the First Name, Last Name, Hourly Rate, YTD Earnings, and Web Page fields by clicking them while holding down the SHIFT key.**

The labels are selected (Figure 5-47).

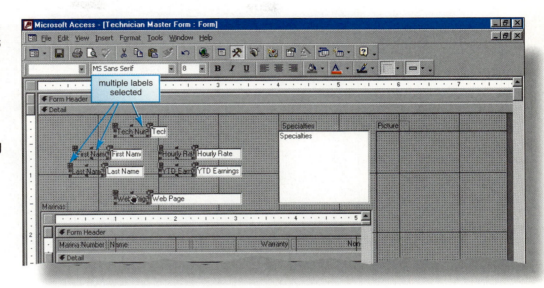

FIGURE 5-47

2 **Right-click the Web Page field. Point to Properties on the shortcut menu.**

The shortcut menu displays (Figure 5-48).

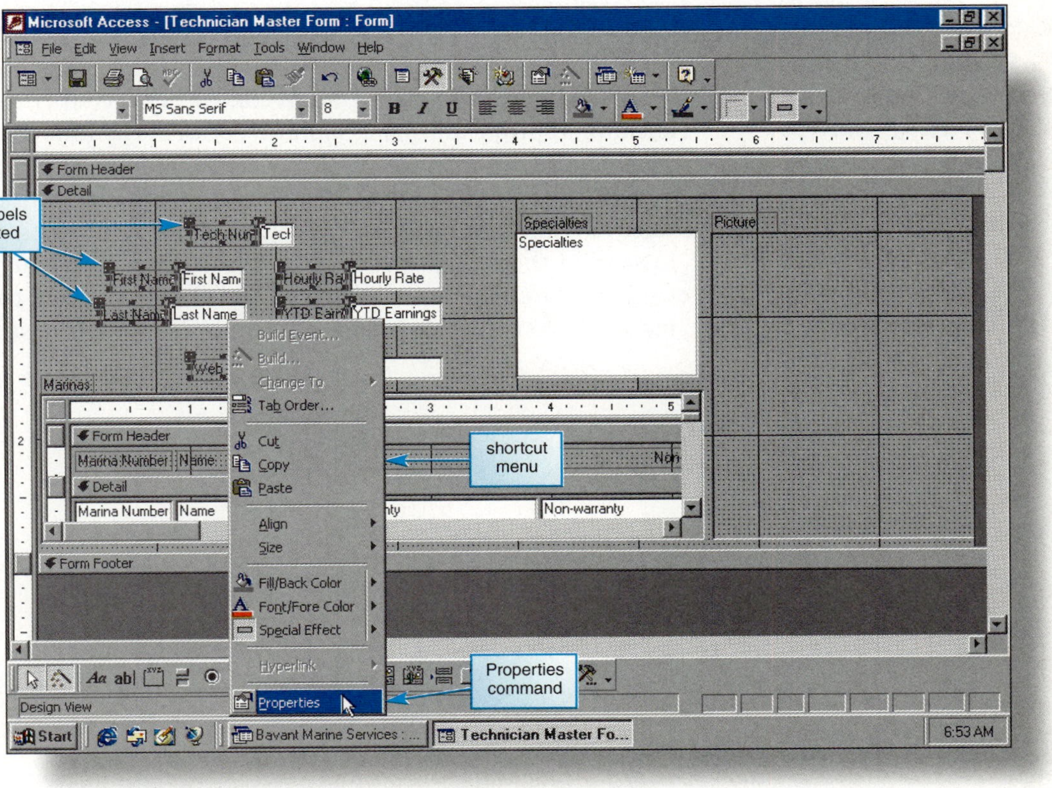

FIGURE 5-48

3 **Click Properties on the shortcut menu and then click the down scroll arrow until the Text Align property displays. Click Text Align, and then click the Text Align arrow.**

The Multiple selection property sheet displays (Figure 5-49). The Text Align property is selected and the list of available values for the Text Align property displays.

4 **Click Right to select right alignment for the labels. Close the Multiple selection property sheet by clicking its Close button.**

The alignment is changed.

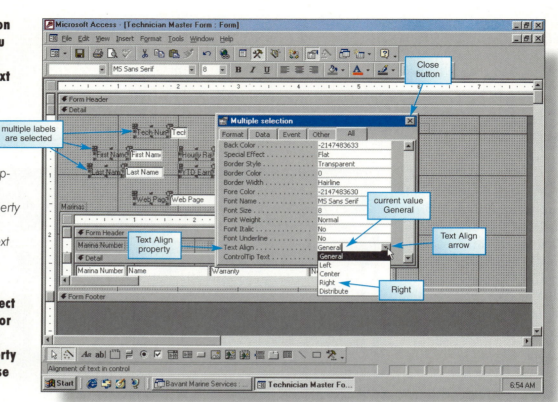

FIGURE 5-49

Resizing the Labels

To resize a label to optimum size, select the label by clicking it, and then double-click an appropriate sizing handle. Perform the following steps to resize the label for the Tech Number, First Name, Last Name, Hourly Rate, YTD Earnings, and Web Page fields just as you resized the label for the Specialties field earlier. The only difference is that you will double-click the sizing handles at the left edge of the labels instead of the right edge. You can resize them individually, but it is easier, however, to make sure they are all selected and then resize one of the labels. Access will automatically resize all the others as demonstrated in the steps on the next page.

To Resize a Label

1 With all the labels selected, point to the handle on the left edge of the Tech Number label (Figure 5-50.

2 Double-click the middle sizing handle on the left edge of the Technician Number label to resize all the labels to the optimal size.

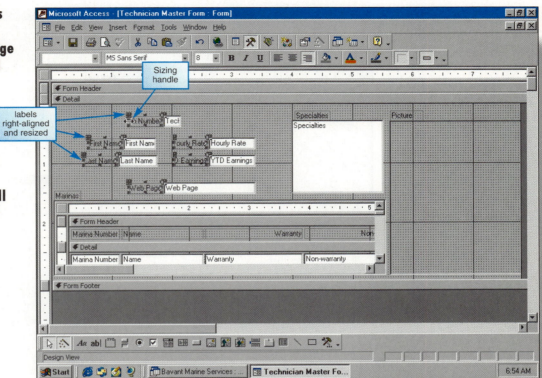

FIGURE 5-50

Changing the Size Mode of a Picture

The portion of a picture that displays as well as the way it displays is determined by the **size mode**. The possible size modes are as follows:

1. **Clip** — Displays only the portion of the picture that will fit in the space allocated to it.
2. **Stretch** — Expands or shrinks the picture to fit the precise space allocated on the screen. For photographs, usually this is not a good choice, because fitting a photograph to the allocated space can distort the image, giving it a stretched appearance.
3. **Zoom** — Does the best job of fitting the picture to the allocated space without changing the look of the picture. The entire picture will display and be proportioned correctly. Some white space may be visible either above or to the right of the picture, however.

Currently, the size mode is Clip, and that is the reason only a portion of the picture displays. To see the whole picture, use the shortcut menu for the picture to change the size mode to Zoom as shown in the steps on the next page.

Steps: To Change the Size Mode of a Picture

1 **Right-click the Picture control to produce its shortcut menu, and then click Properties on the shortcut menu. Click the Size Mode property and then click the Size Mode box arrow. Point to Zoom.**

The Bound Object Frame: Picture property sheet displays (Figure 5-51). The list of Size Mode options displays.

2 **Click Zoom and then close the property sheet by clicking its Close button.**

The Size Mode is changed. The entire picture now will display.

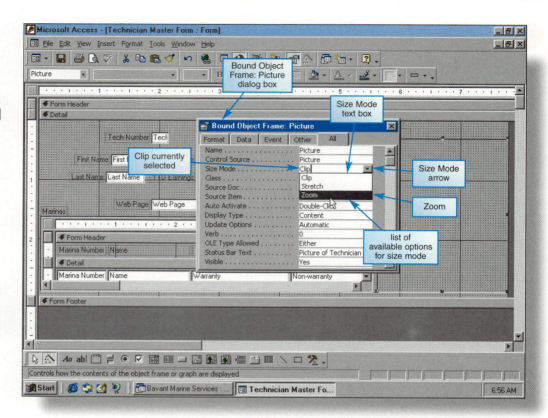

FIGURE 5-51

Colors of Labels

There are two different colors you can change for many objects, including labels. Changing Fore Color (foreground) changes the color of the letters that appear in the label. Changing Back Color (background) changes the color of the label itself.

Changing the Special Effects and Colors of Labels

Access allows you to change a variety of the characteristics of the labels in the form. You can change the border style and color, the background color, the font, and the font size. You also can give the label **special effects**, such as raised or sunken. To change the special effects and colors (characteristics) of a label, perform the steps on the next page.

To Change Special Effects and Colors of Labels

1 **Click the Tech Number label to select it. Then select each of the remaining labels by holding the SHIFT key down while clicking the label. Be sure to include the Marinas label for the subform. Right-click one of the selected labels and then point to Properties.**

All labels are selected (Figure 5-52). The shortcut menu displays.

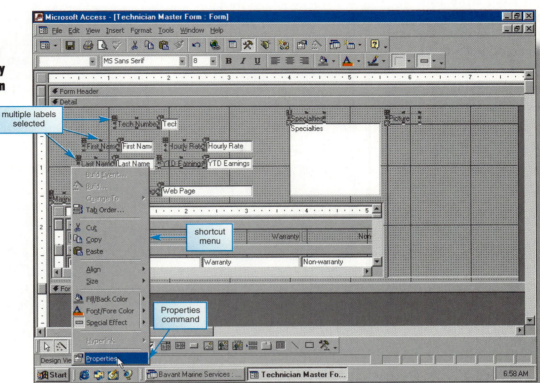

FIGURE 5-52

2 **Click Properties on the shortcut menu that displays. Click the Special Effect property and then click the Special Effect box arrow. Point to Raised.**

The Multiple selection property sheet displays (Figure 5-53). The list of values for the Special Effect property displays, and the Raised Special Effect property is highlighted.

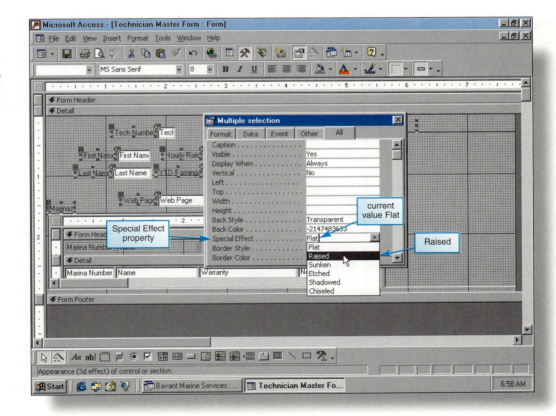

3 **Click Raised. If necessary, click the down scroll arrow until the Fore Color property displays, and then click the Fore Color property. Point to the Build button (the button containing the three dots).**

The Fore Color property is selected (Figure 5-54).

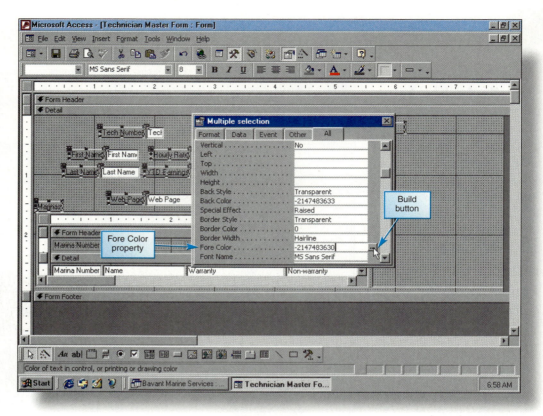

FIGURE 5-54

4 **Click the Build button to display the Color dialog box, and then point to the color blue in row 4, column 5, as shown in Figure 5-55.**

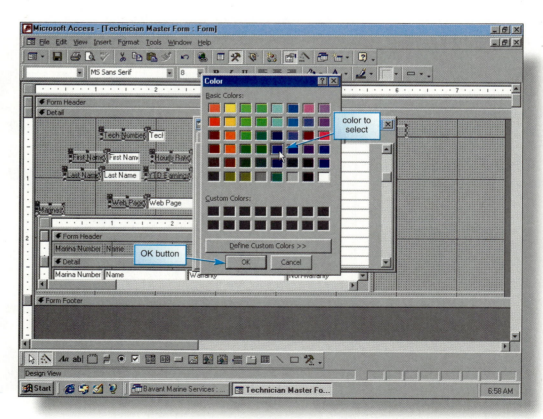

FIGURE 5-55

5 Click the color blue, and then click the OK button. Close the Multiple selection property sheet by clicking its Close button.

The changes to the labels are complete.

6 Click the View button to view the form.

The form displays (Figure 5-56). The fields have been moved and the appearance of the labels has been changed.

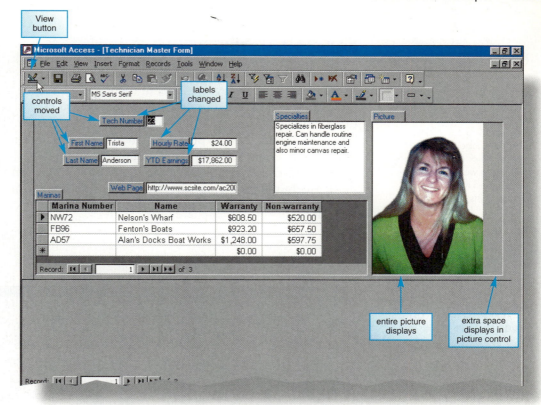

FIGURE 5-56

7 Click the View button a second time to return to the design grid.

The form design displays. Now that the size mode of the picture has been corrected, there is extra space on the right side of the picture, which can be corrected by resizing the picture a final time.

8 Click the Picture control to select it and then point to the right sizing handle (Figure 5-57).

9 Drag the right sizing handle to the left so that the size of the Picture control matches the size of the picture as shown in Figure 5-56.

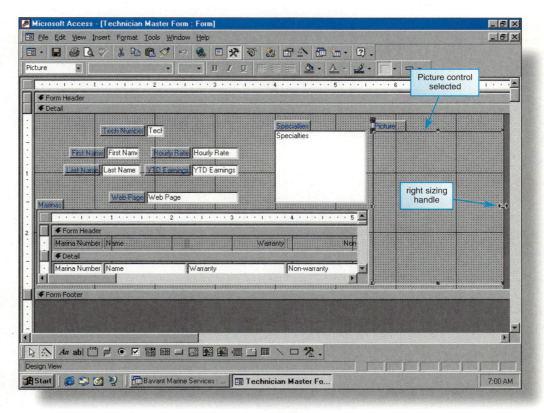

FIGURE 5-57

Microsoft **Access 2000**

More *About* 2000

Form Headers

You may wish to add more than just a title to a form header. For example, you may wish to add a picture such as a company logo. To do so, click the Image button in the toolbox, click the position where you want to place the picture, and then select the picture to insert.

Adding a Form Title

Notice in Figure 5-1 on page A 5.5 that the form includes a title. To add a title to a form, add the title as a label in the Form Header section. To accomplish this task, first you will need to expand the size of the Form Header to accommodate the title by dragging the bottom border of the Form Header. Then, you can use the Label button in the toolbox to place the label. After placing the label, you can type the title in the label. Using the Properties command on the label's shortcut menu you can change various properties to improve the title's appearance, as well.

Perform the following steps to place a title on the form.

Steps **To Add a Form Title**

1 **Point to the line separating the Form Header section from the Detail section.**

The shape of the mouse pointer changes to a two-headed vertical arrow with a horizontal crossbar, indicating you can drag the line to resize the Form Header section (Figure 5-58).

FIGURE 5-58

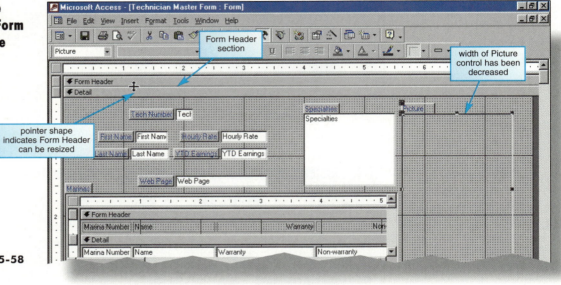

2 **Drag the line down to expand the size of the Form Header section to approximately the size shown in Figure 5-59. Point to the Label button in the toolbox as shown in the same figure.**

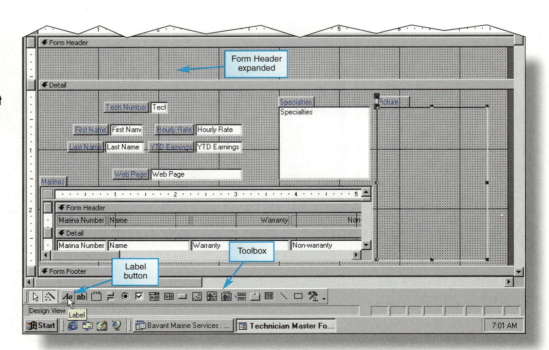

FIGURE 5-59

3 Click the Label button and then position the mouse pointer as shown in Figure 5-60. The shape of the mouse pointer has changed, indicating you are placing a label.

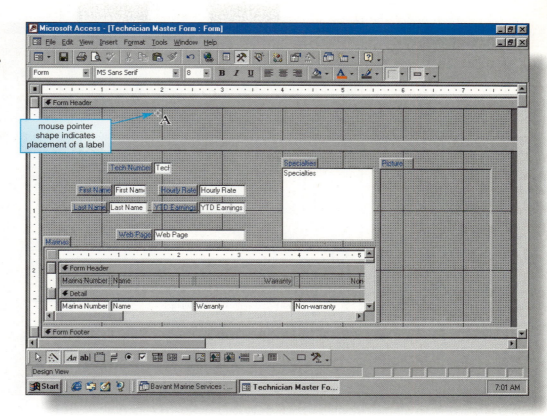

FIGURE 5-60

4 Click the position shown in the figure to place the label on the form. Type Technician Master Form as the title. Click somewhere outside the rectangle containing the title to deselect the rectangle, and then right-click the rectangle containing the title. Click Properties on the shortcut menu that displays, click the Special Effect property, and then click the Special Effect box arrow. Point to Etched.

The property sheet displays (Figure 5-61). The Etched Special Effect property is highlighted.

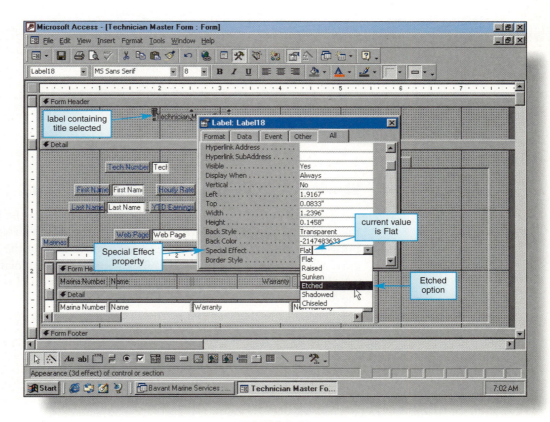

FIGURE 5-61

5 Click Etched. Click the down scroll arrow so the Font Size property displays. Click the Font Size property, click the Font Size box arrow, and then click 12. If necessary, click the down scroll arrow to display the Font Weight property. Click the Font Weight property, click the Font Weight box arrow, and then click Bold. Close the property sheet by clicking its Close button. Resize the label to display the title completely in the larger font size. Move the label so that it is centered over the form.

The Form Header is complete (Figure 5-62).

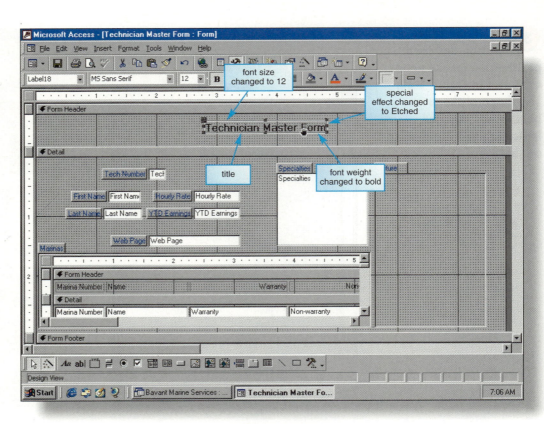

FIGURE 5-62

6 Close the window containing the form. When asked if you want to save the changes to the design of the form, click Yes.

The form is complete.

Viewing Data and Web Pages Using the Form

To use a form to view data, right-click the form in the Database window, and then click Open on the shortcut menu that displays. You then can use the navigation buttons to move among technicians or to move among the marinas of the technician currently displayed on the screen. By clicking the technician's Web Page field, you can display the technician's Web page. As soon as you close the window containing the Web page, Access returns to the form.

Perform the steps on the next page to display data using the form.

Steps: To Use the Form to View Data and Web Pages

1 If necessary, click Forms on the Objects bar. Right-click Technician Master Form and then click Open on the shortcut menu. Be sure the window containing the form is maximized. Point to the Next Record button for the Technician table.

The data from the first record displays in the form (Figure 5-63).

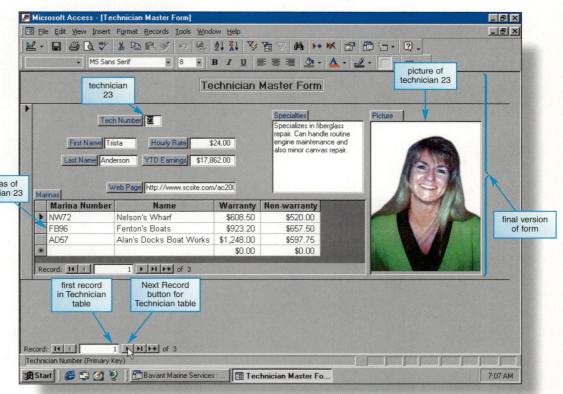

FIGURE 5-63

2 Click the Next Record button to move to the second technician. Point to the Next Record button for the Marinas subform (the Next Record button in the set of navigation buttons immediately below the subform).

*The data from the second record displays (Figure 5-64). (The records in your form may display in a different order.) If more marinas were included than would fit in the subform at a single time, Access would automatically add a **vertical scroll bar** to the Marinas subform. You can use either a scroll bar or the navigation buttons to move among marinas.*

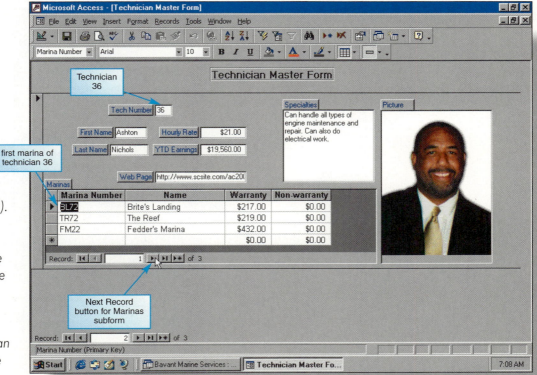

FIGURE 5-64

3 Click the subform's Next Record button twice.

The data from the third marina of technician 36 is selected (Figure 5-65).

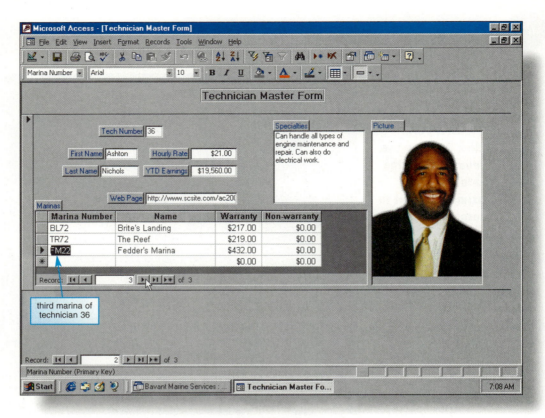

FIGURE 5-65

4 Point to the control for the technician's Web page (Figure 5-66).

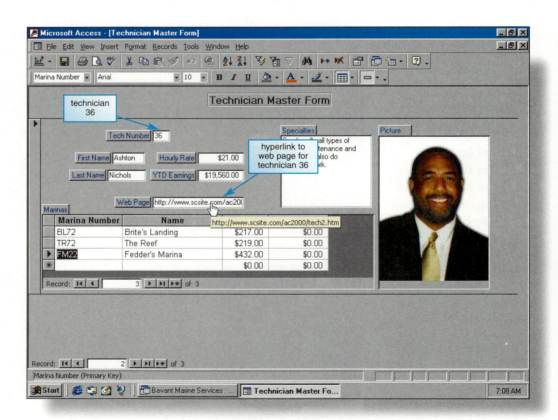

FIGURE 5-66

5 Click the control for the technician's Web Page. If a dialog box displays in either this step or the next, follow the directions given in the dialog box.

The technician's Web page displays (Figure 5-67).

6 When you have finished viewing the technician's Web page, click the Close button to return to the form. Close the form by clicking its Close button.

The form no longer displays.

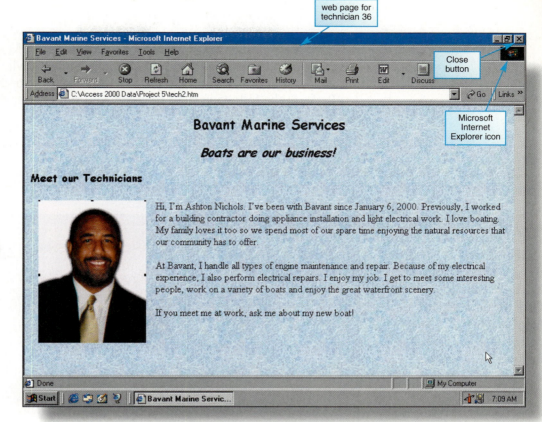

FIGURE 5-67

The previous steps illustrated the way you work with a main form and subform, as well as how to use a hyperlink (the Web Page control in this form). Clicking the navigation buttons for the main form moves to a different technician. Clicking the navigation buttons for the subform moves to a different marina of the technician whose photograph displays in the main form. Clicking a hyperlink moves to the corresponding document or Web Page. The following are other actions you can take within the form:

1. To move from the last field in the main form to the first field in the subform, press the TAB key. To move back to the last field in the main form, press the CTRL+SHIFT+TAB keys.
2. To move from the last field in the subform to the first field in the next record's main form, press the CTRL+TAB keys.
3. To switch from the main form to the subform using the mouse, click anywhere in the subform. To switch back to the main form, click any control in the main form. Clicking the background of the main form will not cause the switch to occur.

Using Date and Memo Fields in a Query

To use date fields in queries, you simply type the dates including the slashes. To search for records with a specific date, you must type the date. You also can use **comparison operators**. To find all the technicians whose start date is prior to November 2, 2000, for example, you type the criterion <11/2/2000.

More About 2000

Date Fields in Queries: Using Date()

To test for the current date in a query, type Date() in the criteria row of the appropriate column. Placing <Date() in the criteria row for Renewal Date, for example, finds those therapists whose renewal date occurs anytime before the date on which you run the query.

More About 2000

Date Fields in Queries: Using Expressions

Expressions have a special meaning in date fields in queries. Numbers that appear in expressions represent numbers of days. The expression <Date()+30 for Renewal Date finds therapists whose renewal date occurs anytime prior to 30 days after the day on which you run the query.

You also can use memo fields in queries. Typically, you will want to find all the records on which the memo field contains a specific word or phrase. To do so, you use wildcards. For example, to find all the technicians who have the word, electrical, in the Specialties field, you type the criterion, like *electrical*.

Perform the following steps to create and run queries that use date and memo fields.

Steps **To Use Date and Memo Fields in a Query**

1 In the Database window, click Tables on the Objects bar, and then, if necessary, select the Technician table. Click the New Object: AutoForm button arrow on the toolbar. Click Query. Be sure Design View is highlighted, and then click the OK button.

2 Maximize the Microsoft Access - [Query1 : Select Query] window that displays. Resize the upper and lower panes and the Technician field list to the sizes shown in Figure 5-68. Double-click the Tech Number, First Name, Last Name, Start Date, and Specialties fields to include them in the query. Click the Criteria row under the Specialties field and then type `like *electrical*` as the criterion. Point to the Run button on the toolbar (Figure 5-68).

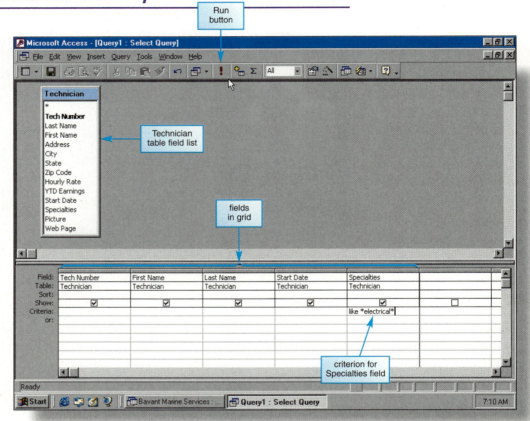

FIGURE 5-68

3 **Click the Run button on the toolbar to run the query.**

The results display in Datasheet view (Figure 5-69). Two records are included.

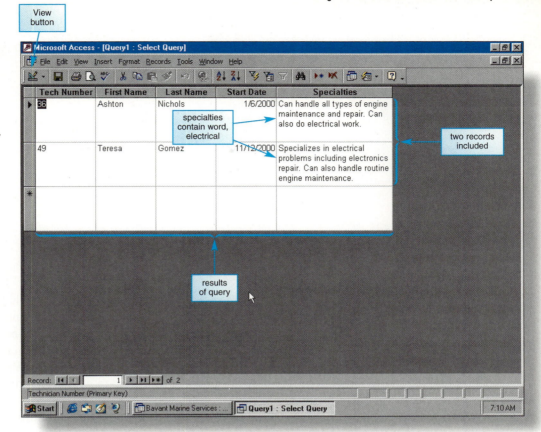

FIGURE 5-69

4 **Click the View button to return to the Select Query window. Click the Criteria row under the Start Date field, and then type** <11/2/2000 **(Figure 5-70).**

5 **Click the Run button on the toolbar to run the query.**

The result contains only a single row, because only one technician was hired before November 2, 2000 and has a specialty entry that contains the word, electrical.

6 **Close the Select Query window by clicking its Close button. When asked if you want to save the query, click the No button.**

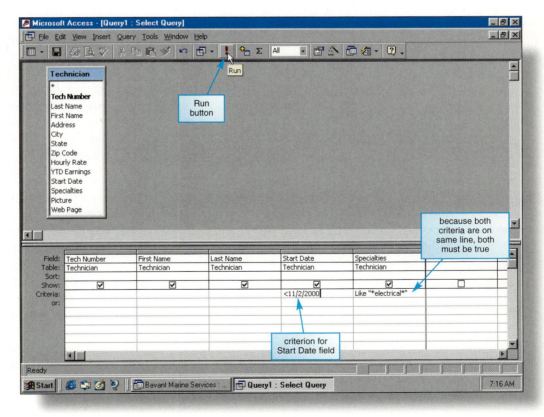

FIGURE 5-70

The results of the query are removed from the screen and the Database window again displays.

Closing the Database

The following step closes the database by closing its Database window.

TO CLOSE A DATABASE

 Click the Close button for the Bavant Marine Services : Database window.

Compacting a Database

As you add more data to a database, it naturally grows larger. Pictures will increase the size significantly. When you delete objects (for example, records, tables, forms, pictures), the space previously occupied by the object does not become available for additional objects. Instead, the additional objects are given new space, that is, space that was not already allocated. If you decide to change a picture, for example, the new picture will not occupy the same space as the previous picture, but instead it will be given space of its own.

In order to remove this wasted space from the database, you must **compact** the database. Compacting the database makes an additional copy of the database, one that contains the same data, but does not contain the wasted space that the original does. The original database will still exist in its unaltered form.

A typical three-step process for compacting a database is as follows:

1. Compact the original database (for example, Bavant Marine Services) and give the compacted database a different name (for example, Bavant Marine Services Compacted).
2. Assuming that the compacting operation completed successfully, use the delete feature of Windows to delete the original database (Bavant Marine Services).
3. Also assuming that the compacting operation completed successfully, use the rename feature of Windows to rename the compacted database (Bavant Marine Services Compacted) with the name of the original database (Bavant Marine Services).

Of course, if there is a problem in the compacting operation, you should continue to use the original database; that is, do not complete steps 2 and 3.

The operation can be carried out on a diskette, provided there is sufficient space available. If the database to be compacted occupies more than half the diskette, there may not be enough room for Access to create the compacted database. In such a case, you should first copy the database to a hard disk or network drive. (You can use whatever Windows technique you prefer for copying files in order to do so.) You can then complete the process on the hard disk or network drive.

Perform the steps on the next page to compact the Bavant Marine Services database after you have copied the database to a hard disk. If you have not copied the database to a hard disk, check with your instructor before completing these steps.

Microsoft Certification

The Microsoft Office User Specialist (MOUS) Certification program provides an opportunity for you to obtain a valuable industry credential - proof that you have the Access 2000 skills required by employers. For more information, see Appendix D or visit the Shelly Cashman Series MOUS Web page at www.scsite.com/off2000/cert.htm.

Quick Reference

For a table that lists how to complete the tasks covered in this book using the mouse, menu, shortcut menu, and keyboard, visit the Office 2000 Web page (www.scsite.com/off2000/qr.htm), and then click Microsoft Access 2000.

To Compact a Database

1 **Be sure the database is closed. Click Tools on the menu bar, click Database Utilities, and then point to Compact and Repair Database (Figure 5-71).**

2 **Click Compact and Repair Database. In the Database to Compact From, select the folder containing the Bavant Marine Services database on the hard disk, select the Bavant Marine Services database and then click the Compact button.**

3 **In the Compact Database Into dialog box, type** Bavant Marine Services Compacted **as the name of the database and then click the Save button.**

The compacted database is stored with the name Bavant Marine Services Compacted.

4 **Assuming the operation is completed successfully, delete the original database (Bavant Marine Services) and rename Bavant Marine Services Compacted as Bavant Marine Services.**

The Bavant Marine Services database now is the compacted form of the original.

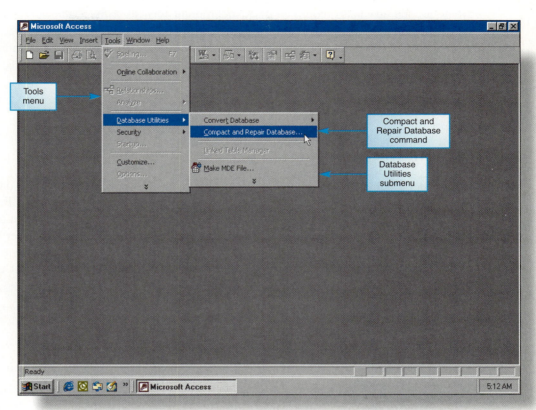

FIGURE 5-71

CASE PERSPECTIVE SUMMARY

You have added the new fields requested by Bavant Marine Services to the Technician table in its database. You have updated the new fields and created a form incorporating some of the new fields. You have also included data about the marinas of the technician on this new form. In addition, you included a link to the technician's Web page on the form. You created queries for Bavant that included criteria based on the new fields. Finally, you compacted the database to remove any wasted space.

Project Summary

Project 5 introduced you to some additional field types. To maintain the additional data required at Bavant Marine Services, you needed to learn how to create and work with date, memo, OLE, and Hyperlink fields. You also learned how to use such fields in a form. You then learned how to build a form on a one-to-many relationship. One technician displayed on the form at the same time as the many marinas serviced by that technician. You learned how to use the form to view technician and marina data as well as to view the technician's Web Page. You saw how to use date and memo fields in queries to answer two important questions for the organization. Finally, you learned how to compact a database to remove any wasted space.

What You Should Know

Having completed this project, you now should be able to perform the following tasks:

- Add a Form Title (A 5.40)
- Add Fields to a Table (A 5.6)
- Change Label Alignment (A 5.33)
- Change Special Effects and Colors of Labels (A 5.37)
- Change the Row and Column Size (A 5.12)
- Change the Size Mode of a Picture (A 5.36)
- Close a Database (A 5.48)
- Close the Table and Save the Properties (A 5.20)
- Compact a Database (A 5.49)
- Create a Form with a Subform Using the Form Wizard (A 5.21)
- Enter Data in Date Fields (A 5.9)
- Enter Data in Hyperlink Fields (A 5.18)
- Enter Data in Memo Fields (A 5.11)
- Enter Data in OLE Fields and Convert the Data to Pictures (A 5.15)
- Modify the Form Design (A 5.28)
- Modify the Subform Design (A 5.26)
- Move Fields (A 5.32)
- Move and Resize Fields (A 5.29)
- Move Labels (A 5.31)
- Open a Database (A 5.5)
- Resize a Label (A 5.31, A 5.35)
- Use Date and Memo Fields in a Query (A 5.45)
- Use the Form to View Data and Web Pages (A 5.43)

Apply Your Knowledge

Project Reinforcement at www.scsite.com/off2000/reinforce.htm

1 Enhancing the Sidewalk Scrapers Database

Instructions: Start Access. Open the Sidewalk Scrapers database that you used in Project 4. Perform the following tasks.

1. Add the fields, Start Date and Notes, to the Worker table structure as shown in Figure 5-72.

2. Save the changes to the structure.

3. Add the data shown in Figure 5-73 to the Worker table. Adjust the row and column spacing for the table.

4. Print and then close the table.

5. Query the Worker table to find all workers who have a driver's license. Include the worker's first name, last name, and pay rate in the query. Print the query results. Do not save the query.

6. Use the Form Wizard to create a form with a subform for the Worker table. Include the Worker Id, First Name, Last Name, Pay Rate, Start Date, and Notes from the Worker table. Include the Customer Number, Name, Telephone, and Balance fields from the Customer table.

7. Modify the form design to create the form shown in Figure 5-74 on the next page.

8. Print the form. To print the form, open the form, click File on the menu bar, click Print, and then click Selected Record(s) as the Print Range. Click the OK button.

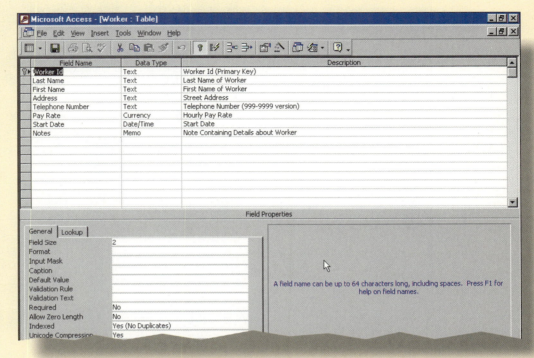

FIGURE 5-72

Data for Worker table

WORKER ID	START DATE	NOTES
03	11/15/1999	Has driver's license. Can operate snowblower and pickup with snowplow attachment.
07	12/02/2000	Can operate snowblower. Available at all hours.
10	01/20/2001	Can work weekends only.
14	12/12/2000	Has driver's license. Can operate snowblower. Prefers to work in the early morning before 7 A.M.

FIGURE 5-73

(continued)

Apply Your Knowledge

➕ **Project Reinforcement at www.scsite.com/off2000/reinforce.htm**

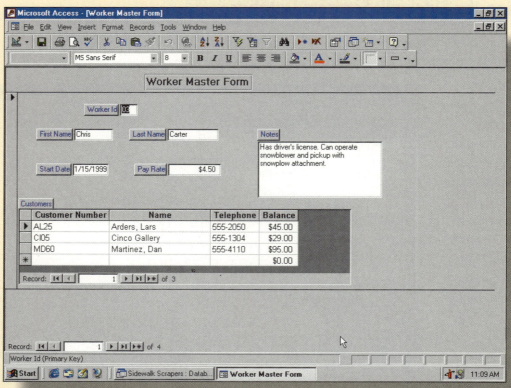

FIGURE 5-74

In the Lab

1 Enhancing the School Connection Database

Problem: The Booster's Club has found that the School Connection database needs to maintain additional data on vendors. They need to know the last date they placed an order with a vendor. They also would like to store some notes about each vendor's return policy as well as store the Web page name of each vendor's Web Page. The club requires a form that displays information about the vendor as well as the products the vendor sells.

Instructions: Open the School Connection database that you used in Project 4. Perform the following tasks.

1. Add the fields, Last Order Date, Notes, and Web Page, to the Vendor table structure as shown in Figure 5-75 and then save the changes to the structure.

In the Lab

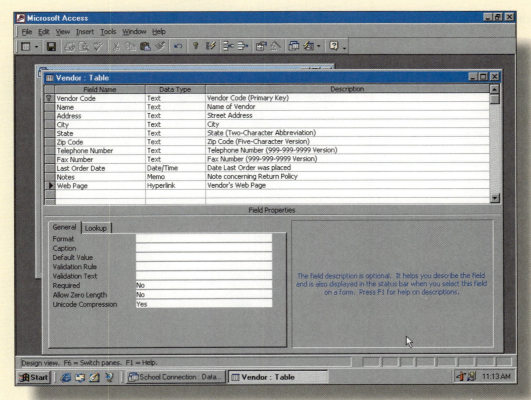

FIGURE 5-75

2. Add the data shown in Figure 5-76 to the Vendor table. Use the same hyperlink files that you used for the Technician table in this project. Adjust the row and column spacing for the table.
3. Print the table.
4. Create the form shown in Figure 5-77 on the next page for the Vendor table. Use Vendor Master Form as the name of the form and Items of Vendor as the name of the subform.
5. Print the form. To print the form, open the form, click File on the menu bar, click Print, and then click Selected Record(s) as the Print Range. Click the OK button.
6. Query the Vendor table to find all vendors that allow all unsold merchandise to be returned. Include the Vendor Code and Name in the query. Print the results. Do not save the query.

Data for Vendor table

VENDOR CODE	LAST ORDER DATE	NOTES
AL	05/20/2001	Can return only those items ordered for the first time. Charges a fee.
GG	06/17/2001	Can return all unsold merchandise. No extra charges.
TM	08/24/2001	Can return all unsold merchandise. Charges a fee.

FIGURE 5-76

(continued)

In the Lab

Enhancing the School Connection Database (continued)

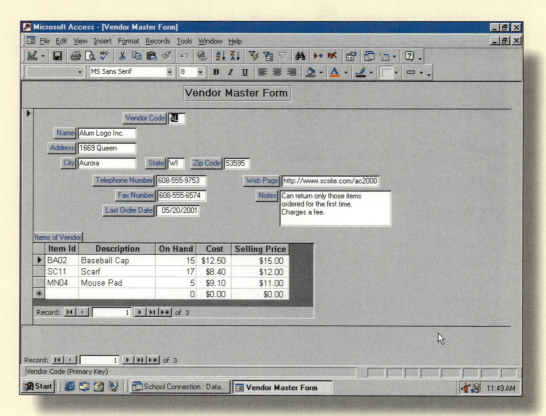

FIGURE 5-77

2 Enhancing the City Area Bus Company Database

Problem: The City Area Bus Company needs to maintain additional data on the advertising sales representatives. The company needs to maintain the date a sales rep started as well as some notes concerning the representative's abilities. They also would like to store a picture of the representative as well as a link to each representative's Web Page. The company wants you to create a form that displays advertising sales representative information and the advertisers for which they are responsible.

Instructions: Open the City Area Bus Company database that you used in Project 4. Perform the following tasks.

1. Add the Start Date, Notes, Picture, and Web Page fields to the Sales Rep table as shown in Figure 5-78. Save the changes to the structure.

In the Lab

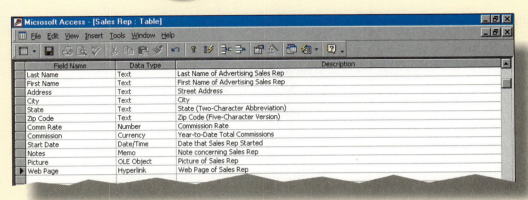

FIGURE 5-78

2. Add the data shown in Figure 5-79 to the Sales Rep table. Add pictures and hyperlinks for each representative. Use the same picture and hyperlink files that you used for the Technician table in this project. Pict1.bmp and pict3.bmp are pictures of females; pict2.bmp is of a male.

3. Print the table.

4. Create the form shown in Figure 5-80. Use Sales Rep Master Form as the name of the form and Advertiser Accounts as the name of the subform.

5. Add the current date to the form. (*Hint*: Use Microsoft Access Help to solve this problem.)

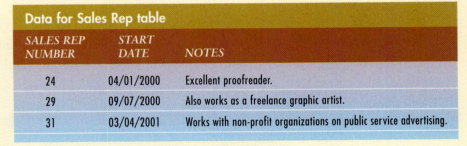

Data for Sales Rep table

SALES REP NUMBER	START DATE	NOTES
24	04/01/2000	Excellent proofreader.
29	09/07/2000	Also works as a freelance graphic artist.
31	03/04/2001	Works with non-profit organizations on public service advertising.

FIGURE 5-79

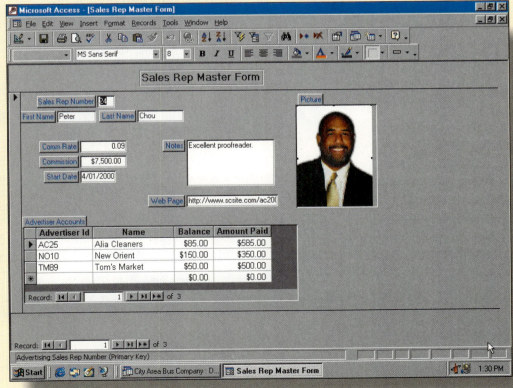

FIGURE 5-80

(continued)

In the Lab

Enhancing the City Area Bus Company Database *(continued)*

6. Print the form. To print the form, open the form, click File on the menu bar, click Print, and then click Selected Record(s) as the Print Range. Click the OK button.

7. Query the Sales Rep table to find all sales reps who also will work as freelance graphic artists. Include the Sales Rep Number, Last Name, and First Name in the query. Print the query results. Do not save the query.

8. Query the Sales Rep table to find all sales reps who started before 2001. Include the Sales Rep Number, Last Name, First Name, Commission, and Comm Rate in the query. Print the query results. Do not save the query.

3 Enhancing the Resort Rentals Database

Problem: The real estate company needs to maintain additional data on the owners. The company needs to maintain pictures of the owners as well as some notes concerning the owner's rental policies. The company wants you to create a form that displays owner information and the rental properties they own.

Instructions: Open the Resort Rentals database that you used in Project 4. Perform the following tasks.

1. Add the fields, Picture and Notes, to the Owner table structure as shown in Figure 5-81. Save the changes to the structure.

2. Add the data shown in Figure 5-82 to the Owner table. Adjust the row and column spacing for the table, if necessary.

3. Print the table.

4. Create the form shown in Figure 5-83. Use Owner Master Form as the name of the form and Rental Properties as the name of the subform.

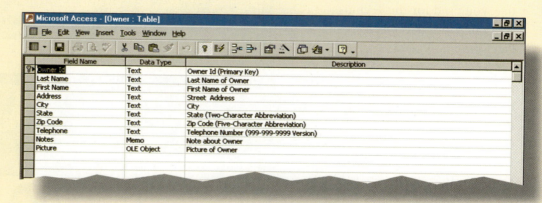

FIGURE 5-81

Data for Owner table

OWNER ID	NOTES
FH15	Has no pets policy. Will not rent to families with children under 12.
LD45	Will rent to families with children. Allows small pets only but requires $100 security deposit.
ML10	Has no smoking policy. Has no pets policy.
PR23	Will rent to families with children. Allows pets but requires $200 security deposit.

FIGURE 5-82

In the Lab

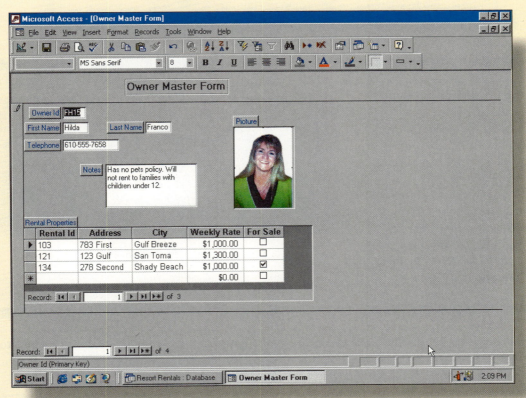

FIGURE 5-83

5. Print the form. To print the form, open the form, click File on the menu bar, click Print, and then click Selected Record(s) as the Print Range. Click the OK button.

6. Query the Owner table to find all owners who allow pets. Include the Owner Id, First Name, and Last Name in the query. Print the results. Do not save the query.

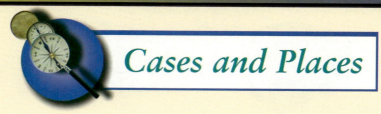

Cases and Places

The difficulty of these case studies varies:
▶ are the least difficult; ▶▶ are more difficult; and ▶▶▶ are the most difficult.

1 ▶ Use the Computer Items database on the Access Data Disk for this assignment. The Computer Club needs additional data on the suppliers. Add the fields and data shown in Figure 5-84 to the Supplier table. Adjust the row and column spacing so that the complete notes about the supplier display. Print the Supplier table. Query the Supplier table to find all suppliers that offer volume discounts.

SUPPLIER CODE	LAST ORDER DATE	NOTES
ER	8/26/2001	Offers volume discounts when more than 12 items are ordered.
HI	9/1/2001	No discounts on any items.
MT	9/9/2001	Logo Mouse Pads are a special order. No discounts.

FIGURE 5-84

2 ▶ Create and print a Supplier Master Form for the Supplier table that is similar in format to Figure 5-77 on page A 5.54. The form should include all the fields from the Supplier table. The subform that displays should include all fields in the Item table except Supplier Code.

3 ▶▶ Use the Galaxy Books database on the Access Data Disk for this assignment. The bookstore owner needs additional data on the publishers. Add the fields and data shown in Figure 5-85 to the Publisher table. Adjust the row and column spacing so that the complete notes about the publisher display. Print the Publisher table. Query the database to find all publishers that will fill single orders.

PUBLISHER CODE	ORDER DATE	NOTES
BB	6/21/2001	Will fill single orders and special requests.
PB	6/30/2001	Will fill single orders on emergency basis only. Ships twice a week.
SI	6/15/2001	Has minimum order requirement of 25 books. Ships weekly.
VN	5/25/2001	Will fill single orders and special requests. Ships daily.

FIGURE 5-85

4 ▶▶ Create and print a Publisher Master Form for the Publisher table. The subform that displays should include all fields in the Book table except Year Published and Publisher Code. Be sure to include a form header and change the special effects and colors of the labels.

5 ▶▶▶ Enhance the Galaxy Books database by adding a summary description for each book. Make up your own summaries. Add a field to the Publisher table that will store a picture of the publisher's sales representative. Use the same picture files used for the Technician table in the project.

Microsoft **Access 2000**

Microsoft Access 2000

Creating an Application System Using Macros, Wizards, and the Switchboard Manager

You will have mastered the material in this project when you can:

OBJECTIVES

- Use the Lookup Wizard to create a lookup field
- Use the Input Mask Wizard to create an input mask
- Update a field using an input mask
- Use a Lookup Wizard field
- Add a control for a single field to a report
- Add a calculated control to a report
- Add a control for a single field to a form
- Create a macro
- Add actions and comments to a macro
- Modify arguments in a macro
- Create a copy of a macro
- Run a macro
- Create a switchboard
- Modify switchboard pages
- Modify switchboard items
- Use a switchboard

Legal Concerns?

Hotlines Offer Speedy Counsel

What are your legal concerns? Do you need to prepare a contract for a job to be done? Are you involved in a dispute with a business partner? Have you been subpoenaed in a litigation? Will you be required to file a new small claims case? With any legal issue facing you for which you are not prepared or informed, you may ask if you have a place to turn for some plain and simple legal guidance. Knowledge of the law empowers you.

You know a lawyer can help you with these problems, but you fear the time and expense of hiring one will really stretch your resources. In response to

these concerns, legal hotlines have sprung up with the goal of providing quick, inexpensive advice. The more efficient hotline systems usually are staffed with experienced attorneys and paralegals who have access to powerful database application systems such as Access 2000 that help organize client information using forms and macros as you will do in this project.

A potential client calling the hotline provides basic information about the legal matter. The hotline staff member answering the telephone selects the client registration form in the database system and begins interviewing the client while simultaneously entering the answers in fields on the form.

Usually, the first field is the client's name. When the name is entered, the database system executes a macro, which is a series of actions designed to carry out a specific task. In this case, the macro searches the client table for a matching name. If a match is found, remaining fields in the registration form are filled in automatically with personal data from the client's previous record. If a match is not found, the hotline staff member interviews the client to obtain the required data.

A second macro is performed when the Social Security number is entered. While a client's last name may change, the Social Security number remains the same. Therefore, the last name macro might not retrieve the client's record if the client has used the hotline service previously using a different name, whereas the Social Security macro would find the record if the same number is used.

After this basic client data has been entered in the registration form, the database application system retrieves another form that includes a field for the name of the person or company causing the conflict. An attorney cannot represent a client if he or she previously has represented the opposing party in a similar case. Then, the database system executes a third macro to check the adverse party table for client conflicts.

If no conflict is found, the hotline worker continues to interview the caller about the case and record the facts and issues in memo fields. Many database application systems integrate with word   processing applications, so the attorney can generate a form letter that merges data from this initial client conversation with prewritten text that confirms the results of this telephone conversation.

With the installation and development of online and legal advice hotlines, trained law office staff are serving more clients and providing direct response at a fraction of the cost for services. Hotlines offer speedy counsel and solutions in an informal setting to resolve legal disputes and concerns.

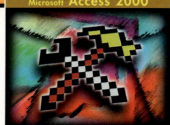

Microsoft Access 2000

Creating an Application System Using Macros, Wizards, and the Switchboard Manager

PROJECT

6

CASE PERSPECTIVE

The management of Bavant Marine Services is pleased with the tables, forms, and reports that you have created thus far. They have additional requests, however. They now realize they should have included phone numbers for marinas in the database. They would like for you to add the phone number field to the Marina table, the Billing Summary report, and the Marina Update Form. They would like to be able to type only the digits in the phone number and then have Access format the number appropriately. If the user enters 6165552312, for example, Access will format the number as (616) 555-2312. Bavant is pleased with the Marina Type combo box you placed in the Marina Update form, which allows users to select a marina type from a list. They realized, however, that this combo box is not visible in Datasheet view. They would like for you to incorporate a similar feature in Datasheet view. Finally, they have heard about switchboard systems that enable users to click a button or two to open any form or table, preview any report, or print any report. They would like for you to create such a system for them because they believe this will increase employee productivity.

Introduction

In previous projects, you created tables, forms, and reports. Each time you wanted to use any of these, however, you had to follow the correct series of steps. To open the Marina Update Form in a maximized window, for example, first you must click Forms on the Objects bar in the Database window, and then right-click the correct form. Next, you had to click Open on the shortcut menu, and then finally click the Maximize button for the window containing the form.

All these steps are unnecessary if you create your own switchboard system, such as the one shown in Figure 6-1a. A **switchboard** is a form that includes buttons to perform a variety of actions. In this system, you just click a button — View Form, View Table, View Report, Print Report, or Exit Application — to indicate the action you wish to take. Other than Exit Application, clicking a button leads to another switchboard. For example, clicking the View Form button leads to the View Form switchboard as shown in Figure 6-1b. You then click the button that identifies the form you wish to view. Similarly, clicking the View Table button would lead to a switchboard on which you would click a button to indicate the table you wish to view. Thus, viewing any form, table, or report, or printing any report requires clicking only two buttons.

In this project, you will create the switchboard system represented in Figures 6-1a and 6-1b. Before doing so, you will create **macros**, which are collections of actions designed to carry out specific tasks, such as opening a form and maximizing the window containing the form. You can run the macros directly from the Database window. When you do, Access will execute the various steps, called **actions**, in the macro. You also can use the macros in the switchboard system. Clicking certain buttons in the switchboard system you create will cause the appropriate macros to be run.

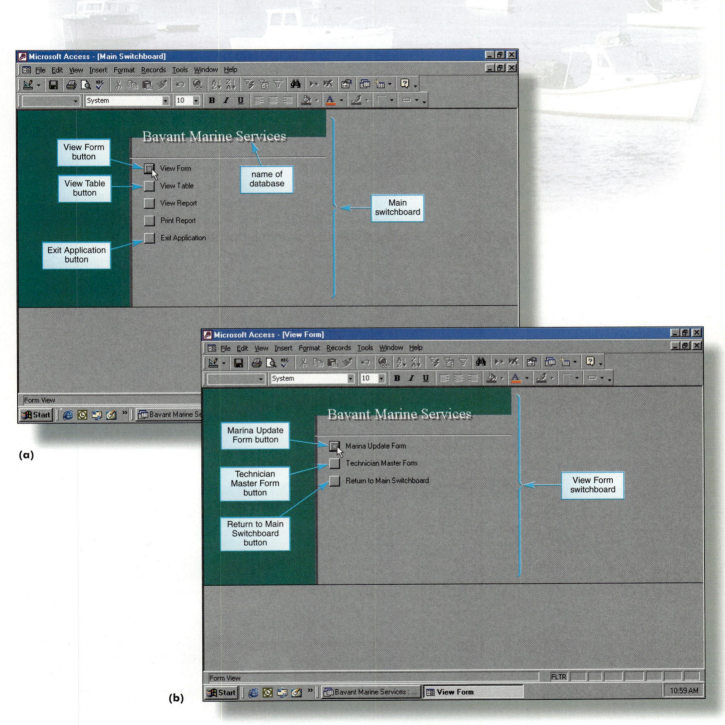

(a)

(b)

FIGURE 6-1

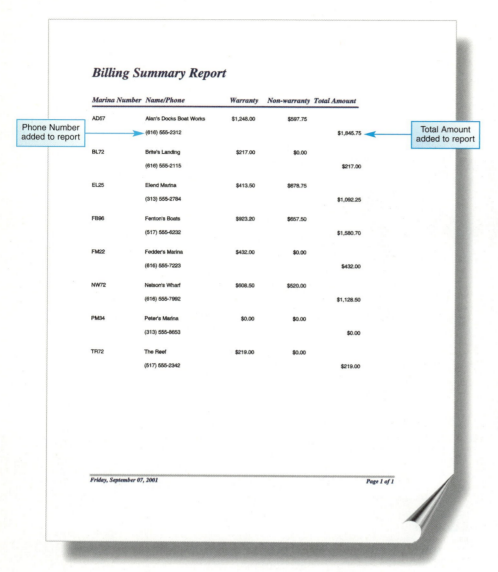

Billing Summary Report

Marina Number	Name/Phone	Warranty	Non-warranty	Total Amount
AD57	Alan's Docks Boat Works	$1,248.00	$597.75	
	(616) 555-2312			$1,845.75
BL72	Brite's Landing	$217.00	$0.00	
	(616) 555-2115			$217.00
EL25	Elend Marina	$413.50	$678.75	
	(313) 555-2784			$1,092.25
FB96	Fenton's Boats	$923.20	$657.50	
	(517) 555-6232			$1,580.70
FM22	Fedder's Marina	$432.00	$0.00	
	(616) 555-7223			$432.00
NW72	Nelson's Wharf	$608.50	$520.00	
	(616) 555-7992			$1,128.50
PM34	Peter's Marina	$0.00	$0.00	
	(313) 555-8653			$0.00
TR72	The Reef	$219.00	$0.00	
	(517) 555-2342			$219.00

Phone Number added to report

Total Amount added to report

Friday, September 07, 2001 — *Page 1 of 1*

(a)

Before creating the switchboard system, you will make two changes to the Marina table. You will convert the data type of the Marina Type field to Lookup Wizard. By doing so, users will be able to select a marina type from a list just as they can when using the combo box on a form. You will also add the Phone Number field to the table and then use the Input Mask wizard to ensure that (1) users need to enter only the digits in the phone number and (2) Access will format the phone numbers appropriately. You will add the phone number to the Billing Summary Report (Figure 6-2a). In addition, you will add the total amount (warranty amount plus non-warranty amount) to the report. You also will add the phone number to the Marina Update Form (Figure 6-2b).

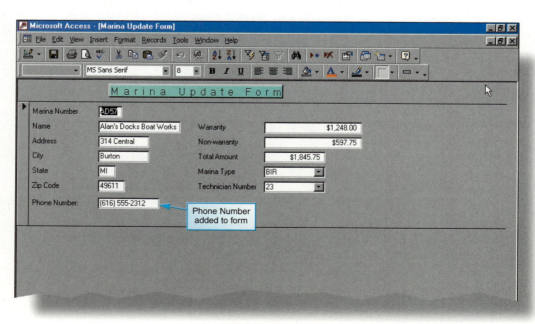

(b)

FIGURE 6-2

Project Six – Creating an Application System for Bavant Marine Services

You will begin this project by changing the data type of the Marina Type field to Lookup Wizard. You then will add the Phone Number field and use the Input Mask Wizard to specify the special format that phone numbers must follow. Next, you will add the phone number to the Billing Summary report. You also will add the total amount (warranty amount plus non-warranty amount) to this report. You will add the phone number to the Marina Update form. Before creating the switchboard system required by the management of Bavant Marine Services, you will create and test the macros that will be used in the system. Finally, you will create the switchboard system that will allow users to access any form, table, or report simply by clicking the appropriate buttons.

Opening the Database

Before completing the tasks in this project, you must open the database. Perform the following steps to complete this task.

TO OPEN A DATABASE

1 Click the Start button on the taskbar.

2 Click Open Office Document on the Start menu, and then click 3½ Floppy (A:) in the Look in box.

3 Click the Open button.

The database opens and the Bavant Marine Services : Database window displays.

Lookup and Input Mask Wizards

As you add the new data in this project, you will need to change the data type for certain fields. You also will need to be able to specify how the data is to be entered and how it will display. To accomplish these tasks, you will use the Lookup Wizard and the Input Mask Wizard.

Using the Lookup Wizard

Currently, the data type for the Marina Type field is text. You need to change the data type to Lookup Wizard. A **lookup wizard** field allows the user to select from a list of values.

To change a data type, click the Data Type column for the field, and then select the desired data type. For many data type changes, no additional action would be required. If the selected type is Lookup Wizard, however, a wizard will guide you through the necessary additional steps. After you complete the wizard, Microsoft Access sets the data type based on the values selected in the wizard. Perform the steps on the next page to change the data type for the Marina Type field.

More About

Switchboards

An application system is simply an easy-to-use collection of forms, reports, and queries designed to satisfy the needs of some specific user or groups of users, such as the users at Bavant Marine Services. A switchboard system is one type of application system that has found widespread acceptance in the Windows environment.

More About

Lookup Wizard Fields

Lookup Wizard fields, which play a role similar to that of combo boxes in forms, are used in a variety of applications. For more information about the uses of Lookup Wizard fields, visit the Access 2000 More About page www.scsite.com/ac2000/more.htm) and then click Lookup Wizard.

Steps To Use the Lookup Wizard

1 **If necessary, click the Tables object. Right-click Marina, and then point to Design View on the shortcut menu.**

The shortcut menu for the Marina table displays, and the Design View command is highlighted (Figure 6-3).

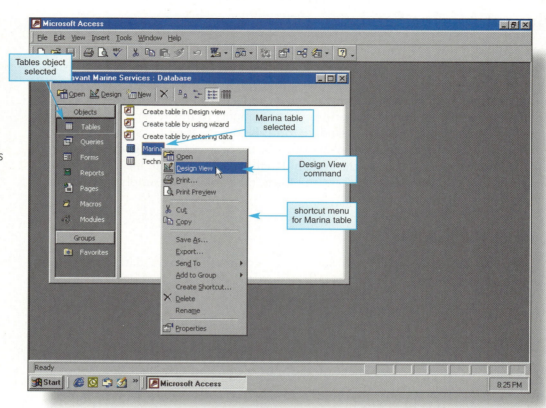

FIGURE 6-3

2 **Click Design View. Click the Data Type column for the Marina Type field, click the arrow, and then point to Lookup Wizard.**

The list of available data types displays (Figure 6-4).

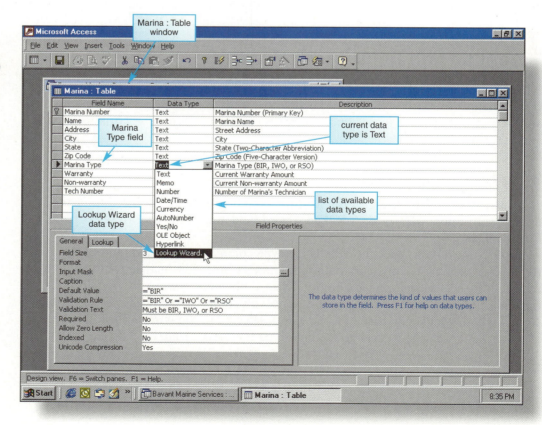

FIGURE 6-4

3 **Click Lookup Wizard, and then point to the I will type in the values that I want option button.**

The Lookup Wizard dialog box displays (Figure 6-5).

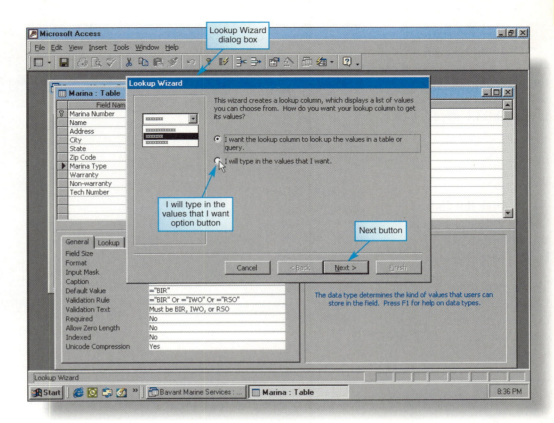

FIGURE 6-5

4 **Click the I will type in the values that I want option button, click the Next button in the Lookup Wizard dialog box, click the first row of the table (under Col1), and then type** BIR **as the entry. Press the DOWN ARROW key and then type** IWO **in the second row. Press the DOWN ARROW key and then type** RSO **in the third. Point to the Next button.**

The list of values for the combo box is entered (Figure 6-6).

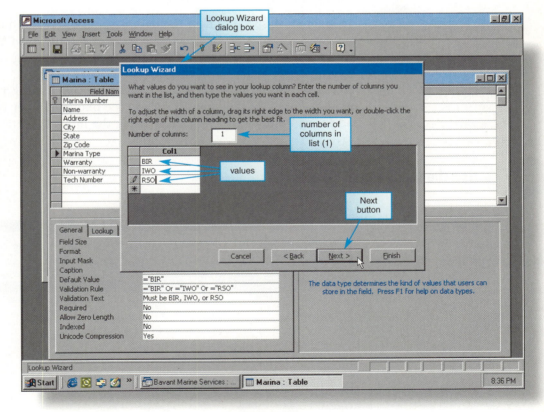

FIGURE 6-6

5 Click the Next button. Ensure **Marina Type** is entered as the label for the lookup column and then point to the Finish button.

The label is entered (Figure 6-7).

6 Click the Finish button to complete the definition of the Lookup Wizard field.

Marina Type is now a Lookup Wizard field, but the data type is still text because the values entered in the wizard were entered as text.

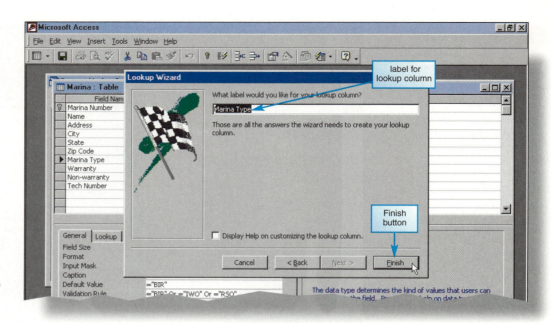

FIGURE 6-7

Input Masks

When you construct an input mask, there are many built-in input masks from which to choose. You can also construct your own input mask. For more information about constructing an input mask, visit the Access 2000 More About page (www.scsite.com/ ac2000/more.htm) and then click Input Mask.

Using the Input Mask Wizard

An **input mask** specifies how the data is to be entered and how it will display. You can enter an input mask directly or you can use the **Input Mask wizard**. The wizard assists you in the creation of the input mask by allowing you to select from a list of input masks you are most likely to want.

To use the Input Mask wizard, select the Input Mask property and then click the build button. The following steps add the phone number field and then specify how the phone number is to appear by using the Input Mask wizard.

 ## To Use the Input Mask Wizard

1 Point to the row selector for the **Marina Type** field.

The mouse pointer changes to a right-pointing arrow (Figure 6-8).

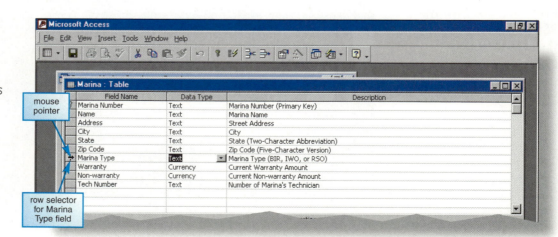

FIGURE 6-8

2 **Click the row selector for the Marina Type field, and then press the INSERT key to insert a blank row. Click the Field Name column for the new field. Type Phone Number as the field name and then press the TAB key. Select the Text data type by pressing the TAB key. Type Phone Number as the description. Click the Input Mask text box, and then point to the Build button (the button containing three dots).**

The data is entered for the field and Build button displays in the Input Mask text box (Figure 6-9).

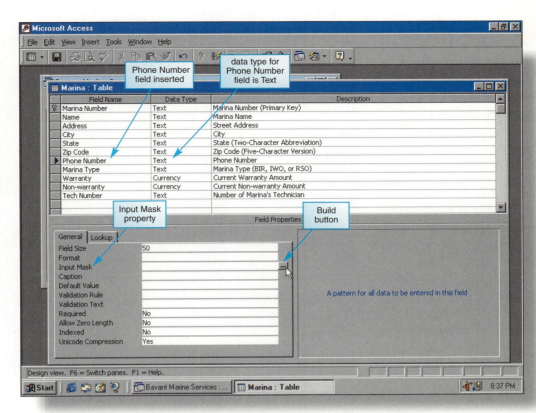

FIGURE 6-9

3 **Click the Build button, and ensure that Phone Number is selected. If a dialog box displays asking you to save the table, click Yes. Point to the Next button.**

The Input Mask Wizard dialog box displays (Figure 6-10). The dialog box contains several common input masks. The Phone Number input mask is highlighted.

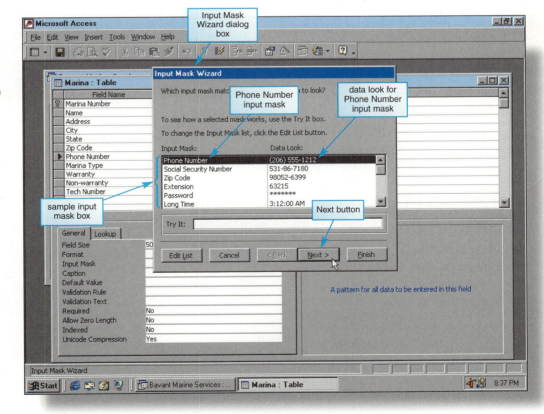

FIGURE 6-10

Microsoft **Access 2000**

4 **Click the Next button. You then are given the opportunity to change the input mask. Because you do not need to change it, click the Next button. Point to the With the symbols in the mask, like this option button.**

The Input Wizard dialog box displays (Figure 6-11). You are asked to indicate whether the symbols in the mask (the parentheses and the hyphen) are to be stored in the database or not. Your dialog box may display different numbers in the examples.

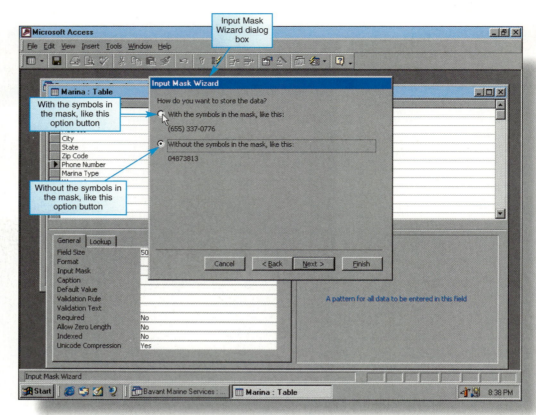

FIGURE 6-11

5 **Click the With the symbols in the mask, like this option button, click the Next button, and then click the Finish button.**

The input mask displays (Figure 6-12).

6 **Close the Marina : Table window by clicking its Close button on the title bar. When the Microsoft Access dialog box displays, click the Yes button to save your changes.**

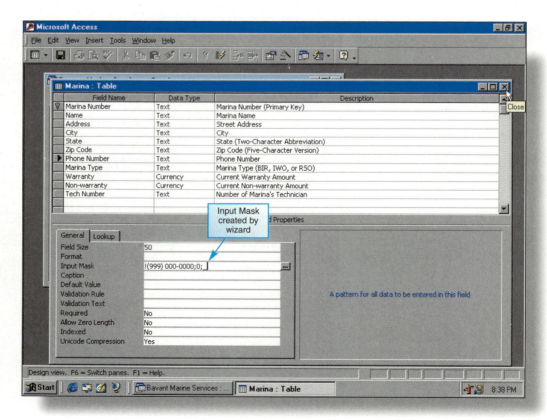

FIGURE 6-12

Entering Data Using an Input Mask

When entering data in a field that has an input mask, Access will insert the appropriate special characters in the proper positions. This means Access will insert the parentheses around the area code, the space following the second parenthesis, and the hyphen automatically in the Phone Number field. Perform the following steps to first resize the Phone Number field so that the entire heading displays and then add the phone numbers.

 To Enter Data Using an Input Mask

1 **If necessary, click the Tables object on the Objects bar. Right-click Marina and then click Open on the shortcut menu. Make sure the window is maximized, and then point to the right boundary of the field selector for the Phone Number field.**

The mouse pointer changes to a two-headed horizontal arrow with a vertical bar (Figure 6-13).

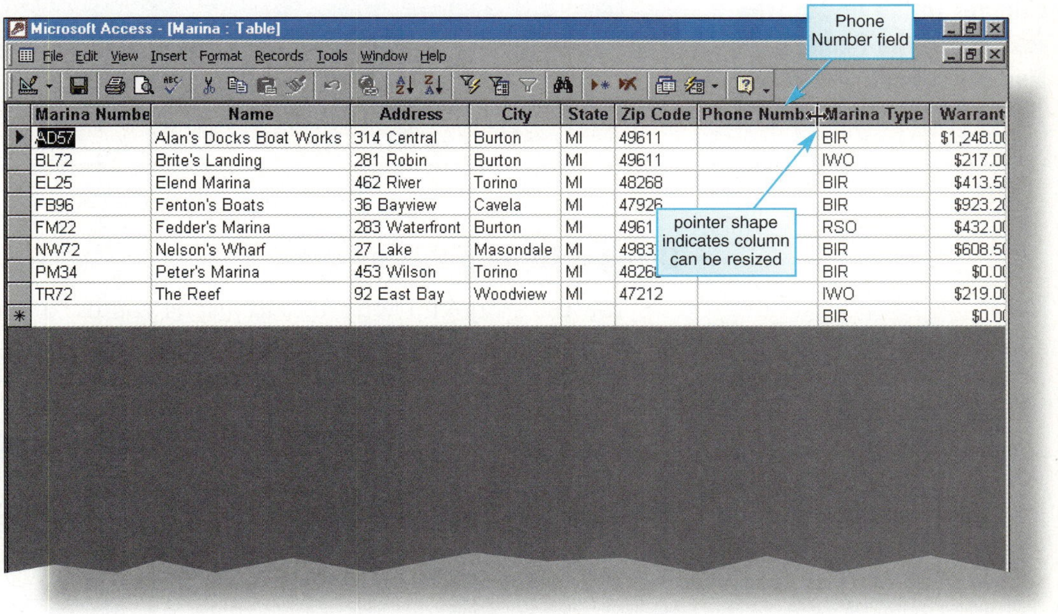

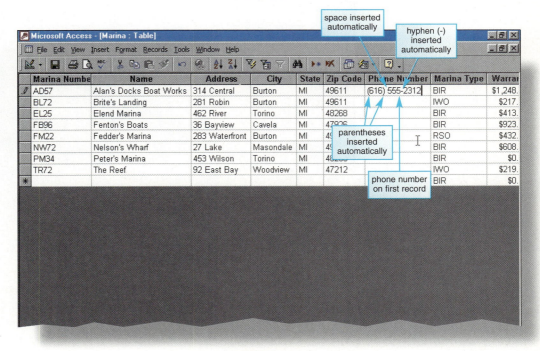

FIGURE 6-13

2 **Double-click the right boundary of the field selector to resize the field. Click the Phone Number field on the first record, and then type 6165552312 as the phone number.**

Access automatically inserts parentheses, a space, and a hyphen and displays under-scores (_) as placeholders when you begin typing (Figure 6-14).

FIGURE 6-14

3 Use the same technique to enter the remaining phone numbers as shown in Figure 6-15.

4 Close the window containing the datasheet by clicking its Close button. When asked if you want to save the changes to the layout (the resizing of the Phone Number column), click the Yes button.

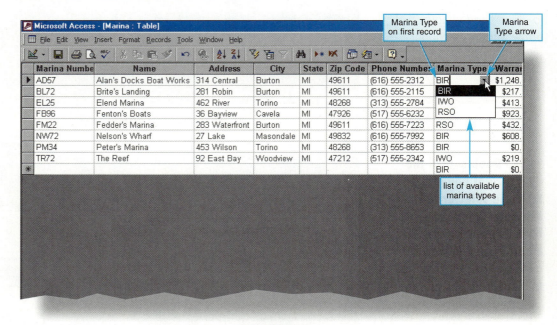

Marina Numbe	Name	Address	City	State	Zip Code	Phone Number	Marina Type	Warrar
AD57	Alan's Docks Boat Works	314 Central	Burton	MI	49611	(616) 555-2312	BIR	$1,248.
BL72	Brite's Landing	281 Robin	Burton	MI	49611	(616) 555-2115	IWO	$217.
EL25	Elend Marina	462 River	Torino	MI	48268	(313) 555-2784	BIR	$413.
FB96	Fenton's Boats	36 Bayview	Cavela	MI	47926	(517) 555-6232	BIR	$923.
FM22	Fedder's Marina	283 Waterfront	Burton	MI	49611	(616) 555-7223	RSO	$432.
NW72	Nelson's Wharf	27 Lake	Masondale	MI	49832	(616) 555-7992	BIR	$608.
PM34	Peter's Marina	453 Wilson	Torino	MI	48268	(313) 555-8653	BIR	$0.
TR72	The Reef	92 East Bay	Woodview	MI	47212	(517) 555-2342	IWO	$219.
*							BIR	$0.

all phone numbers entered

FIGURE 6-15

Using a Lookup Wizard Field

You use a Lookup Wizard field just as you use a Combo box in a form. Click the arrow to display a list of available selections (see Figure 6-16). You can then click one of the items to select it from the list.

Marina Type on first record

Marina Type arrow

Marina Numbe	Name	Address	City	State	Zip Code	Phone Numbe	Marina Type	Warrar
AD57	Alan's Docks Boat Works	314 Central	Burton	MI	49611	(616) 555-2312	BIR	$1,248.
BL72	Brite's Landing	281 Robin	Burton	MI	49611	(616) 555-2115	BIR	$217.
EL25	Elend Marina	462 River	Torino	MI	48268	(313) 555-2784	IWO	$413.
FB96	Fenton's Boats	36 Bayview	Cavela	MI	47926	(517) 555-6232	RSO	$923.
FM22	Fedder's Marina	283 Waterfront	Burton	MI	49611	(616) 555-7223	RSO	$432.
NW72	Nelson's Wharf	27 Lake	Masondale	MI	49832	(616) 555-7992	BIR	$608.
PM34	Peter's Marina	453 Wilson	Torino	MI	48268	(313) 555-8653	BIR	$0.
TR72	The Reef	92 East Bay	Woodview	MI	47212	(517) 555-2342	IWO	$219.
*							BIR	$0.

list of available marina types

FIGURE 6-16

Modifying a Report

The Billing Summary Report shown in Figure 6-2 on page A 6.6 has two additional controls not present in the original version of the report. One of the additional controls contains the Phone Number field that you just added to the Marina table. The other is a calculated control. It displays the total amount, which is the sum of the warranty amount and the non-warranty amount.

Resizing and Moving Controls in a Report

Before adding the additional fields, you need to make changes to the size of the control for the Name field because currently it is not long enough to display all the names. In a previous project, the Name field was expanded after this report was created. You also need to resize and move the controls for the Warranty and Non-warranty fields to allow space to add the Total Amount field. Perform the following steps to resize and move the controls in the Billing Summary Report.

To Resize and Move Controls in a Report

More About 2000

Adding Controls

Even though a control is for a single field, you do not have to use a field list. You also can click the Text Box button on the toolbox, place the text box in the desired location on the report or form, and then type the name of the field in square brackets ([ ]).

1 Click the Reports object in the Database window, right-click Billing Summary Report, and then point to Design View on the shortcut menu.

The Design View command on the shortcut menu is highlighted (Figure 6-17).

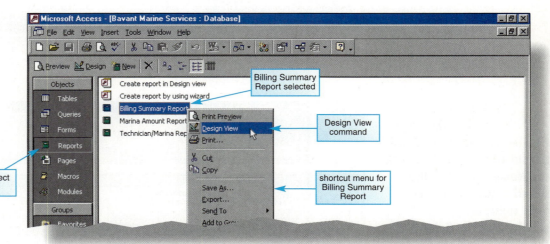

FIGURE 6-17

2 Click Design View. Click the Warranty control in the Page Header section to select the control. Hold down the SHIFT key, and then click the Non-Warranty control in the Page Header section, the Warranty control in the Detail section, and the Non-Warranty control in the Detail section to select all four controls simultaneously. Point to the left sizing handle for the Warranty control in the Page Header section.

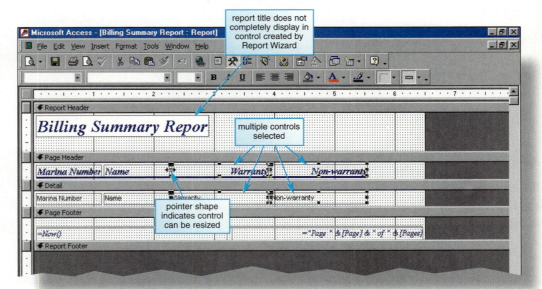

FIGURE 6-18

The report design displays (Figure 6-18). The report title does not completely display in the control, even though it displays correctly when you print or preview the report. (This is the way it was created by the report wizard. Yours may be different. If you would like for it to display completely in the report design, click the control and then drag the right-hand sizing handle.)

3 Drag the handle to the right to resize the controls to the approximate sizes shown in Figure 6-19.

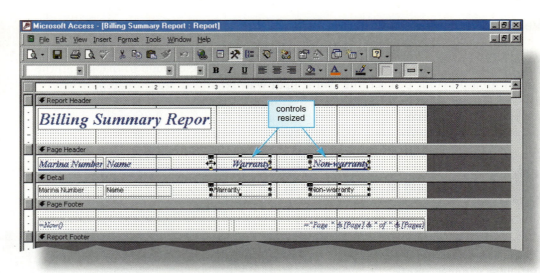

FIGURE 6-19

4 Click the Name control in the Page Header section. Hold down the SHIFT key, and then click the Name control in the Detail section to select both controls simultaneously. Point to the right sizing handle for the Name control in the Detail section.

The Name control in both the Page Header and Detail sections is selected (Figure 6-20).

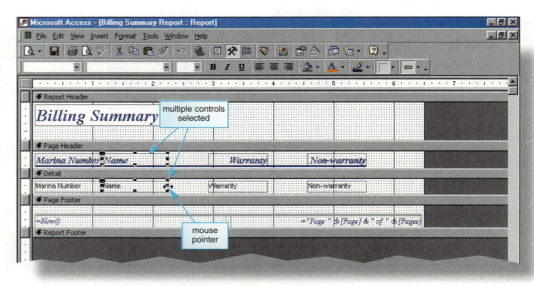

FIGURE 6-20

5 Drag the handle to the right to resize the controls to the approximate sizes shown in Figure 6-21.

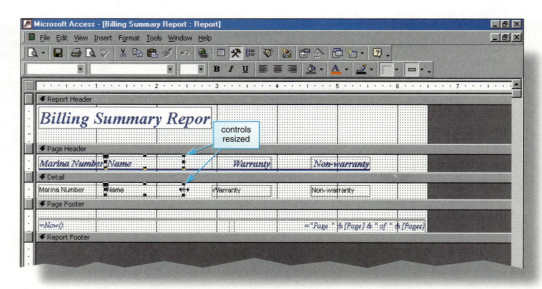

FIGURE 6-21

6 Select the Warranty controls in the Page Header and Detail sections. Point to the border of either control so that the mouse pointer changes shape to a hand and then drag the controls to the approximate position shown in Figure 6-22. Using the same process, move the Non-Warranty controls in the same sections into the approximate positions shown in the figure. Then drag the lower boundary of the Detail section to the position shown in the figure.

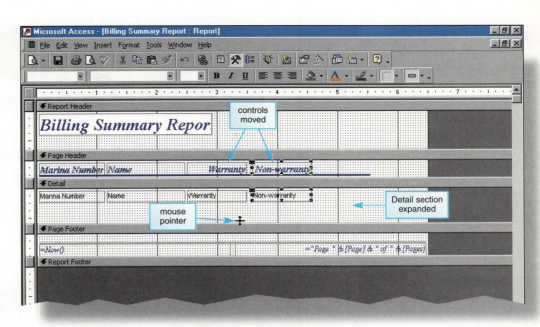

FIGURE 6-22

The Warranty and Non-warranty controls in the Page Header and Detail sections have been repositioned, and the Detail section resized (Figure 6-22).

Adding Controls to a Report

You can add controls to a report just as you added them to a form in Project 4 (pages A 4.34 and A 4.35). You can use either the toolbox or a field list to add various types of controls. If the control is for a single field, using the field list is usually an easier way to add the control. In this section you will add a control for the phone number field. You will also add a control that will display the total amount (warranty amount plus non-warranty amount). Perform the following steps to add the controls and also to make appropriate changes to the column headings.

Adding Controls

Instead of typing an expression in the text box, you can use the text box's Control Source property. Right-click the text box, click Properties, click Control Source, and then type the expression.

 To Add Controls to a Report

1 If the Field list does not already display, point to the Field List button on the Report Design toolbar (Figure 6-23).

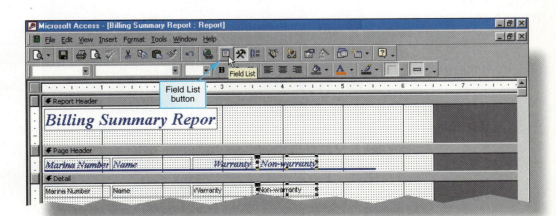

FIGURE 6-23

2 Click the Field List button, if necessary. Point to Phone Number in the Field list.

The Field list displays (Figure 6-24).

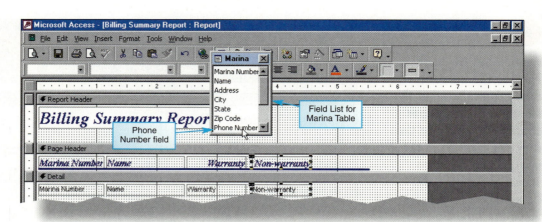

FIGURE 6-24

3 Drag the Phone Number field to the approximate position shown in Figure 6-25.

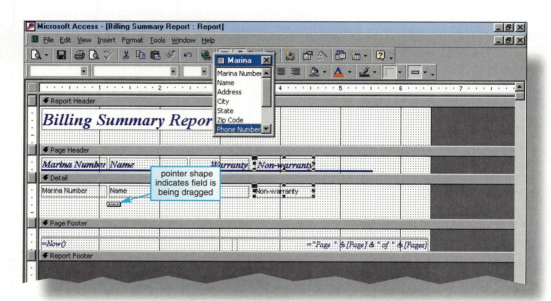

FIGURE 6-25

4 Release the mouse button to complete the placement of the field. Point to the label of the newly placed control (Figure 6-26).

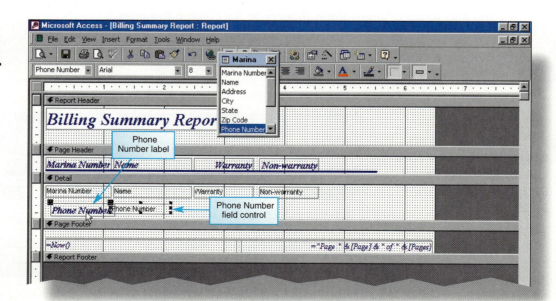

FIGURE 6-26

5 Click the label and then press the DELETE key to delete it. Click the Name control in the Page Header section to select it and then click immediately following the letter e to display an insertion point. Type /Phone to change the contents of the control to Name/Phone.

The contents of the control are changed (Figure 6-27).

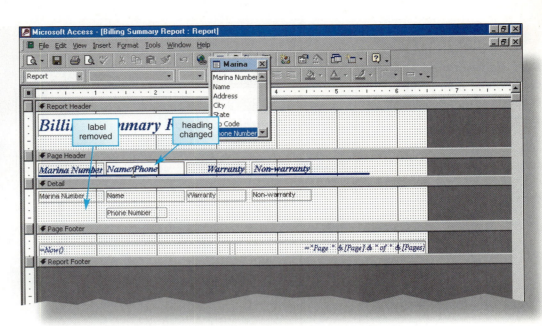

FIGURE 6-27

6 Close the Field list by clicking its Close button. Point to the Text Box button in the toolbox (Figure 6-28).

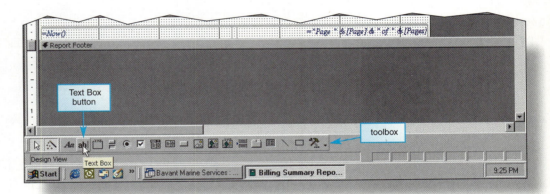

FIGURE 6-28

7 Click the Text Box button and then point to the approximate position shown in Figure 6-29.

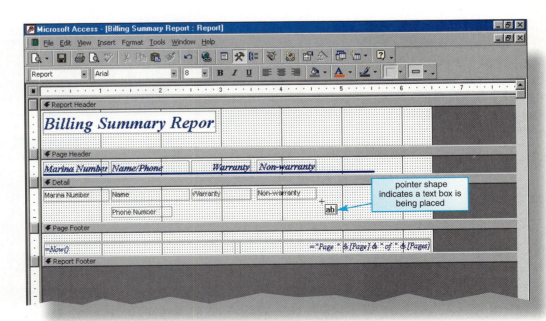

FIGURE 6-29

8 Click the position shown in Figure 6-29, right-click the control, and then point to Properties on the shortcut menu.

The shortcut menu for the control displays, and the Properties command is highlighted (Figure 6-30).

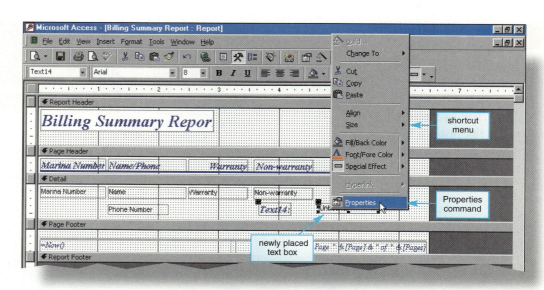

FIGURE 6-30

9 Click Properties, click the Control Source property, and then type =[Warranty]+[Non-warranty] in the Control Source text box.

The final portion of the expression displays in the Control Source text box (Figure 6-31).

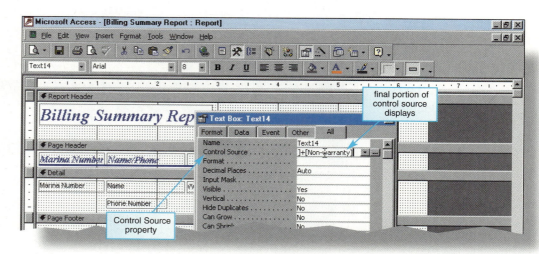

FIGURE 6-31

10 Click the Format property, click the Format arrow, scroll down so that Currency displays, and then point to Currency (Figure 6-32).

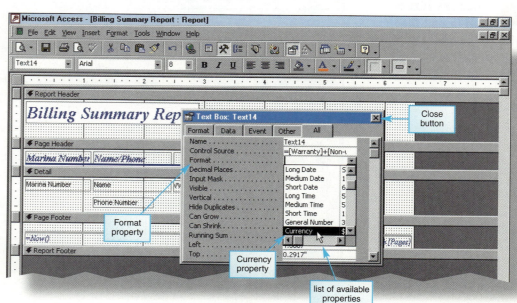

FIGURE 6-32

11 Click Currency to change the Format property. Close the property sheet by clicking its Close button, and then click the label for the text box to select it.

The label is selected (Figure 6-33).

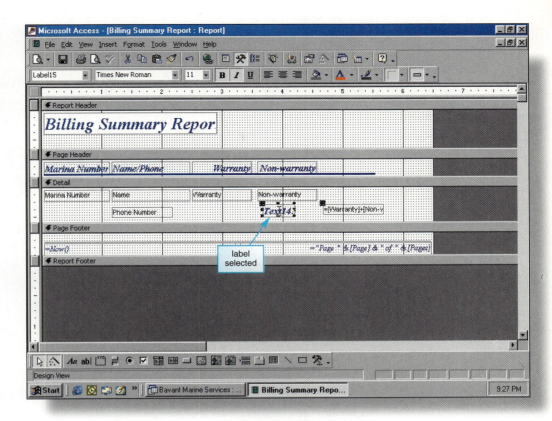

FIGURE 6-33

12 Press the DELETE key to delete the label, and then point to the Label button in the toolbox (Figure 6-34).

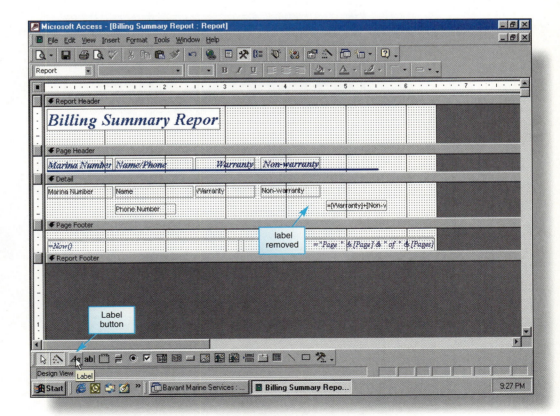

FIGURE 6-34

13 Click the Label button, and then move the pointer, whose shape changes to a small plus sign and label, to the approximate position shown in Figure 6-35.

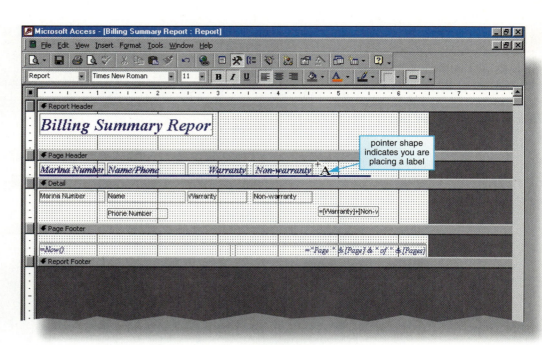

FIGURE 6-35

14 Click the position and then type Total Amount as the entry in the label.

The label displays (Figure 6-36).

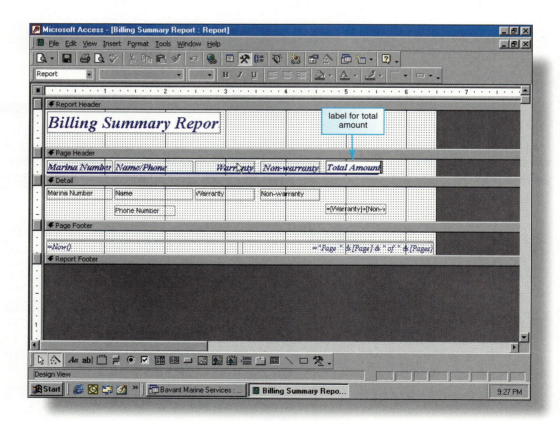

FIGURE 6-36

Previewing a Report

To view the report with sample data, preview the report by clicking the View button on the Report Design toolbar as illustrated in the steps on the next page.

To Preview a Report

1 Point to the View button on the Report Design toolbar (Figure 6-37).

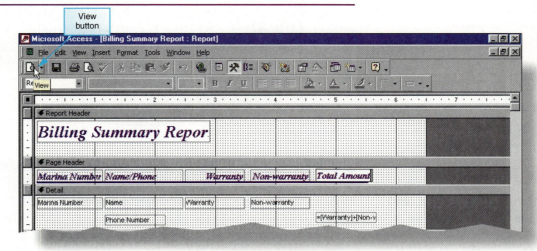

FIGURE 6-37

2 Click the View button to view the report.

The report displays (Figure 6-38). It looks like the one illustrated in Figure 6-2a.

3 Click the Close button to close the report. Click the Yes button in the Microsoft Access dialog box to save the changes to the report.

The report is closed, and the changes to the report are saved.

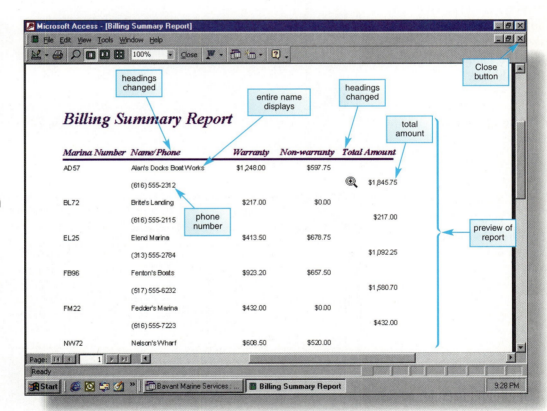

FIGURE 6-38

 Other Ways

1. Click Print Preview button on Report Design toolbar
2. On View menu click Print Preview

Modifying the Form

The Marina Update Form does not contain the Phone Number because there was no Phone Number field when the form was created. To incorporate this field in the form, you must perform the necessary steps to add it to the form.

Adding Controls to a Form

You can add a control to a form by using the toolbox. If the control is for a single field, however, the easiest way to add the control is to use the field list, just as you did with the report. Perform the following steps to add a control for the Phone Number field.

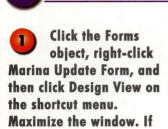

To Add a Control to a Form

1   **Click the Forms object, right-click Marina Update Form, and then click Design View on the shortcut menu. Maximize the window. If the field list does not display, click the Field List button on the Form Design toolbar (see Figure 6-23). Point to Phone Number in the field list.**

The Microsoft Access - [Marina Update Form - Form] displays (Figure 6-39).

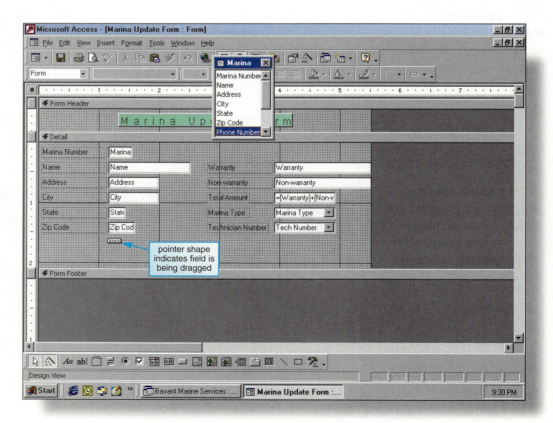

FIGURE 6-39

2   **Drag the Phone Number to the position shown in Figure 6-40.**

FIGURE 6-40

3 **Release the mouse button to place the control. Point to the Move handle of the label for the Phone Number control.**

The mouse pointer changes to a hand indicating the label can be moved (Figure 6-41).

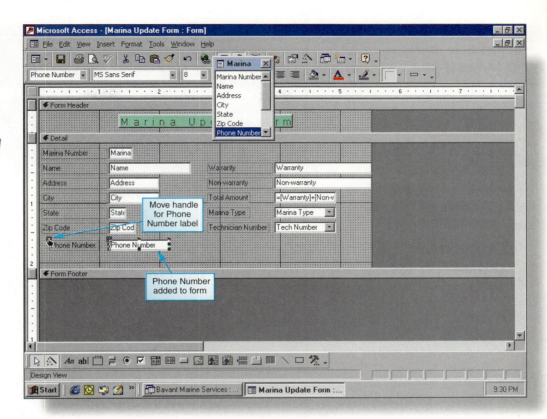

FIGURE 6-41

4 **Drag the label so that it lines up with the labels above it.**

The label is repositioned (Figure 6-42).

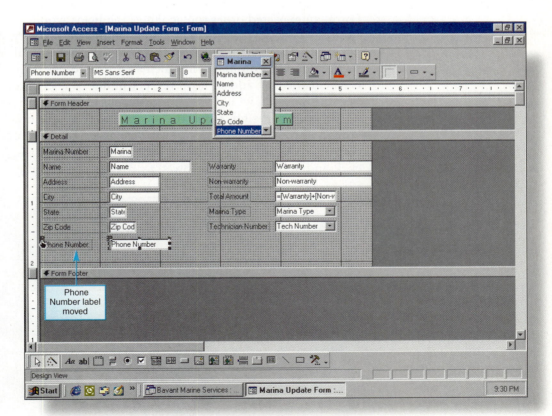

FIGURE 6-42

5 Point to the View button on the Form Design toolbar (Figure 6-43).

6 Click the View button to view the form.

The form displays. It looks like the one illustrated in Figure 6-2b.

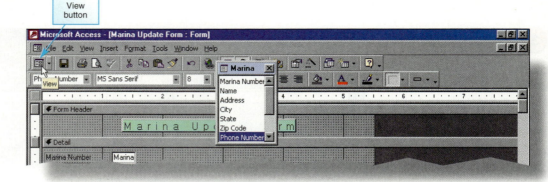

FIGURE 6-43

7 Click the Close button to close the form. Click the Yes button in the Microsoft Access dialog box to save the changes.

The form is closed and the changes are saved.

Changing the Tab Order

Users can repeatedly press the TAB key to move through the fields on a form. When you add new fields to a form, the resulting order in which the fields are encountered in this process may not be the most logical sequence. For example, on the Marina Update Form, an expected order to encounter the fields would be Marina Number, Name, Address, City, State, Zip Code, Phone Number, Warranty, Non-warranty, Marina Type, and Technician Number. This order skips the Total Amount field, because the total amount is automatically calculated from other fields. Because the Phone Number field was just added, however, it will not be encountered between Zip Code and Warranty, as you would like, but instead will be the last field encountered.

To change the **tab order**, that is, the order in which fields are encountered when tabbing through a form, ensure you are in Design view, and then use the Tab Order command on the View menu. When the Tab Order dialog box displays (Figure 6-44), click and drag the selected row(s) to change the tab order.

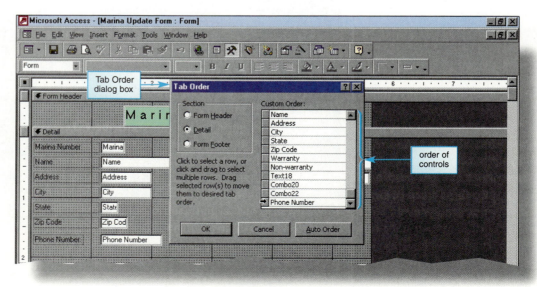

FIGURE 6-44

Creating and Using Macros

A **macro** consists of a series of actions that Access performs when the macro is run; therefore, you will need to specify the actions when you create the macro. The actions are entered in a special window called a **Macro window**. Once a macro is created, you can run it from the Database window by right-clicking the macro and then clicking Run on the shortcut menu. Macros also can be associated with items on switchboards. When you click the corresponding button on the switchboard, Access will run the macro. Whether a macro is run from the Database window or from a switchboard, the effect is the same: Access will execute the actions in the macro in the order in which they are entered.

In this project, you will create macros to open forms and maximize the windows; open tables in Datasheet view; open reports in preview windows; and print reports. As you enter actions, you will select them from a list box. The names of the actions are self-explanatory. The action to open a form, for example, is OpenForm. Thus, it is not necessary to memorize the specific actions that are available.

To create a macro, perform the following steps.

More About

Macros

The actions in a macro are executed when a particular event occurs. The event may be a user clicking Run on the macro's shortcut menu. It also may be clicking a button on a form or switchboard when the macro is associated with the button.

 To Create a Macro

1 **Click the Macros object and then point to the New button.**

The list of previously created macros displays (Figure 6-45). Currently, no macros exist.

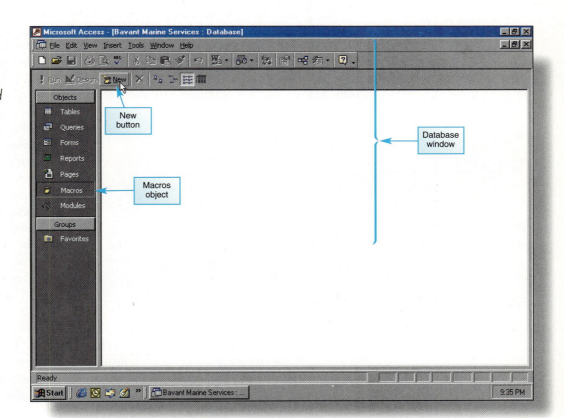

FIGURE 6-45

2 **Click the New button.**

The Microsoft Access – [Macro1: Macro] window displays (Figure 6-46).

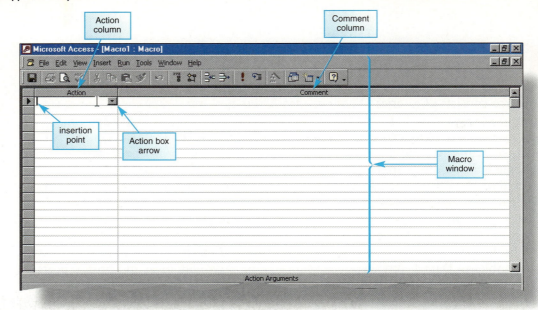

FIGURE 6-46

1. Click New Object: AutoForm button arrow on Database window toolbar, click Macro
2. On Insert menu click Macro

The Macro Window

The first column in the Macro window is the **Action column**. You enter the **actions** you want the macro to perform in this column (Figure 6-46). To enter an action, click the arrow in the Action column and then select the action from the list that displays. Many actions require additional information, called the **arguments** of the action. If you select such an action, the arguments will display in the lower portion of the Macro window and you can make any necessary changes to them.

The second column in the Macro window is the **Comment column**. In this column, you enter **comments**, which are brief descriptions of the purpose of the corresponding action. The actions, the arguments requiring changes, and the comments for the first macro you will create are illustrated in Table 6-1.

The macro begins by turning off the echo. This will eliminate the screen flicker that can be present when a form is being opened. The second action changes the shape of the mouse pointer to an hourglass to indicate that some process is taking place. The third action opens the form called Marina Update Form. The fourth action turns off the hourglass, and the fifth action turns the echo back on so the Marina Update Form will display.

Turning on and off the echo and the hourglass are not absolutely necessary. On computers with faster processors, you may not notice a difference between running a macro that includes these actions and one that does not. For computers with slower processors, however, these actions can make a noticeable difference, so they are included here.

Table 6-1	Specifications for First Macro		
ACTION	**ARGUMENT TO CHANGE**	**NEW VALUE FOR ARGUMENT**	**COMMENT**
Echo	Echo On	No	Turn echo off to avoid screen flicker
Hourglass			Turn on hourglass
OpenForm	Form Name	Marina Update Form	Open Marina Update Form
Hourglass	Hourglass On	No	Turn off hourglass
Echo			Turn echo on

Adding Actions to and Saving a Macro

To continue creating this macro, enter the actions. For each action, enter the action and comment in the appropriate text boxes, and then make the necessary changes to any arguments. When all the actions have been entered, close the macro, click the Yes button to save the changes, and then assign the macro a name. Perform the following steps to add the actions to, and save the macro.

 To Add Actions to and Save a Macro

1 **Click the box arrow in the first row of the Action column. Point to Echo.**

The list of available actions displays, and the Echo action is highlighted (Figure 6-47).

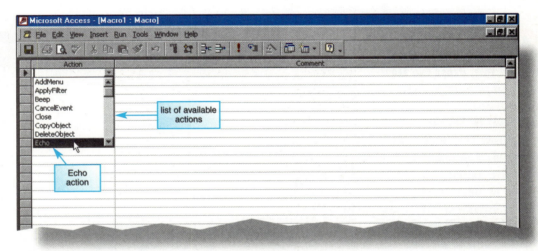

FIGURE 6-47

2 **Click Echo. Press the F6 key to move to the Action Arguments for the Echo action. Click the Echo On box arrow. Point to No.**

The arguments for the Echo action display (Figure 6-48). The list of values for the Echo On argument displays, and the No value is highlighted.

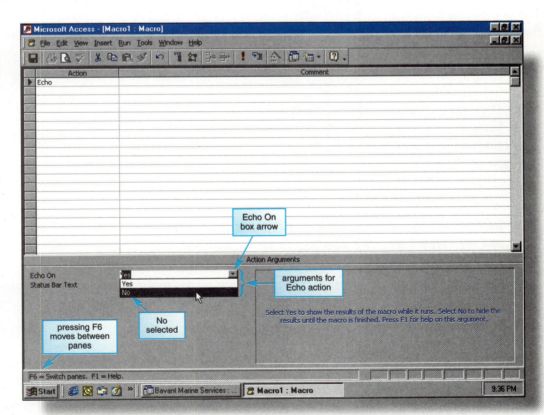

FIGURE 6-48

3 Click No. Press the F6 key to move back to Echo in the Action column. Press the TAB key. **Type** Turn echo off to avoid screen flicker **in the Comment column and then press the TAB key.**

The first action and comment are entered (Figure 6-49).

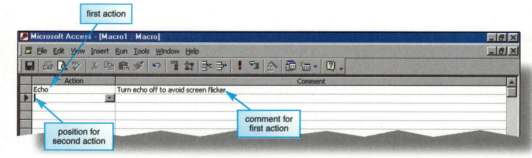

FIGURE 6-49

4 Select Hourglass as the action in the second row. Press the TAB key and then type Turn on hourglass **as the comment in the second row. Press the TAB key and then select OpenForm as the third action. Press the F6 key to move to the Action Arguments and then click the Form Name box arrow. Point to Marina Update Form.**

A list of available forms displays, and Marina Update Form is highlighted (Figure 6-50).

5 Click Marina Update Form, press the F6 key, press the TAB key, and **then type** Open Marina Update Form **as the comment.**

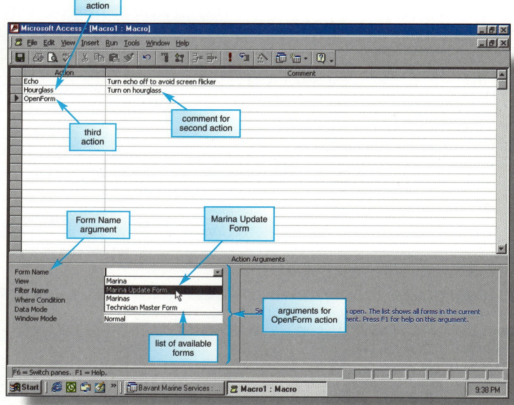

FIGURE 6-50

6 Select Hourglass as the fourth action. Change the Hourglass On argument to No, **and then type** Turn off hourglass **as the comment.**

7 Select Echo as the fifth action. Type Turn echo on **as the comment.**

The actions and comments are entered (Figure 6-51).

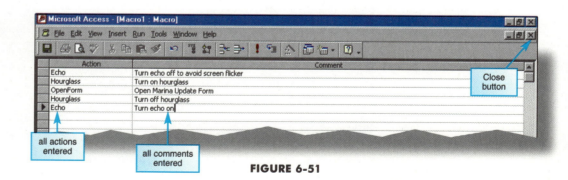

FIGURE 6-51

8 **Click the Close button for the Macro1: Macro window to close the macro, click the Yes button to save the macro, type** Open Marina Update Form **as the name of the macro, and then point to the OK button.**

The Save As dialog box displays (Figure 6-52).

9 **Click the OK button.**

The actions and comments have been added to the macro, and the macro is saved.

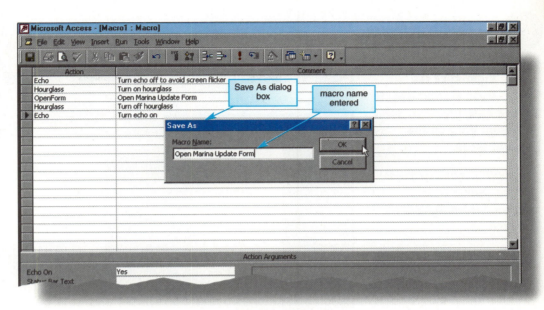

FIGURE 6-52

Running a Macro

To **run a macro**, click the Macros object in the Database window, right-click the macro, and then click Run on the shortcut menu. The actions in the macro will execute. Perform the following steps to run the macro you just created and then close the form.

TO RUN A MACRO AND CLOSE A FORM

1 Right-click the Open Marina Update Form macro and then click Run on the shortcut menu.

2 Close the Marina Update Form by clicking its Close button.

The macro runs and the Marina Update Form displays. The window containing the form is maximized because the previous windows were maximized. The form no longer displays.

If previous windows had not been maximized, the window containing the form also would not be maximized. In order to ensure that the window containing the form is automatically maximized, you can include the Maximize action in your macro.

Modifying a Macro

To **modify a macro**, right-click the macro in the Database window, click Design View on the shortcut menu, and then make the necessary changes. To insert a new action, click the position for the action, or press the INSERT key to insert a new blank row if the new action is to be placed between two actions. Enter the new action, change the values for any necessary arguments, and then enter a comment.

The steps on the next page modify the macro just created, adding a new step to maximize the form automatically.

Steps To Modify a Macro

1 **Right-click the Open Marina Update Form macro, and then point to Design View on the shortcut menu.**

The shortcut menu displays, and the Design View command is highlighted (Figure 6-53).

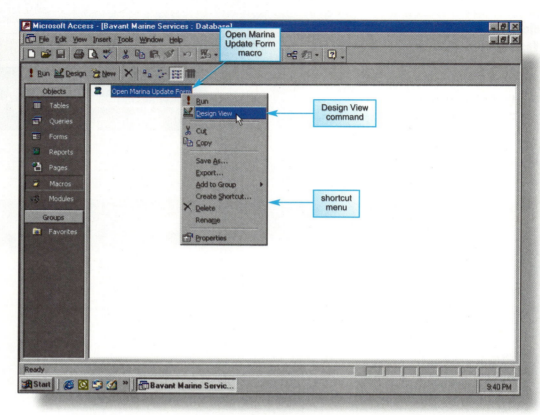

FIGURE 6-53

2 **Click Design View. Point to the row selector in the fourth row, which is directly to the left of the second Hourglass action.**

The Microsoft Access - [Open Marina Update Form : Macro] window displays (Figure 6-54).

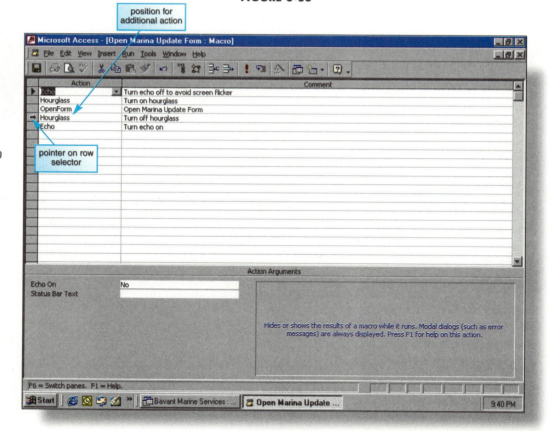

FIGURE 6-54

3 **Click the row selector to select the row, and then press the INSERT key to insert a new row. Click the Action column on the new row, select Maximize as the action, and then type** Maximize the window **as the comment.**

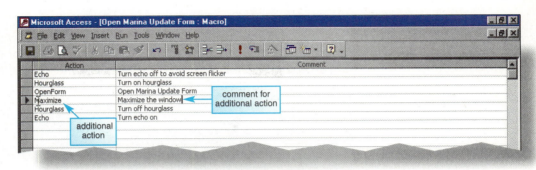

FIGURE 6-55

The new action is entered (Figure 6-55).

4 **Click the Close button, and then click the Yes button to save the changes.**

The macro has been changed and saved.

The next time the macro is run, the form not only will be opened, but the window containing the form also will be maximized automatically.

Errors in Macros

Macros can contain **errors**. For example, if you type the name of the form in the Form Name argument of the OpenForm action instead of selecting it from the list, you may type it incorrectly. Access then will not be able to execute the desired action. In that case, a Microsoft Access dialog box will display, indicating the error and solution as shown in Figure 6-56.

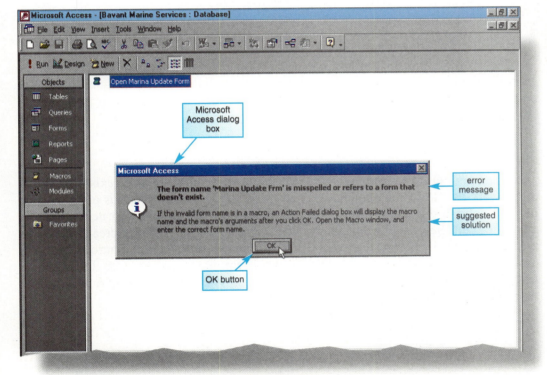

FIGURE 6-56

If such a dialog box displays, click the OK button. The Action Failed dialog box then displays (Figure 6-57). It indicates the macro that was being run, the action that Access was attempting to execute, and the arguments for the action. This information tells you which action needs to be corrected. To make the correction, click the Halt button, and then modify the design of the macro.

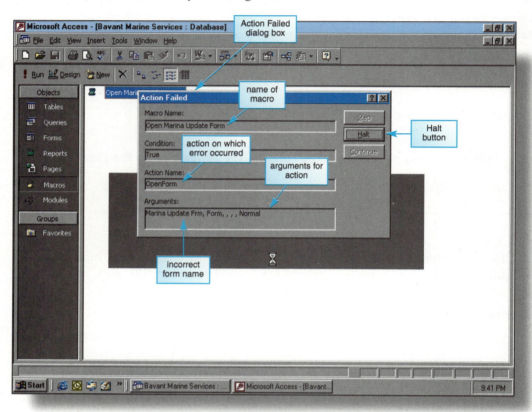

FIGURE 6-57

Additional Macros

The additional macros to be created are shown in Table 6-2. The first column gives the name of the macro, and the second column indicates the actions for the macro. The third column contains the values of the arguments that need to be changed, and the fourth column contains the comments.

Copying a Macro

When you wish to create a new macro, you often find there is an existing macro that is very similar to the one you wish to create. If this is the case, it is often simpler to use a copy of the existing macro and modify it instead of creating a new macro from scratch. The Open Technician Master Form macro you wish to create, for example, is very similar to the existing Open Marina Update Form macro. Thus, you can make a copy of the Open Marina Update Form macro, call it Open Technician Master Form, and then modify it to the new requirements by changing only the portion that differs from the original macro.

To make a copy of a macro, you use the clipboard. First copy the existing macro to the clipboard and then paste the contents of the clipboard. At that point, assign the new name to the macro.

TABLE 6-2   Specifications for additional macros

MACRO NAME	ACTION	ARGUMENT(S)	COMMENT
Open Technician Master Form	Echo	Echo on: No	Turn echo off to avoid screen flicker
	Hourglass	Hourglass On: Yes	Turn on hourglass
	OpenForm	Form Name: Technician Master Form	Open Technician Master Form
	Maximize		Maximize the window
	Hourglass	Hourglass On: No	Turn off hourglass
	Echo	Echo on: Yes	Turn echo on
Open Marina Table	OpenTable	Table Name: Marina	Open Marina Table
		View: Datasheet	
	Maximize		Maximize the window
Open Technician Table	OpenTable	Table Name: Technician	Open Technician Table
		View: Datasheet	
	Maximize		Maximize the window
Preview Billing Summary Report	OpenReport	Report Name: Billing Summary Report	Preview Billing Summary Report
		View: Print Preview	
	Maximize		Maximize the window
Print Billing Summary Report	OpenReport	Report Name: Billing Summary Report	Print Billing Summary Report
		View: Print	
Preview Marina Amount Report	OpenReport	Report Name: Marina Amount Report	Preview Marina Amount Report
		View: Print Preview	
	Maximize		Maximize the window
Print Marina Amount Report	OpenReport	Report Name: Marina Amount Report	Print Marina Amount Report
		View: Print	
Preview Technician/ Marina Report	OpenReport	Report Name: Technician/Marina Report	Preview Technician/Marina Report
		View: Print Preview	
	Maximize		Maximize the window
Print Technician/ Marina Report	OpenReport	Report Name: Technician/Marina Report	Print Technician/Marina Report
		View: Print	

Incidentally, these same techiques will work for other objects as well. If you wish to create a new report that is similar to an existing report, for example, use the clipboard to make a copy of the original report, paste the contents, rename it, and then modify the copied report in whatever way you wish.

Perform the steps on the next page to use the clipboard to copy the Open Marina Update Form macro.

To Copy a Macro

1 **Ensure the Macros object is selected, right-click the Open Marina Update Form macro,** and then point **to Copy on the shortcut menu.**

The shortcut menu for the Open Marina Update Form macro displays, and the Copy command is highlighted (Figure 6-58).

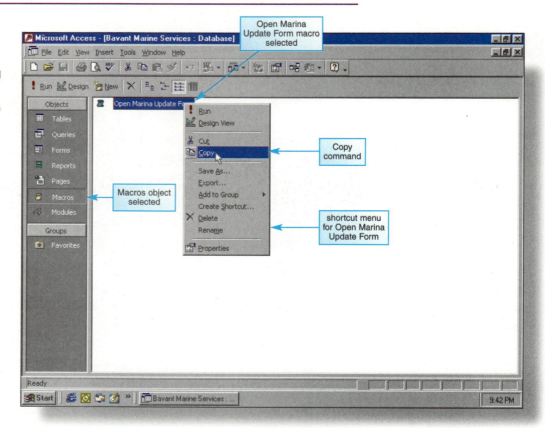

FIGURE 6-58

2 **Click Copy to copy the macro to the clipboard. Right-click any open area of the Database window, and then point to Paste on the shortcut menu.**

The shortcut menu displays, and the Paste command is highlighted (Figure 6-59).

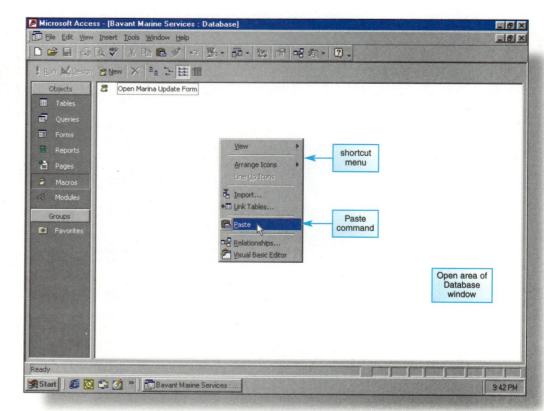

FIGURE 6-59

3 **Click Paste on the shortcut menu,** type Open Technician Master Form **in the Macro Name text box , and then point to the OK button.**

The Paste As dialog box displays, and the new macro name is entered in the text box (Figure 6-60).

4 **Click the OK button.**

The new macro is copied and saved.

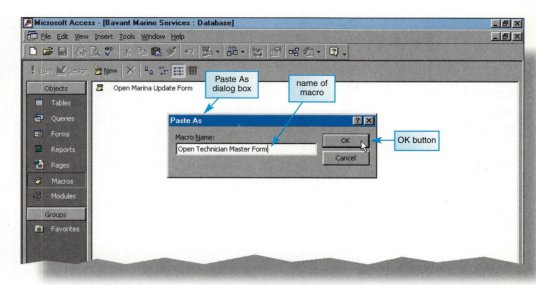

FIGURE 6-60

Modifying the Copied Macro

Once you have copied the macro, you can modify the copy to make any needed changes. The following steps modify the macro just copied by changing the Form Name argument for the OpenForm action to Technician Master Form.

Steps To Modify the Copied Macro

1 **Right-click the Open Technician Master Form macro, and then click Design View on the shortcut menu (Figure 6-61).**

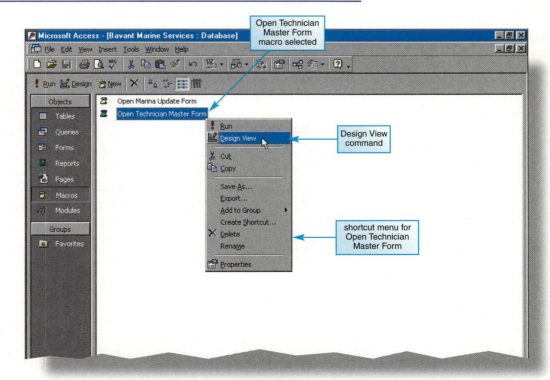

FIGURE 6-61

2 **Click the row selector for the OpenForm action, click the Form Name argument, click the Form Name arrow, and then point to the Technician Master Form.**

The macro displays in Design View. The OpenForm action is selected, the list of available forms displays, and Technician Master Form is highlighted (Figure 6-62).

3 **Click Technician Master Form to change the Form Name argument. Click the Comment text box for the OpenForm action, delete the comment, and type** Open Technician Master Form **as the new comment. Click the Close button for the Open Technician Master Form : Macro window and then click the Yes button to save the changes.**

The changes to the macro have been saved.

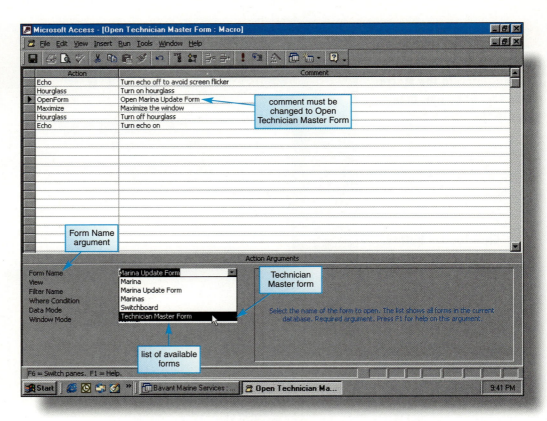

FIGURE 6-62

Macro Arguments

Some macros require a change to more than one argument. For example, to create a macro to preview or print a report requires a change to the Report Name argument and a change to the View argument. In Figure 6-63, the OpenReport action displays Billing Summary Report in the Report Name argument text box and Print Preview is highlighted in the View argument text box.

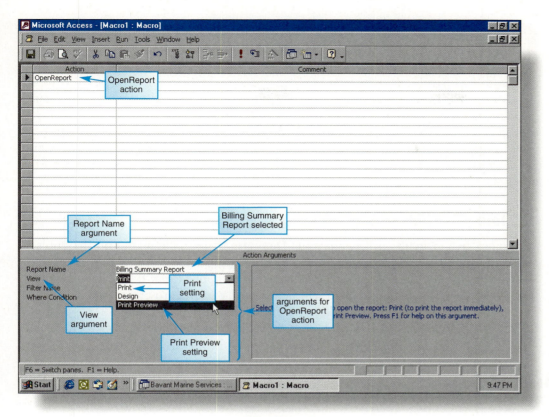

FIGURE 6-63

Creating Additional Macros

You can create additional macros using the same steps you used to create the first macro. You copy an existing macro and then modify the copied macro as needed. Perform the following step to create the additional macros illustrated in Table 6-2 on page A 6.6.

TO CREATE ADDITIONAL MACROS

 Using the same techniques you used to create the Open Marina Update Form macro (page A 6.27), create each of the macros described in Table 6-2.

The Open Technician Master Form, Open Marina Table, Open Technician Table, Preview Billing Summary Report, Print Billing Summary Report, Preview Marina Amount Report, Print Marina Amount Report, Preview Technician/Marina Report, and Print Technician/Marina Report macros are created.

Running the Macros

To run any of the other macros just as you ran the first macro, right-click the appropriate macro in the Database window and then click Run on the shortcut menu. The appropriate actions then are carried out. Running the Preview Billing Summary Report macro, for example, displays the Billing Summary Report in a maximized preview window.

More About

Switchboards

A switchboard is considered a form and is run like any other form. A special tool is used to create it, however, called the Switchboard Manager. Although you can modify the design of the form by clicking Design on its shortcut menu, it is easier to use the Switchboard Manager for modifications.

Creating and Using a Switchboard

A **switchboard** (see Figures 6-1a and 6-1b on page A 6.5) is a special type of form. It contains buttons you can click to perform a variety of actions. Buttons on the main switchboard can lead to other switchboards. Clicking the View Form button, for example, causes Access to display the View Form switchboard. Buttons also can be used to open forms or tables. Clicking the Marina Update Form button on the View Form switchboard opens the Marina Update Form. Still other buttons cause reports to be displayed in a preview window or print reports.

Creating a Switchboard

To create a switchboard, you use the Database Utilities command on the Tools menu and then click **Switchboard Manager**, which is an Access tool that allows you to create, edit, and delete switchboard forms for an application. If you have not previously created a switchboard, you will be asked if you wish to create one. Clicking the Yes button causes Access to create the switchboard. Perform the following steps to create a switchboard for the Bavant Marine Services database.

To Create a Switchboard

1 **With the Database window displaying, click Tools on the menu bar, click Database Utilities on the Tools menu, and then point to Switchboard Manager.**

The Tools menu displays (Figure 6-64). The Database Utilities submenu displays, and the Switchboard Manager command is highlighted.

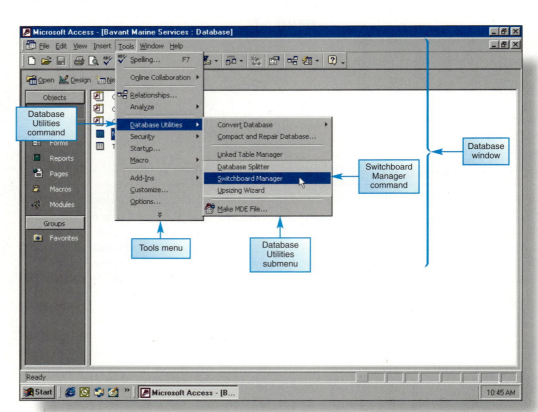

FIGURE 6-64

2 **Click Switchboard Manager and then point to the Yes button.**

The Switchboard Manager dialog box displays (Figure 6-65). The message indicates that no switchboard currently exists for this database and asks whether to create one.

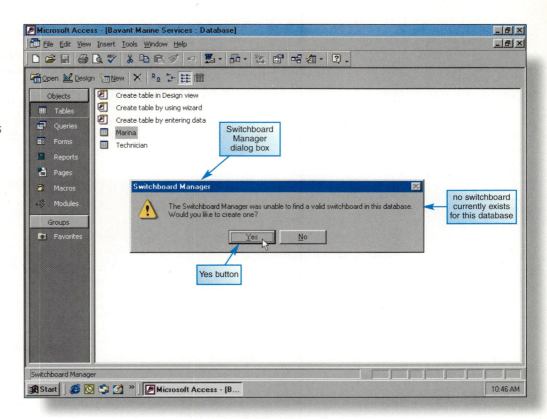

FIGURE 6-65

3 **Click the Yes button to create a new switchboard. Point to the New button.**

The Switchboard Manager dialog box displays and indicates there is only the Main Switchboard at this time (Figure 6-66).

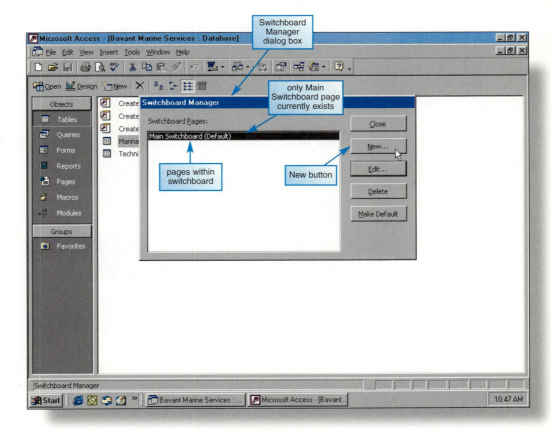

FIGURE 6-66

Creating Switchboard Pages

The next step in creating the switchboard system is to create the individual switchboards within the system. These individual switchboards are called the **switchboard pages**. The switchboard pages to be created are listed in the first column of Table 6-3. You do not have to create the Main Switchboard page because Access has created it automatically (Figure 6-66). To create each of the other pages, click the New button in the Switchboard Manager dialog box, and then type the name of the page.

TABLE 6-3 Specifications for Switchboard Pages and Items			
SWITCHBOARD PAGE	SWITCHBOARD ITEM	COMMAND	ARGUMENT
Main Switchboard	View Form	Go to Switchboard	Switchboard: View Form
	View Table	Go to Switchboard	Switchboard: View Table
	View Report	Go to Switchboard	Switchboard: View Report
	Print Report	Go to Switchboard	Switchboard: Print Report
	Exit Application	Exit Application	None
View Form	Marina Update Form	Run Macro	Macro: Open Marina Update Form
	Technician Master Form	Run Macro	Macro: Open Technician Master Form
	Return to Main Switchboard	Go to Switchboard	Switchboard: Main Switchboard
View Table	Marina Table	Run Macro	Macro: Open Marina Table
	Technician Table	Run Macro	Macro: Open Technician Table
	Return to Main Switchboard	Go to Switchboard	Switchboard: Main Switchboard
View Report	View Billing Summary Report	Run Macro	Macro: Preview Billing Summary Report
	View Marina Amount Report	Run Macro	Macro: Preview Marina Amount Report
	View Technician/Marina Report	Run Macro	Macro: Preview Technician/ Marina Report
	Return to Main Switchboard	Go to Switchboard	Switchboard: Main Switchboard
Print Report	Print Billing Summary Report	Run Macro	Macro: Print Billing Summary Report
	Print Marina Amount Report	Run Macro	Macro: Print Marina Amount Report
	Print Technician/Marina Report	Run Macro	Macro: Print Technician/ Marina Report
	Return to Main Switchboard	Go to Switchboard	Switchboard: Main Switchboard

Perform the steps on the next page to create the switchboard pages.

To Create Switchboard Pages

1 **Click the New button in the Switchboard Manager dialog box. Type** View Form **as the name of the new switchboard page. Point to the OK button.**

The Create New dialog box displays (Figure 6-67). The name of the new page is entered in the Switchboard Page Name text box.

2 **Click the OK button to create the View Form switchboard page.**

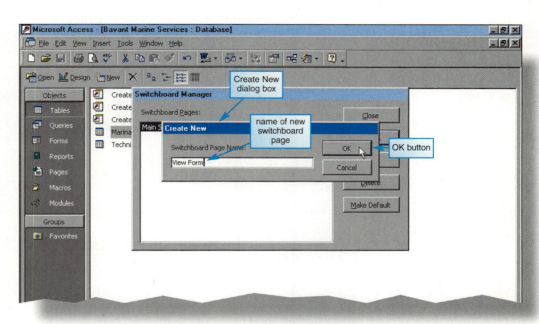

FIGURE 6-67

3 **Use the technique described in Step 1 and Step 2 to create the View Table, View Report, and Print Report switchboard pages.**

The newly created switchboard pages display in the Switchboard Manager dialog box in alphabetical order (Figure 6-68).

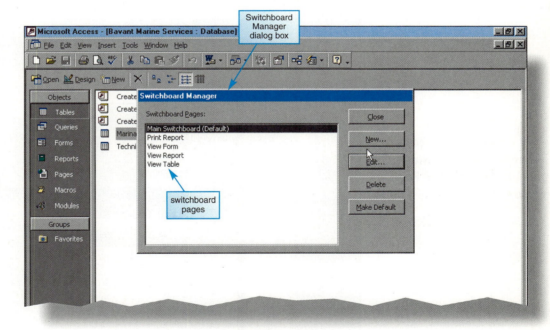

FIGURE 6-68

Modifying Switchboard Pages

You can **modify a switchboard page** by using the following procedure. Select the page in the Switchboard Manager dialog box, click the **Edit button**, and then add new items to the page, move existing items to a different position in the list of items, or delete items. For each item, you can indicate the command to be executed when the item is selected.

Perform the steps on the next page to modify the Main Switchboard page.

To Modify the Main Switchboard Page

1 With the Main Switchboard (Default) page selected, point to the Edit button (Figure 6-69).

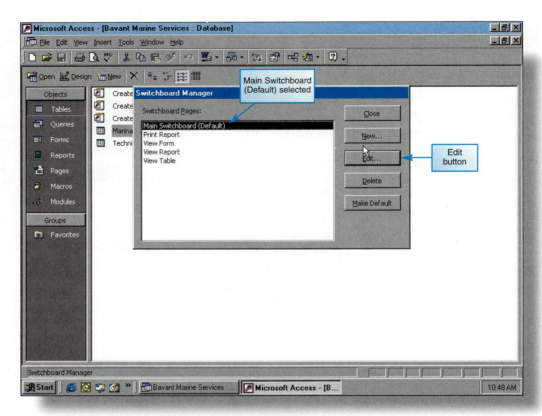

FIGURE 6-69

2 Click the Edit button, and then point to the New button in the Edit Switchboard Page dialog box.

The Edit Switchboard Page dialog box displays (Figure 6-70).

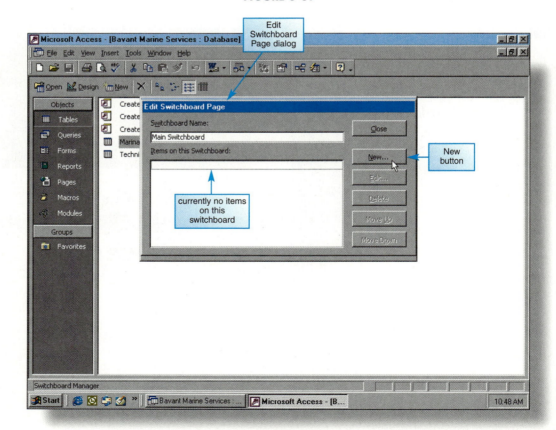

FIGURE 6-70

3 Click the New button, type `View Form` as the text, click the Switchboard box arrow, and then point to View Form.

The Edit Switchboard Item dialog box displays (Figure 6-71). The text is entered, the command is Go to Switchboard, the list of available switchboards displays, and the View Form switchboard is highlighted.

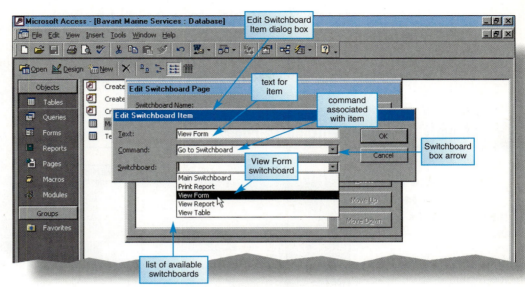

FIGURE 6-71

4 Click View Form, and then click the OK button to add the item to the switchboard.

5 Using the techniques illustrated in Steps 3 and 4, add the View Table, View Report, and Print Report items to the Main Switchboard page. In each case, the command is Go to Switchboard. The names of the switchboards are the same as the name of the items. For example, the switchboard for the View Table item is called View Table.

6 Click the New button, type `Exit Application` as the text, click the Command box arrow, and then point to Exit Application.

The Edit Switchboard Item dialog box displays (Figure 6-72). The text is entered, and the list of available commands displays, and the Exit Application command is highlighted.

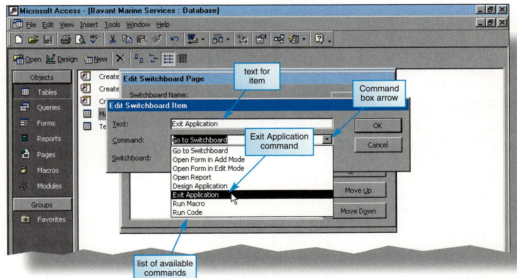

FIGURE 6-72

7 Click Exit Application, and then click the OK button to add the item to the switchboard. Click the Close button in the Edit Switchboard Page dialog box to indicate you have finished editing the Main Switchboard.

The Main Switchboard page now is complete. The Edit Switchboard Page dialog box closes, and the Switchboard Manager dialog box displays.

Modifying the Other Switchboard Pages

The other switchboard pages from Table 6-3 on page A 6.8 are modified in exactly the same manner you modified the Main Switchboard page. Perform the following steps to modify the other switchboard pages.

 To Modify the Other Switchboard Pages

1 **Click the View Form switchboard page, and then point to the Edit button.**

The View Form page is selected (Figure 6-73).

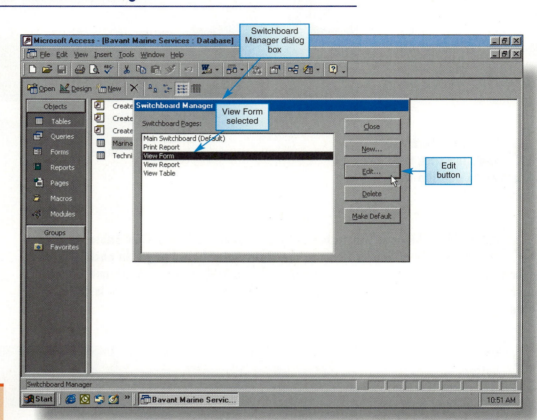

FIGURE 6-73

2 **Click the Edit button, click the New button to add a new item, type** Marina Update Form **as the text, click the Command box arrow, and then click Run Macro. Click the Macro box arrow, and then point to Open Marina Update Form.**

The Edit Switchboard Item dialog box displays (Figure 6-74). The text is entered and the command selected. The list of available macros displays, and the Open Marina Update Form macro is highlighted.

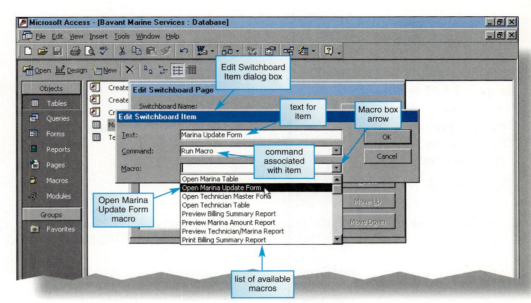

FIGURE 6-74

3 **Click Open Marina Update Form, and then click the OK button.**

The Open Marina Update Form item is added to the View Form switchboard.

4 **Click the New button, type** Technician Master Form **as the text, click the Command box arrow, and then click Run Macro. Click the Macro box arrow, click Open Technician Master Form, and then click the OK button.**

5 **Click the New button, type** Return to Main Switchboard **as the text, click the Command box arrow, and then click Go to Switchboard. Click the Switchboard box arrow, and then click Main Switchboard. Point to the OK button.**

The text is entered, and the command and switchboard are selected (Figure 6-75).

6 **Click the OK button. Click the Close button in the Edit Switchboard Page dialog box to indicate you have finished editing the View Form switchboard.**

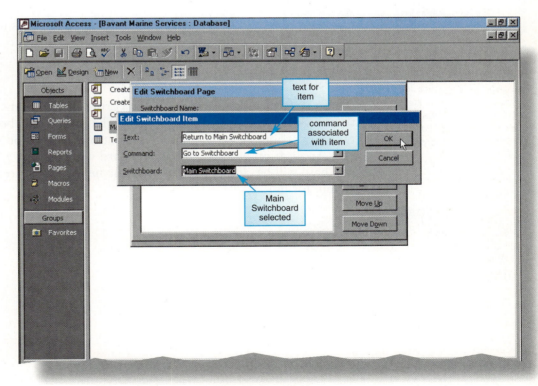

FIGURE 6-75

7 Use the techniques illustrated in Steps 1 through 6 to add the items indicated in Table 6-3 on page A 6.42 to the other switchboards. When you have finished, point to the Close button in the Switchboard Manager dialog box (Figure 6-76).

8 Click the Close button.

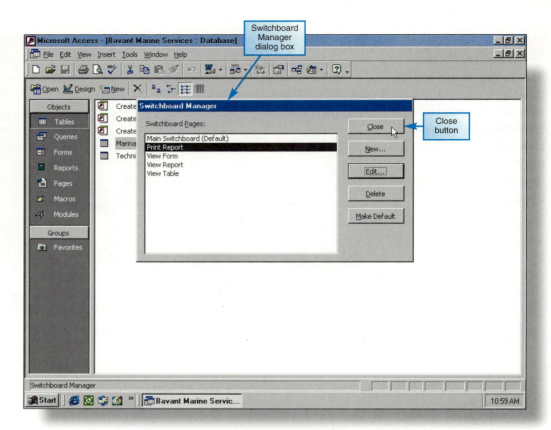

FIGURE 6-76

The switchboard is complete and ready for use. Access has created a form called Switchboard that you will run to use the switchboard. It also has created a table called Switchboard Items. *Do not modify this table.* It is used by the Switchboard Manager to keep track of the various switchboard pages and items.

Using a Switchboard

To use the switchboard, click the Forms object, right-click the switchboard, and then click Open on the shortcut menu. The main switchboard then will display. To take any action, click the appropriate buttons. When you have finished, click the Exit Application button. The switchboard will be removed from the screen, and the database will be closed. The steps on the next page illustrate opening a switchboard system for use.

Displaying Switchboards

It is possible to have the switchboard display automatically when the database is opened. To do so, click Tools on the menu bar, and then click Startup. Click the Display Form box arrow, select the Switchboard form, and then click the OK button.

Closing a Switchboard

The button to close a switchboard is usually labeled Exit Application because a switchboard system is just a special type of application system. Clicking this button will not only close the switchboard, but will also close the database.

To Use a Switchboard

1 **Click the Forms object, and then right-click Switchboard. Point to Open on the shortcut menu.**

The shortcut menu for Switchboard displays (Figure 6-77).

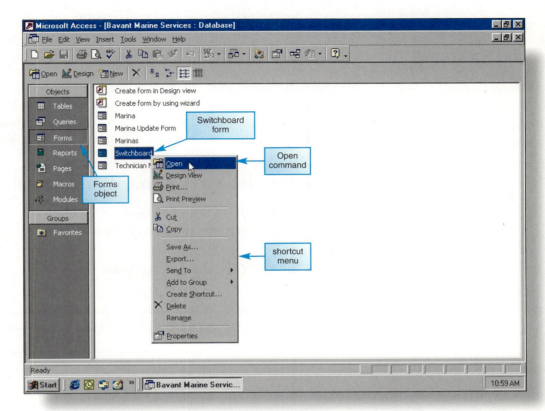

FIGURE 6-77

2 **Click Open.**

The Main Switchboard displays (Figure 6-78).

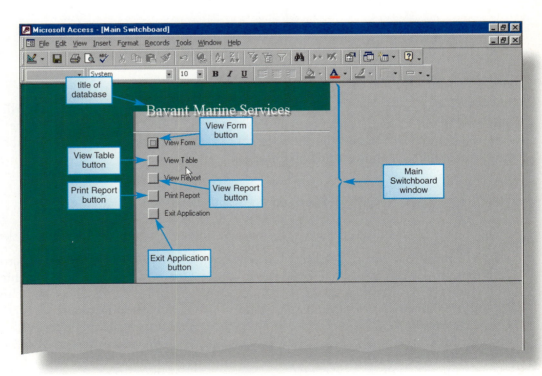

FIGURE 6-78

Quick Reference

For a table that lists how to complete the tasks covered in this book using the mouse, menu, shortcut menu, and keyboard, visit the Office 2000 Web page (www.scsite.com/off2000/qr.htm), and then click Microsoft Access 2000.

Click the View Form button to display the View Form switchboard page. Click the View Table button to display the View Table switchboard page. Click the View Report button to display the View Report switchboard page. Click the Print Report button to display the Print Report switchboard page. On each of the other switchboard pages, click the button for the form, table, or report you wish to view, or the report you wish to print. To return from one of the other switchboard pages to the Main Switchboard, click the Return to Main Switchboard button. To leave the switchboard system, click the Exit Application button.

If you discover a problem with the switchboard, click Tools on the menu bar, click Database Utilities, and then click Switchboard Manager. You can modify the switchboard system using the same techniques you used to create it.

Closing the Switchboard and Database

To close the switchboard and the database, click the Exit Application button. Perform the following step to close the switchboard.

TO CLOSE THE SWITCHBOARD AND DATABASE

 Click the Exit Application button.

The switchboard is removed from the screen. The database closes.

CASE PERSPECTIVE SUMMARY

In Project 6, you modified the Marina Type field, and you added the Phone Number field to the Marina table. You also added the Phone Number field to the Billing Summary Report and to the Marina Update Form. You added the total amount (warranty amount plus non-warranty amount) to the Billing Summary Report, and then you created the macros to be used in the switchboard system. Finally, you created a switchboard system for Bavant Marine Service.

Project Summary

In Project 6, you learned how to use the Lookup Wizard and the Input Mask Wizard. You added controls to both a report and a form. You created and used macros. Using Switchboard Manager, you created the switchboard, the switchboard pages, and the switchboard items. You also used the Switchboard Manager to assign actions to the buttons on the switchboard pages.

What You Should Know

Having completed this project, you now should be able to perform the following tasks:

▶ Add a Control to a Form *(A 6.24)*
▶ Add Actions to and Save a Macro *(A 6.29)*
▶ Add Controls to a Report *(A 6.17)*
▶ Close the Switchboard and Database *(A 6.43)*
▶ Create a Macro *(A 6.27)*
▶ Create a Switchboard *(A 6.40)*
▶ Create Additional Macros *(A 6.39)*
▶ Create Switchboard Pages *(A 6.43)*
▶ Copy a Macro *(A 6.36)*
▶ Enter Data Using an Input Mask *(A 6.13)*
▶ Modify a Macro *(A 6.36)*

▶ Modify the Copied Macro *(A 6.37)*
▶ Modify the Main Switchboard Page *(A 6.44)*
▶ Modify the Other Switchboard Pages *(A 6.46)*
▶ Open a Database *(A 6.7)*
▶ Open a Switchboard *(A 6.49)*
▶ Preview a Report *(A 6.23)*
▶ Resize and Move Controls in a Report *(A 6.15)*
▶ Run a Macro *(A 6.31)*
▶ Use a Switchoard *(A 6.49)*
▶ Use the Lookup Wizard *(A 6.8)*
▶ Use the Input Mask Wizard *(A 6.10)*

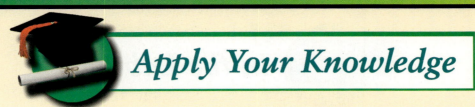

Apply Your Knowledge

1 Creating Macros and Modifying a Report for the Sidewalk Scrapers Database

Instructions: Start Access. Open the Sidewalk Scrapers database that you used in Project 5. Perform the following tasks.

1. Create a macro to open the Customer Update Form you created in Project 4. The macro should maximize the form automatically when it is opened.
2. Save the macro as Open Customer Update Form.
3. Create a macro to print the Worker/Customer Report you created in Project 4.
4. Save the macro as Print Worker/Customer Report.
5. Run the Print Worker/Customer Report macro, and then print the report.
6. Modify the Balance Due Report to include the Telephone Number as shown in Figure 6-79. (*Hint:* The horizontal line underneath the headings is a control that can be resized.)
7. Print the report.

Balance Due Report

Customer Number	Name	Telephone Number	Balance
AL25	Arders, Lars	555-2050	$45.00
AT43	Atari Cleaners	555-7410	$80.00
CH65	Chan's Bootery	555-0504	$70.00
CI05	Cinco Gallery	555-1304	$29.00
JB51	Jordach, Ben	555-0213	$60.00
LK44	Lee, Kim	555-5061	$0.00
MD60	Martinez, Dan	555-4110	$95.00
ME02	Meat Shoppe	555-7557	$0.00
ST21	Styling Salon and Tanning	555-6454	$40.00

Friday, September 07, 2001   *Page 1 of 1*

FIGURE 6-79

In the Lab

1 Creating an Application System for the School Connection Database

Problem: The Booster's Club is pleased with the tables, forms, and reports you have created. The club has some additional requests, however. First, they would like to be able to type only the digits in the Last Order Date field. They also would like to display the profit (selling price – cost) for an item on the Item Update Form. Finally, they would like an easy way to access the various tables, forms, and reports by simply clicking a button or two. This would make the database much easier to maintain and update.

Instructions: Open the School Connection database that you used in Project 5. Perform the following tasks.

1. Open the Vendor table in Design view and create an input mask for the Last Order Date field. Use the Short Date input mask. Save the change.
2. Modify the Item Update Form to create the form shown in Figure 6-80. The form includes a calculated control to display the profit (selling price – cost) on the item. Format the control as currency.

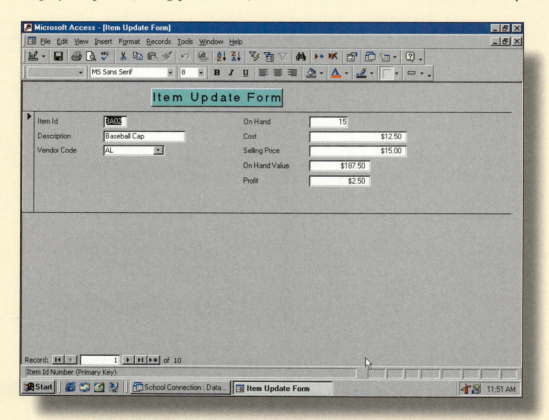

FIGURE 6-80

3. Save and print the form. To print the form, open the form, click File on the menu bar, and then click Print. Click Selected Record(s) as the Print Range. Click the OK button.

In the Lab

4. Create macros that will perform the following tasks:
   a. Open the Item Update Form
   b. Open the Vendor Master Form
   c. Open the Item Table
   d. Open the Vendor Table
   e. Preview the Inventory Report
   f. Preview the Vendor/Items Report
   g. Preview the On Hand Value Report
   h. Print the Inventory Report
   i. Print the Vendor/Items Report
   j. Print the On Hand Value Report

5. Create the switchboard for the School Connection database shown in Figure 6-81. Use the same design for your switchboard pages as the one illustrated in this project. For example, the View Form switchboard page should have three choices: Open Item Update Form, Open Vendor Master Form, and Return to Main Switchboard. Include all the forms, tables, and reports for which you created macros in Step 4.

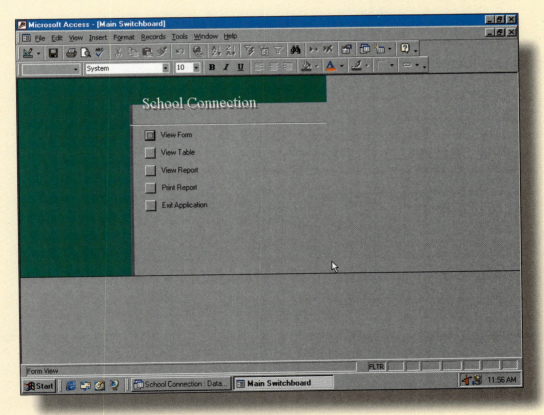

FIGURE 6-81

6. Run the switchboard and correct any errors.

In the Lab

2 Creating an Application System for the City Area Bus Company Database

Problem: The advertising sales manager is pleased with the tables, forms, and reports you have created. He has some additional requests, however. He finds that he needs to include the advertiser's phone number in the database. He also would like an easy way to access the various tables, forms, and reports by simply clicking a button or two.

Instructions: Open the City Area Bus Company database that you used in Project 5. Perform the following tasks.

1. Add the Telephone Number field to the Advertiser table. The field should follow the Zip Code field. Include an input mask for the field. Use the same input mask that was used for Bavant Marine Services.
2. Change the data type for the Ad Type field to a Lookup Wizard field. The values for the Ad Type field are DIN, RET, and SER.
3. Save the changes to the Advertiser table.
4. Open the Advertiser table in Datasheet view and resize the Telephone Number field. Enter the following data in the Telephone Number field:

Advertiser Id	Telephone Number
AC25	2165550987
BB99	3305559876
CS46	3305558765
HC11	3305557654
MC34	2165556543
NO10	3305555432
PJ24	2165554321
PP24	3305554455
TM89	3305558778

Save the changes to the layout of the table.

5. Modify the Advertiser Update Form to include the telephone number. Place the Telephone Number field below the Zip Code field. Be sure to align the Telephone Number label with the Zip Code label. Change the tab order for the form, so that the Telephone Number field immediately follows the Zip Code field and the Ad Type field follows the Telephone Number field. (*Hint:* Ad Type is a combo box control.)
6. Save and print the form. To print the form, open the form, click File on the menu bar and then click Print. Click Selected Record(s) as the Print Range. Click the OK button.
7. Modify the Advertiser Status Report to include the Telephone Number field as shown in Figure 6-82.

Advertiser Status Report

Advertiser Id	Name/Phone	Balance	Amount Paid
AC25	Alia Cleaners (216) 555-0987	$85.00	$585.00
BB99	Bob's Bakery (330) 555-9876	$435.00	$1,150.00
CS46	Cara's Salon (330) 555-8765	$35.00	$660.00
HC11	Hilde's Cards & Gifts (330) 555-7654	$250.00	$500.00
MC34	Mom's Cookies (216) 555-6543	$95.00	$1,050.00
NO10	New Orient (330) 555-5432	$150.00	$350.00
PJ24	Pajama Store (216) 555-4321	$0.00	$775.00
PP24	Pia's Pizza (330) 555-4455	$50.00	$0.00
TM89	Tom's Market (330) 555-8778	$50.00	$500.00

Friday, September 07, 2001   *Page 1 of 1*

FIGURE 6-82

In the Lab

8. Print the report.
9. Create macros that will perform the following tasks:
   a. Open the Advertiser Update Form
   b. Open the Sales Rep Master Form
   c. Open the Advertiser Table
   d. Open the Sales Rep Table
   e. Preview the Advertiser Status Report
   f. Preview the Advertiser Income Report
   g. Preview the Sales Rep/Advertiser Report
   h. Print the Advertiser Status Report
   i. Print the Advertiser Income Report
   j. Print the Sales Rep/Advertiser Report
10. Create the switchboard for the City Area Bus Company database shown in Figure 6-83. Use the same design for your switchboard pages as the one illustrated in this project. For example, the View Form switchboard page should have three choices: Open Advertiser Update Form, Open Sales Rep Master Form, and Return to Main Switchboard. Include all the forms, tables, and reports for which you created macros in Step 9.

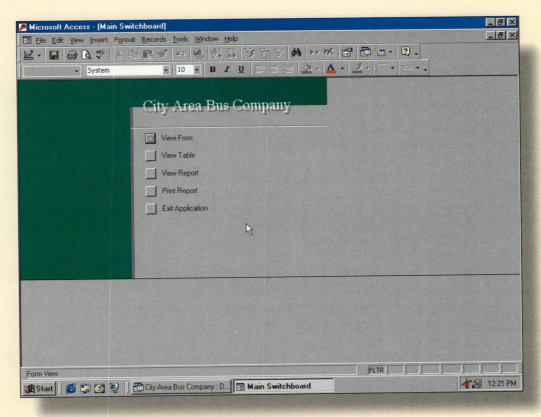

FIGURE 6-83

11. Run the switchboard and correct any errors.

In the Lab

3 Creating an Application System for the Resort Rentals Database

Problem: The real estate company is pleased with the tables, forms, and reports that you have created. The company has some additional requests, however. First, they want to add the sales price to the database. Then, they want an easy way to access the various tables, forms, and reports by simply clicking a button or two.

Instructions: Open the Resort Rentals database that you used in Project 5. Perform the following tasks.

1. Add a Sales Price field to the Rental Units table. Place the field after the For Sale field. Use currency as the data type. Save these changes.

2. Open the Rental Units table in Datasheet view and add the following data to the Sales Price field:

Rental Id	Sales Price
101	$150,000
134	$190,000
148	$165,000

3. Modify the Rental Update Form to create the form shown in Figure 6-84. The form includes the Sales Price field. Change the tab order for the fields to the following: Rental Id, Address, City, For Sale, Sales Price, Weekly Rate, Bedrooms, Bathrooms, Sleeps, Pool, Ocean View, Owner Id.

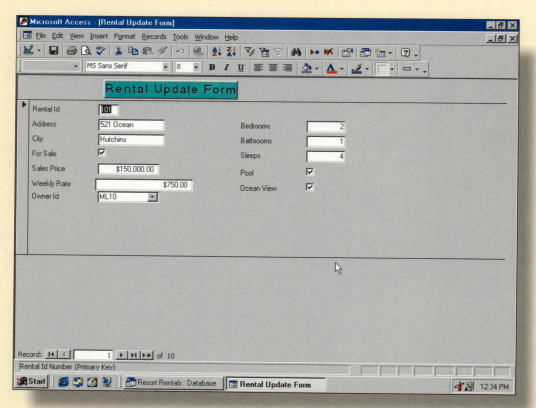

FIGURE 6-84

In the Lab

4. Save and print the form. To print the form, open the form, click File on the menu bar, and then click Print. Click Selected Record(s) as the Print Range. Click the OK button.

5. Add the Sales Price field to the Rental Properties subform you created in Project 5. If necessary, modify the Owner Master Form to ensure that the complete Sales Price field displays on the subform.

6. Save and print the form.

7. Create macros that will perform the following tasks:

   a. Open the Rental Update Form
   b. Open the Owner Master Form
   c. Open the Rental Unit Table
   d. Open the Owner Table
   e. Preview the Available Rental Units Report
   f. Preview the City Rental List
   g. Preview the Owner/Rental Units Report
   h. Print the Available Rental Units Report
   i. Print the City Rental List
   j. Print the Owner/Rental Units Report

8. Create the switchboard for the Resort Rentals database shown in Figure 6-85. Use the same design for your switchboard pages as the one illustrated in this project. For example, the View Form switchboard page should have three choices: Open Rental Update Form, Open Owner Master Form, and Return to Main Switchboard. Include all the forms, tables, and reports for which you created macros in Step 7.

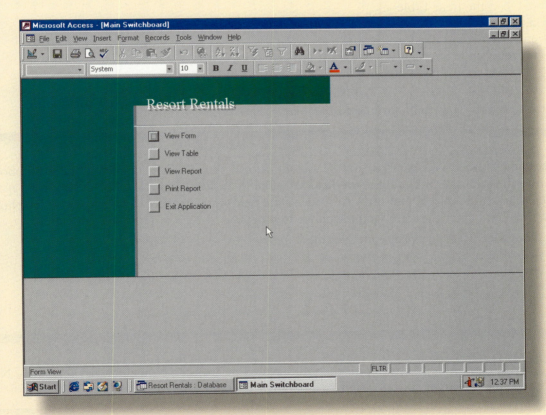

FIGURE 6-85

9. Run the switchboard and correct any errors.

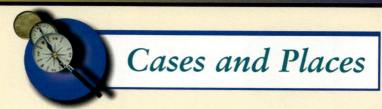

Cases and Places

The difficulty of these case studies varies:
▶ are the least difficult; ▶▶ are more difficult; and ▶▶▶ are the most difficult.

1 ▶ Use the Computer Items database on the Access Data Disk for this assignment. Modify the Item Update Form that you created in Project 4 to include a calculated control called Profit. Profit is the result of subtracting Cost from Selling Price. Place the calculated control below the Selling Price field on the form. Be sure to format Profit as currency. The database includes a report, Inventory Report that contains the item number, description, units on hand, and cost. Modify this report to include a calculated control called On Hand Value. On Hand Value is the result of multiplying units on hand by cost. Be sure to format On Hand Value as currency.

2 ▶ Use the Computer Items database and create macros that will perform the following tasks:
   a. Open the Item Update Form created in Project 4 and modified in Case Study 1
   b. Open the Supplier Master Form created in Project 5
   c. Open the Item Table
   d. Open the Supplier Table
   e. Preview the Inventory Report
   f. Preview the Supplier/Items Report created in Project 4
   g. Print the Inventory Report
   h. Print the Supplier/Items Report
Create and run a switchboard that uses these macros.

3 ▶▶ Use the Galaxy Books database on the Access Data Disk for this assignment. Add a telephone number field to the Publisher table. Place the field after the Publisher Name field. Create an input mask for the Telephone Number field and the Last Order Date field. In Datasheet view, resize the Telephone Number field and enter the following telephone numbers:

Publisher Code	Telephone Number
BB	5125557654
PB	2135559854
SI	2155554329
VN	6105553201

4 ▶▶ Modify the Publisher Master Form that you created in Project 5 to include the Telephone Number field. Change the tab order so that Telephone Number is immediately after Publisher Name.

5 ▶▶▶ Create the appropriate macros to open all forms and tables in the Galaxy Books database. Create macros to preview and to print all reports in the database. Create a switchboard system for the database that uses these macros.

In the Lab

1 Importing an Excel Worksheet

Problem: Literacy Educational Videos has been using Excel for a number of tasks. Literacy uses several worksheets to re-order videos, keep track of carrying costs, graph trends in video buying and maintain employee records. The company realizes that the employee data would be better handled in Access. The company management has asked you to convert its employee data to an Access database.

Instructions: Perform the following tasks:

1. Start Access and create a new database in which to store all the objects related to the employee data. Call the database Literacy Educational Videos.
2. Import the Employee worksheet shown in Figure 13 into Access. The worksheet is in the Literacy workbook on the Data Disk. See the inside back cover of this book for instructions for downloading the Data Disk or see your instructor for information on accessing the files required for this book. When the Import Spreadsheet Wizard dialog box displays, be sure the Employee worksheet is selected.

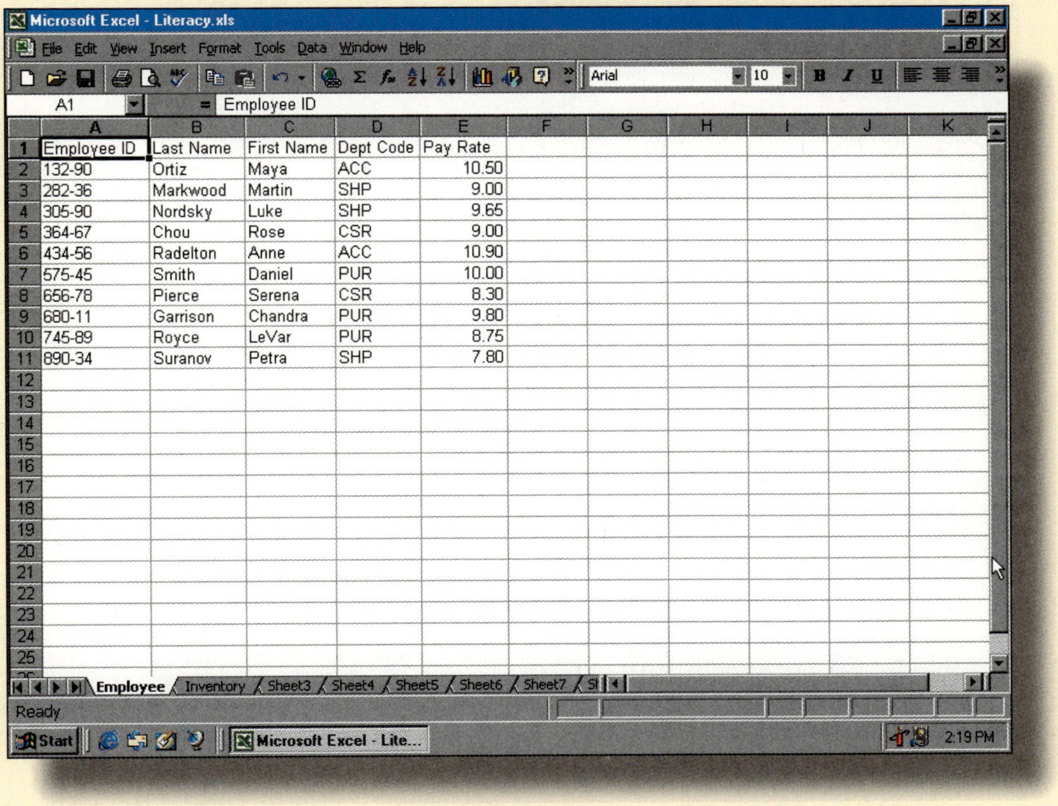

	A	B	C	D	E
1	Employee ID	Last Name	First Name	Dept Code	Pay Rate
2	132-90	Ortiz	Maya	ACC	10.50
3	282-36	Markwood	Martin	SHP	9.00
4	305-90	Nordsky	Luke	SHP	9.65
5	364-67	Chou	Rose	CSR	9.00
6	434-56	Radelton	Anne	ACC	10.90
7	575-45	Smith	Daniel	PUR	10.00
8	656-78	Pierce	Serena	CSR	8.30
9	680-11	Garrison	Chandra	PUR	9.80
10	745-89	Royce	LeVar	PUR	8.75
11	890-34	Suranov	Petra	SHP	7.80

FIGURE 13

3. Use Employee as the name of the Access table and Employee ID as the primary key.
4. Open the Employee table in Design view and change the data type for the Pay Rate field to Currency. Save the change to the table. Be sure to click Yes when a dialog box displays warning you that data may be truncated.
5. Open and print the Employee table

In the Lab

2 Linking an Excel Worksheet

Problem: The management of Literacy Educational Videos is pleased with the benefits they have derived from converting Employee data into an Access database. They now would like to be able to use the Query, Form, and Report features of Access for their inventory data yet still maintain the data in Excel worksheets.

Instructions: Perform the following tasks.

1. Open the Literacy Educational Videos database you created in In the Lab 1.

2. Link the Inventory Worksheet shown in Figure 14 to the database. The worksheet is in the Literacy workbook on the Data Disk. See the inside back cover of this book for instructions for downloading the Data Disk or see your instructor for information on accessing the files required for this book. When the Link Spreadsheet Wizard dialog box displays, be sure the Inventory worksheet is selected.

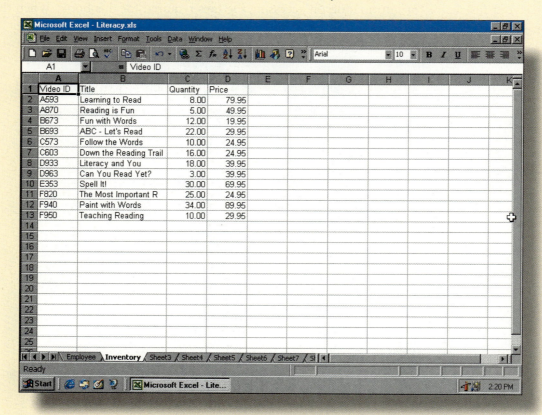

FIGURE 14

3. Open the Inventory table in Access and resize the Title column so that the entire title displays.

4. Print the table.

Microsoft PowerPoint 2000

Microsoft PowerPoint 2000

P R O J E C T

Using Embedded Visuals to Enhance a Slide Show

You will have mastered the material in this project when you can:

O B J E C T I V E S

- Create exciting presentations using embedded visuals
- Import an outline created in Microsoft Word
- Create a slide background using a picture
- Customize graphical bullets
- Create and embed an organization chart
- Insert a table into a slide
- Create and format a table
- Create a PowerPoint clip art object
- Scale objects
- Apply slide transition and text preset animation effects
- Print handouts

Preparation, Palpitations, Exciting & Presentations

I f the thought of getting up to speak in front of a group of strangers gives you palpitations, you are not unusual or in a class by yourself. On the list of the things that individuals fear most, public speaking leads the list.

Although speakers sometimes are faced with obstacles of their own making, if those moments unnerve you out of all proportion, you may think of taking some assertiveness training, or joining groups such as Toastmasters International or Dale Carnegie. An easier way, however, is to personalize your presentations and create a one-of-a-kind, eye-catching look that turns the focus away from your nervousness.

Accomplished speakers agree that the key to overcoming nervousness and hesitation when giving a public speech is preparation. To help you prepare, you can create your presentation with PowerPoint, as you will do in this project. Using a template, you will learn the techniques to enhance your slide show by adding visuals, slide transitions, and animations.

Appropriate visuals help set the tone, which in turn, helps you create a relaxed atmosphere, putting you at ease with your listeners. Then, build your confidence through practice; and you will leave your audience eager for more.

Fortunately, this help is available because leaders in business, government, science, religion, and virtually all vocations agree that the ability to present one's views clearly, while keeping the audience involved, is fundamental to a successful career. Though you probably spend more time in front of the lectern than behind it, your college years are a good time to get a head start on the competition by learning how to develop power presentations on your PC.

Even with this help, however, it is not enough merely to present dry, static details. A presentation needs zest to grab and hold the attention of today's sophisticated audiences.

Among PowerPoint's many features are the capabilities of adding organizational charts, graphs, and tables in a slide show to give the audience a visual association to help assimilate the speaker's words. Going one step further, a variety of pleasing transitions can be achieved to make one image blend into the next, rather than making abrupt frame changes.

Build effects allow a concept to be presented one point at a time, preventing the visual overload that occurs if all the information is presented at once. In psychology, this is called, chunking, recognizing that the human brain absorbs information more readily in small bites than in one huge mass.

Finally, turning your preparation into a successful presentation, the palpitations subside, and the excitement remains.

Using Embedded Visuals to Enhance a Slide Show

CASE PERSPECTIVE

The 1960s film classic *Where the Boys Are* affirmed the fact that students just want to get away and have fun during Spring Break in Ft. Lauderdale. Since that time, millions of young people have made their way to sunny destinations for a week of relaxation and fun. Today, students have a multitude of places from which to choose, most notably Daytona Beach and Key West in Florida and South Padre Island in Texas.

The Student Government Association (SGA) at your school wants to sponsor a college-wide trip to the three destinations. The SGA president, Marla Pervan, has asked you to help with the marketing efforts. She knows you have extensive computer experience and wants you to develop a PowerPoint presentation that advertises the three trips and the highlights of each. She has asked you to use an appropriate photograph as a background and clip art for visual appeal. You agree to create the project, which will be published on your college's intranet for the student body to view.

Create Exciting Presentations Using Embedded Visuals

Bulleted lists and simple graphics are the starting point for most presentations, but they can become boring. Advanced PowerPoint users want exciting presentations — something to impress their audiences. With PowerPoint, it is easy to develop impressive presentations by creating a custom background, customizing bullets, embedding organization charts and tables, and creating new graphics.

One problem you may experience when developing a presentation is finding the proper graphic to convey your message. One way to overcome this obstacle is to modify clip art from the Microsoft Clip Gallery. Another solution is to create a table. PowerPoint design templates offer a limited number of slide backgrounds and allow you to create your own background using a picture or clip art.

This project introduces several techniques to make your presentations more exciting.

Project Three — Fun in the Sun Spring Break

Project 3 expands on PowerPoint's basic presentation features by importing existing files and embedding objects. This project creates a presentation that is used to promote the Student Government Associations' Spring Break trips to Daytona Beach, Key West, and South Padre Island (Figures 3-1a through 3-1e). The project begins by building the presentation from an outline created in Microsoft Word and saved as a Rich Text Format (RTF) file. Then, several objects are inserted to customize the presentation. These objects include customized bullets, an organization chart, a table, and clip art.

(e) Slide 5

(d) Slide 4

(c) Slide 3

(b) Slide 2

(a) Slide 1

FIGURE 3-1

Importing Text Created in Another Application

In your classes, you may be asked to make an oral presentation. For example, in your English composition class, your instructor may require you to summarize a research paper you wrote. You can use a PowerPoint presentation to help you construct and deliver your presentation.

PowerPoint can use text created in other programs to create a new slide show. This text may have originated in Microsoft Word or another word processing program, or it may have appeared in a Web page. Microsoft Word files use the **.doc extension** in their file names. Text originating in other word processing programs should be saved in Rich Text Format (.rtf) or plain text format (.txt), and Web page documents should have an HTML extension (.htm).

An outline created in Microsoft Word or another word processing program works well as a shell for a PowerPoint presentation. Instead of typing text in PowerPoint, as you did in Projects 1 and 2, you can import this outline, add visual elements such as clip art, photos, graphical bullets, animation, and slide transitions, and ultimately create an impressive slide show. If you did not create an outline to help you write your word processing document, you can create one by saving your paper with a new file name, removing all text except the topic heading, and then saving the file again.

The advantage of using an outline saved as a Microsoft Word document is that text attributes and outline heading levels are maintained. Documents saved as plain text files can be opened in PowerPoint but do not maintain text attributes and outline heading levels. Consequently, each paragraph becomes a slide title.

To create a presentation using an existing outline, select All Outlines from the Files of type box in the Open dialog box. When you select **All Outlines**, PowerPoint displays a list of outlines. Next, you select the file that contains the outline. PowerPoint then creates a presentation using your outline. Each major heading in your outline becomes a slide title, and subheadings become a bulleted list.

Opening an Outline Created in Another Application

After starting PowerPoint, the first step in this project is to open an outline created in Microsoft Word. PowerPoint can produce slides from an outline created in Microsoft Word or another word processing program if the outline was saved in a format that PowerPoint can recognize. The outline you import in this project was saved as an RTF file (.rtf extension).

Opening an outline into PowerPoint requires two steps. First, you must tell PowerPoint you are opening an existing presentation. Then, to open the outline, you need to select the proper file type from the Files of type box in the Open dialog box. The following steps summarize how to start a new presentation and open an outline created in Microsoft Word. To reset your toolbars and menus so they display exactly as shown in this book, follow the steps outlined in Appendix C. Perform the following steps to start a new presentation and open an outline.

More About 2000

Constructing Presentations

Mark Twain once said, "The difference between the right word and almost the right word is the difference between 'lightning' and 'lightning bug.'" The goal in constructing powerful, PowerPoint presentations is to convey information precisely. Use the thesaurus, readability statistics, and other tools available in a word processing program, such as Microsoft Word, to help develop effective outlines to import into your slide shows.

Steps **To Start PowerPoint and Open an Outline**

1 **Insert your Data Disk into drive A. Click the Start button on the taskbar. Click New Office Document on the Start menu. If necessary, click the General tab in the New Office Document dialog box.**

2 **Double-click the Blank Presentation icon. Click the Cancel button when the New Slide dialog box displays.**

PowerPoint begins Presentation1 using the Default Design template.

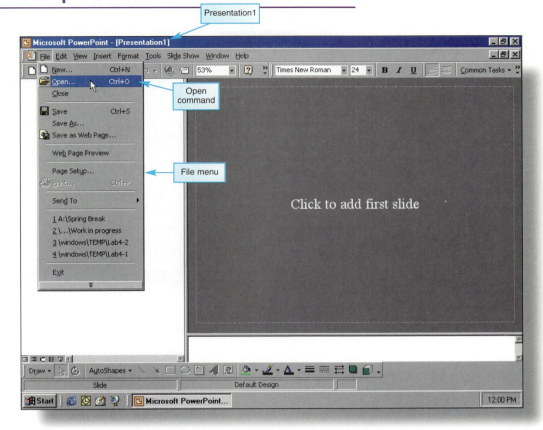

FIGURE 3-2

3 **Click File on the menu bar and then point to Open.**

The File menu displays (Figure 3-2). You want to open the outline created in Microsoft Word and saved on your Data Disk.

4 **Click Open. Click the Look in box arrow and then click 3½ Floppy (A:). Click the Files of type box arrow and then scroll down and click All Outlines.**

The Open dialog box displays (Figure 3-3). A list displays the outline files that PowerPoint can open. Your list may be different depending on the software installed on your computer.

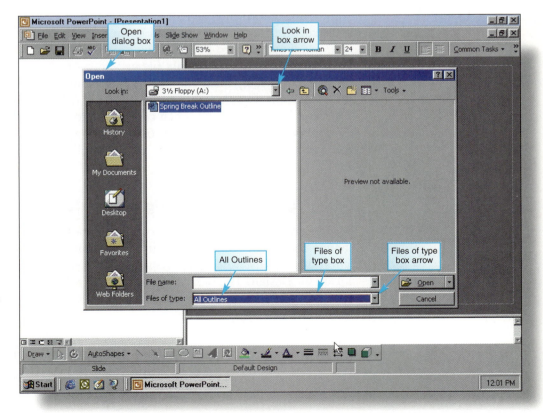

FIGURE 3-3

5 **Double-click Spring Break Outline in the list.**

PowerPoint opens the Spring Break Outline (Figure 3-4). The outline displays in the outline pane, and Slide 1 displays in the slide pane. Bullets display in the outline text, indicating the slide layout is Bulleted List.

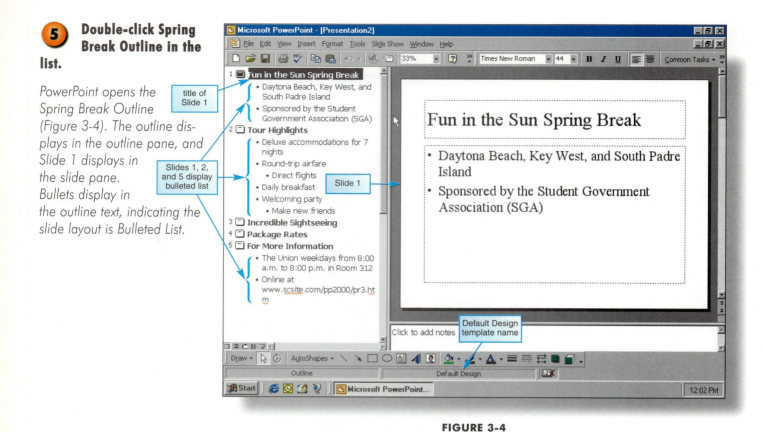

FIGURE 3-4

Copying Slides

Opening a Microsoft Word outline is one way of deriving information for a slide show. Another way is to copy slides from other presentations directly into your new presentation. To do so, display the slide in your presentation that precedes the slide you want to insert, on the Insert menu click Slides from Files, select the presentation containing the slide you want to copy, click Display, select the slide or slides you want to copy to your presentation, and then click Insert. If you want to copy an entire presentation, click Insert All.

When PowerPoint opens a file created in Microsoft Word or a presentation graphics program, such as Harvard Graphics or Lotus Freelance, it picks up the outline structure from the styles used in the file. As a result, heading level one becomes a title, heading level two becomes the first level of text, and so on.

A file saved as a Text Only file in Microsoft Word is saved without formatting. This **plain text file**, which has the **.txt file extension**, does not contain heading styles, so PowerPoint uses the tabs at the beginning of paragraphs to define the outline structure. Imported outlines can contain up to nine outline levels, whereas PowerPoint outlines are limited to six levels (one for titles and five for text). When you import an outline, all text in outline levels six through nine is treated as outline level six.

Changing Presentation Design Templates

Recall that **design templates** format the look of your presentation. You can change the design template any time you want to change the appearance of your presentation, not just when you create a new presentation. The current design template is Default Design. The Whirlpool design template compliments the custom slide background you will create later in this project. Perform this step to change design templates.

TO CHANGE DESIGN TEMPLATES

 Double-click Default Design on the status bar. Scroll down and double-click the Whirlpool design template in the Presentation Designs list in the Apply Design Template dialog box.

PowerPoint applies the Whirlpool design template as indicated by the change to the layout and bullets (Figure 3-5).

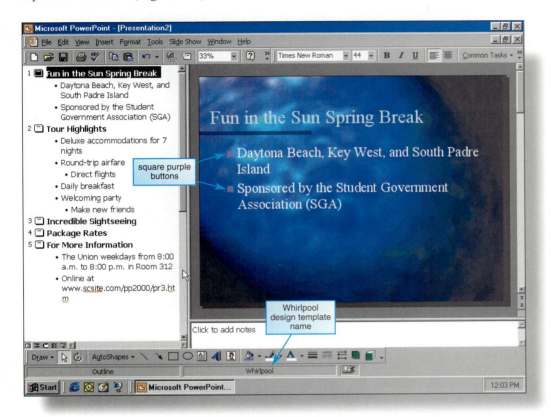

FIGURE 3-5

Recall that slide attributes change when you select a different design template. The Whirlpool design template format determines the slide attributes of the slide master and the title master. For example, when you compare Figure 3-4 with your screen, you see the bullets changed from small black dots to purple squares.

Changing the Font

When you imported the Spring Break Outline file, PowerPoint retained the Times New Roman font used in the Microsoft Word document. You want to change this font to Tahoma, which is the font used in the Whirlpool design template. Perform the steps on the next page to change the font from Times New Roman to Tahoma.

Other Ways

1. Click Common Tasks button on Formatting toolbar, click Apply Design Template, click Whirlpool, click Apply

2. On Format menu click Apply Design Template, scroll down to select Whirlpool, click Apply

To Change the Font

1 **Click Edit on the menu bar and then point to Select All (Figure 3-6).**

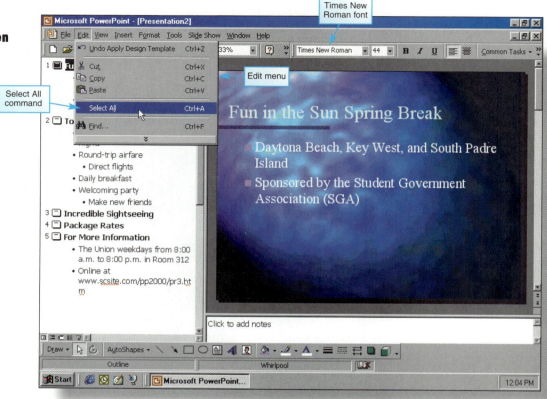

FIGURE 3-6

2 **Click Select All.**

All characters in the outline are selected (Figure 3-7).

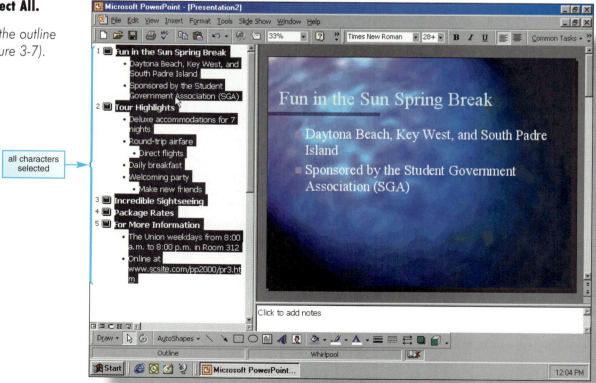

FIGURE 3-7

3 **Click the Font box arrow on the Formatting toolbar, scroll through the list until Tahoma displays, and then point to Tahoma.**

PowerPoint displays a list of available fonts (Figure 3-8). Your list of available fonts may be different depending on the type of printer you are using.

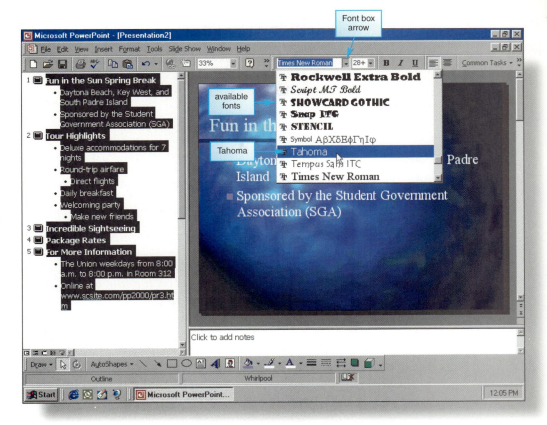

FIGURE 3-8

4 **Click Tahoma.**

Slide 1 displays with the Tahoma font (Figure 3-9).

5 **Click anywhere on Slide 1 except the Title Area or the Object Area placeholders.**

The outline text no longer is selected.

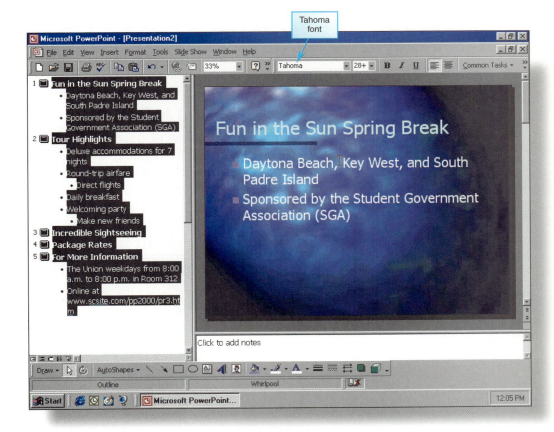

FIGURE 3-9

Saving the Presentation

You now should save your presentation because you created a presentation from an outline file and changed the design template and font. The following steps summarize how to save a presentation.

TO SAVE A PRESENTATION

1 Click the Save button on the Standard toolbar.

2 Type Spring Break in the File name text box.

3 Click the Save in box arrow. Click 3½ Floppy (A:) in the Save in list.

4 Click the Save button in the Save As dialog box.

The presentation is saved on the floppy disk in drive A with the file name Spring Break. This file name displays on the title bar.

Creating a Custom Background

PowerPoint has a variety of design templates in the Presentation Designs folder. Sometimes, however, you may want a background that is not found in one of the design templates, such as the picture of the beach in Figures 3-1a through 3-1e on page PP 3.5. PowerPoint allows you to create that background by inserting a picture. PowerPoint also allows you to customize the background color, shading, pattern, and texture.

You perform two tasks to create the customized background for this presentation. First, you change the slide layout of Slide 1 to the Title Slide AutoLayout. Then, you create the slide background by inserting a picture of a beach.

The next two sections explain how to create a slide background using a picture.

Changing the Slide Layout to Title Slide

When you import an outline to create a presentation, PowerPoint assumes the text is bulleted text. Because Slide 1 is the title slide for this presentation, you want to change the AutoLayout to the Title Slide AutoLayout.

The following steps summarize how to change the layout of Slide 1 to the Title Slide layout.

TO CHANGE THE SLIDE LAYOUT TO TITLE SLIDE

1 Click the Common Tasks button on the Formatting toolbar.

2 Click Slide Layout on the Common Tasks button menu.

3 Double-click Title Slide, the first AutoLayout in the Slide Layout dialog box.

Slide 1 displays with the Title Slide AutoLayout (Figure 3-10).

More About

Backgrounds

Some researchers have determined that audience members prefer viewing photographs instead of line art on a slide, although the line art may be more effective in carrying the desired message. In addition, viewers prefer color graphics as compared to black-and-white objects. The various colors, however, do not affect the amount of information retained. For more information, visit the PowerPoint 2000 Project 3 More About page (www.scsite.com/pp2000/more.htm) and click Backgrounds.

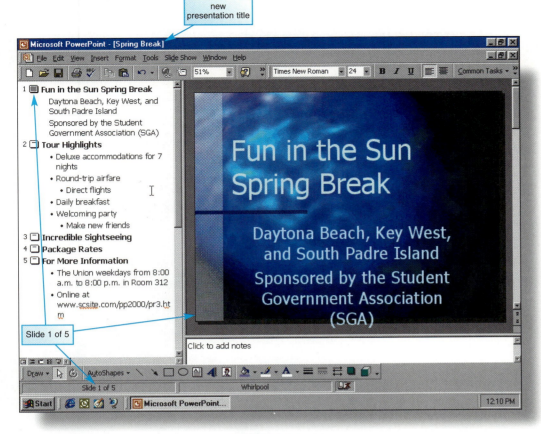

FIGURE 3-10

PowerPoint provides two alternative methods to double-clicking the AutoLayout in Step 3 above. The first alternative is to type the AutoLayout number of one of the 24 AutoLayouts and then press the ENTER key. A layout number corresponds to each AutoLayout, with the four slides in the first row numbered one through four from left to right, the next row of AutoLayouts numbered five through eight, and so on. The second alternative is to type the AutoLayout number and then click the Apply button. PowerPoint interprets the number you type as the corresponding AutoLayout and applies it when you press the ENTER key (alternative one) or click the Apply button (alternative two). For example, the Title Slide AutoLayout is layout number one. When the Slide Layout dialog box displays, you would type the number 1 and then press the ENTER key instead of double-clicking the Title Slide AutoLayout.

Changing the Font Size

When you imported the Spring Break Outline file, PowerPoint placed the first line, Fun in the Sun Spring Break, in the Title Area placeholder and the next two paragraphs in the Object Area placeholder. The text in the Object Area placeholder spills out of the slide, so you want to reduce the font size of the second paragraph, Sponsored by the Student Government Association (SGA).

The steps on the next page summarize how to change the last paragraph on Slide 1 from a font size of 40 to a font size of 24.

AutoLayouts

PowerPoint's AutoLayouts give a balanced, professional look to your presentations. In addition to the AutoLayouts used thus far in this text, additional layouts include areas for media clips, charts, title text, and a maximum of four objects, and one large object. The Blank AutoLayout allows you to add text and graphic elements and place them anywhere on the slide.

TO CHANGE THE FONT SIZE

1 Click to the immediate left of the letter S at the beginning of the second paragraph in the Object Area placeholder, Sponsored by the Student Government Association (SGA). Press the ENTER key to insert a blank line.

2 Triple-click this second paragraph.

3 Click the Font Size box arrow on the Formatting toolbar and then click 24 in the list.

The last paragraph in the Object Area placeholder, Sponsored by the Student Government Association (SGA), moves toward the bottom of the slide and displays in font size 24 (Figure 3-11).

FIGURE 3-11

Inserting a Picture to Create a Custom Background

The next step in creating the Spring Break presentation is to insert a picture of a beach to create a custom background. In PowerPoint, a **picture** is any graphic created in another application. Pictures usually are saved in one of two **graphic formats**: bitmap or vector.

This beach picture is a **bitmap graphic**, which is a piece of art that has been stored as a series of small dots, called pixels, that form shapes and lines. A **pixel**, short for **picture element**, is one dot in a grid. A picture that is produced on the computer screen or on paper by a printer is composed of thousands of these dots. Just as a bit is the smallest unit of information a computer can process, a pixel is the smallest element that can display or that print hardware and software can manipulate in creating letters, numbers, or graphics. The beach picture you use in this project has the dimensions of 600 pixels wide and 396 pixels high.

Customizing Pictures

You can crop pictures added to slides so the focus is on the essential elements of the picture and not the extraneous details. To crop a picture, first select the picture and then click the Crop button on the Picture toolbar. Place the cropping tool over a sizing handle and drag to frame the portion of the picture you want to include on your slide. You also can specify an exact percentage for the object's height and width. If you plan to save your PowerPoint slide show as a Web page, size the picture to a specific dimension less than 50 percent. You later can restore the cropped picture to its original image.

Bitmap graphics are created by digital cameras or in paint programs such as Microsoft Paint. Bitmap graphics also can be produced from **digitizing** art, pictures, or photographs by passing the artwork through a scanner. A **scanner** is a hardware device that converts lines and shading into combinations of the binary digits 0 and 1 by sensing different intensities of light and dark. The scanner shines a beam of light on the picture being scanned. The beam passes back and forth across the picture, sending a digitized signal to the computer's memory. A **digitized signal** is the conversion of input, such as the lines in a drawing, into a series of discrete units represented by the binary digits 0 and 1. **Scanned pictures** are bitmap pictures and have jagged edges. The jagged edges are caused by the individual pixels that create the picture. Bitmap graphics also are known as **raster images**. Pictures in the Microsoft Clip Gallery that have the file extensions of **.jpg** and **.bmp** are examples of bitmap graphic files.

Bitmap files cannot be ungrouped and converted to smaller PowerPoint object groups. They can be manipulated, however, in an imaging program such as Microsoft Photo Editor. This program allows you to rotate or flip the pictures and then insert them in your slides.

The other graphic format in which pictures are stored is vector graphics. A **vector graphic** is a piece of art that has been created by a drawing program such as CorelDRAW or Adobe Illustrator. The clip art pictures used in Project 2 and in this project are vector graphic objects. In contrast to the patterns of individual dots (pixels) that comprise bitmap graphics, vector graphics are created as a collection of lines. Vector graphic files store data either as picture descriptions or as calculations. These files describe a picture mathematically as a set of instructions for creating the objects in the picture. These mathematical descriptions determine the position, length, and direction in which the lines are to be drawn. These calculations allow the drawing program to re-create the picture on the screen as necessary. Because vector graphic objects are described mathematically, they also can be layered, rotated, and magnified with relative ease. Vector graphics also are known as **object-oriented pictures**. Clip art pictures in the Microsoft Clip Gallery that have the file extension of **.wmf** are examples of vector files. Vector files can be ungrouped and manipulated by their component objects. You will ungroup the umbrella clip art used on Slide 5 in this project.

PowerPoint allows you to insert vector files because it uses **graphic filters** to convert the various graphic formats into a format PowerPoint can use. These filters are installed with the initial PowerPoint installation or can be added later by running the Setup program.

The Spring Break presentation will be used to help promote the Student Government Association's trip, so you want to emphasize the beautiful beach scenery. To create the desired effect, you insert a picture of a beach to cover the Whirlpool design template.

Perform the steps on the next page to create a custom background.

More About

Digitizing

Digitizing produces some dazzling objects that add interest to presentations. Many artists have traded their paint brushes and easels for the mouse and monitor. To view some of their creations, visit the PowerPoint 2000 Project 3 More About page (www. scsite.com/pp2000/more.htm) and click Digitizing.

To Insert a Picture to Create a Custom Background

1 **Right-click anywhere on Slide 1 except the Title Area or the Object Area placeholders. Click Background on the shortcut menu. When the Background dialog box displays, point to the Background fill box arrow.**

The Background dialog box displays (Figure 3-12).

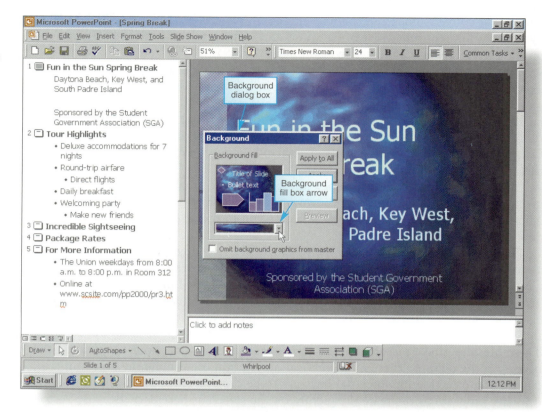

FIGURE 3-12

2 **Click the Background fill box arrow. Point to Fill Effects on the menu.**

The Background fill box menu containing options for filling the slide background displays (Figure 3-13). The current background fill is Automatic, which is the Whirlpool design template default. Fill Effects is highlighted.

FIGURE 3-13

3 Click Fill Effects. If necessary, click the Picture tab, and then click the Select Picture button. Click the Look in box arrow and then click 3½ Floppy (A:). If necessary, click Beach in the list. Point to the Insert button.

The Select Picture dialog box displays (Figure 3-14). The selected file, Beach, displays in the preview box.

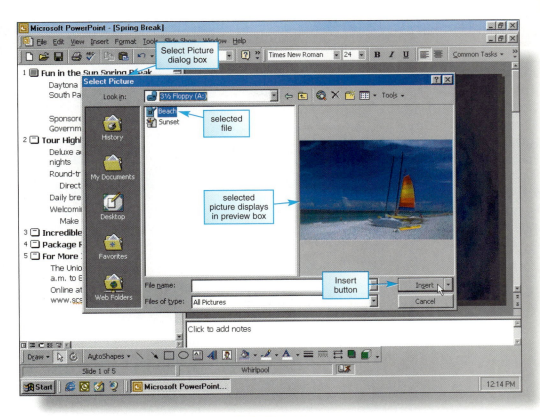

FIGURE 3-14

4 Click the Insert button. When the Fill Effects dialog box displays, click the OK button. When the Background dialog box displays, point to the Apply to All button.

The Background dialog box displays the Beach picture in the Background fill area (Figure 3-15).

FIGURE 3-15

5 **Click the Apply to All button.**

Slide 1 displays the Beach picture as the slide background (Figure 3-16). Although not shown in this figure, the Beach picture is the background for all slides in the presentation. The Whirlpool design template text attributes display on the slide.

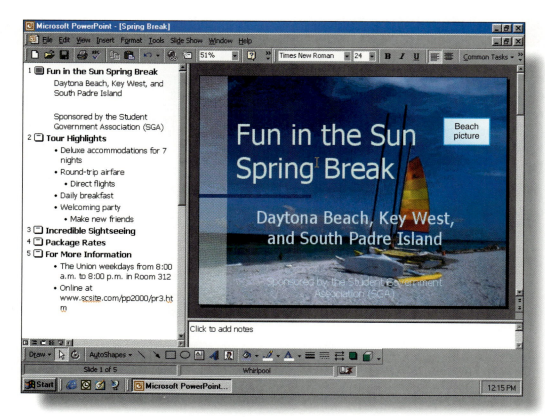

FIGURE 3-16

When you customize the background, the design template text attributes remain the same, but the slide background changes. For example, inserting the Beach picture for the slide background changes the appearance of the slide background but maintains the text attributes of the Whirlpool design template.

Adding Graphical Bullets

PowerPoint allows you to change the appearance of bullets in a slide show. The Bulleted List, Clip Art & Text, and Text & Clip Art AutoLayouts use default bullet characters. You may want to change these characters, however, to add visual interest and variety to your slide show. The graphical character of a beach umbrella fits the theme of your presentation.

The Whirlpool design template uses purple rectangles for the Second level paragraphs and aqua rectangles for the Third level paragraphs. Changing these bullets to graphical characters adds visual interest to your presentation. Creating the graphical bullets requires you to change the default rectangular bullets to the beach umbrella bullets. Perform the following steps to change the bullets from the default rectangles to the graphical umbrellas on Slide 2.

Steps **To Add Graphical Bullets**

1 **Click the Next Slide button on the vertical scroll bar to display Slide 2.**

Slide 2 displays with the Bulleted List AutoLayout (Figure 3-17).

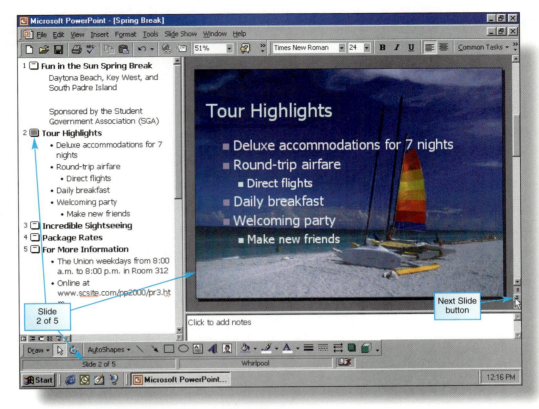

FIGURE 3-17

2 **Click and then drag through all the paragraphs in the Object Area placeholder. Right-click the Object Area placeholder and then point to Bullets and Numbering on the shortcut menu.**

The Object Area placeholder is selected (Figure 3-18). The six paragraphs in the Object Area placeholder are selected.

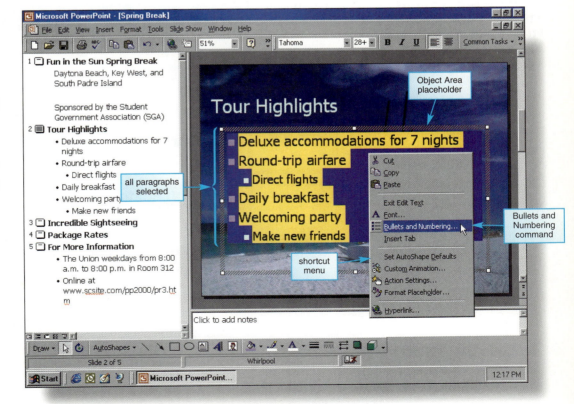

FIGURE 3-18

3 **Click Bullets and Numbering. When the Bullets and Numbering dialog box displays, point to the Character button.**

The Bullets and Numbering dialog box displays (Figure 3-19).

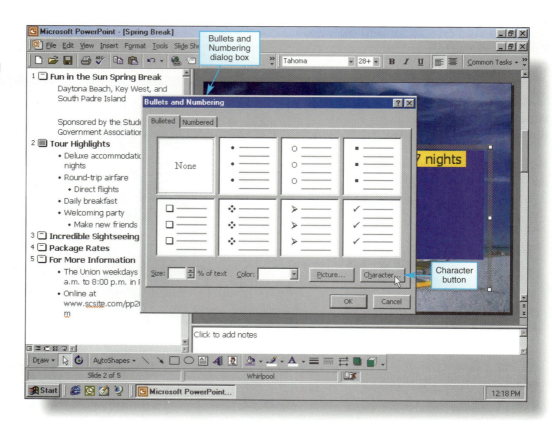

FIGURE 3-19

4 **Click the Character button. When the Bullet dialog box displays, click the Bullets from box arrow. Point to Vacation MT.**

PowerPoint displays a list of available character fonts (Figure 3-20). The character fonts list may differ depending on your system. The default rectangular purple and aqua bullets on Slide 2 are part of the Wingdings character fonts.

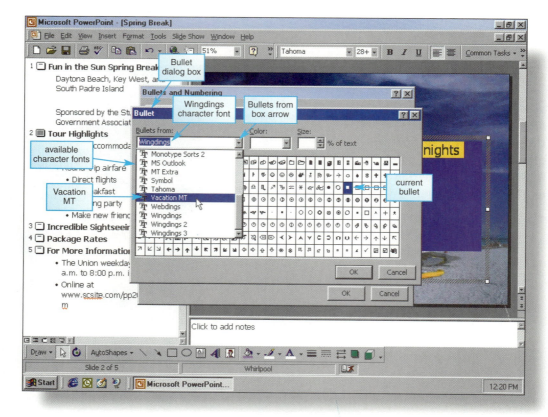

FIGURE 3-20

5 Click Vacation MT. When the Vacation MT character fonts display in the Bullet dialog box, click the beach umbrella bullet (row 2, column 6). Point to the OK button.

The desired beach umbrella bullet enlarges to reveal its shape (Figure 3-21). The Vacation MT bullets are graphical images of activities and symbols related to leisure-time activities.

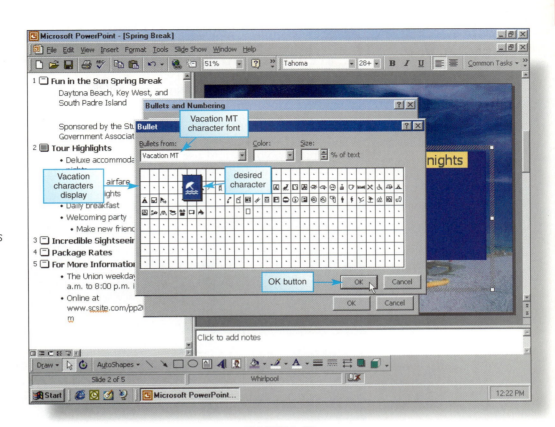

FIGURE 3-21

6 Click the OK button.

The beach umbrella bullets replace the default rectangular bullets (Figure 3-22). The First level paragraphs have a purple bullet that is 80 percent of the text size, and the Second level paragraphs have an aqua bullet that is 70 percent of the text size.

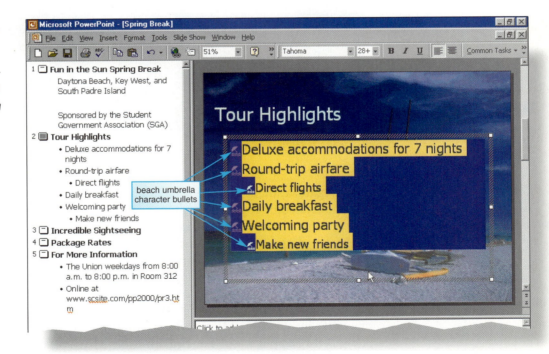

FIGURE 3-22

Other Ways

1. Highlight text, on Format menu click Bullets and Numbering, select character font, click Character, click desired character, click OK button

PowerPoint displays the new character bullets in front of each paragraph on Slide 2. This slide now is complete. The next section describes how to embed an organization chart in a slide.

Creating and Embedding an Organization Chart

Slide 3 contains a chart that elaborates on the sightseeing activities for each of the Spring Break locations, as shown in Figure 3-23. This type of chart is called an **organization chart**, which is a hierarchical collection of elements depicting various functions or responsibilities that contribute to an organization or to a collective function. Typically, you would use an organization chart to show the structure of people or departments within an organization, hence the name, organization chart.

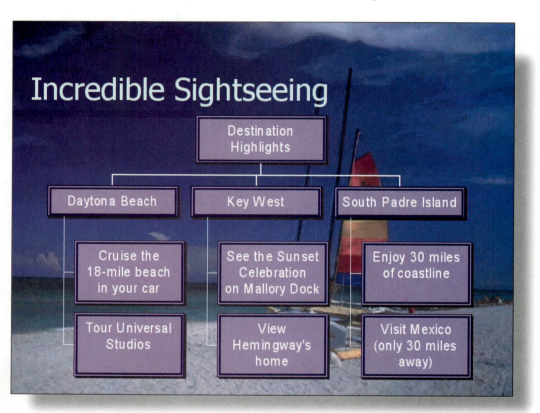

FIGURE 3-23

Organization charts are used in a variety of ways to depict relationships. For example, a company uses an organization chart to describe the relationships between the company's departments. In the information sciences, often organization charts show the decomposition of a process or program. When used in this manner, the chart is called a **hierarchy chart**.

PowerPoint contains a supplementary application called **Microsoft Organization Chart 2.0** that allows you to create an organization chart. When you open Microsoft Organization Chart, its menus, buttons, and tools are available to you directly in the PowerPoint window. Microsoft Organization Chart is an object linking and embedding (OLE) application. The organization chart you create for Slide 3 (Figure 3-23) is an embedded object because it is created in an application other than PowerPoint.

Creating an organization chart requires several steps. First, you display the slide that will contain the organization chart and change the AutoLayout to the Organization Chart AutoLayout. Then, you open the Microsoft Organization Chart application. Finally, you enter and format the contents of the boxes in the organization chart window.

Perform the following steps to create the organization chart for this project.

Changing Slide Layouts

Before you open Microsoft Organization Chart, you need to perform the following steps to display Slide 3 and change the AutoLayout to the Organization Chart AutoLayout.

TO DISPLAY THE NEXT SLIDE AND CHANGE THE SLIDE LAYOUT

1 Click the Next Slide button on the vertical scroll bar to display Slide 3.

2 Click Slide Layout on the Common Tasks button menu.

3 When the Slide Layout dialog box displays, type the number 7 to select the Organization Chart AutoLayout from the 24 available AutoLayouts. Then, click the Apply button.

Slide 3 displays the placeholder for the organization chart and the slide title (Figure 3-24).

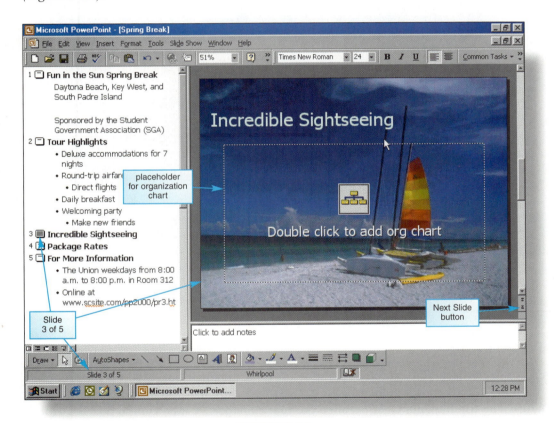

FIGURE 3-24

Slide 3 now displays the placeholder for the organization chart. The next section explains how to open the Microsoft Organization Chart application.

Opening the Microsoft Organization Chart Application

To create the organization chart on Slide 3, you first must open the organization chart application, Microsoft Organization Chart 2.0, which is included within PowerPoint. Recall that when this supplementary application is active, the menus, buttons, and tools in the organization chart application are made available in the

1. Press PAGE DOWN, on Format menu click Slide Layout, double-click Organization Chart AutoLayout

PowerPoint window. Once active, Microsoft Organization Chart displays a sample four-box organization chart in a work area in the middle of the PowerPoint window, as explained in the following step. Perform the following step to open Microsoft Organization Chart.

Steps | To Open Microsoft Organization Chart

1 **Double-click the placeholder for the organization chart in the middle of Slide 3.**

Microsoft Organization Chart displays the Microsoft Organization Chart - [Object in Spring Break] window in a work area in the PowerPoint window (Figure 3-25). Notice the sample organization chart is composed of four boxes connected by lines. When Microsoft Organization Chart is active, the first line of the top box automatically is selected. Depending on the version of Microsoft Organization Chart installed on your computer, the display on the screen may vary slightly.

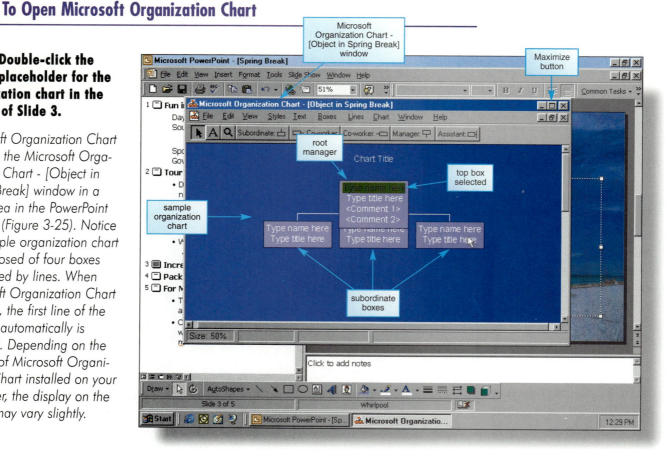

FIGURE 3-25

Microsoft Organization Chart displays a sample organization chart to help you create your chart. The sample is composed of one **manager box**, located at the top of the chart, and three **subordinate boxes**. A manager box has one or more subordinates. The topmost manager is called the **root manager**. A subordinate box is located at a lower level than its manager. A subordinate box has only one manager. When a lower-level subordinate box is added to a higher-level subordinate box, the higher-level subordinate box becomes the manager of the lower-level subordinate box.

In this presentation, each of the three Spring Break trips has two suggested sightseeing activities. As a result, your organization chart will consist of three boxes on level two immediately below the root manager and two boxes immediately under each subordinate manager. These organization chart layouts for each trip are identical, so you create the structure for the Daytona Beach trip, copy it, and make editing changes for the Key West and South Padre Island trips.

Maximizing the Microsoft Organization Chart Window

When Microsoft Organization Chart is active, the Microsoft Organization Chart window is not maximized. Maximizing the Microsoft Organization Chart window makes it easier to create your organization chart because it displays a larger area in which to view the chart. Perform this step to maximize the Microsoft Organization Chart window.

TO MAXIMIZE THE MICROSOFT ORGANIZATION CHART WINDOW

 Click the Maximize button in the upper-right corner of the Microsoft Organization Chart window.

The Microsoft Organization Chart window fills the desktop. Clicking the Restore button returns the Microsoft Organization Chart window to its original size.

Creating the Title for the Root Manager Box

In this presentation, the organization chart is used to describe the various sightseeing activities. The topmost box, the root manager, identifies the purpose of this organization chart: Incredible Sightseeing. Recall that when Microsoft Organization Chart becomes active, the first line in the root manager box is selected. The following step explains how to create the title for the root manager box.

Steps To Create the Title for the Root Manager Box

 **Type** Destination **in the root manager box on level one and then press the ENTER key. Type** Highlights **on the second line.**

Destination Highlights displays in the root manager box (Figure 3-26). Comment 1 and Comment 2 prompts display in brackets under the root manager box title.

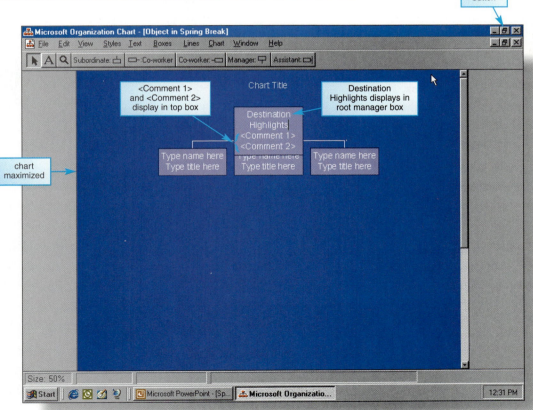

FIGURE 3-26

Titling the Subordinate Boxes

The process of adding a title to a subordinate box is the same as adding the title to the root manager box except that first you must select the subordinate box. The following steps explain how to title subordinate boxes.

  To Title the Subordinate Boxes

1 **Click the left subordinate box.** **Type** Daytona Beach **and then press the ENTER key. Press the DELETE key.**

Daytona Beach displays as the title for the left subordinate box (Figure 3-27). You pressed the DELETE key because only one line of text is needed.

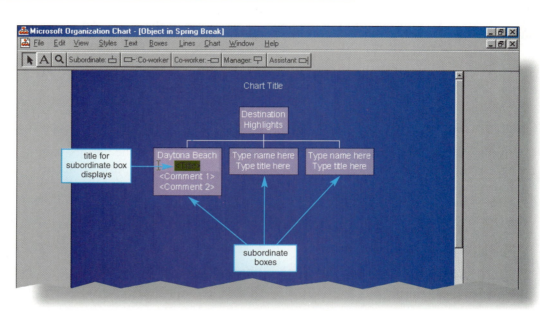

FIGURE 3-27

2 **Click the middle subordinate box.** **Type** Key West **and then press the ENTER key. Press the DELETE key.**

Key West displays as the title for the middle subordinate box.

3 **Click the right subordinate box.** **Type** South Padre Island **and then press the ENTER key. Press the DELETE key.**

South Padre Island displays as the title for the right subordinate box (Figure 3-28).

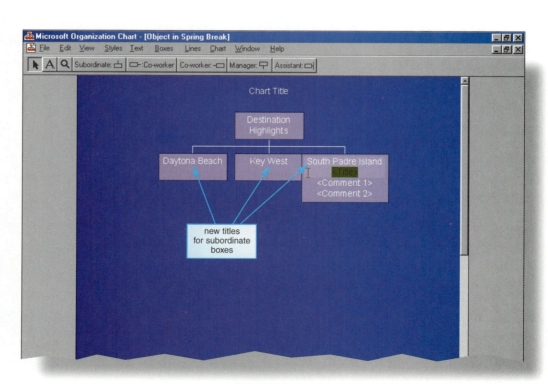

FIGURE 3-28

Adding Subordinate Boxes

Microsoft Organization Chart has five **types of boxes** you can add to a chart. Each box type has a corresponding **box tool** on the Microsoft Organization Chart window **icon bar**. Because each Spring Break trip offers several sightseeing activities, you need to add two subordinate boxes to each of the Spring Break trips.

To add a single subordinate box, click the **Subordinate box tool** and then click the box on the organization chart to which the subordinate reports. When you want to add several subordinate boxes, you can click the Subordinate box tool once for each box you want to add to the organization chart. For example, if you want to add two subordinate boxes, click the Subordinate box tool two times. If the Subordinate box tool is recessed and you decide to not add subordinate boxes, you can deselect the Subordinate box tool by clicking the **Select box tool** on the Microsoft Organization Chart window icon bar or by pressing the ESC key.

The following steps explain how to use the Subordinate box tool to add two subordinate boxes to the Daytona Beach box.

 Steps **To Add Multiple Subordinate Boxes**

1 **Click the Subordinate box tool on the Microsoft Organization Chart window icon bar two times. Point to the Daytona Beach box.**

The Subordinate box tool is recessed (Figure 3-29). The status bar displays the number of subordinate boxes Microsoft Organization Chart is creating, which is two. The mouse pointer changes shape to a subordinate box.

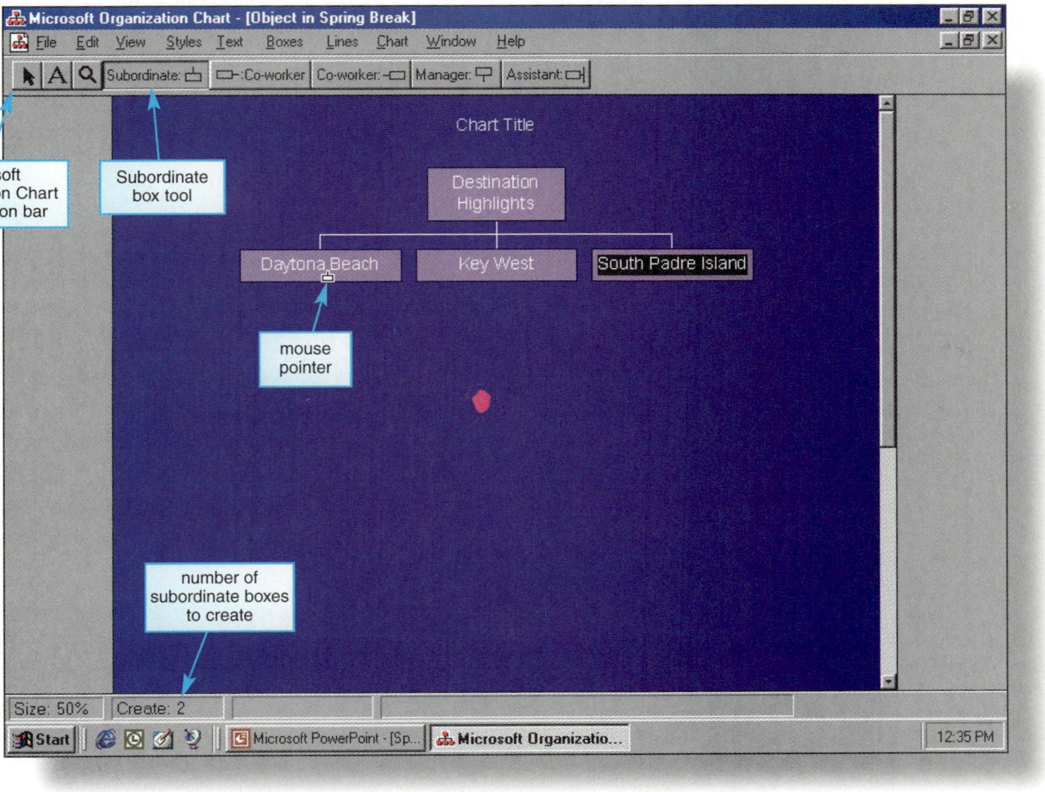

Microsoft Organization Chart - [Object in Spring Break]

File Edit View Styles Text Boxes Lines Chart Window Help

Subordinate: Co-worker Co-worker: Manager: Assistant:

Chart Title

Microsoft Organization Chart window icon bar

Subordinate box tool

Destination Highlights

Daytona Beach   Key West   South Padre Island

mouse pointer

number of subordinate boxes to create

Size: 50%   Create: 2

Start   Microsoft PowerPoint - [Sp...   Microsoft Organizatio...   12:35 PM

FIGURE 3-29

2 Click the Daytona Beach box.

Two subordinate boxes display below the Daytona Beach box (Figure 3-30). The new subordinate boxes display one level lower than the box to which they are attached. Daytona Beach now is the manager to the new subordinate boxes. The left subordinate box on level three is selected.

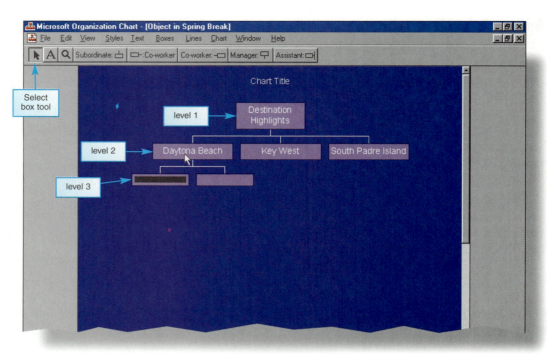

FIGURE 3-30

The basic structure of the left side of the organization chart is complete. The next step is to add titles to the boxes in the chart.

Adding Names to the Subordinate Boxes

To complete the organization chart, you must add names to all subordinate boxes to the Daytona Beach box. After adding the subordinate boxes, the Select box tool is recessed, meaning it is active. When this tool is active, the mouse pointer displays as a left-pointing block arrow. Because the subordinate boxes in this project have names but do not have titles, the Title, Comment 1, and Comment 2 prompts display in brackets under the box name when the box is selected. The brackets indicate the label is optional, and it displays only when replaced by text. The following steps summarize adding a title to each level 3 subordinate box.

TO ADD NAMES TO SUBORDINATE BOXES

1 If necessary, click the left subordinate box on level 3. Type `Cruise the` in the subordinate box and then press the ENTER key. Type `18-mile beach` and then press the ENTER key. Type `in your car` in the subordinate box.

2 Click the right subordinate box on level 3. Type `Tour Universal` in the subordinate box and then press the ENTER key. Type `Studios` and then press the ENTER key.

Both level 3 subordinate boxes under the Daytona Beach box display sightseeing activities (Figure 3-31).

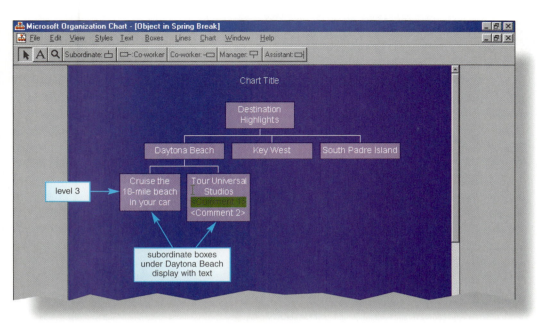

FIGURE 3-31

Changing Organization Chart Styles

Now that the boxes for the Daytona Beach branch are labeled, you want to change the way the organization chart looks. With the addition of each new box, the chart expanded horizontally. Before you add the Key West and South Padre Island activities, you will change the style of selected boxes from horizontal to vertical.

 To Change the Organization Chart Style

1 **Click anywhere outside the organization chart boxes. Press and hold the SHIFT key. Click the two lowest-level boxes: Cruise the 18-mile beach in your car and Tour Universal Studios. Release the SHIFT key.**

The two lowest-level boxes are selected (Figure 3-32).

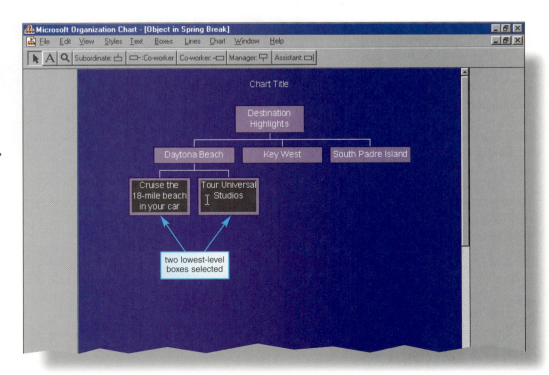

FIGURE 3-32

2 **Click Styles on the menu bar and then point to the vertical styles menu icon (row 1, column 2) in the top set of Groups styles.**

The default group style is selected, which is indicated by the recessed icon (Figure 3-33). The vertical styles menu icon is highlighted.

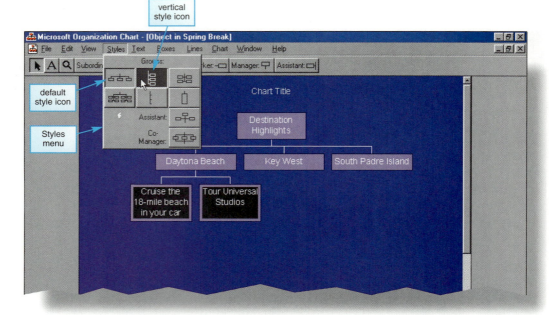

FIGURE 3-33

3 **Click the vertical style icon.**

The organization chart displays the two sightseeing activities vertically under the Daytona Beach box (Figure 3-34).

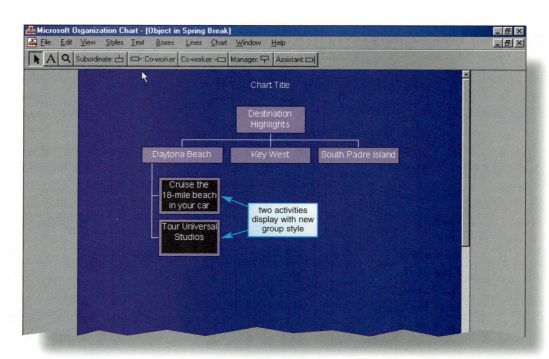

FIGURE 3-34

The **Styles menu** icons allow you to change the arrangement of boxes in your chart. The top set of styles changes the arrangement of boxes in a group. The middle style creates assistant boxes. The bottom style is used to show co-managers. If you select an incorrect style or want to return to the previous style, click the Undo Chart Style command on the Edit menu or press CTRL+Z.

Now that the Daytona Beach activities are complete, you need to compile the Key West and South Padre Island sightseeing lists.

Copying a Branch of an Organization Chart

Instead of creating the Key West and South Padre Island activities by adding and labeling boxes, you copy Daytona Beach's list and add it under the other two Spring Break destinations. When you work with a whole section of an organization chart, it is referred to as working with a **branch**, or an appendage, of the chart. The following steps explain how to copy a branch of the chart.

 Steps To Copy a Branch of an Organization Chart

 1 If not already selected, press and hold the SHIFT key, click the two level 3 boxes, Cruise the 18-mile beach in your car and Tour Universal Studios, and then release the SHIFT key. Right-click one of the selected boxes and then point to Copy on the shortcut menu.

The shortcut menu displays (Figure 3-35).

2 Click Copy.

Microsoft Organization Chart copies the Daytona Beach activities branch of the organization chart to the Clipboard. Recall that the Clipboard is a temporary storage area.

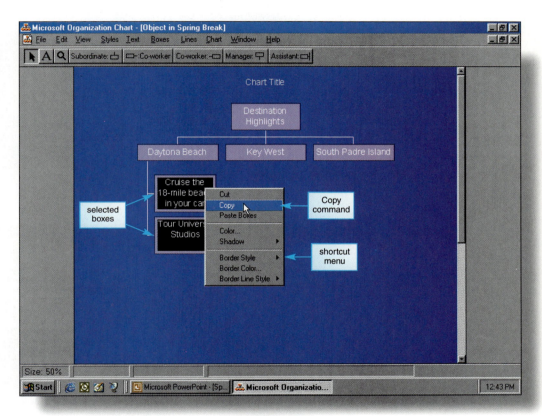

FIGURE 3-35

The next section explains how to paste the Daytona Beach activities branch of the organization chart to two other locations on the chart.

Pasting a Branch of an Organization Chart

Now that a copy of the Daytona Beach branch of the organization chart is on the Clipboard, the steps on the next page are to paste it from the Clipboard to the Key West and South Padre Island areas.

To Paste a Branch of an Organization Chart

 Right-click the middle root manager box, Key West. Then point to Paste Boxes on the shortcut menu.

The shortcut menu displays (Figure 3-36). The Key West box is selected.

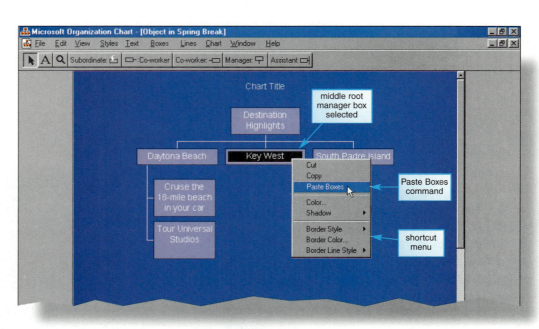

FIGURE 3-36

2 **Click Paste Boxes.**

The organization chart displays the two sightseeing activities under the Key West box.

3 **Right-click the right root manager box, South Padre Island. Click Paste Boxes on the shortcut menu.**

The organization chart displays the two sightseeing activities under the South Padre Island box (Figure 3-37).

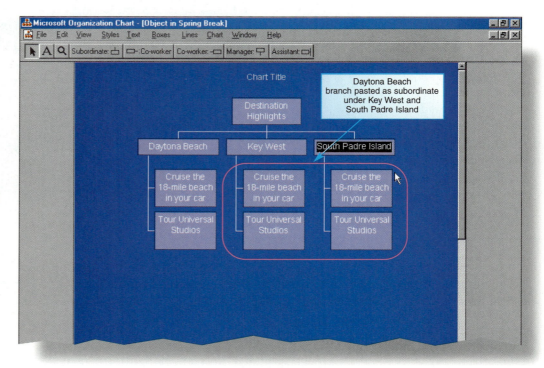

FIGURE 3-37

Editing an Organization Chart

After you have copied and pasted a branch of the organization chart, you need to **edit** the two sightseeing activities for the Key West and South Padre Island trips. Editing a box requires you first to select the box and then make your edits.

Steps: To Edit Text in an Organization Chart

1 **Click the Cruise the 18-mile beach in your car box under the Key West branch of the organization chart. Type** See the Sunset **in the subordinate box and then press the ENTER key. Type** Celebration **and then press the ENTER key. Type** on Mallory Dock **and then point to the Tour Universal Studios box under the Key West branch of the organization chart.**

The three lines of text replace the original wording (Figure 3-38).

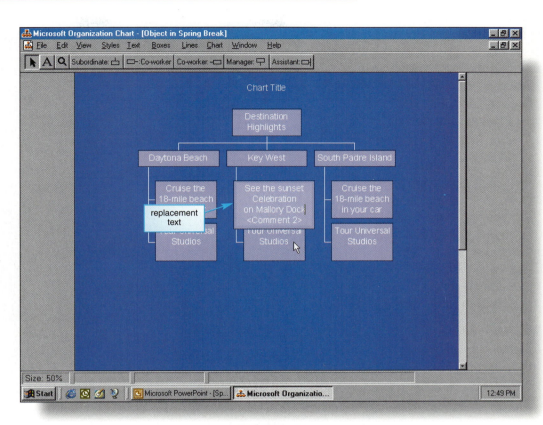

FIGURE 3-38

2 **Click the Tour Universal Studios box under the Key West branch. Type** View **in the subordinate box and then press the ENTER key. Type** Hemingway's **and then press the ENTER key. Type** home **and then point to the Cruise the 18-mile beach in your car box under the South Padre Island branch.**

The editing changes for the Key West branch are complete (Figure 3-39).

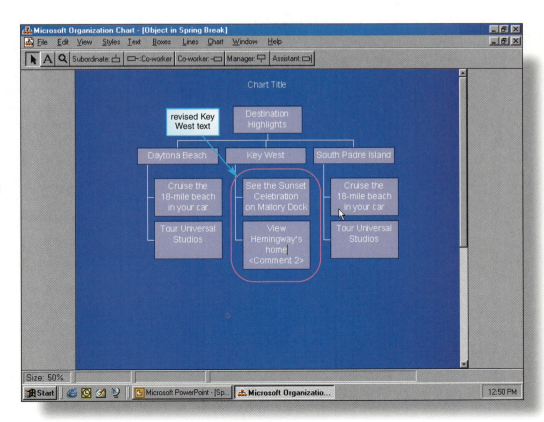

FIGURE 3-39

3 Click the Cruise the 18-mile beach in your car box under the South Padre Island branch. Type Enjoy 30 miles and then press the ENTER key. Type of coastline and then press the ENTER key. Press the DELETE key.

4 Click the bottom-right box, type Visit Mexico and then press the ENTER key. Type (only 30 miles and then press the ENTER key. Type away) and then click anywhere outside the organization chart boxes.

All editing changes for the Destination Highlights organization chart are complete (Figure 3-40).

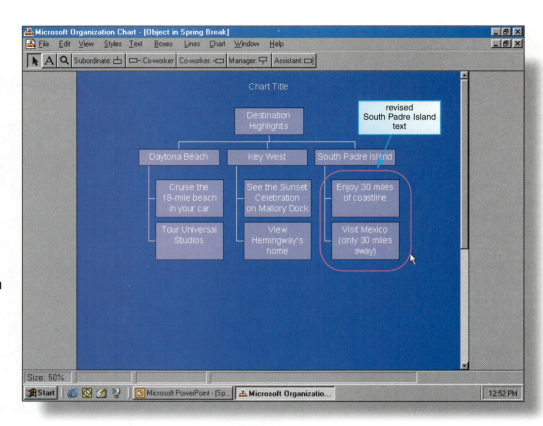

FIGURE 3-40

All the necessary text now appears on the organization chart. The next section explains how to format an organization chart.

Formatting an Organization Chart

Microsoft Organization Chart allows you to format a box simply by selecting it. To make your organization chart look like the chart shown in Figure 3-23 on page PP 3.22, you add shadow effects and a border to every box. The following sections explain how to select all the boxes in the chart and change the shadow and border box attributes.

To Select All Boxes in an Organization Chart

1 Click Edit on the menu bar, point to Select, and then point to All (Figure 3-41).

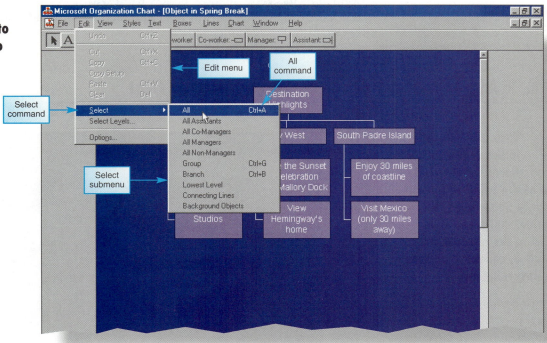

FIGURE 3-41

2 Click All on the Select submenu.

Microsoft Organization Chart selects all the boxes in the chart (Figure 3-42).

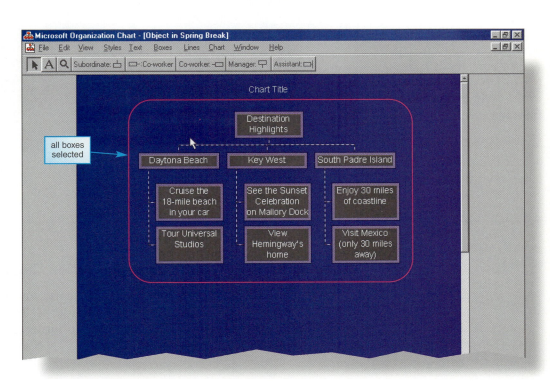

FIGURE 3-42

Other Ways

1. Press CTRL+A

Adding Shadow Effects to Boxes in an Organization Chart

Now that all the boxes are selected, you add shadow effects. Microsoft Organization Chart has eight shadow effects from which to choose. One style is None, which has no shadow. Perform the following steps to add shadow effects to all the boxes in an organization chart.

Steps To Add Shadow Effects to Boxes in an Organization Chart

1 With all the boxes in the organization chart selected, right-click one of the selected boxes. Point to Shadow on the shortcut menu and then point to the shadow style in row 3, column 2 on the Shadow submenu.

Microsoft Organization Chart displays the Shadow submenu (Figure 3-43). The default shadow style for Microsoft Organization Chart is None. The desired shadow style is selected.

2 Click the shadow style on the Shadow submenu.

Microsoft Organization Chart adds the shadow effect to all boxes in the organization chart.

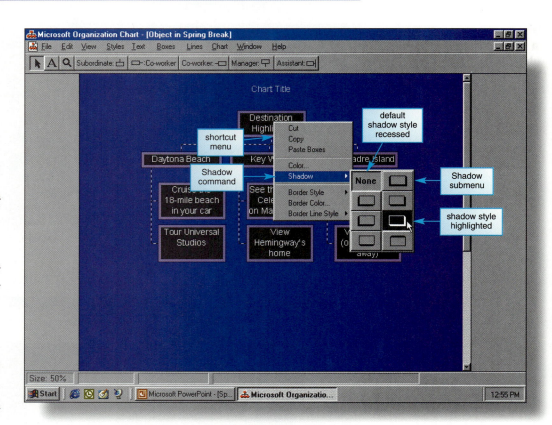

FIGURE 3-43

Changing Border Styles in an Organization Chart

To enhance the boxes in the organization chart, you want to change the border style. Microsoft Organization Chart has 12 border styles from which to choose. One style is None, which has no border. The default border style is a thin line. Perform the following steps to change border styles.

Steps **To Change the Border Style**

1 **With all the boxes in the organization chart selected, right-click one of the selected boxes. Point to Border Style on the shortcut menu and then point to the border style option in row 4, column 1 on the Border Style submenu.**

Microsoft Organization Chart displays the Border Style submenu (Figure 3-44). The default border style for Microsoft Organization Chart is recessed in row 2, column 1. The desired border style is selected.

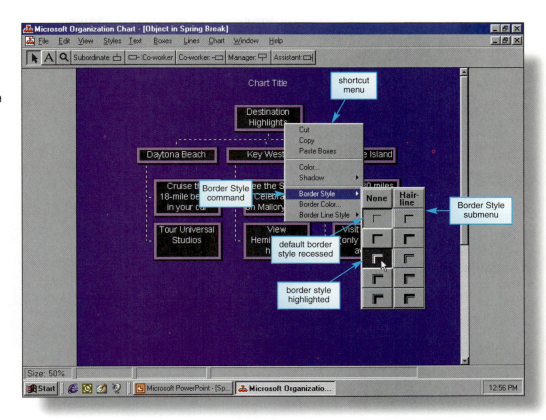

FIGURE 3-44

2 **Click the highlighted border style on the Border Style submenu.**

Microsoft Organization Chart applies the new border style to all boxes in the organization chart (Figure 3-45).

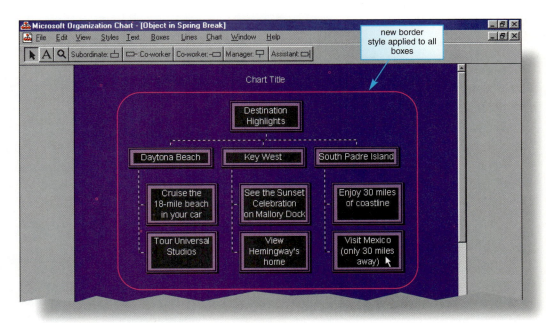

FIGURE 3-45

The organization chart now is complete. The step on the next page is to return to the PowerPoint window.

Quitting Microsoft Organization Chart and Returning to the PowerPoint Window

After you create and format an organization chart, you quit Microsoft Organization Chart and return to the PowerPoint window. The following steps explain how to return to the PowerPoint window.

 ### To Quit Microsoft Organization Chart and Return to the PowerPoint Window

1 **Click the Close button on the Microsoft Organization Chart - [Object in Spring Break] title bar. When the Microsoft Organization Chart dialog box displays, point to the Yes button.**

The Microsoft Organization Chart dialog box warns you that the organization chart object has changed and asks you if you want to update the object in the PowerPoint presentation, Spring Break, before proceeding (Figure 3-46).

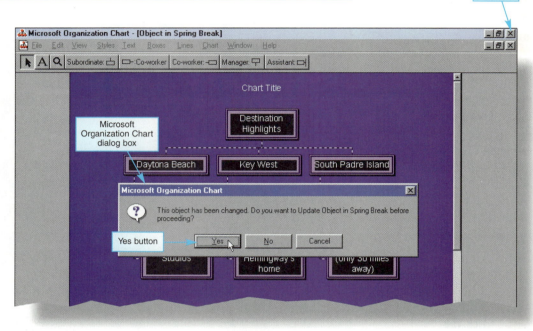

FIGURE 3-46

 2 **Click the Yes button.**

Microsoft Organization Chart updates the organization chart object and closes, and then PowerPoint displays the organization chart on Slide 3 (Figure 3-47).

FIGURE 3-47

Scaling an Organization Chart Object

The organization chart on Slide 3 is sized to fit the placeholder for the organization chart, so it needs to be enlarged. The **Scale command** allows you to enlarge or reduce an object by precise amounts while retaining the object's original proportions.

Perform the following steps to scale an organization chart object.

TO SCALE AN ORGANIZATION CHART OBJECT

1 Right-click the selected organization chart object and then click Format Object on the shortcut menu.

2 Click the Size tab. Click the Height box up arrow in the Scale area until 120% displays.

3 Click the OK button.

The organization chart is scaled to 120 percent of its original size (Figure 3-48).

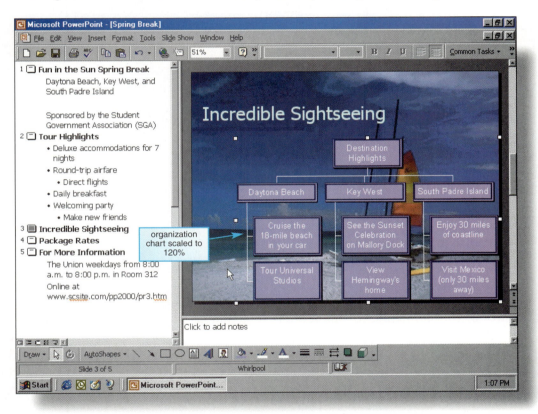

FIGURE 3-48

Other Ways

1. On Format menu click Object, click Size tab, type 120 in Scale Height text box, click OK button

Moving the Organization Chart

Now that the organization chart is scaled to a readable size, you need to move it onto the slide. To move the organization chart, perform the following step.

TO MOVE THE ORGANIZATION CHART

1 Drag the organization chart onto the middle of the blank area of Slide 3.

The organization chart displays in the center of the slide (Figure 3-49 on the next page).

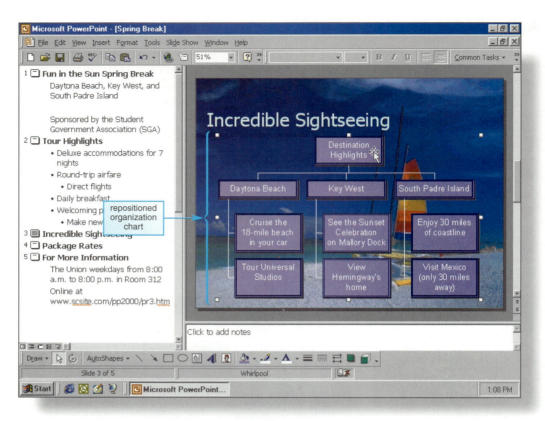

FIGURE 3-49

Slide 3 now is complete. The next section introduces you to inserting a table into a slide.

Inserting a Table into a Slide

Slide 4 is included in this presentation to inform students of the costs of each vacation package. You list each destination and the total package cost. To make this information visually appealing, you arrange the figures in a table. Then you format the table by formatting the column heading font, adding a border, and making the background dark purple.

Inserting a Table into a Slide

The first step is to display the next slide and select the Object Area placeholder.

TO DISPLAY THE NEXT SLIDE AND CHANGE THE SLIDE LAYOUT

1 Click the Next Slide button on the vertical scroll bar to display Slide 4.

2 Click the Common Tasks button on the Formatting toolbar and then click Slide Layout.

3 Double-click the Table slide layout located in row 1, column 4.

Slide 4 displays the Package Rates title and the placeholder for the table with a small table and the words, Double click to add table (Figure 3-50).

Plagiarizing Text

When you gather information for your table or for other aspects of your presentation, be certain to acknowledge the source of this information on the slide or verbally when you give your presentation. The plagiarism rules that you use when writing research papers also apply to your slide shows. Give credit where credit is due. For more information about acknowledging sources, visit the PowerPoint 2000 Project 3 More About page (www.scsite.com/pp2000/more.htm) and click Plagiarism.

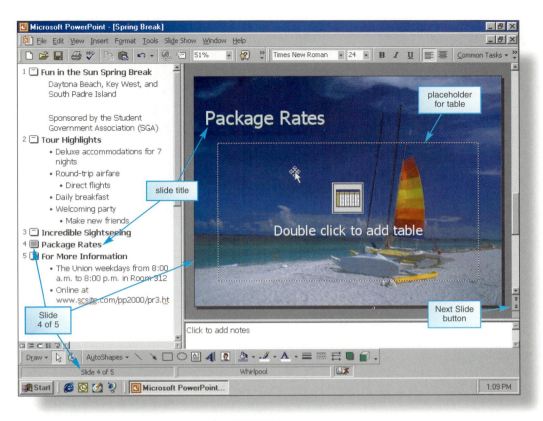

FIGURE 3-50

Now that the AutoLayout is changed to Table and the placeholder for the table is selected, you can insert a table with two columns and four rows. Perform these steps to create the Package Rates table.

Steps: To Create a Table

1 **Double-click anywhere in the placeholder for the table. Point to the Number of rows box up arrow in the Insert Table dialog box.**

The Insert Table dialog box displays. The default settings are two columns and two rows (Figure 3-51).

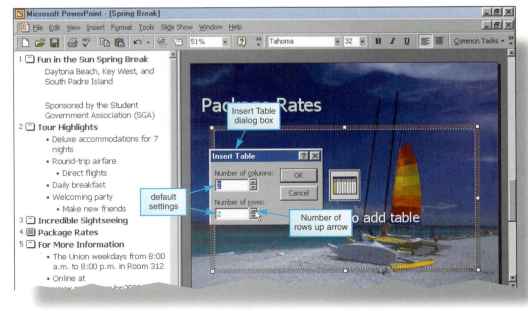

FIGURE 3-51

2 **Click the Number of rows up box arrow twice and then point to the OK button.**

The Number of rows box displays 4 (Figure 3-52).

FIGURE 3-52

3 **Click the OK button.**

PowerPoint displays a table with two columns and four rows (Figure 3-53). The mouse pointer changes to a pencil. The insertion point is in the upper-left cell, which is selected. The Tables and Borders toolbar displays.

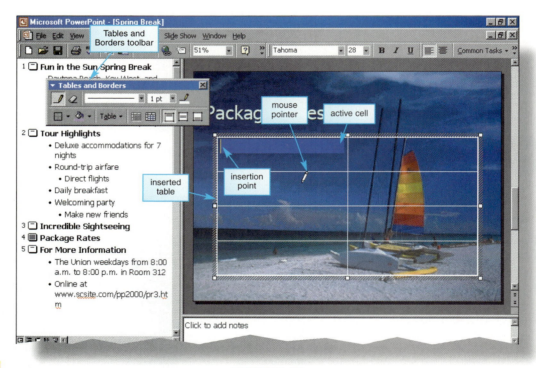

FIGURE 3-53

The Tables and Borders toolbar displays when you insert a table. This toolbar contains buttons and menus that allow you to perform frequent table drawing and formatting functions more quickly than when using the menu bar. Figure 3-54 shows the name of each button on the Tables and Borders toolbar.

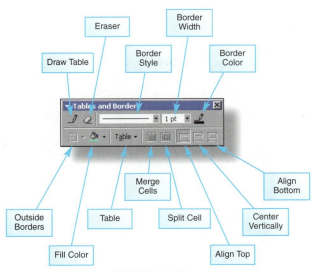

FIGURE 3-54

Entering Data in a Table

The table on Slide 4 has two columns: one for the Spring Break destinations, and one for the package prices. A heading will identify each column. The destinations and prices are summarized in Table 3-1.

Perform the following steps to enter data in the table.

Table 3-1	Destinations and Prices
DESTINATION	**TOTAL COST**
Daytona Beach	$529
Key West	$669
South Padre Island	$549

 To Enter Data in a Table

1 **Type** Destination **and then press the RIGHT ARROW key.**

The first column title, Destination, displays in the top-left cell and the top-right cell is the active cell (Figure 3-55). You also can press the TAB key to advance to the next cell.

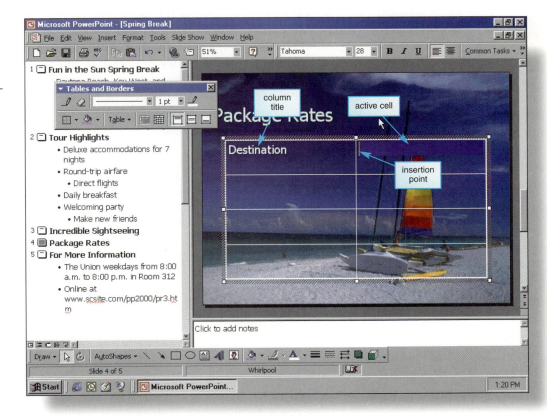

FIGURE 3-55

2 Repeat Step 1 for the remaining column title and for the other table cells by using Table 3-1 as a guide. Enter Total Cost **in row 1, column 2,** Daytona Beach **in row 2, column 1,** $529 **in row 2, column 2,** Key West **in row 3, column 1,** $669 **in row 3, column 2,** South Padre Island **in row 4, column 1, and** $549 **in row 4, column 2.**

The three Spring Break destinations and package rates display (Figure 3-56). All entries are left-aligned and display in 28-point Tahoma font.

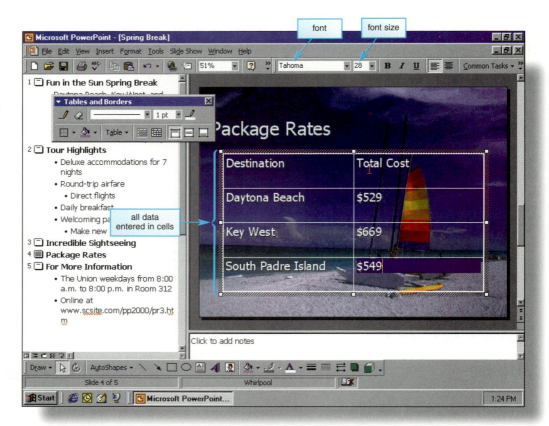

FIGURE 3-56

Table Colors

Graphic artists know that viewers prefer colorful slides. These colors, however, need to be applied to tables and fonts with care. If you are using more than two colors in your table, put the darkest colors at the bottom. When audience members study slides, they will look at the lighter colors at the top, scan naturally to the bottom, and then return their attention to the speaker.

The next step is to format the table. You **format** the table to emphasize certain entries and to make it easier to read and understand. In this project, you will change the column heading alignment and font style and size, add borders, change the border line color, and make the background dark purple. The process required to format the table is explained in the remainder of this section. Although the format procedures will be carried out in a particular manner, you should be aware that you can make these format changes in any order.

Formatting a Table Cell

You format an entry in a cell to emphasize it or to make it stand out from the rest of the table. Perform the following steps to bold and center the column headings and then increase the font size.

Steps: To Format a Table Cell

1 **Click the top-left cell, Destination. Press and hold the SHIFT key and then click the top-right cell, Total Cost. Release the SHIFT key. Click the Font Size box arrow on the Formatting toolbar. Scroll down and then point to 36.**

The two column headings, Destination and Total Cost, are selected and the Font Size list displays (Figure 3-57).

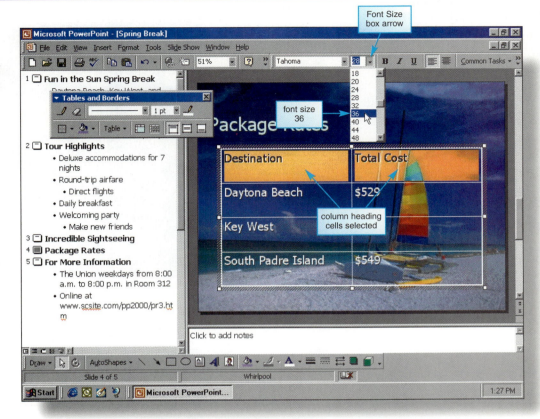

FIGURE 3-57

2 **Click 36. Point to the Bold button on the Formatting toolbar.**

The text in the heading cells displays in 36-point Tahoma font (Figure 3-58).

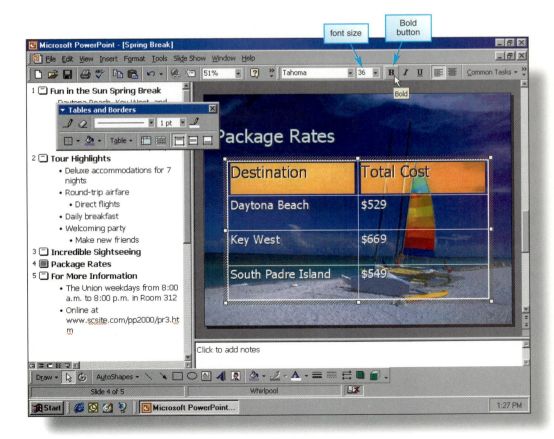

FIGURE 3-58

3   **Click the Bold button and then point to the Center button on the Formatting toolbar.**

The text displays in bold and is left-aligned in the cells (Figure 3-59).

4   **Click the Center button.**

The text is centered in the cells.

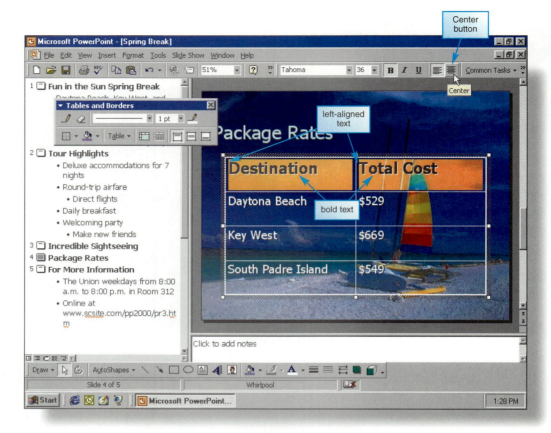

FIGURE 3-59

You can change the font type, size, or style at any time while the table is selected. Some PowerPoint users prefer to change font and cell alignments before they enter any data. Others change the font and alignment while they are building their table or after they have entered all the data.

Formatting a Table

The next step is to format the table by adding borders and a background color. A **border** is the visible line around the edge of an object. The border draws attention to the object by defining its edges. A border has line style and line color attributes. The **line style** determines the line thickness and line appearance of the border. For example, you could choose a thick, solid line for your border. **Line color** determines the color of the line that forms the border. Your table on Slide 4 will have a dashed purple border with a width of three points.

To draw the attention of the audience to the table, add color to the lines of the border. Recall that the design template establishes the attributes of the title master and the slide master. When you click the Border Color button or the Fill Color button arrow on the Tables and Borders or Drawing toolbar, a list displays line color options. A portion of the list includes the eight colors used to create the design template. One of the colors is identified as the line color, and another is identified as the fill color. Both colors are listed as the Automatic option in the color list.

Perform the following steps to format the table on Slide 4 by adding borders, changing the border style, width, and color, and adding a background color.

Line Styles

A border's line style and color affect the attention a viewer gives to a picture or to an object. A thick border draws more attention than a thin border, and warm colors, such as red and yellow, draw more attention than cool colors, such as green or violet.

Steps | **To Format a Table**

1 **Click the Table button on the Tables and Borders toolbar and then point to Select Table.**

The formatting changes will be made to the entire table, so you need to select all the cells and borders (Figure 3-60).

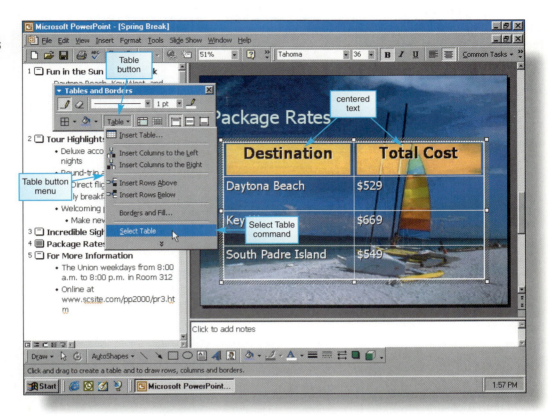

FIGURE 3-60

2 **Click Select Table. Click the Border Style box arrow on the Tables and Borders toolbar and then point to the fifth border style in the list as shown in Figure 3-61.**

PowerPoint provides 10 border styles or a No Border option.

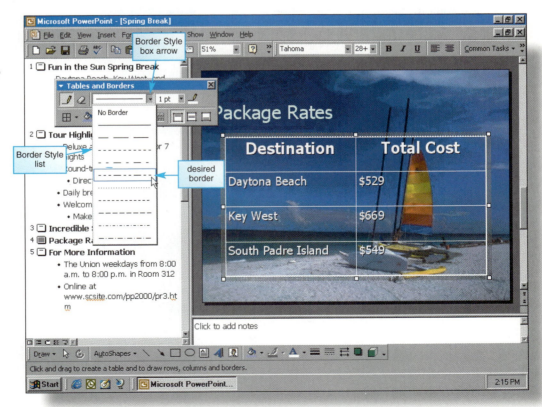

FIGURE 3-61

3 Click the fifth border style. Click the Border Width box arrow on the Tables and Borders toolbar and then point to 3 pt.

The desired border is three-points wide (Figure 3-62). PowerPoint provides nine possible widths in the border list.

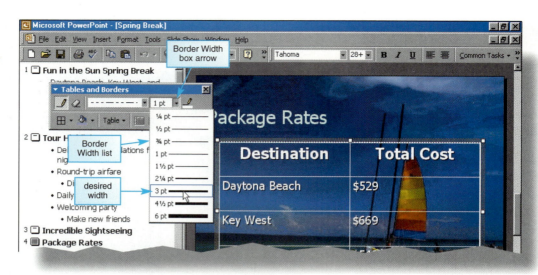

FIGURE 3-62

4 Click 3 pt. Click the Border Color button on the Tables and Borders toolbar and then point to the color purple (color five in the row).

The color purple is the default border color in the Whirlpool design template color scheme (Figure 3-63). The default line color is white.

FIGURE 3-63

5 Click the color purple. Click the Outside Borders button arrow on the Tables and Borders toolbar. Point to the All Borders style in row 1, column 2.

You can choose 12 possible border styles (Figure 3-64). The Outside Borders style is the default border style.

FIGURE 3-64

6 **Click the All Borders style. Click the Fill Color button arrow on the Tables and Borders toolbar. Point to the color dark blue (color one in the row).**

The new purple border style is applied to the table. The default fill color is purple, the same color as the new border (Figure 3-65).

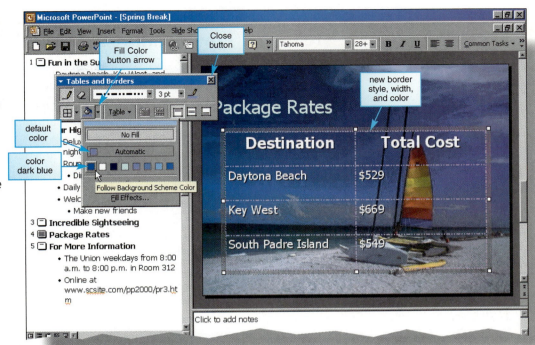

FIGURE 3-65

7 **Click the color dark blue. Click the Close button on the Tables and Borders toolbar title bar.**

The table background is dark blue (Figure 3-66). The Tables and Borders toolbar is not used in the remainder of this project.

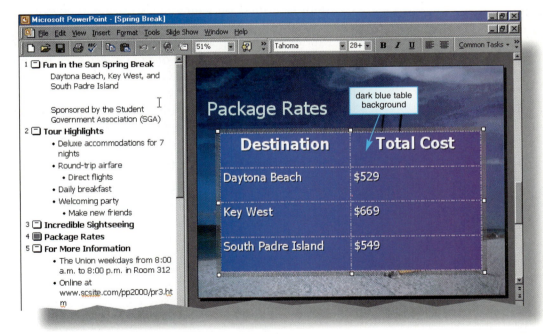

FIGURE 3-66

Slide 4 now is complete. The next section describes how to ungroup clip art and insert pieces of it in your closing slide in the on-screen slide show.

Other Ways

1. On Format menu click Table, click Borders tab, select style, color, and width preferences, click diagram or use buttons to apply borders, click Fill tab, click Fill color arrow, select background color, click OK button

Creating a PowerPoint Clip Art Object

A **clip art picture** is composed of many objects grouped together to form one object. PowerPoint allows you to alter the clip art picture by disassembling it into the objects. **Disassembling** a clip art picture, also called **ungrouping**, separates one object into multiple objects. Once ungrouped, you can manipulate the individual objects as needed to form a new object. When you ungroup a clip art picture in PowerPoint, it becomes a **PowerPoint object** and loses its link to the Microsoft Clip Gallery. Therefore, you cannot double-click the new picture to open the Microsoft Clip Gallery.

Slide 5 contains a modified version of a beach umbrella picture from the Microsoft Clip Gallery. You may want to modify a clip art picture for various reasons. Many times you cannot find a clip art picture that precisely illustrates your topic. For example, you want a picture of a man and woman shaking hands, but the only available clip art picture has two men and a woman shaking hands.

Occasionally you may want to remove or change a portion of a clip art picture or you may want to combine two or more clip art pictures. For example, you can use one clip art picture for the background and another picture as the foreground. Still other times, you may want to combine a clip art picture with another type of object. The types of objects you can combine with a clip art picture depend on the software installed on your computer. The Object type box in the Insert Object dialog box identifies the types of objects you can combine with a clip art picture. In this presentation, the beach umbrella clip art picture contains a beach ball that you do not want to display on your slide, so you will ungroup the clip art picture and remove the ball.

Modifying the clip art picture on Slide 5 requires several steps. First, you display Slide 5 and increase the width of the Object Area placeholder. Then, you insert the beach umbrella clip art picture into the slide. In the next step you scale the clip art picture to increase its size. Finally, you ungroup the clip art picture and delete unwanted pieces. The steps on the following pages explain in detail how to insert, scale, and ungroup a clip art picture.

More About

Objects in Notes

Pictures and objects are not limited to slides; they also can be part of your notes. To add these objects, click Notes Page on the View menu and then add the desired objects. These visuals will print when you specify Notes Pages in the Print dialog box. They will not display in the notes pane, however.

Increasing the Object Area Placeholder Width

For aesthetic reasons, the second bulleted paragraph on Slide 5, Online at www.scsite.com/pp2000/pr3.htm, should display on one line. To change the width of the Object Area placeholder, perform the following steps.

Steps **To Increase the Object Area Placeholder Width**

1 **Click the Next Slide button on the vertical scroll bar to display Slide 5. Click a bulleted paragraph to display the Object Area placeholder and then point to the right-center sizing handle on the right side of the object.**

*The selection rectangle indicates the placeholder is selected (Figure 3-67). Recall that a **selection rectangle** is the box framed by the sizing handles when an image is selected. The mouse pointer displays as a two-headed arrow.*

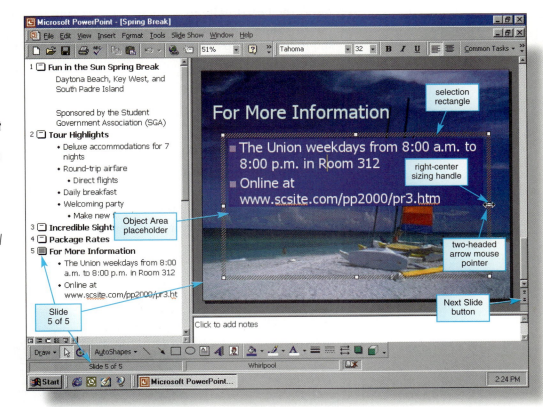

FIGURE 3-67

2 **Drag the sizing handle to the black border along the right edge of the slide.**

The second bulleted paragraph displays on one line (Figure 3-68).

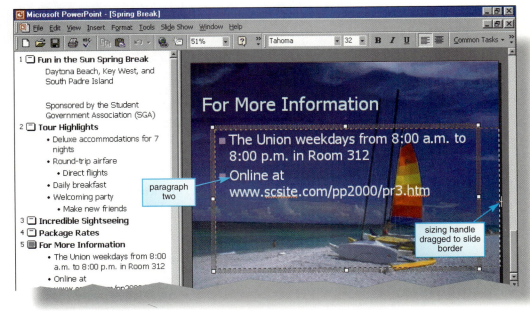

FIGURE 3-68

The area below the bulleted paragraphs is increased to allow more room for the beach umbrella clip art picture. You now can locate and insert the desired picture.

Inserting a Clip Art Picture

The first step in modifying a clip art picture is to insert the picture on a slide. You insert the beach umbrella clip art picture from the Microsoft Clip Gallery. In later steps, you modify the clip art picture.

The following steps explain how to insert the beach umbrella clip art picture on Slide 5 of this presentation.

TO INSERT A CLIP ART PICTURE

1 Click the Insert Clip Art button on the Drawing toolbar.

2 When the Insert ClipArt window displays, type beach umbrella in the Search for clips text box and then press the ENTER key.

3 Click the beach umbrella clip art picture shown in Figure 3-69 and then click the Insert clip button on the shortcut menu.

4 Click the Close button on the Insert ClipArt window title bar.

Slide 5 displays the beach umbrella clip art picture (Figure 3-69). The Picture toolbar displays.

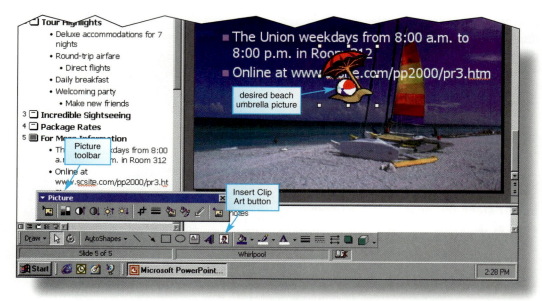

FIGURE 3-69

FIGURE 3-70

The **Picture toolbar** displays when you insert the clip art picture. This toolbar contains buttons and menus that allow you to perform frequent picture formatting functions more quickly than when using the menu bar. Figure 3-70 shows the name of each button on the Picture toolbar.

Scaling and Moving Clip Art

Now that the beach umbrella clip art picture is inserted on Slide 5, you must increase its size by **scaling**. Perform the following steps to scale and move the clip art picture.

TO SCALE AND MOVE A CLIP ART PICTURE

1 If necessary, select the beach umbrella clip art picture and then click the Format Picture button on the Picture toolbar.

2 Click the Size tab in the Format Picture dialog box.

3 Click the Height box up arrow in the Scale area until 185% displays.

4 Click the OK button.

5 Drag the beach umbrella clip art picture to the bottom of the slide near the left corner so the upper-left sizing handle is directly below the bullet for the second paragraph in the Object Area placeholder.

The beach umbrella clip art picture is scaled to 185 percent of its original size and is moved to a desirable location (Figure 3-71).

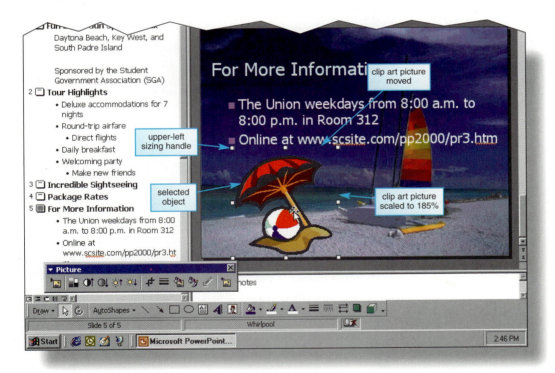

FIGURE 3-71

Ungrouping a Clip Art Picture

The next step is to ungroup the beach umbrella clip art picture on Slide 5. When you **ungroup** a clip art picture, PowerPoint breaks it into its component objects. A clip art picture may be composed of a few individual objects or several complex groups of objects. These groups can be ungrouped repeatedly until they decompose into individual objects.

Perform the steps on the next page to ungroup a clip art picture.

To Ungroup a Clip Art Picture

1 **With the beach umbrella clip art picture selected, right-click the clip art. Point to Grouping on the shortcut menu, and then point to Ungroup on the Grouping submenu (Figure 3-72).**

FIGURE 3-72

2 **Click Ungroup. Click the Yes button in the Microsoft PowerPoint dialog box.**

The clip art picture now displays as many PowerPoint objects and sizing handles display around the ungrouped objects (Figure 3-73). The message in the Microsoft PowerPoint dialog box explains that this clip art picture is an imported picture. Converting it to a Microsoft Office drawing permanently discards any embedded data or linking information it contains.

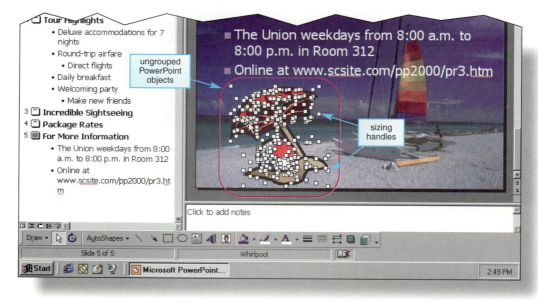

FIGURE 3-73

Other Ways

1. On Draw menu click Ungroup

Because a clip art picture is a collection of complex groups of objects, you may need to ungroup a complex object into less complex objects before being able to modify a specific object. When you ungroup a clip art picture and click the Yes button in the Microsoft PowerPoint dialog box (Step 2 above), PowerPoint converts the clip art picture to a PowerPoint object. The Picture toolbar no longer displays. Recall that a PowerPoint object is an object *not* associated with a supplementary application. As a result, you lose the capability to double-click the clip art picture to open the Microsoft Clip Gallery.

To replace a PowerPoint object with a clip art picture, click the Insert Clip Art button on the Drawing toolbar or click Insert on the menu bar. Click Object and then click Microsoft Clip Gallery. If for some reason you decide not to ungroup the clip art picture, click the No button in the Microsoft PowerPoint dialog box. Clicking the No button terminates the Ungroup command, and the clip art picture displays on the slide as a clip art picture.

Recall that a clip art picture is an object imported from the Microsoft Clip Gallery. Disassembling imported, embedded, or linked objects eliminates the embedding data or linking information the object contains that ties it back to its original source. Use caution when objects are not completely regrouped. Dragging or scaling affects only the selected object, not the entire collection of objects. To **regroup** the individual objects, select all the objects, click the Draw button on the Drawing toolbar, and then click Group.

Deselecting Clip Art Objects

All of the ungrouped objects in Figure 3-73 are selected. Before you can manipulate an individual object, you must **deselect** all selected objects to remove the selection rectangles, and then you must select the object you want to manipulate. For example, in this slide you will remove the beach ball under the umbrella. The following step explains how to deselect objects.

TO DESELECT A CLIP ART OBJECT

 Click outside the clip art object area.

Slide 5 displays without selection rectangles around the objects.

The beach umbrella clip art picture now is ungrouped into many objects. The next section explains how to delete the unwanted beach ball.

Deleting a PowerPoint Object

Now that the beach umbrella picture is ungrouped, you can delete the beach ball object. Perform the steps on the next page to delete the beach ball object.

Printing Speaker Notes

As you add visual elements to your presentations, think about how you are going to discuss these objects in an oral presentation. When you get an idea, type it in the notes pane. Then you can print these speaker notes in a variety of formats. For example, you can add headers and footers that contain page numbers and the current date and time. You specify this information in the speaker notes master, which prints the slide in the upper half of the sheet and your notes in the notes body area in the lower half.

To Delete a PowerPoint Object

1 **Click near the shoreline on the right side of the umbrella pole as shown in Figure 3-74 and then drag diagonally through the beach ball to the lower-left corner of the brown beach blanket.**

A dotted line square displays around the beach ball as you drag. If you inadvertently select a different area, click the shoreline and retry.

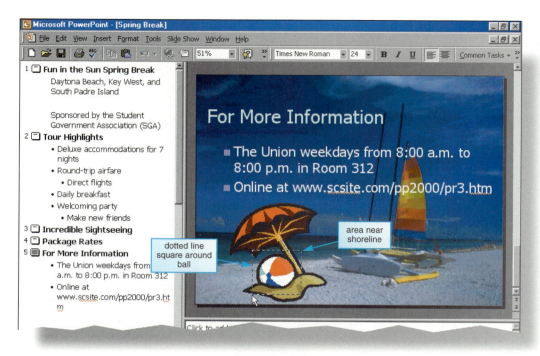

FIGURE 3-74

2 **Release the mouse button. Press the DELETE key.**

The beach ball object is deleted (Figure 3-75). If pieces of the beach ball remain, select each piece and then press the DELETE key.

FIGURE 3-75

1. On Edit menu click Clear

Grouping PowerPoint Objects

All of the ungrouped objects in the beach umbrella picture must be regrouped so they are not accidentally moved or manipulated. Perform the following steps to regroup these objects.

To Group PowerPoint Objects

1 **Click directly below the bullet for the second paragraph in the Object Area placeholder and then drag diagonally to the bottom-right corner of the beach umbrella picture.**

A dotted line rectangle displays around the beach umbrella picture as you drag (Figure 3-76). You want to group the objects within this area.

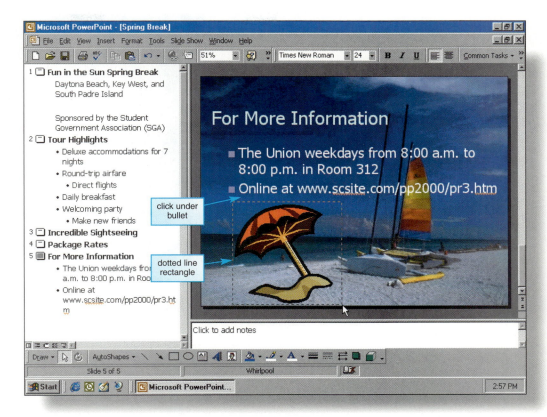

FIGURE 3-76

2 **Release the mouse button. Click the Draw button on the Drawing toolbar and then point to Group.**

Sizing handles display on all the selected components of the beach umbrella picture. You may have to wait a few seconds for the full Draw menu to display (Figure 3-77).

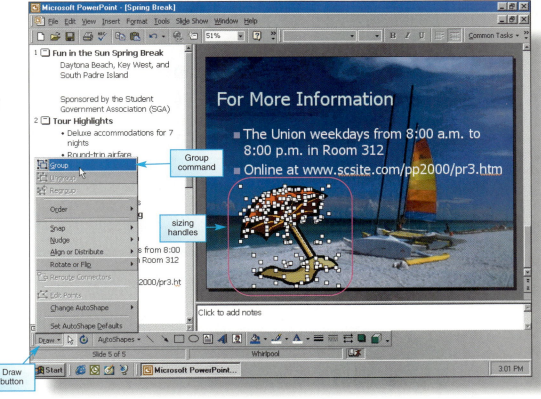

FIGURE 3-77

Click Group on the Draw menu.

The eight sizing handles displaying around the entire beach umbrella picture indicate the object is grouped (Figure 3-78).

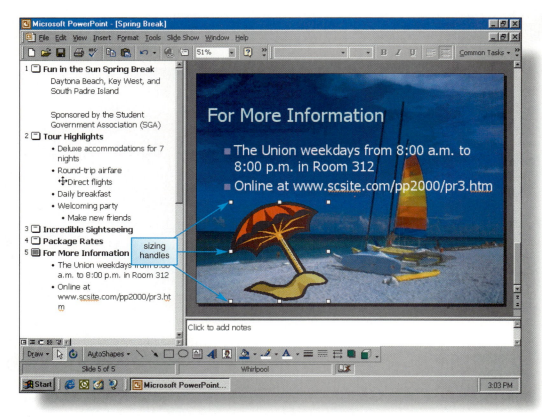

FIGURE 3-78

All the components of the beach umbrella picture now are grouped into one object. Slide 5 now is complete. The next section shows you how to add effects for switching from one slide to the next when you give your presentation.

Adding Slide Transition and Text Preset Animation Effects

The final step in preparing the Spring Break presentation is to add slide transition and text preset animation effects. Perform the following steps to add the slide transition and text preset animation effects.

TO ADD SLIDE TRANSITION AND TEXT PRESET ANIMATION EFFECTS

1 Click the Slide Sorter View button in the lower-left of the PowerPoint window.

2 Press and hold down the SHIFT key and then click Slide 2. Release the SHIFT key.

3 Click the Slide Transition Effects box arrow. Scroll down and then click Strips Right-Down.

4 Click the Preset Animation box arrow. Scroll down and then click Zoom In From Screen Center.

The presentation displays in Slide Sorter View (Figure 3-79). Slide transition effects and preset animation effects are applied to Slides 2, 3, 4, and 5.

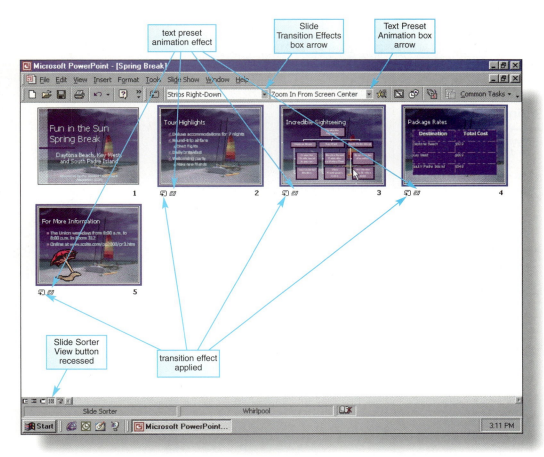

FIGURE 3-79

Printing Slides as Handouts

Perform the following steps to print the presentation slides as handouts, six slides per page.

TO PRINT SLIDES AS HANDOUTS

1 Ready the printer according to the printer manufacturer's instructions.

2 Click File on the menu bar and then click Print on the File menu.

3 Click the Print what box arrow and then click Handouts in the list.

4 Click Pure black and white and then click the OK button.

The handout prints as shown in Figure 3-80 on the next page. The background beach picture does not print.

Other Ways

1. In Slide View or Slide Sorter View, select slide to add transitions, right-click selected slide, click Slide Transition on shortcut menu, click Effect box arrow, choose desired transition, click Apply button

2. Select slide to add transitions, on Slide Show menu click Slide Transition, click Effect box arrow, choose desired transition, click Apply button

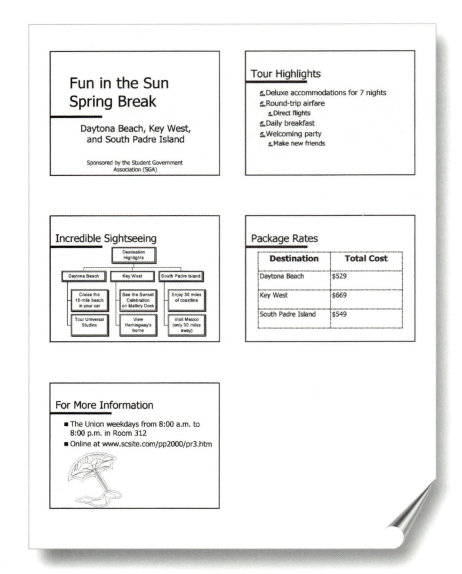

FIGURE 3-80

The Spring Break presentation now is complete. The final step is to make your slide show available to others on an intranet. Ask your instructor how you can publish your presentation.

C A S E   P E R S P E C T I V E   S U M M A R Y

The Spring Break slide show should help generate interest in the three trips. The students viewing your presentation on your college's intranet and receiving a handout available in the Student Union will obtain a good overview of the highlights of each trip, the sightseeing excursions, and the rates. The Student Government Association should expect a complete sellout as students plan for the upcoming Spring Break.

Project Summary

Project 3 introduced you to several methods of enhancing a presentation with embedded visuals. You began the project by creating the presentation from an outline that was created in Word. Then, you learned how to create a special slide background using a picture. When you created Slide 2, you learned how to insert graphical bullets. Slide 3 introduced you to creating and embedding an organization chart using the supplementary application Microsoft Organization Chart. You then learned how to create and format a table on Slide 4. Next, you learned how to ungroup objects on Slide 5. Finally, you learned how to print your presentation slides as handouts.

What You Should Know

Having completed this project, you now should be able to perform the following tasks:

▶ Add Graphical Bullets *(PP 3.19)*

▶ Add Multiple Subordinate Boxes *(PP 3.27)*

▶ Add Names to Subordinate Boxes *(PP 3.28)*

▶ Add Shadow Effects to Boxes in an Organization Chart *(PP 3.36)*

▶ Add Slide Transition and Text Preset Animation Effects *(PP 3.58)*

▶ Change the Border Style *(PP 3.37)*

▶ Change Design Templates *(PP 3.9)*

▶ Change the Font *(PP 3.10)*

▶ Change the Font Size *(PP 3.14)*

▶ Change the Organization Chart Style *(PP 3.29)*

▶ Change the Slide Layout to Title Slide *(PP 3.12)*

▶ Copy a Branch of an Organization Chart *(PP 3.31)*

▶ Create a Table *(PP 3.41)*

▶ Create the Title for the Root Manager Box *(PP 3.25)*

▶ Delete a PowerPoint Object *(PP 3.56)*

▶ Deselect a Clip Art Object *(PP 3.55)*

▶ Display the Next Slide and Change the Slide Layout *(PP 3.23, 3.40)*

▶ Edit Text in an Organization Chart *(PP 3.33)*

▶ Enter Data in a Table *(PP 3.43)*

▶ Format a Table *(PP 3.47)*

▶ Format a Table Cell *(PP 3.45)*

▶ Group PowerPoint Objects *(PP 3.57)*

▶ Increase the Object Area Placeholder Width *(PP 3.51)*

▶ Insert a Picture to Create a Custom Background *(PP 3.16)*

▶ Insert a Clip Art Picture *(PP 3.52)*

▶ Maximize the Microsoft Organization Chart Window *(PP 3.25)*

▶ Move the Organization Chart *(PP 3.39)*

▶ Open Microsoft Organization Chart *(PP 3.24)*

▶ Paste a Branch of an Organization Chart *(PP 3.32)*

▶ Print Slides as Handouts *(PP 3.59)*

▶ Quit Microsoft Organization Chart and Return to the PowerPoint Window *(PP 3.38)*

▶ Save a Presentation *(PP 3.12)*

▶ Scale an Organization Chart Object *(PP 3.39)*

▶ Scale and Move a Clip Art Picture *(PP 3.53)*

▶ Select All Boxes in an Organization Chart *(PP 3.35)*

▶ Start PowerPoint and Open an Outline *(PP 3.7)*

▶ Title the Subordinate Boxes *(PP 3.26)*

▶ Ungroup a Clip Art Picture *(PP 3.54)*

Apply Your Knowledge

Project Reinforcement at www.scsite.com/off2000/reinforce.htm

1 Creating a Presentation from an Outline, Inserting a Clip Art Picture, Changing Bullets, and Changing the Slide Background

Instructions: Start PowerPoint. Open the outline, Hot Outline, from the Data Disk. See the inside back cover of this book for instructions for downloading the Data Disk or see your instructor for information on accessing the files required in this book. Perform the following tasks.

1. Apply the Blue Diagonal design template.
2. Change the AutoLayout for Slide 1 to Title Slide (Figure 3-81a).
3. Create the custom background shown in Figure 3-81a using the Sunset picture file on the Data Disk.
4. On Slide 2, insert the sleeping clip art picture shown in Figure 3-81b. Scale the height of the clip art picture to 110%.
5. Change the bullets to the sun located in the Almanac MT character fonts.
6. Apply the Blinds Vertical slide transition effect. Then apply the Split Vertical In text preset animation effect.
7. Save the presentation with the file name, Heat.
8. Print the presentation.
9. Quit PowerPoint.

FIGURE 3-81a

Apply Your Knowledge

Project Reinforcement at www.scsite.com/off2000/reinforce.htm

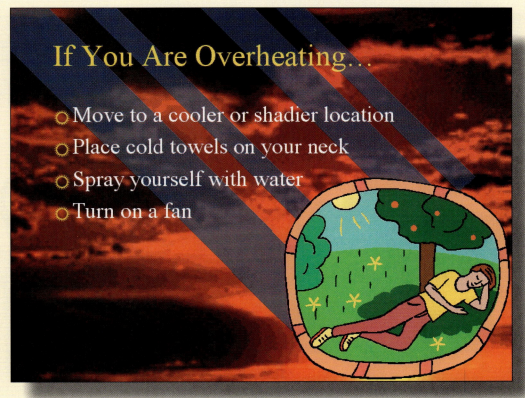

FIGURE 3-81b

In the Lab

1 Creating a Custom Slide

Problem: Communicating effectively among employees is a major problem at your job. Part of the problem stems from reluctance to give and receive instructions. Senior management realizes the problem and wants to schedule a workshop to improve communication skills. Your manager has asked you to prepare a slide show to publicize the goals of the workshop. You want a title slide showing people working together on the job and expressing communication difficulties. You import a picture from the Microsoft Clip Gallery and then modify it to create the slide shown in Figure 3-82 on the next page.

Instructions: Start PowerPoint and perform the following tasks with a computer.

1. Choose the Title Only AutoLayout and then apply the Post Modern design template.
2. Type Communication Skills Workshop for the slide title. Change the font size to 54. Bold this text.

(continued)

In the Lab

Creating a Custom Slide *(continued)*

3. Insert the clip art picture from the Microsoft Clip Gallery with the description, telephones, people. Scale the picture to 300%.

4. Ungroup the picture. Then delete the purple buildings and the blue background. Delete the men's red ties.

5. Insert the clip art picture with the description, communications technology. Scale the picture to 120%.

6. Ungroup this picture and delete the blue background and

FIGURE 3-82

road so that only the three bubbles with the green question mark, the red exclamation point, and the brown exclamation point and plus sign remain. Group each bubble and move them to the locations shown in Figure 3-82.

7. Change the fill effect of the slide background stationery by using the Texture sheet in the Fill Effects dialog box.

8. Group all the PowerPoint objects.

9. Save the presentation with the file name, Workshop.

10. Print the slide using the Pure black and white option.

11. Quit PowerPoint.

2 Embedding an Organization Chart and Inserting a Picture

Problem: Community leaders have announced plans to remodel and upgrade the park district's fitness center. The changes include additional aerobics classes, nutritional counseling, and personal training. The marketing director has asked you to help her publicize the facility, and you want to create a slide show to display at the local mall. Part of your presentation will be the slide shown in Figure 3-83a highlighting the upgrades, and another will be the organization chart shown in Figure 3-83b on page PP 3.66 depicting the individuals involved in organizing the class schedule, the nutrition center, and the personal training workouts.

In the Lab

Instructions: Start PowerPoint and perform the following tasks with a computer.

1. Apply the Text & Clip Art AutoLayout and the LaVerne design template.
2. Type `Coming Soon` in the Title Area placeholder and then press the ENTER key. Type `Your New Fitness Center` on the second line.
3. Type the bulleted text shown in Figure 3-83a.

FIGURE 3-83a

4. Change the bullets to the heart character that is part of the Monotype Sorts character fonts. Change the heart color to pink.
5. Insert the clip art picture shown in Figure 3-83a with the description, fitness. Add a pink border to the picture using the 4½ pt thin-thick line.
6. Insert a new slide and apply the Organization Chart AutoLayout.
7. Type `Meet Your Fitness Center Staff` in the Title Area placeholder. Create the organization chart shown in Figure 3-83b on the next page. Type your name in the Director box.
8. Change the box color for the director to lime green (row 2, column 2). Change the box color for the assistant editor to red (row 1, column 9). Change the box color for the three specialty classes staff members to light green (row 1, column 4). Change the box color for the two nutrition services staff members to yellow (row 2, column 1). Do not change the box color for the four personal training staff members.

(continued)

In the Lab

Embedding an Organization Chart and Inserting a Picture *(continued)*

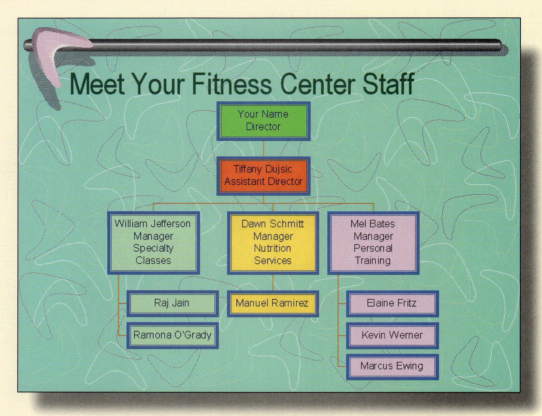

FIGURE 3-83b

9. Add borders to all boxes. Use the border style in the last row, column 2 Border Style submenu. Change the border color for all boxes to royal blue (row 1, column 5).
10. Change the line color to red (row 1, column 9).
11. Quit Microsoft Organization Chart and return to Slide 2. Scale the organization chart to 125%. Then drag the organization chart onto the center of the blank area under the Title Area placeholder.
12. Save the presentation with the file name, Fitness Center.
13. Print handouts (2 slides per page). Quit PowerPoint.

3 Opening an Existing Outline, Adding Graphical Bullets, and Creating a New Clip Art Picture

Problem: Your company softball team is getting organized for the new season, and you have been asked to help with the recruiting efforts. You decide to develop a presentation that includes information about the team. Create the opening slide of the presentation starting with the Softball Outline on your Data Disk. Then add and modify the clip art picture and bullets shown in Figure 3-84.

Instructions: Start PowerPoint and perform the following tasks with a computer.

In the Lab

1. Open the Softball Outline on your Data Disk.
2. Apply the Citrus design template. Change the Auto-Layout to Bulleted List.
3. Select the title text and change the font size to 60.
4. Move the bulleted text to the lower-right corner. Change the bullets to the arrows shown in Figure 3-84 that are part of the Wingdings 3 character fonts. Add a lime green border around the bulleted text using a 1 pt line.

FIGURE 3-84

5. Insert the clip art picture with the description, softball. Enlarge the clip art to 275% and move it to the lower-left corner of the slide.
6. Ungroup the clip art picture. Delete the base. Then, change the color of the shirt to light gray and the shorts to black, which are your team colors. Change the color of the background shape to orange. Enlarge the ball to 120%.
7. Group all the individual objects in the clip art picture into one object.
8. Place the date, your name, and the slide number in the slide footer.
9. Save the presentation with the file name, Play Ball. Print the presentation and then quit PowerPoint.

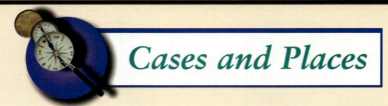

Cases and Places

The difficulty of these case studies varies:
▶ are the least difficult; ▶▶ are more difficult; and ▶▶▶ are the most difficult.

1 ▶ Hiking has become a popular activity for people of all ages. Especially appealing are forest preserves and parks designed for family treks. Families comprise one of the fastest growing hiking groups as parents introduce their children to the wonders of nature. When parents pack the supplies for the hike, they should include water, sunscreen with an SPF of 45 or higher, insect repellent, and the children's favorite wholesome foods, such as fruit and pretzels. They should dress in layers so they can add or peel off layers as conditions change. Hikers also should wear long pants and a long sleeve shirt to protect against ticks and cuts. A hat is a must, as it protects eyes against glare and keeps the body warm in winter. Families can have more fun hiking by singing and doing educational activities such as bird watching, identifying trees and flowers, and looking for animal tracks. It is important to stop frequently and rest. Prepare a presentation that promotes family hiking by describing how to pack, what to wear, and how to enjoy the outing. Create a custom background. Include a title slide and a clip art picture.

2 ▶▶ Car theft is on the rise, so your campus police chief wants to give students some simple tips they can use to protect their cars from thieves. He gives some anti-theft basics, such as installing a good security device and putting stickers on the windows announcing the alarm system. The alarm should sound when the car is tilted or moved. This system will decrease insurance premiums. Another device is a reinforced collar that fits over the steering column casing and has to be removed to start the vehicle. He also gives some parking tips, such as parking in a well-lit area after dark, turning the wheels sharply to the right or left so the car is pointed inward when parking against a curb, and having a panic switch on the remote door opener that triggers the siren and flashes the parking lights to startle potential thieves and attackers. Another technique is etching the vehicle identification number (VIN) on the parts thieves sell to body shops. These parts are windows, doors, fenders, bumpers, and fancy wheels. Also, install a toggle switch on the wire running from the ignition to the starter to deter thieves from starting the car. The switch disables the vehicle's starter circuit. Use the concepts and techniques introduced in this project to create a presentation. Use a title slide and apply slide transition and text preset animation effects. Create handouts to distribute to students.

3 ▶▶▶ Producing your campus' student newspaper is an extraordinary task. Reporters, copy editors, advertising salespeople, and artists must coordinate their activities to generate stories and meet deadlines. Visit the student newspaper office at your school and obtain the names and titles of the editors and their staffs. Then create a presentation that includes a hierarchy chart explaining this chain of command. Format the hierarchy chart to highlight the newspaper's sections, such as news, features, and sports. Include a slide showing the staff's accomplishments, such as awards received in competitions or goals achieved, a short biography of the editor in chief, and appropriate clip art pictures.

Microsoft **PowerPoint 2000**

Microsoft PowerPoint 2000

P R O J E C T

4

Creating a Presentation Containing Interactive OLE Documents

O B J E C T I V E S

You will have mastered the material in this project when you can:

- Open an existing presentation and save it with a new file name
- Create a WordArt object
- Add a special text effect
- Scale a WordArt object
- Create an interactive document
- Create a slide using action buttons and hyperlinks
- Use guides to position and size an object
- Modify an organization chart
- Edit a PowerPoint table
- Hide a slide
- Change the order of slides
- Automatically add a summary slide
- Run a slide show to display a hidden slide and activate an interactive document

Visual Exhilaration

Brings Audiences Back for More

I n the fast-paced world of instant communications and live video-conferencing; multimedia and virtual reality; and the dawn of the twenty-first century, people around the world are networked together for the purposes of exchanging information, providing goods, services and entertainment, reporting global news, and searching the vast resources of the Internet.

Baby boomers and the X Generation both have grown up with technological advances beyond the wildest dreams of former generations. Consider moviegoers of 50 and 60 years ago who viewed reel-to-reel films shot on studio lots projected onto the silver screen in movie palaces such as the Mann's Chinese Theater in Hollywood.

Today's theatergoers sit in stadium seating in mega-theaters that contain custom-designed sound systems and the latest IMAX® theater technology. Incredibly realistic three-dimensional images are projected onto giant screens up to eight-stories high with such realism that you can almost reach out to touch them. Today's audiences are highly educated, informed, and demanding.

Whether the purpose is to dispense entertainment or information, in a universe competing for audiences, higher and more exacting standards have created a

high-tech society that demands excitement and stimulation in everything it sees. Presentations are no exception. In exchange for their time and attention, people expect presentations to be entertaining, as well as informative.

Fortunately for those who face the daunting task of presenting a visually stimulating, rewarding experience to exacting viewers, Microsoft has provided its own answer to theater technology. Far simpler to use than most software in its class, PowerPoint supplies another kind of tool, called Object Linking and Embedding, otherwise known as OLE (pronounced olay). OLE gives users the capability of importing and embedding objects from another source, such as an image on the Web, a Clip Gallery picture, or a scanned-in photo. With the literally thousands of images in commercially available clip art libraries, it is possible to include in a slide any subject whatsoever in the forms of

pictures, sounds, and motion clips with very little effort.

The freedom to create a picture to the author's specifications is a decided plus over other static preparation tools. After embedding a graphics object, the object can be manipulated in several ways: changing its size, extracting part of the image, rearranging the individual components of the image, or adding objects from other sources to the original.

The capability of importing from other applications, such as Excel or Word, adds another powerful tool to the presenter's arsenal. Via this route, interactive documents, graphs, charts, tables, worksheets, and special text effects created with WordArt add to the excitement.

High-tech in the new millennium focuses on the development of advanced information technology such as electronic education and e-commerce. With the excitement derived from a satisfied audience, PowerPoint presentations will be showing well into the new century.

Microsoft PowerPoint 2000

Creating a Presentation Containing Interactive OLE Documents

P R O J E C T

4

C A S E   P E R S P E C T I V E

The PowerPoint presentation for the Fun in the Sun Spring Break trip you created in Project 3 was a great success. Marla Pervan, the Student Government Association (SGA) president, is pleased that your impressive marketing presentation on the three beach destinations gave valuable information and helped recruit students. All three trips were booked solid, and the Student Government Association made a $5,000 profit.

Many students have been discussing cruises as a Spring Break option for next year. Marla thought the initial PowerPoint presentation could be altered to contain marketing information for two cruises. She asked if you would help change the original Spring Break presentation and add information about cruises to the Eastern and Western Caribbean islands. You agree to update the original presentation with the new information. You also create and add a heading using WordArt, replace one slide with another that contains interactive documents, and add the capability of hiding a slide if time limitations occur.

Introduction

Every presentation is created for a specific audience. Occasionally an existing presentation can be modified to fit the needs of a new audience. For example, another audience may have a different knowledge base or have specific interests. Sometimes, when running a slide show, you want to open another application to show more detailed information about a particular topic. For example, when presenting cruise information, you may want to show the cost of the cruise during the slide show without leaving PowerPoint. PowerPoint allows you to do so using interactive documents. An **interactive document** is a file created in another application, such as Microsoft Word, and then opened during the running of a slide show. Other times you may wish to refrain from showing one or more slides because you are short on time or the slides are not applicable to a particular audience.

PowerPoint has the capability of hiding slides. As the presenter, you decide whether to display them. Occasionally, you want to add a more graphical heading to call attention to the slide show topic. Project 4 customizes the Spring Break presentation created in Project 3 (see Figures 3-1a through 3-1e on page PP 3.5) and creates the slide show shown in Figures 4-1a through 4-1h.

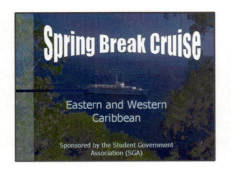

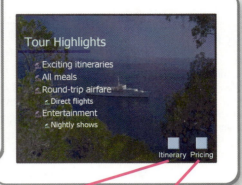

(a) Slide 1

(b) Slide 2

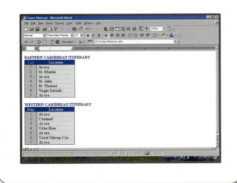

(c) Slide 3

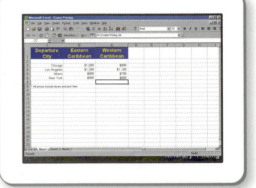

(d) Slide 4

(e) Slide 5

(f) Slide 6

(g) Slide 7

(h) Slide 8

FIGURE 4-1

Project Four — Customizing an Existing Presentation

As the first step in customizing the Spring Break presentation created in Project 3, open the Spring Break file. To ensure that the original presentation remains intact, you must save it using a new file name, Spring Break Cruise. Later in this project, you will modify the new presentation's slides by changing the slide background, replacing bulleted text, changing the chart and table, and adding one new slide. The following steps illustrate these procedures.

Opening a Presentation and Saving It with a New File Name

To begin, open the Spring Break presentation saved in Project 3 and save it with the file name, Spring Break Cruise. This procedure should be done immediately to prevent inadvertently saving the presentation with the original file name. Perform the following steps to open an existing presentation and save it with a new file name. If you did not complete Project 3, see your instructor for a copy of the presentation. To reset your toolbars and menus so they display exactly as shown in this book, follow the steps in Appendix C.

TO OPEN A PRESENTATION AND SAVE IT WITH A NEW FILE NAME

1 Insert your Data Disk into drive A. Click the Start button on the taskbar and then click Open Office Document.

2 Click the Look in box arrow and then click 3½ Floppy (A:).

3 Double-click Spring Break.

4 Click File on the menu bar and then click Save As. Type Spring Break Cruise in the File name text box.

5 Click the Save button in the Save As dialog box.

The presentation is saved on the floppy disk in drive A with the file name, Spring Break Cruise (Figure 4-2).

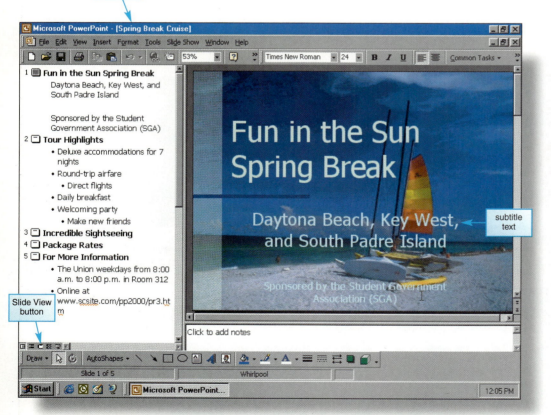

new file name

subtitle text

Slide View button

FIGURE 4-2

Editing the Title Slide

Because the Spring Break location options are changing, you must change the subtitle text in the Object Area placeholder on the title slide. Text that displays on a slide can be edited in the slide or outline panes. Perform the following steps to display the title slide in slide view and then revise the text.

TO CHANGE TEXT

1 Click the Slide View button located at the lower left of the PowerPoint window.

2 Triple-click the text in the Object Area placeholder, Daytona Beach, Key West, and South Padre Island, to select it.

3 Type Eastern and Western Caribbean in place of the highlighted text.

4 Click anywhere on the slide other than the Title Area or Object Area placeholders.

Slide 1 displays the updated Object Area text (Figure 4-3).

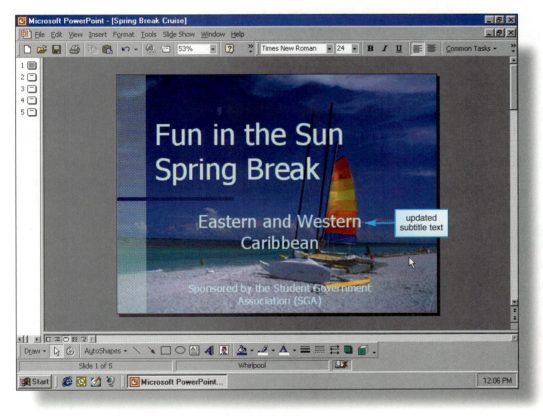

FIGURE 4-3

Changing the Background

The Student Government Association's Spring Break organizing team requests you change the background picture used in Project 3 to something more appropriate for a cruise. You examine various pictures and find one with a ship on the ocean. Perform the steps on the next page to insert this picture and change the slide background.

TO CHANGE THE BACKGROUND

1 Click View on the menu bar, point to Master, and then click Slide Master on the Master submenu.

2 Right-click Slide 1 anywhere except the slide master objects. Click Background on the shortcut menu.

3 Click the Background fill area box arrow. Click Fill Effects in the list.

4 Click the Select Picture button on the Picture tab in the Fill Effects dialog box. Click the Look in box arrow and then click 3½ Floppy (A:).

5 Double-click Ship in the list.

6 Click the OK button in the Fill Effects dialog box and then click the Apply to All button.

7 Click the Slide View button located at the lower left of the PowerPoint window.

FIGURE 4-4

Slide 1 displays the new Ship background picture in slide view (Figure 4-4).

The Spring Break Cruise presentation maintains the same color scheme as the original Spring Break presentation because you are keeping the same design template, Whirlpool. A **color scheme** is a set of eight balanced colors you can apply to all slides, an individual slide, notes pages, or audience handouts. A color scheme consists of colors for a background, text and lines, shadows, title text, fills, accent, accent and hyperlink, and accent and followed hyperlink. Table 4-1 explains the components of a color scheme.

Table 4-1	Color Scheme Components
COMPONENT	**DESCRIPTION**
Background color	The background color is the fundamental color of a PowerPoint slide. For example, if your background color is white, you can place any other color on top of it, but the fundamental color remains white. The white background shows everywhere you do not add color or other objects. The background color on a slide works the same way.
Text and lines color	The text and lines color contrasts with the background color of the slide. Together with the background color, the text and lines color sets the tone for a presentation. For example, a gray background with a black text and lines color sets a dramatic tone. In contrast, a red background with a yellow text and lines color sets a vibrant tone.
Title text color	The title text color contrasts with the background color in a manner similar to the text and lines color. Title text displays in the Title Area placeholder on a slide.
Shadow color	The shadow color is applied when you color an object. This color usually is a darker shade of the background color.
Fill color	The fill color contrasts with both the background color and the text and lines color. The fill color is used for graphs and charts.
Accent colors	Accent colors are designed as colors for secondary features on a slide. Additionally, accent colors are used as colors on graphs.

Creating a WordArt Object

The background picture is changed to differentiate the Spring Break Cruise presentation from the Spring Break presentation created in Project 3. Another way to differentiate the two presentations is by altering the style of the heading. WordArt is used to create the graphical heading that displays on the title slide shown in Figure 4-1a on page PP 4.5.

Creating the Spring Break Cruise heading requires several steps. First, you must delete the heading currently located on the title slide. Next, you use the presentation name to create a WordArt object. Finally, you position and size the heading on the Spring Break Cruise title slide. The next several sections explain how to create the Spring Break Cruise heading object using WordArt.

Deleting the Slide Text

A slide heading is a standard object on a title slide. In this presentation, the slide heading will be replaced with an object created with WordArt. The Florida and Texas destinations will be changed to promote the Eastern and Western Caribbean islands. The following steps show how to delete the title text.

TO DELETE THE SLIDE TEXT

1 Triple-click the title text, Fun in the Sun Spring Break.

2 Double-click the move handle on the Standard toolbar.

3 Click the Cut button on the Standard toolbar.

The title text is deleted (Figure 4-5).

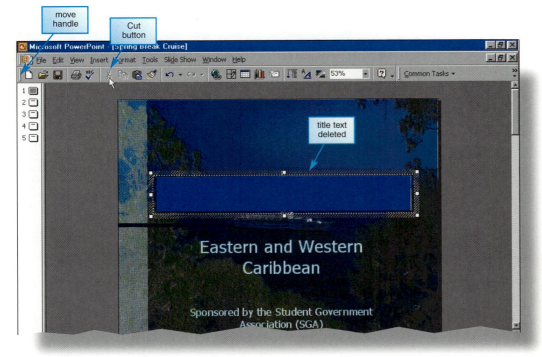

FIGURE 4-5

More About

WordArt Content

Text used in a different application can be copied to your PowerPoint slide and used in a WordArt object. Just select that text, copy it by pressing the CTRL+C keys, and then paste it inside PowerPoint's Edit WordArt Text dialog box by pressing the CTRL+V keys.

Other Ways

1. Highlight title text, on Edit menu click Cut, highlight first subtitle text paragraph, type new text

2. Highlight title text, press CTRL+X, highlight first subtitle text paragraph, type new text

Displaying the Rulers

To help you align objects, PowerPoint provides two **rulers**: a horizontal ruler and a vertical ruler. The **horizontal ruler** displays at the top of the slide window. The **vertical ruler** displays at the left side of the slide window. When the zoom percentage is less than 37 percent, **tick marks** display in one-half-inch segments. When the zoom percentage is 37 percent or greater, tick marks display in one-eighth-inch segments. Your percentages may vary based on your computer system. When you move the mouse pointer, a **pointer indicator** traces the position of the mouse pointer and displays its exact location on both rulers. Perform the following steps to display the horizontal and vertical rulers.

 To Display the Rulers

1 **Right-click anywhere on Slide 1 other than the Title Area and Object Area placeholders, and then point to Ruler on the shortcut menu.**

The shortcut menu displays (Figure 4-6).

 Click Ruler.

Rulers display above and to the left of Slide 1.

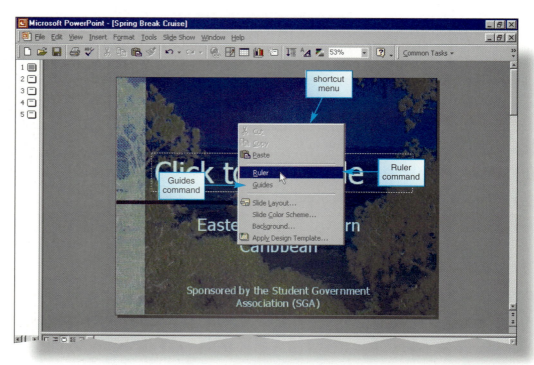

FIGURE 4-6

1. On View menu click Ruler
2. Press ALT+V, press R

When the **Ruler command** is active, a check mark displays in front of the Ruler command on both the shortcut menu and the View menu. When you want to prohibit the rulers from displaying in the PowerPoint window, you **hide the rulers**. To hide the rulers, right-click anywhere in the PowerPoint window except on a placeholder, and then click Ruler.

Displaying the Guides

PowerPoint guides are used to align objects. The **guides** are two straight dotted lines, one horizontal and one vertical. When an object is close to a guide, its corner or its center (whichever is closer) *snaps*, or attaches itself, to the guide. You can move the guides to meet your alignment requirements. Because you are preparing the slide window to create the presentation heading, perform this step to display the guides.

Steps: To Display the Guides

1 **Right-click anywhere on Slide 1 except in the Title Area or Object Area placeholders, and then click Guides on the shortcut menu.**

The horizontal and vertical guides intersect in the middle of the slide window and align with the 0-inch tick marks on the horizontal and vertical rulers (Figure 4-7).

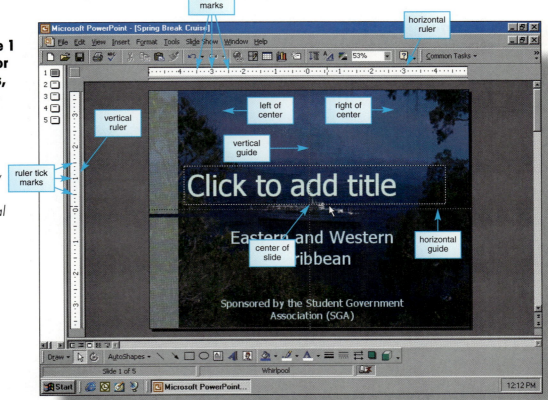

FIGURE 4-7

On the shortcut menu displayed in Step 1, a check mark displays in front of the Ruler command because you activated it in the previous section. Recall that a check mark displays when a command is active, or turned on. In the same manner, when the Guides command is active, a check mark displays in front of the Guides command on both the shortcut menu and the View menu.

Positioning the Guides

The guides can be used to position the WordArt heading. You use the vertical and horizontal guides to help position the heading on the title slide. The center of a slide is 0.00 on both the vertical and the horizontal guides. Position a guide by dragging it to a new location. When you point to a guide and then press and hold the mouse button, PowerPoint displays a box containing the exact position of the guide on the slide in inches. An arrow displays under the guide position to indicate the vertical guide is either left or right of center. An arrow displays to the right of the guide position to indicate the horizontal guide is either above or below center. Perform the steps on the next page to position the guides.

Other Ways

1. On View menu click Guides
2. Press ALT+V, press G

More About 2000

Displaying Guides

At times you may want to display multiple vertical and horizontal guides on your slide. To display an additional guide, press and hold the CTRL key and then drag one of the guides. When the new guide displays, drag it to the position where you want to place an object.

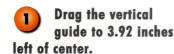 **To Position the Guides**

1 **Drag the vertical guide to 3.92 inches left of center.**

The pointer indicator displays 3.92 inches left of center (Figure 4-8).

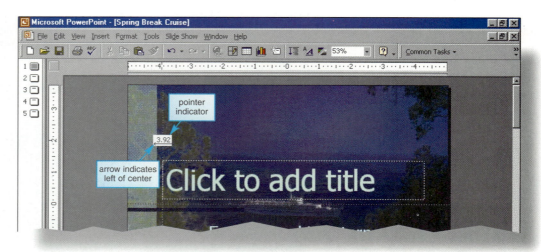

FIGURE 4-8

2 **Drag the horizontal guide to 0.83 inches above center.**

The pointer indicator displays 0.83 inches above center (Figure 4-9).

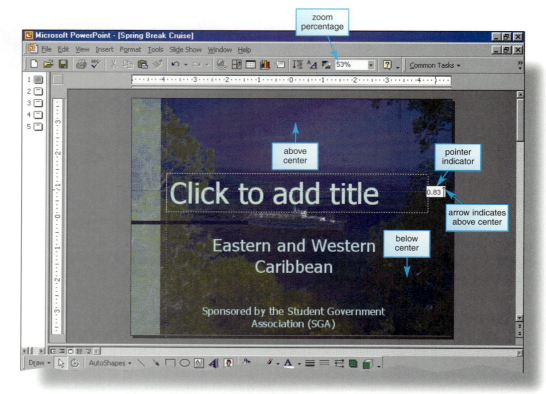

FIGURE 4-9

When you no longer want the guides to display on the screen or want to control the exact placement of objects, you can **hide the guides**. To hide the guides, right-click anywhere in the PowerPoint window except on a placeholder, and then click Guides.

Increasing the Zoom Percentage

Increasing the zoom percentage reduces the editing view of a slide in slide view, but it increases the editing view of individual objects. You increase the zoom percentage to make working with detailed objects or small objects easier. In this project, you increase the zoom percentage to 75 percent because it allows you to work easily with the Title Area object. The following steps summarize how to increase the zoom percentage.

TO INCREASE THE ZOOM PERCENTAGE

1 Click the Zoom box arrow on the Standard toolbar.

2 Click 75% in the list.

The zoom percentage changes to 75% (Figure 4-10). You may drag the vertical or horizontal scroll boxes to display the horizontal and vertical rulers on various areas of the screen.

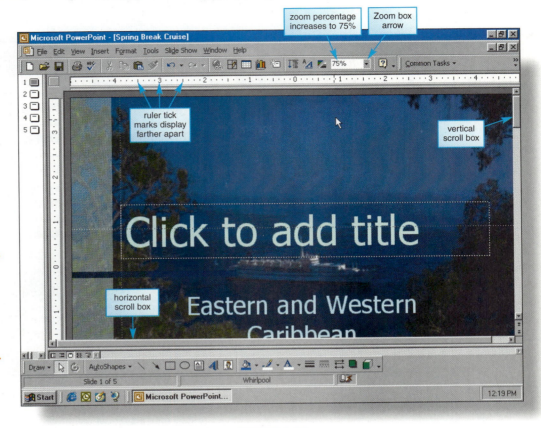

FIGURE 4-10

Adding Special Text Effects

The desired Spring Break Cruise heading contains letters that have been altered with special text effects. Using WordArt, first you will select a letter style for this text. Then you will type the name of the presentation and select a unique shape for their layout, although many other predefined shapes could be used. Buttons on the WordArt toolbar also allow you to rotate, slant, curve, and alter the shape of letters. WordArt also can be used in the other Microsoft Office applications. The next several sections explain how to create the text object shown on the title slide in Figure 4-1a on page PP 4.5.

Selecting a WordArt Style

PowerPoint supplies 30 predefined WordArt styles that vary in shape and color. Perform the steps on the next page to select a style for the Spring Break Cruise text.

To Select a WordArt Style

1 **Click the Insert WordArt button on the Drawing toolbar. When the WordArt Gallery dialog box displays, point to the WordArt style in row 1, column 4.**

The WordArt Gallery dialog box displays (Figure 4-11).

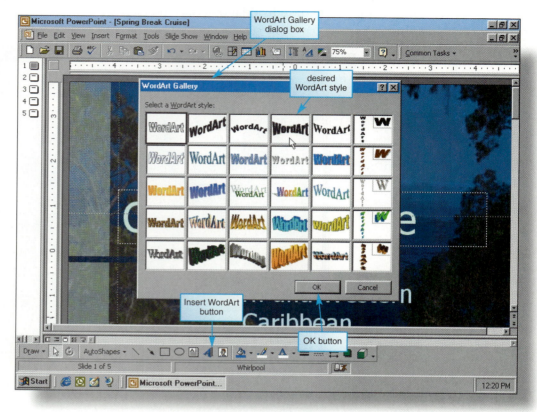

FIGURE 4-11

2 **Click the WordArt style in row 1, column 4. Click the OK button.**

The Edit WordArt Text dialog box displays (Figure 4-12). The default text, Your Text Here, inside the dialog box is highlighted.

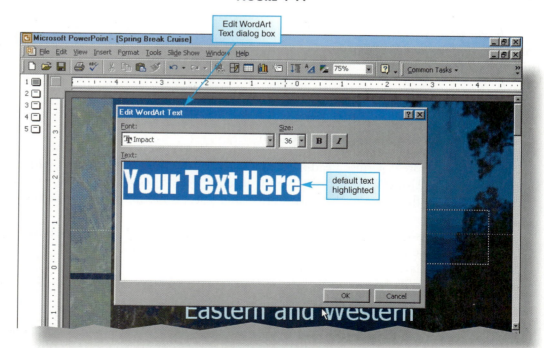

FIGURE 4-12

Entering the WordArt Text

To create a text object, you must enter text in the Edit WordArt Text dialog box. By default, the words, Your Text Here, in the Edit WordArt Text dialog box are highlighted. When you type the text for your title object, it replaces the selected text. When you want to start a new line, press the ENTER key. Perform the following steps to enter the text for the Spring Break Cruise heading.

 To Enter the WordArt Text

1 **If necessary, select the text in the Edit WordArt Text dialog box. Type** Spring Break Cruise **in the box.**

The text displays in the Text text box in the Edit WordArt Text dialog box (Figure 4-13). The default font is Impact, and the font size is 36.

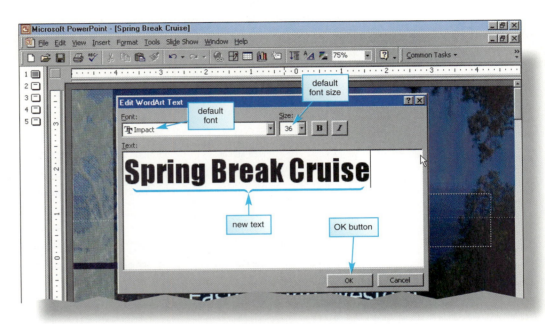

FIGURE 4-13

2 **Click the OK button. If necessary, display the WordArt toolbar by right-clicking a toolbar and then clicking WordArt.**

The Spring Break Cruise text displays (Figure 4-14). The WordArt toolbar displays in the same location and with the same shape as it displayed the last time it was used. You can move the WordArt toolbar by dragging its title bar.

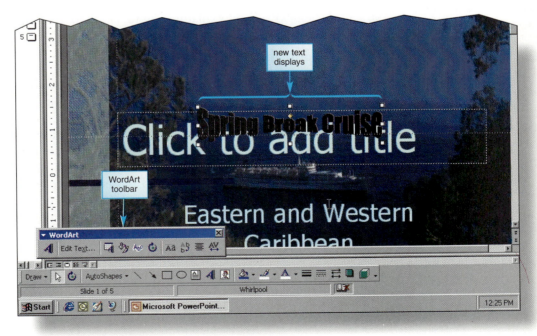

FIGURE 4-14

The WordArt toolbar contains the buttons that allow you to change an object's appearance. For example, you can rotate the letters, change the character spacing and alignment, scale the size, and add different fill and line colors. Table 4-2 explains the purpose of each button on the WordArt toolbar.

Table 4-2	WordArt Toolbar Button Functions	
BUTTON	**BUTTON NAME**	**DESCRIPTION**
	Insert WordArt	Creates a WordArt object
	WordArt Edit Text	Changes the text characters, font, and font size
	WordArt Gallery	Chooses a different WordArt style for the selected WordArt object
	Format WordArt	Formats the line, color, fill and pattern, size, position, and other properties of the selected object
	WordArt Shape	Modifies the text shape
	Free Rotate	Turns an object around its axis
	WordArt Same Letter Heights	Makes all letters the same height, regardless of case
	WordArt Vertical Text	Stacks the text in the selected WordArt object vertically — one letter on top of the other — for reading from top to bottom
	WordArt Alignment	Left-aligns, centers, right-aligns, word-aligns, letter-aligns, or stretch-aligns text
	WordArt Character Spacing	Displays options (Very Tight, Tight, Normal, Loose, Very Loose, Custom, Kern Character Pairs) for adjusting spacing between text

The next section explains how to shape the WordArt text.

Changing the WordArt Height and Width

WordArt objects actually are drawing objects, not text. Consequently, WordArt objects can be modified in various ways, including changing their height, width, line style, fill color, and shadows. Unlike text, however, they neither can display in outline view nor be spell checked. In this project, you will increase the height and width of the WordArt object. The Size tab in the Format WordArt dialog box contains two areas used to change an object's size. The first, the **Size and rotate area**, allows you to enlarge or reduce an object, and turn an object around its axis. The second, the **Scale area**, allows you to change an object's size while maintaining its height-to-width ratio, or **aspect ratio**. If you want to retain the object's original settings, you click the Reset button in the **Original size area**. Perform the following steps to change the height and width of the WordArt object.

More About 2000

Wrapping Text

You can add text to your slide by clicking the Text Box button on the Drawing toolbar and then typing the desired words. If you want the text to wrap to fit the contours of the text box automatically, select the text box, click Format on the menu bar, click Text Box, and then click the Text Box tab. Click Word wrap text in AutoShape.

To Change the WordArt Height and Width

1 **Click the Format WordArt button on the WordArt toolbar. Click the Size tab in the Format WordArt dialog box.**

The Size sheet displays in the Format WordArt dialog box (Figure 4-15).

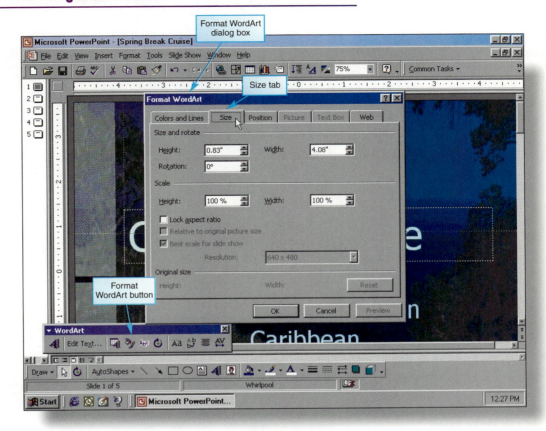

FIGURE 4-15

2 **Triple-click the Height text box in the Size and rotate area. Type 2.4 in the Height text box. Triple-click the Width text box in the Size and rotate area. Type 8.8 in the Width text box. Point to the OK button.**

The Height and Width text boxes display the new entries (Figure 4-16).

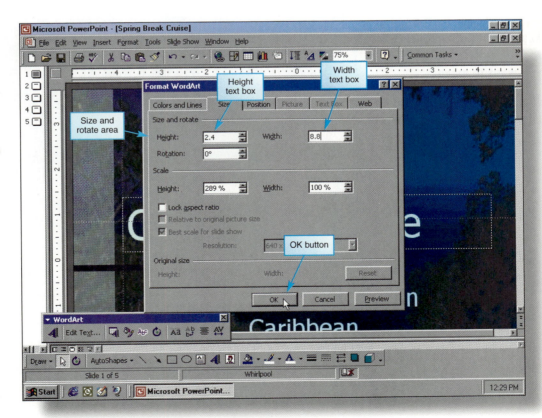

FIGURE 4-16

3 | **Click the OK button.**

The WordArt text object displays over the Title Area placeholder (Figure 4-17).

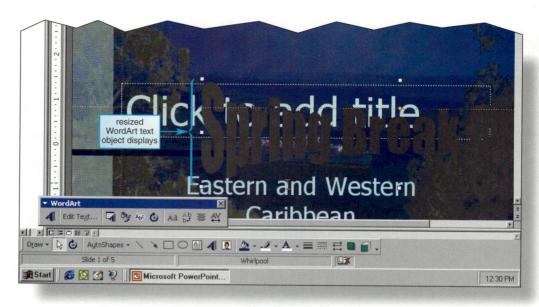

FIGURE 4-17

4 **Drag the text object until the bottom edge snaps to the horizontal guide and the left edge snaps to the vertical guide. If necessary, you can make small adjustments in the position of the object by pressing the ARROW keys on the keyboard that correspond to the direction in which you want to move.**

The WordArt text object is positioned correctly (Figure 4-18).

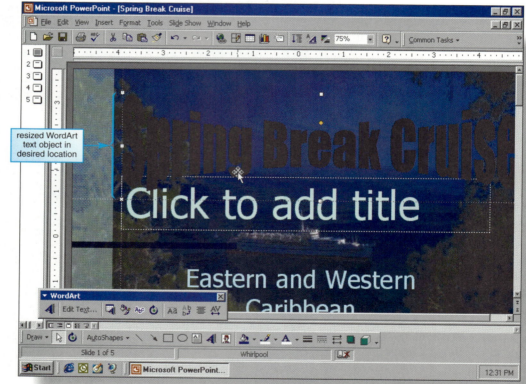

FIGURE 4-18

Changing the WordArt Fill Color

Now that the WordArt object is created, you want to lighten the font color to white. The Colors and Lines sheet in the Format WordArt dialog box contains an area to change the fill color. Perform the following steps to change the fill color.

Steps | To Change the WordArt Fill Color

1 **Click the Format WordArt button on the WordArt toolbar. Click the Colors and Lines tab in the Format WordArt dialog box. Point to the Color box arrow in the Fill area.**

The Colors and Lines sheet displays in the Format WordArt dialog box (Figure 4-19).

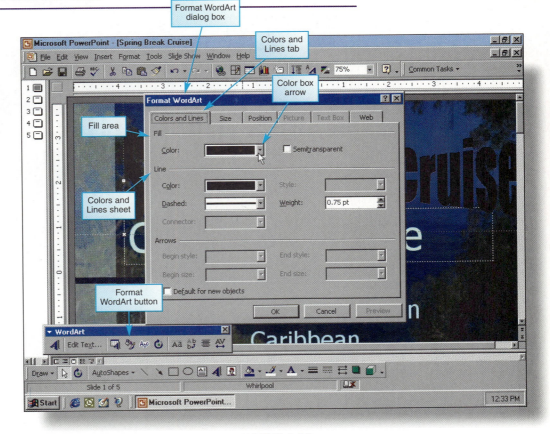

FIGURE 4-19

2 **Click the Color box arrow in the Fill area. Click the color white (row 1, column 2 under Automatic). Click the Weight box down arrow in the Line area once so that 0.5 pt displays.**

The color white displays in the Color box in the Fill area (Figure 4-20). White is the default Follow Text and Lines Scheme color for the Whirlpool template.

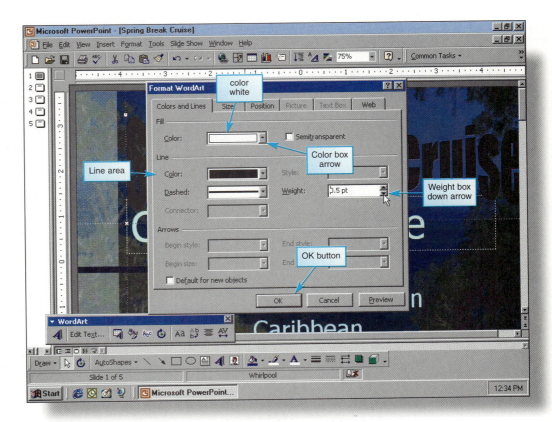

FIGURE 4-20

 **Click the OK button.**

The WordArt text object displays with the color white and a .5 pt solid black border (Figure 4-21).

FIGURE 4-21

The WordArt text object is too large to fit in Slide 1 with the specified height and width. The most effective way to alter the object size is by scaling it. The next section describes how to scale a WordArt object.

Scaling a WordArt Object

The Spring Break Cruise text object is larger than the Spring Break Cruise title slide. To reduce the size of this object, you must scale it to 90 percent of its original size. Perform the following steps to scale the WordArt object.

 **To Scale the WordArt Object**

1 Click the Format WordArt button on the WordArt toolbar. Click the Size tab in the Format WordArt dialog box.

The Format WordArt dialog box displays.

2 Click Lock aspect ratio in the Scale area, and then click the Height text box down arrow until 90% displays. Point to the OK button.

The Height and Width text boxes both display 90% (Figure 4-22). When you change the percentage in the Height text box, the percentage in the Width text box also changes. In addition, the Height and Width text boxes in the Size and rotate area both change. The Lock aspect ratio check box is selected.

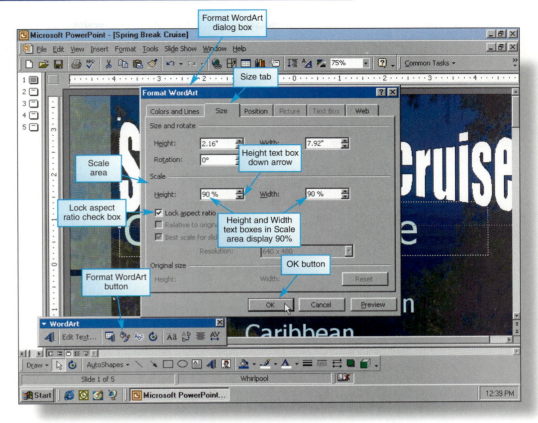

FIGURE 4-22

3 Click the OK button.

The WordArt object is reduced to 90 percent of its original size.

4 Press the RIGHT ARROW key to center the WordArt object in the dark blue portion of the slide.

The scaled WordArt object displays with the desired size in the correct location (Figure 4-23).

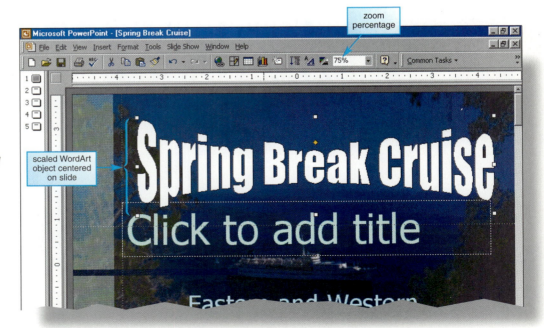

FIGURE 4-23

Hiding the Rulers and Guides

The rulers or guides are not needed when you modify the next slide, so you want to hide them. Recall that a check mark displays in front of the Ruler and Guides commands on the shortcut menu and View menu when the commands are active. Perform the following steps to remove the check mark and deactivate, or hide, the rulers and guides.

TO HIDE THE RULERS AND GUIDES

1 Right-click Slide 1 anywhere except the slide Title Area or Object Area placeholders.

2 Click Ruler on the shortcut menu.

3 Right-click Slide 1 anywhere except the slide Title Area or Object Area placeholders.

4 Click Guides on the shortcut menu.

The rulers and guides no longer display.

Resetting the Zoom Percentage

Zoom also is not needed. This setting can be modified so that PowerPoint determines the best size screen to display for the presentation.

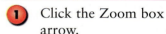
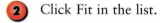
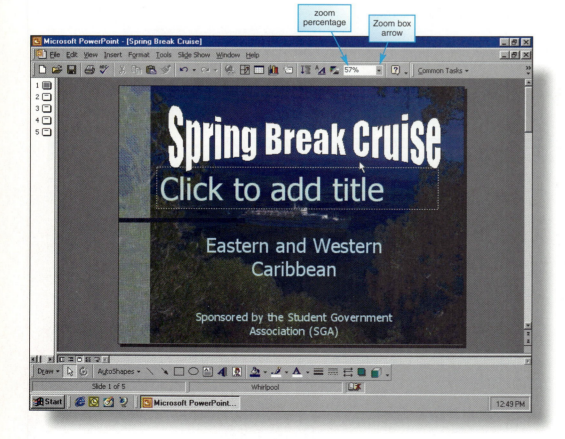

FIGURE 4-24

TO RESET THE ZOOM PERCENTAGE

1 Click the Zoom box arrow.

2 Click Fit in the list.

The WordArt object displays as 57% (Figure 4-24). Your percentage may vary based on your computer system.

The changes to the title slide now are complete. The subtitle text was changed to reflect the purpose of the new presentation. The title text was deleted and replaced with a WordArt object. The next step is to edit Slide 2 to make it an interactive document.

Creating an Interactive Document

The next step in customizing the Spring Break Cruise presentation is to edit a slide so that it connects to two files with additional Spring Break Cruise information. You edit Slide 2 to contain two hyperlinks: one to a Microsoft Word document, Cruise Itinerary, and another to a Microsoft Excel spreadsheet, Cruise Pricing. Both of these files are stored on the Data Disk. Figure 4-25 illustrates the revised Slide 2, which contains two action buttons to reference additional Spring Break Cruise details. An **action button** is a built-in 3-D button that can perform specific tasks such as display the next slide, provide help, give information, and play a sound. In addition, the action button can activate a **hyperlink**, which is a shortcut that allows you to jump to another program, in this case Microsoft Word and Microsoft Excel, and load a specific document. A hyperlink also allows you to move to specific slides in a PowerPoint presentation or to an Internet address. In this slide, you will associate the hyperlink with an action button, but you also can use text or any object, including shapes, tables, or pictures. You specify which action you want PowerPoint to perform by using the **Action Settings** command on the Slide Show menu.

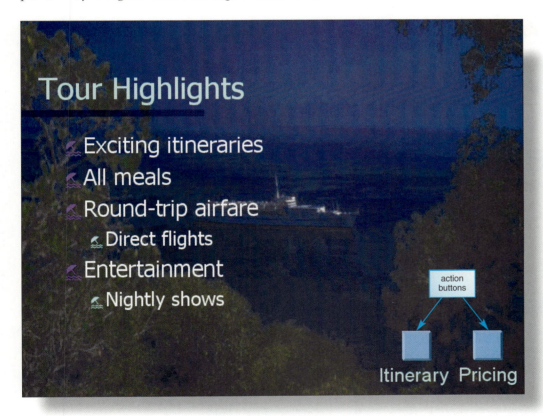

FIGURE 4-25

When you run the Spring Break Cruise presentation and click one of the action buttons in Slide 2, PowerPoint starts Microsoft Word or Excel and loads the designated file. For example, if you click the Itinerary action button, PowerPoint opens the Microsoft Word application and loads the Word document, Cruise Itinerary. Once you have finished viewing the Word document, you want to return to Slide 2. To do so, you will quit Word by clicking the Close button on the title bar, which will return you to the Spring Break Cruise slide show.

Editing Existing Text

Creating the slide shown in Figure 4-25 requires several steps. First, you edit the text in Slide 2 and add some additional text. After the text is edited, you display the guides. Then you add two action buttons and create hyperlinks to a Word document and an Excel spreadsheet. The final step is to scale the buttons and add color and shadows. The next several sections explain how to edit the text in Slide 2 in outline view.

TO EDIT EXISTING TEXT

1 Click the Outline View button at the lower left of the PowerPoint window.

2 Triple-click the first bulleted paragraph in Slide 2, Deluxe accommodations for 7 nights, to highlight it.

3 Type Exciting itineraries as the text.

4 Triple-click the fourth bulleted paragraph, Daily breakfast.

5 Type All meals as the text.

6 Triple-click the fifth and sixth bulleted paragraphs, Welcoming party and Make new friends.

7 Type Entertainment and then press the ENTER key.

8 Press the TAB key and then type Nightly shows as the text.

Slide 2 displays in outline view with the updated information (Figure 4-26).

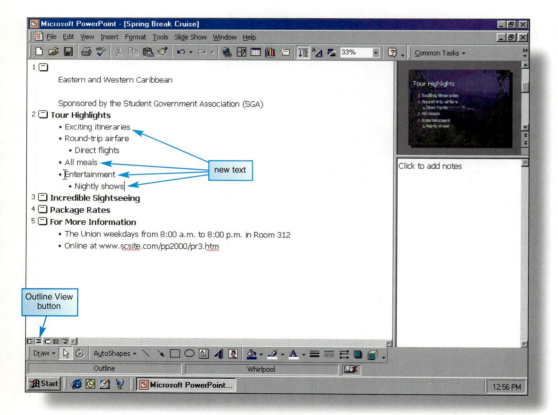

Moving a Slide Bullet within Outline View

In the outline pane, the presentation appears as an outline of titles and text from each slide. Working in the outline view is a good way to develop the content of the presentation because you can see all of the titles and text of the entire presentation on the screen simultaneously. You can rearrange points within a slide, move entire slides from one position to another, and edit titles and text within a slide in outline view.

FIGURE 4-26

An important feature of the cruise pricing is that all meals are included. This aspect should be emphasized near the top of the bullet list, so you want to move the third paragraph, All meals, and make it the second bulleted item on the slide. Bullets can be moved in a presentation by dragging them to the selected location. Perform the following steps to move this paragraph.

 To Move a Paragraph in Outline View

1 **Position the mouse to the left of the fourth bulleted paragraph, All meals.**

The mouse pointer becomes a four-headed arrow (Figure 4-27).

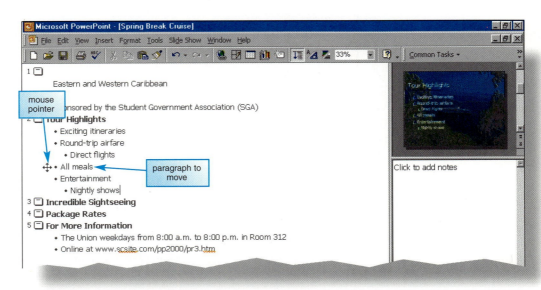

FIGURE 4-27

2 **Drag the third paragraph up directly under the first paragraph, Exciting itineraries.**

A move line helps position the text and the mouse pointer becomes a two-headed arrow (Figure 4-28).

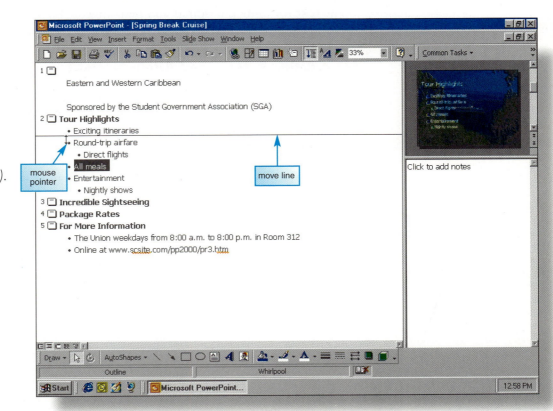

FIGURE 4-28

3 Release the mouse button.

Slide 2 displays in outline view with the newly edited and positioned text, All meals (Figure 4-29).

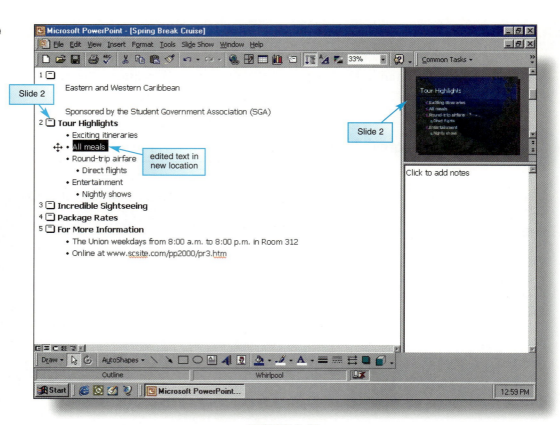

FIGURE 4-29

The text for Slide 2 is edited and rearranged. Perform the following steps to add action buttons and action settings to the slide.

Adding Action Buttons and Action Settings

You want to display additional information about the Spring Break cruise itinerary and pricing by opening files in Word and Excel without quitting PowerPoint. To obtain details on the cruise itineraries, you will click the left action button (Itinerary), and to obtain details on cruise pricing, you will click the right action button (Pricing). When you click a button, a chime sound will play. The next section describes how to create the action buttons and place them in Slide 2. These buttons are added in slide view.

More *About*

Action Buttons

Action buttons are a subset of PowerPoint's AutoShapes, which are convenient visuals designed to enhance your slides. Just click the AutoShapes button on the Drawing toolbar, select one of the categories of shapes on the menu, such as lines, connectors, basic shapes, flowchart elements, stars and banners, and callouts, click an AutoShape, and click the slide in the location where you want the AutoShape to appear. To add text to an AutoShape, just start typing.

To Add an Action Button and Action Settings

1 **Click the Slide View button at the lower left of the PowerPoint window. Click Slide Show on the menu bar, point to Action Buttons, and then point to the first action button, Action Button: Custom, in the list.**

The Action Buttons submenu displays 12 built-in 3-D buttons (Figure 4-30).

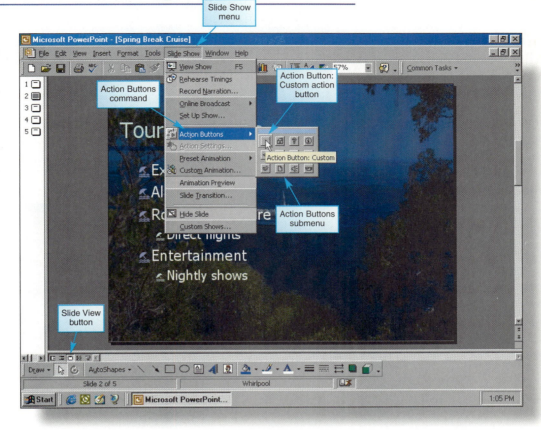

FIGURE 4-30

2 **Click the Action Button: Custom action button (row 1, column 1) in the list. Click the bottom right of Slide 2.**

The Action Settings dialog box displays (Figure 4-31) with the action button placed in Slide 2. None is the default Action on click.

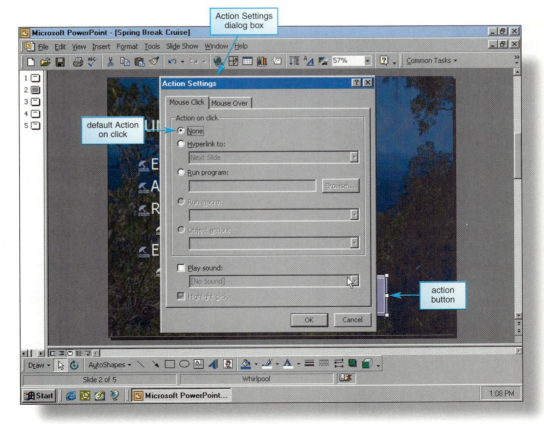

FIGURE 4-31

3 Click the Mouse Click tab. Click the Hyperlink to option button in the Action on click area. Click the Hyperlink to box arrow and then point to Other File in the list.

The list displays the possible locations in the slide show or elsewhere where a hyperlink can be established (Figure 4-32).

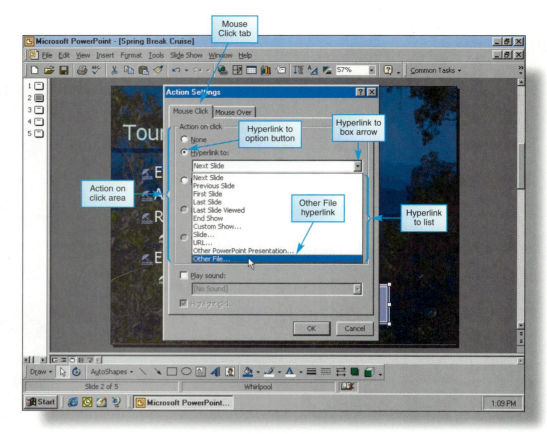

FIGURE 4-32

4 Click Other File. If necessary, click the Look in box arrow, click 3½ Floppy (A:), and then click Cruise Itinerary. Point to the OK button in the Hyperlink to Other File dialog box.

Cruise Itinerary is the Microsoft Word file you will link to the Itinerary action button (Figure 4-33). Your list of file names may vary.

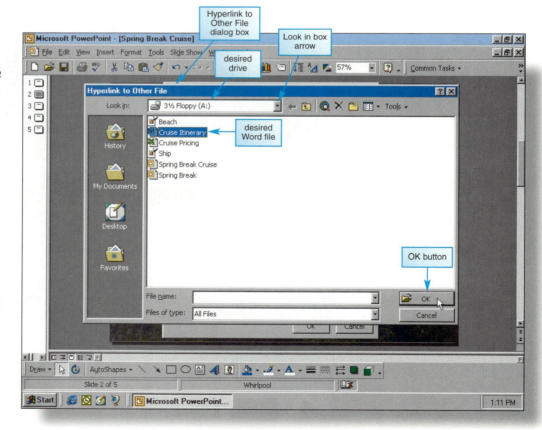

FIGURE 4-33

5 Click the OK button in the Hyperlink to Other File dialog box. Click the Play sound check box, click the Play sound box arrow, and then point to Chime.

The Hyperlink to box displays the Word document file name, Cruise Itinerary (Figure 4-34). A check mark displays in the Play sound check box. The Play sound list displays sounds that can play when you click the action button.

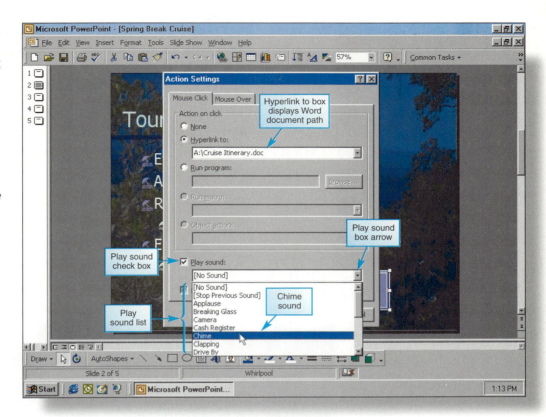

FIGURE 4-34

6 Click Chime. Click the OK button.

The action button is high-lighted in Slide 2 (Figure 4-35).

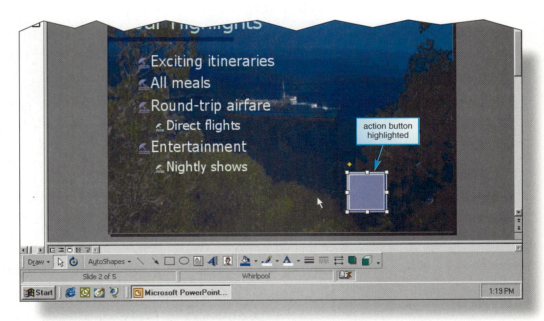

FIGURE 4-35

Now that you have created an action button and linked the Word document, Cruise Itinerary, you need to repeat the procedure for the Excel spreadsheet, Cruise Pricing. Perform the steps on the next page to create another action button and to hyperlink the Excel Cruise Pricing spreadsheet document to the PowerPoint presentation.

TO CREATE A SECOND ACTION BUTTON AND HYPERLINK

1 Click Slide Show on the menu bar, point to Action Buttons, and then click the Action Button: Custom action button (row 1, column 1) in the list.

2 Click to the right of the first action button in Slide 2.

3 Click Hyperlink to in the Action on click area in the Mouse Click sheet in the Action Settings dialog box.

4 Click the Hyperlink to box arrow and then click Other File.

5 Double-click Cruise Pricing in the list.

6 Click Play sound. Click the Play sound box arrow and then click Chime.

7 Click the OK button.

Slide 2 displays with the second action button for the Excel Pricing spreadsheet hyperlink (Figure 4-36). Later in this project you will make small adjustments to align the action button precisely.

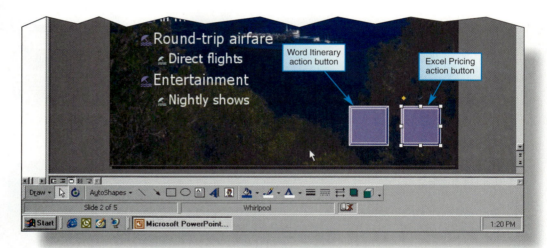

FIGURE 4-36

When you select a file from the Look in box, PowerPoint associates the file with a specific application, which is based on the file extension. For example, when you select the Cruise Itinerary file with the file extension **.doc**, PowerPoint recognizes the file as a Microsoft Word file. Additionally, when you select the Cruise Pricing file with the file extension **.xls**, PowerPoint recognizes the file as a Microsoft Excel file.

Displaying Guides and Positioning Action Buttons

Recall that the guides assist you in placing objects at specific locations on the slide. When an object is close to a guide, it snaps to the guide. In this project, you use the vertical and horizontal guides to help position the action buttons and captions in Slide 2. The center of a slide is 0.00 inches on both the vertical and the horizontal guides. You position a guide by dragging it to a new location. When you point to a guide and then press and hold the mouse button, PowerPoint displays a box containing the exact position of the guide on the slide in inches. An arrow displays under the guide position to indicate the vertical guide either left or right of center. An arrow displays to the right of the guide position to indicate the horizontal guide either above or below center. Perform the following steps to display the guides and position the action buttons.

Sounds

PowerPoint's sounds that play when you click an action button fit a variety of applications. You can, however, add custom sounds, such as a human voice, music, or sound effects, to your slide show. Many sites on the Internet provide these sound files, which have the file extension .wav, and allow you to download them free of charge. For an example of one of these sites, visit the PowerPoint 2000 Project 4 More About page (www.scsite.com/pp2000/more.htm) and click Sounds.

To Display the Guides and Position the Action Buttons

1 **Right-click Slide 2 anywhere except the Title Area or Object Area placeholders or the action buttons. Click Guides on the shortcut menu.**

The horizontal and vertical guides display where they were last positioned in Slide 2.

2 **Drag the vertical guide to 2.58 inches right of center.**

The vertical guide will be used to position the left side of the Microsoft Word action button (Figure 4-37).

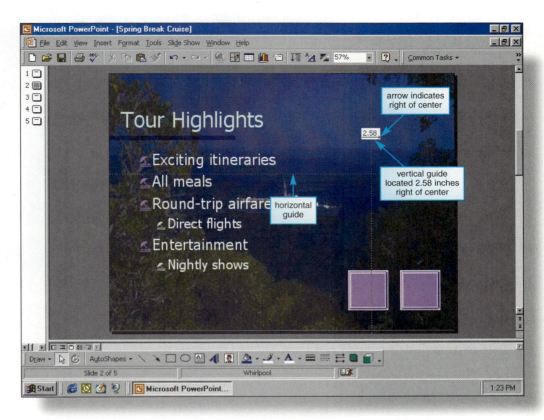

FIGURE 4-37

3 **Drag the horizontal guide to 2.50 inches below center.**

The horizontal guide will be used to position the top side of the Microsoft Word action button (Figure 4-38).

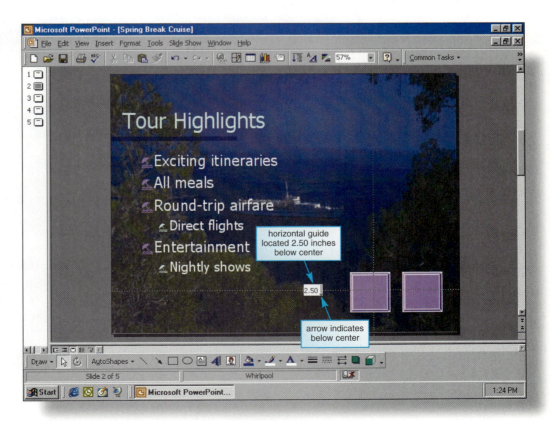

FIGURE 4-38

4 Drag the left action button for the Word document hyperlink until the top edge snaps to the horizontal guide and the left edge snaps to the vertical guide.

The top of the Word document action button aligns with the horizontal guide, and the left side of the button aligns with the vertical guide (Figure 4-39).

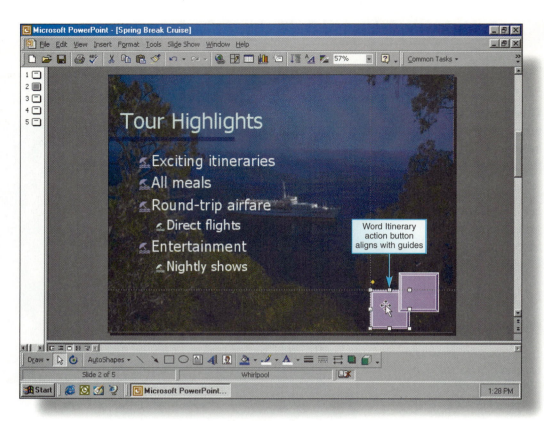

FIGURE 4-39

5 Drag the vertical guide to 4.00 inches right of center.

The vertical guide will be used to align the Excel action button (Figure 4-40).

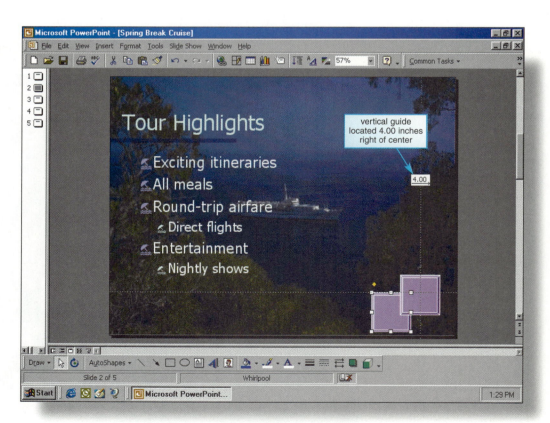

FIGURE 4-40

6 Drag the right action button for the **Excel Pricing spreadsheet hyperlink until the top edge snaps to the horizontal guide and the left edge snaps to the vertical guide.**

The top of the Excel Pricing spreadsheet action button aligns with the horizontal guide, and the left side of the button aligns with the vertical guide (Figure 4-41).

FIGURE 4-41

Scaling Objects

The action buttons in Slide 2 are too large in proportion to the screen. Perform the following steps to scale the two action buttons simultaneously.

TO SCALE ACTION BUTTONS

1 With the Pricing (right) action button still selected, press and hold the SHIFT key. Click the Itinerary (left) action button. Release the SHIFT key.

2 Right-click either action button and then click Format AutoShape on the shortcut menu.

3 If necessary, click the Size tab. Click Lock aspect ratio in the Scale area and then double-click the Height text box. Type 50 in the Height text box.

4 Click the OK button.

Both action buttons are resized to 50 percent of their original size (Figure 4-42).

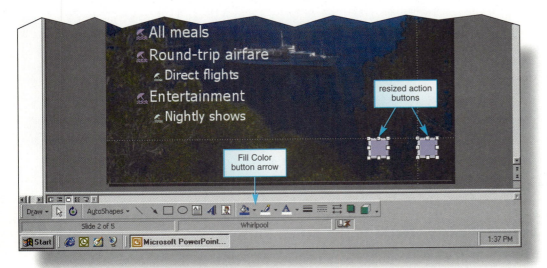

FIGURE 4-42

Adding Fill Color to the Action Buttons

To better identify the action buttons from the slide background, you can add fill color. Recall that fill color is the interior color of a selected object. Perform the following steps to add fill color to the action buttons in Slide 2.

 ### To Add Fill Color to the Action Buttons

1 **With the two action buttons still selected, click the Fill Color button arrow on the Drawing toolbar. Point to the color medium blue (row 1, column 7 under Automatic).**

The Fill Color list displays (Figure 4-43). Automatic is highlighted, indicating that lavender is the current default fill color based on the Whirlpool design template.

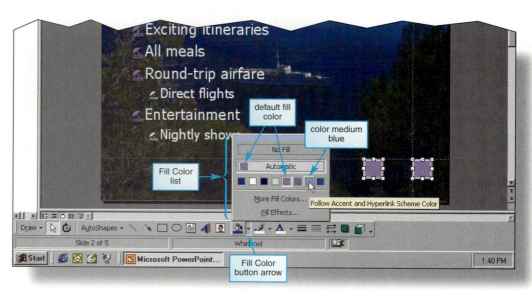

FIGURE 4-43

2 **Click the color medium blue (row 1, column 7 under Automatic).**

Both action buttons display filled with the color medium blue (Figure 4-44). Medium blue is the Follow Accent and Hyperlink Scheme Color in the Whirlpool design template color scheme.

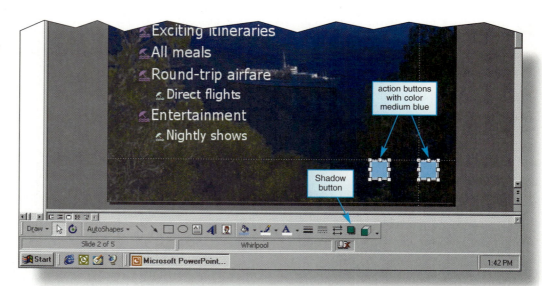

FIGURE 4-44

Adding Shadow Effects to the Action Buttons

To add depth to an object, you **shadow** it by clicking the Shadow button on the Drawing toolbar. Perform the following steps to add shadows to the two action buttons in Slide 2.

TO ADD SHADOWS TO THE ACTION BUTTONS

1 Click the Shadow button on the Drawing toolbar.

2 Click Shadow Style 17 (row 5, column 1) in the style list.

PowerPoint adds the shadow to the two action buttons (Figure 4-45).

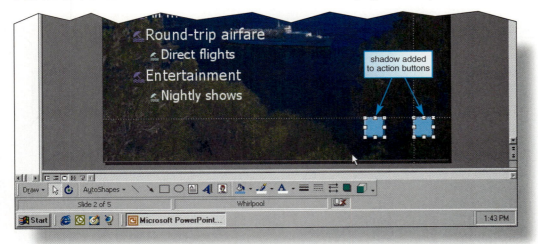

FIGURE 4-45

Adding Captions to the Action Buttons

The final components of Slide 2 that need to be added are the captions under the two action buttons. Perform the following steps to add captions to the action buttons in Slide 2.

TO ADD CAPTIONS TO THE ACTION BUTTONS

1 Click the Text Box button on the Drawing toolbar.

2 Click below the left action button. Type Itinerary as the caption.

3 Click the Text Box button on the Drawing toolbar.

4 Click below the right action button and then type Pricing as the caption.

The captions for the two action buttons display (Figure 4-46).

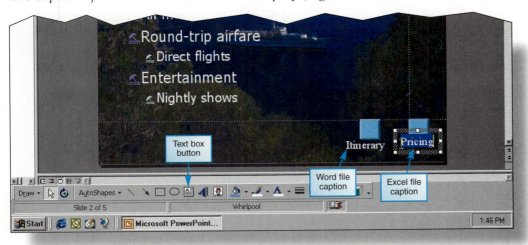

FIGURE 4-46

Formatting Text

To add visual appeal to the captions, you want to change the font to Arial, increase the font size to 28, and change the color to the same color as the title text. Perform the following steps to format the captions for the action buttons in Slide 2.

 To Format Text

1 **Double-click the Pricing caption text, click Edit on the menu bar, and then click Select All.**

2 **Right-click the text, Pricing, and then click Font on the shortcut menu. Click the Font box up arrow, and then click Arial in the Font list. Click the Size box down arrow and then click 28 in the list.**

Arial displays in the Font box, and the font size 28 displays in the Size box (Figure 4-47).

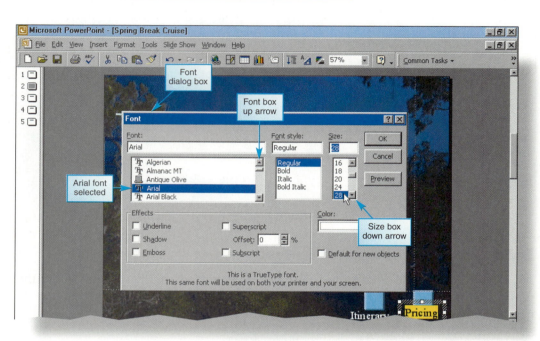

FIGURE 4-47

3 **Click the Color box arrow and then click the color aqua (row 1, column 4 under Automatic).**

The color aqua is the Follow Title Text Scheme Color in the Whirlpool design template color scheme (Figure 4-48). The color aqua displays in the Color box.

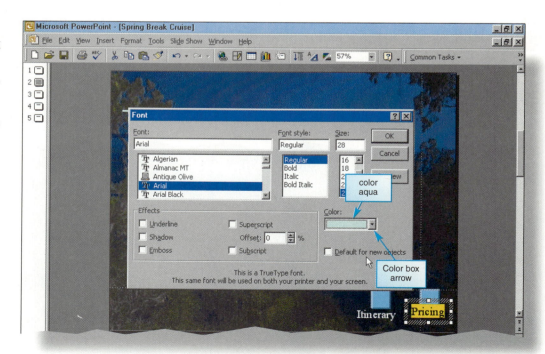

FIGURE 4-48

4 **Click the OK button and then click anywhere on a blank area of the slide.**

PowerPoint displays the Pricing caption with the 28-point Arial font and the color aqua (Figure 4-49).

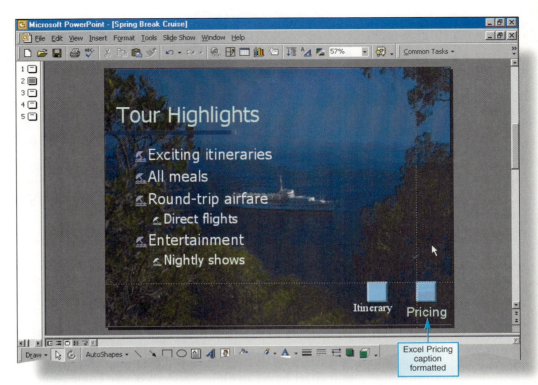

FIGURE 4-49

Now that you have formatted the Pricing caption text, you need to repeat the procedure to format the Itinerary caption text. Perform the following steps to format the Itinerary caption text.

TO FORMAT A SECOND CAPTION TEXT

1 Double-click the Itinerary caption, click Edit on the menu bar, and then click Select All.

2 Right-click the text and then click Font on the shortcut menu. When the Font dialog box displays, click the Font box up arrow, and then click Arial in the list.

3 Click the Size box down arrow and then click 28 in the list.

4 Click the Color box arrow and then click the color aqua (row 1, column 4 under Automatic).

5 Click the OK button and then click anywhere on a blank area of the slide.

Slide 2 is complete (Figure 4-50).

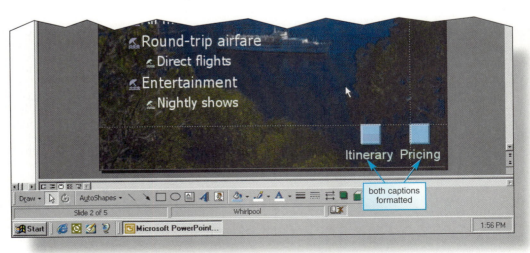

FIGURE 4-50

Now that the captions are added and formatted, you may need to make slight adjustments to their placements under the action buttons. If so, click a caption, click the border, and use the ARROW keys to position the text box as shown in Figure 4-50 on the previous page.

Because you do not need the guides when you modify the next slide, you want to hide them. Recall that a check mark displays in front of the Guides command on the shortcut menu and View menu when the commands are active. Perform the following steps to remove the check mark and deactivate, or hide, the guides.

TO HIDE THE GUIDES

1 Right-click Slide 1 anywhere except the Title Area or Object Area placeholders.

2 Click Guides on the shortcut menu.

The guides no longer display.

The next section explains how to change the organization chart.

More About

Organization Charts

Many companies and municipalities use organization charts to show employees and the public the hierarchical structure. These charts help individuals understand reporting structure and departmental organization. For an example of the New York City organization chart that shows the structure of elected officials, visit the PowerPoint 2000 Project 4 More About page (www.scsite.com/pp2000/more.htm) and click Organization Chart.

Modifying an Organization Chart

Now that you have created aqua action buttons in Slide 2, you want the organization chart boxes in Slide 3 also to be the color aqua. The shadow effects and border style selected in Project 3 can remain. In addition, the Project 3 organization chart depicts the sightseeing excursions available for the three Florida and Texas Spring Break destinations. The organization chart in Project 4, shown in Figure 4-1g on page PP 4.5, displays the itineraries for the Eastern and Western Caribbean island cruises. Consequently, the structure of this organization chart needs to be changed. The next several sections explain how to modify the organization chart.

Changing the Box Color in an Organization Chart

First you will change the color of all the boxes to aqua and the text to red. Perform the following steps to modify the organization chart box and text colors.

TO CHANGE AN ORGANIZATION CHART BOX AND TEXT COLOR

1 Click the Next Slide button to display Slide 3.

2 Double-click an organization chart box to open the Microsoft Organization Chart application.

3 Click the Maximize button in the upper-right corner of the Microsoft Organization Chart window.

4 Click Edit on the menu bar, point to Select, and then click All on the submenu.

5 Click Boxes on the menu bar and then click Color.

6 Click the color aqua (row 2, column 3) and then click the OK button.

7 Click Text on the menu bar and then click Color.

8 Click the color red (row 1, column 9).

9 Click the OK button.

10 Click anywhere in the chart area except a box or line to deselect all.

The Microsoft Organization Chart applies the new color aqua to the boxes and color red to the text (Figure 4-51).

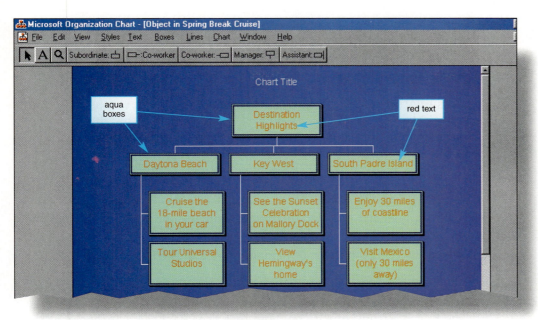

FIGURE 4-51

The organization chart in Project 3 has three branches (Daytona Beach, Key West, and South Padre Island). The Spring Break Cruise presentation only needs two branches (Eastern Caribbean and Western Caribbean). One branch of the organization chart needs to be deleted. The next section explains how to delete a branch.

Deleting a Branch of an Organization Chart

The South Padre Island branch of the organization chart can be removed because it is not needed. Only two branches display in the Spring Break Cruise presentation (Eastern Caribbean and Western Caribbean). The following steps describe how to eliminate a branch of the organization chart.

Other Ways

1. Select branch, press CTRL+B

TO DELETE A BRANCH OF AN ORGANIZATION CHART

1. Click the South Padre Island box.

2. Click Edit on the menu bar, point to Select, and then click Branch.

3. Press the DELETE key.

The South Padre Island branch is deleted, and only the Daytona Beach and Key West branches display (Figure 4-52).

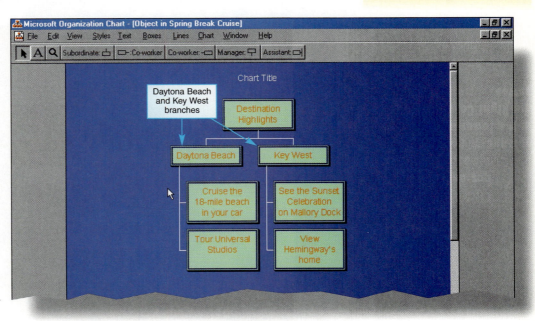

FIGURE 4-52

The text in the chart must be changed to reflect the Caribbean destinations. In the next sections, these editing changes are made.

Editing Text in an Organization Chart

The chart is reformatted for the new presentation. Now the text must be changed to reflect the new items. The two Level 2 subordinate boxes and the four Level 3 subordinate boxes must be changed by highlighting the existing text and then typing the new text. Perform the steps below to edit the text.

TO EDIT TEXT IN AN ORGANIZATION CHART

1. Click the root manager box, Destination Highlights, and type `Islands` as the first line of text.

2. Triple-click Highlights in the root manager box and then press the DELETE key.

3. Click the Daytona Beach subordinate box and then type `Eastern Caribbean` as the text.

4. Click the Key West subordinate box and then type `Western Caribbean` as the text.

5. Click the first box under Eastern Caribbean and then type `St. Martin` in the box.

6. Drag through each line of remaining text in the box and then press the DELETE key.

7. Repeat Steps 5 and 6 to insert the information in Figure 4-53.

The edited organization chart displays.

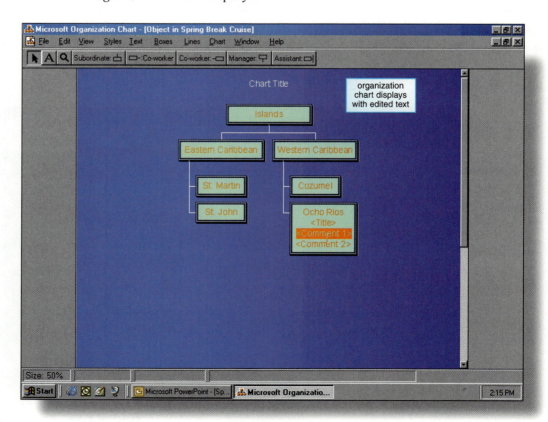

FIGURE 4-53

The seven boxes now reflect the new Caribbean destinations. Three additional subordinate boxes must be added to complete the organization chart. Perform the next steps to insert the remaining boxes.

Adding Co-worker Boxes

Co-workers boxes share the same manager. Three co-workers need to be added to the managers Eastern Caribbean and Western Caribbean. The two types of co-workers are the Left Co-worker, which branches to the left, and the Right Co-worker, which branches to the right. Level 3 of this organization chart has Right Co-worker boxes. Perform the following steps to add three Right Co-workers to Level 3.

 To Add Right Co-worker Boxes

1 **Click the Right Co-worker box tool button on the Microsoft Organization Chart window icon bar two times. Point to the St. John box.**

The Right Co-worker box tool button is recessed (Figure 4-54). The status bar displays the number of subordinate boxes Microsoft Organization Chart is creating, which is two. The mouse pointer changes shape to a Right Co-worker box.

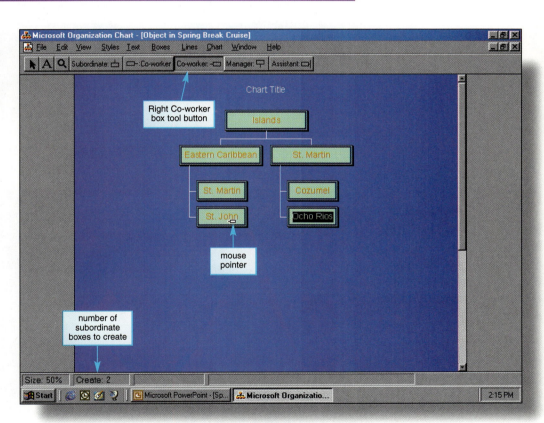

FIGURE 4-54

2 **Click the St. John box and then type** St. Thomas **in the upper box and** Virgin Islands **in the lower box. Point to the Right Co-worker button.**

The new boxes and text display (Figure 4-55).

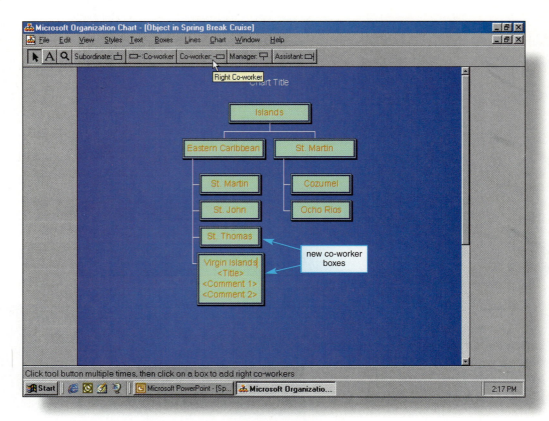

FIGURE 4-55

3 **Click the Right Co-worker box tool button, click the Ocho Rios box, and then type** Great Stirrup Cay **in the new box. Click anywhere in the chart area except on a line or box.**

The chart displays with the three new Level 3 Right Co-worker boxes (Figure 4-56).

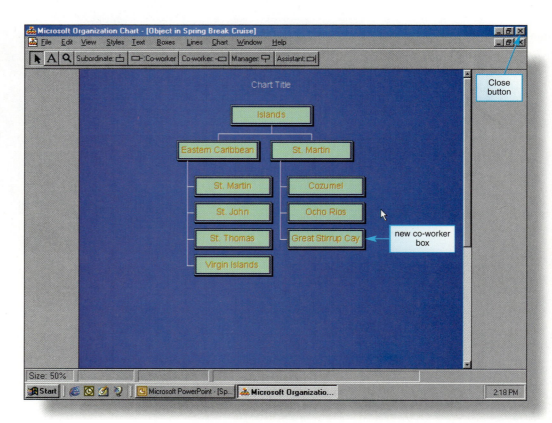

FIGURE 4-56

The organization chart changes now are complete. The text has been updated to reflect the topics of the Spring Break Cruise presentation. The color of the boxes has been changed to differentiate it from the original Spring Break presentation. The organization chart must be saved, and Slide 3 must be updated with the revised chart.

TO SAVE THE CHART AND RETURN TO THE PRESENTATION

1 Click the Close button on the Microsoft Organization Chart – [Object in Spring Break Cruise] title bar.

2 Click the Yes button.

Slide 3 displays the modified organization chart (Figure 4-57).

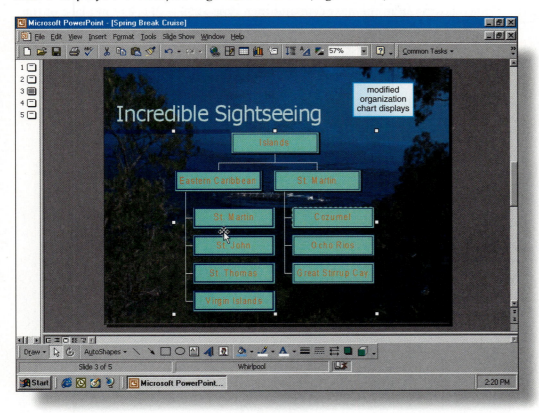

FIGURE 4-57

The organization chart has been updated in Slide 3 with the new colors for the boxes and text and the revised Spring Break Cruise information. The next step is to edit the Slide 4 PowerPoint table.

Editing a PowerPoint Table

The Package Rates slide, Slide 4, discusses the cost of the Florida and Texas travel packages. You want to change that slide to reflect the Eastern and Western Caribbean island prices for the cruises. The prices vary because of multiple departure cities, which is explained in the Excel spreadsheet, Cruise Pricing. The range of prices will be listed in Slide 4. In addition, the third row, South Padre Island, of the table is deleted because it is not needed. Finally, the background color of the slide is changed to better match the presentation's color scheme. The next sections explain how to modify Slide 4 by making these changes.

Other Ways

1. On Microsoft Organization Chart File menu click Update Spring Break Cruise, on Microsoft Organization Chart File menu click Exit and Return to Spring Break Cruise

2. In Microsoft Organization Chart – [Object in Spring Break Cruise] window, press ALT+F, press U, press ALT+F, press X

Editing the Table Text

All of the text in the table must be changed in Slide 4, while the slide title can remain the same. Recall text objects that display on a slide can be edited in slide view or outline view, and you must select text before editing it. Perform the following steps to display the title slide in slide view and then revise the Title Area text.

TO EDIT THE TABLE TEXT

1 Click the Next Slide button to display Slide 4.

2 Triple-click the words, Daytona Beach, in the first table cell, and then type Eastern Caribbean in place of the highlighted text.

3 Triple-click $529 in the next cell, and then type $899 - $1,299 in place of the highlighted text.

4 Triple-click the words, Key West, in the next cell down, and then type Western Caribbean in place of the highlighted text.

5 Triple-click $669 in the next cell, and then type $799 - $1,199 in place of the highlighted text.

Slide 4 displays two rows of updated table text (Figure 4-58).

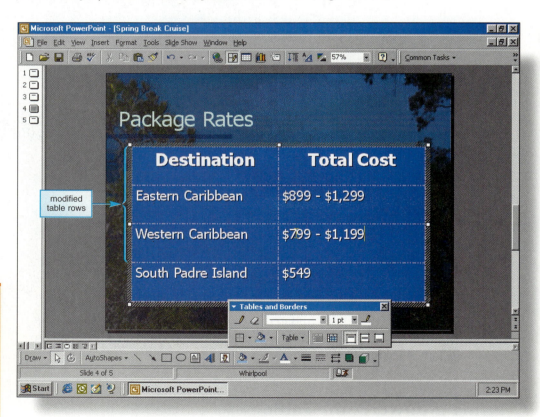

FIGURE 4-58

Modifying Tables

You can add rows or columns to a PowerPoint table. Just select the row above where you want to insert the new row or the column to the left of where you want to insert the new column. Then select the same number of rows or columns you want to insert. Right-click, and then click Insert Rows or Insert Columns on the shortcut menu. You can click the last cell of the last row of the table and then press the TAB key to add a row at the end of the table.

Deleting a Table Row

You need to delete the last row of the table because it is not needed. All text in the row should be highlighted, and then the entire row can be deleted. Perform the following steps to delete the last row of the table in Slide 4.

TO DELETE A TABLE ROW

1 Drag through the text, South Padre Island and $549, in the last row of the table.

2 Right-click anywhere in the selection.

3 Click Delete Rows on the shortcut menu.

Slide 4 displays the edited table with the last row deleted (Figure 4-59).

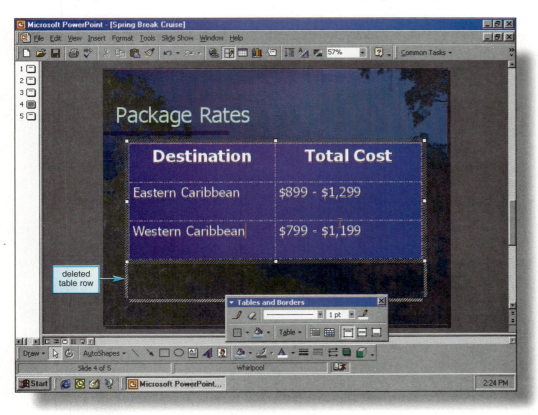

FIGURE 4-59

The final step is to change the table's background fill color. A medium blue color will complement the background picture.

Changing the Table Fill Color

To change the background fill color of the table in PowerPoint, you select the cells and then select a new fill color. Perform the following steps to change the fill color in the table in Slide 4.

TO CHANGE THE TABLE FILL COLOR

1 With the insertion point in the Western Caribbean cell, click Edit on the menu bar, and then click Select All. Right-click anywhere in the selection.

2 Click Borders and Fill on the shortcut menu.

3 Click the Fill tab.

Fill Color

If you want to change the table background fill color to its original default color, select the entire table, click the Fill Color button arrow on the Tables and Borders toolbar, and then click Automatic.

4 Click the Fill color box arrow and then click the color medium blue (row 1, column 7 under Automatic). Click Semitransparent.

5 Click the OK button.

6 Click anywhere in Slide 4 except the table or the Title Area placeholder to deselect all the objects.

The fill color is changed to medium blue (Figure 4-60). The semitransparent color allows some of the slide background to show through.

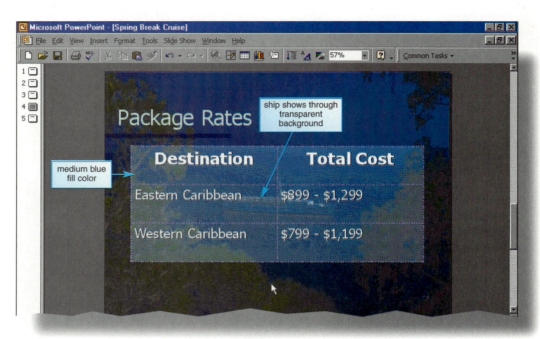

FIGURE 4-60

All the changes have been made to Slide 4. In the next section, a new hidden slide is created.

Hiding Slides

A **supporting slide** provides detailed information to supplement another slide in the presentation. For example, in a presentation to job applicants, a company recruiter displays a graph representing the corporation's current year's profits compared to the previous five years' profits. The supporting slide displays a graph contrasting the competitors' bottom lines.

When running a slide show, you may not always want to display the supporting slide. You would display it when time permits and when you want to show the audience more detail about a topic. You insert the supporting slide after the slide you anticipate may warrant more detail. Then, you use the Hide Slide command to hide the supporting slide. The **Hide Slide command** hides the supporting slide from the audience during the normal running of a slide show. When you want to display the supporting hidden slide, press the H key. No visible indicator displays to show that a hidden slide exists. You must be aware of the content of the presentation to know where the supporting slide is located.

Black Slides

At times you may want your audience to focus on the speaker or on other audience members. A black slide may be helpful to divert the attention away from the slide show and to these individuals. To create a black slide, click the New Slide button on the Standard toolbar, select the Blank AutoLayout, click Format on the menu bar, click Background, click the Background fill box arrow, and then click the color black.

Adding a New Slide

The first step in creating a hidden slide is adding a new slide. Perform the following steps to add a new slide.

TO ADD A NEW SLIDE

1 Click the New Slide button on the Standard toolbar.

2 When the New Slide dialog box displays, type 2 to select the Bulleted List AutoLayout.

3 Click the OK button.

The new Slide 5 displays the Bulleted List AutoLayout with the Ship background graphics (Figure 4-61). PowerPoint automatically renumbers the original Slide 5 as Slide 6.

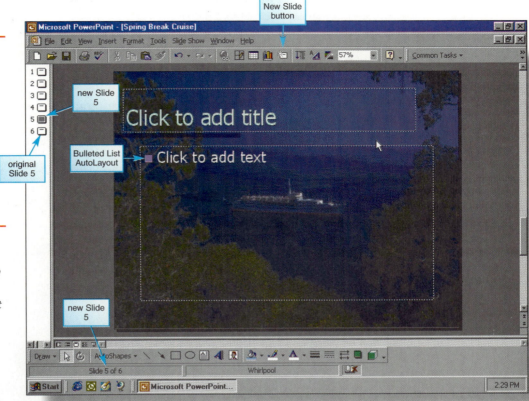

FIGURE 4-61

Adding a Slide Title

The title text for Slide 5 is Special Discounts. Perform the following steps to add a slide title to Slide 5.

TO ADD A SLIDE TITLE

1 Click the slide Title Area placeholder and type `Special Discounts` in the placeholder.

2 Click the Object Area placeholder.

The title, Special Discounts, displays in Slide 5 (Figure 4-62). The Object Area placeholder is selected.

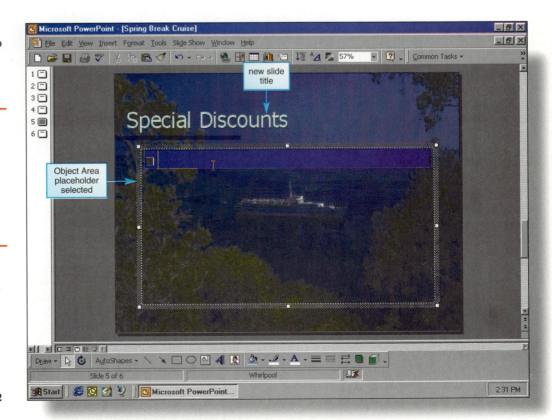

FIGURE 4-62

Adding Text and Removing Bullets

In the next steps, a paragraph of text is inserted in the Title Area placeholder. Because only one paragraph will display, bullets are not needed. The bullet at the beginning of the line of text, therefore, is removed.

TO ADD SLIDE TEXT AND REMOVE BULLETS

1 Type Talk to the cruise sales representative for special discount information. as the information in the Object Area placeholder.

2 Right-click anywhere in the new paragraph of text. Click Bullets and Numbering on the shortcut menu.

3 Click the None bulleted list style and then click the OK button.

4 Click anywhere in Slide 5 except the Title Area or Object Area placeholders.

The new subtitle text displays in the Object Area placeholder with the bullet removed (Figure 4-63).

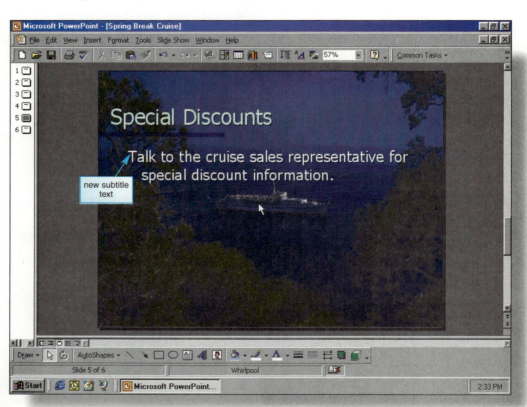

FIGURE 4-63

Hiding a Slide

Slide 5 supports the session information displayed in Slide 4. If time permits, or if the audience requires more information, you can display Slide 5. As the presenter, you decide whether to show Slide 5. You hide a slide in slide sorter view so you can see the **null sign**, which is a slashed square surrounding the slide number, to indicate the slide is hidden. Perform the following steps to hide Slide 5.

Steps **To Hide a Slide**

① **Click the Slide Sorter View button at the lower left of the PowerPoint window. Right-click Slide 5 and then point to Hide Slide on the shortcut menu.**

Slide 5 is selected in slide sorter view (Figure 4-64).

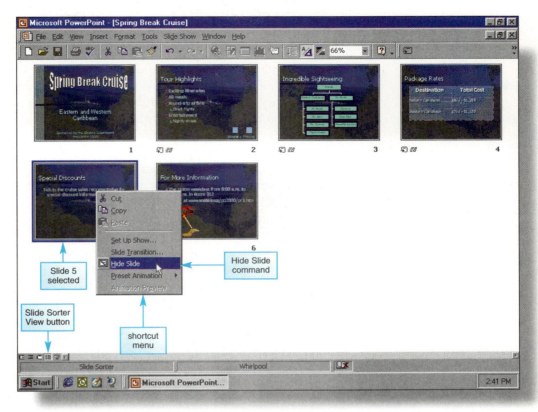

FIGURE 4-64

② **Click Hide Slide.**

The null sign, a square with a slash, displays over the slide number to indicate Slide 5 is a hidden slide (Figure 4-65).

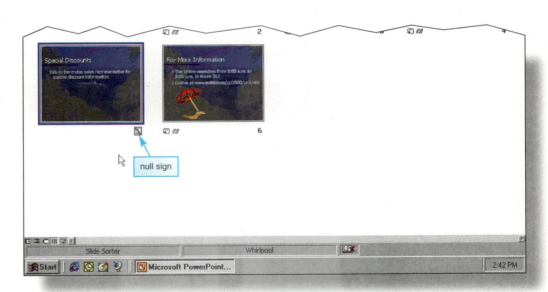

FIGURE 4-65

Other Ways

1. Click Hide Slide button on Slide Sorter toolbar
2. On Slide Show menu click Hide Slide
3. Press ALT+D, press H

The Hide Slide button is a toggle — it either hides or displays a slide. It also applies or removes the null sign. When you no longer want to hide a slide, change views to slide sorter view, right-click the slide, and then click Hide Slide on the short-cut menu. This action removes the square with the null sign.

An alternative to hiding a slide in slide sorter view is to hide a slide in slide view, outline view, or normal view. In these views, however, no visible indication is given that a slide is hidden. To hide a slide in slide view or normal view, display the slide you want to hide, click Slide Show on the menu bar, and then click Hide Slide. To hide a slide in outline view, select the slide icon of the slide you want to hide, click Slide Show on the menu bar, and then click Hide Slide. An icon displays in front of the Hide Slide command on the Slide Show menu, and it is recessed when the slide is hidden. You also can choose not to hide a slide in slide view, normal view, and outline view by clicking Hide Slide on the Slide Show menu. The icon in front of the Hide Slide command no longer is recessed, and the slide then displays like all the other slides in the presentation.

When you run your presentation, the hidden slide does not display unless you press the H key when the slide preceding the hidden slide is displaying. For example, Slide 5 does not display unless you press the H key when Slide 4 displays in slide show view. You continue your presentation by clicking the mouse or pressing any of the keys associated with running a slide show. You skip the hidden slide by clicking the mouse and advancing to the next slide.

Changing the Order of Slides

The presentation changes nearly are complete. Next, the slides are rearranged to highlight the key points early in the presentation. Slides 4 and 5 are moved just after Slide 2. Perform the following steps to reposition Slides 4 and 5.

Action Items

Gathering your audience's comments and reactions while you are giving your presentation is a snap when you use PowerPoint's Meeting Minder. In slide show view, click the right mouse button, click Meeting Minder, and then click the Action Items tab. When your audience members give you some important feedback, type their name, their comments, and, if necessary, a date. When you have recorded all their comments, click the OK button. PowerPoint will create an Action Item slide at the end of your presentation, and these items will display automatically.

 To Change the Slide Order in a Presentation

1 With Slide 5 still selected, press and hold the CTRL key and then click Slide 4. Release the CTRL key.

2 Click Slide 4 or Slide 5 and drag the mouse pointer between Slides 2 and 3.

The move bar displays between Slides 2 and 3 (Figure 4-66). The mouse pointer changes to indicate the slide move.

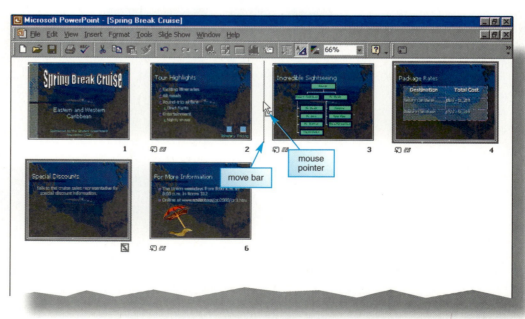

FIGURE 4-66

3 **Release the mouse button.**

The slide show is rearranged and the slides are renumbered automatically (Figure 4-67).

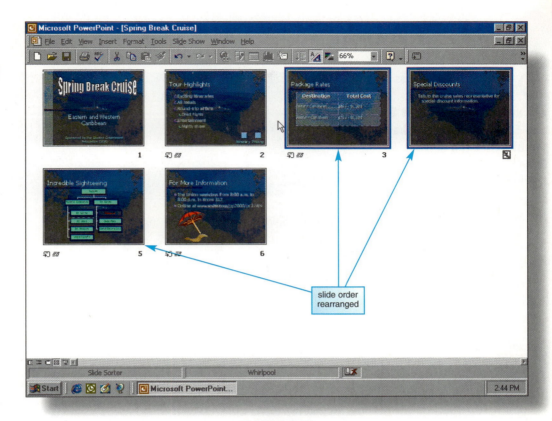

slide order rearranged

FIGURE 4-67

The final step for the Spring Break Cruise presentation is to create a summary slide. The following sections explain how to add this slide to the end of your presentation.

Adding a Summary Slide

The final step in the changes to the Spring Break Cruise presentation is to add a summary slide. A **summary slide** contains bulleted titles from selected slides. The summary slide can be used to summarize the main points of the presentation or as an agenda of topics. Because of this use, the summary slide displays automatically in front of the first selected slide.

In this presentation, only Slides 2, 3, and 5 will be included in the summary slide. The hidden slide, Slide 4, is not included because it is not presented during every presentation. Perform the steps on the next page to add a summary slide.

Other Ways

1. In outline pane, drag slide icon to new position

More About 2000

Creating Slides Automatically

You can use your summary slide to create an agenda slide, which identifies the major presentation items for your audience. When you use an agenda slide, you click each bulleted item to jump to a particular slide, discuss the topic with your audience, and then jump back to your agenda slide. You create a hyperlink from each bulleted item on your summary slide to a corresponding custom show by clicking Action Settings on the Slide Show menu, clicking Hyperlink to, clicking Custom Shows, and then selecting a show. Click Show and return to the agenda slide after viewing the last slide in the custom show.

To Add a Summary Slide

1 **Click Slide 2. Press and hold the CTRL key and then click Slides 3 and 5. Release the CTRL key. Double-click the move handle on the Slide Sorter toolbar. Point to the Summary Slide button on the Slide Sorter toolbar.**

Three slides are selected (Figure 4-68).

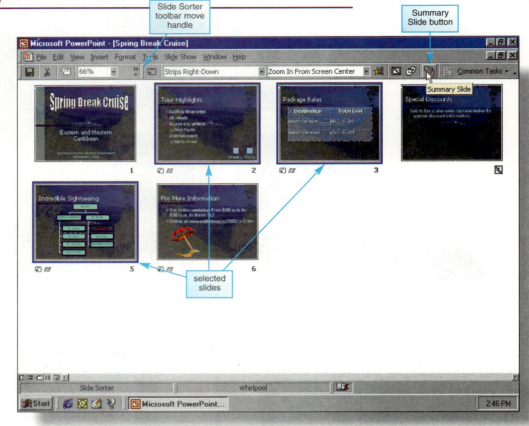

FIGURE 4-68

2 **Click the Summary Slide button.**

The summary slide is inserted as Slide 2 (Figure 4-69). The title text from Slides 2, 3, and 5 displays on this slide.

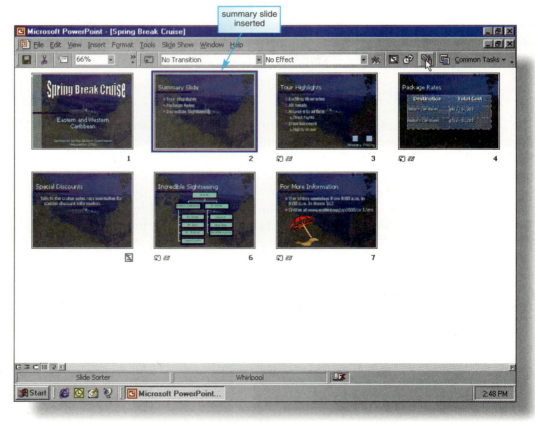

FIGURE 4-69

3 **Double-click Slide 2. Triple-click the Title Object placeholder, and then type** Cruise Summary **as the new title text.**

The summary slide displays in normal view, and the new title text displays (Figure 4-70).

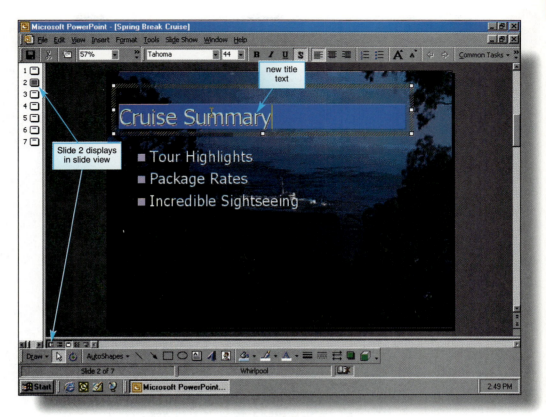

FIGURE 4-70

Deleting a Slide

The last steps in this project are to delete the last slide (Slide 7) and move the summary slide to the end of the presentation. Slide 7 is a slide from the original Spring Break presentation and is not necessary in this slide show. The summary slide ends the presentation conveniently, for it highlights the main topics that are discussed in the slide show. Perform the following steps to delete the last slide from within slide sorter view.

TO DELETE A SLIDE

1 Click the Slide 7 icon in the outline pane.

2 Press the DELETE key.

3 Click the OK button in the Microsoft PowerPoint dialog box.

Slide 7 is deleted from the presentation.

Repositioning the Summary Slide

The summary slide should be the last slide in the presentation before the black slide, which was added in Project 1. With the summary slide, the presenter can highlight the topics discussed previously and summarize them. This is an appropriate ending to the topics explained in the presentation, bringing closure to the sections.

You now are ready to reposition the summary slide to the end of the slide show as described in the steps on the next page.

Exporting to Slides

When your audience exceeds 50 people, you might want to consider using 35mm slides instead of a projection device attached to your computer. These 35mm slides have outstanding clarity, and they are best suited for noninteractive presentations. Memphis-based Genigraphics has teamed with Microsoft to produce these slides directly from a PowerPoint presentation. Click Send to on the File menu and then select Genigraphics. The Genigraphics wizard then steps you through placing an order, which can be filled as quickly as overnight. For more information about Genigraphics, visit the PowerPoint 2000 Project 4 More About page (www.scsite.com/pp2000/more.htm) and click Genigraphics.

Steps **To Reposition the Summary Slide**

1 **Click the Slide 2 icon in the outline pane and drag it below Slide 6.**

The ScreenTip, Cruise Summary, is the Slide 2 title text (Figure 4-71).

2 **Release the mouse button.**

The summary slide now is Slide 6, and the slides in the presentation are renumbered to reflect this change.

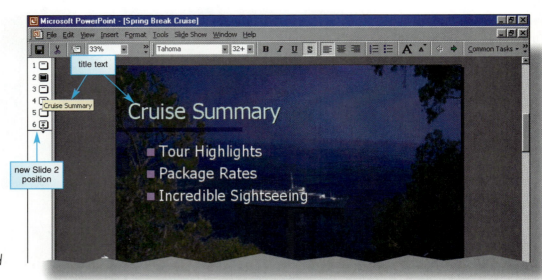

FIGURE 4-71

Applying Slide Transition Effects

Slide 6, the summary slide, was added to the presentation and therefore does not have slide transition effects applied. Recall from Project 3 that the Strips Right-Down slide transition effect was applied to all slides with bullets. The Zoom In From Screen Center preset animation effect also was applied. To keep Slide 6 consistent with the other bulleted slides in the presentation, apply these effects, as described in the following steps.

TO APPLY SLIDE TRANSITION AND TEXT PRESET ANIMATION EFFECTS

1 Click the Slide Sorter View button. If necessary, click Slide 6 to select it.

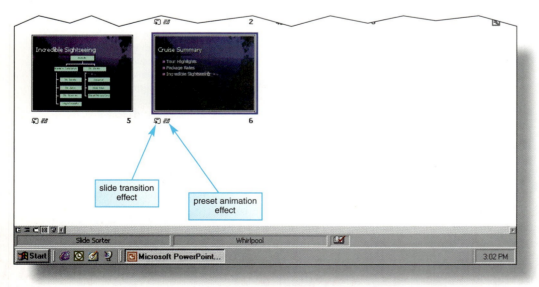

2 Click the Slide Transition Effects box arrow and then click Strips Right-Down in the list.

3 Click the Preset Animation box arrow and then click Zoom In From Screen Center in the list.

PowerPoint applies the Strips Right-Down slide transition and Zoom In From Screen Center preset animation effects to Slide 6 (Figure 4-72).

FIGURE 4-72

Save the Presentation

The presentation is complete. You now should save it again.

Running a Slide Show with a Hidden Slide and Interactive Documents

Running a slide show that contains hidden slides or interactive documents basically is the same as running any other slide show. You must, however, know where slides are hidden. When a slide contains interactive documents, you can activate them by clicking the action button that represents the document. The Cruise Itinerary document displays in Microsoft Word, and the Cruise Pricing spreadsheet displays in Microsoft Excel. When you are finished displaying the interactive document and want to return to the presentation, click the Close button on the title bar of the application. Perform the following steps to run the Spring Break Cruise presentation.

Presentation Guidelines

Graphic designers and speech coaches work together at the corporate level to help senior officials develop effective presentations. The individuals focus on aesthetically pleasing presentations and a fluent delivery. For specific examples of their advice, visit the PowerPoint 2000 Project 4 More About page (www.scsite.com/pp2000/more.htm) and click Guidelines.

TO RUN A SLIDE SHOW WITH A HIDDEN SLIDE AND INTERACTIVE DOCUMENTS

1 Go to Slide 1. Click the Slide Show button at the lower left of the PowerPoint window.

2 Click Slide 1 to display Slide 2.

3 When Slide 2 displays, click four times to display the bulleted list. Click the Itinerary action button. If necessary, maximize the Microsoft Word window when the document displays. Click the Close button on the Cruise Itinerary – Microsoft Word title bar to quit Word.

4 In Slide 2, click the Pricing action button. If necessary, maximize the Microsoft Excel window when the spreadsheet displays. Click the Close button on the Microsoft Excel – Cruise Pricing title bar to quit Excel.

5 Click Slide 2 to display Slide 3.

6 Click Slide 3 to display the table. After viewing Slide 3, press the H key to display the hidden slide, Slide 4.

7 Click the background of Slide 4 to display Slide 5.

8 Click Slide 5 to display the organization chart. Click Slide 5 to display Slide 6.

9 Click Slide 6 three times to display the bulleted summary list. Click Slide 6 again to display the black slide that ends the slide show. Click the black slide to return to the PowerPoint window.

10 Double-click the move handle on the Standard toolbar. Click the Save button on the Standard toolbar.

11 Click the Close button on the title bar.

Slide 1 displays in normal view, PowerPoint quits, and then control returns to the desktop.

C A S E   P E R S P E C T I V E   S U M M A R Y

The revised Spring Break Cruise presentation should pique the students' interest once again in attending the Student Government Association's activity. Your slide show is a versatile method of marketing the cruise, for it contains an interactive slide that provides links to other slides with specific information on the itinerary and pricing for the Eastern and Western Caribbean islands that will be visited. The added slide can be hidden depending on time constraints, and the new WordArt object on the title slide adds visual interest. Running this presentation should result in another sold-out Spring Break Cruise trip for the SGA.

Project Summary

Project 4 customized the Spring Break presentation created in Project 3. The first step was to save the presentation with a new file name to preserve the Project 3 presentation. You then changed the presentation background by adding a new photograph. Next, you used WordArt to create a heading for the title slide. After creating the WordArt object, you added a special text effect to the letters. You repositioned the heading object on the title slide of the Spring Break Cruise presentation. Next, you created a slide containing hyperlinks to a Microsoft Word document and a Microsoft Excel spreadsheet highlighting additional information about the cruise options. Then, you altered a table, inserting a new background color and deleting a row. After completing changes to the table, you created a new slide and marked it hidden because you will display it during the slide show only if time permits or if the audience is interested in the material. Next, you created a summary slide that contains the titles of all selected slides. You repositioned the summary slide and added slide transition effects and preset animation to it. You ran the slide show to display the hidden slide and interactive documents. Finally, you closed the presentation and quit PowerPoint.

What You Should Know

Having completed this project, you now should be able to perform the following tasks:

▶ Add a New Slide *(PP 4.47)*

▶ Add a Slide Title *(PP 4.47)*

▶ Add a Summary Slide *(PP 4.52)*

▶ Add an Action Button and Action Settings *(PP 4.27)*

▶ Add Captions to the Action Buttons *(PP 4.35)*

▶ Add Fill Color to the Action Buttons *(PP 4.34)*

▶ Add Right Co-worker Boxes *(PP 4.41)*

▶ Add Shadows to the Action Buttons *(PP 4.35)*

▶ Add Slide Text and Remove Bullets *(PP 4.48)*

▶ Apply Slide Transition and Text Preset Animation Effects *(PP 4.54)*

▶ Change an Organization Chart Box and Text Color *(PP 4.38)*

▶ Change Text *(PP 4.7)*

▶ Change the Background *(PP 4.8)*

▶ Change the Slide Order in a Presentation *(PP 4.50)*

▶ Change the Table Fill Color *(PP 4.45)*

▶ Change the WordArt Fill Color *(PP 4.19)*

▶ Change the WordArt Height and Width *(PP 4.17)*

▶ Create a Second Action Button and Hyperlink *(PP 4.30)*

▶ Delete a Branch of an Organization Chart *(PP 4.39)*

▶ Delete and Modify the Slide Text *(PP 4.9)*

▶ Delete a Slide *(PP 4.53)*

▶ Delete a Table Row *(PP 4.45)*

▶ Display the Guides and Position the Action Buttons *(PP 4.31)*

▶ Display the Guides *(PP 4.11)*

▶ Display the Rulers *(PP 4.10)*

▶ Edit Existing Text *(PP 4.24)*

▶ Edit Text in an Organization Chart *(PP 4.40)*

▶ Edit the Table Text *(PP 4.44)*

▶ Enter the WordArt Text *(PP 4.15)*

▶ Format a Second Caption Text *(PP 4.37)*

▶ Format Text *(PP 4.36)*

▶ Hide a Slide *(PP 4.49)*

▶ Hide the Guides *(PP 4.38)*

▶ Hide the Rulers and Guides *(PP 4.22)*

▶ Increase the Zoom Percentage *(PP 4.13)*

▶ Move a Paragraph in Outline View *(PP 4.25)*

▶ Open a Presentation and Save It with a New File Name *(PP 4.6)*

▶ Position the Guides *(PP 4.12)*

▶ Reposition the Summary Slide *(PP 4.54)*

▶ Reset the Zoom Percentage *(PP 4.22)*

▶ Run a Slide Show with a Hidden Slide and Interactive Documents *(PP 4.55)*

▶ Save the Chart and Return to the Presentation *(PP 4.43)*

▶ Scale Action Buttons *(PP 4.33)*

▶ Scale the WordArt Object *(PP 4.21)*

▶ Select a WordArt Style *(PP 4.14)*

Apply Your Knowledge

⊕ Project Reinforcement at www.scsite.com/off2000/reinforce.htm

1 Changing a Background and Creating a WordArt Object

Instructions: Start PowerPoint. Open the Crocodile file on your Data Disk. See the inside back cover of this book for instructions for downloading the Data Disk or see your instructor for information on accessing the files required for this book. Perform the following tasks to modify the slide so it displays as shown in Figure 4-73.

1. Click File on the menu bar, and then click Save As. Save the presentation with the file name, Croc Update.
2. Apply the Bamboo design template.
3. Change the background by right-clicking the slide anywhere other than the Title Area or Object Area placeholders and clicking Background on the shortcut menu. Click the Background fill area box arrow and then click Fill Effects in the list. Click the Texture tab in the Fill Effects dialog box. Scroll down and double-click the Water Droplets texture (row 5, column 1).
4. Insert the crocodile clip art shown in Figure 4-73. Scale the crocodile clip art to 200% and drag it to the lower-right corner of the slide.
5. Right-click the crocodile clip art, point to Grouping on the shortcut menu, and then click Ungroup on the Grouping submenu. Click outside the object to deselect the ungrouped objects.
6. Click the green area above the crocodile's head and then press the DELETE key. Click the blue area below the crocodile's head and then press the DELETE key.
7. Regroup the crocodile by dragging the mouse pointer diagonally from the lower-right corner of the slide to above the crocodile's nose. Right-click the crocodile object, click Grouping on the shortcut menu, and then click Group.
8. Animate the crocodile object by right-clicking the object, clicking Custom Animation on the shortcut menu, and then clicking Crawl in the left Entry animation and sound box and From Right in the right Entry animation and sound box.

FIGURE 4-73

9. Click the Insert WordArt button on the Drawing toolbar. Click the WordArt style in row 4, column 4. Type Tales from the Swamp in the Edit WordArt Text dialog box. Scale the WordArt object to 175%.
10. Add your name and today's date to the slide footer.
11. Save the Croc Update file again.
12. Print the slide using the Pure black and white option. Quit PowerPoint.

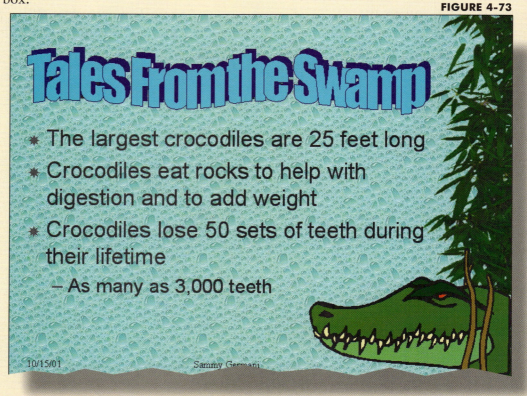

In the Lab

1 Creating a Title Slide Containing WordArt

Problem: Your local park district recently completed clearing a trail for mountain bikers. You have volunteered to help publicize the trail by creating a PowerPoint presentation to load on your school's intranet. The park board commissioners want to approve the title slide before you work on the entire project. The title slide contains a WordArt object and an AutoShape. You create the title slide shown in Figure 4-74.

Instructions: Start PowerPoint and perform the following tasks with a computer.

1. Open a blank presentation and then apply the Title Slide AutoLayout. Insert the Mountain Bike picture on the Data Disk for the background and then apply the Fireball design template. Type the subtitle text in the Object Area placeholder as shown in Figure 4-74.

2. Create the WordArt object by clicking the Insert WordArt button on the Drawing toolbar. In the WordArt Gallery dialog box, select the WordArt style in row 4, column 5. Type Come Play in the Dirt in the Edit WordArt Text dialog box. Scale the object to 160%. Display the guides and rulers. Drag the vertical guide to 4.58 inches left of center and the horizontal guide to 0.50 inches above center. Drag the WordArt object so that the left side of the object snaps to the vertical guide and the bottom of the object snaps to the horizontal guide. Hide the guides and rulers.

3. Click the AutoShapes menu button on the Drawing toolbar. Click Stars and Banners, and then click the Explosion 1 shape (row 1, column 1). Click the lower-left corner of the slide to insert the shape.

4. Scale the Explosion AutoShape to 250%. Type Now Open! in the shape. Change the font to 28-point Tahoma. Click the Free Rotate button on the Drawing toolbar, click one of the green handles on the perimeter of the shape, and rotate the shape to the left so it displays as shown in Figure 4-74.

5. Apply the Spiral animation effect to animate the shape automatically.

6. Save the presentation with the file name, Bike Trail. Print the title slide using the Pure black and white option. Quit PowerPoint.

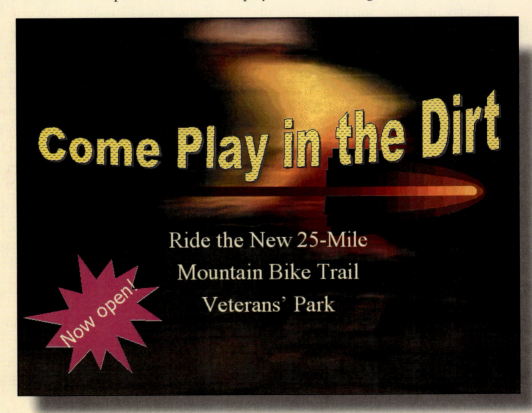

FIGURE 4-74

2 Using the AutoContent Wizard

Problem: Your Introduction to Business instructor, Professor John Fine, has required you to form a group to develop marketing materials for the Tutoring Center. Now he is asking for an oral status report of how the group is progressing and what specific tasks you have accomplished. You decide to create a PowerPoint slide show to accompany your group presentation. You use the AutoContent Wizard to help you develop the key ideas for the slides. You create the presentation shown in Figures 4-75a through 4-75d.

Instructions: Start PowerPoint and perform the following tasks with a computer.

1. Start PowerPoint by opening a new Office document. When the New Office Document dialog box displays, click the AutoContent Wizard icon. When the AutoContent Wizard displays, click the Next button to display the Presentation type panel. Click the Projects button. If necessary, click Reporting Progress or Status, and then click the Next button. If necessary, click On-screen presentation in the Presentation style panel, and then click the Next button. In the Presentation options panel, enter Tutoring Center in the Presentation title text box and BUS 205 in the Footer text box. If necessary, click Date last updated and Slide number. Click the Next button. When the Finish panel displays, click the Finish button.

2. Enter your name as the text in the second paragraph as shown in Figure 4-75a.

3. Click the Insert WordArt button on the Drawing toolbar, and then click the WordArt style in row 4, column 3. Click the OK button in the WordArt Gallery dialog box, and then type Marketing Status Report in the Text text box in the Edit WordArt Text dialog box. Click the OK button.

4. Click Format WordArt on the WordArt toolbar. If necessary, click the Size tab. Click Lock aspect ratio, scale the object to 125%, and then click the OK button.

5. Display the guides and rulers. Drag the vertical guide to 1.83 inches left of center and the horizontal guide to 0.58 inches below center. Drag the WordArt object so that the lower-left corner of the object snaps to the intersection of the guides. Hide the guides and rulers.

6. Click the Slide Sorter View button at the lower left of the PowerPoint window and then delete Slides 4 through 9.

7. Double-click Slide 2, which has the title text Status Summary. Enter the text shown in Figure 4-75b.

8. Click the Next Slide button to display Slide 3, Progress. Create the table shown in Figure 4-75c. Change the column headings to 36 point and change the fill color for those two cells to gold.

9. Click the Next Slide button to display Slide 4, Goals for Next Review. Enter the text shown in Figure 4-75d.

10. Click the Slide Sorter View button at the lower left of the PowerPoint window. Apply the Box Out slide transition effect and the Spiral preset animation effect to Slides 2, 3, and 4. Hide Slide 4.

11. Run the Status Report presentation. When the complete Slide 2 displays, right-click the slide, point to Pointer Options and then click Pen on the Pointer Options submenu. Click and make a check mark in front of the two round bullets, and then circle each group member's name.

12. Press the PAGE DOWN key two times to display Slide 3.

13. Type H and then press the PAGE DOWN key four times to display Slide 4, the hidden slide. Make a check mark in front of the four round bullets.

14. Press the PAGE DOWN key two times to end the presentation.

15. Save the presentation with the file name, Status Report. Print the slides using the Pure black and white option. Quit PowerPoint.

In the Lab

Tutoring Center

Marketing Status Report

Tamara Washington

10/15/01

BUS 205

(a) Slide 1

Project Overview

- **Team goal – to develop marketing materials for Tutoring Center**
- **Team members**
  - **Liz Armstrong**
  - **Marcus Garcia**
  - **Tamara Washington**

10/15/01   BUS 205   2

(b) Slide 2

Project Tasks and Status

Tasks	Status
Interview managers	Complete
Design layout	Complete
Create logo	Complete
Design background	Complete by end month
Develop content	In process
Test	Not started

10/15/01   BUS 205

(c) Slide 3

Group Goals

- **Improve communication skills**
  - **Enhance interviewing abilities**
  - **Prepare written summaries**
- **Develop group cohesiveness**
- **Learn task delegation**
- **Meet most deadlines**

10/15/01   BUS 205   4

(d) Slide 4

FIGURE 4-75

In the Lab

3 Linking PowerPoint Presentations

Problem: Gardening is the favorite pastime of millions of homeowners and apartment dwellers. From huge flower and vegetable gardens in the backyard to compact container gardens on a patio, people have found this hobby a means of relieving stress, getting exercise, and finding rewards. You have offered to create a PowerPoint presentation for the Hometown Gardening Club to help the members with their seminars throughout the community. You decide an interactive slide show would be the best vehicle to answer the home gardeners' questions. Develop the presentation shown in Figures 4-76a through 4-76f on pages PP 4.63 through 4.65.

Instructions Part 1: Perform the following tasks to create three presentations: one consisting of Figures 4-76a and 4-76b, one of Figure 4-76c, and one of Figure 4-76d.

1. Open a new presentation and apply the Bulleted List AutoLayout and the Nature design template. Change the background to the Stationery texture, which is in row 1, column 4 of the Fill Effects dialog box.

2. Create the bulleted list slides shown in Figures 4-76a and 4-76b. Apply the Uncover Down slide transition effect to both slides. Save the presentation with the file name, Gardening Do's and Don'ts. Print the presentation slides using the Pure black and white option. Close the presentation.

3. Open a new presentation, apply the Bulleted List AutoLayout, and then apply the Nature design template. Change the background to the Stationery texture. Create the slide shown in Figure 4-76c. Apply the Split Horizontal Out slide transition effect. Save the presentation with the file name, Fertilizing Guidelines. Print the presentation slide using the Pure black and white option. Close the presentation.

4. Open a new presentation, apply the Table AutoLayout, and then apply the Nature design template. Change the background to the Stationery texture. Create the slide shown in Figure 4-76d. Format the three table headings to 32-point Gill Sans MT. Fill the table with a transparent background that has the color gold (row 1, column 6 under Automatic). Apply the Box Out slide transition effect. Save the presentation with the file name, Conversion Table. Print the presentation slide using the Pure black and white option. Close the presentation.

In the Lab

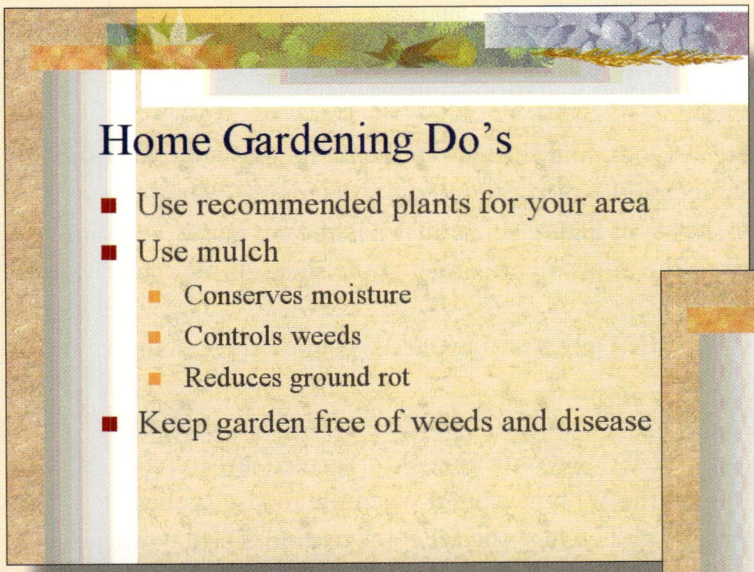

Home Gardening Do's

- Use recommended plants for your area
- Use mulch
  - Conserves moisture
  - Controls weeds
  - Reduces ground rot
- Keep garden free of weeds and disease

(a) Slide 1

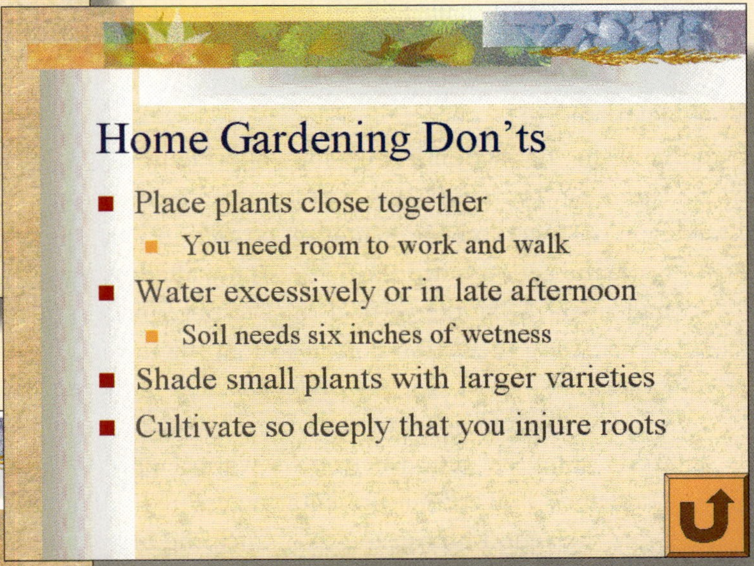

Home Gardening Don'ts

- Place plants close together
  - You need room to work and walk
- Water excessively or in late afternoon
  - Soil needs six inches of wetness
- Shade small plants with larger varieties
- Cultivate so deeply that you injure roots

(b) Slide 2

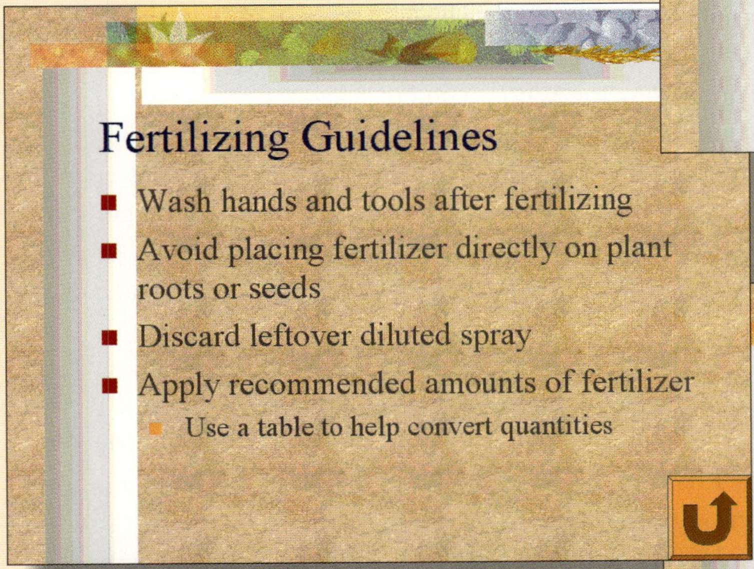

Fertilizing Guidelines

- Wash hands and tools after fertilizing
- Avoid placing fertilizer directly on plant roots or seeds
- Discard leftover diluted spray
- Apply recommended amounts of fertilizer
  - Use a table to help convert quantities

(c) Slide 3

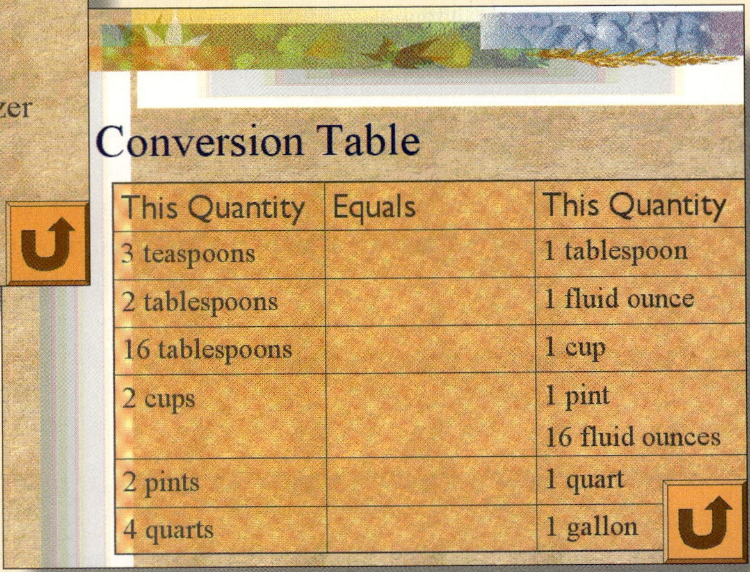

Conversion Table

This Quantity	Equals	This Quantity
3 teaspoons		1 tablespoon
2 tablespoons		1 fluid ounce
16 tablespoons		1 cup
2 cups		1 pint
		16 fluid ounces
2 pints		1 quart
4 quarts		1 gallon

(d) Slide 4

FIGURE 4-76

(continued)

In the Lab

Linking PowerPoint Presentations *(continued)*

Instructions Part 2:   Perform the following tasks to create the presentation shown in Figures 4-76e and 4-76f.

1. Open a new presentation, apply the Title Slide AutoLayout, and then apply the Nature design template. Change the background to the Stationery texture. Create the slide title shown in Figure 4-76e by typing the slide title text and subtitle text. Insert the clip art shown in Figure 4-76e that has the keywords, gardens, light bulbs. Scale the clip art to 125% and drag it to the upper-right corner of the slide. Apply the Dissolve animation effect to animate the flowers automatically.

2. Click the New Slide button and type 11 to apply the Title Only AutoLayout. Type the title text shown in Figure 4-76f.

3. Add the first action button shown in Figure 4-76f, which is in row 1, column 4 of the Action Buttons submenu. Hyperlink this action button to the first slide, Home Gardening Do's, of the Gardening Do's and Don'ts PowerPoint presentation created in Part 1. Play the Whoosh sound when the mouse is clicked.

4. Scale the action button to 75%, apply Shadow Style 2, and change the fill color to gold. Display the guides and rulers. Drag the vertical ruler to 0.42 inches left of center and the horizontal ruler to 0.25 inches above center. Drag the action button so that the lower-left corner snaps to the intersection of the guides. Type the caption Do s and Don ts under this action button, and then change the font to 20-point Gill Sans MT. Change the font color to navy blue. Use the ARROW keys to center the caption under the action button.

5. Add the middle action button shown in Figure 4-76f. Hyperlink this action button to the Fertilizing Guidelines PowerPoint presentation created in Part 1. Play the Whoosh sound when the mouse is clicked.

6. Scale the action button to 75%. Click the first action button, click the Format Painter button on the Standard toolbar, and then click the middle action button. Drag the horizontal ruler to 1.33 inches below center. Drag the second action button so that the lower-left corner snaps to the intersection of the guides. Type the caption Fertilizing Guidelines under this action button, click the caption under the first action button, click the Format Painter button, and then drag through the middle caption text. Use the ARROW keys to center the caption under the action button.

7. Add the bottom action button shown in Figure 4-76f. Hyperlink this action button to the Conversion Table PowerPoint presentation created in Part 1. Play the Whoosh sound when the mouse is clicked.

8. Scale the action button to 75%. Click the first action button, click the Format Painter button, and then click the third action button. Drag the horizontal ruler to 3.00 inches below center. Drag the action button so that the lower-left corner snaps to the intersection of the guides. Type the caption Conversion Table under this action button, click the caption under the first action button, click the Format Painter button, and then drag through the bottom caption text. Use the ARROW keys to center the caption under the action button. Hide the guides and rulers.

9. Apply the Split Vertical Out slide transition effect to Slide 2. Save the presentation with the file name, Bulbs to Blossoms.

10. Add the Return action button (row 3, column 1) to the lower-right corner of each of the three hyperlinked presentations, as shown in Figures 4-76b, 4-76c, and 4-76d. Hyperlink each button to Slide 2, Home Gardening Guide, of the Bulbs to Blossoms presentation. Change the buttons' fill color to gold. Save the three hyperlinked presentations.

In the Lab

11. Print the six presentation slides using the Pure black and white option.

12. Run the Bulbs to Blossoms slide show. Click the Do's and Don'ts action button to display the hyperlinked presentation. Display both slides. Click the hyperlink at the bottom of the second slide to jump to the Bulbs to Blossoms presentation. When the Home Gardening Guide presentation returns, click the Fertilizing Guidelines action button, read the new slide, and click the hyperlink at the bottom of the slide. Repeat this procedure for the Conversion Table action button. Click to display the black closing slide. End the slide shows and quit PowerPoint.

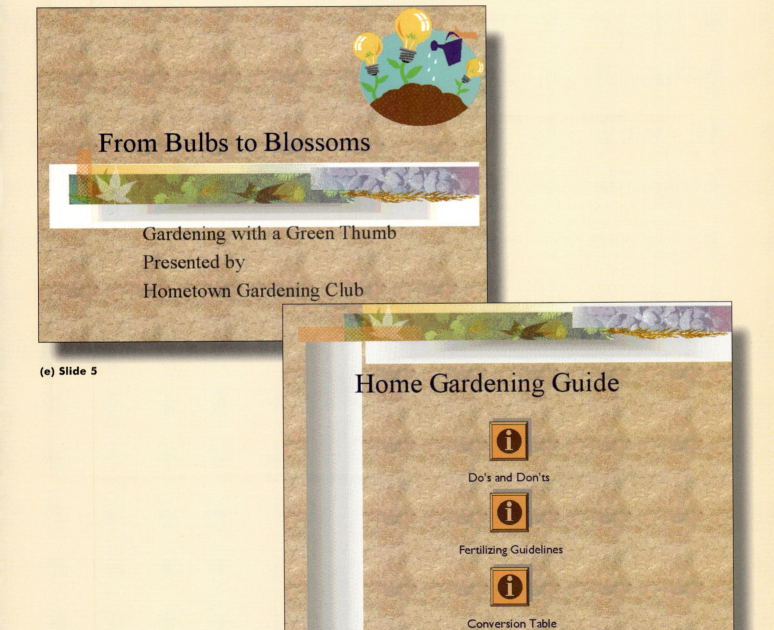

(e) Slide 5

(f) Slide 6

FIGURE 4-76d

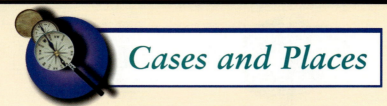

Cases and Places

The difficulty of these case studies varies:
◗ are the least difficult; ◗◗ are more difficult; and ◗◗◗ are the most difficult.

1 ◗ The marketing director of your local food pantry has asked you to help with a holiday food drive on campus. You decide to develop an interactive slide show to run in the cafeteria during the lunch and dinner rush. Prepare a short presentation aimed at encouraging students to bring canned goods and small cash donations to campus next week on Thursday and Friday. One slide should show an Excel worksheet explaining how one dollar can provide three dollars of food because local businesses have agreed to match the contributions. Other slides can feature a list of these participating businesses, statistics on how many people have come to the food pantry for assistance during the past three years, and volunteer opportunities. The title slide should give the dates and hours of the food drive and include WordArt for visual appeal. The final slide should give the address and telephone number of the food pantry.

2 ◗ Computer viruses and worm programs are a major concern in all facets of computing – from the corporate world to the home office. All computer users need to practice safe computing practices; these techniques include not opening or running any executable e-mail file attachment (.exe) sent from an unknown source, installing an anti-virus program on your computer (Norton or McAfee), and ensuring the anti-virus' auto protect feature is enabled (check the tray status area on the taskbar). Computer users should be alert for macro viruses, boot sector viruses, and worms. Macro viruses hide the virus code in the macro language of an application, such as Microsoft Word. When a user opens a document having an infected macro, the macro virus is loaded into memory. Certain actions, such as saving the document, activate the macro virus. Boot sector viruses replace the boot programs, which are used to start the computer systems, with modified, infected versions of the boot programs. When the infected boot programs are run, they load the viruses into the computers' memory. Once the viruses are in memory, they spread to floppy disks inserted into the computers. Unlike viruses, worm programs do not attach themselves to other programs. Instead, they copy themselves repeatedly in memory or on disk drives until no memory or disk space remains. The computers stop working when no memory or disk space exists. Some worm programs copy themselves to other computers on a network. Your school's computer lab supervisors have asked you to prepare a PowerPoint presentation explaining computer viruses and worms to students. Using the techniques introduced in this project, create an interactive short slide show using three buttons that correspond to the two virus types and the worm program. Include WordArt on the title slide, animated text, and slide transition effects.

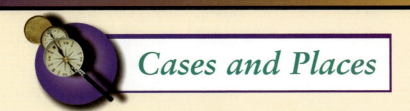

Cases and Places

3 ▶▶ Swing dancing is popular on campus, but very few students know a variety of steps and how to blend them together smoothly. Four of your friends are expert ballroom dancers and have competed in local contests. They have decided to give dance lessons, and they want you to help with their publicity. You decide to create a slide show and want to start by designing a title slide that captures the spirit of swing dancing. Use PowerPoint and WordArt to create the title slide and a short slide show to present to your friends. Enhance the presentation by modifying the slide background and adding graphics, slide transition effects, and a summary slide.

4 ▶▶ Nearly two-thirds of colleges offer personal finance classes, but only one-fourth of the students actually enroll in one. Those who do enroll, however, are no more than nonenrollees to save regularly, comparison shop, or create a budget. Your local credit union realizes this problem that students have with saving routinely, and the managers want to encourage students to take advantage of the services offered at its on-campus branch. You have agreed to develop a persuasive PowerPoint slide show explaining how saving regularly builds a balance that helps with tuition payments. Add other slides featuring additional credit union services, such as certificates of deposit, credit cards with low interest, and vehicle loans. Visit local branches of credit unions or search the Internet to find information for the presentation.

5 ▶▶ Most prospective employees focus on salary and job responsibilities when they consider job offers. One area they often neglect, however, is benefit packages. Career counselors emphasize that these benefits can contribute significantly to salary levels and should be given serious consideration. Specifically, job hunters should investigate retirement plans, stock options, life insurance coverage, health coverage, tuition reimbursement, signing bonuses, and on-site fitness facilities. Visit your campus placement office or search the Internet to find the benefits packages offered by three companies to which you might consider sending a resume and cover letter. Using this information and the techniques introduced in the project, prepare an interactive presentation that compares these benefit packages. Enhance the presentation by modifying the slide background, adding graphics, using text preset animation effects, and applying slide transition effects. Include a hidden slide and a summary slide. Submit all files on a disk to your instructor.

Microsoft PowerPoint 2000

Importing Clips from the Microsoft Clip Gallery Live Web Site

C A S E   P E R S P E C T I V E

The two Spring Break trips to the Florida and Texas beaches and to the Caribbean islands have generated much interest and revenue for the Student Government Association. Now the SGA president, Marla Pervan, wants to add more special effects to your presentation. She suggests you revise the Spring Break presentation created in Project 3 by adding an animated sun and music that has the sound of waves in the background. You review the slide show and decide to add a winking sun and upbeat music to Slide 5. You look at Microsoft Clip Gallery 5.0, but you do not find any appropriate animated clips or music. Knowing that Internet access is built into the Microsoft Clip Gallery, you decide to browse the Microsoft Clip Gallery Live Web site for suitable animated clip art pictures and upbeat music for Slide 5.

Introduction

Although the Microsoft Clip Gallery has a wide variety of picture images, at times it does not have a file that fits your exact needs. Microsoft has created Clip Gallery Live, a source of additional pictures, sounds, and movie clips on the World Wide Web. To access this Web site easily, you click the Clips Online button in the Microsoft Clip Gallery dialog box, and then PowerPoint connects you directly to the Microsoft Clip Gallery Live start page (Figure 1a on the next page).

In this Integration Feature, you modify Slide 5 in the presentation created in Project 3 by adding music and an animated sun from the Web, as shown in Figures 1b and 1c on the next page.

Opening an Existing Presentation and Saving It with a New File Name

Because you are adding clips to the Spring Break presentation created in Project 3, the first step is to open the presentation. To ensure that the original Spring Break presentation remains intact, you save the presentation with a new name; Musical Spring Break. Then you connect to the World Wide Web and import the music and animated sun. The following pages illustrate these steps.

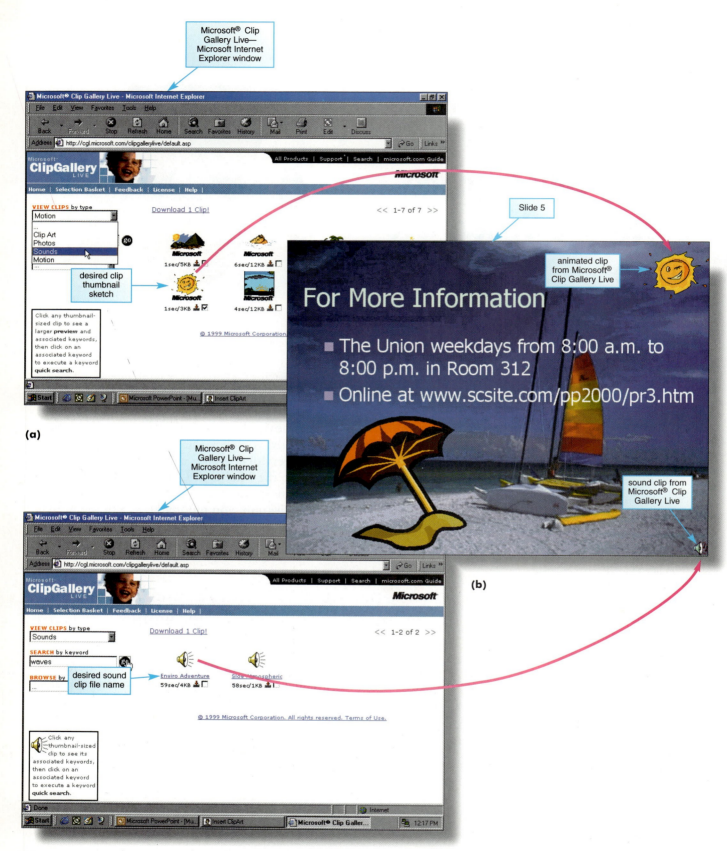

FIGURE 1

TO OPEN AN EXISTING PRESENTATION AND SAVE IT WITH A NEW FILE NAME

1 Insert your Data Disk in drive A. Click the Start button on the taskbar. Click Open Office Document.

2 If necessary, click the Look in box arrow and then click 3½ Floppy (A:).

3 Double-click Spring Break.

4 Click File on the menu bar and then click Save As. Type Musical Spring Break in the File name text box.

5 Click the Save button in the Save As dialog box.

PowerPoint opens the Spring Break file and then saves it with a new file name, Musical Spring Break, on your floppy disk in drive A. The new file name displays on the title bar.

Clip Gallery Live

The clips you download while working on your PowerPoint presentation can be used in other Microsoft Office applications. For example, the sun you import in this project can be part of a flyer created in Microsoft Word, and the music can play while users view a Microsoft Excel chart. The clips also can be used and reused in Microsoft Publisher, Microsoft FrontPage, Microsoft PhotoDraw, and Microsoft Works.

Moving to Another Slide

When creating or editing your presentation, you often want to display a slide other than the current one. Dragging the vertical scroll box up or down displays the slide indicator. Recall the slide indicator displays the slide number and title of the slide you are about to display. Once you see the number of the slide you wish to display, release the mouse button. Perform the following step to move to Slide 5 using the vertical scroll box.

TO MOVE TO ANOTHER SLIDE

1 Drag the vertical scroll box down until Slide: 5 of 5 For More Information displays in the slide indicator.

Slide 5 displays (Figure 2).

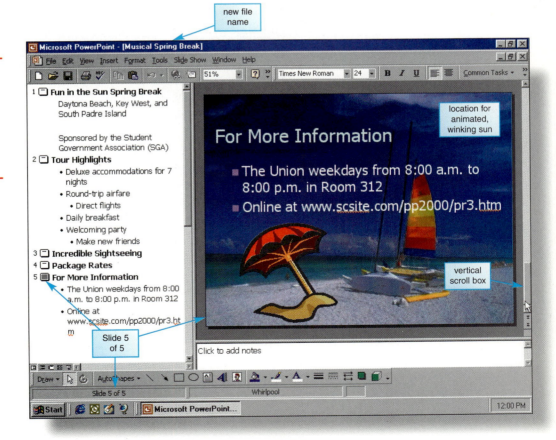

FIGURE 2

Importing Clip Art from Microsoft Clip Gallery Live on the World Wide Web

Recall from Project 2 that one source for additional clip art images is the World Wide Web. Many companies provide clip art images on the Web; some sites offer clips free of charge, and others charge a fee.

Microsoft maintains a Web site called Clip Gallery Live that contains clip art pictures, photographs, sounds, and videos. To use the Microsoft Clip Gallery Live Web site, you must have access to the World Wide Web through an **Internet service provider (ISP)**. Then you use **Web browser** software to find the Microsoft site. This project uses **Microsoft Internet Explorer** for the Web browser. If you do not have Internet access, your instructor will provide the two clips used in this project.

To simplify connecting to the Clip Gallery Live Web site, the Microsoft Clip Gallery dialog box contains a Clips Online button. Your sign-in process depends on your ISP and your computer configuration. For example, some ISPs require users to identify themselves with a name and password. Some schools bypass this window because of the school's Web connection setup. See your instructor for your school's requirements. If you are connecting to the Web at a location other than school, you must know the ISP's sign in requirements.

Connecting to the Microsoft Clip Gallery Live Site

You want to add music that contains the background sound of waves and insert an animated sun on Slide 5. Once you connect to the Web, the Microsoft Clip Gallery Live start page displays. A **start page** is a specially-designed page that serves as a starting point for a Web site. Microsoft updates this start page frequently to reflect seasons, holidays, new collections, artists, special offers, and events.

Perform the following steps to open Microsoft Clip Gallery, connect to the World Wide Web, and then display the Microsoft Clip Gallery Live start page.

More About 2000

The End-User License Agreement

When you view the Microsoft Clip Gallery Live start page for the first time, you may be asked to read the Microsoft End-User License Agreement (EULA). When you click the Accept button, you agree to abide by the copyright restrictions Microsoft imposes to protect the use of its software. Read the EULA to see what rights and restrictions you have to use clips found at this site. For more information, visit the PowerPoint 2000 More About Web page (www.scsite.com/pp2000/more.htm) and click EULA.

Steps ## To Connect to the Microsoft Clip Gallery Live Site

1 **Click the Insert Clip Art button on the Drawing toolbar. Point to the Clips Online button on the Insert ClipArt toolbar.**

Microsoft Clip Gallery 5.0 opens and displays the Pictures sheet in the Insert ClipArt window (Figure 3).

2 **Click the Clips Online button. If necessary, click the OK button in the Connect to Web for More Clip Art, Photos, Sounds dialog box to browse for additional clips. Connect to the World Wide Web as required by your browser software and ISP. When the Microsoft Clip Gallery Live start page displays, if necessary maximize the screen and read the Microsoft End-User License Agreement for Microsoft Software and click the Accept button.**

FIGURE 3

If you are using a modem, a dialog box displays that connects you to the Web via your ISP. If you are connected directly to the Web through a computer network, the dialog box does not display. Once connected to the Web, the Microsoft Clip Gallery Live start page displays the Microsoft End-User License Agreement. When you click the Accept button, the Microsoft End-User License Agreement area no longer displays. The site now displays information about Microsoft® Clip Gallery Live features and text boxes to locate specific types of clips.

Searching for and Downloading Microsoft Clip Gallery Live Clips

Microsoft Clip Gallery Live is similar to Microsoft Clip Gallery 5.0 in that you can search for clip art by keywords. You want to locate a motion clip animating the sun and music containing the sound of waves. You first will search Microsoft Clip Gallery Live for motion files with the keyword, sun. Then, you will search for sound files with the keyword, waves.

Accepting the EULA

When you accept the terms of the Microsoft End-User License Agreement, your computer sends a message to Clip Gallery Live stating that you agree to the licensing restrictions. Microsoft, in turn, sends a message, called a cookie, to your computer so that you will not be asked to accept the EULA each time you visit the Clip Gallery Live site. If you are using Internet Explorer 4.0 or later and are asked to accept the agreement each time you go to this site, your computer probably has been instructed not to accept cookies.

Finding Clips

You may enter a maximum of 36 characters or 6 keywords in the SEARCH by keyword text box. These keywords must be separated by spaces or by commas. Only clips matching all the keywords will display.

When you find a clip to add to your presentation, you can **download**, or copy, it instantly to the Microsoft Clip Gallery on your computer by clicking the Immediate Download icon under the desired clip. You also can select several clips individually and then download them simultaneously. In this project, you want to download motion and sound clips, so you will choose a motion file and then select the check box below the clip to add the file to the selection basket. The **selection basket** holds your selections temporarily until you are ready to add them to your computer. Then, you will add the sound clip to the selection basket. The downloaded clips will be added to the Microsoft Clip Gallery in the Downloaded Clips category. To remove a clip from the selection basket, clear the clip's check box.

Perform the following steps to search for clips in Microsoft Clip Gallery Live.

To Search for and Download Microsoft Clip Gallery Live Clips

1 Click the VIEW CLIPS by type arrow in the Microsoft® Clip Gallery Live window. Point to Motion in the list.

The Selection Basket sheet displays (Figure 4). Microsoft groups the clips in four categories: Clip Art, Photos, Sounds, and Motion.

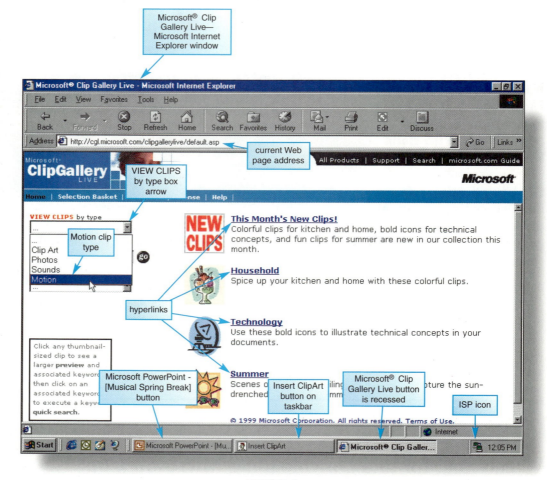

FIGURE 4

2 **Click Motion. Click the SEARCH by keyword text box and type sun in the box. Point to the Go button (Figure 5).**

FIGURE 5

3 **Click the Go button. When the search results display, click the check box below the winking sun clip. Click the VIEW CLIPS by type arrow. Point to Sounds in the list.**

Clip Gallery Live executes the search and displays the results (Figure 6). When you click the check box associated with the thumbnail-sized clip, the motion clip is added to the selection basket, as indicated by the Download 1 Clip! hyperlink. The search status displays at the upper-right corner of the page and indicates the number of clips that match the search criteria. The numbers below the file name are the estimated download time and the clip's file size.

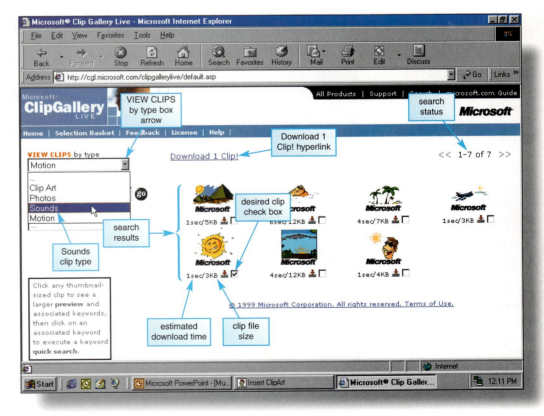

FIGURE 6

4 **Click Sounds. Click the SEARCH by keyword text box, select the text, and type** waves **in the box. Click the Go button.**

Clip Gallery Live executes the search. After a few moments, several thumbnail-sized sound clips with the keyword, waves, display (Figure 7). The speaker icons identify the sound clips. The hyperlink below each clip is its file name.

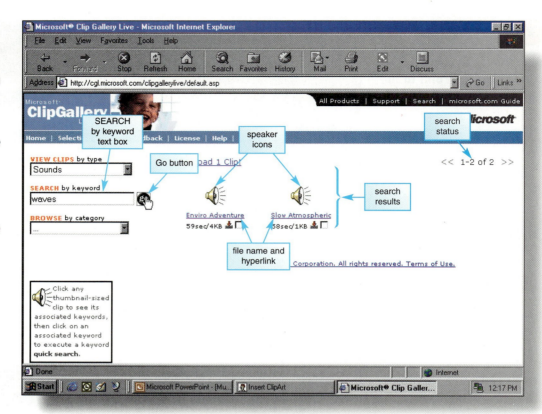

FIGURE 7

5 **Click the check box below the clip with the file name, Enviro Adventure. Point to the Download 2 Clips! hyperlink.**

When you click the check box, the sound clip is added to the selection basket, as indicated by the underlined Download 2 Clips! hyperlink (Figure 8).

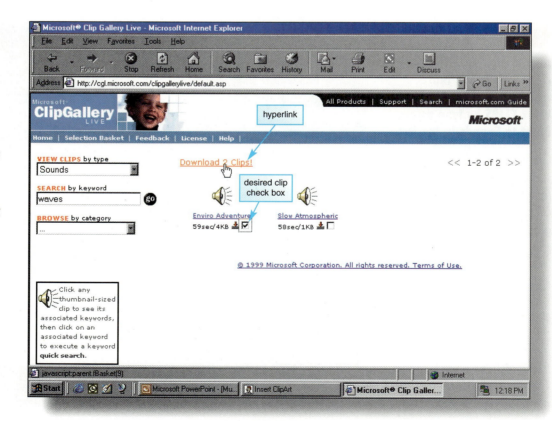

FIGURE 8

6 **Click the Download 2 Clips! hyperlink. Point to the Download Now! hyperlink in the first instruction in the Selection Basket sheet.**

The hyperlink displays with the font color red (Figure 9). Clicking the hyperlink will download the two clips stored temporarily in the selection basket.

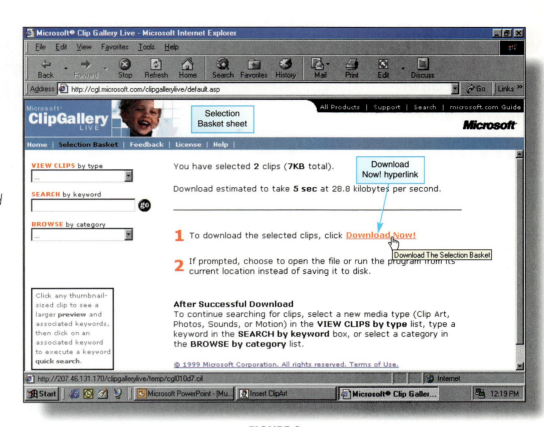

FIGURE 9

7 **Click the Download Now! hyperlink. If necessary, click the Motion Clips tab in the Insert ClipArt window. Click the sun icon and then point to the Insert clip button.**

When you click the sun icon, PowerPoint will insert the sun clip on Slide 5. Slide 5 will not be visible until you close the Insert ClipArt window (Figure 10).

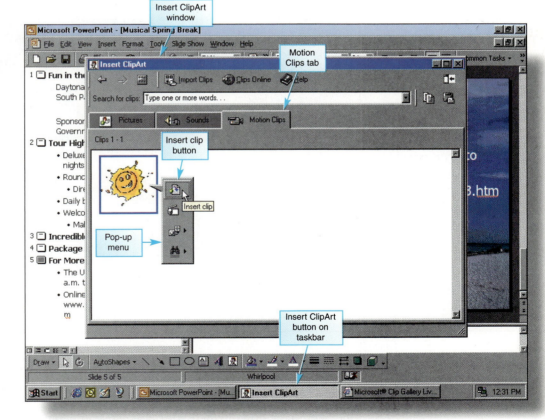

FIGURE 10

8 **Click the Insert clip button on the Pop-up menu. Click the Sounds tab in the Insert ClipArt window. Click the ETHTRK01 icon and then click the Insert clip button on the Pop-up menu. Point to the Close button on the Insert ClipArt window title bar.**

The Enviro Adventure clip, which has the file name ETHTRK01, displays on the Sounds sheet (Figure 11). When you click the Insert clip button, PowerPoint will insert this clip on Slide 5.

FIGURE 11

9 **Click the Close button on the title bar. Click the Yes button in the Microsoft PowerPoint dialog box.**

The animated sun and a speaker icon display on Slide 5 (Figure 12). You want the music to play automatically when your slide show displays Slide 5. Microsoft Clip Gallery Live still is open, and you still are connected to the ISP.

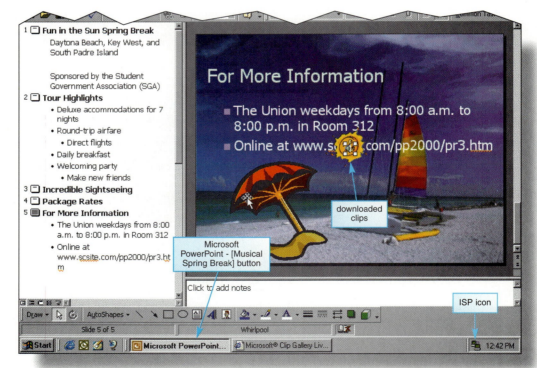

FIGURE 12

Quitting a Web Session

Once you have downloaded your clip art, you want to quit your Web session. Because Windows 98 displays buttons on the taskbar for each open application, you quickly can quit an application by right-clicking an application button and then clicking the Close button on the shortcut menu. Perform the following steps to quit your current Web session.

TO QUIT A WEB SESSION

1 Right-click the Microsoft® Clip Gallery Live – Microsoft Internet Explorer button on the taskbar. If you are not using Microsoft Internet Explorer, right-click the button for your browser.

2 Click Close on the shortcut menu.

3 When the dialog box displays, click the Yes button to disconnect. If your ISP displays a different dialog box, terminate your connection to your ISP.

The browser software closes and the ISP connection is terminated.

Slide 5 displays with the two downloaded objects in the center of the screen. The speaker object represents the Enviro Adventure sound file.

Moving the Clips

You want to move the speaker icon to the lower-right corner of the slide and the sun to the upper-right corner. Perform the following steps to move the clips to these respective locations.

TO MOVE THE CLIPS

1 Drag the speaker icon to the lower-right corner of Slide 5.

2 Drag the sun object to the upper-right corner of Slide 5.

The clips display in the appropriate locations on Slide 5 (Figure 13).

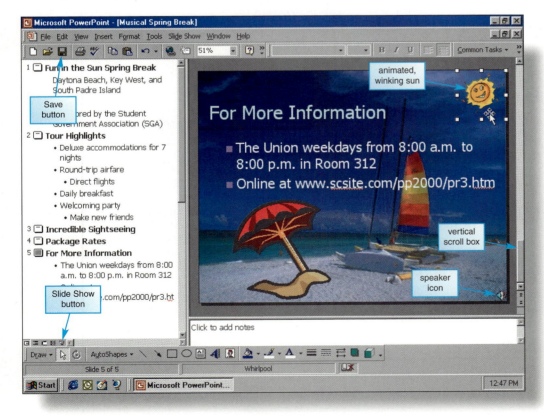

FIGURE 13

Saving the Presentation

The changes to the presentation are complete. Perform the following step to save the finished presentation on a floppy disk before running the slide show.

TO SAVE A PRESENTATION

1 Click the Save button on the Standard toolbar.

PowerPoint saves the presentation by saving the changes made to the presentation since the last save.

Running an Animated Slide Show

To verify that the presentation looks as expected, run the presentation in slide show view. Perform the following steps to run the revised Musical Spring Break slide show.

TO RUN AN ANIMATED SLIDE SHOW

1 Drag the vertical scroll box to display Slide: 1 of 5 Fun in the Sun Spring Break.

2 Click the Slide Show button at the lower left of the PowerPoint window. When Slide 1 displays in slide show view, click the slide anywhere except on the Pop-up menu buttons.

3 Continue clicking the slides to finish running the slide show and return to slide view.

The presentation displays the animated sun and plays the sound file in slide show view and returns to slide view when finished.

Now that the presentation is complete, the last step is to print the presentation slides.

Printing Presentation Slides

Perform the following steps to print the revised presentation.

TO PRINT PRESENTATION SLIDES

1 Click File on the menu bar and then click Print.

2 When the Print dialog box displays, click Pure black and white and then click the OK button.

Quitting PowerPoint

The changes to this presentation are saved. The last step is to quit PowerPoint. Perform the following steps to quit PowerPoint.

TO QUIT POWERPOINT

1 Click the Close button on the title bar.

2 If the Microsoft PowerPoint dialog box displays, click the Yes button to save changes made since the last save.

PowerPoint closes.

CASE PERSPECTIVE SUMMARY

The revised Spring Break presentation now has lively music and an animated, winking sun on Slide 5. These clips from the Microsoft Clip Gallery Live Web site enhance the slide show and should generate additional interest in this popular and profitable event for the Student Government Association.

Integration Feature Summary

This Integration Feature introduced importing sound and animation clips from Microsoft Clip Gallery Live on the World Wide Web to Microsoft Clip Gallery 5.0. You began by opening an existing presentation, Spring Break, and then saving the presentation with a new file name. Next, you accessed the Microsoft Clip Gallery Live start page on the World Wide Web by clicking the Clips Online button on the Insert ClipArt toolbar. Once connected to the Microsoft Clip Gallery Live start page, you searched for an animated sun and upbeat music with waves. Then you imported these clips to the Microsoft Clip Gallery by downloading the files from the Web page. You moved the clips to appropriate locations on Slide 5 and then quit the Web session by closing the browser software and disconnecting from the ISP. Finally, you saved the presentation, ran the presentation in slide show view to check for continuity, printed the presentation slides, and quit PowerPoint.

What You Should Know

Having completed this Integration Feature, you now should be able to perform the following tasks:

▶ Connect to the Microsoft Clip Gallery Live Site *(PPI 1.5)*
▶ Move the Clips *(PPI 1.11)*
▶ Move to Another Slide *(PPI 1.3)*
▶ Open an Existing Presentation and Save It with a New File Name *(PPI 1.3)*
▶ Print Presentation Slides *(PPI 1.12)*
▶ Quit a Web Session *(PPI 1.11)*
▶ Quit PowerPoint *(PPI 1.12)*
▶ Run an Animated Slide Show *(PPI 1.12)*
▶ Save a Presentation *(PPI 1.12)*
▶ Search for and Download Microsoft Clip Gallery Live Clips *(PPI 1.6)*

In the Lab

1 Importing Sound and Motion Clips

Problem: Dr. Mary Halen, the director of the Office of Financial Aid, realizes the importance of informing students of scholarship opportunities, and she wants to enhance the presentation you created in Project 2. Dr. Halen believes the sound of coins dropping into a drawer and an animated clip from the Microsoft Clip Gallery Live Web site would make the slide show even more impressive. She has asked you to find appropriate clips and to modify Slide 1 of the Searching for Scholarships presentation.

Instructions: Start PowerPoint and then perform the following steps with a computer.

1. Open the Searching for Scholarships presentation shown in Figures 2-1a through 2-1f on page PP 2.5 that you created in Project 2. (If you did not complete Project 2, see your instructor for a copy of the presentation.)
2. Save the Searching for Scholarships presentation with the new file name, Motion Scholarships.
3. Display Slide 1, click the Insert Clip Art button on the Drawing toolbar, and then click the Clips Online button on the Insert ClipArt toolbar.
4. Search for motion clips with the keyword, money. Then search for sound clips with the same keyword, money. Download the two clips, and have the sound play automatically.
5. Move the speaker icon to the lower-right corner of Slide 1, and move the money clip to the upper-right corner. Add today's date and your name to the footer.
6. Disconnect from the Web and save the file again.
7. Run the slide show. Print Slide 1. Quit PowerPoint.

2 Importing Motion and Multiple Sound Clips

Problem: The local park board commissioners are pleased that you have volunteered to publicize the new 25-mile mountain bike trail in Veterans' Park. They like the title slide you developed in the In the Lab 1 exercise in Project 4, but they would like you to add an animated bike rider and appropriate sound effects. You decide to search the Microsoft Clip Gallery Live Web site for the bike clips and for sounds of nature that reflect a relaxing outing.

Instructions: Start PowerPoint and then perform the following steps with a computer.

1. Open the Bike Trail presentation shown in Figure 4-74 on page PP 4.59 that you created in Project 4. (If you did not complete this exercise, see your instructor for a copy of the slide.)
2. Save the Bike Trail presentation with the new file name, Musical Biking.
3. Click the Insert Clip Art button on the Drawing toolbar, and then click the Clips Online button on the Insert ClipArt toolbar.
4. Search for a motion clip with the keyword, bike. Then search for sound clips with the keyword, nature, and select two sounds. Download these three clips.
5. If necessary, click the Motion Clips tab in the Insert ClipArt window. Click the bike rider icon, and then click the Insert clip button on the Pop-up menu.
6. Click the Microsoft PowerPoint – [Musical Biking] button on the taskbar. Scale the bike rider clip to 175%, and then apply the Crawl From Left entry animation effect. Move the bike rider clip to the lower-right corner of the slide.

In the Lab

7. Click the Insert ClipArt button on the taskbar. Click the Sounds tab. Click the first sound clip, click the Insert clip button on the Pop-up menu, and then click the Yes button in the Microsoft PowerPoint dialog box to play the first sound automatically. Move the speaker icon to the lower-left corner of Slide 1.

8. Click the Insert ClipArt button on the taskbar. Click the second sound clip, click the Insert clip button on the Pop-up menu, and then click the Yes button in the Microsoft PowerPoint dialog box to play the second sound automatically. Move this speaker icon beside the first speaker in the lower-left corner.

9. Add your name to the footer.

10. Disconnect from the Web and save the file again.

11. Run the slide show. Print Slide 1 using the Pure black and white option. Quit PowerPoint.

3 Modifying a Personal Presentation

Problem: In today's competitive job market, employers are searching for candidates with computer expertise. In addition to sending your cover letter and resume to potential employers, you decide to send a personalized PowerPoint presentation highlighting your computer skills, academic honors, and campus activities.

Instructions: Start PowerPoint and perform the following tasks with a computer.

1. Open the Supplemental Information presentation you created in the In the Lab 3 exercise in the Web Feature 1 project (page PPW 1.14). If you did not complete this exercise, perform Step 1 in that exercise.

2. Search the Microsoft Clip Gallery Live Web site for appropriate motion, picture, and sound clips. Add these clips to your presentation.

3. Save the presentation with the file name, Clip Information.

4. Run the slide show. Print the slides using the Pure black and white option. Quit PowerPoint.

Integration Case Studies

Introduction

In these case studies, you will use the concepts and techniques presented in the projects and integration features in this book to integrate all of the Office 2000 applications. The first case study requires that you link an existing Excel worksheet into a Word document, embed an Excel chart into a PowerPoint presentation, and then insert (attach) the Word document and PowerPoint presentation to an e-mail message. The second case study requires you to use an existing Access database table as the data source for a Word form letter; it also requires you to use WordArt to create the letterhead for the form letter. In the third case study, you will create an Access database table and then convert the table twice, first to a Word document and second to an Excel worksheet. You then will convert the Word document to an Excel worksheet and vice versa. The files for the first and second case studies are provided on the Data Disk for this textbook. See the inside back cover for instructions for obtaining the Data Disk.

Office 2000 Integration Case Studies

1 Integrating Excel, Word, PowerPoint, and E-Mail

Problem: Spring Hill Bottled Water enclosed a survey along with its October invoices, in order to collect data on customer satisfaction. Barbara Swanton, a marketing manager at Spring Hill, has received the completed surveys and summarized the results into an Excel worksheet. She also has charted the results using Excel. The worksheet and corresponding charts are saved in a workbook named Spring Hill Bottled Water.

Barbara would like to schedule a meeting to discuss the survey results with the steering committee of Spring Hill Bottled Water. She plans to send an e-mail message to the committee to schedule the meeting and ask for comments and suggestions. To ensure that the committee can review the results before the meeting, Barbara will attach two documents to the e-mail message: (1) a memo that includes the Excel worksheet summarizing the survey results, and (2) a PowerPoint slide that includes the Excel chart depicting the survey results.

Barbara has asked you, her assistant, to create the memo in Word and the slide in PowerPoint, reminding you to embed the Excel worksheet into the Word document and the Excel chart into the PowerPoint slide. Finally, she wants you to create an e-mail message and insert the Word document and PowerPoint slide.

Part 1 Instructions: *Reviewing the Excel Workbook*

Open the Spring Hill Bottled Water workbook shown in Figures 1a and 1b from the Data Disk. Before you begin creating the memo and slide, familiarize yourself with their contents. Print each sheet of the workbook.

Part 2 Instructions: *Creating a Memorandum in Word with an Embedded Excel Worksheet*

Create a memorandum to schedule the meeting with the steering committee, as shown in Figure 1d. After typing the text in the memo, embed the Customer Survey Results By County worksheet from the Excel workbook into the memo.

Leaving the Excel workbook open, start Word. Use the Professional Memo template to create the memo. Modify the template text so that the memo matches Figure 1d. Next, embed the Customer Survey Results By County worksheet into the memo. (Do not type the worksheet; rather embed it from Excel.) Save the document using the file name Spring Hill Bottled Water. Print the memorandum with the embedded worksheet.

Part 3 Instructions: *Creating a Slide in PowerPoint with an Embedded Excel Chart*

You now are ready to create a slide (Figure 1c) to be used in the presentation that Barbara will make to the board of directors.

Leaving the Excel workbook open, start PowerPoint. Select a blank slide for the slide's layout and use a background color as shown in Figure 1c. Use WordArt to create the title. Embed the Customer Survey Results By County chart into the slide. Save the presentation using the file name Spring Hill Bottled Water.

Part 4 Instructions: *Attaching the Files to an E-Mail Message*

Using Word as your e-mail editor, create the e-mail message (Figure 1e) and attach the Word document and PowerPoint slide to the e-mail message. Print the e-mail message.

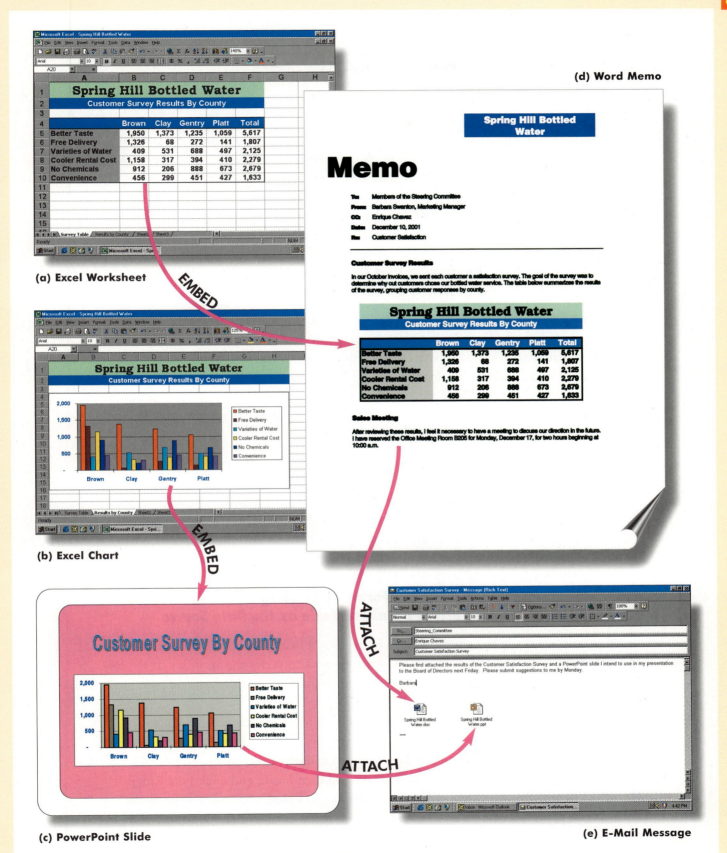

(a) Excel Worksheet

(b) Excel Chart

(c) PowerPoint Slide

(d) Word Memo

(e) E-Mail Message

FIGURE 1

2 Integrating Word, WordArt, and Access

Problem: Every spring, Pine Ridge Health Club sends letters to its clients to verify the Club's internal records. In the past, the Club's director of client services, Antonio Ferraro, has used Word to type these letters to each client individually. This year, he wants to automate the process even further. He has entered the list of clients into an Access table (Figure 2a), which is saved in a database named Pine Ridge Health Club. He has asked you to prepare a form letter to be sent to all clients using the Access database table as a data source. He also would like you to develop a creative letterhead for Pine Ridge Health Club that can be used on all its business correspondence. The completed form letter, with letterhead, is shown in Figure 2b.

Part 1 Instructions: *Reviewing and Maintaining the Access Database Table*

The database table that Antonio created is in a file named Pine Ridge Health Club, which is located on the Data Disk. Open the database and then open the table named Client List. Familiarize yourself with the contents of the Client List table (Figure 2a). Add a record that contains information about yourself to the table — the table then should contain six records. Print the revised table and then close Access.

Part 2 Instructions: *Creating the Letterhead*

Your first task is to develop the letterhead for the correspondence. Start Word and then display the header area. Insert and format a WordArt object, using the text, Pine Ridge, as shown in Figure 2b. Insert the weight-lifting clip art to the right of the WordArt object. Reposition and resize the clip art as shown in Figure 2b. Finally, enter the telephone number and address of the Club, add a bottom border, and color it dark green. When you are finished with the header, save the file as Pine Ridge Letterhead and print a copy.

Part 3 Instructions: *Creating the Form Letter Using an Access Database Table as the Data Source*

You now are ready to create the form letter shown in Figure 2b, which is to be sent to each client in the Client List table. The form letter is to verify the accuracy of the following information for each client: name, address, home and work telephone numbers, fax number, and e-mail address, if applicable.

Using the Pine Ridge Letterhead created in Part 2 above as the main document, create a form letter using the text shown in Figure 2b and the Access database table as the data source. When specifying the data source, change the file type to MS Access Databases in the Open Data Source dialog box and then locate and click Pine Ridge Health Club as the name of the data source. When prompted, click Client List as the table name. When you are finished with the main document, save the document using the file name Pine Ridge Membership Update and then print it. Finally, merge and print the form letters for the six records.

Part 4 Instructions: *Setting Query Conditions*

Antonio Ferraro has requested that you merge and print form letters for only those clients with a home area code of 713. On the resulting printed form letters, hand write the condition you specified. Next, he requests that you merge and print form letters for only those clients that have e-mail addresses. On the resulting printed form letters, hand write the condition you specified.

ID	Title	First Name	Last Name	Address1	Address2	City	State	ZIP Code	Home Phone	Work Phone	Fax Number	Email Address
1	Mr.	Michael	Shank	517 Howard Ave.		Houston	TX	77035	(713) 555-9123	(713) 555-6712	(713) 555-3125	
2	Dr.	Jerad	DeRolf	2510 81st St.		Houston	TX	77038	(713) 555-8282	(713) 555-4523	(713) 555-1111	DeRolf@jet.net
3	Ms.	Hannah	Cameron	312 Douglas St.	Apt. 4A	Houston	TX	77090	(281) 555-3102	(281) 555-9087		Cutie@xyz.com
4	Mr.	Ray	Lykins	4699 Green Ave.		Houston	TX	77031	(713) 555-5209	(713) 555-1523	(713) 555-6653	
5	Mrs.	Marsha	Steiger	P.O. Box 1812	Apt. 16	Houston	TX	77090	(281) 555-2192	(281) 555-6666	(281) 555-8897	MSteiger@bs.edu

(a) Access Table

(b) Word Document

FIGURE 2

3 Integrating Access into Word and Excel

Problem: The owner of Online Investors, Inc., Jasmine Washington, would like to work with the daily stock records. The problem is that the records are stored in an Access database table (Figure 3a) and Jasmine is unfamiliar with Access. Instead, she wants to work with the records in both Word and Excel. Thus, she has asked you to convert the Access table to both a Word document and an Excel worksheet. She also has asked you to show her how to convert in any direction among the three applications, Word, Excel, and Access.

Part 1 Instructions: *Creating the Access Table and Entering the Data*

You are to design and create the Access database table that contains the stock information. The field names for the table are as follows: Stock Symbol, Today's High, Today's Low, Today's Close, 52 Week High, and 52 Week Low. Obtain a recent copy of *The Wall Street Journal* or use the Internet to obtain stock information for five different stocks. Enter the information as records in the table you create. The Access screen in Figure 3a shows a sample of data entered into the Online Portfolio table. The actual data you use will be different. When you finish creating the table, save the database using the file name Online Investors. Print the Access table. Turn in *The Wall Street Journal* pages or printouts of the Web pages you used for stock quotes along with the Access table.

Part 2 Instructions: *Converting an Access Table to a Word Document*

You now are ready to convert the Online Portfolio table to a Word table so that Jasmine can work with it. With the Access table selected in the Online Investors: Database window, click the OfficeLinks button arrow on the Database toolbar and then click Publish It with MS Word. When the Word document window displays the stock information as a Word table, format it so that it is readable and professional, as shown in Figure 3b. Save the document using the file name Online Portfolio. Print the resulting Word table.

Part 3 Instructions: *Converting an Access Table to an Excel Worksheet*

You now are ready to convert the Online Portfolio table to an Excel worksheet for Jasmine. Return to the Access database table. With the Access table highlighted in the Online Investors: Database window, click the OfficeLinks button arrow on the Database toolbar and then click Analyze It with MS Excel. When the Excel window displays the stock information as a worksheet, format it so that it is readable and professional, as shown in Figure 3c. Save the workbook using the file name Online Portfolio. Below the table, add two rows that use Excel's statistical functions to determine the highest and lowest values for each of the numeric columns in the table. (*Note:* you will need to format the stock quotes as numbers rather than text.) Print the resulting Excel worksheet.

Part 4 Instructions: *Converting Between Word, Excel, and Access*

Use the techniques described earlier in this book to convert in any direction among Word, Excel, and Access. For example, open the Excel workbook Online Portfolio and convert it to Word. Next, convert the workbook to Access. Do the same for the Word document Online Portfolio. Print each of the four files created.

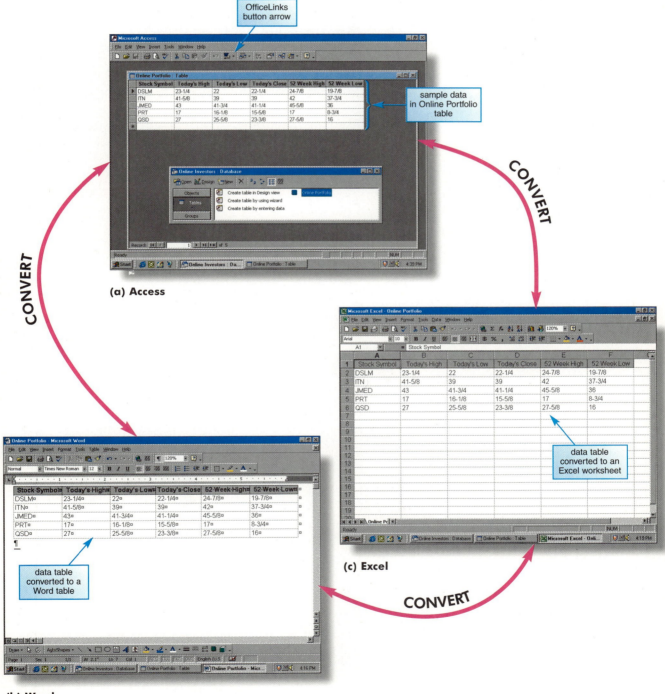

FIGURE 3

APPENDIX A
Microsoft Office 2000 Help System

Using the Microsoft Office Help System

This appendix demonstrates how you can use the Microsoft Office 2000 Help system to answer your questions. At any time while you are using one of the Microsoft Office 2000 applications, you can interact with the Help system to display information on any topic associated with the application. To illustrate the use of the Microsoft Office 2000 Help system, the Microsoft Word 2000 application will be used in this appendix. The Help systems in other Microsoft Office applications respond in a similar fashion.

The two primary forms of Help available in each Microsoft Office application are the Office Assistant and the Microsoft Help window. The one you use will depend on your preference. As shown in Figure A-1, you access either form of Help in Microsoft Word by pressing the F1 key, clicking Microsoft Word Help on the Help menu, or clicking the Microsoft Word Help button on the Standard toolbar. Word responds in one of two ways:

1. If the Office Assistant is turned on, then the Office Assistant displays with a balloon (lower-right side of Figure A-1).
2. If the Office Assistant is turned off, then the Microsoft Word Help window displays (lower-left side of Figure A-1)

Table A-1 on the next page summarizes the nine categories of Help available to you. Because of the way the Word Help system works, please review the rightmost column of Table A-1 if you have difficulties activating the desired category of Help.

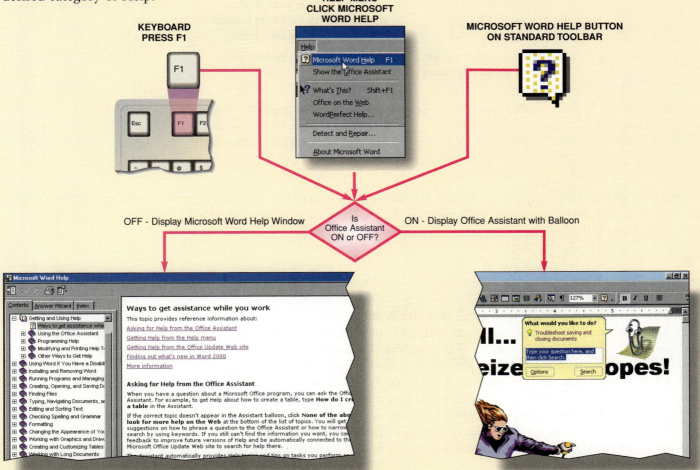

FIGURE A-1

Table A-1 Word Help System

TYPE	DESCRIPTION	HOW TO ACTIVATE	TURNING THE OFFICE ASSISTANT ON AND OFF
Answer Wizard	Similar to the Office Assistant in that it answers questions that you type in your own words.	Click the Microsoft Word Help button on the Standard toolbar. If necessary, maximize the Help window by double-clicking its title bar. Click the Answer Wizard tab.	If the Office Assistant displays, right-click it, click Options on the shortcut menu, click Use the Office Assistant to remove the check mark, click the OK button.
Contents sheet	Groups Help topics by general categories. Use when you know only the general category of the topic in question.	Click the Microsoft Word Help button on the Standard toolbar. If necessary, maximize the Help window by double-clicking its title bar. Click the Contents tab.	If the Office Assistant displays, right-click it, click Options, click Use the Office Assistant to remove the check mark, click the OK button.
Detect and Repair	Automatically finds and fixes errors in the application.	Click Detect and Repair on the Help menu.	
Hardware and Software Information	Shows Product ID and allows access to system information and technical support information.	Click About Microsoft Word on the Help menu and then click the appropriate button.	
Help for WordPerfect Users	Used to assist WordPerfect users who are learning Microsoft Word.	Click WordPerfect Help on the Help menu.	
Index sheet	Similar to an index in a book; use when you know exactly what you want.	Click the Microsoft Word Help button on the Standard toolbar. If necessary, maximize the Help window by double-clicking its title bar. Click the Index tab.	If the Office Assistant displays, right-click it, click Options, click Use the Office Assistant to remove the check mark, click the OK button.
Office Assistant	Answers questions that you type in your own words, offers tips, and provides Help for a variety of Word features.	Click the Microsoft Word Help button on the Standard toolbar or double-click the Office Assistant icon. Some dialog boxes also include the Microsoft Word Help button.	If the Office Assistant does not display, click Show the Office Assistant on the Help menu.
Office on the Web	Used to access technical resources and download free product enhancements on the Web.	Click Office on the Web on the Help menu.	
Question Mark button and What's This? command	Used to identify unfamiliar items on the screen.	In a dialog box, click the Question Mark button and then click an item in the dialog box. Click What's This? on the Help menu, and then click an item on the screen.	

The best way to familiarize yourself with the Word Help system is to use it. The next several pages show examples of how to use the Help system. Following the examples is a set of exercises titled Use Help that will sharpen your Word Help system skills.

The Office Assistant

The **Office Assistant** is an icon that displays in the Word window (lower-right side of Figure A-1 on page MO A.1). It has dual functions. First, it will respond with a list of topics that relate to the entry you make in the What would you like to do? text box at the bottom of the balloon. This entry can be in the form of a word, phrase, or written question. For example, if you want to learn more about saving a file, you can type, save, save a file, how do I save a file, or anything similar in the text box. The Office Assistant responds by displaying a list of topics from which you can choose. Once you choose a topic, it displays the corresponding information.

Second, the Office Assistant monitors your work and accumulates tips during a session on how you might do your work better. You can view the tips at any time. The accumulated tips display when you activate the Office Assistant balloon. Also, if at any time you see a light bulb above the Office Assistant, click it to display the most recent tip.

You may or may not want the Office Assistant to display on the screen at all times. You can hide it, and then show it at a later time. You may prefer not to use the Office Assistant at all. In this case, you use the Microsoft Word Help window (lower-left side of Figure A-1 on page MO A.1). Thus, not only do you need to know how to show and hide the Office Assistant, but you also need to know how to turn the Office Assistant on and off.

Showing and Hiding the Office Assistant

When Word is first installed, the Office Assistant displays in the Word window. You can move it to any location on the screen. You can click it to display the Office Assistant balloon, which allows you to request Help. If the Office Assistant is on the screen and you want to hide it, you click the **Hide the Office Assistant command** on the Help menu. You also can right-click the Office Assistant to display its shortcut menu and then click the **Hide command** to hide it. When the Office Assistant is hidden, then the **Show the Office Assistant command** replaces the Hide the Office Assistant command on the Help menu. Thus, you can show or hide the Office Assistant at any time.

Turning the Office Assistant On and Off

The fact that the Office Assistant is hidden, does not mean it is turned off. To turn the Office Assistant off, it must be displayed in the Word window. You right-click it to display its shortcut menu (right side of Figure A-2). Next, click Options on the shortcut menu. Invoking the **Options command** causes the Office Assistant dialog box to display (left side of Figure A-2).

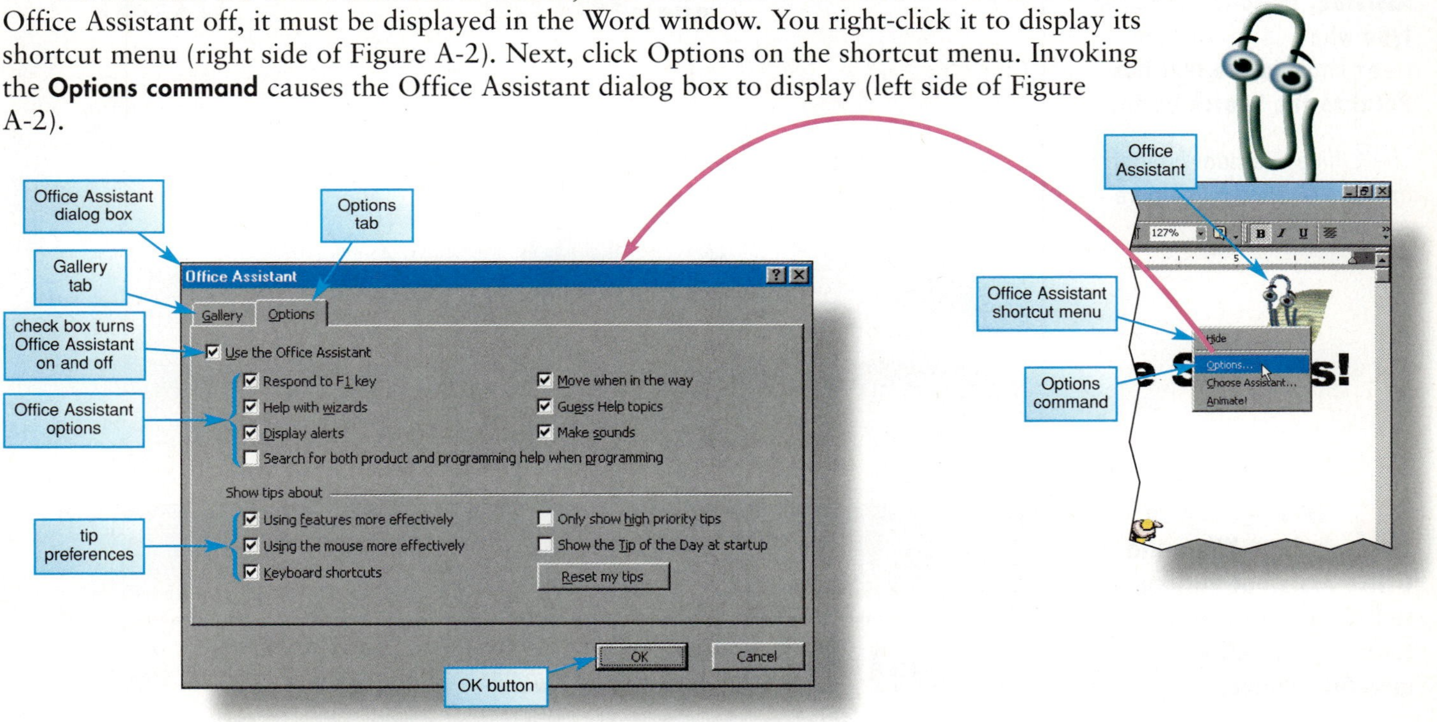

FIGURE A-2

The top check box in the Options sheet determines whether the Office Assistant is on or off. To turn the Office Assistant off, remove the check mark from the **Use the Office Assistant check box** and then click the OK button. As shown in Figure A-1 on page MO A.1, if the Office Assistant is off when you invoke Help, then the Microsoft Word Help window displays instead of the Office Assistant. To turn the Office Assistant on at a later time, click the Show the Office Assistant command on the Help menu.

Through the Options command on the Office Assistant shortcut menu, you can change the look and feel of the Office Assistant. For example, you can hide the Office Assistant, turn the Office Assistant off, change the way it works, choose a different Office Assistant icon, or view an animation of the current one. These options also are available by clicking the Options button that displays in the Office Assistant balloon (Figure A-3 on the next page).

The **Gallery sheet** (Figure A-2) in the Office Assistant dialog box allows you to change the appearance of the Office Assistant. The default is the paper clip (Clippit). You can change it to a bouncing red happy face (The Dot), a robot (F1), a professor (The Genius), the Microsoft Office logo (Office Logo), the earth (Mother Nature), a cat (Links), or a dog (Rocky).

Using the Office Assistant

As indicated earlier, the Office Assistant allows you to enter a word, phrase, or question and then responds by displaying a list of topics from which you can choose to display Help. The following steps show how to use the Office Assistant to obtain Help about online meetings.

Steps To Use the Office Assistant

1 **If the Office Assistant is not turned on, click Help on the menu bar and then click Show the Office Assistant. Click the Office Assistant. When the Office Assistant balloon displays, type** what are online meetings **in the text box. Point to the Search button.**

The Office Assistant balloon displays as shown in Figure A-3.

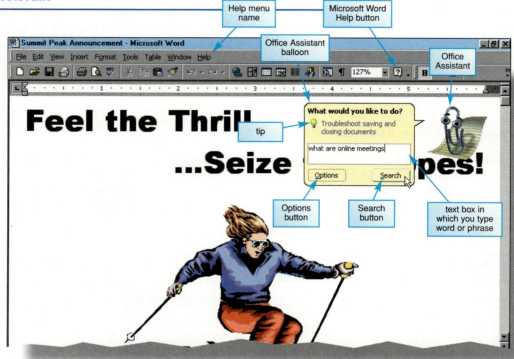

FIGURE A-3

2 **Click the Search button. When the Office Assistant balloon redisplays, point to the topic, About online meetings (Figure A-4).**

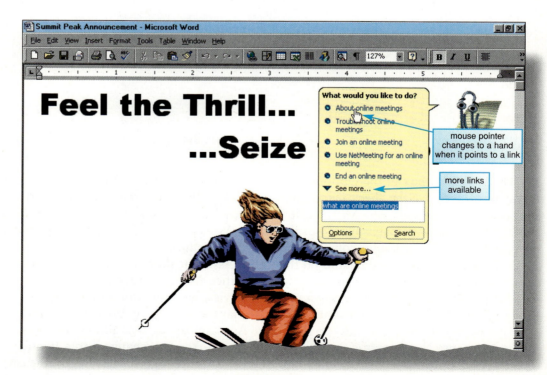

FIGURE A-4

3 ▸ **Click the topic, About online meetings. Double-click the Microsoft Word Help window title bar to maximize it. If necessary, move or hide the Office Assistant so you can view all of the text in the Microsoft Word Help window.**

The Microsoft Word Help window displays the information about online meetings (Figure A-5).

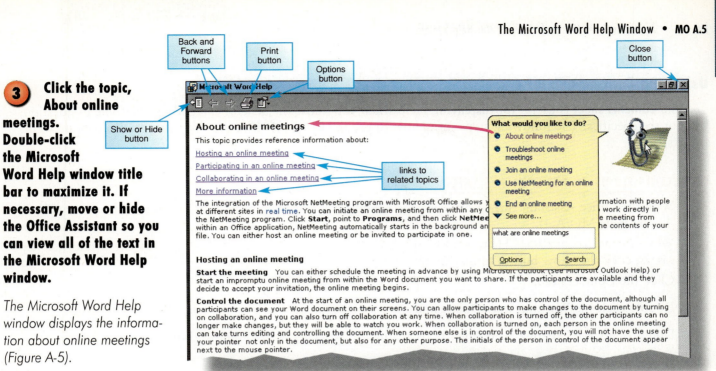

FIGURE A-5

When the Microsoft Word Help window displays, you can choose to read it or print it. To print the information, click the Print button on the Microsoft Word Help toolbar. Table A-2 lists the function of each button on the toolbar in the Microsoft Word Help window. To close the Microsoft Word Help window shown in Figure A-5, click the Close button on the title bar.

Table A-2	Microsoft Word Help Toolbar Buttons	
BUTTON	**NAME**	**FUNCTION**
or	Show or Hide	Displays or hides the Contents, Answer Wizard, Index tabs
	Back	Displays the previous Help topic
	Forward	Displays the next Help topic
	Print	Prints the current Help topic
	Options	Displays a list of commands

Other Ways

1. If Office Assistant is turned on, on Help menu click Microsoft Word Help, or click Microsoft Word Help button on Standard toolbar to display Office Assistant balloon

The Microsoft Word Help Window

If the Office Assistant is turned off and you click the Microsoft Word Help button on the Standard toolbar, the **Microsoft Word Help window** displays (Figure A-6 on the next page). This window contains three tabs on the left side: Contents, Answer Wizard, and Index. Each tab displays a sheet with powerful look-up capabilities. Use the Contents sheet as you would a table of contents at the front of a book to look up Help. The Answer Wizard sheet answers your queries in the same manner as the Office Assistant. You use the Index sheet in the same manner as an index in a book.

Click the tabs to move from sheet to sheet. The five buttons on the toolbar, Show or Hide, Back, Forward, Print, and Options also are described in Table A-2.

Besides clicking the Microsoft Word Help button on the Standard toolbar, you also can click the Microsoft Word Help command on the Help menu or press the F1 key to display the Microsoft Word Help window to gain access to the three sheets. To close the Microsoft Word Help window, click the Close button in the upper-right corner on the title bar.

Using the Contents Sheet

The **Contents sheet** is useful for displaying Help when you know the general category of the topic in question, but not the specifics. The following steps show how to use the Contents sheet to obtain information about Web folders.

TO OBTAIN HELP USING THE CONTENTS SHEET

1 With the Office Assistant turned off, click the Microsoft Word Help button on the Standard toolbar (Figure A-3 on page MO A.4).

2 When the Microsoft Word Help window displays, double-click the title bar to maximize the window. If necessary, click the Show button to display the tabs.

3 Click the Contents tab.

4 Double-click the Working with Online and Internet Documents book on the left side of the window.

5 Double-click the Creating Web Pages book below the Working with Online and Internet Documents book.

6 Click the About Web Folders subtopic below the Creating Web Pages book.

Word displays Help on the subtopic, About Web Folders (Figure A-6).

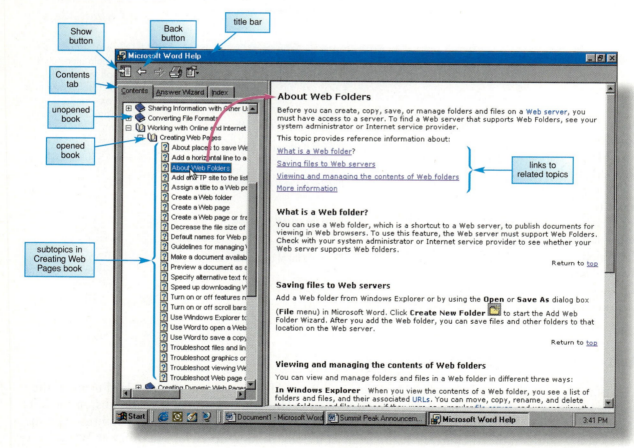

FIGURE A-6

Once the information on the subtopic displays, you can scroll through the window and read it or you can click the Print button to obtain a hard copy. If you decide to click another subtopic on the left or a link on the right, you can get back to the Help page shown in Figure A-6 by clicking the Back button as many times as necessary.

Each topic in the Contents list is preceded by a book icon or question mark icon. A **book icon** indicates subtopics are available. A **question mark icon** means information on the topic will display if you double-click the title. The book icon opens when you double-click the book (or its title) or click the plus sign (+) to the left of the book icon.

Using the Answer Wizard Sheet

The **Answer Wizard sheet** works like the Office Assistant in that you enter a word, phrase, or question and it responds with topics from which you can choose to display Help. The following steps show how to use the Answer Wizard sheet to obtain Help about discussions in a Word document.

TO OBTAIN HELP USING THE ANSWER WIZARD SHEET

1 With the Office Assistant turned off, click the Microsoft Word Help button on the Standard toolbar (Figure A-3 on page MO A.4).

2 When the Microsoft Word Help window displays, double-click the title bar to maximize the window. If necessary, click the Show button to display the tabs.

3 Click the Answer Wizard tab. Type what are discussions in the What would you like to do? text box on the left side of the window. Click the Search button.

4 When a list of topics displays in the Select topic to display list box, click About discussions in Word.

Word displays Help about discussions (Figure A-7).

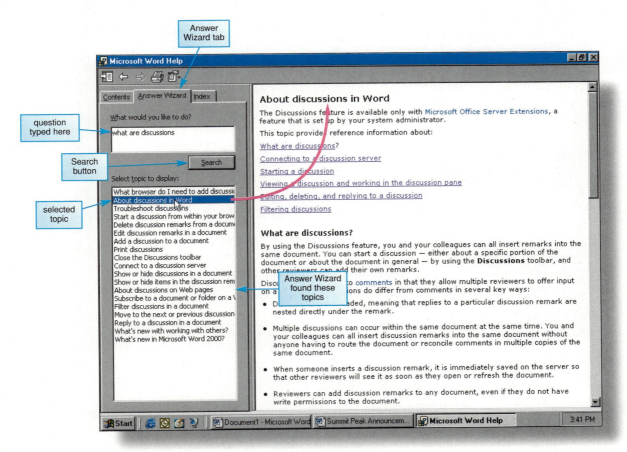

FIGURE A-7

If the topic, About discussions in Word, does not include the information you are searching for, click another topic in the list. Continue to click topics until you find the desired information.

Using the Index Sheet

The third sheet in the Microsoft Word Help window is the Index sheet. Use the **Index sheet** to display Help when you know the keyword or the first few letters of the keyword you want to look up. The following steps show how to use the Index sheet to obtain Help on understanding the readability statistics available to evaluate the reading level of a document.

TO OBTAIN HELP USING THE INDEX SHEET

1 With the Office Assistant turned off, click the Microsoft Word Help button on the Standard toolbar (Figure A-3 on page MO A.4).

2 When the Microsoft Word Help window displays, double-click the title bar to maximize the window. If necessary, click the Show button to display the tabs.

3 Click the Index tab. Type readability in the Type keywords text box on the left side of the window. Click the Search button.

Word highlights the first topic (Readability scores) on the left side of the window and displays information about two readability tests on the right side of the window (Figure A-8).

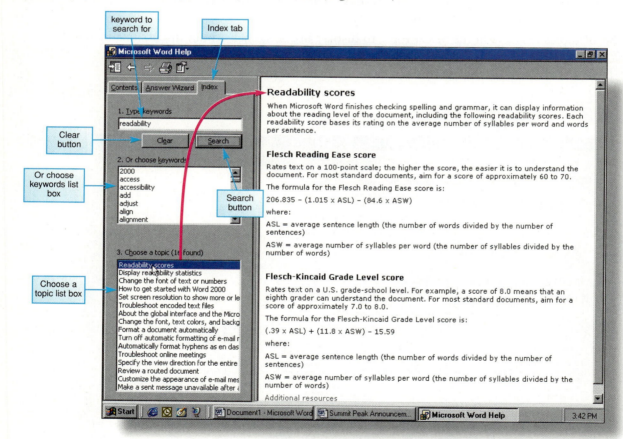

FIGURE A-8

In the Choose a topic list box on the left side of the window, you can click another topic to display additional Help.

An alternative to typing a keyword in the Type keywords text box is to scroll through the Or choose keywords list box (the middle list box on the left side of the window). When you locate the keyword you are searching for, double-click it to display Help on the topic. Also in the Or choose keywords list box, the Word Help system displays other topics that relate to the new keyword. As you begin typing a new keyword in the Type keywords text box, Word jumps to that point in the middle list box. To begin a new search, click the Clear button.

What's This? Command and Question Mark Button • MO A.9

APPENDIX A

What's This? Command and Question Mark Button

Use the What's This command on the Help menu or the Question Mark button in a dialog box when you are not sure what an object on the screen is or what it does.

What's This? Command

You use the **What's This? command** on the Help menu to display a detailed ScreenTip. When you invoke this command, the mouse pointer changes to an arrow with a question mark. You then click any object on the screen, such as a button, to display the ScreenTip. For example, after you click the What's This? command on the Help menu and then click the Zoom box on the Standard toolbar, a description of the Zoom box displays (Figure A-9). You can print the ScreenTip by right-clicking it and clicking Print Topic on the shortcut menu.

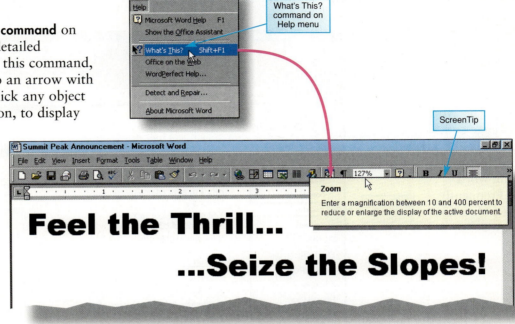

FIGURE A-9

Question Mark Button

In a response similar to the What's This? command, the **Question Mark button** displays a ScreenTip. You use the Question Mark button with dialog boxes. It is located in the upper-right corner on the title bar of dialog boxes, next to the Close button. For example, in Figure A-10, the Print dialog box displays on the screen. If you click the Question Mark button, and then click the Print to file check box, an explanation of the Print to file check box displays in a ScreenTip. You can print the ScreenTip by right-clicking it and clicking Print Topic on the shortcut menu.

If a dialog box does not include a Question Mark button, press the SHIFT+F1 keys. This combination of keys will change the mouse pointer to an arrow with a question mark. You then can click any object in the dialog box to display the ScreenTip.

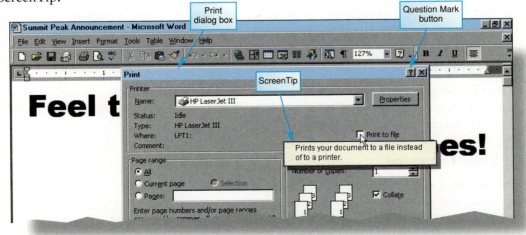

FIGURE A-10

Office on the Web Command

The **Office on the Web command** on the Help menu displays a Microsoft Web page containing up-to-date information on a variety of Office-related topics. To use this command, you must be connected to the Internet. Once the page displays, you can click the Word link on the left side of the window and then click the Assistance link (Figure A-11). The Word Assistance Web page contains several links such as Knowledge Base Articles about Word and Frequently Asked Questions about Word.

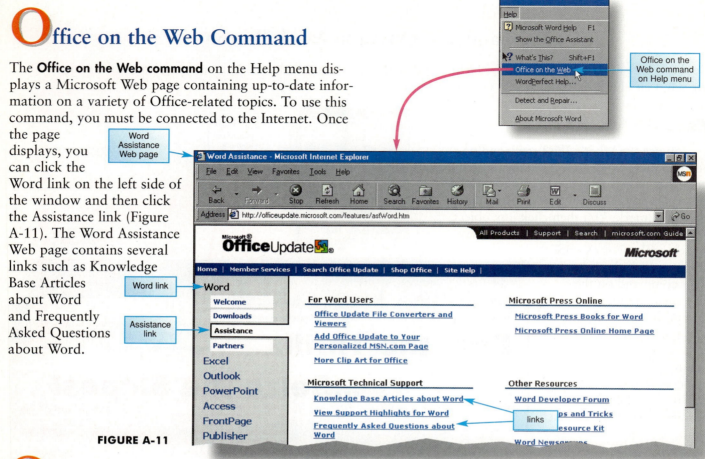

FIGURE A-11

Other Help Commands

Three additional commands available on the Help menu are WordPerfect Help, Detect and Repair, and About Microsoft Word. The WordPerfect Help command is available only if it was included as part of a Custom install of Word 2000. The Help menu of the other Office applications have similar commands that are useful when using each Office application.

WordPerfect Help Command

The **WordPerfect Help command** on the Help menu offers assistance to WordPerfect users switching to Word. When you choose this command, Word displays the Help for WordPerfect Users dialog box. The instructions in the dialog box step the user through the appropriate selections. A similar command is available in each of the other Office applications.

Detect and Repair Command

Use the **Detect and Repair command** on the Help menu if Word is not running properly or if it is generating errors. When you invoke this command, the Detect and Repair dialog box displays. Click the Start button in the dialog box to initiate the detect and repair process.

About Microsoft Word Command

The **About Microsoft Word command** on the Help menu displays the About Microsoft Word dialog box. The dialog box lists the owner of the software and the product identification. You need to know the product identification if you call Microsoft for assistance. The two buttons below the OK button are the System Info button and the Tech Support button. The **System Info button** displays system information, including hardware resources, components, software environment, and applications. The **Tech Support button** displays technical assistance information.

Use Help

1 Using the Office Assistant

Instructions: Perform the following tasks using the Word Help system.

1. If the Office Assistant is turned on, click it to display the Office Assistant balloon. If the Office Assistant is not turned on, click Help on the menu bar, and click Show the Office Assistant.

2. Right-click the Office Assistant and then click Options on the shortcut menu. Click the Gallery tab in the Office Assistant dialog box and then click the Next button to view all the Office Assistants. Click the Options tab in the Office Assistant dialog box and review the different options for the Office Assistant. Click the Question Mark button and then display ScreenTips for the first two check boxes (Use the Office Assistant and Respond to F1 key). Right-click the ScreenTips to print them. Hand them in to your instructor. Close the Office Assistant dialog box.

3. Click the Office Assistant and then type show me the keyboard shortcuts in the What would you like to do? text box at the bottom of the balloon. Click the Search button.

4. Click Keyboard shortcuts in the Office Assistant balloon. If necessary, double-click the title bar to maximize the Microsoft Word Help window. Click the Function keys link and then click the SHIFT+Function key link to view the set of shortcut keys using the SHIFT key and function keys. Click the Print button on the Microsoft Word Help toolbar to print the list of shortcut keys. Hand in the printouts to your instructor.

5. Close all open Help windows.

6. Click the Office Assistant. If it is not turned on, click Show the Office Assistant on the Help menu. Search for the topic, what is a netmeeting. Click the Use NetMeeting for an online meeting link. When the Microsoft Word Help window displays, maximize the window and then click the the Start an impromptu online meeting with Microsoft Word link. Read and print the information. Close the Microsoft Word Help window.

2 Expanding on the Word Help System Basics

Instructions: Use the Word Help system to understand the topics better and answer the questions listed below. Answer the questions on your own paper, or hand in the printed Help information to your instructor.

1. Right-click the Office Assistant. If it is not turned on, click Show the Office Assistant on the Help menu. When the shortcut menu displays, click Options. Click Use the Office Assistant to remove the check mark, and then click the OK button.

2. Click the Microsoft Word Help button on the Standard toolbar. Maximize the Microsoft Word Help window. If the tabs are hidden on the left side, click the Show button. Click the Index tab. Type undo in the Type keywords text box. Click the Search button. Click Reset built-in menus and toolbars. Print the information. Click the Hide button and then the Show button. Click the four links below What do you want to do? Read and print the information for each link. Close the Microsoft Word Help window. Hand in the printouts to your instructor.

3. Press the F1 key. Maximize the Microsoft Word Help window. Click the Answer Wizard tab. Type help in the What would you like to do? text box, and then click the Search button. Click Ways to get assistance while you work. Read through the information that displays. Print the information. Click the first two links. Read and print the information for both.

4. Click the Contents tab. Click the plus sign (+) to the left of the Typing, Navigating Documents, and Selecting Text book. Click the plus sign (+) to the left of the Selecting Text book. One at a time, click the three topics below the Selecting Text book. Read and print each one. Close the Microsoft Word Help window. Hand in the printouts to your instructor.

5. Click Help on the menu bar and then click What's This? Click the E-mail button on the Standard toolbar. Right-click the ScreenTip to print the ScreenTip. Click Format on the menu bar and then click Paragraph. When the Paragraph dialog box displays, click the Question Mark button on the title bar. Click the Special box. Right-click the ScreenTip to print the ScreenTip. Hand in the printouts to your instructor. Close the Paragraph dialog box and the Microsoft Word window.

APPENDIX B
Publishing Office Web Pages to a Web Server

With a Microsoft Office 2000 program, such as Word, Excel, Access, or PowerPoint, you use the **Save as Web Page command** on the File menu to save the Web page to a Web server using one of two techniques: Web folders or File Transfer Protocol. A **Web folder** is an Office 2000 shortcut to a Web server. **File Transfer Protocol (FTP)** is an Internet standard that allows computers to exchange files with other computers on the Internet.

You should contact your network system administrator or technical support staff at your ISP to determine if their Web server supports Web folders, FTP, or both, and to obtain necessary permissions to access the Web server. If you decide to publish Web pages using a Web folder, you must have the Office Server Extensions (OSE) installed on your computer. OSE comes with the Standard, Professional, and Premium editions of Office 2000.

Using Web Folders to Publish Office Web Pages

If you are granted permission to create a Web folder (shortcut) on your computer, you must obtain the URL of the Web server, and a user name and possibly a password that allows you to access the Web server. You also must decide on a name for the Web folder. Table B-1 explains how to create a Web folder.

Office adds the name of the Web folder to the list of current Web folders. You can save to this folder, open files in the folder, rename the folder, or perform any operations you would to a folder on your hard disk. You can use your Office program or Windows Explorer to access this folder. Table B-2 explains how to save to a Web folder.

Using FTP to Publish Office Web Pages

When publishing a Web page using FTP, you first add the FTP location to your computer and then you can save to it. An **FTP location**, also called an **FTP site**, is a collection of files that resides on an FTP server. In this case, the FTP server is the Web server.

To add an FTP location, you must obtain the name of the FTP site, which usually is the address (URL) of the FTP server, and a user name and a password that allows you to access the FTP server. You save and open the Web pages on the Web server using the name of the FTP site. Table B-3 explains how to add an FTP site.

Office adds the name of the FTP site to the FTP locations in the Save As and Open dialog boxes. You can open and save files on this FTP location. Table B-4 explains how to save using an FTP location.

Table B-1   Creating a Web Folder

1. Click File on the menu bar and then click Save As; or click File on the menu bar and then click Open.
2. When the Save As dialog box or the Open dialog box displays, click the Web Folders shortcut on the Places Bar along the left side of the dialog box.
3. Click the Create New Folder button.
4. When the first dialog box of the Add Web Folder wizard displays, type the URL of the Web server and then click the Next button.
5. When the Enter Network Password dialog box displays, type the user name and, if necessary, the password in the respective text boxes and then click the OK button.
6. When the last dialog box of the Add Web Folder wizard displays, type the name you would like to use for the Web folder. Click the Finish button.
7. Close the Save As or the Open dialog box.

Table B-2   Saving to a Web Folder

1. Click File on the menu bar and then click Save As.
2. When the Save As dialog box displays, type the Web page file name in the File name text box. Do not press the ENTER key.
3. Click Web Folders shortcut on the Places Bar along the left side of the dialog box.
4. Double-click the Web folder name in the Save in list.
5. When the Enter Network Password dialog box displays, type the user name and password in the respective text boxes and then click the OK button.
6. Click the Save button in the Save As dialog box.

Table B-3   Adding an FTP Location

1. Click File on the menu bar and then click Save As; or click File on the menu bar and then click Open.
2. In the Save As dialog box, click the Save in box arrow and then click Add/Modify FTP Locations in the Save in list; or in the Open dialog box, click the Look in box arrow and then click Add/Modify FTP Locations in the Look in list.
3. When the Add/Modify FTP Locations dialog box displays, type the name of the FTP site in the Name of FTP site text box. If the site allows anonymous logon, click Anonymous in the Log on as area; if you have a user name for the site, click User in the Log on as area and then type the user name. Type the password in the Password text box. Click the OK button.
4. Close the Save As or the Open dialog box.

Table B-4   Saving to an FTP Location

1. Click File on the menu bar and then click Save As.
2. When the Save As dialog box displays, type the Web page file name in the File name text box. Do not press the ENTER key.
3. Click the Save in box arrow and then click FTP Locations.
4. Double-click the name of the FTP site you want to save to.
5. When the FTP Log On dialog box displays, type your user name and password and then click the OK button.
6. Click the Save button in the Save As dialog box.

Microsoft **Office 2000**

APPENDIX C
Resetting the Menus and Toolbars

When you first install Microsoft Office 2000, the Standard and Formatting toolbars display on one row in some of the applications. As you use the buttons on the toolbars and commands on the menus, Office personalizes the toolbars and the menus based on their usage. Each time you start an application, the toolbars and menus display in the same settings as the last time you used the application. The following steps show how to reset the Word menus and toolbars to their installation settings.

Steps To Reset My Usage Data and Toolbar Buttons

1 **Click View on the menu bar and then point to Toolbars. Point to Customize on the Toolbars submenu.**

The View menu and Toolbars submenu display (Figure C-1).

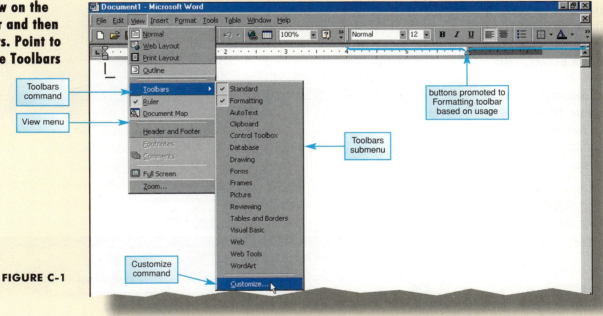

FIGURE C-1

2 **Click Customize. When the Customize dialog box displays, click the Options tab. Make sure the three check boxes in the Personalized Menus and Toolbars area have check marks and then point to the Reset my usage data button.**

The Customize dialog box displays as shown in Figure C-2.

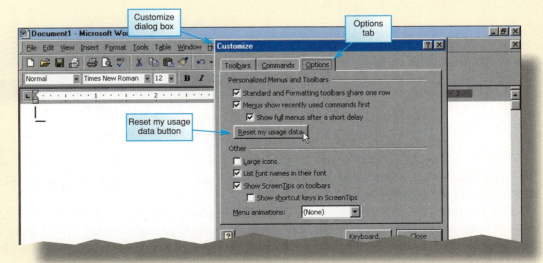

FIGURE C-2

3 Click the Reset my usage data button. When the Microsoft Word dialog box displays explaining the function of the Reset my usage data button, click the Yes button. In the Customize dialog box, click the Toolbars tab.

The Toolbars sheet displays (Figure C-3).

4 Click Standard in the Toolbars list and then click the Reset button. When the Reset Toolbar dialog box displays, click the OK button. Click Formatting in the Toolbars list and then click the Reset button. When the Reset Toolbar dialog box displays, click the OK button.

5 Click the Close button in the Customize dialog box.

The toolbars display as shown in Figure C-4.

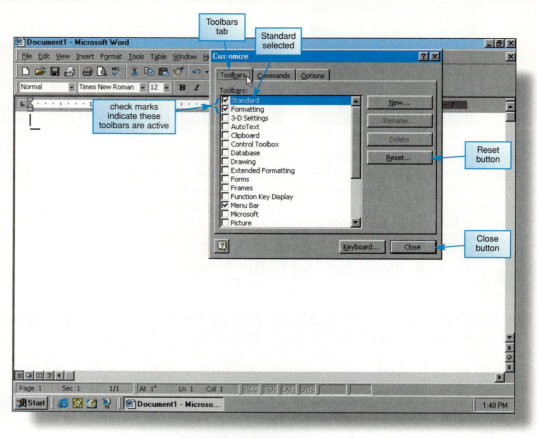

FIGURE C-3

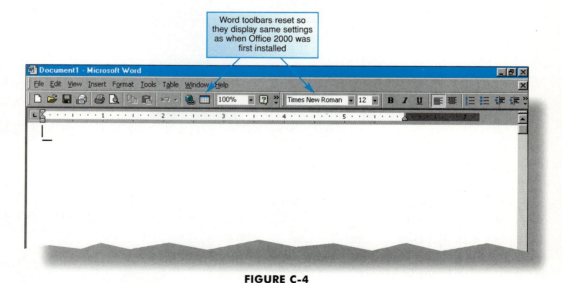

FIGURE C-4

Steps 3 and 4 display or remove any buttons that were added or deleted through the use of the Add or Remove Buttons button on the More Buttons menu.

You can turn off both the toolbars sharing a single row and the short menus by removing the check marks from the two top check boxes in the Options sheet in the Customize dialog box (Figure C-2 on the previous page). If you remove these check marks, Word will display the toolbars on two separate rows below the menu bar and will show only full menus.

Microsoft **Office 2000**

APPENDIX D

Microsoft Office User Specialist Certification Program

The Microsoft Office User Specialist (MOUS) Certification Program provides a framework for measuring your proficiency with the Microsoft Office 2000 applications, such as Word 2000, Excel 2000, Access 2000, and PowerPoint 2000. Three levels of certification are available — Master, Expert, and Core. The three levels of certification are described in Table D-1.

Table D-1	Three Levels of MOUS Certification		
LEVEL	**DESCRIPTION**	**REQUIREMENTS**	**CREDENTIAL AWARDED**
Master	Indicates that you have a comprehensive understanding of Microsoft Office 2000	Pass all FIVE of the required exams: Microsoft Word 2000 Expert Microsoft Excel 2000 Expert Microsoft PowerPoint 2000 Core Microsoft Access 2000 Core Microsoft Outlook 2000 Core	Candidates will be awarded one certificate for passing all five of the required Microsoft Office 2000 exams: Microsoft Office User Specialist: Microsoft Office 2000 Master
Expert	Indicates that you have a comprehensive understanding of the advanced features in a specific Microsoft Office 2000 application	Pass any ONE of the Expert exams: Microsoft Word 2000 Expert Microsoft Excel 2000 Expert	Candidates will be awarded one certificate for each of the Expert exams they have passed: Microsoft Office User Specialist: Microsoft Word 2000 Expert Microsoft Office User Specialist: Microsoft Excel 2000 Expert
Core	Indicates that you have a comprehensive understanding of the core features in a specific Microsoft Office 2000 application	Pass any ONE of the Core exams: Microsoft Word 2000 Core Microsoft Excel 2000 Core Microsoft PowerPoint 2000 Core Microsoft Access 2000 Core Microsoft Outlook 2000 Core	Candidates will be awarded one certificate for each of the Core exams they have passed: Microsoft Office User Specialist: Microsoft Word 2000 Microsoft Office User Specialist: Microsoft Excel 2000 Microsoft Office User Specialist: Microsoft PowerPoint 2000 Microsoft Office User Specialist: Microsoft Access 2000 Microsoft Office User Specialist: Microsoft Outlook 2000

Why Should You Get Certified?

Being a Microsoft Office User Specialist provides a valuable industry credential — proof that you have the Office 2000 applications skills required by employers. By passing one or more MOUS certification exams, you demonstrate your proficiency in a given Office application to employers. With nearly 80 million copies of Office in use around the world, Microsoft is targeting Office certification to a wide variety of companies. These companies include temporary employment agencies that want to prove the expertise of their workers, large corporations looking for a way to measure the skill set of employees, and training companies and educational institutions seeking Microsoft Office teachers with appropriate credentials.

The MOUS Exams

You pay $50 to $100 each time you take an exam, whether you pass or fail. The fee varies among testing centers. The Expert exams, which you can take up to 60 minutes to complete, consist of between 40 and 60 tasks that you perform online. The tasks require you to use the application just as you would in doing your job. The Core exams contain fewer tasks, and you will have slightly less time to complete them. The tasks you will perform differ on the two types of exams.

How Can You Prepare for the MOUS Exams?

The Shelly Cashman Series® offers several Microsoft-approved textbooks that cover the required objectives on the MOUS exams. For a listing of the textbooks, visit the Shelly Cashman Series MOUS Web page at www.scsite.com/off2000/cert.htm and click the Shelly Cashman Office Series 2000 Microsoft-Approved MOUS Textbooks link (Figure D-1). After using any of the books listed in an instructor-led course, you will be prepared to take the MOUS exam indicated.

How to Find an Authorized Testing Center

You can locate a testing center by calling 1-800-933-4493 in North America or visiting the Shelly Cashman Series MOUS Web page at www.scsite.com/off2000/cert.htm and then clicking the Locate an Authorized Testing Center Near You link (Figure D-1). At this Web page, you can look for testing centers around the world.

Shelly Cashman Series MOUS Web Page

The Shelly Cashman Series MOUS Web page (Figure D-1) has more than fifteen Web pages you can visit to obtain additional information on the MOUS Certification Program. The Web page (www.scsite.com/off2000/cert.htm) includes links to general information on certification, choosing an application for certification, preparing for the certification exam, and taking and passing the certification exam.

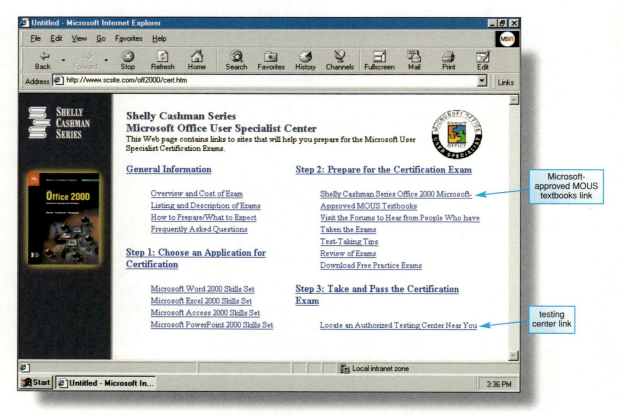

FIGURE D-1

Microsoft Office 2000 User Specialist Certification Map

The tables on the following pages list the skill sets and activities you should be familiar with if you plan to take the Microsoft Office User Specialist Certification examinations for Microsoft Word 2000, Microsoft Excel 2000, Microsoft Access 2000, or Microsoft PowerPoint 2000. Each activity is accompanied by page numbers on which the activity is illustrated in the book.

Microsoft Word 2000 User Specialist Certification Map

The Microsoft Word 2000 portion of *Microsoft Office 2000: Introductory Concepts and Techniques* (ISBN 0-7895-4635-3, 0-7895-4650-7, or 0-7895-5615-4) and *Microsoft Office 2000: Advanced Concepts and Techniques* (ISBN 0-7895-4649-3 or 0-7895-5629-4) used in combination in a two-sequence course has been approved by Microsoft as courseware for the Microsoft Office User Specialist (MOUS) program. After completing the Word 2000 projects and exercises in these two books, students will be prepared to take the Core-level Microsoft Office User Specialist Exam for Microsoft Word 2000. Table D-2 lists the skill sets, activities, and page number where the activity is discussed in the books. You should be familiar with each of the activities if you plan to take the Microsoft Word 2000 Core examination.

Table D-3 on the next page lists the skill sets, activities, and page number where the activity is discussed in the book for the Expert-level Microsoft Office User Specialist Exam for Microsoft Word 2000. POST-ADV in the PAGE NUMBERS column in Table D-3 indicates that the activity is discussed in the textbook *Microsoft Office 2000: Post-Advanced Concepts and Techniques* (ISBN 0-7895-5691-X). This post-advanced textbook is for a third course on Microsoft Office 2000 and is a continuation of *Microsoft Office 2000: Introductory Concepts and Techniques* and *Microsoft Office 2000: Advanced Concepts and Techniques*.

Table D-2   Microsoft Word 2000 MOUS Core Skill Sets, Activities, and Map

SKILL SETS	ACTIVITIES	PAGE NUMBERS
Working with text	Use the Undo, Redo, and Repeat command	WD 1.35, WD 1.36
	Apply font formats (Bold, Italic and Underline)	WD 1.33, WD 1.39, WD 1.42
	Use the SPELLING feature	WD 1.22, WD 1.59, WD 2.50
	Use the THESAURUS feature	WD 2.48, WD 2.61
	Use the GRAMMAR feature	WD 1.22, WD 1.59, WD 2.50
	Insert page breaks	WD 2.31, WD 2.35, WD 4.21
	Highlight text in document	WDW 1.9, WD 6.61
	Insert and move text	WD 1.54, WD 2.46, WD 2.56
	Cut, Copy, Paste, and Paste Special using the Office Clipboard	WD 1.54, WD 2.45, WD 3.33, WD 3.35, WD 6.35
	Copy formats using the Format Painter	WD 6.57
	Select and change font and font size	WD 1.17, WD 1.31, WD 1.32
	Find and replace text	WD 2.43, WD 2.56
	Apply character effects (superscript, subscript, strikethrough, small caps and outline)	WD 2.18, WD 4.16, WD 4.17
	Insert date and time	WD 6.17
	Insert symbols	WD 2.33, WD 3.37, WD 3.46
	Create and apply frequently used text with AutoCorrect	WD 2.20, WD 2.21
Working with paragraphs	Align text in paragraphs (Center, Left, Right and Justified)	WD 1.33, WD 1.35, WD 2.17, WD 2.18, WD 6.26
	Add bullets and numbering	WD 3.50, WD 3.51, WD 4.40, WD 5.30, WD 6.63
	Set character, line, and paragraph spacing options	WD 2.9, WD 2.11, WD 2.18, WD 4.38, WD 6.42

Table D-2   Microsoft Word 2000 MOUS Core Skill Sets, Activities, and Map

SKILL SETS	ACTIVITIES	PAGE NUMBERS
Working with paragraphs (con't)	Apply borders and shading to paragraphs	WD 3.39, WD 4.8, WD 6.37, WD 6.45
	Use indentation options (Left, Right, First Line, and Hanging Indent)	WD 2.18, WD 2.19, WD 2.37, WD 6.43
	Use TABS command (Center, Decimal, Left, and Right)	WD 3.31, WD 3.32, WD 3.43, WD 6.49
	Create an outline style numbered list	WD 3.51, WD 5.30
	Set tabs with leaders	WD 3.31
Working with documents	Print a document	WD 1.50, WD 5.40, WD 6.47
	Use print preview	WD 3.24, WD 4.57
	Use Web Page Preview	WDW 1.11, WDW 1.14
	Navigate through a document	WD 1.25, WD 1.26, WD 1.40, WD 4.25
	Insert page numbers	WD 2.14
	Set page orientation	WD 5.24
	Set margins	WD 2.8, WD 6.7
	Use GoTo to locate specific elements in a document	WD 2.42, WD 2.43
	Create and modify page numbers	WD 2.14, WD 4.29
	Create and modify headers and footers	WD 2.12, WD 2.15, WD 4.28
	Align text vertically	WD 3.35, WD 3.36, WD 4.42
	Create and use newspaper columns	WD 6.23, WD 6.25
	Revise column structure	WD 6.30, WD 6.48, WD 6.51
	Prepare and print envelopes and labels	WD 3.58, WD 5.48, WD 5.54

(Table D-2 continued on the next page)

Table D-2 Microsoft Word 2000 MOUS Core Skill Sets, Activities, and Map

SKILL SETS	ACTIVITIES	PAGE NUMBERS
Working with documents (con't)	Apply styles	WD 2.26, WD 4.19, WD 6.33
	Create sections with formatting that differs from other sections	WD 4.21, WD 4.29, WD 6.24
	Use click & type	WD 2.13
Managing files	Use save	WD 1.26, WD 1.49
	Locate and open an existing document	WD 1.52, WD 4.23
	Use Save As (different name, location, or format)	WD 1.49, WD 3.42, WDW 1.11
	Create a folder	WD 1.49
	Create a new document using a Wizard	WD 3.7, WDW 1.5
	Save as Web Page	WDW 1.3
	Use templates to create a new document	WD 3.18, WD 5.6, WD 5.9
	Create Hyperlinks	WD 2.39, WD 2.53, WDW 1.10

Table D-2 Microsoft Word 2000 MOUS Core Skill Sets, Activities, and Map

SKILL SETS	ACTIVITIES	PAGE NUMBERS
Managing files (con't)	Use the Office Assistant	WD 1.55
	Send a Word document via e-mail	WD 2.54, WDI 1.7
Using tables	Create and format tables	WD 3.52, WD 3.55, WD 4.42, WD 4.49
	Add borders and shading to tables	WD 3.55, WD 4.59, WD 4.61
	Revise tables (insert and delete rows and columns, change cell formats)	WD 3.15, WD 3.62, WD 4.46, WD 4.53
	Modify table structure (merge cells, change height and width)	WD 4.47, WD 4.48, WD 4.53, WD 4.59
	Rotate text in a table	WD 4.50, WD 4.59
Working with pictures and charts	Use the Drawing toolbar	WD 4.15, WD 6.9, WD 6.40
	Insert graphics into a document (WordArt, ClipArt, Images)	WD 1.43, WD 4.12, WD 4.33, WD 4.54, WD 6.9

Table D-3 Microsoft Word 2000 MOUS Expert Skill Sets, Activities, and Map

SKILL SETS	ACTIVITIES	PAGE NUMBERS
Working with paragraphs	Apply paragraph and section shading	WD 4.10, WD 4.51, WD 6.45, POST-ADV
	Use text flow options (Widows/Orphans options and keeping lines together)	WD 2.32, POST-ADV
	Sort lists, paragraphs, tables	WD 2.40, WD 5.45, WD 5.59, POST-ADV
Working with documents	Create and modify page borders	WD 6.59, POST-ADV
	Format first page differently than subsequent pages	WD 4.7, WD 4.21, WD 4.28, POST-ADV
	Use bookmarks	POST-ADV
	Create and edit styles	WD 2.26, POST-ADV
	Create watermarks	WD 4.54
	Use find and replace with formats, special characters, and non-printing elements	WD 2.45, POST-ADV
	Balance column length (using column breaks appropriately)	WD 6.31, WD 6.51
	Create or revise footnotes and endnotes	WD 2.23, WD 2.30, WD 2.61
	Work with master documents and subdocuments	POST-ADV
	Create and modify a table of contents	POST-ADV
	Create cross-reference	POST-ADV
	Create and modify an index	POST-ADV
Using tables	Embed worksheets in a table	POST-ADV
	Perform calculations in a table	WD 3.62, WD 4.59,
	Link Excel data as a table	POST-ADV
	Modify worksheets in a table	POST-ADV

Table D-3 Microsoft Word 2000 MOUS Expert Skill Sets, Activities, and Map

SKILL SETS	ACTIVITIES	PAGE NUMBERS
Working with pictures and charts	Add bitmapped graphics	POST-ADV
	Delete and position graphics	WD 1.46, WD 5.12, WD 6.20, WD 6.46, WD 6.54
	Create and modify charts	WD 4.33, WD 4.35, WD 4.36, WD 4.37
	Import data into charts	POST-ADV
Using mail merge	Create main document	WD 5.14, WD 5.25, WD 5.27, WD 5.29
	Create data source	WD 5.17
	Sort records to be merged	WD 5.45, WD 5.59
	Merge main document and data source	WD 5.41, WD 5.43, WD 5.59
	Generate labels	WD 5.48
	Merge a document using alternate data sources	WDI 1.4
Using advanced features	Insert a field	WD 5.34, WD 5.37
	Create, apply, and edit macros	POST-ADV
	Copy, rename, and delete macros	POST-ADV
	Create and modify form	POST-ADV
	Create and modify a form control (e.g., add an item to a drop-down list)	POST-ADV
	Use advanced text alignment features with graphics	POST-ADV
	Customize toolbars	WD 1.14, POST-ADV
Collaborating with workgroups	Insert comments	POST-ADV
	Protect documents	POST-ADV
	Create multiple versions of a document	POST-ADV
	Track changes to a document	POST-ADV
	Set default file location for workgroup templates	POST-ADV
	Round Trip documents from HTML	WDW 1.12

Microsoft Excel 2000 User Specialist Certification Map

The Microsoft Excel 2000 portion of *Microsoft Office 2000: Introductory Concepts and Techniques* (ISBN 0-7895-4635-3, 0-7895-4650-7, or 0-7895-5615-4) and *Microsoft Office 2000: Advanced Concepts and Techniques* (ISBN 0-7895-4649-3 or 0-7895-5629-4) used in combination in a two-sequence course has been approved by Microsoft as courseware for the Microsoft Office User Specialist (MOUS) program. After completing the Excel 2000 projects and exercises in these two books, students will be prepared to take the Core-level Microsoft Office User Specialist Exam for Microsoft Excel 2000. Table D-4 lists the skill sets, activities, and page number where the activity is discussed in the books. You should be familiar with each of the activities if you plan to take the Microsoft Excel 2000 Core examination.

Table D-5 on the next page lists the skill sets, activities, and page number where the activity is discussed in the book for the Expert-level Microsoft Office User Specialist Exam for Microsoft Excel 2000. POST-ADV in the PAGE NUMBERS column in Table D-5 indicates that the activity is discussed in the textbook *Microsoft Office 2000: Post-Advanced Concepts and Techniques* (ISBN 0-7895-5691-X). This post-advanced textbook is for a third course on Microsoft Office 2000 and is a continuation of *Microsoft Office 2000: Introductory Concepts and Techniques* and *Microsoft Office 2000: Advanced Concepts and Techniques*.

Table D-4 Microsoft Excel 2000 MOUS Core Skill Sets, Activities, and Map

SKILL SETS	ACTIVITIES	PAGE NUMBERS
Working with cells	Use Undo and Redo	E 1.52, E 1.61
	Clear cell content	E 1.53
	Enter text, dates, and numbers	E 1.15, E 1.20, E 2.7, E 3.21
	Edit cell content	E 1.51, E 1.59
	Go to a specific cell	E 1.34, E 1.36
	Insert and delete selected cells	E 3.16, E 3.76
	Cut, copy, paste, paste special, and move selected cells, use the Office Clipboard	E 1.24, E 3.14, E 3.15
	Use Find and Replace	E 6.58
	Clear cell formats	E 1.53
	Work with series (AutoFill)	E 3.8-10
	Create hyperlinks	E 4.42
Working with files	Use Save	E 2.50, E 3.43
	Use Save As (different name, location, format)	E 1.41, E 3.19
	Locate and open an existing workbook	E 1.48, E 3.65
	Create a folder	E 1.44
	Use templates to create a new workbook	E 6.26
	Save a worksheet/workbook as a Web Page	EW 1.3
	Send a workbook via e-mail	E 2.62
	Use the Office Assistant	E 1.55
Formatting worksheets	Apply font styles (typeface, size, color, and styles)	E 2.28, E 2.30, E 3.36
	Apply number formats (currency, percent, dates, comma)	E 2.35, E 2.37, E 2.39, E 3.22
	Modify size of rows and columns	E 2.43, E 2.47, E 3.12
	Modify alignment of cell content	E 2.33
	Adjust the decimal place	E 2.36, E 2.39
	Use the Format Painter	E 3.10
	Apply AutoFormat	E 1.31
	Apply cell borders and shading	E 2.30, E 2.33, E 2.36
	Merge cells	E 1.33, E 2.30
	Rotate text and change indents	E 3.8
	Define, apply, and remove a style	E 6.22

Table D-4 Microsoft Excel 2000 MOUS Core Skill Sets, Activities, and Map

SKILL SETS	ACTIVITIES	PAGE NUMBERS
Page setup and printing	Preview and print worksheets and workbooks	E 2.51, E 3.58
	Use Web Page Preview	EW 1.3
	Print a selection	E 2.54
	Change page orientation and scaling	E 2.56, E 3.58
	Set page margins and centering	E 6.49
	Insert and remove a page break	E 6.56
	Set print, and clear a print area	E 5.22
	Set up headers and footers	E 6.49
	Set print titles and options (gridlines, print quality, row and column headings)	E 6.55
Working with worksheets and workbooks	Insert and delete rows and columns	E 3.16
	Hide and unhide rows and columns	E 2.43, E 2.46
	Freeze and unfreeze rows and columns	E 3.19, E 3.32
	Change the zoom setting	E 3.59
	Move between worksheets in a workbook	E 2.61, E 3.58
	Check spelling	E 2.48, E 3.57
	Rename a worksheet	E 2.61, E 3.56
	Insert and delete worksheets	E 6.27
	Move and copy worksheets	E 6.28
	Link worksheets and consolidate data using 3-D references	E 6.61
Working with formulas and functions	Enter a range within a formula by dragging	E 2.17, E 2.20
	Enter formulas in a cell and using the formula bar	E 2.9, E 2.11, E 3.26
	Revise formulas	E 2.24
	Use references (absolute and relative)	E 3.24
	Use AutoSum	E 1.22, E 2.14, E 3.21, E 3.31, E 3.29
	Use Paste Function to insert a function	E 2.20
	Use basic functions (AVERAGE, SUM, COUNT, MIN, MAX)	E 1.22, E 2.16

(Table D-4 continued on the next page)

Table D-4 Microsoft Excel 2000 MOUS Core Skill Sets, Activities, and Map

SKILL SETS	ACTIVITIES	PAGE NUMBERS
Working with formulas and functions (con't)	Enter functions using the Formula Palette	E 2.18, E 2.20, E 3.28
	Use date functions (NOW and DATE)	E 3.21
	Use financial functions (FV and PMT)	E 4.16
	Use logical functions (IF)	E 3.27

Table D-4 Microsoft Excel 2000 MOUS Core Skill Sets, Activities, and Map

SKILL SETS	ACTIVITIES	PAGE NUMBERS
Using charts and objects	Preview and print charts	E 2.51, E 3.58
	Use Chart Wizard to create a chart	E 1.36, E 3.45
	Modify charts	E 1.36, E 1.40, E 3.49
	Insert, move, and delete an object (picture)	E 4.42
	Create and modify lines and objects	E 6.45

Table D-5 Microsoft Excel 2000 MOUS Expert Skill Sets, Activities, and Map

SKILL SETS	ACTIVITIES	PAGE NUMBERS
Importing and exporting data	Import data from text files (insert, drag and drop)	POST-ADV
	Import from other applications	POST-ADV
	Import a table from an HTML file (insert, drag and drop including HTML round tripping)	POST-ADV
	Export to other applications	POST-ADV
Using templates	Apply templates	E 6.26
	Edit templates	E 6.16
	Create templates	E 6.7
Using multiple workbooks	Use a workspace	POST-ADV
	Link workbooks	E 6.61
Formatting numbers	Apply number formats (accounting, currency, number)	E 2.35, E 2.37, E 2.39, E 3.22
	Create custom number formats	E 6.20
	Use conditional formatting	E 2.40
Printing workbooks	Print and preview multiple worksheets	E 3.58, E 5.22
	Use Report Manager	POST-ADV
Working with named ranges	Add and delete a named range	E 4.12, E 5.19
	Use a named range in a formula	E 4.14
	Use Lookup Functions (HLOOKUP or VLOOKUP)	E 5.15
Working with toolbars	Hide and display toolbars	E 1.14, E 3.37, E 3.43
	Customize a toolbar	POST-ADV
	Assign a macro to a command button	POST-ADV
Using macros	Record macros	POST-ADV
	Run macros	POST-ADV
	Edit macros	POST-ADV
Auditing a worksheet	Work with the Auditing toolbar	POST-ADV
	Trace errors (find and fix errors)	POST-ADV
	Trace precedents (find cells referred to in a specific formula)	E 2.25
	Trace dependents (find formulas that refer to a specific cell)	E 2.25

Table D-5 Microsoft Excel 2000 MOUS Expert Skill Sets, Activities, and Map

SKILL SETS	ACTIVITIES	PAGE NUMBERS
Displaying and formatting data	Apply conditional formats	E 2.40, E 4.27
	Perform single and multi-level sorts	E 5.22, E 5.25
	Use grouping and outlines	E 5.30
	Use data forms	E 5.9
	Use subtotaling	E 5.27
	Apply data filters	E 5.35
	Extract data	E 5.43
	Query databases	E 5.32, E 5.35, E 5.40
	Use data validation	POST-ADV
Using analysis tools	Use PivotTable AutoFormat	POST-ADV
	Use Goal Seek	E 3.65, E 4.52
	Create pivot chart reports	POST-ADV
	Work with Scenarios	POST-ADV
	Use Solver	POST-ADV
	Use data analysis and PivotTables	POST-ADV
	Create interactive PivotTables for the Web	POST-ADV
	Add fields to a PivotTable using the Web browser	POST-ADV
Collaborating with workgroups	Create, edit, and remove a comment	E 6.47
	Apply and remove worksheet and workbook protection	E 4.49
	Change workbook properties	POST-ADV
	Apply and remove file passwords	POST-ADV
	Track changes (highlight, accept, and reject)	POST-ADV
	Create a shared workbook	POST-ADV
	Merge workbooks	POST-ADV

Microsoft Access 2000 User Specialist Certification Map

The Microsoft Access 2000 portion of *Microsoft Office 2000: Introductory Concepts and Techniques* (ISBN 0-7895-4635-3, 0-7895-4650-7, or 0-7895-5615-4) and *Microsoft Office 2000: Advanced Concepts and Techniques* (ISBN 0-7895-4649-3 or 0-7895-5629-4) used in combination in a two-sequence course has been approved by Microsoft as courseware for the Microsoft Office User Specialist (MOUS) program. After completing the Access 2000 projects and exercises in these two books, students will be prepared to take the Core-level Microsoft Office User Specialist Exam for Microsoft Access 2000. Table D-6 lists the skill sets, activities, and page number where the activity is discussed in the books. You should be familiar with each of the activities if you plan to take the Microsoft Access 2000 Core examination.

Table D-7 on the next page lists the skill sets, activities, and page number where the activity is discussed in the book for the Proposed Expert-level Microsoft Office User Specialist Exam for Microsoft Access 2000. POST-ADV in the PAGE NUMBERS column in Table D-7 indicates that the activity is discussed in the textbook *Microsoft Office 2000: Post-Advanced Concepts and Techniques* (ISBN 0-7895-5691-X). This post-advanced textbook is for a third course on Microsoft Office 2000 and is a continuation of *Microsoft Office 2000: Introductory Concepts and Techniques* and *Microsoft Office 2000: Advanced Concepts and Techniques*.

Table D-6 Microsoft Access 2000 MOUS Core Skill Sets, Activities, and Map

SKILL SETS	ACTIVITIES	PAGE NUMBERS
Planning and designing databases	Determine appropriate data inputs for your database	A 1.52
	Determine appropriate data outputs for your database	A 1.53
	Create table structure	A 1.15, A 1.34
	Establish table relationships	A 3.38
Working with Access	Use the Office Assistant	A 1.49
	Select an object using the Objects Bar	A 1.39, A 1.48, A 2.6
	Print database objects (tables, forms, reports, queries)	A 1.31, A 1.48, A 2.12
	Navigate through records in a tables, query, or form	A 1.27, A 1.41
	Create a database (using a Wizard or in Design view)	A 1.9
Building and modifying tables	Create tables by using the Table Wizard	A1.13
	Set primary keys	A 1.14, A 1.17
	Modify field properties	A 3.16, A 3.28
	Use multiple data types	A 1.14
	Modify tables using Design view	A 3.16
	Use the Lookup Wizard	A 6.7
	Use the Input Mask Wizard	A 6.10
Building and modifying forms	Create a form with the Form Wizard	A 4.31, A 5.21
	Use the Control Toolbox to add controls	A 4.34, A 4.37, A 4.43
	Modify format properties (font, style, font size, color, caption, etc.) of controls	A 4.36, A 4.45, A 5.42
	Use form sections (headers, footers, detail)	A 4.43, A 5.40
	Use a calculated control on a form	A 4.34
Viewing and organizing information	Use the Office Clipboard	A 6.36
	Switch between object views	A 1.42, A 3.11
	Enter records using a datasheet	A 1.21, A 1.28

Table D-6 Microsoft Access 2000 MOUS Core Skill Sets, Activities, and Map

SKILL SETS	ACTIVITIES	PAGE NUMBERS
Viewing and organizing information (con't)	Enter records using a form	A 3.8
	Delete records from a table	A 1.29, A 3.14, A 3.26
	Find a record	A 3.9
	Sort records	A 2.26, A 3.43
	Apply and remove filters (filter by form and filter by selection)	A 3.13, A 3.14
	Specify criteria in a query	A 2.17, A 2.19, A 2.21, A 2.24, A 3.26
	Display related records in a subdatasheet	A 3.42
	Create a calculated field	A 2.36
	Create and modify a multi-table select query	A 2.32, A 2.34
Defining relationships	Establish relationships	A 3.38
	Enforce referential integrity	A 3.38
Producing reports	Create a report with Report Wizard	A 1.43, A 4.9, A 4.19
	Preview and print a report	A 1.48
	Move and resize a control	A 4.27, A 6.16
	Modify format properties (font, style, font size, color, caption, etc.)	A 4.16, A 6.20
	Use the Control Toolbox to add controls	A 6.21
	Use report sections (headers, footers, detail)	A 4.14, A 4.25
	Use a calculated control in a report	A 6.20
Integrating with other applications	Import data to a new table	AI 1.3
	Save a table, query, form as a Web page	AW 1.1
	Add hyperlinks	A 5.6, A 5.18
Using Access tools	Print database relationships	A 3.41
	Backup and restore a database	A 3.6
	Compact and repair a database	A 5.48

Table D-7 Microsoft Access 2000 MOUS Proposed Expert Skill Sets, Activities, and Map

SKILL SETS	ACTIVITIES	PAGE NUMBERS
Building and modifying tables	Set validation text	A 3.31
	Define data validation criteria	A 3.28
	Modify an input mask	A 6.10, POST-ADV
	Create and modify Lookup fields	A 6.7, POST-ADV
	Optimize data type usage (double, long, int, byte, etc.)	POST-ADV
Building and modifying forms	Create a form in Design view	POST-ADV
	Insert a graphic on a form	POST-ADV
	Modify control properties	A 4.16, A 5.36, A 5.37, A 5.38
	Customize form sections (headers, footers, detail)	A 4.43, A 5.40, POST-ADV
	Modify form properties	A 4.45, A 5.33, POST-ADV
	Use the subform control and synchronize forms	A 5.26, POST-ADV
	Create a switchboard	A 6.40
Refining queries	Apply filters (filter by form and filter by selection) in a query s recordset	POST-ADV
	Create a totals query	A 2.38
	Create a parameter query	POST-ADV
	Specify criteria in multiple fields (AND vs. OR)	A 2.24, A 2.25
	Modify query properties (field formats, caption, input masks, etc.)	POST-ADV
	Create an action query (update, delete, insert)	A 3.23, A 3.26
	Optimize queries using indexes	A 3.48, POST-ADV
	Specify join properties for relationships	POST-ADV
Producing reports	Insert a graphic on a report	POST-ADV
	Modify report properties	A 4.15, POST-ADV
	Create and modify a report in Design view	POST-ADV
	Modify control properties	A 4.15, A 6.20, POST-ADV
	Set section properties	A 4.15, POST-ADV
	Use the subreport control and synchronize reports	POST-ADV
Defining relationships	Establish one-to-one relationships	POST-ADV
	Establish many-to-many relationships	POST-ADV
	Set Cascade Update and Cascade Delete options	POST-ADV
Utilizing Web capabilities	Create hyperlinks	A 5.6, A 5.18
	Use the group and sort features of data access pages	POST-ADV
	Create a data access page	AW 1.3
Using Access tools	Set and modify a database password	POST-ADV
	Set startup options	POST-ADV
	Use Add-ins (Database Splitter, Analyzer, Link Table Manager)	POST-ADV
	Encrypt and decrypt a database	POST-ADV
	Use simple replication (copy for a mobile user)	POST-ADV
	Run macros using controls	POST-ADV
	Create a macro using the Macro Builder	POST-ADV
	Convert a database to a previous version	POST-ADV
Data integration	Export database records to Excel	POST-ADV
	Drag and drop tables and queries to Excel	POST-ADV
	Present information as a chart (MS Graph)	POST-ADV
	Link to existing data	AI 1.3, POST-ADV

Microsoft PowerPoint 2000 User Specialist Certification Map

The Microsoft PowerPoint 2000 portion of *Microsoft Office 2000: Introductory Concepts and Techniques* (ISBN 0-7895-4635-3, 0-7895-4650-7, or 0-7895-5615-4) and *Microsoft Office 2000: Advanced Concepts and Techniques* (ISBN 0-7895-4649-3 or 0-7895-5629-4) used in combination in a two-sequence course has been approved by Microsoft as courseware for the Microsoft Office User Specialist (MOUS) program. After completing the PowerPoint 2000 projects and exercises in these two books, students will be prepared to take the Core-level Microsoft Office User Specialist Exam for Microsoft PowerPoint 2000. Table D-8 lists the skill sets, activities, and page number where the activity is discussed in the books. You should be familiar with each of the activities if you plan to take the Microsoft PowerPoint 2000 Core examination.

Table D-9 on the next page lists the skill sets, activities, and page number where the activity is discussed in the book for the Proposed Expert-level Microsoft Office User Specialist Exam for Microsoft PowerPoint 2000. POST-ADV in the PAGE NUMBERS column in Table D-9 indicates that the activity is discussed in the textbook *Microsoft Office 2000: Post-Advanced Concepts and Techniques* (ISBN 0-7895-5691-X). This post-advanced textbook is for a third course on Microsoft Office 2000 and is a continuation of *Microsoft Office 2000: Introductory Concepts and Techniques* and *Microsoft Office 2000: Advanced Concepts and Techniques*.

Table D-8 Microsoft PowerPoint 2000 MOUS Core Skill Sets, Activities, and Map

SKILL SETS	ACTIVITIES	PAGE NUMBERS
Creating a presentation	Delete slides	PP 4.53
	Create a specified type of slide	PP 1.33, PP 1.40-42, PP 2.7, PP 2.11, PP 2.13, PP 2.15, PP 2.18
	Create a presentation from a template and/or a Wizard	PP 1.8, PP 2.7, PPW 1.1
	Navigate among different views (slide, outline, sorter, tri-pane)	PP 1.13, PP 2.8, PP 2.20, PP 2.21, PP 2.46
	Create a new presentation from existing slides	PP 4.6
	Copy a slide from one presentation into another	PP 3.8
	Insert headers and footers	PP 2.35
	Create a blank presentation	PP 1.10, PP 2.6, PP 3.7
	Create a presentation using the AutoContent Wizard	PP 1.8
	Send a presentation via e-mail	PP 2.55
Modifying a presentation	Change the order of slides using Slide Sorter view	PP 4.50-51
	Find and replace text	PP 1.57, PPW 1.10, PP 4.7, PP 4.24
	Change the layout for one or more slides	PP 2.22, PP 2.27-28
	Change slide layout (Modify the Slide Master)	PP 1.57-63, PP 2.42, PP 3.14-18, PP 4.8
	Modify slide sequence in the outline pane	PP 2.10, PP 4.25-26, PP 4.49, PP 4.54
	Apply a design template	PP 1.18, PP 2.7, PP 3.9
Working with text	Check spelling	PP 1.54
	Change and replace text fonts (individual slide and entire presentation)	PP 1.24, PP 1.27, PP 2.47, PP 3.10
	Enter text in tri-pane view	PP 1.21, PP 1.23, PP 1.35, PP 1.37-42, PP 2.11-12 PP 2.14-19
	Import text from Word	PP 3.7-8
	Change the text alignment	PP 1.59
	Create a text box for entering text	PP 4.35, PP 4.37
	Use the Wrap text in AutoShape feature	PP 4.59
	Use the Office Clipboard	PP 3.34
	Use the Format Painter	PP 4.64

Table D-8 Microsoft PowerPoint 2000 MOUS Core Skill Sets, Activities, and Map

SKILL SETS	ACTIVITIES	PAGE NUMBERS
Working with text (con't)	Promote and Demote text in slide and outline panes	PP 1.37-41, PP 2.11, PP 2.14-19
Working with visual elements	Add a picture from the ClipArt Gallery	PP 2.24, PP 2.27-30, PP 3.16-18, PP 3.52, PP 4.8
	Add and group shapes using WordArt or the Drawing toolbar	PP 3.53-58, PP 4.13-21
	Apply formatting	PP 1.25, PP 1.27, PP 2.47, PP 3.14, PP 3.45-49, PP 4.34-38
	Place text inside a shape using a text box	PP 4.35
	Scale and size an object including ClipArt	PP 2.32, PP 3.39, PP 3.53, PP 4.21, PP 4.33
	Create tables within PowerPoint	PP 3.41-49
	Rotate and fill an object	PP 4.19-20, PP 4.34
Customizing a presentation	Add AutoNumber bullets	PP 3.18
	Add speaker notes	PPW 1.4
	Add graphical bullets	PP 3.19-21
	Add slide transitions	PP 2.38, PP 3.58, PP 4.54
	Animate text and objects	PP 2.50-51, PP 3.58, PP 4.54
Creating output	Preview presentation in black and white	PP 1.63
	Print slides in a variety of formats	PP 1.64, PP 2.51, PP 2.54
	Print audience handouts	PP 1.64, PP 2.5, PP 3.59
	Print speaker notes in a specified format	PP 3.55
Delivering a presentation	Start a slide show on any slide	PP 1.46, PP 1.48, PP 2.49
	Use on-screen navigation tools	PP 1.48, PP 2.50, PP 3.40 PP 3.41, PP 4.38, PP 4.44
	Print a slide as an overhead transparency	PP 1.67
	Use the pen during a presentation	PP 4.60
Managing files	Save changes to a presentation	PP 1.51, PP 1.65, PP 1.69, PP 2.35, PP 2.49, PP 2.57, PPW 1.4, PP 3.12, PP 4.6
	Save as a new presentation	PP 1.28, PP 2.19
	Publish a presentation to the Web	PPW 1.3
	Use Office Assistant	PP 1.67
	Insert hyperlink	PP 2.35, PP 4.27-30

Table D-9 Microsoft PowerPoint 2000 MOUS Proposed Expert Skill Sets, Activities, and Map

SKILL SETS	ACTIVITIES	PAGE NUMBERS
Creating a presentation	Automatically create a summary slide	PP 4.52-53
	Automatically create slides from a summary slide	PP 4.51
	Design a template	POST-ADV
	Format presentations for the Web	PPW 1.3
Modifying a presentation	Change tab formatting	POST-ADV
	Use the Wrap text in AutoShape feature	PP 4.16
	Apply a template from another presentation	PP 3.9
	Customize a color scheme	POST-ADV
	Apply animation effects	PP 2.37, PP 2.46-48, PP 3.58, PP 4.54
	Create a custom background	PP 3.12-18, PP 4.8
	Add animated GIFs	PPI 2.8
	Add links to slides within the presentation	PP 4.64
	Customize clip art and other objects (resize, scale, etc.)	PP 2.33, PP 3.39, PP 3.53, PP 3.54-58
	Add a presentation within a presentation	POST-ADV
	Add an action button	PP 4.27-30
	Hide slides	PP 4.49
	Set automatic slide timings	POST-ADV
Working with visual elements	Add textured backgrounds	PP 4.58
	Apply diagonal borders	POST-ADV
Using data from other sources	Export an outline to Word	PP 2.51
	Add a table (from Word)	POST-ADV
	Insert an Excel chart	POST-ADV
	Add sound	PP 4.27-30, PPI 2.6-8
	Add video	PPI 2.1
Creating output	Save slide as a graphic	POST-ADV
	Generate meeting notes	POST-ADV
	Change output format (Page setup)	PP 2.51, PP 3.59
	Export to 35mm slides	PP 4.53
Delivering a presentation	Save presentation for use on another computer (Pack 'N Go)	POST-ADV
	Electronically incorporate meeting feedback	POST-ADV
	Use presentations on demand	POST-ADV
Managing files	Save embedded fonts in presentation	POST-ADV
	Save HTML to a specific target browser	PPW 1.6
Working with PowerPoint	Customize the toolbar	PP 2.22, POST-ADV
	Create a toolbar	POST-ADV
Collaborating with workgroups	Subscribe to a presentation	POST-ADV
	View a presentation on the Web	PPW 1.6
	Use Net Meeting to schedule a broadcast	POST-ADV
	Use NetShow to deliver a broadcast	POST-ADV
Working with charts and tables	Build a chart or graph	POST-ADV
	Modify charts or graphs	POST-ADV
	Build an organization chart	PP 3.22-40
	Modify an organization chart	PP 4.38-43

Index

Microsoft Office 2000

Microsoft Office 2000
Quick Reference Summary

In the Microsoft Office 2000 applications, you can accomplish a task in a number of ways. The following five tables (one each for Word, Excel, Access, PowerPoint, and Outlook) provide a quick reference to each task presented in this textbook and its companion textbook *Microsoft Office 2000: Introductory Concepts and Techniques*. Any task with a page number reference beginning with 1, 2, or 3 is from the companion textbook. Any page number reference beginning with 4, 5, or 6 is from this textbook. You can invoke the commands listed in the MENU BAR and SHORTCUT MENU columns using either the mouse or keyboard.

Table 1 Microsoft Word 2000 Quick Reference Summary

TASK	PAGE NUMBER	MOUSE	MENU BAR	SHORTCUT MENU	KEYBOARD SHORTCUT
1.5 Line Spacing	WD 2.18		Format | Paragraph | Indents and Spacing tab	Paragraph | Indents and Spacing tab	CTRL+5
AutoCorrect Entry, Create	WD 2.21		Tools | AutoCorrect | AutoCorrect tab		
AutoText Entry, Create	WD 3.45		Insert | AutoText | New		ALT+F3
AutoText Entry, Insert	WD 3.47		Insert | AutoText		Type entry, then F3
Blank Line Above Paragraph	WD 2.18		Format | Paragraph | Indents and Spacing tab	Paragraph | Indents and Spacing tab	CTRL+0
Bold	WD 1.33	Bold button on Formatting toolbar	Format | Font | Font tab	Font | Font tab	CTRL+B
Border, Bottom	WD 3.39	Border button arrow on Formatting toolbar	Format | Borders and Shading | Borders tab		
Border, Outside	WD 4.8	Border button arrow on Tables and Borders toolbar	Format | Borders and Shading | Borders tab		
Border, Page	WD 6.59		Format | Borders and Shading | Page Border tab	Borders and Shading | Page Border tab	
Bulleted List	WD 3.50	Bullets button on Formatting toolbar	Format | Bullets and Numbering | Bulleted tab	Bullets and Numbering | Bulleted tab	* and then space followed by text, then ENTER
Capitalize Letters	WD 2.18		Format | Font | Font tab	Font | Font tab	CTRL+SHIFT+A
Case of Letters	WD 2.18				SHIFT+F3
Center	WD 1.35	Center button on Formatting toolbar	Format | Paragraph | Indents and Spacing tab	Paragraph | Indents and Spacing tab	CTRL+E
Center Vertically	WD 4.17		File | Page Setup | Layout tab		
Character Formatting, Remove	WD 2.18		Format | Font	Font	CTRL+Q
Character Spacing	WD 6.42		Format | Font | Character Spacing tab	Font | Character Spacing tab	
Chart, Format Axis Numbers	WD 4.35	Click axis, Increase or Decrease Decimals button on Formatting toolbar	Click axis, Format | Format Axis	Right-click axis, click Format Axis on shortcut menu	
Chart, Move Legend	WD 4.36		Click legend, Format | Format Legend	Right-click legend, click Format Legend on shortcut menu	
Chart Table	WD 4.33		Insert | Picture | Chart		
Clip Art, Insert	WD 1.43		Insert | Picture | Clip Art		
Clip Gallery Live	WD 4.12		Insert | Picture | Clip Art		
Close All Documents	WD 3.60		SHIFT+File | Close All		
Close Document	WD 1.54	Close button on menu bar	File | Close		CTRL+W

(continued)

Table 1 Microsoft Word 2000 Quick Reference Summary *(continued)*

TASK	PAGE NUMBER	MOUSE	MENU BAR	SHORTCUT MENU	KEYBOARD SHORTCUT
Color Characters	WD 3.28	Font Color button arrow on Formatting toolbar	Format | Font | Font tab	Font | Font tab	
Column Break	WD 6.31		Insert | Break		CTRL+SHIFT+ENTER
Columns	WD 6.25	Columns button on Standard toolbar	Format | Columns		
Columns, Balance	WD 6.51		Insert | Break		
Columns, Format	WD 6.25		Format | Columns		
Copy	WD 3.33	Copy button on Standard toolbar or Clipboard toolbar	Edit | Copy	Copy	CTRL+C
Count Words	WD 2.49		Tools | Word Count		
Current Date, Insert	WD 6.17		Insert | Date and Time		
Data Source, Add Field	WD 5.23	Manage Fields button on Database toolbar			
Data Source, Add Record	WD 5.24	Add New Record button on Database toolbar			
Data Source, Change Designation	WDI 1.4	Mail Merge Helper button on Mail Merge toolbar	Tools | Mail Merge		
Data Source, Create	WD 5.17	Mail Merge Helper button on Mail Merge toolbar	Tools | Mail Merge		
Data Source, Delete Record	WD 5.24	Delete Record button on Database toolbar			
Delete Text	WD 1.54	Cut button on Standard toolbar	Edit | Cut	Cut	DELETE or BACKSPACE
Demote List Item	WD 3.51	Decrease Indent button on Formatting toolbar			
Distribute Columns Evenly	WD 4.48	Distribute Columns Evenly button on Tables and Borders toolbar	Table | AutoFit | Distribute Columns Evenly		
Distribute Rows Evenly	WD 4.47	Distribute Rows Evenly button on Tables and Borders toolbar	Table | AutoFit | Distribute Rows Evenly		
Document Window, Open New	WD 3.27	New Blank Document button on Standard toolbar	File | New | General tab		
Double Strikethrough, Characters	WD 4.17		Format | Font | Font tab	Font | Font tab	
Double-Space Text	WD 2.9		Format | Paragraph | Indents and Spacing tab	Paragraph | Indents and Spacing tab	CTRL+2
Double-Underline	WD 2.18		Format | Font | Font tab	Font | Font tab	CTRL+SHIFT+D
Drop Cap	WD 6.28		Format | Drop Cap		
E-mail Document	WD 2.54	E-mail button on Standard toolbar	File | Send To | Mail Recipient		
Emboss, Characters	WD 4.17		Format | Font | Font tab	Font | Font tab	
Engrave, Characters	WD 4.17		Format | Font | Font tab	Font | Font tab	
Envelope	WD 3.58		Tools | Envelopes and Labels		
Envelopes Using Data Source	WD 5.54	Mail Merge Helper button on Mail Merge toolbar	Tools | Mail Merge		
Erase Table Lines	WD 4.45	Eraser button on Tables and Borders toolbar			
Field Codes, Display	WD 5.39		Tools | Options | View tab		ALT+F9
Field Codes, Print	WD 5.40		Tools | Options | Print tab		
Fill-in Field	WD 5.37	Insert Word Field button on Mail Merge toolbar	Insert | Field		
Find	WD 2.45	Select Browse Object button on vertical scroll bar	Edit | Find		CTRL+F
Find and Replace	WD 2.43	Select Browse Object on vertical scroll bar	Edit | Replace		CTRL+H

Table 1 Microsoft Word 2000 Quick Reference Summary *(continued)*

TASK	PAGE NUMBER	MOUSE	MENU BAR	SHORTCUT MENU	KEYBOARD SHORTCUT
First-Line Indent	WD 2.19	Drag First Line Indent marker on ruler	Format	Paragraph	Indents and Spacing tab	Paragraph	Indents and Spacing tab	
Floating Graphic	WD 6.20	Text Wrapping button on Picture toolbar	Format	Picture	Layout tab	Format Picture	Layout tab	
Folder, Create	WD 1.49		File	Save As		
Font	WD 1.31	Font button on Formatting toolbar	Format	Font	Font tab	Font	Font tab	CTRL+SHIFT+F
Font Size	WD 1.17	Font Size box arrow on Formatting toolbar	Format	Font	Font tab	Font	Font tab	CTRL+SHIFT+P
Footnote, Create	WD 2.23		Insert	Footnote		
Footnote, Delete	WD 2.30	Delete note reference mark in document window			
Footnote, Edit	WD 2.30	Double-click note reference mark in document window	View	Footnotes		
Footnotes to Endnotes, Convert	WD 2.30		Insert	Footnote		
Format Painter	WD 6.57	Format Painter button on Standard toolbar			
Formatting Marks	WD 1.20	Show/Hide ¶ button on Standard toolbar	Tools	Options	View tab		CTRL+SHIFT+*
Formatting Toolbar, Display Entire	WD 1.13	Double-click move handle on Formatting toolbar			
Full Menu	WD 1.12	Double-click menu name	Click menu name, wait few seconds		
Go To	WD 2.42	Select Browse Object button on vertical scroll bar	Edit	Go To		CTRL+G
Hanging Indent, Create	WD 2.37	Drag Hanging Indent marker on ruler	Format	Paragraph	Indents and Spacing tab	Paragraph	Indents and Spacing tab	CTRL+T
Hanging Indent, Remove	WD 2.18	Drag Hanging Indent marker on ruler	Format	Paragraph	Indents and Spacing tab	Paragraph	Indents and Spacing tab	CTRL+SHIFT+T
Header, Different from Previous	WD 4.28	In print layout view, double-click header area	View	Header and Footer		
Header, Display	WD 2.12	In print layout view, double-click header area	View	Header and Footer		
Help	WD 1.55	Microsoft Word Help button on Standard toolbar	Help	Microsoft Word Help		F1
Hidden Characters	WD 4.17		Format	Font	Font tab	Font	Font tab	
Highlight Text	WD 6.61	Highlight button on Formatting toolbar			
HTML Source	WDW 1.11		View	HTML Source		
Hyperlink, Add	WDW 1.10	Insert Hyperlink button on Standard toolbar		Hyperlink	
Hyperlink, Create	WD 2.39	Insert Hyperlink button on Standard toolbar		Hyperlink	Web address then ENTER or SPACEBAR
Hyperlink, Edit	WDW 1.10	Insert Hyperlink button on Standard toolbar		Hyperlink	
IF Field	WD 5.34	Insert Word Field button on Mail Merge toolbar	Insert	Field		
Insert File	WD 4.23		Insert	File		
Insert Merge Fields	WD 5.27	Insert Merge Field button on Mail Merge toolbar			
Italicize	WD 1.39	Italic button on Formatting toolbar	Format	Font	Font tab	Font	Font tab	CTRL+I
Justify	WD 6.26	Justify button on Formatting toolbar	Format	Paragraph	Indents and Spacing tab	Paragraph	Indents and Spacing tab	CTRL+J
Landscape Orientation	WD 5.24		File	Page Setup	Paper Size tab		

(continued)

Table 1 Microsoft Word 2000 Quick Reference Summary *(continued)*

TASK	PAGE NUMBER	MOUSE	MENU BAR	SHORTCUT MENU	KEYBOARD SHORTCUT
Last Editing Location	WD 4.25				SHIFT+F5
Leader Characters	WD 3.31		Format | Tabs		
Left-Align	WD 2.17	Align Left button on Formatting toolbar	Format | Paragraph | Indents and Spacing tab	Paragraph | Indents and Spacing tab	CTRL+L
Line Break, Enter	WD 3.22				SHIFT+ENTER
Link	WD 6.34		Edit | Paste Special		
List Item, Demote	WD 5.32	Increase Indent button on Formatting toolbar			SHIFT+TAB
List Item, Promote	WD 5.32	Decrease Indent button on Formatting toolbar			TAB
Mailing Label	WD 3.58		Tools | Envelopes and Labels		
Mailing Labels Using Data Source	WD 5.48	Mail Merge Helper button on Mail Merge toolbar	Tools | Mail Merge		
Main Document, Identify	WD 5.14	Mail Merge Helper button on Mail Merge toolbar	Tools | Mail Merge		
Margins	WD 2.8	In print layout view, drag margin boundary	File | Page Setup | Margins tab		
Menus and Toolbars, Reset	WD 2.7		View | Toolbars | Customize | Options tab		
Merge Certain Records	WD 5.43	Merge button on Mail Merge toolbar			
Merge to E-mail Addresses	WDI 1.4	Merge button on Mail Merge toolbar			
Merge to Printer	WD 5.40	Merge to Printer button on Mail Merge toolbar			
Merged Data, View	WD 5.47	View Merged Data button on Mail Merge toolbar			
Move Selected Text	WD 2.46	Drag and drop	Edit | Cut; Edit | Paste		CTRL+X; CTRL+V
Nonbreaking Hyphen	WD 3.46		Insert | Symbol | Special Characters tab		CTRL+SHIFT+HYPHEN
Nonbreaking Space	WD 3.46		Insert | Symbol | Special Characters tab		CTRL+SHIFT+SPACEBAR
Normal Style, Apply	WD 4.19	Style box arrow on Formatting toolbar	Format | Style		CTRL+SHIFT+N
Note Pane, Close	WD 2.29	Close button in note pane			
Numbered List	WD 3.51	Numbering button on Formatting toolbar	Format | Bullets and Numbering | Numbered tab	Bullets and Numbering | Numbered tab	1. and then space followed by text, then ENTER
Open Document	WD 1.52	Open button on Standard toolbar	File | Open		CTRL+O
Orphan	WD 2.32		Format | Paragraph | Line and Page Breaks tab	Paragraph | Line and Page Breaks tab	
Outline Numbered List	WD 5.30		Format | Bullets and Numbering | Outline Numbered tab		
Outline, Characters	WD 4.17		Format | Font | Font tab	Font | Font tab	
Page Break	WD 2.35		Insert | Break		CTRL+ENTER
Page Numbers, Insert	WD 2.14	Insert Page Number button on Header and Footer toolbar	Insert | Page Numbers		
Page Numbers, Modify	WD 4.29		Insert | Page Numbers		
Paragraph Formatting, Remove	WD 2.18		Format | Paragraph	Paragraph	CTRL+SPACEBAR
Paste	WD 3.35	Paste button on Standard toolbar or click icon on Clipboard toolbar	Edit | Paste	Paste	CTRL+V
Picture Bullets	WD 4.40		Format | Bullets and Numbering | Bulleted tab	Bullets and Numbering | Bulleted tab	
Picture, Insert	WD 6.53		Insert | Picture | From File		
Print Document	WD 1.50	Print button on Standard toolbar	File | Print		CTRL+P

Table 1   Microsoft Word 2000 Quick Reference Summary *(continued)*

TASK	PAGE NUMBER	MOUSE	MENU BAR	SHORTCUT MENU	KEYBOARD SHORTCUT
Print Preview	WD 3.24	Print Preview button on Standard toolbar	File | Print Preview		CTRL+F2
Promote List Item	WD 3.51	Increase Indent button on Formatting toolbar			
Quit Word	WD 1.51	Close button on title bar	File | Exit		ALT+F4
Redo Action	WD 1.35	Redo button on Standard toolbar	Edit | Redo		
Repeat Command	WD 1.36		Edit | Repeat		
Resize Graphic	WD 1.47	Drag sizing handle	Format | Picture | Size tab		
Restore Graphic	WD 1.48	Format Picture button on Picture toolbar	Format | Picture | Size tab		
Right-Align	WD 1.33	Align Right button on Formatting toolbar	Format | Paragraph | Indents and Spacing tab	Paragraph | Indents and Spacing tab	CTRL+R
Rotate Text in Table	WD 4.50	Change Text Direction button on Tables and Borders toolbar	Format | Text Direction	Text Direction	
Ruler, Show or Hide	WD 1.11		View | Ruler		
Save as Web Page	WDW 1.3		File | Save as Web Page		
Save Document— New Name	WD 1.49		File | Save As		F12
Save Document— Same Name	WD 1.49	Save button on Standard toolbar	File | Save		CTRL+S
Save New Document	WD 1.26	Save button on Standard toolbar	File | Save		CTRL+S
Section Break, Continuous	WD 6.24		Insert | Break		
Section Break, Next Page	WD 4.21		Insert | Break		
Select Document	WD 2.46	Point to left and triple-click	Edit | Select All		CTRL+A
Select Graphic	WD 1.46	Click graphic			CTRL+SHIFT+RIGHT ARROW
Select Group of Words	WD 1.41	Drag through words			CTRL+SHIFT+RIGHT ARROW
Select Line	WD 1.37	Point to left of line and click			SHIFT+DOWN ARROW
Select Multiple Paragraphs	WD 1.30	Point to left of paragraph and drag down			CTRL+SHIFT+DOWN ARROW
Select Paragraph	WD 2.46	Triple-click paragraph			
Select Sentence	WD 2.45	CTRL+click in sentence			CTRL+SHIFT+RIGHT ARROW
Select Table	WD 3.56	Drag through table	Table | Select | Table		ALT+5 (on numeric keypad)
Select Word	WD 1.38	Double-click word			CTRL+SHIFT+RIGHT ARROW
Shade Graphic	WD 6.21	Format Picture button on Picture toolbar	Format | Picture | Colors and Lines tab	Format Picture | Colors and Lines tab	
Shade Paragraph	WD 6.45	Shading Color button on Tables and Borders toolbar	Format | Borders and Shading | Shading tab	Borders and Shading | Shading tab	
Shadow, on Characters	WD 4.17		Format | Font | Font tab	Font | Font tab	
Single-Space Paragraph	WD 4.31		Format | Paragraph | Indents and Spacing tab	Paragraph | Indents and Spacing tab	CTRL+1
Small Uppercase Letters	WD 2.18		Format | Font | Font tab	Font | Font tab	CTRL+SHIFT+K
Sort Data Records	WD 5.45	Merge button on Mail Merge toolbar			
Sort Paragraphs	WD 2.40		Table | Sort		
Spelling Check as You Type	WD 1.22	Double-click Spelling and Grammar Status icon on status bar		Right-click flagged word, click correct word on shortcut menu	
Spelling Check At Once	WD 2.50	Spelling and Grammar button on Standard toolbar	Tools | Spelling and Grammar	Spelling	F7
Standard Toolbar, Display Entire	WD 1.15	Double-click move handle on Standard toolbar			
Strikethrough, Characters	WD 4.17		Format | Font | Font tab	Font | Font tab	

(continued)

Table 1 Microsoft Word 2000 Quick Reference Summary (continued)

TASK	PAGE NUMBER	MOUSE	MENU BAR	SHORTCUT MENU	KEYBOARD SHORTCUT
Style, Apply	WD 6.33	Style box arrow on Formatting toolbar	Format | Style		
Style, Modify	WD 2.26		Format | Style		
Subscript	WD 2.18		Format | Font | Font tab	Font | Font tab	CTRL+=
Superscript	WD 2.18		Format | Font | Font tab	Font | Font tab	CTRL+SHIFT+PLUS SIGN
Switch from Data Source to Main Document	WD 5.25	Mail Merge Main Document button on Database toolbar			
Switch to Open Document	WD 3.33	Program button on taskbar	Window | document name		
Symbol, Insert	WD 3.37		Insert | Symbol		ALT+0 (on numeric keypad)
Synonym	WD 2.48		Tools | Language | Thesaurus	Synonyms | desired word	SHIFT+F7
Tab Stops, Insert	WD 3.31	Click location on ruler	Format | Tabs		
Table AutoFormat	WD 3.55	AutoFormat button on Tables and Borders toolbar	Table | Table AutoFormat		
Table, Create	WD 3.52	Insert Table button on Standard toolbar	Table | Insert | Table		
Table, Draw	WD 4.42	Tables and Borders button on Standard toolbar	Table | Draw Table		
Template	WD 3.42, WD 5.6		File | New		
Text Box, Format	WD 6.41	Double-click text box	Format | Text Box	Format Text Box	
Text Box, Insert	WD 6.40	Text Box button on Drawing toolbar	Insert | Text Box		
Top Alignment	WD 4.22		File | Page Setup | Layout tab		
Underline	WD 1.42	Underline button on Formatting toolbar	Format | Font | Font tab	Font | Font tab	CTRL+U
Underline Words, not Spaces	WD 2.18		Format | Font | Font tab	Font | Font tab	CTRL+SHIFT+W
Undo Command or Action	WD 1.36	Undo button on Standard toolbar	Edit | Undo		CTRL+Z
Unlink a Field	WD 5.28				CTRL+SHIFT+F9
Vertical Rule	WD 6.37		Format | Borders and Shading | Borders tab		
Watermark	WD 4.54	In print layout view, double-click header area	View | Header and Footer		
Web Page Frame, Resize	WDW 1.9	Drag frame border	Format | Frames | Frame Properties | Frame tab		
Web Page, View	WDW 1.11		File | Web Page Preview		
Web Page Wizard	WDW 1.5		File | New | Web Pages tab		
Widow	WD 2.32		Format | Paragraph | Line and Page Breaks tab	Paragraph | Line and Page Breaks tab	
Wizard, Resume	WD 3.7		File | New | Other Documents tab		
WordArt Drawing Object, Format	WD 6.12	Format WordArt button on WordArt toolbar	Format | WordArt	Format WordArt	
WordArt Drawing Object, Insert	WD 6.9	Insert WordArt button on Drawing toolbar	Insert | Picture | WordArt		
WordArt Drawing Object, Shape	WD 6.14	WordArt Shape button on WordArt toolbar			
Wrap Text Around Graphic	WD 6.54	Text Wrapping button on Picture toolbar	Format | Picture | Layout tab	Format Picture | Layout tab	
Zoom Page Width	WD 1.15	Zoom box arrow on Formatting toolbar	View | Zoom		
Zoom Text Width	WD 3.17	Zoom box arrow on Formatting toolbar	View | Zoom		
Zoom Whole Page	WD 6.32	Zoom box arrow on Formatting toolbar	View | Zoom		

Table 2   Microsoft Excel 2000 Quick Reference Summary

TASK	PAGE NUMBER	MOUSE	MENU BAR	SHORTCUT MENU	KEYBOARD SHORTCUT
Arrow, Add	E 6.45	Arrow button on Drawing toolbar			
AutoFilter	E 5.35		Data | Filter | AutoFilter		ALT+D | F | F
Advanced Filter	E 5.41		Data | Filter | Advanced Filter		ALT+D | F | A
AutoFormat	E 1.31		Format | AutoFormat		ALT + O | A
AutoSum	E 1.22	AutoSum button on Standard toolbar	Insert | Function		ALT+=
Bold	E 1.29	Bold button on Formatting toolbar	Format | Cells | Font tab	Format Cells | Font tab	CTRL+B
Borders	E 2.30	Borders button on Formatting toolbar	Format | Cells | Border tab	Format Cells | Border tab	CTRL+1 | B
Center	E 2.33	Center button on Formatting toolbar	Format | Cells | Alignment tab	Format Cells | Alignment tab	CTRL+1 | A
Center Across Columns	E 1.33	Merge and Center button on Formatting toolbar	Format | Cells | Alignment tab	Format Cells | Alignment tab	CTRL+1 | A
Chart	E 1.37	Chart Wizard button on Standard toolbar	Insert | Chart		F11
Clear Cell	E 1.53	Drag fill handle back	Edit | Clear | All	Clear Contents	DELETE
Close All Workbooks	E 1.46		SHIFT+File | Close All		SHIFT+ALT+F | C
Close Workbook	E 1.46	Close button on menu bar or workbook Control-menu icon	File | Close		CTRL+W
Color Background	E 2.30	Fill Color button on Formatting toolbar	Format | Cells | Patterns tab	Format Cells | Patterns tab	CTRL+1 | P
Column Width	E 2.44	Drag column heading boundary	Format | Column | Width tab	Column Width	ALT+O | C | W
Comma Style Format	E 2.32	Comma Style button on Formatting toolbar	Format | Cells | Number tab | Accounting	Format Cells | Number tab | Accounting	CTRL+1 | N
Comment	E 6.47		Insert | Comment	Insert Comment	ALT+I | M
Conditional Formatting	E 2.40		Format | Conditional Formatting		ALT+O | D
Copy and Paste	E 3.14	Copy button and Paste button on Standard toolbar	Edit | Copy; Edit | Paste	Copy to copy | Paste to paste	CTRL+C; CTRL+V
Currency Style Format	E 2.35	Percent Style button on Formatting toolbar	Format | Cells | Number tab | Currency	Format Cells | Number tab | Accounting	CTRL+1 | N
Custom Formats	E 6.20		Format | Cells | Number tab | Custom	Format Cells | Number tab | Custom	CTRL+1 | N
Cut	E 3.16	Cut button on Standard toolbar	Edit | Cut	Cut	CTRL + X
Data Form	E 5.9		Data | Form		ALT+D | O
Data Table	E 4.19		Data | Table		
Date	E 3.22	Paste Function button on Standard toolbar	Insert | Function		CTRL+ SEMICOLON
Decimal Place, Decrease	E 2.36	Decrease Decimal button on Formatting toolbar	Format | Cells | Number tab | Currency	Format Cells | Number tab | Currency	CTRL+1 | N
Decimal Place, Increase	E 2.36	Increase Decimal button on Formatting toolbar	Format | Cells | Number tab | Currency	Format Cells | Number tab | Currency	CTRL+1 | N
Delete Rows or Columns	E 3.18		Edit | Delete	Delete	DELETE
Draft Quality	E 6.55		File | Page Setup | Sheet tab		ALT+F | U | S
Drop Shadow	E 3.39	Shadow button on Drawing toolbar			
Embed a Clip Art Graphic	E 4.44		Insert | Picture | Clip Art		ALT+I | P | C
E-mail from Excel	E 2.63	E-mail button on Standard toolbar	File | Send To | Mail Recipient		ALT+F | D | A
Find	E 6.58		Edit | Find		CTRL+F
Fit to Print	E 2.56		File | Page Setup | Page tab		
Font Color	E 2.30	Font Color button on Formatting toolbar	Format | Cells | Font tab	Format Cells | Font tab	CTRL+1 | F

(continued)

MICROSOFT EXCEL 2000 QUICK REFERENCE SUMMARY

Table 2   Microsoft Excel 2000 Quick Reference Summary (continued)

TASK	PAGE NUMBER	MOUSE	MENU BAR	SHORTCUT MENU	KEYBOARD SHORTCUT
Font Size	E 1.30	Font Size box arrow on Formatting toolbar	Format | Cells | Font tab	Format Cells | Font tab	CTRL+1 | F
Font Type	E 2.28	Font box on Formatting toolbar	Format | Cells | Font tab	Format Cells | Patterns tab	CTRL+1 | F
Footer	E 6.49		File | Page Setup | Header/Footer tab		ALT+F | U | H
Formula Palette	E 2.18	Edit Formula box in formula bar	Insert | Function		CTRL+A after typing function name
Formulas Version	E 2.56		Tools | Options | View | Formulas		CTRL+ SINGLE LEFT QUOTATION MARK
Freeze Worksheet Titles	E 3.20		Windows | Freeze Panes		ALT+W | F
Function	E 2.20	Paste Function button on Standard toolbar	Insert | Function		SHIFT+F3
Gridlines	E 6.55		File | Page Setup | Sheet tab		ALT+F | U | S
Go To	E 1.36	Click cell	Edit | Go To		F5
Goal Seek	E 3.65		Tools | Goal Seek		ALT+T | G
Header	E 6.49		File | Page Setup | Header/Footer tab		ALT+F | U | H
Help	E 1.54	Microsoft Excel Help button on Standard toolbar	Help | Microsoft Excel Help		F1
Hide Column	E 2.46	Drag column heading boundary	Format | Column	Column Height	CTRL+0 (zero) to hide CTRL+SHIFT+) to display
Hide Row	E 2.48	Drag row heading boundary	Format | Row	Row Height	CTRL+9 to hide CTRL+SHIFT+(to display
In-Cell Editing	E 1.51	Double-click cell			F2
Insert Rows or Columns	E 3.16		Insert | Rows or Insert | Columns	Insert	ALT+I | R or ALT+I | C
Italicize	E 3.42	Italic button on Formatting toolbar	Format | Cells | Font tab	Format Cells | Font tab	CTRL+I
Link Update	E 6.63		Edit | Links		ALT+E | K
Link Worksheet to Word Document	EI 1.4		Edit | Copy; Edit | Paste Special	Copy to copy | Paste Special to paste	CTRL+C; ALT+E | S
Margins	E 6.49		File | Page Setup | Margins		ALT+F | U | M
Move	E 3.15	Point to border and drag	Edit | Cut; Edit | Paste		CTRL+X; CTRL+V
Name Cells	E 4.12	Click in Name box and type name	Insert | Name | Create or Insert | Name | Define		CTRL+SHIFT+F3
Name Cells, Redefine	E 5.18		Insert | Name | Define		ALT+I | N | D
New Workbook	E 1.54	New button on Standard toolbar	File | New		CTRL+N
Open Workbook	E 1.48	Open button on Standard toolbar	File | Open		CTRL+O
Outline a Range	E 4.9	Borders button on Formatting toolbar	Format | Cells | Border tab	Format Cells | Border tab	CTRL+1 | B
Outline a Worksheet	E 5.30		Data | Group and Outline		ALT+D | G | A
Page Break	E 6.56		Insert | Page Break		ALT+I | B
Percent Style Format	E 2.39	Percent Style button on Formatting toolbar	Format | Cells | Number tab | Percentage	Format Cells | Number | Percentage	CTRL+1 | N
Preview Worksheet	E 2.51	Print Preview button on Standard toolbar	File | Print Preview		ALT+F | V
Print Row and Column Headings	E 6.55		File | Page Setup | Sheet tab		ALT+F | U | S
Print Row and Column Titles	E 6.55		File | Page Setup | Sheet tab		ALT+F | U | S
Print Worksheet	E 2.51	Print button on Standard toolbar	File | Print		CTRL+P
Protect Worksheet	E 4.49		Tools | Protection | Protect Sheet		ALT+T | P | P
Quit Excel	E 1.46	Close button on title bar	File | Exit		ALT+F4
Redo	E 1.52	Redo button on Standard toolbar	Edit | Redo		ALT+E | R

Table 2 Microsoft Excel 2000 Quick Reference Summary *(continued)*

TASK	PAGE NUMBER	MOUSE	MENU BAR	SHORTCUT MENU	KEYBOARD SHORTCUT
Remove Auditing Arrows	E 2.23	Remove All Arrows button on Auditing toolbar	Tools | Auditing | Remove All Arrows		ALT+T | U | A
Remove Splits	E 3.62	Double-click split bar	Window | Split		ALT+W | S
Rename Sheet Tab	E 2.61	Double-click sheet tab		Rename	
Replace	E 6.58		Edit | Replace		CTRL+H
Rotate Text	E 3.8		Format | Cells | Alignment tab	Format Cells | Alignment tab	ALT+O | E | A
Row Height	E 2.47	Drag row heading boundary	Format | Row	Row Height	ALT+O | R | E
Save as Web Page	EW 1.3		File | Save as Web Page		ALT+F | G
Save Workbook—New Name	E 1.41		File | Save As		ALT+F | A
Save Workbook—Same Name	E 2.50	Save button on Standard toolbar	File | Save		CTRL+S
Select All of Worksheet	E 1.54	Select All button on worksheet			CTRL+A
Select Multiple Sheets	E 3.57	CTRL and click tab or SHIFT and click tab		Select All Sheets	
Series	E 3.8	Drag fill handle	Edit | Fill | Series		ALT+E | I | S
Shortcut Menu	E 1.51	Right-click			SHIFT+F10
Sort	E 5.22	Click Sort Ascending button or Sort Descending button on Standard toolbar	Data | Sort		ALT+D | S
Spell Check	E 2.49	Spelling button on Standard toolbar	Tools | Spelling		F7
Split Window into Panes	E 3.61	Drag vertical or horizontal split box	Window | Split		ALT+W | S
Stock Quotes	E 2.58		Data | Get External Data | Run Web Query		ALT+D | D | D
Style, Add	E 6.22		Format | Style | Add button		ALT+O | S
Style, Apply	E 6.25		Format | Style		ALT+O | S
Subtotals	E 5.27		Data | Subtotals		ALT+D | B
Subtotals, Remove	E 5.31		Data | Subtotals | Remove All button		ALT+D | B | R
Text Box, Add	E 6.45	Text Box button on Drawing toolbar			
Trace Dependents	E 2.25	Trace Dependents button on Auditing toolbar		Tools | Auditing | Trace Dependents	ALT+T | U | D
Trace Precedents	E 2.25	Trace Precedents button on Auditing toolbar		Tools | Auditing | Trace Precedents	ALT+T | U | T
Toolbar, Reset	E 1.14		View | ToolBars | Customize | Toolbars tab	Customize | Toolbars tab	ALT+V | T | C | B
Toolbar, Show Entire	E 1.28	Double-click move handle			
Toolbar, Show or Hide	E 3.38		View | Toolbars	Customize	ALT+V | T
Underline	E 3.42	Underline button on Formatting toolbar	Format | Cells | Font tab	Format Cells | Font tab	CTRL+U
Undo	E 1.52	Undo button on Standard toolbar	Edit | Undo		CTRL+Z
Unfreeze Worksheet Titles	E 3.32		Windows | Unfreeze Panes		ALT+W | F
Unlock Cells	E 4.49		Format | Cells | Protection tab	Format Cells | Protection	CTRL+1 | SHIFT+P
Unprotect Worksheet	E 4.51		Tools | Protection | Unprotect Sheet		ALT+T | P | P
WordArt	E 6.41	Insert WordArt button on Drawing toolbar	Insert | Picture | WordArt		ALT+I | P | W
Web Page Preview	EW 1.3		File | Web Page Preview		ALT+F | B
Zoom	E 3.59	Zoom box on Standard toolbar	View | Zoom		ALT+V | Z

Table 3   Microsoft Access 2000 Quick Reference Summary

TASK	PAGE NUMBER	MOUSE	MENU BAR	SHORTCUT MENU	KEYBOARD SHORTCUT
Add Combo Box	A 4.37	Combo Box button			
Add Field	A 3.17	Insert Rows button	Insert	Rows	Insert Rows	INSERT
Add Label	A 4.43	Label button			
Add Record	A 1.21, A 1.28	New Record button	Insert	New Record	New Record	
Add Switchboard Item	A 6.44	New button			
Add Switchboard Page	A 6.43	New button			
Add Table to Query	A 2.32	Show Table button	Query	Show Table	Show Table	
Add Text Box	A 4.34	Text Box button			
Apply Filter	A 3.13	Filter by Selection or Filter by Form button		Records	Filter	
Calculate Statistics	A 2.40	Totals button	View	Totals	Totals	
Change Group of Records	A 3.23	Query Type button arrow	Update Query	Query	Update Query	Query Type	Update Query	
Change Property	A 4.16	Properties button	View	Properties	Properties	
Clear Query	A 2.16		Edit	Clear Grid		
Close Database	A 1.25	Close button	File	Close		
Close Form	A 1.38	Close button	File	Close		
Close Query	A 2.14	Close button	File	Close		
Close Table	A 1.25	Close button	File	Close		
Collapse Subdatasheet	A 3.42	Expand indicator (−)			
Compact a Database	A 5.48		Tools	Database Utilities	Compact and Repair		
Copy Object to Clipboard	A 6.36	Copy button	Edit	Copy	Copy	CTRL+C
Create Calculated Field	A 2.36			Zoom	SHIFT+F2
Create Data Access Page	AW 1.3	New Object button arrow	Page	Insert	Page		
Create Database	A 1.9	Start button	New Office Document	File	New		CTRL+N
Create Form	A 1.37, A 4.31	New Object button arrow	AutoForm	Insert	Form		
Create Index	A 3.48	Indexes button	View	Indexes		
Create Input Mask	A 6.10	Input Mask text box			
Create Lookup Wizard Field	A 6.8	Text arrow	Lookup Wizard			
Create Macro	A 6.27	New Object button arrow	Macro	Insert	Macro		
Create Query	A 2.6	New Object button arrow	Query	Insert	Query		
Create Report	A 1.43	New Object button arrow	Report	Insert	Report		
Create Switchboard	A 6.40		Tools	Database Utilities	Switchboard Manager		
Create Table	A 1.14	Tables object	Create table in Design view or Create table by using Wizard	Insert	Table		
Default Value	A 3.31	Default Value box			
Delete Field	A 1.19, A 3.19	Delete Rows button	Edit	Delete Rows	Delete Rows	DELETE
Delete Group of Records	A 3.26	Query Type button arrow	Delete Query	Query	Delete Query	Query Type	Delete Query	
Delete Record	A 3.14	Delete Record button	Edit	Delete Record	Delete Record	DELETE
Exclude Duplicates	A 2.29	Properties button	View	Properties	Unique Values Only	Properties	Unique Values Only	
Exclude Field from Query Results	A 2.20	Show check box			

Table 3 Microsoft Access 2000 Quick Reference Summary (continued)

TASK	PAGE NUMBER	MOUSE	MENU BAR	SHORTCUT MENU	KEYBOARD SHORTCUT
Expand Subdatasheet	A 3.42	Expand indicator (+)			
Field Size	A 1.17, A 3.16	Field Size text box			
Field Type	A 1.16	Data Type arrow | appropriate type, appropriate letter			
Format	A 3.33	Format box			
Import Worksheet	AI 1.3		File | Get External Data | Import		
Include All Fields in Query	A 2.15	Double-click asterisk			
Include Field in Query	A 2.10	Double-click field in field list box			
Key Field	A 1.17	Primary Key button	Edit | Primary Key	Primary Key	
Link Worksheet	AI 1.3		File | Get External Data | Link Tables		
Modify Switchboard Page	A 6.44, A 6.46	Edit button			
Move Control	A 4.33	Drag control		Properties | All tab | Top and Properties | All tab | Left	
Move to Design View	A 5.39	View button	View | Design View	Design View	
Move to First Record	A 1.27	First Record button			CTRL+UP ARROW
Move to Last Record	A 1.27	Last Record button			CTRL+DOWN ARROW
Move to Next Record	A 1.27	Next Record button			DOWN ARROW
Move to Previous Record	A 1.27	Previous Record button			UP ARROW
Open Database	A 1.26	Start button | Open Office Document	File | Open Database		CTRL+O
Open Form	A 3.7	Forms object | Open button		Open	Use arrow keys to move highlight to name, then press ENTER key
Open Table	A 1.21	Tables object | Open button		Open	Use arrow keys to move highlight to name, then press ENTER key
Preview Table	A 1.31	Print Preview button	File | Print Preview	Print Preview	
Print Relationships	A 3.38		File | Print Relationships		
Print Report	A 1.48	Print button	File | Print	Print	CTRL+P
Print Results of Query	A 2.12	Print button	File | Print	Print	CTRL+P
Print Table	A 1.31	Print button	File | Print	Print	CTRL+P
Quit Access	A 1.25	Close button on title bar	File | Exit		ALT+F4
Relationships (Referential Integrity)	A 3.38	Relationships button	Tools | Relationships		
Remove Control	A 4.24	Cut button	Edit | Cut	Cut	DELETE
Remove Filter	A 3.14	Remove Filter button	Records | Remove Filter/Sort		
Resize Column	A 3.21, A 5.13	Drag right boundary of field selector	Format | Column Width	Column Width	
Resize Control	A 5.29	Drag sizing handle	View | Properties | All tab | Width and View | Properties | All tab | Height	Properties | All tab | Width and Properties | All tab | Height	
Resize Row	A 5.13	Drag lower boundary of row selector	Format | Row Height	Row Height	
Resize Section	A 4.43	Drag section boundary	View | Properties | All tab | Height	Properties | All tab | Height	
Restructure Table	A 3.16	Tables object | Design button		Design View	
Return to Design View	A 2.12	View button	View | Design View		
Run Query	A 2.11	Run button	Query | Run		
Save Form	A 1.38	Save button	File | Save		CTRL+S
Save Query	A 2.42	Save button	File | Save		CTRL+S
Save Table	A 1.19	Save button	File | Save		CTRL+S
Search for Record	A 3.9	Find button	Edit | Find		CTRL+F

(continued)

Table 3 Microsoft Access 2000 Quick Reference Summary *(continued)*

TASK	PAGE NUMBER	MOUSE	MENU BAR	SHORTCUT MENU	KEYBOARD SHORTCUT
Select Fields for Report	A 1.45	Add Field button or Add All Fields button			
Sort Data in Query	A 2.26	Sort row | arrow | type of sort			
Sort Records	A 3.43	Sort Ascending or Sort Descending button	Records | Sort | Sort Ascending or Sort Descending	Sort Ascending or Sort Descending	
Switch Between Form and Datasheet Views	A 1.42, A 3.11	View button	View | Datasheet View		
Update Hyperlink Field	A 5.18		Insert | Hyperlink	Hyperlink | Edit Hyperlink	CTRL+K
Update OLE Field	A 5.15		Insert | Object	Insert Object	
Use AND Criterion	A 2.24				Type criteria on same line
Use OR Criterion	A 2.25				Type criteria on separate lines
Validation Rule	A 3.30	Validation Rule box			
Validation Text	A 3.30	Validation Text box			

Table 4   Microsoft PowerPoint 2000 Quick Reference Summary

TASK	PAGE NUMBER	MOUSE	MENU BAR	SHORTCUT MENU	KEYBOARD SHORTCUT
Action Button, Add	PP 4.27	AutoShapes button on Drawing toolbar	Action Buttons	Slide Show	Action Buttons		ALT+D	I
Action Button, Add Caption (Text Box)	PP 4.35	Text Box button on Drawing toolbar	Insert	Text Box		ALT+I	X
Action Button, Fill Color	PP 4.34	Fill Color button on Drawing toolbar	Format	AutoShape	Colors and Lines tab	Format AutoShape	Colors and Lines tab	ALT+O	O	Colors and Lines tab
Action Button, Scale	PP 4.33	Drag sizing handle	Format	AutoShape	Size tab	Format AutoShape	Size tab	ALT+O	O	Size tab
Action Button, Shadow	PP 4.35	Shadow button on Drawing toolbar			
Animate Text	PP 2.48	Custom Animation button on Animation Effects toolbar	Slide Show	Custom Animation	Effects tab	Custom Animation	Effects tab	ALT+D	M
Apply Design Template	PP 1.18	Apply Design Template button on Standard toolbar; Apply Design Template on Common Tasks button menu on Formatting toolbar	Format	Apply Design Template	Apply Design Template	ALT+O	Y
Bullets, Remove	PP 4.48	Bullets button on Formatting toolbar	Format	Bullets and Numbering	Bulleted tab	None	Bullets and Numbering	Bulleted tab	None	ALT+O	B	SPACEBAR
Change Design Templates	PP 3.9	Double-click design template name on status bar; Apply Design Template button on Standard toolbar	Format	Apply Design Template	Apply Design Template	ALT+O	Y
Change Font Color	PP 1.24	Font Color button arrow on Drawing toolbar	color sample	Format	Font	Font	Color	ALT+O	F	ALT+C	DOWN ARROW
Change Slide Layout	PP 2.22	Slide Layout on Common Tasks buttons menu on Formatting toolbar	Format	Slide Layout	Slide Layout	ALT+O	L	RIGHT ARROW
Change Slide Order	PP 4.50, PP 4.54	Drag			
Change the Font	PP 3.10	Font box arrow on Formatting toolbar	Format	Font	Font	ALT+O	F
Check Spelling	PP 1.55	Spelling button on Standard toolbar	Tools	Spelling		F7
Choose a Design Template	PP 1.18	Common Tasks button on Formatting toolbar	Apply Design Template	Format	Apply Design Template	Apply Design Template	ALT+C	Y
Clip Art, Animate	PP 2.47		Slide Show	Preset Animation		ALT+D	P
Clip Art, Change Size	PP 2.33	Format Picture button on Picture toolbar	Size tab	Format	Picture	Size tab	Format Picture	Size tab	ALT+O	I	Size tab
Clip Art, Insert	PP 2.25	Insert Clip Art button on Drawing toolbar	Insert	Picture	Clip Art		ALT+I	P	C
Clip Art, Move	PP 2.32	Drag			
Clip Art, Ungroup	PP 3.54	Draw button on Drawing toolbar	Ungroup		Grouping	Ungroup	SHIFT+F10	G	U
Connect to Microsoft Clip Gallery Live Site	PPI 1.4	Insert Clip Art button on Drawing toolbar	Clips Online button on Insert ClipArt toolbar	Insert	Picture	Clip Art	Clips Online button on Insert ClipArt toolbar		ALT+I	P	C	ALT+C
Create a Table	PP 3.41	Insert Table button on Standard toolbar	Insert	Table		ALT+I	B
Custom Background, Insert Picture	PP 3.16		Format	Background	Background	ALT+O	K
Decrease Font Size	PP 1.25	Decrease Font Size button on Formatting toolbar	Format	Font	Font	Size	CTRL+SHIFT+<
Delete an Object	PP 3.56	Select object	Cut button on Standard toolbar	Edit	Clear or Edit	Cut	Cut	ALT+E	A or DELETE or CTRL+X

(continued)

MICROSOFT POWERPOINT 2000 QUICK REFERENCE SUMMARY

Table 4 Microsoft PowerPoint 2000 Quick Reference Summary *(continued)*

TASK	PAGE NUMBER	MOUSE	MENU BAR	SHORTCUT MENU	KEYBOARD SHORTCUT
Delete Slide	PP 4.53	Click slide icon, press DELETE	Edit | Delete Slide		ALT+E | D
Delete Text	PP 4.9	Cut button on Standard toolbar	Edit | Cut	Cut	CTRL+X
Demote a Paragraph	PP 1.34	Demote button on Formatting toolbar			TAB or ALT+SHIFT+ RIGHT ARROW
Deselect a Clip Art Object	PP 3.55	Click outside clip art object area			
Display Guides	PP 4.11		View | Guides	Guides	ALT+V | G
Display Rulers	PP 4.10		View | Ruler	Ruler	ALT+V | R
Edit Web Page Through Browser	PPW 1.9	Edit button on Internet Explorer Standard Buttons toolbar			
E-mail from PowerPoint	PP 2.56	E-mail button on Standard toolbar	File | Send To | Mail Recipient		ALT+F | D | A
Graphical Bullets, Add	PP 3.19	Bullets button on Formatting toolbar	Format | Bullets and Numbering | Bulleted tab | Character	Bullets and Numbering | Bulleted tab | Character	ALT+O | B | ALT+H
Group Objects	PP 3.57	Drag through objects | Draw button on Drawing toolbar | Group		Grouping | Group	
Header and Footer, Add to Page	PP 2.36		View | Header and Footer | Notes and Handouts tab		ALT+V | H
Header and Footer, Add to Slide	PP 1.75		View | Header and Footer | Slide tab		ALT+V | H
Help	PP 1.67	Microsoft PowerPoint Help button on Standard toolbar	Help		F1
Hide Guides	PP 4.38		View | Guides	Guides	ALT+V | G
Hide Rulers	PP 4.22		View | Ruler	Ruler	ALT+V | R
Hide Slide	PP 4.49	Hide Slide button on Slide Sorter toolbar	Slide Show | Hide Slide	Hide Slide	ALT+D | H
Increase Font Size	PP 1.25	Increase Font Size button on Formatting toolbar	Format | Font	Font | Size	CTRL+SHIFT+>
Increase Zoom Percentage	PP 4.13	Zoom box arrow on Standard toolbar	View | Zoom		ALT+V | Z
Italicize Text	PP 1.27	Italic button on Formatting toolbar	Format | Font | Font style	Font | Font style	CTRL+I
Microsoft Organization Chart, Add Co-worker Boxes	PP 4.41	Co-worker box tool on Microsoft Organization Chart icon bar			
Microsoft Organization Chart, Add Shadow Effects	PP 3.36		Boxes | Shadow	Shadow	ALT+B | W
Microsoft Organization Chart, Add Subordinate Boxes	PP 3.27	Subordinate box tool on Microsoft Organization Chart icon bar			
Microsoft Organization Chart, Change Border Style	PP 3.37		Boxes | Border Style	Border Style	ALT+B | B
Microsoft Organization Chart, Change Style	PP 3.29		Styles		ALT+S
Microsoft Organization Chart, Copy a Branch	PP 3.31		Edit | Copy	Copy	CTRL+C
Microsoft Organization Chart, Delete a Branch	PP 4.39		Edit | Select | Branch | Edit | Clear		CTRL+B | DELETE
Microsoft Organzation Chart, Open	PP 3.24		Insert | Picture | Organization Chart		ALT+I | P | O
Microsoft Organization Chart, Paste a Branch	PP 3.32		Edit | Paste Boxes	Paste Boxes	CTRL+V
Microsoft Organization Chart, Quit	PP 3.38	Close button on Microsoft Organization Chart title bar	File | Close and Return to presentation		ALT+F | C